THE OLD TESTAMENT

THE
OLD TESTAMENT

Newly translated from the Vulgate Latin by Msgr.
Ronald Knox at the Request of His Eminence
The Cardinal Archbishop of Westminster

VOLUME II

JOB TO MACHABEES

With Appendix
(Alternative Version of The Psalms)

Issued by
SHEED & WARD, Inc.
NEW YORK · 1950

IMPRIMATUR

✠ E. Morrogh Bernard
Vic. Gen.

Westmonasterii, die 2 Maii 1949

CONTENTS

CONTENTS

THE BOOK OF JOB

CHAPTER ONE

THERE was a man dwelling in the land of Uz once, Job was the name of him, that was true and honest; ever he feared God, and kept far
2 from wrong-doing. Seven sons he had, and three daughters; and for wealth, he had seven thousand sheep, three thousand camels, five hundred yoke of oxen, five hundred she-asses, and servants a many; in all the East
4 none was Job's rival. And this custom his sons had in feasting, each invited the rest in turn; at such times they would send for their three
5 sisters to eat and drink beside them. And ever when their week of feasting was over, Job would send for them,[1] and have them rid of all defilement; next morning, it was his first care to offer burnt-sacrifice for each of them. Who knows, thought he, but they may have committed some fault, these children of mine? Who knows but they may have slighted God in their secret thoughts? Never would he let the day pass without burnt sacrifice.
6 One day, when the heavenly powers stood waiting upon the Lord's
7 presence, and among them, man's Enemy, the Lord asked him, where he had been? Roaming about the earth, said he, to and fro about the earth.
8 Why then, the Lord said, thou hast seen a servant of mine called Job. Here is a true man, an honest man, none like him on earth; ever he fears his God,
9 and keeps far from wrong-doing. Job fears his God, the Enemy answered,
10 and loses nothing by it. Sheltered his life by thy protection, sheltered his home, his property; thy blessing on all he undertakes; worldly goods that
11 still go on increasing; he loses nothing. One little touch of thy hand, assailing all that wealth of his! Then see how he will turn and blaspheme
12 thee. Be it so, the Lord answered; with all his possessions do what thou wilt, so thou leave himself unharmed. And with that, the Enemy left the Lord's presence, and withdrew.
13 And now it was the turn of Job's children to sit over their feasting
14 and their wine at the house of the eldest brother. That day, a messenger brought Job news of his oxen and asses. The oxen were a ploughing, said
15 he, and the asses grazing near them, when on a sudden a band of Sabæans swept down on them, and carried all away. As for thy men, the Sabæans
16 put them to the sword, and none lives to tell the tale but I. Even as he spoke, another messenger came in with news of the sheep, how God's lightning had fallen, devouring sheep and shepherd, so that none was left
17 to tell the tale but he. And upon the heels of that, in came a third to say

---

[1] Or possibly, 'Job would send (a priest) to them.'

that robbers from Chaldæa, in three several bands, had closed in upon the camels and driven them away, killing the men who tended them, so that

18 none was left to tell the tale but he. And before this one had finished his story, a fourth messenger came in. I come, said he, from thy eldest son's house, where but now thy sons and daughters sat at their feasting and

19 their wine. All on a sudden, came a tempestuous wind from across the desert, and beat so on every corner of the house that it fell in, crushing thy children to death amid the ruins of it; none lives to tell the tale but I.

20 Then rose up Job, and rent his garments about him; and he shaved his

21 head bare, and fell down to earth to do reverence. Naked I came, said he, when I left my mother's womb, and whence I came, naked I must go. The Lord gave, the Lord has taken away; nothing is here befallen but

22 what was the Lord's will; blessed be the name of the Lord.[1] In all this, Job guarded his lips well, nor challenged with human folly God's wisdom.[2]

CHAPTER TWO

ONCE again the heavenly powers came to wait upon the Lord's presence; and there, waiting with the rest of them, was the Enemy of

2 man. And of his travels he still said the same; he had been roaming about

3 the earth, to and fro about the earth. Why then, the Lord said, thou hast seen for thyself that this servant of mine, Job, has not his like on earth; a man so true and honest, ever fearing his God, and keeping far from wrong-doing. And still he maintains his innocence.[3] Shame it is that thou

4 wouldst set me on to do him a mischief, and all to no purpose. Nay, answered the Enemy, skin must suffer before skin grieves.[4] Nothing a

5 man owns, but he will part with it to keep his skin whole. That hand of thine, let it fall on bone of his, flesh of his; see if he does not turn and

6 blaspheme thee. And thereupon said the Lord to man's Enemy, Have

7 what power over him thou wilt, so his life be kept safe in him. And with that, the Enemy left the Lord's presence, and withdrew.

And cruelly he smote Job; smote him with the foul scab from head to

---

[1] The words 'Nothing is here befallen but what was the Lord's will' are found in the Septuagint Greek, but not in the Hebrew text.

[2] Literally, in the Latin, 'nor said anything foolish against God.' The sense of the Hebrew text seems to be, 'nor charged God with senseless procedure.'

[3] This may mean that he continued to shew correct behaviour (cf. 1.22), but more probably that he would not admit he had done anything to deserve his sufferings (cf. 27.6, where the same words are used, and the argument of the book generally).

[4] Literally, 'Skin on behalf of skin.' The rendering given assumes that a proverb, couched in elliptical language, is best interpreted by reference to the context.

8 foot, so that he was fain to sit him down on the dung-hill, and scratch
9 himself with a shard where he itched. Little comfort his own wife gave
  him; What, she said, still priding thyself on thy innocence? Better thou
10 shouldst renounce God, and have done with living. Spoken like a foolish
   wife, Job answered. What, should we accept the good fortune God sends
   us, and not the ill? So well, even now, did Job guard his lips.
11   News of the calamity that had befallen him reached three of his friends,
   Eliphaz the Themanite, Baldad the Suhite, and Sophar the Naamathite.
   From their far homes all, by agreement made, came to visit him, and give
12 him comfort. Scarcely, upon a distant view, could they recognize him;
   loud they cried out, and sore they wept, tore their garments about them
13 and heaped the dust high on their heads. And for seven days and seven
   nights they sat there on the ground beside him, and no word spoken;
   here, they saw plainly, was overmastering grief.

CHAPTER THREE

  A T last, Job himself broke into utterance, and fell to cursing the day
2   on which he was born. And this was his plaint: Blotted out for
   ever be the day of my birth; that night, too, which gave word that a human
4 life had been conceived in the womb! Plunged be that day in darkness;
5 may God on high forget it, and grant it never shine of sun; shades, like
   the shades of death, claim it for their own; deep gloom lie heavy on it, and
6 wrap it all in desolation. Shrouded be that night in a black storm, neither
7 mark nor reckoning let it have in the moon's calendar; a night doomed
8 to exile, a night that never wakes the sound of praise. Wizards that can
   overcast the sun, and rouse old Chaos from his lair, on that night lay
9 your ban; blacken its starlight, let it await the coming of dawn; the night
   that should have closed the doors of the womb against me, shut these
   eyes for ever to sights of woe!
11   Had but the womb been the tomb of me, had I died at birth, had no
13 lap ever cherished me, no breast suckled me, all would be rest now,
14 all would be silence. Deeply I would take my repose, with the old kings
15 and senators, that once restored cities for their whim,[1] the chieftains that
16 had such wealth of gold, houses full of silver; with babe still-born and
17 babe unborn, hidden away in the sunless grave. There the unquietness of
18 the wicked is stilled, and the weary are at rest; untroubled the thrall
19 sleeps, his tyrant's bidding cannot reach him now; master and slave are
   there, and the slave masterless.

---

[1] 'Restored cities'; this is sometimes rendered, 'built mausoleums,' but the
meaning should probably be determined by passages like Is. 58.12.

20 Why should they see the light, that groan to see it; why should they
21 live, that must live in bitterness of soul? Why should they long for
22 death, like treasure-seekers, a grave the prize they covet? Such men
24 as I, that must tread blindfold in a maze of God's making! Ever as I sit
25 down to meat the sighs come, grief floods over me unrestrained. Must I
   have nothing left to daunt me? Must each calamity be felt as soon as
26 feared? And still I kept my own counsel, still patient and silent I, till my
   angry mood overcame me at last.[1]

CHAPTER FOUR

2 THEREUPON Eliphaz the Themanite made answer: Speak we, it
3 may be thou wilt take our words amiss, yet speech will out. Well
4 thou knewest how to teach others, strengthen the drooping hands, give
5 courage to the waverer, support to flagging knees, by counsel of thine. Now
   the blow has fallen on thyself, and thy strength is gone; the nearer neigh-
6 bourhood of misfortune unmans thee. No more we hear now of that fear
   of God, that life perfectly lived, which once gave thee confidence, gave
7 thee strength to endure! And, sure enough, ruin never fell yet on the
8 innocent; never yet was an upright soul lost to memory.[2] The men that
   traffic in wrong-doing, that sow a crop of mischief they themselves must
9 reap at last, these I have seen undone; one breath, one blast of the divine
   anger withers them quite, and they are gone.
10 Roar lion and growl lioness, the fangs of the lion-cubs will yet be
11 shattered. For lack of prey, the tiger goes his way at last, the young lions
   wander wide.[3]
12 Listen; here is a secret that was made known to me; it was but the
13 breath of a whisper overheard. It was the hour when night visions breed
14 disquiet, as men lie chained by sleep; fear took hold of me, a fit of trem-
15 bling that thrilled my whole frame, and made every hair bristle. All at
16 once a spirit came beside me; no face I knew, yet I could see the form of
17 it, and catch its voice, light as a rustling breeze. Can man have right on

---

[1] The Hebrew text is ordinarily understood as meaning, 'I have no ease,
no quiet, no rest; nothing but turmoil is my lot.'

[2] The argument here may be understood in either of two ways; it may be,
'You, Job, are innocent, therefore you cannot be wholly condemned to misfortune,' or it may be, 'You, Job, are condemned to misfortune, therefore you
cannot be wholly innocent.' Perhaps both lines of thought were in the speaker's
mind.

[3] These two sentences are evidently proverbs, and it is difficult to determine
their relevance here with certainty. 'Lioness' and 'tiger' in the Latin version
should be 'lion' according to the Hebrew text; five different words are here
used to describe the same animal.

his side, the voice asked, when he is matched with God? Can a mortal
18 creature shew blameless in its Creator's presence? Nay, in his own retinue
19 God finds loyalty wanting; angels may err. What, then, of Man, earth-
20 bound in his house of clay, eaten away by the moth of time? What of Man,
21 cut down between morn and eve, doomed to perish unregarded, even
the straggler marching on at last?[1] Will he not die before he learns
wisdom?

CHAPTER FIVE

WHO will listen to thy plaint against God? Wilt thou turn to one of
2 his angels for redress? This impatience of thine is a great murderer
of fools; in their simpleness of heart, they repine at the injury, to their
3 ruin. Never yet did I see a fool secure in his possessions but I prophesied
4 disaster, there and then, for his fair prospects. And still would I see his
children bereft of hope, ground down by false judgement, and none to
5 bring redress; his harvest a prey for hungry neighbours, himself for the
armed robber, his wealth drunk up by thirsty mouths.[2]
6 Never was ill without a cause; never did mischief spring up self-sown.
7 Man's bent is for mischief, as sure as birds will fly.[3]
8 Wiser counsels for me; to the Lord himself my plaint shall be made,
9 of God himself I will seek audience. His magnificent counsels none may
10 fathom, none reckon up his marvellous deeds. His to grant the parched
11 earth rain, watering the countryside; his to exalt men of low esteem, to
12 comfort the mourner with new hope. Through him the crafty schemer
13 is baulked of his aims; cunning overreaches itself, and knavish plots are
14 scattered to the winds; wise fools, that blink in daylight, and grope their
way blindly at full noon!
15 So, from their slander and their violence, he rescues the poor and the
16 unbefriended; now, misery, take heart, now, malice, hide thy face
abashed!
17 Happy the man, whom God chastens for his faults! The correction
18 he sends thee never, on thy life, refuse. Wounds he, it is but to heal;
19 the same hand, which smote, shall medicine thee. So in six perils thou

---

[1] 'Even the stragglers marching on at last'; or perhaps, according to the
Hebrew text, 'their excellency deserting them at last.' Some think we should
read, by a very slight alteration in the text, 'when their tent-peg is taken out,'
a metaphorical description of Man's impermanency.
[2] The text and interpretation of this verse are uncertain.
[3] 'Mischief'; literally, in the Latin version, 'trouble,' but the context seems
to shew that the other meaning of the Hebrew noun is to be preferred. The
troubles man undergoes do not spring up haphazard; they are the fruit of his
proneness to sin. 'As sure as birds will fly'; some interpret the Hebrew text
as meaning 'as sure as sparks will fly upwards.'

20 shalt go unharmed, and find yet one deliverance more; hunger shall not
21 starve thee, sword wound thee, slander find thee out, havoc reach thee;
22 rapine and dearth thou shalt defy. And besides all this, ravening beasts
23 shall not daunt thee; friendly soil for thee are the desert rocks, and the
24 wild things are in league with thee; secure thou shalt keep thy tent, or
25 visit thy fair lands, and nought shall go amiss. Be sure that thy posterity
26 will increase; like the green grass thy race shall flourish; and when go to
   the grave thou must, it shall be with strength undiminished, like ripe
27 corn at harvest-home. Here are thoughts tested and found true; well for
   thee if thou wilt heed them, and ponder them in thy heart.

CHAPTER SIX

2 BUT Job answered: Oh that I had such a pair of scales as might weigh
3   provocation of mine against the ills I suffer! [1] The sand on the shore
   of ocean could not match the burden of them, and do you wonder that my
4 utterance is all reproach? Deep the Lord's arrows rankle in me, draining
5 my life; all his terrors are arrayed against me. Brays the wild ass, be sure
6 he lacks pasture; lows the ox, he stands before an empty crib. Would
   you have me relish food unseasoned, lick my lips over the taste that
7 brings death? The food I had no stomach for, in my hard straits eat I
   must. [2]
8   Might it be granted, this is the boon I long for, this the request I would
9 make of God, that he would finish what he has begun, crush me alto-
10 gether, strike a full blow and make an end of me! Consolation enough,
   if he will but torment me to my death; no repining, then, against his
11 will! In what strength should I hold out? In what hope repose? Have I
13 the endurance of flint? Is my flesh brass? Help in myself is none; human
14 aid keeps its distance from me now. Nay, who defies the Lord's ven-
15 geance more surely than friend who refuses compassion to a friend? See
   how the men that are my brothers have failed me, fickle as the mountain
16 brooks that run headlong down their ravines; first shrivelled with frost,
17 then piled high with snow, then, when the snows melt, gone, vanished
18 away at the first touch of the heat! This way and that their winding chan-
19 nels turn, but all to no purpose, all are lost to view. [3] Nay, fickle streams,

---

[1] 'Provocation of mine'; it is not certain whether this means 'wrong-doing by which I have provoked God to punish me,' or 'the sense of provocation which I feel.'

[2] In verses 6 and 7, the sense of the original is very doubtful.

[3] The Latin version here, taken by itself, yields no tolerable sense. The rendering given above interprets it in the light of the Hebrew text, from which it differs considerably.

bethink you of the wayfarers from Thema, the thirsty pilgrims of
20 Saba! Some hope I had in my friends, but all is disappointment; with
eyes that will not meet mine, they come to visit me.[1]
21   Ay, you have come, but finding me so sorely smitten you dread my
22 company. It was little enough I asked; I never bade you diminish your
23 own wealth by bringing gifts to me, never begged your aid to rid me of
24 some enemy that was too strong for me. Come, be my instructors; I will
hear you out in silence; tell me what is the fault I have committed, all
25 unknowing? Ill fare the claims of truth with such as you; not one of you
26 can shew me in the wrong, yet for very love of reproof you must be
27 reproving still, all your words wasted on the air. Is it well done, to make
a prey of the defenceless, to conspire against the good name of your
28 friend? Browbeat me, then, at your pleasure; try if close scrutiny can
29 prove me false; only let there be no contentiousness in your pleadings;
30 in all honesty bring your complaint. You will not fasten guilt on any
word of mine; reckless utterance never these lips shall frame.[2]

CHAPTER SEVEN

WHAT is man's life on earth but a campaigning? Like a hired drudge,
2   he passes his time away; nor ever was slave so weary, longing for
3 the shade, or drudge so weary, waiting to earn his hire, as I have been,
counting these months of emptiness, these nights that never brought
4 rest. Lie I down to sleep, I weary to be up with the day; comes the day,
5 I weary for the evening, comfortless until dark. Overgrown my flesh
6 with worms, matted with dust; my skin dried up and shrivelled. Frail
as the weaver's thread my years vanish away, spent without hope.
7   Bethink thee, Lord, it is but a breath, this life of mine, and I shall look
8 on this fair world but once; when that is done, men will see me no more,
9 and thou as nothing. Like a cloud dislimned in passing, man goes to his
10 grave never to return; never again the home-coming, never shall tidings
11 of him reach the haunts he knew. And should I utter no word? Nay, the
crushed spirit will find a voice, the embittered heart will not keep its own
12 counsel. Am I a raging sea, a ravening monster, that thou guardest me so
13 close? When I would find rest on my pillow, take refuge in night
14 thoughts, what dreams thou sendest to daunt me, what sights of terror
to unman me!
15   The rope for me! Death only will content this frame. To despair I

---

[1] The sense of the Hebrew text is that the travellers (not the friends) come
hopefully looking for the streams, and are disappointed.
[2] The Hebrew text of verses 25–30 is largely different, and its interpretation
largely doubtful.

yield myself, I will live on no more; loose thy hold of me; this life of
17 mine is but the shadow of a life. Why is it that thou wilt make so noble
18 a thing of man, wilt pay so much heed to him? Never a day dawns but
   thou wilt surprise him at his post; never a moment when thou art not
19 making proof of him. Nay, gaze on me no more; leave me, though it were
20 but for a breathing-space, to myself! If sinned I have, does human act
   of mine claim thy divine regard? Must my path always cross thine, my
21 life always be a burden to me? [1] Would it cost thee much to forgive sin
   of mine, pass over fault of mine, when I, so soon, shall be lying in the dust,
   missing at my post, as thou makest thy rounds at dawn?

CHAPTER EIGHT

2 THEN answered Baldad the Suhite: What, still at thy old complaining;
3   blustering still, like a high wind, in vain? Can sentence undeserved
4 come from God, unjust award from the Almighty? What if these children
  of thine committed some fault, and he allowed justice to take its course?
5 For thyself, thou hast but to keep early tryst with God, make thy
6 plea to his omnipotence. Then, if thou comest before him innocent and
  upright, he will give thee audience betimes; he will establish thee in thy
7 possessions again, as one that enjoys his favour. A poor thing thy old
  prosperity will seem, matched with the abundance he gives thee now.
8   Ask counsel of the ages that are long past; let the experience of former
9 men overrule thee. How blind are we, creatures of a day, whose time on
10 earth passes like a shadow! Those fathers of ours will be thy best
11 teachers, and this is the advice their wisdom offers thee: Never yet grew
12 bulrush without moisture, nor reed-bed that lacked water; fade it must,
13 no leaf so soon, in its first flower, before men have time to gather it. So
  frail their happiness, who leave God unremembered; so fade the hopes
14 of the false heart. Little shall their recklessness avail them; in threads
15 of gossamer they put their trust. Or say they are like a climbing plant, that
  clings to a falling house; come down it must, for all the support they give
16 it, [2] a plant that seems well watered enough, spreads abroad its early shoots,
17 but only till the sun rises; wrapped about stones are the roots of it, and
18 stones all its dwelling-place; yonder sun must needs drain its life, and the

---

[1] The Hebrew tradition is that the text originally ran, 'Must I always be a
burden to thee?' but was altered by the copyists as a disrespectful phrase. There
is, however, no trace of any such older reading in any of the versions.
   [2] This verse, in the original, begins simply 'They lean on a falling house,'
but the context shews that the speaker has transferred his thought from one
plant-metaphor to another.

19 garden will keep no memory of its passage. So brief its pride; they are
waiting even now underground, the shoots that will fill its place.
20   Trust me, God will not cast off the innocent, will not lend his aid to
21 the malice of their enemies. Ere long, he will teach those lips to smile,
22 that mouth to sing praise; brief shall be the triumph of thy foes, brief
the security of the wrong-doer.

CHAPTER NINE

1 B UT Job answered: No need to teach me that; how should a man win
3   his suit, matched against God? Who would go to law, where one
4 plea on this side is arrayed against a thousand on that? His all-knowing
mind, his all-conquering arms, what man ever throve yet that defied
5 them? God, the unseen power that can thrust mountains this way and
6 that, uproot them in his anger, can move earth from its place, and set all
7 its pillars quaking, can prevent, with a word, the sun's rising, or imprison,
8 under his royal seal, the very stars? He it was that spread out heaven to be
9 his covering, made ocean a floor under his feet; that created Arcturus,
10 and Orion, and the Hyades, and the nooks of the south; [1] great wonders
11 he does, beyond all our understanding and all our reckoning. Hidden
12 from my sight, hidden from my thought, he comes and goes; comes
suddenly, and how should I defend my doings? goes suddenly, and how
13 should I question his? There is no braving the anger of such a God,
14 when even the Titanic powers obey him; [2] and should I defend myself, in
phrases of studied eloquence, being what I am?
15   Nay, though I had right on my side, I would not plead against him
16 as an adversary, I would sue to him for mercy as a judge. Summon him
to law if I might, and he should answer my summons, well I know he
17 would listen to no pleadings of mine; his storms would overwhelm me,
18 faster than ever the unmerited blows would fall; never a breathing-space,
19 never a draught but of poison! Nought avails might, when a giant
threatens me; nought avails right, when none dares to support my
20 quarrel. Would I plead in defence, he turns my own words against me;
21 be I never so upright, he will prove me hypocrite. And innocent I am,
but of that I take regard no longer; I am aweary of life itself.

---

[1] 'The nooks of the south'; this is presumably some astronomical allusion to
which we have lost the key.
[2] 'The Titanic powers'; literally, in the Latin version 'those who hold up the
earth.' The Hebrew text is generally understood as referring to the powers of
Chaos over which, by an allegory, Almighty God is pictured as triumphing
at the Creation.

22   Still unchanged is the burden of my complaint; innocent and guilty,
23 he sweeps all away.[1] If his scourge must fall, should not a single blow
      suffice? Why does he look on and laugh, when the unoffending, too, must
24 suffer? So the whole world is given up into the power of wrong-doers;
      he blinds the eyes of justice. He is answerable for it; who else?
25   Swift as a royal courier my days pass, and joyless each one,   like a
27 pinnace gliding down stream,[2] or an eagle swooping on its prey. Ere now,
      I have been minded to put away such talk as this, wear a sad face and
28 live on the rack no more; but ever the warning came, fresh pains were
      in store for me; still thou wouldst hold me guilty, wouldst not spare.[3]
29 Blamed I must be, in spite of all; vain was my striving,   vainly I washed
31 me in water pure as snow, kept my hands shining clean; thy con-
      demnation must roll me in the mire again, till the very clothes I wear
32 shun the touch of me! I cannot meet him in judgement as man to man,
33 claim an impartial hearing for my plea;   there can be no arbiter between
34 us, to claim jurisdiction over both. Let him lay by his rod, let his terrors
35 cease to daunt me;   then I will speak out bravely to his face; it is fear
      that holds me dumb.

CHAPTER TEN

O H, I am weary of life; I will speak out, come what may; my soul is
2   too embittered for silence. I will protest against my sentence,
3 demand to know why his judgement is so cruel. Is it well done in thee to
   play the tyrant, to spurn me, the creature of thy own hands, to smile on
4 the ill designs of the godless? Are those eyes of thine human after all; is
5 thy sight, too, blinded, like the sight of men? Hast thou a mortal's span
6 of life, is thy reign brief like the reign of a mortal king,   that thou must
7 search for faults in me, labour to convict me of wrong done,   when thou
   knowest full well that I am innocent, knowest that I am in thy power
   beyond hope of rescue?
8   It was thy hand that made me, no part of me but is thy fashioning; and
9 wilt thou cast me aside all in a moment? Thou the craftsman, though

---

[1] The Hebrew text of this verse opens with the words, 'It is one thing,' a
phrase which is generally interpreted, 'It is all one' (whether I live or die; or
perhaps, whether a man is guilty or innocent). But there is no evidence that
this English idiom was familiar to the Hebrew mind.

[2] Literally, in the Latin version, 'ships carrying fruit'; the phrase in the
Hebrew text is usually rendered, 'skiffs made of papyrus.'

[3] In verses 27 and 28, the Latin as it stands does not yield any natural sense
that is appropriate to the context; the rendering given above interprets it in
the light of the Hebrew text.

10 of clay thy handiwork, and must all be ground to dust again? Milk of thy
11 milking, cheese of thy pressing, were flesh and skin that clothed me,
12 bone and sinew that built up my frame; the life given by thee, by thee
13 was spared; thy vigilance was all my safety. Only in thy heart the mem-
14 ory of this is stored, but I know thou hast not forgotten. And was it thy
15 purpose to spare me for a little, if I sinned, but absolve me never? Woe
to me, if I rebelled against thee! And if I remained innocent, what then?
Why, I would be drowned in misery and despair till I could lift up my
16 head no more! Or if I did, that were pride in me, to be hunted down as a
17 lioness is hunted; thou wouldst devise fresh miracles of torment; wouldst
bring fresh witnesses against me, redouble thy vengeful strokes, array
against me a new host of punishments.
18   Why didst thou ever take me from the womb; why could I not perish
19 there, never to meet men's eyes; a being without being, carried from
20 womb to tomb? Brief, brief is my span of days; for a little leave me to
21 myself, to find some comfort in my misery. Soon I must go to a land
whence there is no returning, a land of darkness, death's shadow over
22 it; a land of gloomy night, where death's shadow lies over all, and no
peace haunts it, only everlasting dread.

CHAPTER ELEVEN

2 THEN answered Sophar the Naamathite: So ready to speak, be ready
in thy turn to listen; glibness will not make an innocent man of thee.
3 Must all keep silence till thou hast done; shall none make answer to thy
4 raillery? Still thou wilt have it that all thy dealings [1] are upright, that thy
5 heart, as God sees it, is pure. Would he but speak one word in thy ear,
6 make thee his confidant! Would he but reveal to thee the secrets of his
wisdom, in its ordered variety! Then wouldst thou learn that the penalty
7 he is exacting of thee is less, far less, than thy sins deserve. What, wouldst
thou search out the ways of God, have knowledge unconfined of his
8 omnipotence? High as heaven is that wisdom, and thy reach so small;
9 deep as hell itself, and thy thought so shallow! Far as earth it stretches,
10 wide as ocean; will he sweep them all away, or confine them all in a little
11 space, there is no gainsaying him. [2] He knows the false hearts of men, sees
12 wickedness there, and wouldst thou have him overlook it? Poor fools,

---

[1] 'Thy dealings'; the Hebrew text gives 'thy doctrine,' but this is not in point.
Job has claimed to be innocent, not to be infallible. The Latin word used here
means 'dealings' generally in such passages as III Kings 1.7, Heb. 4.13.
[2] The Latin version differs here from the Hebrew text, the meaning of which
is quite uncertain.

that will have a mind of their own, and think they were born free as the wild ass!

13   But see, thy heart once guided aright, thy hands outspread to him in
14 prayer, thou hast but to cleanse thy hands of their wrong-doing, rid thy
15 dwelling-place of the guilt that defiles it. Then thou mayst lift up thy
16 head again, free from reproach, waver no more, tremble no more. These
miseries of thine shall be forgotten, or remembered gratefully, like floods
17 that are overpast. Radiance of noon shall dispel twilight, dawn shall rise
18 where darkness seemed to envelop thee; fresh confidence shall be thine,
19 fresh hope; hidden away in safety [1] thou shalt sleep secure; and that rest
of thine, none shall disturb, suitors a many shall come to court thy favour.
20   The godless another doom awaits; their eyes shall grow faint with
watching, and no rescue shall ever reach them; no other prospect they
have but despair.

CHAPTER TWELVE

2 BUT Job answered: Strange, that you alone should have the gift of
3 reason; that when you die, wisdom must die too! Well, I too have
my thoughts; I will yet try a fall with you; this knowledge you bring me
4 is knowledge common to all. For all his friends' raillery, a man such as I
will still summon God to answer for his doings; [2] the simplicity of the
5 upright was ever a laughing-stock, and indeed, it is but a rushlight,
6 despised by shrewd and prosperous folk, but it waits its turn. [3] Meanwhile, see how well the robbers store their houses, braving God's anger,
7 and yet in all things he lets them have their way! Dost thou doubt it?
8 The very beasts will tell thee, the birds in air will be thy counsellors; the
secret is known in every cranny of the earth, the fish in the sea will make
9 it known to thee; none doubts, I tell thee, that all this is the Lord's
10 doing; all living things that breathe, all the spirits of all mankind, lie in
11 the hollow of his hand. As surely as the ear judges words, and the mouth
12 relishes the taste of food, so surely is there truth in ancient sayings; it is
time brings experience.

---

[1] 'Hidden away in safety'; literally 'dug in.' It can hardly be supposed that the Latin version intends an allusion to burial.

[2] 'Summon God to answer for his doings'; literally, 'call on God and he will answer him,' but it seems likely that Job is referring to judicial interrogations; cf. 5.1, 9.16, 13.22.

[3] Two words in the Hebrew text here are susceptible of other interpretations than those given by the Latin version; and its sense is probably better rendered 'The shrewd and prosperous make light of a man's ruin, when his feet are just ready to stumble.'

13 All God's doing; his are the wisdom and the power; to him belong
14 prudence in act and discernment. The ruins he makes, none can rebuild,
15 his imprisonment none can escape; withholds he the rain, all is dried
16 up; sends he rain, it floods all the ground. Yes, he is strong, he is wise;
17 reads the knave's heart as easily as the fool's. He can thwart the coun-
18 sellor, bemuse the judge, exchange the king's baldric for the rope of a
19 prisoner, lead the priest away unfrocked, disseise the noble, bewitch the
21 lips that never erred, rob the elder of his prudence, bring princes into
22 disgrace, relieve the oppressed.[1] Things deep hidden in darkness he
23 reveals, kindles the light where death's shadow lay, brings growth or
24 ruin to a people, and what he has ruined restores. The hearts of chief-
25 tains he bewilders, leading them by false paths to vain ends, till all light
    fails, and they grope about in darkness, wander aimless like a drunkard
    after his wine.

CHAPTER THIRTEEN

2 EYES nor ears nor wits are wanting to me, and I know all this as
3 well as you, but I will still try a fall with you. Or rather, it is to God,
4 the omnipotent, I will speak; against him lies my complaint; but first I
   would prove you what you are, unskilful plasterers all of you, that follow
5 false rules of your craft. Would you but hold your tongues once for all!
6 It were your best wisdom. Listen while I refute you; mark well what are
7 my pleadings. Do you think God stands in need of your shifts, your
8 lying advocacy? Are you God's hired partisans, resolved to acquit
9 him? Why then, beware of his own infallible scrutiny; think you he will
10 be blinded, as men are blinded, by your sophistries? Nay, he himself will
11 be the first to blame you for wrongful attachment to his cause; your
12 turn, then, to fear his offended majesty, to cower before his terrors! Your
   wise memories will vanish into dust, your blustering contentions prove to
   be things of clay.
13 Nay, hold your tongues for a little, while I say out my mind. Do not
15 ask why I set my teeth so firmly,[2] take my life in my hand; let him slay
   me if he will! I await his decree;[3] needs must that I should make my

---

[1] 'Relieve the oppressed'; according to the Hebrew text, 'loosen the girdle of
the strong'; the Latin rendering is quite out of keeping with the context.

[2] Literally 'tear (in the Hebrew text, carry) my flesh in my teeth'; evidently
this was a proverbial way of expressing rashness, like that in the second half
of the verse.

[3] Literally, 'even if he slays me, I will hope in him.' But the true sense of the
verse is hard to determine; there are two traditions of the Hebrew text, one
reading 'I will wait' and the other 'I will not wait.'

16 defence before him, and spare me he will; let the guilty shun his presence,
17 not I. Nay, hear me out; let me open my mind in full; should I stand my
19 trial, I know that I must be found innocent! Only let me meet my
accuser! Why must I die unheard?[1]
20   But two rights I claim, if I am to face thee openly; withdraw thy
22 chastising hand, and daunt me with thy terrors no longer. Then, if thou
wilt call me in question, I will make reply; or let me speak, and be thou
23 ready with thy answer. Tell me, what are all these transgressions, these
24 faults thou findest in me? What crime, what wrong-doing is mine? Why
25 is it that thou turnest thy back on me, and wilt treat me as an enemy? As
26 well wrestle with a flying leaf, chase a wisp of straw, as keep this jealous
27 record against me, tax me with the offences of my youth! To hold me so
28 close a prisoner, watch me wherever I go, track my foot-prints, when I
am no better than rotting carrion, than a garment fretted away by the
moth!

CHAPTER FOURTEEN

2 SO frail man's life, woman-born, so full of trouble, brief as a flower
that blooms and withers, fugitive as a shadow, changing all the
3 while; and is he worth that watchfulness of thine, must thou needs call
4 him to account? (Who can cleanse what is born of tainted stock, save
5 thou alone, who alone hast being?) [2] Brief, brief are man's days; thou
keepest count of the months left to him, thou dost appoint for him the
6 bound he may not pass. And wilt thou not leave him undisturbed, to
enjoy his little day of drudgery? [3]
7   Were he but as the trees are! A tree has hope to live by: pollarded, it
8 still grows green, and fresh branches spring from it. Root and stock old
9 and withered, down in the dusty earth, but at the breath of water it
10 revives, and the leaves come, as they came when it first was planted. For
us mortal men, death; a stripping, and a breathing out of the soul, and all
11 is over. Where is the sea, when its waters dry up, the river when its bed
12 is empty? So man falls asleep, never to rise again while heaven endures;
13 from that sleep there is no waking, there is no rousing him. Ah, if the

---

[1] It is possible to interpret the Hebrew text as meaning, 'Who is there that will accuse me? If anybody can, then I will remain silent and go to my death'; but this fits the context less naturally.

[2] In the Hebrew text, this verse reads simply, 'Who can bring the clean from the unclean? Not one'; there is no agreement either as to the meaning of the phrase or as to its relevance in the discussion, and some think it has been accidentally misplaced.

[3] Or possibly, 'Wilt thou not leave him undisturbed for a little, poor drudge, until his welcome day (of release) comes to him?'

grave were only a place of shelter, where thou wouldst hide me away until thy anger was spent, with a time appointed when thou wouldst bethink
14 thyself of me again! [1] Strange thought, if the dead could rise! Then I could wait willingly enough, all the time of my campaigning, till I were
15 relieved at my post; thou wouldst summon me at last, and I would answer thy summons, thy creature, safe in thy loving hand! [2]
16 So jealous a record thou keepest of every step I take, and hast thou no
17 pardon for my faults? Instead, must thou seal up every wrong-doing of mine, as in a casket; cover away, as with a plaster, my transgressions? [3]
18 Nay there is no help for it; mountain-side or cliff that begins to crumble
19 scales away and vanishes at last, water hollows into the hard rock, and floods wear away the firm ground at last, and thou hast made no less
20 inevitable man's doom. His brief mastery thou takest away for ever; the
21 lively hue changes, and he is gone. His children rise to honour, sink to
22 shame, and he none the wiser; nothing man feels save the pains that rack him in life, the griefs that fret his soul. [4]

CHAPTER FIFTEEN

2 THEN answered Eliphaz the Themanite: This is not a wise man's way, to answer with windy sophistries, as if thou hadst the sirocco in
3 thy blood, ill matched for the contest, prating to thy hurt. Worse, if thou hadst thy way, all reverence should be abolished, all devotion at an
5 end. Thy tongue takes its instructions from a sinful heart; this is rebel
6 speech. No need for me to prove thee a guilty man, thy words prove it; thy own lips arraign thee.
7 Tell me, was thine some primeval birth; wast thou made before the
8 hills? Hast thou overheard the secrets of God's council-chamber, that
9 thou thinkest him no match for thee in wisdom? What knowledge hast

---

[1] Cf. Gen. 8.1.

[2] The unfulfilled condition here expressed is represented in the Latin version as if it were something which is actually happening, but such a rendering is plainly out of harmony with the context.

[3] There has been much discussion over the meaning of these two verses, and over the position which they occupy in the argument. Some think they are part of the unfulfilled condition which goes before, and that the hiding away of man's sin is represented as something desirable; others, that they express the actual condition of things, and that man's sins are represented as treasured up against him, *i.e.*, remaining unforgiven. Once again the suspicion arises that they really belong to a different context.

[4] The words 'in life' do not occur in the Hebrew text, and some think that the verse refers to the (entirely self-regarding) unhappiness of the soul after death.

10 thou but we share it, what discernment greater than ours? We too have
   ancients among us, grey-headed men that have seen more days than any
11 father of thine. It should be no great matter for God to comfort thee, if
12 thy untimely speech did not forbid it;[1] what mean these transports, why
13 does that eye roll so wildly? What pride is this that would cross God
14 himself, moving thee to rash utterance? It is not in man to live a life all
15 blameless; never son of woman yet found acquittal. Fickle natures God
   finds among his very angels; the purity of heaven itself does not suffice
16 him; what of man, the abominable, the defiled, athirst ever for wrong-
   doing?
17   Listen, while I tell thee my mind; thou shalt hear what my own eyes
18 have witnessed; thou shalt hear what wise men have said, making known
19 the tradition of their fathers, that dwelt ever in their own land, and held
   no commerce with strangers.
20   Proudly though he carry himself all his days, the godless man is on the
21 rack; how long will his tyrannous reign last? All the while, terror whis-
22 pers in his ear; danger there is none, but he sees plots everywhere. Treads
   he by dark ways, he never hopes to see light again, swords here, swords
23 there to threaten him; ventures he out in search of food,[2] he doubts not
24 his last hour is at hand; dangers threaten him, difficulties hedge him
25 round, as though he were a king making ready for battle. And all because
26 he chose God for his enemy, matched himself against omnipotence; head
27 high in air he made the onslaught, proud of his strong sinews, like a bull
   with hanging dewlap and well-covered flanks.[3]
28   Now he is like some plant that grows[4] amid deserted streets, upon
29 houses uninhabited that lie in ruins; no root shall he strike into the earth,
30 of true wealth or abiding prosperity; never leave the shadows, but he
31 is withered up by the heat or carried away by the blast. Let no fond
32 hope delude him that he can buy off his doom; fall he must before his

---

[1] The Hebrew text here is usually understood as meaning, 'Art thou not
content with God's consolations, his word spoken gently to thee?'

[2] The Hebrew text here may be corrupt, and has to be rendered with considerable interpolations: 'He (imagines himself at some future time) wandering
(to look) for food, (and saying to himself) Where (is any to be found)?' In
any case, it is probable that Eliphaz is still describing the tortures of a bad
conscience, not some actual punishment of the wicked.

[3] The words 'like a bull' are not in the original; but the Hebrew notion of
fat as a symbol of arrogance cannot well be reproduced in English without
the use of simile.

[4] In the original, simply 'he dwells.' Some have imagined that the wicked
man lives among the ruins of his victims' estates; others, that he is represented
as daring God's vengeance by rebuilding accursed cities (cf. Jos. 6.26). But in
view of the plant-metaphors which follow, it seems more probable that Eliphaz
is comparing the wicked to an ill-rooted plant, like Baldad in 8.11–19.

33 time; withered the palm, despoiled the vine with clusters yet unripe,
34 shed the olive's flower. Barren, barren the schemer's plot; the house
35 of the perjured man shall burn about his ears. Vainly engendered, borne
in the womb, brought forth, their load of misery and infamy and shame.

CHAPTER SIXTEEN

2 BUT Job answered: Old tales and cold comfort; you are all
3 alike. Words are but wind; there is no end to them, and they cost
4 thee nothing. Believe me, I could do as well, were you in my case, talk
6 the language of consolation, and mock you all the while, speak of en-
7 couragement, and make mouths at you under a show of pity.[1] But here is
8 grief words cannot assuage, nor silence banish; grief that bows me down
9 till my whole frame is lifeless; these furrowed cheeks are the witness of it.
10   And now a false accuser dares me to my face and baits me![2] One that
vents all his spite against me, gnashes his teeth malignantly, watches
11 me with fierce eyes like an enemy. Mouths that deride me, hands that
12 smite me on the cheek in reproof, hearts that delight in my anguish, to
what ill neighbourhood God has condemned me, what tyrants hold me
in their grip!
13   So free from care my life was, and now, suddenly as a wild beast that
fastens on its prey, dashes it to the ground, he has broken that life to
14 pieces. I am a mark for his archery, his arrows are all about me; still they
15 pierce me to the marrow, drain my life,[3] wound upon wound; giant hands
16 assail me. No wonder if I go clad in sackcloth, disfigured with ashes, if
my face is swollen with weeping, and on my eyelids the darkness falls.
18   Such is the reward of a guiltless life, of prayer offered without stain. I
charge thee, earth, to leave my blood unburied, never to muffle the
20 echoes of my protest; there is one in high heaven that knows the truth

---

[1] Both in the Hebrew text and in the Latin version, the exact train of thought
may be variously interpreted.

[2] 'And now a false accuser dares me to my face and baits me'; according
to some the meaning is, 'My leanness gives open proof of it,' which corresponds
well with the former half of the verse. For those who adopt this rendering,
it is possible to understand the verbs in verse 10 as referring to God himself.
The 'false accuser' can hardly refer to God; and only by a strong rhetorical
exaggeration could it refer to Eliphaz. It seems more likely that in this section
Job is thinking of his spiritual enemies, perhaps as he has seen them in night
visions (7.14).

[3] 'Still they pierce me to the marrow, drain my life'; literally, 'without respite
he wounds my loins (in the Hebrew, kidneys), and pours out my bowels (in
the Hebrew, gall) upon the ground.'

21 and must bear witness. Friends, prate on; these tears of mine issue their
22 challenge to a God! Ah, could but a mortal bring God to justice, as man
23 impleads man! Mortal am I; swiftly my years pass, and by the road I
tread there is no returning.

CHAPTER SEVENTEEN

BROKEN my will to live, shortened my days, the grave my only pros-
2 pect; my eye lingers on sights of bitterness, never through my
3 fault![1] Lord, wouldst thou but vindicate me, and set me right with thee!
4 I care not who else is for or against me.[2] For these, at least, I care not;
thou hast robbed their hearts of all discernment, and they shall have
5 no cause for boasting. Small thanks a man has for counting out the
spoils, while his children go hungry![3]
6 A public by-word God has made me, a warning in all men's sight, my
8 eyes grown dim, my whole frame wasted away, in my resentment. Here
is sore bewilderment for honest hearts; angrily do innocent men complain,
9 to see knaves prosper; will the just be true to their resolve any longer?
10 Will they be encouraged to keep their hands clean?[4] Nay, sirs, return
to the charge as often as you will; I do not look to find a wise man
among you.
11 Swift pass my days, my mind distracted with whirling thoughts, that
make night into day for me, as through the hours of darkness I await
13 the dawn. Waiting for what? The grave is my destined home; among the
14 shadows I must make my bed at last; only from corruption I claim a
father's welcome, mother's and sister's greeting the worms shall offer
16 me; what hope is this? Wait I patiently or impatiently, who cares? Into
the deep pit I must go down, all of me; even there, in the dust, shall I
find rest?[5]

---

[1] The Hebrew text here is generally understood as meaning, 'There are
mockers at my side, and my eye dwells on their provocations.'

[2] Literally, in the Latin version, 'Deliver me, Lord, and set me close to thee,
and let who will fight against me'; in the Hebrew text, 'Go bail for me, Lord;
who (else) will be my security?'

[3] Literally, 'He promises spoils to his companions, and the eyes of his children
will languish.' The Hebrew text is very obscure, and is thought by many to
be corrupt; the copyist may have been baffled by the unexpected appearance
of a proverb, perhaps on the subject of boasting.

[4] This verse fits best into the context if it is understood as a question; those
who take it as a statement regard it as an allusion to Job himself.

[5] The Hebrew text here is largely different and wholly obscure.

CHAPTER EIGHTEEN

2 THEN answered Baldad the Suhite: Ah, you word-mongers, you have
      never had enough! First grasp our meaning, and we might argue to
3 some purpose; but no, to men like thee we are worthless as dumb
4 beasts.[1] See with what fury he rends his own bosom! Must earth be
   dispeopled, must the rocks be torn from their place, to gratify one man's
   despairing mood?
5 Nay, the hopes of the wicked man are a light that shall be put out; a very
6 will of the wisp; darkness shall fall over his dwelling-place, and the lamp
7 that shone there will shine no more. The boldness of his own stride takes
8 him prisoner; his own devices recoil against him; into the trap he walks,
9 struggles vainly with its meshes; now he is laid by the heels! Mounts ever
10 higher his burning thirst.[2] The ground sown with snares, pit-falls about
11 his path, fears attend him everywhere, catch everywhere at his feet.
12 His strength brought low by famine, hunger gnawing at his sides and
13 wasting all his beauty, death in its primal guise shall devour those
14 limbs.[3] Gone the security of his home, now its master lies under the heels
15 of tyrant death; in his house strangers [4] shall dwell, on his lands brimstone
16 be scattered, root never grow beneath nor harvest rise from it.[5] Gone
   the fame of him, gone the name of him, from street and country-
18 side,[6] eclipsed in utter darkness, lost to the world. Root nor branch of
   his posterity shall remain among his folk, vanished every trace of him
20 from the lands he knew. That doom with terror and amazement high and
21 low shall witness.[7] Here (they will say) was a home of wrong-doing; he
   who lived here, lived a stranger to God.

---

[1] Job is here addressed in the plural. Some picture the scene of the whole
book as a kind of public debate (cf. 32.2) and suppose that the audience was
divided in its sympathies. But it seems more likely that 'you' means 'thou and
people like thee,' 'you critics of Providence.'

[2] The word rendered 'thirst' in the Latin is of uncertain meaning.

[3] Literally, 'first-born death,' in the Hebrew text, 'the first-born of death.'
This is usually interpreted of fever or some other kind of disease, but without
evidence. The context here would suggest rather starvation.

[4] Literally, in the Latin version, 'the dead man's fellows.' The phrase in
the Hebrew text is of doubtful meaning; some think that weeds are referred
to. 'On his lands'; the Latin version repeats 'in his house,' but two different
words are used in the Hebrew text, and the latter is a more general word for
the place where a man lives.

[5] Or possibly 'from him,' cf. verse 19.

[6] *vv.* 12–17. The verbs of this passage are represented by the Latin, unsuit-
ably, as expressing a wish.

[7] 'High and low'; literally 'the last and the first,' which may also be explained
as meaning 'later generations and earlier generations.' Some interpret the
Hebrew text as meaning 'men of the west and men of the east.'

CHAPTER NINETEEN

1 BUT Job answered: What, will you torment me still? Every word of
3 yours a fresh blow of the hammer? How many times is this you have
4 fallen on me, trampled me down without ruth? If, unawares, I have com-
5 mitted some fault, it concerns none but myself; not for you to claim
authority over me, bring home to me my disgrace!
6 How to make you understand that God has misjudged me, caught me
7 in his toils! If I cry out upon that my wrongs, there is none to hear me,
8 none to take cognisance of my plea; my path hedged in, so that there is
9 no escape, my direction lost, and I benighted. By him discredited, dis-
10 crowned, by him left defenceless on every side, I go my ways; a tree torn
11 up by the roots has more to hope for than I. Against me all his anger is
12 aroused; I am that enemy against whom he musters all his forces, to ride
13 over me, to beleaguer my dwelling place. Sundered am I from my
14 brethren, a stranger to all that knew me, forsaken by my kindred, by
15 my friends forgotten. Guests that dwell in my house, ay, and the very
16 serving-women, stare at me, the alien, the unknown; my servants do not
17 come at my call, I must speak them fair; my wife shuns the breath of me,
18 to my own flesh and blood [1] I am a suppliant. The very innocents [2] despise
19 me, jeer at me when my back is turned; no counsellor so trusted but he is
20 weary of me, no friend so loved but he abandons me now. And I so
wasted! Skin clinging to bone, save where the lips cover my teeth, is all
that is left of me.[3]
21 Friends, friends, do you at least have pity, now when God's hand has
22 fallen on me! Would you take part in God's hue and cry against me,
23 slander me to your hearts' content? [4] Could but these words of mine be
24 written down in a book, graven with a pen of iron upon tablets of lead,
chiselled on hard flint! [5]
25 This at least I know, that one lives on who will vindicate me, rising up

---

[1] Literally, 'the sons of my womb.' This may be taken as meaning 'sons of my body' (Job's description of his loneliness being only rhetorical; cp. 1.19), or as meaning 'sons of the same mother as myself.'

[2] In the Latin version, 'fools,' in the Hebrew text, 'little children.'

[3] The Hebrew text appears to run: 'To my skin, to my flesh, my bones cling; I have escaped by the skin of my teeth.' It is difficult to see how the English phrase (derived from this passage) fits in here.

[4] 'Slander me'; literally, 'eat my flesh,' a well known Hebrew idiom.

[5] The word *celte*, said to mean 'a chisel,' does not occur anywhere else in Latin literature, and is thought by some to be a misprint in our Bibles for *certe;* 'Upon tablets of lead, or perhaps upon flint.'

26 from the dust when the last day comes.¹ Once more my skin shall clothe
27 me, and in my flesh I shall have sight of God.² I myself, with my own
eyes; it will not be something other than myself that sees him. Deep in
my heart is this hope reposed.³
28 You that would raise the hue and cry, finding matter of complaint
29 against me, should rather take flight yourselves, the sword at your heels;
the sword that avenges wrong, proof to you that justice shall be done.

CHAPTER TWENTY

2 THEN answered Sophar the Naamathite: Strange hesitation thy words
3 breed in me; my thoughts veer to and fro. Not deaf am I to thy
4 pleadings, but there is a voice in my heart gives me pause. Certain it is
5 that never since man found a place on earth did the wrong-doer win
lasting triumph; only for a little time does knavery bring him content.
6 Let his pride overtop heaven itself, his head be lifted high as the
7 clouds, he is for the dung-hill at last; none knows what has become of
8 him. Vanished and gone like a dream, the phantom of yesternight,
9 unmarked by human eyes, lost to the scenes he knew! Crushing poverty
shall be his children's lot; his acts shall yield their own harvest of
11 shame, all the lusty vigour of his frame doomed, like himself, to silence
12 and the dust. Sweet in the mouth is the taste of evil-doing; how the
13 tongue cherishes it! How he treasures it, loth to lose the secret pleasure
14 of his palate! But once let that food reach his belly, not the gall of adders
15 is so venomous. The wealth he loved to swallow, disgorge he must; God
16 will make his belly return it; poisonous as the asp's head or the viper's
17 tongue were those juices he sucked, when he thought to enjoy streams of
plenty; honey and cream should have been his in rich abundance.
18 Endlessly he shall pay for the wrong he did, plagued in the measure
19 of his own false dealings. He who oppressed and robbed the poor shall
20 never prosper with his ill-gotten fortunes; he, the insatiable, will not
21 keep what he so coveted; he, that never had a crust to spare, will be
22 stripped now of all his goods. Once so full fed, now he goes in need;

---

¹ In the Hebrew text, it is the Vindicator himself, not Job, who will 'stand
up over the dust hereafter.'
² The first part of this verse is unintelligible in the Hebrew text; it appears
to mean 'And after (or, afterwards) they will strip my skin, this.' Probably
the reading is corrupt, but the other versions do not bear out the sense given
by the Latin. 'In my flesh'; literally 'from my flesh,' which some would interpret
as meaning, 'deprived of my flesh.'
³ *v.* 27. 'Something other than myself'; literally, 'a stranger.' The end of the
verse, in the Hebrew text, reads 'My inmost thoughts die away in my bosom.'

23 stands in doubt, with distress crowding in on every side; ah for a meal
to fill his belly with! But no, God's angry vengeance is let loose on him,
24 raining down all its weapons; shuns he the steel, to the bow of bronze
25 he falls a prey. Bright and bitter the drawn sword threatens; about him,
26 dread warriors come and go.[1] He hides away, where thick darkness
broods over him;[2] straightway a fire no human hand has kindled threatens
to devour him; woe betide any that would take refuge in that dwell-
27 ing! Heaven will reveal the story of his crimes, earth itself rise in revolt
28 against him; all the promise of his race will be laid bare and torn away,
in that hour of the Lord's vengeance.[3]
29   Such is the lot God sends to the wicked, such their divinely appointed
doom.

CHAPTER TWENTY-ONE

2 B UT Job answered: Listen, do but listen to me, and then, if you will,
3 repent of your charity; let me have my say, and then mock on. It
is not as if I bore a grudge against man; I have better reason than that
5 to be indignant. Mark my complaint well, and you shall be astonished,
6 hold your breath[4] in amazement, as I too tremble with dismay at the
thought of it.

7   How is it that godless men live on, meet with advancement, enjoy their
8 riches undisturbed? Long they live, to see their posterity thrive about
9 them, kinsmen and grandsons thronging all around. Safe and sound their
10 dwelling-place; God's scourge passes them by; never bull of theirs failed
11 to gender, cow to calve; blithe as lambs the little children go out to
12 play; everywhere is tambour and harp-playing, everywhere the pipe's
13 merry note. So, full of ease, their life passes, and they go down at last
without a struggle to the grave.

14   And these are the men who bade God keep his distance from them,
15 refused to learn his will;[5] what right had he, the Omnipotent, to their

---

[1] This sentence has, in the original, no subject. The Hebrew text is usually
interpreted as referring to the act of drawing the arrow out of a wound.

[2] Literally, 'all darkness is concealed in his hidden things.'

[3] 'The promise of his race'; literally, 'the bud of his house,' a phrase not
elsewhere paralleled. 'Be laid bare'; in the Hebrew text, 'go into exile.'

[4] Literally, 'put your hands on your mouths.'

[5] *vv.* 14–33. The interpretation here given to this passage is designed to make
Job's remarks consistent with each other and with his general line of argument.
Several of them would appear at first sight (especially as read in the Latin
version) to favour the notion that God inflicts signal punishment on evil-doers.
But it seems clear that these do not reflect Job's own sentiments; they are an
ironical presentation of his opponents' point of view, *e.g.*, verse 16 and the
first half of verse 19.

obedience, what advantage would they gain by offering prayer to him?
16 These are the godless folk whose counsel I must shun because they
17 cannot command their own good fortune! Tell me, how often in very
deed are the hopes of the wicked extinguished, engulfed by the flood?
18 Does God's vengeance often deal out misfortune to them, sweeping
them away like chaff before the wind, ashes beneath the storm?
19 But perhaps God is reserving for the children punishment of their
father's sins? Nay, let the sinner himself feel the retribution when it
20 comes; his own eyes must see the blow fall, his own lips drink in the
21 divine vengeance! Little he cares what befalls his posterity after he is
gone, though halved be the time of its continuance.

22 The God that passes judgement on his angels needs none to instruct
23 him![1] It is man's lot in life that signifies;[2] one man goes to his death
24 sound and strong, rich and happy, well covered with flesh, his bones full
25 of marrow; another, all misery and poverty, and he, no less than the
other, has dust for bed, worms for coverlet.

27 Spare me those thoughts I know already, those reasons that would
28 crush me! What becomes of the tyrant's palace, of the evil-doer's home,
29 at last? Ask any wayfarer (you say) that knows them, and you shall hear
30 the same account of the matter: The rogue's villainy is being reserved
31 for future punishment, he is being slowly drawn on to his doom. Fools,
how can anyone bring home his guilt to him now, punish the wrong he
32 did? He is being slowly drawn on to burial, with men to keep watch over
33 his tomb, an honoured guest in the valley's stony bed,[3] with a throng of
mourners behind and before, past all counting.

34 Vain is all your consolation, while the answer you give me matches
so ill with truth.

---

[1] It is hard to see how this verse fits into the context, and some think it has
been misplaced. The idea seems to be that Job's comforters are offering an
apology for the Providential order such as God himself would not approve of.

[2] 'It is man's lot in life that signifies'; these words are not in the original,
they have been supplied so as to make the argument easier to follow. Nobody
will be deterred from sinful ways by the fear of what may happen to his children, if he thinks that his own happiness will be unaffected by his behaviour.

[3] The Latin here gives the strange rendering, 'the gravel of Cocytus.' In
pagan mythology, Cocytus was a river flowing through the underworld.

CHAPTER TWENTY-TWO

2 THEN answered Eliphaz the Themanite: A man cannot hope to
3 implead God, even a man of perfect wisdom. Just though thou be,
how is God the better for knowing thou art just? Can stainless life of
4 thine advantage him? Or dost thou think that fear of thee will persuade
5 him to appear in court, and prove thee in the wrong? [1] Must he browbeat
6 thee over a long record of guilt,[2] over many heinous deeds done; remind
thee of the usurer's pledge needlessly taken, of thy brother left to go naked
while thou hadst his garment by thee, of water grudged to thirsty men,
8 bread refused to the hungry? Must he tell the story of a rich tyrant that
9 had lands and held to them; of widows sent away without redress,
10 orphans left without support, through thy means? Must he say, that
11 is why thou art caught in the snare, dismayed by sudden peril, left
benighted when thou thoughtest to see day, overwhelmed by the unexpected flood?
12   Bethink thee, God is high as heaven itself, reaches beyond the utter-
13 most star. Wouldst thou tell us that he has no knowledge of what passes,
14 that he issues his decree blindly, gives no heed to our mortal doings,
15 there where he walks above heaven's vault, all wrapped in cloud? That
were to follow old paths of error, trodden long ago by impious feet.
16 Snatched away before their time were the men that reasoned so; a flood
17 engulfed the solid ground beneath them. These, beyond doubt, were
men who bade God keep his distance from them, thought the Omnipotent
18 could give them no aid, when he had filled their abode with blessings!

---

[1] *vv.* 2–4. The Hebrew text is ordinarily understood as meaning: 'Can a man
render useful service (by living an innocent life) to God? No, it is of service
only to himself. Can the Almighty take any pleasure in the fact that thou art
upright, is it any gain to him if thou followest honest paths? Is it because of
thy fear of him that he finds fault with thee, comes to court as thy adversary?'
But, although this apparently gives a satisfactory account of the various
sentences, it leaves an unbridgeable gulf in logic between verse 3 and verse 4.
The Latin version yields a greatly preferable sense: God cannot be expected
to answer Job's summons to trial, since he has no motive, whether of interest
or of fear, for doing so.

[2] The Latin version begins the sentence with the words 'Is it not rather
because of . . .' But this seems due to an erroneous apprehension of the Hebrew
original. The Hebrew text reads simply, 'Are not thy wickednesses many and
thy faults endless?' This is generally understood as a charge brought by Eliphaz
against Job; but such a sudden attack on Job's character would be out of
keeping with the rest of the chapter, and indeed of the book. Verses 5–11 fall
better into place if they are understood as an imaginary address by Almighty
God to an imaginary sinner (cf. Ps. 49.16–21).

19 Not for nothing do I shun their counsels! Here was a sight to make the
20 just triumphant, make innocent folk laugh aloud in scorn, to see how
their proud hopes vanished, and all that was left of them perished in the
flames.[1]
21   Make thy peace with him, as thou lovest thy own well-being; so shall
22 fair hopes attend thee. Let his lips be thy oracle, his words written on
23 thy heart. Turn back to the Almighty for thy healing, and rid thy
24 dwelling-place of guilt. Firm rock thou shalt have for shifting dust,
25 and for firm rock streams of gold; the Almighty himself will be thy
26 shield, and silver thou shalt never lack.[2] In those omnipotent arms
27 thou shalt rest content, thy face upturned towards God himself, thy
28 prayer heard as soon as offered, thy vows paid as soon as due; all thy
29 desire thou shalt have, and all thy paths will be sunshine. He that was
once brought low shall be high in renown; the downcast eye shall win
deliverance.
30   But the innocent shall be kept safe; in a pair of clean hands there was
safety ever.[3]

CHAPTER TWENTY-THREE

2 BUT Job answered: And still I repine bitterly as ever, no groaning
3 too heavy for the wounds I bear. Ah, if I could but find my way to
4 God, reach his very throne, in reproachful accents plead my suit before
5 him, and learn what he would say in his defence, grasp the meaning of
6 it! Must his great power still be used to crush me, silence my plea by
7 constraint? The justice of my cause once made known to him, I should
triumph at last.
8   But no; travel I east or west, I find no trace of him, turn I left or
10 right, I have no skill to catch sight of him. And he, all the while, keeps
11 watch over my doings, tests me like gold the fire assays; he knows how
12 close I have kept to the path he traced for me, swerving never aside, true

---

[1] *vv.* 15–20. Some definite historical situation seems to be envisaged, but
it cannot be identified with certainty. The Deluge has been suggested in view
of verse 16, the destruction of Sodom in view of verse 20; the death of Core
and his companions (Num. 16) is also a possible solution.

[2] *vv.* 24, 25. The Hebrew text here is usually interpreted, 'Put (thy) gold-
ore upon the dust, and thy (gold of) Ophir upon the rocks of the valleys; then
the Almighty will be thy gold-ore . . .,' &c. The Latin version has probably
failed to recognize the word for gold-ore, rendering it in one verse 'flint-stone'
and in the other 'against thy enemy.' But it is doubtful whether our present
Hebrew text is genuine; it is not easy to see why Eliphaz should encourage
a man who has just lost all his possessions to throw away his gold.

[3] *vv.* 29, 30. The sense of the Hebrew text here is doubtful.

to every command of his, every utterance of his cherished in my heart.
13 But what of that? He reigns without a rival, none can cross his purposes;
14 he does what likes him best. His will once fully accomplished in me,
15 he has many another like purpose to fulfil. What wonder if I am all
16 adread in his presence, if the thought of him racks me with terror? It
is God that melts my heart with fear, his omnipotence that daunts
17 me; that thought unmans me, not the surrounding darkness, not the
mists which hide my view.[1]

CHAPTER TWENTY-FOUR

SINCE he, who is omnipotent, determines every event, how is it that
those who know him wait in vain for his doom to fall?[2]
2   Here are men that alter their neighbour's landmark, drive stolen
3 cattle to pasture, rob the orphan of his ass, take the widow's ox in
4 pawn, shoulder the poor aside, conspire to oppress the friendless; leave
others to make their living as best they may, like the wild ass in the
6 desert, waking betimes to scrape food for hungry mouths at home. Reap
they the field that is none of theirs, strip they the vineyard wrongfully
7 seized from its owner; let men go bare, their garments snatched away,
8 defenceless against cold and rain on the mountain side, so that they are
9 fain to hug the rocks for lack of shelter. Their violence robs the helpless
10 children, despoils the poor and simple; back and side must go bare, and
11 never a stalk left for hungry men to glean; huddled they must lie under
12 the noon's heat that trod the wine-press, and still are thirsty![3] A cry goes
up from the city streets, where wounded men lie groaning; tell me, does
not God allow it to pass unheeded?[4]
13   How they shun the light, these rebels who ignore God's precepts,
14 leave his paths untrodden! The murderer must be stirring before daybreak, to catch his helpless prey, or prowl, as the thieves prowl, at
15 night. For darkness, too, the adulterer waits, no eye must scan his muffled
16 features; under cover of darkness he will break into the house, to keep the

---

[1] *v.* 17. This somewhat forced rendering seems to be the only way of reading
this obscure passage, if the text is sound.
[2] Literally, 'Times are not hidden from the omnipotent, but those who know
him are ignorant of his days.'
[3] *vv.* 2–11. The Latin version is here in disagreement, occasionally, with
the Hebrew text, which is itself very difficult. It is not always easy to see
whether the subject of a particular sentence is the wicked, or their victims.
[4] It seems necessary to understand the end of this verse as a question; otherwise the Latin flatly contradicts the meaning, both of the Hebrew text and of
the Septuagint Greek, nor can we easily suppose it to have been Job's opinion.

17 tryst made yesterday; no light for him. To him, the first flush of dawn
is death's shadow; deep gloom is the light he walks by.

18   Light as foam on the waters, surely he is doomed to a life of misery;
19 not for him the vineyard's sunny slope! Swift as snow melts under the
20 noon-day heat, let his guilty soul pass to the grave, unpitied, with worms
for its boon-companions, forgotten, overthrown like an unfruitful tree!
21 The childless woman was his prey; [1] in vain the widow looked to him for
22 redress; now, surely, God has pulled the tyrant down; firm he has stood,
23 but now he despairs of life itself! Time for repentance God gave him,
24 by his pride misused, but ever on his doings kept a watchful eye; now,
their brief renown over, such men must pass, as all things pass, into the
dust, be carried off, swept away like ears of corn! [2]
25   But no, never the day comes! Who dares give me the lie, challenge me
in God's sight? [3]

CHAPTER TWENTY-FIVE

2 THEN answered Baldad the Suhite: Ay, but what power, ay, but what
3 terrors he wields, who reigns peacefully, there in high heaven! He,
4 the lord of countless armies, he, whose light dazzles every eye! And shall
man, born of woman, win his suit, prove his innocence, when he is
5 matched with God? Dim shews the moon, tarnished the stars, under
6 his eye; poor worm that breeds corruption, what is mortal man in his
presence?

CHAPTER TWENTY-SIX

2 BUT Job answered: Bravely spoken, for a cause that so much needed
3 it! That arm of thine ever upheld the weak. Brave advice offered in
4 that great discernment of thine, to one who so lacks wisdom! A fine
lesson thou hast read him, the God who gave thee breath!
5   Sure enough, there is none but trembles before him; even the old
heroes, and those who share their dwelling-place under the lower depths;
6 bare to his eyes is the place of shadows, oblivion lies revealed. He it

---

[1] 'Was his prey'; the Latin word used can mean either 'fed' or 'fed upon.'

[2] *vv.* 18–24. These verses, with their threat of calamity to the wicked, should
perhaps be understood as an ideal consummation which, as verse 25 points
out, does not seem to be verified in fact. Their exact sense is largely open to
dispute.

[3] The meaning of the Hebrew text is probably, 'reduce my words to nothingness.'

was spread out the northern skies over emptiness, poised earth on
8 nothing; cloud-bound he holds the rain, that else would spill on earth
9 all at once, veiled and shut in with cloud his unseen throne. While day
11 and night last, the waters keep the bounds he has decreed for them; the
12 very pillars of heaven tremble awe-struck at his will. His the power that
drew the seas together all in a moment, his the wisdom that struck the
13 rebellious dragon down; his the spirit that clothed the heavens, his the
14 hand that drew yonder writhing serpent from the womb.[1] Here is but a
small part of his doings, here is but the whisper of his voice; who dares
to contemplate the thunder of his full magnificence?

CHAPTER TWENTY-SEVEN

2 AND thus Job continued to lay bare his thought: As sure as he is a
living God, he, the omnipotent, who so refuses me justice, who
3 makes my lot in life so bitter; while life is in me, while he still grants me
4 breath, never shall these lips condone the wrong, never this tongue utter
5 the lie! Gain your point with me you shall not; I will die sooner than
6 abandon my plea of innocence. That claim, once made, I will not forgo;
7 not one act in all my life bids conscience reproach me. Count him a
knave that is my enemy, every detractor of mine a friend of wrong![2]
8 (What is the sinner's hope worth after all, when God takes the life
9 away from him?[3] In that hour of need, his cry for reprieve will go
10 unheard; he cannot go on for ever basking in the Almighty's favour,

---

[1] 'Drew . . . from the womb'; rather, 'pierced through'; see Is. 51.9, where
the same verb is used in the Hebrew text. Here, as in that passage, the power
of the sea is allegorically described as a proud monster, the darkness of night
(perhaps) as a writhing serpent.

[2] This verse may be taken, instead, with what follows, and interpreted as
meaning, 'May the sinner, the wrong-doer, fare as I would have my own
enemies and detractors fare.'

[3] *vv.* 8–23. These verses, or most of them, are thought by some scholars
to have been accidentally misplaced, belonging properly to Baldad's speech
in ch. 25, or to some other utterance by Job's interlocutors. It is undeniable
that upon first reading they seem to tell against, not for, the point of view Job
has hitherto supported; and it is curious that Job should be the speaker all
through chapters 26–31 inclusive. If our present text is accurate, the following
observations may be made on it. Verses 8–23 are probably concerned only with
what happens after the sinner's death; Job's complaint has been that the sinner
is not punished during life. Possibly, then, Job's speculations here take on a
new turn. Still maintaining that virtue is not rewarded or vice punished in
this life (and therefore that his own sufferings do not prove him guilty) he
asks what is the value of the brief prosperity which ends with the sinner's life-
time (cf. Luke 12.16–21). The secret of life must, after all, be something other
than the acquisition of worldly advantage. What that secret is, he proceeds to
examine in the next chapter.

11 calling God to his aid. Now be God's hand laid bare, now let me
12 acknowledge openly the counsels of omnipotence! Not one of you but
knows the truth of it already; yet one and all you must be urging a false
plea, without the need for it!
13   What spoil, after all, does God grant to the wicked? From his almighty
14 hand, what abiding possession does the man of violence receive? Sons
beget he never so many, what avails it, when the sword overtakes them,
15 and their children in turn must go wanting bread, when the plague gives
all the rest of his line their burial, and never a widow to bemoan them?
16 What avails it, to heap up silver like the sand, buy fine clothes, too,
17 and think such treasures cheap as dirt, if more upright men than he,
more innocent than he, must wear out those clothes, share out that silver
18 at last? Light as the moth he builds; not so frail a shelter the vineyard-
19 watcher weaves about him. Rich he is laid to rest, but nothing takes with
20 him; rich he shall wake no more.[1] Helpless in the flood, driven in dark-
21 ness by the storm, carried off, as if sirocco or whirlwind had swept him
23 away, he is routed before the pitiless onslaught, hands clapped in
triumph, tongues hissing in derision as he goes.)

CHAPTER TWENTY-EIGHT

WHERE, then, does wisdom lie? Easy to trace where the veins of
2 silver run, where gold-ore is refined, where iron is dug from the
3 depths of earth, and rocks must be melted to yield copper. See how man
has done away with the darkness, has pierced into the very heart of
4 things, into caves under ground, black as death's shadow! Where yonder
ravine cuts them off from the shepherd-folk, the miners toil, forgotten;
5 lost to all track, far from the haunts of men.[2] That earth, from whose

---

[1] Literally, in the Latin version, 'The rich man when he goes to sleep will
take nothing with him; he will open his eyes and find nothing.' The Hebrew
text seems to mean, 'Rich he shall lie down, and it shall not continue (or, he
shall never lie down again); he will open his eyes, and—nothing.' Conceivably this refers to a situation in which ruin comes upon the sinner in a single
night. But more probably it refers to his death, and the words 'he will open
his eyes' are only figurative.

[2] In the Hebrew text, this verse runs 'The ravine divides (or, he divides
the ravine) from a foreign resident the forgotten ones from the foot they
have languished from mankind they have wandered (or, tottered).' The Latin
version gives, 'The torrent divides from the exiled people those whom the
foot of the poor man has forgotten, those who are far from the beaten track.'
The guess of modern scholars which would identify the ravine as a pit-shaft,
and sees a reference to miners swinging to and fro in hanging cages, does justice
neither to the usage of words nor to the requirements of the context. The text
is probably corrupt, but we may presume that it refers to the remoteness and
hiddenness of mining operations, not to contemporary conditions of labour.

6 surface our bread comes to us, must be probed by fire beneath, till the
7 rocks yield sapphires, and the clods gold. Here are passages no bird
8 discovers in its flight, no vulture's eye has seen; that never gave roving
9 merchant shelter, or the lioness a lair. Boldly man matches himself against
10 the flint, uproots the mountain, cuts channels through the rock, where
11 things of price have dazzled his eye; narrowly he scans the river's depths,
12 and brings to light all they hide. But wisdom, tell me where to search
   for wisdom; tell me in what cache discernment lies?
13   How should man set a price on it? This earth, our pleasant home,
14 yields no return of it; Not here, cries the abyss beneath us, and the sea
15 echoes, Not here. Not for pure gold is it bartered, or weighed against
16 silver in the balance; not the bright wares of the Indies, nor jewel of
17 sardonyx, nor sapphire can vie with it; it is not to be matched with
   treasures of glass or gold, rivalled by all the goldsmith's workmanship.
18 Do not talk of coral or of crystal;[1] for wisdom you must make deeper
19 search still; with wisdom the topaz from Arabia and the finest gold-leaf
   cannot compare.
20   Whence, then, does wisdom come to us; where is discernment to be
21 found? That is the secret kept hidden from beast on earth and bird in
22 heaven; the shadow-world of death claims no more than to have heard
23 the rumour of it. Only God knows the way to it, only God can tell
24 where it lies, he whose view reaches to the world's end, sees all that
25 passes under the wide heavens. He, when first he took scale and
26 measuring-line to set wind and water their task, when he appointed a
27 time for the rain's abating, and a track for the whistling storm, descried
   wisdom already; traced its plan, and set all in order, and mastered it.
28   To man, he has told this much, that wisdom is fearing the Lord; there
   lies discernment, in refusing the evil path.

CHAPTER TWENTY-NINE

2 AND thus Job continued to lay bare his thought: Alas for the changes
   the months have brought with them! Alas for the old days, when
3 God was my protector, when his light shone above me, its rays guiding
4 me through the darkness! Days of ripe manhood, when God was my
5 home's familiar guest, he, the Almighty, at my side! I had my children
6 still about me; the milk frothed in pools at my feet, no rock so hard but
7 my olives bathed it in oil. Went I to the city gate, there was my seat

---

[1] Literally, in the Latin version, 'things high and things jutting out.' In
the Hebrew text, the second half of the verse refers to a third kind of jewel,
perhaps pearls.

8 ready for me in the open square; rose the young men to make place for
9 me, rose the aged to do me honour; nobles fell silent, and waited, finger
10 on lip, words failed the chieftains, and counsel they gave no more.
11 None heard the fame of me then, but called me a happy man; none
12 watched my doings then, but spoke in my praise. Poor man nor helpless
13 orphan cried to me in vain; I was the welcome refuge of the doomed,
14 the solace of the widow. Dutiful observance was still the vesture I wore,
15 my robe and crown integrity; in me, the blind found sight, the lame
16 strength, the poor a father. None so ready to give the stranger's cause a
17 hearing, break open the fangs of the wrong-doer and snatch the prey
   from his teeth.
18 Here, thought I, I have built myself a nest to die in; here, like some
19 palm-trunk, I shall defy the years, like a tree that spreads out its roots
20 to the river-bank, on whose leaves lodges the dew; my fame never
21 diminishing, never worn out the bow I bear. How eagerly men hung
22 upon my words, intent to learn what counsel I would give, nor ventured
23 to speak when I had done! A gracious influence my words fell, like
24 autumn rain or the spring showers on lips athirst. I smiled on them
   though they were never so ill at ease, and the encouragement of my glance
25 never failed them. Deigned I to be their leader, the first place was mine;
   yet ever when I sat like a king with his retinue about him, I would comfort the mourner's tears.

CHAPTER THIRTY

   AND now? Now I am a laughing-stock, even to younger men; a flock
2 of such base breed as theirs sheep-dog of mine never tended![1] So
   profitless their puny strength, I would have let them die before ever they
3 came to maturity. Starveling creatures, they should browse in the waste,
4 unkempt, haggard and woe-begone, cropping mallow and tree-bark and
5 juniper-root for their diet, and making great hue and cry after such
6 dainties, as they pluck them from the hill-slopes! Barren ravine and
7 cave and rock their dwelling-place, they were glad of so much shelter;
8 a bramble thicket should be their welcome refuge. A senseless and a
9 nameless breed, earth is well rid of them. O that I should be a song
10 and a by-word on such lips as these! That they loathe and shun me, and
11 make bold to spit in my face, being what they are! Now God has made
12 me a mark for his archery, now he has put a bit in my mouth; when my

---

[1] *vv.* 1–31. All through this chapter, the expressions are forced, and the con-
nexions of thought difficult to follow; it seems doubtful, in some cases, whether
the true text has been preserved to us.

fair spring was overcast by calamity,[1] every passer-by might throw me
13 down; like a flood they swept over me, trampled down my path, took me
14 unawares and overcame me, when there was none to bring rescue. One
breach made, one gate forced, they might fall upon me all at once, and add
their weight to my misery.

15 All that I was, is gone, the ambition, the happiness that was mine
16 swept away like clouds before the storm; my heart is dead within me, a
17 prey to long despairs. By night, anguish racks my frame; sleepless the
18 cares that consume me, their poison[2] seems to eat away the very garments
19 I wear, clings fast about me like the collar of my coat. No better I than
20 mud in the streets, little thought of as dust or ashes; unheard I cry to
21 thee, unregarded I stand in thy presence; so hardened is thy heart, so
22 pitilessly thy blows fall upon me. Didst thou exalt me, lift me so high
23 in air, only to hurl me down in ruin? I know well enough that thou wilt
bring me to the grave at last; it is the home thou hast appointed for all
24 living men; but surely thou dost not exert thy power only to destroy,
25 surely thou hast mercy on the fallen? I myself know what it is to pity the
26 afflicted, to shed tears over human need! But no, hope I for better things,
I hope in vain; ever deeper the darkness shews to eyes straining for the
27 light. Still my heart is in turmoil, greeted still by fresh despairs; I go
mourning, my face blacker than ever the sun's heat made it, rise up in
29 public, and claim audience for my wrongs; crying so dismally as if I had
30 jackals[3] for my brothers, ostriches for my company. And all the while,
31 fever to discolour this flesh, to shrivel this frame! What wonder if all,
with me, is mourning and lament, if the music of harp and flute is heard
no more?

CHAPTER THIRTY-ONE

AND this was a man that had bound his eyes over by covenant; never
2 should even his fancy dwell upon the thought of a maid! Well I
knew that God Almighty in high heaven would have neither part nor
3 lot with me else; ruin for the sinner his doom is, oblivion for the wrong-
4 doer. Tell me, does not this God watch over every path I take, trace my
5 footsteps one by one? Walk I by crooked ways, run I eagerly after false

---

[1] Literally, 'calamities arose at the right hand of me sprouting.' The Hebrew text is usually interpreted as meaning, 'the rabble rose up to attack me on my right hand.'

[2] Literally, 'their multitude'; the sense of the Hebrew text is quite uncertain here.

[3] 'Jackals'; in the Latin text literally 'dragons.'

6 dealing, he can weigh my offence with true scales; let God himself bear
7 witness to my innocence! Have I strayed from my course; has my heart
8 followed the lure of my eyes; are my hands stained with wrong? Then
let another man enjoy the harvest I have sowed, then let my race be
9 doomed to extinction! Have wiles of woman entangled my heart; did I
10 lie in wait under my neighbour's window? Then be my own wife
11 another's whore, strangers be her bedfellows! That were sin in me, and
12 foul wrong done; that fire, once lighted, will rage till all is consumed,
never a crop shall escape it.

13   Did I refuse justice to manservant of mine or woman servant, when
14 they had complaint to bring? Then it shall go hard with me when it is
15 God's turn to pronounce judgement; how shall I meet his scrutiny, who
16 fashioned in the womb this one and that, man and master alike? Did I
deny some poor man the alms he craved, keep the widow waiting for her
17 pittance, sit over my meal alone, and never an orphan boy to share
18 it? That were an ill return for the loving care that has borne me company
19 as I grew up from childhood, ever since I left my mother's womb.[1] Did
I spurn the naked that were ready to perish of cold, too poor to find
20 clothing; did I never earn thanks from the back that went bare till fleece
21 of my flock warmed it? Did I threaten the friendless, when I could
22 secure judgement against them in the market-place? Then let shoulder
23 of mine hang from shoulder-blade, every bone in my arm broken! Nay,
but God's terrors overwhelmed, his majesty overbore me.

24   In wealth did I put my trust, hail the bright gold as my life's pro-
25 tector; doted I upon my great riches, upon all my toil had earned? When
I gazed on the sun in its splendour, on the moon in her royal pro-
27 gress, did these things steal my heart away, so that mouth kissed hand
28 in adoration? That were great wrong done, to deny the God who is higher
29 than all. Did I triumph over a fallen foe, rejoice at his ruin; lend my
31 lips to ill uses, cursing my enemy's life away? Rather, it was of myself
men were fain to speak evil, men of my own household, and to their
32 hearts' content.[2] Never had the stranger to lodge in the open, my doors
were open to every wayfarer that passed.

33   Men are frail; does sin lie on my conscience undisclosed, does the

---

[1] Literally, 'For mercy grew up with me from my childhood, and came out
of my mother's womb with me'; the sense may be that Job himself was always
a merciful man, but the parenthesis is awkward. There is no mention of
mercy in the Hebrew text.

[2] Literally, 'If the folk of my tabernacle did not say, who will give us of his
flesh, that we may be glutted?' This is usually interpreted, in various ways,
as if 'his flesh' could mean 'the dishes of meat which he provides,' but this
is very improbable. For 'eating a man's flesh' in the sense of traducing him,
see 19.22 above.

34 memory of guilt rankle in my bosom? Was I daunted by fear of the
throng, of my neighbours' contemptuous looks? Did I hold my tongue,[1]
35 and keep within doors? O that my cause might be tried; that he, the
Almighty, would grant my request, that he, my judge, would write my
36 record down;[2] how proudly I would bear it with me, shoulder-high,
37 wear it as a crown! I would proclaim it wherever I went, fit for a king's
38 eyes to read. Can these lands of mine bear testimony against me, can
39 their furrows tell a sad tale of harvests enjoyed, and no price paid for
40 them, of labourers cruelly treated? Then thistles for wheat, thorns for
barley may it yield me.

Ended herewith are the sayings of Job.

CHAPTER THIRTY-TWO

SO they answered Job no more, those others, a man persuaded of his
2 own innocence. But there was one who stood by in anger and
thought scorn of them, Eliu the Buzite, son of Barachel, of Ram's
kindred. Angry he was with Job, for claiming that God did him an
3 injury, and thought scorn of those friends of his, that could find no
4 reasonable answer, but were content to find Job a guilty man. Eliu,
then, waited till Job had finished speaking; was he not younger than the
5 rest? But when he found that the other three had no answer to give, he
could contain himself no longer.
6 Thus, then, spoke Eliu the Buzite, son of Barachel: Late in time was
I born, and you are older men than I; with bowed head I kept my own
7 counsel, ready to listen, while old age spoke, and learn from you the
8 garnered wisdom of years. But I see now that man speaks by inspiration;
9 only the breath of the most High can grant discernment; long life does
10 not make men wise, it is not always the aged that give true award. So
it is that I would fain have you listen while I make known my thought
11 to you. I have waited long on your words, heard you out, while you
12 searched about for reasons, attentive enough, while I still hoped to
hear the truth from you; but no, not one of you has convinced Job, or
13 answered his riddle. Do not flatter yourselves that you have tracked
14 down the truth; God must put him down, not man.[3] Not against me has

---

[1] Literally, according to the Latin version, 'And did I not rather hold my
tongue,' but this obscures the sense of the passage.
[2] The Latin version here gives what is perhaps the most coherent rendering
of a sentence which presents much difficulty in the original.
[3] Literally, 'Lest perhaps you should say, We have found wisdom; God
not man, has cast him (in the Hebrew text, will thrust him) away.' It is not
clear whether the wisdom is that of Job or his friends, nor whether the second
half of the verse is part of their supposed utterance.

he drawn up these pleadings of his; not with your shiftless answers will I meet him.

15 What, all abashed, these wise men, no answer ready, the words driven
16 from their lips? I have had enough of waiting for them to speak, and
17 seeing them stand dumb; I will take my turn at pleading, tell out my
18 thoughts. I am full of matter, in labour with ripe utterance; fresh wine
20 that has no vent will burst even a new wine-skin. Speak I must, if I
21 would get relief, unburden my lips of their answer. Human respect shall
22 not daunt me; how should I match man with God?[1] Uncertain my span
of days; what if he should call me suddenly to account, he, my Creator?

CHAPTER THIRTY-THREE

2 LISTEN, then, Job, to my remonstrances, and hear me out; flows my
3 speech free, tongue and throat are loosed; here be plain words,
4 uttered in all honesty. A creature I; God's spirit made me, the breath
5 of omnipotence woke me to life; if answer thou hast, thou canst meet
6 me fearlessly, since God made us both, and we were fashioned of one
7 clay; here are no terrors to daunt thee, no threats to overbear thee.

8 Openly thou hast said, with my own ears to witness it, Innocent
10 though I be of all wrong, free from the stain of guilt, God has picked
a quarrel with me; that is the reason, and no other, why he treats me
11 as an enemy, holds me so close a prisoner, and watches me wherever
12 I go. But there is no substance in thy plea; I tell thee, man cannot be
13 matched with God. What, wouldst thou complain that he does not meet
14 these charges of thine? Know, then, that God warns us once, but does
15 not repeat his warning.[2] Sometimes in visions of the night, when deep
16 sleep falls upon men as they lie abed, he speaks words of revelation, to
17 teach them the lesson they need. This is one means by which he will
18 turn a man away from his designs, purge him of his pride; and so the
19 grave is disappointed, the sword misses its prey. Or else he will use the
pains of the sick-bed for a man's correction, and leave his whole frame
wasted with disease.

20 Evil days, when he sickens at the thought of food, of all the dainties
21 he once loved so well; when the flesh pines and the bones have nought
22 to cover them, when death encroaches on life, and the powers of darkness

---

[1] According to the Hebrew text, 'I cannot give flattering titles to men,' a phrase which is repeated in the next verse, where the Latin has 'I do not know how long I shall last.'

[2] The Hebrew text is usually interpreted as meaning, 'God warns us once and a second time (or, warns us in one of two ways) without our perceiving it.'

23 daunt his spirits! Then it is an angel's [1] task, as many angels there be,
24 to interpret his need, and shew him where man's good lies; and the word
    of mercy will be spoken, Let be, the grave is not for him; I have found
25 the secret of his ransoming; [2] enough, now, torment has racked him, let
26 him return to the vigour of his youth! So, God's pardon wooed and won,
    the sick man stands in his presence once more, all thankfulness, restored
27 to favour. He turns to the bystanders and makes acknowledgement,
    A sinner I, no doubt but I have greatly offended, my punishment was less
28 than I deserved! Now God has reprieved me from death's exile, I am to
    live still, and see the light.
29   Such mercy, not once or twice, God shews to man, rescuing him from
31 the grave, rekindling the lamp of life for him. Listen to me, then, Job,
32 and hear me out; make answer to me, if answer thou canst, for I would
33 fain see thee acquitted. If answer thou hast none, listen to me in silence
    while I unfold the truth. [3]

CHAPTER THIRTY-FOUR

2   AND Eliu spoke on: A word for the wise; listen, you that are the
3   world's sages; for food, the discerning palate, for wisdom, the
4 discerning ear. Award we must give, this way or that; of two ways we
5 must choose the better. Here is Job telling us that he is innocent, that
6 God denies him his rights, judges him falsely, and plies him with
7 punishment undeserved. Are there many such; many that thirst so
8 greedily for the opportunity to cavil? See how pat his conclusions fall
9 for every sinner that would have an excuse for wrong-doing, when he
    complains that there is no pleasing God, however ready a man is to do
    his will!
10   Listen to me, then, discerning hearts! From God, the Almighty, far
11 removed is all wickedness, is every thought of wrong; he treats men
12 only as they deserve, giving due reward to each. What, should Almighty
13 God pervert justice by condemning the innocent? Is the care of the
    wide earth entrusted to some other; is not the maker of the world himself
14 the world's judge? He has but to turn his thought towards men, reclaim-

---

[1] The word used in the Hebrew text may also be rendered, 'a messenger's.'

[2] It is not certain here whether it is the angel that speaks, or God himself.

[3] *vv.* 27–33. Eliu does not, like the three friends, suspect Job of some special
fault which has called down God's punishment upon him. He explains human
suffering as sent by God not for vengeance but for correction. Only, since
we are all sinners, we have to confess that our suffering was (incidentally)
deserved.

15 ing the spirit he once breathed into them, and all life would fail everywhere; mankind would return to its dust.

16   Is Job wise? Then let him listen to these words of mine, heed well
17 my warning. Can there be healing,[1] where there is no love of right?
18 Wouldst thou find fault with him whose justice runs so deep? He it is
that says Traitor to a crowned king, and finds princes themselves guilty
19 of rebellion. Nothing cares he for royal dignity, nor takes the oppressor's
20 part against the friendless; are not all alike his creatures? Suddenly dies
the tyrant; there is stir and bustle about the court, as they carry him off
21 to burial, and yet no hand laid on him! Still God's eye watches over men,
22 whatever they do, wherever they take their path; darkness is none,
though it were the shadow of death itself, that can hide the wrong-
23 doer; not at a time of his own choosing man meets God in judgement. A
25 whole world of men he will destroy, and put others in their place; weary
26 of their ill deeds, he bids darkness fall, and there is an end of them. In
some place where many triumph at the sight, he beats down the
27 rebels [2] that hitherto of set purpose defied him, recked nothing of his
28 commandments, till at last the despairing cry of poor folk unbefriended
29 reached his ears. So long as he grants prosperity, redress there is none;
30 it is when he frowns upon man or nation that no eye can meet him. Yet
for a people's sins, he will appoint a false-hearted king to rule them.

31   Such is the testimony I give to God; now let us hear thine; shew me
my error, and if thou canst prove that I have spoken amiss, I will speak
33 no more. Perhaps thou thinkest it part of the punishment God asks of
thee, hearing what it pains thee to hear? But it was thou, not I, wert
the first to speak. If thou hast better advice to offer, say on.[3]

34   O for wise tongues to speak, for discerning ears to listen! This Job
36 has spoken as fools do; no word of his that echoes true doctrine! Father,[4]
let Job be tried still, tried to the uttermost; have no patience with a man
37 so perverse, that sets a crown on his sins by blasphemy! For a while, let
us see all ease denied him; and let him cite God to judgement if he will!

---

[1] Rather, according to the Hebrew text, 'governance'; Eliu's argument seems
to be that right itself can have no other source than him who is the world's
supreme Ruler.

[2] Literally, 'He smites them as if they were wicked in the dwelling-place of (or
perhaps, instead of) those who see'; it is probable that the text here is corrupt.

[3] *vv.* 31–33. It is not easy to be certain what is the sense of the Latin version
here. The Hebrew text differs from it considerably; but the interpretations
given of this are so forced and so various as to make it doubtful whether the
true reading has been preserved.

[4] 'Father'; the Hebrew word so rendered in the Latin can also be interpreted,
'I would that . . .'

CHAPTER THIRTY-FIVE

2 AND Eliu spoke on: What substance is there in this contention of
3 thine, when thou claimest to have right on thy side against God? He
cares nothing (so runs thy complaint) for man's good deeds; they are of
4 no advantage to him, that he should care for sin of mine![1] Here is my
5 answer, to thee, Job, and to thy friends alike. Look heavenward, mark
6 how the skies tower above thee, and read thy lesson there. Multiply thy
7 wrong-doing as thou wilt, no sin of thine can harm or touch him; be
honest as the day, no gift thou makest him, he is none the richer for thy
8 pains. Only to thy fellow man thy malice does a hurt; only Adam's children profit by thy uprightness.
9 . . . Cries and groans there are in plenty when oppression abounds,
10 when tyranny holds unchecked sway;[2] Where is God? men ask; yet
never did they seek to find him when he brought triumph in the hour of
11 distress, the God who teaches them such lessons as he never gave to
12 beast or bird. Only then, only when the wicked lord it over them, men
13 cry out, but their cry goes unheard; should God concern himself with
these random complaints, he, the Almighty, examine their pleadings one
14 by one? Nay, when he seems to take no heed, submit thyself to his judge-
15 ment and await his hour; thy present sufferings do not betoken his
anger, he is not taking vengeance to the full.
16 See, then, how all Job's utterance misses the mark; glib words with
no tincture of knowledge!

CHAPTER THIRTY-SIX

2 AND still Eliu would have his say: Bear with me a little while I
declare my thought to thee; I have more to say yet on God's
3 behalf. From a deep source I will draw my reasons, proving him, my
4 Maker, to be just; here is no delusive eloquence, the full truth shall be
5 made known to thee. He, the all-powerful, does not grudge men power;
6 it is only to the wicked he denies his aid; the friendless shall have

---

[1] Literally, 'For thou hast said, Thou (God) takest no pleasure in the right,
or what advantage will it be to thee if I sin?'—it seems necessary to suppose
that there is an ellipsis in the thought of the sentence here. In the Hebrew text,
Job is probably represented as asking how upright behaviour on his part could
be of more advantage to God than if he should sin.

[2] At verse 9, there is such a sudden break in the argument of the chapter
that it is difficult to believe the text has come down to us without omission.

7 redress. Never from the just is his favour withdrawn; a royal throne is
8 theirs for ever, so high he exalts them. If he should leave them in chains,
9 caught in the toils of sore need, it is but to apprise them of their own ill
10 deeds, their own tyrannous deeds; he will speak home to them for their
11 correction, warn them to turn back from their guilty ways. Hear they and
12 heed, they shall live long in ease and renown; if hear they will not, it
13 is the sword's point for them, to their last gasp fools still. It is the
   cunning, the false-hearted, that are God's sworn enemies; from them no
14 cry comes when the chains close about them; the storm sweeps them
15 away, forgotten in death as the temple minions are forgotten;[1] it is the
   friendless he rescues in their need, speaks home to them through the
16 afflictions they endure. From the pit's mouth, where the ground seems
   lost under thy feet, he will bring thee out into full freedom; thou shalt
   take thy ease at a table loaded with dainties.

17   Is sentence passed on thee such as rebels undergo? Thou shalt have
18 justice yet, and a true award. Never let the thought that God is angry
19 lure thee into tyranny and corruption; lay aside thy greatness, forbear
20 to oppress, away with the body-guard which attends thee; put an end to
21 the dark time when nations must march under their orders. Do not
   yield to the rebellious mood thou hast cherished since affliction came
   upon thee.[2]

22   God, that is so great and powerful, man's sovereign teacher, how
24 should anyone fathom his designs, or charge him with injustice? Bethink
   thee, how high beyond thy thought are those creatures of his which men
25 praise; how mortals see, but see, like mortals, from afar. Truly there
27 is no measuring God's greatness, no reckoning his length of days. He
28 hoards up the rain-drops, or showers them down in full flood from the
29 cloud-fountains that curtain us overhead. With those clouds, when it is
30 his pleasure, he spreads his pavilion, flashes his lightning on high, brings
31 darkness on the depths of the sea. Has he not a whole world to rule,
32 a whole race of mortals to supply with food? Now he hides the light
33 away with the shadow of his hand, now he bids it shine out again, as if
   to shew a friend at his side that he is the owner of it, that he can reach
   its high fastness when he will.[3]

----

[1] It is doubtful whether the second half of this verse has been correctly
transmitted to us. If it has, the enemies of God are perhaps compared to the
temple-prostitutes of heathen worship as persons unlikely to beget any posterity.

[2] *vv.* 16–21. Throughout this passage, both the Hebrew text and the Latin
version are hopelessly obscure.

[3] *vv.* 22–33. While the general sense of these verses can be roughly inferred,
the expressions used are very confusing, and it is probable that the passage
has suffered from errors in transmission.

CHAPTER THIRTY-SEVEN

1 WHAT wonder if my heart trembles and fails me at the thought?
2 Listen to the bruit of it, the voice that speaks amid such terrors,
3 the dread accents of that utterance! Under what part of heaven, into
4 what corner of earth does he not look, do not his lightnings flash? Then
what a crash resounds, the magnificent peal of his thunder; a voice
5 heard, and none can tell whence it comes! God's voice in the thunder,
a marvel worthy of him, whose deeds are so great and so unsearchable.
6 He it is that bids the snows fall over earth, and winter sleet, and his
7 fierce storms of rain. No hand of man but is shut up close now under his
8 seal; cowers the beast in its lair, or lurks in its cave; from his treasure-
10 house in the cold north tempest comes and cold. At God's breath the
11 frost binds fast, till he bids the waters flow again in plenty. And now the
crops must have rain; far and wide the clouds scatter their rays of
12 hope; [1] this way and that they turn at the guidance of his will, to do their
13 appointed task on earth, among distant tribes, or here in his own land,
let his mercy bid them appear where it may.
14 Matter enough, Job, for thy heeding! Halt where thou standest, and
15 consider the marvellous acts of God. Canst thou tell us when it was
16 God bade the rain bring hope to us from those clouds of his, tell us the
17 course of their journeyings? Is thy knowledge so perfect? See if thy
garments do not cling warm about thee when the south wind cheers the
18 earth! And was it with help of thine God fashioned the heavens, firm
19 as cast bronze? Tell us, what words we shall use to him, we, shut up in
20 our darkness? What messenger shall deliver my complaint to him, a
human messenger that will bring on himself only ruin?
21 Light fails men's eyes; all of a sudden, the air is thick with clouds;
22 then a breath of passing wind has driven them away! As well search for
the treasures of the north, as for the majestic praise which is God's
23 due; find speech worthy of it we cannot, so great he is in strength, so
prudent in counsel, so faithful in right dealing, past all that tongue can
24 tell. Well may men fear him; none that think themselves wise but will
tremble to meet his look.

---

[1] According to the Hebrew text, this verse should begin, 'He loads the clouds with moisture.' 'Their rays of hope'; literally, 'their brightness,' which is usually interpreted of the lightning, but the allusion seems out of place here, and also in verse 15 below.

CHAPTER THIRTY-EIGHT

THEN, from the midst of a whirlwind, the Lord gave Job his answer:
2 Here is one that must ever be clouding the truth of things with words
3 ill considered! Strip, then, and enter the lists; it is my turn to ask
4 questions now, thine to answer them. From what vantage-point wast
thou watching, when I laid the foundations of the earth? Tell me, whence
5 comes this sure knowledge of thine? Tell me, since thou art so wise, was
6 it thou or I designed earth's plan, measuring it out with the line? How
7 came its base to stand so firm, who laid its corner-stone? To me, that day,
all the morning stars sang together, all the powers of heaven uttered their
8 joyful praise. Was it thou or I shut in the sea behind bars? No sooner
9 had it broken forth from the womb than I dressed it in swaddling-
10 clothes of dark mist, set it within bounds of my own choosing, made
11 fast with bolt and bar; Thus far thou shalt come, said I, and no further;
here let thy swelling waves spend their force.
12   Dost thou, a mortal, take command of the day's breaking, and shew
13 the dawn its appointed post, twitching away earth's coverlet, scaring
14 away the ill-doers? The dawn, that stamps its image on the clay of earth;
15 stands there, flung over it like a garment,[1] taking away from the ill-doers
the darkness that is their light, so that all their power goes for nothing.
16 Didst thou ever make thy way into the sea's depths, walk at thy ease
17 through its hidden caverns? When did the gates of death open to thee,
18 and give thee sight of its gloomy threshold? Nay, hast thou viewed the
whole surface of earth itself? Tell me, if such knowledge is thine, all
19 its secrets; where the light dwells, where darkness finds its home; hast
thou followed either of these to the end of its journey, tracked it to its
21 lair? Didst thou foresee the time of thy own birth, couldst thou foretell
the years of life that lay before thee? [2]
22   Hast thou found thy way in to see the chambers where snow and
23 hail lie stored, my armoury against the times of stress, when there are
24 wars to be fought, battles to be won? Tell me by what means the light
25 is scattered over earth, the heat diffused; tell me what power carved
out a channel for the tempestuous rain, a vent for the echoing thunder-
26 storm, that they should fall on some lonely desert where foot of man
27 never trod, water those trackless wastes, and make the green grass
28 spring? What sire gendered the rain, or the drops of dew; what mother's

---

[1] The grammar of the Hebrew text is obscure; it runs, literally, 'It turns about as clay (of?) the signet-ring; they stand like a garment.'

[2] The sense of the Hebrew text is rather, 'Wast thou born so long ago, are thy years so many, that thou hast knowledge of all this?'

30 womb bore the ice, the frost that comes from heaven to make water hard as stone, imprison the depths beneath its surface?

31   Is it at thy command the glittering bright Pleiads cluster so close, and

32 Orion's circlet spreads so wide? Dost thou tell the day-star when to shine

33 out, the evening star when to rise over the sons of earth? [1] Is it thine to understand the motions of the heavens, and rule earth by their influence?

34 Can thy voice reach the clouds, and bid their showers fall on thee; canst thou send out lightnings that will do thy errand, and come back to await

36 thy pleasure? What power gives either man's heart its prescience, or the

37 cock its sure instinct,[2] knows all the motions of heaven, and lulls the

38 music of the spheres? [3] When was it that earth's dust was piled, and the solid ground was built up?

39   Is it thou or I that finds the lioness her prey, to satisfy those hungry

40 whelps of hers, where they lie in rocky caves, their lurking-places?

41 Which of us feeds the ravens? Is it not to God their nestlings cry so shrilly, homeless for want of food?

CHAPTER THIRTY-NINE

NOT thine to know when the wild goats give birth on their high crags,
2 to watch the hinds in their throes; count the months while they
3 carry their young, and know the time of their delivery. Without thy aid
4 they travail; born of those pangs, the calves are soon weaned, and make
5 for the pastures, go out to return no more. Who gives the wild ass
6 untrammelled liberty to roam the wilderness, and make the salt plains
7 his dwelling-place; to spurn the din of cities, no driver crying after
8 him, and look about him at the slopes where he feeds, all that green world
9 his pasturage? Canst thou tame the wild ox [4] to thy service, feed him at
10 thy stall, bind him to the plough with thongs and lead him out to break
11 clods in the valley? Wouldst thou trust that great strength of his to do
12 thy work for thee, bring in thy harvest and fill thy threshing-floor?
13   Here is the ostrich, of one feather with heron and hawk, yet she will leave her eggs on the bare earth; and canst thou give warmth to the dust

---

[1] The constellations mentioned cannot be identified with certainty.

[2] The two words represented here by 'heart' and 'the cock' are variously interpreted by Hebrew scholars.

[3] In the Hebrew text, 'Who is wise enough to count the stars, or can lay down the water-skins of heaven?'

[4] Literally, in the Latin version 'rhinoceros' here, and elsewhere 'unicorn.' The word occurs frequently in Scripture, but the exact meaning of it remains in dispute.

15 to hatch them? [1] Heedless, though foot of man should trample or wild
16 beast devour them, she steels herself to pity as if the brood was none of
17 hers; throws away all her hopes in causeless alarm. God's will it was to
18 deny her sense; wisdom she might have none, though she were swift,
at need, to hoist her wings aloft, mocking the pains of horse and rider.
19   Ay, and what of the horse? Is it of thy gift his great strength comes,
20 was it thou didst caparison him with terrors? [2] Thou wilt not scare him
21 away like a locust; fiercely he breathes, deeply he paws the ground,
22 bravely he prances, as he goes out to meet the shock of battle. Fear
23 cannot daunt him, nor the sword drive him back; clang quiver, let shield
24 and spear dazzle as they may, he swallows up the intervening distance,
25 all heat and rage. Little recks he of the trumpet's blast; echoes exultantly
the bugle's note, while he scents from afar the combat, hears the shouting
of captains, and the din of armies.
26   Is it of thy devising the hawk grows full-fledged, in time to spread her
27 wings for the southward journey? Is it at thy bidding the eagle soars,
28 to make her eyrie in the heights, cave and crag and inaccessible rock her
29 familiar home, whence her far-seeing eyes look round, searching for
30 prey? Blood-thirsty her brood, and where the carcase waits, waits she.
31   All this the Lord said to Job, and added besides, Here is one that
brought a charge against God easily put down! Nay, God thou didst
33 challenge, God thou must refute. And thus Job made the Lord answer:
34 So vain a pleader, I have no suit to make; finger on lip I will listen.
35 Once and again I have spoken the word I would fain unsay; more I
dare not.[3]

CHAPTER FORTY

A ND once more, from the midst of a whirlwind, the Lord gave Job
2   his answer: Strip, then, and enter the lists; it is my turn to ask
3 questions, thine to impart knowledge. My awards thou wouldst fain
4 reverse; wouldst prove me unjust, to prove thyself innocent; why then,
let us see thee shew strength like the strength of God, let us hear thee
5 thunder as God thunders. Come, deck thyself with glory, up with thee to
the heights; shew all thy splendours, robe thyself in dazzling array!
6 Scatter the proud in that indignation of thine, with thy frown abase the
7 tyrant; here is an oppressor for thee to thwart; here is one that defies

---

[1] *vv.* 13, 14. The Latin here does not tally with the Hebrew text, the sense
of which is by no means certain.

[2] Literally, 'clothe his neck with neighings (or perhaps, with thunders).'

[3] *vv.* 31–35. In the Hebrew text, these are marked as the first five verses of
chapter 40.

8 thee, crush him! Bury them in the dust, one and all, hide them from
9 sight, deep in the abyss; then I will acknowledge thee for one whose
   own strength can bring him victory.
10   Here is Behemoth,[1] my creature as thou art, fed on the same grass the
11 oxen eat; yet what strength in his loins, what lustihood in the navel of
12 his belly! Stiff as cedar-wood his tail, close-knit the sinews of his
13 groin, bones like pipes of bronze, gristle like plates of steel! None of
   God's works can vie with him, no weapon so strong in the hands of its
15 maker;[2] whole mountain-sides, the playground of his fellow beasts, he
16 will lay under tribute,[3] as he lies there under the close covert of the
17 marsh-reeds, thick boughs for his shadow, among the willows by the
18 stream. The flooded river he drinks unconcerned; Jordan itself would
19 have no terrors for that gaping mouth. Like a lure it would charm his
   eye, though it should pierce his nostrils with sharp stakes.[4]
20   Or Leviathan, wilt thou find a hook that will draw him to land, a line
21 that will hold his tongue fast? Canst thou ring him, or pass a chain
22 through his jaw? Will he importune thee with entreaties, or cajole thee
23 with blandishments, till thou makest a covenant that binds him to be
24 thy servant for ever? Wilt thou caress him like a tame bird, chain him
25 up to make sport for thy maid-servants? Is he to be divided up among
26 fellow fishermen, sold piece-meal to the merchants? Is that skin a spoil
27 for the net, that head for the fishermen's cabins? Do but try conclusions
   with him, and see if the memory of the combat does not keep thee
28 dumb! Fond hope, that must be dashed to the ground for all to see it!

CHAPTER FORTY-ONE

IT is in mercy that I forbear to make him a plague for mankind. But
2 indeed, there is no resisting me, nor can any deserve my thanks by
3 lending me the aid I lacked; nothing on earth but is at my disposal. I

---

[1] Behemoth is usually identified with the hippopotamus, sometimes with the elephant; Leviathan with the crocodile, sometimes with the whale. But both may be allegorical representations of the hostile powers overcome by the Creator.

[2] Literally, 'He is the beginning of the works of God; he who made him will bring near his sword,' a phrase variously interpreted by commentators.

[3] The Latin version represents the mountains as giving Behemoth grass, but the word used in the Hebrew text means produce of any kind, and it seems possible, in view of what follows, that mountain streams are referred to.

[4] This seems to be the best way of taking the Latin; exactly the same expression is used in Judith 10.17, and the river forms the natural subject of the sentence. The Hebrew text runs: 'By his eyes he captures him, by snares he pierces his nostrils'; and the words are commonly taken, not without hesitation, as alluding to the difficulty, or perhaps the ease, with which the animal is caught.

give him no quarter, for all his boastful, all his flattering words.[1]

4 Who can strip the skin of him, who can penetrate into the cavern of
5 his mouth, forcing the gates that guard it, the terrors of his teeth? The
7 body of him is like shields of cast metal, scale pressing on scale, so close
8 to one another as to leave no vent between; so well joined that nothing
9 will part them. Let him but sneeze, the fire flashes out; let him open his
10 eyes, it is like the glimmer of dawn; flames come from his jaws, bright
11 as a burning torch, smoke from his nostrils, thick as the fumes of a
12 seething pot; his very breath will set coals aflame, such fire issues from
13 that mouth. What strength dwells in that neck of his, what terrors play
14 about him! Firm-set are the folds of his flesh, unyielding though a
15 thunder-bolt should strike them;[2] firm-set, too, is the heart of him,
16 firm as ever stone was, or smith's anvil. Rises he up, angels themselves
17 are afraid, and take sanctuary in their dread.[3] Sword-thrust, nor spear,
18 nor breast-plate can hold their own against him; to him, steel is but
19 chaff, bronze but tinder-wood, nor fears he the archer; sling-stones he
20 counts as straw, as straw the hammer-blow, laughs at the brandished
21 spear. Sunlight flashes beneath him as he goes, a path of gold through
22 the slimes;[4] he makes the deep sea boil like a pot where ointment sim-
23 mers; how it shines in his wake, as though ocean itself had grown hoary
with age!

24 He has not his like among the strong things of earth, that fearless
25 nature, that heaven-confronting eye. Over all the pride of earth he reigns
supreme.

CHAPTER FORTY-TWO

2 AND thus Job answered the Lord: I acknowledge it, thou canst do
3 all thou wilt, and no thought is too difficult for thee. Here indeed
is one that clouds over the truth with his ignorance! I have spoken as fools

---

[1] *vv.* 1–3. The Latin version here differs widely from the Hebrew text, which
itself gives a questionable sense. If we follow the Latin it seems impossible
to suppose that any creature in the natural order, such as the crocodile, is
envisaged. But indeed there are many allusions in this chapter which cannot,
without considerable ingenuity, be referred to the crocodile.

[2] There is no reference to a thunder-bolt in the Hebrew text.

[3] 'Take sanctuary'; literally, in the Latin version, 'purify themselves.' The
Hebrew word used is commonly interpreted as meaning 'are bewildered' in
this context; and the Hebrew word rendered 'angels' perhaps only means
'strong men.'

[4] The Hebrew text is different here, and apparently compares the scales of
Leviathan to potsherds.

4 speak, of things far beyond my ken. Henceforth it is my turn to speak,
5 thine to listen; my turn to ask questions, thine to impart knowledge! I
6 have heard thy voice now; nay, more, I have had sight of thee; now I am
all remorse, I do penance in dust and ashes.[1]
7   And now, his converse with Job finished, the Lord said to Eliphaz
the Themanite, You have earned my displeasure, thou and these two
8 friends of thine, by speaking amiss of me as my servant Job never did. To
Job you must go for your ransoming, with seven bulls and seven rams to
offer in burnt-sacrifice; he, my servant, shall intercede for you, and for
his sake your folly shall be pardoned, that spoke amiss of me when he
spoke the truth.
9   So away they went, Eliphaz the Themanite, Baldad the Suhite, and
Sophar the Naamathite, and did the Lord's bidding. For Job's sake the
10 Lord pardoned them; and, as he prayed for these friends of his, the Lord
relented at the sight of his penitence. So he gave back to Job twice over
11 all that he had lost.   Clansmen and clanswomen and all his old acquaintances gathered about him now, and sat down as guests in his house, and
made great ado bemoaning all the afflictions the Lord had sent him;
not one of them but gave him presents, a sheep and a gold ear-ring
12 apiece.   A richer man the Lord made Job now than ever he had been in
old days; fourteen thousand sheep he had, and six thousand camels, and
13 a thousand yoke of oxen, and a thousand she-asses.   Seven sons he had,
14 and three daughters,   the first he called Fair as the Day, and the second
15 Sweet as Cassia, and the third Dark Eye-lids.[2] Nowhere might women
be found fair as Job's daughters, and each had the same patrimony as
her brothers.
16   Job himself lived on for a hundred and forty years, to see sons and
grandsons and a new generation yet of his descendants; so he died at last
as old men die, that have taken their full toll of the years.

---

[1] The text of this passage is not above suspicion. Neither the beginning
of verse 3 nor the end of verse 4 can be said to suit Job's own position; even
if we regard them as quotations (the one from 38.2 and the other from 40.2)
they have no obvious relation to the context. Nor is the sense of the contrast
in verse 5 by any means clear.
[2] 'Dark Eye-lids'; literally 'Pot of Antimony,' which was used as a cosmetic.

THE BOOK OF PSALMS *

PSALM ONE

B LESSED is the man who does not guide his steps by ill counsel,
or linger where sinners walk, or, where corrupt souls [1] gather, sit
2 down to rest; the man whose heart is set on the law of the Lord, on that
3 law, day and night, his thoughts still dwell. He stands firm as a tree
planted by running water, ready to yield its fruit when the season comes,
4 and never shedding its leaf; all that he does will prosper. Not such, not
such the wicked; the wicked are like dust, swept away by a wind from the
5 face of the earth. Not for the wicked, when judgement comes, to rise up
and plead their cause; sinners will have no part in the reunion of the
6 just. They walk, the just, under the eye of the Lord's favour; the path
of the wicked, how soon is it lost to sight!

PSALM TWO

W HAT means this turmoil among the nations? Why do the peoples
2 cherish vain dreams? See how the kings of the earth stand in array,
how its rulers make common cause, against the Lord, and against the
3 King he has anointed, crying, Let us break away from their bondage,
4 let us throw off their yoke! He who dwells in heaven is laughing at
5 their threats, the Lord makes light of them; and at last, in his displeasure,
6 he will speak out; his fierce anger will hurl them into confusion. To me,
he has given a kingly throne upon mount Sion, his sanctuary,[2] there to
7 proclaim his edict; how he told me, Thou art my son, I have begotten
8 thee this day. Ask thy will of me, and thou shalt have the nations for thy
9 patrimony; the very ends of the world for thy domain. Thou shalt herd
them like sheep [3] with a crook of iron, break them in pieces like earthen-
10 ware. Princes, take warning; learn your lesson, you that rule the world.
11 Tremble, and serve the Lord, rejoicing in his presence, but with awe

---

★ A new Latin translation of the Hebrew text, published by the Pontifical
Biblical Institute, was approved by Pope Pius XII in 1945. An English rendering of this is given in an Appendix on p. 1535.
    [1] Literally 'pestilence'; the Greek has 'pestilent fellows,' the Hebrew text
'scoffers.'
    [2] Another version of the Hebrew text makes God the speaker here, 'I have
enthroned (or perhaps, anointed) my king upon the hill of Sion, my sanctuary.'
    [3] 'Herd them like sheep'; or, according to another reading, 'shatter them.'

12 in your hearts. Kiss the rod;[1] do not brave the Lord's anger, and go
13 astray from the sure path. When the fire of his vengeance blazes out
suddenly, happy are they who find their refuge in him.

PSALM THREE

(A psalm David wrote, when he fled before his son Absalom.)

2 SEE how they surround me, Lord, my adversaries, how many rise up
3 in arms against me; everywhere voices taunting me, His God cannot
4 save him now. Yet, Lord, thou art the shield that covers me, thou art the
5 pride that keeps my head erect. I have but to cry out to the Lord, and my
6 voice reaches his mountain sanctuary, and there finds hearing. Safe in
7 God's hand I lay down, and slept, and have awoken; and now, though
thousands of the people set upon me from every side, I will not be afraid
8 of them. Bestir thyself, Lord; my God, save me; thine to smite down the
9 foes that wantonly assail me,[2] thine to break the fangs of malice. From
the Lord all deliverance comes; thy benediction, Lord, rests upon thy
people.

PSALM FOUR

(To the end among the songs; a psalm of David.)[3]

2 WHEN I call on his name, God listens to me and grants redress;
still, in time of trouble, thou hast brought me relief; have pity on
3 me now, and hear my prayer. Great ones of the world, will your hearts
always be hardened,[4] will you never cease setting your heart on shadows,
4 following a lie? To the souls he loves, the Lord shews wondrous favour;
5 whenever I call on his name, the Lord will hear me. Do not let anger
betray you into sin;[5] be ashamed, when you lie down to rest, of the
6 thoughts that were in your hearts. Offer sacrifices with due observance,
and put your trust in the Lord. There are many that languish for a sight
7 of better times, but already, Lord, the sun of thy favour shines out clear

---

[1] The word given in the Hebrew text should mean either 'purity,' or 'the Son.'
[2] The Hebrew text has, 'smitten the cheeks of all who assailed me.'
[3] This is a rendering of the Latin; but all these titles prefixed to various
psalms are very obscure, and there is little agreement about their meaning
except that they refer to the musical and liturgical setting.
[4] Our Hebrew text has, 'Will my honour always be turned into reproach?'
[5] Literally, 'Be angry, and do not sin.' Some would render 'be frightened'
instead of 'be angry.'

8 above us; thou hast made me glad at heart, like men who are enriched [1]
9 by the yield of their corn, and wine, and oil. In peace and friendliness
10 I will sleep and take my rest; [2] thou, Lord, hast bidden me repose in confidence unprotected.

PSALM FIVE

(To the end; for the heiress; a psalm of David.)

2 LORD, listen to my plea, let me not sigh in vain; pay heed to my
4 cry of petition, my King, my God. To thee, Lord, my prayer goes
5 up, early to win thy audience; early in the morning I present myself
6 before thee and watch. No evil thing claims thy Divine assent; with thee
7 baseness cannot dwell; nor rebellion hold its ground at thy coming. Thou
8 hatest the wrong-doer, and wilt bring the liar to destruction; bloodthirsty and treacherous men the Lord holds in abhorrence. I, then, encompassed by thy mercy, will betake myself to thy house, and in reverence of thee bow down before thy sanctuary.
9 Lord, do thou lead me with faithful care; guide me lovingly, where
10 I walk [3] beset by enemies. In their speech no truth can be found; their
11 hearts are emptiness, their mouths gaping tombs; flattering is ever on their lips. Thy sentence, O God! cheat them of their hopes, cast them out
12 in all their wickedness; Lord, have they not defied thee? But for all those who trust in thee there is joy and everlasting triumph; thou wilt dwell
13 among them; all true lovers of thy name will boast of thee, who givest thy benediction to the just. Lord, thou dost throw thy loving-kindness about us like a shield.

PSALM SIX

(To the end among the songs; a psalm of David; for the octave.)

2 LORD, when thou dost reprove me, let it not be in anger; when thou
3 dost chastise me, let it not be in displeasure. Lord, pity me; I have
4 no strength left; Lord, heal me; my limbs tremble; my spirits are

---

[1] Literally, 'They have been enriched'; but the sense given may be inferred from the Hebrew.

[2] Others would render, 'I will both sleep and take my rest in peace; thou only, Lord, hast bidden me repose in confidence.' But the Latin interpretation suits the context well, if we accept the common opinion that this psalm, like the one before, refers to the defeat of Absalom's revolt.

[3] Literally, 'direct my way in thy sight.' The Hebrew text has 'direct thy way in my sight.'

5 altogether broken; Lord, wilt thou never be content? Lord, turn back,
   and grant a wretched soul relief; as thou art ever merciful, save me.
6 When death comes, there is no more remembering thee; none can praise
7 thee in the world beneath. I am wearied out with sighing; every night
8 I lie weeping on my bed, till the tears drench my pillow. Grief has
   dimmed my eyes, and made an old man of me, so many are the adver-
9 saries that surround me. Depart from me, all you that traffic in iniquity;
10 the Lord has heard my cry of distress. O prayer divinely heard, O boon
11 divinely granted! All my enemies will be abashed and terrified; taken
   aback, all in a moment, and put to shame.

PSALM SEVEN

(A psalm of David; one which he sang to the Lord over the words of
Chusi, the Benjamite.)

2 O LORD my God, my confidence is in thee; save me from all my
3   pursuers, and grant me deliverance: must I fall a helpless prey to
4 the lion, with none to rescue me, none to bring me aid? O Lord my
5 God, if I too have been at fault, if these hands are stained with guilt; if
   I have avenged myself on the man who wronged me, then indeed let me
   go away from my adversary's presence empty-handed; [1] it is all I have
6 deserved. Then indeed let some enemy overtake me with his relentless
7 pursuit, trample me to earth, and level my pride with the dust! Lord,
   rise up in thy anger, make thyself feared in the lands of my enemies;
   bestir thyself, O Lord my God, in defence of the laws thou thyself hast
8 given us. All the nations will gather about thee, if thou wilt come back
9 to thy throne and rule them, the Lord judging the nations! Give me
   redress, Lord, in my uprightness, in all the innocence that clothes me.
10 Surely thou wilt put an end to the wrong-doing of the wicked, and
   prosper the innocent; no thought or desire of ours can escape thy Divine
   scrutiny.
11   From the Lord, refuge of true hearts, my unfailing [2] protection
12 comes. How just a judge God is, how strong, how patient; [3] and must he

---

[1] Others would render the Hebrew, 'That I have wronged the man who
was at peace with me, that I have wantonly despoiled my adversary'; or, 'That
I have wronged the man who was at peace with me, (nay, I have been at pains
to rescue those who wantonly attacked me).' In either case, the sentence will
then end with a comma, not with a full stop.

[2] Literally 'just'; some think the word belongs to verse 10 and agrees with 'God.'

[3] The words 'strong' and 'patient' are not in the Hebrew text. The Latin
has, in the second half of the verse, 'Is God indignant every day?', the Greek,
'God is not indignant every day,' the Hebrew, 'God is indignant every day.'

13 be daily provoked to anger? If you do not repent, his sword will flash
14 bright; he has bent his bow in readiness, and deadly are the weapons
15 he has fitted to it; he has barbed his arrows with fire. Here was a heart
   pregnant with malice, that conceived only spite, and gave birth only to
16 shame! [1] Here was one who dug a pit and sunk it deep, and fell into a
17 snare of his own setting! All his spite will recoil on himself, all his
18 violence will fall on his own head. I will ever thank the Lord for his
   just retribution, singing praises to the name of the Lord, the most High.

PSALM EIGHT

(To the end; for the winepresses; a psalm of David.)

2 O LORD, our Master, how the majesty of thy name fills all the
3   earth! Thy greatness is high above heaven itself. Thou hast made
   the lips of children, of infants at the breast,[2] vocal with praise, to confound
4 thy enemies; to silence malicious and revengeful tongues. I look up at
   those heavens of thine, the work of thy hands, at the moon and the stars,
5 which thou hast set in their places; what is man that thou shouldst
   remember him? What is Adam's breed, that it should claim thy care?
6 Thou hast placed him only a little below the angels,[3] crowning him with
7 glory and honour, and bidding him rule over the works of thy hands.
8 Thou hast put them all under his dominion, the sheep and the cattle,
9 and the wild beasts besides; the birds in the sky, and the fish in the sea,
10 that travel by the sea's paths. O Lord, our Master, how the majesty of
   thy name fills all the earth!

PSALM NINE

(To the end; for the son's mysteries; a psalm of David.)

2 LORD, I give thee all the thanks of my heart, recounting thy won-
3   derful doings; glad and triumphant in thee, I will sing psalms to
4 thy name, O God most high. See how my enemies turn back, how they
5 faint and melt away at the sight of thee! Thou hast given me redress
   and maintained my cause; thou art there on thy throne, seeing justice

---

[1] 'Shame,' that is, according to the Latin, sin; the Hebrew word has rather
the sense of disappointment, frustration (cf. verse 16).

[2] Some would interpret the Hebrew here, 'thou hast founded strength through
the lips of children and infants at the breast.'

[3] The Hebrew can also be translated 'below God.'

6 done. Thou hast checked the heathen in their course; thou hast brought
the wicked to nothing, blotting out their name endlessly, for all time.
7 The swords of the enemy have lost their edge for ever; thou hast rooted
up their cities, and the memory of them died with the crash of their
8 ruin.[1] But the Lord abides for ever on the throne of judgement he has
9 prepared, still judging the world rightly, still awarding each people
10 its due: the Lord is a stronghold to the oppressed, a refuge in time of
11 peril. Those who acknowledge thy name, Lord, can trust in thee; never
was man forsaken that had recourse to thee.

12 Sing, then, to the Lord, who dwells in Sion, tell the Gentiles of his
13 love; how he, the avenger of blood, cares for the afflicted, does not forget
14 them when they cry to him. Have pity on me, Lord, look upon all that
15 I suffer at my enemies' hands; thou who didst ever rescue me from the
16 gate of death, to proclaim thy praises at the gate of thy loved Sion, to
exult in thy saving power. The heathen have been caught in their own
deadly devices; their feet have been trapped in the very toils they had
17 laid; now it will be seen how the Lord defends the right, how the wicked
18 contrive their own undoing. To the place of death the wicked must
19 return, heathens that have no thought of God. He does not forget the
helpless; their time will come; the patience of the afflicted will not go for
20 nothing. Bestir thyself, Lord, let not human strength prevail; let the
21 heathen stand upon their trial before thee; let the heathen, too, have a
law-giver,[2] to teach them that they are but men.

(Here, in the Hebrew text, Psalm 10 begins.)

22 Lord,[3] why dost thou stand far off? In days of peril and affliction, why
23 dost thou make no sign? The heart of the oppressed burns within them,
24 so triumphant is the schemer that has entrapped them; so proud of his
25 wicked end achieved, so well content with his knavery.[4] What wonder
if the sinner defies the Lord, thinking, for all his anger,[5] he will never

---

[1] The Latin here differs from the Hebrew text, which has no reference to
swords, or to a noise of ruin.

[2] The Hebrew text has 'bring terror upon them' instead of 'appoint a law-
giver over them.'

[3] The numbering of the Psalms here corresponds with that of the Vulgate.
In the Hebrew text, which is followed by some modern versions, verses 22–30
of this Psalm are treated as a separate psalm and numbered 10; while Psalms
146 and 147 are given as one psalm. Thus the Vulgate numbers 10 to 147
correspond to 11–147 of the alternate reckoning.

[4] The meaning here is very obscure; it is not clear whether the wicked themselves are entrapped by their own guile, or entrap their victims by guile,
whether the sinner congratulates himself, or receives congratulation from others.

[5] 'For all his anger'; according to the Hebrew text 'in his (the sinner's) contempt.'

26 make strict enquiry? A heart that has no thought of God, a life ever
   stained with crime, eyes that are blind to thy judgements; and still he has
27 the mastery of his enemies! Endless time, he thinks, cannot shake his
28 untroubled existence. His mouth overflows with curses, and calumny,
29 and deceit; his tongue is a store-house of misery and shame. He will
   agree with the rich [1] to lie in wait at dark corners, and kill the man who
30 never wronged him; his eyes are continually on his prey; like a lion in
   its lair, he watches from his hiding-place, to surprise his defenceless foe,
31 safe in the net. So he catches him in the toils; and see how he bows
32 and scrapes,[2] now that he is master of his prey! Why not? he thinks to
   himself, God has forgotten about it; God still turns his face away, and
   sees nothing.
33   O Lord God, bestir thyself, lift up thy hand; do not forget the
34 helpless. Why is the sinner allowed to defy God, to think he will never
35 make enquiry? But in truth thou seest it; thou hast eyes for the misery
   and shame; thou wilt give them up to vengeance.[3] The destitute are cast
36 on no care but thine; to thee only the orphan looks for redress. Break
   down the power of the wicked oppressor, till men look [4] for a sign of his
37 wickedness, and look in vain. The Lord will reign for ever and ever,
38 while you, the heathen, will vanish from the land he loves. The sighing
   of the defenceless has found audience; thou dost listen to the prayer of
39 the well ordered heart, dost give redress to the fatherless and the poor;
   mortal man shall make himself feared no longer.

PSALM TEN   (11)

(To the end; a psalm of David.)

2 MY trust is in the Lord; how is it that you say to your friend, Escape,
3   like a frightened sparrow, to the hill-side? Escape; the rebels
   have strung their bows, have arrows ready in the quiver, to shoot from
4 their hiding-places at an unoffending heart; they have thrown down all
5 thou hadst built; what hope, now, for the just man? Yes, but the Lord
   is in his holy shrine, the same Lord whose throne is in heaven, whose

---

[1] The Hebrew text has 'in the villages.'
[2] *v.* 31. This seems the most natural way of taking a much-disputed sentence.
It is not clear whether the wicked man does this before God, or before his rich
employers.
[3] Or perhaps 'thou wilt take them (the misery and shame) into thy keeping.'
[4] The Hebrew has 'Thou wilt look,' that is, make enquiry, as in verses 25 and
34 above, but it is hard in that case to make any natural sense of what follows,
'thou wilt not find.'

eye looks on the helpless, whose glance scrutinizes the deeds of men.
6 Innocent or sinful, he reads every heart, and the friends of wrong-doing
7 are the enemies of their own souls.[1] He will rain down sudden destruction
on sinners; fire, and brimstone, and stormy wind, such is the draught
8 he brews for them. The Lord is just, and just are the deeds he loves;
who deals uprightly, deserves the favour of his smile.[2]

PSALM ELEVEN (12)

(To the end; for the octave, a psalm of David.)

2 LORD, come to my rescue; piety is dead; in a base world, true hearts
3 have grown rare. None but exchanges empty forms of speech with
4 his neighbour; everywhere false hearts and their treacherous lips. Those
treacherous lips, that tongue with high-sounding phrases, Lord, rid the
5 earth of them! With our tongues, they say, we can do great things; our
6 lips are good friends to us; we own no master. Now, says the Lord, I will
bestir myself, on behalf of the helpless who are so ill used, of the poor
who cry out so bitterly; I will win them redress, speak out for their cause.
7 The promises of the Lord are true metal, like silver that is melted down
in the crucible to purify it, and runs to the ground seven times refined.[3]
8 Yes, Lord, thou wilt watch over us, and keep us ever safe from these evil
days.
9 See how the wicked come and go all around us! How high thou art
above us, and yet how great is the increase thou givest to a base breed
of men![4]

PSALM TWELVE (13)

(To the end; a psalm of David.)

2 LORD, must I still go all unremembered, must thy look still be
3 turned away from me? Each day brings a fresh load of care, fresh
4 misery to my heart; must I be ever the sport of my enemies? Look
upon me, O Lord my God, and listen to me; give light to these eyes,
5 before they close in death; do not let my enemies claim the mastery,

---

[1] In the Hebrew text, 'His soul hates the friends of wrong-doing.'

[2] In the Hebrew text, 'the upright shall see his face.'

[3] It is not certain what the end of this verse means. Some commentators think there is a reference to coin 'current in the land.'

[4] Literally 'sons of Adam,' a term which is sometimes used slightingly, to mean 'men of inferior degree.' This last sentence of the psalm is very obscure in the Hebrew text.

6 my persecutors triumph over my fall! I cast myself on thy mercy; soon
may this heart boast of redress granted. Then my song shall be of the
goodness the Lord has shewn me, my psalms shall honour the name of
the Lord, the most High.[1]

PSALM THIRTEEN   (14)
(To the end; a psalm of David.)

THERE is no God above us, is the fond thought of reckless hearts;
2 false aims and hateful, never a man but lives amiss. The Lord looks
down from heaven at the race of men, to find one soul that reflects,
3 and makes God its aim; but no, all have missed the mark and disappointed him; a life well lived is nowhere to be found. Their mouths are
gaping tombs; they use their tongues to flatter; under their lips the poison
of asps is hidden. Their mouths overflow with curses and calumny. They
run hot-foot to shed blood; havoc and ruin follow in their path; the
way of peace is unknown to them. They do not keep the fear of God
4 before their eyes. What, can they learn nothing, all these traffickers in
iniquity, who feed themselves fat on this people of mine, as if it were
5 bread for their eating, and never invoke the Lord's name? What wonder
6 if fear unmans them, where they have no cause to fear? Just souls the
Lord comforts with his presence; but you have thwarted the hopes of the
7 oppressed; it is for the just to put their confidence in the Lord. Oh, that
it might dawn over Sion, Israel's deliverance! Day of gladness for Jacob,
day of Israel's triumph, when the Lord restores the fortunes of his own
people.[2]

PSALM FOURTEEN   (15)
(A psalm of David.)

WHO is it, Lord, that will make his home in thy tabernacle, rest
2 on the mountain where thy sanctuary is? One that guides his
3 steps without fault, and gives to all their due; one that tells the truth
in his own heart, utters no treacherous word, never defrauds a friend,
4 or believes ill of his neighbour. He scorns the reprobate, keeping his

---

[1] The last twelve words are wanting in the Hebrew text.

[2] This psalm is a curious literary problem; the whole of it can be found elsewhere in the Bible. Verses 1 and 2, with the first sentence of verse 3, and verses
4–7, reappear in Psalm 52, with some variation in verse 6. The remainder of
verse 3 is found in the Greek and Latin, but not in the Hebrew text. It corresponds exactly with verses 10–18 in the third chapter of St. Paul's Epistle to the
Romans, and appears to be a canto of Scriptural quotations taken from the
following sources: Ps. 5.10, 139.4, 9.28, Is. 59.7, Ps. 35.2.

reverence for such as fear God, abides by the promise he made to his
5 neighbour;[1] lends without usury, and takes no bribe to condemn the
innocent. He who so lives will stand firm for ever.

PSALM FIFTEEN   (16)

(An inscription for a monument; for David himself.)

2 KEEP me safe, Lord; I put my trust in thee. The Lord, whom I own
3 as my God! all the good I possess is nothing to him.[2] There are
faithful souls in this land of his; wondrous love he gives me of their com-
4 panionship. But many have sinned, and been quick to follow their own
ways;[3] I will not join with such as these in holding the assemblies where
5 they drink blood; I will not take forbidden names on my lips. No, it is
the Lord I claim for my prize, the Lord who fills my cup; thou, and no
6 other, wilt assure my inheritance to me. Portion is none were more to
7 my liking; welcome the lot's choice! Blessed be the Lord, who schools
8 me; late into the night my inmost thoughts chasten me. Always I can
keep the Lord within sight; always he is at my right hand, to make me
9 stand firm. Glad and merry I am, heart and lips of me, my body, too,
10 shall rest in confidence that thou wilt not leave my soul in the place of
11 death, or allow thy faithful servant to see corruption. Thou hast shewn
me the way of life; thou wilt make me full of gladness in thy presence;
at thy right hand are delights that will endure for ever.

PSALM SIXTEEN   (17)

(A prayer of David.)

LORD, to my just complaint give ear; do not spurn my cry for aid.
Listen to this prayer of mine; they are no treacherous lips that make
2 it. At thy judgement-seat I claim award, look for unerring justice

---

[1] In the Latin, 'when he has sworn to his neighbour,' in the Hebrew text,
'when he has sworn to (his own) disadvantage.'

[2] That is, in the Latin, 'is unnecessary to him'; according to the Hebrew text,
it more probably means 'is nothing as compared with him.'

[3] Literally, 'their infirmities were multiplied; afterwards they made haste.'
But it is evident from what follows that this refers to other Israelites, not to
those mentioned in the previous verse. Some have rendered 'their idols were
multiplied,' or 'they ran after other gods' from the Hebrew; but the Latin
is not patient of this interpretation. The Hebrew word for 'infirmities' comes
from a verb which is sometimes used of provoking God to anger (Ps. 77.40,
Is. 63.10). 'Forbidden names'; literally, 'their names'; but it can hardly be
doubted that the names of false gods are referred to. Cf. 1 Cor. 10.21.

3 from thy scrutiny. Hast thou not read my heart, drawing near in the
4 darkness to test me as if by fire, still no treachery found in me? Never
   may I share the base thoughts of men; still mindful of thy warnings,
5 I have kept to the paths that are hard to follow.[1] Do thou maintain
6 my steps firm in thy own ways, never allowing my feet to stumble. And
   now I cry to thee, the God who ever hearest me; turn thy ear towards
7 me, and listen to my plea. Thy mercy, thy signal mercy shew; none ever
8 trusted thy help in vain. From the rebels that defy thy will [2] protect me
   as a man protects the apple of his eye; hide me under the shelter of thy
9 wings, safe from the evil-doers who wrong me. See how my enemies
10 close about me mercilessly, their hearts shut to pity,[3] a boast on their
11 lips! Even now they have pulled me down, and are closing in about me,
12 their eyes fixed on the ground, avoiding mine; [4] better had a lion caught
13 me, eager for his prey, a young lion that waits hidden in its lair. Bestir
   thyself, Lord; forestall him and throw him to the ground; deliver me from
   the evil-doer, me, thy chosen weapon, from the enemy that defies thee! [5]
14 Lord, shall they live to share the favours thou grantest to so few on earth;
   whose desires thou dost satisfy with treasures from thy store, who are
   enriched with offspring, and can leave their inheritance to their own
15 children? [6] As for me, I will come with upright heart into thy presence
   innocent; and when thy glory dawns, I shall be well content.[7]

---

[1] 'I have kept to the paths that are hard to follow'; the Hebrew text more
probably means, 'I have shunned the paths of the violent.'

[2] It is possible that the words 'from the rebels that defy thy will' belong not to
this sentence but to the last.

[3] Literally, 'shutting up their own fat,' that is, around their hearts.

[4] Others would interpret this phrase (in the Hebrew) as meaning 'they have set
their eyes (or, as we should say, their minds) on casting us down to the ground.'

[5] Others would render the Latin, 'deliver me from the power of the evil-
doer, and deliver thy sword from the enemy,' but the sense of this is hard to
determine. The Hebrew probably means 'deliver me *with* thy sword.'

[6] Both the Hebrew and the Latin (which may have arisen from a false reading in the Greek) are very obscure. The rendering here given seems the best
way of taking the Latin; it is difficult to believe that the wicked are described
as people whom God enriches, even in this life, with his store of treasures.

[7] 'When thy glory dawns, I shall be well content'; it is possible to interpret the
Hebrew as meaning, 'when I wake up, I shall be well content with thy likeness.'

PSALM SEVENTEEN (18)

(To the end; a psalm for David, the servant of the Lord. He addressed to the Lord the words of this song, on the day when God delivered him from the hand of Saul, and from the hands of all his enemies; as follows:) [1]

2 SHALL I not love thee, Lord, my only defender? The Lord is my rock-fastness, my stronghold, my rescuer; it is my God that brings me aid, and gives me confidence; he is my shield, my weapon of
4 deliverance, my place of refuge. Praised be the Lord! when I invoke
5 his name, I am secure from my enemies. Death's terrors were near at
6 hand, deep flowed the tide of wrong, to daunt me; the terror of the
7 grave was all about me, deadly snares had trapped my feet. One cry to the Lord, in my affliction, one word of summons to my God, and he, from his sanctuary, listened to my voice; the complaint I made before him found a hearing.
8 Earth thereupon shivered and shook, the very foundations of the
9 hills quailed and quaked before his anger; smoke went up before his indignant presence, and a consuming fire; burning coals were kindled
10 as he went. He bade heaven stoop, and came down to earth, with mist
11 at his feet; he came, mounted on the cherubim, borne up on the wings
12 of the wind, shrouded in darkness, canopied with black rain-storms that
13 fell from the clouds of heaven. The clouds, too, at the brightness of his
14 coming, parted in a storm of hail and burning coals; hail and burning coals, as the Lord sent his thunder from heaven, as the Most High let his
15 voice be heard. How they scattered when he rained down his arrows on
16 them, how they fled in confusion before the volleys of his lightning! The secret springs of the rivers came to light, the very foundations of the world were laid bare, when thou didst threaten them, Lord, when thou
17 didst blow upon them with the breath of thy anger. Then he reached
18 down from heaven, caught hold of me, rescued me from that flood, saved me from triumphant malice, from the enemies that held me at their
19 mercy. Evil days, when they faced me at every turn! Yet the Lord stood
20 by me, and brought me out into freedom again; his great love befriended me.
21 And still as he sees me dutiful, the Lord will requite me, as he sees me
22 guiltless in act, he will make return. Have I not kept true to the Lord's

---

[1] The whole of this psalm has been preserved for us independently among the records of King David's reign, with very slight variations (1 Kg. 22).

23 paths? Have I not been ever loyal to my God? No law of his, but I have
24 kept it before my eyes; no task he laid upon me have I refused; ever
   stainless in his presence, ever watchful to keep myself clear of wrong,
25 ever faithful, ever found guiltless in act, the Lord will requite me. Lovingly dost thou treat those who love thee, and biddest the innocent go
27 unharmed; he that is thy own shall find thee his very own, from the man
28 who turns against thee thou wilt turn away. To humble folk thou wilt
   bring deliverance; the proud, with their haughty looks, thou wilt bring
29 down to earth. It is thou, Lord, that keepest the lamp of my hopes still
30 burning; shine on the darkness about me, O my God. In thy strength I
   shall be proof against all attack; in my God's strength their defences overleap.

31   Such is my God, unsullied in his dealings; his promises are like metal
32 tested in the fire; he is the sure defence of all who trust in him. Who
33 but the Lord is God? What other God can there be, except our God? It
   is he that girds me with strength; he that makes me go on my way
34 untroubled. He makes me sure-footed as the deer, and gives me the
35 freedom of the hills; these hands, through him, are skilled in battle,
36 these arms are a match for any bow of bronze. Thy saving power, Lord,
   is my defence, thy right hand supports me; and still thou humblest me
37 for my correction, I am schooled by thy chastisement.[1] Through thee,
38 my steps are untrammelled as I go, my tread never falters; I can overtake
   the enemies I pursue, and never turn home till I have made an end of
39 them; I can beat them to their knees, and hurl them down at my feet.
40 Thou girdest me about with a warrior's strength; whatever power chal-
41 lenges me, thou dost subdue before me, putting my enemies to flight,
42 and throwing all their malice into confusion. Loudly they cry out to the
43 Lord, bereft of aid, but he makes no answer to their cries. I can crush
   them to pieces, like the dust which the wind blows along; I can brush
   them away like mire from the streets.

44   Nor was it enough, of domestic broils to rid me; a world should be my
45 vassal; new realms should pay me homage, quick to do my bidding. See
   where they come, the alien born, come hobbling out of their deserted
47 streets, enfeebled men, to cringe before me![2] Blessed be the living Lord
48 who is my God, praised be the God who rescues me! It is thou, my God,
   that bringest me redress, that grantest me dominion over my people, that
49 savest me from the spite of my enemies; so that I am high above the
50 reach of their assaults, proof against their violence. Then, Lord, I will

---

[1] In the Hebrew text the second half of this verse reads 'And thy condescen-
sion has exalted me.'

[2] 'Their deserted streets'; the Hebrew text has 'prisons' (or perhaps 'strongholds').

give thee thanks in the hearing of all the nations, singing in praise of thy
51 name. What victory thy mercy grants to the king thou hast anointed, to
David, and David's line for ever.

PSALM EIGHTEEN   (19)

(To the end ; a psalm of David.)

2 SEE how the skies proclaim God's glory, how the vault of heaven
3 betrays his craftsmanship! Each day echoes its secret to the next,
4 each night passes on to the next its revelation of knowledge; no word,
5 no accent of theirs that does not make itself heard,[1] till their utterance
6 fills every land, till their message reaches the ends of the world. And
where the sun is, there he sets up his tabernacle; the sun, which comes
out as a bridegroom comes from his bed, and exults like some great
7 runner who sees the track before him.[2] Here, at one end of heaven, is its
starting-place, and its course reaches to the other; none can escape its
burning heat.

8   The Lord's perfect law, how it brings the soul back to life; the Lord's
9 unchallengeable decrees, how they make the simple learned! How plain
are the duties which the Lord enjoins, the treasure of man's heart; how
clear is the commandment the Lord gives, the enlightenment of man's
10 eyes! How sacred a thing is the fear of the Lord, which is binding for
ever; how unerring are the awards which the Lord makes, one and all
11 giving proof of their justice! All these are more precious than gold, than
12 a hoard of pure gold, sweeter than the honey, dripping from its comb. By
these I, thy servant, live; none ever lived by them that was not richly
13 rewarded. And yet, who knows his own frailties? If I have sinned
14 unwittingly, do thou absolve me. Keep me ever thy own servant, far from
the worship of other gods ; [3] so long as these do not lord it over me, I will
15 yet be without fault, I will yet be innocent of the great sin. Every word
on my lips, every thought in my heart, what thou wouldst have it be, O
Lord, my defender, my redeemer!

---

[1] The meaning of the Hebrew text here is quite uncertain; the literal sense
of the Latin is probably, 'there are no words or utterances (of theirs) whose
sound is not heard.'

[2] The Hebrew text has 'He has made a tabernacle for the sun in them'; the
Latin, 'He has put his tabernacle in the sun,' probably in the sense that the sun
in the heavens is his abiding witness (Ps. 88.38) as the tabernacle was to his
people in the wilderness.

[3] Or perhaps 'from men of a strange race'; the Hebrew text has, 'from the
proud,' or perhaps 'from sins of pride.'

PSALM NINETEEN   (20)

(To the end ; a psalm of David.)

2 THE Lord listen to thee in thy time of need, the power of Jacob's
3 God be thy protection! May he send thee aid from his holy place,
4 watch over thee, there on mount Sion ; may he remember all thy offerings,
5 and find savour in thy burnt-sacrifice. May he grant thee what thy
6 heart desires, crown thy hopes with fulfilment. So may we rejoice at
7 thy deliverance, extolling the name of the Lord our God ; abundantly
may he grant thy prayer. Shall I doubt that the Lord protects the king
he has anointed, will listen to him from his sanctuary in heaven? Is
8 not his right hand strong to save? Let others talk of horses and chariots ;
9 our refuge is the name of the Lord our God. See how they are caught
10 in the toils, and brought low, how we keep our feet, and stand erect! O
Lord, save the king,[1] and hear us in the hour when we call upon thee.

PSALM TWENTY   (21)

(To the end ; a psalm of David.)

2 WELL may the king rejoice, Lord, in thy protection, well may he
3 triumph in thy saving power! Never a wish in his heart hast thou
4 disappointed, never a prayer on his lips denied. With abundant blessing
thou dost meet him on his way, dost set a jewelled crown on his head.
5 Prays he for life? Long continuance of his reign thou dost grant him ;
6 to last unfailing till the end of time. Great is the renown thy protection
7 has won for him ; glory and high honour thou hast made his. An everlasting monument of thy goodness, comforted by the smile of thy
8 favour, he stands firm, trusting in the Lord ; the mercy of the most
High is with him.
9 Ay, but thy enemies—they shall feel thy power ; that right hand will
10 not leave their malice unpunished. At thy frown, they will wither away
like grass in the oven ; whirled away by the Lord's anger, burnt up in its
11 flames. Thou wilt rid the land of their breed, their race will vanish from
12 the world of men. See how all their false designs against thee, all their

---

[1] Some would understand the Hebrew text as meaning, 'O Lord, our King,
save us.'

[801]

13 plots come to nothing! Thou wilt put them to flight, drive them back
where thy auxiliaries await them.[1]

14 Stand high above us, Lord, in thy protecting strength; our song, our
psalm, shall be of thy greatness.

PSALM TWENTY-ONE   (22)

(To the end, to be accepted in the morning; a psalm of David.)

2 MY God, my God, look upon me; why hast thou forsaken me? Why
3 cannot my sinful words reach thee, who art my salvation? Thou
dost not answer, my God, when I cry out to thee day and night, and I am
4 patient still.[2] Thou art there none the less, dwelling in the holy place;
5 Israel's ancient boast. It was in thee that our fathers trusted, and thou
6 didst reward their trust by delivering them; they cried to thee, and
7 rescue came; no need to be ashamed of such trust as theirs. But I, poor
worm, have no manhood left; I am a by-word to all, the laughing-stock
8 of the rabble. All those who catch sight of me fall to mocking; mouthing
9 out insults, while they toss their heads in scorn, He committed himself
to the Lord, why does not the Lord come to his rescue, and set his
favourite free?
10 What hand but thine drew me out from my mother's womb? Who else
11 was my refuge when I hung at the breast? From the hour of my birth,
thou art my guardian; since I left my mother's womb, thou art my God!
12 Do not leave me now, when trouble is close at hand, when I have none to
13 help me. My enemies are all about me, hemming me in, packed close as
14 a herd of oxen, strong as bulls; so might a lion threaten me with its
15 jaws, roaring for its prey. I am spent as spilt water, all my bones out of
16 joint, my heart turned to molten wax within me; my strength has
shrivelled up, like clay in the baking, and my tongue sticks fast in my
17 mouth; thou hast laid me in the dust, to die. Prowling about me like a
pack of dogs, their wicked conspiracy hedges me in; they have torn holes

---

[1] Verses 9–13 are perhaps addressed to God, more probably to the psalmist
himself. The second half of verse 13 appears to mean, in the Hebrew text,
'Thou wilt shoot (arrows) with thy bowstrings against their faces,' but the
rendering is somewhat doubtful. The Latin clearly depends on a different
reading of the text; the sense seems to be 'Thou wilt direct their faces among
(or by means of) thy men (or things) left over.' Possibly the picture is that of
a commander who reserves his second-best troops to intercept a fleeing enemy,
or 'heads off' the enemy into an ambush.

[2] Literally, 'and (it does) not (lead) to rash folly for me.' The Hebrew text
has, 'and not to my silence,' which some interpret as meaning, 'and it gives
me no respite.'

18 in my hands and feet; they mark every bone in my body, as they stand
19 there watching me, gazing at me. They divide my spoils among them,
20 cast lots for my garments. Then, Lord, do not stand at a distance, if
21 thou wouldst aid me; look to my defence. Only life is left me; save that
22 from the sword, from the clutches of these dogs; rescue me from the
very mouth of the lion, the very horns of the wild oxen that have brought
me thus low.

23   Then I will proclaim thy renown to my brethren; where thy people
24 gather, I will join in singing thy praise, Praise the Lord, all you that
are his worshippers; honour to him from the sons of Jacob, reverence
25 to him from Israel's race! He has not scorned or slighted the appeal of the
friendless, nor turned his face away from me; my cry for help did not go
26 unheeded. Take what I owe thee, my song of praise before a great
assembly. I will pay my vows to the Lord in the sight of his worshippers;
27 the poor shall eat now, and have their fill, those who look for the Lord
28 will give him thanks, their hearts refreshed eternally. The furthest
dwellers on earth will bethink themselves of the Lord, and come back to
29 him; all the races of the heathen will worship before him; to the Lord
30 royalty belongs, the whole world's homage is his due. The great ones
of the earth feast in his presence, and adore; men brought low, even to the
31 dust, bow down at his feet.[1] I, too, shall live on before him,[2] and beget
32 children to serve him; the Lord will claim for his own a generation still
to come; heaven itself will make known his faithfulness to a people yet
to be born, a people of the Lord's own founding.[3]

PSALM TWENTY-TWO   (23)

(A psalm of David.)

2 THE Lord is my shepherd; how can I lack anything? He gives me
a resting-place where there is pasture, and leads me out by cool
3 waters, to make me live anew. As in honour pledged, by sure paths he
4 leads me; what though I walk with the shadow of death all around me?
Hurt I fear none, while thou art with me; thy rod, thy crook are my
5 comfort. What though my enemies trouble me? Full in their view thou
dost spread a banquet before me; richly thou dost anoint my head with

---

[1] The meaning of this verse is quite uncertain.

[2] 'I, too, shall live on before him'; according to the Hebrew text, this should
be 'and their souls have no life,' belonging to verse 30 as part of the description that verse gives of the unfortunate.

[3] In the Hebrew text the sense is quite different; it is generally taken as meaning,
'tidings shall be given to the (coming) generation about the Lord; they will come
and tell a people yet to be born about his faithfulness, that he has accomplished it.'

6 oil, generous the cup that steals away my senses! All my life thy goodness pursues me; through the long years, the Lord's house shall be my dwelling-place.

PSALM TWENTY-THREE   (24)

(On the first day of the week. A psalm of David.)

THE Lord owns earth, and all earth's fulness, the round world, and
2 all its inhabitants. Who else has built it out from the sea, poised it on the hidden streams?
3 Who dares climb the mountain of the Lord, and appear in his
4 sanctuary? The guiltless in act, the pure in heart; one who never played fast and loose with his soul,[1] by swearing treacherously to his neighbour.
5 His to receive a blessing from the Lord, mercy from God, his sure
6 defender; his the true breed that still looks, still longs for the presence of the God of Jacob.
7 Swing back the doors,[2] captains of the guard; swing back, immemorial
8 gates, to let the King enter in triumph! Who is this great King? Who
9 but the Lord, mighty and strong, the Lord mighty in battle? Swing back the doors, captains of the guard; swing back, immemorial gates, to let the
10 King enter in triumph! Who is this great King? It is the Lord of Armies that comes here on his way triumphant.

PSALM TWENTY-FOUR   (25)

(To the end; a psalm of David.)

2 ALL my heart goes out to thee, O Lord my God. Belie thou never the
3 trust I have in thee, let not my enemies boast of my downfall. Can any that trust in thee be disappointed, as they are disappointed, who
4 wantonly forsake the right? Direct my way, Lord, as thou wilt, teach me
5 thy own paths. Ever let thy truth guide and teach me, O God, my
6 deliverer, my abiding hope. Forget not, Lord, thy pity, thy mercies of
7 long ago. Give heed no more to the sins and follies of my youth, but
8 think mercifully of me, as thou, Lord, art ever gracious. How gracious is the Lord, how faithful; light of the traveller that has missed his path!
9 In his own laws he will train the humble; in his own paths the obedient
10 he will guide. Jealous be thy keeping of covenant and ordinance, and the

---

[1] Some authorities give 'with *my* soul'—that is, taken God's name in vain. But the Hebrew text is generally understood as meaning 'one who has not lifted up his heart to vain things,' that is, to false gods.
[2] In verses 7, 9, the Hebrew text has 'Lift up your heads, you gates.'

11 Lord's dealings will be ever gracious, ever faithful with thee. **K**indly be
thy judgement of my sin, Lord, for thy own honour's sake, my grievous
sin.

12 **L**et a man but fear the Lord, in the path chosen for him he shall find
13 guidance enough. **M**uch joy he shall have of his lands, and to his sons
14 leave them. **N**o man ever feared the Lord, but found support in him,
15 and revelation in his covenant. **O**n the Lord I fix my eyes continually,
16 trusting him to save my feet from the snare. **P**ity me, Lord, as thou
17 seest me friendless and forlorn. **Q**uickly as my troubles increase do thou,
18 Lord, save me from my distress. **R**estless and forlorn, I claim thy pity,
19 to my sins be merciful. **S**ee how many are my foes, and how bitter is the
20 grudge they bear me. **T**ake my soul into thy keeping; come to my rescue,
21 and do not let me be disappointed of my trust in thee. **U**prightness
22 and purity find a friend in me, as I wait patiently for thy help. **W**hen
wilt thou deliver Israel, my God, from all his troubles?

PSALM TWENTY-FIVE   (26)

(To the end; a psalm of David.)

LORD, be thou my judge; have I not guided my steps clear of wrong?
2 Have I trusted in the Lord, only to stumble on my path? Test
me, Lord, put me to the proof; assay my inmost desires and thoughts.
3 Ever I keep thy mercies in mind, thy faithfulness commands my love.
4 I have not consorted with false men, or joined in plotting evil; I have
shunned the company of the wicked, never sat at my ease with sinners.
6 With the pure in heart I will wash my hands clean, and take my place
7 among them at thy altar, listening there to the sound of thy praises,
8 telling the story of all thy wonderful deeds. How well, Lord, I love thy
9 house in its beauty, the place where thy own glory dwells! Lord, never
count this soul for lost with the wicked, this life among the bloodthirsty;
10 hands ever stained with guilt, palms ever itching for a bribe! Be it mine
12 to guide my steps clear of wrong; deliver me in thy mercy. On sure
ground my feet are set; where thy people gather, Lord, I will join in blessing thy name.

PSALM TWENTY-SIX   (27)

(A psalm of David before he was anointed.)

THE Lord is my light and my deliverance; whom have I to fear?
2 The Lord watches over my life; whom shall I hold in dread? Vainly
the malicious close about me, as if they would tear me in pieces, vainly

3 my enemies threaten me; all at once they stumble and fall. Though a
  whole host were arrayed against me, my heart would be undaunted;
  though an armed onset should threaten me, still I would not lose my
4 confidence. One request I have ever made of the Lord, let me claim it
  still, to dwell in the Lord's house my whole life long, gazing at the beauty
5 of the Lord, haunting his sanctuary. In his royal tent he hides me, in the
6 inmost recess of his royal tent, safe from peril. On a rock fastness he
  lifts me high up, see how far above my enemies' reach! I will join with the
  throng, and make an offering of triumphant music in this tabernacle of
  his, singing and praising the Lord.
7   Listen to my voice, Lord, when I cry to thee; hear and spare. True
  to my heart's promise, I have eyes only for thee; [1] I long, Lord, for thy
9 presence. Do not hide thy face, do not turn away from thy servant in
  anger, but give me still thy aid; do not forsake me, do not neglect me,
10 O God, my defender. Father and mother may neglect me, but the Lord
11 takes me into his care. Lord, shew me the way thou hast chosen for me,
12 guide me into the right path, beset as I am with enemies; do not give me
  over to the will of my oppressors, when false witnesses stand up to accuse
13 me, with malice self-betrayed.[2] My faith is, I will yet live to see the
14 Lord's mercies. Wait patiently for the Lord to help thee; be brave, and
  let thy heart take comfort; wait patiently for the Lord.

PSALM TWENTY-SEVEN   (28)

(A psalm of David.)

·

T O thee, Lord, I cry; my God, do not leave my cry unanswered; speak
    to me, or I am no better than a dead man, sinking to the grave.
2 Listen, Lord, to my plea, as I raise my hands in prayer towards thy
3 holy temple. Do not summon me, like the wicked, before thy judgement-
  seat; let me not share its doom with men who traffic in iniquity, men
  who talk of peace to their neighbours, while their hearts are full of
4 malice. For them, the reward of their own acts, their own evil ways;
5 as they did, be it done to them, in their own coin repaid. Of the Lord's
  acts, the Lord's ways, they took no heed; ruin be theirs, ruin irreparable.
6   Blessed be the Lord's name, my plea is heard; the Lord is my strength
  and shield. Trusting in him, I found redress, and with health renewed
8 right heartily I praise him. The Lord defends his own, protects and

---

[1] Literally, 'My heart has said, My face has sought thee.' The Hebrew text
has, 'My heart has said, Seek my face.'
[2] In the Hebrew text perhaps rather 'who breathe out violence.'

9 delivers the king he has anointed. Lord, save thy people, bless thy own chosen race; be their shepherd, evermore in thy arms upholding them.

PSALM TWENTY-EIGHT (29)

(A psalm of David; at the finishing of the tabernacle.) [1]

SONS of God, make your offering to the Lord, an offering to the
2 Lord of yearling rams. Make an offering to the Lord of honour and glory, an offering to the Lord of the glory that befits his name; worship
3 the Lord, here, in his holy precincts.[2] The voice of the Lord is heard over the waters, when the glorious God thunders, the Lord, thunder-
4 ing over swollen waters; the Lord's voice in its power, the Lord's voice
5 in its majesty. The Lord's voice, that breaks the cedars; the Lord breaks
6 the cedars of Lebanon; the Holy One throws them down, as some calf
7 on Lebanon is thrown down by the breed of the wild ox.[3] The Lord's
8 voice cleaves those shafts of flame; the Lord's voice makes the wilderness
9 rock; the Lord, rocking the wilderness of Cades. The Lord's voice puts the hinds in travail; who but the Lord strips the deep forest bare. Mean-
10 while, in his sanctuary, there is no sound but tells of his glory. Out of a raging flood, the Lord makes a dwelling-place; the Lord sits enthroned
11 as king for ever. And this Lord will give strength to his people; the Lord will give his people his own blessing of peace.

PSALM TWENTY-NINE (30)

(The psalm of a song at the dedication of David's house.)

2 PRAISE to thee, Lord, thou hast taken me under thy protection,
3 and baulked my enemies of their will; I cried out to the Lord my
4 God, and thou didst grant me recovery. So didst thou bring me back,

---

[1] 'The finishing of the Tabernacle' is generally taken as referring to the close of the Feast of Tabernacles (the psalm is still used among the Jews in their liturgy of Pentecost). In the Hebrew text, there is no mention of offering rams.
[2] 'His holy precincts'; the Hebrew text has 'the beauty of holiness.'
[3] The Latin here reads literally, 'and he will throw them down like a calf of Lebanon, the Beloved One, (acting) like the young of unicorns.' 'The beloved one' is a title elsewhere given to God's people, but nowhere to himself; its sense in Hebrew is rather 'the upright one.' It seems clear that the Septuagint, and the Latin in translating it, have mistaken one of the Hebrew words; the Hebrew text has 'he makes them leap like a calf, Lebanon and Sirion (that is, Hermon) leap like a young unicorn.' The unicorn means either the buffalo or some kind of antelope, according to the common opinion.

Lord, from the place of shadows, rescue me from the very edge of the
5 grave. Sing praise to the Lord, then, faithful souls, invoke his name
6 with thankfulness. What if his vengeance falls swift when he is angry? [1]
With his favour life returns; sorrow is but the guest of a night, and joy
comes in the morning.

7 I, too, had thought, in the time of my prosperity, Nothing can shake
8 me now; so firmly, Lord, hast thou established my kingship.[2] Then thou
9 didst turn thy face away from me, and I was at peace no more. Lord,
10 I was fain to cry aloud to thee, to plead with my God, How will it profit
thee to take my life? I can but go down into the grave; and will this dust
11 give thanks to thee, or acknowledge, there, thy faithfulness? With pity
12 the Lord heard me; the Lord himself, now, took my part. Thou hast
turned my sadness into rejoicing; thou hast undone the sackcloth I wore,
13 and girded me about with gladness. So may this heart never tire of singing praises; O Lord my God, I will give thanks to thee for ever.

PSALM THIRTY   (31)

(To the end, a psalm of David; for bewilderment.)

2 TO thee, O Lord, I look for refuge, never let me be ashamed of my
3 trust; in thy faithful care, deliver me. Grant me audience, and make
haste to rescue me; my divine protector, my stronghold of defence, to
4 save me from peril. Thou dost strengthen and defend me; thou, for thy
5 own honour, dost guide and nurture me; by thee protected, I shall
6 escape from the snare that lies hidden in my path. Into thy hands I
commend my spirit; thou, God ever faithful, hast claimed me for thyself.
7 Let fools provoke thee by wasting themselves on false dreams;[3] for me
8 no refuge but the Lord. I will triumph and exult in thy mercy; it was
thou that didst pity my weakness, and save me when I was hard bestead;
9 before the enemy's toils could close around me, the open plain lay at my
feet.
10 And now, Lord, have compassion on my distress; vexation has dimmed
11 my eyes, frets me away, soul and body. My life is all grief, my years are
but sighs; for very misery,[4] my strength ebbs away, my frame is wasted.
12 Openly my foes deride me; even to my neighbours I am a thing of
utter scorn; my friends are adread, and the passer-by shuns my contact;

---

[1] In the Hebrew text, 'His anger lasts but a moment.' To match this, some
would render what follows, 'and his favour lasts a lifetime.'

[2] According to the Hebrew text, 'my hill (fastness).'

[3] 'False dreams'; the reference is probably to heathen worship.

[4] In the Hebrew text 'through my sin.'

13 I am lost to memory, like a dead man, discarded like a broken pitcher.
14 On every side their busy whispering comes to my ears,[1] so powerful the
15 conspiracy that threatens my life. And still, Lord, my trust in thee is
16 not shaken; still I cry, Thou art my God, my fate is in thy hand; save
17 me from the enemy's power, save me from my pursuers! Smile on thy
18 servant once more, and deliver me in thy mercy; Lord, do not let me
   plead in vain. Disappoint the wicked of their hopes, hurl them down into
19 the abyss; let silence fall on those treacherous lips, that spoke maliciously
   of the innocent, in the days of their pride and scorn!
20   What treasures of loving-kindness, Lord, dost thou store up for the
   men who fear thee, the men who trust thee, made known in act, for all
21 the world to see! Thy presence is a sanctuary, to hide them away from
22 the world's alarums; thy tabernacle a refuge from its noisy debate. Blessed
   be the Lord; so wondrous is his mercy, so strong the wall of his pro-
23 tection. I thought, bewildered, that thy watchful care had lost sight of
   me; but I cried out to thee, and thou thereupon didst listen to my plea.
24 Love the Lord well, you who worship him; the Lord keeps faith with
25 his servants, and repays the actions of the proud above measure. Take
   heart, keep high your courage, all you that wait patiently for the Lord.

PSALM THIRTY-ONE   (32)

(For David himself; of understanding.)

   B LESSED are they who have their faults forgiven, their trans-
2   gressions buried deep; blessed is the man who is not guilty in the
3 Lord's reckoning, the heart that hides no treason. While I kept my
   own secret, all day long I cried to thee in vain; still my strength pined
4 away, bowed down day and night by thy chastisement; still I tossed
5 about in pain, so deep did the thorn rankle.[2] At last I made my transgression known to thee, and hid my sin no longer; I will be my own
   accuser, I said, and confess my fault to the Lord; and with that, thou
6 didst remit the guilt of my sin. Let every devout soul, then, turn to thee
   in prayer while it has time to reach thee; none will find access,[3] when the
7 waters are running deep in flood. Thou art my hiding-place, when
   oppression rings me round; of thee is my triumph-song, rescue me from
   my besiegers.

---

[1] In the Hebrew text, 'and fear is round about me,' cf. Jer. 20.10.
[2] The Hebrew text in the second half of this verse appears to mean, 'all my
freshness was withered away (as if) by summer drought.'
[3] Literally 'they will not approach him.' Probably, in the Hebrew text, this
means the waters will not approach the devout soul.

8   Friend, let me counsel thee, trace for thee the path thy feet should
9 tread; let my prudence watch over thee. Do not be like the horse and the
mule, that are senseless things; hold them in thou must with bit and
10 bridle, so obstinately they shun thee.¹ Again and again the sinner must
feel the lash; he who trusts in the Lord finds nothing but mercy all
11 around him. Just souls, be glad, and rejoice in the Lord; true hearts,
make your boast in him.

PSALM THIRTY-TWO   (33)

(A psalm of David.)

T RIUMPH, just souls, in the Lord; true hearts, it is yours to praise
2   him. Give thanks to the Lord with the viol's music, praise him with
3 a harp of ten strings. For him let a new song be sung; give him of your
4 best, sound the harp lustily. The Lord's word is true, he is faithful in all
5 his dealings; compassion he loves, and the just award, the whole earth
6 overflows with the Lord's goodness. It was the Lord's word that made
7 the heavens, the breath of his lips that peopled them; he it is who stores
up the waters of the sea as in a cistern, and makes a cellar of its deep
8 caverns. Let the whole earth hold the Lord in dread, let all the inhabi-
9 tants of the world stand in awe of him; he spoke, and they were made,
10 he gave his command, and their frame was fashioned. At the Lord's
bidding, a nation's purposes come to nothing, a people's designs are
11 thwarted, kings are baulked of their will: his own designs stand firm for
ever; generation after generation, his will does not swerve.
12   Blessed the nation that calls the Lord its own God, the people he
13 has chosen out to be his! Looking down from heaven, he watches all
14 mankind, his immovable dwelling has the whole world in view; he has
16 fashioned each man's nature, and weighs the actions of each. There is
no protection for kings in powerful armies, for great warriors in abundant
17 prowess; nor shall horses avail thee against peril, brute strength that
18 cannot save. It is the Lord, watching over those who fear him and trust
19 in his mercy, that will protect their lives, will feed them in time of
20 famine. Patiently we wait for the Lord's help; he is our strength and our
21 shield; in him our hearts will find contentment, in his holy name we
22 trust. Lord, let thy mercy rest upon us, who put all our confidence in
thee.

---

¹ Some understand the Hebrew text here as meaning that the horse or mule
will turn on its rider unless it is bridled. The sense of the Latin is uncertain;
it can be taken as addressed to Almighty God, 'Hold them in with bit and
bridle, the men who will not approach thee!'

PSALM THIRTY-THREE   (34)

(For David, when he disguised himself at the court of Achimelech, so that Achimelech sent him away, and he escaped.) [1]

2 AT all times I will bless the Lord; his praise shall be on my lips
3 continually. Be all my boasting in the Lord; listen to me, humble
4 souls, and rejoice. Come, sing the Lord's praise with me, let us extol his
5 name together. Did I not look to the Lord, and find a hearing; did he
6 not deliver me from all my troubles? Enter his presence, and find there
7 enlightenment; here is no room for downcast looks. Friendless folk may
   still call on the Lord and gain his ear, and be rescued from all their
8 afflictions. Guardian of those who fear the Lord, his angel encamps at
9 their side, and brings deliverance. How gracious the Lord is! Taste and
10 prove it; blessed is the man that learns to trust in him. It is for you, his
   chosen servants, to fear the Lord; those who fear him never go wanting.
11 Justly do the proud fall into hunger and want; [2] blessing they lack not
   that look to him.
12 Know, then, my children, what the fear of the Lord is; come and listen
13 to my teaching. Long life, and prosperous days, who would have these
14 for the asking? My counsel is, keep thy tongue clear of harm, and thy
15 lips free from every treacherous word. Naught of evil cherish thou, but
16 rather do good; let peace be all thy quest and aim. On the upright the
   Lord's eye ever looks favourably; his ears are open to their pleading.
17 Perilous is his frown for the wrong-doers; he will soon make their name
18 vanish from the earth. Roused by the cry of the innocent, the Lord
19 sets them free from all their afflictions. So near is he to patient hearts,
20 so ready to defend the humbled spirit. Though a hundred trials beset
21 the innocent, the Lord will bring him safely through them all. Under
   the Lord's keeping, every bone of his is safe; not one of them shall suffer
22 harm. Villains will come to an evil end; the enemies of innocence will
   bear their punishment.
23 The Lord will claim his servants as his own; they go unreproved that
   put their trust in him.

---

[1] See I Kg. 21.10 and following. The Hebrew text here gives Abimelech instead of Achimelech; in the Book of Kings, he is called Achish.
[2] For 'the proud,' the Hebrew text has 'the young lions.'

PSALM THIRTY-FOUR (35)

(David's own.)

1 LORD, redress my wrongs; disarm the enemies who rise in arms
2 against me; grip thy weapons and thy shield, bestir thyself in my
3 defence. Unsheathe thy sword, and bar the way against my pursuers;
4 whisper in my heart, I am here to save thee. For my mortal enemies,
shame and disappointment, for my ill-wishers one and all, ruin and re-
5 morse; dust before the wind, with the angel of the Lord to scatter
6 them, benighted and bemired on their way, with the angel of the Lord
7 in pursuit! Wantonly they have laid their deadly snares for me, wantonly
8 they have laughed at my misfortune; [1] now let the net overtake them
unawares, now let the snare they laid close round them; their own net,
9 see how they fall into it! Mine to triumph in the Lord, to take delight
10 in his saving power; this be the cry of my whole being, There is none
like thee, Lord; who else rescues the afflicted from the hand of tyranny,
the poor, the destitute, from his oppressors?
11 See how false witnesses have come forward, to browbeat me over
12 charges of which I know nothing; how they have repaid my kindness
13 with cruelty, and left me friendless! What did I do, when they began
to trouble me thus? [2] I went clad in sackcloth, and humbled my pride with
14 fasting; and all my prayer hid itself in my own bosom. I went on my
way peaceably, treating them like friends and brothers; I humbled
15 myself, as a mourner humbles himself for grief.[3] Now they met to
triumph over my misfortune, when punishments crowded in upon me,
16 that meant no harm.[4] Now they would scatter,[5] but still gave me no
respite, baiting me, heaping mockery on mockery, gnashing their teeth
17 at me. Lord, wilt thou never have eyes to see it? Wilt thou leave my life
18 unprotected at the mercy of these roaring lions? Let me live to praise
and thank thee before the multitude that throngs thy courts.

---

[1] The Hebrew text has, 'they have dug a pit for me.'

[2] 'When they began to trouble me thus'; the Hebrew text has 'when they were in sickness,' as if King David were recalling his earlier kindness to these enemies of his. 'My prayer hid itself in my own bosom,' either in the sense that it made no impression on his enemies (cf. Mt. 10.13), or merely in the sense that he bowed himself double in the intensity of his prayer (cf. III Kg. 28.42).

[3] The sense of this verse is not certain; in the second part of it, the Hebrew text has 'I went bowed in mourning as one that weeps for his mother.'

[4] Some would render, 'when punishments crowded in upon me unexpectedly.'

[5] In the Hebrew text, 'they tore me to pieces.'

19 No more the leer of triumph in the eye of yonder treacherous foe, that
20 wantonly assails me! Time was when they talked to me peaceably enough,
    yet all the while they were plotting, and their talk bred quarrels in the
21 land. Now they cry out against me openly, Joy, joy that we should
22 have lived to see this![1] Thou too, Lord, hast seen it, do not pass it by in
23 silence; Lord, do not abandon me. Bestir thyself and take my part, give
24 me speedy redress, my Lord and my God. As thou art just, O Lord my
25 God, give thy award for me, never let them triumph over me; never let
    them think, All goes well, and boast that they have made a prey of me.
26 Fill them with shame and with awe, the men who delight in my mis-
    fortune; cover them with confusion and self-reproach, the enemies that
27 triumph over me. Joy and gladness be theirs, who applaud my innocence;
28 Praise to the Lord! be their cry, who wish well to his servant. And all
    day long, for thy just awarding, this tongue shall make known thy praise.

PSALM THIRTY-FIVE   (36)

(To the end; for David himself, the Lord's servant.)

2 THE sinner thinks to keep his evil ways secret, forgetting that he
3   has God to fear; plans treacherously under that watchful eye, till at
4 last his sin comes to light in all its hatefulness.[2] No word on his lips
   but is cruel and false; never a wholesome thought his mind harbours.
5 He lies awake plotting mischief, and lends himself to every evil course,
   never weary of wrong-doing.
6 Lord, thy mercy is high as heaven; thy faithfulness reaches to the
7 clouds; thy justice stands firm as the everlasting hills,[3] the wisdom of
8 thy decrees is deep as the abyss. Lord, thou dost give protection to
   man and beast, so rich is thy divine mercy; under the shelter of those
9 wings the frail children of earth will find confidence. Their senses will be
   ravished with the treasures of thy house; thou wilt bid them drink deep
10 at thy fountain of contentment. In thee is the source of all life; thy
11 brightness will break on our eyes like dawn. Give proof, then, of thy

---

[1] In verses 20 and 21, the Latin seems to imply that there were two different
stages in King David's persecution, one of treacherous friendship, and one
of open hostility. But the Hebrew text has 'they did not talk to me peaceably.'
The second half of verse 20 is obscure; the Hebrew text has, 'their talk was
against those who are quiet in the land.'

[2] In verses 2 and 3 the Hebrew text is obscure, and probably corrupt. The
sense of the Latin appears to be that given above, though possibly 'in all its
hatefulness' should be 'in the form of hatred.'

[3] Literally 'the hills of God,' a Hebrew form of speech for what is magnificent in nature.

12 mercy to those who acknowledge thee, of thy favour to upright hearts; do
13 not suffer the proud to trample on me, the wicked to dispossess me. See
what a fall awaits the wrong-doers, how they lose the path, and can keep
their feet no more!

PSALM THIRTY-SIX   (37)

(A psalm for David himself.)

ART thou jealous when the wicked thrive, dost thou envy the lot of
2 evildoers? They will soon fade like the grass, wither away like the
3 green leaf. Be content to trust in the Lord and do good; live on thy land,
4 with its riches to sustain thee, all thy longing fixed in the Lord; so he will
5 give thee what thy heart desires. Commit thy life to the Lord, and trust
6 in him; he will prosper thee, making thy honesty clear as the day, the
7 justice of thy cause bright as the sun at noon. Doom the Lord sends thee
accept, and pray to him, never fretting over the man that has his own way,
8 and thrives by villainy. End thy complaints, forgo displeasure, do not
9 fret thyself into an evil mood; the evil-minded will be dispossessed, and
10 patient souls, that wait for the Lord, succeed them. Forbear yet a little,
and the sinners will be seen no more; thou wilt search in vain to find
11 them, while patient souls are the land's heirs, enjoying great peace.
12 Gnashing his teeth with envy, the wrong-doer lies in wait for the
13 innocent, and cannot see his own turn coming; but the Lord sees it, and
14 laughs at his malice. How they draw the sword, how they bend the bow,
these sinners, to overthrow the poor in their helplessness, to murder the
15 upright; swords that will pierce their own hearts, bows that will break
16 in pieces! Innocence, little endowed, has the better of the wicked in
17 their abundance; soon fails the strength of their arms, and still the
18 Lord has the just in his keeping. Jealously the Lord watches over the
19 lives of the guiltless; they will hold their lands forever, undismayed
20 by adversity, in time of famine well content. Knavery will yet come to
an end; proud and powerful the Lord's enemies may be,[1] but soon they
21 will vanish, vanish like smoke. Let the sinner borrow, and never repay,
22 still the good man will be a generous giver;[2] bless the Lord, and the land
23 is thine, blaspheme him, and thy name will be forgotten. Man's feet
24 the Lord must guide, if he would be sped on his journey; stumble he

---

[1] The Hebrew text has 'are like the beauty of the field' instead of the words
'proud and powerful (the Lord's enemies) may be.'

[2] It is difficult to see the connexion between this verse and the next, unless
we suppose that it indicates a reversal of fortunes, in which the wicked will always be defaulting borrowers, and good men will be in a position to help them.

25 may, but fall never, with the Lord's hand to uphold him. **N**ow youth
is past, and I have grown old; yet never did I see the good man forsaken,
26 or his children begging their bread; still he lends without stint, and men
27 call down blessings on his posterity. **O**ffend no more, rather do good,
28 and be at rest continually; the Lord is ever just, and will not abandon
his faithful servants. **P**erish the sinner, forgotten be the name of the evil-
29 doer, but these will hold their land, and live on it always at rest.
30   **R**ight reason is on the good man's lips, well weighed are all his
31 counsels; his steps never falter, because the law of God rules in his
32 heart. **S**inners lie in wait, plotting against the life of the innocent;
33 but the Lord will never leave him in their power, never find him guilty
34 when he is arraigned. **T**rust the Lord, and follow the path he has chosen;
so he will set thee up in possession of thy land, and thou wilt live to see
35 the wicked come to ruin. **U**ntil yesterday, I saw the sinner enthroned
36 high as the cedars of Lebanon; then, when I passed by, he was there no
37 longer, and I looked in vain to find him. **V**igilantly preserve innocence,
and keep the right before thy eyes; he that lives peaceably will leave
38 a race behind him, while the sinners are rooted out every one, and their
39 graceless names forgotten. **W**hen affliction comes, the Lord is the refuge
40 and defence of the innocent; the Lord will aid and deliver them, and
preserve them from the power of wickedness, because they put their trust
in him.

PSALM THIRTY-SEVEN   (38)

(A psalm of David; for a memorial concerning the sabbath.)

2 THY reproof, Lord, not thy vengeance; thy chastisement, not thy
3   condemnation! Thy arrows pierce me, thy hand presses me hard;
4 thy anger has driven away all health from my body, never a bone sound
5 in it, so grievous are my sins. My own wrong-doing towers high above
6 me, hangs on me like a heavy burden; my wounds fester and rankle,
7 with my own folly to blame. Beaten down, bowed to the earth, I go
8 mourning all day long, my whole frame cruelly buffeted,[1] my whole
9 body diseased; so spent, so crushed, I groan aloud in the weariness of
10 my heart. Thou, Lord, knowest all my longing, no complaint of mine
11 escapes thee; restless my heart, gone my strength; the very light that
shone in my eyes is mine no longer.
12   Friends and neighbours that meet me keep their distance now;[2] old

---

[1] *v.* 7. In the Hebrew text, 'full of burning.'
[2] *v.* 12. In the Hebrew text, 'Friends and neighbours kept their distance from
my punishment,' cf. Apoc. 18.10.

13 companions shun me. I am assailed by enemies that grudge me life
itself; night and day, with false whispering, their malice plots against
14 me. And I, all the while, am deaf to their threats, dumb before my
15 accusers; mine the unheeding ear, and the tongue that utters no defence.
16 On thee, Lord, my hopes are set; thou, O Lord my God, wilt listen
17 to me. Such is the prayer I make, Do not let my enemies triumph
18 over me, boast of my downfall. See, I bow before the lash,[1] ever mindful
19 of my wretchedness, ever ready to publish my guilt, ever anxious
20 over my sin. And still they live, these enemies of mine, and still they
21 have the mastery; so many that bear me a grudge so wantonly, ever
rewarding good with evil, and for the very rightness of my cause assailing
22 me. Do not fail me, O Lord my God, do not forsake me; hasten to
my defence, Lord God, my only refuge.

PSALM THIRTY-EIGHT   (39)

(To the end, for Idithun himself; a psalm of David.)

2 IT was my resolve to live watchfully, and never use my tongue amiss;
still, while I was in the presence of sinners, I kept my mouth gagged,
3 so dumb and patient that I would not speak even to good purpose.
4 But indignation came back, and my heart burned within me, the
5 fire kindled by my thoughts, so that at last I kept silence no longer.[2]
Lord, warn me of my end, and how few my days are; teach me to
6 know my own insufficiency. See how thou hast measured my years
with a span, how my life is nothing in thy reckoning! Nay, what is
7 any man that lives, but nothingness? Truly man passes through the
world like a shadow; with what vain anxiety he hoards up riches, when
8 he cannot tell who will have the counting of them! What hope then
9 have I? What but thyself, Lord? All that I am is from thee. Clear
me of that manifold guilt which makes me the laughing-stock of fools,
10 tongue-tied and uncomplaining, because I know that my troubles
11 come from thee; spare me this punishment; I faint under thy powerful
12 hand. When thou dost chasten man for his sins with thy reproof, his
life melts away like gossamer;[3] all he once cared for seems worthless
13 then. Listen, Lord, to my prayer, let my cry reach thy hearing, and

---

[1] In the Hebrew text, 'I am ready to fall.'

[2] It is not clear what is the connexion between the two parts of this psalm.

[3] The words 'with thy reproof' can also be taken as part of the preceding
sentence. 'His life melts like gossamer'; in the Hebrew text, 'thou consumest
(literally, meltest) all the desire of his heart as a moth would.'

my tears win answer. What am I in thy sight but a passer-by, a wanderer,
14 as all my fathers were? Give me some respite,[1] some cool breath of
comfort, before I go away and am known no more.

PSALM THIRTY-NINE   (40)

(To the end; a psalm for David himself.)

2 PATIENTLY I waited for the Lord's help, and at last he turned
3 his look towards me; he listened to my plea, drew me up out
of a cheerless pit, where the mire had settled deep, and gave me a
4 foothold on the rock, with firm ground to tread. He has framed a
new music on my lips, a song of praise to our God, to fill all that stand
5 by with reverence, and with trust in the Lord. Happy the man whose
trust is there bestowed, who pays no heed to false gods, and lying dreams.[2]
6 O Lord my God, how long is the story of thy marvellous deeds! There
is no wisdom like thy wisdom. Mine to proclaim it, mine to utter it, great
7 beyond all our measuring. No sacrifice, no offering was thy demand;
enough that thou hast given me an ear ready to listen. Thou hast not
8 found any pleasure in burnt-sacrifices, in sacrifices for sin. See then,
I said, I am coming to fulfil what is written of me, where the book lies
9 unrolled;[3] to do thy will, O my God, is all my desire, to carry out that
10 law of thine which is written in my heart. And I told the story of thy
just dealings before a great throng; be witness, Lord, that I do not seal
11 my lips. Thy just dealings are no secret hidden away in my heart; I
boast of thy faithful protection, proclaim that mercy, that faithfulness of
thine for all to hear it.

12 Lord, do not withhold thy pity from me; thy mercy and faithfulness
13 that have ever been my shield. I am beset with evils past numbering,
overtaken by my sins; they fill my prospect, countless as the hairs on
14 my head; my courage fails me. Deign, Lord, to set me free; Lord,
15 give heed and help. Disappointment and shame be theirs, who lay plots

---

[1] In the Hebrew, 'Look away from me.'

[2] 'False gods, and lying dreams'; in the Hebrew text, 'the proud, and those
who fall into error.'

[3] vv. 7–8. Heb. 10.5. 'Thou hast given me an ear ready to listen'; literally, in
the Latin, 'thou hast perfected ears for me.' In the Hebrew text, this is 'thou
hast pierced ears for me.' But the Septuagint Greek has 'thou hast fitted a
body for me,' and this is the form in which the Epistle to the Hebrews (10.5)
quotes the passage: 'Where the book lies unrolled'; literally 'In the head-part'
(or, according to the Hebrew text, the volume) 'of the book.' This is often
identified as the book of the Law; but the context suggests rather a metaphorical
reference to David's own destiny (cf. Ex. 32.32; I Kg. 13.14).

16 against my life; let them slink away in confusion, my ill-wishers. Joy,
17 joy, is their cry now; ere long they will be blushing in their turn.[1] Rejoicing and triumph for all the souls that look to thee; Praise to the Lord,
18 will ever be their song, who rejoice in thy saving power. I, so helpless,
   so destitute, and the Lord is concerned for me! Thou art my champion
   and my refuge; do not linger, my God, do not linger, on the way.

PSALM FORTY   (41)

(To the end; a psalm for David himself.)

2 BLESSED is that man who takes thought for the poor and the
3   destitute; the Lord will keep him safe in time of trouble. May
   the Lord watch over him, and give him long life and happiness on
4 earth, and baulk his enemies of their will. May the Lord sustain him
   when he lies bed-ridden; ease thou canst give abundantly to the fever-
   tossed.
5   Lord have mercy on me, is my prayer; bring healing to a soul that
6 has sinned against thee. Bitterly my enemies taunt me; How long,
7 they ask, ere he will die, and his name be forgotten? When one comes
   to visit me, he comes with smooth words, his heart full of malice;
8 ready to go out and plot against me in secret. There they stand, my
9 enemies talking of me in whispers, devising my hurt, pitiless in their
10 resolve; He sleeps now, but what is to prevent his waking?[2] Why, the
   very man I trusted most, my own intimate friend, who shared my
11 bread, has lifted his heel to trip me up.[3] Lord, have mercy on me;
12 give me back life, and let me requite them! Proof of thy favour, my
13 enemies are baulked of their triumph; thou dost befriend my innocence;
14 nevermore wilt thou banish me from thy presence. Blessed be the Lord
   God of Israel, from the beginning to the end of time, Amen, Amen.

---

[1] Literally, 'let them quickly carry their own confusion'; in the Hebrew
text, 'let them be desolate because of their confusion.'

[2] 'Pitiless in their resolve'; the Hebrew text has 'an evil thing is poured into
him (or perhaps, fixed upon him),' as part of what the conspirators said. 'What
is to prevent his waking?' The sense of the Hebrew text is, 'Shall he (be allowed to) rise up?'; the Latin seems to express the same idea more allusively.

[3] Jn. 13.18.

PSALM FORTY-ONE (42)

(To the end; of understanding; for the sons of Core.)

2 O GOD, my whole soul longs for thee, as a deer for running water;
3 my whole soul thirsts for God, the strong, the living God; shall
4 I never again make my pilgrimage into God's presence? Morning
and evening, my diet still of tears! Daily I must listen to the taunt,
5 Where is thy God now? Memories come back to me yet, melting the
heart; I am back at God's house, his majestic tabernacle, amid the
6 cries of joy and thanksgiving, and all the noise of holiday![1] Soul, art
thou still downcast? Wilt thou never be at peace? Wait for God's help;
I will not cease to cry out in thankfulness, My champion and my God.
7 In my sad mood I will think of thee, here in this land of Jordan
8 and Hermoniim, on these stunted hills.[2] One depth makes answer to
another[3] amid the roar of the floods thou sendest; wave after wave,
9 crest after crest overwhelms me. Such mercy the Lord has shewn me
while day lasted; and have I no song for him, here in the night, no
10 prayer to the God who is life for me?[4] Thou art my stronghold, I will
tell him; hast thou never a thought for me? Must I go mourning, with
11 enemies pressing me hard; racked by the ceaseless taunts of my per-
12 secutors, Where is thy God now? Soul, art thou still downcast? Wilt
thou never be at peace? Wait for God's help; I will not cease to cry out
in thankfulness, My champion and my God.

---

[1] 'I am back at God's house, his majestic tabernacle'; this seems to be the
sense of the Latin, referring to an exile's day-dreams. The Hebrew text is
usually rendered, 'I passed on with the crowd, and led them to the house of
God'; but the word translated 'crowd' is not found elsewhere.

[2] The psalm seems to have been written by an exile from Jerusalem, living
to the east of Jordan, at its northern end, on the foot-hills of the Hermon
range. These low hills are described by a word which ordinarily expresses
insignificance, perhaps by way of contrasting them with mount Sion.

[3] These 'depths' are ordinarily understood as being waterfalls; but the second part of the verse would seem to be a metaphor derived from storms at
sea. Cf. Jon. 2.4.

[4] The exact sense here is doubtful; so is the exact punctuation. But it looks
as if 'day-time' was used by a metaphor for the writer's former prosperity, and
'night' for his present unhappy condition.

PSALM FORTY-TWO (43)

(A psalm of David.)

O GOD, sustain my cause; give me redress against a race that
2 knows no piety; save me from a treacherous foe and cruel. Thou,
O God, art all my strength; why hast thou cast me off? Why do I go
3 mourning, with enemies pressing me hard? The light of thy presence,
the fulfilment of thy promise, let these be my escort, bringing me
safe to thy holy mountain, to the tabernacle where thou dwellest.
4 There I will go up to the altar of God, the giver of youth and happiness;
5 thou art my own God, with the harp I hymn thy praise. Soul, art thou
still downcast? Wilt thou never be at peace? Wait for God's help; I will
not cease to cry out in thankfulness, My champion and my God.[1]

PSALM FORTY-THREE (44)

(To the end; for the sons of Core, for understanding.)

2 O God, the tale has come to our ears—have not our fathers told
it?—of the great things thou didst in their time, in days long ago;
3 it was thy power that gave them a home by rooting out the heathen,
4 crushing and dispossessing nations before them. It was not by their
own sword that our fathers won the land, it was not their own strength
that brought them victory; it was the work of thy hand, thy strength;
5 thy smile shone upon them, in proof of thy favour. I too have no King,
6 no God, save thee; it is thou that sendest deliverance to Israel. Through
thee we shew a bold front to our enemies;[2] under thy protection we
7 reck little of their onslaught. Not in my bow I trust, not to my sword
8 I look for safety; it is thou that savest us from our enemies, and coverest
9 their malice with confusion. In God at all times is our boast; his name we
praise eternally.
10 And now? Now, O God, thou hast disowned us, and put us to shame,
11 by refusing to go into battle with our armies. Thou dost put us to
flight before our enemies; our ill-wishers plunder us as they will.
12 Thou hast made us like sheep sold for food, scattered here and there

---

[1] The repetition here of the refrain used in Psalm 41 makes it probable that these two were originally a single psalm.
[2] 'Shew a bold front'; literally 'toss with one's horns.'

13 among the heathen; thou hast bartered away thy people without profit,
14 asking no rich amends for thy loss. Thou hast turned us into a laughing-
stock for our neighbours, mocked and derided by all who dwell around;
15 till the heathen make a by-word of us, and Gentiles toss their heads
16 at us in scorn. All day long my disgrace confronts me; my cheeks
17 are covered with blushes, as I hear nothing but reproach and reviling,
see none but enemies, none but persecutors.
18   All this has come upon us, and it was not that we had forgotten thee.
19 We have not been untrue to thy covenant, or withdrawn our hearts
from thee, that thou shouldst let our steps wander away from thy
20 paths.[1] Why hast thou brought us so low, with misery all around us,[2]
21 and the shadow of death hanging over us? If we had forgotten the
name of our own God, and spread out our hands in prayer to the gods
22 of the alien, would not he know of it? He can read the secrets of men's
hearts. How is it, then, that we face death at every moment for thy
23 sake, reckoned no better than sheep marked down for slaughter? Bestir
thyself, Lord, why dost thou sleep on? Awake, do not banish us from
24 thy presence for ever. How canst thou turn thy face away, without
25 a thought for our need and our affliction? Our pride is bowed in the
26 dust; prostrate, we cannot lift ourselves from the ground. Arise, Lord,
and help us; for thy honour's sake, claim us for thy own.

PSALM FORTY-FOUR   (45)

(To the end, for those who will be transformed; to the sons of Core,
for understanding; a song for a man beloved.)

2 JOYFUL the thoughts that well up from my heart, the King's honour
for my theme; my tongue flows readily as the pen of a swift writer.
3 Thine is more than mortal beauty, thy lips overflow with gracious
4 utterance; the blessings God has granted thee can never fail. Gird
5 on thy sword at thy side, great warrior, gird thyself with all thy majesty
and all thy beauty; make ready, ride on in triumph, and take thy crown,
in the name of faithfulness, and mercy, and justice. Thy own wonderful
6 deeds shall be thy passport;[3] so sharp are thy arrows, subduing nations
7 to thy will, arrows aimed at the hearts of the king's enemies. Thy

---

[1] In the Hebrew text, 'that our step should wander away.'

[2] In the Hebrew text, 'in a place of monsters.'

[3] *v.* 5. 'Make ready'; literally, 'bend thy bow,' but the reading here is uncertain.
'Take thy crown' (literally, 'reign') is not in the Hebrew text. At the end of the
verse, the Hebrew text has, 'Thy right hand shall teach thee terrible lessons.'

throne, O God, endures for ever and ever, the sceptre of thy royalty
8 is a rod that rules true;[1] thou hast been a friend to right, an enemy
to wrong, and God, thy own God, has given thee an unction to bring
9 thee pride beyond any of thy fellows. Thy garments are scented with
myrrh, and aloes, and cassia, stored till now in ivory palaces, whence
the daughters of kings have brought them as gifts to do thee honour.[2]
10 At thy right hand stands the queen in a vesture of gold, all hung about
11 with embroidery.[3] (Listen, my daughter, and consider my words
attentively; thou art to forget, henceforward, thy own nation, and
12 the house of thy fathers; thy beauty, now, is all for the king's delight;
13 he is thy Lord and God,[4] and worship belongs to him.) The women
of Tyre, too, will have their presents to bring; all that are rich among
14 the citizens will be courting thy favour. All her splendour is the
15 splendour of a princess through and through;[5] so bedecked is she
with embroidery, and tassels of gold. Maidens will follow in her retinue
16 into the King's presence, all rejoicing, all triumphant, those com-
17 panions of hers, as they enter the king's palace! Thou shalt have sons
worthy of thy own fathers, and divide a world between them for their
18 domains. While time lasts, thy name will never be forgotten; nations
will do thee honour, age after age, for ever.

PSALM FORTY-FIVE (46)

(To the end; to the sons of Core for hidden things; a psalm.)

2 GOD is our refuge and stronghold; bitter the trial that has over-
3 taken us, but he can save. Not for us to be afraid, though earth
should tumble about us, and the hills be carried away into the depths

---

[1] 'Thy throne, O God'; various other ways of taking these words have been
suggested, as, for example, 'God is (the support of) thy throne.' None of these
has met with general acceptance. This verse and the following are applied
to our Lord in the Epistle to the Hebrews (1.8).

[2] Both the interpretation of these words, and their division into sentences,
have been the subject of dispute. Some think the Hebrew text should be rendered, 'Thy garments are scented with myrrh, aloes, and cassia; music from
the ivory palaces brings thee delight.'

[3] The words 'all hung about with embroidery' are not in the Hebrew text.

[4] The Hebrew text has simply 'thy Lord.'

[5] 'Through and through,' literally 'within,' a word elsewhere used only of
the insides of buildings. The rendering given above seems to represent the
literal meaning of the Latin. The whole passage is very difficult, and some
think that the word translated 'within' is a mistake for the word 'pearls,' which
may have stood in the original text.

4 of the sea. See how the waters [1] rage and roar, how the hills tremble
5 before his might! But the city of God, enriched with deeply flowing
6 rivers, is the chosen sanctuary of the most High,[2] God dwells within her,
  and she stands unmoved; come dawn,[3] he will grant her deliverance.
7 Nations may tremble, and thrones totter, earth shrink away before his
8 voice; but the Lord of hosts is with us, the God of Jacob is our refuge.
9 Come near, and see God's acts, his marvellous acts done on earth;
10 how he puts an end to wars all over the world, the bow shivered, the
11 weapons shattered, the shields burnt to ashes! Wait quietly, and you
   shall have proof that I am God, claiming empire among the nations,
12 claiming empire over the world. The Lord of hosts is with us, the God
   of Jacob is our refuge.

PSALM FORTY-SIX (47)

(To the end; for the sons of Core; a psalm.)

2 CLAP your hands, Gentiles, in applause; acclaim your God with
3 cries of rejoicing. The Lord is high above us, and worthy of dread;
4 he is the sovereign Ruler of all the earth; he has tamed the nations
5 to our will, bowed the Gentiles at our feet, claimed us for his own
6 portion, Jacob the fair, the well beloved. God goes up, loud are the
7 cries of victory; the Lord goes up, loudly the trumpets peal. A psalm,
8 a psalm for our God, a psalm, a psalm for our King! God is King
9 of all the earth; ponder well, the praise you bring him. God reigns over
10 the heathen, God sits enthroned in holiness. The rulers of the nations
   gather before him, the God of Abraham; men high in honour, powerful
   lords [4] of the earth.

PSALM FORTY-SEVEN (48)

(A psalm of music for the sons of Core on the second day of the week.)

2 THE Lord is great, great honour is his due here in the city where
3 he, our God, dwells, here on his holy mountain. Boldly stands
the hill of Sion, the pride of the whole earth, where it slopes northward,

---

[1] In the Latin, 'their waters,' as if the mountain torrents were referred to, but it would appear from the Greek and the Hebrew that the waters are those of the sea.

[2] There may be a reference here to II Par. 32.4.

[3] Literally 'very early in the morning'; which sense may be intended if those scholars are right who connect this psalm with the defeat of Sennacherib (cf. IV Kg. 19.35).

[4] Literally 'gods.' The Hebrew text seems to mean: 'the rulers of the nations have been reckoned as a people belonging to the God of Abraham; God holds the shields of the earth; he is greatly exalted.' It is difficult to believe that either version fully represents the original.

4 the city of the great King; within those walls, God is made known in
5 his protecting care. See, how the kings of the earth have made common
6 cause, and met there in arms! At the sight of her, all was bewilderment,
7 and confusion, and dismay; fear took hold of them, sudden as the
8 throes of a woman in travail: was not thine the power that wrecks
9 the ocean-going ships in the storm? Here, in this city of the Lord
of hosts, the city of our own God, we have proved the tale long since,
10 God has built her to endure for all eternity; sheltered in his temple, we
11 sought and found deliverance. O God, wherever thy name is known on
12 earth, thy praise is told, ever just in thy dealings; well may the hill of
Sion rejoice, well may the women of Juda triumph, at the decrees which
13 thou, Lord, hast executed. Walk about Sion, make the round of her
14 towers, and tell the story in each of them; mark well the defences that
are hers, pass all her strongholds in review; then give the word to the next
15 generation, Such is the God, who is our God for ever and ever; our
Shepherd eternally.[1]

PSALM FORTY-EIGHT   (49)

(To the end, for the sons of Core; a psalm.)

2 LISTEN, you nations far and wide; let all the world give hearing,
3 poor clods of earth, and men nobly born, for rich and poor the
4 same lesson. Here are wise words, thoughts of a discerning heart;
5 mine to overhear mysteries, and reveal, with the harp's music, things
of deep import.

6   What need have I to be afraid in troubled times, when malice dogs
7 my heels [2] and overtakes me, malice of foes who trust in their own
8 strength and boast of their great possessions? What, can brother pay
the penalty instead of brother; [3] must not each pay his own? Man cannot
9 buy God off, and give a ransom for his own life, so that he should be
10 able to scheme on continually, live to eternity,[4] and never meet death.

---

[1] 'Eternally'; the Hebrew text reads 'Until death,' but there is some doubt
of its genuineness.

[2] Literally, 'the wrong-doing of my heels.' The sense of the Hebrew text is
probably 'the wickedness of those who supplant me.'

[3] The Latin here can also be translated, 'Brother cannot ransom brother;
shall a man, then, be able to ransom himself?' The Hebrew text appears to
mean, 'It is quite certain no man can ransom his brother,' which is simpler,
but does not fit in well with the context.

[4] The Latin here can also be translated, 'His life is too precious a thing for
that; he will labour for ever in vain (trying to find the ransom needed), even
though he should live eternally.' This is nearer to the sense of the Hebrew
text, which has 'he must give up that hope once and for all,' instead of 'he will
labour for ever in vain.'

11 True it is, wise men die; but reckless fools perish no less; their riches
12 will go to others, and the grave will be their everlasting home. Generation will follow generation, and they will live on there, under the fields
13 they once called their own. Yet man, in his self-esteem, will not reflect
on what he is;[1] match him with the brute beasts, and he is no better
than they.[2]
14 Fatal path, that ensnares both themselves and those who follow,
15 trusting their advice! There they lie in the world beneath, huddled like
sheep, with death for their shepherd. By tomorrow's dawn, the just
will be triumphing over them; helpless, their pride fades away in the
16 world beneath.[3] But my life God will rescue from the power of that
17 lower darkness, a life that finds acceptance with him. Do not be disturbed, then, when a man grows rich, and there is no end to his house-
18 hold's magnificence; he cannot take all that with him when he dies,
19 magnificence will not follow him to the grave. While life lasts, he
calls himself happy, and gives thanks to thee, O God, for blessing
20 him,[4] but soon he will be made one with the line of his fathers, never
21 again to see the light. Man, in his self-esteem, will not reflect on what
he is; match him with the brute beasts, and he is no better than they.

PSALM FORTY-NINE (50)

(A psalm of Asaph.)

IT is the Lord, the God of gods, that speaks; his message goes out
2 to all the earth, from the sun's rise to its setting. Out of Sion,
3 in perfect beauty, God comes, revealed; he will keep silence no longer.
Before him goes a raging fire; there is a whirling storm round about
4 him. So, from on high, he will summon heaven and earth to witness
5 the judgement pronounced on his people. Muster in his presence
his faithful servants, who honour his covenant still with sacrifice.

---

[1] *v.* 13 (also *v.* 21). 'Man, in his self-esteem, will not reflect on what he is;'
The meaning of the Hebrew text is, 'The honours men enjoy will not last.'
[2] In verses 11–13 the Latin can also be translated, 'He cannot grasp (the
meaning of death) though he sees that,' &c. Instead of 'the grave will be their
everlasting home,' &c., the Hebrew text seems to read, 'their innermost thought
is, that their homes will last for ever, that their brief abodes will go on from
generation to generation, and so they call their fields by their own names.'
[3] The Hebrew text probably means, 'their outward form will be a prey to
the world beneath, and have no habitation left for it,' but the expression is
awkward, and it seems likely that the true reading has been lost.
[4] The Hebrew text reads, 'and men will praise thee (that is, the rich,
thoughtless man) for managing thy affairs successfully.'

6 The heavens themselves pronounce him just, God who is our judge.
7 Listen, my people, to these words of mine, listen, Israel, to the assurance
8 I give thee, I, the God thou ownest as God. I do not find fault with
thee over thy sacrifices; why, all day long thy burnt-offerings smoke
9 before me. But the gifts I accept are not cattle from thy stock, or
10 buck-goats from thy folds; I own already every wild beast in the forest,
11 every drove and herd on the hills; I know every bird that flies in heaven;
12 mine is all the verdure of the fields.[1] If I am hungry, I will not complain of it to thee, I, who am master of earth and all that earth con-
13 tains. Wouldst thou have me eat bull's flesh, and drink the blood of
14 goats? The sacrifice thou must offer to God is a sacrifice of praise,
15 so wilt thou perform thy vows to the most High. So, when thou criest
to me in time of trouble, I will deliver thee; then thou shalt honour
me as thou wilt.

16 But thus, to the sinner, God speaks: How is it that thou canst repeat
17 my commandments by rote, and boast of my covenant with thee, and
thou, all the while, hast no love for the amendment of thy ways, casting
18 every warning of mine to the winds? Swift thou art to welcome the
thief who crosses thy path, to throw in thy lot with the adulterers.
19 Malice wells up from thy lips, and thy tongue is a ready engine of
20 deceit; thou wilt sit there in conclave, speaking evil of thy brother,
21 plotting against thy own mother's son. Such were thy ways, and I made
no sign, till the wicked thought came to thy heart that I was such as
thou art. Here is thy reproof; here is thy indictment made plain to
22 thee. Think well on this, you that forget God, or his hand will fall
23 suddenly, and there will be no delivering you. He honours me truly,
who offers me a sacrifice of praise; there lies your path, who would see the
saving power of God.

PSALM FIFTY (51)

2 (To the end; a psalm of David, on the occasion of Nathan's coming
to reproach him for his adultery with Bethsabee.)

3 HAVE mercy on me, O God, as thou art ever rich in mercy; in
the abundance of thy compassion, blot out the record of my
4 misdeeds. Wash me clean, cleaner yet, from my guilt, purge me of
5 my sin, the guilt which I freely acknowledge, the sin which is never

---

[1] 'The verdure'; this is probably a mistake in the Greek, owing to the use in
Hebrew of a very rare word, which refers to some (unidentified) class of
animal creatures.

6 lost to my sight. Thee only my sins have offended; thou wast the
witness of my wrong-doing; thy warnings were deserved, and if thou
7 art called in question, thou hast right on thy side. For indeed, I was
born in sin; guilt was with me already when my mother conceived
8 me. But thou art ever faithful to thy purpose; and now, in deep parables,
9 thy wisdom has instructed me. Thou wilt sprinkle me with a wand
of hyssop, and I shall be clean; washed, I shall be whiter than snow;
10 a message thou wilt send me of good news and rejoicing, and the body
that lies in the dust shall thrill with pride.
11   Turn thy eyes away from my sins, blot out the record of my guilt;
12 my God, bring a clean heart to birth within me; breathe new life, true
13 life, into my being. Do not banish me from thy presence, do not take
14 thy holy spirit away from me; give me back the comfort of thy saving
15 power, and strengthen me in generous resolve. So will I teach the
wicked to follow thy paths; sinners shall come back to thy obedience.
16 My God, my divine Deliverer, save me from the guilt of bloodshed!
17 This tongue shall boast of thy mercies; O Lord, thou wilt open my
18 lips, and my mouth shall tell of thy praise. If thou hadst a mind for
sacrifice, sacrifice I would have given thee, but thou takest no pleasure
19 in burnt-offerings; the sacrifice God loves is a broken spirit; a heart
20 that is humbled and contrite thou, O God, wilt never disdain. Lord,
in thy great love send prosperity to Sion, so that the walls of Jerusalem
21 may be built.[1] Then indeed thou wilt take pleasure in solemn sacrifice,
in gift and burnt-offering; then indeed bullocks will be laid upon thy
altar.[2]

PSALM FIFTY-ONE   (52)

2 (To the end. Of understanding, for David; when Doeg, the Edomite,
came and told Saul, David went into Achimelech's house.)

3 WILT thou take pride, tyrant, in thy own malice, in thy own
4   ill-doing, all the long day?[3] Thy tongue is skilled in mischief,
5 thy wits razor-edged for treachery. Cruelty, never kindness, is thy
6 study, treason, never honest speech; well thy false lips love the word

---

[1] It seems certain that David built a great part of the defences of Jerusalem
(Josephus, *Antiquities,* VII. iii. 2). But some scholars think that these last two
verses were added to the original psalm, after the capture of Jerusalem by the
king of Babylon.

[2] If this verse is part of the original psalm, it seems to imply that the sacrifice
of beasts, though of no avail in reparation for grievous sin (verse 18), was a
legitimate form of thanksgiving ceremony. (cf. Ps. 49.15).

[3] The words 'all the long day' may be attached, not to what goes before,
but to what follows.

7 that brings men to ruin. And will not God destroy thee utterly, root
thee up, drive thee from thy home, till thy stock is known among
8 living men no more? Honest folk will watch, and wonder, and taunt
9 him then; So much for the man who would have none of God's help,
but relied on his store of riches, and found his strength in vain hopes!
10 And I? rooted like a fruitful olive-tree in the house of my God, I will
11 trust for ever and for ever in his divine mercy; I will give thee eternal
thanks for all thou hast done, and put my trust in thy name, as they ever
love to do, that are thy true servants.

PSALM FIFTY-TWO (53)

1   (To the end, for Maeleth. Of understanding, for David.) [1]

2 THERE is no God above us, is the thought of reckless hearts. Warped
natures everywhere, and foul wrong done; there is not an innocent
3 man among them. God looks down from heaven at the race of men, to
4 find one soul that reflects, and goes in search for him; but no, all have
missed the mark and disappointed him; a life well lived is nowhere to be
5 found. What, can they learn nothing, all these traffickers in iniquity, who
feed themselves fat on this people of mine, as if it were bread for their
6 eating, and never invoke God's name? What wonder if fear assails them,
where they have no cause for fear? Man's friends, God's foes, they fell
7 back routed,[2] and he has scattered their bones far and wide. Oh, may
Sion bring deliverance to Israel! Day of gladness for Jacob, day of Israel's
triumphs, when God brings his exiled people home!

PSALM FIFTY-THREE (54)

2 (To the end among the songs; of understanding, for David. Upon
the occasion when the men of **Ziph** told Saul that David was in hiding
among them.)

3 LORD, by the virtue of thy name deliver me, let thy sovereign
4 power grant me redress; give a hearing, Lord, to my plea; let
5 me speak, and know thou art listening. Alien foes take arms against

---

[1] *vv*. 1–7. See notes on Ps. 13. In the part common to the two Psalms, this
one uses 'God' where the earlier psalm uses 'the Lord,' but otherwise there
is no substantial variation except in verse 6.

[2] In the Hebrew text, 'they encamped against thee.' Some think that this
verse was inserted to celebrate the destruction of Sennacherib's army (IV Kg.
19.35).

me, strong foes that grudge me life itself, with no thought of God
6 to check them. Ah, but God is here to help me; the Lord has my safety
7 in his keeping. Let the blow recoil on my persecutors; ever faithful to
8 thy word, do thou overthrow them. So will I joyfully offer thee sacrifice,
9 and praise thy name, Lord, as praised it must be,   that hast so delivered
me from all peril, and let me see the downfall of my enemies.

PSALM FIFTY-FOUR   (55)

(To the end among the songs. Of understanding, for David.)

2 GIVE audience to my prayer, O God; do not spurn this plea of
3   mine;   hear and grant relief. I am spent with anxiety, bewildered
4 by the outcry of my enemies, by the malice which persecutes me; their
5 sidelong thrusts of injury, their spiteful rage against me. My heart is
6 full of whirling thoughts; the fear of death stands over me; trembling
7 and terrified, I watched the darkness closing about me. Had I but wings,
8 I cry, as a dove has wings, to fly away, and find rest! How distant would
my journey be, how long I would remain there, out in the wilderness!
9 Vainly I wait for rescue from the fears that daunt me,[1] from the storm
around me.
10   Plunge them deep, Lord, in ruin, bring dissension into their councils!
11 Do I not see, already, violence and sedition in the city? Does not
12 wrong stalk about the walls of it night and day, do not misery and
crime occupy its citadel? Oppression and treason are ever busy in
13 its streets. Had it been some enemy that decried me, I could have
borne it patiently; some open ill-wisher, I could have sheltered myself
14 from his scorn. But thou, who hadst known my thoughts, my captain,
15 my familiar friend! How pleasant was the feast when we shared it,
16 thou and I; how lovingly we walked together in the house of God![2] May
death overtake them, may the abyss swallow them up alive, their homes,
their hearts so tainted with evil!
17   Still I will call upon God, and the Lord will save; still at evening
and morn and noon I will cry aloud and make my plea known; he
19 will not be deaf to my appeal. He will win my soul peace, will rescue
20 me from their onset, though so few among many take my part.[3] He,

---

[1] 'From the fears that daunt me'; in the Hebrew text, 'from the raging wind.'
[2] In the Hebrew text, 'We held pleasant converse together, and walked
(together) into God's house with the throng (of worshippers).'
[3] Literally, 'among many they were with me.' The Hebrew text is generally
construed as meaning, 'those against me amounted to many,' but the phrase is
awkward.

the God who reigned before time was, will listen to me, will bring
21 them low. So long unpunished,[1] they have had no fear of God; his
22 hand is raised, now, to do justice. They violated his covenant, and
still his frown was hidden from them, but his heart watched them narrowly; his words were so gentle, they soothed like oil, but in truth they
23 are weapons of destruction.[2] Cast the burden of thy cares upon the Lord,
and he will sustain thee; never will he let thee stumble, his servant if thou
24 be. These, O God, thou wilt sink in a pit of ruin; the blood-thirsty, the
treacherous, will not live out half their days; but I, Lord, will put my
trust in thee.

PSALM FIFTY-FIVE   (56)

(To the end, for the people which is far removed from God's faithful
servants. For David, for the inscription of a monument, when the
Philistines held him prisoner in Geth.)

2 HAVE mercy on me, O God, downtrodden evermore by man's
3 cruel oppression; evermore my enemies tread me under foot,
4 so many there are to make war upon me. Day is no sooner up,[3] than
5 terror surrounds me, but I will still put my confidence in thee; I boast
aloud of God's help, My trust is in God, no mortal design can daunt
6 me. Evermore they shun my converse, have no thought but for my
7 undoing. Ill neighbours,[4] that hide their thoughts from me, watching
8 my steps as they plot against my life! So worthless,[5] and wilt thou

---

[1] This is probably the sense of the Latin, and certainly of the Septuagint
Greek. But it would be possible to render, either from the Hebrew or from
the Latin, 'they never alter their ways.'

[2] *vv.* 21, 22. The Greek and Latin renderings here differ greatly from the
Hebrew text, which perhaps gives a better sense, though it involves much
confusion of pronouns. It appears to mean, 'He (the sinner) raises his hand
against one who is at peace with him, in violation of the covenant between
them; his speech was smooth as butter, when thoughts of war were in his
heart,' &c. 'They are weapons of destruction,' in that case, will refer to the
sinner's words. The Latin version, translated above, has the advantage that
'he' refers to God, and 'they' to the sinners, in verse 22 and in verse 21. 'His
words,' that is, God's commandments, which are urged upon us persuasively,
but bring destruction if they are disobeyed. 'His frown was hidden from them'
may also be rendered, 'they were scattered by his frown.'

[3] Literally 'from the height of the day.' The meaning of the Hebrew text
here is uncertain.

[4] This is probably the sense of the Latin, and certainly of the Septuagint
Greek. The Hebrew verb is better translated, 'they gather themselves together.'

[5] *v.* 8. Literally 'in return for their nothingness.' The Hebrew text has, 'in
return for their sinfulness.'

be their protector? Thou, who dost bring nations to ruin when thou
9 art angry? No, indeed; my life has no secrets from thee, my God;
no tear of mine but is recorded in thy sight; faithful is thy promise,[1]
10 and my enemies will turn their backs when I call upon thee; I know
11 well that thou, God, art on my side. This is the watchword of my
boast in God, the burden of my song of triumph to the Lord, My
12 trust is in God, man's designs cannot daunt me. The vows which
13 thou claimest from me, O God, my praise shall fulfil; hast thou not
saved my life from every peril, my feet from every slip? And shall I
not enjoy God's favour, while the light of life is with me?

PSALM FIFTY-SIX   (57)

(To the end; do not destroy. For David, for the inscription of a
monument, on the occasion when he took refuge in a cave at the approach
of Saul.)

2 HAVE mercy on me, O God, have mercy on me; here is a soul
that puts its trust in thee; I will take refuge under the shelter
3 of thy wings, and let tyranny pass me by. I will cry out to the most
4 high God, the God who has ever befriended me, ever sent aid from
heaven to deliver me, and thrown my oppressors into confusion. His
5 mercy, his faithfulness came to my aid; rescued me from a very den of
lions, where I fainted with fears;[2] from the base breed, whose envious
tooth bites deeper than spears or arrows, whose tongue is sharp as a
6 sword. O God, mount high above the heavens, till thy glory over-
7 shadows the whole earth. See where they have laid a snare for my
feet, to bring me low, dug a pit in my path, and fallen into it them-
8 selves! A heart to serve thee, my God, a heart ready to serve thee;
9 its song, its music are for thee! Wake, all my skill,[3] wake, echoes
10 of harp and viol; dawn shall find me watching; so will I give thee
thanks, Lord, for all the world to hear it, sing psalms while the Gentiles
11 listen, of thy mercy, high as heaven itself, of thy faithfulness, that
12 reaches to the clouds. O God, mount high above the heavens, till thy
glory overshadows the whole earth.

---

[1] The Hebrew text has 'my wanderings' instead of 'my life,' and 'treasured
in thy cruse' instead of 'recorded in thy sight.' Some would connect the words
'faithful is thy promise' with what goes before, rather than with what follows.

[2] Literally, 'I slept in confusion.' The Hebrew text seems to mean, 'I lay
down amidst flaming ones'; the original reading has perhaps been lost.

[3] 'All my skill'; literally, 'my glory,' a term by which the psalmist sometimes
refers to himself, *e.g.*, 29.13.

PSALM FIFTY-SEVEN   (58)

(To the end; do not destroy. For David, for the inscription of a monument.)

2 A ND are your thoughts indeed honest thoughts? If you would but
3 judge uprightly, base breed of men![1] See how you devise treachery
4 in your hearts, cover the land with a web of oppression! Sinners that
left the womb only to go a-straying; renegades and liars their mothers
5 bore them! They are venomous as serpents, as the asp that turns a deaf
6 ear and will not listen to the snake-charmer's music, magician and skilful
7 enchanter though he be. And now God will break their cruel fangs; the
8 Lord will shatter their jaws, strong as the jaws of lions. They will
vanish away like spilt water; when he bends his bow, they will be
9 powerless before him. They will melt like wax,[2] one touch of the
10 flame, and they will see the sun no more; the flame will burn them
11 alive, like young thorns that grow into a thicket never.[3] The innocent
man will triumph at the sight of their punishment, as he dips his hands
12 in the blood of the evil-doer; Sure enough, men will say, innocence has
its reward, sure enough, there is a God who grants redress here on earth.

PSALM FIFTY-EIGHT   (59)

(To the end; do not destroy. For David, for the inscription of a monument, on the occasion when Saul had his house watched, so as to kill him.)

2 O God, deliver me from my enemies, rescue me from their assaults;
3 thwart their treacherous designs, disappoint their lust for blood. See
how they have taken me at a disadvantage, mustering all their strength
5 to overwhelm me! Yet never, Lord, through any fault or offence of mine;

---

[1] The Hebrew text in the first half of the verse is doubtful; some think that the oppressors are addressed by a name which may mean either 'judges' or 'gods.'

[2] The Hebrew text is usually rendered, 'like a snail,' but it is difficult to see in what sense.

[3] The sense appears to be, that the ungodly will be cut off while they are still vigorous, like young thorns which are consumed by a forest fire before they have turned into the withered bush commonly used for kindling-wood (cf. Jg. 9.15). The literal sense of the Latin is, 'Just as they are alive, so it (or he) will devour them angrily, before your thorns have ever understood (what it was to be) a thorn-bush.' The word 'them' is probably a mistake for 'you,' which is found in the Septuagint Greek. The Hebrew text is equally obscure; the Hebrew word rendered 'thorns' in the Latin is usually given the sense of 'cooking-pots.'

6 I have kept steadfastly on my way,[1] doing injury to no man. Bestir
thyself, come to my side and witness my wrongs; Lord God of hosts,
God of Israel, haste thee, visit mankind, and shew the sinner no mercy.
7 See them come back at night-fall, like hungry dogs,[2] to prowl about the
8 city! Hark, how those cruel tongues blurt out their secrets! They think
9 none can hear them, and all the while thou, Lord, makest light of them,
thou, in whose esteem all the nations are as nothing.
10   In thee evermore I find my stronghold; the God who upholds me,[3]
11 the God whose love meets me on the way, the God who bids me
triumph over my enemies. Not for their destruction I pray; should
my own people be lost to man's remembrance? Only let thy power
13 disperse them; crush them down, my protector, my Master![4] Down
with the guilty tongues, the boastful lips; let their own pride ensnare
14 them; let their cursing and lies mark them out for defeat; thy vengeance
will defeat them, and bring their power to an end. Shew them that
there is a God who rules over Jacob, rules over the utmost ends of the
15 earth.[5] Back come they at nightfall, like hungry dogs, and prowl about
16 the city; far and wide they will roam in search of their prey, and snarl
17 with rage when they go unfed at last.[6] And I, ere long, will be thanking
thee for thy protection, will be triumphing in the mercy thou hast shewn
18 me, thou, my stronghold and my refuge in the hour of peril. To thee
I will sing, the God who delivers, the God who upholds me, my God,
and all my hope of mercy.

---

[1] In the Hebrew text, 'they run about and make themselves ready.'

[2] 'Hungry dogs;' in the Hebrew text, 'howling dogs.'

[3] The Hebrew text is usually rendered, 'O my defence, I will wait for thee,'
but some think we should read 'I will sing a psalm to thee,' as in verse 18 below.

[4] The Hebrew text may also be rendered, 'Do not slay them, lest my people
forget it,' but the thought seems difficult to follow. The Septuagint Greek
has, 'lest they forget my law'; the Hebrew may, and the Latin must, be translated, 'lest they (mankind) should forget my people,' *i.e.*, lest this wholesale
destruction should depopulate the kingdom of Israel altogether.

[5] *vv*. 13, 14. The Hebrew text appears to mean, 'With the cursing and the
lying words they utter. Destroy them in thy vengeance, destroy them.'

[6] *vv*. 15, 16. The enemies of the Psalmist, who are patrolling the city to keep
him in, will find that he has escaped, and will be scattered (as in verse 12)
far and wide in their disappointed search for him.

PSALM FIFTY-NINE   (60)

(To the end, for those who will be transformed; for the inscription
2 of a monument, for David himself, with a view to instruction. On
the occasion when he was laying waste Syria of the two rivers, and Sobal;
and Joab turned back and defeated the Edomites, twelve thousand strong,
in the valley of Salt.)

3 TOO long, O God, hast thou disowned us and taken toll of us; now,
4   instead of anger thou shewest mercy. Heal the wounds of the land
5 thou hast shaken and torn asunder, the land that trembles still. Cruel
sights thou hast made us witness; such a draught thou didst brew for us
6 as made our senses reel. But now thou hast set up a standard to rally
thy faithful servants, and to protect them from the archers' onset; [1] now
7 bring aid to the men thou lovest, give my prayer answer, and lift thy
right hand to save.

8   God's word came to us from his sanctuary, I mean to divide up
9 Sichem, and parcel out the valley of Tents; to me Gilead, to me
Manasses belongs; Ephraim is my helmet, Juda issues my commands;
10 Moab, one day, shall be a vessel in my service; I will cast out my shoe
over Edom to claim possession; the Philistines will bow before me.[2]
11 Such was the oracle; but now who is to lead me on my march against
12 this fortress, who is to find an entrance for me into Edom, when thou,
O God, hast disowned us, and wilt not go into battle with our armies?
13 It is thou that must deliver us from peril; vain is the help of man.
14 Only through God can we fight victoriously; only he can trample our
oppressors in the dust.

PSALM SIXTY   (61)

(To the end, among the hymns; for David.)

2 LISTEN, Lord, to this cry of appeal; do not let my prayer go
       unheeded, though it be from the ends of the earth that I call upon
3 thee. Full of misgiving was my heart; but thou hast set me high up

---

[1] Literally 'thou hast given a sign to those who fear thee, that they should
escape from the presence of the bow.' Probably the 'sign' is meant to be a standard, as in the Hebrew; some would read 'truth' instead of 'bow' in the
Hebrew text, and interpret the second half of the sentence differently.

[2] *vv.* 8–10. This would seem to be a quotation from some old prophecy,
referring to the conquest of Chanaan. For 'cast out my shoe,' cf. Ru. 4.7.

4 on a rock, thou hast escorted me on my way, thou, my only hope,
5 my strong tower against the assault of my enemies. Oh let me dwell
for ever in thy tabernacle, let me take refuge under the shelter of thy
6 wings! Lord, thou hast listened to my prayer, thou hast given thy
7 worshippers a home to dwell in. Year upon year thou wilt add to the
8 king's reign; while generations come and go, his life will last. He
will stand firm for ever in the presence of God, the God whose mercy
9 and faithfulness are beyond all reckoning.[1] Eternally I will sing thy
praises, day after day perform my vows.

PSALM SIXTY-ONE (62)

(To the end; for Idithun; a psalm of David.)

2 MY soul, do but leave thyself in God's hands; to him I look for
3 deliverance. I have no other God, no other deliverer but him;
4 safe in his protection, I fear no deadly fall. Still one man my enemies
single out for their murderous attack, all swept one way, like cattle
5 at hedge's gap or wall's breach.[2] Still I must go on uncomforted,[3] while
these conspire to dishonour me, men that once used to speak me fair, but
6 ever with a curse in their hearts. Yet even now, my soul, leave thyself in
7 God's hands; all my trust is in him. He is my God and my deliverer, my
8 protector, bidding me stand unmoved. God is all my defence and all my
9 boast; my help, my hope come from God. Israelites one and all, put your
confidence in him, and lay the homage of your hearts at his feet; God is
our defence for ever.
10 Man is but emptiness, light weigh the sons of Adam as false coin in
11 the scales; vain are all their conspiracies to deceive.[4] Hope no more for

---

[1] It is not clear, in the Latin, whether the mercy and faithfulness referred
to are those of God, or those of the king; the former explanation seems more
likely, since David himself is traditionally the author of the psalm. The Hebrew
text has, 'appoint thy mercy and thy faithfulness as his protectors.'

[2] Literally, 'How long do you rush upon a man? You are all murderers; as
if to a leaning hedge or a broken wall.' It is not clear, either in the Hebrew
or in the Latin, how the words 'like a bowed wall or a broken-down fence'
are to be fitted into the grammar of the sentence. It is perhaps easiest to
think of the Psalmist's enemies as compared to a herd of cattle, rushing for a
gap in a wall or hedge.

[3] Literally, 'thirsty.' This is probably a misunderstanding of the Septuagint
Greek, 'they run in thirst,' itself a corrupt reading for 'they run in falsehood,'
which (according to the Hebrew text) should be 'they take pleasure in falsehood.'

[4] In the Hebrew text this verse seems to run, 'The sons of Adam are emptiness,
the sons of man are but a cheat; they rise high, for very emptiness, in the scales.'

wrongful gains, sigh for plunder no more; on mounting store of riches
12 set never your heed. Not once, but twice I have heard God's voice of
13 warning; all power is God's. To thee, Lord, mercy belongs; thou wilt
repay every man the reward of his deeds.

PSALM SIXTY-TWO   (63)

(A psalm of David, composed when he was in the desert of Edom.)

2 O GOD, thou art my God; to thee at dawn I keep vigil, body and soul
3   athirst for thee, a hundred ways, in this parched, this trackless
wilderness! See, I have made pilgrimage to thy sanctuary, scene of thy
4 great acts, scene of thy glory! To win thy mercy is dearer to me than
5 life itself; my songs of praise can no more be withheld. So all my life
6 long, I will bless thee, holding up my hands in honour of thy name; my
heart filled, as with some rich feast, my mouth, in joyful accents, singing
7 thy praise. My thoughts shall go out to thee at dawn, as I lie awake
8 remembering thee, and the protection thou hast given me. Gladly I
9 take shelter under thy wings, cling close to thee, borne up by thy pro-
10 tecting hand. In vain do my enemies plot against my life, soon to be
11 swallowed up in the depths of earth, a prey to the sword, carrion for
12 jackals! The king shall triumph in God's protection, blessed as they are
ever blessed who take their vows in his name;[1] silence shall fall on the
lips that muttered treason.

PSALM SIXTY-THREE   (64)

(To the end, a psalm of David.)

2 O GOD, listen to my prayer when I call for aid, save me from the
3   threats of my mortal foe. Thine to defend me from this con-
4 spiracy of malice, this throng of evil-doers; the tongues that wound like
a sharpened sword, the bitter hatred aimed at me, like a bow ready bent.
5 Stealthily they shoot their arrows at the innocent; suddenly, from a safe
vantage-point, they wound him. See them pledged to an infamous
7 resolve, plotting to lay snares for me, sure that they will go unseen. With
what care they hatch their treason, redoubled care that defeats its pur-

---

[1] Or the meaning may be, 'All who swear by the king's name shall be blessed.'

8 pose! ¹ Let man's thoughts be deep as they will, yet God must triumph;
9 their arrows do no more harm than children's toys, and all their con-
10 spiring plays them false. A sight to strike men with amazement, and fill
their hearts with dread; who but will acclaim God's power, who but will
11 ponder his great acts? Honest men will rejoice and put their trust in the
Lord; upright hearts will find their recompense.

PSALM SIXTY-FOUR   (65)

(To the end, a psalm of David. A song made by Jeremy and Ezechiel
for the people of the exile, when they began their outward journey.)

2 O GOD, thou shalt yet have praise in Sion; Jerusalem shall yet pay
3   her vows to thee. Listen to my prayer, thou to whom all mankind
4 must look for pardon; and though the cause of the wicked has prevailed
5 against us, a sinful people to thy favour restore. Blessed the man on
whom thy choice falls, whom thou takest to dwell with thee in thy own
domain! Thy house has treasures to content our hearts; holy is thy
6 temple, wonderful in its ordered worship. Listen to us, O God our
Saviour; at the bounds of earth, far over the seas, in thee we hope.²
7   What power girds thee about! Thy strength bids the mountains stand
8 firm, stirs up the depths of the sea,³ and sets its billows roaring; thy
9 portents fill the heathen with dismay, strike terror at the world's end,
10 fill the lands of sunrise and sunset with rejoicing. And now thou hast
brought relief to this land of ours, hast watered and greatly enriched it.
Deep flows the stream whence thy divine providence grants us food;
11 long time thou dost prepare it. Make earth's channels dance, make its
fruits abound with the showers that fall on it, till it blossoms forth joy-
12 fully.⁴ So thou wilt bless us with plenty, to crown the year; the fields,

---

¹ Literally, 'they have failed through scrutinizing with scrutiny.' In the
Hebrew text, the meaning seems to be 'they have finished their careful search.'
² This verse, in the Hebrew text, begins 'Thou, in thy faithfulness, didst
answer our prayer with terrible portents, O God our Saviour,' perhaps with
a reference to the plagues of Egypt.
³ 'Stirs up' is 'stills,' according to the Hebrew text.
⁴ The Hebrew text has, 'thou dost water its furrows, and smooth out its
ridges; thou dost soften it with showers, and bless its yield'; the following
sentence begins 'thou dost crown the year with plenty.'

13 through thee, will be thick with harvest, the fair desert pastures will
14 bear richly, and the hill-sides be gaily clad. No flock but will boast of
its ram's fleece, no valley but will stand deep in corn; the shout of joy
everywhere, everywhere the hymn of praise.

PSALM SIXTY-FIVE (66)

(To the end; a psalm-song of resurrection.)

2 LET the whole world keep holiday in God's presence, sing praise
3 to his name, pay homage to his glory! Cry out to God, What dread,
Lord, thy acts inspire! How great is that might of thine, which makes
4 thy enemies cringe before thee! Let the whole earth worship thee, sing
5 of thee, sing praises to thy name. Come near, and see what God does,
6 how wonderful he is in his dealings with human kind, how he turns the
sea into land, and lets men cross a river dry-shod; ours to rejoice in his
7 mercy. In that power of his he reigns for ever, and has eyes for what the
8 Gentiles do; let rebellious souls tame their pride. Bless the name of our
God, you Gentiles, echo the sound of his praise.
9 God's will is I should live yet; he does not allow my steps to falter.[1]
10 Yes, Lord, thou hast put us to the proof, tested us as men test silver in
11 the fire; led us into a snare, and bowed our backs with trouble, while
human masters rode us down; our way led through fire and water, but
13 now thou hast brought us out into a place of repose. See, I come into thy
14 house with burnt-offerings, to pay thee all the vows these lips have
15 framed, this mouth has uttered, when trouble came upon me. Fat burnt-
offerings shall be thine, and the smoke of ram's flesh; bullocks and goats
16 shall be thy sacrifice. Come and give ear, all you who worship God, while
17 I tell of the great mercies he has shewn me; how this voice of mine cried
18 out to him, this tongue did him honour. Would God listen to me, if my
19 eyes were set on wrong? And God has listened to me; given heed to my
20 cry for succour. Blessed be God, who does not reject my prayer, does not
withhold his mercy from me.

---

[1] The Hebrew text has 'we should live' and 'our steps.'

PSALM SIXTY-SIX   (67)

(To the end, in hymns; a psalm-song of David.)

2 MAY God be merciful to us, and bless us; may he smile graciously
3 on us, and shew us his mercy.   Make known thy will,[1] O God,
4 wide as earth; make known among all nations thy saving power.   Honour
5 to thee, O God, from the nations, honour from all the nations!   The
  Gentiles, too, may rejoice and be glad; the whole earth abides thy
6 judgement, and the Gentiles, too, obey thy sovereignty.   Honour to
7 thee, O God, from the nations, honour from all the nations!   The earth
8 has yielded its harvest;   may God, our own God, bless us; may God
  grant his blessing, and may earth, far and wide, do him reverence.

PSALM SIXTY-SEVEN   (68)

(To the end. For David; a psalm to be sung.)

2 LET God bestir himself now, and rout his enemies, confront his ill-
3 wishers and put them to flight.   Let the wicked vanish as smoke
  vanishes, consumed by God's presence, as the wax melts at the presence
4 of fire,   while honest men keep holiday and rejoice in sight of him, glad
5 and content.   Sing, then, in God's honour, praise his name with a psalm;
  a royal progress for the God whose throne is the sunset, whose name is
6 Javé.   Triumph in his presence; let the wicked tremble at his frown;   he
  is a father to the orphan, and gives the widow redress, this God who
7 dwells apart in holiness.   This is the God who unites in peace the
  families that were scattered,[2] brings the prisoners back in the flower of
  their manhood; the outlaws, too, that lurked in barrows among the hills.
8   O God, when thou didst go forth at the head of thy people, on that
9 royal progress of thine through the desert,   how the earth shook, how
  the sky broke at God's coming, how even Sinai shook, when the God of
10 Israel came!   And on this thy own land, O God, thou sendest rain to be
  a mark of thy favour; all parched it lies, and thou dost bring it relief.
11 All living things that dwell in it are thy pensioners; so kindly, O God,
  is the provision thou hast made for the poor.

---

[1] Literally, in the Latin, 'that we may know thy will'; but this variation
from the Hebrew and the Greek interrupts the world-wide sweep of the psalm.

[2] 'Unites in peace the families that were scattered'; the Hebrew text more
probably means 'Turns lonely people into heads of households.' In the rest
of this verse, the Hebrew text is generally read as meaning that God leads
back prisoners into prosperity, while the outlaws are left in the wilderness.

12   Here are bringers of good news, with a message the Lord has given
13   them, from the army he leads;[1] a king, leading the armies of a beloved
      people; a people how well beloved! He bids the favourites of his court
14   divide the spoil between them. Live at peace in the midst of your
      inheritance, and riches shall be yours like the silver that covers the
15   dove's wings, like the sheen of gold on its back. He who dwells in
      heaven has strewn the ground with the wealth of kings, like the snow
16   that lies white on Salmon.[2] God's mountain, how fruitful it is, how
17   rugged, yet how fruitful it is! What need to look up enviously at the
      mountain heights? It is this mountain God has chosen for his dwelling-
      place; on this mountain the Lord will dwell for ever.[3]
18   See where God comes, with chariots innumerable for his escort;
      thousands triumph with him; the Lord is their leader, as at Sinai, so here
19   on his holy mountain.[4] Thou dost mount up on high, thou dost capture
      thy spoil, and men must pay thee tribute; the heathen must make way
20   for the Lord God to dwell in their midst.[5] Blessed be the Lord now and
21   ever, the God who protects us, and prospers our journey. Our God is a
      God of deliverance; Javé is a Lord who saves from peril of death.

---

[1] In the Hebrew, the bringers of good news are women; it is not clear what
is the grammar of the word 'army,' at the end of the sentence.

[2] In verses 13–15 the sense of the Latin here can only be guessed at; the
Hebrew text probably means, 'Kings at the head of their armies fled away,
fled away, while she who waited at home divided (in anticipation) the spoils.
Surely you will not lie at ease among the sheep-folds? (The spoils are like)
the wings of a dove covered with silver, its pinions with the sheen of gold.
When he who rules in heaven scatters kings upon it, (it is as when) it snows
on Salmon.' But the word 'scatters' should more properly be rendered 'spreads
out,' and the words 'upon it' (feminine) are difficult to understand. The rendering given in the text assumes that 'they' refers to God's inheritance (verses
10 and 11), and thus by inference to God's people, who are described in the second half of the verse as 'snowed white' with spoil. The early part of this psalm
clearly refers to the victory of Barac over King Sisera; verses 8 and 9 being
actually repeated from Jg. 5.28, and verse 14 of the Hebrew from Jg. 5.16.

[3] *vv.* 16, 17. The Hebrew text has, 'Why do you look up enviously, you (other)
rugged hills?' and instead of 'fruitful hill' it has 'hill of Basan' throughout.

[4] The Hebrew text here has 'the Lord is among them, Sinai, in holiness
(or, in a holy place).' The Latin has 'the Lord is among them, in Sinai, in the
holy (place),' but it seems clear that Sinai is only introduced by way of comparison, the scene of the picture being in Palestine itself.

[5] S. Paul in Eph. 4.5, apparently using some other text, has 'gave gifts to
men' instead of 'received gifts among men.' In the second half of the verse,
a verb has to be supplied to make sense of 'yes, unbelievers (nominative),
that the Lord might dwell.'

22 God will smite the heads of his enemies, smite the proud locks of the men
23 who live at ease in their wickedness. I will restore my people, the Lord
   says; I will restore them to their land, from Basan to the shore of the high
24 seas.[1] Soon the blood of thy enemies will stain thy feet, never a jackal
25 that follows thee but shall lick its prey. Thou comest, O God, a mark
   for all eyes; he comes, my God and my king, the dweller in the sanctuary.
26 Before him go the chieftains, and the minstrels with them, while the
27 maids play on their tambours round about. Give praise to the Lord God
28 in this solemn assembly, meeting-place of all the streams of Israel! Here
   is Benjamin, youngest of the tribes, rapt in worship;[2] here are the chieftains of Juda, leading the rest, chieftains, too, from Zabulon, chieftains
   from Nephtali.
29   O God, give thy power full play, perfect thy own achievement among
30 us; so, in thy temple at Jerusalem, kings shall offer gifts before thee. Take
   the wild beasts of the marshes, fierce bulls that lord it over the peaceful
   herd of nations, ready to shut out thy loyal tributaries from their lands;[3]
32 scatter the nations that delight in war, till Egypt sues for pardon, till
33 Ethiopia hastens to make her peace with God. Kingdoms of the earth,
   raise your voices in God's honour, sing a psalm to the Lord; a psalm to
34 God, who mounts on the heaven of heavens, over against the dawn,[4] and
35 utters his word in a voice of thunder. Pay honour to God in the name of
   Israel, the God whose splendour and majesty reach up to the clouds.
36 How wonderful God is in his holy place! The God of Israel will give his
   people strength and courage; blessed be God!

PSALM SIXTY-EIGHT (69)

(To the end, for those who will be transformed; for David.)

2 O GOD, save me; see how the waters close about me, threatening my
3   very life! I am like one who sticks fast in deep mire, with no
   ground under his feet, one who has ventured out into mid-ocean, to be

---

[1] God says that he will bring back (his people, is presumably understood)
from Basan, from the depths of the sea, according to the Hebrew text; the
Latin version has 'to the depths.' The sense is in any case obscure; but the
Latin is perhaps best understood as a mere geographical description of Northern Palestine, which lay between the Basan country and the Mediterranean.

[2] The Hebrew word here used might also be translated, 'ruling over them.'

[3] The sense of this verse is far from certain, but it is generally agreed that
the wild beast of the marshes (literally, 'reeds') is a symbol of the power of
Egypt. 'Ready to shut out thy loyal tributaries,' literally (in the Latin), 'that
they may shut out those who are approved by silver'; there is no agreement
about the meaning of the Hebrew text.

[4] The Hebrew text probably means 'from the beginning.'

4 drowned by the storm. Hoarse my throat with crying wearily for help;
5 my eyes ache with looking up for mercy to my God. Countless as the
  hairs on my head are my wanton enemies, powerful the oppressors that
6 wrong me. I have made amends to them, I, that never robbed them; O
  God, thou knowest my frailties, no fault of mine is hidden from thy
7 sight. Master, Lord of hosts, shall ill fortune of mine bring shame to
  those who trust in thee, make men repent of looking for aid to thee, the
8 God of Israel? It is for thy sake that I have met with reproach, that I
9 have so often blushed with confusion, an outcast among my own
10 brethren, a stranger to my own mother's children. Was it not jealousy
  for the honour of thy house that consumed me; was it not uttered against
  thee, the reproach I bore?

11   What more could I do? I humbled myself before them by fasting;
12 and that, too, was matter for finding fault; I dressed in sackcloth, and
13 they made a by-word of me. Idlers in the market-place would taunt
14 me; the drunkards would make a song of me over their wine. To thee,
  Lord, I make my prayer; never man more needed thy good will. Listen
  to me, O God, full of mercy as thou art, faithful as thou art to thy pro-
15 mise of aid. Save me from sinking in the mire, rescue me from my
16 enemies, from the deep waters that surround me; let me not sink
  under the flood, swallowed up in its depths, and the well's mouth close
17 above me. Listen to me, Lord, of thy gracious mercy, look down upon
18 me in the abundance of thy pity; do not turn thy face away from thy
19 servant in this time of trouble, give a speedy answer to my prayer. Take
  heed of my distress, and grant deliverance; relieve me, so hard pressed
  by my enemies.

20   Lord, thou knowest how they reproach me, how I blush with shame;
21 thou seest how many are my persecutors. Naught else but shame and
  misery does my heart forebode; [1] I look round for pity, where pity is
22 none, for comfort, where there is no comfort to be found. They gave
  me gall to eat, and when I was thirsty they gave me vinegar to drink. [2]
23 Let their feast be turned into a trap, a snare to recoil on them; [3] ever
25 the blind eye be theirs, the bowed back. Pour out thy anger upon them,
26 let them be overtaken by thy avenging wrath; let their dwelling-place be
27 deserted, their tents for ever uninhabited. [4] Who is it they persecute? A
  man already afflicted by thee; hard was my hurt to bear, and these have
28 added to it. Do thou add guilt to guilt in their reckoning; let them never

---

[1] The meaning of the Hebrew text is probably 'Reproach has broken my
heart; I languish in sickness.'
[2] Mt. 27.48.
[3] Rom. 11.9.
[4] Ac. 1.20.

29 find their way back to thy favour; let their names be blotted out from the
record of the living, and never be written among the just.
30   See how friendless I am, and how distressed! But thy help, O God,
31 sustains me. I will sing in praise of God's name, exalt him with all my
32 homage; a more acceptable sacrifice, this, to the Lord than any young
33 bullock, for all its promise of horn and hoof. Here is a sight to make the
afflicted rejoice; do you, too, search after God, and it will be life to your
34 hearts. The Lord listens to the prayer of the destitute; he does not forget
35 his servants in their chains. To him be praise from sky, earth and sea,
36 and from all the creatures that move about them. God will grant
deliverance to Sion; the cities of Juda will rise from their ruins, inhabited
37 now and held firmly in possession, an inheritance for the race that serves
him, a home for all true lovers of his name.

PSALM SIXTY-NINE   (70)

(To the end; a psalm of David. In commemoration of the deliverance
God brought him.) [1]

2 O GOD, take heed, and save me; O Lord, make haste to help me.
3   Disappoint them, put them to the blush, the enemies who plot
4 against my life! Baffled let them go their way, that rejoice at my mis-
5 fortune, slink away in confusion, that crowed over me so loud! Triumphant joy be theirs who long for thee; Praise to the Lord, be ever their song,
6 who rejoice in thy saving power. Thou seest me helpless and destitute;
my God, help me. Thou art my champion and my deliverer; Lord, do not
delay thy coming.

PSALM SEVENTY   (71)

(A psalm of David; concerned with Jonadab and the first who were
taken captive.)

2 IN thee, O God, I put my trust; may I never be disappointed! Rescue
and deliver me, faithful as thou art; listen to my cry for succour.
3 Let me find in thee a Divine protector, a stronghold; I have no other
4 support, no other refuge, but thee. Rescue me, Lord, from the power
5 of the wicked, from the grasp of lawlessness and oppression; thou, my
6 Lord and Master, the hope and confidence of my youth. Thou hast
upheld me from birth, thou hast guarded me ever since I left my

---

[1] This psalm is nearly a repetition of Ps. 39.14–18.

7 mother's womb; and shall I weary of praising thee, I, that am a portent
8 now in the eyes of the multitude? [1] Thou art strong to aid; fill these lips
   with praise, to sing all day long of the glory and the splendour that is
9 thine; do not cast me off now, in my old age; my strength ebbs, do not
10 thou forsake me. A mark thou seest me for envious tongues; mortal
11 enemies conspire together, and whisper, God has abandoned him; now
   is the time to overtake and seize him; no one can bring him rescue now.
12 O God, do not keep thy distance from me; be on the watch, my God, to
13 aid me. Defeat their plot against my life, and bring it to nothing; cover
   my ill-wishers with confusion and shame.
14   Still will I hope on, praising thee ever more and more. Day in, day
   out, these lips shall tell of thy faithfulness, of thy saving power. All
16 unskilled in learning, [2] I will make the great acts of God my theme, thy
17 matchless justice, Lord, proclaim. It is thou, O God, that hast inspired
   me ever since the days of my youth, and still I am found telling the tale
18 of thy wonders. O God, do not fail me, even now when I am old and
   grey-headed, until I have made known the proofs of thy power to all the
19 generations that will follow; thy majesty, and that faithfulness of thine
   which reaches up, O God, to the heavens. What great deeds are thine!
20 There is none like thee, O God, none like thee. Ah, how often thou
   hast made me see times of bitter trouble! And still thou wouldst relent,
   and give me back life, and bring me up again from the very depths of the
21 earth; still thou wouldst give fresh proof of thy greatness, and turn back,
22 and comfort me. [3] So true to thy word, and shall I not give thee thanks
   with psalm-music, praise thee on the harp, O God, the Holy One of
23 Israel? Gladly these lips will sing of thee, this heart, which owes thee
24 its deliverance. Day in, day out, I will repeat the story of thy faithfulness, and how disappointment and confusion fell on the men who sought
   to wrong me.

---

[1] It is not clear in what sense the Psalmist was a portent or sign to his contemporaries, but the context suggests that he may be referring to his great
age, and God's long preservation of him.

[2] The Hebrew text here is usually translated as meaning, 'I cannot reckon
the sum' (of God's faithfulness and power), but this interpretation is very far
from certain.

[3] *vv.* 20, 21. In the Hebrew text we find 'us' where the Latin has 'me'; it is
probable, too, that the verbs should be read as futures.

PSALM SEVENTY-ONE　　　　　(72)

(A psalm; for Solomon.)

G RANT to the king, O God, thy own skill in judgement; the
2 inheritor of a throne, may he be just, as thou art just; may he give
3 thy people right awards, and to thy poor, redress. Such be the harvest
his subjects shall reap, peace on every mountain, justice on every hill-side.
4 Right award he will give to friendless folk; protect the children of the
5 poor, and crush the oppressor. Ageless his reign, while sun lasts or
6 moon shines down; kindly as the rain that drops on the shorn fleece, as
7 the showers that water the earth. Justice in his days shall thrive, and the
blessings of peace; and may those days last till the moon shines no more!
8 　From sea to sea, from the great river to the ends of earth, his sway
9 shall reach. In his presence the Ethiopians will bow down; all his
10 enemies will be humbled in the dust; gifts shall flow in from the lords
of Tharsis and the islanders, tribute from the kings of Arabia and of
11 Saba; all the kings of the earth must needs bring their homage, all the
12 nations serve him. He will give the poor redress when they cry to him,
13 destitute folk, with none to befriend them; in their need and helplessness,
they shall have his compassion. Their lives he will take into his keeping,
14 set them free from the claims of usury and oppression; no name of theirs
15 unhonoured in his sight. Long life shall be his, and gold from Arabia
shall be given him; [1] men will pray for him continually, bless his name
16 evermore. The land shall have good store of corn,[2] high up the hill-
sides, springing up like the trees of Lebanon; shall multiply its citizens
17 like grass on the ground. For ever let his name be used in blessing, a
name to endure while the sun gives light; in him all the tribes of the
18 earth shall be enriched, all the nations shall extol him. Blessed be the
19 Lord God of Israel, who does wonderful deeds as none else, and blessed
for ever be his glorious name; all the earth shall be filled with his glory,
20 Amen, Amen. (Here end the praises [3] of David the son of Jesse.)

---

[1] Some interpreters would make this mean that the poor man (previously
referred to in the plural) will be saved from death, and will be given gold by
the king—or perhaps that he will give the king gold; but these suggestions
have little to recommend them.

[2] Literally, 'a sustainment'; the Hebrew text makes the meaning of this clear.

[3] In the Hebrew text, 'the prayers.' It is the general opinion of commentators, that one section or volume of the Psalms ended here. In the second half
of the Psalter, as in the first, many Psalms are to be found which claim King
David as their author.

PSALM SEVENTY-TWO   (73)

(A psalm of Asaph.)

2 WHAT bounty God shews to Israel, to all upright hearts! Yet I came near to losing my foothold, felt the ground sink under
3 my steps, so indignant was I at seeing the good fortune of sinners that
4 defy his law; men that have no hope in death, no comfort to support
5 them in calamity.[1] Not for these to share man's common lot of trouble;
6 the plagues which afflict humankind still pass them by? No wonder if
7 they are overcome with pride, flaunt their lawlessness and impiety. How
malice distils[2] from those pampered lives; how easily they attain the
8 desire of their hearts! On mischief they brood, of mischief they talk;
9 throned on high they preach injustice; their clamour reaches heaven, and
their false tales win currency on earth.
10 Enviously the men of my own race look on, to see them enjoying
11 their full span of life;[3] Can God, they ask, be aware of this? Does
12 the most High know of all that passes? Look at these sinners, how
13 they prosper in the world, how they gain mastery of riches! Why
then, thought I, it is to no purpose that I have kept my heart true,
14 and washed my hands clean among pure souls; still, all day long,
I am plagued for it, and no morning comes but my scourging is renewed.
15 Was I to utter that thought? Nay, that were to put the whole company
16 of thy children in the wrong. I set myself to read the riddle, but it
17 proved a hard search, until I betook myself to God's sanctuary,[4] and
18 considered, there, what becomes of such men at last. The truth is,
thou dost repay their treacheries, thou, at the height of their fortune,
19 dost overthrow them; what a ruin is theirs! How suddenly they vanish
20 away, cut off in their sinfulness! The very memory of them, Lord,
is like a waking dream, heard of in thy holy city no more.[5]
21 My heart so full of bitterness, my inmost thoughts so deeply moved,
22 I am brought to nothing, I am all ignorance, standing there like a

---

[1] The meaning of the Hebrew text is very uncertain; the rendering given above is most probably the meaning of the Latin, which is sometimes rendered, 'they do not think about death, their chastisement is feeble.'

[2] 'Malice distils'; the sense of the Hebrew text is, 'their eyes stand out,' or possibly, 'their eyes look out.'

[3] The Hebrew text has, 'So many people turn (pay attention) to them, and drink their fill of water,' it is not clear in what sense.

[4] The Hebrew text can also be understood as meaning, 'entered into God's mysteries.'

[5] 'In thy holy city'; the Hebrew text may mean, 'when thou art aroused.'

24 dumb beast before thee; yet am I ever close to thee, and thou dost hold
   me by my right hand. Thine to lead me in a way of thy own choosing,
25 thine to welcome me into glory at last. What else does heaven hold
   for me, but thyself? What pleasure should I find in all thy gifts on
26 earth? This frame, this earthly being of mine must come to an end;
   still God will comfort my heart, God will be, eternally, my inheritance.
27 Lost those others may be, who desert thy cause, lost are all those who
28 break their troth with thee; I know no other content but clinging to God,
   putting my trust in the Lord, my Master; within the gates of royal Sion
   I will be the herald of thy praise.

PSALM SEVENTY-THREE   (74)

(Of understanding; for Asaph.)

O GOD, hast thou altogether abandoned us? Sheep of thy own
2 pasturing, must we feel the fires of thy vengeance? Bethink thee
   of the company thou hast gathered, brought them in, long ago, claimed
   them for thyself, to be the stock of thy chosen race; where but on
3 mount Sion wouldst thou have thy dwelling-place? Lift up thy hand,
   to crush human pride for ever! See what havoc thy enemies have wrought
4 in the holy place, how their malice has triumphed in thy very precincts,[1]
5 setting up its emblems, strange emblems, over gate-way and stair-
6 head. Blow after blow, like woodman in the forest, they have broken
   through its doors with axes, brought it down, with pick and hatchet,
7 to the ground. They have set fire to thy sanctuary, sullied the dwelling-
8 place of thy glory in the dust. They have but one thought, the whole ·
9 brood of them, to sweep away all God's worship [2] from the land; our
   own emblems are nowhere to be seen, there are no prophets now; none
10 will acknowledge us.[3] O God, shall our enemy taunt us everlastingly,
11 shall blasphemy still defy thy name? Why dost thou withhold thy
   hand? That right hand of thine, must it always lie idle in thy bosom?
12 Ours is a King who reigned before time was; here on earth he has the
13 means to bring deliverance. What power but thine could heap up the
14 shifting sea, crush the power of the monster beneath its waters; shatter

---

[1] Literally, 'thy solemn feast.' The words which follow are difficult to translate, whether in the Latin or in the Hebrew text.

[2] Literally 'festivals.'

[3] 'None will acknowledge us'; literally 'he will not recognize us'; which may
refer either to God or (by a Hebrew usage) to men generally. The Hebrew
text here probably means, 'there is none of us who can tell how long' (the
tyranny will last).

Leviathan's power, and give him up as prey to the dwellers in the
15 desert? Thou didst open up fountains and streams of water; thou, too,
16 madest the rivers of Ethan run dry.[1] Thine is the day, thine the night;
17 dawn and sun are of thy fashioning; thou hast fixed all the bounds
18 of earth, madest the summer, madest the cool of the year. Wilt thou
   pay no heed, when thy enemies taunt thee, and in their recklessness
19 set the name of Javé at defiance? Wilt thou throw us to wild beasts,
   the souls that still acknowledge thee?[2] Souls unbefriended, but for
20 thee, wilt thou leave us quite forgotten? Bethink thee of thy covenant;
   darkness has fallen on the land, and the lairs of oppression are all
21 about us. Do not let the humble go away disappointed; teach the
22 poor and the helpless to exalt thy name. Bestir thyself, O God, to
   vindicate thy own cause; do not forget the taunts which reckless men
23 hurl at thee all day long; do not overlook them, the triumphant cries
   of thy enemies, the ever growing insolence that here defies thee.

PSALM SEVENTY-FOUR   (75)

(To the end; do not destroy; a psalm-song of Asaph.)

2 WE will praise thee, O God, and, praising thee, call upon thy
3   name; we will tell the story of thy wondrous deeds. When the
4 time is ripe, I will judge strictly; faint grows the earth, and all that
5 dwell on it; I alone support its fabric.[3] Rebel no more, I cry to the
6 rebels, Abate your pride, to the transgressors, Abate your overweening
7 pride, that hurls defiance at God himself. No need to look eastward
8 or westward, or to the desert mountains of the south; it is God who
9 rules all, humbling one man and exalting another. In the Lord's hand
   is a cup of strong wine, brewed till it overflows; he holds it to one
   man's lips, then to another's; but the dregs are not drained yet, sinners

---

[1] *vv.* 12–15. Some think these verses refer to the escape of Israel from Egypt
and the miracles done in the wilderness, Leviathan (perhaps the crocodile)
being used as a symbol of Egypt. Ethan, in that case, may be the same as
Etham (Ex. 13.20); but the Hebrew text is generally rendered 'thou madest
everflowing rivers run dry.' Others think the whole is an allegorical account
of the Creation.
[2] According to the Hebrew text, 'souls that still acknowledge thee' should
be 'thy dove.'
[3] *vv.* 3, 4. It is not clear whether the speaker is God or man, nor whether he
is still the speaker in verses 5 sqq. The two verses are ordinarily interpreted
as God's own utterance, but a comparison of verse 11 below suggests that an
earthly judge may be intended; 'the earth' in verse 4 may also be translated
'the land.'

10 everywhere must drink them. Mine it is to bear everlasting record,
11 singing praises to the God of Jacob; mine to crush the pride of every
sinner, and raise high the courage of the just.

PSALM SEVENTY-FIVE   (76)

(To the end, with praises; a psalm of Asaph; a song against the
Assyrians.) [1]

2 IT is in Judaea God makes himself known, in Israel that his name
3 is extolled; and there, in the city of peace, he makes his abode,
4 dwells in Sion. It was there he broke the power of the archers, broke
5 shield, and sword, and battle array. How wonderful was thy dawning
6 over the everlasting hills! Routed, their rash design; there they sleep on,
7 empty-handed, the warriors in their pride; there they sleep on, the
horsemen, overthrown, God of Jacob, at thy word of rebuke.
8 Who can resist thee, so terrible, so sudden in thy anger? Loud
10 rings in heaven the doom thou utterest; earth trembles and is silent
when God rouses himself to execute his sentence, giving redress to
11 those who are scorned on earth. Then, human malice itself falls to
praising thee; men that were rebels once make pilgrimage in thy honour.[2]
12 To the Lord your God let your vows be made and paid, tributary
13 nations on every side; to God that is feared by awestricken princes,
feared among all the kings of the earth.

PSALM SEVENTY-SIX   (77)

(To the end, for Idithun; a psalm of Asaph.)

2 TO the Lord I cry aloud for succour, cry aloud to the God who
3 will not refuse a hearing. To God I look when distress comes
upon me; in his presence I lift up my hands amid the darkness, not in
4 vain.[3] My heart is steeled against all consolation; it is to God my thoughts
turn, in him lies all my content, all my study. So I wait, with fainting

---

[1] If the traditional title of this Psalm gives the true account of it, the reference is probably to the defeat of Sennacherib (II Par. 32.21).
[2] The sense of this verse is very uncertain; in the Hebrew text, God is
spoken of as 'girding himself' with what is left of human malice.
[3] Or perhaps, 'and I am not disappointed'; literally, 'I was not deceived.'
The Hebrew text has, 'I did not cease.'

5 spirits, my eyes straining for the dawn,[1] silent and bewildered. I reflect
7 upon days long past, the immemorial years possess my mind; lonely
musings occupy my thoughts at midnight, stir my heart to its depths.
8 Can it be that God will always leave us forsaken, will never shew us again
9 his old kindness? Will he shut us out for ever, generation after genera-
10 tion, from his pity? Can God forget to be gracious, can anger move him
11 to withhold his mercy? And now I resolve to begin afresh; it is at such
times that the Most High relents in his dealings with men.[2]
12   Now to remember all the Lord has done, now to recall those wonder-
13 ful acts of thine, since first the world was; to ponder over all thy
14 dealings, to make thy secret designs my study! Thy path, O God, is
15 hedged about with holiness; what God is great as our God is great? Thy
own wonderful acts acclaim thy Deity; even to the Gentiles thou wouldst
16 make thy power known, by forcing them to set free thy people, the
17 sons of Jacob and of Joseph. The waters saw thee, O God, the waters
18 trembled at the sight of thee, moved to their inmost depths; how
the waves roared unceasingly, what tumult among the clouds! To and
19 fro thy arrows passed, thy thunders whirled round about, till all the
20 world shone with thy lightning, and the troubled earth shook. Thy
way led through the sea, the deep tide made a road for thee, and none
21 may read the traces of thy passage, where thou, with Moses and Aaron
for thy shepherds, didst bring thy people out on their journey.

PSALM SEVENTY-SEVEN   (78)

(Of understanding; for Asaph.)

L ISTEN, my people, to this testament of mine, do not turn a deaf
2   ear to the words I utter as I declare my meaning to you under a
3 figure, taking my theme from days long ago.[3] It is a story often heard,
4 well known among us; have not our fathers told it to us, a thing not
to be kept back from their children, from the generation which follows?
Their talk was of God's praise, of his power often made known, of the
5 wonderful deeds he did. He made a covenant with Jacob, gave Israel
his law, commanding our fathers to make it known to their children,

---

[1] Literally, 'my eyes forestall the night-watches.' The Hebrew text probably
means, 'Thou dost hold my eye-lids awake.'

[2] 'I resolve to begin afresh'; the Hebrew text seems to mean, 'I tell myself,
This is my weakness.' In the second half of the sentence, the Hebrew text
has 'the years of the right hand of the most High.'

[3] In the Hebrew text, 'I will utter age-long riddles'; cf. Mt. 13.35, where
the Hebrew text is evidently followed.

6 so that a new generation might learn it; sons would be born to them to
7 take their place, and hand it on to their own sons after them. They were
to put their trust in God, ever remembering his Divine dealings with
8 them, ever loyal to his commands; they were not to be like their fathers,
a stubborn and defiant breed, a generation of false aims, of a spirit that
broke faith with God.

9 So it was that the sons of Ephraim cast away their bows,[1] already
10 bent, shrinking from the day of battle when it came. They were false
11 to God's covenant, refused to follow his law, as if they had forgotten
all his mercies, all those wonderful deeds of his they had witnessed.
12 Had not their fathers seen wonders enough in Egypt, on the plains
13 of Tanis, when he parted the sea to let them pass through it, making
14 its waters stand firm as though in a cistern;[2] when he led them with a
15 cloud by day, with glowing fire all through the night? He pierced
the rock, too, in the desert, and slaked their thirst as if from some deep
16 pool, bidding the rock yield water, till fountains gushed from it,
abundant as rivers.

17 And still they went on offending him, there in the wilderness,
18 rebelling against the Most High, challenging God in their thoughts
19 to give them the food they craved for. Bitterly they asked, Can God
20 spread a table for us in the wilderness? True, he smote the rock, and
made water flow from it, till the stream ran in flood, but can he give
21 bread too, and make a feast for his people? All this the Lord heard,
and waited a while;[3] but already a fire was lit among the sons of Jacob,
22 already his anger was mounting against Israel. What, had they no
23 faith in God, no trust in his power to save? He laid his command
24 upon the clouds above them, threw open the doors of heaven, and
rained down manna for them to eat. The bread of heaven was his
25 gift to them; man should eat the food of angels,[4] and so their want
26 should be supplied abundantly. Next, he swept away the south wind
from the sky;[5] it was his power that sent them a south-west wind,
27 raining down meat on them thick as dust, birds on the wing, plentiful
28 as the sea-sand. Into their very camp it fell, close about their tents;

---

[1] 'Ephraim' is probably used here to represent the people of Israel, as often
in the prophets, who contrast it with 'Juda' (cf. *v.* 67). The Hebrew text may
imply that the Israelites shot with their bows, not that they threw them away.
The reference may be to the refusal to invade Palestine (Num. 14), but the
chronology of this psalm is difficult to disentangle.

[2] Literally 'water-bottle'; in the Hebrew text, 'in a heap.'

[3] In the Hebrew text, 'was angry.' The same is true of 'passed them by'
in *v.* 59.

[4] Literally 'of the strong,' according to the Hebrew text.

[5] The Hebrew text gives 'moved an easterly wind across the sky.'

29 and they ate, and took their fill. All they asked, he granted them;
30 he would not disappoint them of their longing. But while the food
31 was yet in their mouths God's anger against them rose, and slew their
   lordliest, caught them unawares, all the flower of Israel.

32   Yet, with all this, they continued to offend him; all his wonderful deeds
33 left them faithless still. And ever their lives passed away like a breath,
34 still the end of their years was hastened on. When he threatened them
   with death, they would search after him, coming back betimes to
35 look for him; they would remind themselves that it was God who had
36 protected them, his almighty power that had delivered them. Loving
   professions were on their lips, but they were false tongues that spoke
37 to him; their hearts were not true to him, no loyalty bound them
38 to his covenant. Yet, such is his mercy, he would still pardon their
   faults, and spare them from destruction; again and again he turned
39 his vengeance aside, let his anger die down. He would not forget
   that they were flesh and blood, no better than a breath of wind, that
40 passes by and never returns. How often the desert saw them in revolt
41 against him, how often, in those solitudes, they defied his anger! Always
   new challenges to God's power, new rebellions against the Holy One of
   Israel!

42   Had they forgotten all he did for them, that day when he set them
43 free from the power of their oppressor, all those miracles among the
44 men of Egypt, those portents in the plain of Tanis, when he turned
   all their streams, all their cisterns into blood, so that they could not
45 drink? He sent out flies, to their ruin, frogs to bring devastation on
46 them, gave all their harvest over to the mildew,[1] their tillage to the
47 locust, sent hail on their vineyards, frost on their mulberry-trees,
48 let the hail have its way with their cattle, the fire with their flocks.
49 He let his anger loose on them in all its vehemence; what rage, what
50 fury, what havoc, as the angels of destruction went on their errand! So,
   the way made ready for his vengeance, he took toll of their lives, doomed
51 even their cattle to death; on every first-born creature in Egypt, on the
52 first-fruits of increase in all the dwellings of Cham, his stroke fell. Then,
   like a shepherd, he rescued his own people, led them, his own flock,
53 through the wilderness; guided them in safety, free from all alarm, while
54 the sea closed over their enemy. So he brought them to the mountain
   which is his sanctuary, the mountain he took, with his own right hand
55 for title; so he drove out the heathen at their onset, parcelled out the
   land to them by lot, to each his own inheritance, bidding the tribes of
   Israel dwell where the heathen had dwelt before them.

---

[1] In the Hebrew text, 'the caterpillar.'

56 These were the men who defied the most high God, and rebelled
57 against him; would not observe his decrees, but turned away and
    broke faith with him as their fathers had done, like a bow that plays
58 the archer false; made mountain shrines, to court his anger, carved
59 images, to awake his jealousy! The Lord heard the bruit of it, and
60 passed them by, rejecting Israel in utter scorn; he forsook his tabernacle
61 in Silo, that tabernacle where once he dwelt among men. A prey,
    now, to the captor, all that once was strong, a prey now, all that once
62 was fair, to the power of the enemy; he would leave his people at the
63 mercy of the sword, reject his own inheritance. Their young men
    fed the flames, and where were the maidens to mourn for them? [1]
64 Their priests fell by the sword, and none was left to lament over their
    widows.[2]
65   Then suddenly, like a man that wakes up from sleep, like some
    warrior that lay, till now, bemused with wine, the Lord roused himself;
66 he smote his enemies as they turned to flee,[3] branded them for ever
67 with shame. But he refused, now, to make his dwelling with Joseph;
68 it was not the tribe of Ephraim he would choose; he chose the tribe
69 of Juda, and the hill of Sion, there to bestow his love. And there,
    on soil for ever undisturbed, he built his sanctuary, terrible as the
70 pasture-grounds of the wild oxen.[4] He chose David, too, for his
    servant; took him away from herding the sheep, bade him leave off
71 following the ewes that were in milk, and be the shepherd of Jacob's
72 sons, his own people, of Israel, his own domain. His was the loyal
    heart that should tend them, his the skilful hand that should be their
    guide.

PSALM SEVENTY-EIGHT   (79)

(A psalm of Asaph.)

O GOD, the heathen have broken into thy inheritance; they have
  profaned the temple, thy sanctuary, and brought Jerusalem low
2 as an orchard wall. They have thrown the corpses of thy servants to
  feed all the birds of heaven; wild beasts prey on the carrion of the

---

[1] The Hebrew text has 'their maidens were not given in marriage' (literally,
'had no song of praise sung over them').

[2] The Latin text here has, 'their widows were not mourned for'; the Hebrew
'their widows could not mourn.'

[3] Or possibly 'in their buttocks' (I Kg. 5.9).

[4] 'Terrible as the pasture grounds of the wild oxen'; the Hebrew text has
simply 'exalted on high.'

3 just; blood has flowed like water on every side of Jerusalem, and there
4 was none to bury the dead. What a triumph was this for the nations
   that dwell around us; how have our neighbours mocked and derided
5 us! Lord, must we always taste thy vengeance, must thy jealous anger
6 still burn unquenched? Pour out this indignation of thine upon the
   nations that do not acknowledge thee, on the kingdoms that never
7 invoke thy name; see how they have made Israel their prey, and left
8 his dwelling-place in ruins! Forget the long record of our sins, and
   haste in mercy to our side; never was need so sore as this.

9 O God, our Saviour, help us; deliver us, Lord, for the glory of thy
10 name, and pardon our sins for the sake of thy own renown! Shall
   the heathen ask, What has become of their God? Shall our eyes never
   witness thy vengeance upon the Gentiles, that vengeance thou wilt
11 take for thy servants' blood? Could but the groaning of the captive
   reach thy presence! Thy arm has not lost its strength; claim for thy own
12 the children of the slain![1] Pour out seven-fold retribution into the
   laps of our neighbours, for all the insults, Lord, which they have put
13 upon thee; and we, thy own people, sheep of thy pasturing, will give
   thee thanks for ever, echoing, from one generation to the next, the story
   of thy renown.

PSALM SEVENTY-NINE   (80)

(To the end, for those who will be transformed; the testimony of
Asaph; a psalm.)

2 GIVE audience, thou that art the guide of Israel, that leadest Joseph
   with a shepherd's care. Thou who art enthroned above the
3 Cherubim, reveal thyself to Ephraim, Benjamin, and Manasse; exert
4 thy sovereign strength, and come to our aid. O God, restore us to
5 our own; smile upon us, and we shall find deliverance. Lord God of
6 hosts, wilt thou always turn away in anger from thy servant's prayers;
   wilt thou allot us nothing but tears for our daily food and drink?
7 Thou hast made us a coveted prize to our neighbours, enemies mock at
8 our ill fortune! O God of hosts, restore us to our own; smile upon us,
   and we shall find deliverance.

9 Long ago, thou didst bring a vine out of Egypt, rooting out the
10 heathen to plant it here; thou didst prepare the way for its spreading,
   and it took root where thou hadst planted it, filled the whole land.
11 How it overshadowed the hills, how the cedars, divinely tall, were
12 overtopped by its branches! It spread out its tendrils to the sea, its

---

[1] For 'the children of the slain' the Hebrew text has 'men doomed to death.'

13 shoots as far as the great river. Why is it that in these days thou hast
14 levelled its wall, for every passer-by to rob it of its fruit? See how
    the wild boar ravages it, lone dweller in the woods, and finds pasture
15 in it![1] God of hosts, wilt thou not relent, and look down from heaven,
16 look to this vine that needs thy tending? Revive this stock which thy
    hand has planted, offspring that by thee throve, and throve for thee.
17 Blackened with fire is that stock, and near uprooted; there is death in thy
18 frown.[2] Thy chosen friends, a race [3] by thee thriving, and thriving for
19 thee, O let thy hand protect them still! Henceforth we will never forsake
20 thee; grant us life, and we will live only to invoke thy name. Lord God
    of hosts, restore us to our own; smile upon us, and we shall find deliver-
    ance.

PSALM EIGHTY (81)

(To the end, for the wine-presses; a psalm of Asaph's own.)

2 R EJOICE we all in honour of the God who aids us; cry out with
3   gladness to the God of Jacob; take up the psalm. The tambour,
4 there! The harp, sweetly sounding, and the zither! The new moon
5 has come; blow the trumpet loud, to grace our festival! Duty demands
6 it of Israel; it was a decree the God of Jacob made, bidding Joseph
    remember the day when he escaped from Egypt. The alien speech heard
7 no more,[4] his shoulder eased of the burden, his hands free, at last,
8 from the slavery of the hod! Such deliverance I brought, when thou
    didst cry out to me in thy misery; then gave thee audience under a canopy
    of cloud, and tested thy loyalty at the Waters of Rebellion.
9   Give heed, my people, to this warning of mine; Israel, wilt thou
10 listen? Then let no strange worship find a home with thee; never let
11 thy knees be bowed to an alien god; am not I the Lord thy God, I, who
    rescued thee from Egypt? Open thy mouth wide, and thou shalt have
12 thy fill. So I spoke, but my people would not listen; Israel went on

---

[1] The Hebrew text probably means, 'the boar from the woods ravages it, and
the wild beast devours it.'
[2] Literally, 'they will perish before thy threatening face,' referring either
to the people of Israel, or (more probably) to those in general who incur
God's anger.
[3] Literally, 'the man of thy right hand, the son of man.' This probably refers
to Israel personified.
[4] Literally, 'He had (till then) been hearing a language he did not know.'
The Hebrew text gives, 'I heard a language I did not know'; it is not clear in
what sense; some think a human speaker is intended, the rest of the psalm
being the content of his mysterious audition.

13 unheeding, till I was fain to let them have all they had set their hearts
14 on, following their own devices. Ah, if my people had but listened
15 to me! If Israel had but taken me for their guide! How lightly, then,
would I have brought their enemies low, smitten their persecutors!
16 But now, the Lord's enemies have won him over; age after age their
17 prosperity endures; full ears of wheat are still the nourishment he
gives them, and honey dripping from the rock to their heart's content.[1]

PSALM EIGHTY-ONE   (82)

(A psalm of Asaph.)

SEE, where he stands, the Ruler of all, among the rulers [2] assembled,
comes forward to pronounce judgement on the rulers themselves!
2 Will you never cease perverting justice, espousing the cause of the
3 wicked? Come, give redress to the poor and the friendless, do right
4 to the afflicted and the destitute; to you need and poverty look for
5 deliverance, rescue them from the hand of the oppressor. But no,
ignorant and unperceiving, they grope their way in darkness; see how
6 unstable are the props of earth! Gods you are, I myself have declared
7 it; favoured children, every one of you, of the most High; [3] yet the
doom of mortals awaits you, you shall fall with the fall of human princes.
8 Bestir thyself, Lord, bring the world to judgement; all the nations
are thy own domain.

PSALM EIGHTY-TWO   (83)

(A psalm-song of Asaph.)

2 O GOD, who can compare with thee? O God, do not keep still
3 now, do not hold back now! What turmoil among thy enemies;
4 how their malice lifts its head! Maliciously they plot against thy people,
5 compass the ruin of the men thou hast set apart for thyself; Come,

---

[1] *vv.* 16 and 17. In the Hebrew text, the former verse and perhaps the latter
also must be taken as referring to what *would* have happened; 'the enemies of
the Lord would have come cringing before him, and their (ill) fortune would
have lasted for ever; God would have fed them (*i.e.,* the Israelites) with full
ears of wheat,' &c. But it is difficult to make the Latin version yield any other
sense than that given above.

[2] Literally 'gods' as in verse 6, the Divine name being specially applied in
this way to judges (cf. Ex. 21.6).

[3] Jn. 10.34.

they whisper, let us put an end to their sovereignty, so that the very
6 name of Israel will be remembered no more. All are agreed, all alike
7 are ranged in confederacy against thee; here Edom lies encamped,
8 there Ismael; Moab, too, and the Agarenes; Gebal, Ammon and
9 Amelec, the Philistines, and the folk that dwell at Tyre. Even Assyria
has made common cause with them, lends her aid to these children of
Lot.[1]
10   Do to these what thou didst to Madian, to Sisara and Jabin at the
11 brook of Cisson; the men who died at Endor, rotted there like dung
12 on the ground.[2] May their princes fare as Oreb fared, and Zeb; may
the doom of Zebee and Salmana be the doom of all their chieftains.
13 And did they think to make God's sanctuary their spoil? My God,
send them whirling this way and that, like straws before the wind.
15 See how the fire burns up the forest, how its flames scorch the mountain-
16 side! So the storm of thy onset will rout them, thy fury will dismay
17 them. Let their cheeks blush crimson with shame, Lord, as they come
18 to sue for thy favour; confusion and dismay be theirs for ever, for
19 ever let them be abashed and brought to nothing, till they, too, know
the meaning of Javé's name, acknowledge thee as the most high God,
the Overlord of earth.

PSALM EIGHTY-THREE   (84)

(To the end, for the wine-presses; to the sons of Core, a psalm.)

2 LORD of hosts, how I love thy dwelling-place! For the courts
of the Lord's house, my soul faints with longing. The living God!
4 at his name my heart, my whole being thrills with joy. Where else
should the sparrow find a home, the dove a nest for her brood, but
5 at thy altar, Lord of hosts, my king and my God? How blessed, Lord,
are those who dwell in thy house! They will be ever praising thee.
6 How blessed is the man who finds his strength in thee! He sets his
7 heart on an upward journey, that leads through a valley of weeping,
8 but to his goal.[3] Strong in their Master's blessing, the pilgrims go on
from height to height, till they meet him in Sion, the God of all gods.
9   Lord God of hosts, listen to my prayer; God of Israel, grant me

---

[1] *vv.* 7–9. It is not certain what was the occasion of this psalm. The names
given suggest a simultaneous attack on the Jews by all their neighbours; the
children of Lot are the Moabites and the Ammonites (Gen. 19.37).

[2] *vv.* 10–12. See Jg. 4; 7.25; 8.

[3] In the Hebrew text, 'When he passes through a valley of weeping, he
turns it into a well.'

10 audience! God, ever our protector, do not disregard us now; look
11 favourably upon him whom thou hast anointed![1] Willingly would
   I give a thousand of my days for one spent in thy courts! Willingly
   lie there forgotten, in the house of my God, so I might dwell no more
12 in the abode of sinners! God loves mercy and faithfulness;[2] all favour,
13 all honour, come of the Lord's gift. To innocent lives he will never
   refuse his bounty; Lord of hosts, blessed is the man who puts his confidence
   in thee.

PSALM EIGHTY-FOUR   (85)

(To the end, for the sons of Core, a psalm.)

 2 WHAT blessings, Lord, thou hast granted to this land of thine,
 3   restoring Jacob from captivity, pardoning thy people's guilt,
 4 burying away the record of their sins, all thy anger calmed, thy fierce
 5 displeasure forgotten! And now, God of our deliverance, do thou
 6 restore us; no longer let us see thy frown. Wouldst thou always be
    indignant with us? Must thy resentment smoulder on, age after age?
 7 Nay, thou wilt relent, O God, and give fresh life, to rejoice the spirits
 8 of thy people. Shew us thy mercy, Lord; grant us thy deliverance!
 9   Let me listen, now, to the voice of the Lord God within me; it is
    a message of peace he sends to his people; to his loyal servants, that
10 come back, now, to take counsel of their hearts.[3]   For us, his wor-
    shippers, deliverance is close at hand; in this land of ours, the divine
11 glory is to find a home.[4] See, where mercy and faithfulness meet in
12 one; how justice and peace are united in one embrace! Faithfulness
13 grows up out of the earth, and from heaven, justice looks down. The
    Lord, now, will grant us his blessing, to make our land yield its harvest;
14 justice will go on before him, to make the way ready for his progress.

---

[1] It is not certain whether King David, or the people of Israel, is here referred to as the anointed (or Christ) of God.

[2] In the Hebrew text, 'the Lord is a sun and a shield.'

[3] Literally, in the Latin, 'who turn back to the heart,' cf. Is. 46.8; the Septuagint Greek has, 'to those who turn their hearts back to him.' The Hebrew
text is quite different, 'let them not turn back to their folly.'

[4] *vv*. 11, 12. These verses perhaps imply that God's fidelity to his promises
and God's mercy have combined to restore the Jewish people; that his justice,
satisfied with the expiation of their sins, no longer grudges them peace and
well-being; that loyalty to the old covenant is once more a native growth in
the land of Israel, and that God looks down to reward it. But the picture may
be a more general one.

PSALM EIGHTY-FIVE   (86)

(A prayer of David's own.)

TURN thy ear, Lord, and listen to me in my helplessness and my
2 need. Protect a life dedicated to thyself; rescue a servant of thine,
3 my God, that puts his trust in thee. Have mercy, O Lord; for mercy
4 I plead continually; comfort thy servant's heart, this heart that aspires,
5 Lord, to thee. Who is so kind and forgiving, Lord, as thou art, who
6 so rich in mercy to all who invoke him? Give a hearing, then, Lord,
7 to my prayer; listen to my plea when I cry out to thee in a time of
8 sore distress, counting on thy audience. There is none like thee, Lord,
9 among the gods; none can do as thou doest. Lord, all the nations
   thou hast made must needs come and worship thee, honouring thy
10 name, so great thou art, so marvellous in thy doings, thou who alone
   art God.
11   Guide me, Lord, thy own way, thy faithful care my escort, make this
12 heart thrill with reverence for thy name. O Lord my God, with all my
13 heart I will give thee thanks, eternally hold thy name in honour for the
   greatness of the mercy thou hast shewed me, in rescuing me thus from
14 the lowest depths of hell. And now, O God, see how the despisers of thy
   law have set upon me, how their dread conspiracy threatens my life, with
15 no thought of thee to restrain it! But thou, Lord, art a God of mercy and
16 pity, patient, compassionate, true to thy promise. Look upon me and be
   merciful to me; rescue, with thy sovereign aid, one whose mother bore
17 him to thy service! Shew me some token of thy favour; let my enemies
   see, abashed, how thou dost help me, how thou, Lord, dost comfort me.

PSALM EIGHTY-SIX   (87)

(For the sons of Core; a psalm-song.)

2 HIS own building amidst the inviolate hills, the Lord loves Sion
3 walls better than any other home in Israel. City of God, how
4 high the claim that is made for thee: I can tell of Egypt and of Babylon
   as peoples that know me well. The Philistines, too, and the Tyrians,
5 and the Ethiopian tribes, all have visited her. Not for Sion to boast
   that this man or that man was born in her, when she was founded
6 by no other than the Most High. So the Lord proclaims, telling the

7 tale of nations and princes that have visited her. All the world, rejoicing,
finds its dwelling-place in thee.[1]

PSALM EIGHTY-SEVEN   (88)

(A psalm-song for the sons of Core; to the end, for an answer for
Maheleth; of understanding, for Eman the Ezrahite.)

2 LORD God, my deliverer, day and night I cry aloud to thee; let
4 my prayer reach thy presence, give audience to my entreaty, for
indeed my heart is full of trouble. My life sinks ever closer to the grave;
5 I count as one of those who go down into the abyss, a man past all help,
6 there among the lordless dead. It is with me as with men laid low in the
grave, men thou rememberest no longer, cast away, now, from thy
7 protecting hand. Such is the place where they have laid me, in the
8 depths of earth, amidst darkness and in the shadow of death; heavily
thy anger weighs down on me, and thou dost overwhelm me with
9 its full flood. Thou hast estranged all my acquaintance from me,
so that they treat me as a thing accursed; I lie in a prison whence there
10 is no escape, my eyes grow dim, waiting for the help that does not
come. So, all day long, I call upon thee, all day long stretch out my
hands to thee.

11   Not for the dead thy wonderful power is shewn; what physician can
12 bring him back alive to give thee thanks? There in the grave, how
shall he recount thy mercies; how shall he tell of thy faithfulness,
13 now that life is gone? How can there be talk of thy marvels in a world
14 of shadows, of thy goodness in a land where all is forgotten? To prayer,
15 Lord, fall I lustily; it shall reach thee while there is yet time. Why dost
16 thou reject my plea, Lord, and turn thy face away from me? Ever since
youth, need and sorrow have been my lot; lifted up only to be cast down
17 and left bewildered; and now I am overwhelmed with thy anger, dis-
18 mayed by thy threats, that still cut me off like a flood all at once sur-
19 rounding me. Never a friend or a neighbour but has left me, never an
acquaintance to comfort my distress.

---

[1] *vv.* 4–7. The sense of this passage is very obscure, and the versions differ
both from the Hebrew text and from one another. In the Hebrew text, the
words 'This man was born there' appear in verse 4, instead of 'all have visited
her'; and verse 6 reads 'The Lord, keeping record of the nations, will reckon,
This man was born there.' Verse 5 begins simply 'It shall be Sion's boast,' and
the last verse appears to run 'The singers, like the dancers, (shall say) All my
fountains are in thee.' The Greek Septuagint, in verse 4, has 'I will make mention to my familiars of Egypt and of Babylon'; and in verse 5, 'Men will say,
Sion is a mother, and, A man has been born in her.'

PSALM EIGHTY-EIGHT (89)

(Of understanding; for Ethan the Ezrahite.)

2 HERE is a song to put the Lord's mercies on record for ever; ages will pass, and still these words of mine shall proclaim thy faithful-
3 ness. There, in the heavens, thou hast framed a design of everlasting
4 mercy [1]; there thy faithful promise rests; I have made a covenant with
5 my chosen people, sworn an oath to my servant David: To all time I will make thy posterity continue, age after age I will bid thy throne endure.

6 And are not those heavens, Lord, witnesses of thy wonderful power,
7 of thy faithfulness, before the court of the holy ones? Who is there above the clouds to rival the Lord; where is God's like among all his
8 sons? How honoured is God, in that assembly of the holy ones; how
9 great he is, how reverenced by all that stand about him! Lord God of hosts, who can compare with thee; in the power, Lord, that is thine,
10 in the faithfulness that everywhere attends thee? It is thou that dost
11 curb the pride of the sea, and calm the tumult of its waves; insolence lies crushed at thy feet,[2] where thy strong arm has routed thy enemies.
12 Thine are the heavens, thine the earth; author, thou, of the world and
13 all it holds. The north wind and the sea are of thy fashioning; [3] thy
14 name wakes the glad echoes of Thabor and Hermon. Thine is a warrior's
15 arm; shew the strength of that hand, lift it on high! Right and justice are the pillars of thy throne; mercy and faithfulness the heralds of thy coming.

16 Happy is the people that knows well the shout of praise, that lives, Lord,
17 in the smile of thy protection! Evermore they take pride in thy name,
18 rejoice over thy just awards. What else but thy glory inspires their
19 strength? What else but thy favour bids us lift our heads? The help of the Lord, our King, the Holy One of Israel, is ours.

20 Long ago, in a vision, thou didst make a promise to thy faithful ser- vants. To a warrior, thou saidst, I have committed your safety, chosen
21 out among the common folk a man to honour. Here was my servant
22 David; on him my consecrating oil has been poured. My hand shall

---

[1] 'There in the heavens,' &c., literally, 'Thou hast said, Mercy shall be built up.' The Hebrew text has, 'I have said.'

[2] The word translated 'insolence' may, in the Hebrew, be a proper noun, Rahab; either meaning Egypt (as in 86.4), or personifying the principle of Chaos which was destroyed by the Creation (cf. 73.13).

[3] 'The sea'; in the Hebrew text, 'the south wind.'

23 strengthen him, my arm shall give him courage; foe is none shall make
head against him, nor champion of wrong have power, henceforth, to
24 injure him; I will crush the enemies that confront him, put all their
25 malice to rout. My faithfulness and mercy shall go with him; by my
26 favour he shall rise to pre-eminence. I will make his power rest on the
27 sea; to the streams of the great river his hand shall reach out.[1] Thou art
my Father, he will cry out to me, thou art my God, my stronghold and
28 my refuge; and I will acknowledge him as my first-born, overlord to all
29 the kings of earth. I will continue my mercy towards him for ever, my
30 covenant with him shall remain unbroken; I will give him a posterity
31 that never fails, a throne enduring as heaven itself. Do his children for-
32 sake my law, instead of following the law I have given them; do they
33 violate my decrees, neglect my commandments? Then I will punish
34 their transgressions, scourge them for their sin, but I will not cancel my
35 gracious promise to him; never will I be guilty of unfaithfulness, never
36 will I violate my covenant, or alter the word once spoken. Once for all
37 I have sworn it on my holy throne, I will never be false to David; his
38 posterity shall continue for ever, his royalty, too, shall last on in my
presence like the sun, like the moon's eternal orb; that bears witness in
heaven unalterable.

39 And now? Now thou hast only loathing and scorn for us; thou dost
40 refuse audience to him thou hast anointed. Thou hast annulled the
covenant thou didst make with thy servant, dishonoured his royalty[2]
41 in the dust, broken down all the walls about him, and thrown his
42 stronghold into confusion: till he is plundered by every passer-by,
43 a laughing-stock to all his neighbours. Thou hast granted aid to the
44 men who conspire against him, triumph to all his enemies, foiling the
45 thrust of his sword, and denying him thy aid in battle. Thou hast
robbed him of the bright glory[3] that once was his, thou hast cast down
46 his throne to earth, cut short the days of his prosperity, and covered
him with shame.

47 Lord, wilt thou always turn away so obdurately, will the flame of
48 thy anger never be quenched? Remember how frail a thing I am,
49 how brief the destiny of all Adam's sons. Where is the man that can
live on, and leave death untasted; can ransom his life from the power
50 of the world beneath? Lord, where are those mercies of an earlier
51 time, promised so faithfully to David? Remember how a world's

---

[1] 'The great river' is Euphrates, as in 71.8, 79.12.

[2] The Latin word used here is sometimes translated 'shrine,' but refers,
where kings are concerned, to their secret archives. In the Hebrew text, the
sense is 'crown.'

[3] Literally, 'purification.'

52 taunts assail thy people, and this one heart must bear them all; the
   taunts, Lord, of thy enemies, reviling, in thy stead, the man whom thou
   hast anointed!
53   Blessed be the Lord for ever. Amen, Amen.

PSALM EIGHTY-NINE   (90)

(A prayer of Moses, the man of God.)

L ORD, thou hast been our refuge from generation to generation.
2 Before the hills came to birth, before the whole frame of the
   world was engendered, from eternity to eternity, O God, thou art.
3 And wilt thou bring man to nothing, that thou sayest, Return, children
4 of Adam, to what you were? In thy sight, a thousand years are but
   as yesterday, that has come and gone, or as one of the night-watches;
5 what is man's life-time, then, but a thing not worth the reckoning? [1]
6 So be it; let him be grass that fades with the morning, blooms with
   the morning, only to fade; by evening it lies drooping, all dry and
7 withered. Still thy anger takes toll of us, thy displeasure denies us rest,
8 so jealous thy scrutiny of our wrong-doing, so clear our lives shew
9 in the light of thy presence. Day after day vanishes, and still thy anger
10 takes toll of us; the work of a life-time is only gossamer.[2] What is our
    span of days? Seventy years it lasts, eighty years, if lusty folk we be;
    beyond that, all is toil and sorrow; and at last thy hand comes upon us in
11 mercy, for our correction.[3]   Alas, that so few heed thy vengeance,
12 measure thy anger by the reverence we owe thee! With such correction
    thou must needs assert thy power, chasten us and make us wise.[4]
13   Relent, Lord; must it be for ever? Be gracious to thy servants.
14 For us thy timely mercies, for us abiding happiness and content;
15 happiness that shall atone for the time when thou didst afflict us, for
16 the long years of ill fortune. Look upon thy servants, thy own fashion-

---

[1] In the Hebrew text, 'thou carriest them away like a flood; they become
like a sleep.'

[2] In the Hebrew text, 'Day after day is consumed through thy anger; we
bring our years to an end like a sigh.'

[3] 'If we count among the heroes'; the Latin version possibly implies a reference
to Gen. 6.4. The sense of the Hebrew text is, 'if they reach fulness,' or perhaps
'if they are eighty, by reason of our strength.' According to the same text, the
last clause of the verse should mean, 'so swiftly it passes, and we are gone.'

[4] The Hebrew text is usually understood as meaning, 'And measure thy
anger by the reverence we owe thee. Teach us so to count our days, that we may
come by a wise heart.'

17 ing, and be the guide of their posterity;[1] brightly may the splendour of the Lord shine upon us! Prosper our doings, Lord, prosper our doings yet.

PSALM NINETY (91)

(A song of praise for David.)

2 HE who lives under the protection of the most High, under his heavenly care content to abide, can say to the Lord, Thou art my
3 support and my stronghold, my God, in whom I trust. It is he that rescues me from every treacherous snare, from every whisper of harm.[2]
4 Sheltered under his arms, under his wings nestling, thou art safe; his faithfulness will throw a shield about thee. Nothing shalt thou have to
6 fear from nightly terrors, from the arrow that flies by day-light, from trouble that infests the darkness, from the assault of man or fiend under
7 the noon. Though a thousand fall at thy side, ten thousand at thy right
8 hand, it shall never come next or near thee; rather, thy eyes shall look about thee, and see the reward of sinners.
9 Yes, Lord, thou art my hope; my soul, thou hast found a strong-
10 hold in the most High.[3] There is no harm that can befall thee, no
11 plague that shall come near thy dwelling. He has given charge to his angels concerning thee, to watch over thee wheresoever thou goest;
12 they will hold thee up with their hands lest thou shouldst chance to
13 trip on a stone. Thou shalt tread safely on asp and adder,[4] crush lion and serpent under thy feet.
14 He trusts in me, mine it is to rescue him; he acknowledges my name,
15 from me he shall have protection; when he calls upon me, I will listen;
16 in affliction I am at his side, to bring him safety and honour. Length of days he shall have to content him, and find in me deliverance.

---

[1] According to the Hebrew text, this verse means 'Shew thy servants thy action, and their children thy glory.'

[2] vv. 3, 6. The 'whisper of harm' and the 'trouble that infests the darkness' should be, according to the most probable interpretation of the Hebrew text, 'the destroying pestilence' and 'the pestilence that infests the darkness.' According to the same text, 'the assault of man or fiend' (literally 'assault or the fiend') should be 'the destruction that lays waste.'

[3] The words 'my soul' are not in the original; they are inserted here so as to soften the sudden transition from a phrase addressed to God to one which is addressed to the Psalmist himself.

[4] For 'the asp' the Hebrew text has 'the lion.'

PSALM NINETY-ONE   (92)

(A psalm-song on the sabbath day.)

SWEET it is to praise the Lord, to sing, most high God, in honour
3 of thy name; to proclaim thy mercy and faithfulness at day-break
4 and at the fall of night. Here is a theme for ten-stringed harp and
5 viol, for music of voice and zither; so delightsome, Lord, is all thou
6 doest, so thrills my heart at the sight of all thou hast made. How
magnificent is thy creation, Lord, how unfathomable are thy purposes!
7 And still, too dull to learn, too slow to grasp his lesson, the wrong-
8 doer goes on in his busy wickedness. Still he thrives, still he makes
a brave show like the grass in spring, yet is he doomed to perish eternally,
9 whilst thou, Lord, art for ever exalted on high. Vanished away thy
enemies, Lord, vanished away, and all their busy wickedness scattered
to the winds!
11 He gives me strength, that gives strength to the wild oxen; even
12 in my grey hairs his mercy is rich towards me.[1] Blessed are these
eyes with the sight of my enemies' downfall, these ears with the tidings
13 of insolent malice defeated. The innocent man will flourish as the
palm-tree flourishes; he will grow to greatness as the cedars grow
14 on Lebanon. Planted in the temple of the Lord, growing up in the
15 very courts of our God's house, the innocent flourish in a green old
16 age, still in good heart;[2] theirs to proclaim how just is the Lord our
God, his dealings how clear of wrong.

PSALM NINETY-TWO   (93)

(A psalm-song for David himself on the day before the sabbath, the day
on which the earth was established.)

THE Lord reigns as king, robed in majesty; royalty the Lord has
for robe and girdle. He it was that founded the solid earth, to abide
2 immovable. Firm stood thy throne ere ever the world began; from all
3 eternity, thou art. Loud the rivers echo, Lord; loud the rivers echo;

---

[1] In the Hebrew text, 'So rich is the oil with which I am anointed.'
[2] In the Hebrew, 'Will not the innocent yet flourish in old age, vigorous
and fresh?'

4 rivers that rise in flood, with a roar of eddying waters; [1] magnificent
the sea's rage; magnificent above these, the Lord reigns in heaven.
5 How faithful, Lord, are thy promises! Holy is thy house, and must needs
be holy until the end of time.

PSALM NINETY-THREE   (94)

(A psalm of David's own, for the fourth day of the week.)

THE Lord is a God who takes vengeance, and now in vengeance
2 he is made manifest. Judge of the world, mount thy throne,
3 and give the proud their deserts! Must it be the sinners still, Lord,
4 the sinners still that triumph? Shall there be no end to the prating,
5 the rebellious talk, the boastfulness of wrong-doers? See, Lord, how
6 they crush down thy people, afflict the land of thy choice, murder
7 the widow and the stranger, slay the orphan! And they think, The
8 Lord will never see it, the God of Israel pays no heed. Pay heed, rather,
yourselves, dull hearts that count among my people; fools, learn your
9 lesson ere it is too late. Is he deaf, the God who implanted hearing
10 in us; is he blind, the God who gave us eyes to see? He who punishes
nations, who taught man all that man knows, will he not call you to
11 account? The Lord looks into men's hearts, and finds there illusion.
12 Happy, Lord, is the man whom thou dost chasten, reading him the
13 lesson of thy law! For him, thou wilt lighten the time of adversity,
14 digging a pit all the while to entrap the sinner. God will not abandon
15 his people, will not desert his chosen land; ere long,[2] his justice will
16 reappear in judgement, claiming all upright hearts for its own. Who
takes my part against the oppressor? Who rallies to my side against the
17 wrong-doers? It is the Lord that helps me; but for that, the grave
18 would soon be my resting-place. Still, when my foothold seemed lost,
19 thy mercy, Lord, held me up; amid all the thronging cares that filled
20 my heart, my soul thrilled with thy consolation. What part have these
unjust judges with thee? Thy punishments are for the breakers of thy

---

[1] Literally 'as the result of (or perhaps, in comparison with) the voice of many
waters.' It is not certain whether these words should be taken with what goes
before, or with what follows; the meaning of the Hebrew text is much in doubt.
[2] This verse simply begins, in the original, with the word 'until,' but some
words evidently must be supplied to trace the connexion of thought with what
goes before.

21 law;[1]   these plot against upright lives, it is the innocent they condemn
22 to death.   In the Lord I find my stronghold, in my God's help I trust;
23 he will punish the wrong done, destroy them in their wickedness, doubt
   not the Lord our God will destroy them.

PSALM NINETY-FOUR   (95)

(A psalm-song of David's own.)

2 COME, friends, rejoice we in the Lord's honour; cry we out for
   gladness to God, our deliverer; the first to court his presence with
3 thanksgiving, greet him with a joyful psalm!   A high God is the Lord,
4 a king high above all the gods;[2]   beneath his hand lie the last bounds
5 of earth, his are the mountain peaks;   his the ocean, for who but he
6 created it? What other power fashioned the dry land?   Come in, then,
   fall down before him, bow the knee; plead [3] we with the God who made
7 us.   Who but the Lord is our God? And what are we, but folk of his
   pasturing, sheep that follow his beckoning hand?
8   Would you but listen to his voice today! Do not harden your hearts,
   as they were hardened once when you provoked me, and put me to
9 the test, in the wilderness.[4]   Your fathers put me to the test, challenged
10 me, and had proof of my power,   for forty years together. From that
   generation I turned away in loathing; [5] These, I said, are ever wayward
11 hearts,   these have never learned to obey me. And I took an oath in
   anger, They shall never attain my rest.[6]

---

[1] The Latin here runs, literally, 'Does the (judgement) seat of iniquity cleave
to thee, thou who dost fashion misfortune (or perhaps, toil) in accordance with
precept?' Some such rendering as that given above seems to be demanded by
the context. Instead of 'thou who dost fashion,' the Hebrew text has 'which
fashions,' referring to the 'seat of iniquity'; and the second half of the sentence is generally understood as meaning, 'which makes iniquity its law.'

[2] The Gallican Psalter, which is used in the liturgical recitation of the psalms,
adds at the end of this verse 'God will not abandon his people' (cf. 93.14).

[3] In the Hebrew text, 'kneel down.'

[4] 'When you provoked me and put me to the test'; in the Hebrew text, proper
names may be understood here, 'at Massa and at Meriba' (Ex. 17.7).

[5] The Gallican Psalter has, 'When I lived close to that generation.'

[6] *vv.* 8–11. See Heb. 3.7–19.

PSALM NINETY-FIVE (96)

(A song of David's own, when the house was being built after the captivity.) [1]

SING the Lord a new song; in the Lord's honour, let the whole
2 earth make melody! Sing to the Lord, and bless his name; never
3 cease bearing record of his power to save. Publish his glory among
4 the heathen; his wonderful acts for all the world to hear. How great
is the Lord, how worthy of honour! What other god is to be feared
5 as he? They are but devils [2] whom the heathen call divine; the Lord,
6 not they, made the heavens. Honour and beauty wait on his presence;
worship and magnificence are the attendants of his shrine.
7 Lands of the heathen, make your offering to the Lord, an offering
8 to the Lord of glory and praise, an offering of glory to the Lord's
9 name; bring sacrifice, come into his courts, worship the Lord in his
holy temple.[3] Before the Lord's presence let the whole earth bow in
10 reverence; tell the heathen, The Lord is king now, he has put the
world in order, never to be thrown into confusion more; he will give
11 the nations a just award. Rejoice, heaven, and let earth be glad; let the
12 sea, and all the sea contains, give thunderous applause. Smiling the
fields, and all the burden they bear; no tree in the forest but will rejoice
13 to greet its Lord's coming. He comes to judge the earth; brings the world
justice, to every race of men its promised award.

PSALM NINETY-SIX (97)

(For him, David, when his land was restored.)

THE Lord reigns as king; let earth be glad of it, let the furthest
2 isles rejoice! See where he sits, cloud and darkness about him,
3 justice and right the pillars of his throne; see where he comes, fire sweep-
4 ing on before him burning up his enemies all around! In the flash of his

---

[1] This psalm is to be found in a slightly altered form in I Par. 16 (*vv.* 23 and following). The 'captivity' referred to in the title is not that of Israel, but that of the Ark, which had been taken by the Philistines (I Kg. 4.11), and seems not to have been a centre of worship for Israel until David brought it back to Jerusalem.

[2] The word used in the Hebrew text rather signifies nothingness, worthlessness.

[3] The Hebrew text has 'in holy beauty,' (cf. Par. 16.29); some think the meaning is, 'in holy vestments.'

lightning, how shines the world revealed; how earth trembles at the
5 sight! The hills melt like wax at the presence of the Lord; at its Master's
6 presence, the whole earth shrinks away.[1] The very heavens proclaim his
7 faithfulness; no nation but has witnessed his glory. Shame upon the men
that worship carved images, and make their boast of false gods! Him only
all you powers of heaven prostrate adore!
8   Glad news for Sion, rejoicing for Juda's townships, when thy judge-
9 ments, Lord, are made known. Art thou not sovereign Lord of all the
10 earth, beyond measure exalted above all gods? Lovers of the Lord, hate
the evil things; souls that are true to him he guards ever, rescues them
11 from the hand of the wrong-doer. Dawn of hope [2] for the innocent, dawn
12 of gladness for honest hearts! Rejoice and triumph, just souls, in the
Lord, of his holy name published everywhere the renown.

PSALM NINETY-SEVEN   (98)

(A psalm of David's own.)

SING the Lord a new song, a song of wonder at his doings; how
2 his own right hand, his own holy arm, brought him victory. The
Lord has given proof of his saving power, has vindicated his just dealings,
3 for all the nations to see; has remembered his gracious promise, and
kept faith with the house of Israel; no corner of the world but has
4 witnessed how our God can save. In God's honour let all the earth
5 keep holiday; let all be song and rejoicing and festal melody! Praise
6 the Lord with the harp, the harp that has a psalm for its music; with
trumpets of metal, and the music of the braying horn! Keep holiday
7 in the presence of the Lord, our King; the sea astir, and all that the
8 sea holds, the world astir, and all that dwell on it; the rivers echoing
9 their applause, the hills, too, rejoicing to see the Lord come. He comes
to judge the earth; brings the world justice, to every race of man its
due award.

---

[1] In the Hebrew text, the last clause of this verse is more naturally rendered,
'at the presence of the Master of the whole earth.'
[2] Literally 'light has dawned.' The Hebrew text has, 'light has been sown.'

PSALM NINETY-EIGHT (99)

(A psalm of David's own.)

THE Lord is king; let the heathen chafe as they will; he is throned
2 above the Cherubim; let the earth tremble before him.[1]   Great
3 is the Lord who dwells in Sion, sovereign ruler of all peoples!   Let them
4 all praise that great name of thine, a name terrible and holy.   Dearly
thy kingly heart loves justice; thou dost bring redress to all, giving the
5 sons of Jacob doom and award.   Praise, then, the Lord our God, and bow
6 down before his footstool; that, too, is holy.[2]   Remember Moses and
Aaron, and all those priests of his, Samuel and those others who have
called on his name, how he listened to them when they called upon
7 him.   His voice came to them from the pillar of cloud; faithfully they
8 kept the decrees, kept the command he gave them.   And thou, O Lord
our God, didst listen to them, and they found thee a God of pardon; yet
when they followed their own false conceits, thou wert quick to punish.[3]
9 Praise the Lord our God, and do worship on the holy mountain where
he dwells; the Lord our God is holy.

PSALM NINETY-NINE (100)

(A psalm for thanksgiving.)

2 LET the whole earth keep holiday in God's honour; pay to the
Lord the homage of your rejoicing, appear in his presence with
3 glad hearts.   Learn that it is the Lord, no other, who is God; we did
not make ourselves, it was he that made us.[4] You that are his people,
4 sheep of his own pasturing,   pass through these gates, enter these
courts of his, with hymns of praise; give him thanks, and bless his name.
5 Gracious is the Lord, everlasting his mercy; age succeeds age, and he
is faithful to his promise still.

---

[1] The Latin here represents the nations as being angry at the thought of God's sovereignty; but the word used in the Hebrew text means rather, 'be dismayed.'

[2] The Hebrew text may mean 'for he is holy' at the end of the verse.

[3] Literally 'thou wert (an) avenging (God) towards all their false conceits.' The sense of the verse is not altogether clear, and some commentators believe that the text is corrupt.

[4] There is a different tradition of the Hebrew text which gives, 'He made us, and we belong to him.' If this other tradition is right, it is best to join the rest of verse 3 to what precedes, rather than to what follows.

PSALM ONE HUNDRED   (101)

(A psalm of David's own.)

OF mercy and of justice my song shall be; a psalm in thy honour,
2 Lord, with a life of holiness for its theme. Ah, when wilt thou grant
me thy presence? Here in my house I would live[1] with stainless heart;
3 no ill purpose clouding my view, the transgressors of the law my
4 enemies. Never was false heart bosom friend of mine; the wicked part
5 company with me, and are none of my acquaintance. From me, the
whisper of calumny wins no forgiveness; proud looks, and grasping
6 ambition, find no place at my table. To plain, honest folk I look for my
7 company; my servants are such as follow the path of innocence. No
welcome here for rebellious spirits, no standing in my presence for men
8 who talk deceitfully. Mine, ere long, to root out from the land every
guilty soul, till I purge the Lord's city of all evil-doing.

PSALM ONE HUNDRED AND ONE   (102)

(A prayer for the friendless man, when he is troubled, and is pouring
out his petition before the Lord.)

2 O LORD, hear my prayer, and let my cry come unto thee. Do
not turn thy face away from me, but lend me thy ear in time
4 of affliction; give me swift audience whenever I call upon thee. See
how this life of mine passes away like smoke, how this frame wastes
5 like a burning faggot! Drained of strength, like grass the sun scorches,
6 I leave my food untasted, forgotten; I am spent with sighing, till my
7 skin clings to my bones. I am no better than a pelican out in the desert,
8 an owl on some ruined dwelling; I keep watch, lonely as a single
9 sparrow on the house top. All day long my enemies taunt me; even
10 those who once flattered me curse me now. Ashes are all my food,
11 I drink nothing but what comes to me mingled with my tears; I shrink
before thy vengeful anger, so low thou hast brought me, who didst

---

[1] This verb, and all the verbs which follow, up to the end of the psalm, are
given by the Latin in a past tense, which seems meant to describe the daily habits
of the psalmist. The Hebrew verbs in question may, however, be understood
as verbs referring to the future, describing what the course of the Psalmist's
life will be when God has 'granted his presence.' This last phrase is thought
by some commentators to mean the coming of the Ark to Jerusalem (II Kg. 6).

12 once lift me so high. Like a tapering shadow my days dwindle, wasting away, like grass in the sun!

13 Lord, thou endurest for ever, thy name, as the ages pass, is not
14 forgotten; surely thou wilt bestir thyself, and give Sion redress! It
15 is time, now, to take pity on her, the hour has come. See how' the
servants love her even in ruin, how they water her dust with their
16 tears! Will not the heathen learn reverence, Lord, for thy glorious
17 name, all those monarchs of the earth, when they hear that the Lord
18 has built Sion anew, ready to be revealed there in glory, that he has
given heed to the prayer of the afflicted, and neglects their appeal
19 no more? Such legend inscribe we for a later age to read; a new people
20 that has come into being shall praise the Lord, the Lord who looks down
from his sanctuary on high, viewing, as the Lord can, earth from
21 heaven, listening to the groans of the prisoners, delivering a race
22 that was doomed to die. There will be talk of the Lord's name in
23 Sion, of his praise in Jerusalem, when peoples and kings meet there,
24 to pay the Lord their homage; has he not answered the prayer of his
own people, come mightily to their aid? [1]

25 Give me warning of the time I have left; do not call me away sud-
26 denly, my life half done. Age after age thy years endure; it was thou,
Lord, that didst lay the foundations of earth when time began, it was
27 thy hand that built the heavens. They will perish, but thou wilt remain;
they will all be like a cloak that grows threadbare, and thou wilt lay
28 them aside like a garment, and exchange them for new; and thou, all the
29 while, art what thou art, unalterably; thy years can never fail. The posterity of thy servants shall yet have a home to dwell in; their race shall
thrive endlessly.

PSALM ONE HUNDRED AND TWO   (103)

(For David himself.)

BLESS the Lord, my soul, unite, all my powers, to bless that holy
2 name. Bless the Lord, my soul, remembering all he has done
3 for thee, how he pardons all thy sins, heals all thy mortal ills, rescues
thy life from deadly peril, crowns thee with the gifts of his kindness

---

[1] The first half of this verse, in the Latin, means literally, 'he has answered him (or, it) in the journeying of his strength.' With this reading, it seems best to understand God as the subject, and his people (referred to in verse 19 above) as receiving an answer from him. In the Hebrew text, the sense is quite different, and the whole verse reads 'he has brought my strength (according to another reading, his strength) low in the course of the journey; he has shortened my days'; the next verse begins, 'I have said, O my God, do not call me away,' &c.

5 and compassion; how he contents all thy desire for good, restores thy
6 youth, as the eagle's plumage is restored. The Lord's acts are acts
7 of mercy, to every wronged soul he gives redress. The Lord, who told
his secrets, shewed the sons of Israel his will!

8   How pitying and gracious the Lord is, how patient, how rich in
9 mercy! He will not always be finding fault, his frown does not last for
10 ever; he does not treat us as our sins deserve, does not exact the penalty
11 of our wrong-doing. High as heaven above the earth towers his mercy
12 for the men that fear him; far as the east is from the west, he clears
13 away our guilt from us. For his own worshippers, the Lord has a
14 father's pity; does he not know the stuff of which we are made, can
15 he forget that we are only dust? Man's life is like the grass, he blooms
16 and dies like a flower in the fields; once the hot wind has passed over
17 it, it has gone, forgets the place where it grew.[1] But the Lord's worshippers know no beginning or end of his mercy; he will keep faith
18 with their children's children, do they but hold fast by his covenant,
19 and live mindful of his law. The Lord has set up his throne in heaven,
20 rules with universal sway. Bless the Lord, all you angels of his; angels
of sovereign strength, that carry out his commandment, attentive
21 to the word he utters; bless the Lord, all you hosts of his, the servants
22 that perform his will; bless the Lord, all you creatures of his, in every
corner of his dominion; and thou, my soul, bless the Lord.

PSALM ONE HUNDRED AND THREE   (104)

(For David himself.)

B LESS the Lord, my soul; O Lord my God, what magnificence
2   is thine! Glory and beauty are thy clothing. The light is a garment
thou dost wrap about thee, the heavens a curtain thy hand unfolds.
3 Thou hast roofed it in with the upper waters; the clouds are thy stair-
4 way; on the wings of the wind thou dost come and go. Thou wilt have
thy angels [2] be like the winds, the servants that wait on thee like a flame
of fire.
5   The earth thou hast planted on its own firm base, undisturbed for
6 all time. The deep once covered it, like a cloak; see how the waters

---

[1] The more probable meaning of the Hebrew text is, 'the place where it
grew forgets it.'

[2] The word 'angels,' in the Hebrew or in the Greek, might be translated
'messengers.' Some would translate the Hebrew text, 'who makes messengers
of the winds, servants out of the flaming fire.' But see Heb. 1.7, which plainly
supports the sense given above.

7 stand high above the mountains,[1] then cower before thy rebuking word,
8 flee away at thy voice of thunder, leaving the mountain-heights to
9 rise, the valleys to sink into their appointed place! And to these waters
    thou hast given a frontier they may not pass; never must they flow back,
10 and cover the earth again. Yet there shall be torrents flooding the glens,
11 water-courses among the hills that give drink to every wild beast;
12 the hope of the wild asses in their thirst. The birds of heaven, too,
    will roost beside them, and the rocks echo with their music.
13   From the divine store-house comes rain to water the hills; it is
14 thy hand gives earth the plenty she enjoys. Grass must grow for the
    cattle; those faithful servants of men must have their fresh feed, if
15 thou art to bring corn out of the earth; if there is to be wine that will
    rejoice man's heart, oil to make his face shine, and bread that will
16 keep man's strength from failing. Moisture, too, for the forest trees,[2]
17 for the cedars of Lebanon, trees of the Lord's own planting. Here
    it is the birds build their nests, with the eyrie of the stork overtopping
18 them all, refuge such as the deer find in the high hills, the hedge-hog
    in its cave.
19   We should have the moon for our calendar; the sun knows well
20 the hour of his setting. Thou dost decree darkness, and the night
21 falls; in the night all the forest is astir with prowling beasts; the young
    lions go roaring after their prey, God's pensioners, asking for their
22 food. Then the sun rises, and they meet to lie down in their dens,
23 while man goes abroad to toil and drudge till the evening. What
    diversity, Lord, in thy creatures! What wisdom has designed them
    all. There is nothing on earth but gives proof of thy sovereignty.
25   There lies the vast ocean, stretching wide on every hand; this, too,
    is peopled with living things past number, great creatures and small;
26 the ships pass them on their course. Leviathan himself is among them;
27 him, too, thou hast created to roam there at his pleasure.[3] And all
28 look to thee to send them their food at the appointed time; it is through
    thy gift they find it, thy hand opens, and all are filled with content.
29 But see, thou hidest thy face, and they are dismayed; thou takest their
    life from them, and they breathe no more, go back to the dust they
30 came from. Then thou sendest forth thy spirit, and there is fresh
    creation; thou dost repeople the face of earth.
31   Glory be to the Lord for ever, the Lord who takes delight in his

---

[1] See Gen. 1.9.
[2] 'The forest trees'; in the Hebrew text, 'the trees of the Lord.'
[3] It is possible to read another sense, whether in the Hebrew, in the Greek,
or in the Latin; namely, that God has made the whale (or whatever creature
Leviathan represents) as a jest for his own enjoyment.

32 creatures. One glance from him makes earth tremble; at his touch,
33 the mountains are wreathed in smoke. While life lasts, I will sing
   in the Lord's honour; my praise shall be his while I have breath to praise
34 him; Oh, may this prayer with him find acceptance in whom is all my
35 content! Perish all sinners from the land, let the wrong-doers be forgotten! But thou, my soul, bless the Lord

PSALM ONE HUNDRED AND FOUR   (105)

(Alleluia.)

P RAISE the Lord, and call upon his name; tell the story of his
2   doings for all the nations to hear; [1]   greet him with song and psalm,
3 recount his acts of miracle. Triumph in that holy name; let every heart
4 that longs for the Lord rejoice. To the Lord betake you, and in him
5 find strength, evermore court his presence. Remember the marvel-
6 lous acts he did, his miracles, his sentences of doom; are you not the
   posterity of Abraham, his own servant, sons of that Jacob on whom
7 his choice fell? And he, the Lord, is our own God, wide though his
8 writ runs through all the world. He keeps in everlasting memory that
   covenant of his, that promise which a thousand generations might not
9 cancel. He gave Abraham a promise, bound himself to Isaac by an oath;
10 by that law Jacob should live, his Israel, bound to him with an eternal
11 covenant. To thee, he said, I will give the land of Chanaan, as the
12 portion which thou and thine must one day inherit. So few they were
13 in number; only a handful, living there as strangers! And ever they
14 passed on from country to country, the guests of king or people; but
   he suffered none to harm them; [2] to kings themselves the warning came;
15 Lay no hand on them, never hurt them, servants anointed and true
   spokesmen of mine.
16   And now he brought famine on the land, cutting off all their supply
17 of bread. But he had sent an envoy to prepare the way for them, that
18 very Joseph, who was sold as a slave. Grievously his feet had been
19 galled in the stocks, till the iron pierced his very soul; but he proved
20 a true prophet at last, when an oracle from the Lord inspired him. [3] Then
   the king sent to release him; the proud ruler of many peoples set him

---

[1] In the Hebrew text, the word Alleluia is the last word of the psalm preceding this, of this psalm, and of the psalm which follows.

[2] See Gen. 12.17.

[3] See Gen. 40, 41, 'Inspired him'; literally 'inflamed him'; the Hebrew text
here is generally rendered 'the word of the Lord tried him as if by fire.'

21 free, and appointed him master of his household, lord of all the posses-
22 sions that were his. Joseph should teach his courtiers to be as Joseph
23 was,[1] should train his aged counsellors in wisdom. So it was that Israel
    came into Egypt, that Jacob dwelt as an alien in the country of Cham.
24   Time passed, and he gave his people great increase of numbers,
25 till it outmatched all its rivals, and so changed their hearts, that they
    grew weary of his people, and were treacherous enemies to these,
26 his worshippers. Then he sent his servant Moses, and Aaron the
27 man of his choice, to be the authors of those signs, those miracles
28 which the country of Cham would witness. Dark night he sent to
29 benight them, still keeping his worst threat in store.[2] He turned all
30 their supply of water into blood, killing all the fish; frogs swarmed
31 out of their land, even in their royal palaces; at his word, flies attacked
32 them, gnats, too, all their land over; hail was the rain he gave them, and
33 it brought fire that burned up their countryside, till he had shattered
    their vines and fig-trees, broken down all the wood that grew in their
34 domains. He gave the word, and locusts came, grass-hoppers, too,
35 past all numbering, eating up all the grass in their country, eating
36 up all the crops their land yielded. Then, his hand fell upon Egypt's
37 first-born, on the first-fruits of all they had engendered; and so he
    brought his people out, enriched with silver and gold, no foot that
    stumbled among all their tribes.
38   Glad indeed was Egypt at their going, such fear of them had over-
39 taken it. He spread out a cloud to cover them, that turned to fire in
40 the darkness, lighting their journey. Quails came, when they asked
41 for food; he satisfied their desire, too, with bread from heaven, and
    pierced the rock so that water flowed down, running streams in the
42 wilderness. So well did he remember that holy promise of his, made
43 to her servant Abraham; in joy and triumph he led them out, his chosen
44 people, and gave them the lands of the heathen for their own. There,
45 on soil Gentile hands had tilled, his commandments should be kept
    sacred, his law should reign.

---

[1] In the Hebrew text, 'bind his courtiers at his (Joseph's) pleasure.'
[2] The Hebrew text has, in the second half of this verse, 'and they did not
rebel against his word.' The sense is difficult, and the Septuagint Greek gives,
'and they rebelled against his word.' The Latin appears to mean 'and he did
not embitter his words'; a form of phrase which occurs nowhere else, and
seems best interpreted as above.

PSALM ONE HUNDRED AND FIVE   (106)

(Alleluia.)

PRAISE the Lord, the Lord is gracious; his mercy endures for
2   ever; what tongue can recount all the great deeds of the Lord, can
3 echo all his praise? Blessed are they who abide ever by his decrees,
4 ever do the right! Remember us, Lord, with loving thoughts towards
5 thy people, come among us with thy saving power, to witness [1] the
prosperity of thy chosen servants, to share the happiness of thy people,
to glory in the glory of thy own inheritance.
6   We have taken part in our fathers' sins; we are guilty men, rebels
7 against thee. So it was with our fathers in Egypt, unremarked, thy wonderful doings, unremembered, thy abundant mercies; even at the Red
8 Sea's brink they must prove rebellious. Yet, for his own honour, to make
9 known his power, he delivered them, checking the Red Sea, so that it
dried up, and leading them through its depths as safely as if they still trod
10 the desert sands. From a cruel enemy's grasp he rescued them, claimed
11 them for his own, and the water overwhelmed their oppressors, till
12 not one of them was left. They believed, then, in his promises, sang
13 song, then, in his honour, but soon they forgot what he had done,
14 and could not wait for the accomplishment of his will. They must
needs give way to their cravings in the wilderness, challenge God's
15 power, there in the desert, till he granted their demand, and plagued
16 their appetites with satiety.[2] Faction raised its head in the camp against
17 Moses, against Aaron, whom the Lord had sanctified; and now earth
gaped, swallowing up Dathan, overwhelming Abiron and his conspiracy;
18 fire broke out in their company, and the rebels perished by its flames.
19 They made a calf, too, at Horeb, moulding an image and worshipping
20 it, as if they would exchange the glory that dwelt among them for
21 the semblance of a bullock at grass. So little they remembered the
22 God who had delivered them, those portents of his in Egypt, strange
things seen in the land of Cham, terrible things done by the Red Sea!
23 What wonder if he threatened to make an end of them? But Moses, the
man of his choice, stood in the breach to confront his anger, to ward off
destruction.
24   And now they poured scorn on the land of their desire, distrusting

---

[1] 'To witness' in the Latin has the sense of 'that thou mayest witness'; the
Hebrew text (which has 'Remember me' above, instead of 'Remember us')
more probably means 'that I may witness.'

[2] 'Satiety'; in the Hebrew text, 'leanness.'

25 his promise; and the camp was all disaffection. So the Lord, finding they
26 would not listen to his voice, lifted his hand and threatened to smite
27 them down, there in the wilderness, to make them the lowest of the
28 peoples, scatter them abroad among the nations of the world. They
     dedicated themselves to Beelphegor, in honour of the dead gods sat down
29 to feast; till their wicked ways roused God's anger, and a fierce plague
30 fell upon them. Nor might the destruction cease, till Phinees rose up and
31 made amends, winning himself such title to God's favour as shall be
32 remembered, age after age, eternally. They provoked his anger, too, at
     the waters of Rebellion, so that Moses was punished for their sake;
33 because in his heart's bitterness, he broke out into open complaint.
34   Not theirs to root out the heathen, as the Lord had bidden them;
35 they mingled with the heathen instead, and learned their ways; wor-
37 shipping carved images of alien gods, to their own undoing, sacrificing
38 their sons and daughters in honour of devils. Innocent blood, the
     blood of their own sons and daughters, was poured out in worship
39 to the idols of Chanaan; with blood the whole land was polluted, so
40 heinous the guilt of its people, so wanton their ways. Then God's anger
     blazed up against his people, his chosen race became abominable
41 to him, and he handed them over to the Gentiles, to serve hated
42 masters; they were oppressed by their enemies, bowed down under
43 the yoke. Again and again he brought them deliverance, but ever
     there were fresh shifts to provoke him, there was fresh guilt to drag
44 them in the dust. And still, when he saw their distress, when he heard
45 their appeals to him, he bethought him of his covenant, and in his
46 great mercy would relent; their very captors should be moved to pity
     them.
47   Deliver us, O Lord our God, and gather us again, scattered as we
     are among the heathen, to praise thy holy name, to triumph in thy
48 renown. Blessed be the God of Israel from all eternity to all eternity;
     let all the people cry, Amen, Amen.

PSALM ONE HUNDRED AND SIX   (107)

(Alleluia.)

PRAISE the Lord, the Lord is gracious; his mercy endures for
2   ever; be this the cry of men the Lord has rescued, rescued them
     from the enemy's hand, and gathered them in from far-off countries,
3 from sunrising and sunset, from northern lands and from the sea.
4   Some have wandered in parched deserts, missing the way to the
5 city that was their home, hungry and thirsty, so that their spirits

6 died within them. So they cried out to the Lord in their trouble, and
7 he relieved their distress, guiding them surely to the place where they
8 should find a home. Praised be the Lord in his mercies, in his wondrous
9 dealings with mortal men; [1] poor souls that were thirsty, contented now,
poor souls that were hungry, satisfied now with all good.

10   Some lay in darkness, overcast with the shadow of death, helpless
11 in bonds of iron; their punishment for rebelling against God's decrees,
12 for thwarting the will of the most High. Their hearts bowed down
13 with sorrow, none else to aid their mortal weakness, they cried out
14 to the Lord in their trouble, and he relieved their distress, rescuing
them from darkness, from death's shadow, tearing their chains asunder.
15 Praised be the Lord in his mercies, in his wondrous dealings with
16 mortal men; the Lord who has shattered the gates of brass, riven the
bonds of iron.

17   Some for their own fault must needs be humbled; from their own
18 guilt's consequence he saved them; [2] they lay sick, with no stomach
19 for food, [3] close to death's door. So they cried out to the Lord in their
20 trouble, and he relieved their distress, giving the command that they
21 should be healed, and saving them from their peril. Praised be the
22 Lord in his mercies, in his wondrous dealings with mortal men; theirs
to offer him sacrifice in thanksgiving, and proclaim joyfully what
he has done for them.

23   Some there were that ventured abroad in ships, trafficking over the
24 high seas; these are men that have witnessed the Lord's doings, his
25 wonderful doings amid the deep. At his word the stormy wind rose,
26 churning up its waves; high up towards heaven they were carried, then
27 sank into the trough, with spirits fainting in their peril; see them reeling
and staggering to and fro as a drunkard does, all their seamanship
28 forgotten! So they cried out to the Lord in their trouble and he relieved
29 their distress, stilling the storm into a whisper, till all its waves were
30 quiet. Glad hearts were theirs, when calm fell about them, and he
31 brought them to the haven where they longed to be. Praised be the

---

[1] Here, and elsewhere, the Hebrew text probably means, 'Let them (the rescued) give thanks to God for his mercy and his wonders'; but the Latin version seems to personify the mercy and the wonders, directing *them* to give thanks to God.

[2] In the Hebrew text, 'Fools are brought low because of their wrong-doing and of their guilt'; but some think the original word must have been 'sick men' instead of 'fools.' In any case it is clear that this section of the psalm deals with relief in sickness, and (in the Latin) 'from the way of their own guilt' must be understood as meaning 'from the punishment of their own guilt,' perhaps on the analogy of passages like Ez. 9.10.

[3] Literally, 'their soul loathed every kind of food.'

32 Lord in his mercies, in his wondrous dealings with mortal men; let
them extol his name, where the people gather together, glorify him
33 where the elders sit in council. Here, he turns rivers into desert, wells
34 into dry ground; land that once was fruitful into a salty marsh, to
35 punish its people's guilt. There, he changes the wilderness into pools
36 of water, desert ground into springs; and establishes hungry folk
37 there, so that they build themselves a city to dwell in, sow fields,
38 and plant vineyards, and reap the harvest; he blesses them, so that
their numbers increase beyond measure, and takes no toll of their
39 cattle. Here, men grow few, and are worn down by stress of need
40 and ill fortune;[1] scorn overwhelms them now, those proud chieftains,
41 as he keeps them wandering in a pathless desert. There, he rescues
the poor from need, their households thrive like their own flocks.
42 Honest men will rejoice to witness it, and malice will stand dumb
43 with confusion. Heed it well, if thou wouldst be wise; be these thy
study, the mercies of the Lord.

PSALM ONE HUNDRED AND SEVEN (108)

(A psalm-song of David's own.)

2 A HEART to serve thee, O God, a heart ready to serve thee; I
3 will sing of thee and praise thee with all my skill. Wake, all my
skill, wake, echoes of harp and viol; dawn shall find me watching.
4 Let me give thanks, Lord, for all the world to hear it, sing psalms
5 while the Gentiles listen, of thy mercy, high above heaven itself,
6 of thy faithfulness, that reaches the clouds! O God, mount high above
7 the heavens,[2] till thy glory overshadows the whole earth. Now, bring
aid to the men thou lovest, give my prayer answer, and lift thy right hand
8 to save. God's word came to us from his sanctuary: In triumph I will
9 divide up Sichem, and parcel out the valley of Tents; to me Gilead,
to me Manasses belongs; Ephraim is my helmet, Juda issues my com-
10 mands. Moab, one day, shall be my drudge; over Edom I will claim
11 my right, God says; the Philistines will bow before me. Such was the
oracle, but now who is to lead me on my march against this fortress,

---

[1] This verse reads at first sight as if it (and the verse following) referred
to the same people who are mentioned in verse 38. But the context seems to
demand that they should be the people mentioned in verse 34 (which is really
part of the same sentence). The whole of this concluding paragraph shews
the contrast between God's treatment of the proud and his treatment of the
oppressed.

[2] *vv.* 2–6. See Ps. 56.8–12.

12 who is to find an entrance for me into Edom, when thou, O God, hast
13 disowned us, and wilt not go into battle with our armies? It is thou that
14 must deliver us from peril; vain is the help of man. Only through God
can we fight victoriously; only he can trample our oppressors in the dust.[1]

PSALM ONE HUNDRED AND EIGHT (109)

(To the end, for David; a psalm.)

2 O GOD, do not leave my good name unbefriended; there are malicious
3 lips, treacherous lips, that decry me; false tongues are whispering
against me, hedging me about with a conspiracy of hatred, in unprovoked
4 attack. On their side, all calumny in return for love, on mine all prayer;
5 kindness is repaid with injury, love with ill will.

6   Give him over to the power of wickedness, let an evil spirit [2] stand
7 at his right hand to accuse him; let him leave the court of judgement
8 a doomed man, every prayer of his reckoned as guilt. Swiftly let his
9 days come to an end, and his office be entrusted to another; [3] orphancy
10 for the children, widowhood for the wife! Far let his cowering children
11 wander to beg their bread, exiled from home, while creditors eagerly
count up his possessions, and strangers divide the fruits of his toil.
12 May no friend be left to take his part, none to have pity on his defence-
13 less kin; a speedy end to his race, oblivion for his name before a genera-
14 tion passes! Still may the sin of his fathers be remembered in the
15 Lord's sight, his mother's guilt remain indelible; still may the Lord
16 keep it in mind and wipe out their memory from the earth. Did he
17 himself keep mercy in mind, when he persecuted the helpless, the
18 destitute, the grief-stricken, and marked them down for death? Cursing
he loved, and a curse shall come upon him; for blessing he cared little,
and blessing shall keep its distance from him. Cursing was the livery
of his choice; it sank like water into his inmost being, soaked, like oil,
19 into the marrow of his bones! Now let it be the garb he wears, cling to
him like a girdle that he can never take off.[4]
20   Such are the men[5] that calumniate me in the Lord's presence, the

---

[1] See Ps. 59.6–14.

[2] 'An evil spirit'; the Hebrew word may also be translated simply 'an accuser.'

[3] Ac. 1.20.

[4] In the Hebrew text, all the verbs of this verse express a wish for the future. It is possible to understand these verses (*vv.* 6–19 or *vv.* 6–17) as spoken, not by the Psalmist, but of the Psalmist by his detractors.

[5] Literally, 'these are the doings of the men.' Some would translate the Hebrew text 'This is the recompense of the men'; but the word here used, though it sometimes means 'reward,' is nowhere else found in the sense of 'punishment.'

21 men that defame me so cruelly. But do thou, my Lord and Master,
   take my part, to defend thy own honour; no mercy is so tender as
22 thine. Deliver me in my helpless need; my heart is dismayed within
23 me. Like a tapering shadow I depart, swept away like a locust on the
24 wing. My knees are weak with fasting, my strength pines away un-
25 nourished.[1] They make a laughing-stock of me, nod at me in derision
26 as they pass by. Help me, O Lord my God; deliver me in thy mercy;
27 prove to them that my woes are a visitation from thee, sent by no
28 hand but thine. Bless me, thou, and let them curse as they will; dis-
29 appoint my adversaries, and grant thy servant relief. Let these, my
   accusers, be covered with shame, wrapped in the mantle of their own
30 confusion. Loudly will I give the Lord thanks, praise him before
31 multitudes that listen; the Lord who has stood at the right hand of
   the friendless, brought redress to an innocent soul misjudged.

PSALM ONE HUNDRED AND NINE   (110)

(For David; a psalm.) [2]

TO the Master I serve the Lord's promise was given, Sit here at
   my right hand while I make thy enemies a footstool under thy
2 feet. The Lord will make thy empire spring up like a branch out of Sion;
3 thou art to bear rule in the midst of thy enemies. When thou shewest
   thy power, princely state shall be thine,[3] amid the splendour of the
4 holy places; thou art my son, born before the day-star rises. The
   Lord has sworn an oath there is no retracting, Thou art a priest for
5 ever in the line of Melchisedech.[4] At thy right hand, the Lord beats
6 down kings in the day of his vengeance; he will pass sentence on the
   nations, and accomplish their ruin; assail a well-peopled land [5] and

---

[1] 'Unnourished'; literally 'for the sake of oil,' either in the sense of 'fatness,'
or because the Psalmist was denying himself the use of oil while keeping a fast.

[2] This psalm, the meaning of which is in any case obscure, is further confused in the Latin, and in the Septuagint Greek, by the use of the same rendering for two different words in the Hebrew, here translated by 'Lord' and
'Master' respectively. Cf. Mt. 22.44, Mk. 12.36, Lk. 20.42, Ac. 2.34.

[3] In the Hebrew text, 'thy people offers itself willingly.' Some would translate the words which follow, 'in holy garments'; it is possible that there was a
manuscript error, and the original line ran, 'upon the holy mountains.' The
second half of the verse, as it is given in the Hebrew text, is traditionally
rendered 'the dew of thy birth is of the womb of the morning,' a phrase of
which many different explanations have been given.

[4] See Heb. 5.6, and elsewhere.

[5] Some think that the Hebrew text conceals a proper name, 'in the land of
Rabbah' (the capital of Ammon).

7 smite down its princes. Let him but drink of the brook by the wayside,
he will lift up his head in victory.[1]

PSALM ONE HUNDRED AND TEN (111)

(Alleluia.)

A LL my heart goes out to thee, Lord, in thanksgiving, before
2 Athe assembly where the just are gathered. Chant we the Lord's
3 wondrous doings, decreed to fulfil all his purposes.[2] Ever his deeds are
4 high and glorious, faithful he abides to all eternity. Great deeds, that
he keeps still in remembrance! How kind the Lord is, how merciful!
5 If men will fear him, still he feeds them, keeping his covenant unfor-
6 gotten. Lordly the power he shewed his people, making the lands of
the heathen their possession. No act but shews him just and faithful;
8 of his decrees there is no relenting. Perpetual time shall leave them
9 changeless; right and truth are their foundation. So he has brought
his people deliverance; to all eternity stands his covenant. Unutterable
10 is his name and terrible; vain without his fear is learning. Wise evermore are you who follow it; yours the prize that lasts for ever.

PSALM ONE HUNDRED AND ELEVEN (112)

(Alleluia; of the return of Aggaeus and Zachary.)

A BLESSED man is he, who fears the Lord, bearing great love to
2 Ahis commandments. Children of his shall win renown in their
3 country; do right, and thy sons shall find a blessing. Esteem dwells
with such a man, and great prosperity; fame shall ever record his bounty.[3]
4 Good men see a light dawn in darkness; his light, who is ever merciful,
5 kind and faithful. It goes well with the man who lends in pity; justice
6 shall be found in all his pleadings. Length of days shall leave him still
7 unshaken; men will remember the name of the just for ever. No fear

---

[1] There is no agreement as to the precise meaning of this verse; some would render, 'they will drink,' understanding the first half as an ironic reference to the princes lying slaughtered by the road side.

[2] 'Decreed to fulfil all his purposes'; the Hebrew text is usually rendered, 'searched out by those who delight in them.'

[3] In the first half of this verse, the Hebrew text has 'There is affluence and prosperity in his household.'

shall he have of evil tidings; on the Lord his hope is fixed unchangeably.
8 Patient his heart remains and steadfast, quietly he waits for the downfall
9 of his enemies. Rich are his alms to the needy; still, through the years,
his bounty abides in memory.[1] The Lord will lift up his head in triumph,
10 ungodly men are ill content to see it. Vainly they gnash their teeth in
envy; worldly hopes must fade and perish.

PSALM ONE HUNDRED AND TWELVE (113)

(Alleluia.)

PRAISE the Lord, you that are his servants, praise the name of
2 the Lord together. Blessed be the Lord's name at all times, from
3 this day to all eternity; from the sun's rise to the sun's setting let the
4 Lord's name be praised continually. The Lord is sovereign king over
5 all the nations; his glory is high above the heavens. Who is like the
6 Lord our God, so high above us, that stoops to regard lowly things
7 in heaven and earth, lifting up the poor man from the dust he lay
8 in, bidding the beggar leave his dung-hill, to find him a place among
9 the princes, the princes that rule over his people? He gives the barren
woman a home to dwell in, a mother rejoicing in her children.

PSALM ONE HUNDRED AND THIRTEEN (114)

(Alleluia.)

WHEN Israel came out of Egypt, and the sons of Jacob heard no
2 more a strange language, the Lord took Juda for his sanctuary,
3 Israel for his own dominion. The seas fled at the sight they witnessed,
4 backward flowed the stream of Jordan; up leapt, like rams, the startled
5 mountains, up leapt the hills, like yearling sheep. What ailed you,
seas, that you fled in terror; Jordan's stream, what drove thee back?
6 Why did you leap up like rams, you mountains, leap up, you hills,
7 like yearling sheep? The whole earth thrilled at its Master's presence;
8 it was he that came, the God of Jacob, who turned the rock into pools
of water, the flint-stone into a springing well.

(115)

9 Not to us, Lord, not to us the glory; let thy name alone be honoured;
10 thine the merciful, thine the faithful; why must the heathen say, Their

---

[1] II Cor. 9.9.

11 God deserts them? Our God is a God that dwells in heaven; all that his
12 will designs, he executes. The heathen have silver idols and golden,
13 gods which the hands of men have fashioned. They have mouths, and
14 yet are silent; eyes they have, and yet are sightless; ears they have, and
15 want all hearing; noses, and yet no smell can reach them; hands un-
16 feeling, feet unstirring; never a sound their throats may utter. Such be
the end of all who make them, such the reward of all who trust them.
17 It is the Lord that gives hope to the race of Israel, their only help, their
18 only stronghold; the Lord that gives hope to the race of Aaron, their
19 only help, their only stronghold; the Lord that gives hope to all who
20 fear him, their only help, their only stronghold. The Lord keeps us in
mind, and grants us blessing, blesses the race of Israel, blesses the race
21 of Aaron; all those who fear the Lord, small and great alike, he blesses.
22 Still may the Lord grant you increase, you and your children after you;
23 the blessing of the Lord be upon you. It is he that made both heaven
24 and earth; to the Lord belongs the heaven of heavens, the earth he gives
25 to the children of men. From the dead, Lord, thou hast no praises,
26 the men who go down into the place of silence; but we bless the Lord,
we, the living, from this day to all eternity.

PSALM ONE HUNDRED AND FOURTEEN

(Alleluia.)   (116.1–9)

M Y heart is aflame, so graciously the Lord listens to my entreaty;
2 to the Lord, who grants me audience, I will offer prayer all my
3 life long. Death's pangs about me, overtaken by all the terrors of
4 the grave, ever I found distress and grief at my side, till I called upon
5 the Lord, Save me, Lord, in my peril. Merciful the Lord is, and just,
6 and full of pity; he cares for simple hearts, and to me, when I lay
7 humbled, he brought deliverance. Return, my soul, where thy peace
8 lies; the Lord has dealt kindly with thee; he has saved my life from
9 peril, banished my tears, kept my feet from falling. I will be the Lord's
servant henceforward in the land of the living.

PSALM ONE HUNDRED AND FIFTEEN

(Alleluia.)   (116.10–19)

I TRUSTED, and trusting found words to utter in my abasement;
2 bewildered, I said, Man's faith is false; but the Lord's mercies
3 have never failed me; what return shall I make to him?[1] I will take
the cup that is pledge of my deliverance, and invoke the name of the
5 Lord upon it; I will pay the Lord my vows in the presence of all his
6 people. Dear in the Lord's sight is the death of those who love him;
7 and am not I, Lord, thy servant, born of thy own handmaid? Thou
8 hast broken the chains that bound me; I will sacrifice in thy honour,
9 and call on the name of the Lord. Before a throng of worshippers
10 I will pay the Lord my vows, here in the courts of the Lord's house,
here, Jerusalem, in thy heart.

PSALM ONE HUNDRED AND SIXTEEN (117)

(Alleluia.)

PRAISE the Lord, all you Gentiles, let all the nations of the world
2 do him honour. Abundant has his mercy been towards us; the
Lord remains faithful to his word for ever.

PSALM ONE HUNDRED AND SEVENTEEN (118)

GIVE thanks to the Lord; the Lord is gracious, his mercy endures
2 for ever. Echo the cry, Israel; the Lord is gracious, his mercy
3 endures for ever. His mercy endures for ever, echo the cry, race of
4 Aaron; his mercy endures for ever, echo the cry, all you who are the
5 Lord's worshippers. I called on the Lord when trouble beset me, and
6 the Lord listened, and brought me relief. With the Lord to aid me,
7 I have no fear of the worst man can do; with the Lord to aid me, I
8 shall yet see the fall of my enemies. Better trust the Lord than rely on

---

[1] *vv.* 1–3. The sense here is obscure, and much disputed. It is usually supposed that what the Psalmist said comes to an end with verse 1; but it is difficult to see how this could be described as a confident utterance (see II Cor. 4.13), and it seems best to take verse 2, and part or the whole of what follows, as falling within the quotation.

9 the help of man; better trust the Lord than rely on the word of princes.
10 Let all heathendom ring me round, see, in the power of the Lord I crush
11 them! They cut me off from every way of escape, but see, in the power
12 of the Lord I crush them! They swarm about me like bees, their fury
blazes up like fire among thorns, but see, in the power of the Lord I
13 crush them. I reeled under the blow, and had well-nigh fallen, but still
14 the Lord was there to aid me. Who but the Lord is my protector, the
pride of my song; who but the Lord has brought me deliverance?
15 The homes of the just echo, now, with glad cries of victory; the
16 power of the Lord has triumphed. The power of the Lord has brought
17 me to great honour, the power of the Lord has triumphed. I am
reprieved from death, to live on and proclaim what the Lord has done
18 for me. The Lord has chastened me, chastened me indeed, but he
19 would not doom me to die. Open me the gates where right dwells;
20 let me go in and thank the Lord! Here is the gate that leads to the
21 Lord's presence; here shall just souls find entry. Thanks be to thee,
22 Lord, for giving me audience, thanks be to thee, my deliverer. The
very stone which the builders rejected has become the chief stone
23 at the corner; this is the Lord's doing, and it is marvellous in our
24 eyes.[1] This day is a holiday of the Lord's own choosing; greet this day
with rejoicing, greet this day with triumph!
25 Deliverance, Lord, deliverance; Lord, grant us days of prosperity!
26 Blessed is he who comes in the name of the Lord! A blessing from
27 the Lord's house upon your company! The Lord is God; his light
shines out to welcome us; solemnize this day, with a screen of boughs
28 that reaches to the very horns of the altar.[2] Thou art my God, mine to
acknowledge thee, thou art my God, mine to extol thee; thanking thee for
29 giving me audience, thanking thee, my deliverer.[3] Give thanks to
the Lord; the Lord is gracious, his mercy endures for ever.

PSALM ONE HUNDRED AND EIGHTEEN (119)

AH, blessed they, who pass through life's journey unstained, who
2 follow the law of the Lord! Ah, blessed they who study his
3 decrees, make him the whole quest of their hearts! As for the wrong-

---

[1] *vv.* 22, 23. Mt. 21.42.

[2] The interpretation of this verse, in the Hebrew text, is uncertain. Some
would translate, 'Bind the sacrifice with cords, close up to the horns of the
altar.' The rendering in the Latin version evidently supposes an allusion to the
Feast of the Tabernacles (Lev. 23.40).

[3] The repetition of verse 21 appears in the Septuagint Greek, but not in the
Hebrew text as we have it.

4 doers, they leave his ways untrodden. **A**bove all else it binds us, the
5 charge thou hast given us to keep. **A**h, how shall my steps be surely
6 guided to keep faith with thy covenant? **A**ttentive to all thy com-
7 mandments, I go my way undismayed. **A** true heart's worship thou shalt
8 have, thy just awards prompting me. **A**ll shall be done as thy laws
demand, so thou wilt not forsake me utterly.

9   **B**est shall he keep his youth unstained, who is true to thy trust.
10 **B**e thou the whole quest of my heart; never let me turn aside from
11 thy commandments. **B**uried deep in my heart, thy warnings shall
12 keep me clear of sin. **B**lessed art thou, O Lord; teach me to know
13 thy will. **B**y these lips let the awards thou makest ever be recorded.
14 **B**lithely as one that has found great possessions, I follow thy decrees.
15 **B**ethinking me still of the charge thou givest, I will mark thy foot-
16 steps. **B**e thy covenant ever in my thoughts, thy words kept in memory.

17   **C**rown thy servant with life, to live faithful to thy commands. **C**lear
19 sight be mine, to contemplate the wonders of thy law. **C**omfort this
20 earthly exile; do not refuse me the knowledge of thy will. **C**rushed
21 lies my spirit, longing ever for thy just awards. **C**hastener of the proud,
22 thy curse lies on all who swerve from thy covenant. **C**lear me of the
23 reproach that shames me, as I was ever attentive to thy claims. **C**loseted
together, princes plot against me, thy servant, that thinks only of thy
24 decrees. **C**laims lovingly cherished, decrees that are my counsellors!

25   **D**eep lies my soul in the dust, restore life to me, as thou hast prom-
26 ised. **D**eign, now, to shew me thy will, thou who hast listened when
27 I opened my heart to thee. **D**irect me in the path thou biddest me
28 follow, and all my musing shall be of thy wonderful deeds. **D**espair
29 wrings tears from me; let thy promises raise me up once more. **D**eliver
30 me from every false thought; let thy covenant be my comfort. **D**uty's
31 path my choice, I keep thy bidding ever in remembrance. **D**isappoint
32 me, Lord, never, one that holds fast by thy commandments. **D**o but
open my heart wide, and easy lies the path thou hast decreed.

33   **E**xpound, Lord, thy whole bidding to me; faithfully I will keep it.
34 **E**nlighten me, to scan thy law closely, and keep true to it with all my
35 heart. **E**agerly I long to be guided in the way of thy obedience. **E**ver
37 let my choice be set on thy will, not on covetous thoughts. **E**yes have
I none for vain phantoms; let me find life in following thy way.
38 **E**stablish now the truth of thy promise to one that serves and fears
39 thee. **E**ase me of the reproach my heart dreads, thou, whose awards
40 are gracious. **E**ach command of thine I embrace lovingly; do thou
in thy faithfulness grant me life.

41   **F**or me too, Lord, thy mercy, for me too the deliverance thou hast
42 promised! **F**it answer for those who taunt me, that I rely on thy truth.

43 Faithful thy promise, let me not boast of it in vain; in thy covenant lies
44 my hope. For ever and for evermore true to thy charge thou shalt find
45 me. Freely shall my feet tread, if thy will is all my quest. Fearlessly
   will I talk of thy decrees in the presence of kings, and be never abashed.
47 Fain would I have all my study in the law I love. Flung wide my
   arms to greet thy law, ever in my thoughts thy bidding.

49   Go not back on the word thou hast pledged to thy servant; there
50 lies all my hope. Good news in my affliction, thy promises have brought
51 me life. Ground down by the scorn of my oppressors, never from thy
52 law I swerve aside. Gracious comfort, Lord, is the memory of thy
53 just dealings in times long past. Great ruth have I to see wrong-doers,
54 and how they abandon thy law. Gone out into a land of exile, of thy
55 covenant I make my song. Gloom of the night finds me still thinking
56 of thy name, Lord, still observant of thy bidding. Guerdon I ask no
   other, but the following of thy will.

57   Heritage, Lord, I claim no other, but to obey thy word. Heart-deep
59 my supplication before thee for the mercies thou hast promised. Have
60 I not planned out my path, turned aside to follow thy decrees? Haste
61 such as mine can brook no delay in carrying out all thy bidding. Hemmed
   in by the snares which sinners laid for me, never was I forgetful of
62 thy law. Hearken when I rise at dead of night to praise thee for thy
63 just dealings. How well I love the souls that fear thee, and are true
64 to thy trust! How thy mercy fills the earth, Lord! Teach me to do thy
   will.

65   In fulfilment of thy promise, Lord, what kindness thou hast shewn
66 thy servant! Inspire, instruct me still; all my hope is in thy covenant.
67 Idly I strayed till thou didst chasten me; no more shall thy warnings
68 go unheeded. Indeed, indeed thou art gracious; teach me to do thy
69 bidding. In vain my oppressors plot against me; thy will is all my quest.
70 Inhuman hearts, curdled with scorn! For me thy law is learning enough.
71 It was in mercy thou didst chasten me, schooling me to thy obedience.
72 Is not the law thou hast given dearer to me than rich store of gold
   and silver?

73   Jealous for the handiwork thou hast made, teach me to understand
74 thy commandments. Joy shall be theirs, thy true worshippers, to see
75 the confidence I have in thy word. Just are thy awards; I know it
76 well, Lord, it was in faithfulness thou didst afflict me. Judge me no
77 more; pity and comfort thy servant as thou hast promised. Judge
78 me no more; pardon and life for one that loves thy will! Just be their
79 fall, who wrong me scornfully; thy law is all my study. Joined to my
   company be every soul that worships thee and heeds thy warnings.
80 Jealously let my heart observe thy bidding; let me not hope in vain.

81 Keeping watch for thy aid, my soul languishes, yet I trust in thy
82 word. Keeping watch for the fulfilment of thy promise, my eyes
83 languish for comfort still delayed. Keen frosts shrivel the wine-skin;
84 so waste I, yet never forget thy will. Knowest thou not how short are
85 thy servant's days? Soon be my wrongs redressed. Knaves will be
86 plotting against me still, that are no friends to thy law. Knaves they
87 are that wrong me; bring aid, as thy covenant stands unchanging. Keep
88 thy bidding I would though small hope of life they had left me. Kind as
thou ever wert, preserve me; then utter thy bidding, and I will obey.

89 Lord, the word thou hast spoken stands ever unchanged in heaven.
90 Loyal to his promise, age after age, is he who made the enduring earth.
91 Long as time lasts, the day keeps its appointed course, obeying thy
92 decree, Master of all. Lest I should sink in my affliction, thou hast
93 given thy covenant to be my comfort. Life-giving are thy commands,
94 never by me forgotten. Lend me thy aid, for thine I am, and thy
95 bidding is all my quest. Let sinners go about to destroy me, I wait
96 on thy will. Look where I may, all good things must end; only thy law
is wide beyond measure.

97 My delight, Lord, is in thy bidding; ever my thoughts return to it.
98 Musing still on thy commandments, I have grown more prudent than my
99 enemies. More wisdom have I than all my teachers, so well have I
100 pondered thy decrees. More learning have I than my elders, I that
101 hold true to thy charge. Mindful of thy warnings, I guide my steps
102 clear of every evil path. Meek under thy tuition, thy will I keep ever
103 in view. Meat most appetizing are thy promises, never was honey
104 so sweet to my taste. Made wise by thy law, I shun every path of
evil-doing.

105 No lamp like thy word to guide my feet, to shew light on my path.
106 Never will I retract my oath to give thy just commands observance.
107 Nothing, Lord, but affliction, never the saving help thou didst promise
108 me? Nay, Lord, accept these vows of mine; teach me to do thy bidding.
109 Needs must I carry my life in my hands, yet am I ever mindful of thy
110 law. Nearly the snares of the wicked caught my feet, yet would I not
111 swerve from my obedience. Now and ever thy covenant is my prize,
112 is my heart's comfort. Now and ever to do thy will, to earn thy favour,
is my heart's aim.

113 Out upon the men that play traitor to the law I love! Other defence,
115 other stronghold have I none; in thy law I trust. Out of my path,
116 lovers of wrong; I will keep my God's commandments. Only let thy
promised aid preserve me; do not disappoint me of the hope I cherish.
117 Only do thou sustain me in safety, looking ever to thy will. Obey
thee who will not, shall earn thy disdain; idle is all their scheming.

119 Outcasts, they are that profane the land with wrong; for me, thy law
120 is enough. Overcome my whole being with the fear of thee; I am adread
of thy judgements.

121   Protect the justice of my cause; never leave me at the mercy of my
122 oppressors.   Pledge thyself still to befriend me; save me from the
123 scorn of my enemies.   Pining away, I look for thy saving help, the
124 faithful keeping of thy promises.   Pity thy own servant, and teach
125 him thy decrees.   Perfect in thy own servant's heart the knowledge
126 of thy will.   Put off the hour, Lord, no more; too long thy command-
127 ment stands defied.   Precious beyond gold or jewel I hold thy law.
128 Prized be every decree of thine; forsworn be every path of evil-doing.
129   Right wonderful thy decrees are, and well my heart heeds them.
130 Revelation and light thy words disclose to the simple.   Rises ever
132 a sigh from my lips as I long after thy covenant.   Regard and pity
133 me, as thou hast pity for all that love thy name.   Rule thou my path
134 as thou hast promised; never be wrong-doing my master.   Rescue me
135 from man's oppression, to wait henceforth on thy bidding. Restore to thy
servant the smile of thy loving favour, and teach him to know thy
136 will.   Rivers of tears flow from my eyes, to see thy law forgotten.

137   So just, Lord, thou art, thy awards so truly given!   Strict justice
139 and utter faithfulness inspire all thy decrees.   Stung by love's jealousy,
140 I watch my enemies defy thy bidding.   Shall not I, thy servant, love
141 thy promises, tested and found true?   Still, despised and disinherited,
142 I do not forget thy charge.   Stands thy faithfulness eternally, thy law
143 for ever changeless.   Sorrow and distress have fallen on me; in thy
144 commandments is all my comfort.   Sentence eternal is thy decree;
teach me the wisdom that brings life.

145   Thy audience, Lord, my whole heart claims, a heart true to thy
146 trust.   To thee I cry, O grant deliverance; I will do all thy bidding.
147 Twilight comes, and I come to plead with thee, hoping ever in thy
148 promises.   Through the night my eyes keep watch, as I ponder thy
149 sayings.   Thine, Lord, to listen in thy mercy, and grant life according
150 to thy will.   Treacherous foes draw near, that are strangers to thy
151 covenant.   Thou, Lord, art close at hand; all thy awards are true.
152 Taught long since by thy decrees, I know well thou hast ordained them
everlastingly.

153   Unblessed is my lot; look down and rescue me, that still am mindful
154 of thy law.   Uphold my cause, and deliver me; true to thy promise,
155 grant me life.   Unknown thy mercy to the sinner that defies thy bidding.
156 Unnumbered, Lord, are thy blessings; as thy will is, grant me life.
157 Under all the assaults of my oppressors, I keep true to thy charge.
158 Unhappy I, that watch thy warnings to the sinner go unheeded!   Up,

Lord, and witness the love I bear thy covenant; in thy mercy bid me
160 live! Unchanging truth is thy word's fountain-head, eternal the force
of thy just decrees.
161 Vexed by the causeless malice of princes, my heart still dreads thy
162 warnings. Victors rejoice not more over rich spoils, than I in thy
163 promises. Villainy I abhor and renounce; thy law is all my love. Votive
thanks seven times a day I give thee for the just awards thou makest.
165 Very great peace is theirs who love thy law; their feet never stumble.
166 Valiantly, Lord, I wait on thee for succour, keeping ever true to thy
167 charge. Vanquished by great love, my heart is ever obedient to thy
168 will. Vigilantly I observe precept and bidding of thine, living always
as in thy sight.
169 Wilt thou not admit my cry, Lord, to thy presence, and grant me
170 thy promised gift of wisdom? Wilt thou not countenance my plea,
171 redeem thy pledge to deliver me? What praise shall burst from my
172 lips, when thou makest known thy will! What hymns of thankfulness
173 this tongue shall raise to the author of all just decrees! Wouldst thou
174 but lift thy hand to aid me, that take my stand on thy covenant! Weary
175 it is, Lord, waiting for deliverance, but thy law is my comfort. When
176 will thy just award grant redress, that I may live to praise thee? Wayward thou seest me, like a lost sheep; come to look for thy servant, that
is mindful still of thy bidding.

PSALM ONE HUNDRED AND NINETEEN (120)

(A song of ascents.)

1 NOT unheeded I cry to the Lord in the hour of my distress. Lord,
have pity and deliver me from the treacherous lips, the perjured
3 tongue. Perjurer, he will give thee all thy deserts and more; sharp
5 arrows from a warrior's bow, coals that spread desolation. Unhappy
6 I, that am still doomed to exile; still dwell where Cedar dwells, my
7 heart sick for home! Among the enemies of peace, for peace I labour;
no word of mine but provokes their wanton attack.

PSALM ONE HUNDRED AND TWENTY (121)

(A song of ascents.)

2 I LIFT up my eyes to the hills, to find deliverance; from the Lord
deliverance comes to me, the Lord who made heaven and earth.
3 Never will he who guards thee allow thy foot to stumble; never fall

4 asleep at his post! Such a guardian has Israel, one who is never weary,
5 never sleeps; it is the Lord that guards thee, the Lord that stands
6 at thy right hand to give thee shelter. The sun's rays by day, the moon's
7 by night, shall have no power to hurt thee. The Lord guard thee
8 from all evil; the Lord protect thee in danger; the Lord protect thy
journeying and thy home-coming, henceforth and for ever.

PSALM ONE HUNDRED AND TWENTY-ONE

(A song of ascents. Of David.)   (122)

W ELCOME sound, when I heard them saying, We will go into
2   the Lord's house! Within thy courts, Jerusalem, our feet stand at
3 last; Jerusalem, built as a city should be built that is one in fellowship.
4 There the tribes meet, the Lord's own tribes, to give praise, as Israel is
5 ever bound, to the Lord's name; There the thrones are set for judge-
6 ment, thrones of authority over the house of David. Pray for all that
7 brings Jerusalem peace! May all who love thee dwell at ease! Let there
8 be peace within thy ramparts, ease in thy strongholds! For love of my
brethren and my familiar friends, peace is still my prayer for thee;
9 remembering the house of the Lord our God, I long for thy happiness.

PSALM ONE HUNDRED AND TWENTY-TWO

(A song of ascents.)   (123)

U NTO thee I lift up my eyes, unto thee, who dwellest in the heavens.
2   See how the eyes of the servants are fixed on the hands of their
masters, the eyes of a maid on the hand of her mistress! Our eyes,
too, are fixed on the Lord our God, waiting for some sign of his mercy.
3 Have mercy on us, Lord, have mercy on us; we have had our fill of man's
4 derision. Our hearts can bear no more to be the scorn of luxury, the
derision of the proud.

PSALM ONE HUNDRED AND TWENTY-THREE

(A song of ascents. Of David.)   (124)

2 I F the Lord had not been on our side, Israel may boast, if the Lord
3   had not been on our side when human foes assailed us, it seemed
as if they must have swallowed us up alive, so fierce their anger threatened

4 us. It seemed as if the tide must have sucked us down when we ven-
5 tured our lives on that flood; an overbearing tide, and our lives ventured
6 on it! Blessed be the Lord, who has not let us fall a prey to those
7 ravening mouths! Safe, like a bird rescued from the fowler's snare; the
8 snare is broken now, and we are safe! Such help is ours, the Lord's help,
that made heaven and earth.

PSALM ONE HUNDRED AND TWENTY-FOUR

(A song of ascents.)   (125)

THOSE who trust in the Lord are strong as mount Sion itself.
2 Unmoved for ever is he who dwells at Jerusalem; as the hills protect
3 it, so the Lord protects his people, now and for ever. Domain of the
just! No longer shall godless men bear rule in it; else the just, too, might
4 soil their hands with guilt. Deal kindly, Lord, with the kindly, with the
5 true-hearted. Feet that stray into the snare the Lord will punish, as he
punishes wrong-doers; but upon Israel there shall be peace.

PSALM ONE HUNDRED AND TWENTY-FIVE

(A song of ascents.)   (126)

WHEN the Lord gave back Sion her banished sons, we were like
2 men refreshed; [1] in every mouth was laughter, joy was on every
tongue. Among the heathen themselves it was said, What favour the
3 Lord has shewn them! Favour indeed the Lord has shewn us, and
4 our hearts are rejoiced. Our withered hopes, Lord, like some desert
5 watercourse renew! [2] The men who are sowing in tears will reap, one day,
6 with joy. Mournful enough they go, but with seed to scatter; trust me,
they will come back rejoicing, as they carry their sheaves with them.

---

[1] In the Hebrew text, 'like men who dream.'
[2] Some commentators think that the process of deliverance was still incomplete, only a small number of exiles (for example) having returned from
captivity; others, that verse 1 expresses, not something which had actually
happened, but an imaginary picture.

PSALM ONE HUNDRED AND TWENTY-SIX

(A song of ascents. Of Solomon.)   (127)

VAIN is the builder's toil, if the house is not of the Lord's building;
vainly the guard keeps watch, if the city has not the Lord for
2 its guardian. Vain, that you should be astir before daybreak; rest
awhile before you stir abroad, you whose bread is so hardly won; is
3 not sleep his gift to the men he loves?[1] Fatherhood itself is the Lord's
4 gift, the fruitful womb is a reward that comes from him. For the dis-
5 inherited, children are like arrows in a warrior's hand.[2] Happy the
man who has his heart's fill of these;[3] his cause will not be set aside
when he pleads against his enemies at the gate.

PSALM ONE HUNDRED AND TWENTY-SEVEN

(A song of ascents.)   (128)

BLESSED are all those who fear the Lord, and follow his paths!
2 Thyself shall eat what thy hands have toiled to win; blessed
3 thou art; all good shall be thine. Thy wife shall be fruitful as the vine
that grows on the walls of thy house, the children round thy table
4 sturdy as olive-branches.[4] Let a man serve the Lord, such is the
5 blessing that awaits him. May the Lord who dwells in Sion bless thee;
6 mayest thou see Jerusalem in prosperity all thy life long. Mayest
thou live to see thy children's children, and peace resting upon Israel.

---

[1] The Hebrew text is generally interpreted as meaning, 'Vain that you should
rise before daybreak, and sit on late at night, winning your bread so hardly;
he provides as well for us in our sleep,' or, as some would translate the latter
part 'he provides equally well for the men he loves while they lie asleep.' The
verse is not, in any case, an incitement to idleness; the gist of the psalm lies in
what follows. What is the use of a house to a childless man, of a well-built
city with a dwindling number of inhabitants; what is the use of toiling day and
night, unless you have a family to provide for?

[2] The Hebrew text probably means, 'The children of a young man are like
arrows in a warrior's hand,' since they have grown to manhood before he is
enfeebled with old age.

[3] 'His heart's fill'; in the Hebrew text, 'his quiver full.'

[4] The Hebrew text probably means, 'Thy wife shall dwell in the innermost
part of thy house, like a fruitful vine.'

PSALM ONE HUNDRED AND TWENTY-EIGHT

(A song of ascents.)   (129)

OFTEN have they assailed me even from my youth (let this be Israel's
2 boast); often have they assailed me even from my youth, but
3 never once outmatched me. I bent my back, and sinners mishandled
4 me; long their tyranny lasted, but the Lord proved faithful, and broke the
5 sinners' necks in pieces. Let them be dismayed and routed, all these
6 enemies of Sion. Let them be like the stalks on a house-top, that wither
7 there unharvested; never will they be grasped in the reaper's hand,
8 or fill the gleaner's bosom, no passer-by will say, The Lord's blessing
on you; we bless you in the name of the Lord.[1]

PSALM ONE HUNDRED AND TWENTY-NINE

(A song of ascents.)   (130)

2 OUT of the depths I cry to thee, O Lord; Master, listen to my
voice; let but thy ears be attentive to the voice that calls on thee
3 for pardon. If thou, Lord, take heed of our iniquities, [2] Master, who
4 has strength to bear it? Ah, but with thee there is forgiveness; I will
wait for thee, Lord, as thou commandest. My soul relies on his promise,
5 my soul waits patiently for the Lord. From the morning watch till
7 night has fallen, let Israel trust in the Lord; [3] the Lord, with whom
8 there is mercy, with whom is abundant power to ransom. He it is that
will ransom Israel from all his iniquities.

---

[1] Cf. Ru. 2.4.

[2] Some authors would translate 'retain' or 'store up,' rather than 'take heed of.'

[3] *vv*. 4–6. The Hebrew text here is usually rendered, 'Ah, but with thee there
is forgiveness, therefore thou shalt be feared. I rely upon the Lord, my soul
relies upon him. In his promise I trust. My soul looks towards the Lord, more
eagerly than the watchmen look for the morning.'

PSALM ONE HUNDRED AND THIRTY   (131)

(A song of ascents. Of David.)

LORD, my heart is not lifted up, my eyes not raised from the earth;
my mind does not dwell on high things, on marvels that are
2 beyond my reach.   Bear me witness that mine were humble thoughts,[1]
that my soul was never exalted with pride.   The thoughts of a child
newly weaned towards its mother, this is all my soul knows of recom-
3 pense.   Let Israel trust in the Lord, henceforth and for ever.

PSALM ONE HUNDRED AND THIRTY-ONE

(A song of ascents.)   (132)

2 LORD, remember David, and all his patient endurance,   the oath
he swore to the Lord, the vow he made to the God of Jacob:
3 Never will I come beneath the roof of my house, or climb up into
4 the bed that is strewn for me;   never shall these eyes have sleep, these
5 eyelids close,   this brow take any rest, until I find the Lord a home,
6 the God of Jacob a dwelling-place.   And now, at Ephrata, we have
heard tidings of what we looked for; we have found it in the woodland
7 plains;[2]   we will make our way into his tabernacle, pay reverence at
8 the place where he halted on his journey.   Up, Lord, and take pos-
9 session of thy resting-place, thou and the ark which is thy shrine!   Let

---

[1] Literally, 'If I did not think humbly,' some such words as 'may the Lord
punish me for it' being understood. This was a frequent form of oath-taking
among the Jews, cf. Ps. 94.11. But some authors would translate literally, and
make the whole verse into one sentence. The second part of it has been very
variously interpreted, 'recompense' being sometimes understood as 'revenge.'
But it seems simpler to interpret the Latin as meaning that the Psalmist has no
more thought of making a return to God for his favours, than a weaned child
has of making return to its mother. The Hebrew text is generally rendered,
'Like a weaned child with its mother, like a weaned child my soul is with me,'
but here too the significance of the words is variously interpreted.

[2] Literally, 'Behold, we have heard of it at Ephrata, and found it in the
plains of the wood (or, of Jaar)'. If this psalm was composed for the dedication
of Solomon's Temple (II Par. 6.41, 42) and commemorates the bringing back
of the Ark to Jerusalem (I Par. 13), we should naturally suppose that 'it'
means the Ark. It is not clear that the Ark ever rested at Bethlehem-Ephrata;
but some think that Ephrata here is another name for Silo (I Kg. 4.3), and
that the other half of the verse refers to Cariathiarim, the 'city of the woods'
(I Par. 13.5).

thy priests go clad in the vesture of innocence, thy faithful cry aloud
with rejoicing.
10   Think of thy servant David, and do not refuse audience to the king
11 thou hast anointed. Never will the Lord be false to that inviolable
oath he swore to David: I will raise to thy throne heirs of thy own
12 body; if thy sons hold fast to my covenant, to the decrees which I
make known to them, their sons too shall reign on thy throne for ever.
13 The Lord's choice has fallen upon Sion, this is the dwelling he longed
14 for: Here, for ever, is my resting-place, here is my destined home.
15 Trust me, I will give my blessing to the widow,[1] the poor shall have
16 bread to their hearts' content. I will clothe her priests in the vesture
of triumph, cries of rejoicing shall echo among her faithful people.
17 There the stock of David shall bud, there the lamp burn which I have
18 lit for my anointed.[2] I will cover his enemies with confusion; on his
brow my holy unction shall be bright.

PSALM ONE HUNDRED AND THIRTY-TWO

(A song of ascents. Of David)   (133)

GRACIOUS the sight, and full of comfort, when brethren dwell
2 united. Gracious as balm poured on the head till it flows down
on to the beard; balm that flowed down Aaron's beard, and reached
3 the very skirts of his robe. It is as if dew like the dews of Hermon
4 were falling on this hill of Sion;[3] here, where the Lord has promised
to grant benediction and life everlastingly.

PSALM ONE HUNDRED AND THIRTY-THREE

(A song of ascents.)   (134)

COME, then, praise the Lord, all you that are the Lord's servants;
you who stand in the house of the Lord, in the courts where
2 our God dwells. At midnight lift up your hands towards the sanctuary

---

[1] In the Hebrew text, 'Here will I make abundant provision.'

[2] Literally, 'There will I make a horn grow for David, I have trimmed a
lamp for my anointed,' both metaphors for the continuance of his royal
dynasty (III Kg. 15.4, Lk. 1.69).

[3] Literally, 'like the dew of Hermon that falls on the hill of Sion,' which,
however, was more than a hundred miles distant. It seems clear, therefore,
that the dews of Hermon are only mentioned here as typical of exceptionally
heavy dews; unless those authors are right who suspect that the reference is
to a mount Sion, differently spelt in Hebrew, which was part of the Hermon
range (Deut. 4.48).

3 and bless the Lord. May the Lord who dwells in Sion bless thee, the Lord who made heaven and earth!

PSALM ONE HUNDRED AND THIRTY-FOUR

(Alleluia.) (135)

PRAISE the Lord's name; praise the Lord, you that are his servants,
2 you who stand in the house of the Lord, in the courts where
3 our God dwells. Praise to the Lord, a Lord so gracious, praise to
4 his name, a name so well-beloved. Has not the Lord made choice of Jacob, claimed Israel for his own?
5 Doubt it never, the Lord is great; he, our Master, is higher than
6 all the gods. In heaven and on earth, in the sea and in the deep waters
7 beneath us, the Lord accomplishes his will; summoning clouds from the ends of the earth, rain-storm wedding to lightning-flash, bringing
8 winds out of his store-house. He it was that smote the first-born of
9 the Egyptians, man and beast alike; what wonders and portents, Egypt, thou didst witness, sent to plague Pharaoh and all his servants!
10 He it was that smote nation after nation, and slew the kings in their
11 pride, Sehon king of the Amorrhites, and Og the king of Basan, and
12 all the rulers of Chanaan, and marked down their lands for a dwelling-place where his own people of Israel should dwell.
13 Lord, thy name abides for ever; age succeeds age, and thou art ever
14 unforgotten. The Lord defends his people, takes pity on his servants.
15 What are the idols of the heathen but silver and gold, gods which the
16 hands of man have fashioned? They have mouths, and yet are silent;
17 eyes they have, and yet are sightless; ears they have, and want all
18 hearing, never a breath have they in their mouths. Such the end of all
19 who make them, such the reward of all who trust them. Bless the
20 Lord, sons of Israel, bless the Lord, sons of Aaron, bless the Lord, sons of Levi, bless the Lord, all you that are the Lord's worshippers.
21 Here, in Sion, his dwelling-place, here, in Jerusalem, let the Lord's name be blessed.

PSALM ONE HUNDRED AND THIRTY-FIVE

(Alleluia.) (136)

GIVE thanks to the Lord for his goodness, his mercy is eternal;
2 give thanks to the God of gods, his mercy is eternal; give thanks
4 to the Lord of lords, his mercy is eternal. Eternal his mercy, who does

5 great deeds as none else can; eternal his mercy, whose wisdom made
6 the heavens; eternal his mercy, who poised earth upon the floods.
7 Eternal his mercy, who made the great luminaries; made the sun
9 to rule by day, his mercy is eternal; made the moon and the stars to
 rule by night, his mercy is eternal.
10 Eternal his mercy, who smote the Egyptians by smiting their first-
11 born; eternal his mercy, who delivered Israel from their midst, with
 constraining power, with his arm raised on high, his mercy is eternal.
13 Eternal the mercy that divided the Red Sea in two, eternal the mercy
15 that led Israel through its waters, eternal the mercy that drowned in the
16 Red Sea Pharao and Pharao's men. And so he led his people through the
 wilderness, his mercy is eternal.
17 Eternal the mercy that smote great kings, eternal the mercy that
19 slew the kings in their pride, Sehon king of the Amorrhites, his mercy
20 is eternal, and Og the king of Basan, his mercy is eternal. Eternal the
22 mercy that marked down their land to be a dwelling-place; a dwelling-
23 place for his servant Israel, his mercy is eternal. Eternal the mercy
24 that remembers us in our affliction, eternal the mercy that rescues
25 us from our enemies, eternal the mercy that gives all living things
26 their food. Give thanks to the God of heaven, his mercy is eternal,
 give thanks to the Lord of lords, his mercy is eternal.

PSALM ONE HUNDRED AND THIRTY-SIX

(A psalm of David; of Jeremias.) (137)

 WE sat down by the streams of Babylon and wept there, remembering
2 Sion. Willow-trees grow there, and on these we hung up our
3 harps when the men who took us prisoner cried out for a song. We
 must make sport for our enemies; A stave, there, from the music they
4 sing at Sion! [1] What, should we sing the Lord's song in a strange land?
5 Jerusalem, if I forget thee, perish the skill of my right hand! [2] Let
 my tongue stick fast to the roof of my mouth if I cease to remember
 thee, if I find in aught but Jerusalem the fountain-head of my content!
7 Remember, Lord, how the sons of Edom triumphed when Jerusalem
 fell; Strip it, they cried, strip it, till the very foundation is left bare.
8 Babylon, poor withered queen, [3] blessed be the man who deals out to

---

[1] The Hebrew text of this verse probably means 'When the men who took
us prisoners asked us for a stave of a song, those who laid us waste asked us
for joyful music, Sing us one of the melodies of Sion.'
[2] The Hebrew text has 'Let my right hand forget'; the Latin version, 'Let
my right hand be given over to forgetfulness.'
[3] Literally, 'Wretched (in the Hebrew text, devastated) daughter of Babylon'.

9 thee the measure thou hast dealt to us; blessed be the man who will
catch up thy children, and dash them against the rocks!

PSALM ONE HUNDRED AND THIRTY-SEVEN

(For David himself.)   (138)

2 MY heart's thanks, Lord, for listening to the prayer I uttered;
angels for my witnesses,[1] I will sing of thy praise. I bow down
in worship towards thy sanctuary, giving thanks to thy name for thy
mercy and faithfulness; thou hast made thy name reverenced above
3 all things else.[2] Do thou but listen to me when I call upon thee, thou
4 wilt fill my heart with courage. All the kings of the earth will praise
5 thee now; were not thy promises made in their hearing? Let their
6 song be of the Lord's doings, how great is his renown, the Lord,
who is so high above us, yet looks upon lowly things, looks upon the
7 proud, too, but from far off. Though affliction surround my path, thou
dost preserve me; it is thy power that confronts my enemies' malice,
8 thy right hand that rescues me. My purposes the Lord will yet speed;
thy mercy, Lord, endures for ever, and wilt thou abandon us, the
creatures of thy own hands?

PSALM ONE HUNDRED AND THIRTY-EIGHT

(To the end; of David, a psalm.)   (139)

2 LORD, I lie open to thy scrutiny; thou knowest me, knowest when
3 I sit down and when I rise up again,[3] canst read my thoughts
4 from far away. Thou dost map out the path I take, the lot I inherit, dost
5 foresee all my journeyings, and yet no word of mine spoken. And
indeed, Lord, thou knowest all things, new and old;[4] it is thou that
6 hast fashioned me, thy hand that has been laid upon me. Such wisdom
as thine is far beyond my reach, no thought of mine can attain it.

---

[1] The Hebrew word here translated 'angel' means literally 'gods.' Some
think it refers, as in Ps. 81, to earthly rulers, cf. verse 4 below.

[2] The last sentence of this verse is probably corrupt: literally, 'thou hast
exalted thy holy name above all things else'; the Hebrew text has, apparently,
'thou hast exalted thy word above all thy name.'

[3] In the Hebrew text, 'Thou dost examine my journey and my resting.'

[4] *vv*. 4, 5. The Hebrew text is probably to be interpreted, 'There is no word
on my tongue which thou, Lord, dost not know. Thou dost hedge me in behind
and before,' &c.; but the sense of the last verb is uncertain.

7   Where can I go, then, to take refuge from thy spirit, to hide from
8 thy view? If I should climb up to heaven, thou art there; if I sink
9 down to the world beneath, thou art present still. If I should take
   flight at dawn of day, and come to rest at the furthest ends of the sea,
10 still would I find thee beckoning to me, thy right hand upholding
11 me. Or perhaps I would think to bury myself in darkness; night should
12 be the only witness of my pleasures;[1] but no, darkness is no hiding-
   place from thee, with thee the night shines clear as the day itself; light
   and dark are one.
13   Thine are my inmost thoughts. Didst thou not form me in my
14 mother's womb? I praise thee for thy awful majesty,[2] for the wonders
15 of thy creation, which my own being must needs acknowledge. This
   mortal frame has no mysteries for thee, who didst contrive it in secret;
16 all that I am was once hidden in the dark recesses of the earth. Thy
   eyes looked upon me, when I was yet unformed; all human lives are
   already written in thy record, brought to birth through the long days
   when they had no being.[3]
17   Great reverence have I for thy friends, O God;[4] sovereign power
18 is theirs in abundance; they are numberless as the sand, past all my
19 counting. I awake from sleep, and thou art still with me.[5] O God, wouldst
   thou but make an end of the wicked! Murderers, keep your distance
20 from me! You are ever whispering in your hearts, They shall have no
21 advantage from the cities thou gavest them.[6] Lord, do I not hate the
22 men who hate thee, am I not sick at heart over their rebellion? Sur-
23 passing hatred I bear them, count them my sworn enemies. Scrutinize
   me, O God, as thou wilt, and read my heart; put me to the test, and
24 watch the steps I take. See if on any false path my heart is set, and
   thyself lead me in ways immemorial.

------

[1] Literally, 'Night (should be all) my illumination in my pleasures.'

[2] Literally, 'because thou art fearsomely exalted.' The Hebrew text has,
'because fearsome wonders went to my making.'

[3] The sense here is very uncertain, but a comparison with the Septuagint Greek
shews that the rendering here given is the sense intended by the Latin version.

[4] The word translated 'friends' in the Latin version is more commonly
interpreted as meaning 'thoughts,' 'wise counsels,' as in verse 3 above.

[5] The second part of this verse is usually interpreted as meaning that the
Psalmist falls into a trance while trying to reckon up the sum of God's wise
counsels, and comes to himself finding the sum still incalculable. But it may
be questioned whether the sense is not more general; cf. Ps. 3.6 above.

[6] The intention of the Latin seems to be, that the enemies of Israel are determined not to leave it in peaceful possession of the cities God has given it for
an inheritance. The sense of the Hebrew text is doubtful, but it is generally
interpreted as meaning that the wicked make mention of God (or, rebel against
God) craftily, and take his name in vain.

PSALM ONE HUNDRED AND THIRTY-NINE

(To the end; a psalm; of David.)   (140)

2 RESCUE me, Lord, from human malice, save me from the lovers
3 of oppression,   always plotting treachery in their hearts, always
4 at their quarrelling, tongues sharp as the tongues of serpents, lips that
5 hide the poison of adders.   Preserve me, Lord, from the power of
sinful men, save me from these lovers of oppression who are plotting
6 to trip my feet.   What hidden snares they set for me, these tyrants,
what nets they spread to catch me, what traps they lay in my path!
7 To the Lord I make my appeal, Thou art my God, listen to the
8 voice that pleads with thee.   My Lord, my Master, my strong deliverer,
9 it is thou that shieldest my head in the day of battle.   Do not betray
my hopes, Lord, into the hands of the wicked; do not forsake me, and
10 let the schemers triumph.   This be the fruit of their conspiracy, that
11 all their busy whispering should recoil upon themselves.[1] Let burning
coals fall upon them; down into the fire thou wilt hurl them, to anguish
12 insupportable.   Glib tongues will not always have their way on earth;
13 misfortune will overtake the oppressors and destroy them.   Can I
doubt that the Lord will avenge the helpless, will grant the poor redress?
14 Honest men will yet live to praise thy name, upright hearts enjoy
the smile of thy favour.

PSALM ONE HUNDRED AND FORTY   (141)

(A psalm. Of David.)

COME quickly, Lord, at my cry for succour; do not let my appeal
2 to thee go unheard.   Welcome as incense-smoke let my prayer
rise up before thee; when I lift up my hands, be it as acceptable as the
3 evening sacrifice.   Lord, set a guard on my mouth, a barrier to fence
4 in my lips.   Do not turn my heart towards thoughts of evil, to cover
sin with smooth names; not mine to take part with wrong-doers; not
5 mine to mingle with the company they keep.[2]   Rather in love let some

---

[1] Literally, 'The head of their going about, the labour of their lips will cover
them.' It seems that the Latin and Greek versions mean to give some such
interpretation as that suggested above. The Hebrew text appears to mean 'As
for the head of those who compass me about, the mischief of their own lips
shall overwhelm them.'

[2] The Hebrew text is usually rendered 'Not mine to share in their choice
dainties.'

just man chastise me, reprove me; never shall the sinner sleek this head
with the oil of his flattery. My prayer is still unabated while they have
their will. . . .[1]

6   . . . Here are men who have seen their rulers swallowed up by
death, doomed to the precipice. Listen to me they [2] shall, while listen they
7 may.[3] The bones of our countrymen lie scattered at the foot of the abyss,
like the ruins of a landslip that has fallen to earth.

8   And yet, these eyes look to thee, my Lord, my Master; in thee I
9 trust; let not my life be forfeit. Preserve me from the ambush they
10 have laid for me, from the snares of the wrongdoers. Into his net
the sinner shall fall, while I, all unprotected, go safe on my journey.[4]

PSALM ONE HUNDRED AND FORTY-ONE (142)

(Of understanding; for David, when he was in the cave; a prayer.)

2 L OUD is my cry to the Lord, the prayer I utter for the Lord's
3   mercy, as I pour out my complaint before him, tell him of the
4 affliction I endure. My heart is ready to faint within me, but thou art
watching over my path. They lie in ambush for me there by the way-
5 side; I look to the right of me, and find none to take my part; [5] all hope
6 of escape is cut off from me, none is concerned for my safety. To
thee, Lord, I cry, claiming thee for my only refuge, all that is left
7 me in this world of living men. Listen, then, to my plea; thou seest

---

[1] In the Hebrew text, there is no reference to the 'oil of the sinner'; the
Psalmist says that he will not refuse correction from the upright, but will treat
it as 'oil poured on the head.' He adds at the end of the verse, 'my prayer is
unabated by their wickedness,' apparently in reference to verse 4.

[2] It does not seem likely that the word 'they' in this verse refers to the
sinners just mentioned; it is more naturally interpreted of the Jewish people
generally. This verse, and the verse which follows, are obscure both in the
Hebrew text and in the Latin rendering; the sense is probably that certain
leading men were thrown down a precipice; but the words which follow are
difficult to connect with the context.

[3] For 'now the opportunity is theirs' the Hebrew text (as ordinarily translated) gives 'for they (*i.e.*, my words) are pleasant to them.' At the ending of
the next verse the Hebrew text is usually translated 'as when a man ploughs
and cleaves the earth.'

[4] 'His net' according to some interpreters means 'their own net.' In the
Hebrew text the word 'unprotected' in the second half of the verse should
rather be translated 'together' (in reference to the sinners) or 'at the same time'
(in reference to the Psalmist himself).

[5] The Hebrew text is understood by some as meaning 'Look to the right
of me, and thou wilt find none to take my part.'

me all defenceless. Rescue me from persecutors who are too strong
8 for me; restore liberty to a captive soul. What thanks, then, will I give
to thy name! Too long have honest hearts waited to see thee grant
me redress.[1]

PSALM ONE HUNDRED AND FORTY-TWO (143)

(A psalm. Of David, when his son Absalom was in pursuit of him.)

L ISTEN, Lord, to my prayer; give my plea a hearing, as thou art
2 ever faithful; listen, thou who lovest the right.   Do not call thy
servant to account; what man is there living, that can stand guiltless
3 in thy presence?   See how my enemies plot against my life, how they
have abased me in the dust, set me down in dark places, like the long-
4 forgotten dead!   My spirits are crushed within me, my heart is cowed.
5 And my mind goes back to past days; I think of all thou didst once,
6 dwell on the proofs thou gavest of thy power.   To thee I spread out
my hands in prayer, for thee my soul thirsts, like a land parched with
drought.
7   Hasten, Lord, to answer my prayer, my spirit grows faint. Do not
turn thy face away from me, and leave me like one sunk in the abyss.
8 Speedily let me win thy mercy, my hope is in thee; to thee I lift up
9 my heart, shew me the path I must follow;   to thee I fly for refuge,
10 deliver me, Lord, from my enemies.   Thou art my God, teach me to
do thy will; let thy gracious spirit lead me on, till I find sure ground
11 under my feet.   For the honour of thy own name, Lord, thou wilt grant
12 me life; in my sore need, thy mercy will bring deliverance.   Thou wilt
have pity, and rout my enemies; thy servant I; make an end of my cruel
persecutors.

PSALM ONE HUNDRED AND FORTY-THREE

(A psalm of David against Goliath.)   (144)

B LESSED be the Lord, my God, who makes these hands strong
2 for battle, these fingers skilled in fight;   the Lord who pities me
and grants me safety, who shelters me and sets me at liberty, who
protects me and gives me confidence, bowing down nations to my
3 will.   Lord, what is Adam's race, that thou givest heed to it; what

---

[1] In the second part of this sentence, the Hebrew text has, 'Honest folk will
gather round me (or, perhaps, will be crowned with joy) when thou rewardest
me with thy favour.'

4 is man, that thou carest for him. Like a breath he comes and goes, like a shadow his days pass.

5 Bid heaven stoop, Lord, and come down to earth; at thy touch, the
6 mountains will be wreathed in smoke. Brandish thy lightnings, to rout my enemies; shoot thy arrows, and throw them into confusion!
7 With heavenly aid, from yonder flood deliver me; save me, rescue me
8 from the power of alien foes, who make treacherous promises, and lift
9 their hands in perjury. Then, O my God, I will sing thee a new song, on a
10 ten-stringed harp I will sound thy praise; the God to whom kings must look for victory, the God who has brought his servant David rescue.
11 Save me from the cruel sword, deliver me from the power of alien foes, who make treacherous promises, and lift their right hands in perjury.
12 Happy is their lot, whose sons grow to manhood, tall as the saplings, their daughters fair of form, gaily decked to match the temple itself
13 for beauty; their garners full to bursting on this side and that, their
14 sheep bearing fruitfully, thronging the pasture-land, sturdy their
15 cattle, no ruined walls, no farewell, no lamenting in their streets. Happy men call such a people as this; and is not the people happy, that has the Lord for its God? [1]

PSALM ONE HUNDRED AND FORTY-FOUR

(Praise of David's own.)   (145)

A ND shall I not extol thee, my God, my king; shall not I bless
2 thy name forever and for evermore. Blessing shall be thine, day
3 after day; for ever and for evermore praised be thy name. Can any praise be worthy of the Lord's majesty, any thought set limits to his
4 greatness? Down the ages the story of thy deeds is told, thy power
5 is ever acclaimed; each magnifies thy unapproachable glory, makes
6 known thy wonders. Fearful are the tales they tell of thy power, pro-
7 claiming thy magnificence; grateful their memory of all thy goodness,
8 as they boast of thy just dealings. How gracious the Lord is, how
9 merciful, how patient, how rich in pity! Is he not a loving Lord

---

[1] *vv.* 12–15. The Greek and Latin versions seem to suggest that the prosperity here described is experienced by the Psalmist's enemies, mentioned in verse 11. In that case, the latter half of verse 15 must be understood as instituting a contrast between temporal and spiritual well-being. The Hebrew text, however, has 'our' instead of 'their' throughout this passage, and is generally understood as a prayer for the happiness of God's own people. The meaning of verse 12 in the Hebrew text is uncertain; in verse 13 it has 'with every kind (of grain),' instead of 'on this side and on that.'

to his whole creation; does not his mercy reach out to all that he has made?

10 Joining, then, Lord, in thy whole creation's praise, let thy faithful
11 servants bless thee; let them publish the glory of thy kingdom, and
12 discourse of thy power, making that power known to the race of men,
13 the glory, the splendour of that kingdom! No age shall dawn but shall
see thee reigning still; generations pass, and thy rule shall endure. O
how true the Lord is to all his promises, how high above us in all his
14 dealings! [1] Prostrate though men may fall, the Lord will lift them up,
will revive their crushed spirits.

15 Quietly, Lord, thy creatures raise their eyes to thee, and thou grantest
16 them, in due time, their nourishment, ready to open thy hand, and
17 fill with thy blessing all that lives. So faithful the Lord is in all he
18 does, so high above us in all his dealings. The Lord draws near to every
man that calls upon him, will he but call upon him with a true heart.
19 Utter but the wish, you that fear the Lord, and he will grant it; will
20 hear the cry and bring aid. Vigilantly the Lord watches over all that
21 love him, marks down the wicked for destruction. While these lips tell of
the Lord's praise, let all that lives bless his holy name, for ever, and for
evermore.

PSALM ONE HUNDRED AND FORTY-FIVE

(Alleluia. Of Aggaeus and Zachary.)   (146)

2 PRAISE the Lord, my soul; while life lasts, I will praise the Lord;
of him, my God, shall my songs be while I am here to sing them.
3 Do not put your trust in princes; they are but men, they have no
4 power to save. As soon as the breath leaves his body, man goes back
to the dust he belongs to; with that, all their designs will come to
5 nothing. Happier the man who turns to the God of Jacob for help,
6 puts no confidence but in the Lord his God, maker of heaven and
7 earth and sea and all they contain; the God who keeps faith for ever,
8 who redresses wrong, and gives food to the hungry. The Lord, who
brings release to the prisoner, the Lord, who gives sight to the blind,
the Lord, who raises up the fallen, the Lord who befriends the innocent!
9 The Lord, who protects the stranger, who defends orphan and widow,
10 who overturns the counsel of the wicked. The Lord, reigning for ever,
thy God, Sion, reigning from age to age! [2]

---

[1] The second half of this verse is wanting in the Hebrew text.
[2] The Hebrew text prints here the Alleluia which, in the Greek and Latin versions, begins the following psalm.

PSALM ONE HUNDRED AND FORTY-SIX

(Alleluia.)   (147.1–11)

PRAISE the Lord, a gracious thing is a psalm; cheerfully and worthily
2 let us give our God praise. The Lord is rebuilding Jerusalem,
3 calling the banished sons of Israel home; he it is that heals the broken
4 heart, and binds up its wounds. Does he not know the number of the
5 stars, and call each by its name? How great a Lord is ours, how mag-
6 nificent his strength, how inscrutable his wisdom! The Lord is the
7 defender of the oppressed, and lays the wicked low in the dust. Strike
up, then, in thanksgiving to the Lord, with the harp's music praise
8 our God; the God who curtains heaven with clouds, and lays up a
store of rain for the earth, who clothes the mountain-sides with grass,
9 with corn for man's need,[1] gives food to the cattle, food to the young
10 ravens that cry out to him. Not the well-mounted warrior is his choice,
11 not the swift runner wins his favour; the Lord's favour is for those
who fear him, and put their trust in his Divine mercy.

PSALM ONE HUNDRED AND FORTY-SEVEN

(Alleluia.)   (147.12–20)

2 PRAISE the Lord, Jerusalem; Sion, exalt thy God! He it is that
bolts thy gates fast, and blesses thy children, who dwell safe
3 in thee; that makes thy land a land of peace, and gives thee full ears
4 of wheat to sustain thee. See how he issues his command to the earth,
5 how swift his word runs! Now he spreads a pall of snow, covers the
6 earth with an ashy veil of mist,[2] doles out the scattered crusts of ice,
7 sends the frost there is no enduring. Then, at his word, all melts away;
8 a breath from him, and the waters flow! This is the God who makes
9 his word known to Jacob, gives Israel ruling and decree. Not such his
dealings with any other nation; nowhere else the revelation of his
will. Alleluia.

---

[1] The last five words of this verse are wanting in the Hebrew text.

[2] According to the Hebrew text, it is not the dark mists that are compared
with ashes, but the hoar-frost lying white on the ground.

PSALM ONE HUNDRED AND FORTY-EIGHT

(Alleluia.)

GIVE praise to the Lord in heaven; praise him, all that dwells
2 on high. Praise him, all you angels of his, praise him, all his
3 armies. Praise him, sun and moon; praise him, every star that shines.
4 Praise him, you highest heavens, you waters beyond the heavens.
5 Let all these praise the Lord; it was his decree that fashioned them,
6 his command that gave them birth. He has set them there unaging
for ever, given them a law which cannot be altered.[1]
7 　Give praise to the Lord on earth, monsters of the sea and all its
8 depths; fire and hail, snow and ice,[2] and the storm-wind that executes
9 his decree; all you mountains and hills, all you fruit-trees and cedars;
10 all you wild beasts and cattle, creeping things and birds that fly in
11 air; all you kings and peoples of the world, all you that are princes
12 and judges on earth; young men and maids, old men and boys together;
13 let them all give praise to the Lord's name. His name is exalted as
14 no other, his praise reaches beyond heaven and earth; and now he
has given fresh strength to his people. Shall not his faithful servants
praise him, the sons of Israel, the people that draws near to him?

PSALM ONE HUNDRED AND FORTY-NINE

(Alleluia.)

SING the Lord a new song; here, where the faithful gather, let his
2 praise be heard. In him, the maker of Israel, let Israel triumph;
3 for him, the ruler of Sion, let Sion's children keep holiday; let there
be dancing in honour of his name, music of tambour and of harp,
4 to praise him. Still the Lord shews favour to his people, still he relieves
5 the oppressed, and grants them victory. In triumph let thy faithful
6 servants rejoice, rejoice and take their rest. Ever on their lips they
bear the high praise of God, ever in their hands they carry two-edged
7 swords, ready to take vengeance upon the heathen, to curb the nations,
8 to chain the kings and bind princes in fetters of iron. Long since their
9 doom is written; boast it is of his true servants that doom to execute.
Alleluia.

---

[1] The last six words of this verse are wanting in the Hebrew text.
[2] For 'ice' the Hebrew text has 'smoke.'

PSALM ONE HUNDRED AND FIFTY

(Alleluia.)

PRAISE God in his sanctuary, praise him on his sovereign throne.
2 Praise him for his noble acts, praise him for his surpassing great-
3 ness. Praise him with the bray of the trumpet, praise him with harp
4 and zither. Praise him with the tambour and the dance, praise him
5 with the music of string and of reed. Praise him with the clang of the
cymbals, the cymbals that ring merrily. All creatures that breath have,
praise the Lord. Alleluia.

THE BOOK OF PROVERBS

CHAPTER ONE

THESE proverbs were written by David's son Solomon, that was king
2 of Israel, for the better understanding of true wisdom, and self-com-
3 mand. Here is made known the secret of discernment; here men may
learn the lesson of insight, the dictates of duty and right and honour.
4 Here simplicity is put on its guard; here youth may find instruction and
5 advice both together. The wise, too, may be the wiser for hearing them;
6 they will aid even the discerning to guide his course aright; he will read
both parables and the interpretation of parables, both wise words and the
hidden thoughts they signify.

7 True wisdom is founded on the fear of the Lord; who but a fool
would despise such wisdom, and the lessons she teaches?

8 Heed well, my son, thy father's warnings, nor make light of thy
9 mother's teaching; no richer heirloom, crown or necklace, can be
10 thine. Turn a deaf ear, my son, to the blandishments of evil-doers
11 that would make thee of their company. There are lives to be had
for the ambushing, the lives of unsuspecting folk whose uprightness
12 shall little avail them; there are fortunes to be swallowed up whole,
13 as a man is swallowed up by death when he goes to his grave. No
lack of treasures here, they say, rich plunder that shall find its way
14 into our houses; thou hast but to throw in thy lot with us; every man
15 shares alike. Such errands, my son, are not for thee; never stir a foot
16 in their company; thou knowest well how eager they are for mischief,
17 how greedy for blood, and the snare is laid to no purpose if the bird
18 is watching. What do they, but compass their own ruin, plot against
19 their own lives? Such is ever the end of greed; he who cherishes it
must fall by it at last.

20 And all the while Wisdom is publishing her message, crying it aloud
21 in the open streets; never a meeting of roads, never a gateway, but
22 her voice is raised, echoing above the din of it. What, says she, are
you still gaping there, simpletons? Do the reckless still court their
23 own ruin? Rash fools, will you never learn? Pay heed, then, to my
protest; listen while I speak out my mind to you, give you open warning.
24 Since my call is unheard, since my hand beckons in vain, since my
26 counsel is despised and all my reproof goes for nothing, it will be
mine to laugh, to mock at your discomfiture, when perils close about
27 you. Close about you they will, affliction and sore distress, disasters
that sweep down suddenly, gathering storms of ruin.

28 It will be their turn, then, to call aloud; my turn, then, to refuse
an answer. They will be early abroad looking for me, but find me
29 never; fools, that grew weary of instruction, and would not fear the
30 Lord. Well for them, if they had followed my counsel, if they had
31 not spurned all the warnings I gave! Now they must eat of the harvest
their own wickedness has reaped, make the best of the cheer their own
32 knavish schemes have brought them. Ah, silly souls, what a perilous
refusal, what fatal foolhardiness was here!
33   But let a man give heed to me, peace undisturbed shall be his, happiness shall be his, free from all threat of danger.

CHAPTER TWO

HERE, then, my son, is counsel for thee; take this bidding of mine to
2 heart; ever be thy ear attentive to wisdom, thy mind eager to attain
3 discernment. Wisdom if thou wilt call to thy side, and make discern-
4 ment welcome, as thou wouldst fain hoard riches, or bring hidden
5 treasure to light, then thou wilt learn what it is to fear God, make trial
6 of what it is to know God. Wisdom is the Lord's gift; only by his word
7 spoken comes true knowledge, true discernment. So it is that he watches
8 over the lives of the upright, bids the innocent walk unharmed; safe and
9 sound the chosen friends of God come and go. Duty and right and
10 honour thou shalt discern, and see ever where the best course lies, if
once wisdom finds a lodgement in thy heart, if knowledge once casts her
11 spell upon thee. Watch and ward right counsel shall keep over thee; it
shall save thee from the wrong choice, save thee from the false counsellor.
13 False counsellors there are, that leave the high road to walk by dark alleys;
14 for sin and shame is all their love and liking; ill guides on a wrong path
16 all of them! And from her, too, right counsel shall protect thee, the
woman that is no daughter of Israel, with her mincing foreign ways,
17 that has forsaken the love of her youth, forgotten the troth once plighted
to her God. The house she dwells in is death's antechamber, the road by
19 which she beckons leads to the grave; never man went in there that
came back and set his face towards life.[1]
20   Thine to choose a nobler course, keeping ever the path of duty;
21 the upright, the innocent, shall have lands of their own and long enjoy
22 them; the godless, the wrong-doer will be lost for ever to the scenes
they knew.

---

[1] *vv*. 16–19. Some take this as a literal reference to the habits of light women,
as in ch. 7 below; but it is more probably an allegorical reference to apostasy
from the Jewish religion.

CHAPTER THREE

FORGET not then, my son, the teaching I give thee; lock these
2 words of mine close in thy bosom; long years they shall bring
3 thee of life well spent, and therewith prosperity. Two things must
never leave thee, kindness and loyalty; be these the seals that hang
about thy neck, graven be this inscription with thy heart for tablet;
4 so both to God and man thou shalt be friend and confidant. Put all
thy heart's confidence in the Lord, on thy own skill relying never;
6 wilt thou but keep him in thy thoughts wherever thou goest, he will
7 shew thee the straight path. Do not give thyself airs of wisdom; enough
8 that thou shouldst fear God and shun ill-doing; here is health for the
9 midmost of thy being, here is sap for the marrow of thy bones. Pay
the Lord his due with what goods thou hast, letting him share the
10 first-fruits of every crop; so shall plenty fill thy barn, so shall thy wine-
press overflow at the vintage.
11   My son, do not undervalue the correction the Lord sends thee,
12 do not be unmanned when he reproves thy faults. It is where he loves
that he bestows correction, like a father whose son is dear to him.
13   Happy the man whose treasure-trove is wisdom, who is rich in
14 discernment; silver and finest gold are less profitable in the handling.
15 More rare is it than all things else; no prize thou covetest that can
16 match it. Long life wisdom holds out to thee in one hand, riches and
17 glory in the other; where she guides, journeying is pleasant, where
18 she points the way, all is peace. Take hold of her, clasp her to thee,
19 and the Tree of Life itself could not make thee more blessed. Not
without these, wisdom and discernment, the Lord based earth, the Lord
20 framed heaven; not without skill of his did the waters well up from
21 beneath us, or the dews fall in mist. My son, never lose sight of what
22 I am telling thee; cling to the wholesome dictates of prudence, that will
23 quicken life within thee, sparkle like jewels on thy breast. Securely thou
24 shalt walk, with no fear of stumbling, fearlessly thou shalt lie down to
25 rest, and enjoy untroubled sleep; let no sudden alarm affright thee,
26 though godless enemies press thee hard; the Lord will be at thy side, and
keep thy feet clear of the snares they lay for thee.
27   Suffer him to do kindness who may, and thou thyself, when thou
28 mayest, do kindness; [1] never bid a friend come back to-morrow for
29 the gift that might be made to-day. Never plot harm against the friend
30 that suspects no harm of thee, or pick a quarrel with one who has

---

[1] The meaning of the Hebrew text is doubtful.

31 done thee no injury. Do not envy the prosperity of the wrong-doer,
32 and be led away by his example; knavery the Lord hates, and keeps
33 for honest men his familiar friendship. Still on the home of the wicked
34 the Lord's ban falls, his blessing where uprightness dwells; he laughs
35 at the mocker, grants his favours to the humble, and the wise shall
win renown; only to their shame are fools exalted.

CHAPTER FOUR

SONS of mine, take a lesson from your father; a lesson that will
2 make discerning men of you, will you but heed it. A precious
heirloom it is, the tradition I teach, not to be lightly bartered away.
3 Time was when I had a father of my own; and when I was but a
4 boy, my mother's darling, in such words as these he would teach me:
Ever be thy heart true to my bidding; if thrive thou wouldst, hold fast
5 the charge I give thee. Wisdom be thy quest, thy quest discernment
6 still; thy father's apt and faithful pupil, keep her at thy side, thy
7 guardian; cherish her, thy preserver. Wisdom be thy chief thought,
8 make discernment thine at all hazards; her attainment exalts, her em-
9 brace ennobles thee; a wreath of fresh graces she will give thee, a crown
of glory, to overshadow thy brow.
10 Listen, then, my son, and master the charge I give thee, as thou
11 wouldst have long life. Here lies the road to wisdom, here is the path
12 that will bring thee straight to thy goal; here thou mayst walk un-
13 hampered, run without fear of stumbling. Hold fast by the instruction
thou hast received, and never let it go; guard it as thou wouldst guard
14 thy life. For godless ways and the example of sinful men have thou
15 neither love nor liking; shun their haunts and turn thy back upon
16 them. Rest they never without some ill deed done; some traveller's
17 feet must stumble, or they lie sleepless on their beds; godlessness is the
18 very bread they eat, they crave for wrong-doing as for wine. See how the
path of the just grows ever brighter, like the light of dawn opening out
19 into full day! But these, the sinners, are fain to walk on in darkness, surprised by every fall.
20 Hear then and heed, my son, these words of warning; never lose
22 sight of them, cherish them in thy inmost heart; let a man master
23 them, they will bring life and healing to his whole being. Use all thy
watchfulness to keep thy heart true; that is the fountain whence life
24 springs. Far, very far from thy tongue be the cheating word, from thy
25 lips the whisper of calumny; let thy eyes see straight, thy gaze ever scan

26 the path that lies before thee. Consider [1] that path well, and on safe
27 ground thou shalt journey still; swerving neither to right nor left, but
keeping thy steps ever clear of wrong-doing. (To the right lie such ways
as win the Lord's favour, to the left such as miss the goal. He it is that will
guide thy course aright, and set thy journey forward in peace).[2]

CHAPTER FIVE

2 MY son, here is good advice for thy heeding; listen to wise counsel,
if thou wouldst be circumspect, if thou wouldst have ever on
thy lips the maxims of prudence. First, give no credence to the wiles
3 of woman; honey-sweet words the temptress [3] may use, all her talk be
4 soothing as oil, but oh, the dregs of that cup are bitter; a two-edged
5 sword brings no sharper pang. Death's road she follows, her feet set
6 towards the grave; far from the highway that leads to life is the maze
7 she treads. Heed, then, my warning, and depart from it never; shun
9 her company, do not go near her doors. Wouldst thou squander the
pride of thy manhood upon heartless strangers like these?
10 If thus thou wilt spend all thy hopes, bestow all thy pains, upon
11 an alien home that is no home of thine, a time will come at last when
health and strength shall be wasted away. Then thou wilt complain
12 bitterly, Alas, why did I spurn every precept, reject every warning,
13 unheard, unheeded, every lesson I was taught? No marvel, had I paid
the last penalty, with the assembled people for my judges! [4]
15 Nay, drink, and drink deep, at thy own well, thy own cistern; thence
let thy offspring abound, like waters from thy own fountain flowing
17 through the public streets; [5] only let them be thy own, let there be no
18 commerce between thyself and strangers. A blessing on that fountain
of thine! take thy pleasure with the bride thy manhood wins for thee.

---

[1] Literally 'direct' in the Latin version, 'weigh' in the Hebrew text. The
Hebrew verb is ordinarily interpreted 'smooth out,' but it is difficult to see the
relevance of such a metaphor here.

[2] The words enclosed in brackets are found in the Septuagint Greek, but
not in the Hebrew text. They have perhaps been misplaced by accident; evidently they do not suit the thought of the present passage.

[3] Literally 'harlot,' but it would appear from what follows, especially verse
14, that the warning here given is one against adultery, not fornication. It is
uncertain, both here and elsewhere in the book, how much the Hebrew term
'strange woman' is meant to convey the sense of foreign birth.

[4] Lev. 20.10; cf. Jn. 8.5.

[5] Literally, 'Let thy fountains be carried out in channels abroad; distribute
thy well-water through the streets'; but the phrase evidently refers to a numerous family born in lawful wedlock.

19 Thy own bride, gentle as a hind, graceful as a doe; be it her bosom that
20 steals away thy senses with the delight of a lover that loves still. What,
   my son, wouldst thou yield to the wiles of a stranger, dally with her
21 embraces that is none of thine? The Lord is watching, and knows
22 what a man's errand is, let him betake himself where he will. The
   sinner will be ensnared by his own guilt, caught in the toils of his own
23 wrong-doing; doomed by his own incontinence, by his own great
   folly bemused.

CHAPTER SIX

MY son, has some friend persuaded thee to be his surety? Hast thou
2 pledged thyself for a bond which is none of thine? Believe me, that
   word of assent has caught thee in a snare, thou art the prisoner of thy
3 own promise made. Do then, my son, as I bid thee; obtain thy freedom;
   it is ill done to fall into another man's power. Quick, no time to lose; wake
4 up this neighbour of thine from his bed, ere thou thyself close an eye-lid
5 in sleep; deer from captivity nor bird from fowler's hand so swift to
   escape!
6 Up with thee, idleness, go to school with the ant, and learn the lesson
7 of her ways! Chief or ruler she has none to give her commands; yet in
   summer hours, when the harvest is a-gathering, she ever lays up food
9 for her own nourishment. And thou, idleness, art still a-bed; wilt thou
10 never wake? What, thou wouldst sleep a little longer, yawn a little longer;
11 a little longer thou must pillow head on hand? Ay, but poverty will not
   wait, the day of distress will not wait, like an armed vagabond it will fall
   upon thee! (Wouldst thou see the good grain flow like water, wouldst
   thou see poverty take wing, thou must be up and doing).[1]
12 Worthless men there be, sinners there be, that go ever with a cunning
13 smile on their lips; a wink here, there a pressure of the foot, there a
14 beckoning finger; all the while their wicked hearts are plotting mischief,
15 are sowing the causes of strife. Such men will be overtaken by their
   doom ere long, crushed all of a sudden beyond hope of remedy.
16 Six things I will tell thee, and name a seventh for good measure, the
17 Lord hates and will never abide; the haughty look, the lying tongue, the
18 hands that take innocent life, the heart that ever devises thoughts of mis-
19 chief, the feet that hasten upon an ill errand, the false witness whose
   every breath is perjury, and the sower of strife among brethren.

---

[1] The words enclosed in brackets appear in the Septuagint Greek, but not
in the Hebrew text.

20   Keep true, my son, to the charge thy father gives thee, nor make
21 light of thy mother's teaching; wear them ever close to thy heart,
22 hang them like a locket upon thy breast; be these, when thou walkest
    abroad, thy company, when thou liest asleep, thy safeguard, in waking
23 hours, thy counsellors. That charge is a lamp to guide thee, that
    teaching a light to beckon thee; the warnings correction gave thee are a
    road leading to life.
24   Here is protection for thee against the temptress that would lure
25 thee away with her seductions. Never let her beauty win thy heart,
26 never let her bold glance deceive thee. A harlot's pay is but the price
    of a meal; the adulteress costs dearer, her price is a man's whole life.
27 Who can carry fire in his bosom, without singeing the clothes he wears,
28 or walk on hot coals without burning his feet? No more can a man
30 mate with his neighbour's wife, and not be defiled by her touch. Small
31 blame to the thief, when he steals to fill his hungry belly, and if he
32 be caught, why, he can pay sevenfold, or yield up all that he has; the
33 adulterer, in the hunger of his heart, must risk losing life itself. Scathe
34 and scorn he wins for himself, and shame there is no blotting out; no
    mercy for him, when the day of reckoning comes, from the anger of a
35 jealous husband   that will listen to no man's entreaties, will refuse ransom
    never so abundant.

CHAPTER SEVEN

M Y son, do not forget these warnings; let this charge of mine be an
2   heirloom, kept jealously, as thou lovest thy own life; precious to
3 thee as the apple of thy eye be the teaching I give thee. Bind it fast about
4 thy fingers, write it, as upon a tablet, on thy heart; give to wisdom a
    sister's welcome, and hail discernment as thy friend.
5   So wilt thou learn to shun the temptress with her honeyed words,
6 the wife that is no wife of thine. Ere now, looking down from my
7 window through the lattice, I have watched the thoughtless crowd,
8 and seen some gallant, more insensate than the rest, crossing the street
    at the corner where such a woman dwells. Now his steps are taking
9 him near that abode of hers; the day wanes, and the light fades; night
10 spreads her pall of darkness. Who comes to meet him? A woman in right
11 harlot's guise, that goes out, ready of speech, to hunt men's lives. No
12 rest for her, stay at home she cannot; ever in street and market-place
13 she lies in ambush, at some corner of the ways. She draws him to herself
14 and kisses him, flattering him with her bold speech: Only to-day I have
    paid a vow that I owed for my preservation, and here are my victims

15 freshly killed; so I came out to find thee, longing for the sight of thee,
16 and here thou art! Soft, soft I have made my bed, spread it with em-
17 broidered tapestries of Egyptian woof; freshly scented is that bower of
18 mine with myrrh, and aloes, and cinnamon. Come, let us lose ourselves
   in dalliance, all the night through let us enjoy the long desired embrace.
19 My home stands masterless, my husband far away, and his purse with
   him; no fear of his returning till the moon is full.
21   Alas, the ready speech that beguiles him, the seducing lips that lead
22 him captive away! He follows without more ado, unwitting as the ox
   that goes to the shambles, or a frisking lamb;[1] nor knows what fetters
23 await him, till the shaft is already deep in his bosom. So joyfully flies
24 bird into snare, heedless of its life's peril. Heed me well, my son; let not
25 this warning be given in vain; do not let her steal thy heart away, do not
26 be enticed by her beckoning. Many the wounds such a woman has dealt;
27 a brave retinue she has of men murdered; truly her house is the grave's
   ante-chamber, opens the door into the secret closet of death.

CHAPTER EIGHT

AND, all the while, the wisdom that grants discernment is crying
2 aloud, is never silent; there she stands, on some high vantage-
3 point by the public way, where the roads meet, or at the city's approach,
4 close beside the gates, making proclamation. To every man, high
5 and low, her voice calls: Here is better counsel for the simpleton;
6 O foolish hearts, take warning! Listen to me, I have matters of high
7 moment to unfold, a plain message to deliver. A tongue that speaks
8 truth, lips that scorn impiety; here all is sound doctrine, no shifts,
9 no evasions here. No discerning heart, no well-stored mind, but will
10 own it right and just. Here is counsel, here is instruction, better worth
11 the winning than silver or the finest gold; wisdom is more to be coveted
   than any jewel; there is no beauty that can be matched with hers.
12   What am I, the wisdom that speaks to you? To shrewdness I am
13 a near neighbour, and I occupy myself with deep designs; but, since
   they must hate evil that fear the Lord, all pride and boastfulness,
14 every mischievous design and every treacherous word I shun. Good
   counsel is mine, and honourable dealing, self-command and high
15 courage are my gifts; through me kings learn how to reign, law-givers
16 how to lay down just decrees; through me chieftain and magistrate
17 exercise their power aright. Love me, and thou shalt earn my love;
18 wait early at my doors, and thou shalt gain access to me. The gifts

---

[1] The sense of the Hebrew text here is uncertain.

I bring with me are riches and honour, princely state and the divine
19 favour. Mine is a yield better than gold or jewels, mine are revenues
20 more precious than the finest silver. A faithful course I tread, nor
21 exceed the bounds of just retribution, failing never to enrich the souls
that love me with abundant store.
22   The Lord made me his [1] when first he went about his work, at the birth
23 of time, before his creation began. Long, long ago, before earth was
24 fashioned, I held my course. Already I lay in the womb, when the
depths were not yet in being, when no springs of water had yet broken;
25 when I was born, the mountains had not yet sunk on their firm founda-
26 tions, and there were no hills; not yet had he made the earth, or the
27 rivers, or the solid framework of the world.[2] I was there when he
built the heavens, when he fenced in the waters with a vault inviolable,
28 when he fixed the sky overhead, and levelled the fountain-springs of
29 the deep. I was there when he enclosed the sea within its confines,
forbidding the waters to transgress their assigned limits, when he poised
30 the foundations of the world. I was at his side, a master-workman,
my delight increasing with each day, as I made play before him all the
31 while; made play in this world of dust, with the sons of Adam for
32 my play-fellows. Listen to me, then, you that are my sons, that follow,
33 to your happiness, in the paths I shew you; listen to the teaching
34 that will make you wise, instead of turning away from it. Blessed
are they who listen to me, keep vigil, day by day, at my threshold, watch-
35 ing till I open my doors. The man who wins me, wins life, drinks deep
36 of the Lord's favour; who fails, fails at his own bitter cost; to be my
enemy is to be in love with death.

CHAPTER NINE

SEE, where wisdom has built herself a house, carved out for herself
2 those seven pillars of hers! And now, her sacrificial victims slain,
3 her wine mingled, her banquet spread, this way and that her maidens
are dispatched, to city keep and city wall, bidding her guests make
4 haste. Simple hearts, she says, draw near me; and to all that lack learning
5 this is her cry, Come and eat at my table, come and drink of the wine
6 I have brewed for you; say farewell to your childishness, and learn to
live; follow all of you in the path that leads to discernment.

---

[1] Some would give 'made me' as the right translation of the verb used in
the Hebrew text. But it is doubtful whether it really has this meaning in the
passages cited (*e.g.*, Gen. 14.19), and all through the book of Proverbs it is
regularly used in the sense of 'acquiring' wisdom.

[2] In the Hebrew text, 'the open spaces, or the beginnings of the world's dust.'

7   (Rash souls there are, godless souls, that will not be taught or trained;
who makes the attempt, gets only injury and abuse for his thanks.
8 With a rash fool never remonstrate; it will make him thy enemy; only
9 the wise are grateful for a remonstrance.   Ever the wise profit by the
opportunity to become wiser yet; ever the godly are the best learners.) [1]
10   True wisdom begins with the fear of the Lord; he best discerns,
11 who has knowledge of holy things.   Long life I bring thee, and a full
12 tale of years;   wisdom thyself shall profit, and misfortune fall only on
the rash fools that earned it.
13   Out upon her silly clamour, the woman that is so crafty, yet knowl-
14 edge has none!   At her door she sits, her chair commanding the city's
15 height,   and cries aloud to such as pass by on their lawful errands.
16 Simple hearts, she says, draw near me, and to all that lack learning
17 this is her cry,   Stolen waters are sweetest, and bread is better eating
18 when there is none to see.   Who shall warn them that dead men are
her company, no guest of hers but is guest of the dark world beneath?

CHAPTER TEN

Proverbs of Solomon.

A FATHER'S smile, a mother's tears, tell of a son well schooled
or ill.
2   No good ever came of money ill gotten; honest living is death's
3 avoiding.   Still the Lord gives honesty a full belly, and on the knave's
scheming shuts his door.
4   Idle hand, empty purse; riches come of hard work. (Who trusts in
false promises, throws his food to the winds; as well may he chase
5 bird in flight).[2]   Wilt thou gather in harvest time, a son well schooled?
Or sleep the summer round, to thy father's great shame?
6   Shines the Lord's favour on the just man's head; the sinner in his
7 violence must walk blindfold.   When blessings are given, the just
are remembered still; it is the sinner's name that rusts.
8   Warning the wise man hears; the fool talks on, and is ruined.
9   He walks secure, who walks pure; cunning will yet be found out.
10   It needs no more than a wink of the eye to bring trouble; what wonder

---

[1] *vv.* 7–9. There is some reason to suspect dislocation in the text here. These
verses do not fit naturally into the speech of Wisdom, who is making an
express appeal (verse 4) to the foolish.
[2] The second half of this verse is not found in the Hebrew text; the Septuagint
Greek gives it immediately after verse 12 of ch. 9.

11 if the fool who talks earns a beating? [1] The mouth, for the just man
12 a life-giving well, for the wicked an arsenal of harm. [2] Hatred is ever
13 ready to pick a quarrel; love passes over all kinds of offence. Never
wise man's lips but found the right word, or fool's back but felt the
14 rod. Wise men treasure up their knowledge; a fool's talk is ready
to mar all.
15 As the rich man's wealth is his stronghold, and the poor man's
16 need his peril, so the doings of the just evermore win fresh life, the
17 sinner's increase his guilt. Who lives by the lessons he has learned
finds life; the way is lost when warnings go unheeded.
18 Lying lips that hide malice, foolish lips that spread slander, what a
19 world of sin there is in talking! Where least is said, most prudence is.
20 Silver refined is the just man's every word, and trash the sinner's every
21 thought. The just man's talk plays the shepherd to many, while the fool
dies of his own starved heart.
22 Of the Lord's gift comes wealth without drudgery.
23 For the fool, it is but a pastime to make mischief; to act prudently
needs all a man's wisdom.
24 Not in vain the sinner fears, the just man hopes; vanished, like
the storm of yesterday, or secure eternally.
26 What irks a man more than vinegar on the tooth, or smoke in the
eyes? A lingering messenger.
27 If fear of the Lord brings life, few years shall the wicked have; die
29 their hopes must while honest folk wait on contentedly. The Lord's
judgements, what comfort they bring to the innocent, what terrors to
30 the evil-doer! An abiding home never the just lacked yet, or the guilty
31 found. A just man's talk breeds wisdom, while the sinner's tongue
32 dies barren; welcome ever the one, cross-grained the other.

CHAPTER ELEVEN

A FALSE balance the Lord hates; nothing but full weight will
content him.
2 Pride is neighbour to disesteem; humility to wisdom.
3 The innocence of the upright guides them safely; the treacherous
4 by their own plots are destroyed. When the time for reckoning comes,
5 little shall wealth avail; right living is death's avoiding. An honest
purpose clears a man's path; the wicked are entangled by their own

---

[1] *vv.* 8, 10. The second half of either verse is the same in the original.

[2] *vv.* 6, 11. In the Hebrew text, both verses end with the same formula, which
the Latin interprets in verse 6 'iniquity covers the mouth of the godless' and
in verse 11 'the mouth of the godless covers iniquity.'

6 scheming. For his honesty, the upright man shall go free; not so the
7 wrong-doer, caught in the meshes of his own net. No hope follows the
godless to the grave; nothing left, now, of all their anxious longing.
8 Honesty shall yet go free, and a knave be heir to its troubles. False
speech the hypocrite will use to ruin his neighbour; true knowledge is the
10 saving of the just. Thrive honest men, come ruin on knaves, there is
11 huzza'ing all through the city; how should a city stand or fall, but by
good words from the one, ill counsel from the other?

12 He mocks loud, who lacks wit; discernment holds her tongue. Who
bears ill tales, keeps no secrets; trust none with thy confidence but a loyal
friend.

14 Ill fares the people, that guidance has none; safety reigns where
counsel abounds.

15 He who goes bail for a stranger has great harm of it; that snare avoid,
and sleep sound.

16 Gracious ways may win a woman renown; man never grew rich
but by hardiness.[1]

17 A kindly man is the friend of his own well-being; cruelty will not
spare its own flesh and blood.

18 Precarious livelihood the godless man wins; wouldst thou be sure
19 of thy revenue, let honest doings be thy crop; mercy breeds life, evil
20 ambitions death. A false heart the Lord cannot endure; nothing but
21 honest dealing will content him. Depend upon it, the sinner shall
never be held guiltless; the race of the just shall find acquittal.

22 A woman fair and fond, a sow ringed with gold.

23 In the desires of the just only good dwells; frantic dreams are for
24 the wicked. One spares, and has more to spend, another grudges what
25 he owes, and is a poor man still; give and thou shalt thrive; he shall
26 have abundance, that bestows abundantly. Corn hoarded shall win thee
a curse, corn sold freely a blessing, from the lips of a whole people.
27 Plan thou good, thou canst not be afoot too early; plan thou evil, on
28 thy own head it shall recoil. Fall he must, that relies on riches; never
29 shall the just fade or fail. He shall feed on air, that misrules his own
household; the fool will be slave and the wise man master in the end.
30 Where right living bears its fruit, a tree of life grows up; the wise man's
31 reward is living souls.[2] Even honest men cannot go through the world
unpunished; what, then, of the godless, what, then, of the sinner?

---

[1] The word used in the Hebrew text means 'ruthlessness,' but is perhaps a
false reading for the very similar word meaning 'diligence' (cf. 10.4).

[2] In the second half of the verse, the text is possibly corrupt; as it stands,
it should mean either that the wise man takes other people's lives, or that he
receives the persons of others as his captives (Gen. 14.14,21). The exact sense
is not clear.

CHAPTER TWELVE

EVER the friend of admonition is the friend of knowledge; only fools are impatient of warning.

2   A kindly man wins the Lord's favour, a schemer is his enemy.
3   Wickedness shall never thrive; the just have roots immovable.
4   Crowned is his brow, who wins a vigorous wife; sooner let thy bones rot than marry one who shames thee.
5   Honourable thoughts the just conceive, the wicked are all double-
6   dealing; yet, when the accusations of the wicked lay a fatal snare,
7   the just shall find words to deliver them. A turn in their fortunes, and no more is heard of the wicked; only the just have abiding prosperity.
8   Good sense is the measure of a man's repute; fond fancies are ever despised.
9   Better be poor, and toil to support thyself, than play the great lord with an empty belly.
10   A just man cares for the safety of the beasts he owns; the wicked are heartless through and through.
11   Till field and fill belly; idle pursuits are but foolishness. (Sit long enjoying thy wine, and there is no strong fortress will win thee renown).[1]
12   In unholy ambitions the wicked put their trust, but it is honesty
13   that strikes deep root. Ruin comes upon the sinner for a word spoken
14   amiss, while honest men find acquittal. When a man is blessed, it is his own words that bear fruit; never son of Adam but had the lot his deeds deserved.
15   A fool is ever right to his own thinking; the wise listen to advice.
16   Fools betray anger on the instant, when prudence would pass the insult by.
17   Nothing but his honest thought a lover of truth declares, a false
18   witness nothing but lies. Rash promises can stab the heart with remorse;[2]
19   wise words bring healing. Lips that speak the truth shall fade never; a lie serves but the haste of the moment.
20   The schemer's thoughts dwell ever on treachery; for peace be all
21   thy plotting, if thou wouldst have a contented heart. Nothing can befall the just man to do him hurt; the wicked shall have their fill of mischief.

---

[1] The second half of this verse is found in the Septuagint Greek, but not in the Hebrew text.
[2] The meaning of the Hebrew text is perhaps rather, 'he who speaks rashly can wound like a sword.'

22   Lying lips the Lord cannot abide; keep faith if thou wouldst content him.

23   Prudence says less than it knows; the fool's heart cannot contain its folly.

24   Busy hands, hands that shall bear the sceptre; idle hands, hands that shall bring tribute.

25   A heart bowed down with anxiety, how a kind word can refresh it!

26   It is well done to put up with loss for a neighbour's need; the cal-
27 culations of the sinner do but lead him astray.   Never yet did cunning achieve the gains it hoped for; a contented heart is precious as fine
28 gold.[1]   Wouldst thou attain life, honesty is the high road; by-way there is none but leads to death.

CHAPTER THIRTEEN

B Y his father's teaching a son grows wise; only the headstrong will not listen to a warning.

2   Fair words yield a crop to content a man's heart; but not for the
3 treacherous; they have no stomach but for wrong-doing.   Guard thy tongue, guard thy soul; thoughtless speech may bring ruin.

4   Idleness will and will not, both at once; it is hard work that gives a full belly.

5   Honesty shuns the false word; the sinner disappointment gives and
6 gets.[2]   The upright heart is protected by its own innocence; guilt trips the heel of the wrong-doer.

7   Some are rich that nothing have; some with a well-lined purse are
8 yet poor.   A man's wealth may be his own life's ransom; yet will not the poor man be chidden for his poverty.[3]

9   Welcome the shining beams of a life well lived; the rush-light of the wicked glimmers and is gone.

10   Ever there is wrangling among the proud; wisdom's part is to be guided by other men's counsel.

11   Riches soon won are soon spent; the patient hoard breeds best.

12   Hope deferred, how it crushes a man's spirits! The granted wish, a tree of life-giving fruit!

---

[1] The Latin version here disagrees with the Hebrew text, which is obscure and perhaps corrupt.

[2] 'Disappointment gives and gets'; according to the Hebrew text, 'behaves vilely and shamefully.'

[3] The second half of this verse is difficult, and perhaps corrupt.

13   Neglect thy errand, whatever it be,[1] and thou art in default; carry out thy orders, and be at peace.

Faithless hearts wander far in their transgressions, but the just are ever pitying, ever merciful.

14   The teaching of the wise is a fountain where men may drink life
15   far removed from all mortal perils. Good instruction breeds gracious
16   thoughts; the headstrong are for the morass. For the prudent, skill guides every action; ignorance betrays the fool.

17   Who runs a sinner's errand, falls into mischief by the way; a faithful envoy mends all.

18   Comes want, comes shame from warnings unheeded; he achieves great things who will accept reproof.

19   A man ever loves his own way best; no wonder fools cannot abide
20   it when ill is averted. Wise company brings wisdom; fool he ends that fool befriends.

21   Calamity is hard on the heels of wickedness, and honest men shall
22   yet be rewarded. Son and grandson shall be the good man's heirs;
23   the sinner lays up wealth for nobler men; the rich harvest of those ancestral fields, lack he honest worth, shall be reaped for strangers.[2]

24   Spare the rod, and thou art no friend to thy son; ever a kind father is quick to punish.

25   The just man eats his fill; the godless craves and never has enough.

CHAPTER FOURTEEN

IT is by woman's wisdom a home thrives; a foolish wife pulls it down about her ears.

2   Does a man fear the Lord? He holds an even course; the knave has little regard for him.[3]

3   Pride burgeons from the lips of fools; in modesty of speech the wise find safety.

4   No need for a full crib, where oxen are none; yet ever rich harvest tells of the ox at work.

---

[1] 'Thy errand, whatever it be'; the sense of the Hebrew text is probably 'the word of command.'

[2] The Latin appears to connect this verse with the preceding one; the Hebrew text has 'There is much food in the fallow-lands of the poor, but there are some who are swept away, not by just judgement.'

[3] The sense of the Hebrew text is plain; the God-fearing are the right-living, the despisers of God are revealed by their treacherous conduct. The Latin version makes the whole verse into a single sentence, which says that the God-fearing and right-living man is despised by, or (possibly) despises, the treacherous.

5   It is a faithful witness that never lies; the perjurer breathes out lies continually.

6   Vainly the rash aspire to wisdom; the discerning come by their
7   knowledge with little pains. Go thy way, and let the fool go his; good
8   sense is a strange language to him. Prudence picks its way wisely; the
9   fool blunders and is lost. Fools make light of the guilt that needs atonement, and leave honest men to enjoy the Lord's favour.[1]

10 Heart's bitterness none may know but the heart that feels it; no prying stranger can tell when it finds relief.

11 Fall it must, the house of the wicked; where the upright dwell, all is increase.

12 The right road in a man's thinking may be one whose goal is death.
13 Joy blends with grief, and laughter marches with tears. The incorrigible shall have a taste of his own ill-doings, and honest men shall have the better of him.

15 The simpleton takes all on trust; wisdom considers each step. (A treacherous son no part shall have; better shall a wise servant thrive
16 and prosper).[2] Caution teaches the wise to shun danger; the fool is
17 carried away by rash confidence. The impatient man blunders, as
18 surely as the schemer makes enemies. Folly is the simpleton's heirloom; skill crowns the wise.

19 Vice lies prostrate before virtue, the sinner at the gates of the just.

20 Of the beggar, his own neighbours grow weary; wealth never lacks
21 friends. Shame on the man who holds his neighbour in contempt; mercy to the poor brings a blessing. (Mercy he loves, who puts his
22 trust in the Lord).[3] They follow a false path, that plot mischief; mercy and faithfulness mercy and faith shall find.

23 Hard work is sure wealth; of chattering comes only poverty.

24 Made rich, the wise are crowned, the folly of the thoughtless will be folly yet.

25 Men owe their lives to truthful witnesses; the very breath of the perjurer is treason.

26 The fear of the Lord gives strong confidence, bequeaths hope from the
27 father to the children. The fear of the Lord is a fountain where men may drink life, far removed from all mortal peril.[4]

28 Great people, great king; it is for want of men crowns are lost.

---

[1] The first half of this verse is obscure in the Hebrew text. 'The Lord's favour'; literally, 'favour'; if the two halves of the verse are to be parallel, divine favour must be meant.

[2] The words enclosed in brackets do not appear in the Hebrew text; they occur in the Septuagint Greek after verse 13 of the foregoing chapter.

[3] The words printed in brackets are peculiar to the Latin.

[4] Cf. 13.14 above.

29 Patience comes of sovereign prudence, impatience of unchecked
30 folly. Peace of mind is health of body; more than all else, envy wastes
the frame.
31 He who oppresses the poor, insults man's Maker; him if thou wouldst
honour, take pity on human need.
32 When the wicked is paid in his own coin, there is an end of him;
at death's door, the just still hope.
33 In the discerning heart, wisdom finds a resting-place; even among
fools it can impart learning.[1]
34 Duty well done, a whole nation becomes great; suffer whole peoples
for guilt incurred.
35 A king shews favour to a wise servant; disappoint him, and thou
shalt feel his anger.

CHAPTER FIFTEEN

A GENTLE answer is a quarrel averted; a word that gives pain
2 does but fan the flame of resentment. The speech of the wise is
3 learning's ornament; the fool babbles on. Go where thou wilt, the Lord's
4 eye is watching; good nor evil escapes his scrutiny. Tongue that speaks
peaceably is a tree whose fruit gives life; tongue undisciplined can break
hearts.
5 He is a fool that makes light of his father's warnings; would he but
listen to reproof, he should be prudent yet.
(Might is most where right is most; root and branch the sinner
6 shall be plucked up.) [2] The just man's home guards its treasure well;
the hopes of the wicked are all confusion.
7 The talk of the wise is a seed-ground of learning; the thoughts of
fools are ill matched with it.
8 From the wicked man's sacrifice the Lord turns away with loathing;
9 only the just with their vows win his favour. The whole course of the
sinner's life he cannot brook; pursue the right, if thou wouldst win
10 his love. Forsake the right path, and correction shall seem hard to
11 thee; grow weary of reproof, and thy life shall pay for it. Shall the
Lord read the secrets of the devouring grave, and not men's hearts?
12 Warn the headstrong, and thou wilt get no thanks for it; not for him
the company of the wise.

---

[1] In the second half of the verse, the Hebrew text appears to mean, 'and
in the inmost being of fools it makes itself known'; it is perhaps corrupt. The
Latin version runs 'and it will instruct all fools,' probably a copyist's error for
'And it will instruct even fools.'

[2] The words enclosed in brackets occur in the Septuagint Greek, but not
in the Hebrew text.

13 Gay heart, gay looks; sad thoughts crush the spirit.
14 Truth is the quest of discerning minds, trifling the pasture-ground of the foolish.
15 To the friendless, every day brings trouble, but every day is a feast-
16 day to a contented heart. Better a humble lot, and the fear of the Lord
17 present, than great riches that leave a man unsatisfied. Better sit down to a dish of herbs seasoned with charity, than feast on a fattened ox in ill will.
18 Any brawler can provoke a quarrel; it needs a patient man to lay it by.
19 Idleness finds ever a hedge of thorns in its path; the man of duty walks on unhampered.
20 A father well content, a mother slighted, tell of a son's wisdom or mortal folly.
21 A man of little sense is in love with his follies; prudence keeps to
22 its chosen path. Counsel lacking, all designs go amiss; with the advice
23 of many, they should have thriven. There are times when a counsellor has good cause to be proud; nothing better than the right word spoken.
24 A mind well schooled sees the way of life stretching upwards, leading away from the pit beneath.
25 A house where pride reigns the Lord will pull down at last; will
26 have no encroaching on the lands of the friendless widow. The schemes of wickedness he abhors; the dreams of innocence he loves, and brings
27 true.[1] Let avarice lead thee away, thy home shall be ruined; long life is his, who scorns the bribe. (Kindness and honour are sin's purging; ever it is the fear of the Lord turns men away from harm).[2]
28 Attentive and docile is the upright heart; from the lips of the wicked
29 comes mischief in full flood. From the wicked, the Lord withholds his presence, listens only to the prayer of the just.
30 The dawn of hope, how it cheers the heart! Good news, how it lends vigour to a man's frame!
31 A man's ear once attentive to the discipline that brings life, no com-
32 pany shall be welcome thenceforward, but the wise. He holds his life cheap, that will not listen to a warning; heed reproof, and be master
33 of thy soul. It is the fear of the Lord teaches the lessons of wisdom; humility goes first, and honour comes in her train.

---

[1] The second half of this verse reads, in the Hebrew text, 'but pleasant words are pure'; it is not certain in what sense.
[2] The Latin version gives the second maxim twice over (see 16.6 below).

CHAPTER SIXTEEN

MAN'S heart is ever full of devising; from the Lord comes the
2 ordering of right speech.[1] His own path man scans, and nothing
3 sees amiss, but the divine balance weighs our thoughts; share with the
Lord the burden of all thy doings, if thou wouldst be sincere in thy
intent.
4   God, who made all, made all for his own purposes, even the godless
man, with doom awaiting him.
5   A proud man the Lord holds in abhorrence; depend upon it, no
acquittal shall he find. (To do right, that is the first step on the way
of blessedness, a more welcome thing in God's sight than any sacrifice
6 a man can offer).[2] Kindness and honour are sin's purging; ever it is the
7 fear of the Lord turns men away from harm. Live as the Lord would
have thee live, and he will make even thy enemies into well-wishers.
8   Better a penny honestly come by than great revenues ill gotten.
9   Heart of man must plan his course, but his steps will fall as the
Lord guides them.
10   Speaks king, speaks oracle; never a word amiss. Scale and balance
are emblems of the Lord's own justice; no weight in the merchant's
12 wallet but is of divine fashioning. Wrong-doing the king will not
13 abide; on right his own throne rests. Kings are for honest talk; free-
14 spoken is well loved. The king's frown is death at thy door; wisdom
15 will appease it; his smile is life; not more welcome the spring rains,
than royal favour.
16   Not of gold or silver be thy hoard; make wisdom thine, discernment
thine, more precious than these.
17   The just man travels by the high road, safe from harm, watching
his path anxiously, as he values his life.
18   Presumption comes first, and ruin close behind it; pride ever goes
19 before a fall. Better a humble lot among peaceful folk, than all the
spoil a tyrant's friendship can bring thee.
20   Well versed in doctrine, happiness thou shalt win; trust in the Lord,
21 and find a blessing. Good judgement a wise heart can claim; winning
22 words bring greater prizes yet. The prudent man drinks from a living
23 fountain; fools only learn the lessons of their folly. Wisdom distils
24 from heart to mouth, and lends the lips persuasion. Honey itself

---

[1] The bearing of this maxim is uncertain.
[2] The second half of this verse is found in the Septuagint Greek, but not
in the Hebrew text.

cannot vie with well-framed words, for heart's comfort and body's
25 refreshment. The right road in a man's thinking may be one whose
goal is death.

26   No better friend drudgery has than appetite; hunger drives a man to
his task.

27   Ever the godless man digs a well of mischief, ever his lips are aflame.

28 His the scheming that breeds quarrels, the whispering that divides his

29 clan, the love of wrong that misleads his neighbours and carries them off

30 into evil ways; spell-bound with dreams of treachery, he shuts his lips
tight and goes about his false errand.[1]

31   No prize so honourable as old age, and it is won by innocence of life.

32   Patience is worth more than valour; better a disciplined heart than
a stormed city.

33   Into the lap's fold the lot falls hap-hazard, but the Lord rules the
issue.

CHAPTER SEVENTEEN

BETTER dry crust and gay heart, than a house where all is feasting
and all is quarrelling.

2   Where sons are fools, slaves will be masters, and share the inheritance
like heirs born.

3   For silver and gold, furnace and crucible; men's hearts are for the
Lord's assaying.

4   Ever ill will gives heed to injurious talk, false faith listens to the
slander.

5   He who shews contempt to the poor, insults man's Maker; at thy
own peril thou wilt take delight in another's ruin.

6   Crown of old age, when a man sees his children's children; pride of
youth, when a man can boast of the fathers that begot him.

7   Solemn talk matches ill with folly, lying speech with royalty.

8   When a man has hope in view, like a jewel it shines before him; look
where he will, his way lies clear.[2]

9   If good will be thy quest, hide the wrong done; gossip unknits the
bond of friendship.

10   One word of warning in a prudent man's ear does more than a

11 hundred lashes given to a fool. Still the godless man will be for stirring

---

[1] In the first half of this verse, the Hebrew text is usually understood to
mean 'He plots treachery with a wink of the eye.'

[2] The sense of the Hebrew text seems to be, 'A bribe is a talisman for him
who owns it; wherever he turns, he prospers.'

12 up strife, till at last an angel visits him with no kindly message. Better
meet the she-bear reft of her cubs, than a fool in his blind confidence.
13   Evil shall still haunt his dwelling, that repays kindness with injury.
14   Who began the quarrel? He who let loose the flood-gates of it; and
before he can suffer injury, he stands aside from the debate.[1]
15   Misjudgement the Lord will never abide, whether the guilty go free,
or the innocent are condemned.
16   Little the fool's wealth avails; he may not buy wisdom if he would.
(Build high, and court thy ruin; despise learning, and thou shalt come
to mischief).[2]
17   He is thy friend, who is thy friend at all times; of a brother's love
there is no test like adversity.
18   He is a fool, that lightly goes bail for his friend.
19   He loves a feud, that loves contention; build high, and court thy
20 ruin.   False heart never found happiness, nor lying tongue escaped
mischief.
21   A fool's birthday is a day of shame; never father had joy of a reckless
son.
22   A cheerful heart makes a quick recovery; it is crushed spirits that
waste a man's frame.
23   Out comes bribe from bosom, and the godless man turns justice
aside from its course.
24   Wisdom is a beacon-light to the discerning; the fool's eyes roam this
. 25 way and that, as wide as earth.   Poor fool, his father's bane, sorrow of the
mother that bore him!
26   Foul shame it is to make the innocent suffer, to strike a blow against
the chieftain that gives redress.
27   Skilful is he who has skill to check his tongue; learned he is that
28 knows how to spare his breath.   Let him keep his own counsel, a fool
may pass for a wise man; shut lips can claim discernment.

CHAPTER EIGHTEEN

NONE so quick to find pretexts,[3] as he that would break with a
friend; he is in fault continually.
2   For prudent warnings a fool has no stomach; nothing will serve but
to echo his own thought.

---

[1] The Hebrew text is commonly interpreted as meaning, 'The beginning
of a quarrel is as when a man opens a sluice; let it alone, before trouble
breaks out.'
[2] The second part of this verse is found in the Septuagint Greek, but not
in the Hebrew text.
[3] 'Quick to find pretexts'; in the Hebrew text, 'selfish.'

3   Little the godless man recks of it, when he falls into sin's mire, but shame and reproach go with him.

4   Man's utterance has currents like the waters that run deep; from wisdom's well flows a stream in full flood.[1]

5   Foul shame it is to court favour with the wrong-doer by turning justice aside from its course.

6   A fool's talk is for ever embroiling him; let him but open his mouth,
7   blows will follow. From his own words his undoing comes, from his own
8   lips the snare. Innocent enough seem the words of the back-biter, yet their poison sinks deep into a man's belly.

      (Slow natures every fear disarms; womanish souls shall go hungry.)[2]

9   Dainty and listless go to work, thou art own brother to that work's undoer.

10   No stronghold like the Lord's name; there the just take refuge, high
11   above reach. What citadel has the rich man? His own possessions; he
12   seems shut in by a wall impregnable; yet hearts are proudest when ruin is nearest; humility is the ante-chamber of renown.

13   Let a man hear the tale out before he answer, or he is a fool manifest, marked out for shame.

14   All mortal ills the spirit of man can bear; if the spirit itself be impatient, there is no lightening his lot.

15   Prize of the discerning heart, quest of the wise man's ear, is to learn truth.

16   The gift made, how it opens a man's path for him, wins him access to the great!

17   An innocent man is the first to lay bare the truth; let his neighbour come and search him as he will.[3]

18   The lot brings feuds to an end; greatness itself must bow to the lot's decision.

19   When brother helps brother, theirs is the strength of a fortress; their cause is like a city gate barred, unassailable.[4]

20   As mouth speaks, belly shall find its fare; a man's own words bear

---

[1] The sense and the bearing of this maxim are open to dispute.

[2] The words printed in brackets are found in the Septuagint Greek, but not in the Hebrew text.

[3] Literally, 'A just man is the first to accuse himself'; but this can hardly mean that he confesses his guilt, since there would be no need, in that case, for investigation by his neighbours. The sense will be rather that he makes admissions which at first sight tell against his innocence. The Hebrew text is obscure; with some difficulty, it is interpreted as meaning, 'He who speaks first is always (apparently) in the right.'

[4] The Hebrew text here is usually rendered, 'A brother trespassed (against) is (harder to win over) than a strong city; (such) contentions are like the bars of a fortress.'

21 the fruit that must needs content him. Of life and death, tongue holds the keys; use it lovingly,[1] and it will requite thee.

22 A good wife found is treasure found; the Lord is filling thy cup with happiness. (A good wife cast away is treasure cast away; leave to fools, and godless fools, the adulterous embrace).[2]

23 Poor men must cringe, for the rich to rate them.

24 A man endeared to thee by fellowship will prove a better friend to thee than thy own kin.[3]

CHAPTER NINETEEN

BETTER the poverty which keeps to honest ways, than the lot of a
2 rich man who never learned to speak truth.[4] Lack learning, all is not
3 well within; ever the hasty stumble. Tripped by his own folly, a man eats his heart out, finding fault with the Lord.

4 Riches will make thee new friends a many, poverty rob thee of the old.

5 Perjury will bring its own punishment; never was liar yet that escaped his doom.

6 Suitors a many the princely heart shall have; give, and thou shalt
7 find friends. The beggar wearies out his kinsmen; his friends, too, will shun him.

8 Who hunts idle talk, comes home empty-handed; as thou lovest thy life get wisdom; discernment at thy side, thou shalt speed well.

9 Perjury will bring its own punishment; never was liar but met his doom.

10 Ill days, when fools live in comfort; worse yet, when servants sway their own masters.

11 Patience is wisdom's livery; there is no such boast as a wrong overlooked.

12 Of the king's frown beware, as of lion roaring; welcome as dew on the grass his smile.

13 Great hurt it is to be a fool's father; he has a roof that drips un-
14 endingly, who is husband to a scold. House and hoard a man may inherit; it is the Lord's gift only, if he have a wife that minds her ways.

15 Sloth brings the sleep that has no awaking; idle hands, empty belly.

---

[1] 'Lovingly' is usually interpreted as meaning 'lavishly,' but 'with due reverence' may be meant.

[2] The second part of this verse is found in the Septuagint Greek, but not in the Hebrew text.

[3] This verse is very obscure, and perhaps corrupt; some infer from the Hebrew text a contrast between fair weather and genuine friends.

[4] The word 'rich' does not occur in the Hebrew text.

16   Law observed is life preserved; the careless step leads the way to death.

17   Befriend the poor, and lend to the Lord; he will repay faithfully.

18   Chasten thy son still, nor despair of his amendment; reconcile thyself never to his loss.

19   He injures himself, that is ungovernable in rage; every advantage
20   he takes does but injure him the more.[1]   Give heed to counsel, accept
21   correction, and thou shalt be wise at last.   Thought jostles thought in man's heart; the Lord's will stands firm.

22   Poverty is the school of piety; better need than knavery.   Fear of the Lord leads on to life, life where all is contentment, and no ill may come.

24   With folded hands the sluggard sits by, and never puts hand to mouth.[2]

25   The lash for the reckless, if thou wouldst turn a fool into a wise man; only cool heads will profit by a rebuke.

26   Shame on the wretch that brings ruin on his own father, drives his own mother out of doors.

27   Never weary, my son, of giving heed to warnings; never let the counsels of experience pass thee by.[3]

28   Out on the faithless witness that scorns right; the sinful souls that
29   are ever greedy for wrong-doing!   There is a doom awaits the reckless; there are thick cudgels ready for the fool's back.

CHAPTER TWENTY

A RECKLESS counsellor is wine, strong drink a riotous friend; the
2   man who is swayed by these, call not wise.   Beware of the king's
3   power, as of lion roaring; challenge it, and thy life is forfeit.   Well may he boast, that keeps clear of strife; every fool will be quarrelling.

4   Too cold to plough, says Sloth; vainly, when harvest comes, he will go a-begging.

5   Prudent counsel is a well buried deep in man's heart; but the wise
6   know how to draw from it.   Many there are that pass for kindly souls,
7   but a faithful friend is hard to come by.   An upright man that goes
8   armed with honest intent, leaves a blessing to his children.   Let a

---

[1] This verse, in the Hebrew text, is of very disputable interpretation. The same is true of verse 22.

[2] According to the Latin version, the sluggard hides his hands under his arm-pits; according to the Hebrew text, he buries them in the dish that lies in front of him.

[3] The Hebrew text here lacks the negative, and yields no good sense as it stands.

king rule justly, wrong-doing shall be winnowed away under his scrutiny.

9   Who dares to boast, My heart is unsullied now, I have cleansed myself of every fault?

10   One balance for getting and one for giving, one yard-wand for selling and one for buying, the Lord will not endure.

11   Watch a boy even at his play, thou canst tell whether his heart is
12   pure and true. The ear that listens, the watchful eye, are both of the Lord's fashioning.

13   Love not thy sleep, or poverty will overtake thee unawares; the open eye means a full belly.

14   A poor thing, says the buyer, a poor thing! Then off he goes, and boasts of it.

15   Gold thou mayst have in abundance, and jewels a many, but the finest ware of all is wise speech.

16   Does a man go bail for a stranger? Without more ado, take his garment from him; who trusts without knowledge, forfeits the pledge.

17   Ill-gotten wealth is bread most appetizing, that will yet turn to grit in the mouth.

18   Counsel is the sure buttress of determination; wars must ever be won by statecraft.

19   With the whisperer, that goes about open-mouthed on his errand of gossip, never throw in thy lot.

20   In deepest night the lamp of his hopes shall be quenched, that turns
21   upon father or mother with a curse. The inheritance too soon come
22   by, too late thou shalt find unblessed. Never promise thyself vengeance;
23   await the Lord's hour, and redress shall be thine. One weight for getting and one for giving, the Lord cannot endure; a false balance is
24   great wrong. Every step man takes is of the Lord's choosing; and thou, poor mortal, wouldst thou plot out thy path?

25   Some, to their ruin, invoke [1] the Holy Ones with vows they afterwards repent.

26   Fan and flail a wise king has for the ill-doer.

27   Man's spirit is a lamp the Lord gives, to search out the hidden corners of his being.

28   What is a king's best body-guard? Mercy and faithfulness; on mercy his throne rests.

29   Youth has strong arms to boast of, old age white hairs for a crown.

30   Hurts that bruise cruelly, chastisement felt deep within, are sin's best remedy.

---

[1] Our present text of the Vulgate, probably through a copyist's error, has 'devour.' There is no reference in the Hebrew text to the invoking of angels, but cf. Job. 5.1.

CHAPTER TWENTY-ONE

THE thoughts of a king are in the Lord's hand, streams he can sluice
2   which way he wills. His own path man scans, and nothing sees amiss,
3 but the divine balance weighs our thoughts. Mercy shewn and justice
4 done win the Lord's favour beyond any sacrifice. Lordly looks, proud
   heart; the hopes [1] of the wicked are all at fault.
5   Ever diligence plans for plenty; sloth must be content to starve.
6   Illusion it is and madness, wealth to win by perjury; death has caught
7 thee in his snare. Wicked men, that refuse the right, by their own
8 violence come to ruin. Crooked is man's course, and belies his own
   nature, but pure souls there are whose life runs true.
9   Better lodge in a garret than share thy house with a scold.
10   A godless man has set his heart on ill-doing; no ruth has he for
11 his fellows. The lash for the reckless, if thou wouldst turn a fool into
12 a wise man; a wise master, and he shall learn yet. Good heed the just
   man gives to the sinner's household, in hope of diverting sinners from
   harm.[2]
13   Who shuts his ear to the poor man's plea, himself one day shall
   plead in vain.
14   Carry a secret gift in thy bosom for thy enemy's appeasing; the
   open hand no grudge will ever resist.
15   Right done, honest folk rejoice, and knaves tremble.
16   Stray from the path thou wast taught, and thou shalt lodge with the
   dead.
17   Of greed comes want; he grows not rich that loves wine and roast.
18   The wicked is still the price of the just man's ransom; for honest
   folk, treachery pays the score.[3]
19   Better dwell in a wilderness than with a scold who rails at thee.
20   Precious store there is and good cheer where justice dwells; [4] the
   fool devours all at once.

---

[1] Literally, 'the lamp,' or (according to the Hebrew text) 'the untilled
ground.' The sense is doubtful; nor is it clear whether 'at fault' refers to sinful actions or has its literal sense of missing a mark.

[2] There is no agreement as to the meaning of this verse; the Hebrew text
has 'drag down to' instead of 'divert from,' and some think that 'the Just' refers
not to a just man but to Almighty God.

[3] Some think this means that in periods of general calamity the wicked suffer,
while the just go free; but even so the phrasing of the verse would be obscure.

[4] The Hebrew text has 'wisdom' instead of 'justice,' and the reference is
presumably to material (not spiritual) blessings, which the fool squanders
and the wise man saves up.

21 Honest living be thy quest and kindly deeds, life shall be thine,
22 and blessing, and honour. Wisdom can scale the fortress great warriors
23 hold, and bring low its boasted strength. Guard lips and tongue, as
24 thou wouldst guard thy life from peril. I know one, Sir Reckless is
the name of him, that is all proud airs, and does nothing but in a great
taking of scorn.

25 Day-dreams are the sluggard's downfall; work his hands will not; all
day long dreaming and scheming, while honest men never spare themselves, nor take their ease.

27 Tainted is the sinner's sacrifice; the hand that offers it is stained
28 with guilt. The false witness shall meet his doom; obey the com-
29 mandment, and thy pleadings shall triumph. The ill-doer has eyes
for nothing but his wanton designs; the upright scans well his path.

30 Wisdom is none, prudence is none, counsel is none that can be
31 matched against the Lord's will; well armed thy horse may be on
the eve of battle, but the Lord sends victory.

CHAPTER TWENTY-TWO

PRECIOUS beyond all treasure is good repute; not gold or silver is so
2   worth the winning, as to be loved. Rich and poor dwell ever side by
side, God's creatures both of them.

3   When ill times come, prudence is on its guard, and takes refuge;
the unwary march on, and pay the penalty.

4   Humility brings fear of the Lord, and therewith riches, honour
and long life.

5   Stake and caltrop beset the path of the wicked; as thou lovest life,
keep thy distance.

6   There is a proverb, Youth will be served; and when a man has grown
old, he will have his own way still.[1]

7   Rich rules poor, debtor must wait on creditor.

8   Who sows mischief, reaps a sorry crop; ere long, the flail of his
9 tyranny will have done its work.[2] For every loaf of bread given to the
hungry, blessing shall be the reward of kindly hearts. (A renowned
victory he wins, that is a bestower of gifts, and living men are the
spoils of it.) [3]

---

[1] The sense of the Hebrew text is different: 'Train a boy in the way that
is best for him, and when he is old he will not leave it.'
[2] In the second half of this verse, the Latin (not the Hebrew) would allow
us to translate, 'he will be brought to an end by the flail of his own violence.'
[3] The sentence in brackets is found in the Septuagint Greek, but not in the
Hebrew text. The sense of its second half is uncertain, but cf. Gen. 14.21.

10   Banish the reckless spirit, and strife goes out with him; thou art
rid of quarrelling and of disgrace.

11   Love purity of heart, and thou shalt find such gracious words as shall
12   win thee a king's friendship. True knowledge has the Lord's smile for
its protection; the schemer's cause he will overthrow.

13   Out? says Sloth; why, there is a lion without; wouldst thou have
me slain in the open street?

14   Like a deep pit is the flattery of wanton wife; they only are ensnared,
whom the Lord loves little.

15   Boyhood's mind is loaded with a pack of folly, that needs the rod
of correction to shift it.

16   Oppress the poor for thy enrichment, and ere long a richer man's
claim shall impoverish thee.[1]

17   Wouldst thou but give heed, and listen to wise counsels, take these
18   my warnings to heart! Digest them well, and they shall bring back a
19   sweet taste to thy lips; to fill thy own heart too with confidence in the
20   Lord, is the sum of my present teaching. Not once nor twice have
21   I warned thee and instructed thee, so as to ground thee in true doctrine,
and send thee home supplied with ready answers concerning it.

22   Never oppress the poor; his poverty protects him; never bear hard on
23   the friendless at law; be sure the Lord will grant them redress, and
24   claim life for life. Never let a quarreller, a man of angry moods, be thy
25   friend; go thy way, and let him go his; ill habits are soon learned, to the
26   sudden peril of thy life. Leave it to others to engage themselves, and go
27   bail for their neighbour's debts; for thyself, thou hast no means of pay-
28   ment; wouldst thou see the clothes stripped from thy bed? Pass not
29   beyond the ancient bounds which thy fathers have set. Mark me the man
whose task is deftly done; he is for the court, no common service shall
be his.

CHAPTER TWENTY-THREE

WHEN thou art sitting at table with a prince, mark well what is set
2   before thee, and, have thou thy appetite under control, guard as
3   with a drawn knife thy gullet. Hanker thou never after those good things
of his; they are bait to lure thee.[2]

---

[1] The Latin version here gives the most intelligible account of a maxim
whose meaning has been much disputed.

[2] At first sight, this passage suggests the danger of poisoning; but since no
such occurrences are mentioned in the Old Testament, we should perhaps
understand that the prince is trying to extort some advantage out of his guest
by taking him off his guard.

4   Do not be at pains to amass riches; let thy scheming [1] have its bounds.
5   Never let thy eyes soar to the wealth that is beyond thy reach, eagle-
winged against thy pursuit.
6   Shun the niggard's table; not for thee his dainties. Abstracted he
sits, like soothsayer brooding over false dreams; Eat and drink, he
8 tells thee, but his mind is far away. For that grudged food thou wilt
have no stomach; all gracious speech will die away on thy tongue. [2]
9   Speak not with fools for thy hearers; of thy warning utterance they
will reck nothing.
10   Leave undisturbed the landmarks of friendless folk, nor encroach
11 on the orphan's patrimony; a strong Champion they have, to grant
them redress.
12   Still let thy heart be attentive to warnings, open be thy ear to words
13 of instruction. Nor ever from child of thine withhold chastisement;
14 he will not die under the rod; rather, the rod thou wieldest shall baulk
15 the grave of its prey. Wise heart of thine, my son, is glad heart of
16 mine; speak thou aright, all my being thrills. Do not envy sinners
18 their good fortune, but abide in the fear of the Lord continually; the
future holds blessings for thee, never shall that hope play thee false.
19   Listen, then, my son, and shew thyself wise, keeping still an even
20 course. Be not of their company, that drink deep and pile the dishes
21 high at their revels; ruined they shall be, sot and trencherman, and
wake from their drunken sleep to find themselves dressed in rags.
22 Thine to obey the father who begot thee, nor leave thy mother without
23 reverence in her gray hairs; truth to covet, hold wisdom, and self-
24 command, and discernment for treasured heirlooms. Joy there is and
pride in an upright man's begetting for the glad father of a wise son;
25 such joy let thy father have, such pride be hers, the mother who bore
thee!
26   My son, give me the gift of thy heart, scan closely the path I shew
27 thee. What pit so deep as the harlot's greed, what snare holds so close
28 as wanton wife? Like a footpad she lurks beside the way, a deadly
peril to all that forget their troth.
29   Unhappy son of an unhappy father, who is this, ever brawling, ever
30 falling, scarred but not from battle, blood-shot of eye? Who but the
31 tosspot that sits long over his wine? Look not at the wine's tawny
glow, sparkling there in the glass beside thee; how insinuating its address!
32 Yet at last adder bites not so fatally, poison it distils like the basilisk's
33 own. Eyes that stray to forbidden charms, a mind uttering thoughts that

---

[1] Literally 'prudence.'
[2] *vv.* 6–8. The language of this passage is strained throughout, and it is hard
to feel certain that we have found the right clue to its meaning.

34 are none of thine, shall make thee helpless as mariner asleep in mid ocean,
35 when the tiller drops from the helmsman's drowsy grasp. What! thou
wilt say, blows all unfelt, wounds that left no sting! Could I but come to
myself, and be back, even now, at my wine!

CHAPTER TWENTY-FOUR

2 NOT for thee to emulate wrong-doers, and aspire to be of their company; what minds are theirs, who think only of men's undoing,
what talk, whose every word is treachery!

3   No foundation for a house like wisdom, no buttress like discernment;
4 no furnishing may be found for the rooms of it so rare and so pleasant,
5 as true knowledge. Only the wise are strong; well taught is firm of
6 sinew. War must be planned first, before thou wage it, and he will
7 prosper best who most takes counsel; wisdom hangs high beyond the
fool's reach; tongue-tied he stands when there are consultations at
the gate.[1]

8   Consecrate close thought to evil ends, and thou wilt earn no better
9 name than mischief-maker. Craft of his own the fool has, but all used
amiss; the insidious rogue [2] no man can stomach.

10   What, hang thy hands down in time of peril? Little shalt thou avail.
11 Thine to rescue the doomed, to cheat the gallows of its prey; not
plead thy lack of strength, when he, the Searcher of all hearts, the
Saviour of thy life, knows all, sees all, and requites the actions of men.

13   Sweet to thy palate, my son, is honey from the comb; why then, eat;
14 but wise teaching is no less thy soul's food, to-morrow's resource, and a
resource unfailing.

15   Lie not in wait, treacherously, to despoil the homes where honest
16 men take their ease; seven times the just may stumble, and rise to
17 their feet again, it is the wicked fall headlong into ruin. Not thine to
triumph over a fallen foe; that thrill of rejoicing in thy heart over his
18 calamity the Lord will see, and little love; his vengeance may yet change
19 its course. Do not be impatient when the wicked thrive, do not envy the
20 lot of evil-doers; villainy has no hope in store, its light flickers and is
gone.

21   Fear God, my son, and fear the king; have nothing to do with mal-
22 contents. How sudden their ruin, how swift falls, from either hand,
the blow!

23   More maxims of the wise. It is ill done, to let partiality sway thy

---

[1] The meaning of the Hebrew text here is doubtful.
[2] 'The insidious rogue'; literally, 'the calumniator.' The word used in the
Hebrew text commonly implies rash folly, and is here inappropriate.

24 judgement; if thou acquit the guilty, what race will have a good word
25 for thee, what people will love thee? Condemn him, and thou shalt
have renown, blessings shall fall on thy head.
26   The right word spoken seals all like a kiss on the lips.[1]
27   Be thy first care what lies without; till thy lands first with all diligence;
then build up thy home.
28   Do not come forward as a witness against thy neighbour; wouldst
29 thou spread lying tales? Nor be content to say, I am but serving him
as he served me; I pay off old scores.
30   Passing by field or vineyard where idleness reigned and improvidence,
31 what sights I have seen! Nettles were everywhere, briers had covered
32 the ground, the stone wall was ruinous. That sight I took to heart,
33 found a warning in that ill example. Sleep on (thought I) a little longer,
34 yawn a little longer, a little longer pillow head on hand; ay, but poverty
will not wait, the day of distress will not wait; like an armed vagabond
it will fall upon thee! [2]

CHAPTER TWENTY-FIVE

HERE are more of Solomon's proverbs, copied out by Ezechias'
men, that was king of Juda.
2   For mysteries unfathomable, praise God; for mysteries revealed, the
3 king. High as heaven thou must look, deep as earth, ere the mind of kings
4 shall be made known to thee. Rid silver of dross, and the cup shines
5 bright; rid the court of knaves, and the throne stands firm. Never play
7 the great lord at court, and mingle with men of rank; who would not
rather be beckoned to a higher place, than be put to the blush, and in the
king's presence? [3]
8   When men go to law, do not disclose hastily what thy eyes have witnessed; [4] it may be thou hast tainted a friend's name, and there is no un-
9 doing the mischief. To thy friend's private ear open thy wrongs; vent the
10 secret abroad, and he, hearing it, will turn on thee with reproaches, nor
wilt thou lightly recover thy good name. (Favour and friendship are thy
protection; to lose them is a foul blot.) [5]

---

[1] The phrase, in the original, runs simply 'Who returns right words kisses
lips'; the exact bearing of it can only be conjectured.
[2] *vv.* 33, 34. See 6.10,11 above.
[3] Lk. 14.8–10.
[4] 'What thy eyes have witnessed'; some interpreters of the Hebrew text
would connect the words so rendered with the preceding sentence.
[5] The words enclosed in brackets are found in the Septuagint Greek, but not
in the Hebrew text.

11 Like a boss of gold amid silver tracery it shines out, the right word
12 spoken. Golden ear-ring nor pearl drop fits so well, as wise reproof
13 given to a wise listener. Find a trusty messenger; not snow in harvest-
14 time will bring thee more relief. Storm-wrack and cloud and no rain
to follow; such thanks he wins that boasts much, and nothing
accomplishes.

15 A prince, in his forbearance,[1] may yet be won over to thy cause;
hard heart gives place to soft tongue.

16 Honey if thou find, eat thy fill and no more; nothing comes of surfeit
17 but vomiting. Rare be thy visits to a neighbour; he will soon have
enough, and weary of thee.

18 What is worse than javelin, sword, and arrow all at once? One that
19 bears false witness against his neighbour. What is more frail than
rotting tooth, or sprained foot? A false friend trusted in the hour of
20 need; as well lose thy cloak in mid winter. Vinegar goes ill with natron,
and song with a discontented heart. (Moth cannot fret garment, or
worm wood, as care the heart).

21 Hungers thy enemy? Here is thy chance; feed him. Thirsts he?
22 Of thy well let him drink. So doing, thou wilt heap burning coals
upon his head, and for thyself, the Lord will recompense thee.[2]

23 The north wind stops rain, and a frown the backbiter.

24 Better lodge in a garret than share thy house with a scold.[3]

25 Good news from a far land, refreshing as cold water to parched lips.

26 Fouled the spring, poisoned the well, when honest men bow down
before knaves.

27 A surfeit harms, though it be of honey; search too high, and the
28 brightness shall dazzle thee.[4] Like a city unwalled he lies defenceless,
that cannot master himself, but ever speaks his mind.

CHAPTER TWENTY-SIX

AS well snow in summer or rain in harvest, as honour paid to a fool.
2 Light as a bird of passage, light as sparrow on the wing, the curse
that is undeserved shall reach thee.

3 Whip for horse, bridle for ass, and never a rod for the fool's back?

---

[1] Some would render 'through thy forbearance,' but we should hardly expect
a subject's attitude towards his prince to be so described.

[2] *vv.* 21, 22. See Rom. 12.20 and note there.

[3] Repeated from 21.9 above.

[4] The second half of this verse has given rise to much conjecture. It runs,
literally, in the Hebrew, 'and the searching out of their glory, glory.' The
rendering given above is that presumably intended by the Latin, but it is difficult to derive this or any meaning from the Hebrew text as it stands.

4   Leave the fool's challenge unanswered, and prove thyself wise; or
answer it, if thou wilt, and prove him fool.
6   Send a fool on thy errand, thou hast a lame journey, and mischief
7 brewing for thee. Give a fool leave to speak, it is all fair legs and no
8 walking. Pay a fool reverence, thou hast wasted one more stone on
9 Mercury's cairn. Speech fits as well in a fool's mouth as branch of bramble
10 in the hand of a drunkard. The law settles quarrels at last, yet silence
11 the fool, and feud there shall be none.[1] Like a dog at his vomit, the
12 fool goes back ever to his own folly.[2] Who is in more perilous case
than the fool himself? The man who lays claim to wisdom.
13   What, go abroad? says Sloth; there is a lion there; trust me, a lion's
14 dam loose in the street. Sloth turns about, but keeps his bed, true as the
15 door to its hinge. With folded hands the sluggard sits by, too idle to put
16 hand to mouth.[3] Wiser than seven sages is the sluggard in his own
thought.
17   Better pull a dog by the ears than meddle in another's quarrels;
pass on in quiet.
18   No excuse he finds, that deadly brand and arrow casts about him;
19 nor he either, that hurts a friend by treachery and pleads that it was
done in jest.
20   No fuel, no fire; no tell-tale, no quarrel. Coal needs ember, and
22 fire tinder, and strife a quarreller, for their kindling. Innocent enough
seem the words of the backbiter, yet their poison sinks deep into a
23 man's belly.[4] When the heart is wicked, fine talk is but lustre ware.
24 The enemy that has treacherous thoughts is betrayed by his friendly
25 talk;[5] trust him not when he speaks thee fair; here are seven depths
26 of wickedness in a single heart. Vain the pretences that cloak his malice;
27 before the whole assembly it shall be made known; dig pit, and thou
28 shalt fall into it, shift rock, and it shall roll back on thee. Fie on the
glib tongues that hate all honesty, the treacherous lips that plot men's
downfall!

---

[1] *vv.* 6–10. The meaning of all these verses is obscure, and the Hebrew text,
perhaps, not above suspicion. In verse 8, the Latin follows a rather far-fetched
interpretation given by the Talmud; there is no reference to heathen worship
in the original. Verse 10 is very variously interpreted; the sense offered by the
Latin is perhaps simpler than any other available, but it is not easy to guess
what reading it represents in the Hebrew.

[2] See II Pet. 2.22.

[3] *vv.* 13, 15. See 22.13, 19.24 above.

[4] See 18.8.

[5] In the Hebrew text, 'dissembles in his talk.'

CHAPTER TWENTY-SEVEN

DO not flatter thyself with hopes of to-morrow; what lies in the womb of the future thou canst not tell.

2   Seek praise, but not of thy own bestowing; another's lips, not thine, must sound it.

3   What is more crushing than stone, more burdensome than sand?
4   A fool's ill humour. Fierce, fierce is rage, and indignation mounts like a flood, but the pangs of jealousy, these there is no resisting.

5   Better open reproof than the love that gives no sign. Better the love that scourges, than hate's false kiss.

7   Full-fed spurns the honeycomb; to Hunger's lips, bitter is sweet.

8   When bird leaves nest, let a man leave his home.

9   Sweeter than ointment, sweeter than any perfume, when man's
10   heart talks to heart of friend. Friend of thine, and friend that was thy father's, never forsake; so, in thy sore need, no kinsman's door thou shalt need to enter.
     Neighbour over the way is better than kinsman at a distance.

11   My son, wouldst thou be thy father's pride? Court wisdom, and silence thy detractors.

12   When ill times come, prudence is on its guard, and takes refuge; the unwary march on, and pay the penalty.[1]

13   Does a man go bail for a stranger? Without more ado, take his garment from him; who trusts without knowledge, forfeits the pledge.[2]

14   So early abroad, so loudly wishing thy neighbour well? This is curse, not blessing.[3]

15   Between a scold and a roof that drips in winter there is nothing to
16   choose. As well store up the wind in thy house, though thou call her the marrow of thy right hand.[4]

17   Iron whets iron, friend shapes friend.

18   If figs thou wouldst eat, tend thy fig-tree well; if honour thou wouldst have, wait well on thy master.

19   Clear as a face mirrored in water, the wise see men's hearts.[5]

20   Death and the grave were never yet content, nor man's eyes with gazing.

---

[1] See 22.3.
[2] See 20.16.
[3] The precise bearing of this proverb remains in doubt.
[4] The whole of this verse is obscure, and the second half of it probably corrupt.
[5] The Hebrew text reads simply, 'As water face to face, so heart of man to man,' it is not clear in what sense.

21   Silver and gold are judged by furnace and crucible, man by his repute.[1] (Heart of knave is ever set on mischief, heart of true man on wisdom).

22   Bray a fool like corn, with pestle and mortar, he will be a fool still.

23   Spent be thy care, thy eyes watchful, over flock and herd of thine;
24   riches will slip from thy grasp, and crowns, will they last for ever?[2]
25   See, where the meadows are laid bare, and the aftermath is springing,
26   the hay all carried, now, from the hill-slopes! Pasture for the lambs that shall clothe thee, for the goats that shall be the price of more
27   fields yet; goat's milk, too, shall suffice to feed thee, give life and strength to thy men and thy serving-maids.

CHAPTER TWENTY-EIGHT

BAD conscience takes to its heels, with none in pursuit; fearless as a lion the unreproved heart.

2   Short reigns and many, where a land is plagued for its guilt; by wise counsel, and men's talk overheard, long lives the king.

3   Tempest threatens and famine when poor men oppress the poor.

4   Sound teaching is forgotten, where the wrong-doer is well spoken
5   of; honest folk will still be up in arms. No skill the knave has to discern
6   the right; quest of the Lord's will makes that craft perfect. Better
7   a poor life lived honestly than crooked ways that bring riches. A son's wisdom is to obey his father's teaching, not to shame him by keeping
8   riotous company. Wealth that the usurer by extortion amassed, a
9   more generous than he shall have the spending of. Turn a deaf ear
10   to thy teachers, and thy prayer shall be all sacrilege. Ruin he brings on himself, that leads the innocent into ill ways, and honest men shall
11   be the heirs of him. Wisdom he claims, that wealth has; yet there is many a poor man will put him down.

12   A fair sight it is, to see honest folk rejoicing; knaves' rule is the people's ruin.

13   Never shalt thou thrive by keeping sin hidden; confess it and leave
14   it, if thou wouldst find pardon. Blessed evermore is the timorous conscience; it is hardened hearts that fall to their ruin.

---

[1] That common repute should be regarded as a test of what a man really is, seems unlikely (cp., especially 17.3 above). Some think the Hebrew text means a man should be judged by what he holds in repute, and this would fit in well with the second part of the verse (which is found in the Septuagint Greek, but not in the Hebrew text itself). Others would read, instead of 'repute,' 'adversity,' and this would lead on well to verse 22.

[2] The Latin version here ignores the question, and runs 'but a crown shall be granted for ever'; a rendering which yields no good sense in the context.

15 Nation without bread and prince without scruple, here is ravening
16 lion and hungry bear all at once. Let prince lack prudence, everywhere
is wrongful oppression; less covetous, he should have lived longer.
17 Compass thou a man's death, thou mayst flee to the depths of earth,
none will shield thee.
18 Keep the path of innocence, and thou shalt be safe; at one blow
the double-dealer shall fall.
19 Till field and fill belly; idleness shall have a bellyful of nothing
20 but want.[1] Of honesty comes much honour, and how shall wealth
21 reach thee suddenly, yet leave thy hands clean? Great wrong it is to
sell judgement; wouldst thou barter truth away for a mouthful of
22 bread? Eye on his rivals in the race for wealth, a man sees nothing,
when want is hard at his heels.
23 More thanks thou wilt have, in the end, for honest reproof than for
designing flattery.
24 Shall he who robs father or mother make light of it? He is next door
to a murderer.
25 Jostling pride it is that stirs up enmity; trust in the Lord, and thou
26 shalt prosper. He is a fool that trusts his own wit; follow the rule of
wise men, if thou wouldst reach safety.
27 Give to the poor, and nothing lack; turn away from their plea, and
blessing thou shalt have none.
28 When knaves flourish, all the world takes to hiding; come they by
their end, thou shalt see honest folk abroad.

CHAPTER TWENTY-NINE

WHO spurns the yoke of correction shall meet sudden doom, and
past all remedy.
2 When right thrives, the city is all rejoicing; when there be knaves
that rule it, all lament.
3 Glad the father's heart, when the son takes wisdom for his mistress,
nor spends on wantons his patrimony.
4 Kings by justice or exaction make the fortunes of a state or mar
them.
5 By empty flattery thou mayst lay a snare for thy friend's feet.
6 By his own false steps the sinner is entangled; innocence goes singing
7 and rejoicing on its way. An eye the upright man has for the friendless cause; the sinner is all darkness.
8 Rashness in a city ruins all; that madness, wisdom must turn aside.

---

[1] See 12.11.

9   Alas for the wise man that goes to law with a fool! Between bluster and mockery, there is no end to it.[1]

10   He makes murderous enemies, that lives innocently . . . and honest men demand his life.[2]

11   Folly blurts out its whole mind; wise men reserve utterance till by and by.

12   King that listens to false rumour has a worthless court. Poor men and their masters dwell side by side, sharing the Lord's sunlight.

14 King that gives due redress to the poor has a throne unshakeable.

15   Wisdom comes of reproof, comes of the rod; leave a child to go its own way, and a mother's care is wasted.

16   Thrive the godless, there will be wrongs a many; but the just will yet see them put down.

17   A son well schooled is rest well earned; great joy thou shalt have of him.

18   What revel among the host,[3] the power of prophecy once withdrawn! Happy is he that keeps the law unbroken.

19   Word was never yet that would check a slave; he listens only to defy it.

20   Who is in more perilous case than the fool himself? The man who speaks too soon.[4]

21   Pamper thy slave young, and breed a pert manservant.

22   Ever the quarreller breeds strife; quick temper is ever at fault.

23   Pride will come low; honour awaits the humble.

24   As thou lovest thy life, aid thieves never; wouldst thou hear appeal made, and keep thy own counsel?[5]

25   Fear of man's judgements will bring thee quickly to ruin; in the
26 Lord put thy trust, and rise high above them. Suitors a many an earthly prince has for his favour; but it is God that judges all.

---

[1] The Latin version (strangely misunderstood by modern editors) gives no indication whether it is the wise man or the fool who blusters and laughs; the latter is evidently meant.

[2] 'Demand his life,' according to Hebrew usage, can only mean 'demand that he should be put to death.' It seems clear, therefore, that our present text is either faulty or defective.

[3] The uncommon Hebrew verb here rendered by 'revel' occurs in Ex. 32.25; which makes it probable that the absence of Moses on Mount Sinai is here referred to. Otherwise, it is hard to establish any connexion between the two halves of the verse.

[4] The form of this verse is exactly the same as that of 26.12 above; but here (perhaps through an error) our present Latin text gives 'folly' instead of 'fool,' and obscures the evident meaning of the sentence.

[5] See Lev. 5.1.

27   Eyesores alike, the rogue to honest men, the plain-dealer to villains.
(Let the son heed a father's warning, he shall fear no ruin).[1]

CHAPTER THIRTY

HERE are the words of Agur, son of Jacé.[2] Here is revelation made
known by one that had God with him, God's near presence to comfort him, as he spoke.
2   What though I be ignorant, beyond human wont? What though the
knowledge of man has passed me by, wisdom's dull pupil, without skill
4 in holy lore? Who may he be that has scaled heaven, and come back to
tell its secrets; held the winds in the hollow of his hand, wrapped away the
storm-clouds under his mantle, fixed the bounds of earth? Tell me his
name; tell me, if thou canst, where son of his may be found?[3]
5   All God's promises are like metal tested in the fire; he is the sure
6 defence of all who trust in him. Add to his word no word of thine;
speedily thy practices shall come to light.
7   Two requests I would make of thee; be they mine while life lasts.
8 Keep my thoughts ever far from treachery and lying; and for my state
of life, be neither poverty mine nor riches. Grant me only the livelihood
9 I need; so shall not abundance tempt me to disown thee, and doubt
if Lord there be, nor want bid me steal, and dishonour my God's name
with perjury.
10   Never accuse a slave to his master; curse thee he may, and to thy
undoing.
11   A bad breed it is, that curse their fathers and for their mothers
12 have no good word. A bad breed, that owns no blot, yet is all unpurged
13 from its defilement. A bad breed, all haughty looks and scornful brow.
14 A bad breed, that has teeth sharp as swords, jaws that grind slowly
on, till poor folk none are left, their friendless neighbours.
15   Two sisters there are, men say, brood of the leech, that still cry,
Give us more, give us more! But stay, there is a third Insatiable; nay,
16 a fourth I can name that never says, Enough! The grave, and the

---

[1] The bracketed words occur neither in the Hebrew text nor in the Septuagint
Greek.
[2] The Latin version here translates the two proper names, Agur and Jacé,
as He who gathers and He who vomits. The latter part of the verse is wholly
obscure, and is generally thought to include more proper names, Ithiel and
Ucal. It is not clear whether Agur's prophecy forms a part or the whole of
this chapter.
[3] See Ps. 17.31.

barren womb, and earth that soaks up the rain, and fire; did fire ever say, Enough?

17 Proud looks, that tell of a father mocked, a mother's right despised! That eye the ravens shall pick out on the hill-side, the vulture's brood shall prey on it.

18 Three mysteries there are too high for me, and a fourth is beyond
19 my ken; eagle that flies in air, viper that crawls on rock, ship that
20 sails the sea, and man that goes courting maid.[1] Nor less I marvel at wanton wife that licks her greedy lips, and will have it that she did no harm.

21 Three sights there are set earth trembling, and a fourth it cannot
22 endure; slave turned king, churl full fed, a scold married, and a maid that supplants [2] her mistress.

24 Of four little things in nature, wise men cannot match the skill.
25 How puny a race the ants, that hoard their food in harvest time; how defenceless the rock-rabbits, that hide their burrows in the clefts!
27 No prince have the locusts, yet ever they march in rank; the lizard climbs high, and makes its home in the palaces of kings.

29 Three creatures there are that walk majestically, and a fourth goes
30 proudly on his way; bravest of beasts, the lion, that fears no encounter,
31 the cock, (Loins-girt they call him),[3] and the ram; and the king, too, for who can say him nay?

32 Fool that thrusts himself forward will prove a fool;[4] he had been better
33 advised to hold his tongue. First milk, then butter thou mayst have for the wringing; blow thy nose lustily, and blood shall flow at last; how then canst thou press thy quarrel home, and no strife come of it?

CHAPTER THIRTY-ONE

HERE are words of king Lamuel; here is revelation his mother made known to him for his instruction.
2 What word have I for my son, the child of my own womb, the ful-
3 filment of my prayers? Wouldst thou give thyself up to the love of

---

[1] The fourth mystery is given in the Hebrew text as 'the way of a man with a maid'; the Latin version, evidently in the same sense, has 'the way of a man in his manhood.'

[2] Literally, according to the Latin, 'inherits from,' but the other sense of the Hebrew verb is clearly more appropriate.

[3] The second majestic beast is given in the Hebrew text simply as 'the girt of loins,' and cannot be certainly identified. The greyhound, or some other creature with a thin waist, seems more likely than the cock.

[4] 'Thrusts himself forward' appears to be the sense of the Hebrew verb here, which is rendered in the Latin 'meets with advancement.'

4 women, spend thy all on a king's undoing? Wine was never made for
kings, Lamuel, never for kings; carouse befits ill thy council-chamber.
5 Not for them to drink deep, and forget the claims of right, and mis-
6 judge the plea of the friendless. Strong drink for the mourner, wine
7 for the afflicted heart; deep let them drink, and forget their need,
8 and think of their misery no more. Do thou, meanwhile, give thy
9 voice for dumb pleader and for doomed prisoner; ever let that voice
of thine pronounce true sentence, giving redress to the friendless and
the poor.
10   A man who has found a vigorous wife has found a rare treasure,
11 brought from distant shores. Bound to her in loving confidence, he
12 will have no need of spoil. Content, not sorrow, she will bring him
13 as long as life lasts. Does she not busy herself with wool and thread,
14 plying her hands with ready skill? Ever she steers her course like
15 some merchant ship, bringing provision from far away. From early
dawn she is up, assigning food to the household, so that each waiting-
16 woman has her share. Ground must be examined, and bought, and
17 planted out as a vineyard, with the earnings of her toil. How briskly
18 she girds herself to the task, how tireless are her arms! Industry, she
knows, is well rewarded, and all night long her lamp does not go out.
19 Jealously she sets her hands to work, her fingers clutch the spindle.
20 Kindly is her welcome to the poor, her purse ever open to those in
21 need. Let the snow lie cold if it will, she has no fears for her household;
22 no servant of hers but is warmly clad. Made by her own hands was
the coverlet on her bed, the clothes of lawn and purple that she wears.
23 None so honoured at the city gate as that husband of hers, when he
24 sits in council with the elders of the land. Often she will sell linen
of her own weaving, or make a girdle for the travelling merchant to
25 buy. Protected by her own industry and good repute, she greets the
26 morrow with a smile. Ripe wisdom governs her speech, but it is kindly
27 instruction she gives. She keeps watch over all that goes on in her
28 house, not content to go through life eating and sleeping. That is
why her children are the first to call her blessed, her husband is loud
29 in her praise: Unrivalled art thou among all the women that have
30 enriched their homes. Vain are the winning ways, beauty is a snare;
31 it is the woman who fears the Lord that will achieve renown. Work
such as hers claims its reward; let her life be spoken of with praise
at the city gates.

THE BOOK OF ECCLESIASTES

CHAPTER ONE

WORDS of the Spokesman,[1] king David's son, that reigned once at Jerusalem.
2 A shadow's shadow, he tells us, a shadow's shadow; a world of
3 shadows! How is man the better for all this toiling of his, here under
4 the sun? Age succeeds age, and the world goes on unaltered. Sun
6 may rise and sun may set, but ever it goes back and is reborn. Round
to the south it moves, round to the north it turns; the wind, too,
though it makes the round of the world, goes back to the beginning
7 of its round at last. All the rivers flow into the sea, yet never the sea
grows full; back to their springs they find their way, and must be
8 flowing still. Weariness, all weariness; who shall tell the tale? Eye
9 looks on unsatisfied; ear listens, ill content. Ever that shall be that
ever has been, that which has happened once shall happen again;
10 there can be nothing new, here under the sun. Never man calls a
thing new, but it is something already known to the ages that went
11 before us; only we have no record of older days. So, believe me,
the fame of to-morrow's doings will be forgotten by the men of a
later time.
12 I was a king in my day, I, the Spokesman; Israel my realm,
13 Jerusalem my capital. And it was my resolve to search deep and
find out the meaning of all that men do, here under the sun; all that
curse of busy toil which God has given to the sons of Adam for their
14 task. All that men do beneath the sun I marked, and found it was
15 but frustration and lost labour, all of it; there was no curing men's
cross-grained nature, no reckoning up their follies.
16 I at least (so I flattered myself) have risen above the rest; a king
so wise never reigned at Jerusalem;[2] here is a mind has reflected much,
17 and much learned. And therewith I applied my mind to a new study;
what meant wisdom and learning, what meant ignorance and folly?
18 And I found that this too was labour lost; much wisdom, much woe;
who adds to learning, adds to the load we bear.

---

[1] The word Ecclesiastes, like the Hebrew word it renders, should mean one
who convokes an assembly, or addresses it, or both.
[2] The Hebrew text here seems to imply that king Solomon was wiser than
anyone who had reigned *before* him at Jerusalem, whereas David was in fact
his only (Israelite) predecessor. But we need not attach too much importance
to a conventional turn of phrase; cf. III Kg. 14.9.

CHAPTER TWO

2 NEXT, I thought to give the rein to my desires, and enjoy pleasure,
until I found that this, too, was labour lost. Wouldst thou know
how I learned to find laughter an empty thing, and all joy a vain
3 illusion; how I resolved at last to deny myself the comfort of wine,
wisdom now all my quest, folly disowned? For I could not rest until
I knew where man's true good lay, what was his life's true task, here
4 under the sun.¹ Great plans I set on foot; I would build palaces, I
5 would plant vineyards, I would have park and orchard, planted with
6 every kind of tree; and to water all this greenery there must be
7 pools of water besides. Men-slaves I bought and women-slaves, till I
had a great retinue of them; herds, too, and abundance of flocks, such
8 as Jerusalem never saw till then. Gold and silver I amassed, revenues
of subject king and subject province; men-singers I had and women-
singers, and all that man delights in; beakers a many, and jars of wine
9 to fill them.² Never had Jerusalem known such wealth; yet in the
10 midst of it, wisdom never left my side. Eyes denied nothing that
eyes could covet, a heart stinted of no enjoyment, free of all the
pleasures I had devised for myself, this was to be my reward, this
11 the fruit of all my labours. And now, when I looked round at all I had
done, all that ungrateful drudgery, nothing I found there but frustration and labour lost, so fugitive is all we cherish, here under the sun.
12   Then my mind went back to the thought of wisdom, of ignorance,
too, and folly. What (thought I), should mortal king strive to imitate
13 the sovereign power that made him?³ I saw, indeed, that wisdom
14 differed from folly as light from darkness; the wise man had eyes
in his head, while the fool went his way benighted; but the ending of
15 them? In their ending both were alike. Why then (I said to myself),
if fool and I must come to the same end at last, was not I the fool,
that toiled to achieve wisdom more than he? So my thoughts ran, and

---

¹ In the Hebrew text, the first part of this verse refers not to the second
thoughts which recalled the author to a simpler way of living, but to those first
thoughts of which he afterwards repented: 'I considered how best to pamper
my body with wine, how best to cling to my follies, yet retaining wisdom all
the while.'

² The last ten words of this verse represent, in the Hebrew text, a passage
of uncertain significance.

³ The Hebrew text, in the latter half of this verse, runs: 'For what (shall)
the man (do) that comes after the king? Why, what they have already done',
perhaps a footnote recalling the follies of king Roboam (see verse 19 below).
The literal sense of the Latin is: 'What (said I) is man, that he should be able
to follow the King, his Maker?'

16 I found labour lost, here too. Endlessly forgotten, wise man and fool alike, since to-morrow's memory will be no longer than yesterday's; wise man and fool alike doomed to death.

17 Thus I became weary of life itself; so worthless it seemed to me, all that man does beneath the sun, frustration all of it, and labour

18 lost. And I, beneath that same sun, what fond labours I had spent! I hated the thought of them now; should heir of mine succeed to

19 them? An heir, would he be wise man or fool? None could tell; but his would be the possession of all I had toiled for so hard, schemed

20 for so anxiously; could there be frustration worse than this? I would

21 hold my hand; no more should yonder sun see labours of mine. What, should one man go on toiling, his the craft, his the skill, his the anxious care, leaving all to another, and an idler? That were frustration surely, and great mischief done.

22 Tell me, how is a man the richer for all that toil of his, all that lost

23 labour of his, here under the sun? His days all painfulness and care,

24 his very nights restless; what is here but frustration? Were it not better to eat and drink, and toil only at his own pleasures? These,

25 too, come from God's hand; and who has better right to food tasted

26 and pleasure enjoyed than I? Who wins God's favour, has wisdom and skill for his reward, and pleasure too; it is the sinner that is doomed to hardship and to thankless care, hoarding and scraping, and all to enrich some heir God loves better! For him frustration, for him the labour lost.

CHAPTER THREE

EVERYTHING must be done by turns; no activity, here beneath the heavens, but has its allotted time for beginning and coming to an end.

2 Men are born only to die, plant trees only to displant them. Now we take life, now we save it; now we are destroying, now building.

4 Weep first, then laugh, mourn we and dance; the stones we have scattered we must bring together anew; court we first and then shun

6 the embrace. To-day's gain, to-morrow's loss; what once we treasured,

7 soon thrown away; the garment rent, the garment mended; silence

8 kept, and silence ended; love alternating with hatred, war with

9 peace. For all this toiling of his, how is man the richer? [1] Pitiable

---

[1] *vv.* 1–9: These verses are ordinarily understood as implying that man's varied activities have to be carried on at a time of God's, not of his own, choosing. But, if so, the instances are strangely chosen, nor is it even clear why a series of contrasts should have been instituted at all. The context suggests (cf. especially verse 9) that we are meant to think of life as a monotonous alternation of opposite activities; in that case, the passage has the same note of frustration as 4–7 above.

11 indeed I found it, this task God has given to mankind; and he, meanwhile, has made the world, in all its seasonable beauty, and given us the contemplation[1] of it, yet of his own dealings with us, first and last,
12 never should man gain comprehension. To enjoy his life, to make
13 the best of it, beyond doubt this is man's highest employment; that gift at least God has granted him, to eat and drink and see his toil
14 rewarded. But be sure all God has made will remain for ever as he made it; there is no adding to it, no taking away from it; so he will
15 command our reverence. Nothing that has been, but lasts on still; nothing that will be, but has been already; he is ever repeating the history of the past.
16   I marked, too, how wrong was done instead of right, injustice
17 instead of justice, there under the sun's eye; and I told myself that God would give judgement one day between the just and the sinners,
18 and all things would reach their appointed end then.[2] I told myself that God's purpose with the sons of men was to test them . . .
19   . . . And that they might see they were only like the beasts . . .[3] After all, man comes to the same ending as the beasts; there is nothing to choose between his lot and theirs; both alike are doomed to die. They are but a breath, all of them; what has man that the beasts have not?
20 Frustration everywhere; we are all making for the same goal; of
21 earth we were made, and to earth we must return. Who has a right to tell us that the spirit of man mounts upwards, and the spirit of a
22 beast sinks down to the depth? So I became aware that it is best for man to busy himself here to his own content; this and nothing else is his allotted portion; who can show him what the future will bring?

CHAPTER FOUR

AND then my thoughts would turn back to all the wrongs that are done under the sun's eye. Innocent folk in tears, and who is to comfort them? Who is to comfort them, powerless against their oppres-

---

[1] Literally 'the discussion'. The Hebrew text gives a more mysterious phrase: 'He has set eternity (or perhaps, the world) in their hearts.'

[2] The Hebrew text has 'For there is a time for every purpose and for every deed there', it is not clear in what sense.

[3] The end of this verse, in the Hebrew text, is commonly suspected of corruption. But it seems doubtful whether there has not been some wider dislocation; the want of logical connexion between the two halves of this verse is unmistakable. Those editors who would strike out verse 18 as an insertion do not mend matters; it leaves a hopeless gap between the thought of verse 17 and that of verse 19.

2 sors? The dead, it seemed, were more to be envied than the
3 living; better yet to be still unborn, never to have known the shameful deeds that are done, out here in the sunlight.

4   I thought, too, of human toil and striving; how much it owed to man's rivalry with his fellows! All was frustration and lost labour
5 here. What wonder if the fool sits idle, and starves to death? Better a handful (says he) quietly come by, than a whole armful that is all striving and labour lost.[1]

7   And there was another kind of frustration I marked, here under
8 the sun. Here is one that works alone, partner nor son nor brother to aid him, yet still works on, never content with his bright hoard, never asking, as he toils and stints himself, who shall gain by it. Frustration and lost labour, here too.

9   Better to be in partnership with another, than alone; partnership
10 brings advantage to both. If one falls, the other will give support; with the lonely it goes hard; when he falls, there is none to raise
11 him. Sleep two in one bed, each shall warm the other; for the lonely,
12 there is no warmth. Two may withstand assault, where one is no match for it; a triple cord is not lightly broken.

13   There is more hope for a wise servant[2] that is in hard straits, than
14 for a dotard king that foresight has none. Men have risen to a throne that till now were bound in prison; men born to rule a kingdom have
15 died of want. I have seen the whole world, from east to west, take part with the young man, the usurper that rises in the old king's stead.
16 The old king, that had an immemorial line of ancestors;[3] and now posterity shall take no pride in him! All is frustration, and labour lost.
17   Look well what thou art doing when thou goest into God's house; present thyself there in a spirit of obedience. Obedience is far better than the sacrifice made by fools, that are guilty of unwitting sacrilege.[4]

---

[1] *vv.* 5, 6: It is the Latin version, not the Hebrew text, that puts verse 6 into the mouth of the fool. Some think that verse 5 is misplaced here, and belongs to another context.

[2] Or perhaps 'boy'.

[3] 'The old king, that had an immemorial line of ancestors'; literally, 'The number of the people of those who were before him is infinite'. The Hebrew text has, 'The number of the people who followed his leadership was infinite', referring evidently to the usurper; the Latin gives a better sense. The language of the whole passage is strained, and perhaps in part corrupt; there is no reason to think that any particular historical situation is referred to.

[4] The allusion is perhaps in the first instance to ceremonial defilement, such as might disqualify the worshipper from bringing his offering until he had been purified. But evidently it may be interpreted of moral disqualification; cf. Mt. 5.23.

CHAPTER FIVE

WHEN thou standest in God's presence, do not pour out with rash haste all that is in thy heart. God sees as heaven sees, thou as earth;
2 few words are best. Sure as dreams come from an overwrought brain,
3 from glib utterance comes ill-considered speech. Vow to God if thou utterest, without delay perform it; he will have no light and rash
4 promises; vow made must be vow paid. Far better undertake
5 nothing than undertake what thou dost not fulfil. Wouldst thou defile thy whole nature through the tongue's fault? Wouldst thou find thyself saying, with God's angel to hear thee, No thought I gave to it? [1] Little wonder if God disappoints every ambition of the
6 man who speaks so. Dreams, empty dreams, led to those glib promises of thine; content thyself rather with the fear of God. [2]
7 Thou seest, it may be, in this province or that, oppression of the poor, false award given, and wrong unredressed? Let not such things bewilder thee; trust me, authority is watched by higher authority,
8 subject in turn to higher authority yet; and, above them all, the
9 King of the whole earth rules the wide spaces of it. [3] What is his decree? Why, that covetousness should never fill its own maw; never did he that loved money taste the enjoyment of his money; [4] here is
10 frustration once again. Richer if thou grow, riches will give thee more mouths to feed; profit he has none that owns them, save the
11 feasting of his eyes on them if he will. Full belly or empty, sound is the cottar's sleep; sleep, to the pampered body of the rich still denied.
12 Another evil I have found past remedy, here under the sun; riches
13 that a man hoards to his own undoing. By cruel misadventure they are lost to him, and to the son he has begotten nothing he leaves but
14 poverty. Naked he came, when he left his mother's womb, and

---

[1] *v.* 5: 'No thought I gave to it'; literally, 'There is no foresight'. A comparison with the Hebrew text makes it clear that there is no question of denying God's Providence.

[2] *vv.* 1–6: It is perhaps best to understand the whole of this passage as referring to rash vows. In that case, the words in verse 1, 'God is in heaven, and thou art on earth', will not be a mere assertion of the divine dignity, but a reminder that God knows, better than we ourselves, what is best for us.

[3] There can be little doubt that the old Douay translators were right in interpreting the Latin as a reference to divine, not to earthly kingship. The meaning of the Hebrew text is quite uncertain.

[4] In the original, this verse begins simply, 'The covetous man will never have his fill of money'; the rendering given above assumes that there is a tacit connexion between this verse and what went before.

naked still death finds him; nothing to show for all his long endeavour.
15 Alas, what ailed him, that he should go away no richer than he came?
16 Nothing left of all those wasted labours of his; all his life long the
cheerless board, the multitudinous cares, the concern, the melan-
17 choly! Better far, by my way of it, that a man should eat and drink
and enjoy the revenues of his own labour, here under the sun, as long
18 as God gives him life; what more can he claim? God's gift it is, if
a man has wealth and goods and freedom to enjoy them, taking what
19 comes to him and profiting by what he has earned. Few be his days
or many, he regards little, so long as God gives his heart content.

CHAPTER SIX

WITH another hardship I have seen men visited here beneath the
2 sun, and commonly. God gives a man wealth, and goods, and
state, till there is nothing more left for his appetites to desire; and then
God denies him the enjoyment of all this, throws the coveted morsel to a
3 stranger instead; here is frustration, here is cold comfort indeed. Ay,
let a man have a hundred children to his name, years let him have a
many, and be near his end; yet, if he is not to enjoy the revenues of
his land still, and lay his bones in it,[1] I say it were better for him never
4 to have come to the birth. Well made, the empty passage from light
5 to darkness, well lost, the chance of earthly renown, if only a man
never sees the sun, never learns the meaning of good fortune and ill!
6 Though he should have lived two thousand years, he were none the
better for it, if he might not continue in the enjoyment of his goods.
Do we not all reach the same goal at last?[2]
7 What is all our striving, but a full mouth and an empty belly? Is
wise man more to be envied than fool? Where should a man go when
he is poor, save where he can find a livelihood?[3]
9 Better aim at what lies in view than hanker after dreams. But indeed
all is frustration, and labour lost.
10 He is known already by name, that is still unborn; and this at least

---

[1] Literally, 'and lack burial', but it is difficult to believe that the author of
these chapters would regard the lack of funeral rites as a significant misfortune.
[2] *vv.* 1–6: It is not clear how this situation differs from that described in
5.12–16; unless perhaps the difference is between confiscation of a man's
riches, and their accidental loss.
[3] The second half of this verse, in the Latin, is literally: 'And what (advantage has) the poor man, save to go where there is life?' The true reading has
perhaps been lost; the Hebrew text, 'What (has) the poor man who has
knowledge to walk in the presence of the living?' yields no satisfactory sense.

is known of him, that he is but man, and cannot plead his cause, matched against too strong an adversary.

11 Words, they be spun endlessly; yet what should lie at the heart of our reasoning, but frustration?

CHAPTER SEVEN

WHAT need for man to ask questions that are beyond his scope? There is no knowing how best his life should be spent, this brief pilgrimage that passes like a shadow, and is gone. And what will befall after his death, in this world beneath the sun, who can tell?

2 There is no embalming like a good name left behind; man's true birthday is the day of his death.

3 Better a visit paid where men mourn, than where they feast; it will put thee in mind of the end that awaits us all, admonish the living
4 with the foreknowledge of death. Frown ere thou smile; the down-
5 cast look betokens a chastened heart. Home of sadness, home of gladness; haunt of the wise mind, haunt of the foolish.

6 Better receive a wise man's rebuke, than hear thy praises sung by
7 fools. Loud but not long the thorns crackle under the pot, and fools make merry; for them, too, frustration.

8 Oppression bewilders even a wise man's wits, and undermines his courage.

9 Speech may end fair, that foul began; patience is better than
10 resentment. Never be quick to take offence; it is a fool's heart that harbours grudges.

11 Never ask why the old times were better than ours; a fool's question.

12 Great worth has wisdom matched with good endowment; more advantage it shall bring thee than all the rest, here under the
13 sun. Wealth befriends whom wisdom befriends; better still, who learns wisdom wins life.

14 Mark well God's doings; where he looks askance, none may set the crooked straight.

15 Come good times, accept the good they bring; come evil, let them never take thee unawares; bethink thee, that God has balanced these against those, and will have no man repine over his lot.

16 In my days of baffled enquiry, I have seen pious men ruined for
17 all their piety, and evil-doers live long in all their wickedness. Why then, do not set too much store by piety, nor play the wise man to
18 excess, if thou wouldst not be bewildered over thy lot. Yet plunge not deep in evil-doing; folly eschew; else thou shalt perish before

19 thy time. To piety thou must needs cling, yet live by that other
caution too; fear God, and thou hast left no duty unfulfilled.[1]

20 Wisdom is a surer ally than ten city magistrates; there is no man
on earth so exact over his duties that he does ever the right, never
commits a fault.

22 The chance words men utter, heed but little; how if thou shouldst
23 hear thy own servant speaking ill of thee? Thy own conscience will
tell thee how often thou too hast spoken ill of other men.

24 Thus, by the touchstone of my wisdom, I would test all
things; Wisdom, cried I, I must have; yet all the while she withdrew
25 from me, further away than ever. Deep, deep is her secret; who shall
read it?

26 Here is a mind that has passed the whole world of things in review,
examining everything, weighing everything, so as to have a wise
estimation of them, eager to understand the fool's rebelliousness,
27 the false calculations of rash souls. And this I have ascertained;
death itself is not so cruel as woman's heart that wheedles and beguiles,
as woman's clutches that release their captive never. God's friends
28 escape her; of sinners she makes an easy prey. I weighed this against
that (he, the Spokesman, tells us), and the sum of my enquiry was
29 this. One thing I ever longed to find, and found never, a true woman.
One true man I might find among a thousand, but a woman never.
30 Of this, beyond all else, I have satisfied myself; man's nature was
simple enough when God made him, and these endless questions are of
his own devising.
31 The wise man, there is none like him. O for one who should read
the riddle!

CHAPTER EIGHT

WHEN a man is given wisdom, it shines out in his face; the
stamp of Omnipotence is on his brow.
2 Mine to do a king's bidding, to hold fast by an oath taken in the
3 name of God. Do not hasten away from his presence, or rebelliously
4 withstand him; he can do all he will, with such authority his word
5 runs; none may call his acts in question. Do as thou art bidden,
and fear no harm. A time will come, the wise man knows, when he

---

[1] *vv.* 16–19: The author here appears to recommend taking a middle course
between excessive piety and excessive ill-doing. Some think this was part of
his immature speculations (verse 16); others, that the 'justice' which can be
excessive is censoriousness about our fellow men, or scrupulous observance of
ceremonial detail.

6 shall win a hearing; time brings every man his chance, be his business
7 what it may, only this curse lies upon man, that he cannot learn from
the past, cannot get word of the future.[1]
8 The winds man may not hold in check; the day of his death he
cannot determine; nor ever does war give release from service, nor
sin discharge to the sinner.
9 This, too, I have marked, as I gave heed to all that befalls us, here
beneath the sun. There are times when man rules over man to his
10 undoing.[2] I have seen godless men go peacefully to the grave, that
had lived their lives out in haunts of holiness, and won the name of
11 good men from their fellow citizens; here, too, is frustration.[3]
Because sentence is not pronounced upon the evil-doers without
12 more ado, men are emboldened to live sinfully. And yet, though
the sinner presume on the Divine patience that has borne with a
hundred misdeeds, I know well enough that blessings are for those
13 who fear God, who fear his vengeance. Never a blessing for sinners;
never be it said they lived out their full span of days! Reckless of
God's vengeance, see, they pass like a shadow, and are gone!
14 Another kind of frustration, too, earth sees; there are upright men
that are plagued as though they lived the life sinners live, just as there
are sinners who take no more harm than if they could plead innocence;
I say this is frustration indeed.
15 For me, then, mirth! No higher blessing could man attain, here
under the sun, than to eat and drink and make merry; nothing else
has he to shew for all those labours of his, for all that life-time God
has given him, here under the sun.
16 Should I cudgel my wits to grow wise, and know the meaning of all
earth's tasks; be like the men that allow their eyes no sleep, day or
17 night? Nay, I understood too well that God's dealings with man,
here under the sun, are past all accounting for; the more a man labours
to read that riddle, the less he finds out, and he least of all, that boasts
himself wise in the reading of it.

---

[1] *vv.* 2–7: It is not clear whether we are concerned, in this passage, with an
earthly king or a heavenly.

[2] 'His undoing'; according to the Latin, the ruler's own; more probably, in
the original, the reference was to that of the subject.

[3] The Hebrew text here is obscure, and the Latin differs from it in some
points.

CHAPTER NINE

A LL this, too, I pondered in my heart, and would spare no pains to find out the meaning of it. Here are upright men and wise; and it is a drudge's task they do; all in God's keeping, and yet men have no means of telling whether they have earned his love, or his displeasure!
2 This remains as yet uncertain, and meanwhile all have the same lot, upright and godless, good and wicked, clean and unclean alike. Brought they offerings or brought they none, well did they or ill, true swore
3 they or false, it is all one. Of all that goes amiss, here under the sun, nothing does more hurt than this equality of fortunes; what wonder if men's hearts, while yet they live, are full of malice and defiance?
4 And so they journey on to the grave. Were but immortality the prize! But no, hope of that is none; living dog is better off than dead
5 lion. They live under sentence of death; and when death comes, of nothing will they be aware any longer; no reward can they receive,
6 now that every trace of them has vanished away; no love, no hatred, no envy can they feel; they have said good-bye to this world, and to all its busy doings, here under the sun.
7 Go thy ways, then, eat thy bread with a stout heart, and drink wine
8 to thy contenting; that done, God asks no more of thee. Ever be thy
9 garments of white, ever let thy brow glisten with oil; live at ease with the wife that is thy heart's love, long as this uncertain life is granted thee; fugitive days, here beneath the sun. Live thou and labour thou under the sun as thou wilt, this thy portion shall be, and nothing
10 more. Whatever lies in thy power, do while do it thou canst; there will be no doing, no scheming, no wisdom or skill left to thee in the grave, that soon shall be thy home.
11 Then my thought took a fresh turn; man's art does not avail, here beneath the sun, to win the race for the swift, or the battle for the strong, a livelihood for wisdom, riches for great learning, or for the
12 craftsman thanks; chance and the moment rule all. Nor does man see his end coming; hooked fish or snared bird is not overtaken so suddenly as man is, when the day of doom falls on him unawares.
13 And here, too, is wise warning, most wise, as I judge it. There was a small city once, with few men to hold it; and there was a great king that marched out against it, raised a mound and ringed it with siege-
15 works, till it was beleaguered on every side. To such a city, how came relief? By the wise counsel of one poor man that had his wits about him. And was there anyone, think you, that remembered the

16 poor man afterwards? Not one. Sure enough, said I, wisdom has the
better of valour; but see how the poor man's wisdom goes for nothing,
and no one listens to him now!

17   A wise man's whisper carries further than great outcry from a king
18 of fools. Arms cannot match wisdom; by one slip,[1] what great advantage is lost!

CHAPTER TEN

NO ointment can perfumer brew so sweet, but it grows foul when
dead flies are lodged in it. And wouldst thou barter away wisdom
and honour both, for a moment's folly?

2   The fool's wits are astray; the wise man's right is to him left.[2] By
his way of it, every passer-by on the road is a fool, save he.

4   Though a prince's anger should mount against thee, do not desert
thy post; great harm by thy healing touch may yet be assuaged.

5   This is a source of trouble I have marked, here under the sun; the
causeless whim of tyrants.

6   Fools come to the top, down go rank and riches; slaves you will
see riding on horseback, and princes going afoot at their bridle-rein.

8   Fall into pit thou shalt not, if thou dig none; breach no walls, if
9 thou wouldst avoid the adder's sting. Stone crushes his foot that
stone carries, and wood scratches him that wood cuts.

10   Blunt tool that has grown dull from long disuse shall cost thee
pains a many;[3] if thou hadst been wise sooner, thou shouldst have
11 toiled less.[4] Bite snake ere the spell begins, he is no better off that
has the master-word.[5]

12   Wise utterance wins favour; the fool that opens his mouth does but
13 ruin himself, his preface idle talk, his conclusion madness. Of
words a fool has no stint . . .

---

[1] The rendering 'one sin' is here less appropriate; the verb used, in the Latin
as in the Hebrew, has the root meaning of 'making a mistake'.

[2] Literally, 'The wise man's heart is towards the right, the fool's towards
the left'.

[3] The Latin version obscures the sense of the proverb by adding 'in sharp-
ening it'—the sense is rather 'in using it'.

[4] Literally, 'thy wisdom follows thy striving'. The Hebrew text, which is
perhaps corrupt, gives the lame ending, 'wisdom is a useful guide'.

[5] This seems the best interpretation of the Hebrew text, which runs, literally,
'The owner of the tongue has no advantage'. Cf. Ps. 57.6. The Latin rendering
here, 'No worse off is he who backbites in secret', yields no appropriate sense.

. . . What went before, is lost to man's view, and what shall befall when he is gone, none can tell him.[1]

15 He is on a fool's errand, that does not even know his way to town.[2]

16 Woe to the land that has young blood on the throne, whose court
17 sits feasting till daybreak! And happy the land whose king is of true princely breed, whose courtiers feast when feast should be, to comfort their hearts, not all in revelry.

18 Roof sags where idleness dwells; a leaking gutter means nerveless hands within.

19 Food will cheer thee, wine bring thee gladness, but money, it answers every need.

20 Of the king, no treasonable thought; of the nobles, no ill word even in thy bed-chamber; the very birds in heaven will catch the echoes of it, and fly off to betray thy secret.

CHAPTER ELEVEN

2 HERE, on the stream's bosom, venture thy livelihood; wait long thou mayst, but be sure thou shalt recover it at last. Seven claims thou hast satisfied, do not refuse the eighth. Not thine to foresee what
3 general calamities the future holds in store; there the rain comes, where the clouds gather; north or south as the tree falls, north or
4 south the trunk will lie. Still waiting for a wind? Never shall thy seed be sown. Still watching the clouds? Never shall thy harvest be
5 carried. What guides the wind's course, how man's frame is fashioned in the womb, thou canst not tell; and thinkest thou to
6 understand God's doings, that is Maker of all? Early abroad, to sow thy seed, and let evening find thee still at work; which sowing shall speed better, none knows, or whether both shall thrive to thy profit.[3]
7 Ay, it is good to look upon, the light of day; never was eye yet but
8 loved to see the sun. Only be thy years never so many, never so happy, do not forget the dark days that are coming, the long days, when
9 frustration will be the end of it all. While thou art young, take thy fill of manhood's pride, let thy heart beat high with youth, follow where thought leads and inclination beckons, but remember that for

---

[1] It seems probable that there has been some dislocation of the text here. The latter part of the verse is practically a repetition of 8. 7.

[2] The exact bearing of this proverb can no longer be identified.

[3] *vv.* 1–6: These verses evidently teach that action is worth while, in spite of all the pessimistic considerations hitherto adduced. But commentators are not agreed whether they refer expressly to charitable actions (cf. Lk. 16. 9), or (at least in the first instance) to commercial ventures, or to action in general.

10 all this God will call thee to account. Rid thy heart, then, of resentment, thy nature of ill humours; youth and pleasures, they are so quickly gone!

CHAPTER TWELVE

DO not forget thy Maker, now, while youth lasts; now, while the
2 evil days are still far off, the years that pass unwelcomed. Not yet the obscuration of sun and moon and starlight; and the clouds that still
3 gather when the rainy season is done. One day, palsy will shake those door-keepers, those stalwart guards will be bowed with age; rarer, now, the busy maidens at the mill, dimmer, now, those bright glances
4 from the windows. The street-doors shut, muffled the hum of the
5 mill, bird-song for waking-time, and all the echoes [1] of music faint! Fear upon every height, terrors on the road; almond-blossom matched for whiteness; the grasshopper's weight a burden now; the spiced food untasted! [2] Man is for his everlasting home, and already the mourners
6 are astir in the streets. That, or else yonder cord of silver will be loosed, yonder golden skein unravelled; pitcher broken beside
7 the fountain, wheel lost in the well; [3] with that, back goes dust to its parent earth, and the spirit [4] returns to God who gave it.

8   A shadow's shadow, he, the Spokesman, tells us, a world of shadows!
9   Abundant wisdom the Spokesman had, to be the oracle of his people; the story of his life he made known to them, laid secrets bare, and
10 proverbs framed a many. Sayings of much import he devised, and
11 nothing his pen set down but was truth unalloyed. Sharp goads they are to sting us, sharp nails driven deep home, these wise words
12 left to us by many masters, but all echoing one shepherd's voice. Let these, my son, be all the wisdom thou cravest; this writing of books is an endless matter, and from overmuch study nature rebels.
13   Conclude we then thus in general; Fear God, and keep his command-
14 ments; this is the whole meaning of man. No act of thine but God will bring it under his scrutiny, deep beyond all thy knowing, and pronounce it good or evil.

---

[1] Literally, 'daughters'.

[2] Literally, 'Also they shall fear what is high, and be afraid on the road. The almond-tree will flourish, the locust will grow fat, and the caper-berry will be scattered to the winds, because man is . . .'

[3] *vv.* 2–6: The allegory of these verses has been the subject of much dispute among commentators; but it is probable that they describe, first the loss of physical and nervous strength which accompanies old age, and then (in verse 6) the sudden accidents which may cause death. The rendering above tries to indicate the lines of the interpretation commonly given, without insisting on its details.

[4] Or perhaps, 'the breath'.

THE SONG OF SONGS

THAT OF SOLOMON

CHAPTER ONE

A KISS from those lips!¹ Wine cannot ravish the senses like that
2 embrace, nor the fragrance of rare perfumes match it for delight.
Thy very name spoken soothes the heart like flow of oil; what wonder
3 the maids should love thee? Draw me after thee where thou wilt;
see, we hasten after thee, by the very fragrance of those perfumes
allured! To his own bower the king has brought me; he is our pride and
boast, on his embrace, more ravishing than wine, our thoughts shall
linger. They love truly that know thy love.

4 Dark of skin, and yet I have beauty, daughters of Jerusalem.²
Black are the tents they have in Cedar; black are Solomon's own
5 curtains; then why not I? Take no note of this Ethiop colour; it was
the sun tanned me, when my own brothers, that had a grudge against
me, set me a-watching in the vineyards. I have a vineyard of my own
6 that I have watched but ill. Tell me, my true love, where is now thy
pasture-ground, where now is thy resting-place under the noon's
heat? Thou wouldst not have me wander to and fro where the flocks
graze that are none of thine?

7 Still bewildered, fairest of woman-kind?³ Nay, if thou wilt, wander
abroad, and follow with the shepherds' flocks; feed, if thou wilt, those
8 goats of thine beside the shepherds' encampment. My heart's love,
prized above all my horsemen, with Pharao's wealth of chariots
9 behind them! Soft as doves are thy cheeks, thy neck smooth as coral.
10 Chains of gold that neck must have, inlaid with silver.
11 Now, while the king sits at his wine, breathes out the spikenard of

---

¹ It is not certain, here or throughout the book, whether we are dealing with
a series of disconnected love-songs, or with a continuous drama. The present
rendering has been divided up into paragraphs on the assumption that a kind
of dramatic unity is present, though we cannot always be certain who is the
speaker. The first three verses are perhaps flattery addressed to king Solomon
by the women of his court.
² *vv.* 4–6: The speaker seems to be a village girl, newly brought to the palace,
and still thinking of her absent lover. 'A vineyard', i.e., a sweetheart, cf. 8.12
below.
³ *vv.* 7–10: Spoken to her by king Solomon.

12 my thoughts![1] Close my love is to my heart as the cluster of myrrh
13 that lodges in my bosom all the night through. Close he clings as a
tuft of cypress in the vine-clad rocks of Engedi.

14 See how fair is the maid I love! Soft eyes thou hast, like a dove's
eyes.

15 And see how fair is the man I love, how stately! Green grows that
16 bower, thine and mine, with its roof of cedars, with a covert of cypress
for its walls.

CHAPTER TWO

COUNT me no more than wild rose on the lowland plain, wild
lily on the mountain slopes.[2]

2 A lily, matched with these other maidens, a lily among the brambles,
she whom I love!

3 An apple-tree in the wild woodland, shade cool to rest under, fruit
sweet to the taste, such is he my heart longs for.

4 Into his own banqueting-hall the king has brought me, shewn me
5 the blazon of his love. Cushioned on flowers, apples heaped high
6 about me, and love-sick all the while! His left hand pillows my head;
his right hand, even now, ready to embrace me.

7 An oath, maidens of Jerusalem! By the gazelles and the wild fawns
I charge you, wake never from her sleep my heart's love, till wake
she will![3]

8 The voice I love! See where he comes, how he speeds over the
9 mountains, how he spurns the hills![4] Gazelle nor fawn was ever so
fleet of foot as my heart's love. And now he is standing on the other
side of this very wall; now he is looking in through each window in

---

[1] *vv.* 11–16: 'The spikenard of my thoughts'; in the original, simply 'my
spikenard'. But it has been suggested that the words are meant to introduce a
new access of reverie. The interruption in verse 14 may be either spoken words
from Solomon, or an imagined address by the absent lover.

[2] *vv.* 1–6: The village girl appears to be speaking, except in verse 2, which
may be attributed to Solomon. 'He' is the country lover in verse 3, Solomon in
verse 6.

[3] The end of this verse is sometimes taken literally in the Hebrew text, as
meaning 'do not arouse or excite (the sentiment of) love (in me) until it
pleases to awake of its own accord'. But the Latin rendering, which interprets
'love' as 'the loved one' seems far simpler. If it is right, Solomon is the
speaker; the village girl has fallen asleep over the banquet.

[4] *v.* 8 to *v.* 4 of the next chapter. Since this passage begins and ends with a
warning that the sleeper must not be awoken, the pictures recorded in it are
evidently those of a dream. In verse 9, the dreamer seems to echo the half-heard
utterance of verse 7.

10 turn, peering through every chink. I can hear my true love calling to
   me: Rise up, rise up quickly, dear heart, so gentle, so beautiful, rise
11 up and come with me. Winter is over now, the rain has passed by. At
   home, the flowers have begun to blossom; pruning-time has come;
13 we can hear the turtle-dove cooing already, there at home. There
   is green fruit on the fig-trees; the vines in flower are all fragrance.
   Rouse thee, and come, so beautiful, so well beloved, still hiding thyself
14 as a dove hides in cleft rock or crannied wall. Shew me but thy face,
   let me but hear thy voice, that voice sweet as thy face is fair.
15 How was it they sang? Catch me the fox, the little fox there, thieving
   among the vineyards; vineyards of ours, all a-blossoming! [1]
16 All mine, my true love, and I all his; see where he goes out to pasture
17 among the lilies, till the day grows cool, and the shadows long. Come
   back, my heart's love, swift as gazelle or fawn out on the hills of Bether.

CHAPTER THREE

IN the night watches, as I lay abed, I searched for my heart's love,
2 and searched in vain. Now to stir abroad, and traverse the city,
   searching every alley-way and street for him I love so tenderly! But
3 for all my search I could not find him. I met the watchmen who go
4 the city rounds, and asked them whether they had seen my love; then,
   when I had scarce left them, I found him, so tenderly loved; and now
   that he is mine I will never leave him, never let him go, till I have
   brought him into my own mother's house, into the room that saw my
   birth.
5 An oath, maidens of Jerusalem! By the gazelles and the wild fawns
   I charge you, wake never from her sleep my heart's love, till wake
   she will!
6 Who is this that makes her way up by the desert road, erect as a
   column of smoke, all myrrh and incense, and those sweet scents the
   perfumer knows? [2]
7 See now the bed whereon king Solomon lies, with sixty warriors
8 to guard him, none braver in Israel; [3] swordsmen all, well trained for

---

[1] This is usually thought to be the text of some country song; the words 'How
was it they sang?' have been inserted above, so as to prepare the reader for this.

[2] It is difficult to see how this verse fits into its surroundings. Some would
translate 'What is it that makes its way up . . .' and treat verse 7 as the
answer; but the analogy of 8, 5 suggests that the reference is somehow to the
heroine of the poem.

[3] *vv.* 7–11: These verses are plainly an interlude, in the form of a song (perhaps chanted by the women of Jerusalem) in honour of king Solomon's state litter.

battle, and each with his sword girt about him, against the perils of
9 the night! A litter king Solomon will have, of Lebanon wood; a
golden frame it must have, on silver props, with cushions of purple;
within are pictured tales of love, for your pleasure, maidens of
11 Jerusalem.[1] Come out, maidens of Sion, and see king Solomon
wearing the crown that was his mother's gift to him on his day of
triumph, the day of his betrothal.

CHAPTER FOUR

HOW fair thou art, my true love, how fair![2] Eyes soft as dove's
eyes, half-seen behind thy veil; hair dazzling as the goats have,
2 when they come flocking home from the Galaad hills; teeth white
as ewes fresh from the washing, well matched as the twin lambs that
3 follow them; barren is none. Thy lips a line of scarlet, guardians of
that sweet utterance; thy cheeks shew through their veil rosy as a
4 halved pomegranate. Thy neck rising proudly, nobly adorned, like
David's embattled tower, hung about with a thousand shields, panoply
5 of the brave; graceful thy breasts as two fawns that feed among
the lilies.
6 Till the day grows cool, and the shadows long, myrrh-scented
mountain and incense-breathing hill shall be my home.
7 Fair in every part, my true love, no fault in all thy fashion-
8 ing! Venture forth from Lebanon, and come to me, my bride, my
queen that shall be! Leave Amana behind thee, Sanir and Hermon
heights, where the lairs of lions are, where the leopards roam the hills.[3]
9 What a wound thou hast made, my bride, my true love, what a
wound thou hast made in this heart of mine! And all with one glance
10 of an eye, all with one ringlet straying on thy neck! Sweet, sweet
are thy caresses, my bride, my true love; wine cannot ravish the senses
like that embrace, nor any spices match the perfume that breathes
11 from thee. Sweet are thy lips, my bride, as honey dripping from its

---

[1] Literally, 'Within, it was inlaid with love, on account of (in the Hebrew text, from) the daughters of Jerusalem'.

[2] These verses form a love-song which has no special reference to any particular situation; they may be understood as words addressed to the village girl by her lover, and heard either literally or in the imagination.

[3] 'My queen that shall be'; literally, 'thou shalt be crowned'. The Hebrew text has simply 'Look down', or perhaps, 'Make thy way down'. It is difficult to see why the various heights of the Lebanon range should be mentioned here; unless, indeed, we may suppose that the house called 'the Forest of Lebanon' (III Kg. 7. 2 and elsewhere) had its different parts or rooms named after these peaks.

comb; honey-sweet thy tongue, and soft as milk; the perfume of thy
12 garments is very incense. My bride, my true love, a close garden;
13 hedged all about, a spring shut in and sealed! Well-ordered rows of
14 pomegranates, tree of cypress and tuft of nard; no lack there whether
of spikenard or saffron, of calamus, cinnamon, or incense-tree,[1] of
15 myrrh, aloes or any rarest perfume. A stream bordered with garden;
water so fresh never came tumbling down from Lebanon.
16 North wind, awake; wind of the south, awake and come; blow
through this garden of mine, and set its fragrance all astir.

CHAPTER FIVE

INTO his garden, then, let my true love come, and taste his fruit.[2]
The garden gained, my bride, my heart's love; myrrh and spices
of mine all reaped; the honey eaten in its comb, the wine drunk and
the milk, that were kept for me! Eat your fill, lovers; drink, sweet-
hearts, and drink deep!
2 I lie asleep; but oh, my heart is wakeful! A knock on the door, and
then my true love's voice: Let me in, my true love, so gentle, my bride,
so pure! See, how bedewed is this head of mine, how the night rains
3 have drenched my hair! Ah, but my shift, I have laid it by: how
can I put it on again? My feet I washed but now; shall I soil them
4 with the dust? Then my true love thrust his hand through the lattice,
5 and I trembled inwardly at his touch. I rose up to let him in; but my
hands dripped ever with myrrh; still with the choicest myrrh my fingers
6 were slippery, as I caught the latch. When I opened, my true love
was gone; he had passed me by. How my heart had melted at the sound
of his voice! And now I searched for him in vain; there was no answer
7 when I called out to him. As they went the city rounds, the watchmen
fell in with me, that guard the gates; beat me, and left me wounded,
8 and took away my cloak. I charge you, maidens of Jerusalem, fall
you in with the man I long for, give him this news of me, that I pine
away with love.[3]

---

[1] 'Incense-tree'; the Latin version here transliterates, 'trees of Lebanon',
instead of translating the second noun.

[2] *vv.* 1–7: The first of these verses may describe a reunion which presents
itself to the imagination of the village girl as she falls asleep; the remainder
are evidently a dream, which repeats, with variations, the dream of 3. 1–3.

[3] *vv.* 8–17: These verses, with the first two of the following chapter, form a
dialogue in which the village girl, now awake, satisfies the curiosity of her
companions about her lover's appearance, but puts them off with vague guesses
as to his whereabouts.

9   Nay, but tell us, fairest of women, how shall we know this sweetheart of thine from another's? We must know him from another's sweetheart, if we are to join in the search with thee.

10   My sweetheart? Among ten thousand you shall know him; so white
11 is the colour of his fashioning, and so red. His head dazzles like the purest gold; the hair on it lies close as the high palm-branches, raven
12 hair. His eyes are gentle as doves by the brook-side, only these are
13 bathed in milk, eyes full of repose.[1] Cheeks trim as a spice-bed of the perfumer's own tending; drench lilies in the finest myrrh, and you
14 shall know the fragrance of his lips. Hands well rounded; gold set with jacynth is not workmanship so delicate; body of ivory, and veins
15 of sapphire blue; legs straight as marble columns, that stand in sockets of gold. Erect his stature as Lebanon itself, noble as Lebanon
16 cedar. Oh, that sweet utterance! Nothing of him but awakes desire. Such is my true love, maidens of Jerusalem; such is the companion I have lost.

17   But where went he, fairest of women, this true love of thine? Tell us what haunts he loves, and we will come with thee to search for him.

CHAPTER SIX

W̶HERE should he be, my true love, but among the spices; where
2 but in his garden, gathering the lilies? All mine, my true love, and I all his; ever he would choose the lilies for his pasture-ground.[2]
3 Fair thou art and graceful, my heart's love; for beauty, Jerusalem itself is not thy match; yet no embattled array so awes men's hearts.[3]
4 Turn thy eyes away, that so unman me! Hair dazzling as the goats
5 have, when they come flocking home from the Galaad hills; teeth white as ewes fresh from the washing, well matched as the twin lambs
6 that follow them; barren is none; thy cheeks shew through their veil
7 rosy as skin of pomegranate! What are three score of queens, and
8 eighty concubines, and maids about them past all counting? One there is beyond compare; for me, none so gentle, none so pure! Only once her mother travailed; she would have no darling but this. Maid

---

[1] 'Eyes full of repose'; we can only make guesses at the meaning of the Hebrew phrase, 'reposing upon fullness', which the Latin version renders 'residing by the floods'.

[2] *vv*. 1, 2 evidently continue the thought of the preceding chapter.

[3] *vv*. 3–9: The allusions in *vv*. 4–6 (cf. 4. 1–3 above) suggest that the village girl is being addressed; but this time, it would seem, by king Solomon (cf. *vv*. 7, 8). That he should hit upon the same terms of comparison is perhaps a stroke of deliberate art.

was none that saw her but called her blessed; queen was none, nor
9 concubine, but spoke in her praise. Who is this, whose coming
shews like the dawn of day? No moon so fair, no sun so majestic, no
embattled array so awes men's hearts.
10   But when I betook me to the fruit garden, to find apples in the
hollows, to see if vine had flowered there, and pomegranate had
11 budded,   all unawares, my heart misgave me . . . beside the chariots of
Aminadab.[1]
12   Come back, maid of Sulam, come back; let us feast our eyes on
thee. Maid of Sulam, come back, come back![2]

CHAPTER SEVEN

WHAT can the woman of Sulam give you to feast your eyes on,
if it be not the dance of the Two Camps?[3]
   Ah, princely maid, how dainty are the steps of thy sandalled feet!
Thighs well shaped as the beads of a necklace, some master-craftsman's
2 work;   navel delicately carved as a goblet, that has ever its meed of
3 liquor, belly rounded like a heap of corn amid the lilies. Graceful
4 thy breasts are as two fawns of the gazelle. Thy neck rising proudly
like a tower, but all of ivory; deep, deep thy eyes, like those pools at
Hesebon, under Beth-rabbim Gate; thy nose imperious as the keep
5 that frowns on Damascus from the hill-side. Thy head erect as
6 Carmel, bright as royal purple the braided ripples of thy hair. How
7 graceful thou art, dear maiden, how fair, how dainty! Thy stature

---

[1] *vv.* 10, 11: There is no clue to the speaker; naturally we assume that it is still
king Solomon. A comparison of the words used with verse 1 above and 7.8 below
suggests that it was his intention to make the village girl his bride. At this point,
the text seems to play us false; the statement (both in the Hebrew and in the
Septuagint Greek), 'My soul made me into the chariots of Aminadab' (or, of my
noble people), is one which gives no tolerable sense. It is probably implied that
the speaker swooned away, but the exact meaning of the verse is irrecoverable, and
it is not even certain that there may not be a serious gap in the text of the poem.

[2] This verse, in which the word 'Sulamite' occurs for the first time, belongs
in its context to the succeeding chapter.

[3] *vv.* 1–9: The first sentence is presumably spoken by the Sulamite herself,
the rest by Solomon. It is commonly assumed that this woman of Sulam (or
Sunam, III Kg. 1. 3) is the village girl who was the heroine of the preceding
chapters. But this is not stated; and we are free, if we will, to regard her as a
new character in the drama; a dancer whose charms, lavishly displayed,
distract king Solomon from his former love. At the end of verse 5 the Hebrew
text probably means 'a king is held captive by thy ringlets', which confirms the
impression that king Solomon is the speaker.

8 challenges the palm tree, thy breasts the clustering vine. What thought should I have but to reach the tree's top, and gather its fruit?
9 Breasts generous as the grape, breath sweet as apples, mouth soft to my love's caress [1] as good wine is soft to the palate, as food to lip and tooth.
10 My true love, I am all his; and who but I the longing of his
11 heart? [2] Come with me, my true love; for us the country ways, the
12 cottage roof for shelter. Dawn shall find us in the vineyard, looking to see what flowers the vine has, and whether they are growing into fruit; whether the pomegranates are in blossom. And there thou shalt be
13 master of my love. The mandrakes, what scent they give! Over the door at home there are fruits of every sort a-drying; I put them by, new and old, for my true love to eat.

CHAPTER EIGHT

WOULD that thou wert my brother, nursed at my own mother's breast! Then I could meet thee in the open street and kiss thee,
2 and earn no contemptuous looks. [3] To my mother's house I will lead thee, my captive; there thou shalt teach me my lessons, and I will give
3 thee spiced wine to drink, fresh brewed from my pomegranates. His left hand pillows my head; his right hand, even now, ready to embrace
4 me! An oath, maidens of Jerusalem! Never wake from her sleep my heart's love, till wake she will! [4]
5 Who is this that makes her way up by the desert road, all gaily clad, leaning upon the arm of her true love? [5]

---

[1] *v.* 9: 'To my love's caress'; in the original, the phrase is 'to him whom I love', but this introduces utter confusion into the passage, and the change of a single vowel-point gives us 'my caresses' as in 1.1 and elsewhere.

[2] *vv.* 10–13: The village girl, who has now evidently said good-bye to the court, rejoins her lover.

[3] *vv.* 1–14: Although the transitions of thoughts are not always easy to follow, this chapter can be read without difficulty as lovers' talk, following on the reunion implied in the foregoing chapter. So read, it is curiously graphic, from verse 1, in which the village girl complains of prying eyes, to verse 14, in which her lover complains of being overheard.

[4] *vv.* 3, 4: The bride, in a drowsy ecstasy, repeats both her own words and Solomon's words from 2. 6, 7.

[5] It is not clear whether the first half of this verse is spoken by the bride, or by onlookers; cf. 3. 6. The words 'all gaily clad' are in the Septuagint Greek, but not in the Hebrew text. In the second half, the bride speaks, reminding her lover that their trysting-place has been the actual place in which he was born; this is the sense both of the Hebrew text and of the Septuagint Greek, though

When I came and woke thee, it was under the apple-tree, the same where sore distress overtook thy own mother, where she that bore
6 thee had her hour of shame. Hold me close to thy heart, close as locket or bracelet fits; not death itself is so strong as love, not the grave itself cruel as love unrequited; the torch that lights it is a blaze of
7 fire. Yes, love is a fire no waters avail to quench, no floods to drown; for love, a man will give up all that he has in the world, and think nothing of his loss.
8 A little sister we have, still unripe for the love of man;[1] but the day will come when a man will claim her; what cheer shall she have from
9 us then? Steadfast as a wall if she be, that wall shall be crowned with silver; yield she as a door yields, we have cedar boards to fasten
10 her. And I, I am a wall; impregnable this breast as a fortress; and the man who claimed me found in me a bringer of content.
11 Solomon had a vineyard at Baal-Hamon; and when he gave the care of it to vine-dressers, each of these must pay a thousand silver pieces
12 for the revenue of it. A vineyard I have of my own, here at my side; keep thy thousand pieces, Solomon, and let each vine-dresser have his two hundred; not mine to grudge them.[2]
13 Where is thy love of retired garden walks? All the countryside is
14 listening to thee. Give me but the word to come away, thy bridegroom, with thee; hasten away, like gazelle or fawn that spurns the scented hill-side underfoot.

---

the Latin version curiously has: 'There thy mother was ravished; there she who bore thee was violated'.

[1] *vv.* 8, 9 are evidently a countryside song or proverb, which the bride quotes here so as to emphasise (in verse 10) her own faithfulness.

[2] *vv.* 11, 12: (Cf. Mt. 21.34.) The Latin version here has translated the proper names as common nouns, which yields no good sense.

BOOK OF WISDOM

CHAPTER ONE

LISTEN, all you who are judges here on earth. Learn to love justice; learn to think high thoughts of what God is, and with
2 sincere hearts aspire to him. Trust him thou must, if find him thou wouldst; he does not reveal himself to one that challenges his power.
3 Man's truant thoughts may keep God at a distance, but when the
4 test of strength comes, folly is shewn in its true colours; never yet did wisdom find her way into the schemer's heart, never yet made
5 her home in a life mortgaged to sin. A holy thing it is, the spirit that brings instruction; how it shrinks away from the touch of falsehood, holds aloof from every rash design! It is a touchstone, to betray the
6 neighbourhood of wrong-doing. A good friend to man is this spirit of wisdom, that convicts the blasphemer of his wild words; God can witness his secret thoughts, can read his heart unerringly, and shall
7 his utterance go unheard? No, the spirit of the Lord fills the whole world; bond that holds all things in being, it takes cognisance of every
8 sound we utter; how should ill speech go unmarked, or the scrutiny of
9 justice pass it by? The hidden counsel of the godless will all come to light; no word of it but reaches the divine hearing, and betrays their
10 wicked design; that jealous ear man's lowest whisper cannot escape.
11 Beware, then, of whispering, and to ill purpose; ever let your tongues refrain from calumny. Think not that the secret word goes for nought;
12 lying lips were ever the soul's destroying. Death for its goal, is not life's aim missed? Labours he well, that labours to bring doom about
13 his ears? Death was never of God's fashioning; not for his pleasure
14 does life cease to be; what meant his creation, but that all created things should have being? No breed has he created on earth but for its thriving; none carries in itself the seeds of its own destruction.
15 Think not that mortality bears sway on earth;[1]   no end nor term is
16 fixed to a life well lived . . .[2]   It is the wicked that have brought death on themselves, by word and deed of their own; court death, and melt away in its embrace, keep tryst with it, and lay claim to its partnership.

---

[1] What is said here is understood by some as referring only to human life; others take it as implying that mortality in general owes its origin to the fall of Adam.

[2] This verse seems to be incomplete; the old Sixtine Vulgate adds, on the authority of certain Latin manuscripts, the phrase 'death is earned only by wrong-doing'.

CHAPTER TWO

REASON they offer, yet reason all amiss. Their hearts tell them.
So brief our time here, so full of discomfort, and death brings no
remedy! Never a man yet made good his title to have come back from
2 the grave! Whence came we, none can tell; and it will be all one
hereafter whether we lived or no. What is our breath, but a passing
vapour; what is our reason, but a spark that sets the brain whirling?
3 Quench that spark, and our body is turned to ashes; like a spent sigh,
our breath is wasted on the air; like the cloud-wrack our life passes
away, unsubstantial as the mist yonder sun disperses with its ray,
4 bears down with its heat. Time will surely efface our memory, and
5 none will mark the record of our doings. Only a passing shadow, this
life of ours, and from its end there is no returning; the doom is sealed,
and there is no acquittal.
6   Come then (they say), let us enjoy pleasure, while pleasure is ours;
7 youth does not last, and creation is at our call; of rich wine and well
spiced take we our fill. Spring shall not cheat us of her blossoming;
8 crown we our heads with roses ere they wither; be every meadow the
9 scene of our wanton mirth. Share we the revels all alike, leave traces
everywhere of our joyous passing; no part or lot have we but this.
10   Helpless innocence shall lie at our mercy; not for us to spare the
11 widow, to respect the venerable head, grown white with years. Might
12 shall be our right, weakness count for proof of worthlessness. Where
is he, the just man? We must plot to be rid of him; he will not lend himself to our purposes. Ever he must be thwarting our plans; transgress
we the law, he is all reproof, depart we from the traditions of our race,
13 he denounces us. What, would he claim knowledge of divine secrets,
14 give himself out as the son of God? The touchstone, he, of our
15 inmost thoughts; we cannot bear the very sight of him, his life so
different from other men's, the path he takes, so far removed from
16 theirs! No better than false coin he counts us, holds aloof from our
doings as though they would defile him; envies the just their future
17 happiness, boasts of a divine parentage. Put we his claims, then, to
18 the proof; let experience shew what end awaits him. If to be just is
to be God's son indeed, then God will take up his cause, will save him
19 from the power of his enemies.[1] Outrage and torment, let these be
the tests we use; let us see that gentleness of his in its true colours,

---

[1] Cf. Mt. 27. 43.

20 find out what his patience is worth. Sentenced let him be to a shameful death; by his own way of it, he shall find deliverance.[1]
21   So false the calculations that are blinded by human malice! The
secret purposes of God they might not fathom; how should they foresee that holiness is requited, how should they pass true award on a
23 blameless life? God, to be sure, framed man for an immortal destiny,
24 the created image of his own endless being; but, since the devil's
25 envy brought death into the world, they make him their model that
take him for their master.[2]

CHAPTER THREE

BUT the souls of the just are in God's hands, and no torment, in
2   death itself, has power to reach them. Dead? Fools think so;
3 think their end loss, their leaving us, annihilation; but all is well
4 with them. The world sees nothing but the pains they endure; they
5 themselves have eyes only for what is immortal; so light their suffering, so great the gain they win! God, all the while, did but test them,
6 and testing them found them worthy of him. His gold, tried in the
crucible, his burnt-sacrifice, graciously accepted, they do but wait
7 for the time of their deliverance; then they will shine out, these just
souls, unconquerable as the sparks that break out, now here, now
8 there, among the stubble.[3] Theirs to sit in judgement on nations, to
subdue whole peoples, under a Lord whose reign shall last for ever.
9 Trust him if thou wilt, true thou shalt find him;[4] faith waits for him
calmly and lovingly; who claims his gift, who shall attain peace, if not
they, his chosen servants?[5]
10   But dearly shall the wicked pay for their error,[6] for the claims of
11 right forgotten, for the Lord's will defied. Their case is pitiable
indeed, who make light of true wisdom and of ordered living; vain
12 their hope, profitless their toil, barren their achievement. Light
13 women are the wives they wed, worthless is their brood; a curse
lies on their begetting. Blessed, rather, her lot, that childless is, yet

---

[1] Some would render, less plausibly, 'he shall be judged by his words'.

[2] 'They make him their model'; the Greek text has, 'they experience it', i.e.,
death.

[3] Mt., 13.43.

[4] 'Trust him if thou wilt, true thou shalt find him'; literally, 'those who trust
in him shall understand truth'. The word 'truth' in the Old Testament refers,
as a rule, either to human loyalty or to divine fidelity.

[5] 'His chosen servants'; the Greek text gives, 'His holy ones; who shall find
deliverance, if not his chosen servants?'

[6] Or perhaps, 'The scheming of the wicked shall recoil on them in punishment'.

chaste, that never knew the bed of shame; offspring she will not lack,
14 when holy souls have their reward. Nay, let there be some eunuch
that has kept his hands clear of wrong, has never harboured treasonable thought against the Lord; he too with rare gifts shall be faithfully
rewarded, shall have the portion that most contents him in God's
15 holy place.[1] A noble harvest good men reap from their labours;
16 wisdom is a root which never yet cast its crop. Not so the adulterers; never look for children of theirs to thrive; the offspring of the
17 unhallowed wedlock will vanish away.[2] Live they long, they shall
18 be held in no regard, in their late age unhonoured; die they soon,
they shall die without hope, no comfort to sustain them in the day
19 when all comes to light. Bitterly they shall rue it hereafter, the race
of the evil-doers.

CHAPTER FOUR

HOW fair a thing is the unwedded life [3] that is nobly lived! Think
not the memory of it can fade; God and man alike preserve the
2 record; in life how eagerly imitated, in death how long regretted,
in eternity how crowned with triumph, the conquest gained in fields
3 of honourable striving! Let the wicked gender as they will, it shall
nothing avail them; what, should those bastard slips ever strike their
4 roots deep, base the tree firm? Burgeon they may for a little, but
the wind will shake their frail hold; root and all, the storm will carry
5 them away. Half-formed, the boughs will be snapped off, and their
6 fruit go to waste, unripe, unprofitable. And indeed, when the day
of reckoning comes, needs must they should be cited as witnesses
against their own parents, these, the children of their shame, by
unlawful dalliance begotten.[4]

7 Not so the innocent; though he should die before his time, rest
8 shall be his. A seniority there is that claims reverence, owing nothing
to time, not measured by the lapse of years; count a man grey-
9 haired when he is wise, ripe of age when his life is stainless. Divine
favour, divine love banished him from a life he shared with
11 sinners; caught him away, before wickedness could pervert his
12 thoughts, before wrong-doing could allure his heart; such witchery

---

[1] Cf. Deut. 23.1; Is. 56.3. 'He too with rare gifts shall be faithfully rewarded'; literally, 'He too shall be given a rare gift of fidelity'.

[2] Some think that adultery, here as often in the Old Testament, is used by a
metaphor for the worship of false gods.

[3] In the Greek text, 'even a childless life'.

[4] Some think that the author is condemning, not literal adultery, but marriage
with the heathen.

evil has, to tarnish honour, such alchemy do the roving passions exer-
13 cise even on minds that are true metal. With him, early achievement
14 counted for long apprenticeship; so well the Lord loved him, from
a corrupt world he would grant him swift release.
15   The world looks on, uncomprehending; a hard lesson it is to learn,
that God does reward, does pity his chosen friends, does grant his
16 faithful servants deliverance. Did they know it, the death of the
just man, with its promise early achieved, is a reproach to the wicked
17 that live yet, unregarded in their late old age. But what see they?
Here is a man dead, and all his wisdom could not save him. That
the Lord planned all this, and for the saving of him, does not enter
18 their minds. What wonder if the sight fills them with contempt?
And they themselves, all the while, are earning the Lord's contempt;
they themselves, doomed to lie there dishonoured among the dead,
19 eternally a laughing-stock! How they will stand aghast, when he
pricks the bubble of their pride![1] Ruins they shall be, overthrown
from the foundation, land for ever parched dry; bitter torment shall
20 be theirs, and their name shall perish irrecoverably. Alas, the long
tally of their sins! Trembling they shall come forward, and the
record of their misdeeds shall rise up to confront them.

CHAPTER FIVE

H OW boldly, then, will the just man appear, to meet his old
2 persecutors, that thwarted all his striving! And they, in what
craven fear they will cower at the sight of him, amazed at the sudden
3 reversal of his fortunes! Inward remorse will wring a groan from
those hearts: Why, these were the men we made into a laughing-stock
4 and a by-word! We, poor fools, mistook the life they lived for
5 madness, their death for ignominy; and now they are reckoned as
God's own children, now it is among his holy ones that their lot is cast.[2]
6   Far, it seems, did our thoughts wander from the true path; never
7 did the ray of justice enlighten them, never the true sun shone. Weary
it proved, the reckless way of ruin, lonely were the wastes we travelled,
8 who missed the path the Lord meant for us. What advantage has it
brought us, all our pomp and pride? How are we the better for all
9 our vaunted wealth? Nothing of that but is gone, unsubstantial as
10 a shadow, swift as courier upon his errand. The ship that ploughs

---

[1] Literally, 'when he breaks them asunder, all puffed up as they are'. The
sense of the Greek text is probably, 'When he throws them down headlong'.
   [2] *vv.* 3–5: 'These were the men' . . . in the Greek text, 'This is the man'. . .
the singular being used throughout.

angry waves, what trace is left of her passage? How wilt thou track
11 her keel's pathway through the deep? The bird's flight through air
what print betrays? So fiercely lashed the still breeze with the beating
of her pinions, as she cleaves her noisy way through heaven, wings
12 flapping, and is gone; and afterwards, what sign of her going? Or be
it some arrow, shot at a mark, that pierces the air, how quick the
13 wound closes, the journey is forgotten! So with us it was all one,
our coming to birth and our ceasing to be; no trace might we leave
behind us of a life well lived; we spent ourselves on ill-doing.
14   (Such is the lament of sinners, there in the world beneath.) [1] Short-
lived are all the hopes of the godless, thistle-down in the wind, flying
spray before the storm, smoke that whirls away in the breeze; as soon
16 forgotten as the guest that comes for a day, and comes no more. It
is the just that will live for ever; the Lord has their recompense waiting
17 for them, the most high God takes care of them. How glorious is
that kingdom, how beautiful that crown, which the Lord will bestow
on them! His right hand is there to protect them, his holy arm to be
18 their shield. Indignantly he will take up arms, mustering all the
19 forces of creation for vengeance on his enemies. His own faithfulness is the breast-plate he will put on, unswerving justice the helmet
20 he wears, a right cause his shield unfailing. See, where he whets the
sword of strict retribution, and the whole order of nature is banded
22 with him against his reckless foes! Well-aimed fly his thunder-bolts,
sped far and wide from yonder cloud-arch, never missing their
23 mark. Teeming hail-storms shall whirl about them, the artillery of
his vengeance; fiercely the sea's waves shall roar against them, pitilessly
24 the floods cut them off; the storm-wind shall rise in their faces, and
scatter them as the gust scatters chaff. The whole earth ransacked,
and the thrones of the mighty pulled down, by their own disobedience,
their own malignancy!

CHAPTER SIX

WISDOM more avails than strength; for a man of prudence, the
2   warrior is no match.[2] A word, then, for kings' ears to hear,
kings' hearts to heed; a message for you, rulers, wherever you
3 be! Listen well, all you that have multitudes at your command,
4 foreign hordes to do your bidding. Power is none but comes to you
from the Lord, nor any royalty but from One who is above all. He

---

[1] The words enclosed in brackets are not found in the Greek text.
[2] Verses 1 and 23 are not found in the Greek text.

it is that will call you to account for your doings, with a scrutiny that
5 reads your inmost thoughts; you that held his commission and
were false to it, justice neglected, the law set aside, his divine will
6 transgressed. Swift and terrible shall be his coming; strictly his
7 doom falls where heads rise high. For the meanest, there may be
8 pardon, for greatness, greater torment is reserved. What, should he
cringe before high rank, stand in awe of a name, he, the Lord of a
9 universe, that made great and little alike, that cares alike for all? Who
10 most has power, him the sharpest pains await. Do you, then, royal
sirs (for my warning touches none so nearly), learn wisdom's lesson,
11 and save yourselves from ruin. He that would find health, holy must
be and hallowed precepts observe; master these he must, if he would
12 make good his defence. Cherish these warnings of mine, and greedily
devour them for your instruction.
13   The bright beacon of wisdom, that never burns dim, how readily
14 seen by eyes that long for it, how open to their search! Nay, she is
beforehand with these her suitors, ready to make herself known to
15 them; no toilsome quest is his, that is up betimes to greet her; she is
16 there, waiting at his doors. Why, to entertain the very thought of
her is maturity of the mind; one night's vigil, and all thy cares are over.
17 She goes her rounds, to find men worthy of her favours; in the open
street unveils that smiling face of hers, comes deliberately to meet
18 them. The very first step towards wisdom is the desire for dis-
19 cipline, and how should a man care for discipline without loving it,
or love it without heeding its laws, or heed its laws without winning
20 immortality, or win immortality without drawing near to God? A
22 royal road it is, then, this desire for wisdom; and you, that have
nations under your sway, as you value throne and sceptre, must hold
23 wisdom in honour; how else shall your reign be eternal? (A welcome
light hers should be to the world's princes.)
24   What wisdom is, whence came its birth, I will now make known
to you. Not for me to withhold the secret; from first to last I will tell
the story of her origin, bring to light all that may be known of her,
25 no word of the truth passed by. Withhold it? Nay, the pale miser
that grudges his store was never friend of mine; no such character
26 befits the wise. Wide let wisdom be spread, for the more health of
mankind; what better security for a people, than prudence on the
27 throne? Learn, then, who will, the lesson of discernment; at my
charges, and to his profit.

CHAPTER SEVEN

W̲HAT of myself? Was not Solomon a mortal man like the rest of you, come down from that first man that was a thing of clay? [1]
I, too, was flesh and blood; ten months I lay a-fashioning in my
2 mother's womb; of woman's body my stuff came, and of man's
3 procreation; midnight joys went to the making of me. Born was I, and born drew in the common air; dust amid the dust I fell, and, baby-
4 fashion, my first utterance was a cry; swaddled I must be, and cared
5 for, like the rest. Tell me, was ever king had other manner of coming
6 to be? By one gate all enter life, by one gate all leave it.
7 Whence, then, did the prudence spring that endowed me? Prayer brought it; to God I prayed, and the spirit of wisdom came upon
8 me.[2] This I valued more than kingdom or throne; I thought nothing
9 of my riches in comparison. There was no jewel I could match with it; all my treasures of gold were a handful of dust beside it, my silver
10 seemed but base clay in presence of it. I treasured wisdom more than health or beauty, preferred her to the light of day; hers is a flame
11 which never dies down. Together with her all blessings came to me;
12 boundless prosperity was her gift. All this I enjoyed, with wisdom to prepare my way for me, never guessing that it all sprang from her.
13 The lessons she taught me are riches honestly won, shared without
14 stint, openly proclaimed; a treasure men will find incorruptible. Those who enjoy it are honoured with God's friendship, so high a value he sets on her instruction.
15 God's gift it is, if speech answers to thought of mine, and thought of mine to the message I am entrusted with. Who else can shew wise
16 men the true path, check them when they stray? We are in his hands, we and every word of ours; our prudence in act, our skill in craftsman-
17 ship. Sure knowledge he has imparted to me of all that is; how the
18 world is ordered, what influence have the elements, how the months [3] have their beginning, their middle, and their ending, how the sun's
19 course alters and the seasons revolve, how the years have their
20 cycles, the stars their places. To every living thing its own breed, to every beast its own moods; the winds [4] rage, and men think deep

---

[1] Solomon's name is not mentioned in the original; but it is certainly he who is represented as speaking in this and the following chapters.
[2] Cf. III Kg. 3. 9.
[3] Literally, 'The times'.
[4] Or perhaps 'the spirits', either human or diabolic.

thoughts; the plants keep their several kinds, and each root has its
21 own virtue; all the mysteries and all the surprises of nature were
made known to me; wisdom herself taught me, that is the designer
of them all.
22   Mind-enlightening is the influence that dwells in her; set high
apart; one in its source, yet manifold in its operation; subtle, yet
easily understood. An influence quick in movement, unassailable,
persuasive, gentle, right-thinking, keen-edged, irresistible, beneficent,
23 kindly, proof against all error and all solicitude. Nothing is beyond
its power, nothing hidden from its view, and such capacity has it
that it can pervade the minds of all living men; so pure and subtle an
24 essence is thought. Nothing so agile that it can match wisdom for
25 agility; nothing can penetrate this way and that, etherial as she. Steam
that ascends from the fervour of divine activity, pure effluence of his
26 glory who is God all-powerful, she feels no passing taint; she, the
glow that radiates from eternal light, she, the untarnished mirror of
27 God's majesty, she, the faithful echo of his goodness. Alone, with
none to aid her, she is all-powerful; herself ever unchanged, she makes
all things new; age after age she finds her way into holy men's hearts,
28 turning them into friends and spokesmen of God. Her familiars it
29 is, and none other, that God loves. Brightness is hers beyond the
brightness of the sun, and all the starry host; match her with light
30 itself, and she outvies it; light must still alternate with darkness,
but where is the conspiracy can pull down wisdom from her throne?

CHAPTER EIGHT

BOLD is her sweep from world's end to world's end, and everywhere her gracious ordering manifests itself.
2   She, from my youth up, has been my heart's true love, my heart's
true quest; she was the bride I longed for, enamoured of her
3 beauty. Was I moved by noble birth? No better claim than hers,
who dwells in God's palace, marked out by the Ruler of the world
4 as his favourite; the mistress of his craftsmanship, the arbiter of
5 his plans.[1] Or should life's dearest aim be wealth? Why then, who has
more wealth at her disposal than wisdom, that turns all to account?
6 Or if sound judgement is man's business, who else on earth goes to
7 work so skilfully as she?[2] If thy desire be for honest living, man's
excellences are the fruit she labours to produce; temperance and

---

[1] The exact meaning of verses 3 and 4 is uncertain.
[2] Or perhaps, 'Who but she is the contriver of all that is?'

prudence she teaches, justice and fortitude, and what in life avails
8 man more? Or if wide knowledge be thy ambition, she can inform
thee of what is past, make conjecture of the future; she is versed in
the subtleties of debate, in the reading of all riddles; marvels and
portents she can foretell, and what events time or season will bring.
9   Her, then, I would take to myself, to share my home; to be my
10 counsellor in prosperity, my solace in anxiety and grief. Through
her (said I) I shall win fame in the assembly, find honour, though so
11 young, amidst the elders. When I sit in judgement, quick wit I needs
must shew, strike awe into the princes when I appear before them;
12 silent they wait my leisure; speak I, they take heed; flows my speech
13 on, they listen, hand on lip. She, too, will bring me immortality;
14 imperishable the name I shall leave to after ages. Mine to rule
15 peoples, and have nations at my call; dread tyrants to daunt by the
very name of me, the name of a king so loved by his people, so brave
16 in battle. Then home again, to rest upon her bosom; no shrewish
mate, no tedious housewife, joy and contentment all of her.
17   So ran my thoughts, and well in my heart I pondered them.
18 Wisdom, that brought such kinship with immortality, whose friendship was such dear delight, whose wages earned were riches inexhaustible, her daily comradeship a training in sound judgement, the
eloquence she inspired an earnest of renown; win her for myself I must,
19 and went about to attain my purpose. I was, indeed, a boy of good
20 parts, and nobility of nature had fallen to my lot; gentle birth above
21 the common had endowed me with a body free from blemish.[1] But
to be master of myself was a thing I could not hope to come by,
except of God's bounty; I was wise enough already to know whence
the gift came. So to the Lord I turned, and made my request of him,
praying with all my heart in these words following:

CHAPTER NINE

GOD of our fathers, Lord of all mercy, thou by thy word hast made
2 all things, and thou in thy wisdom hast contrived man to rule
3 thy creation, to order the world by a law of right living and of just
dealing, and give true award in the honest purpose of his

---

[1] The Greek would naturally be taken to mean, 'Or rather, gentle birth had
endowed me. . .' But it is impossible to institute the desired contrast between
this and the preceding verse, whatever rendering of them is adopted. The
translation given above assumes that 'good' means 'nobly born', which is the
primary sense of the word in Greek. Literally, 'And being more good I came
into an undefiled body'.

4 heart. Wisdom I ask of thee, the same wisdom that dwells so near
5 thy throne; do not grudge me a place among thy retinue. Am I not
thy servant, and to thy service born? Mortal man thou seest me, the
puny creature of an hour, a mind unapt for judgement and the making
6 of laws. Grow man to what perfection he will, if he lacks the wisdom
7 that comes from thee, he is nothing; and me thou hast chosen to
reign over thy people; from me sons and daughters of thine must seek
8 for redress! More than this, thou hast bidden me raise thee temple
and altar, upon the holy mountain where thou dwellest, model of that
holy tabernacle, made long ago, whose pattern was of thy own
9 devising.[1] Wisdom was with thee then,[2] privy to all thy designs,
she who stood by thee at the world's creation, and knows thy whole
10 will, the whole tenour of thy commandments. Let her be thy envoy
still out of thy heavenly sanctuary; send her out still upon thy errand,
to be at my side too, and share my labours! How else should thy will
11 be made clear to me? For her, no secret, no riddle is too dark; her
12 prudent counsel will be my guide, the fame of her my protection. So
shall my task be accomplished as thou wouldst have it be; so shall I
give this people of thine just awards, no unworthy heir of the throne
my father left me.
13 What God's purpose is, how should man discover, how should his
14 mind master the secret of the Divine will? So hesitating our human
15 thoughts, so hazardous our conjectures! Ever the soul is weighed
down by a mortal body, earth-bound cell that clogs the manifold
16 activity of its thought. Hard enough to read the riddle of our life
here, with laborious search ascertaining what lies so close to hand;
17 and would we trace out heaven's mysteries too? Thy purposes none
may know, unless thou dost grant thy gift of wisdom, sending out
18 from high heaven thy own holy spirit. Thus ever were men guided
19 by the right way, here on earth, and learned to know thy will; ever
since the world began wisdom was the salve they used, that have won
thy favour.[3]

---

[1] Literally, 'Which thou didst make ready beforehand from the beginning'.
The rendering given assumes a reference to the tabernacle in the desert, and
the pattern of it shewn to Moses on Mount Sinai. Others would interpret the
verse as alluding to God's dwelling-place in heaven.

[2] Or perhaps, 'Wisdom is ever at thy side'.

[3] This verse is represented in the Greek text by four words, meaning 'And
were saved (or, healed) by wisdom'.

CHAPTER TEN

WHEN man was but newly made, the lonely father of this created world, she it was that watched over him, and set him free from
2 wrong-doing of his own,[1] and gave him the mastery over all things
3 else. Against her Cain rebelled,[2] when he did foul wrong, and by
4 murderous spite against his brother compassed his own ruin. Who but she, when the world was a-drowning for Cain's fault,[3] gave it a second term of life, steering, on a paltry raft, one innocent man to
5 safety? And when the nations went their several ways,[4] banded in a single conspiracy of wickedness, of one man's innocence she still took note; Abraham must be kept irreproachable in God's service,
6 and steeled against pity for his own child. Here was another innocent man, Lot, that owed his preservation to Wisdom, when godless folk were perishing all around him. Escape he should, when fire came
7 down upon the Cities of the Plain; those five cities whose shame is yet unforgotten, while smoke issues from the barren soil, and never tree bears seasonable fruit, and the pillar of salt stands monument to
8 an unbelieving soul. Fatal neglect of Wisdom's guidance, that could blind their eyes to the claims of honour, and leave the world such a memorial of their folly, as should make the record of their sins unmistakable!
9 But those who cherish her, Wisdom brings safely out of all their
10 striving. When Jacob, her faithful servant, was in flight from his brother's anger, she guided him straight to his goal, and on the way shewed him the heavenly kingdom, gave him knowledge of holy things. She enriched him by his toil, and gave all his labours a happy issue.
11 Knavery went about to get the better of him, but she stood by him
12 and prospered him; kept him safe from his enemies, protected him from their scheming. She would have him wrestle manfully, and
13 prove that there is no strength like the strength of wisdom. When

---

[1] It is not clear whether the final words of this verse refer to Adam's original innocence, or to his deliverance from the death-penalty after he had sinned.

[2] This chapter, in the original, mentions no proper names; a few of them have here been supplied, in accordance with modern usage.

[3] 'For Cain's fault' is an expression difficult to account for, except on the view that the 'sons of God' mentioned in Gen. 6. 2, are the descendants of Seth, the 'children of men' those of Cain.

[4] The Latin here obscures the sense of the original, by describing the nations as 'coming together'. According to the Greek text, they 'were confounded', almost certainly a reference to Gen. 11.7, where the same verb is used. Mankind, for its sin, was split up into a multitude of nations, but Wisdom saw to it that one of these, with Abraham as its founder, should be different from the rest.

Joseph, in his innocence, was sold for a slave, Wisdom did not desert him, did not leave him among the guilty, but went down with him
14 into his dungeon. Fast he was bound, but she had not finished with him till she gave him dominion over a whole kingdom, and power to do what he would with his persecutors. So she brought home the lie to those who had traduced him, and won him everlasting fame.

15 So, too, with that innocent people of Israel, that unoffending race;
16 did she not deliver them from the nations that kept them under? Did she not enter into the heart of God's servant, confronting dread rulers
17 with portent and with miracle? Did she not restore to men ill-used the just reward of their labours? She, too, led them out on their miraculous journey, affording them shelter by day and starry radiance at
18 night. She made a passage for them through the Red Sea, brought
19 them safely through those leagues of water, and churned up the
20 bodies of their drowned enemy from those unfathomed depths. So, enriched by the spoils of the godless, they extolled, O Lord, thy holy
21 name, proclaimed with one voice thy sovereign power; Wisdom opened the dumb mouths, and made the lips of infants [1] vocal with praise.

CHAPTER ELEVEN

WITH Moses set apart for his spokesman, [2] to what good issue he
2 brought all their enterprises! Through desert solitudes they
3 journeyed on, pitching their camp far from the haunts of men; boldly
4 they confronted their enemy, and overcame his malice. When they were thirsty, on thy name they called, and out of the rocks's sheer face
5 water was given to heal their thirst, out of the hard flint. Strange likeness between the punishment that befell their enemies, [3] who went
6 thirsty while Israel had drink to their heart's content, and the relief
7 of their want Israel now experienced! Thou who once, into defiling
8 blood, hadst troubled the sources of a living stream, to avenge a murderous edict against new-born children, didst now give thy
9 people abundant water to drink, by means unlooked for. How ill it

---

[1] Unless the word 'infants' is to be understood metaphorically (of the Jews, as a people newly born by their ransoming from Egypt), this verse seems to preserve a tradition not found in Ex. 15.1, that even little children took part in the song of Moses.

[2] The word 'Moses', here and in verse 14, like the names of Egyptian and Israelite, has been inserted for the sake of clearness.

[3] *vv.* 5–14: The thought of this whole passage is obscurely expressed in the original, and it is still further obscured by the Latin translation in verses 8 and 13, where the Greek has to be used as a guide, if we are to obtain any tolerable sense.

had gone with their adversaries in Egypt, that thirst of theirs in the
10 desert plainly shewed them; in mercy schooled, yet sorely tried, they
learned to know what torments the wicked had undergone, forfeit to
11 thy vengeance. For Israel, only a test of their faith, only a father's
correction; for Egypt, as from a king, stern scrutiny and stern doom.
12 Tidings from far away, that racked the Egyptians no less than their
13 own former sufferings; anguish redoubled, as they groaned over the
14 memory of things past! That the same plague of thirst which had
tortured themselves should be the source of Israel's rejoicing! Then
indeed they felt the Lord's power, then indeed they wondered at
15 the revenge time had brought; wondered at Moses, whom their
insolence had long ago disinherited, when they exposed him with
the other children. Thirst, that had been Egypt's enemy, had no terrors
for the just.
16 So lost to piety were these Egyptians, such foolish reasonings led
them astray, that they worshipped brute [1] reptiles, and despicable
vermin. And swarms of brute beasts thou didst send to execute thy
17 vengeance, for the more proof that a man's own sins are the instrument
18 of his punishment. Thy power knows no restraint, the power that
created an ordered world out of dark chaos. It had been easy to send
19 a plague of bears upon them, or noble lions; or to form new creatures,
of a ferocity hitherto unknown, breathing fiery breath, churning out
20 foul fumes, terrible sparks darting from their eyes, so that men would
die of fear at their very aspect, without waiting for proof of their
21 power to do harm. Nay, without more ado thou mightest have
overthrown them with a single blast; all at once thy justice might
have tracked them down, thy fierce breath whirled them away; but no,
all thou doest is done in exact measure, all is nicely calculated and
weighed.
22 No moment passes but thou, if thou wilt, canst shew thyself supreme;
23 that arm has power there is no withstanding; the whole world,
matched against thee, is but a scruple on the balance, is but a drop of
24 dew, falling to earth at sunrise. Only thou art all-merciful, as befits
the Almighty, and dost overlook our human slips, in hope of our
25 repentance. All things thou lovest, nor holdest any of thy creatures
26 in abhorrence; hate and create thou couldst not, nor does aught
abide save at thy will, whose summoning word holds them in being.
27 They are thine, and thou sparest them; all things that live thou lovest,
thou, the Master of them all.

---

[1] It seems likely that the author meant rather, 'inconsiderable'; cf. verse 17.
The Egyptians, who were credited with worshipping beetles, were punished
by plagues of insects.

CHAPTER TWELVE

2 THY kindly influence, Lord, thy gracious influence is all about us. At the first false step, none is so ready to rebuke us, to remind and warn us of our error, bidding us come back and renew 3 our loyalty to thee. So it was with the former inhabitants of this 4 thy holy land. Good reason thou hadst to be their enemy; of what detestable practices were they not guilty, with those sorceries and 5 unhallowed rites of theirs! Murderers that would not spare their own children, that feasted on human flesh, human entrails and blood, 6 were they to take part in thy ceremonies? No, thy will was that our fathers should root them out, the unnatural parents of a race past all 7 aid;[1] and this land, dear to thee as no other, should be more worthily peopled by the sons of God. Yet they, too, were men, and thou 8 wouldst deal gently with them; thou wouldst send hornets as the van- 9 guard of thy invading host, to wear them down gradually.[2] Not that it was beyond thy power to give piety the mastery over godless- ness by victory in battle, by some plague of ravening monsters, or 10 by one word of doom. But no, their sentence should be executed by degrees, giving them opportunity to repent; though indeed thou knewest well that theirs was a worthless breed, of a malice so ingrained, 11 that they would turn aside from their ill devices never; from its beginnings, an accursed race.

Nor, if thou wast patient with the sinner, was it human respect 12 that persuaded thee to it. Thy acts who shall question, thy doom who shall gainsay? Will some champion arise to challenge thee on behalf of these rebels, tax thee with unmaking the peoples thou hast 13 made? God there is none save thou, that hast a whole world for thy 14 province; and shall thy justice abide our question? Punish thou mayst as punish thou wilt; king nor emperor can be bold to outface 15 thee. So high beyond our censure, and therewithal so just in thy dealings! To condemn the innocent were unworthy of such majesty as 16 thine; of all justice, thy power is the true source, universal lordship 17 the ground of universal love! Only when thy omnipotence is doubted wilt thou assert thy mastery, their rashness making manifest, who will 18 not acknowledge thee;[3] elsewhere, with such power at thy disposal,

---

[1] *vv.* 5, 6: The Greek text is here almost certainly corrupt, and the words rendered 'Were they to take part in thy ceremonies?' do not correspond to the existing Greek, or to any probable emendation of it.

[2] See Ex. 23.28.

[3] The Greek text, probably by an error, gives 'who acknowledge thee'.

a lenient judge thou provest thyself, riding us with a light rein, and keeping thy terrors in reserve.

19   Two lessons thy people were to learn from these dealings of thine; ever should justice and mercy go hand in hand, never should thy own

20 children despair of forestalling thy justice by repentance. What, so patient, so unhurrying, in thy vengeance on the doomed enemies of thy chosen race; always delay, always the opportunity given them

21 to repent of their misdeeds; and wouldst thou shew less anxious care in trying the cause of thy own children, bound to thee from of

22 old by a sworn covenant so rich in mercies? It is for our instruction, then, that thou usest such exquisite care in the punishing of our enemies;[1] judge we, let us imitate thy clemency, abide we judgement, let us ever hope for pardon.

23   And so it was that thou didst plague the Egyptians,[2] that were knaves and fools both; their own false gods should be the undoing of

24 them. This was the worst error of all their erring, that they worshipped the meanest of beasts as gods; silly children had been no

25 more credulous. Why then, these silly children should have play-

26 time penalties first; of those play-time penalties if they took no

27 heed, then at last they should feel how a God can punish. Humiliated they well might be at those sufferings of theirs, the very gods they worshipped the instruments of their distress; a sight enough to convince them that he was the true God, whom all this while they had rejected! But no, they must needs bring upon themselves the full rigours of justice.

CHAPTER THIRTEEN

WHAT folly it argues in man's nature, this ignorance of God! So much good seen, and he, who is existent Good,[3] not known! Should they not learn to recognise the Artificer by the contemplation of his

2 works? Instead, they have pointed us to fire, or wind, or to the nimble air, wheeling stars, or tempestuous waves, or sun and moon,

3 and made gods of them, to rule the world! Perhaps the beauty of such

---

[1] The first half of this verse is ordinarily rendered, 'In chastening us, thou dost scourge our enemies ten thousandfold'; but it will be seen that such considerations are out of harmony with the rest of the sentence.

[2] The word 'Egyptians' does not occur in the original, but the reference of this passage is almost certainly to them; cf. 11. 15 above. For 'didst plague' the Latin version has, 'didst inflict the utmost torments upon', but this misses the sense. The plagues of lice, flies, locusts, etc., are here contrasted, as being comparatively light, with the last two plagues, to be mentioned in ch. 17 and 18.

[3] Or perhaps simply, 'who is'.

things bewitched them into mistaking it for divinity? Ay, but what of him who is Master of them all; what excellence must be his, the
4 Author of all beauty, that could make them! Or was it power, and power's exercise, that awoke their wonderment? Why then, how many
5 times greater must he be, who contrived it! Such great beauty [1] even creatures have, reason is well able to contemplate the Source from which these perfections came.
6   Yet, if we find fault with men like these, their fault is little by comparison; err they may, but their desire is to find God, and it is in
7 that search they err. They stop short in their enquiry at the contemplation of his creatures, trusting only in the senses, that find
8 such beauty there. Excuse them, then, we may not; if their thoughts could reach far enough to form a judgement about the world around them, how is it they found, on the way, no trace of him who is Master
10 of it? But there are men more wretched yet, men who repose all their confidence in a world of shadows. They give the name of god to what is made by human art, gold and silver that human workmanship has turned into the likeness of living things, blocks of senseless stone that human hands have carved, long ago.
11   What would you? Here is a craftsman in wood has been to the forest and sawed off a fine straight branch; deftly he strips off the bark, and fashions, with patient skill, some piece of carpentry apt for man's
12 needs. As for the chips in his workshop, they cook his meal for him,
13 to eat and take his fill. But one more piece of refuse wood is left, that is fit for nothing; so crooked is it and so gnarled. See him, in an idle moment, pick it up and spend his leisure carving it! A master craftsman this; ere long it has taken shape, made into a man's like-
14 ness; or it may be he gives it the form of a senseless beast. And now he paints it with ochre; ruddled it must be till all its native colour
15 is lost, all its faults hidden away. That done, he must find a suitable room to house it, and there lets it into the wall, making it fast with
16 iron clamps. No pains does he spare to keep it from falling; fall if it does, it shall find no remedy; please you, this is but an image, and cannot shift for itself!
17   And so, unashamed, for home and children and wife he utters his
18 prayer, addressing himself all the while to a senseless thing. A weak, foolish thing, and for health he asks it; dead, and he will have life of
19 it; shiftless, and he will have aid of it. How should it set forward his journeyings, that cannot walk? What service should it do, if trade he want, or skill, or good fortune, that is every way unserviceable?

---

[1] Some manuscripts of the Greek read, 'such greatness and beauty'.

CHAPTER FOURTEEN

NAY, here is one that will go a-voyaging, the wild waves for his pathway, and perishable wood to carry him, yet he makes his
2 prayer to a piece of wood more perishable yet! As for the ship's timbers, it was man's covetousness that made the need for them, and
3 man's skill that fashioned them; but it is thy fatherly Providence that brings her safe to port; thou hast made the sea into a high road
4 men may travel by without harm, as if thou wouldst prove to us how
5 strong is thy protection, though the sailor have little skill. So careful art thou that the gifts thy wisdom affords us should not go unused; man ventures his life on a few planks, and the frail barque gives him
6 safe conduct across the waves. And what marvel? At the beginning of all, when the giants perished in their pride, was not such a barque the refuge of all the world's hopes? Yet thy hand was at the helm, and
7 the seed of life was saved for posterity. A blessing on the wood that
8 can so procure salvation! But yonder idol is accursed, no less than the man who made it; he for his wicked design, and the lifeless thing
9 for the legend of divinity that was attached to it. Sinner and sin,
10 God hates both; pardon is none for deed or doer. Thus it is that a time of reckoning will come for these idols the Gentiles make; part of God's creation though they be, he detests them, so have they entangled men's souls, and laid a trap for fools.
12 When idols were first devised, then began unfaithfulness; there was
13 death in the invention of them. For indeed they were no part of
14 man's life from the first, nor shall be at the last; it was but man's folly brought them into the world, and there shall be a short way with
15 them yet. Here was some father, bowed with sorrow before his time, his child untimely lost; of those features, mortal and now dead, he must have the likeness made, and with that, rites of initiation must
16 become the tradition of his clan. As time went on, impious habit grew into impious custom. A king would have his own likeness
17 carved, and his subjects, living far away, so that they could not do obeisance to him in person, would have his present image set up in
18 their view, eager to pay his absent royalty their adulation. And if any spur were needed yet for their ignorant superstition, the rivalry
19 of craftsmen afforded it; each of these sought to please his master
20 by improving the portrait, with the utmost abuse of his skill, till at last the vulgar, carried away by so much grace of art, would account
21 him a god whom yesterday they reverenced as mortal man. So, unawares, the world was caught in the ambush; under the stress, now

of bereavement, now of royal policy, men imparted to stocks and stones the incommunicable name of God.

22 Nor were they content with these false notions of God's nature; living in a world besieged by doubt, they misnamed its innumerable
23 disorders a state of peace. Peace, amidst their rites of child-murder,
24 their dark mysteries, their vigils consecrated to frenzy! Peace, while there is no respect for life, or for wedlock undefiled; always the
25 murderous ambush, the jealous pangs of a husband betrayed! All is a welter of bloodshed and murder, theft and fraud, corruption and
26 disloyalty, sedition and perjury; honest men are assailed, kindnesses forgotten, souls defiled, breeds confused, marriages unsettled; adultery
27 reigns and wantonness. Name we all these, name we never the idols whose worship is the cause, the beginning and end, of all these!
28 Their ecstasies are but raving, their prophecies are but lies; ill live
29 their worshippers, and lightly forswear themselves. And no marvel; what hurt should they take from the oath falsely sworn, since all their
30 faith is in dead gods? But indeed they shall pay both scores, idolaters that thought so ill of God, and perjurers that by their treason slighted
31 all honour; not the power he swore by, but the justice that keeps watch over sinners, calls ever the rogue to account.

CHAPTER FIFTEEN

FOR us, thou art God; thou, beneficent and truthful, thou, always
2 patient and merciful towards the world thou governest. Sin we, still we are thy worshippers; have we not proof of thy power? Sin we not, of this, too, we have proof, that thou wilt count us for thy own.
3 To know thee as thou art, is the soul's full health; to have proof of thy
4 power, is the root whence springs immortality. Not for us to be led astray by foolish tales of man's imagining, by the sculptor's barren
5 art, as he picks out some image with motley colours, to set fools gaping
6 at the sight of a lifeless shadow, all seeming and no breathing. Lovers they are of their own ruin, worthy of the fond hopes they cherish, that make such things, or sigh after them, or do them reverence.
7 Despise we not the potter's toil, that works the pliant earth between his fingers, and makes a cup here, a dish there for our use. Serve they noble ends or base, all alike come from the same clay, and what employment each of them shall find, it is the potter's right to deter-
8 mine. But very ill is that toil bestowed, when he uses the same clay to fashion some god that is no god. Bethink thee, potter, that it is but a little while since thou thyself wast fashioned out of the same earth,

and ere long, when the lease of thy soul falls due, to that earth thou
9 shalt return. But no, he never looks forward to the day when he will
be past work; how short life is, he recks not; he must vie with goldsmith and silversmith, he must be even with his neighbour that works
in bronze; in puppet-making [1] all his hope lies of winning fame.
10 O heart of dust, O ambition worthless as the sand, life than his own
11 clay more despicable! No thought for the God that was his own
fashioner, quickened him with the pulse of energy, breathed into him
12 a living spirit! Existence, for him, only a toy to be played with; our
life here, only a market-place, where a man must needs get his living
13 by fair means or foul! Such a man, as no other, sins with his eyes
open; from the same earthenware he will make you fragile pot or
carved effigy as you will.
14 　　Fools all, and doomed to misery beyond the common doom of
tyrants,[2] were the enemies that from time to time have lorded it over
15 thy people. Gods, for them, were all the idols of the heathen, with
their sightless eyes, their nostrils that never drew breath, deaf ears,
16 unfeeling hands, and feet that still would walk, yet still tarry; gods
man-made, gods of his fashioning that is a debtor for the very breath
he draws. For indeed, the gods man fashions are less than himself;
17 vain his impiety, since he is but mortal, they already dead; better he
18 than they, since he lived once, and they never. And what beasts
are these they worship? Of all beasts, the most hateful; such models
19 they have foolishly chosen as cannot vie with the others;[3] as have no
beauty, even beast-fashion, to make them desirable; the least honourable of God's creatures and the least blessed.

CHAPTER SIXTEEN

FITTINGLY, then, were the Egyptians plagued by such beasts
2 as these, that swarmed to their undoing.[4] Thy own people no
plague befell; pined their queasy stomach for dainties, thou wouldst
3 feed them on quails. Though hunger drove them to food, the men of
Egypt turned away with loathing from the necessaries they craved,

---

[1] Rather, according to the Greek text, 'in passing false coin'. The imputation
seems to be that such workmen covered over their clay figures with metal leaf;
even as images, they were false; how much more as gods!

[2] According to the Greek text (itself probably corrupt), 'of infants'.

[3] The sense of the original is here highly doubtful.

[4] The names 'Egypt' and 'Egyptian' have, as before, been inserted to make
the sense of the original plainer. The same is to be said of the following words:
'frogs' in verse 3, 'brazen serpent' in verse 7, and 'manna' in verse 27.

so foul the sight of the frogs that came to punish them. Thy own people should go wanting for a little, only so as to prepare them for
4 the dainties that would follow. Their oppressors must feel the pinch of poverty; for themselves, the sight of another's chastisement should
5 be lesson enough. When they themselves encountered brute malice, and the bites of writhing serpents threatened them with de-
6 struction, thy vengeance did not go to all lengths; enough that they should be warned by a brief experience of distress; they should be put in mind of thy law, yet have the assurance that thou wouldst come to
7 their rescue. For indeed, he who turned to look did not win safety from the brazen serpent which met his eyes, but from thee, who alone canst save.

8   No better proof could our enemies have, that from all peril thou
9 alone deliverest. Bite of locust or sting of fly was the undoing of them; no salve could be found against the mortal punishment they had
10 deserved. And here were these sons of thine, unvanquished even by the teeth of venomous serpents, because thy mercy came out to meet
11 them and gave relief. They must feel the prick, to remind them of the commandments they had from thee, and then quickly be rescued before they sank into deep lethargy, beyond the reach of thy succour.
12 Herb nor plaster it was that cured them, but thy word, Lord, that all
13 healing gives. Lord of life as of death, thou canst bring us down to
14 the grave and back from the grave; thine is not the fatal stroke man deals in anger, that banishes life beyond recall, imprisons the soul for ever.

15   Truly, thine is a power there is no escaping; the uplifted arm that plagued impious Egypt, where thou wast treated as a stranger. Strange, indeed, to that country were the rains that hunted them down, the
17 fierce hail-storms; the fire, too, that wasted them. Wonder beyond all wont, that in water, the all-quenching, fire should rage its fiercest;
18 no element but must rally in the cause of right. Here the flame would burn low, to spare those creatures a scorching, that were thy emissaries against the godless; doubt there should be none, for any
19 who saw it, but divine justice was at his heels. Here, in the very midst of the water it would burn as never fire burned yet, to blast all
20 the fruits of that accursed land. And thy own people, Lord? Them thou didst foster with the food of angels; bread from heaven thou didst set before them, which no labour of theirs had made ready, every taste uniting that could bring content, of every appetite the welcome
21 choice. So would thy own nature manifest a father's universal love; this food should humour the eater's whim, turning itself into that
22 which he craved most. In Egypt, snow and ice had resisted the fire,

never melting; plain it was that this fire, which shone out amid the
hailstones and the rain, was in alliance with them to burn up and
23 destroy the enemy's harvest.   Now, once again, fire forgot its own
24 nature, this time, to give faithful souls their nourishment![1]   So well
does thy creation obey thee, its author, now exerting all its powers to
punish the wicked, now abating its force to do thy loyal followers a
service!
25   Why should nature, seconding that universal bounty of thine, go to
26 all shifts to meet the needs of thy suppliants, but for the instruction
of thy own children, Lord, children so well beloved? They were to
learn that man lives, not by the ripening of crops, but by thy word,
27 ever protecting the souls that trust in thee. This manna, that never
shrank from the fire while it was a-cooking, would melt before the
28 heat of the sun's first feeble ray. What meant this, but that we must
be up before the sun to give thee thanks, seeking thy audience with
29 day's earliest light? Thankless if a man be, like the hoar frost of
winter his hopes shall dissolve; like water that goes to waste they
shall vanish.

CHAPTER SEVENTEEN

HIGH above us, Lord, are thy judgements, mysterious thy dealings; no skill had those Egyptian hearts to understand them.
2 They had thought to exercise barbarous tyranny over a nation consecrated to thee. And now they lay, shut close under their own roofs,
darkness their dungeon, their sentence a long-drawn night, exiled
3 from the gifts of thy eternal Providence. Did they hope, under that
dark veil of oblivion, to find a cloak for secret sinning? Nay, they
were scattered far apart, and in grievous dread of the terrors that came
4 to daunt them. Lie snug in their hidden lairs they might not;
noises swept down, echoing about their affrighted ears, and boding
5 visions of sad faces cowed their spirits. Fire itself no light could give
6 them, nor star's clear beam illuminate that hideous night; only now
and again a blaze shone out, not of their kindling, terrible to behold;
and fear of this unseen radiance lent fresh horror to the sights it
shewed.[2]

---

[1] *vv.* 22, 23: The meaning here is not very clearly expressed; it is, that fire
twice failed to produce its natural effect, once when it did not melt the hail-
stones which fell in Egypt, and again when it did not melt the manna in the
cooking-pots of the Israelites (see verse 27 below, and Ex. 16.21).

[2] The original is here very obscure; it runs, literally, 'Only a self-lighted
beacon shone upon them at intervals, full of terror, and being afraid of that
vision which escaped their observation, they thought the things seen worse'.

7 A mockery, now, seemed those magic arts of theirs; ignominious
8 the rebuff to their boasted cunning. The very men who had pro-
fessed to rid ailing minds of all discomposure and disquiet, were now
9 themselves sick with apprehension, to their great discomfiture. Even
when no alarms were present to disturb them, the memory of prowling
10 beast and hissing serpent filled them with mortal tremors, till they
shut their eyes against the sight of empty air, reason there is none to
dread.[1] Nothing gives such proof of cowardice as wickedness detected;
hard pressed by conscience, it will meet all its troubles half-way.
11 What else is timorousness, but a betrayal of the vantage-ground
12 reason gives us? Imagination, already defeated within its own
stronghold, fears the unknown more than it fears the true source of
13 its misery. Whether the darkness that held them bound were true
night, or that darkness which comes up from the lowest depths of the
14 grave, their bemused senses could not well distinguish;[2] now monstrous apparitions came indeed to scare them, now it was but their
own faint hearts made cowards of them; in a moment dismay was all
about them, and took them unawares.
15 Into this prison, then, that needed no bars to secure it, all fell alike,
16 whatever their condition; tiller of the fields, or shepherd, or workman
that plied his task out in the desert, each was caught at his post, each
17 must abide the inevitable lot, by darkness, like all his fellows, held in
thrall. Did the wind whistle, or bird utter tuneful notes deep amid
18 the boughs; were it the dull roar of some waterfall, or the sudden
crash of tumbling rocks, or the padding feet of beasts that gambolled
past them unseen, or the howl of wild things ravening, or a booming
echo from the mountain hollows, it was all one; it would startle them
19 into a great quaking of fear. All around them the world was bathed
20 in the clear sunlight, and men went about their tasks unhindered; over
them alone this heavy curtain of night was spread, image of the darkness that should be their next abode. Yet each man had a burden
heavier to bear than darkness itself, the burden of his own companionship.

---

[1] 'Reason there is none to dread'; the common philosophical meaning of the
participle used in the Greek text is 'worthy to be avoided'. It is commonly taken
here as meaning 'avoidable', but this gives a less apposite sense.

[2] *vv.* 11–14: There is much obscurity here, and perhaps some corruption in
the text. Of verse 13, only conjectural interpretation is possible; it runs, literally,
'sleeping the same sleep the really impossible night and (the night) coming
upon them from the depths of an impossible lower world'.

CHAPTER EIGHTEEN

BRIGHTEST of all, that light shone on thy chosen people. These neighbours of theirs, heard but not seen, the Egyptians must con-
2 gratulate on their escape from the common doom, thank them for
3 letting vengeance be, and ask forgiveness for past ill-will.[1] To these thou gavest, not darkness, but a pillar of burning fire, to be the guide of their unfamiliar journey, to be the sun whose gracious welcome should preserve them from harm.[2]
4   A fitting punishment it was for the Egyptians, this loss of light; fitting that they should be imprisoned in darkness, who had kept thy own sons in prison; thy own sons, through whom that law, which is
5 light unfailing, was to be given to the world. It was their purpose, besides, to slay all the children born of that holy stock; but one child survived exposure and lived to rebuke them; through him thou didst destroy Egypt's own children in their thousands, and drown its
6 assembled host in the rushing waves. Of what should befall that night, our fathers had good warning; confidence in thy sworn protection
7 should keep them unafraid. A welcome gift it was to thy people,
8 when at one stroke thou didst punish our enemies, and make us proud men by singling us out for thyself!
9   In secret they offered their sacrifice, the children of a nobler race, all set apart; with one accord they ratified the divine covenant, which bound them to share the same blessings and the same perils; singing
10 for prelude their ancestral hymns of praise. But music was none in the enemy's cry that answered them; here all was dirge for children
11 untimely mourned. Slave and master, prince and peasant, a common
12 doom met them, and a common loss; death levelled all under one title; unnumbered everywhere the slain, nor might the living suffice to bury
13 them; all in one moment, the flower of their race had perished. Against

---

[1] *vv.* 1, 2: The Greek text (which is rendered above) has here been mis-understood by the Latin translator, and the version he gives altogether mis-represents the sense of the passage; it runs: 'Brightest of all the light shone on thy chosen people. They did not hear the voice of these, but saw their form. And they glorified thee for their escape from the common doom, thanking that they were not now, as they had been formerly, the sufferers; and they made a request of thee, that thou wouldst distinguish' (between themselves and the Egyptians). The words 'Egypt', 'Egyptians', 'Israel', and 'Aaron', though not in the original, have been supplied in this chapter as before.
[2] The Greek text probably means, 'which should preserve them from harm during their ambitious travels'.

those earlier plagues, sorcery had hardened their hearts; Israel they recognised for God's children only when the first-born died.

14 There was a hush of silence all around, and night had but finished
15 half her swift journey, when from thy heavenly throne, Lord, down leaped thy word omnipotent. Never lighted sterner warrior on a
16 doomed land; never was sword so sharp, errand so unmistakable;
17 thy word that could tread earth, yet reach up to heaven. All at once came terror in their dreams; phantoms dismayed, and sudden alarms
18 overtook them; and when they lay a-dying, each fallen where fall
19 he must, they confessed what fault it was they expiated; all was foretold by the dreams that so disquieted them; they were not suffered to perish ignorant of their offence.
20 There was a time, too, when God's own people tasted the bitterness of death; out there in the desert a plague fell upon the common folk;
21 but not for long this vengeance lasted. A peerless champion they found in Aaron, that quickly took up the shield of his appointed ministry, the power of intercession that was his, and the atoning incense, held thy wrath in check, and brought the calamity to an end; none could
22 doubt now he was the man of thy choice! Not by strength of body, not by prowess in arms, he won the victory; [1] by persuasion he disarmed
23 resistance, calling to mind the sworn covenant of our race. Already the corpses were piled thick one on another; but he kept vengeance at bay, standing in between to breach the path between dead and
24 living. Such blazonings he bore; what meant that long robe of his but the whole world's orbit, the four rows of gems but the great deeds
25 of our first fathers, the mitre on his head but thy own greatness? In awe of these shrank the destroying angel away; for thy own people, some taste of thy vengeance should be enough.

CHAPTER NINETEEN

IT was not so with their impious enemies; with them, God decreed that pitiless justice should run its course, knowing well what ill-doing
2 of theirs lay yet in store; how the very men who had allowed the Israelites to depart, nay, set them eagerly on their way, would soon
3 repent of it and march out in pursuit.[2] The business of mourning still in hand, the grave-sides of the dead still calling for their tears,

---

[1] That is, according to the Latin version, 'he overcame the multitude', but some manuscripts of the Greek text give, 'he overcame the (divine) anger'.

[2] The word 'Israelites', like the other proper names used in this chapter, has been supplied so as to make the original text less obscure.

they must needs betake themselves to a fresh desperate shift; they would hunt down as fugitives the unwelcome guests of yester-
4 day. Fitting destiny, that lured them to a fitting doom, made them forget the past, and led them on to complete their tale of suffering
5 and of punishment! For thy people, a strange sea-faring; for those others, an unexampled manner of death!
6 Each form of nature, in its own proper sphere, was formed anew as from the beginning, obedient to the new laws thou hadst given it, for
7 the greater safety of thy children. Such was the cloud that overshadowed their camp; such the dry land that appeared where water stood before; the Red Sea unlaboriously crossed, a grassy floor spread
8 out amid the surging billows! So, sheltered by thy hand, they passed on their way, a whole nation of them, strange marvels seen in their
9 passage; lighthearted as horse at pasture or frisking lamb, they
10 chanted praises to thee, Lord, their rescuer. Such, too, were their memories of Egypt itself; memories of the land that bred lice and could breed no beasts else, the river where no fish lived that could yet
11 spawn frogs. Later on, they were to see how birds could be the subject of a new creation, when their appetites craved for richer fare, and quails came up from the sea to content them.
12 Nor were the Egyptians punished without warning; the thunders that terrified them were but echoes of the past. Did not their own
13 wickedness deserve the pains they suffered, a race even more inhospitable than the men of Sodom before them? These did but refuse a welcome when strangers came to their doors; the Egyptians con-
14 demned their own guests, their own benefactors, to slavery. It is one thing to be called to account for unfriendly treatment of alien
15 folk; but these Egyptians had received the Israelites into their midst with rejoicing, had admitted them to rights of citizenship, and then
16 turned on them with savage ill-treatment. No wonder blindness fell on them, as upon the men of Sodom at Lot's door! But in Egypt the darkness was so bewildering that a man could not find his way through the doors of his own house.
17 All the elements may be transposed among themselves, keeping up the same answering rhythm, like the notes of a harp altering their mood; so much we may infer with certainty from the sights that have
18 been witnessed in the past.[1] Land-beasts turned to water-beasts,
19 and the firm ground was trodden by creatures born to swim. Fire

---

[1] The meaning of this passage is highly doubtful, and it is possible that the text has been badly transmitted. But the notion seems to be that the history of miracle shews a kind of reciprocity between the elements, earth yielding to water and then water to land, ice to fire and then fire to ice.

20 surpassed its own nature, when water forgot to quench it; then fire, in its turn, could not waste the frail flesh of living creatures that traversed it, nor melt that heavenly food that melted easily as ice. No means wouldst thou neglect, Lord, to magnify thy people and win them renown; never wouldst thou leave them unregarded, but always and everywhere camest to their side.[1]

----

[1] *vv.* 18–20: It is not certain, from the context, whether these verses refer entirely to the period of the Exodus.

BOOK OF ECCLESIASTICUS

PREFACE

MANY are the important truths conveyed to us by the law, by the prophets and those other writers who have followed them. Israel can boast of its own philosophical tradition, suited not only to instruct those who talk its language, but to reach, in spoken or written form, the outside world too, and bring it great enlightenment. No wonder if my own grandfather, Jesus, who had devoted himself to the careful study of the law, the prophets, and our other ancestral records, had a mind to put something in writing himself that should bear on this philosophical tradition, to claim the attention of students who had already mastered it, and to encourage their observance of the law.

I must beg its readers to come well-disposed to their task, and to follow me closely, making allowances for me wherever I seem to have failed in the right marshalling of words, as I pass on wisdom at second hand. Hebrew words lose their force when they are translated into another language; moreover, when the Hebrews read out the law, the prophets, and the other books among themselves, they read them out in a greatly different form.

It was in my thirty-eighth year,[1] in the reign of Euergetes, that I went to Egypt and spent some time there. When I found writings preserved there which were of high doctrinal value, it seemed to me right and fitting that I, too, should be at some pains; I would set about translating this book. Learning I gave to the task and long labour, and so brought it to an end; who will apply their minds to it, shall find out how a man must frame his conduct if he would live by the divine law.

CHAPTER ONE

2 ALL wisdom has one source; it dwelt with the Lord God before ever time began. Sand thou mayst count, or the rain-drops, or the days of the world's abiding; heaven-height thou mayst measure,
3 or the wide earth, or the depth of the world beneath, ere God's wisdom
4 thou canst trace to her origin, that was before all. First she is of all

---

[1] In the original, 'the thirty-eighth year'; some think that the author refers to 132B.C., the thirty-eighth regnal year of Ptolemy Euergetes II. If the year meant is that of his own age, he may equally well have lived under Ptolemy Euergetes I (247–222B.C.).

created things; time was never when the riddle of thought went
5 unread. (What is wisdom's fount? God's word above. What is her
6 course? His eternal commandments).[1] Buried her roots beyond all
7 search, wise her counsels beyond all knowing; (too high her teaching
to be plainly revealed, too manifold her movements to be understood).
8 There is but one God, high creator of all things, sitting on his throne
9 to govern us, a great king, worthy of all dread; he it was that created
her, through his holy Spirit. His eye could take in the whole range of
10 her being; and so he poured her out upon all his creation, upon all
living things, upon all the souls that loved him, in the measure of his
gift to each.
11   To fear the Lord is man's pride and boast, is joy, is a prize to be
12 coveted; comfort it brings to the heart, happiness and content and a
13 long life bestows; well it is, at his last hour, for the man who fears the
14 Lord; his day of death shall be a day of blessing. (Love of God is
15 wisdom worth the having; welcome the sight when it shews itself,
16 when it gives proof of its wondrous power.) Wouldst thou be wise,
the first step is fear of the Lord; to his chosen servants, a gift connatural from the womb; it goes with holy motherhood, and sets its
17 mark on his true worshippers. (The fear of the Lord lends wisdom
18 that piety which is hers; such piety as shall keep the heart safe and
19 make it acceptable, bring it joy and content. Well it shall be indeed
for the man who fears the Lord; at his last end he shall win blessing.)
20 God's fear is wisdom's fulfilment, yields the deep draught that satis-
21 fies; never a nook or cranny in thy house but shall be filled with the
22 store of its harvesting. The fear of the Lord is wisdom's crown;
23 with this, peace and health are thine to enjoy; (this fear itself is God's
gift, no less than the wisdom which is counted out under his eye).
24 Wisdom it is that imparts to us all our knowledge, all our powers of
discernment; hold her fast, and she will set thee on a pinnacle of
25 renown; yet rooted this wisdom must be in fear of the Lord, or
long life shall never burgeon from it.
26   (True insight wisdom has in her treasure-house, and the knowledge that sanctifies; no wonder if sinners hate the name of her.
27 The fear of the Lord drives out sin); the rash soul shall never find

---

[1] The verses printed in brackets, here and in later chapters, are either not
found in the Greek text at all, or found only in certain manuscripts of it. There
are many other differences of detail between the Greek and the Latin, too
numerous to be mentioned in these notes. The Hebrew original (which has been
preserved to us only in small part) must have been current in several different
forms at the time when our versions were made; and it seems probable that
the Latin has sometimes included two alternatives side by side (cf. verses 26
and 31, 32 of this chapter).

29 pardon, its own wild mood overbalances it. Patience bides her time,
30 and with time, content comes back to her; praise shall be upon
every lip for the wise thought that checked, for a while, her utterance.
31 Deep in wisdom's treasure-house is buried the secret of all knowledge;
32 no wonder if sinners hate the name of piety. My son, if on wisdom
thy heart is set, keep the commandments, and God will grant· thy
34 wish; fear of the Lord is true wisdom, true learning, and his will is
35 to see thee loyal and patient; thou shalt have no empty coffers then.
36   Let not thy fear of the Lord be overcast with doubt; never come
to him with a heart that hesitates.
37   Do not play false in thy dealings with men, and suffer thy own
38 words to ensnare thee. Watch those words well, or they may trip
39 thee up; thou wilt have compassed thy own disgrace, if God should
reveal thy secret thoughts at last. Wouldst thou be thrown down,
40 to be mocked by all thy neighbours, a heart that came to meet the
Lord grudgingly, full all the while of treachery and deceit?

CHAPTER TWO

M Y son, if thy mind is to enter the Lord's service (wait there in
his presence, with honesty of purpose and with all reverence,
2 and) prepare thyself to be put to the test. Submissive be thy heart,
and ready to bear all (to wise advice lend a ready ear), and be never
3 hasty when ill times befall thee. Wait for God, cling to God and wait
4 for him; at the end of it, thy life shall blossom anew. Accept all that
5 comes to thee, patient in sorrow, humiliation long enduring; for
gold and silver the crucible, it is in the furnace of humiliation men
6 shew themselves worthy of his acceptance. Trust in him, and he will
lift thee to thy feet again; go straight on thy way, and fix in him thy
hope; (hold fast thy fear of him, and let that fear be the habit of thy
later age).
7   All you that fear the Lord, wait patiently for his mercies; lose
8 sight of him, and you shall fall by the way. Fear him? Ay, and trust
9 him; you shall not miss your reward. Fear him? Ay, and fix your
10 hope in him; his mercy you shall find, to your great comfort. (Fear
11 him? Ay, and love him; your hearts shall be enlightened.) My sons,
look back on the ages that are past; was ever man yet that trusted in
12 the Lord, and was disappointed, held fast to his commandments,
13 and was forsaken, prayed to him, and found the prayer unregarded? A
gracious God and a merciful; in times of affliction, he leaves our sins
unpunished, watches over all that with true hearts turn to him.

14 Out upon the false heart, the cheating lips, the hands busy with
ill-doing; upon the sinner that will go two ways about it, to enter the
15 land of his desire. Out upon the unnerved will, that trust in God has
16 none, and from him shall have no succour. Out upon the men who
have given up hope (forsaking the right path, and to false paths
17 betaking them); what shift will they make when the Lord calls them
18 to account? Fear the Lord, and doubt his promises? Love him, and
19 not keep true to the way he shews us? Fear the Lord, and not study
20 to know his will? Love him, and not find contentment in his law?
21 Fear God, and not keep the will alert, the soul set apart for him? (To
fear God is to keep his commandments, and wait patiently until he
22 comes to relieve us.) Be this our thought, that it is God's power we
23 have to reckon with, not man's, if there is no penance done. And he
has mercy ever at his side, a God merciful as he is great.

CHAPTER THREE

WHEREVER choice souls are found, wisdom is the mother of
2 them; loyalty and love went to the making of them. Speak we
now of a father's rights; do you, sons, give good heed, and follow
3 these counsels, if thrive you would. God will have children honour
4 their fathers; a mother's rights are his own strict ordinance. (A lover
of God will fall to prayer over his sins and sin no more; so, all his life
5 long, his prayer shall find audience.) . . . riches he lays up for himself,
6 that gives his mother her due.[1] As thou wouldst have joy of thy own
children, as thou wouldst be heard when thou fallest to praying,
7 honour thy father still. A father honoured is long life won; a father
8 well obeyed is a mother's heart comforted. None that fears the Lord
but honours the parents who gave him life; slave to master owes no
9 greater service. Thy father honour, in deed and in word and in all
10 manner of forbearance; so thou shalt have his blessing, a blessing
11 that will endure to thy life's end. What is the buttress of a man's
house? A father's blessing. What tears up the foundations of it? A
12 mother's curse. Never make a boast of thy father's ill name; what,
13 should his discredit be thy renown? Nay, for a father's good repute
14 or ill, a son must go proudly, or hang his head. My son, when thy
father grows old, befriend him; long as he lives, never of thee be his
15 repining. Grow he feeble of wit, make allowance for him, nor in

---

[1] *vv.* 4, 5: The Latin version here inserts a sentence which seems out of place
(perhaps belonging to the end of the foregoing chapter); it omits the words
given in the Greek text: 'He who honours his father will atone for his own sins'.

thy manhood's vigour despise him. The kindness shewn to thy father
16 will not go forgotten; favour it shall bring thee in acquittal of thy
17 mother's guilt.[1] Faithfully it shall be made good to thee, nor shalt
thou be forgotten when the time of affliction comes; like ice in summer
18 the record of thy sins shall melt away. Tarnished his name, that
leaves his father forsaken, cursed his memory, that earns a mother's ban.
19 My son, go about thy own business with a quiet mind; men's love
20 is worth more than their praise. The greater thou art, the more in
21 all things abase thyself; so thou shalt win favour with God . . .[2] Sovereignty belongs to God and no other; they honour him most that most
22 keep humility. Seek not to know what is far above thee; search not
beyond thy range; let thy mind ever dwell on the duty God has given
23 thee to do (content to be ignorant of all besides). Things thou seest
24 not, what need is there for thee to know? Leave off, then, thy much
questioning about such things as little concern thee (and be content
25 with thy ignorance); more lies in thy view than lies within human
26 ken. By such fancies, many have been led astray, and their thoughts
chained to folly.[3]
27 . . . Heart that is obstinate shall thrive ill at the last; danger loved
28 is death won. (Heart that will try both ways shall prosper little; he
29 falls into the snare that goes a-straying.) Heart that will not mend
shall be weighed down by its own troubles; the sinner is ever ready for
30 one sin more. For one sort of men there is no remedy, the proud;
31 too deep a root the evil has taken, before they knew it. Heart that is
wise will prove itself in wise company; ever greedy of wise talk is the
32 ear that knows how to listen. (Heart that is wise and discerning will
keep clear of wrong, and by honest dealings prosper yet.)
33 No fire burns so high but water may quench it; alms-giving was
34 ever sin's atoning. God marks the grateful eye, and remembers it;
here is sure support won against peril of falling.

CHAPTER FOUR

MY son, do not grudge a poor man the alms he asks, nor pass him
2 by, with averted look, in his need. Wouldst thou despise his
3 hungry glance, and add to the burden of his distress? Wouldst thou

---

[1] In the Greek text, the giver of alms atones not for his mother's sin, but for
his own. Cf. however Ps. 50.7.

[2] Some manuscripts and versions add, at the end of this verse, 'Men's esteem
and honour is to be had for the asking, but it is to the humble that hidden
things are revealed'.

[3] Some manuscripts and versions add, at the end of this verse, 'Want eyes,
want light; boast not that thou hast knowledge, where knowledge is none'.

4 disappoint his eagerness by bidding him wait for the gift? Nay,
spurn thou never the plea of the friendless; look thy suppliant in the
5 face, and of his poverty take good heed; shall his baffled rage curse
6 thee behind thy back? The curse of a despairing man does not go
unheard; his Maker is listening.

7 To the common sort of men give friendly welcome; before an elder
8 abate thy pride, and to a man of eminence bow meekly thy head. If
a poor man would speak to thee, lend him thy ear without grudging
9 (give him his due), and let him have patient and friendly answer. If
he is wronged by oppression, redress thou needs must win him, nor
10 be vexed by his importunity. When thou sittest in judgement, be a
11 father to the orphans, a husband to the widow that bore them; so
the most High an obedient son shall reckon thee, and shew thee more
than a mother's kindness.

12 New life wisdom breathes into her children, befriends all that have
13 recourse to her (and guides them in the right way). Love her, as thou
lovest life; wait early at her doors, if thou wouldst win her sweet
14 embrace. Life the prize, if thou hold her fast; come she in at the
15 door, God's blessing comes with her; court paid to her, worship
paid to the Holy One; love given to her, God's love made thine in
16 return for it! A word from her, and the world is at thy feet, a sight of
17 her face, and thou shalt dwell ever secure; trust her, and she will
18 be thy inheritance, settled on the heirs of thy body. When first she
19 chooses a man out, she does but make trial of his company; she puts
him to the proof, threatening him with her frown, teasing him with
her difficult lore, until at last she has explored his every thought, and
20 can trust him perfectly. Then she gives him confidence, coming out
21 openly to meet him; gladdens him with her smile, and tells him all
her secrets; (makes him rich with store of true knowledge, and enables
22 him to discern the right). Only if he strays away from her does she
abandon him, and leave him at the mercy of his foes.

23 My son, watch well for thy opportunity, ever on thy guard against
24 wrong-doing; though life itself were in peril, never be ashamed to
25 speak the truth. Shame, that is the grace and glory of a man, may
26 yet make a sinner of him. Wouldst thou hold another man's honour
27 dearer than thy own, and swear the lie at thy soul's peril? (Nay,
speak out without shame, though thy own neighbour should be
28 threatened with ruin.) Withhold not thy counsel while safety may
yet be won; thy wisdom is not to be hidden away like a veiled beauty.
29 Wisdom still needs a tongue to disclose it; no discernment or knowledge
or shrewd counsel but waits on the apt word; (how else should men be
30 encouraged in well doing?) Speak thou never against the known

31 truth; and if thy ignorance has erred, own thy error. Be never ashamed to confess thy faults, nor, for thy fault, put thyself in any man's power.

32   Wouldst thou defy, and openly, a ruler's authority? Thou hadst better swim against the stream's force.[1]

33   Do battle for the right, all thy life long, and with thy last breath do battle for the right still; God, in thy cause, will overcome thy enemies.

34   A glib tongue, and hands that hang down idle; such be not thine.

35   Lion if thou must be, let not thy own house feel the brunt of it, thy own servants harried, thy own slaves beaten to the earth.

36   Open hand when the word is Take, shut when the word is Give; such be not thine.

CHAPTER FIVE

WILT thou look round at ill-gotten gains, and tell thyself thou hast enough for all thy needs? (Trust me, when vengeance
2 finds thee out, all this shall nothing avail thee.) In manhood's vigour,
3 do not follow the lust of thy heart, boasting of thy strength, and asking who will call thee to account for thy doings; God will find a way to
4 punish thee. Nor ever flatter thyself that thou hast sinned and came
5 away scot-free; the eternal justice waits its time. Ill were it that
6 sin's pardon should embolden thee to sin afresh. Dost thou tell thyself God's mercies are great, and he will overlook thy sins for all
7 they are so many? Bethink thee that his vengeance follows swiftly
8 on the heels of his mercy; it is a jealous eye that watches the sinner. Or wouldst thou make slow work of turning to the Lord, and put it off
9 from day to day? Swift falls his anger and perilous, when the time
10 for vengeance is ripe. And must thy thoughts still dwell on the ill-gotten gains, that shall nothing avail thee when vengeance finds thee out?

11   Turn not with every wind, nor walk in every way that offers; that
12 sinners do, till their hypocrisy is found out. Firm let thy feet be set on the path the Lord has chosen for thee; be true to thy own thought and to the knowledge thou hast, and ever let the counsels of peace and justice guide thee on thy way.

---

[1] *vv.* 31, 32. The Greek text here varies considerably from the Latin version. It runs: 'Be never ashamed to confess thy faults; wouldst thou swim against the stream's force? Never put thyself in the power of a fool, and never flatter a ruler's greatness'. Throughout the last fourteen verses of this chapter, the Latin and the Greek have many different twists of meaning, and neither can be interpreted with much certainty.

13 True answer and wise answer none can give but he who listens patiently, and learns all.

14 If discernment thou hast, give thy neighbour his answer; if none,
15 tongue held is best, or some ill-advised word will shame thee; speech uttered was ever the wise man's passport to fame, the fool's undoing.

16 Never win the name of back-biter, by thy own tongue entrapped
17 into shame. A thief must blush and do penance, a hypocrite men will mark and avoid; the back-biter earns indignation and enmity and disgrace all at once.

18 For all men, high and low, make the same excuses.

CHAPTER SIX

WOULDST thou rather have thy neighbour enemy than friend? Wouldst thou earn, by ill-nature, an ill name, and be despised for such faults as these, envy and hypocrisy?
2 Wilt thou toss thy head, bull-fashion, and glory in thy own strength?
3 What if that strength should be brought down by thy own folly? Then wilt thou be no better than some dry tree-stump out in the desert,
4 its leaves withered, its hope of fruit all gone. Ill nature brings a man to an ill end, the scorn of his enemies and a prey to iniquity.
5 Gentleness of speech, how it wins friends everywhere, how it disarms its enemies! Never was a good man wanting for a gracious
6 word. Be on good terms with all, but for thy trusted counsellor,
7 choose one in a thousand. Friends are best made in the hour of trial;
8 do not bestow thy confidence lightly; some men are but fair-weather
9 friends, and will not stand the test of adversity. Some will veer from friend to foe, and lay bare old grudges, old quarrels, to reproach thee;
10 some will be thy boon companions, but desert thee when trouble is
11 afoot. Or else, though he be a true friend, one will set himself up to
12 be thy rival, and play the master among thy servants; let him learn to behave modestly, and rid thee of his presence, before there can be
13 true and tried friendship between you.[1] From enemies thou mayst
14 keep thy distance; against friends be on thy guard. True friend-
15 ship, sure protection and rare treasure found; true friendship, a thing beyond compare, its tried loyalty outweighing gold and
16 silver; true friendship, in life and death the salve thou needest!
17 Only those who fear God will come by it; the fear of God gives friendship evenly shared, friend matched with friend.

---

[1] *vv.* 11, 12: The sense of these verses is doubtful. The Greek text has, for verse 12, '(But) if thou art brought low, he will turn against thee, and hide his presence away from thee'.

18 My son, learn the lessons of youth, and garner wisdom against thy
19 grey hairs; ploughman and sower thou must come to the task, and
20 wait patiently for the harvest; how light the toil wisdom claims, the
21 fruits of her how soon enjoyed! Only to undisciplined minds she
    seems an over-hard task-mistress; not for long will the fool endure her
22 company; here is a weight (says he) that tries my strength too much,
23 and away he casts it. The enlightenment which comes with wisdom
    is true to its name; known to so few, yet where men are acquainted
24 with it, it waits to light them into the presence of God.[1] My son, give
    good heed to the warnings of experience, do not spurn this counsel of
25 mine. Yield foot of thine to wisdom's fetters, neck of thine to her
26 collar, shoulder of thine to her yoke; do not chafe at her bonds. Make
    her thy whole heart's quest, follow, as best thou canst, the path she
28 makes known to thee; search, and thou wilt find her, hold fast, and
29 never let her go; in good time, thou shalt repose in her, and find her
30 all delight. In time, those fetters of hers shall prove a strong pro-
    tection, a sure support, that halter of hers a badge of honour about thy
31 neck; there is life in those trappings, healing virtue in those bonds.
32 Robe is none shall do thee more honour, crown is none shall rest more
    radiant on thy brow.
33 My son, mark well and learn, take heed and be wise; here is true
    knowledge for the listening, here is wisdom if thou wilt lend an ear.
35 Where older men than thou are met, and wiser, take thou thy place,
    and give thy whole heart to their teaching; old tales of God's wonders
36 thou shalt hear, and sayings of much renown. A man of discernment
    if thou find, wait on him at day-break, and wear out his door-step with
37 thy often visiting. Think ever upon God's commandments, and be
    constant in the following of his will; be sure he will give thee courage,
    and all thy desire for wisdom shall be granted thee.

CHAPTER SEVEN

2   HARM if thou do none, harm shall none befall thee; clear of
3   wrong is clear of mishap. What need, my son, to sow in the
    furrow of mischief, and reap a sevenfold harvest?
4   Never ask of God high station, or of the king preferment.

---

[1] The Greek text runs, 'Wisdom is true to her name, she is revealed to few',
which seems to imply a play upon words quite foreign to Hebrew vocabulary.
The Latin version runs literally, 'The wisdom of doctrine is true to its name;
it is revealed to few, but for those to whom it is known, it abides even to the
sight of God'. There is an accidental resemblance in Hebrew between the noun
'wisdom' and the verb 'to wait'.

5 Never try to prove thy innocence before God, who knows all, nor thy subtlety before the king.

6 Do not sit in judgement, unless thou hast enough courage to crush the wrong; if thou favour the rich, what else is thy award but a snare for thy own virtue?

7 Let not fault of thine be the source of public calamity; no need to embroil thyself with thy own neighbours.

8 Never tack sin to sin; for the first thou art in arrears.

9 Do not lose confidence in thy praying, or leave almsgiving undone.

11 Do not flatter thyself that God will look favourably on thy many offerings, as if he, the most High, could not refuse thy gifts.

12 Do not triumph over the disconsolate; God, who sees all, casts men down and lifts them up.

13 Not against thy own brother trump up the charge; nor thy neighbour either.

14 Any the least falsehood avoid in thy speech; so ill grows the habit of it.

15 Idle talk becomes thee not, when thou sittest with the elders in council, nor, when thou prayest, repetition of thy prayer.

16 At toil repine not; the farmer's trade is of divine appointment.

17 Think not to pass unnoticed, where sinners are so many; bethink
19 thee rather, how swiftly comes vengeance, and so curb thy unruly spirits; for sinful flesh, fire and worm.

20 Thou hast a friend who is over-long in thy debt; still do not wrong
21 him; dear to thee as a brother, and shall gold count more? Thou hast a good wife, a thrifty woman that has thrown in her lot, in the fear of the Lord, with thine; do not leave her; that modesty of hers is
22 a grace gold cannot buy. The slave that works for thee faithfully,
23 the hireling that depends on thee for his livelihood, injure not; a thrifty slave thou shouldst love as thy own self, not baulking him of
24 liberty or leaving him to starve. Cattle thou hast; tend them well,
25 nor part with them while they do thee good service. Thou hast
26 sons; train them to bear the yoke from their youth up. Thou hast daughters; keep them chaste, and do not spoil them with thy smile;
27 a daughter wed is great good done, if a thrifty husband thou find her.
28 And thy own wife, if thou lovest her, never do thou forsake, trusting thy happiness to some other that shall be little to thy mind.

29 And oh, with thy whole heart honour thy father, nor forget thy
30 mother's pangs; bethink thee, that without them thou hadst had no being, and repay the service they have done thee.

31 With all thy soul fear God, and reverence his priests. He made thee; wilt thou not devote all thy powers to his love? Wilt thou leave

33 his ministers unbefriended? Rather, with all thy soul fear God, and to
    his priests give their due; with gift of the consecrated shoulder clear
34 thyself of what is owing. The priests must have their share, by law
    prescribed, of first-fruits and of offering for transgression; even if thou
    hast committed a fault in ignorance, a little is claimed for thy cleansing.
35 The gift of the consecrated shoulder thou must make to the Lord,
    and the offering of all that is dedicated, and the holy first-fruits;
36 moreover, thou must open thy hand to the poor; so thy atonement
    shall be perfect, and perfect thy blessing.
37 No living man but is thankful for the gift given; and it is ill done
38 to withhold thy favours even from the dead. Fail not to comfort the
39 distressed, let the mourner have thee for his escort. Without qualm
40 visit the sick; no surer way of winning thy neighbour's love. Re-
    member at all times what thou must come to at the last, and thou shalt
    never do amiss.

CHAPTER EIGHT

    IF quarrel thou hast, let it not be with a prince, that may attach
2   thy person; nor with a rich man, that may implead thee, with all
    the power there is in silver and gold to corrupt men, and sway even
4   the hearts of kings; nor with a glib talker; thou dost but add fuel to
    his fire.
5   Be not familiar with a boor; thou wilt hear no good of thy ancestry.
6   Scorn not the sinner that would amend his ways; reproach comes
7   amiss, where all stand in need of correction. Nor fail in respect for
8   the aged; it is of our stuff grey hairs are made.[1] Rejoice not over thy
9   enemy's death; we all die, not for other men's rejoicing. Do not be
    contemptuous of what older and wiser men have to tell thee; by their
10 lore live thou, if wise thou wouldst be, and have the secret of dis-
11 cernment, and win favour in the service of the great. Do not let them
    pass thee by, these traditions older men have inherited from their
12 fathers; they will turn thee into a man of judgement, that answer
    can make when answer is needed.
13 Wouldst thou remonstrate with a sinner? Make sure thou art not
    fanning the flame of his passions, thyself in peril of a scorching.
14 Wouldst thou make reply to the railing accuser? Make sure he is
    not baiting a trap to ensnare thee.
15 Lend to one who can master thee? Then lent is lost. Pledge not
17 thyself beyond thy means; count ever thy pledge forfeit. Dispute
18 not a judge's award; who judges by right rule if not he? Travel not

---

[1] Literally, 'men grow old out of (people like) us'.

with a rash companion, if thou wouldst not shoulder all his misfortune;
19 he will go his own way, and thou share the reward of his folly. Quarrel
not with a man of quick moods; on a desert road he is no companion for
thee; he cares nothing for bloodshed, and none shall aid thee in thy
20 fall. Take not counsel with a fool; he knows none but his own way
21 of it. Share not thy secret plans with a stranger; thou knowest not
22 what trouble he may breed. Never open to any man thy whole heart;
an ill requital he may make, by bringing shame on thee.

CHAPTER NINE

NEVER shew thyself a jealous husband to the wife thou lovest;
2 she may learn too well the ruinous lesson. Never give thy soul
into a woman's power, and let her command the fortress of it, to thy
3 shame. Never turn to look at the wanton, that would catch thee in
4 her snare, nor spend thy attentions upon some dancing woman,
5 that has power to be thy undoing; nor let thy eyes linger on a maid
6 unwed, whose very beauty may take thee unawares. And for harlots,
7 let nothing tempt thee to give way to them, as life and patrimony thou
holdest dear; look not round thee in the city streets, nor haunt the
8 alley-ways. From a woman bravely decked out turn away; have no
9 eyes for her beauty that is none of thine. Woman's beauty has been
10 the ruin of many ere now, a spark to light the flame of lust. (A
11 harlot? Then trample her down like mire in thy path. The love of
stolen sweets has been the undoing of many; a word with her, and
12 the spark is lit.) Sit down never with a wedded wife, nor lean thy
13 elbow upon table of hers, nor bandy words with her over the wine;
steal she thy heart away, thy life is forfeit.
14   An old friend leave not; the new is not his like. New friendship,
new wine; it must ripen ere thou canst love the taste of it.
16   Envy not the wrong-doer his wealth and state; beyond all expecta-
17 tion of thine it shall come to ruin. For his ill-gotten gains have
neither love nor liking; be sure he will not die unpunished.
18   From one that has the power of life and death keep thy distance;
19 so thou shalt be free from mortal alarms. If dealings thou hast with
him, keep clear of all offence, or thou shalt pay for it with thy
20 life. Death has become thy familiar; pit-falls encompass thy path;
thou art making the rounds of a beleaguered city.[1]

---

[1] This seems to be the meaning of the Greek, although the text is perhaps
corrupt. The Latin gives no good sense: 'Thou wilt be walking on the weapons
of grieving men'.

21   Be at pains to avoid ill neighbourhood; be wise and prudent men
22   thy counsellors, honest men thy guests.
23   Be the fear of God all thy boast, the thought of God all thy thinking,
the commandments of the most High all the matter of thy discourse.
24   By skilful handiwork the artist is known, the ruler of a people by
the prudence of his counsel (the good sense of the aged by their
word spoken).
25   No such peril to a city as a great talker; for his rash utterance, no
man so well hated as he.

CHAPTER TEN

A WISE ruler, a folk well disciplined; firm sits prudence on the
2   throne. Like king, like court; like ruler, like subjects. Royal
folly is a people's ruin; where prudence reigns, there cities thrive most.
4   God's will it is, then, that rules a nation; when the time comes, he
5   will give it the prince it needs. God grants prosperity where he will;
divine authority is stamped on the scribe's brow.
6   Forget the wrong done, nor enrol thyself among the doers of it.
7   Pride God hates, and his ban lies on all the world's iniquities, wrong
and crime and outrage and treacherous shift, that he punishes by
passing on the sceptre of empire into new hands; but worse sin is
9   none than avarice. See how man, for all his pride, is but dust and
10 ashes! This love of money is of all things the most perverse; what
does the miser but sell his own soul? As well be bowelled alive!
11 Why be tyrannies short-lived? Why, it is a wearisome thing to the
12 physician, a long illness, so he is fain to cut it short, and the king
13 that reigns to-day will be dead to-morrow. And what is the new
kingdom he inherits? Creeping things, and carrion beast, and worm.[1]
14 Pride's beginning is man's revolt from God, when the heart
forgets its Maker; and of all sin pride is the root. Leave it, or a tempest
16 of blasphemy shall follow, and thou thyself be ruined at the last. Un-
looked-for humiliation the Lord has in store; vanished utterly is
17 yonder confederacy; proud thrones cast down, to make room for
18 the oppressed, proud nations withered from the root, and a humbled
19 race of exiles planted anew! Whole nations of the world the Lord has
20 overthrown, rased them to the ground; shrivelled and vanished away,
21 they have left no trace of their passage. (The proud forgotten, the

---

[1] *vv*. 7–13: A comparison of the Latin with the Greek suggests that the order
of these verses differed in different manuscripts of the original, and their sense
cannot be certainly established. It seems likely that in *vv*. 11–13 the physician
referred to is Providence.

22 humble kept in memory; such was the Lord's will.) Pride was meant
for beasts, not men; never woman bore child that had that fierce mood
for its birthright.

23 There are two breeds of men; one fears God and wins renown, the
24 other passes his commandments by, and is forgotten. Let clansmen
honour a chieftain's gifts; it is humble fear wins the divine regard.
25 For riches and renown, as for the lowly born, there is one boast worth
26 having, the fear of God. Honest poverty never despise, nor flatter,
27 for all his wealth, the evil-doer; prince nor ruler nor nobleman can
win any higher title than the fear of God.

28 Of his master's sons a prudent servant shall yet be master. Only
the fool, that is ill trained, takes punishment amiss; and a fool will
never rise to greatness.

29 Do not boast of thy fine craftsmanship and then, in time of urgent
30 need, stand idle;[1] better fall to work and have a full belly than keep
31 thy pride and go fasting. Abate thy pride, keep body and soul together;
32 value thy life as it deserves. There is no excusing the man who is
his own enemy, no worth in the man who thinks his life worth nothing.

33 One man, that little wealth has, may boast of his skill (and the fear of
34 God), another of his riches. Grow he rich, the poor man shall boast
indeed; grow he poor, the other has good cause to fear his poverty.

CHAPTER ELEVEN

A MAN may be lowly born, and yet rise high through the wisdom
that is in him, till at last he takes his seat among men of rank.
2 Esteem no man for his good looks, nor for his outward show despise
3 him; yonder bee is an inconsiderable creature, and yet there is a
4 world of sweetness in the harvest he wins. Plume not thyself when
thou goest bravely clad, nor pride thyself in thy brief hour of greatness.
Of wonder and of praise what else is worthy, but the doings of the most
5 High? And these, how hedged about with secrecy! Kings a many
6 have lost their thrones,[2] to pretenders they never dreamed of; great
ones a many have fallen full low, and their glory has passed to others.
7 Blame not, till thou hast heard the excuse; more just thy reproof
8 shall be when thou hast learnt all. Listen first, then answer, never
breaking in when the tale is half told.

---

[1] This seems, in view of the context, the best account to give of a verse which
is difficult in the Latin, and in the Greek almost untranslatable.

[2] Literally, in the Greek text, 'have sat on the ground'. The Latin version,
perhaps through an error, reads 'have sat on their thrones'.

9   Quarrel not, where thou thyself art not concerned; leave judgement
of the offender to others.

10   Do not be entangled, my son, in too many enterprises. The rich
man pays forfeit, chasing what overtake he may not, or fleeing what
he may not shun.

11   Some men's lives are all toil and haste and anxiety; yet the more
12   they toil, the less advantage they win (for want of piety). And others
are backward folk, that cannot hold their gains, men of little power
13   and much poverty; and yet such a man the Lord will look upon with
favour, rescue him from neglect and greatly advance him, to the
14   world's amazement, and the greater honour of God. From God
all comes, good fortune and ill, life and death, poverty and riches;
15   in God's keeping are wisdom and temperance and knowledge of the
law, charity and the good life.

16   Sinners if blindness mislead, that blindness is connatural to them;
yet it is by making evil their delight that men grow hardened in evil.

17   No momentary blessing it is, God's largesse to his faithful servants;
18   that seed bears an eternal crop. No such boast has the man of thrift,
19   that by his own effort wins wealth. Does he tell himself that he has
found security at last; nothing remains but to glut, with his own
20   earnings, his own greed? He forgets that time flies, and death draws
21   near; die he must, and leave all he has to another. Be true to thy
covenant with God; its words to thy own ears repeat; to that, and
22   thy enjoined duty, inure thyself. Wouldst thou stand there gaping
at the doings of sinners? Nay, trust in God, and keep to thy appointed
23   task. Dost thou think God finds it hard to enrich the beggar, and
24   in a moment? Swift, swift comes the blessing that rewards faithful
service; in one short hour its fruits ripen.

25   Never tell thyself, need thou hast none, there is no more good can
26   befall thee; never flatter thyself, thou art master of thy own lot, no
27   harm can touch thee now. Rather, bethink thyself of foul weather in
28   fair, of fair weather in foul; on the very day of a man's death God
29   can give him his deserts. One hour of misery, how it can efface in
the memory long years of ease! Only a man's death-bed brings the
full history of his fortunes to light.

30   Never call a man happy until he is dead; his true epitaph is written
in his children.

31   Do not keep thy house open to every comer; knaves have many
32   shifts. (Foul breath lurks in a diseased body); the partridge a hidden
lure awaits, a hidden snare the doe; so there be unquiet hearts, ever on
33   the watch for a neighbour's downfall, ready to interpret good things
34   amiss, and cast blame on the innocent. One spark is enough to

spread a fire, and one man's treachery may be the cause of bloodshed;
35 (such villains as these plot against life itself). Against such a plague
be thou timely on thy guard, or it may prove thy eternal disgrace.
36 Alien let in is whirlwind let in, that shall alienate from thee all thou
hast.[1]

CHAPTER TWELVE

FAVOUR if thou grantest, look well to whom thou grantest it; so
2 shall thy favours earn abundant gratitude. A good turn done to
an honest man is well rewarded; if not he, then the Lord will repay
3 thee. It goes ill with the man who spends all his time courting the
wicked, and alms gives none; does not the most High himself treat
4 sinners as his enemies, never sparing them till they repent? (. . . For
rebellious sinners he has nothing but punishment, although he may
5 save up the day of their punishing).[2] Keep thy favours for the kind-
6 hearted, and let the sinners go without their welcome. The friendless man deserves thy alms; to the godless give nothing; nay, prevent
7 food reaching him, or he will have the mastery of thee. All his gain
will be doubly thy loss; and so it is that the most High both hates
sinners and will bring retribution on their impiety.
8   Prosperity will not shew thee who are thy friends. In bad times, thy
9 enemies may triumph openly, that till now were grieved at thy good
fortune; but it is these bad times will shew thee thy friends too.
10   Never trust an enemy; deep as verdigris on copper his malice is
11 ingrained. Lout he never so low, look to it well and be on thy guard
12 against him; never let him attend on thee, or sit at thy right hand.
His eyes are on thy place; a time will come when he will sit where thou
sittest, when thou wilt recognize the truth of my warning, and be
13 stung by the memory. Who shall pity snake-charmer or beast-tamer
for the fatal blow? And he deserves no less, who consorts with rogues
14 and is entangled in their sinful ways. This false friend will be thy

---

[1] *vv.* 31–36: The exact bearing of these verses cannot be determined. In
verse 32, 'unquiet hearts' is literally 'proud hearts'; but pride seems irrelevant
to the present context, and it is likely that the original Hebrew text had
'hearts of aliens' (as in verse 36). In that case the whole passage may be a
warning against undue fraternization with Gentiles.

[2] At the beginning of this verse, the Latin inserts the words, 'Keep thy
favours for the merciful, and let the sinners go without their entertainment',
which appears to be a duplicate of verse 5, included by error. It has been
omitted in the rendering given above, as fatally disturbing to the order of the
sentence. There was no doubt some dislocation of the text here; the Greek,
too, has a duplicate of verse 5 immediately after verse 7.

companion for an hour, then, if thou art for altering thy course, he
15 will not hear of it; all those honeyed words do but mask a plot to lure
16 thee into some ditch. How he weeps for thee, this enemy of thine!
Yet, if his chance comes, there will be no glutting him with thy blood;
17 come thou into mischief, he is there already waiting for thee. How
he weeps for thee, this enemy of thine! If he makes to aid thee, it is
19 only to trip thy heel; then what mopping and mowing, what clapping
of the hands and whispering, what a change of mien!

CHAPTER THIRTEEN

WHO handles pitch, with pitch is defiled; who throws in his lot
2 with insolence, of insolence shall have his fill. A heavy burden
thou art shouldering, if thou wouldst consort with thy betters; not for
3 thee the company of the rich. Pot and kettle are ill matched; it is
4 the pot breaks when they come together; wealth has more than its
5 share, and must be fretting still, while poverty suffers in silence. If
thou hast favours to bestow, thy rich friend will make use of thee; if
6 none, he bids thee farewell; thy guest, he will eat up all thou canst
7 give, and have no pity to waste on thee. Has he need of thee? Then,
to be sure, he will ply his arts, all smiles and fair speeches, and eager-
8 ness to know what thy need is; he encumbers thee, now, with hospitality. So, twice and three times, he will drain thee dry; then he
will turn on thee with a laugh, and if he meets thee again, it will be to
pass thee by with a toss of the head.
9 (Learn to abase thyself before God, and wait for his hand to beckon
10 thee), instead of courting false hopes, that bring their own abasement.
11 (For all thy wisdom, do not hold thyself too cheap, or thou wilt lower
12 thyself the fool's way.) If a great man bids thee come close, keep thy
13 distance; he will but bid thee the more; do not court a rebuff by
14 wearying him, nor yet withdraw altogether, and be forgotten. Affable
though he should be, treat him never familiarly; all his friendly talk
15 is but a lure to drag thy secrets out of thee. All that thou sayest his
pitiless heart will hold against thee; never a blow, never a chain the
16 less. Have a care of thyself, give good heed to this warning, thou
17 that walkest with ruin ever at thy side; (wake from sleep at the hearing
18 of it, and see thy peril. Love God all thy days, and pray that he will
send thee good deliverance).
19 Every beast consorts with its own kind, and shall not man with his
20 fellow? Like to like is nature's rule, and for man like to like is still
21 the best partnership; as well match wolf with lamb as rogue with

22 honest liver. Consecrated person [1] and prowling dog, what have they
in common? And what fellowship can there be between rich man and
23 poor? Poor man is to rich as wild ass is to lion out in the desert, his
24 prey; wealth hates poverty, as the proud heart scorns humble rank.
25 Totters the lordly house, it has friends to sustain it; the poor man in
26 his ruin is driven from familiar doors. Trips the rich man, he has
many to keep him in countenance; his insolent talk finds acquittal;
27 trips the poor man, he is called to account for it; even for what he
28 said to the purpose, no allowance is made him. Speaks the rich man,
all must listen in silence, and afterwards extol his utterance to the
29 skies; speaks the poor man, Why, say all, who is this? And if his words
offend, it is the undoing of him.
30   Yet, where there is no sin to smite a man's conscience, a full purse
is a blessing, and poverty itself is a great evil when it goes with a
31 blasphemer's mouth.[2] Heart of man changes his mien, for good or
32 ill, but where that pleasant mien is, that comes of a generous heart,
no short or easy way there is to discover.[3]

CHAPTER FOURTEEN

BLESSED the man whose lips have never betrayed him into a
2 fault, who has never known the sting of remorse, never felt conscience condemning him, and the hope he lived by, his no more!
3   Vain is that store the miser cherishes; wasted on his distrustful
4 nature, the bright gold! See how he wrongs himself to hoard up
goods for others; to let his heirs keep high revel when he is gone!
5 Whose friend is he, that is his own enemy, and leaves his own cheer
6 untasted? This is the last villainy of all, that a man should grudge
7 himself his own happiness; fit punishment for his poverty of soul
that never did good except by oversight, and to his manifest remorse!
8 A diseased eye has the niggard, that will turn away and let hunger go
9 unsatisfied; and for the covetous man, he has an eye that ever sees
his own share less, till his very nature dries up from continual pining.
10 An eye jaundiced with its own passions, and never a full meal, but
always he must sit hungry and pensive at his own table!

---

[1] Or perhaps 'holy person'. The Greek text has, 'hyena'.
[2] Literally, 'in the mouth of a sinner'. This would naturally be interpreted
as meaning 'in the estimation of a sinner', but such a rendering would give no
parallel of thought between the two halves of the verse.
[3] Or possibly the sense is that it is difficult to find instances of the pleasant
mien that results from a generous heart, because they are so rare. If so, the
first two verses of ch. 14 should be taken as part of this chapter.

11 My son, if wealth thou hast, eat well, and make thy offering to God
12 proportionable. Bethink thee that death waits not; there is no putting off thy tryst with the grave; nothing in this world, but its death-
13 warrant is out already. While life still holds, make thy friends good
14 cheer, and to the poor be open-handed as thy means allow thee; stint
not the feast, nor any crumb put by of the blessings granted thee;
15 wouldst thou have thy heirs wrangling over the fruits of thy bitter
16 toil? Much give, much take, set thy soul at ease; while life still
holds, do thy duty of almsgiving; feasting there shall be none in the
18 grave. No living thing but fades as the grass fades, as the leaves fade
19 on a growing tree, some sprouting fresh and some a-dying; so it is
20 with flesh and blood, one generation makes room for the next. All
the works of man are fugitive, and must perish soon or late, and he,
21 the workman, goes the same way as the rest. (Yet shall their choicest
works win favour, and in his work he, the workman, shall live.)
22 Blessed the man that dwells on wise thoughts, musing how to
23 acquit himself well, and remembering the all-seeing eye of God; that
can plan out in his heart all wisdom's twists and turns, fathom her
24 secrets! Like a spy he follows her, and lingers in her tracks, peers
25 through her window, listens at her doors, by her house takes up his
abode, driving his nail into the walls of it, so as to build his cabin at
her very side, cabin that shall remain for ever a home of blessing!
26 Wisdom shall be the shade under which his children find their
27 appointed resting-place; her spreading boughs shall protect them
from the noon-day heat; wisdom shall be the monument of his glorious
repose.

CHAPTER FIFTEEN

IF a man fears the Lord, he will live an upright life. If a man holds fast
2 to innocence, he will find wisdom [1] ready to his embrace, welcoming him as a mother welcomes the son who cherishes her, greeting
3 him like a maiden bride. Long life and good discernment are the
bread this mother will provide for him, truth the refreshing draught
she will give him to drink. She will take firm hold of him, so that he
4 never wavers, restrain him, so that he is never disgraced. She will
5 raise him to high repute among his neighbours; she will move him to
speak before the assembled people (filling him with the spirit of
6 wisdom and discernment, clothing him in magnificent array). Joy
and triumph she has in store for him, and will enrich him with a name

---

[1] Literally, 'will find her'. Grammatically, this might refer to 'innocence', but
it is fairly certain we are meant to think of Wisdom, alluded to in 14. 22 above.

7 that shall never be forgotten. Not for the fools her embrace, only apt pupils encounter her; how should the fools catch sight of her,
8 that is so far removed from proud and treacherous ways? Nay, she is beyond the deceiver's ken; (true hearts alone are her company, and
9 these shall profit by it till they are fit for God's scrutiny). Praise is
10 but praise deformed when it is uttered by the lips of a sinner; wisdom comes from God only, and of this divine gift praise must ever be at the beck and call. Praise on the lips of one who trusts God is rich in meaning; the Ruler of all inspires it.
11 This wisdom lackest thou?[1] Do not blame God for the want of it;
12 learn to shun the deeds God hates. Do not complain that it was he led thee into false paths; what need has God, thinkest thou, of
13 rebels? No foul misdeed there is but God hates it; there is no loving
14 it and fearing him. When men first came to be, it was God made them, and, making them, left them to the arbitrament of their own
15 wills; yet giving them commandments to be their rule. Those commandments if thou wilt observe, they in their turn shall preserve
17 thee, and give thee warrant of his favour.[2] It is as though he offered
18 thee fire and water, bidding thee take which thou wouldst; life and death, blessing and curse, man finds set before him, and the gift
19 given thee shall be the choice thou makest; so wise God is, so con-
20 straining his power, so incessant the watch he keeps over mankind. The Lord's eye is watching over the men who fear him, no act of ours
21 passes unobserved; upon none does he enjoin disobedience, none
22 has leave from him to commit sin. (A brood of disloyal sons and worthless, how should this be the Lord's desire?)

CHAPTER SIXTEEN

A BROOD of disloyal sons, let not thy eye dwell on these with pleasure; the fear of God lacking, let not the multitude of them be
2 thy consolation. Not on such lives as these set thy hopes, little
3 regard have thou for such doings as theirs; better one man who fears
4 God than a thousand who grew up rebellious; better die childless
5 than have rebels to succeed thee. Through one man that is well-minded a whole country may thrive, and of sinners a whole race may
6 be extinguished; much proof of this my own eyes have seen, and

---

[1] 'This wisdom lackest thou?'; according to the Greek text, 'Hast thou rebelled against him?'

[2] The rendering given above is an attempt to combine the Greek and the Latin versions, either of which, taken by itself, is untranslatable.

7 stronger proof yet are the tales that have come to my hearing, of fire
breaking out where sinners were met in company, fires of vengeance
8 to consume a disobedient race. Those old giants who perished in
the pride of their strength, did they find means for the pardon of their
9 guilt? Lot's neighbours, did God spare them? Did he not attest his
10 hatred of their insolence, destroying a whole nation without pity,
11 for the sinfulness that defied him? And what of those six hundred
thousand that marched out into the desert, men of stubborn heart?
Stiff-necked if he had been like the others, Caleb himself should not
12 have had God's pardon.[1] His to pity, his to punish; intercession avails
13 with him, but in full flood comes his vengeance; his severity, no less
14 than his clemency, judges men by their deeds. Never may sinner
enjoy his ill-gotten gains in safety, nor the hope of the generous be
15 disappointed. No generous act but shall win God's consideration;
he weighs each man's merits, knows how each passed his time on
earth.
16   Never think to hide thyself away from God; never tell thyself, from
17 that great height none shall regard thee; that thou wilt pass unnoticed
amidst the throng of humanity, thy soul a mere speck in the vast
18 fabric of creation. Why, the very heavens, and the heavens that are
above the heavens, the great deep, and the whole earth with all it
19 contains, shrink away at the sight of him; mountains and hills and
20 earth's foundations tremble at his glance; all these have a heart,
though it be a heart void of reason [2] (and there is no heart but its
21 secrets are known to him). There is no fathoming his ways, no
22 piercing the dark cloud man's eyes have never seen; all but a few of
his doings are hidden away. His acts of retribution [3] who can understand, or who can bear? Far, far removed is that covenant of his (from
some men's thoughts; and yet in the end all shall undergo his
23 scrutiny).[4] Away with these fancies of shallow minds, these fond
dreams of error!

---

[1] The words 'into the desert' have been inserted to make it clear that the
Exodus is alluded to; they are not in the text. Nor is the name 'Caleb', but the
grammar of the Latin version necessarily implies that one person was excepted
from the general doom, cf. Num. 14.24 and elsewhere. The Greek text has,
'And if there is one stiff-necked person, it is a marvel if he escapes'.

[2] 'All these have a heart, though it be a heart void of reason'; or perhaps,
'and in all these matters, the (human) heart is powerless to reason', which is
the sense of the Greek text.

[3] The sense of the Greek text is probably rather 'the acts which win his
approval'.

[4] *vv.* 18–22: In the Latin version, this is apparently regarded as an answer
to the notions mentioned in *vv.* 16, 17; in the Greek text, it seems to be a
continuation of them, the answer being delayed till verse 24.

24 Wilt thou but listen to me, my son, thou shalt learn a wiser lesson.
25 Give me thy heart's heeding, and instruction thou shalt have in full
measure (wisdom both profound and clear. Give me thy heart's
heeding, and thou shalt share with me knowledge of the wonderful
endowments God gave his creatures when first he made them); all
26 the lore I have shall be truly told thee. From the first, all God's
creatures are at his beck and call; to each, when he first made it, he
gave its own turn of service, the power of motion that belonged to its
27 own nature. To each, for all time, its own office is assigned, nor
28 lack they, nor tire they, nor cease they from work, nor, for all time,
29 can any of them infringe upon its neighbour's rights; his word there
30 is no gainsaying.[1] This done, on earth he let fall his regard, and
31 filled earth with his blessings; covered the face of it [2] with the living
things that breathe there, and into its bosom bade them return.

CHAPTER SEVENTEEN

MAN, too, God created out of the earth (fashioning him after his
2 own likeness), and gave him, too, earth to be his burying-place
3 (for all the divine power that clothed him); man, too, should have
his allotted toll of years, his season of maturity, and should have
4 power over all else on earth; no living thing, beast or bird, that should
5 not fear him and be subject to his rule. To him (and to that partner
of his, created like himself and out of himself), God gave will and
speech and sight and hearing; gave them a heart to reason with, and
6 filled them with power of discernment; (spirit itself should be within
their ken, their hearts should be all sagacity). What evil was, what
7 good, he made plain to them; gave them his own eyes to see with, so
8 that they should keep his marvellous acts in view, praise that holy
name of his, boast of his wonders, tell the story of his renowned
9 deeds. Warnings, too, he gave them; the law that brings life should
be a cherished heirloom; and so he made a covenant with them which
10 should last for ever; claim and award of his he would make known
11 to them. Their eyes should see him in visible majesty, their ears
catch the echo of his majestic voice. Keep your hands clear, he told
12 them, of all wrong-doing, and gave each man a duty towards his
neighbour.

---

[1] That is, according to the Greek text, the forces of nature are bound to obey
it; the Latin version represents it as a warning against human disobedience.
[2] This is the meaning of the Greek text. The Latin version has 'denounced
before the face of it', which yields no satisfactory sense.

13 Ever before his eyes their doings are; nothing is hidden from his
14 scrutiny. To every Gentile people he has given a ruler of its own;
15 Israel alone is exempt, marked down as God's patrimony. Clear as
the sun their acts shew under his eye; over their lives, untiring his
17 scrutiny. Sin they as they will, his covenant is still on record; no
misdeed of theirs but he is the witness of it.
18 Alms if thou givest, thou hast the sign-manual of his favour;
treasured as the apple of his eye is the record of man's deserving.[1]
19 . . . A day will come when he rouses himself and requites them,
one by one, for their misdoing (overwhelms them in the depths of
20 earth). Yet, to such as repent, he grants the means of acquittal, and
makes their fainting hearts strong to endure; (for them, too, he has a
21 share in his promised reward). Turn back to the Lord, and let thy
22 sins be; a suppliant before him, thou mayest rob the snare of its
23 fangs. Come back to the Lord, from wrong-doing turn away, and
24 thy foul deeds hate; (in all his decrees and awards own God just,
stand in thy appointed place to make intercession to him, the most
25 High), and take thy part with a race of men sanctified, living men
26 that still give thanks to God.[2] (Linger not in the false path of
wickedness; give thanks while breath is in thee); the dead breathe no
27 more, give thanks no more. Thanks while yet thou livest, thanks
while health and strength are still with thee, to praise God and to take
28 pride in all his mercies! The Lord's mercy, that is so abundant,
the pardon that is ever theirs who come back to him!
29 Think not man is the centre of all things;[3] no son of Adam is im-
30 mortal, for all the delight they take in their sinful follies. Nought
brighter than the sun, and yet its brightness shall fail; nought darker
than the secret designs of flesh and blood, yet all shall come to light.
31 God, that marshals the armies of high heaven, and man, all dust and
ashes!

---

[1] It seems possible that this verse has been misplaced, since it breaks into the
connexion of thought between verse 17 and verse 19.

[2] *vv.* 24, 25: The Latin here reads very unnaturally, and is perhaps the
rendering of a corrupt Hebrew original. In the first half of verse 25, the Greek
text has, 'Who will give praise to the most High in the grave?' The word
rendered 'give thanks', here and in the following verses, may also, according
to Hebrew usage, mean 'confess'. But cf. Is. 38.19.

[3] Literally, 'it is not possible that all things should be in man'.

CHAPTER EIGHTEEN

NAUGHT that is, but God made it; he, the source of all right,
2 the king that reigns for ever unconquerable. And wouldst thou
3 tell the number of his creatures, trace his marvellous doings to their
4 origin, set forth in words the greatness of his power, or go further
5 yet, and proclaim his mercies? God's wonders thou shalt learn to
understand, when thou hast learned to increase the number of them,
6 or diminish it. Reach thou the end of thy reckoning, thou must
needs begin again; cease thou from weariness, thou hast nothing
7 learnt. Tell me, what is man, what worth is his, what things are
8 they that are boon and bane to him? What is his span of life? Like a
drop in the ocean, like a pebble on the beach, seem those few years of
9 his, a hundred at the most matched with eternity. What wonder if
God is patient with his human creatures, lavishes mercy on them?
10 (If none reads, as he, their proud heart,) none knows, as he, the cruelty
11 of their doom; and so he has given his clemency full play, and shewed
12 them an even path to tread. Man's mercy extends only to his neigh-
13 bour; God has pity on all living things. He is like a shepherd who
14 cares for his sheep, guides and controls all alike; welcome thou this
merciful discipline of his, run thou eagerly to meet his will, and he
will shew pity on thee.

15 My son, bestow thy favours ungrudgingly, nor ever mar with harsh
16 words the gladness of thy giving. Not more welcome the dew, tem-
pering the sun's heat, than the giver's word, that counts for more than
17 the gift. Better the gracious word than the gracious gift; but, wouldst
18 thou acquit thyself perfectly, let both be thine. Folly must be railing
still; never yet did eye brighten over a churl's giving.

19 First arm thyself with a just cause, then stand thy trial; first learn,
20 then speak. Study thy health before ever thou fallest sick, and thy
own heart examine before judgement overtakes thee; so in God's sight
21 thou shalt find pardon. While health serves thee, do penance for
thy sins, and then, when sickness comes, shew thyself the man thou
22 art.[1] From paying thy vows [2] let naught ever hinder thee; shall death
find thee still shrinking from acquitting thyself of the task? (God's
23 award stands for ever.) And before ever thou makest thy petition,

---

[1] Literally, 'shew thy conversation', or perhaps, 'shew thy conversion'—the point is the same in either case. The Greek has, 'shew thy conversion at the time of transgressions', it is not clear in what sense.

[2] The Latin has simply 'praying', but this misses the emphasis of the context, this paragraph being evidently concerned with getting things done in good time.

count well the cost.[1] Let it not be said of thee that thou didst defy
24 God's anger. When his vengeance is satisfied, bethink thee of his
vengeance still; of his retribution, when his glance is turned away.[2]
25 When all abounds, bethink thee of evil times; of pinching poverty,
26 when thou hast wealth in store. Between rise and set of sun the face
27 of things alters; swiftly God changes all; and he is wisest who walks
timorously, shunning carelessness in a world where sins abound.
28   They are well advised that master wisdom's secret; much cause for
29 thankfulness she bestows on him who finds her. Wise man that has
the gift of utterance does more than wisely live; (no stranger to truth
and right), he is a fountain of true sayings and of right awards.
30   Do not follow the counsel of appetite; turn thy back on thy own
31 liking. Pamper those passions of thine, and joy it will bring, but to
32 thy enemies. Love not the carouse, though it be with poor men;
33 they will be vying still one with another in wastefulness. And
wouldst thou grow poor with borrowing to pay thy shot, thou with
thy empty coffers? That were to grudge thy own life.

CHAPTER NINETEEN

LET him toil as he will, the sot's purse is empty; little things
2 despise, and little by little thou shalt come to ruin. Wine and
women, a trap for the loyalty of the wise, the touchstone of good
3 sense! He will go from bad to worse, that clings to a harlot's love;
waste and worm shall have him for their prize; one gibbet the more,
one living soul the less.
4   Rash heart that lightly trusts shall lose all; forfeit thy own right to
5 live, and none will pity thee. (A foul blot it is, to take pride in wrong-
doing; a courting of death, to despise reproof; a riddance of much
6 mischief, to forswear chattering. Who forfeits his own right to live,
will live to rue it; who loves cruelty, blots his own name.)

---

[1] Literally 'prepare thy mind' (for the fulfilment of the vow with which the
petition was accompanied).

[2] Literally, this verse reads: 'Remember anger in the day of the end, and a
time of retribution in the turning of the face'. It is ordinarily interpreted as
meaning, 'Remember the anger (which God will shew) at the end of the world
(or, at the time of thy death), and the time of retribution (which will consist)
in the turning away of his face'. But it is surely incredible that verse 24 should
have exactly the same grammatical appearance as verse 25, and yet a totally
different grammatical construction. Nor is God said to 'turn away his face'
when he punishes men, but, on the contrary, when he seems to 'look the other
way' and leaves them unpunished; cf. Ps. 9 (*b*). 11.

7 Malicious word if thou hear or harsh, do not repeat it; never wilt
8 thou be the loser. Speak not out thy own thought for friend and foe
to hear alike, nor ever, if thou hast done wrong, discover the secret.
9 He that hears it will be on his guard, and eye thee askance, as if to
avert fresh fault of thine; such will be all his demeanour to thee thence-
10 forward.[1] Hast thou heard a tale to thy neighbour's disadvantage?
11 Take it to the grave with thee. Courage, man! it will not burst thee. A
fool with a secret labours as with child, and groans till he is delivered
12 of it; out it must come, like an arrow stuck in a man's thigh, from
that reckless heart.
13 Confront thy friend with his fault; it may be he knows nothing of
the matter, and can clear himself; if not, there is hope he will amend.
14 Confront him with the word spoken amiss; it may be, he never said it,
15 or if say it he did, never again will he repeat it. Be open with thy
16 friend; tongues will still be clattering,[2] and thou dost well to believe
less than is told thee. Slips there are of the tongue when mind is
17 innocent; what tongue was ever perfectly guarded? Confront thy
18 neighbour with his fault ere thou quarrellest with him, and let the
fear of the most High God do its work.
What is true wisdom? Nothing but the fear of God. And since the
fear of God is contained in it, all true wisdom must be directed by
19 his law; wisdom is none in following the maxims of impiety, prudence
20 is none in scheming as the wicked scheme. Cunning rogues they
may be, yet altogether abominable; a fool he must ever be called, that
21 lacks the true wisdom.[3] Better a simpleton that wit has none, yet
knows fear, than a man of great address, that breaks the law of the
22 most High. It is one thing to be exact and adroit, another thing to
23 utter the plain word that tells the whole truth. Here is one that
24 wears the garb of penance for wicked ends, his heart full of guile; here
is one that bows and scrapes, and walks with bent head, feigning not to
25 see what is best left aside, and all because he is powerless to do thee

---

[1] *vv.* 8, 9: The sense of the Greek text is: 'Do not tell tales about friend or
foe; bring nothing to light, unless it were sin in thee (to keep silent). Friend
or foe will hear of it, and will keep thee under his eye, waiting for the opportunity to shew his hatred of thee'.

[2] Literally, 'for often there is competition', i.e., in the retailing of scandal;
the same word is used by the Latin version as in 18. 32 above. The Greek text
has, 'often there is slander'.

[3] The first half of this verse runs, both in the Greek and in the Latin, 'There
is a wickedness (or, worthlessness), and it is an abomination'; a phrase which
means little and does not suit the context. Evidently the Hebrew original
contained some word which might be interpreted either as 'prudence' or as
'wickedness'; e.g., the word used in the former sense by Prov. 1.4, and in the
latter sense by Jer. 11. 15.

26 a harm; if the chance of villainy comes, he will take it. Yet a man's
looks betray him; a man of good sense will make himself known to thee
27 at first meeting; the clothes he wears, the smile on his lips, his gait,
will all make thee acquainted with a man's character.
28   Reproof there is that no good brings, as the event shews; the mistaken reproof that anger prompts in a quarrel. And a man may shew
prudence by holding his tongue.

CHAPTER TWENTY

BETTER the complaint made than the grudge secretly nursed.
2 When a man confesses his fault, do not cut him short in mid
utterance.
3   Redress [1] sought by violence no more content shall bring thee than
eunuch's lust for maid.
4   Well it is to be reproved, and to confess thy fault, and be rid of all
such guilt as thou hast incurred knowingly.
5   A man may be the wiser for remaining dumb, where the glib talker
6 grows wearisome; the silent man, has he nothing to say? Or is he
7 waiting for the right time to say it? Wisdom keeps its utterance in
8 reserve, where the fool's vanity cannot wait. The babbler cuts his
own throat; claim more than thy right, and all men are thy enemies.
9   For a mind ill trained, success is failure, winning is losing. Gift
11 given may bring thee nothing in return, or twice its worth. Honour
12 achieved may belittle a man, and modesty bring him renown. What
use to make a good bargain, if thou must pay for it sevenfold?
13   Word of wise man endears him; the fool spends his favours in vain.
14 Little will the fool's gift profit thee; seven times magnified is all he
15 sees.[2] The paltrier the gift, the longer the admonitions that go with
16 it, and every word of his an incitement to anger. Out upon the man
17 who lends to-day, and will have the loan restored to-morrow! The
18 fool has no friends, nor can win love by all his favours; they are but
parasites that eat at his table; loud and long they will laugh over him;
19 (so injudiciously he bestows gifts worth having, and gifts nothing
worth).

---

[1] The Latin version substitutes 'false award' for 'redress', but it is doubtful
whether this interpretation improves the sense of a passage already obscure.
[2] Literally, 'his eyes are sevenfold', a phrase which is sometimes understood
as meaning that he expects a sevenfold return for his gift. But this meaning
does not seem to be borne out either by usage or by the context, which empha-
sizes only the self-importance of the clumsy giver. But it must be admitted that
the interpretation of this whole paragraph cannot be reached with certainty.

20   Slip of a liar's tongue is like slip from roof to ground; a villain's end is not long a-coming.

21   An ungracious man is no more set by than some idle tale that is ever on the lips of the ill-bred.

22   No weighty saying but offends in a fool's mouth; sure it is that he will bring it out unseasonably.

23   Some avoid wrong only because they lack the means to do it; idle they remain, yet conscience-stricken.[1]

24   Some for very shame have courted their own ruin, resolved, though that opinion were worthless enough, to sacrifice themselves for another's
25   good opinion. Some, too, for shame, make their friends high-sounding promises, and thereby gain nothing, but lose a friend.

26   A lie is a foul blot upon a man's name, yet nothing so frequent on
27   ill-guarded lips. Worse than a thief is one who is ever lying, and
28   to no better end may he look forward. He lives without honour that lies without scruple, and shame is at his side continually.

29   The wise word brings a man to honour; prudence will endear thee
30   to the great. Till ground, and fill barn; (live uprightly, and attain honour); win prince, and shun harm.

31   Hospitality here, a gift there, how they blind the eyes of justice! With these, though thy lips be dumb, thou mayst escape censure.[2]

32   Wisdom hidden is wasted, is treasure that never sees the light of
33   day; silence is rightly used when it masks folly, not when it is the grave of wisdom.

CHAPTER TWENTY-ONE

SINNED if thou hast, my son, be not emboldened to sin further; to
2   prayer betake thee, and efface the memory of sins past. Sin dread
3   thou not less than the serpent's encounter; its fangs will not miss thee, if once thou come close. Teeth so sharp no lion ever had, to catch
4   human prey, nor ever two-edged sword gave wound so incurable
5   as the law's defiance. Browbeat and oppress the poor, thy own wealth shall dwindle; riches that are grown too great the proud cannot long
6   enjoy; pride shrivels wealth. Swiftly comes their doom, because the poor man's plea reached their ears, but never their hearts.[3]

---

[1] Literally, 'he will be conscience-stricken in his repose'. The Greek inserts a negative.

[2] The Greek gives a different turn to the second half of the verse, 'no better gag to silence reproof'.

[3] Literally, 'The plea of the poor man will come from the mouth as far as his ears'. Some interpret this as meaning the ears of divine justice, but there is no hint of this in the text.

7   Where reproof is unregarded, there goes the sinner; no God-fearing man but will pass his own conscience under review.

8   To the glib speaker, fame comes from far and wide; only the wise man knows the slips of his own heart.

9   Wouldst thou build thy fortunes on earnings that are none of thine? As well mightest thou lay in stones for winter fuel.

10   When knaves come together, it is like heaping up tow; the flame burns all the brighter.

11   How smoothly paved is the path of sinners! Yet death lies at the end of it, and darkness, and doom.

12   If thou wouldst be master of thy own thought, first keep the law; no
14   wisdom or discernment but is the fruit of God's fear. Without shrewd-
15   ness [1] thou wilt never advance in the school of virtue; yet shrewdness there is that breeds abundance of mischief; where the stream runs
16   foul, there can be no rightness of mind. Where true wisdom is, there discernment flows in full tide, there prudence springs up, an inexhaustible fountain of life.

17   Heart of fool is leaking bucket, that loses all the wisdom it learns.
18   Truths that wisdom will prize and cherish, the profligate hears no less,
19   but hearing despises, and casts them to the winds. Listening to a fool is like journeying with a heavy pack; there is no pleasing the ear,
20   where sense is none. How they hang on the lips of a wise man, the
21   folk assembled, ay, and ponder in their hearts over the word said! A fool takes refuge in wise talk as a man takes shelter in a ruin; learning
22   without sense, that cannot abide scrutiny. To the fool, instruction
23   seems but a fetter to clog him, gyves that cramp his wrist. A fool
24   laughs loud; smiling, the wise compress their lips. Precious as an ornament of gold, close-fitting as a bracelet to the right arm, is
25   instruction to a wise man. Folly sets foot over every threshold, where
26   the experienced mind stands, as in a royal presence, abashed; folly
27   peeps in at windows, where experience waits patiently without; listens thoughtlessly behind open doors, where prudence hangs back for
28   very shame.[2] Fools break out into rash utterance, where the prudent
29   are at pains to weigh their words; with the one, to think is to speak, with the other, to speak is to think.

30   Let the sinner curse the foul fiend that spites him,[3] on his own head
31   the curse shall recoil. The tale-bearer is his own enemy, shunned by

---

[1] In the Latin version, 'wisdom', in the Greek text, 'knavery'; cf. note on 19. 20.

[2] *vv.* 25–27: These verses are usually understood as an instruction in the usages of polite society. It is more probable that the sacred author is denouncing, under a metaphor, the habit of rash enquiry.

[3] 'The foul fiend' may, in the Hebrew text, have meant simply 'his enemy'.

all; court his friendship, and thou wilt court hatred; shut lips and calm judgement shall bring thee a good name.

CHAPTER TWENTY-TWO

WHAT ill names shall we hurl at the sluggard? Stone from the
2   sewers, that has no man's good word; dung from the midden, for all to wash their hands of him.
3   Spoilt son thou shall beget to thy shame, spoilt daughter to thy
4 great loss; bring she to her husband no dower of modesty, her shame
5 shall cost thee dear. Shame the father shall have, shame the husband; fit company for sinners, she will have no good word from either of these.
6   Speech may be out of season, like music in time of mourning; not
7 so the rod, not so chastisement; there lies ever wisdom.[1] Teach a
8 fool, and mend a pot with glue; better audience thou shalt have from
9 the sleeper thou wouldst awake from a deep dream; thy speech ended, Why, what's to do?[2] ask fool and dreamer alike.
10   For the dead that lacks light, for the fool that lacks wit, never cease
11 to mourn; yet not for the dead overmuch, since rest is his, but the
13 fool's life is empty beyond the emptiness of death; seven days the dead are mourned, but the fool, the godless fool, all his life long.
14   Linger never with a fool in talk, nor cast in thy lot with his; keep clear of him, as thou wouldst keep clear of mischief, and of sin's pol-
16 lution; go thy way, and let him go his; thou shalt sleep the sounder,
17 for having no folly of his to cloud thy spirits. Nought like lead for
18 heaviness? Ay, but its name is fool. With sand or salt or iron bars burden thyself, not with rash and godless company, not with a fool.
19   Tie fast the foundations with timber baulks, thy house shall with-
20 stand all shock; nor less shall he, whose heart stands resolved in the counsels of prudence; no hour of peril can daunt that steadfast heart.
21 Palisade set on high ground, with no better protection against the
22 wind's fury than cheap rubble, is but of short endurance; faint heart that thinks a fool's thoughts will not be proof against sudden terror. Faint heart that thinks a fool's thoughts . . .
23   . . . shall never be afraid; no more shall he, that still keeps true to God's commandments.[3]

---

[1] The use of words in this verse is very strained, and it is likely that the Hebrew text was corrupt.
[2] The Greek text here has, 'What is it?' The Latin version ('Who is it?') would apply to the sleeper, but gives no satisfactory sense as applied to the fool.
[3] The Latin text here is evidently confused, and perhaps defective.

24   Chafed eye will weep, chafed heart will shew resentment. One
stone flung, and the birds are all on the wing; one taunt uttered, and
26 the friendship is past repair. Hast thou drawn sword against thy
27 friend? Be comforted; all may be as it was. Hast thou assailed
him with angry words? Thou mayst yet be reconciled. But the taunt,
the contemptuous reproach, the secret betrayed, the covert attack,
all these mean a friend lost.

28   Keep faith with a friend when his purse is empty, thou shalt have
29 joy of his good fortune; stand by him when he falls upon evil times,
thou shalt be partner in his prosperity.

30   Chimney-fumes and smoke rising, of fire forewarn thee; curse
uttered, and threat, and insult, of bloodshed.

31   Never will I be ashamed to greet friend of mine, never deny myself
to him; let harm befall me for his sake, I care not.

32   . . . All that hear of it will keep their distance from him.[1]

33   Oh for a sentry to guard this mouth of mine, a seal to keep these
lips inviolate! Were I but safe from that snare, might but my tongue
never betray me!

CHAPTER TWENTY-THREE

LORD, that gavest my life and guidest it, never may these lips of
mine have me at their mercy, never let them betray me into a fall!
2 Be my thoughts ever under the lash, my heart disciplined by true
wisdom; let it never deal gently with their unwitting offences, or gloss
3 over the wrong they do! What if my transgressions should go, all
unobserved, from bad to worse, if I should grow hardened in wrong-
doing, and add fault to fault? What humiliation were this, in full view
4 of my enemies; how would my ill-wishers triumph at the sight! Lord,
that gavest my life and guidest it (let them not have me at their mercy);
5 never let haughty looks be mine, never the assaults of passion come
6 near me. Let the itch of gluttony pass me by, nor ever carnal lust
overtake me; do not leave me, Lord, at the mercy of a shameless, an
unprofitable mind!

7   Here is the lore, my sons, of the tongue's use; hold fast by it, and
8 thy own lips shall never be thy undoing. What is it but his lying that
entraps the sinner, what snare but their own speech catches the
9 proud, the slanderers? That mouth of thine do not inure to oath-
10 taking; therein lie many perils; wilt thou take God's name often on

---

[1] *vv.* 31, 32: It is impossible to make these verses into a continuous sentence;
to render 'let harm befall me through his agency' is a mistranslation of the
Greek. There has perhaps been an omission in the text.

thy lips, and bind thyself by invocation of the holy ones, thy word is
11 forfeit to them. Slave that is ever under the lash cannot escape
without bruises in the end; thy often swearing, thy often invoking,
12 shall lead thee into guilt at last. Oaths a many, sins a many; punish-
13 ment shall be still at thy doors. Forswear thyself, thou shalt be held
14 to account for it; forget the oath, it is at thy double peril; and though
it were lightly taken, thou shalt find no excuse in that; plague shall
light on all thou hast, in amends for it.

15   Sin of speech there is, too, that has death for its counterpart; God
16 send it be not found in Jacob's chosen race;[1] from men of tender
conscience every such thought is far away, not theirs to wallow in
evil-doing.

17   Beware of habituating thy tongue to lewd talk; therein is matter of
offence.

18   Treat not father and mother with disregard. There are great ones
19 all around thee; what if thyself God should disregard, when thou
art arraigned before them? Then shall this ill custom of thine strike
thee dumb[2] and bring thee to great dishonour; thou wilt wish thou
hadst never been, and rue the day of thy birth.

20   Let a man grow into a habit of railing speech, all his days there is
no amending him.

21   Two sorts of men are sinners above measure, and a third I can name
22 that calls down vengeance. There is a hot temper, all fire and fury,
23 that cannot die down till it has had its fill. A man that is corrupted
by the prompting of his own lust[3] will not be content until it bursts
24 into flame. To the fornicator, one pasture-ground is as good as
25 another; there is no wearying him till he has tried all. Out on the
man that takes his life in his hands and comes between another's
26 sheets! There is none to witness it, thinks he; darkness all about,
and walls to shelter me, and none watching; what have I to fear? Of
27 sins like mine the most High lets the record pass. Of that all-seeing
eye no heed takes he; fear of a man has driven the fear of God from
28 his thoughts; of human eyes only he shuns the regard.[4] What, are

---

[1] There can be little doubt that the reference is to blasphemy (see Lev. 24. 16).

[2] 'What if thyself God should disregard, when thou art arraigned before
them? Then shall this ill custom of thine strike thee dumb'; literally, 'Lest by
chance God should forget thee (in the Greek, thou shouldst forget) in their
presence, and be made foolish by thy habit'. It is difficult to be certain either of
the exact meaning of the passage, or of its relevance to the context.

[3] Literally, 'by the mouth of his flesh'. It would be easiest to understand what
are the three sins mentioned in verse 21, if we could suppose that the Hebrew
text intended, in verse 23, the sin of gluttony (cf. verse 6 above).

[4] The Latin version, evidently by an error, gives at the end of the verse 'the
eyes of men fear him', instead of 'the eyes of men frighten him'.

not God's eyes a thousand times more piercing than the sun's rays? Do they not watch all the doings of men (the depths of earth, and man's
29 heart), every secret open to their scrutiny? God, that knows all he means to make, does he not watch over all he has made?
30   In full view of the open street the adulterer shall pay the penalty; (loud, as for a runaway horse, the hue and cry;) where he thought to
31 escape, justice outruns him. (All the world shall witness his shame,
32 that left the fear of the Lord unregarded). Nor less guilty is she who plays her husband false, giving him for heir a child that is no son of
33 his. Broken, the law of the most High; her plighted troth forsaken; has she not thrice played the wanton, that bears sons to a paramour?
34 Needs must she confront the folk assembled, nor shall those sons of
35 hers be spared; such roots must not burgeon, such boughs never
36 bear fruit; she leaves but the memory of an accursed name, a name
37 for ever dishonoured. Warning she gives to after ages that God's fear is best, nor sweeter lot is any than the divine law well observed.
38 (Follow the Lord, and it shall be thy renown; a long life is the reward it shall bring thee.)

CHAPTER TWENTY-FOUR

HEAR now how wisdom speaks in her own regard (of the honour God has given her), of the pride she takes in the nation that is
2 her home. In the court of the most High, in the presence of all his
3 host, she makes her boast aloud (and here, amid the holy gathering
4 of her own people, that high renown of hers is echoed; praise is hers from God's chosen, blessing from blessed lips).
5   I am that word, she says, that was uttered by the mouth of the
6 most High (the primal birth before ever creation began. Through me light rose in the heavens, inexhaustible); it was I that covered, as
7 with a mist, the earth. In high heaven was my dwelling-place, my
8 throne a pillar of cloud; none but I might span the sky's vault, pierce
9 the depth of the abyss, walk on the sea's waves; no part of earth but gave a resting-place to my feet.
10   People was none, nor any race of men, but I had dominion there;
11 (high and low, my power ruled over men's hearts). Yet with all these I sought rest in vain; it is among the Lord's people that I mean to
12 dwell. He who fashioned me, he, my own Creator, has taken up his
13 abode with me; and his command to me was that I should find my home in Jacob, throw in my lot with Israel, take root among his chosen
14 race. From the beginning of time, before the worlds, he had made me, unfailing to all eternity; in his own holy dwelling-place I had

15 waited on his presence; and now, no less faithfully, I made Sion my
16 stronghold, the holy city my resting-place, Jerusalem my throne. My
roots spread out among the people that enjoys his favour, my God has
granted me a share in his own domain; (where his faithful servants are
gathered I love to linger).

17   I grew to my full stature as cedar grows on Lebanon, as cypress on
18 Sion's hill; or a palm tree in Cades, or a rose bush in Jericho; grew
like some fair olive in the valley, some plane-tree in a well-watered
20 street. Cinnamon and odorous balm have no scent like mine; the
21 choicest myrrh has no such fragrance. Perfumed is all my dwelling-
place with storax, and galbanum, and onycha, and stacte, and frank-
22 incense uncrushed; (the smell of me is like pure balm). Mastic-
tree spreads not its branches so wide, as I the hopes I proffer of glory
23 and of grace. No vine ever yielded fruit so fragrant; the enjoyment
of honour and riches is the fruit I bear.

24   It is I that give birth to all noble loving, all reverence, all true know-
25 ledge, and the holy gift of hope. (From me comes every grace of
26 faithful observance, from me all promise of life and vigour.) Hither
turn your steps, all you that have learned to long for me; take your fill
27 of the increase I yield. Never was honey so sweet as the influence I
28 inspire, never honey-comb as the gift I bring; (mine is a renown
29 that endures age after age). Eat of this fruit, and you will yet hunger
for more; drink of this wine, and your thirst for it is still un-
30 quenched. He who listens to me will never be disappointed, he who
31 lives by me will do no wrong; (he who reads my lesson aright will
find in it life eternal).

32   What things are these I write of? What but the life-giving book
that is the covenant of the most High (and the revelation of all
33 truth?) What but the law Moses enjoined, with the duties it prescribes,
34 the inheritance it bestows, the promises it holds out? (Afterwards,
he pledged himself to give his servant David an heir most valiant,
35 that should hold his royal throne for ever.) Who but he [1] can make
wisdom flow, deep as the stream Phison sends down, or Tigris, in the
36 spring, make the tide of prudence run, strong as Euphrates' own, or
37 Jordan's tide in the month of harvest, make obedience rise to its full
38 height, like Nile [2] or Gehon when men gather the vintage? He it was
that first attained to wisdom's secret, never since made known to any

---

[1] Some would render, 'What but this . . .', referring to the Law of Moses.
[2] Both the Latin and the Greek have, 'like the light'; but the context makes it
clear that they have overlooked a single vowel in the word which must have
stood in the Hebrew original.

39 less than himself; so deep are her thoughts, sea-deep, so dark her
counsels, dark as the great abyss.

40   (From me rivers flow, says Wisdom, deep rivers.)

41   And what am I?[1] A conduit that carries off the river's overflow, its
42 channel, the aqueduct that waters a park. I thought to refresh my
43 well-set garden, give drink to the fruits that fringe its border; and all
at once my channel overflowed, this stream of mine had nigh turned
44 into a sea! Teaching is here like the dawn for brightness, shedding
45 its rays afar. (Nay, I will make my way down to the depths of earth,
and visit those who sleep there, and to such as trust in the Lord I
46 will bring light.) My teaching shall yet flow on, faithful as prophecy,
heirloom to all such as make wisdom their quest, and to their children
47 yet, until the holy days come. See how I have toiled, not for my
own sake merely, but for all such as covet wisdom!

CHAPTER TWENTY-FIVE

T HREE sights warm my heart; God and man wish them well;
2 peace in the clan, good will among neighbours, man and wife
3 well matched. Three sorts of men move my spleen, so that I am fain
4 to grudge them life itself; poor man that is proud, rich man that is
a liar, old man that is fond and foolish.

5   The store youth never put by, shall old age enjoy? Good judgement
7 well matches grey hairs, for still the elders must give advice; wisdom
8 for the old, discernment for senators, and the gift of counsel! No
crown have old men like their long experience, no ornament like the
fear of God.

9   Nine envious thoughts came suddenly into my mind, and a tenth
10 I will add for good measure. Happy is he that has joy of his children;
11 that lives to see his enemies' downfall. Happiness it is to share thy
home with a faithful wife; to have a tongue that never betrays thee; to
12 serve only thy betters. Happiness it is to have a true friend . . .[2]
13 and to speak the right word to an ear that listens. Happy is he that
wisdom gains and skill; yet is he no match for one who fears the Lord.
14 The fear of God, that is a gift beyond all gifts; (blessed the man that

---

[1] *vv.* 41–46: Commentators are not agreed whether these words are to be
understood as spoken by Wisdom, like verse 40, or by Ecclesiasticus himself,
like verse 47 (cf. 33. 18 below).

[2] It seems possible that one of the nine beatitudes has fallen out through a
textual error, unless we reckon wisdom and skill in verse 13 as separate sources
of happiness.

16 receives it), he has no equal. (Fear the Lord, and thou shalt learn to love him; cling close, and thou shalt learn to trust him.)

17 (There is no sadness but what touches the heart, no mischief but
18 what comes from woman.) A man will endure any wound but the
19 heart's wound, and any malice but a woman's; just so he will
21 endure any annoyance but from his ill-wishers, any sentence imposed
22 on him but by his enemies.[1] No head so venomous as the viper's,
23 nor any anger like a woman's. Better share thy home with lion and
24 serpent both, than with an ill woman's company. A woman's ill will changes the very look of her; grim as a bear's her visage, and she goes
25 like one mourning. See where he sits among his neighbours, that
26 husband of hers, groaning deep and sighing as he listens to them! All other mischief is a slight thing beside the mischief an ill woman does;
27 may she fall to a sinner's lot! Better climb sandy cliff in thy old age,
28 than be a peace-loving man mated with a scold. Let not thy eye be
29 caught by a woman's beauty; not for her beauty desire her; think of
30 woman's rage, her shamelessness, the dishonour she can do thee, how
31 hard it goes with a man if his wife will have the uppermost. Crushed spirits, a clouded brow, a heavy heart, all this is an ill woman's
32 work; faint hand and flagging knee betoken one unblessed in his
33 marriage. Through a woman sin first began; such fault was hers, we
34 all must die for it. Thy cistern thou wouldst not let leak, ever so
35 little; and wouldst thou let a wanton wife roam at large? Leave she
36 once thy side (thou shalt be the laughing-stock of thy enemies); best cut away the ill growth from thy flesh; (she will ever be taking advantage of thee).

CHAPTER TWENTY-SIX

HAPPY the man that has a faithful wife; his span of days is doubled.
2 A wife industrious is the joy of her husband, and crowns all his
3 years with peace. He best thrives that best wives; where men fear
4 God, this is the reward of their service, given to rich and poor alike; day in, day out, never a mournful look.

5 Three things daunt me somewhat, a fourth I dare not face. Gossip
7 of the streets, the judgement of the rabble, and the false charge
8 preferred, all these make death itself seem a light thing. But there

---

[1] *vv.* 20, 21: It is difficult to feel certain that our versions have preserved the exact sense of the original. These two verses entirely break up the continuity of the context; in verse 23 the Greek makes matters worse by giving us 'like an enemy's' instead of 'like a woman's'. The word translated 'sentence' in verse 21 is literally 'vengeance'; and it is hard to see from what other class of people than one's enemies vengeance could reasonably be expected.

9 is no affliction wrings the heart like a woman's jealousy; once a woman
10 grows jealous, her tongue is a scourge to all alike. Easier to guide
an unsteady team of oxen than an ill woman; easier to hold a snake
11 than to manage her. Woman that is a sot vexation shall bring thee
12 and great dishonour; there is no hiding her shame. Haughty gaze
13 and lowered eye-lid, there goes a wanton. Headstrong daughter
must be held with a tight rein, or she will find opportunity to bestow
14 her favours; beware of that shameless eye; it shall go hard but she
15 will defy thee. Reckless thou wilt find her as thirsty traveller that
puts his mouth to the spring and drinks what water he can get; no
stake but she will make fast by it, no arrow comes amiss to her archery,
till of dalliance she has had enough.

16   Great content an industrious wife brings to her husband; health to
17 every bone of his body is that good sense of hers. No better gift of
18 God to man than a prudent woman that can hold her tongue; a soul
19 well disciplined is beyond all price. Grace so gracious is none as
20 woman's faithfulness and woman's modesty; woman's continence
21 there is no valuing. Sun dawning in heaven cannot match the lustre
22 a good wife sheds on her home, and that beauty lasts into ripe age,
23 like the glow of lights on the holy lamp-stand. Firm as golden pillar
in silver socket rest the feet of steadfast woman on the ground she
24 treads; (and firm as foundations built for all time on solid rock is
holy woman's loyalty to God's commandments).[1]

25   Two sad sights my heart knows, and one more that fills it with
26 indignation; warrior left to starve, and wise counsellor unregarded,
27 and a man that leaves right living for ill-doing, ripe for God's vengeance.

28   (Two dangers I see that are hard to overcome.) How shall a merchant
be cured of careless dealing, or a huckster for his lying talk find
pardon?

CHAPTER TWENTY-SEVEN

SIN comes often of an empty purse; nothing distorts the eye like
2 the love of riches. Baulk of timber pressed either way by a stone
wall cannot escape; nor yet sinful dealing when there is seller on this
3 side, buyer on that. (Wrong done shall be undone, and the doer of
4 it as well;) hold fast to thy fear of the Lord, or thy wealth shall soon
come to ruin.

---

[1] A few Greek manuscripts insert here nine more verses upon the subject of
women.

5   The sieve shaken, nothing is left but refuse; so thou wilt find a
man's poverty in his thought.[1]

6   Pottery is tested in the furnace, man in the crucible of suffering.

7   Good fruit comes from a tree well dressed, and a man will be in
8   word what he is in thought; do not give thy opinion of a man till he
has spoken; there lies the proof.

9   Make right-doing thy quest, and thou wilt not miss the mark; this
shall be a robe of honour to clothe thee (a welcome guest in thy house,
to watch over thee continually and to be thy stronghold at the hour
when all is made known).

10   Bird mates with bird, and he that shews faithfulness faithfulness
shall meet.

11   The lion waits in ambush for his prey; leave the right path, and
sin shall be ever at thy heels.

12   Unfailing as the sun is the wisdom of a devout mind; moon and
fool change continually.

13   When thou hast fools for thy company, thy word can wait; be
closeted continually with the wise.

14   Out upon the wearisome talk of sinners, that of sin and its dalliance
15   makes a jest! Out upon the man that uses oaths lightly; hair stands
16   upright at his blaspheming, and ears are stopped. Out upon the
proud, that provoke bloodshed with their quarrelling, and by their
cursing offend all who listen.

17   Betray thy friend's secret, and all confidence is lost; never more
18   shalt thou have friend to comfort thee. Use such a man lovingly,
19   and keep faith with him; if once thou hast betrayed him, court no
20   more his company. Friendship thus killed, thy friend is dead to thee;
21   bird let go from the hand is not lost more irretrievably; he is gone,
like hind released from the snare, gone beyond thy pursuit. The
23   wound that hurts a man's soul there is no healing; the bitter taunt
24   may yet be unsaid, but once the secret is out all is misery, all is despair.
25   Sly glance of the false friend! How shall a man be rid of him?
26   Here in thy presence, he smooths his brow, and is all in wonderment
at thy wise sayings; but ere long he will change his tune, and lend thy
27   words an ill colour. Above all else, he earns my hatred; God's hatred
too, I doubt not.

28   At thy own head's peril thou throwest stone in air; the traitor's
29   treacherous attack will deal wounds all around; a man may fall into

---

[1] This obscure maxim may be interpreted in several ways, none of which
is quite satisfactory. There may have been an error in the text; 'poverty' is
represented in the Greek by a second word for 'refuse', and in the Latin by an
abstract noun which signifies 'not knowing which way to turn'.

the pit he dug, (trip on the stone he set in his neighbour's path), perish
30 in the snare he laid for another. Plot ill, and the ill shall recoil on
thyself, springing up beyond all thy expectation.

31　For the proud, mockery and shame! Vengeance, like a lion, couches
in wait for them.

32　For all who triumph at the ill fortune of the just, a snare to catch
them, and a long remorse before death takes them!

33　Rancour and rage are detestable things both; and the sinner has
both in store.

CHAPTER TWENTY-EIGHT

HE that will be avenged brings on himself the Lord's vengeance;
2　watch and ward shall be kept over his sins continually. Forgive
thy neighbour his fault, and for thy own sins thy prayer shall win
3 pardon; should man bear man a grudge, and yet look to the Lord for
4 healing? Should he refuse mercy to his fellow man, yet ask forgive-
5 ness, should he think to appease God, while he, a mortal man, is
6 obdurate? Who shall plead for his acquittal? Look to thy last end,
7 and leave thy quarrelling; with the grave's corruption God's com-
8 mandments threaten thee.[1] Thy God fear, thy neighbour forgive;
9 the covenant of the Most High remember, thy neighbour's slip forget.
10　Keep clear of quarrelling, and sin shall less abound. Quick temper
sets feuds a-raging, and wicked men there are that will embroil fast
12 friends, and stir up strife among folk that lived at peace. More fuel,
more fire; strong man will rage the more, rich man push his vengeance
further.[2]

13　Heat is gendered by the haste of rivalry, and bloodshed by hot
14 blood; (but it is tongue of witness that brings death). Spark blown
upon will blaze, spat upon will die out; see how of both the mouth is
15 arbiter! A curse on every tale-bearer and traducer that disturbs the
16 world's peace! Tongue that comes between two friends, how many
17 it has exiled, sent them to wander far away, how many rich cities
18 dismantled, great houses demolished, (what armies it has routed,
19 what proud nations brought to ruin), what noble women it has driven
20 out from their homes, and left all their toil unrewarded! Pay heed to
it, and thou shalt never rest more, never find friend in whom thou

---

[1] Literally, in the Latin, 'Corruption and death threaten in his commandments'; in the Greek '(look to) corruption and death, and abide in his commandments'.

[2] *vv.* 12, 13: The exact sense of these verses cannot be determined with
certainty.

21 canst trust. Whip that lashes does but bruise the skin; tongue that
22 lashes will break bones; the sword has killed many, the tongue more.
23   Blessed is he that is preserved from the tongue's wickedness, that
24 has never felt its fury, never borne its yoke or worn its chains; that
25 yoke of iron, those chains of bronze! Here is death worse than death
26 itself, here is loss the grave cannot outvie. (Not for ever shall its
    reign persist, but where wicked men go it still follows); the just it
27 cannot consume, but if thou forsake God thou shalt encounter it,
    a fire that burns thee and will not be quenched, an assault more peri-
28 lous than assault of lion or pard. Fence thy ears about with thorns,
    and give the wicked tongue no hearing; make fast thy mouth with bolt
29 and bar. Melt down gold and silver of thine, and get thee a balance
    that shall weigh thy words, a bridle that shall be the rule of thy
30 mouth;[1] do all that lies in thee to keep thy tongue from speaking
    amiss, lest lurking enemies triumph over thy ruin, the fatal and final
    ruin that shall be thine.

CHAPTER TWENTY-NINE

HEART full of kindness and hand full of comfort will keep the
2   commandment, Lend to thy neighbour. Neighbour must borrow
3 easily when he needs, must repay readily when his need is over. Keep
4 thy bond, deal faithfully, and thou shalt never lack. Out upon the man
   that treats loan as treasure trove, and is a burden to his benefactor!
5 What, kiss the hand that gives, and make humble promises of repay-
6 ment; then, when the debt falls due, ask for grace, and complain
7 peevishly of hard times? Pay grudgingly when pay thou canst, offer
8 but half the sum, and think the lender lucky? Or, if thou canst not,
9 disown the debt and make an enemy of him, rewarding thy benefactor
10 not with due honour, but with angry curse and reproach? What
   wonder if many refuse to lend, not churlishly but for fear of wilful
11 wrong? Yet I would have thee patient with needy folk; do not keep
12 them waiting for thy charity; befriend them, as the law commands,
13 nor ever send them away in their misery empty-handed. It is thy
   brother, thy friend that asks; better lose thy money than leave it to
14 rust in a vault. Lay up store for thyself by obeying the command-
15 ments of the most High; more than gold it shall profit thee; the good
   deed treasured in poor men's hearts shall ransom thee from all

---

[1] *vv.* 28, 29: The Greek here differs from the Latin considerably, but its
effect is the same, and makes it clear that the sacred author is alluding, all
through this paragraph, not to the danger of incurring calumny, but to the
danger of falling into a habit of calumniating others.

16 harm, shall more avail than stout shield or lance to ward off thy enemies.
18   Kindness bids thee go bail for thy neighbour; for very shame, thou
19 canst not leave him to his own devices.[1] And if another goes bail for thee, do not forget the benefit done thee; he gave his life for
20 thine. It is right foully done to play a surety false; (wouldst thou treat his goods as if they were thy own?). Wouldst thou, ungrateful
22 wretch, leave thy ransomer to suffer for it? (Men have gone bail ere
23 now for shameless friends that so abandoned them.) By going bail for scoundrels, men of good fortune have fallen upon ruin and ship-
24 wreck; men that held their heads high must now wander far and wide,
25 exiles in strange countries. Leave godless sinners to become sureties to their ruin; men that take rash ventures to fall into the law's
26 clutches. For thyself, relieve thy neighbour as thy means allow, but never to thy own entanglement.
27   What are man's first needs? Water, and bread, and clothing, and the
28 privacy of a home. Better the poor man's fare under his roof of bare boards, than to be guest at a splendid banquet, and home have none.
29 Make much of the little thou hast; (never be it thine to bear the
30 reproach of a wanderer). A wretched life it is, passing on from house to house to find a welcome; that welcome found, thou wilt lack all
31 confidence, and sit there mumchance. Then, when thou hast helped to entertain, with food and drink, the guests that owe thee no thanks,
32 thou wilt have a poor reward for it: Up, wanderer! Lay me a fresh
33 table, and what lies before thee leave for others; I have honoured guests coming, and thou must make way for them; a kinsman of mine
34 stands in need of my hospitality! Bitter words for an honest man to hear; shall he owe his bread to one that calls him homeless?

CHAPTER THIRTY

INURE thy son to the rod, as thou lovest him; so shalt thou have comfort of him[2] in thy later years (nor go about knocking softly at
2 thy neighbours' doors). Discipline thy son, and thou shalt take pride
3 in him; he shall be thy boast among thy familiars. Discipline thy son, if thou wouldst make thy ill-wishers envy thee, wouldst hold thy

---

[1] *vv.* 19 sqq.: In Prov. 17.18, and elsewhere a warning is given against the folly of becoming surety for a friend, and *vv.* 26, 27 of the present chapter seem to imply the same moral. These warnings perhaps refer to rash commercial speculations; where it is a question of charity, we may have the duty of making ourselves responsible on behalf of some poor man, at the risk of his defrauding us.

[2] Or possibly, 'so shall he have comfort'.

4 head high among thy friends. Father that dies lives on, if a worthy
5 son he has begotten; here is a sight to make life joyous for him, and
  death not all unhappiness (and a bold front he keeps before his ill-
6 wishers); such an heir will shew loyalty to his race, its foes warding
7 off, its friends requiting. Let a man pamper his children, binding
8 up every wound, his heart wrung by every cry,[1] and he shall find
9 spoilt son headstrong and stubborn as a horse unbroken. Cosset thy
  son and make a darling of him, it shall be to thy own anxiety, thy
10 own remorse. Smile at his follies now, and the bitter taste of it shall
11 set thy teeth on edge hereafter. Thou canst not afford to give him
12 freedom in his youth, or leave his thoughts unchecked; none is too
  young to be bent to the yoke, none is too childish to be worth a
  drubbing, if thou wouldst not see him wilful and disobedient, to thy
13 heart's unrest. Discipline thy son, be at pains with him, or his shameless ways will be thy downfall.
14   Poor man sound and strong of body is better off than rich man
15 enfeebled, and racked with disease. Health (of the soul, that lies in
  duty done faithfully,) is more worth having than gold or silver; no
16 treasure so rare that it can match bodily strength. Health is best
17 wealth; no comfort wilt thou find like a merry heart. Better the
  endless repose of death, than life by lingering sickness made irk-
18 some. For mouth that refuses nourishment what use in dainties?
19 They are no better than the banquet left on a tomb, little availing
20 yonder idol, that cannot taste or smell. Once the Lord has laid thee
21 by the heels, to do penance for thy sins, thou shalt hanker and sigh
  for these dainties but as eunuch that fondles maid.
22   Nor let anxious thoughts fret thy life away; a merry heart is the
  true life of man, (is an unfailing store of holiness); length of years is
24 measured by rejoicing. Thy own self befriend (doing God's will
  with endurance, and giving all thy heart to the holiness he enjoins),
25 and banish thy sad thoughts; sadness has been the death of many,
26 and no good ever came of it. Jealousy and peevishness shorten a
27 man's days; cares bring old age untimely; gay and gallant heart is
  ever feasting, sets to and makes good cheer.

---

[1] The sense given here is that of the Greek; the Latin version, apparently
through misunderstanding a rare word in the Greek, gives us the meaningless
phrase, 'he will bind up his own wounds for the souls of his sons'.

CHAPTER THIRTY-ONE

2   WILT thou pine away with scheming to grow rich, lose thy sleep
for thinking of it? These solicitudes breed a madness in the
3   brain, such as only grave sickness can expel.[1]   Toils rich man for
4   gain, and when he ceases wealth brings satiety; toils poor man to
5   fend off need, and when he ceases he is a poor man still. Love money,
and thou shalt be called to account for it; thy quest corruption, of
6   corruption thou shalt have thy fill. Many have given themselves up
7   to the lure of gold, and in its beauty found their ruin; its worship
was a snare to catch their feet; alas, poor fools that went searching for
it, and themselves were lost!
8   Blessed is the man who lives, for all his wealth, unreproved, who
9   has no greed for gold (and puts no trust in his store of riches)! Shew
us such a man, and we will be loud in his praise; here is a life to wonder
10 at. A man so tested and found perfect wins eternal honour; he kept
clear of sin, when sinful ways were easy, did no wrong, when wrong
11 lay in his power. His treasure is safely preserved in the Lord's keeping
and wherever faithful men are met, his alms-deeds will be remembered.
12   Sit thou at table with the great, be not quick to remark upon it; it
14 is ill done to cry out, Here is a table well spread! Be sure a covetous
15 eye shall do thee no good; eye is a great coveter, and for that, like no
16 other part of thy face, condemned to weep. Be not quick to reach
17 out thy hand, and be noted, to thy shame, for greed; haste goes ill
18 with a feast. Learn from thy own conjecture thy neighbour's need;
19 share honestly the good things set before thee, nor court ill-will by thy
20 gluttony. For manner's sake, leave off eating betimes, or thy greed
21 shall give offence. Even though there be many about thee, do not be
22 quick to stretch out thy hand, (quick to call for wine). For a man
well disciplined a little wine is enough; spare thyself the uneasy sleep,
23 the pains that shall rack thee; wakeful nights come of excess, and
24 bile and griping pains. For the temperate man, there is sound sleep;
25 sleep that lasts till morning, and contents his whole being; though
thou have been constrained to eat beyond thy wont, thou hast but to
leave the table and vomit, and thou shalt find relief, (nor come to any
bodily harm).[2]

---

[1] This appears to be the meaning of the Latin, but the language seems
forced. The Greek yields no tolerable sense, and the text may well be corrupt.
[2] The Greek contains no allusion to vomiting. The sense of the Latin seems
to be, that over-eating will do a man no harm unless it is accompanied by
excessive drinking.

26 Take good heed, my son, do not belittle this advice of mine; thou
27 shalt live to prove it true. Put thy heart into all thou doest, and no
28 infirmity of purpose shall hinder thee.[1] The generous host is on all
29 men's lips; ever they bear witness to his loyal friendship; the niggard
has the ill word of a whole city; men form shrewd judgement of a
niggard.
30 Never challenge hard drinker to a drinking-bout; wine has been the
31 ruin of many. Fire tests the strength of steel; and a proud man fuddled
32 with wine betrays the secrets of his bosom. Easy flow wine, easy flow
life, but to men of sober habit; sobriety must drink within measure.
33 To the drunkard,[2] life is no life at all; (wine is death, when it so
35 deprives a man of life). Wine was made for mirth (never for drunken-
36 ness); drink wisely, and it shall rejoice thy heart and thy whole
37 being; (health it brings to mind and body, wine wisely taken). Wine
39 drunk in excess brings anger and quarrelling and calamities a many; it
40 is the poison of a man's life. What does the false courage of the
drunkard? It takes him unawares, and makes him less a man; grievous
41 wounds come of it. When the wine goes round, do not find fault
42 with thy neighbour, or think the worse of him for being merry; never
taunt him, never press him to repay the debt.

CHAPTER THIRTY-TWO

I F they will make thee master of the feast, do not give thyself airs;
2 bear thyself as an equal. Make good provision for the guests, and
3 so take thy place among them; thy duty done, recline at ease, and
enjoy thy sovereignty; the crown that marks their favour, the honour
4 bestowed by their gifts. Speak first, as becomes thy seniority, but
with due choice of thy words; and do not break in when music is a-
6 playing; no need for thy words to flow when none is listening, for
7 thy wisdom to be displayed unseasonably. Music and wine, carbuncle
8 set in gold, music and wine, signet ring of gold and emerald, so the
wine be good, and taken in due measure.
9 (Keep silence, and give others a hearing; it shall win thee a name
10 for modesty;) if thou art but a young man, be loth to speak even of

---

[1] The bearing of this maxim is very doubtful; we may translate 'sickness'
instead of 'infirmity of purpose'.

[2] *v*. 33: 'To the drunkard'; literally, 'to him who is lessened by (or, in respect
of) wine'. Elsewhere in this book this verb expresses some deficit in personal
qualities. The sense 'to him who must go without wine' is admissible, and if it
is adopted, the next verse will refer not to immoderate drinking, but to an
empty cellar.

11 what concerns thee, and if thou art pressed for an answer, give it in
12 brief. For the most part keep thy knowledge concealed under a mask
13 of silence and enquiry; nor ever be familiar among great men, nor
14 garrulous among the wise. Sure as the lightning is sign of a storm,
men's good word is the sign of a modest nature; they will love thee
15 all the better for thy bashfulness. When the time comes for going,
do not linger; get thee gone speedily to thy home, there to divert
16 thyself, and take thy ease, and follow the whim of thy own thoughts,
17 yet innocently and with no word proudly said. And for all this give
thanks to God thy maker, that so contents thee with his gifts.
18 If thou fearest the Lord, thou wilt accept the schooling he gives
19 thee, waiting early at his door to win his blessing. In the law, the
law's follower finds deep content, the false heart nothing but a snare
20 to catch it. Those who fear the Lord will discover where right lies,
21 the light of truth shall shine from their awards; [1] the sinner fears to
have his life reproved, and will ever be finding precedents for grati-
22 fying his own whim. A man of prudence will never throw caution to
23 the winds; his proud enemy feels no dread even upon rashly pro-
24 voking him, (but shall live to rue the assault). [2] Do nothing, my son,
save with consideration, and thy deeds shall not bring thee repentance.
25 Take not some ruinous road that shall trip thee with its boulders;
some road where all journeying is difficult [3] (and thou mayst expose
26 thy life to sudden dangers). Turn away from thy own children,
27 (pay no heed to thy own household); be it thine to trust with all thy
28 soul's confidence, [4] and thou hast kept the commandments. Who
trusts in God, keeps well God's command; confidence in him was
never disappointed.

CHAPTER THIRTY-THREE

IF a man fears the Lord, he shall meet with no disaster; God will be
watching over him, even when his faith is put to the test, and from
such disaster will preserve him. A wise man does not grow weary of

---

[1] Or perhaps 'examples of obedience' (to the Law).

[2] *vv.* 22, 23: The language here is very confused, and it seems likely that the
true text may have been lost.

[3] In the Greek, 'where there is no danger of stumbling'.

[4] Or perhaps, 'to trust with all confidence in thy own soul', that is, in thyself; this is probably the meaning of the Greek. But, in these later chapters, we
have a Hebrew text to consult, which doubtless goes back (though with certain
alterations) to the original manuscript from which Jesus, son of Sirac, made
his Greek translation. And this, supported by the Syriac version, gives us
'keeps watch over his own soul' instead of 'trusts his own soul'.

2 the law, and the duties it enjoins, and no shipwreck can befall him.
3 If thou art a man of judgement, thou hast only to trust God's com-
4 mandment, and it will not fail thee ; . . . giving a true answer to the
question asked . . .[1] thou wilt prepare thy plea, and find audience
(for thy prayer) ; wilt recollect the teaching given thee, and so satisfy
5 thy questioner. A fool's heart is but a wheel that turns ; his are
6 whirling thoughts. Hast thou a friend that will ever be mocking?
Be comforted ; stallion will ever neigh, ride him who will.
7 Why is it that one day, one dawn, one year, takes precedence of
8 another, when all come of the same sun? God's wisdom it was that
so divided them (when he made the sun, and gave it a law to keep) ;
9 made a succession of seasons, a succession of feast days (when at
10 stated times men must keep holiday). To some he would assign high
dignity ; others should be lost in the common rabble of days. So
it is that all men are built of the same clay ; son of Adam is son of
11 earth ; yet the Lord, in the plenitude of his wisdom, has marked them
12 off from one another, not giving the same destiny to each. There are
those he has blessed with high station ; there are those he has set apart
and claimed for himself ; there are those he has put under a ban and
turned them into humble folk, or degraded them from their former
13 distinction. Clay we are in the potter's hands ; it is for him who made
14 us to dispose of us ; clay is what potter wills it to be, and we are in
15 our maker's hands, to be dealt with at his pleasure. Evil matched
with good, life matched with death, sinner matched with man of
piety ; so everywhere in God's works thou wilt find pairs matched,
one against the other.
16 Think of me as one that has been last of all to leave his bed,
and goes about gleaning a fruit here, a fruit there, after the vintagers
17 have done. Yet did I trust that I, too, might have God's blessing, and I,
18 too, have filled my wine-press, a vintager like the rest. See how I
have toiled, not for my own sake merely, but for all such as covet
19 wisdom! Words for the hearing of all, high and low ; you that hold
high place in the assembly, never disdain to listen.
20 Long as thou livest, do not put thyself in the power of others, though
it be son or wife, kinsman or friend ; do not make over thy goods to
21 another ; it is ill to go a-begging for what is thy own. While life and
22 breath is in thee, never change places with another ; it is for thy
children to ask thee for what they need, not to have thyself for their
23 pensioner. Be at the head of thy own affairs, nor ever tarnish thy

---

[1] There may be some confusion in the text here ; the words 'giving a true answer to the question asked' are connected by the Greek with what goes before, by the Latin with what follows.

renown, until thy days are finished; then, at the hour of thy death, make thy bequests.

25 Fodder thy ass must have, and the whip, and a pack to bear; thy
26 slave, too, needs food and discipline and hard work. Under duress he toils, what marvel if ease should tempt him? Leave his hands idle,
27 and he will seek to be his own master. The stubborn ox yoke and rein
28 will subdue; (slave held to his task is slave bowed to thy will;) keep rack and stocks for one that is bent on mischief. To the task, no hours
29 of leisure! Idleness is a great teacher of ill habit. Toil first assign to him; toiling is his lot; then, if he disobeys thee, with the stocks thou mayst tame him. Yet do not burden flesh and blood more than it can
31 bear, nor inflict grave sentence while the plea is still unheard. Faithful slave if thou hast, make much of him as of thy own self; treat him as if he were thy brother, as if thy own life were [1] the price of his
33 purchase. Wrong him, and he may run away from thy service; once he takes to his heels, who can tell thee where or in what guise thou mayst discover him?

CHAPTER THIRTY-FOUR

FOOLS are cheated by vain hopes, buoyed up with the fancies of
2 a dream. Wouldst thou heed such lying visions? Better clutch at
3 shadows, or chase the wind. Nought thou seest in a dream but
4 symbols; man is but face to face with his own image. As well may
5 foul thing cleanse, as false thing give thee a true warning. Out upon the folly of them, pretended divination, and cheating omen, and
6 wizard's dream! Heart of woman in her pangs is not more fanciful. Unless it be some manifestation the most High has sent thee, pay no
7 heed to any such; trust in dreams has crazed the wits of many, and
8 brought them to their ruin. Believe rather the law's promises, that cannot miss their fulfilment, the advice of some trusty counsellor that shall prove its wisdom.

9 A man will not learn until he is tested by discipline.[2] That experience (gained, he will think deeply, and the many lessons he has learned)
10 will make him a wise talker. Without experience, a man knows little; yet, if he is too venturesome, he reaps a rich harvest of mischief. . .
11 (A man will not learn until he is tested by discipline . . . and if he is

---

[1] Literally, 'since thy own life is'. Different versions have different variants of the phrase, and it is not certain what meaning should be assigned to it.
[2] 'Tested by discipline'; some of the Greek manuscripts have 'chastised', or perhaps simply 'schooled'; others, more plausibly 'a travelled man'.

12 led astray he will be full of knavery . . .) [1] I myself have seen much in
my wanderings; I could tell of much I have grown accustomed
13 to.[2] Sometimes, by this means, I have been in danger of death, and
only the Divine favour has preserved me from it.

14   The life of such as fear the Lord is held precious (and wins a
15 blessing from his regard); they have a deliverer they can trust in,
16 (and God's eye watches over them in return for their love). Fear the
Lord, and thou shalt never hesitate; nothing may daunt thee, while
17 such a hope is thine. Blessed souls, that fear the Lord! They know
19 where to look for refuge. Fear the Lord, and his eyes watch over
thee; here is strong protection, here is firm support; shelter when the
20 hot wind blows, shade at noon-day; here is reassurance when a man
stumbles, support when he falls; soul uplifted, eyes enlightened, health
and life and blessing bestowed.

21   Tainted is every sacrifice that comes of goods ill gotten; a mockery,
22 this, of sacrifice, that shall win no favour. (For those who wait upon
23 him in loyal duty, the Lord alone is God.) [3] Should the most High
accept the offerings of sinners, (take the gifts of the wrong-doer into
his reckoning), and pardon their sins because their sacrifices are many?
24 Who robs the poor and then brings sacrifice, is of their fellowship
that would immolate some innocent child before the eyes of his
25 father. Poor man's bread is poor man's life; cheat him of it, and thou
26 hast slain him; sweat of his brow, or his life's blood, what matters?
27 Disappoint the hireling, and thou art own brother to a murderer. Build
29 while another pulls down, and toil is its own reward. Pray while
another curses, and which of you shall find audience with
30 God? Cleanse thyself from dead body's contamination, and touch
31 it again, what avails thy cleansing? So it is when a man fasts for his
sins, yet will not leave his sinning; vain is the fast, the prayer goes
unanswered.

CHAPTER THIRTY-FIVE

2 LIVE true to the law, and thou hast richly endowed the altar. Let
this be thy welcome-offering, to heed God's word and keep clear
3 of all wickedness; this thy sacrifice of amends for wrong done, of

---

[1] *vv.* 10, 11: The Latin here seems to have suffered from much confusion.
'Mischief' and 'knavery' in the Greek are 'discernment' and 'resourcefulness';
'if he is led astray' is 'when he has travelled'. The Latin translator seems to have
given two separate renderings of the same verse, neither of them accurate.

[2] In the Greek, 'I know more than I am ready to tell'.

[3] It is difficult to see the appositeness of this phrase. The rendering 'The
Lord is only (approachable) for those who wait upon him in loyal duty' does
not represent the Latin.

4 atonement for fault, to shun wrong-doing. Bloodless offering wouldst
thou make, give thanks;[1] victim wouldst thou immolate, shew
5 mercy. Wickedness and wrong-doing to shun is to do God's will,
is to win pardon for thy faults.

6 Yet do not appear in the Lord's presence empty-handed; due
8 observance must be paid, because God has commanded it. If thy
heart is right, thy offering shall enrich the altar; its fragrance shall
9 reach the presence of the most High; a just man's sacrifice the Lord
10 accepts, and will not pass over his claim to be remembered. Generously
pay the Lord his due; do not grudge him the first-fruits of thy earn-
11 ings; all thou givest, give with a smiling face, gladly bring in the
12 tithe. In his own measure God's gift repay; grudge thou must not
13 what afford thou canst; the Lord is a good master, and thou shalt
have sevenfold in return.

14 But think not to bribe his justice; he will have none of thy
15 bribery. Never pin thy hopes on the power of wealth ill gotten; the
16 Lord is a true judge, not swayed by partiality, and thou canst not
make interest with him against the friendless, turn him deaf to the
17 plea of the wronged. Prayer of the orphan, eloquent sigh of the
18 widow, he will not disregard; see the tears on yonder widow's cheeks,
19 accusing tears! (From her cheeks they mount to heaven; the Lord
loves to answer prayer, and will the author of her misery find favour
20 with him?) None but his true worshippers he makes welcome; for
21 their supplication the clouds give passage. Pierce those clouds if
thou wouldst, thou must humble thyself, inconsolable till that
prayer finds audience, unwearying till it wins redress.

22 Trust me, the Lord will not keep us waiting long. (Hearing and
redress he will grant to the innocent;) strong as of old, patient no
23 longer, he will crush the backs of our oppressors. The Gentiles
punished, scattered the hordes of insolence, broken the sceptre of
24 wrong! Men called to account everywhere for their doings, the
25 harvest of their mortal pride, and his own people vindicated at last,
26 triumphing in his mercy at last! God's mercy, welcome to the
afflicted as rain-clouds are welcome in time of drought!

---

[1] This would more naturally be rendered from the Latin, 'If thou wouldst
give thanks, make a bloodless offering', but the context seems to indicate that
this is a misinterpretation of the Greek.

CHAPTER THIRTY-SIX

GOD of all men, have mercy on us; look down, (and let us see the
2 smile of thy favour).   Teach them to fear thee, (those other
nations that have never looked to find thee; let them learn to recognize
3 thee as the only God, and to acclaim thy wonders).   Lift up thy hand,
4 to shew these aliens thy power; let us see them, as they have seen us,
5 humbled before thee; let them learn, as we have learnt, that there
6 is no other God but thou.   Shew new marvels, and portents stranger
7 still; win renown for that strength, that valiant arm of thine; rouse
9 thyself to vengeance, give thy anger free play; away with the oppressors,
10 down with thy enemies!   Hasten on the time, do not forget thy pur-
11 pose; make them acclaim thy wonders.   Let none of them escape
their doom, the oppressors of thy people; let there be a raging fire
12 ready to devour them; heavy let the blow fall on the heads of those
13 tyrants, that no other power will recognize but their own.   Gather
anew all the tribes of Jacob (for all the world to know that thou alone
art God, to acclaim thy wonders), and make them thy loved possession
14 as of old.   Have compassion on the people that is called by thy own
15 name, on Israel, owned thy first-born; have compassion on Jerusalem,
16 the city thou hast set apart for thy resting-place; fill Sion's walls,
fill the hearts of thy people, with promises beyond all telling come
17 true, with thy glory made manifest. Vindicate the race that was from
the first thy chosen; wake echoes of the old prophecies uttered in thy
18 name; have we waited for thee to no purpose? Shall thy prophets be
19 proved false?   Listen to thy servants' plea, that claim the blessing
Aaron pronounced over thy people; (guide us into the right path); let
all the world know that thou art God, watching us eternally.
20   Take what food thou wilt, belly is content; yet meat and meat
21 differ.   The savour of venison only palate can reach; only wise heart
can discern lying tongue.
22   False heart breeds dismal thoughts; mind well schooled keeps them
at bay.[1]
23   Any woman is a mate for any man; yet maid and maid differ.
24   Fair wife, blithe husband; as no other lure, beauty draws us.   What
of her tongue? If that, too, has power to charm, if that is soft and
26 gentle, never was man so blessed.   Good wife won is life well begun;
27 a comforter thou hast, of thy own breed, a stay to support thee.   No
28 hedge, no heritage; alas, poor vagabond, that wife hast none!   Trust

---

[1] The meaning of this verse is uncertain.

him never, that has not found a nest to dwell in, and does but lodge where night overtakes him, cut-purse that travels light from city to city.

CHAPTER THIRTY-SEVEN

FRIENDS every man has that will say, I love him well; yet friends
2 they may be in name only. Death itself cannot match it for sadness,
3 when friend and companion becomes thy enemy. Cruel pretence, what
mind first conceived thee, to turn solid earth into a morass of foul
4 treachery? A companion, how he will enjoy the delights of his
5 friend's prosperity, and turn against him in the hour of need! A
companion, how he will share a friend's griefs if he may share his bake-
6 meats; use him as a shield against some enemy! [1] Never let friend of
thine be far from thy thoughts; in thy prosperity never forget him.
7   (Never take counsel with one who may be laying a trap for thee;
8 from his envy hide thy purpose); advice every counsellor will give
9 thee, but some will be keeping their own counsel all the while. Be on
thy guard, then, against him who advises thee; how is his own turn
10 best served? What is his secret mind? It may be, he will hide stake
11 in pit for thee, crying, Thy course lies clear; then stand at a
12 distance to see what becomes of thee. Consult, if thou wilt,[2] (un-
believer about holiness, knave about justice), woman about her rival,
dastard about war, merchant about value, buyer about price, cynic
13 about gratitude, (scoffer about piety, rogue about honesty), farm
14 labourer about work to be done, yearman about year's end, idle
servant about great undertakings; but all the advice they give thee heed
15 thou never. Closet thyself rather with some man of holy life, known
16 to thee as God's worshipper, some soul well matched with thine, such
17 as would grieve to see thee stumbling in darkness. And thy own
heart enthrone as thy best counsellor; nothing may compare with that;
18 there are times when a man (of piety) sees truth clearer than seven
19 sentinels high in a watch-tower. With all this, entreat the most High
to guide thy steps in the right path.
20   For every undertaking, every act of thine let just consideration
21 prepare thee, and firm resolve. Ill counsel may make the heart veer

---

[1] This is usually rendered, 'he will take up his shield against an enemy', but this, without further qualification, seems meaningless.

[2] The words 'if thou wilt' are not in the original; but the context evidently demands them in the Latin version; the Greek provides no difficulty; since it gives a negative, 'Do not consult . . .'

round; four points its compass has, good and evil, life and death; and
of these, day after day, the tongue is arbiter.[1]

22   Shrewdness there is that can much impart, yet is its own enemy.
23 (The experience that imparts much is its own friend besides.) There
24 is quibbling talk that will earn thee enemies, and an empty belly; no
power to win men the Lord has given it, so empty is it of all wisdom.
25 But there is wisdom that befriends the owner of it, earning high meed
26 of praise; if thus thou art wise, wisdom thou shalt impart to thy
27 fellows, and shalt not miss thy own reward; blessings the wise man
28 reaps from all around, to see him is to praise him. Man's days are
29 numbered, Israel's none can number, and among our people the
wise man wins an inheritance of honour, a deathless renown.
30   Son, as thy life goes on, make trial of thy appetites, and if harmful
31 they be, give them no liberty; not all things all men suit, nor please.
32 When there is feasting, thy greed restrain; do not fall upon all the
33 meats thou seest; much feasting breeds infirmity, gluttony the bile,
34 and many have died of surfeiting; the temperate live long.

CHAPTER THIRTY-EIGHT

D ENY not a physician his due for the service he has done thee; his
2   task is of divine appointment, since from God all healing comes,
3 and kings themselves must needs enrich him. High rank his skill
4 gives him; of great men he is the honoured guest. Medicines the most
High has made for us out of earth's bounty, and shall prudence shrink
5 from the use of them? Were not the waters of Mara made wholesome
6 by the touch of wood?[2] Well for us men, that the secret virtue of such
remedies has been revealed; skill the most High would impart
7 to us, and for his marvels win renown. Thus it is that the
physician cures our pain, and the apothecary makes, not only perfumes to charm the sense, but unguents remedial; so inexhaustible is
8 God's creation, such health comes of his gift, all the world over.
9   Son, when thou fallest sick, do not neglect thy own needs; pray to
10 the Lord, and thou shalt win recovery. Leave off thy sinning, thy
11 life amend, purge thee of all thy guilt. With frankincense and rich oil
12 make bloodless offering of meal; and so leave the physician to do his
13 work. His task is of divine appointment, and thou hast need of him;
14 let him be ever at thy side. Needs must, at times, to physicians thou

---

[1] The text here is uncertain, and the meaning obscure. The Latin seems to
demand some such rendering as that given above.
[2] See Ex. 15.23.

shouldst have recourse; and doubt not they will make intercession with the Lord, that they may find a way to bring thee ease and remedy,
15 by their often visiting thee. Offend thou thy maker by wrong-doing, much recourse thou shalt have to physicians.

16   When a man dies, my son, let thy tears flow, and set up a great lamenting, as for thy grievous loss; shroud him according to his
17 quality, and grudge him no pomp of funeral; then, (to be rid of gossip, bemoan him bitterly for a day's space, ere thou wilt be comforted in
18 thy sorrow); one day or two, as his worth claims, bemoan him; no
19 need to win thyself an ill name. Grief will but hasten thy own death, (will be the grave of thy own strength); where heart goes sad, back goes
20 bowed. So long as thou withdrawest thyself, sad thy heart will be;
21 and what patrimony but heart's mirth is left to the poor? Why then, do not give thyself over to regrets; put them away from thee, and
22 bethink thee rather of thy own end. Do not fancy that the dead can
23 return; by torturing thyself thou canst nothing avail him. Remember, he tells thee, this doom of mine; such shall thine be; mine yesterday,
24 thine to-day. Let his memory rest, as he rests, in death; enough for thee that thou shouldst comfort him in the hour when his spirit leaves him.

25   The wisdom of a learned man is the fruit of leisure; he must starve
26 himself of doing if he is to come by it. How shall he drink full draughts of wisdom that must guide the plough, that walks proud as any spear-man while he goads on his team, all his life taken up with their labours,
27 all his talk of oxen? His mind all set on a straight furrow, the feeding
28 of his cows an anxiety to deny him sleep? So it is with every work-man and master-workman, that must turn night into day. Here is one that cuts graven seals; how he busies himself with devising some new pattern! How the model he works from claims his attention, while
29 he sits late over his craft! Here is blacksmith sitting by his anvil, intent upon his iron-work, cheeks shrivelled with the smoke, as he battles
30 with the heat of the furnace, ears ringing again with the hammer's
31 clattering, eyes fixed on the design he imitates. All his heart is in the finishing of his task, all his waking thoughts go to the perfect achieving
32 of it. Here is potter at work, treadles flying, anxious continually over
33 the play of his hands, over the rhythm of his craftsmanship; arms
34 straining at the stiff clay, feet matching its strength with theirs.[1] To finish off the glaze is his nearest concern, and long he must wake to
35 keep his furnace clean. All these look to their own hands for a living,
36 skilful each in his own craft; and without them, there is no building

---

[1] Literally, 'bowing down his strength before his feet,' but the Greek has, 'its strength'.

37 up a commonwealth. For them no travels abroad, no journeyings
from home; they will not pass beyond their bounds to swell the
38 assembly,[1] or to sit in the judgement-seat. Not theirs to sift evidence
and give verdict, (not theirs to impart learning or to make award);
39 they will not be known for uttering wise sayings. Theirs it is to support this unchanging world of God's creation; craftsmanship is their
title to live; . . . lending themselves freely and making their study
in the law of the most High.[2]

CHAPTER THIRTY-NINE

BUT the wise man will be learning the lore of former times; the
2 prophets will be his study. The tradition handed down by
famous men will be in his keeping; his to con the niceties of every
3 parable, learn the hidden meaning of every proverb, make himself
4 acquainted with sayings hard to understand. To great men he will
render good service, will be summoned to the prince's own council;
5 will go upon his travels in foreign countries, to learn by experience
6 what the world offers of good and of harm. With dedicated heart, he
will keep early vigil at the Lord's gates, the Lord that made him, to win
7 audience for his plea from the most High. His lips will be eloquent
8 in prayer, as he entreats pardon for his sins. At the Lord's sovereign
9 pleasure, he will be filled with a spirit of discernment, so that he pours
out showers of wise utterance, giving thanks to the Lord in his prayer.
10 His plans and thoughts guided from above, he will have skill in the
11 divine mysteries; will make known to all the tradition of teaching he
has received, and take pride in that law which is the Lord's covenant
12 with man. This wisdom of his, extolled on every side, will never fall
13 into oblivion; the memory of him, the renown of him, will be held in
14 honour from age to age. His wise words will become a legend among
15 the nations; where faithful men assemble, his praise will be told. A
life that shall leave such fame as one man wins in a thousand; a death
not unrewarded.

16   And still I have thoughts worth the telling; madman as easily might
17 contain himself. A voice proclaims, Give heed to me, you that are
scions of the Divine stock; yours to burgeon like a rose-bush that is
18 planted by running water; yours to yield the fragrance of incense;

---

[1] The interpretation of this verse is uncertain.
[2] The last fourteen words of the chapter really belong, as the Greek shews,
to the beginning of the next chapter. As applied to the manual labourers described above, they give exactly the wrong sense.

19 yours to blossom like the lily, and smell sweet, and put forth leaves for
your adornment; yours to sing songs of praise, and bless the Lord for
20 all things he has made. His name extol; songs of praise let your lips
utter, and let harp's melody mingle with the song. And you shall
praise him in these words following.

21 Good, wondrously good, is all the Lord has made.[1] Piled high the
waters stand at his command, shut in by cisterns of his appointing.[2]
23 All-sufficient is his will, unfailing his power to save; open to his
view are all deeds of mortal men, nothing can escape that scrutiny.
25 On every age of time his glance rests; marvel is none beyond his com-
26 pass. There is no asking what this or that may be, each shall be needed
27 in its turn. His blessings flow like a stream in full flood, like rain
pouring down to refresh the parched earth. But the nations that never
29 look to find him, shall be the prey of his vengeance; did he not turn
the waters into firm ground, and dry up the floor of them, so that it
made a path for the passage of his own people,[3] and yet a trap to
punish the wicked?

30 From the first, good things were made for good men to enjoy; for
31 sinners, they are good and evil at once. What are the first needs of
man's life? Water, fire, iron, salt, milk, wheat-meal, honey, the grape-
32 cluster, oil, and clothing. Thereby, for just men, nought but good
33 is intended, yet for sinners they turn to evil. Some powers [4] there be
that are created for wreaking of vengeance, and sternly they wield the
34 lash in their raging; when the time for reckoning comes, they will
35 put out all their force, until their Maker's anger is appeased. Fire,
hail, hunger and death, all these were made for wreaking of vengeance;
36 ravening beasts, too, and scorpions, and serpents, and the sword that
37 punishes the wicked till there are none left. All these hold high
revel as they perform his will; ready they stand till earth has need of
them, and when the need comes, they will obey.

38 From the first, all my questioning and all my thought confirms me
39 in what I have written, all things God has made are good, and each of
40 them serves its turn; nor ever must we complain things have hap-

---

[1] It is not clear how many of the remaining verses in this chapter the hymn
of praise includes.
[2] Cf. Ps. 32. 7 (33. 7 in the Hebrew text).
[3] In the original, simply 'their passage'; but it seems clear that the Latin
intends an allusion to the crossing of the Red Sea. The other versions would
rather suggest a reference to the destruction of Sodom.
[4] Literally, 'some spirits'. It may be that diabolical agencies are referred to;
but the word 'spirits' may mean simply 'winds'; or (perhaps with greater
probability) it may be taken as describing the forces of nature which are to be
mentioned in verse 35.

pened for the worse, since each has its own occasion to justify it.
41 With full hearts, then, and full voice, praise we and bless the Lord's name.

CHAPTER FORTY

GREAT is the anxiety all men are doomed to, heavy the yoke each son of Adam must bear, from the day when he leaves his mother's womb to the day when he is buried in the earth, that is mother of all.
2 What solicitude is his, what fears catch at his heart; how quick his mind runs out to meet coming events! And the term of it all is death.
3 What matter, whether a man sit on a throne, or grovel in dust and
4 ashes; whether he goes clad in purple and wears a crown, or has but coarse linen to wear? Anger he shall know, and jealousy, and concern, and bewilderment, and the fear of death, and the grudge that rankles,
5 and rivalry. Rest he on his bed at night, sleep comes to fashion his
6 thinking anew; even there, the rest he wins is but little or none at all, and thereupon, in his dreams, he is anxious as sentry waiting to be
7 relieved, his are such whirling thoughts as fugitive has, just escaped from the battle. Then, at the moment of deliverance, comes waking;
8 and he marvels to find his fears all vain. This lot he shares with all living things; beast has it as well as man, but for the sinner it is multi-
9 plied sevenfold. There is more besides, mortal sickness, bloodshed,
10 quarrelling, the sword, oppression, famine, devastation and plague; all such things are designed for the punishing of the wicked; was it not from wickedness the flood came?
11 All that is of earth, to earth must needs return, and all waters find
12 their way back to the sea; what shall become of bribery and oppression? The memory of them shall vanish; faithfulness will endure for
13 ever. All the riches of the wrong-doer will disappear, like stream that runs dry, will die away, like roll of thunder in a storm-
14 cloud; open-handed is merry-hearted, the sinners it is that shall
15 pine away at the last. Branches the posterity of the wicked shall never put forth; dead roots they are that rattle on the wind-swept
16 rock. How green yonder rushes grow by the river's bank! But they
17 shall be plucked up before hay-harvest. But kindliness, like the garden trees, lasts on, remembered in blessing; charity remains unforgotten.
18 Sweet is his lot, that toils and is contented; here is hidden treasure for thy finding.[1]

---

[1] The other versions assimilate this maxim to the formula observed in *vv.* 19–25; 'Contentment and hard work (in the Hebrew, a life of wine and strong drink) may be sweet, but best of all is finding a treasure'—an observation so little worth making, that it looks as if the Latin had preserved the true text.

19   Children born, and a city founded, will bring thee a great name;
20   best of all, a woman without spot.   Wine and music make heart
21   glad; best of all, the love of wisdom.   Flute and harp make sweet
22   melody; best of all, a kindly tongue.   Grace and beauty charm the
23   eye; best of all, the green wheat.   Friend and friend, gossip and gossip,
24   are well met; best of all, man and wife.   Kinsmen . . .[1] will help thee
25   in hard times; best of all, thy alms-deeds to deliver thee.   Gold and
26   silver give thee sure vantage-ground; best of all, right counsel.   Riches
      and strength make the heart beat high; best of all, the fear of the
      Lord.
27   Fear the Lord, lack thou shalt have none, help need none;   the
      fear of the Lord is a garden that yields blessing . . . and in splendour
      above all splendour they have clothed him.[2]
29   Long as thou livest, my son, never turn beggar; die is better than
30   beg.   Look thou for thy meat to another's table, I count thy life no
31   life at all; what, owe thy very being to another man's larder?   From
      such a chance, good teaching and good training shall keep thee safe.
32   Poverty, on a fool's lips, will pass for a thing desirable; but trust
      me, he has a fire raging within.

CHAPTER FORTY-ONE

OUT upon thee, death, how bitter is the thought of thee to a man
2   that lives at ease in his own home,   a man untroubled by care,
3   no difficulties in his path, that his food still relishes!   Hail, death!
4   Welcome is thy doom to a man that is in need, and lacks vigour;   worn
    out with age and full of anxieties, that has no confidence left in him,
5   no strength to endure.   Never fear death's doom; bethink thee of the
    years that went before thee, and must come after thee.   One sentence
6   the Lord has for all living things.   What the will of the most High
    has in store for thee, none can tell; what matter, whether it be ten
7   years, or a hundred, or a thousand?   Once thou art dead, thou wilt
    take no grudging count of the years.
8   The children wicked men beget are born under a curse, familiars of
9   a godless home;   all they inherit is soon lost to them; reproach dogs
10 the footsteps of their posterity.   How bitter their complaints against
11 the father who is the author of their ill fame!   Woe to you, rebels,

---

[1] It seems clear that something has fallen out here; probably the original
had 'Kinsmen and neighbours'.
[2] The last clause of this verse does not fit on to what precedes it, either in
sense or in grammar; once more, it seems likely that the text is defective.

12 that have forsaken the law of the Lord, the most High, born of an
13 unholy birth, an unholy death your destiny! All that is of earth, to
   earth must needs return; from ban to bale is the cycle of a life ill lived.
14   Man sighs over his body's loss; what of his name? The wicked are
15 lost to memory. Of thy good name heed take thou; it shall remain
16 thine longer than thousand heaps of rare treasure. Life is good, but
   its days are numbered; a good name lasts for ever.
17   My sons, here is wholesome teaching.[1] Wisdom hidden, I told you,
18 is wasted, is treasure that never sees the light of day; silence is rightly
19 used when it masks folly, not when it is the grave of wisdom. Yet
20 sometimes bashfulness is no fault, as I will now make known to you. It
   is ill done to be abashed on every occasion; but yet neither is self-
21 confidence for all and every use. Of these things, then, be ashamed;[2]
   that thy parents should find thee a fornicator, ruler or prince a liar,
22 magistrate or judge a wrong-doer, assembly of the people a law-
23 breaker, partner or friend a knave, or thy neighbour a thief.
24 . . . concerning the faithfulness of God, and his covenant; concerning
   thy sitting over meat . . . Ashamed be thou of belittling the gift
25 received, of leaving the greeting unreturned, of letting thy eyes
26 stray after harlots, of denying thyself to kinsman that has a near
27 claim on thy regard, of property fraudulently shared. Let not thy
   eye fall on woman wed to another, nor ever exchange secrets with
28 handmaid of hers, nor come between her sheets. Be ashamed of
   uttering reproach against thy friends, nor insult the receiver of thy
   gift.

CHAPTER FORTY-TWO

NOR ever do thou repeat gossip to the betraying of another's
  secret. If of such things thou art ashamed, shame thou shalt
never feel, and thou shalt have all men's good word besides.
   And other dealings there are over which thou must never be
abashed,[3] nor, through respect for any human person consent to

---

[1] *vv.* 17–20: The order of the text here seems to be confused both in the
Greek and in the Latin; they are here interpreted in the light of the Hebrew.
The words, 'I told you', are not in the original, but there seems to be a delib-
erate quotation from 20.32, 33.

[2] *vv.* 21–28: There is further confusion here, as even the grammar of the
sentences shews, and several phrases cannot be interpreted with certainty.

[3] *vv.* 1–8: Once more the text seems curiously confused. Verse 2 ought, judging by its form, to be a list of things we ought never to be ashamed of; 'Concerning the law of the most High, and his covenant, and acquitting the guilty'
yields no tolerable sense. Verses 6, 7 look as if they had been displaced, and
belonged to some quite different context. The explanation of verse 8 is perhaps
to be found in Deut. 21.18.

2 wrong, defying law and covenant of the most High, and by thy
3 award acquitting the sinner. Such are, a matter between some partner
of thine and strangers from far off, the apportioning of an inheritance
4 among thy friends, the trueness of weight and balance, profit
5 overmuch or too little, the exchange between buyer and seller, the
strict punishing of children, the cudgelling of a wicked slave till
6 he bleeds . . . Thriftless wife if thou hast, seal is best; and lock
all away in some place where many hands are at work; nothing but
must be counted and weighed before thou hand it over, and account
8 kept in writing of all she had from thee . . . Nor be thou abashed,
when there is question of chastising reckless folly, and the complaints
of old men against the young. So thou shalt shew prudence in all thy
dealings, and win the good word of all.

9   Daughter to her father is ever hidden anxiety, a care that banishes
sleep. Is she young? Then how if age creep on too soon? Is she wed?
10 Then how if her husband should tire of her? Is she maid? Then
how if she were disgraced, and in her own father's house brought to
bed? Once more, is she wed? Then how if she were false to her
11 husband? How if she prove barren? Over wanton daughter of thine
thou canst not keep watch too strict; else she will make thee the
scorn of thy enemies, the talk of the city; strangers will point the
12 finger at thee, and all the rabble know thy shame. Gaze not on
13 the beauty of human kind, nor occupy thyself much with women; gar-
14 ment breeds moth, and woman wickedness in man. Man's wickedness
is too strong for woman at her best;[1] and a woman that plays thee
false brings thee only disgrace.

15   Recount we now what things the Lord has made; his visible
16 creation be our theme; work of the Lord is word of the Lord. Just
as yonder sun that looks down on all gives light to all, so the glory of
17 the Lord shines through all his creation; how should his faithful
servants herald them enough, these marvels of his, enabled by Divine
18 omnipotence in that glory to endure? Nothing is hidden from him,
the deepest depths of earth or of man's heart; he knows our most
19 secret designs. All knowledge is his; does he not hold the clue of
eternity, making plain what has been and what is yet to be, laying
20 bare the track of hidden things? No thought of ours escapes him,

---

[1] The Greek is just patient of the rendering given above; but the natural
sense of all the versions is 'Man's wickedness is better than a woman who does
good'—a sentiment which could have little meaning, even in the mouth of the
most determined cynic. Probably the true text is lost in this passage; the Greek
in verse 13 has 'wickedness in woman', and the Hebrew in verse 12 has 'let her
not shew her beauty to male eyes'.

21 never a whisper goes unheard. How great the wisdom that so
ordered all things, his wisdom who has neither beginning nor end;
22 nothing may be added, nothing taken away from them, nor needs he
23 any man's counsel. How lovely is all he has made, how dazzling to
24 look upon![1] Changeless through the ages, all of it is alive and respon-
25 sive to his calls. All things he has made in pairs, balanced against
26 one another; never a fault of symmetry;[2] to each one its own well-
being assured. His glory contemplating, thou shalt never have thy fill.

CHAPTER FORTY-THREE

LIKE a jewel the vault of heaven is set above us; the sight of it is
2 glory made visible. Plain to our view is the sun's passage as it
shines out, a very masterpiece of his workmanship, who is the most
3 High. How it burns up the earth at noon-day! How fierce its glow,
beyond all endurance! Tend thou the furnace, heat is thy daily
4 portion; yet three times hotter the sun, as it burns up the hill-side,
scorching all with its fiery breath, blinding men's eyes with its glare.
5 Swiftly it speeds on its course, to do the bidding of the Lord, its
6 glorious maker. The moon, too, whose changes serve mankind for a
calendar, to mark the passing of time, and give the signal when feast
7 days come round! The moon, whose light must decrease till it
8 vanishes, and then increase to the full circle, the month its name-
9 child; cresset of a watch-fire that lights up the high vault of heaven
10 with its radiant glow. And the stars that deck the sky with their
11 splendour, a beacon-light the Lord kindles high above us; the summons of his holy word answering so loyally, watching so patiently
at their post!
12   Look up at the rainbow, and bless the maker of it; how fair are those
13 bright colours that span heaven with a ring of splendour, traced by an
14 almighty hand. Swift comes the snow at his word, swift flashes the
15 fire that executes his vengeance; he has but to unlock his store-house,
16 and the clouds hover, bird-fashion, arsenals of his might, whence the
17 pounded hail-stones fall. How his glance makes the hills tremble!
18 Blows the south wind at his bidding, earth echoes with the crash of
his thunder; blows the north wind, and there is whirling storm.
19 Soft as roosting bird falls the snow, spread all around; not more
20 silently comes locust-swarm to earth; what eye but is captivated by

---

[1] Literally, 'and like a spark which is to consider'; the Greek is hardly more
intelligible.
[2] Cf. 33.15.

21   its pale beauty, what heart but is filled with terror at the darkness of its descending? He it is pours out the frost, that lies white as salt on the earth, the frozen earth that seems covered with thistle-down.

22   Cold blows the north wind, and ice forms on the water; no pool but

23   it rests there, arming the water as with a breast-plate; frost gnaws at the mountain-side, parches the open plains, strips them, as fire might

24   have stripped them, of their green. Remedy for all these is none, but the speedy coming of the mist; frost shall be overmastered by the

25   showers the sirocco drives before it [1] (and at the Lord's word the chill blast dies away).

What else but divine wisdom tamed the rising of the seas,[2] and

26   planted the islands there? Hear we what perils in the deep mariners

27   have to tell of, and wonder at the tale; of the great marvels it contains, living things a many, both fierce and harmless, and monstrous

28   creatures besides. Who but the Lord brought the venture to a happy issue? His word gives all things their pattern.

29   Say we much as we will, of what needs to be said our words come

30   short; be this the sum of all our saying, He is in all things.[3] To what end is all our boasting? [4] He, the Almighty, is high above all that

31   he has made; he, the Lord, is terrible, and great beyond compare,

32   and his power is wonderful. Glorify him as best you may, glory is

33   still lacking (such is the marvel of his greatness; praise him and

34   extol him as you will, he is beyond all praising); summon all your strength, the better to exalt his name, untiring still, and you shall not

35   reach your goal. Who can tell us what he is from sight seen of him?

36   Who can magnify his eternal being? Much more lies beyond our

37   ken; only the fringe of creation meets our view; and of all things the Lord is maker. Yet, live thou in the worship of him, wisdom thou shalt have for thy reward.

CHAPTER FORTY-FOUR

NOW let us call the roll of famous men that were our fathers, long

2   ago. What high achievements the Lord has made known in them,

3   ever since time began! Here were men that had power and bore rule,

---

[1] *vv.* 23, 24: It is possible, both in the Greek and in the Hebrew, to interpret verse 23 as referring to drought, with Almighty God himself as the subject of the sentence; verse 25 will then mean that the showers save the grass from the effects of the sirocco.

[2] Literally, 'pacified the abyss', but it seems clear that the reference is to Gen. 1.9 and kindred passages.

[3] Both the Greek and the Hebrew give, 'He is all'.

[4] In the Greek and in the Hebrew, 'our glorifying of him'.

men that excelled in strength, or in the wisdom that dowered them;
4 prophets that worthily upheld the name of prophecy, issuing to the
people the commands their times needed, uttering, through their
5 foresight, a sacred charge to the nations. Here were men that had
skill to devise melodies, to make songs and set them down in writing.
6 Here were men rich in ability, (noble of aim), that dwelt peacefully
7 in their homes. These were the glories of their race, the ornament
8 of their times; and the sons they begot have left a memory that adds
9 to the recital of their praise. Not like those others, who are forgotten
in death as if they had never been; nameless, they and their children,
10 as if they had never lived; no, these were men of tender conscience;[1]
11 their deeds of charity will never be forgotten. Blessings abide with
12 their posterity; their descendants are a race set apart for God, the
13 pledged heirs of his promises. For their sakes this line of theirs will
endure for all time; their stock, their name, will never be allowed to
14 die out. Their bodies lie in peace; their name lasts on, age after age.
15 Their wisdom is yet a legend among the people; wherever faithful
men assemble, their story is told.
16   Enoch there was, that did God's will, and was taken away to Para-
17 dise, repentance his gift to mankind.[2] Noe, too, blameless lived and
faithful proved; when the day of retribution came, he made amends
18 for all;[3] so it was that earth had a stock left to breed from when the
19 flood came; with him God's covenant was made, never again should
20 all living things be drowned together. What greatness was Abraham's,
to be the father of so many nations! Where shall we find another that
can boast he kept the law of the most High as Abraham kept it? He,
21 too, entered into a covenant with God, and was bidden to bear on his
own body the record of it. Once he had put him to the test and found
22 him obedient, God took an oath that this should be the father of a
renowned posterity; their numbers should rival the dust on the
23 ground, should match the stars in heaven, stretching from southern
24 to western sea, from Euphrates to the ends of earth. Isaac, the son
25 of such a father, fared no worse; to him the Lord gave that blessing
which should extend to all nations. In Jacob's person, too, the cove-
26 nant should be revived; the blessings Jacob uttered should be rati-

---

[1] Here, and in verse 27, we may translate 'men well beloved'; that is, God's favourites.

[2] This is commonly interpreted by the Fathers in connexion with Apoc. 11.3. In the Greek, Enoch is represented as an *example* of penitence; in the Hebrew, of wisdom.

[3] The Greek word thus translated might also mean, 'was (allowed to survive) in exchange for all'.

fied, and the lands promised him should be divided among twelve
tribes of his own begetting.

27   Him a posterity of famous sons awaited,[1] men of tender conscience,
that had the good word of all their fellows.

CHAPTER FORTY-FIVE

2   WELL loved by God, well loved among men, on the name of
Moses a benediction rests. The Lord gave him such honour
as he gives to his holy ones; gave him renown by striking terror into his
enemies, and then, at his word, abated the prodigies that had befallen
3   them.   He made him great in the eyes of kings, entrusted commandments to him in full view of the chosen people, made a revelation to
4   him of the divine glory.   The Lord set him apart, chosen out from
5   the rest of mankind, so loyal he was and so gentle;   answered his
6   prayer by taking him up into a cloud,   and there, face to face,
imparting commandments to him, the law that gives life and wisdom;
here, Jacob, was thy covenant, here, Israel, the rule thou wast to
live by.

7   Of Levite blood, too, sprang another renowned as Moses himself,
8   his brother Aaron. To Aaron the Lord gave high office,   making an
eternal covenant with him, investing him with the priesthood of the
9   chosen race, enriching him with his own glory.   Bright was the
cincture that girded him, bright the robe that clothed him; no
10   ornament he wore but spoke of majesty. The long tunic, the breeches,
11   the sacred mantle, and golden bells a many compassing him about,   that
tinkled still as he walked, echoing through the temple to keep Israel's
12   name unforgotten! The hallowed robe, all gold and blue and purple,
work of a master weaver, that lacked neither skill nor faithful-
13   ness![2]   What craftsmanship of twisted thread dyed scarlet, of rare
stones in a gold setting, engraved with all the gem-cutter's art,
14   twelve of them to commemorate the twelve tribes of Israel!   The
gold finishing, too, of his mitre, engraved with the legend, Holiness;
so proud an adornment, so noble a work of art, such a lure for men's
15   eyes in its ordered beauty! Never vesture till then was seen so fair;
16   and, from time immemorial, no other might put it on,   only the sons
of Aaron's line, in undying succession.

---

[1] The Greek and the Hebrew give 'him a descendant awaited'; that is, Moses.
[2] The Latin translator has probably missed the meaning of the original. It
seems clear from the other versions that a reference is made here to the
oracular burse described in Ex. 28.30.

17 Day in, day out the fire should consume his sacrifice; when Moses
19 consecrated him with the holy oil's anointing, this was a right
granted in perpetuity, long as the heavens should last. His to perform
the priest's office, to echo God's praise, to bless the people in his
20 name. Alone of living men, he was chosen out to offer sacrifice, and
the sweet-smelling incense that is a people's plea for remembrance,
21 a people's atonement. Power was his to administer the divine law,
a justiciary by right, handing on to Jacob its tradition, interpreting
22 the law Israel must needs obey. Once, out in the desert, that right
was challenged; with envious cries, men of another clan surrounded
him, Dathan and Abiron for their leaders, espousing Core's quarrel.
23 Ill content was the Lord God at the sight of it; his vengeance swept
24 them away; by no common doom, a raging flame devoured
25 them. Fresh privileges for Aaron were kept in store; he must share
26 in the conquest by receiving all the land's first-fruits; his clan first
of all must have bread enough and to spare, his children should
27 inherit the eating of the Lord's own sacrifice. But he must have
no lands in the conquered territory, no share like the rest of his race;
the Lord should be his wealth, the Lord his portion.
28 Next to these two, Phinees the son of Eleazar won high renown;
29 like Aaron, with the fear of God to guide him, he stood firm while
the people shrank away; a loyal and a willing heart that made amends
30 for Israel. For his reward, he received assurance of the divine
favour; command he should have of sanctuary and of people both,
and the high priesthood that was his should descend to his heirs for
31 ever. David the son of Jesse, of Juda's tribe, should bequeath to his
children a legacy of kingship . . .
. . . with wise hearts endowing us, to preserve justice among his
people, and keep safe the blessings he has given to it; and this pre-
eminence over his people he has settled on them in perpetuity.[1]

CHAPTER FORTY-SIX

NEXT to Moses in the line of prophets comes Josue the son of
Nave, that fought so well. With him, name and renown are
2 one; who is more renowned for the deliverance he brought to God's

---

[1] A comparison with the other versions confirms the impression, which the
incoherence of the Latin would in any case suggest, that several words have
been omitted. Both the Hebrew and the Greek indicate that King David was
introduced into the narrative only by way of contrast; the sacred author is
pointing out an analogy between the ecclesiastical and the secular government
of Israel. In the Hebrew, the concluding words of the chapter form part of a
doxology, which begins, 'And now bless the Lord, that is so bountiful'.

chosen people, beating down the enemies that defied him until Israel
3 made their land its own? What fame he won by those valiant blows
4 he dealt, hurling his armed strength at city after city! What chieftain
had ever stood his ground so manfully? And still the Lord brought
5 enemies to confront him. On his fierce resolve the sun itself must
6 wait, and a whole day's length be doubled. Let enemies attack him
on every side, he would invoke the most High, to whom all strength
belongs, the great God, the holy God, and his prayer was answered.[1]
7 Hail-stones came down in a storm of wondrous violence, that fell on
the opposing army and shattered the menace of it, there on the hill-
8 side. So the Gentiles should feel God's power, and learn that it is a
hard matter to fight against him. Ever had Josue followed in that
9 Prince's retinue, since the days when Moses yet lived; he it was,
and Caleb the son of Jephone, that took a generous part together;
they would have engaged the enemy, and saved their own people
10 from guilt by hushing the murmurs of rebellion. These two alone,
out of six hundred thousand warriors, survived the perils of the
journey; these two were appointed to lead Israel into the land, all
milk and honey, that was its promised home.
11 On Caleb, too, the Lord bestowed such vigour, that in his old age
he was a warrior still, and made his way up into the hill country,
12 where his descendants held their lands after him; no doubt should
Israel have that he rewards his servants bountifully, the God who
13 dwells apart. The judges, too, have their glorious muster-roll, men
14 of resolute heart, that God's cause never forsook; be their names,
too, remembered in blessing, and may life spring from their bones,
15 where they lie buried; undying be their memory, in their own
posterity continued, undying be the sacred record of their renown.
16 Dearly the Lord God loved his prophet Samuel, that restored Israel's
17 fortunes and anointed kings to rule over it. Well was the divine law
kept, when he ruled our commonwealth, and the God of Jacob was
18 gracious to it; here was a prophet of proved loyalty, and ever his
19 word came true, such vision had he of the God that gives light. With
foes about him on every side, he invoked the Lord, the Almighty,
20 with an unblemished lamb for sacrifice; and therewith came thunder,
21 sent from heaven, loud echo of the divine voice,[2] that overthrew
22 all the princes of the sea coast, all the captains of the Philistines. There
must be an end at last to his life, and to the age he lived in; but first
he would make profession, with the Lord and the new-anointed king
for his witnesses, bribe he had never taken from any living man,

---

[1] *vv.* 5, 6: See Josue 10.10–14.
[2] See I Kg. 7.10.

though it were but a gift of shoe-leather; and none might gainsay
23 him.[1] Even when he had gone to his rest, he had a revelation for the
king's ear, and gave warning of the death that awaited him; a prophet,
even in the tomb, while there was yet guilt among his people to be
effaced.

CHAPTER FORTY-SEVEN

AMONG prophets, Nathan was the next to arise; and it was then
2 the reign of David began. Only the fat from the sacrifice, only
3 David out of all Israel; the Lord must have ever the best! Here was
one that would use lion or bear as playthings for his sport, tussle
with them as if they had been yearling lambs. Such was his boy-
4 hood; and who but he should save the honour of his people, by
5 slaying the giant? He had but to lift his hand, and the stone aimed
6 from his sling brought low the pride of Goliath; prayer to the Lord,
the Almighty, gave him the mastery over a brave warrior, and retrieved
7 the fortunes of his race. Ere long, they had given him the title,
Slayer of ten thousand, and sang his praises, blessing the Lord's name;
8 kingly honours they accorded him. He it was that laid their enemies
low all about them, extirpating, to this day, the malice of the
9 Philistines, shattering their power for ever. Yet there was no feat
of David's but made him thank the most High, the most Holy, and
10 to him give the glory; still with all his heart he praised the Master
he loved so well, the God who had created him (and endowed him
11 with strength to meet his enemies). He would have musicians wait
12 around the altar, and rouse sweet echoes with their chant; feast-
days should be kept with splendour, times and seasons duly observed,
all his life long; morning after morning the Lord's holy name should
13 be praised, God should receive his full tribute of worship. So it was
that the Lord pardoned his sins, and bade him carry his head high
evermore; his by right was the kingship, and the proud throne of
Israel.
14   To a wise son of his that throne passed; for David's sake all the
15 threats of the enemy were stilled,   and Solomon might reign undisturbed. If God gave him mastery all around, it was because he
would have a temple built in his honour, to be his sanctuary for all
16 time. Ah, Solomon, how well schooled in thy youth! Deep as a
river flowed thy wisdom; thy ambition it was to lay bare all the secrets
17 of earth; full scope thou wouldst have for riddle and proverb. Even

---

[1] See I Kg. 12.3.

to the distant isles thy renown spread, and everywhere thy peaceful
18 reign made thee beloved. The whole earth stood in awe of song and
19 proverb and parable and interpretation of thine; in awe, too, of the
name of Javé, the God who is known among men as the God of
20 Israel. Gold thou didst amass in such plenty, as it had been orichalc;
21 silver was abundant in thy domains as lead. Yet women bowed thee
22 to their will; of body's appetites thou wouldst brook no restraint, and
thus thy renown was tarnished with the gendering of a breed unhallowed. So it was that vengeance fell upon thy children, that must
23 rue thy folly in after times; the kingdom divided, and in Ephraim a
rebel dynasty exercising dominion, through thy fault.
24   Yet God is ever merciful; his own design he will not mar fruit-
lessly, nor undo; should he destroy it root and branch, the posterity
of his chosen servant? Should the man that so loved him have begotten
25 sons in 'vain? Jacob must have a stock to breed from; the root of
26 David should burgeon yet. Solomon once laid to rest with his
27 fathers, what heirs left he? A man of his own blood, born to infatuate
28 a nation, insensate Roboam, whose ill counsel drove the people to
29 rebellion; and that other, Jeroboam son of Nabat, who taught Israel
to sin. All Ephraim followed the example of his misdoing; high rose
30 the tide of their sins, till it swept them away altogether from their
own country.
31   For all this wickedness of theirs God held them to account, waiting
till the time should come for punishing them, and purging them of
their guilt.

CHAPTER FORTY-EIGHT

AND now another prophet arose, Elias, a man of flame; blazed, like
2   a fire-brand, his message. This man it was brought down a
famine to punish them, till few were left of the enemies that bore him
3 a grudge, (and found the Lord's commandment too hard for them). At
the Lord's word, he laid a ban on heaven itself, and three times brought
4 fire down from it; such was the fame of Elias' miracles. Who else
5 could boast, as thou, of calling back the dead from the tomb, by the
6 power of the Lord God, and to life restoring them; of kings brought
to ruin (and all their power lightly shattered), proud kings, that
7 might leave their sick-beds no more? Sinai should tell thee, Horeb
8 should tell thee, of award made, and doom pronounced; kings thou
shouldst anoint, to be the redressers of wrong, and prophets to come
9 after thee; then, amidst a flaming whirlwind, in a chariot drawn by
10 horses of fire, thou wast taken up into heaven. Of thee it stands

written in the decrees of doom, that thou shouldst appease the Divine
anger, by reconciling heart of father to heart of son, and restore the
11 tribes of Israel as they were. Ah, blessed souls that saw thee, and
12 were honoured with thy friendship! We live only for a life-time;
and when death comes, we shall have no such renown as thine.

13   In that whirlwind Elias was lost to view, bequeathing his spirit of
prophecy in full measure to Eliseus. Here was a man that in all his
life never held prince in awe, never made way for human great-
14 ness. Difficulty there was none could overreach him; was not his
15 dead body prophetic still, to prove him a wonder-worker in death,
16 that in life was marvellous? Yet the nation for whom all this was done
would not amend, nor leave its sinning, until all the inhabitants of the
17 land were driven out, and scattered through the world; only that
18 little kingdom remained that was ruled by the heirs of David, and
of these rulers, though some did God's will, there were some that had
sins a many to answer for.

19   Well did Ezechias fortify his city, and brought a running stream
into the midst of it, breaking through the rock with tools of iron,
20 and building a cistern for the water. In his reign Sennacherib
marched against the country, and sent Rabsaces to threaten it; Sion
itself he threatened with attack, so proudly he trusted in his own
21 strength. Heart and hand were unnerved at his coming; worse
22 anguish woman in labour never knew. Yet they cried out upon
God for pity, with hands outstretched heavenwards; and he, the holy
23 One, he, the Lord God, was not slow to answer them. (Their sins
he would remember no more; he would not leave them at the mercy
of their enemies); by means of his holy prophet Isaias they should find
24 release. With that, the Lord's angel fell on the camp of Assyria, and
25 brought its armies to nothing. So faithfully Ezechias did the Lord's
will, following boldly the example of his father, king David, with
Isaias to encourage him, a great prophet and a faithful interpreter of
26 the vision the Lord gave him. In Isaias' days it was that the sun
27 went back, in token that the royal life should be prolonged; Isaias
it was that saw things far distant, by the power of inspiration, and
28 comforted mourning hearts in Sion. Without end or limit   future
things he foretold, that still lay hidden in the womb of time.

CHAPTER FORTY-NINE

JOSIAS, too, is still remembered; a memory grateful as some mingled
2 scent, pride of the perfumer's art, or the honey that tastes sweet
3 in all men's mouths, or music over the wine. A king divinely

ordained to make a nation's amends, how he swept away all the foul
4 idols of the law-breakers; how true he kept his heart to the
Lord's bidding, what comfort he gave to piety, when wickedness
5 abounded! David, Ezechias, Josias, these three only were exempt
6 from the guilt of their line; the other kings of Juda forsook the law
7 of the most High, and counted the fear of God a light matter. What
wonder if they were doomed to bequeath all the glories of their
8 kingdom to strangers, to princes of an alien race, who set fire to the
city that was God's chosen sanctuary, and left the ways unfrequented?
9 . . . By means of Jeremias;[1] so ill they used him, that was set apart
to be a prophet when he was yet in his mother's womb, empowered to
overthrow, to uproot, to destroy, then to rebuild and to plant
10 anew. And next Ezechiel, to whose eyes God shewed the vision of
glory, by wheeling cherubs borne aloft . . .
11 And in storm he remembered the enemy . . . to reward all such as
pointed men to the right path.[2]
12 The twelve prophets, too, put heart into the sons of Jacob, and by
trusting in his power won deliverance.
13 The fame of Zorobabel what words of ours shall enhance? The jewel
14 God wore on his right hand for signet-ring; he, with Josue son of
Josedec, rebuilt God's house that then lay ruined; raised up a holy
15 temple, of the divine glory the eternal dwelling-place. Nor shall
Nehemias be soon forgotten, that mended these ruined walls of ours,
our gates built and barred, our homes restored to us.
16 Enoch no man born on earth can match, that from earth was taken
17 away; nor Joseph, that was born to be his brethren's master, and the
18 bulwark of a great nation. (Lord of his brethren, stay of a people, he
left his bones to await the day of God's deliverance, in death prophetic
19 still.) Among the races of mankind, Seth and Sem have the pre-
eminence; but from the stock of Adam we all descend alike.

---

[1] It is very doubtful whether the words 'in the hand of Jeremias' can be construed so as to form a single sentence with verse 8; a gap in the text seems
more probable.
[2] A further gap should perhaps be indicated here; Ez. 13.13 hardly justifies
us in making Ezechiel the subject of verse 11. The Hebrew and the Syriac
have 'he remembered (or, made mention of) Job', which again would not
naturally apply to Ezechiel, in spite of Ez. 14.14.

CHAPTER FIFTY

A GREAT priest was Simon, son of Onias;[1] in his day the house of God was repaired, to make the temple strong was his life's task.
2 The high part of the temple, where the building was of double thick-
3 ness, and the towering walls about it, he underpinned; in his day, too, the cisterns received their full flow of water, rose beyond all measuring,
4 sea-deep. So well he cared for his fellow citizens; no enemy should
5 be able to compass our ruin. (Means he found to enlarge the city's span); the common life of the people should be the theatre of his
6 renown; to temple and temple-court he gave wider entrance. This man was the light of his times, bright as day-star or full moon amid
7 the clouds; nor sun ever shed on our own temple such generous
8 rays as he. What shall recall his memory? Rainbow that lights up the clouds with sudden glory, rose in spring-time, lilies by the water-side,
9 scent of olibanum on the summer air? Fire that glows brightly, and
10 glow of incense on the fire? Ornament of pure gold, set with what-
11 ever stones are rarest; olive-tree that burgeons, tall cypress pointing to the sky? Such was he when he put on his robe of office, clad himself
12 with the full majesty of his array; sacred the garments in which he went up to the sacred altar, yet were they ennobled by the man that wore them.
13 There he stood, by the altar, with the priests handing him their portions, every one, for sacrifice; and all these standing about him
14 were but Lebanon cedars standing about Lebanon, were but as palm branches growing from their parent stem, all these sons of
15 Aaron in the splendour of their attire. Theirs to hold out, before assembled Israel, the offerings made to the Lord; and he, completing his task at the altar, for the due observance of the great King's sacri-
16 fice, would reach out his hand for the cup, and with the grape's blood
17 offer libation. And as he poured out at the altar's foot its consecrated
18 fragrance, loud shouted the sons of Aaron, loud the silver trumpets
19 blew; great was the cry raised to win God's audience. And with that, down fell all the people, face to earth, worshipping the Lord their God and pouring out their prayers to him, the Almighty, to him, the
20 most High. The singers, too, broke out into chants of praise; sweetly

---

[1] There were two high priests who could be described as 'Simon the son of Onias'. One of these flourished about three hundred, the other about two hundred years before Christ. The former is probably the one here alluded to. We have no information elsewhere about the improvements which are described, somewhat obscurely, in verses 2–5.

21 their voices echoed through the wide courts; nor would the people leave off their praying to the Lord, the most High, till the divine
22 praise was completed, and all their duty done. And then Simon would come down, his hand outstretched over the assembly of Israel,
23 a blessing on his lips, and his heart proud to serve such a Master; and so fell to prayer again, for the better manifesting of God's power.
24 Bless we now his name who is God over all; [1] wide as earth is his wondrous power, the God that has granted us life since first we were
25 borne in the womb, and most mercifully used us. Gladness of heart may he give us, and send Israel in our time peace that shall last for
26 ever; and still may it be Israel's faith that God's mercy is with us, ready, when his time comes, to grant us deliverance.
27 Two nations with all my heart I loathe; and a third I can name,
28 that nation indeed is none; the hill-tribes of Edom, and the Philistines, and the miscreant folk that dwell at Sichem.
29 The lessons of discernment and of true knowledge in this book contained were written down by Jesus, the son of Sirach, of Jerusalem;
30 one that had set his heart on the reviving of wisdom. Blessed is he who lingers in these pleasant haunts, and treasures the memory of
31 them; wisdom he shall never lack; and if by these precepts he live, nothing shall avail to daunt him; God's beacon-light shews the track he shall tread.

CHAPTER FIFTY-ONE

A PRAYER uttered by Jesus, son of Sirach. O Lord, my king, I
2 give thee thanks, O God, my deliverer, I praise thee; I extol
3 thy name, for all the succour and protection thou hast given me, saving my life from deadly peril, when calumny lay in wait, and lying tongues assailed me. In full sight of all that stood by thou didst come to my
4 rescue; roaring lions stood ready to devour me, and thou in that
5 great mercy, that renowned mercy of thine, didst deliver me. I was in the hands of my mortal enemies, shut in on every side by mis-
6 fortune; there were stifling flames all round me, and I stood in the
7 heart of the fire uninjured. I looked down into the deep womb of the grave, when foul lips brought lying accusations, and cruel king
8 gave unjust sentence. And still I would praise the Lord, long as I
9 had breath to praise him, though death's abyss yawned at my very
10 feet, though I was cut off on every side, with none to aid me. Man's
11 help I looked for, and could not find; yet I bethought me, Lord, of

---

[1] *vv.* 24–26: It is not clear whether this is the formula of blessing used by Simon, or an epilogue written in the person of the author.

12 thy mercy, thy deeds of long ago; if men will but wait for thee
patiently, thou, Lord, dost deliver them, dost rescue them from the
13 power of the heathen.   It was thou who hadst prospered my life on
14 earth, and now, death ready to overwhelm me,   to the Lord, Father of
the Master I serve,[1] I made my plea. Would he leave me unaided when
15 I was in distress, when my enemies were triumphing over me?   I
will extol thy name unceasingly, with grateful praise; my prayer did
16 not go unregarded.   Thou didst rescue me from deadly peril, didst
17 save me in the hour of defeat; shall I not give thanks, shall I not
praise and bless thy name?

18   **A** young man still, ere ever my wanderings began, I made my
19 prayer for wisdom.[2]   **B**efore the temple I asked for this, my life's
20 quest to the end.   **C**ame early the ripening of those grapes, and my
21 heart rejoiced at it.   **D**own a straight path I sped, the ardour of youth
22 to aid my search.   **E**ar that little listens shall yet hear; much wisdom
23 that little listening gave.   **F**urther and further yet I travelled, thanks
24 be to the God that all wisdom bestows.   **G**ood use to make of her
25 was all my love and longing; never was that hope disappointed.   **H**ard-
26 ily I strove to win her, put force on myself to keep her rule;   **I**
stretched out my hands towards heaven, and grieved for the want of
27 her.   **K**ept I but true to the search for her, I found and recognized
28 her still.   **L**ong since trained by her discipline, I shall never be left
29 forsaken.   **M**uch heart-burning I had in the quest for her, but a rich
30 dowry she brought me.   **N**ever shall this tongue, with utterance
31 divinely rewarded, be negligent of praise.   **O** hearts untutored, come
32 near, and frequent the school of learning!   **P**arley at the gates no more,
33 complaining of thirst ever unsatisfied.   **R**ather, to my proclamation
34 give heed; win the treasure that is to be had without price paid.   **S**uffice
it that you bow your necks to her yoke, are content to accept her
35 schooling.   **T**o find her, needs no distant travel. . .[3]   **U**nlaborious days,
36 as all can testify, what a harvest they have won me of repose!   **W**ould
you grudge free expense of silver in the search for wisdom, that shall
37 make you ample returns in gold?   **Y**our hearts shall yet triumph in
his mercy, nor ever rue the day when you learned to praise him.

38   Do, while time serves, what needs doing; when the time comes, he
will reward you.

---

[1] It is not easy to see what the sacred author meant by 'the Master whom I
serve'; the obscure words used in Ps. 109.1 are only an incomplete parallel.
[2] It is not clear whether we are to understand the word 'wanderings' literally (cf. 34.12) or metaphorically.
[3] It seems clear that some words have dropped out at the end of this verse;
the Hebrew gives 'and the man who is intent upon her will discover her'.

THE PROPHECY OF ISAIAS

CHAPTER ONE

THIS is the revelation made to Isaias, son of Amos, about Juda and Jerusalem, during the reigns of Ozias, Joatham, Achaz and Ezechias
2 in Juda. Listen, you heavens, and let earth attend to this, the Lord's complaint; my own sons, that I reared and brought to manhood, think to
3 defy me! Ox recognizes its owner, ass knows the way to its master's crib; and I? I go unacknowledged; my own people of Israel gives me never a
4 thought. Woe to a sinful nation, a people bowed with guilt, a rebellious race, a thankless brood! They have forsaken God, they have spurned the
5 Holy One of Israel, turned strangers to me. Would you have me smite you again, that you shew yourselves ever more faithless? Everywhere
6 bowed heads, and faint hearts; no health anywhere, from sole to crown, nothing but wounds, and bruises, and swollen sores, that none binds up,
7 or medicines, or anoints with oil! Your land a desert, your cities burnt to ashes, your fields ravaged before your eyes by strangers, desolation every-
8 where, as if an enemy had plundered you! Poor Sion, forlorn as vineyard
9 watch-tower, summer-house in a herb-garden, a beleaguered city! A stock to breed from, so much the Lord of hosts has left us; but for that, we should be as Sodom is, Gomorrha's doom should be ours.
10 Listen, then, to this, chiefs of the Sodom-city; people of a new
11 Gomorrha, here is a command from the Lord for your hearing. What do I care, the Lord says, how you multiply those victims of yours? I have had enough and to spare. Burnt offerings of rams, and the fat of stall-fed beasts, and the blood of calves and lambs and goats are nothing to me.
12 Think you it is a welcome sound, the tramp of your feet in my courts,
13 bringing worship such as yours? Vain offerings, bring them no more; your very incense is an abomination. Enough of new moons and sabbaths,
14 of thronged assemblies where none but sinners meet! The new month begins, the feast day comes round, stale and wearisome, cloying the
15 appetite. Hold out your hands as you will, you shall get no heed from me; add prayer to prayer, I will not listen; are not those hands stained with blood?
16 Wash yourselves clean, spare me the sight of your busy wickedness,
17 keep holiday from wrong-doing. Learn, rather, how to do good, setting your hearts on justice, righting the wrong, protecting the orphan, giving
18 the widow redress; then come back, says the Lord, and make trial of me. Then, the scarlet dye of your guilt will show snow-white, the crimson
19 stains will be like clean wool. Will you think better of it, and listen, and

20 have rich harvests to feed you? Or will you refuse, and defy me, and yourselves be food for the sword? The Lord's warrant is out against you.
21 Strange, that the city once so faithful, once so dutiful, has turned harlot;
22 the haunt of murderers, that was the home of right! The silver in thee
23 turned to dross, the wine grown watery to the taste, thy law-givers wanting loyalty, so that they make common cause with thieves! None of them but takes bribe and looks for profit, none will give the orphan redress, none listen to the plaint of the widow.
24   What, then, does the Lord proclaim; he, the God of hosts, he, the Prince of Israel? Out upon it, I will rid myself of these rebels, my enemies shall
25 have their deserts. And then I will take thee in hand again, smelting thee
26 till thou art free from dross, purging away all that base alloy. Once more I will give thee judges like the judges of old, counsellors like the counsellors of past days, and thou shalt be called the home of right, the faithful
27 city. Sion shall be won back, dutiful once again; her exiles shall be
28 brought home, doers of right; with one blow, the wayward sinner shall
29 be overthrown, by the Lord he has forsaken doomed to perish. Tree-idols that have played you false, fond trust in your garden-shrines, you
30 shall learn to rue them; yourselves but an oak-tree whose leaves are fall-
31 ing, a garden unwatered; when all your strength is like smouldering tow, and the idols you have made but a spark to set light to it, until both burn together, with none to quench them.

CHAPTER TWO

THIS is a message which was revealed to Isaias, the son of Amos, about
2 Juda and Jerusalem. In the days that are still to come, the mountain where the Lord dwells will be lifted high above the mountain-tops, look-
3 ing down over the hills, and all nations will flock there together. A multitude of peoples will make their way to it, crying, Come, let us climb up to the Lord's mountain peak, to the house where the God of Jacob dwells; he shall teach us the right way, we will walk in the paths he has chosen. The Lord's commands shall go out from Sion, his word from Jerusalem,
4 and he will sit in judgement on the nations, giving his award to a multitude of peoples. They will melt down their swords into plough-shares, their spears into pruning-hooks, nation levying war against nation and
5 training itself for battle no longer. Come you too (they will say), children of Jacob, let us walk together in the path where the Lord shews us light.
6   And still they are cast off, these children of Jacob, the Lord's own people; ever since they grew rich, like the men who went before them,[1]

---

[1] 'Like the men who went before them'; the Hebrew text more probably means 'from the east.' But the whole of the verse is very obscure, and perhaps corrupt.

and began to trust in divination, like the Philistines, and to ally themselves
7 with men of alien breed. A land full of silver and gold, with no end to its
8 treasures, a land full of horses and chariots innumerable; a land full of
9 idols, where men worship the devices their own hands have made. High
and low they fall to earth, abate their human pride to worship dumb
things; and shall they find forgiveness?
10 See where the Lord comes, in all his terrors, in all the glory of his
majesty; take refuge, now, in some rock-cavern, hide thee in some pit!
11 Now indeed man's haughty looks must fall to earth, human pride must be
abated; no room for any greatness but the Lord's, when that day comes.
12 With the dawn of it all human pomp and state must be overshadowed,
13 all human magnificence grow dim. High it will rise above the cedars of
14 Lebanon, that grow so straight and tall, above the oaks of Basan; above
15 aspiring mountain and swelling hill; above every topless tower, every
16 impregnable citadel, above all the navies of Tharsis, above every sight
17 that is fair to see. Shall not man's greatness fall to earth, shall not human
18 pride be abated then? Vanished the false gods, only cave in the rock,
crevice in the ground will afford shelter, when the Lord comes, great and
20 terrible, rises up to smite earth with dread! Flung away, when that day
comes, idols of silver and gold they once made and worshipped; moles
21 and bats all their worship now, as they slink into clefts of the hills, into
rocky caverns, to hide themselves from the terrors of the Lord's coming,
22 from this sublime majesty that daunts the earth! Trouble mankind no
more; [1] this at least man can boast, he has the breath of life in his nostrils.

CHAPTER THREE

SEE where the Lord of hosts, our Master, takes away from Jerusalem
and from Juda all that was valiant and strong, all the support they had
2 against famine and thirst! Gone the hero and the warrior, judge and pro-
3 phet, diviner and senator, captain of the watch, and nobleman, and coun-
4 sellor, and skilful workman, and master of charms. Only boys will be left
5 to rule, and all shall be wantonness; the citizens coming to blows, neighbour falling out with neighbour; for age and rank shall be no reverence.
6 Here is one saying to his own brother, his own house-mate, What, hast
thou a coat to thy back? Be our chieftain, then; take these ruins into thy
7 keeping. So hard the times! And the other answers, Who, I? Nay, I have
no doctor's skill. As for my house, there is neither bread nor coat in it;

---

[1] This verse seems to be addressed to the false gods. But the Hebrew text is
best translated, 'Cease from man, whose breath is in his nostrils; what claim
has he to regard.' The sense is not clear, and the Septuagint Greek omits the
whole verse.

8 ruler thou shalt never make of me. Jerusalem in ruins, Juda lying prostrate! Whispering and scheming of theirs defied the Lord, challenged his
9 divine scrutiny. Their hang-dog looks betray them; they publish their
guilt abroad, like the men of Sodom, making no secret of it. Alas, poor
souls, retribution has come upon them.

10 For the just man have no fears; all is well, his reward is earned; but woe
12 betide the sinner! He shall be repaid for his ill deeds. My people has been
despoiled by the tyrants that rule it; women have gained power over it;
those who call thee happy, my people, are deceiving thee, are luring thee
13 into false paths. Even now the Lord stands ready to hold his assize, waits
14 there to pass judgement on all nations. The Lord will enter into a reckoning with the senators and the rulers of his people: You have made spoil
of the vineyard, your houses are full of the plunder you have taken from
15 the oppressed; what means it, that you ride roughshod over my people,
that you spurn the right of friendless folk? The Lord, the God of hosts,
will have his answer.

16 This, too, the Lord says: See what airs they put on, the women-folk of
Sion, walk with heads high, look about them with glancing eyes, click the
trappings on their feet with mincing steps. Ay, but the Lord has his doom
17 ready for them; bald of head and bare of temple the women of Sion shall
18 know it. In one day the Lord will sweep away all their finery, the shoes
19 with the rest; locket, and collar, necklace and bracelet and veil; hair-pin,
21 ankle-ring, chain, scent-box, pendant, signet-ring and nose-ring; gala
23 dress and gown and scarf, bodkin and mirror and shawl and riband and
24 kerchief. There will be new fashions then; stench for scent, hempen rope
for waist-band, baldness for curls, and hair shirt for stomacher.

25 Of the men-folk, too, all that is fairest shall fall by the sword, all that
26 is bravest, slain in battle. See where she sits on the ground desolate,
every gateway of hers full of sorrow and lament!

CHAPTER FOUR

DAY of desolation! Here are seven women catching hold of one man,
and promising, We will earn our bread, find ourselves in clothing;
only let us bear thy name, and be saved from the reproach of barrenness!
2 When that day comes, bud and fruit there shall be, of the Lord's foster-
ing; burgeoning of glory made manifest, and fruit piled high, the trophy
3 of Israel's gleanings.[1] Set apart for him, all that dwell in Sion now, all

---

[1] Literally, 'In that day there will be a bud (or, according to the Hebrew,
a burgeoning) of the Lord, for magnificence and glory, and fruit of the earth
high uplifted, a source of triumph to those in Israel who are saved.' Scholars
are not agreed whether this is a direct or only an indirect reference to the
coming of the Messias.

that survive the city's purging; none else will be left alive in Jerusalem,
4 when the Lord sweeps away the guilt of Sion's women-folk, washes
Jerusalem clean from the blood that stains her, with the searing breath of
5 his judgement. And over mount Sion, the shrine of his name, cloud shall
6 hang by day, glowing haze by night, a veil for glory. Canopy they shall
have, to shade them from the day's heat, a refuge to give them shelter
from storm and rain.

CHAPTER FIVE

A SONG, now, in honour of one that is my good friend; a song about a
near kinsman of mine, and the vineyard that he had. This friend,
that I love well, had a vineyard in a corner of his ground, all fruitfulness.[1]
2 He fenced it in, and cleared it of stones, and planted a choice vine there;
built a tower, too, in the middle, and set up a wine-press in it. Then he
3 waited for grapes to grow on it, and it bore wild grapes instead. And now,
citizens of Jerusalem, and all you men of Juda, I call upon you to give
4 award between my vineyard and me. What more could I have done for
it? What say you of the wild grapes it bore, instead of the grapes I looked
5 for? Let me tell you, then, what I mean to do to this vineyard of mine.
I mean to rob it of its hedge, so that all can plunder it, to break down its
6 wall, so that it will be trodden under foot. I mean to make waste-land of
it; no more pruning and digging; only briars and thorns will grow there,
7 and I will forbid the clouds to water it. Alas, it is the house of Israel that
the Lord once called his vineyard; the men of Juda are the plot he once
loved so. He looked to find right reason there, and all was treason; to find
plain dealing, and he heard only the plaint of the oppressed.
8 Woe upon you, that must ever be acquiring house after house, field
after neighbouring field, till all the world goes wanting! Would you have
9 the whole land to yourselves to live in? The news of all this has reached
me, says the Lord of hosts; see if I do not leave these many houses, these
10 fine great houses of yours, lonely and untenanted. Wait, till you find
thirty acres of vine-land yielding but one flagon of wine, thirty bushels of
11 seed-corn yielding but three. Woe upon you, the men who must be up
betimes to go a-drinking, and sit late into the evening, till you are heated
12 with wine! Still you must have zither and harp, tambour and flute and
wine for your entertainment; you give no thought to God's dealings, to
13 the world his hands have made. It is this inconsiderateness that has made
my people homeless exiles, their nobles starving, and common folk

---

[1] Literally, 'a horn, the son of oil.' The word 'horn' is generally interpreted
here as a hill; but a rocky crag such as the word would indicate would be no
place for a vineyard.

14 parched with thirst; that is why the abyss hungers for you, opens its greedy jaws, till all alike, the nobles of Sion and her common sort, that

15 boast and triumph now, go down to its depths. The low-born must fall, the high-born abate his pride; the eyes of the boaster will be downcast;

16 doom, by which the Lord of hosts will be exalted, just award, by which

17 the God of holiness will shew holier yet! There, with his flocks browsing undisturbed, the stranger shall enjoy the rich pastures you left a wilderness.

18 Woe upon you, that sin yet, and draw down sin's punishment on your-

19 selves, wilful as high-mettled steed straining at the traces! What is this, you say, that the Holy One of Israel threatens? Quick, no waiting; let us

20 know the worst, and with all speed! Woe upon you, the men who call evil good, and good evil; whose darkness is light, whose light darkness;

21 who take bitter for sweet, and sweet for bitter! Woe upon you, that think

22 yourselves wise, and boast of your own foresight! Woe upon you, heroes

23 of the tankard, brave hearts round the mixing bowl, that take bribes to acquit the guilty, and rob the innocent of his rights!

24 See how stubble is eaten away by the fire that licks round it, melting away into the heat of the flame; so the root of them will turn to smoulder-ing embers, and the fruit of them will go up like flying ashes; men who reject the law of the God of hosts, who defy every warning from the Holy

25 One of Israel. That is why the Lord's anger against his people has been so fierce; that is why his hand has been raised to smite them, so that the mountains trembled at it, and corpses lay unregarded like dung in the streets. But even so his anger is not yet appeased, his hand threatens us still.

26 And now he will raise up among the distant nations one people to be a signal to the rest; he will whistle it up from the ends of the earth, swiftly

27 and suddenly it will answer his call. Not a man in those ranks that will faint or lag behind; none grows weary or falls asleep; never a belt is

28 unbuckled, never a shoe-string loosed. Sharp arrows this people has, and all its bows are ready bent; it has horses with hoofs like flint, and chariot-

29 wheels like the rushing of the storm. No lion roars so loud; it will roar as lion-cubs do, growling and holding its prey fast, encircling it so that

30 none can bring rescue. Sounds of dread shall usher in that day, loud as the roaring of the sea; look where you will, all shall be dark with misery; light itself will be darkened by the shadow of its coming.

CHAPTER SIX

IN the year of king Ozias's death, I had a vision. I saw the Lord sitting on a throne that towered high above me, the skirts of his robe filling
2 the temple. Above it rose the figures of the seraphim, each of them six-winged; with two wings they veiled God's face, with two his feet, and the
3 other two kept them poised in flight.[1] And ever the same cry passed between them, Holy, holy, holy, is the Lord God of hosts; all the earth
4 is full of his glory. The lintels over the doors rang with the sound of that cry, and smoke went up, filling the temple courts.
5 Alas, said I, that I must needs keep silence;[2] my lips, and all my neighbours' lips, are polluted with sin; and yet these eyes are looking upon their
6 King, the Lord of hosts. Whereupon one of the seraphim flew up to me,
7 bearing a coal which he had taken with a pair of tongs from the altar; he touched my mouth with it, and said, Now that this has touched thy lips,
8 thy guilt is swept away, thy sin pardoned. And now I heard the Lord say, Who shall be my messenger? Who is to go on this errand of ours? And I said, I am here at thy command; make me thy messenger.
9 Go then, said he, and give a message to this people of mine: Listen as you will, but ever without understanding; watch all, and nothing perceive!
10 Thy office is to dull the hearts of this people of mine, deaden their ears, dazzle their eyes, so that they cannot see with those eyes, hear with those ears, understand with that heart, and turn back to me, and win healing.[3]
11 For how long, Lord? I asked. And he said, Till the cities are left unpeopled, and the houses untenanted, and the whole land a wilderness.
12 The Lord will send its people into exile far away; wider, ever wider
13 desolation must spread over it. Though a tenth of their number remain, it is but empty show,[4] like leafage of terebinth or oak that needs pruning; only a remnant of it will be left, the true stock of holiness.

---

[1] The Hebrew text here is ambiguous, and may mean that the seraphim veiled their own faces and their own feet (cf. Ez. 1.11), but the sense given above is that of the Latin version.

[2] 'I must needs keep silence'; in the Hebrew text, 'I am lost!'; cf. Ex. 33.20.

[3] The effect of prophecy or preaching, if it is met by an impenitent attitude, is to put the hearer in a worse frame of mind than ever, since the message has become staled by repetition. Cf. Mt. 13.14; where, however, our Lord quotes the prophecy in a milder form.

[4] 'It is but empty show'; in the Hebrew text, 'it will once again be destroyed.'

CHAPTER SEVEN

AFTERWARDS, in the reign of Achaz, whose father was Ozias's son Joathan, an attack was made upon Jerusalem by Rasin, king of Syria, and Phacee, son of Romelia, king of Israel. As it proved, they were not
2 strong enough to take it; but when the news reached David's palace that Syria had gained a footing in Ephraim, the hearts of Achaz and his people
3 trembled like forest trees before the wind. Then it was that the Lord said to Isaias, Take with thee thy son, Jashub the Survivor,[1] and go out to the end of the aqueduct that feeds the upper pool in the Fuller's Ground.
4 There thou wilt meet Achaz, and this shall be thy message to him, Shew a calm front, do not be afraid. Must thy heart fail thee because Rasin king of Syria and the son of Romelia are thy sworn enemies? What is either of
5 them but the smouldering stump of a fire-brand? What if Syria, what if
6 Ephraim and the son of Romelia are plotting to do thee an injury? They think to invade Juda and strike terror into it, so that they can bring it into
7 their power, and set up the son of Tabeel as its ruler; a vain errand, the
8 Lord says; it shall not be. As surely as Damascus rules Syria,[2] and Rasin rules Damascus, within sixty-five years Ephraim will be a people no
9 longer. As surely as Samaria rules Ephraim, and the son of Romelia rules Samaria, if you lose courage, your cause is lost.
10   The Lord sent, besides, this message to Achaz, Ask the Lord thy God to give thee a sign, in the depths beneath thee, or in the height above thee.
12 But Achaz said, Nay, I will not ask for a sign; I will not put the Lord to
13 the test. Why then, said Isaias, listen to me, you that are of David's race. Cannot you be content with trying the patience of men? Must you try my
14 God's patience too? Sign you ask none, but sign the Lord will give you. Maid shall be brought to bed of a son,[3] that shall be called Emmanuel.
15 On butter and honey shall be his thriving, till he is of age to know good
16 from harm;[4] already, before he can tell this from that, king they shall have none, the two kingdoms that are thy rivals.

---

[1] The full name of the prophet's son would seem to have been Shearjashub, 'a remnant shall return' (10.22).

[2] The words 'as surely as' are not expressed in the original; but it seems very difficult to explain the context if they are not understood.

[3] 'Maid shall be brought to bed'; cf. Mt. 1.23. The Hebrew text, but not the Greek, would admit 'a maid' instead of 'the maid.' In the Hebrew text, the word translated 'virgin' should perhaps be 'maiden,' since it refers rather to a time than to a state of life; but in view of the event, we cannot doubt that this prophecy looks forward to the Virgin Birth. No very successful attempt has been made to explain its relevance to contemporary happenings.

[4] Probably, both here and in verse 22 below, butter and honey signify not prosperity, but privation, the arable lands of Judaea having been turned into pasture.

17 As for thee, and for thy people, and for thy father's house, the Lord
means to bring upon thee such days of trouble as have not been seen since
18 Ephraim parted from Juda, with the coming of the king of Assyria. Days
when the Lord will whistle up those plagues of his, yonder flies that hatch
by the last rivers of Egypt; yonder bees, that hive in the land of Assur.
19 Invading swarms, that settle even upon mountain gully and rock cavern;
20 thicket is none, nor underground pit shall be safe from them. Hard times,
when the Lord will be hiring mercenaries from beyond Euphrates, the
king of Assyria's men, and will leave you quite bare, hair of head and legs
21 shaved close with this hired razor of his, and the beard too! Hard times,
22 when one heifer and a pair of sheep are all the stock a man has; milk
plentiful, so that he has butter to eat; of butter and honey the survivors
23 will have no lack; but where once a thousand vines grew, each worth a
24 silver piece, all will be thorns and brushwood. Covert of thorns and
25 brushwood, where men go armed with bow and arrows; only the hill-
sides, that have felt the hoe, shall be free from the terrors of the covert,
and these the cattle shall graze, the sheep trample under foot.

CHAPTER EIGHT

THEN the Lord said to me, Take a great scroll, and write on it, in thy
human penmanship,[1] the words, Spoiler, haste; there's plunder afoot.
2 I took care to have men of credit for my witnesses, the priest Urias and
3 Zacharias, son of Barachias. Afterwards, when the prophetess conceived
and bore me a son, the Lord said to me, Call him by this name, Spoiler,
4 haste; there's plunder afoot. This boy will not have learned to use the
words Father and Mother, before the king of Assyria comes to carry off
the wealth of Damascus, the spoils of Samaria.
5 And the Lord went on to say to me, This people of mine has cut itself
off from the gently-flowing waters of Siloe, to welcome Rasin and the son
7 of Romelia instead;[2] and now the Lord will bring the waters of Euphrates
upon it, in full flood; I mean the king of the Assyrians, in all his greatness.
This flood will fill up all the channels of the river, overflow all its banks,

---

[1] Literally, 'the pen of a man.' This has often been translated 'with an ordinary
pen' or 'in the common speech of the country,' but it is difficult to see why either
direction should be necessary. In Deut. 3.11 'the cubit of a man' is evidently a
measurement taken from the arm of an ordinary man, not from that of a giant.
[2] The people of Juda are blamed for cutting themselves off from the holy
city (here represented by the pool of Siloe, its water-supply), and permitting
the son of Romelia to enter their country (II Par. 28.6). They will be punished
by a flood, that is, the invasion of Juda by Sennacherib (IV Kg. 18); it will
drown them only up to the neck, because Jerusalem will remain unconquered.

8 till it pours over Juda, overwhelming her and reaching up to her very
neck. Wings spread out wide, till they cover the whole breadth of thy own
land, Emmanuel, the God who is with us!

9   Muster, then, you peoples, to your own overthrow; obey the call, dis-
10 tant lands, in vain; arm yourselves in vain! All your scheming baffled,
11 all your boasts belied; God is with us![1] Strict warning the Lord has given
12 me, I must not fall in with the fashion of Israel; Not thine to go about
crying Treason; this people is for ever crying treason.[2] Not for thee and
13 thine to go in fear, dismayed like these others; enthrone the Lord of
14 hosts above all else, him you must fear, of him stand in awe. Let the hour
of peril consecrate you to him; for the rest, both in Israel and in Juda, it
will be a stone to trip men's feet, a boulder that catches them unawares.[3]
15 A trap, a fine snare, for the citizens of Jerusalem; and there are many of
them that will stumble, and fall, and bruise themselves, caught in its
16 meshes. (Guard close the prophetic record, you that are my disciples,
17 put a seal on these instructions I give you. What though the Lord hide
his face from the men of Israel? To him will I look, and wait patiently
18 for him; here stand I, and these children[4] the Lord has given me, a warn-
19 ing sent to Israel by the Lord of hosts, a beacon-light from Sion. Men
will bid you consult wizard and diviner, that talk in ghostly voices over
their enchantments; Who doubts God will send his own people answer,
20 an oracle from the dead to the living? By these instructions rather abide,
this record of prophecy; who follows other inspiration, shall not see the
dawn.)
21 . As for the invader,[5] he shall meet with disaster, and then famine.
Famine-stricken, he will turn with curses against his king, his god; first
22 looking upwards and then to earth, to find nothing but distress and dark-

---

[1] *vv.* 9, 10. These verses are evidently addressed to the defeated forces of
Sennacherib.

[2] The Latin (though not the Hebrew text) would also yield the sense 'it is
rather the (alarmist) language of these people themselves that should be
accounted treason.'

[3] It is commonly assumed that Almighty God himself will be a stone, a
boulder, &c.; but the sense of this is not evident, and there is no reason, either
in the Latin or in the Hebrew, why the subject of the verb should not be
neuter. This national crisis will be a means of sanctification to Isaias and his
disciples; others, taken unawares by it, will involve themselves in ruin (*e.g.*,
by taking flight and falling into the hands of the Assyrians).

[4] The word 'children' may be taken literally (cf. 7.3 and 8.3 above); St
Jerome, however, understands it of the prophet's disciples.

[5] Literally, 'he will go through it' (the land). Verses 21, 22 probably relate
to the position of Sennacherib after his defeat (IV Kg. 19.35), the prophet's
thought having gone back to verse 8 above. The invasion is there described as
a spreading out of wings, and here, in verse 22, Sennacherib is warned that he
will not be able to 'fly away' from his calamity.

ness, ruin and want, with night pressing hard upon him; from his calamity there is no escaping.

CHAPTER NINE

L AND of Zabulon and Nephthali, its burden at first how lightly borne! but the time came when affliction weighed heavily on it, Galilee,
2 where the Gentiles dwell west of Jordan.[1] And now the people that went about in darkness has seen a great light; for men abiding in a land where
3 death overshadowed them, light has dawned. Their number thou didst increase, but gavest them no joy of it;[2] now, they shall rejoice in thy presence, as men rejoice when the harvest is in, as men triumph when victory is won, and booty taken, and they fall to dividing up the spoils.
4 Yoke that fixed the burden, shaft that galled the shoulder, rod of the
5 tyrant, all lie broken now, as they did long ago, when Madian fell. All the trophies of the old tumultuous forays,[3] all the panoply stained with blood,
6 will be burnt up now, will go to feed the flames. For our sakes a child is born, to our race a son is given, whose shoulder will bear the sceptre of princely power. What name shall be given him? Peerless among counsellors, the mighty God, Father of the world to come, the Prince of peace.
7 Ever wider shall his dominion spread, endlessly at peace; he will sit on David's kingly throne, to give it lasting foundations of justice and right; so tenderly he loves us, the Lord of hosts.
8 Meanwhile, the Lord has issued his sentence against Jacob, his writ is
9 out against Israel: Ephraim will soon know of it, all the citizens of
10 Samaria. Fools, that boast in the pride of their hearts: The brick houses have fallen, we must build them up in stone; the sycamores have been cut
11 down, we must plant cedars instead! The Lord will make Rasin's rivals more powerful than Rasin himself;[4] all the enemies of Israel he will set
12 astir, Syria on the East, and the Philistines in the south, that will fall upon him wide-mouthed. And even so the Lord's anger is not appeased;

---

[1] In the Hebrew text, this is given as verse 23 of ch. 8, and connected with verse 22 by the words, 'Yet that ruin shall not be like the (former) straits.' But the transition here to Messianic rejoicing, and back again to lamentation in verse 8, perhaps represents a shifting current of prophetic inspiration, rather than any connexion of thought; a principle which deserves to be remembered all through the writings of the prophets. Cf. Mt. 4.15.

[2] The negative here is of doubtful authority in the Hebrew.

[3] Literally, 'every violent foray accompanied by tumult.' The Hebrew text is generally understood as meaning 'the boots whose tramping was so loud.'

[4] The sense here is very confused, and some think the word 'Rasin' has crept in by error; in which case the original meaning was, that Israel's own enemies were exalted above him. As the text stands, the rivals of Rasin will be the Assyrians (IV Kg. 16.9).

13 his hand threatens us still. Alas for the people that will not come back to
God, who chastens it; that leaves the Lord of hosts unregarded as ever!
14   And now, in one day, the Lord will cut off from Israel both head and
15 tail, both pliant reed and stubborn bough.[1] (What is the head, but the
senator that holds his head so high? What is the tail, but the prophet that
16 gives lying assurances?) False guides, that promised all was well; fools
17 that gave them credence, to their own undoing! Pride in their warriors
the Lord has none, pity for orphan and widow has none; all are false and
worthless, no mouth but talks presumptuously. Even so the Lord's anger
18 is not appeased, his hand threatens us still. Our wickedness is like a raging
fire, that will devour brushwood and thornbush, then set light to the
forest's tangled boughs; see how proudly yonder column of smoke whirls
19 upward! Fiery vengeance of the Lord of hosts, that ravages countryside
20 and devours citizen! Brother shews brother no mercy; turn he to the right,
nought but famine is there; eat he what comes to his left hand, he is yet
hungry, so that at last he will fall on his own flesh and blood,[2] Manasses
on Ephraim and Ephraim on Manasses, and both will be banded together
21 against Juda. And even so the Lord's anger is not appeased; his hand
threatens us still.

CHAPTER TEN

O UT upon you, that enact ill decrees, and draw up instruments of
2   wrong; suppress the claims of the poor, and refuse redress to humble
3 folk; the widow your spoil, the orphan your prey! What shifts will you be
put to, when the day of reckoning comes, when the ruin that is still distant overtakes you? With whom take refuge, where hide away your
4 treasures? Yours to crouch down in chains, or fall among the massacred.
And even so the Lord's wrath is not appeased, his hand threatens us still.
5   Woe, too, upon the Assyrian! What is he but the rod that executes my
6 vengeance, the instrument of my displeasure? I have sent him to punish
one nation that has proved false to me; against one defiant people he holds
my warrant; let him prey on it as he will, carry off what spoils he will,
7 trample it like the mire in the streets. Not such are his own thoughts, not

---

[1] 'Pliant reed and stubborn bough'; literally, 'him who bends down and him
who holds back.' The Hebrew text has, 'both the palm-branch and the reed,'
which is commonly understood as meaning 'both high and low,' but seems
to be interpreted by the Latin translator as meaning 'both the stubborn (senator) and the pliant (prophet),' so as to correspond with the 'head' and the
'tail,' as explained in verse 15.
[2] Literally, 'the flesh of his own arm,' but the context seems to shew that
the words are used metaphorically.

such the dreams he cherishes; he dreams of extermination, of realm after
8 realm dispeopled. Are not my chieftains, he says, as good as kings, every
9 one of them? What difference between Charcamis and Calano, between
10 Arphad and Emath, between Damascus and Samaria? I have had my
way with the kingdoms that worship false gods; shall it not be the same
11 with the images they worship at Jerusalem and Samaria? May I not treat
Jerusalem and her images as I treated Samaria and her false gods? [1]
12   Wait we, till the Lord has carried out all his designs upon mount Sion
and Jerusalem. Then he means to reckon with the boastful ambition of
13 Sennacherib, with the proud glance of those scornful eyes. My own
strength (the king says to himself) has done all this, my own wisdom has
planned it; I have removed the frontiers of nations, I have robbed princes
of their treasure, with a strong hand I have pulled down rulers from their
14 thrones. Mighty peoples, and my hand closed over them like a nest; I
gathered up a whole world, as a man gathers up eggs that lie abandoned;
15 no flapping of wings, no angry screech to forbid me. Poor fool, can axe
set itself up against woodman, saw defy carpenter? Shall the rod turn on
him who wields it, the staff, that is but wood, try conclusions with a living
man?
16   What says our Master, the Lord of hosts? He will send a wasting sickness into that gorged frame; beneath that pride a living firebrand shall
17 burn, burn deep. He who is our light will turn into a fire, the Holy One
of Israel will be a flame, that will burn up suddenly; in one day those
18 thorn-bushes, that dry brushwood shall be consumed. Like a proud
forest, or a garden plot, he shall be eaten up, body and soul; see where he
19 flies in terror! Of all the trees in that forest so few shall be left, a child
20 might count them. And when that day comes, the remnant of Israel,
the survivors of Jacob's line, will learn to trust, not in the staff that turns
rod to smite them,[2] but in the Lord, the Holy One of Israel; who claims
21 their loyalty but he? A remnant will turn back, only a remnant of Jacob,
22 to God, the Mighty One. Countless though Israel be as the sea sand, only
a remnant of it will return; there must be a sharp reckoning first, before
23 we are restored, abundantly, to his favour.[3] Short and sharp is the

[1] *vv.* 10, 11. Cf. IV Kg. 18.34, 35. Sennacherib is represented as supposing
that the God of Israel would have images like the gods of the neighbouring
countries; in calling these 'false gods,' he is using the prophet's language, not
his own.
[2] Literally, 'in him who smites them.' The sense is, that Achaz, instead of
trusting in God, had put his trust in the king of Assyria to help him against
his own neighbours (IV Kg. 16.7), and this staff on which he had leaned was
to turn into a rod which would chastise him.
[3] This is the general sense of the Hebrew text, which seems to mean, 'there
is (to be) a decisive bringing-to-an-end, which will produce an overflow of

reckoning the Lord, the God of hosts, will make, with the whole world for the scene of it.

24   Here, then, is a message for you from the Lord, the God of hosts: Never lose heart, men of Sion, my own people, before the Assyrian, rod though he have to smite thee, staff to chastise thee, when thou meetest him on
25 the road to Egypt. Wait for a little, for a short moment wait, and my
26 angry vengeance for his ill doings shall find full scope. The Lord of hosts will bring the lash down upon him, as he did once on Madian at the rock Oreb; by the sea-shore, on the road to Egypt, his rod will be uplifted.
27 And with that, thy shoulder will be eased of the burden, the yoke will fall from thy neck, yoke that has gone rotten for want of oil.[1]
28   See where he enters Aiath, crosses to Magron, halts his baggage-train
29 at Machmas! Already the pass lies behind them; Geba will be theirs by nightfall. In Rama; what terror! Saul's own city of Gabaa is in flight.
30 Cry aloud, maidens of Gallim, and listen, Laisa, to the cry; woe upon
31 thee, poor Anathoth! Medemena stands empty; now, men of Gabim, you
32 need courage! Daylight still! Why, he will make his halt at Nobe, threaten the mountain where queen Sion stands, the very hill of Jerusalem!
33   Then, as we look, our Master, the Lord of hosts, will spread terror among them, and break them like earthenware.[2] Yield greatness, and
34 pride topple; axe-iron for yonder tangled forest, the strength of Lebanon outmatched!

CHAPTER ELEVEN

    FROM the stock of Jesse a scion shall burgeon yet; out of his roots a
2   flower shall spring. One shall be born, on whom the spirit of the Lord will rest; a spirit wise and discerning, a spirit prudent and strong, a spirit

---

rightness of heart'; that is, God will leave in Juda a remnant that is pleasing to himself, only at the price of destroying many other lives first. The Latin version means literally, 'An abbreviated consummation will overflow with rightness of heart'—perhaps in the sense given above, but not necessarily. The Septuagint Greek has, '(God is) consummating and cutting short his word (that is, his action upon the world) in rightness of heart (or perhaps, in justice).' This Greek version is the basis of the quotation which St Paul makes in Rom. 9.27.

[1] Literally, 'from the face of oil.' If the text is sound, it seems necessary to interpret the phrase here as meaning 'away from,' 'deprived of' oil, not in its usual sense, 'as the result of.'

[2] Literally, 'break an earthen vessel in (an atmosphere of) terror.' Cf. Ps. 2.9. The Hebrew text is generally understood as meaning 'lops off branches terribly.'

3 of knowledge and of piety,[1] and ever fear of the Lord shall fill his heart. Not his to judge by appearances, listen to rumours when he makes award;
4 here is judgement will give the poor redress, here is award will right the wrongs of the defenceless. Word of him shall smite the earth like a rod,
5 breath of him destroy the ill-doer; love of right shall be the baldric he
6 wears, faithfulness the strength that girds him. Wolf shall live at peace with lamb, leopard take its ease with kid; calf and lion and sheep in one
7 dwelling-place, with a little child to herd them! Cattle and bears all at pasture, their young ones lying down together, lion eating straw like ox;
8 child new-weaned, fresh from its mother's arms, playing by asp's hole,
9 putting hand in viper's den! All over this mountain, my sanctuary, no hurt shall be done, no life taken. Deep as the waters that hide the sea-floor, knowledge of the Lord overspreading the world!
10 There he stands, fresh root from Jesse's stem, signal beckoning to the peoples all around; the Gentiles will come to pay their homage, where he
11 rests in glory.[2] Then, once again, the Lord's hand at work! From Assyria, from Egypt, Pathros and Ethiopia, from Elam and Sennaar, from Emath, from the islands out at sea, his people, a scattered remnant, shall return.
12 High lifted, for a world to see it, the standard that shall call Israel home,
13 gather in the exiled sons of Juda from the four corners of the earth. Gone, Ephraim's envious looks, vanished away Juda's enemies; Ephraim shall
14 hate Juda, Juda harry Ephraim, no more. Together they will sweep down on Philistia's neck, there by the western sea; plunder the children of the east, Edom and Moab in their grasp, the sons of Ammon pliant to their
15 will. And the Lord will make a desert out of the tongue of sea that flanks Egypt; with the blast of his breath he will threaten Euphrates, dividing
16 it into seven streams, that a man can cross dry-shod. And so the remnant of my people which is left among the Assyrians will find a path made for it, as a path was made for it when it came up out of Egypt, long ago.

CHAPTER TWELVE

ANGRY with me, Lord? thou wilt say, when that day comes; ay, thou wast angry with me, but now, praised be thy name, the storm has
2 passed; all is consolation. God is here to deliver me; I will go forward confidently, and not be afraid; source of my strength, theme of my praise,
3 the Lord has made himself my protector.[3] So, rejoicing, you shall drink

---

[1] The Hebrew text does not make any mention of the gift of piety; perhaps through a corruption, it seems to introduce 'fear of the Lord' twice over.

[2] 'Where he rests in glory'; the Latin understands this of resting in the tomb, but this is not suggested by the Hebrew text.

[3] The second half of this verse is a quotation from Ex. 15.2; cf. 11.16 above.

4 deep from the fountain of deliverance; singing, when that day comes,
  Praise the Lord, and call upon his name, tell the story of his doings among
  all the nations, keep the majesty of his name in grateful remembrance.
5 Sing in honour of the great deeds the Lord has done, make them known
6 for all the world to hear. Cry aloud in praise, people of Sion; great is the
  Holy One of Israel, that dwells among you.

CHAPTER THIRTEEN

THE burden [1] that awaits Babylon, as it was revealed to Isaias, son of
  Amos.
2   A signal raised amid the shadow of the mountain, voices lifted, and a
  waving of hands; all is ready for the captains to march in through the city
3 gates. These are my chosen warriors, doing my bidding; my champions,
  whom I have summoned to execute my vengeance; they boast of my
4 renown. The hills echo with the voices of a multitude, as if a host had
  gathered; voices of assembled kings, of whole peoples mustered there;
5 the Lord of hosts is marshalling his troops for battle. They come from
  far away, from the most distant region under heaven; the Lord is angry,
  and these are the instruments of his vengeance, to lay a whole world
6 waste. Cry aloud, for the day of the Lord is coming; his the dominion,
7 his the doom. No hand now but will hang useless, no heart but will be
8 fainting with dismay; tortures and pangs will seize them, throes as of
  a woman in travail; each man looks at his neighbour in bewilderment,
  their faces ashy pale.[2]
9   Yes, the day of the Lord is coming, pitiless, full of vengeance and bitter
  retribution, ready to turn earth into a wilderness, ridding it of its sinful
10 brood. The stars of heaven, its glittering constellations, will shed no ray;
11 sunrise will be darkness, and the moon refuse her light. I will punish the
  world's guilt, and tax the wicked with their misdoings, stilling the rebel's
12 pride, crushing the haughtiness of tyrants, till a man is a rarer sight than
13 gold, and a slave cannot be bought with all the treasure of Ophir. So
  terribly will I shake the heavens, and move earth from its place, to shew
  that the Lord of hosts will be patient no longer, and the hour of his bitter
14 vengeance has come. Men will take to flight as deer or sheep would,
  with none to marshal them, each turning towards his own home, seeking

---

[1] The word in the Hebrew text which is translated 'burden,' here and in
the following chapters, is understood by some as meaning 'utterance,' 'oracle.'
[2] Literally, 'burnt up'; in the Hebrew text, 'faces of flame.' This is understood by many commentators as meaning 'red with excitement,' but St. Jerome
interprets it as pallor.

15 refuge in his own country. Whoever is found left behind will be slain,
16 and those who come back will fall at the sword's point; their children
   will be dashed to pieces before their eyes, their houses plundered, their
   wives ravished.
17   With such an enemy I mean to embroil them; the Medians, who reck
18 nothing of silver, who are not to be tempted with gold; they will make
   young boys a target for their arrows, have no pity for pregnant mothers,
19 no kindly glance for children. So Babylon, the pride of many nations,
   glory and boast of the Chaldeans, will go the way of Sodom and Gomor-
20 rha, cities which the Lord overthrew. It shall remain forever uninhabited;
   generation after generation will pass, but it will not be founded again;
   even the Arabs will not pitch their tents, wandering shepherds will not
21 find a lodging there. Wild beasts will make their lairs in it, its houses will
22 be tenanted by serpents; ostriches will nest there, and satyrs dance; the
   owls will hoot to one another in its palaces, birds of ill omen in its temples
   of delight.[1]

CHAPTER FOURTEEN

THE day of her doom is close at hand, not long the respite that will be
granted her.
   And now the Lord will have pity on Jacob; on the sons of Israel, his
chosen people still. On their own lands they shall live undisturbed, whose
new inhabitants will make common cause with them, and throw in their
2 lot with Jacob's race. Alien peoples will take them by the hand, to escort
   them back to their home; content now to be Israel's servants and hand-
3 maidens, the captors captive, the oppressors tributary now. When that
   time comes, when the Lord gives thee respite from all the hardship and
4 uneasiness and drudgery of old days, it will be thy turn to have thy say
   against the king of Babylon. Can it be (thou wilt say) that the tyranny is
5 over, the exactions at an end? The Lord has broken the staff in the hands
6 of the wicked, the rod that oppressed us; the rod whose mortal stroke
   once fell on the peoples so angrily, tamed the nations so cruelly, perse-
7 cuted, and would not spare. The whole earth, now, sinks back into ease;
8 listen to its cry of rejoicing! The very fir-trees and the cedars of Lebanon
   triumph over thee; no woodman comes near us any longer, since thou
9 wast laid to rest. The shadow world beneath is astir with preparation
   for thy coming; wakes up its giants to greet thee. The great ones of the

---

[1] *vv.* 21, 22. The creatures here mentioned cannot be certainly identified;
according to some, the 'wild beasts' are wild cats; the 'serpents,' 'owls' and
'birds of ill-omen' may also be jackals, hyenas, wolves, &c. The 'satyrs' are
perhaps wild goats.

world, that ruled the nations, rise up from the thrones where they sit,
10 hailing thee with a single voice, Thou too in the same case as we, thou
11 too like us! All thy pride sunk down into the world beneath, and there
thy corpse lies, with the moth for its shroud, worms for its cerecloth.
12 What, fallen from heaven, thou Lucifer, that once didst herald the
dawn? Prostrate on the earth, that didst once bring nations to their knees?
13 I will scale the heavens (such was thy thought) ; I will set my throne higher
than God's stars, take my seat at his own trysting-place, at the meeting of
14 the northern hills ; [1] I will soar above the level of the clouds, the rival of
15 the most High. Thine, instead, to be dragged down into the world
16 beneath, into the heart of the abyss. Who that sees thee there, but will
peer down at thee and read thy story: Can this be the man who once
17 shook the world, and made thrones totter ; who turned earth into a desert,
18 its cities into ruins ; never granted prisoner release? For those others,
19 honourable burial, each in his own palace ; thee the grave itself rejects,
like a withered root, like a thing unclean. Rots thy corpse unrecognized,
beneath yonder coverlet of men slain, that went down to the deep pit
20 together ; no fellowship hast thou with those others, no share in their
sepulture, thou who didst lead thy country to ruin, thou, who didst bring
destruction on thy people. The posterity of the wicked shall be nameless
21 for ever ; for the guilt they have inherited, his sons too must be slain,
they must not live to make the land their own, and people the world with
22 cities. A message from the Lord of hosts : Now I mean to take arms against
23 them, to destroy Babylon name and fame, root and branch. I will make
the place over to the hedge-hog,[2] turn it into standing pools ; I will sweep
it clean, the Lord of hosts says, sweep it clean away.
24 And now the Lord of hosts has taken an oath, his doom shall be exe-
25 cuted, his design shall stand : In this my own land I will break the power
of Assyria,[3] upon these hills I will trample him under foot. Gone his yoke ;
26 there shall be no more shouldering his burden ; such purpose I have for
27 the world's ordering ; my hand once lifted, all the nations must bow. The
Lord's decree, who shall annul it? The Lord's oath, who shall set it aside?

---

[1] Literally, 'on the hill of the covenant, on the northern slopes.' This may
have some reference to the situation of Jerusalem (cf. Ps. 47.2, and note there) ;
but it is more generally understood by modern scholars as a reference by the
King of Babylon to those northern hills upon which, according to his own
mythology, the gods were supposed to meet.

[2] The word here translated 'hedge-hog' is found nowhere else, and some
think it is the name of a bird, perhaps the bittern.

[3] *vv.* 24–32. Hitherto this chapter, like the last, has dealt with the destruction
of Babylon by the Medes, about two centuries after Isaias' own time. Here
the prophecy abruptly returns to contemporary events ; the destruction of the
Assyrians when they invaded Juda, and the ill fortune which nevertheless
awaits the neighbouring country of the Philistines.

28   And in the year of king Achaz's death, a fresh burden was imposed:
29   Too soon, Philistia, thou wouldst make public holiday over the breaking
of the rod that smote thee. The serpent has gone, but he has left a basilisk
30   stock behind him; a race that can catch birds on the wing. The poorest
of my pensioners will find nourishment, and rest securely; thee I will
destroy with famine root and branch, slay all the remnant that is left in
31   thee. All thy gates, now, must echo with lament, all thy cities ring with
cries; all Philistia swoons away. From the north a smoke comes ever
nearer, signal of an army none may escape.
32   Our news when the world asks, what message? Tell them Sion never
rested in the Lord so surely; here be friendless folk that trust in him.

CHAPTER FIFTEEN

WHAT burden for Moab? Ar Moab has fallen in a night, remembered no more; Moab's battlements have fallen in a night, remem-
2   bered no more! Prince [1] and people of Dibon have gone up to the hill-
shrines to lament; on Nabo and on Medaba, Moab cries aloud, every
3   head cropped, every beard shaved in mourning. In the streets, men walk
girded with sackcloth; housetop and square echo with loud crying, that
4   breaks into tears. The dirge goes up from Hesebon and Eleale, so loud
that Jasa hears it; well may the warriors of Moab cry out; the very soul
of Moab utters a cry.
5   My heart laments for Moab, once ringed with walled cities as far as
Segor; Segor that now moans like a full-grown heifer.[2] There is weeping
on the slopes of Luith; along the Oronaim road they wail aloud for
6   misery. The waters of Nemrim will turn into desert; old grass has
withered, new grass has failed, and their banks are green no more.
7   Heavy their reckoning, to match the abundance of their riches; a nation
8   in exile, carried away to the Vale of Willows.[3] A cry goes up all about
the frontiers of Moab; Gallim echoes the lament, and the well of Elim
9   hears the sound of it. Dibon's waters already swollen with blood; and

---

[1] 'Prince'; literally, 'the house,' unless the word conceals a proper name,
but it seems likely that the text here is corrupt.

[2] Literally, in the Latin, 'My heart laments for Moab; its bars reach as far
as Segor, a calf of three years old.' Some think the word 'bars' should be 'fugitives,' by a different understanding of the Hebrew text, and it is possible that
the 'calf of three years old' conceals a proper name.

[3] In the Hebrew text, the first half of this verse is generally understood to
mean 'What remains of their abundance, their store,' and it is this which is
carried away to the 'Vale of Willows' in an effort to save it. St Jerome understands that the inhabitants themselves are carried away to the 'Vale of Willows,' possibly with a reference to Ps. 136.2.

still for Dibon I have perils in store, lions to meet the fugitives, the remnant that is left in the land of Moab.[1]

CHAPTER SIXTEEN

SEND forth (O Lord) a lamb to be ruler of the land,[2] from Petra in the
2 desert to the hill where queen Sion reigns. There they will be, the
women-folk of Moab, waiting at the ford of Arnon, like fluttered birds,
3 fledglings that have taken wing from the nest; there are plans to be
made, deliberations to be held, Shelter us, like the shadow, dark as night,
that gives shelter at noonday; hide these fugitives of ours, do not betray
4 them in their wanderings; let them dwell as exiles in your land; poor
Moab,[3] give it sanctuary from threat of the invader! And all the while,
the dust of armies has died down, the guilty wretch has met his end;
5 vanished and gone, who trampled the world under foot! Mercy and
faithfulness return; a throne set up in David's dwelling-place, for a judge
that loves right and gives redress speedily!
6   The boasting of Moab has long been in our ears, as it was ever
boastful; proud, and scornful, and quick to take offence, with dreams
7 that came to nothing. So, from one end of Moab to the other, there is
a dirge, everywhere a dirge; for yonder folk, that live content behind
8 walls of hardened brick, tidings of ruin.[4] The fields about Hesebon
lie deserted; alien chieftains have rooted up the vineyard of Sabama,
whose shoots once reached as far as Jazer, strayed through the wilder-
9 ness;[5] forlorn, now, its tendrils, wandering overseas. I will weep,
then, as Jazer weeps, for the vineyard of Sabama, water Hesebon

---

[1] The reference to fresh troubles soon to arise may be compared with 14.29
above, though it is not certain that the events dealt with in the two passages
are contemporary.

[2] The word 'Lord' is lacking in the Hebrew text, and the verb 'send' is in
the plural; many modern scholars omit the word 'be' and think the allusion
is to the old tribute of lambs paid to Samaria. But the prophet is interested in
Juda rather than in Israel, and Petra was in Edom, not in Moab. There may be
corruption in the text; the Septuagint Greek has 'I will send forth as it were
creeping things on the land.' For the whole of this chapter, cf. Jer. 48.29–37.

[3] The word Moab has the appearance of a vocative in the Latin; but the
Hebrew idiom makes it probable that the refugees are coming out of Moab,
not going into it, and the context implies as much.

[4] The Hebrew text, in the second half of this verse, is usually interpreted
as meaning, 'You will lament, all stricken, for the raisin-cakes (or perhaps,
the foundations) of Cir-chareset.'

[5] According to the Hebrew text, the end of this verse may also be rendered,
'its tendrils spread out, they crossed the seas,' perhaps with the implication
that the Moabite wine was good enough for export.

and Eleale with my tears. That thy vineyard, thy vintage-time should
10 be disturbed by the cry of trampling armies! All joy, all triumph gone
from that land of thine, fruitful as Carmel; no mirth, no gaiety left;
the presses shall be trampled, but not by the labourers we knew; forgotten, now, the cry that used to go up when they trod the grapes.
11 For Moab, my inmost being thrills like a harp's strings; my heart
12 goes out to those brick-walled cities of hers. What shift will she make,
when all goes ill with her on the heights? Prayer of hers, recourse to
those shrines of hers, shall nothing avail her?
14 Such was the word the Lord spoke to Moab, long since, and now
he declares his purpose: In three years, by the time a labourer's contract
is out, Moab, so populous now, shall be shorn of her glory; shall be
left small and weak, a thriving nation no longer.

CHAPTER SEVENTEEN

WHAT burden for Damascus? Damascus, too, shall cease to be a
2 city, shall become a heap of stones in ruin: the cities of Aroer will
3 lie, now, abandoned to flocks, that take their ease undisturbed. When
Ephraim is robbed of her defences, Damascus too will be robbed of
her place among the kingdoms, and what is left of Syria will enjoy no
more renown than Israel itself; such is her doom from the Lord of hosts.
4 The renown of Jacob, little enough will it be when that day comes;
5 nothing but skin and bone will be left. Scanty as the corn a man gathers
in his arm when he picks up what is left after the harvest, some gleaner
6 in the valley of Rephaim. Such is all the crop his race will yield; a
cluster here and there, a few olives still to be shaken off, two or three
at the end of a branch, four or five on the top branch of all; that is what
7 the Lord, the God of Israel, has decreed. Then at last helpless man will
8 turn to his Maker, will look towards the Holy One of Israel. He will
turn no longer towards altars of his own designing, have eyes no longer
9 for pillar and shrine of his own fashioning. The cities he had fortified
will be abandoned then, as ploughs and crops [1] were abandoned when
10 Israel itself was the invader, and thou shalt be left forlorn. Thou didst
forget the God who delivered thee, and gavest no thought to thy strong
protector; thou art like one who plants hopefully enough, but all the
11 while is putting in bastard shoots. Wild grapes they were when thou
didst plant them, and soon this planting of thine will begin to bud;

---

[1] The meaning of the words in the Hebrew text is uncertain, and many
modern scholars follow the Septuagint Greek, which has 'the Amorrhites and
the Hevites'—that is, the old inhabitants of Chanaan.

and now, when the time comes to enjoy it, here is all thy harvest lost to thee, and bitterly thou dost repine.[1]

12 Doom goes with it, this swollen multitude of nations, like the swollen seas that go roaring past; like the roar of those swollen seas is the stir
13 of such a throng. Nations roaring with the roar of waters in full flood; and then, God will rebuke him, and in a moment he is far away, swept like the dust when a wind blows on the hills, or the whirl of leaves
14 before the storm. Night comes, and there is terror all around; day breaks, and it is seen no more. Such the invader's doom, so evermore shall they speed, that come to despoil us.[2]

CHAPTER EIGHTEEN

WOE to the land that has the whirring of wings for its music, there
2 beyond the Brook of Egypt! Lightly they come and go, skiffs of papyrus reed that carry your ambassadors to the sea-coast! Ay, speed on your errand, but to a people far away, sundered from you by leagues of travel, dreaded people at the end of the earth, race that bears a tyrant's yoke, in a land that is all rivers like your own.[3]

3 All you peoples of the world, all you that dwell on earth, wait till you see the signal raised on the mountains, till you hear the trumpet
4 sound. Such warning the Lord has given me: I will keep silent and watch, here in my dwelling-place, as still as the bright sunshine of
5 noon-day, or the haze that comes with the dew in harvest time. What a blossoming was here before the time of harvest, how fully formed the unripe buds! But its boughs shall be cut back with the pruning-
6 knife, its straying tendrils shall be torn off and thrown away. All alike will be left a prey to the mountain birds, and the beasts that roam

---

[1] *vv.* 10, 11. The text here is difficult, and variously explained; but all are agreed on the general meaning, which is, that the Ten Tribes, in adopting the worship of false gods, were like men who are deceived, until it is too late, about the quality of the plants they put into the ground.

[2] *vv.* 12–14. These verses are generally interpreted as a doom pronounced against the Assyrians, as if the subject were abruptly changed. But it is possible that it is Israel who will be 'rebuked' in verse 13, and will disappear in verse 14, with the Assyrians as the cause of his downfall.

[3] *vv.* 1, 2. Almost every word in these two verses is interpreted by scholars in a variety of ways; nor is there any agreement as to the bearing of what is said. The race referred to may be the Egyptians, or the Ethiopians, or some nation still more distant; and it is not clear whether the messengers in verse 2 are being sent back to give a message to their own race, or sent on their way to give a message to some other race, for example the Assyrians. Some think the prophet is discouraging an Egyptian offer of alliance (IV Kg. 18.24).

through the land; all through summer the birds will hover about it,[1]
7 and the beasts flock to it in winter. And then the people that is sundered far away, dreaded nation at the ends of the earth, land of the tyrant's yoke, land of the branching rivers, will bring gifts to the Lord of hosts, betaking itself to mount Sion, where the name of the Lord of hosts is worshipped.

CHAPTER NINETEEN

WHAT burden for Egypt? See where the Lord comes into Egypt, with the cloud-drift for his chariot, and all the false gods of Egypt
2 tremble, the very heart of Egypt melts away! Egyptians I will embroil with Egyptians; each man will turn on his neighbour, one city, one
3 kingdom on another. The spirit of Egypt shall fail her, and I will daze her wits, till men go about consulting oracle and diviner, wizard and
4 soothsayer. Tyrants for Egypt's masters, a fierce king to rule over it;
5 the Lord of hosts has decreed it. Waters of the sea shall ebb, river
6 waters retreat, be parched and dried up, the brooks failing, the channels, with their high banks,[2] flowing in a thin stream, reed and sedge withered
7 away. Laid bare, yonder river-bed, from its source; fade the crops
8 its moisture nourished, fade and dwindle to nothing. Sad days for the fisher-folk; never a hook cast, never a net sunk, all is repining and
9 ill-content. Disappointed of their trade, the men who worked in flax,
10 combing and weaving it so cunningly; in those brackish swamps there are no fish-ponds a-making now.[3]
11 Nonplussed, all the princes of Tanis; all Pharao's wise counsellors must needs give him a fool's answer. Where is that inheritance of
12 learning they boast, come down from ancient kings? What has become of thy wise men, Pharao? Let them give thee news, let them tell thee
13 what the Lord means to do with Egypt. No, the princes of Tanis are nonplussed; degenerate, the lords of Memphis; Egypt is deceived in her great men, that should have been the corner-stone of her common-
14 wealth.[4] The Lord has mazed her wits; fuddled brains of drunkard

[1] Owing to the doubts alluded to above, it is difficult to say what nation is referred to by the 'it' of this verse.

[2] 'The channels, with their high banks'; or perhaps (according to the Hebrew text) 'the channels of Egypt.'

[3] *vv.* 7–10. Several phrases in this passage are of doubtful interpretation, particularly the last verse; the Hebrew text here being understood by some as meaning 'The pillars of the land (that is, the nobles) shall be crushed, and those who work for hire will grieve.'

[4] The Latin implies that Egypt is the corner-stone of her own commonwealth, but the Hebrew text can equally well be interpreted as applying that description to the great men of the country.

15 had given as good advice;   head from tail, pliant reed from stubborn
16 branch, in Egypt's troubled counsels who shall distinguish? [1]   Dazed
   and terrified Egypt will be, as woman when her time comes, to see
   the Lord of hosts lift his hand so threateningly.
17   Upon Juda Egypt must needs look with awe; fear is in the very name
18 of it; what means the Lord of hosts now?   Cities five there shall be in
   the land of Egypt that talk with the speech of Chanaan, and take oaths
   in the name of the Lord of hosts; a city that bears the sun's name among
19 them.   There will be an altar set up to the Lord for all Egypt to see,
20 and at its frontier a pillar dedicated to him,   a trophy, there, in Egypt,
   of his renown. Cry they out to him, when they suffer oppression, he
21 will give them a saviour, a champion, to deliver them.   Thus the Lord
   will reveal himself to Egypt; the Egyptians, when that day comes, will
   acknowledge him, doing him worship with sacrifices and offerings, will
   make vows to the Lord and perform them.
22   First calamity, then healing; when they come back to the Lord, he will
23 relent and restore.   There will be a high-road, then, between Egypt
   and the Assyrians; either shall visit other, and Egypt under Assyria
24 be at peace.[2]   And with these a third people shall be matched; who
25 but Israel, source of the whole world's happiness?   Such blessing the
   Lord of hosts has pronounced upon it, Blessed be my people in Egypt,
   and the home I have made for the Assyrian to dwell in, and Israel, the
   land of my choice.

CHAPTER TWENTY

IT was in the year when Tharthan, at the bidding of king Sargon of
Assyria, invaded the territory of Azotus, and captured it by assault,
2 that the Lord sent out a message through Isaias, son of Amos.   Up,
   said he, and undo the sackcloth that girds thee, and take off thy shoes.
3 This Isaias did, and went bare and unshod.   Whereupon the Lord
   said, Look, how my servant Isaias goes bare and unshod; that is a sign
   and a portent of what must come upon Egypt and Ethiopia when
4 three years are past.[3]   It is thus that the king of Assyria will lead away
   the prisoners he takes in Egypt, the exiles from Ethiopia, young and
   old alike. Bare and unshod they shall go, with their buttocks exposed,
5 to the shame of Egypt.   A time of dismay and confusion for those who

---

[1] See note on 9.14 above.
[2] The Hebrew text here may mean, not that the Egyptians will serve the
Assyrians, but they will serve (*i.e.,* worship, the true God) *with* the Assyrians.
[3] Literally, 'a sign and portent of three years.' It is not clear whether the
prophet was ordered to go half-clad and barefoot during all that time.

6 put their trust in Ethiopia, who boasted of Egypt's power! Dwellers
in this nook of earth, they will cry out, Here lay all our hope; these
were to be our protectors, and bring us deliverance when the king
of Assyria came! What refuge is left us now?

CHAPTER TWENTY-ONE

WHAT burden for the desert by the sea? [1] From the desert it comes,
from a land full of terrors, like the storm-wind rising from the south.
2 Here be stern threats revealed to me: the faithless one still faithless, the
plunderer still at his plundering! Elam, to the attack! Lay siege to him,
3 Medians! From yonder desert there shall be groaning no more! What
wonder if pain gripped the loins of me, sudden as woman's pangs in
4 travail? What wonder if sight and sound of it daunt and daze me, if
heart fails and I grope in darkness, bewildered over her ruin, the Babylon [2] I love?
5 What, the banquet spread? From yonder post of vantage look down
on them, where they sit at their meat and drink! Now, captains, to arms!
6 The Lord's word came to me, Go and bid the watchman stand at
7 his post, to give tidings of all he sees. A chariot he saw, with two outriders, one that rode on an ass, and one that rode on a camel; looked
8 long at them, watching them eagerly. Then he cried, Lonely as lion
am I, that have charge of the Lord's watch-tower; day after day I
9 stand here, night after night I keep my post. Nearer now, the chariot
and its two outriders; Tidings! cries charioteer. Babylon has fallen,
has fallen; images of the gods she worshipped have come crashing
10 to the ground. [3] My countrymen, winnowed with me in the same
threshing-floor of trial, from the Lord of hosts, the God of Israel, such
tidings I bring.
11 What burden for Duma? [4] A cry comes to me from Seir, How goes the
12 night, watchman? How goes the night? Morning is on its way, says
he, but with morning, the night. Come back again and enquire, if
enquire you must.

---

[1] The desert by the sea is evidently Babylon. Some think this prophecy refers
to the defeat of Merodach-Baladan, who was friendly to Juda (see ch. 39
below), which would explain the prophet's sympathy. Others connect it with
the defeat of Baltassar (Dan. 5), supposing verse 5 here to be an allusion to
Baltassar's feast; in that case, the prophet must be speaking in an assumed
character, or perhaps in irony.

[2] 'Babylon'; the Hebrew text has 'twilight.'

[3] It is not clear how much of this verse, if any, is spoken by the watchman.

[4] Duma, which is the Hebrew word for silence, is here used to represent
Idumaea, or Edom; some think, by a play upon words.

13   What burden for the Arabs?[1] Come evening, sleep in the woods
14 you must, you that travel to Dedanim. Dwellers in the south, bring
15 out water to meet the thirsty, bread to meet fleeing men. They have
    fled to escape the sword, the drawn sword, to escape the bow already
16 bent against them, the stress of battle. In a year's time, the Lord says,
    when labourer comes back for his hire, Cedar shall be robbed of all
17 its glory;[2] of all the brave archers that were Cedar's sons, only a
    dwindling remnant shall be left; the Lord, the God of Israel has decreed
    it.

CHAPTER TWENTY-TWO

WHAT burden for the Valley of Revelation?[3] Here is great stir among
2   the townspeople, climb they eagerly to the house-tops. What
means this shouting everywhere, these thronged streets, as of a city that
makes holiday? Alas for thy dead, that were never slain by the sword,
3 never died in battle; alas for rulers of thine, who with one accord have
fled, or else been cruelly bound? Chains for all that were left, and distant
4 exile. Leave me, sirs, leave me alone, to weep bitterly; never try to com-
5 fort me, now that this people of mine is widowed. Day of doom, when
the Lord of hosts will have yonder Valley of Revelation defeated, overrun, thrown into confusion; a day to test its ramparts, and threaten its
6 citadel;[4] to archer, to chariot, to horseman, Elam sends out her challenge,
7 bids shield come down from its place on the wall. Chariots up and down
all the valleys thou lovest, horsemen halted at thy gate!
8   Here is Juda, then, stripped bare; quick, to the armoury, there in the
9 Forest House,[5] bring weapons at need. How many breaches, already, in
the wall of David's city! Water you must bring in from the lower pool;
10 take count of the houses in Jerusalem, pulling down some to build up

---

[1] The Hebrew forms 'in Arabia' and 'at evening' differ from one another
only minutely. The Hebrew text reads 'in Arabia' twice over; some modern
scholars, on the contrary, give this prophecy the heading 'A burden (or, oracle)
at evening.'
[2] Cf. 16.14 above; the reference is perhaps to the time of year at which
labourers were paid off.
[3] The Valley of Revelation is clearly Jerusalem itself; but it is not clear to
what period in its history the prophet refers, nor whether the disasters of
which the Jews shew so little consciousness are already past, or still to come.
[4] 'A day to test its ramparts, and threaten its citadel'; in the Hebrew text,
it is possible to read proper names here, 'Cir is undermining, and Shoa is on
the mountain side'—the two names being those of countries subject to Assyria.
Similarly in verse 6 we may understand, 'Cir is laying bare (that is, is getting
ready) the shield.'
[5] See III Kg. 7.2.

11 the defences; you must find a bed between the two walls for the water
     of the old pool to run. And all the while, no thought of him who made it
12 all, no eyes for him who fashioned it, long ago. On such a day as this the
     Lord, the God of hosts, summons you to mourn and lament, to shave your
13 heads and wear sackcloth; and instead all is mirth and gladness, oxen
     killed here, rams slaughtered there, meat being eaten and wine drunk;
14 come, let us eat and drink, for tomorrow we die! Plain it rings in my
     ear, the voice of the Lord of hosts, Never while you live shall this sin of
     yours be pardoned.

15   A message from the Lord God of hosts; Up, to my house betake
     thee, and find Sobna, that has charge of the temple.[1] This be thy
16 word to him, What claim or kindred hast thou here, that thou shouldst
     hew out a burying-place for thyself? A tomb carefully hewed out on
17 the hill side, an eyrie for thyself among the rocks? Wait till the Lord
18 trusses thee like a trussed fowl, folds thee like a cloak, twines thee
     about with misfortune, and tosses thee like a ball into the great open
     plain! There shalt thou lie, and there that chariot which is thy pride,
19 which is the shame of thy master's house. I mean to expel thee from
20 the rank thou holdest, deprive thee of thy office. And when that time
     comes, I will summon one who is a true servant of mine, Eliacim the
21 son of Helcias, clothe him with thy robe, gird him with thy girdle,
     entrust him with the power that once was thine; to rule all the citizens
22 of Jerusalem, all Juda's race, with a father's care. I will give him the
     key of David's house to bear upon his shoulder; none may shut when
23 he opens, none open when he shuts.[2] I will fix him securely in his
     place, like a peg that is to carry all the honour of his father's house;
24 all the honour of his father's house will rest upon him, as a man's goods
     rest on a peg, the smaller of them, here a cooking-pan, there an instru-
25 ment of music. A day is coming, says the Lord of hosts, when the peg
     that was once securely fixed will be dislodged from its place; suddenly
     it must break and fall, and all that hung from it be ruined; the Lord
     decrees it.[3]

---

[1] 'Of the temple'; in the Hebrew text, 'of the house,' that is, probably, the
royal palace.

[2] Apoc. 3.7.

[3] In the Hebrew text, the meaning of verses 23–25 is obscure; nor are scholars agreed, whether the peg that is to be dislodged from its place is Eliacim
himself, at a later time, or Sobna, his predecessor in office.

CHAPTER TWENTY-THREE

WHAT burden for Tyre? Mourn aloud, ocean-going ships,[1] that
2 reach Cyprus to learn that the home you left is in ruins! Stand they
aghast, dwellers in the coast land that once was thronged with Sidonian
3 merchants, that gathered its revenue from far over seas; grain of Egypt's
4 sowing, of the Nile's ripening, bartered they among the nations. Poor
Sidon, by false hopes betrayed! A cry comes up from the sea, from her
that was guardian of the sea, Not for me a mother's joys, a mother's
5 pangs; never a son reared, never a maid brought to womanhood. Here is
6 news for Egypt, news from Tyre that shall grip her with despair! Go out
7 on your ocean voyage, dwellers on the coast land, mourning aloud; your
city fallen, the same city that had so long boasted of her ancientry. For
8 her townsfolk there is a journey to make on foot, a distant journey. Who
was it plotted the downfall of Tyre, a city once so rich in crowns, whose
merchants were princes, whose traffickers were among the great men of
9 the earth? He, the Lord of hosts, designed it; who else drags in the mire
the boaster's pride, brings all the great men of the earth into derision?
10 Daughter of ocean,[2] flooded thy land must be as Egypt is; the girdle
11 of strength thou hadst is thine no more. The Lord's hand, now, is
stretched out over the sea itself, throwing all the kingdoms into dismay;
his writ has gone out against Chanaan, that all its strongholds should
12 be brought to nothing. Sidon, poor queen (he says), boast no more
of thy virginity; thy name is tarnished now. Cross the sea, and betake
13 thyself to Cyprus if thou wilt; even there thou shalt find no rest. Her
resting-place is the land of the Chaldeans, where Assur has founded
a nation strong as no nation ever was; nation that has carried off her
warriors into captivity, undermined her palaces, made her into a heap of

---

[1] 'Ocean-going ships'; in the Hebrew text, 'ships of Tharsis,' and so in verses
10 and 14 below. The position of Tharsis is uncertain, but it is generally identified with Tartessus, on the Western coast of Spain. In that case a 'ship of
Tharsis' would have to be one capable of resisting the seas of the Atlantic.

[2] In the Hebrew text, 'daughter of Tharsis.' This is understood by some as
meaning that Tharsis, once Tyre had fallen, could enjoy complete liberty (the
'girdle' being interpreted as meaning the restraint of foreign domination).
But there is no evidence that Tartessus was in any sense a colony of Tyre;
it was only a trading station. The prophet, then, seems to be condoling with
Tartessus on the loss of her imports, as he condoled with Egypt in verse 5
on the loss of her exports. Tharsis will now have to grow her own food; this
is the sense implied by the rendering given in the Septuagint Greek, 'Till thy
own land, for no more vessels will come to thee from Carthage.'

14 ruins.[1]   Mourn aloud, ocean-going ships; your stronghold is laid waste.
15   After this thou wilt be forgotten, thou city of Tyre, for seventy
     years, long as the life-time of one of thy kings. At the end of those
16 seventy years, Tyre will know the meaning of the harlot's song,   Take
     thy harp and go round the streets, poor harlot forgotten; now for thy
     best notes, now for thy whole store of music, to bring thee back into
17 remembrance! At the end of those seventy years, the Lord will relent
     towards Tyre, and send her back to her trafficking; all the world over,
     with all the world's kingdoms, she shall play the harlot once more.
18 But now the revenues of her trafficking shall be devoted to the Lord's
     use, not hoarded up and laid by; revenue she shall earn, but for Sion's
     folk, the Lord's servants, to give them food in abundance, and durable
     clothing.

CHAPTER TWENTY-FOUR

L OOK you, the Lord means to make earth a void, a wilderness; twist
2 it out of shape, and scatter its inhabitants far and wide. One law for
priest and people, for master and servant, for mistress and maid; for
seller and buyer, for borrower and lender, for debtor and exactor of debts.
3 Earth drained to its dregs, earth ravaged and ransacked; such decree the
4 Lord has uttered. Earth woebegone and withered, a world that withers
    and grows feeble; how feeble they have grown now, the great ones of the
5 earth! Poor earth, polluted by the men that dwell on it; they have broken
    God's law, traversed the decree he made for them, violated his eternal
6 covenant with men; cankered it lies by a curse, peopled with guilty men,
7 only a frantic remnant left [2] of its inhabitants.   Woebegone the vintage,
8 withered now the vine, hearts sighing that once were merry;   silent the
    gay tambour, hushed the noise of holiday-making, silent the harp's mirth.
9 No more feasting and song; the wine turns bitter in their mouths.   The
    whole earth is like a city ransacked and ruined, where every house denies
11 entrance,   and a cry goes up in the streets because all the wine is spent,
12 the mirth forsaken, the joy vanished;   a city left to desolation, with ruin
    fallen upon its gates.
13   In the midst of the wide earth, among those many peoples, what
    shall be left? A remnant, the last olives that are shaken from the tree,
14 the gleanings that remain when vintage-time is over. Few only, but they
    shall lift up their voices in praise; God's honour vindicated, their

---

[1] The Hebrew text here is different, and the interpretation of it is much
disputed. It gives 'has raised towers' for 'has carried off her warriors.'
[2] 'A frantic remnant left'; in the Hebrew text, 'they will be burned up till
few of them are left.'

15 rejoicing shall be heard across the sea,   Give glory to God, where
knowledge of him is revealed; [1] praise to the God of Israel among the
16 distant isles;   here at the ends of the earth his song of triumph has
reached us, the boast of his elect.[2] Heart, keep thy secret, heart, keep
thy secret; no more of that.

But alas, the traitors still betray his cause; treachery is treachery still,
17 and its fruit is treason.   For the dwellers on earth, dismay; pit and
18 snare await them;   flee they from peril, they shall fall into the pit,
flee they from the pit, they shall be held fast in the snare. The flood-
19 gates of heaven will be opened, and the foundations of earth rock;   earth
must be rent and riven, earth torn and tattered, earth must quiver and
20 quake;   earth rolling and reeling like a drunkard, earth tottering like
some frail shelter that is gone in a night, bowed down by the weight
21 of its own guilt, till it falls, never to rise again.   When that day comes,
the Lord will hold a reckoning with the hosts of heaven, there above,
22 with the kings of the earth, here on earth;   huddled together, as captives
are huddled together in a dungeon, they shall remain prisoners; so,
23 at last, the reckoning will be held.   And then the Lord of hosts will
reign at Jerusalem, on mount Sion; and the moon will be put to shame,
and the sun hide his face, before the glory in which he will appear then,
with the elders of his people about him.

CHAPTER TWENTY-FIVE

L ORD, thou art my God; I extol thee and praise thy name for thy
wonderful doings; for thy designs, so long prepared, so faithfully
2 executed; see, it is done! A heap of stones where, but for thy decree, a
town stood; a crumbling ruin, all that is left of a walled city; a fortress of
3 the invader, dismantled now and never to be built again. What wonder
great nations should do thee homage, embattled cities hold thee in dread?
4 Stronghold thou art of the poor, stronghold of the helpless in their affliction, refuge from the storm, shade in the noonday sun; against that wall
5 the rage of tyrants blusters in vain. Uproar of the invader stilled, as it

---

[1] 'Where knowledge of him is revealed'; literally 'in the doctrines,' the
Hebrew word being that used for the oracular adornment of the high priest's
breastplate. Its literal meaning is 'lights,' and some think it is here used poetically for 'the east.'
[2] 'His elect'; that is, either the Messias, or the redeemed people generally.
The words which follow are obscure in the Hebrew, and some think the meaning is, 'My weakness, my weakness' (literally, 'my leanness'). If this translation is right, the words are more naturally taken with what follows than with
what precedes them.

were the breathless summer of a parched land; oppression withered up
from the roots, like haze of burning heat! [1]

6   A time is coming when the Lord of hosts will prepare a banquet
on this mountain of ours; no meat so tender, no wine so mellow, meat
7 that drips with fat, wine well strained.   Gone the chains in which he
has bound the peoples, the veil that covered the nations hitherto; on
8 the mountain side, all these will be engulfed;   death, too, shall be
engulfed for ever. No furrowed cheek but the Lord God will wipe away
its tears; gone the contempt his people endured in a whole world's
eyes; the Lord has promised it.

9   When that day comes, men will be saying, He is here, the God to
whom we looked for help, the Lord for whom we waited so patiently;
10 ours to rejoice, ours to triumph in the victory he has sent us.   On
yonder mountain the divine deliverance shall rest, and by his power
11 Moab shall be crushed, like straw ground in the chaff-cutter; [2]   Moab
shall stretch out his hands, like a man swimming, and low shall his
12 pride fall when they crash down to earth! [3]   Down they must come,
the battlements that crown those walls, lie inglorious in the dust.

CHAPTER TWENTY-SIX

BUT in the land of Juda, when that day comes, what shall their song
be? Sion is ours, an impregnable fortress; divine protection it has for
2 wall and breast-work;   wide let its gates be opened, to welcome true
3 hearts that still keep troth with him.   Our thoughts wayward no longer,
thou wilt maintain us in peace, peace that comes surely to those who
4 trust in thee.   Yours to trust in the Lord continually, the Lord that is
5 evermore your protection.   Mountain-dwellers he can bring low, towering city walls he can level, level them with the ground, drag them down
6 to the dust.   There they lie, trodden under foot; poor folk trample on
them now, the disinherited spurn them as they pass.

7   Where heart is true, path lies plain; level the road he treads that
8 wins acceptance with thee.   And we, Lord, we have kept to the path
thou hadst decreed for us, waiting for thee still; longing we had none

---

[1] The Hebrew text here is difficult, and may perhaps be corrupt; for 'oppression withered up from the roots' it has 'bring low the song of the oppressor.'

[2] For 'ground in the chaff-cutter' the Hebrew text has 'trodden down in the
dung-hill' (or perhaps, the cess-pool).

[3] It is not easy, either in the Latin or in the Hebrew text, to be certain what
the subject of the verbs is, or what the precise picture is meant to be. In the
Latin it is, apparently, that of a man who puts out his hands to save himself
from falling, but unsuccessfully.

9 but for thy greater renown. All through the night my soul has yearned for thee, to thee my heart aspires, watching for the dawn; soon thou wilt execute thy decrees on earth, and the whole world shall know how
10 just thou art. The godless will not learn that lesson from mercy shewn him; in a land that is all holiness, they will pervert justice still, no eyes
11 for the Lord's majesty. Hand of thine which threatened them, heed they would not; heed now they must, those envious eyes, and to their
12 own confusion; they shall see fire consume thy enemies! Thou wilt busy thyself, Lord, to make peace for us; what achievement of ours but the doing of it is thine?

13 O Lord our God, masters we have had a many in place of thee,
14 but only thy name shall be held in remembrance; live they cannot nor revive, gone down to death with the heroes of long ago; thou hast called them to account, and made an end of them, till the very memory
15 of their names has vanished. Didst thou win thyself honour, Lord, when thou didst shew favour, such high favour, to thy people, when
16 thou didst enlarge all the frontiers of its land? [1] No, Lord, it was in affliction they turned back to thee; in silent hours of suffering thy
17 chastisement reached them.[2] We were no better than woman with child that is near her time, ready to cry out dolorously in her pangs;
18 such lot thou hast given us. Conceived we, aye, and travailed, yet nothing brought forth but wind; not through us came deliverance to our country, not through us were the peoples of the world cast down.[3]
19 Fresh life they shall have, Lord, that are thine in death; lost to us, they shall live again. Awake and utter your praises, you that dwell in the dust. The dew thou sendest, Lord, shall bring light to them; only the land of dead heroes thou wilt doom to overthrow.
20 Up then, my people, to your innermost chambers betake you; shut yourselves within doors; hide for a little, until the time of retribution
21 is past. See, where the Lord comes out from his dwelling-place, holds the nations of the world to account for their guilt! Earth shall disclose the blood spilt on it, and no more cover its dead.

---

[1] In the Hebrew text, there is no sign that this is meant to be a question; but the statement 'Thou didst win honour' is more difficult to fit into the context.

[2] 'In silent hours of suffering thy chastisement reached them'; this is the sense indicated by St Jerome. The phrase runs, literally, 'Thy chastisement (came) to them in the tribulation of a whisper'; the Hebrew text gives the equally difficult sense, 'they poured out a whisper; thy chastisement (came) to them.'

[3] The last clause in this verse is understood by some as meaning 'not through us were (new) inhabitants born to the land'; the sense suggested is that the small numbers of the surviving Jews will be supernaturally recruited by a resurrection. But there is no other instance of the word 'to fall' meaning 'to be born'; unless in the next verse, where the same scholars would translate 'thou wilt cause the land of dead heroes to be reborn.'

CHAPTER TWENTY-SEVEN

Hard and heavy and strong that sword is which the Lord carries;
shall he not wreak his vengeance, in due time, upon the monstrous
serpent that bars the gate, and the monstrous serpent that coils up
2 yonder;[1] shall he not deal death to the great beast of the sea? And
the praise of his doings shall be sung by his own vineyard, a vineyard
rich in wine.
3   I, the Lord, am the keeper of this vineyard; I come soon to water
4 it. Day by day I watch over it, to shield it from attack,   nor any grudge
my heart bears it. Would I were an enemy as relentless as thorns and
briars are![2] Then I would trample it down and make a bonfire of it.
5 But now, see how it clings to my protection! Ay, it shall have peace,
6 it shall make its peace with me.   Israel shall flourish and put forth
shoots, multitudes that shall be added to the number of Jacob; with
its offspring the wide face of earth shall be peopled.
7   What, should the Lord smite Israel as he smote his enemies? Destroy
8 it, like those others he doomed to overthrow?   Nay, cast her away
he might, but there should be due measure in her punishment; not
9 for nothing did he expose her to cruel wind and burning heat;[3]   so
should the race of Jacob find pardon for its sins. Cleansed now from
guilt, to bear fruit in full abundance; ground fine as chalk the altar-
stones, pillar and shrine raised up no more!
10   Meanwhile, the city that once was fortified must lie desolate, forsaken, that fair dwelling-place, abandoned, part of the wilderness;
11 cattle will browse and lie down, and crop the tall bushes on it;   nothing
that grows there but will wither and be snapped off. Women shall
be their teachers,[4] so foolish has this nation grown, too foolish for
12 its own maker to pity, for its own creator to spare.   But a time is coming,

---

[1] The enemies of Israel are probably alluded to here under symbolic names,
but they cannot be identified with any certainty.

[2] So the Latin version, which seems to suggest, rhetorically, that God is
reluctantly unable to abandon his people. Some, supposing a very unusual
construction in the Hebrew, translate, 'Would that I had thorns and briars
for my enemies.'

[3] In the Latin, the second half of this verse reads literally, 'he meditated
with his hard breath in the day of heat.' The Hebrew seems to mean, 'he removed (her) with his fierce wind, at the season of the sirocco.'

[4] 'Women shall be their teachers'; in the Hebrew text, the meaning generally
understood is 'women shall come and set it (*i.e.,* the vegetation just mentioned) on fire.'

when the Lord will beat the fruit from his trees,[1] as far away as the bed of Euphrates and the river of Egypt, and you, sons of Israel, shall
13 be gathered in one by one. That day, a call will be sounded on a great trumpet, and men long lost will come from Assyria, and exiles from Egypt, to worship the Lord on his holy mountain, in Jerusalem.

CHAPTER TWENTY-EIGHT

OUT upon the drunken lords of Ephraim, and the city that is their boast, their crown! Quickly shall it fade, this flower, in the pride of its beauty. Careless they dwell at the head of yonder fruitful valley, all
2 besotted with their wine; and the Lord will come upon them like a rough, boisterous hail-storm, like a destroying whirlwind, like a swift flood that
3 rises and spreads out over the plain. Trodden under foot it shall lie, the
4 crown that was drunken Ephraim's boast; that flower, whose brief bloom once delighted him, shall look down over the fruitful valley no more. Fig ripens to its cost, that ripens ere autumn brings the harvest, no sooner seen than plucked and eaten by the first that passes by!
5   But the Lord has his own people still left him; to these he shall
6 be a crown to boast of, a garland of pride; his the justice inspires them when they sit in judgement; his the courage that rallies them when they fall back, fighting to the gates.
7   What, these too? These too fuddled with wine, bemused with their revelling? High revel they hold, priest and prophet together, till all are fuddled and sodden with wine, their wits bemused; what wonder
8 if the true seer goes unrecognized, if justice is forgotten? No room
9 is left at their tables for aught but filth and vomit. Here is one (they say) has knowledge to impart,[2] has a message to make known, to whom? Does he think we are children new-weaned, fresh from their mothers'
10 milk? It is ever, Pass the word on, pass the word on, Wait a while yet, wait a while yet, A word with you, here, A word with you, there!
11 Here is stammering speech, here is outlandish talk for our folk to listen
12 to! Yet he did but counsel rest and repose; rest none other, repose none other, than to give respite to a weary nation. And listen they would

---

[1] Or possibly 'beat out (instead of threshing) his ears of corn.'

[2] In verses 9–13, the prophet evidently relates a personal experience. It seems as if the dissolute notables of Jerusalem had taunted him, over their wine, with always repeating the same 'catch' phrases, like one teaching children to spell, or a stammerer who can get no further with his sentence, or a foreigner who cannot express himself. Some think that 'he' in verse 11 is Almighty God, who will 'speak to' his people through a foreign invasion, but it seems simpler to understand it of the prophet himself.

13 not; to them, the Lord's message was all Pass the word on, pass the
word on, Wait a while yet, wait a while yet, A word with you, here,
and a word with you, there! And so they will go on their way, to stumble
backwards and break their bones, to fall into a trap and lie there caught.
14 Hear the Lord's word, then, you mockers, that bear rule over my
15 people in Jerusalem. Did you think to make terms with death, enter
into alliance with the grave itself, that the flood of ruin should pass
16 you by, so confident in your vain hopes, so armed with illusion? A
message to you, then, from the Lord God, See, I am laying a stone
in the foundations of Sion that has been tested and found true, a corner-
stone, a stone of worth, built into the foundations themselves.[1] Hurry
17 to and fro who will; faith knows better. You shall have justice dealt
out to you by weight, your sentence shall be strictly measured; shattered,
the vain hopes, as by a storm of hail, buried the illusion as by a deluge.
18 Hold they shall not, your terms with death, your compact with the grave;
19 when the flood of ruin sweeps past, it shall leave you prostrate. It
will carry you away as it passes; pass it will, suddenly, in the space of a
day and a night, and the very alarm of it will make you understand
20 the revelation at last. Too narrow a bed, and one or the other must
21 fall out; a short cloak is no covering for two.[2] Who stands there? None
other than the Lord himself, as he stood once on the mountain of
Disruption,[3] vengeful still, as when he stood in the valley at Gabaon;
but now, his own purpose to achieve, he lends himself to the purpose
22 of another, now his will is, to let the alien have his will. Mock, then,
no more, if you would not see your chains riveted tighter; the Lord
God of hosts is my witness, he means to make a short and sharp reckoning
with the whole earth.
23 Listen now, and give me a hearing, mark well the message I bring.
24 Plough the farmer must, ere he sow, but will he be ever ploughing?
25 For hoe and harrow is there no rest? Nay, he will water it anon, plant
fennel, sow cummin, with a border of wheat or barley, millet or vetch;
26 such lore he has learned, such prudence his God has given him. What,
shall sledge crush the fennel seed, threshing-wheel pass to and fro

[1] In verses 15 and 16 the reference, according to some, is to those Jews who
put their trust in a projected alliance with Egypt against Assyria (cf. ch. 31
below). We know nothing about the corner-stone, except that the prophet
refers here, at least indirectly, to our Lord's coming. Cf. Rom. 9.33, where
the verse ends 'The believer will not be disappointed' instead of 'Hurry to and
fro who will; faith knows better.'
[2] This is clearly a proverb, intended to justify God's design in saving some
of the Jewish people, rejecting others.
[3] 'The mountain of Disruption,' that is, Baal Parasim, II Kg. 5.20; for Gabaon,
see Jos. 10.10. The same God who once fought for his people will now carry
out his purposes by granting success, for the time being, to foreign invaders.

over the cummin? A switch for the fennel, a rod for the cummin,
28 and they shall be beaten enough. Thrashed the corn must be, sure
enough, yet not for ever does the wheel harry it, do the spikes wear
29 it down.[1] This lesson, too, the Lord would teach us; learn we how
wonderful are his designs, how high above us his dealings.

CHAPTER TWENTY-NINE

OUT upon her, Ariel,[2] the lion-city King David stormed long ago!
This year once added to the tale of years, feast-days of it over and
2 gone, I will lay siege to Ariel, that shall roar and roar again, a lion-city
3 indeed. Trust me, I will ring thee round, throw up earth-works against
4 thee, set engines in place to besiege thee. Cower down thou must, and
offer parley from the earth where thou liest; from the ruins thy voice
will make itself heard, no better than a muttering from the ground,
as it were some ghost that moaned there under the earth.
5 Then, like fine dust, the hordes that routed thee shall vanish; like
6 a spark that smoulders, thy conquerors shall die away. Suddenly,
in a moment, the Lord will sweep down upon them in thunder, and
earthquake, in a storm of roaring wind, in fire that devours all before
7 it; gone, the thronging nations that fought against Ariel, like a dream
that passes with the night; gone, the fighting, and the siege, and their
8 triumph. Dreams hungry man of a full belly, then wakes empty as
ever; dreams thirsty man of a cool draught, then wakes weary, and
thirsty, and still unsatisfied! Such comfort shall be theirs, the many
folk that beleaguered Sion.
9 Ay, gape and gaze as you will; hum and haw you, bemused ere you
lifted cup, besotted ere you have been at your wine, besotted with
10 never a taste of drink! So deep a lethargy the Lord instils, blinding
the prophets that should be your eyes, muffling with a veil the wise
11 heads that should see visions for you. What is revelation to you, but
12 a sealed book, offered as vainly to scholar that finds it sealed, as to
13 yonder simpleton, that vows he never learned his letters? This people,
the Lord says, makes profession of worshipping me, does me honour
with its lips, but its heart is far from me.[3] If they fear me, it is a lesson

---

[1] It is not certain whether this parable in verses 23–28 is meant to explain
the merciful gradation God shews in his judgements, or to recommend a less
oppressive policy to the Jewish rulers (cf. verse 12 above).
[2] Ariel is generally interpreted as meaning, Lion of God. It is nowhere else
used as a name for Jerusalem, and no certainty can be felt about the sense of
the passage.
[3] Cf. Mt. 15.8.

14 they learned from human precepts. What remains but some great, some resounding miracle, to strike awe into such hearts as these? Bereft of wisdom their wise men shall be, cunning of their counsellors vanish.
15 Out on you, that would hide your designs from the Lord in the depth of your hearts, plotting on in the dark and telling yourselves none
16 can see, none can find you out! What a strange thought is this! As well might clay scheme against the potter; handicraft disown its crafts-man, or thing of art call the artist fool.
17 Short the time shall be, and quickly fled, ere Lebanon forest shall be fruitful as Carmel, ere land fruitful now shall be reckoned as forest.
18 Then this book will have a message for deaf ears to hear, for blind
19 eyes to see through the mist that darkens them; humble folk shall yet learn to rejoice in the Lord, poor clods of earth triumph in the
20 Holy One of Israel. Vanished, the triumphant foe, scornful incredulity is silenced; where are they now, that spent themselves on wrong-
21 doing, watching a man's words to convict him of guilt, defrauding him of justice at the city gate, setting aside, with a quibble, the plea
22 of the innocent? Here is a message to the race of Jacob from the Lord, that was Abraham's deliverer: No longer shall Jacob be disappointed,
23 no longer put to the blush. He shall see children of his, my gift, doing honour publicly to my name; honour to the Holy One of Jacob, homage
24 to the God of Israel! Restless hearts will attain true knowledge then, and the murmurers learn wisdom.

CHAPTER THIRTY

OUT upon you, the Lord says, what treason is this? Here be plans afoot that were never mine, webs a-weaving, and the pattern none of
2 my choice. Trust me, you do but add to your guilt. What are these journeyings down into Egypt, and I never consulted? Think you to find
3 refuge in the strength of Pharao, look you to Egypt for shelter? Strength of Pharao shall play you false, nor shelter Egypt bring you, but shame.
4 Princes of thine in Tanis, ambassadors from thee making their way to
5 Hanes! Fruitless errand to a folk that could not save them; no help, no comfort there, only failure and mockery.
6 What burden for the cattle-droves in the south? Here is a land of difficulty and danger, home of lion and lioness, of viper and flying serpent; and through it, goods piled on asses' backs, treasures stored on the humps of camels, go men asking for help where help is none.
7 From Egypt's protection you shall have neither gain nor good; my
8 word has been said about her, There goes Pride, let her alone. Go

home, then, and engrave it on a tablet of box-wood for their instruction; write it down, too, carefully on a scroll, to be an abiding record
9 in after days. So rebellious a people is this, so treacherous a breed,
10 refusing, my own children, to listen to the law of their God; forbidding
the prophet to prophesy, the man of vision to have vision of the truth.
Ever they must be told what likes them best, comforted in their illusions;
11 for them no marching orders, no prescribed path; he, the Holy One of
Israel, must be kept far from their view.

12   From him, the Holy One of Israel, this message: Warning of mine
you have rejected, so blindly you trust your own cunning, your own
13 headstrong will. Sudden and swift shall be your punishment, as the
crash of a high wall that has long gaped ruinously, long been anxiously
14 watched. So shrewd a blow potter never dealt, shivering earthen
pot into fragments, till no shard is left that will carry a lighted coal
15 from the hearth, or a mouthful of water from the cistern. From the
Lord God, the Holy One of Israel, word was given you, Come back
and keep still, and all shall be well with you; in quietness and in con-
16 fidence lies your strength. But you would have none of it; To horse!
you cried, We must flee! and flee you shall; We must ride swiftly,
17 you said; but swifter still ride your pursuers. Be you a thousand to
one, yet at the challenge of five men you shall take to flight; nought
left of you but a remnant, lonely as flag-staff on the mountain top, as
beacon on the hill.

18   What if the Lord waits his time before he will have mercy on you?
The more glorious, when it comes, his deliverance. The Lord is a God
19 who makes award justly, blessed they shall be that wait for him. In
Jerusalem they only will be left, true citizens of Sion. And thou, Jerusalem, tears shalt have none to shed; mercy is none he shall withhold.
20 Soon as he hears thee crying out to him, the answer will come. Bread
the Lord will grant, though it be sparingly, water, though it be in short
measure. Birds of passage they shall be no longer,[1] the men he gives
thee for thy teachers; always thou wilt have a true counsellor in sight,
21 always hear his voice in thy ear as he warns thee, This is the true
path, follow it; no swerving to right or left!

22   Silver leaf on thy graven images defaced now, defaced the sheaths of
gold; thou wilt cast all away, as a woman casts away defiled clouts of
23 hers, and bid it begone. And thereupon, sow where thou wilt all over
the land, rain shall be granted to thy crops; rich and full shall be thy
harvest of wheat; thou shalt have pasture, then, for lambs to browse
24 in at liberty. Ox and ass on thy farm shall have mixed feed, pure grain

---

[1] 'Birds of passage they shall be no longer'; the Hebrew text is more commonly interpreted as meaning, 'no longer hide away in corners.'

25 fresh winnowed on the threshing-floor; never a mountain top, never
a high hill, but will flow with torrents of water, when that day comes.
The dead shall lie in heaps that day, and towers come crashing down;
26 moon's light will be like the light of the sun, and the sun will shine
in sevenfold strength, as if the light of seven days were joined in one,
when the time comes for the Lord to bind up his people's hurt, and heal
their grievous wound.

27   See where the majesty of the Lord comes from far away; his anger
is aflame, and there is no withstanding it! There is menace on his lips,
28 his tongue is like a consuming fire, and his breath like a mountain
stream that floods over till it is neck-deep. He will sweep away whole
nations into oblivion, sweep away the bridle of false fears that curbed
29 the peoples till now.[1]   But, you, that night, will be singing for joy,
as if it were the night when a solemn feast begins; your hearts will
be light, as men's hearts are light when they go up, with the flutes
playing about them, to the mountain of the Lord, where he dwells,
30 the strong God of Israel. The Lord will make his dread voice heard,
will lay bare his terrible arm, volleying out his anger in flashes of
devouring fire, laying all low with his whirlwind, with his hail-stones;
31 and Assur will shrink in fear from the Lord's voice, and will feel his
32 rod. So it is decreed that the rod should pass over him, brought down
on him by the Lord's hand to the music of your tambours and harps;
33 a strange warfare this,[2] that shall quell them! In these times a new
Topheth[3] has been made ready; this, too, made ready by a king. It is
deep and wide, fed with flaming brands in abundance; and the breath
of the Lord comes down like a stream of brimstone, to kindle it.

CHAPTER THIRTY-ONE

OUT upon you, that betake yourselves to Egypt for succour! Horses
must be your speed in the hour of peril; great array of chariots you
must have, and horsemen without number, to bring you confidence; to
the Holy One of Israel turn you never, confidence in the Lord is none.
2 And yet he too is a wise counsellor; brings he trouble to a man's door, he

---

[1] It is not certain, here, what is meant by a 'bridle of false fears'; nor is it
clear from the Hebrew text whether it is something the Lord will destroy
(literally, 'winnow away'), or something which he will impose.

[2] 'A strange warfare'; in the Hebrew text, 'a warfare of waving.'

[3] Topheth was the name given to a place where human sacrifices were burned
to Moloch, 'the King.' The burning of Sennacherib's dead soldiers will be a new
Topheth, prepared (according to the Hebrew text) 'for a king'; but the Latin
version gives a better sense, if we understand the King to be Almighty God.

does not lightly change his purpose; doubt not he will take arms against a
3 rebellious race, the unholy alliance bring to nothing.   Strength of Egypt
is human, not divine; its horses are weak flesh, not immortal spirit; one
movement of the Lord's hand, and down comes rescuer, down falls the
4 rescued, to lie there forgotten.   A promise from the Lord God! Here is
lion, or cub of a lion, growling over his prey; what though the shepherds
rally, and go out to meet him? Nothing cares he for their shouts, is not
awed by their numbers. So it will be with the Lord of hosts, when he
comes down to war, here on mount Sion, with his own hill-side for battle-
5 ground. As parent bird hovers over nest, so will the Lord of hosts protect
Jerusalem; protect her and bring her safe through, grant signal deliver-
6 ance.   Come back, sons of Israel, that have hidden yourselves away so
deep.
7   Time, then, for each man to cast away his idols of gold and silver,
8 idols your guilty hands have made.   Not by the sword of man Assur
shall fall, earthly weapon is none shall boast it slew him. Flee he must
ere sword threaten him, and never warrior of his be left, but to slavery.
9 All that stubborn strength of his by terror unmanned, all his princes
fled away! Such comfort the Lord sends to Sion, where his fire is lit,
to Jerusalem, where glows his furnace.

CHAPTER THIRTY-TWO

SEE, where a king rules his folk justly! His nobles, too, make right
2 award; [1] to them men look, as for shelter against the wind, cover in a
storm; for running streams in drought, shade of towering rock in a
3 parched land.   Eyes they will have to see with, no darkness there; ears
4 that are strained to listen attentively;   rude minds shall learn wise
5 thoughts, the stammering tongue speak out readily and clear.   Noble rank
6 shall no longer be for the reckless, or lordly titles for the crafty.   The
reckless man, that speaks ever recklessly, his heart set on mischief, still
full of empty show, and blasphemy against the Lord; food to the hungry,
7 drink to the thirsty denying still!   And the crafty man, an ill craft is his,
false pleas devising to ruin harmless folk, cheat the poor of their rights!
8 From a noble nature spring noble acts; title is none to greatness higher
than this.
9   Bestir you, fine ladies, and listen; for ears untroubled by alarm

---

[1] Verses 1–8 are generally understood as a prophecy, *e.g.*, of the reforming
activities of king Ezechias. But they may be read simply as an expression of
proverbial truths; and indeed the whole tone of them recalls that of the Wisdom literature.

10 I have a message. Swiftly the days pass, the year goes round, and
you shall have trouble enough, anxious foreboding, when the vintage
11 fails, and no fruit-harvest comes. Bewildered, the minds that were
once at ease, full of foreboding, those untroubled hearts; you must
go stripped and shame-faced now, with sackcloth about your loins,
12 mourn for lost fruitfulness, for the fields once so smiling, for the vine-
13 yards that bore so well. That thorns and briers should come up in
these lands of yours; come up over haunts you loved in the city that was
14 all mirth! Empty, now, the palace, forgotten, the hum of yonder streets;
nothing but gloom, where a man must pick his way through caverns [1]
endlessly; loved haunts of the wild ass, a pasture-ground for the flock.
15 All this, until the spirit is poured out on us from above; fruitful
as Carmel then the wilderness, to make your well-tilled lands seem
16 but waste. Alike desert and fruitful field the home, now, of innocence,
17 the abode of loyalty; loyalty, that has peace for its crown, tranquility for
18 its harvest, repose for ever undisturbed. In quiet homes this people of
mine shall live, in dwelling-places that fear no attack; all shall be ease
19 and plenty. But first the hail-storm must do its work, forest be laid low,
20 city levelled with the ground. Ah, blessed race, their seed sowing, their
oxen and asses driving, by every stream that flows! [2]

CHAPTER THIRTY-THREE

WHAT, plunderer of the nations, unplundered still? Proud lord of
others, does none dispute thy lordship? A time comes when thou
must cease plundering, and thyself be plundered, when of lordship thou
2 hast had enough, and others lord it over thee. Have mercy on us, Lord,
that wait for thee so patiently; day after day be our stronghold, our
deliverer thou in time of trouble!
3 Fled, the alien host, scattered the heathen, thy angel's voice [3] once
4 heard, thy power made manifest! Your spoils, Gentiles, how easily
amassed! Easily as the locusts, where they swarm in the trenches.
5 The Lord's power made manifest, that is throned high in heaven!
6 With his just award Sion shall be well content; still in these times
of ours [4] the promise well kept, the full deliverance. Knowledge and
wisdom and the fear of the Lord, what treasure like these?

---

[1] Literally, 'gloom and a groping over caverns.' The Hebrew text seems
rather to mean, 'Ophel and the watch-tower shall be turned into caverns.'
[2] It is not clear whether this refers to the security which God's people are
later to enjoy, or whether it is a proverb whose meaning is now lost to us.
[3] 'Thy angel'; in the Hebrew text, 'a rumour.'
[4] 'Of ours'; literally, 'of thine,' the prophet addressing (it seems) an imaginary contemporary of his own.

7   See, where they stand at the gates, the men we sent out to report,[1] hailing us; the messengers we sent to ask for peace,[2] weeping bitterly;
8 Deserted, the highways, the lanes untravelled; the enemy has broken the truce, making no terms with the cities, not sparing the lives of
9 men; widowed the countryside and lifeless, Lebanon shrunken and withered, Saron a wilderness, Basan and Carmel quaking with fear.
10 Now, the Lord says, to bestir myself, now to rise up in arms against them, now to make them feel my power! A raging fire conceived in the
11 womb, and nothing but stubble brought to the birth; your own
12 impetuous spirit shall be a fire, Gentiles, to devour you; like ashes in a kiln they shall be left, the alien hordes, bundles of brushwood eaten up by the fire.
13   Listen then, you that live far off, to the story of my doings; and you,
14 who dwell close to me, learn the lesson of my power. In Sion itself there be guilty folk that tremble, false hearts full of dismay; who shall survive this devouring flame, the near presence of fires that burn
15 unceasingly? He only, that follows the path of innocence, tells truth, ill-gotten gain refuses, flings back the bribe; his ears shut to murderous
16 counsels, his eyes from every harmful sight turned away. On the heights his dwelling shall be, his eyrie among the fastnesses of the rocks,
17 bread shall be his for the asking, water from an unfailing spring. Those eyes shall look on the king in his royal beauty, have sight of a land whose frontiers are far away.
18   Of those old fears, how thou wilt recall the memory! Where are they now, the learned men, that could weigh each phrase of the law,
19 that taught us like children?[3] No longer wilt thou see before thee a rebellious people,[4] all profound talk that passes thy comprehension,
20 and no wisdom. Look around thee at Sion, goal of our pilgrimage, see where Jerusalem lies, an undisturbed dwelling-place; here is tent securely fixed, its pegs immovable, its ropes never to be broken.
21 Here, as nowhere else, our Lord reigns in majesty; a place of rivers, of wide, open streams, yet no ship's oar will disturb it, no huge galleon
22 pass by; the Lord our judge, the Lord our lawgiver, the Lord our

---

[1] 'The men we sent out to report'; literally, 'those who see,' but it does not seem probable that the phrase refers here, as it often does, to the prophets. The Hebrew text differs, and its meaning is much disputed.

[2] Literally, 'The angels (or messengers) of peace.'

[3] According to the Hebrew text, the prophet asks what has become of the notaries, the men who weighed (out money, to buy off Assyria), the men who counted the towers of Jerusalem.

[4] 'A rebellious people'; this word, nowhere else found, is understood by some modern scholars in the sense of 'barbarous,' and the whole verse is taken as referring to the Assyrians.

23 king, will himself be our deliverance. Now, thy tackle hangs loose
and unserviceable, too weak thy mast is to display thy pennon; then,
thou wilt have the spoil of many forays to divide, even lame folk shall
24 carry plunder away. No more shall they cry out on their helpless
plight, these, thy fellow citizens; none dwells there now but is assoiled
of his guilt.

CHAPTER THIRTY-FOUR

NATIONS, come near and listen, here is news for all mankind; give
heed the whole world must, and all that lives on it, earth and all
2 earth breeds. On all nations the Lord will be avenged, never an armed
host but must feel the blow, forfeit, all of them, and doomed to perish.
3 See where they lie slain, their carrion polluting the air, the very hills
4 rotted away with their blood! Fade they into nothing, yonder heavenly
powers; shrivel, like a scroll, the heavens themselves, nor any star there
5 but must wither, as leaf withers on vine or fig-tree; in the very heavens
my sword shall drink deep of blood. On Edom doubt not it shall fall,
6 death-sentence to execute, the sword of the Lord, glutted with blood!
Well nourished with fat, where it drank the blood of lambs and goats, of
stalled rams! There are victims ready for the Lord in Bosra; great
7 slaughter then shall be in the land of Edom. Down go the wild bulls with
the rest, the bullocks, leaders of the herd; earth must be sodden with
8 their blood, rich grow the soil with fat of their pampered kings. Swiftly
it comes, the day of the Lord's vengeance, the year that shall see Sion's
9 wrongs redressed. Pitch they shall be henceforward, the brooks of Edom,
10 its soil brimstone; a land of burning pitch, never quenched night or day,
its smoke going up eternally; age after age it shall yet be desolate, un-
11 travelled for ever by the foot of man. Pelican and hedge-hog shall claim
it, ibis and raven be its tenants; plotted with the Lord's measuring-line,
12 an empty void, tried with his plummet, a hanging ruin. Cry they for a
king to govern it, that has no chieftain now; all its princes have vanished.
13 Thorns and nettles shall grow in its palaces, briers over its battlements; it
14 shall be the lair of serpents, the pasture-ground of the ostrich. Devils and
monstrous forms shall haunt it, satyr call out to satyr; there the vampire
15 lies down and finds rest. Hedge-hog makes a nest to rear its young,
nurtured safely in yonder shade; vulture there with vulture meets.[1]

---

[1] The names of the beasts and monsters mentioned in verses 11–15 cannot
be given with certainty. Some would understand a bird (perhaps the bittern)
in place of the hedge-hog in verse 11; and in verse 15, where a different and
very rare word is used in the Hebrew text, there is no clear agreement what
animal, bird, or reptile is meant.

16   Turn back, when the time comes, to this record of divine prophecy,[1]
and read it afresh; you shall learn, then, that none of these signs was
lacking, none waited for the coming of the next. The Lord it was
entrusted me with the prophecies I utter; by his Spirit that strange
17 company was called together. For each its own dwelling-place; in his
hand was the line that measured it out to them; there they shall live
on for ever, to all ages undisturbed.

CHAPTER THIRTY-FIVE

THRILLS the barren desert with rejoicing; the wilderness takes heart,
2   and blossoms, fair as the lily. Blossom on blossom, it will rejoice and
sing for joy; all the majesty of Lebanon is bestowed on it, all the grace of
Carmel and of Saron. All alike shall see the glory of the Lord, the majesty
3 of our God. Stiffen, then, the sinews of drooping hand and flagging knee;
4 give word to the faint-hearted, Take courage, and have no fear; see where
your Lord is bringing redress for your wrongs, God himself, coming to
5 deliver you! Then the eyes of the blind shall be opened, and deaf ears
6 unsealed; the lame man, then, shall leap as the deer leap, the speechless
tongue cry aloud. Springs will gush out in the wilderness, streams flow
7 through the desert; ground that was dried up will give place to pools,
barren land to wells of clear water; where the serpent had its lair once,
8 reed and bulrush will show their green. A high road will stretch across it,
by divine proclamation kept holy; none that is defiled may travel on it;
and there you shall find a straight path lying before you, wayfarer is none
9 so foolish he can go astray. No lions shall molest it, no beasts of prey
10 venture on it. Free men shall walk on it, coming home again to Sion, and
praising the Lord for their ransoming. Eternal happiness crowns them,
joy and happiness in their grasp now, sorrow and sighing fled far away.

CHAPTER THIRTY-SIX

IT was in the fourteenth year of Ezechias' reign that Sennacherib, king
of Assyria, marched on the fortified cities of Juda, and took them.[2]
2 And the king of Assyria, who was then at Lachis, sent Rabsaces at the

---

[1] 'Turn back, when the time comes, to this record of divine prophecy'; literally 'search carefully in the book of the Lord.' The sense given above is that
commonly adopted, but the text of the passage is uncertain; the Septuagint
Greek has, 'there the hinds gather, and meet face to face.'
[2] The whole of this chapter is to be found, with slight variations, in the
fourth book of Kings (ch. 18).

head of a strong force to Jerusalem, where king Ezechias was. This Rabsaces took up his stand on the aqueduct that fed the upper pool, on the
3 way that brings you to the Fuller's Field, and there he was met by
Eliacim, son of Helcias, the controller of the royal household, and Sobna,
4 the scribe, and Joahe, son of Asaph, the recorder. So he bade them tell
Ezechias, Here is a message to thee from the great king, the king of
5 Assyria. What confidence is this that makes thee so bold? By what cunning or what force dost thou hope to meet me in arms? On whose help
6 dost thou rely, that thou wouldst throw off my allegiance? What, wilt
thou rely on Egypt? That is to support thyself on a broken staff of cane,
that will run into a man's hand, if he presses on it, and pierce him
through; such does Pharao, king of Egypt, prove himself to all those who
7 rely on him. Or wilt thou answer, We trust, I and my people, in the
Lord our God? Tell me, who is he? Is he not the God whose hill-shrines
and altars their king, Ezechias, has cleared away, bidding Juda and Jeru-
8 salem worship at one altar here? Come now, if thou wert to make terms
with my master, the king of Assyria, by which I must hand over to thee
two thousand horses, wouldst thou be able to do thy part by putting
9 riders on them? Why, thou art no match even for a city prefect, the least
of my master's servants. Trust if thou wilt in Egypt, its chariots and
10 its horsemen; but dost thou doubt that I have the Lord's warrant
to come and subdue this land? It was the Lord himself who sent word
to me, Make war on this land, and subdue it.
11   At this, Eliacim and Sobna and Joahe said to Rabsaces, My lord,
pray talk to us in Syriac; we know it well. Do not talk to us in the
Hebrew language, while all these folk are standing on the walls within
12 hearing. What, said Rabsaces, dost thou think my master hath sent
me with this message for thee only, and for that master of thine? It
is for the folk who man the walls, these companions of yours that
have nothing left to eat or drink but the ventings of their own bodies.
13 Then Rabsaces stood up and cried aloud, in Hebrew, Here is a message
14 to you from the great king, the king of Assyria! This is the king's
warning, Do not be deluded by Ezechias, he is powerless to save you;
15 do not let Ezechias put you off by telling you to trust in God; that
the Lord is certain to bring you aid, he cannot allow the king of Assyria
16 to become master of your city. No, do not listen to Ezechias; here are the
terms the king of Assyria offers to you. Earn my good will by surrendering
to me, and you shall live unmolested; to each the fruit of his own vine
17 and fig-tree, to each the water from his own cistern. Then, when I come
back, I will transplant you into a land like your own, which will grudge
you neither wheat nor wine, so rich is it in cornfields and vineyards.
18 No, do not let Ezechias stir you to action by telling you that the Lord

will deliver you. What of other nations? Were their countries delivered,
19 by this god or that, when the king of Assyria threatened them? What
gods had Emath and Arphad, what god had Sepharvaim? Did any power
20 rescue Samaria from my attack? Which of all the gods in the world has
delivered his country when I threatened it, that you should trust in the
Lord's deliverance, when I threaten Jerusalem?
21   But all kept silence, and gave him no word in answer; the king had sent
22 orders that they were not to answer him. So Eliacim, son of Helcias,
the controller of the royal household, and Sobna, the scribe, and Joahe,
son of Asaph, the recorder, went back to Ezechias, with their garments
torn about them, to let him know what Rabsaces had said.

CHAPTER THIRTY-SEVEN

NO sooner had king Ezechias heard it, than he tore his garments
open, and put on sackcloth, and went into the house of the Lord.[1]
2 Meanwhile, he sent word to the prophet Isaias, son of Amos. Eliacim,
the controller of the household, and Sobna, the scribe, and some of
3 the older priests, went on this errand. Here is a message for thee,
they said, from Ezechias. Troublous times have come upon us; times
to make us mend our ways, or else blaspheme God.[2] What remedy,
when children come to the birth, and the mother has no strength to
4 bear them? Unless indeed the Lord God should take cognizance of
what Rabsaces has been saying, Rabsaces, who was sent here by his
master, the king of Assyria, to blaspheme the living God. Surely the
Lord thy God has listened to the reproaches he uttered. Raise thy voice,
then, in prayer for the poor remnant that is left.
5   Thus visited by the servants of Ezechias, Isaias answered, Give
your master this message. Do not be dismayed, the Lord says, at hearing
the blasphemies which the courtiers of the Assyrian king have uttered
7 against me. See if I do not put him in such a mind, see if I do not
make him hear such news, as will send him back to his own country.
And when he reaches his own country, I will give the word, and the
sword shall make an end of him.
8   And now Rabsaces went back to find the king of the Assyrians before
9 Lobna, hearing that he had raised the siege of Lachis. News had
come that Taracha, king of the Ethiopians, was on his way to do battle
with him. And the king, when he heard the report, despatched mes-
10 sengers to Ezechias; Give this warning, he said, to Ezechias, king of

---

[1] *vv.* 1–38. See IV Kg. 19.
[2] Literally, 'times of reproof and of blasphemy.'

Juda. Do not let the God in whom thou puttest such confidence deceive thee with false hopes, telling thee that Jerusalem will never be allowed
11 to fall into the hands of the Assyrian king. What, hast thou not heard what the kings of Assyria have done to the nations everywhere, destroy-
12 ing them utterly? And what hope hast thou of deliverance? What saving power had the gods of those old peoples my fathers overthrew, Gozam, and Haram, and Repheth, and the race of Eden who lived in Thalassar?
13 Where are they, the kings of Emath, and Arphad, the kings who governed the city of Sepharvaim, and Ana, and Ava?

14 These despatches were handed by the messengers to Ezechias, and when he had read them, he went up into the house of the Lord,
15 and held them out open in the Lord's presence. And this was the
16 prayer which Ezechias made to the Lord: Lord of hosts, God of Israel, who hast thy throne above the cherubim, thou alone art God over all the kingdoms of the world, heaven and earth are of thy fashioning.
17 Give ear, Lord, and listen; open thy eyes, Lord, and see; do not let Sennacherib's words go unheard, these blasphemies he has uttered against
18 the living God. It is true, Lord, that the kings of Assyria have brought
19 ruin on whole nations, and the lands they lived in, and thrown their gods into the fire; but these were in truth no gods; men had made
20 them, of wood or stone, and men could break them. Now it is for thee, O Lord our God, to rescue us from the invader, and shew all the kingdoms of the world there is no other Lord, save thee.

21 Then Isaias, son of Amos, sent word to Ezechias, A message to thee from the Lord, the God of Israel, in answer to the prayer thou
22 hast made to him about Sennacherib, king of the Assyrians. This is what the Lord has to say of him: See how she mocks thee, flouts thee, Sion, the virgin city! Jerusalem, proud maiden, follows thee with
23 her eyes and tosses her head in scorn. So thou wouldst hurl insults, and blaspheme, and talk boastfully, and brave it out with disdainful
24 looks, against whom? Against the Holy One of Israel. In thy name, these servants of thine have hurled insults at the Lord. It was thy dream that thou hadst scaled, with those chariots of thine, the mountain heights, the slopes of Lebanon; and now thou wouldst cut down its tall cedars, its noble fir-trees, till thou couldst reach the very summit
25 of the ascent, the garden its woods enclosed. Thou wouldst dig wells and drink wherever it pleased thee, thou wouldst dry up, in thy march, the banked channels of the Nile.[1]

26 What, hast thou not heard how I dealt with this people in time past? This present design, too, is one I have formed long since, and am now carrying out; such a design as brings with it ruin for the

---

[1] Literally, 'the channels of earthworks,' but see 19.6, and note there.

27 mountain-fastnesses, the walled cities that fight against thee. Sure
enough, they were overawed and discomfited, the puny garrisons
that held them; frail as meadow grass or mountain pasturage, or the
28 stalks that grow on the house-top, withering before they can ripen. But
I am watching thee where thou dwellest, thy comings and goings, thy
29 raving talk against me. Yes, I have listened to the ravings of thy pride
against me, and now a ring for thy nose, a twitch of the bridle in thy
mouth, and back thou goest by the way thou didst come.
30   Here is a test for thee, Ezechias, of the truth of my prophecy; this
year thou must be content to eat the aftergrowth, and next year wild
things shall be thy food; in the third year you may sow and reap, plant
31 vineyards and eat the fruit of them.[1] A remnant of Juda's race will be
saved, and this remnant will strike root deep in earth, bear fruit high
32 in air; yes, it is from Jerusalem the remnant will come, from mount
Sion that we shall win salvation; so tenderly he loves us, the Lord
33 of hosts. This, then, is what the Lord has to tell thee about the king
of the Assyrians; he shall never enter this city, or shoot an arrow into
it; no shield-protected host shall storm it, no earthworks shall be cast
34 up around it. He will go back the way he came, and never enter into
35 this city, the Lord says; I will keep guard over this city and deliver it,
for my own honour and for the honour of my servant David.
36   It was after this that an angel of the Lord went out on his errand,
and smote down a hundred and eighty-five thousand men in the Assyrian
camp; when morning came, and men were astir, nothing was to be seen
37 but the corpses of the dead. So Sennacherib, king of the Assyrians,
broke up camp, and took the road, and was gone; nor did he leave
38 Nineve again. And one day, when he was at worship in the temple
of his god Nosroch, two sons of his, Adramelech and Sarasar, drew
their swords on him, and so escaped into the land of Ararat; and the
kingdom passed to his son Asarhaddon.

CHAPTER THIRTY-EIGHT

A ND now Ezechias fell sick, and was at death's door;[2] indeed, the
prophet Isaias, son of Amos, visited him with this message from the
Lord, Put thy affairs in order; it is death that awaits thee, not recovery.
2 At this Ezechias turned his face towards the wall, and prayed to the Lord

---

[1] Some think that this prophecy was made three years before the events
described in 5.36, Sennacherib having been engaged meanwhile in an attack
on Egypt. But the exact bearing of the 'sign' is not certain.
[2] *vv.* 1–8. See IV Kg. 20.1–11.

3 thus: Remember, Lord, I entreat thee, a life that has kept true to thee, an
innocent heart; how I did ever what was thy will. And Ezechias wept
4 bitterly. And thereupon the word of the Lord came to Isaias, Go and
tell Ezechias, Here is a message to thee from the Lord, the God of thy
father David. I have listened to thy prayer, and marked thy tears; be it so,
6 I will add fifteen years to thy life. And I will save thee and thy city from
7 the power of the Assyrian king; I will be its protector. This sign, too, the
8 Lord gives thee, in proof that he will make his promise good; see how
low the shadow has fallen, with sun-down, where the dial of Achaz marks
the hours! I will make it go ten hours back. And with that the sun retraced
ten hours of its descent.

9   These are the words Ezechias king of Juda wrote, upon falling sick
10 and recovering of his illness. It seemed as if I must go down to the
gates of the world beneath, in the noontide of my years; the remnant
11 of life that I hoped for, hoped for in vain. No more (thought I) to
lift up my eyes to the Lord God in this land of the living, to see men's
12 faces, and quiet homes, no more![1] This familiar world [2] taken away
from me, folded up like a shepherd's tent, my life cut short like the
weaver's thread! And he had cut me off while the web was still in the
making; before the day reached its evening, he would make an end
13 of me. All night long I lay still, as if he had been a lion that had broken
all my bones; before the day reached its evening he would make an
14 end of me. My voice was as feeble as the voice of a nestling swallow
or murmuring dove; my eyes wearied out with ever straining upwards.
15 Lord, I am in hard straits; win my release for me! And yet, what words
can I use, what answer can I expect, when it is he himself that has
brought this upon me? With bitter heart I pass all my years in review.[3]
16 Lord, so frail a thing is life; on so little does my mortal breath depend!
17 Thou canst chastise me, thou canst make me live.[4] Bitter, bitter the
discipline that brings me peace!
   And now thou hast saved the life that was in peril, thrusting away

---

[1] Literally, 'I shall no more see man, nor the dweller in quiet.' The reference seems to be to the years of peace promised after the failure of Sennacherib's invasion. But some, by a slight change in the Hebrew text, would read
'the world' instead of 'quiet'; others interpret the Hebrew text as meaning,
'I shall be deprived of the sight of man, as those who dwell in quiet (that is,
in the grave) are.'

[2] The Hebrew word here used may mean 'my contemporaries,' or 'my dwelling,' or perhaps simply 'my life.'

[3] The Hebrew text appears to mean, 'I will walk as if in procession all my
years in the bitterness of my soul.'

[4] Literally, 'Lord, if it is thus men live, and the breath of my life is such,
thou wilt correct me and make me live.' The Hebrew text has 'grant me recovery' instead of 'correct me.'

18 all my sins out of thy sight. Thou hast no praise in the world beneath,
death cannot honour thee; those who go down into the grave have
19 no promise of thine to hope for; it is living men, as I am a living man
to-day, that give thee thanks, pass on from father to son the story
20 of thy faithfulness. Lord, be my saviour still; so, all day long, the
Lord's house shall ring with the music of our psalms.
21   Note that Isaias bade them take a lump of figs, and make a plaster
22 of it for the king's ulcer, and this is how he was healed. And note
that Ezechias had asked what sign should be given him, in proof that
he would set foot in the Lord's house again.[1]

CHAPTER THIRTY-NINE

A ND now, hearing of his sickness and recovery, the king of Babylon, Merodach Baladan, son of Baladan, sent a letter and gifts to
2 Ezechias.[2] Ezechias was delighted at the coming of these envoys, and
shewed them his scented treasure-house,[3] with its silver and gold and
spices and rich ointments; the rooms where his ornaments were kept; all
the wealth of his store-house. There was nothing in palace or domain but
he showed it to them.
3   Then the prophet Isaias gained audience of king Ezechias, and
asked him, What message did these men bring, and whence had they
come? They came to see me, said Ezechias, from a country that is
4 far away, from Babylon. And when Isaias asked what they had seen
in his palace, he told him, They saw everything in my palace; I have
5 no treasures I did not shew them. And at that Isaias said to Ezechias,
6 I have a message for thy hearing from the Lord of hosts. Behold,
a time is coming when all that is in thy house, all the treasures which
thy fathers have amassed there in times past, will be taken away to
7 Babylon; nothing shall be left of it, the Lord says. And sons of thine,
men of thy own line, of thy own stock, shall be carried off to be eunuchs
8 in the palace of the king of Babylon. Why then, Ezechias said to Isaias,
welcome be the word the Lord has spoken! In my time at least, he said,
may there be peace, may the promise hold good.

---

[1] We should expect verses 21 and 22 to occur between verse 6 and verse 7
above (as they do in IV Kg. 20). It seems probable that they dropped out by
accident, and were replaced here as a footnote to the story.
[2] *vv.* 1–8. See IV Kg. 20.12–19.
[3] Literally, 'his house of perfumes,' according to the Latin version. The
Hebrew text is generally understood as meaning 'his house of treasures.' The
word translated 'ornaments' probably means, according to the Hebrew text,
'armour.'

CHAPTER FORTY

2 TAKE heart again, my people, says your God, take heart again. Speak
Jerusalem fair, cry aloud to her that her woes are at an end, her guilt
3 is pardoned; double toll the Lord has taken for all her sins. A cry, there,
out in the wilderness, Make way for the Lord's coming; a straight road
4 for our God through the desert! Bridged every valley must be, every
mountain and hill levelled; windings cut straight, and the rough paths
5 paved; the Lord's glory is to be revealed for all mankind to witness; it is
6 his own decree.[1] A voice came, bidding me cry aloud; asked I in what
words, in these: Mortal things are but grass, the glory of them is but grass
7 in flower; grass that withers, a flower that fades, when the Lord's breath
8 blows upon it. The whole people, what is it but grass? Grass that withers,
9 a flower that fades; but the word of our Lord stands for ever. Good news
for Sion, take thy stand, herald, on some high mountain; good news for
Jerusalem, proclaim it, herald, aloud; louder still, no cause now for fear;[2]
10 tell the cities of Juda, See, your God comes! See, the Lord God is coming, revealed in power, with his own strong arm for warrant; and see, they
come with him, they walk before him, the reward of his labour, the
11 achievement of his task,[3] his own flock! Like a shepherd he tends
them, gathers up the lambs and carries them in his bosom, helps the
ewes in milk forward on their way.
12 Who was it measured out the waters in his open hand, heaven
balanced on his palm, earth's mass poised on three of his fingers?
Who tried yonder mountains in the scale, weighed out the hills?
13 No aid, then, had the spirit of the Lord to help him, no counsellor
14 stood by to admonish him. None other was there, to lend his skill;
15 guide to point out the way, pilot to warn him of danger. What are
whole nations to him but a drop of water in a bucket, a make-weight
16 on the scales? What are the islands but a handful of dust? His altar-
hearth Lebanon itself could not feed, victims could not yield enough
17 for his burnt-sacrifice. All the nations of the world shrink, in his
18 presence, to nothing, emptiness, a very void, beside him. And will
19 you find a likeness for God, set up a form to resemble him? What
avails image the metal-worker casts, for goldsmith to line with gold,

---

[1] Cf. Lk. 3.4.

[2] In the Hebrew text, it is Sion (or Jerusalem) itself that is represented as
the bringer of good news, according to the most probable interpretation.

[3] Literally, 'his reward is with him, and his task (or perhaps, the wages of
his task) is before him.' It seems likely that the Israelites returning from exile
are here compared to the flocks and herds with which Jacob returned from
Mesopotamia (Gen. 31.18).

20 silversmith plate with silver? What avails yonder wood, hard of fibre, proof against decay; the craftsman's care, that his statue should stand immovable? [1]

21   What ignorance is this? Has no rumour reached you, no tradition from the beginning of time, that you should not understand earth's

22 origin? There is One sits so high above its orb, those who live on it seem tiny as locusts; One who has spread out the heavens like gossamer,

23 as he were pitching a tent to dwell in. The men who can read mysteries, how he confounds them, the men who judge on earth, what empty

24 things he makes of them! Saplings never truly planted, or laid out, or grounded in the soil, see how they wither at his sudden blast, how

25 the storm-wind carries them away like stubble! What likeness, then,

26 can you find to match me with? asks the Holy One. Lift up your eyes, and look at the heavens; who was it that made them? Who is it that marshals the full muster of their starry host, calling each by its name, not one of them missing from the ranks? Such strength, such vigour, such spirit is his.

27   What, then, is this thought of thine, Jacob, what is this complaint of thine, Israel, that the Lord does not see how it fares with thee,

28 that thy God passes over thy wrongs? What ignorance is this? Has not the rumour of it reached thee? This Lord of ours, who fashioned the remotest bounds of earth, is God eternally; he does not weaken

29 or grow weary; he is wise beyond all our thinking. Rather, it is he who gives the weary fresh spirit, who fosters strength and vigour

30 where strength and vigour is none. Youth itself may weaken, the

31 warrior faint and flag, but those who trust in the Lord will renew their strength, like eagles new-fledged; hasten, and never grow weary of hastening, march on, and never weaken on the march.

CHAPTER FORTY-ONE

L ET the islands cease their clamour, and come to me, let the peoples of the world take heart afresh; [2] and so let them come and plead their

2 cause; we will submit the question to an arbiter, they and I. Tell me, who was it summoned his faithful servant [3] from the east, beckoned him to

---

[1] The Hebrew text differs here, but its sense is obscure, and perhaps corrupt.

[2] 'Take heart afresh'; the same words are used for 'renew their strength' in 40.31 above, and some think they have been written in here by an error, since they are not clearly suitable to the context.

[3] Literally, 'a just man.' The Hebrew text has 'justice,' and some modern

follow? Whole nations should be at his mercy, kings be subdued at his coming; flying like dust before his sword, scattered like chaff in the wind
3 at the threat of his bow. He should rout them in battle, and pass through
4 their country unmolested, leaving not a footprint behind him. Who was the author, the doer of all this, but I, the Lord, who summon all the ages
5 into being? Before all, and at the end of all, I am. The islands have seen it, and trembled at the sight; the remotest parts of the world have been smitten with dismay; they draw near, and obey the summons.

6   (And still each abets his neighbour; Courage, says one to another,
7 The metal-worker, plying the hammer, encourages his fellow that is smiting the anvil; all goes well, he says, with the soldering. And he fastens it with nails, immovable.) [1]

8   But thou, Israel, my servant, thou, Jacob, on whom my choice has
9 fallen, art sprung from that Abraham, who was my friend; in his person, I led thee by the hand from the ends of the earth, beckoning thee from far away, and still I whispered to thee, My servant thou
10 art, chosen, not rejected. Have no fear, I am with thee; do not hesitate, am I not thy God? I am here to strengthen and protect thee; faithful
11 the right hand that holds thee up. Thou shalt see all thy enemies disappointed and put to the blush; what are they? A very nothing,
12 those adversaries of thine; they must vanish away; thou wilt look in vain for the men who troubled thee, fought against thee; thy search
13 is for a very nothing, a memory of the past. It is I, the Lord thy God, that hold thee by the hand and whisper to thee, Do not be afraid, I am here to help thee.

14   Jacob, poor worm, poor ghost of Israel, do not be afraid; I am here, says the Lord, to help thee; I am here, says the Holy One of Israel,
15 to ransom thee. I mean to go a-threshing, and thou my sledge, newly made; teeth like saws to thresh the mountains and crush them down,
16 turn the hills into chaff; ay, and winnow them, till wind carries them away and storm scatters them! Thou shalt yet make thy boast of the
17 Lord, triumph in the Holy One of Israel. Poor vagrants that long

---

scholars would interpret: 'Who summoned from the east (a certain person whom) justice (that is, victory) meets (that is, attends) at his heels?' It is a matter of much disagreement, who is the person so referred to. St Jerome and others think it is the Messias; but the context seems to suggest that the event lies in the past, not in the future. It may perhaps be Cyrus, king of Persia, who is described as God's chosen emissary in 44.48, 45.1. But it can also be understood of Abraham and his descendants, taken in conjunction, verse 2 referring to Abraham himself and verse 3 to the Exodus. The text of verse 9 below seems to favour this last interpretation.
[1] Verses 6 and 7 are generally understood as referring to the making of idols; but their connexion with the context is so obscure that some think they have been misplaced, and stood originally after verse 20 of the foregoing chapter.

for water, where water is none, how dry their tongues with thirst!
And shall I, the Lord, refuse them a hearing, I, the Holy One of Israel,
18 leave them forsaken? I will open springs on the hill-slopes, wells
in the open plain, turn the wilderness into pools, the trackless desert
19 into running streams. I will plant those wastes with cedar and acacia,
myrtle and olive, rear, in that desert soil, fir and elm and box besides;
20 proof for all to see and recognize, for all to mark and to consider, that
the Lord's hand was there; who but he, the Holy One of Israel, creates?
21 Come then, says the Lord, your pleadings! Let the King of Jacob
22 hear your contentions; let them come forward, these other gods, and
tell us the future.¹ So read the past for us, that the study of it may
23 disclose what needs must follow; coming events make known. Foretell
you what is yet to be, we shall know you are gods indeed. Then, if
you have the power, grant good or ill fortune to mankind; confer we,
24 and pass judgement on it! Why, you are all empty air, a nothing that
nothing can effect; he courts his own shame, that makes choice of you.
25 I summoned one from the north country; from the east his coming
should be, and ever he should invoke my name.² Princes he should
26 harry to and fro, lightly as potter treads out his clay. Which of you
foretold this from the first? Let us recognize it. Which of you knew
it from the beginning? We must needs say, His plea is just. But no,
none gave tidings of it, none foretold it; there was no word came from
27 you. Who will be the first ³ to tell Sion, Here, here they are? He shall
28 carry my good news to Jerusalem. But when I looked, there was none
of them that could offer counsel, or give a word in answer when I
29 questioned him. None of them has right on his side; all their doings
are nothingness; no better than empty air the images men make of them.

---

¹ The words 'these other gods' are not expressed in the original, but are
inserted for the sake of clearness, being easily deducible from the context.
² There is the same uncertainty here about the person alluded to, as in verse
2 above.
³ In the Hebrew text, the verb is not expressed, and it is generally understood
as meaning, 'I will be the first.' In that case, the following clause should read,
'and I will send a messenger with good news to Jerusalem.'

CHAPTER FORTY-TWO

A ND now, here is my servant,[1] to whom I grant protection, the man
of my choice, greatly beloved. My spirit rests upon him, and he will
2 proclaim right order among the Gentiles. He will not be contentious or a
3 lover of faction; none shall hear his voice in the streets. He will not snap
the staff that is already crushed, or put out the wick that still smoulders;
4 but at last he will establish right order unfailingly.[2] Not with sternness,
not with violence; to set up right order on earth, that is his mission. He
5 has a law to give; in the far-off islands men wait for it eagerly. Thus says
the Lord God, he who created the heavens and spread them out, craftsman of the world and all the world affords, he who gives being and breath
6 to all that lives and moves on it: True to my purpose, I, the Lord, have
summoned thee, taking thee by the hand and protecting thee, to make,
through thee, a covenant with my own people, to shed, through thee,
7 light over the Gentiles: to give sight to blinded eyes, to set the prisoner
8 free from his captivity, from the dungeon where he lies in darkness. I am
Javé; that is the name I bear; I will not let the boast that is mine pass to
9 another, or share my renown with graven gods. What I told you long
since,[3] has proved true under your eyes; I tell you now what is still to be;
you shall hear of it before ever it comes to light.
10 Sing the Lord a new song; let his praise sound from end to end
of the earth. Praise him from the sea, all men that sail on it, and all
11 creatures the sea contains; the islands and the island-dwellers. Let
the wilderness, now, lift up its head,[4] and the desert cities; the men
of Cedar shall have villages to dwell in.[5] Give praise, then, rock-dwellers;

---

[1] The servant of the Lord, frequently mentioned in these later chapters
of the prophecy, is beyond doubt a type of our Lord (cf. Mt. 12.18). It is not so
clear whether Isaias was speaking directly of him, or referring in the first
instance to events nearer his own time. Some think the Servant means primarily
the people of Israel, or at any rate that portion of it which returned from the
exile at Babylon (cf. verse 19 below). Others would identify him with some
individual figure, as king Ezechias, Zorobabel (who brought back the exiles),
or Cyrus king of Persia; many other names have been suggested.
[2] Cf. Mt. 12.18, where the text (quoted from the Septuagint Greek) differs
considerably from the text here. 'A lover of faction'; literally, 'an accepter
of persons'; the Hebrew text here is obscure, but it is generally taken to mean
'lift up his voice' (as in St Matthew).
[3] Literally, 'the things which were first,' but the context makes the meaning
clear.
[4] The Hebrew text probably implies 'its voice,' as in verse 2 above.
[5] According to the Hebrew text, 'and those, too, who dwell in the settlements
of Cedar.'

12 the mountain-tops shall ring with their cries. All shall give God his praise, till the renown of him reaches the islands far away.

13   Like a giant the Lord shall go out to battle, like a warrior that stirs
14 up his own rage, with hue and cry, flouting his enemies.[1] Too long I have been dumb, eaten my heart out, held myself in like a woman in labour;[2] now I will have my say, I will destroy, and as I destroy,
15 devour! I will turn mountain and hill into a waste, withering all their
16 verdure, make barren islands of the rivers, dry up the marshes; and I will lead men blindfold by unfamiliar ways, guide their steps by paths unknown to them; I will make the darkness light, and the winding ways straight for them. Such was my promise to them, and were they
17 disappointed of it? See how they are routed, how they blush and blench, the men who trust in graven images, and say to the idols they have cast, You are gods of ours!

18   Listen now, you that are deaf; look up, blind eyes, and see. Who so blind as my servant, who so deaf as he, to whom my messengers were sent?[3] Who so blind, as he that has forfeited his liberty? Who
20 so blind, as the Lord's servant is? Eyes that have seen so much, must they be still unheeding; ears open to every rumour, will they never
21 hear? It was ever the Lord's will to sanctify him; so great, so glorious
22 the law he gave him; yet here is a people robbed and spoiled, caught by warriors that have hidden it away in dungeons, a prey there is none
23 to deliver, spoil none bids them restore. Which of you will listen
24 to this, and mark it, and give a hearing to prophecy? Who was it that made Jacob a spoil, gave Israel up into the hands of the conqueror? It was that Lord, against whom we have sinned. Because his ways
25 lay untrodden, his laws went unheeded, he poured out on Israel his angry retribution, war without mercy; and he? The flames burned round him, and he could not read their lesson, scorched him, and still he could not understand.

---

[1] Some think that verses 13–17 allude to the events of the Exodus (see verses 15, 16); if so, they should probably be enclosed in inverted commas, as a quotation, as far as the words, 'such was my promise.'

[2] It is not certain whether the words 'like a woman in labour' should be taken with the verb which precedes, or with the verb which follows them. The second part of the sentence, according to the Hebrew text is generally interpreted as meaning, 'I will cry out, and gasp, and pant, all at once'; but the verbs used are rare, and their meaning is somewhat doubtful.

[3] According to the Hebrew text, 'he whom I sent as a messenger.'

CHAPTER FORTY-THREE

AND now, here is a message from the Lord to Jacob, his creature, to the Israel he fashioned: Do not be afraid, I have bought thee for
2 myself, and given thee the name thou bearest: thou belongest to me. Pass through water, and I will be with thee, so that the flood shall not drown thee; walk amid the flames, and thou shalt not be burnt, the fire shall have
3 no power to catch thee. I am the Lord thy God, the Holy One of Israel, thy deliverer; I have bartered away Egypt to win thee, Ethiopia and Saba
4 for thy ransom. So prized, so honoured, so dearly loved, that I am ready
5 to give up mankind in thy place, a world to save thee. Do not be afraid, I am with thee; I will restore thy sons from the east, the west shall hear
6 the calling of their muster-roll; I will say to the north wind, Give them back; to the south wind, Restrain them no more; bring back these sons of
7 mine from far away, these daughters of mine from the world's end. Whoever owns my name [1] is my creature, made and fashioned for my glory.
8   Bring them out, then, into the light of day, this people of mine
9 that have eyes, and still cannot see, have ears, and cannot hear. Round about us, all the nations of the world are gathered, all its tribes assemble. And now, which among you can make this claim, give us an account of events foretold long ago? [2] Let them produce witnesses to justify
10 their claim, so that all may listen and say, It is the truth. I call you to witness, the Lord says, you and this servant of mine, on whom my choice has fallen; will you not recognize the truth, and believe me? Will you not learn to understand that I am the God you seek? [3]
11 None ever came into being before me, or will after me. It is I, I, the
12 Lord; no other can bring deliverance. It was I who promised that deliverance, I who bought it; I told you of it, when there was no alien god worshipped among you; you are my witnesses to that, the Lord
13 says. I am God, and what I was, I am; [4] from my power there is no escaping; when I execute my designs, none can avert them.
14   Thus says the Lord, your ransomer, the Holy One of Israel, If I send my emissaries to Babylon, casting down all its barriers,[5] casting

---

[1] Literally, 'calls upon my name'; in the Hebrew text, 'is called by my name.'
[2] Literally, 'the first things'; cf. note on 42.9 above.
[3] Literally, 'I am he'; cf. note on John 9.24.
[4] Literally, 'I am he,' as in verse 10, but here the predominant sense is perhaps 'I am the same God who brought you out of Egypt,' cf. verses 16, 17.
[5] The word in the Hebrew text which the Latin translates 'barriers' is understood by some as meaning fugitives; it is also possible, in the Hebrew text, to interpret what follows as meaning, 'I cast down the Chaldeans into the ships which are their pride.'

down the Chaldeans, with all the pride of their navies, it is for your
15 sakes. I, the Lord, am your Holy One, I, the maker of Israel, am
16 your king. A message to you from that same Lord, who could once
lead you through the sea, make a passage for you through the foaming
17 waters; could bring out chariots and horses, rank and file and chieftain
together in pursuit, to fall there and never to rise again, crushed like
18 a wick, and their light quenched. Do not remember those old things,
he says, as if you had eyes for nothing but what happened long ago;
19 I mean to perform new wonders; even now they are coming to the
birth; surely you will understand at last? I mean to make a causeway
20 over the desert, with streams flowing beside it in the waste. The wild
things will do me honour, the serpents and the ostriches, for thus
giving them water in the desert, streams in the waste; but it was for
21 my people's sake that I did it, to give drink to my chosen people. I
made them for myself, surely they too will have praise to give me!
22   Alas, Jacob, that my name should be forgotten, alas, Israel, that
23 thou shouldst have troubled thyself about me so little! No ram of
thine offered in burnt-sacrifice to me, no victims of thine to do me
honour; little burden have my offerings been to thee, little trouble
24 my meed of incense! Scented cane [1] thou wouldst not buy to burn
for me, nor think to cheer me with the fat of sacrifice; rather, it was
I that was burdened, burdened with thy sins; I that was troubled,
25 troubled with thy faithlessness. It was I, ever I, that must be blotting
26 out thy offences, effacing the memory of thy sins. Time, now, thou
shouldst remember me; come, let us settle the matter by arbitration,
27 thou and I; tell me what plea thou hast to bring forward. For the
guilt of thy first father, for the rebellions of thy own spokesmen against
28 me, [2] I brought thy inviolable princes to dishonour, gave up Jacob
to destruction, Israel to the scorn of his enemies.

CHAPTER FORTY-FOUR

L ISTEN, then, Jacob, my servant, Israel, the people of my choice.
2   Here is a message to thee from the Lord that made and fashioned thee
in the womb, thy protector: do not be afraid, my servant, Jacob, my true,
3 my chosen people. I will pour out water on the thirsty plain, streams over

---

[1] The scented cane was used in making holy oils for the service of the
Temple, cf. Ex. 30.23.
[2] Since Adam was the first father of the whole human race, not merely of the
Jews, the reference here is probably to one of the later patriarchs; the 'spokesmen'
may be Moses and Aaron (cf. Num. 20.12), or the false prophets of a later time.

the land that once was dry; I will pour out my spirit upon thy race, my
4 blessing on all thy line, and where the grass springs up they shall spring
5 up too, like willows by running water. Now, a man will say openly, The
Lord's servant I; make his boast of Jacob's name; write with his own
6 hand,[1] Dedicated to the Lord, and lay claim to the title of Israelite. Thus
says the Lord, Israel's king and ransomer, the Lord of hosts: I am before
7 all; there is no other God but I. What other is like me? Let me proclaim
it, tell us of it; let him expound the history of the past, ever since I established the primal race of man; then let him make known the future that is
8 yet to come.[2] Do not be afraid, or bewildered; you can bear me witness
that from the first I proclaimed it in your hearing, there is no other God
but I, no other Powers to rival me.

9 What empty minds be theirs, that idols fashion! What help found
any of them yet in his own darling inventions? Confess they, and to
10 their shame, that these have neither sight nor thought. Who was
11 it framed this god, moulded this image that nothing avails? What
can they do, yonder whole conspiracy, but stand there blushing? They
are but craftsmen with human power. See them met there in a body,
12 all struck dumb, every one abashed as his neighbour! Here is blacksmith that works away with his file, beats out image with furnace
and hammer, his strong arm the whole author of it; faints he, like other
men, if he be hungry, tires at his task if water he have none to drink!
13 Here is carpenter unfolding his rule; plane smoothes the wood, square
and compasses must do their work; and what has he made for you?
A figure fair enough, yet a man that must have roof to shelter him!
14 For this, cedar must fall, ilex and oak be cut away from their place
in the forest; for this, pine-tree was planted where rains should nourish
it.

15 Logs yonder carpenter will cut, a human hearth to feed; some he
brings in to warm himself, kindles more when the bread is a-baking;
and the rest? With the rest he makes himself a god to worship, bows
16 down before the thing his own hands have carved! Claims hearth,
claims oven its share; the broth brewed, the full belly none grudges
him, nor the fire's glow that cheers him with the sight of his own
17 chimney corner. But that he should take the rest to make a god for
himself! That he should fall down before an image, worship it, cry
18 out to it, Save me, thou art my god! Ignorance and folly, bleared
19 eyes that cannot see, dull hearts that cannot understand! Minds with-

---

[1] Or possibly 'on his own hand,' as if branding himself with the mark of the
divine service.

[2] The text of this verse seems confused, and it seems possible that the
heathen gods are once more being challenged to produce proofs of successful
prophecies; cf. 42.9; 43.9 above.

out reason, or sense, or thought, that cannot learn their lesson! Logs that fed the flame, embers that baked for me, now that my dinner is cooked and eaten, shall I take the rest and make an idol of it, fall
20 down before a stump of wood? Dust and ashes are his portion; the fool goes on worshipping, cannot free his own soul from bondage, nor ask if he shelters himself under a lie.[1]
21 Remember it, Jacob, remember it, my servant Israel; it was I, Israel,
22 that made thee; thou art my servant, and wilt thou forget me? The cloud of thy guilt, the haze of thy sinfulness, I have swept away; come
23 back to me, thy ransomer. The Lord has been merciful; you heavens, sing your praises; depths of the earth, rejoice; echo the song of praise, mountain and forest and every forest tree; the Lord has ransomed
24 Jacob, Israel shall make his boast in him. Thus says the Lord, thy ransomer, he who fashioned thee in the womb: I am the Lord, the author of all things; alone I spread out heaven's canopy, looked for no
25 help when I laid the floor of the earth. Mine to disappoint the sooth-sayers of their prophecies, and bewilder the diviner's wits, send the
26 wise men back to school, their wisdom all exposed as folly, vindicate my own servant, and justify the counsel my own messengers have given. It is my voice that bids Jerusalem grow populous, and the cities
27 of Juda rise again, while I restore their ruins; my voice that bids the
28 deep turn into a desert, and threatens to dry up all its floods; my voice that says to Cyrus, I give thee a shepherd's part to play; it is for thee to carry out my whole purpose. And to Jerusalem it says, Thou shalt be built up; and to the Temple, Thou shalt be founded again.

CHAPTER FORTY-FIVE

A MESSAGE from the Lord to the king he has anointed, to Cyrus. I have caught him by his right hand, ready to subdue nations at his coming, put kings to flight, open every gateway before him, so that no
2 door can keep him out. And now (says the Lord) I will still lead thee on thy way, bending the pride of earth low before thee; I will break open
3 gates of bronze, and cleave through bars of iron; their hidden treasures, their most secret hoards, I will hand over to thee. Know by this that it is I, the Lord, the God of Israel, who am calling upon thee by thy name;
4 and that I do it for love of my servant Jacob, of Israel, my chosen people. Yes, I have called thee by thy name; I have found a title for thee,[2] when

---

[1] Literally, 'if there is a lie at his right hand'; it was the right side that was exposed in ancient warfare.
[2] Literally, 'a comparison for thee,' *i.e.,* in describing Cyrus as his shepherd (44.28).

5 thou of me hadst no knowledge as yet. My name is Javé, and there is no
other to rival me, no God but I; I, still unknown to thee, was fain to make
6 thee strong, to what end? Because I would proclaim it from east to west
that there is no other God. My name is Javé, and there is no other to
7 rival me; I, the fashioner of darkness, the creator of light, I, the maker
of peace, the author of calamity. I, the Lord, am the doer of all this.

8   (You heavens, send dew from above, you skies, pour down upon
us the rain we long for, him, the Just One; may he, the Saviour, spring
from the closed womb of earth, and with him let right order take its
being.) [1]

9   I, the Lord, have made my servant what he is. At his peril does
man, poor shard of earthly clay, bandy words with his own Fashioner;
shall the clay dare ask the potter who moulds it, What ails thee? Or tell
10 him he is no craftsman? Strange, if a man should be asked by his
11 own son, why he begot him, or a woman, why she gave birth! [2] Thus
says the Lord, the Holy One of Israel, and Israel's maker, Of me you
must learn, what times they be that are coming; mine to do what I
12 will with my sons, with my own creatures. It was I framed the earth,
and created man to dwell in it; it was my hands that spread out the
13 heavens, my voice that marshalled the starry host; I, too, have summoned this man to perform my designs faithfully; go he where he will,
my guidance shall be his. He shall build up my own city, he shall let
my captives go free, without bribe or ransom, says the Lord of hosts.
14   This, too, the Lord says: all the toil of Egypt, all the merchandize
of Ethiopia, and tall slaves from Sabaea shall come into thy power
and be thine; they shall walk behind thee, their hands manacled as
they go, paying thee reverence, and crying out, God is with thee, with
thee only; there is no God where thou art not.[3]

15   Truly, God of Israel, our Saviour, thou art a God of hidden ways!
16 All the makers of false gods must needs be disappointed, must go
17 away ashamed and abashed. Israel has found deliverance in the Lord,
eternal deliverance; while ages last, no shame, no disappointment
18 for you. The Lord has pronounced it; the Lord who made the heavens,

---

[1] The Hebrew text has, not 'the Just One,' but 'justice' (that is, God's faithful mercies to his people, or their acquittal from sin); not 'the Saviour,' but
'salvation.' This verse seems to interrupt the thread of the argument; unless
indeed it is put in the mouths of those Jews who would not expect deliverance
from the king of Persia, but only from a Messias. Some would include the first
sentence of verse 9 within the parenthesis.

[2] 'Why he begot him,' 'why she gave birth'; it is equally possible to translate,
both from the Hebrew and from the Latin, 'what he has begotten' and 'to what
she has given birth.'

[3] It is not certain whether this promise relates to the people of Israel or to
king Cyrus.

and the whole frame and fashion of earth, moulded to his will. He did not create it to lie idle, he shaped it to be man's home. And he 19 says, My name is Javé, there is no other to rival me; it was not in secret, not in some dark recess of earth, that my word was spoken. Not in vain I bade the sons of Jacob search for me; I am the Lord, 20 faithful to my promises, truthful in all I proclaim. Gather yourselves and come near, flock together to my side, heathen men that have found deliverance; who still, in your ignorance, set up wooden images of your 21 own fashioning, and pray to a god that cannot save. Tell us your thoughts, come, take counsel among yourselves; who was it that proclaimed this from the first, prophesied it long ago? Was it not I, the Lord? There is no God where I am not. Was it not I, the faithful God? 22 There is no other that can save. Turn back to me, and win deliverance, all you that dwell in the remotest corners of the earth; I am God, there 23 is no other. By my own honour I have sworn it, nor shall it echo in 24 vain, this faithful promise I have made, that every knee shall bow 25 before me, and every tongue swear by my name. Then shall men say of the Lord, that redress and dominion come from him;[1] all those 26 who rebelled against him shall appear in his presence abashed. Through the Lord, the whole race of Israel shall be righted and brought to honour.

CHAPTER FORTY-SIX

HERE is Bel fallen in pieces, Nabo shattered;[2] their idols a gazing-stock for wild beasts and cattle! Heavy enough the burden you had 2 to carry; these must be left to moulder in a common ruin; comfort they had none for their toiling worshippers,[3] living souls that have gone off 3 into captivity. Listen to me, sons of Jacob, you whose weight has ever 4 been my burden, like an unborn child, a babe in the womb. You grow old, but I am still the same; the grey hairs come, but I ever uphold you; I must carry you, I that created you, I must bear you away to safety. 5 What comparison, what match will you find for me, what likeness to 6 resemble me? Fools that fetch gold out of a sack, weigh silver in the balance, bid some craftsman make a god they should fall down and wor-

---

[1] The Latin version is here somewhat confused, and reads, 'Therefore in the Lord he shall say mine are deeds of justice and empire,' but the sense intended is probably that given above; the Hebrew text, also, is obscure.

[2] The verbs used in the Hebrew text do not bear any stronger sense than that of 'fall down,' or even 'stoop down.' Some would interpret this verse as meaning that the idols of Babylon have been loaded on pack-animals, but proved too heavy to carry away.

[3] Literally, 'for him who was carrying'; in the Hebrew text, 'for the burden.'

7 ship! Shoulder-high it must be borne, set down on its pedestal; there it stands, powerless to move from its place, deaf to their cry, and in their need bringing no deliverance.

8 This, for your confusion, call to mind; think well on it, unbelieving
9 hearts. Remember the lesson of times long since, that I am God,
10 and there is no other, none to rival me; did I not tell you from the first the events of latter days, from the beginning what had not yet come to be? My purpose, I promised, should not fail, my whole will
11 must needs be done. See where I have summoned a bird of prey from the east, a man from a distant country, to do this will of mine! I, that spoke, will make my word good; I, that purposed it, my purpose will
13 accomplish. Redress far off? Nay, faithless hearts, listen to me; here is redress I bring you, close at hand. Distance there is none to be travelled, nor lingers deliverance on the way. Delivered Sion's mountain shall be, Jerusalem have sight of my glory.

CHAPTER FORTY-SEVEN

COME down, sit in the dust, poor maid of Babylon; the ground thy seat shall be; no throne any longer for that queen of the Chaldean
2 folk we knew once, so dainty, so delicate. Get thee to the millstones and grind there, ready to expose thy nakedness; off with thy veil, here are
3 streams to be crossed bare of leg. Thou shalt be exposed to shame, thy naked form uncovered; I mean to take vengeance on thee, and no man shall stay my hand.

4 (But we have one to ransom us; who but the Lord of hosts, the Holy One of Israel?)[1]

5 Sit dumb, bury thyself in darkness, lady of Chaldea; thou shalt
6 rule the nations no longer. Angry with my people, turned enemy against the land of my choice, I gave them into thy power; and thou, what mercy didst thou shew them? Heavy the yoke thou didst lay on
7 aged shoulders. Thou wouldst surely be a queen for ever; thou didst
8 it light-heartedly, not recking what the end should be. And now, here is a word for those delicate ears, lady of the careless heart, who sittest there telling thyself, I am Babylon, I have no rival; no lonely
9 widowhood, no childless lot for me. These two things shall fall on thee suddenly in a single day, childlessness and widowhood; fall upon

---

[1] It is difficult to see either what is the relevance of this verse in its present context; or how it could have strayed into that context from elsewhere. As it stands, it appears to be a triumphant refrain sung by the Israelites, interrupting God's message to the Babylonians.

thee in full measure, so blind amid all thy sorceries, through the crass
folly of thy wizards so blind.
10   Such was thy trust in these wicked arts of thine, thou hadst no fear
of discovery; thy very wisdom, thy very knowledge were a snare; I
11 am Babylon, thy heart told thee, rival I have none.   And now comes
ruin unforeseen, comes doom no sacrifice can avert; sudden and strange
12 thy encounter with sorrow.   What ails thee? All that multitude of
wizards, and wilt thou not persevere with thy enchantments, the hard-
earned lore of thy youth? Maybe it will turn to thy advantage; thou
13 shalt be formidable yet!   But no, thou art wearied of those many consultations. Let them come to thy side now and save thee if they can,
diviners that gaze up at the stars, count days of the month, to tell
14 thy future for thee!   Like stubble burn they one and all; their own lives
they cannot rescue from the flame. Here is no brazier to warm them,
15 no ingle-nook to sit by! And this is the end of all thy long study; trusted
counsellors of thy youth, all have gone astray in their reckoning;
deliverance for thee is none.

CHAPTER FORTY-EIGHT

A MESSAGE for you, sons of Jacob, heirs of Israel's name, sprung
from the stock of Juda, that take oath in the Lord's name, of Israel's
2 God the memory preserve, but not in faith, but not in loyalty! Townsmen
they are still reckoned of a holy city; still on Israel's God, the Lord of
3 hosts, lean they for support.   What happened in times past, I had foretold
long before; warning was uttered, and in the public ear; then, suddenly, I
4 would set to work, and the prophecy was fulfilled.   I knew well what an
untamed creature thou art, neck stubborn as an iron hawser, forehead
5 intractable as bronze; I would warn thee from the first, tell thee what was
coming before it came; never shouldst thou say this was the work of thy
6 false gods, the will of idols thou didst carve and cast.   Consider closely the
things I warned thee of, was there any foretelling them? Ever I reveal to
7 thee, long before, things kept secret from thy knowledge;   events that are
coming about now, unheard of then.[1] When they are yet beyond know-
8 ledge, I reveal them; not thine to boast, it was no news to thee.   And
still thou wouldst not listen, thou wouldst be ignorant still; when I prophesied to thee in times past, I could get no hearing; what hope from
9 the traitor but of treason? I know thee a rebel from thy birth.   If I

---

[1] The exact sense of verses 6 and 7 is doubtful; both the Hebrew text and
the Latin version, which differs from it considerably, give 'then' instead of
'now' as the time when the 'things kept secret' were revealed.

reprieve thee from my vengeance, it is my own honour demands it;
curb thee I must, for my own sake, or wouldst thou rush to thy doom.
10 I have tested thee, but not as silver is tested; even in the furnace of
11 affliction, thou wast already my choice. Honour, my own honour
demands it; how should I suffer my name to be reviled, or the worship
that belongs to me given to another?

12   Listen then, Jacob; listen to me, thou Israel to whom my call was
13 sent. I am still the same; before all, and at the end of all, I am. My
hand fashioned the heavens, my fingers measured the span of earth;
14 it is my command holds them in their place. Assemble, all you nations,
and listen to me; tell me which of your gods has prophesied it,[1] The
Lord, in his great love for Israel,[2] means to subdue Babylon to his will,
15 to bare his arm among the Chaldeans? But I did, I foretold it; it was
I that brought the conqueror on his way, so that it lay smooth before
him.

16   Gather round me and listen; from the first I have been telling you
this openly enough; was I not there among you long since, before
it happened? And now that it is happening, it is the Lord God, it is the
17 spirit of the Lord God, that sends me to you.[3] Here is a message from
the Lord, thy ransomer, the Holy One of Israel: I am the Lord thy God,
ever ready to teach thee what it concerns thee to know, guide thee on
18 the path thou treadest. If thou hadst but heeded my warnings! Then
had a flowing stream of peace been with thee, a full tide of the Lord's
19 favour; thy own race, thy own stock, should have been numberless
as the sand or the pebbles on the sea-beach; the remembrance of thee
20 should never have been cut off from my merciful regard.[4] Away from
Babylon, have done with Chaldea, let this be your triumphant watchword; make it heard everywhere, publish it to the ends of the earth,
21 tell them the Lord has ransomed his servant Jacob; they did not go
thirsty when he led them through the desert; he could bring water
out of the rock for them, cleave the hard rock and make the water flow.
22 But for the rebellious, the Lord says, there is no peace.

---

[1] Or perhaps, 'assemble, all you Israelites, and listen to me, tell me which
of the heathen gods.' The context makes it clear that one sense or the other
is intended by the original text, which gives simply, 'assemble, all of you, and
listen to me, tell me which of them.'

[2] In the original, simply 'him.'

[3] It is presumably the prophet who speaks here in his own person.

[4] In the Latin version, these sentences express regret for the past; in the
Hebrew text, they might express a hope for the future.

CHAPTER FORTY-NINE

LISTEN, remote islands; pay heed to me, nations from far away. Ere
ever I was born, the Lord sent me his summons, kept me in mind
2 already, when I lay in my mother's womb.[1] Word of mine is sword of his,
ready sharpened, under cover of his hand; arrow he has chosen out care-
3 fully, hidden yet in his quiver. Thou art my servant, he whispers, thou
4 art the Israel I claim for my own.[2] To me, all my labour seemed useless,
my strength worn out in vain; his to judge me, he, my God, must reward
5 my work as he would. But now a new message he sends me; I am his
servant, appointed ever since I lay in the womb, to bring Jacob back to
him. What if Israel will not answer the summons? None the less, the
6 Lord destines me to honour; none the less, he, my God, protects me. Use
thee I will, he promises, nor with thy service be content, when the tribes
of Jacob thou hast summoned, brought back the poor remnant of Israel;
nay, I have appointed thee to be the light of the Gentiles, in thee I will
send out my salvation to the furthest corners of the earth.

7   A message from the Lord, Israel's ransomer, Israel's Holy One,
to the despised one, to the nation that is abhorred,[3] to the slave of
tyrants: Kings, when they see this, shall rise up from their thrones,
princes too, and fall down to worship, in honour of the Lord, that
keeps his promise so faithfully, the Holy One of Israel, that claims
thee still.

8   Thus says the Lord, Here is a time of pardon, when prayer of thine
shall be answered, a day of salvation, when I will bring thee aid. I
have kept thee in readiness, to make, by thy means, a covenant with
my people.[4] Thine to revive a ruined country, to parcel out the for-
9 feited lands anew, men that are bound in darkness restoring to freedom
and to the light. There shall be pasture for my flock by the wayside,
10 feeding-grounds they shall have on all the barren uplands; they will

---

[1] It is not certain whether the speaker here is the prophet himself, or the
servant of the Lord referred to in 42.1 and elsewhere.

[2] Perhaps in the sense that this one man is all the Israel left, at a time of
general apostasy. The sentence may also be rendered, 'Thou, Israel, art my
servant'; but verse 6 below seems also to indicate that the person addressed is a
messenger sent to Israel, not the people itself.

[3] In the Hebrew text, the probable meaning is 'to him that is abhorred by
the nation.' This would mean that the promise is made to the Servant of the
Lord (or perhaps to the prophet), not to the Jewish nation. Whatever explanation be given, it is not easy to be sure of the connexion of this verse either with
what precedes it or with what follows it.

[4] Cf. II Cor. 6.2.

hunger and thirst no more, noonday heat nor sun overpower them;
theirs is a merciful shepherd, that will lead them to welling fountains
11 and give them drink.   And I will turn all these mountains of mine
into a highroad for you; safe through the uplands my path shall lead.
12 See how they come from far away! Exiles from north and west, exiles
13 from the south country return.   Ring out, heaven, with praise; let earth
keep holiday, and its mountains echo that praise again; the Lord brings
consolation to his people, takes pity on their need.

14   Did Sion complain, the Lord has forsaken me, my own Master
15 gives me never a thought?   What, can a woman forget her child that
is still unweaned, pity no longer the son she bore in her womb? Let
16 her forget; I will not be forgetful of thee.   Why, I have cut thy image
on the palms of my hands; those walls of thine dwell before my eyes
17 continually.   Here are craftsmen ready to build thee again; vanished,
18 now, the spoilers that plundered thee.   Look about thee, and see thy
children met together, coming back to thee; As I am living God, the
Lord says, all these shall be a robe to deck thee, shall ring thee round
19 like a bride's jewels; the silent homes, the lonely places of a ruined
countryside, shall have no room, now, for thy many inhabitants, when
20 all that robbed thee of thy lands have fled far away.   Sons born to
thee in the days of thy barrenness shall cry out, Here all is confined,
21 give me room to live! Who has begotten me these? thou wilt ask.
Barren days of exile, when I could not give birth; who has reared
me these, when I was left solitary? Where were these all the while?
22 Even now, says thy Lord God, I will beckon to the nations, lift up a
signal for all the world to see; son and daughter of thine shall be nursed
23 in their arms, carried on their shoulders.   Thou shalt have kings to
foster them, queens to nurse them for thee; kings and queens shall
bow to earth before thee, kissing the dust thy feet have trodden. And
thou shalt know at last what a Lord I am, a Lord none ever trusted
in vain.
24   Shall the strong be robbed of his spoil? Who shall deliver the captives
25 from a warrior's hand? [1]   Captives of the strong, the Lord says, shall
be taken away from him, the valiant warrior shall lose his spoil. I will
pass judgement on the men who have been thy judges, and thy own
26 children shall escape.   I will feed thy enemies on their own flesh,
give them their own blood to make them drunk, and all mankind shall
know that I, the Lord, have delivered you, that I, the Prince of Israel,
have brought thee rescue.

---

[1] Cf. Mt. 12.29.

CHAPTER FIFTY

THUS says the Lord, Who can shew writ of separation your mother had from me when I sent her away? Was I in debt, that I must needs sell you as slaves? Nay, if I sold you, it was for your disobedience; it was 2 wanton wife I thrust out of doors. And now must I come to you, and find none to greet me,[1] call you, and hear no answer to my call? What, has arm of mine grown shrunk and shrivelled, lost its power to save? Have I strength no longer to set men free? Nay, with a word I can yet turn sea into desert, dry up rivers, till the fish lie rotting on the banks, dead of 3 thirst; cover I can yet the heavens with darkness, and give them mourning weeds to wear.

4 Ever the Lord schools my tongue to utterance that shall refresh the weary; awakes my dull ears, morning after morning, their Master's 5 bidding to heed. An attentive ear the Lord has given me; should I 6 withstand him? Should I shrink from the task? I offered my body defenceless to the men who would smite me, my cheeks to all who plucked at my beard; I did not turn away my face when they reviled 7 me and spat upon me. The Lord God is my helper; and that help cannot play me false; meet them I will, and with a face unmoved as 8 flint; not mine to suffer the shame of defeat; here is One stands by 9 to see right done me. Come, who pleads? Meet me, and try the issue; let him come forward who will, and accuse me. Here is the Lord God ready to aid me; who dares pass sentence on me now? Shrivels it away, their malice, like garment the moth has eaten!

10 Who is here that fears the Lord, listens to his servant's message? Who would make his way through dark places, with no glimmer of light? Let him trust in the name of the Lord, and lean upon his God. 11 For you others, with brand at girdle, that your own fire would make, with fire your own brands have kindled light the path if you can; this is all the gift I have for you, a bed of anguish.[2]

---

[1] 'I find none to greet me'; literally, 'there was not a man.'

[2] The meaning of this verse is very obscure, and is variously explained. The context is perhaps best suited if we understand it of such Jews as were plotting rebellion against the governing powers, instead of waiting confidently for God's help, like those referred to in the previous verse.

CHAPTER FIFTY-ONE

LISTEN to me, then, you who follow the true path, you that have recourse to the Lord. Think of the rock you were quarried from, of
2 the hidden depths whence you came, of Abraham that begot you, of Sara that was your mother; he was a childless man when I called him, and
3 blessed him, and granted him a posterity. And has the Lord no pity for Sion, left desolate, no pity on her ruined state? Doubt not he will turn that wilderness into a garden of delight, that loneliness into a paradise; in her, too, mirth and gladness shall be found, there shall be thanksgiving
4 and songs of praise. People of mine, men of a chosen race, give heed and hearing! Henceforth, my law shall be promulgated, my decrees be ratified,
5 for a whole world's enlightening. Soon, now, my faithful servant will come, even now he is on his way to deliver you; these arms of mine shall execute judgement on the nations; the remote islands are waiting for me,
6 are looking for my aid. Lift up your eyes to the heavens, cast them down to earth again; those heavens shall vanish like smoke, that earth be fretted away like a garment, and all who dwell on it share the same destruction;
7 my saving power is eternal, my faithfulness inexhaustible. Listen to me, you that can discern the right, my own people, with my law written in your hearts; not yours to be afraid of men's taunts, shrink from
8 them when they revile you; crumble away they must, like garment the worms have eaten, like wool fretted by the moth; my saving power is eternal, my faithfulness lives on from age to age.
9 Up, up, arm of the Lord, array thyself in strength; up, as in the days that are past, long ages since. What other power was it that smote
10 our insolent enemy,[1] wounded the dragon; what other power dried up the sea, with its deep rolling waters, made the sea's caverns a high-
11 way, for a ransomed people to cross? Now, too, men the Lord has ransomed will come home again to Sion, praising him as they go. Eternal happiness crowns them, joy and happiness in their grasp now, sorrow and sighing fled far away.
12 It is I, still it is I, that will bring thee consolation. And it is thou that
13 art afraid of mortal man, of earth-born things that die like grass? Is it thou that dost forget the Lord, thy maker, who spread out the heavens and laid the foundations of the earth? What, go in fear all day long of yonder angry tyrant, sworn to undo thee? What of the tyrant's anger

---

[1] Literally, 'the proud one,' but the word used in the Hebrew text is probably a proper name, Rahab. This is used as a title for Egypt, as in Ps. 88.11; and 'the dragon' is no doubt another symbol of the Egyptian power, as perhaps in Ps. 73.14.

14 now? Comes he [1] with hurried step to release his prisoner, persecuted
15 to the death till now, or suffered to starve for want of bread! I am
    the Lord thy God, the same power that stirs up the sea till waves rise
16 high on it; the Lord of hosts is the name I bear. To thy lips I have
    entrusted my message, kept thee under cover of my hand, to replant
    heaven and refound earth, to tell Sion, Thou art my people.[2]
17   Up, up, Jerusalem, bestir thyself! It was a draught of his vengeance
    the Lord gave thee to drink; ay, thou hast drunk deep of a cup that
18 numbs the senses, drained it to the dregs. So many children she has
    borne and reared, and none to give her support, none to take her by
19 the hand! Who is to mourn for thee, the sport of a double calamity,
    by want and war dismantled and unmanned? Who is here to console
20 thee? They are left to lie at every street corner, those sons of thine,
    dazed as wild bull caught in a net, brought down by the Lord's anger,
21 by the punishment he, thy God, has sent them. Listen thou, the
22 unbefriended, thy wits bemused with sorrow, not with wine, here
    is the message thy master has for thee, thy Lord and God, ready to
    fight in his people's cause! I am taking it away from thy hand, this
    draught that numbs the senses, the dregs of the vengeance I had poured
23 out for thee; thou shalt drink it no longer. Cruel oppressors that bade
    thee lie down and let them walk over thee, dust under their feet, a
    pathway for them to tread, shall find the cup has passed from thy hand
    to theirs.

CHAPTER FIFTY-TWO

UP, up, array thyself, Sion, in all thy strength; clothe thyself as befits
    thy new glory, Jerusalem, city of the Holy One! The uncircumcised,
2 the unclean, shall enter thee no more. Shake the dust from thee, Jeru-
    salem, rise up and take thy throne; rid thy neck of the chains that bound
3 it, Sion, once captive queen! This is the Lord's promise, You were
    bartered away for nothing, and you shall be ransomed without cost.[3]
4 Time was, the Lord God says, long ago, when my people went down into
    Egypt and dwelt among strangers there; time was, since then, they were

---

[1] Or possibly 'One is coming.'

[2] From this verse it appears that the dialogue, verses 9–16, is either between
the Lord and his prophet, or between the Lord and his Servant, cf. 49.2.

[3] The sense is probably, 'I gained nothing in return when I sent you into
exile at Babylon' (cf. 50.1 above, Ps. 43.13); 'I did not engage the gratitude
of the Chaldeans, who remain idolaters; I am free therefore, to remit your
sentence of exile whenever I will.' The interpretation, 'You were sent into exile
for no fault of your own, and you shall be reprieved for no merits of your own'
is neither probable in itself nor suited to the context.

5 oppressed, beyond all reason, by the Assyrians; what needs it,[1] the Lord says, then or now, my people should be carried off thus wantonly into exile? Their new masters sin defiantly, bring my name continually into

6 reproach. The day comes when my own people my own name will recognize, nor doubt that I, who promised to be with them, am with them now.

7 Welcome, welcome on the mountain heights the messenger that cries, All is well! Good news brings he, deliverance cries he, telling

8 Sion, Thy God has claimed his throne! A shout goes up from the watchmen; they are crying out all at once, all at once echoing their praise; their own eyes shall witness it, when the Lord brings Sion

9 deliverance. Rejoice, echo all at once with rejoicing, ruined homes of Jerusalem; comfort from the Lord for the Lord's people, Jerusalem

10 redeemed! The Lord bares his holy arm for all the nations to see it; to the remotest corners of earth he, our God, makes known his saving

11 power. Return, return; no more of Babylon; touch nothing defiled as you come out from the heart of her, keep yourselves unsullied,

12 you that have the vessels of the Lord's worship in your charge. No need for confusion at the time of your going; this shall be no hasty flight, with the Lord himself to march before you, the God of Israel to rally you.

13 See, here is my servant, one who will be prudent in all his dealings.

14 To what height he shall be raised, how exalted, how extolled! The world stands gazing in horror; was ever a human form so mishandled,

15 human beauty ever so defaced? Yet this is he that will purify a multitude of nations; kings shall stand dumb in his presence; seen, now, where men had no tidings of him, made known to such as never heard his name.[2]

---

[1] 'What needs it, then or now?' Literally, 'And now, what is to me here?'—though this is less accurate as a rendering of the Hebrew text. The idiomatic sense which this phrase commonly has (cf. 22.16 above, and many other passages) would be 'And what business have I to interfere here?' But this is evidently inappropriate, and it is best to take the words literally, as in Gen. 19.12. Cf. note on verse 3.

[2] 'Purify'; literally 'sprinkle', but wherever this word occurs elsewhere, the thing, not the person, is its object (*i.e.*, you sprinkle something on a person), and various attempts have been made to amend the Hebrew text, *e.g.*, 'startle.' The end of this verse, in the Hebrew text, will equally well yield the sense, 'they shall see that of which they had no tidings, that which they had never heard shall be made known to them.' But the other sense, which is given by the Latin version, is clearly assumed by St. Paul in Rom. 15.21.

CHAPTER FIFTY-THREE

WHAT credence for such news as ours? Whom reaches it, this new
2 revelation of the Lord's strength? [1] He will watch this servant of
his appear among us, unregarded as [2] brushwood shoot, as a plant in
waterless soil; no stateliness here, no majesty, no beauty, as we gaze upon
3 him, to win our hearts. Nay, here is one despised, left out of all human
reckoning; bowed with misery, and no stranger to weakness; how should
we recognise that face? [3] How should we take any account of him, a man
4 so despised? Our weakness, and it was he who carried the weight of it,
our miseries, and it was he who bore them. [4] A leper, so we thought of him,
5 a man God had smitten and brought low; and all the while it was for our
sins he was wounded, it was guilt of ours crushed him down; on him the
punishment fell that brought us peace, by his bruises we were healed.
6 Strayed sheep all of us, each following his own path; and God laid on his
shoulders our guilt, the guilt of us all.
7   A victim? Yet he himself bows to the stroke; [5] no word comes from him.
Sheep led away to the slaughter-house, lamb that stands dumb while
8 it is shorn; no word from him. Imprisoned, brought to judgement,
and carried off, he, whose birth is beyond our knowing; numbered
among the living no more! Be sure it is for my people's guilt I have
9 smitten him. [6] Takes he leave of the rich, the godless, to win but a
grave, to win but the gift of death; [7] he, that wrong did never, nor had

---

[1] Cf. Rom. 10.16.

[2] 'Unregarded as'; in the original, simply 'like,' but this sense appears most
probable, in view of what follows. The second part of the verse may also be
interpreted as meaning, 'there is no stateliness, no majesty here to catch our
eyes, no beauty to win our hearts.'

[3] Literally, 'his face was as it were hidden.' In the Hebrew text, it is not
clear whether the face of the Servant is hidden from the onlookers, or theirs
(in disgust) from him.

[4] Mt. 8.17.

[5] Literally, according to the Latin version, 'He has been offered up because
he himself willed it.' The meaning of the Hebrew text seems to be rather, 'he
has been cruelly treated, and all the while he abased himself.'

[6] The beginning of this verse in the Hebrew text runs literally, 'He was taken
away from the restraint and from judgement, and his generation—who will
meditate?' The meaning usually given to the passage uses almost every word
in a strange sense, and it seems probable that there has been a corruption in
the text; cf. the Septuagint Greek version, quoted in Ac. 8.33.

[7] The Hebrew text here yields a more simple translation, 'He (God) gave
him burial with the wicked, and with the rich (man) in his death'; but the
bearing of the phrase is difficult to determine. The Latin can only be interpreted
(on the lines of verse 3 above) as meaning that the Servant renounced all
fellowship with the wicked and the rich in order to win himself a felon's grave.

10 treason on his lips! Ay, the Lord's will it was, overwhelmed he should
be with trouble. His life laid down for guilt's atoning, he shall yet
be rewarded; father of a long posterity, instrument of the divine purpose;
11 for all his heart's anguish, rewarded in full. The Just One, my servant;
many shall he claim for his own, win their acquittal, on his shoulders
12 bearing their guilt. So many lives ransomed, foes so violent baulked
of their spoil! Such is his due, that gave himself up to death, and would
be counted among the wrongdoers; bore those many sins, and made
intercession for the guilty.

CHAPTER FIFTY-FOUR

SING with praise, barren city that art childless still; echo thy praise,
cry aloud, wife that wast never brought to bed; forsaken, she is to have
more children now, the Lord says, than wife whose husband remains with
2 her.[1] Make more room for thy tent, stretch wide—what hinders thee?—
the curtains of thy dwelling-place; long be the ropes, and firm the pegs
3 that fasten them. Right and left thou shalt spread, till thy race dis-
4 possesses the heathen, peoples the ruined cities. Not thine to fear disappointment, not thine to blush for hopes unfulfilled; forget, henceforward,
the shame of younger days, the reproach of thy widowed state; think upon
5 it no more. Husband now thou hast, and the name of him is the Lord of
hosts, thy creator; he, the Holy One of Israel, that will now be called God
6 of the whole earth, makes thee his own. The Lord calls thee back, a
woman forsaken and forlorn, the wife of his youth, long cast away; thy
7 God sends thee word, if I abandoned thee, it was but for a little moment,
8 and now, in my great compassion, I bring thee home again. Hid I my
face from thee, it was for a short while, till my anger should be spent; love
9 that takes pity on thee shall be eternal, says the Lord, thy ransomer. The
days of Noe have come again; I swore to Noe that I would bring no
more floods on the earth such as his; thou, too, hast my oath for it,
10 I will be angry with thee no more, rebuke thee no more. Let the mountains be moved, the hills shake; my compassion towards thee stands
immovable, my promise still unshaken, says the Lord, thy comforter.
11   Thou, the friendless, the storm-beaten, the inconsolable, shalt have
a pavement of patterned stones, and thy foundations shall be of sapphire;
12 thou shalt have turrets of jasper, and gates of carved gems, and all
13 thy boundary stones shall be jewels. All thy children, then, shall
be disciples of the Lord; thy children, blessed how abundantly with
14 peace! Justice shall be thy sure foundation; far from thy thoughts

---

[1] Gal. 4.27.

be all oppression, now thou hast nothing to fear, all tumult of the
15 mind,[1] when peril is none to threaten thee. Aliens that had no part
with me shall come to thy side; strangers shall throw in their lot with
16 thine.[2] See where the smith blows the coals at his forge, fashioning
each weapon according to its use! Who but I made him? And who
17 but I made the slayer that goes out to destroy? No weapon that is
forged against thee shall go true; no voice that is raised to condemn
thee, but thou shalt give it the lie. Such their lot shall be that are the
Lord's servants; such protection shall they have of me, says the Lord.

CHAPTER FIFTY-FIVE

SO many athirst; who will not come to the water? So many destitute;
who will come and get him food, get wine and milk free, no price to be
2 paid? What, always spending, and no bread to eat, always toiling, and
never a full belly? Do but listen, here you shall find content; here are
3 dainties shall ravish your hearts. To my summons give heed and hearing;
so your spirits shall revive; a fresh covenant awaits you, this time eternal;
gracious promise of mine to David shall be ratified now.[3]
4   Before all the world my witness thou, a prince and a ruler among
5 the nations![4] Summons of thine shall go out to a nation thou never
knewest; peoples that never heard of thee shall hasten to thy call; such
the glory thy God, the Holy One of Israel, has bestowed on thee.[5]
6   To the Lord betake you, while he may yet be found; cry out, while
7 he is close at hand to hear. Leave rebel his ill-doing, sinner his guilty
thoughts, and come back to the Lord, sure of his mercy, our God,
8 so rich in pardon. Not mine, the Lord says, to think as you think,
9 deal as you deal; by the full height of heaven above earth, my dealings
10 are higher than your dealings, my thoughts than your thoughts. Once

---

[1] 'Tumult of the mind'; the word in the Hebrew text means either 'dismay'
or 'ruin'; neither seems a very good parallel for the word 'oppression,' and
some have suspected corruption in the text.
[2] The Latin version, probably through misunderstanding a word that is three
times repeated, differs widely here from the Hebrew text, whose meaning
seems to be 'Let men strive against thee as they will, it is with no sanction of
mine; whoever strives against thee shall fall because of thee (or perhaps, shall
be compelled to fall in with thee).'
[3] Cf. Ps. 88.35–38; Ac. 13.34.
[4] This is ordinarily assumed to refer to David, but the description is not
very suitable, and it seems possible that the prophet, with one of his sudden
transitions, has gone back to the Lord's Servant here.
[5] The person mentioned in verse 4 is more probably the subject of this
address, than the people of Israel.

fallen from the sky, does rain or snow return to it? Nay, it refreshes earth, soaking into it and making it fruitful, to provide the sower with
11 fresh seed, the hungry mouths with bread. So it is with the word by these lips of mine once uttered; it will not come back, an empty echo, the way it went; all my will it carries out, speeds on its errand.
12 Doubt not, then, yours shall be a happy departure, a peaceful return; doubt not mountain and hill shall escort you with their praises, and
13 the woods echo their applause. Tall pine-trees then shall grow where valerian grew, and myrtles spring from yonder nettle-beds; great glory the Lord shall win, such a blazon as eternity cannot efface.

CHAPTER FIFTY-SIX

KEEP right order, the Lord says, faithful to your duty still; ere long I will send deliverance, my own faithfulness shall be revealed.
2 Blessed, every man that so lives, every mother's son that by this rule holds fast, keeps the sabbath holy, and his own hands clear of mischief.
3 Proselyte let him be, of alien birth, will the Lord deny him citizenship? Eunuch let him be, is he no better than a barren trunk, cut down
4 as worthless? Nay, for yonder eunuch the Lord has this message: Who keeps my sabbath? Who makes my will his choice, true to my
5 covenant? A place he shall have in this house, within these walls of mine a memorial; son nor daughter his name could so perpetuate; such a memorial I will grant him as time shall never efface.
6 And so it shall be with the alien born, will they but throw in their lot with the Lord's worshippers, that cherish the love of his name; the Lord's servants that keep the sabbath inviolate, and are true to
7 his covenant. Free of the mountain that is my sanctuary, welcome guests in the house where men pray to me, not vainly to my altar they shall bring burnt-offering and sacrifice. Claimed my house shall be,
8 for a house of prayer, by all the nations.[1] Such promise the Lord God makes, that now brings home the exiled sons of Israel: I have others to bring, that must yet rally to thy side.
9 Come, all you wild things, all you beasts of the forest, your prey
10 awaits you! Here are none but blind watchmen, all unawares; here are dumb dogs that cannot bark, false seers that lie sleeping, in love
11 with their dreams; shameless dogs that cannot tell when they are gorged with food. The very shepherds have forgotten their craft; see them go their ways, each busy, first and last, with gorging his own

---

[1] Mt. 21.13.

12 appetite: Fetch we wine, and drink ourselves drunk! To-morrow
shall be as to-day was, and braver, braver yet! [1]

CHAPTER FIFTY-SEVEN

ALAS, that none takes warning! See how good men die, how the
friends of God are borne away from us; and none has the wit to see
2 trouble is coming, and the good must be spared the sight of it! [2] Peace
be his lot, easy let him rest, that followed ever the straight path.
3   But you, come and answer for yourselves, brood of the sorceress,
4 children of the adulterer and the harlot! Over whom would you make
merry, with open mouth and hanging tongue? What are you but the
5 sons of shame, a bastard race? You, that dally with idols under the
first spreading tree, that sacrifice little children in the rock-caves among
the glens?
6   Where the valleys part,[3] there is thy part and lot; to those thou
wilt pour out libations, wilt offer sacrifice; and must I look on unmoved?
7 Thou hast set down thy bed on the peak of a high mountain; there
8 thou hast gone up to offer victims. Keepsake of mine must be put
behind the door, where the posts should hide it, now thou wouldst
strip thee naked and let in a gallant in my place, make free with my
marriage-bed! With such as these thou didst exchange vows, greedily
9 thou didst buy their good will. A king's favour to win,[4] with ointments
thou wouldst cover thee, wouldst spare no kind of perfume; on a far
errand thy envoys went out, and ever thy pride was humbled, low
10 as hell itself. So wearied with long journeying, and never didst thou
11 cry, Enough; still obstinate, confess thy need thou wouldst not. Alas,
what anxious fears were these, that to my service made thee false, of
me no memory left thee, no thought? And all because I nothing said,

---

[1] The denunciations in verses 9–12 would be suitable to Babylon on the
eve of its capture by the Persians (Dan. 5); but they are usually regarded as
continuous with the succeeding chapter, which seems to be addressed to unworthy rulers of God's own people.

[2] There is no agreement among scholars, what is the situation here alluded
to. Some think the prophecies are made against the half-heathen remnant of
Israelites which occupied Samaria when the Jews returned from exile; others
would identify the 'good man' of verses 1 and 2 as king Ezechias, and apply
what follows to the idolatry of Manasses.

[3] Some would interpret the Hebrew text as meaning 'in the smooth stones
of the valleys,' which lends more force to the play upon words.

[4] The king is identified by some with the god Moloch (whose name means
'king'); by others with the king of Assyria. From the context, some reference
to foreign alliances seems probable.

12 made as if I nothing saw, till at last thou hadst forgotten me! Yet, wouldst thou regain thy strength, from me, no other, thou must have
13 news of it; thy own striving is all in vain. Let them deliver thee, if they can, at thy summons, these new allies thou hast made! See how they are carried away on the wind, how a breath will scatter them! His the prize, that in me has confidence; on my holy mountain he
14 shall find a resting-place. Hark, how the cry goes up, A road, there, a road; let them have free passage! These are my people; clear of every hindrance be their path!

15 A message from the high God, the great God, whose habitation is eternity, whose name is hallowed! He, dwelling in that high and holy place, dwells also among chastened and humbled souls, bidding
16 the humble spirit, the chastened soul, rise and live! I will not be always claiming my due, I will not cherish my anger eternally; what soul but takes its origin from me? Am I not the maker of all that breathes? [1]
17 Greedy wrongdoer that defies me I must needs smite down; hide my face from him in anger, let him follow the path his own erring
18 will has chosen. Now to pity his plight, now to bring him remedy! Home-coming at last, consolation at last, for him and all that bemoan
19 him! The harvest of men's thanks, it is I that bring it to the birth. [2] Peace, the Lord says, peace to those who are far away, and to those
20 who are near at hand; I have brought him remedy. But rebellious hearts are like the tempestuous sea that can never find repose; its waters
21 must ever be churning up mire and scum. For the rebellious, the Lord says, there is no peace.

CHAPTER FIFTY-EIGHT

CRY aloud, never ceasing, raise thy voice like a trumpet-call, and tell my people of their transgressions, call the sons of Jacob to account.
2 Day after day they besiege me, arraign my dealings with them, a nation, you would think, ever dutiful, one that never swerved from the divine will. Proof they ask of my faithfulness, would fain bring a plea against
3 their God. [3] Why hadst thou no eyes for it, say thy, when we fasted; why

---

[1] The latter part of this verse, in the Hebrew text, is usually interpreted, 'for the (human) spirit would faint away, (and) the breathing souls which I have made'; but this rendering lacks the parallelism we should expect in Hebrew poetry. The Latin reads literally, 'a spirit shall go out from my face, and I will give breaths'; the interpretation offered above is that of St. Jerome and other Fathers.

[2] Literally, 'I have created the fruit of the lips'; cf. Heb. 13.15.

[3] 'Bring a plea against,' literally, 'approach,' but the context shows that the verb is used in a legal sense, as in 57.3 above and elsewhere.

didst thou pass by unheeding, when we humbled ourselves before thee?
Fasting, when you follow your own whim, distrain upon all your
4 debtors! Naught comes of it but law-suit and quarrelling; angry blows
profane it. A better fast you must keep than of old, ere plea of yours
5 makes itself heard above. With such fasting, with a day's penance,
should I be content? Is it enough that a man should bow down to
earth, make his bed on sackcloth and ashes? Think you, by such a
6 fasting day, to win the Lord's favour? Nay, fast of mine is something
other. The false claim learn to forgo, ease the insupportable burden,
7 set free the over-driven; away with every yoke that galls! Share thy
bread with the hungry, give the poor and the vagrant a welcome to
thy house; meet thou the naked, clothe him; from thy own flesh and
8 blood turn not away. Then, sudden as the dawn, the welcome light
shall break on thee, in a moment thy health shall find a new spring;
divine favour shall lead thee on thy journey, brightness of the Lord's
9 presence close thy ranks behind. Then the Lord will listen to thee
when thou callest on him; cry out, and he will answer, I am here at thy
side.

Banish from thy midst oppression, and the finger pointed scornfully,
10 and the plotting of harm, spend thyself giving food to the hungry,
relieving the afflicted; then shall light spring up for thee in the darkness,
11 and thy dusk shall be noonday; the Lord will give thee rest [1] continually,
fill thy soul with comfort, thy body with ease.[2] Not more secure the
12 well-watered garden, the spring whose waters never fail. Rebuilt,
in thy land, the immemorial ruins; restored, the foundations of long
ago; this thy task shall be, to repair the broken walls, to reclaim the
13 by-ways. Walk warily, keep my sabbath unprofaned. Here is a day
I have sanctified, not for thy self-pleasing; a precious thing the Lord
has made holy and honourable; and wilt thou dishonour it? Wilt thou
go thy own way, use it for thy own pleasure, while it away in gossip?
14 Thou shalt yet have joy in the Lord; I will carry thee aloft, high above
the high places of the land, satisfy thy longing for Jacob's patrimony;
the Lord's lips have promised it.

---

[1] The sense of the Hebrew text is, 'guide thee.'

[2] Literally, 'he will fill thy soul with brightness and deliver thy bones.'
But the Hebrew text means rather, 'he will satisfy thy desire in time of drought,
and refresh thy bones,' though the authority for this last verb is uncertain.

CHAPTER FIFTY-NINE

D OUBT you the Lord's hand can reach far as ever, to bring deliverance? Think you his ear has grown deaf, that you cry out in vain?
2 Nay, sin of yours has come between you and your God; guilt of yours has
3 estranged him that he denies you audience; the bloodstained hands, the
4 itching fingers, lying lips, and tongues that whisper of treachery. Who owns the claim of justice, who judges honourably? A lie their confidence, folly their watchword, they carry mischief in the womb, bring shame to
5 birth. Eggs the cockatrice may hatch, yet there is death in the taste of
6 them, a brood of basilisks; deftly the spider weaves, yet web of hers will never make cloth, none will be the warmer for her toil; so it is with these;
7 all unprofitable their schemes, their doing all undoing. Swift ministers of evil, hot-foot they scent down the blood of innocence,[1] their aim ever
8 to destroy, leave a trail of havoc and ruin. Where peace should be found they know not, nor ever set their hearts on right; still stray by crooked paths where safety is none.
9   What wonder if redress is still far from us, if reprieve linger on its way? Crave we light, and nothing see but darkness, hope we for dawn,
10 and walk in dusk. Blind men that grope along a wall, hands, not eyes, to shew the way, stumble we at noonday as though benighted; we
11 are dead men in a world of shadows. No better than growling bears, or doves that moan and mourn, still we hope for the redress that never
12 comes, the deliverance that is far away. Our guilt mounts up before thee, our sins accuse us; shame ever at our side, we confess the wrong
13 done. Heinous our treason against the Lord, that turn away from his divine leading to plan cruelty and rebellion; false thoughts we
14 conceive in our hearts that still find utterance. Redress is withheld from us, because loyalty lies neglected in our streets, and honour finds
15 no entrance; alas that loyalty should be forgotten, innocence marked down for spoil!
    All this the Lord has seen, and shame he thought it there should
16 be no redress. Was there no champion to come forward? None found he, and his heart misgave him. And so his own arm must bring the
17 deliverance he intended, his own faithfulness held him to it.[2] That faithfulness is the breastplate that arms him, that saving power the

---

[1] Rom. 3.15.

[2] The second part of this verse reads literally, 'His own arm delivered him, and his own justice strengthened him.' The notion is that of Almighty God interfering in person to help men because they cannot help themselves; cf. 63.5 below (where, however, 'indignation' takes the place of 'justice').

helmet that guards his head; vengeance the garment he wears, jealous
18 love the mantle that wraps him round.[1]   Doubt not he will repay,
wreak his anger upon the rebels, give his enemies their due; no island
19 so far off but it shall have its punishment,   till the name of the Lord
strikes terror into western lands, and the east stands in awe of his
fame. Here is a river coming upon them in full flood, driven on by
20 the Lord's breath;   here is one that brings deliverance to Sion, and
to all Jacob's children that turn away from their sins; the Lord has
21 promised it.   This covenant I will make with them, the Lord says:
Spirit of mine that dwells in thee, words of mine entrusted to thy lips,
on thy lips shall I dwell, on the lips of thy children and thy children's
children, henceforth and for ever.

CHAPTER SIXTY

RISE up, Jerusalem, and shine forth; thy dawn has come, breaks the
2 glory of the Lord upon thee!   What though darkness envelop the
earth, though all the nations lie in gloom? Upon thee the Lord shall dawn,
3 over thee his splendour shall be revealed.   Those rays of thine shall light
the Gentiles on their path; kings shall walk in the splendour of thy sun-
4 rise.   Lift up thy eyes and look about thee; who are these that come flocking to thee? Sons of thine, daughters of thine, come from far away, or
5 rising up close at hand.[2]   Heart of thee shall overflow with wonder and
gratitude, to see all the riches of ocean, all the treasure of the Gentiles
6 pouring into thee!   A stream of camels thronging about thee, dromedaries
from Madian and Epha, bringing all the men of Saba[3] with their gifts of
7 gold and incense, their cry of praise to the Lord!   Into thee all the herds
of Cedar shall be driven, the rams of Nebaioth shall be thy victims; gifts
at my altar accepted, to make the fame of my temple more famous yet.
8 Who are these that come, swift as the cloud-wrack, as doves flying home
9 to the dove-cot?   These, too, are thy sons; long since, the islands and the
ocean-going ships have awaited my signal, when I would bring them
home from far away, their silver and their gold with them, for the honour

---

[1] Eph. 6.14, 17; I Thess. 5.8.
[2] The second part of this verse reads literally, 'Thy sons shall come from far,
and thy daughters shall arise from the side'; it seems clear that St. Jerome
wrote, not 'arise,' but 'suck,' agreeing substantially with the Hebrew text,
which has 'and thy daughters shall be carried at the side.' But this makes a
weak parallel, and it is hard to see why infant daughters should come into the
picture; it is possible that there was a corruption in the text.
[3] 'All the men of Saba'; in the Hebrew text, 'All of them (*i.e.,* the riders
on the camels) from Saba.'

of the Lord thy God, the Holy One of Israel, that has bestowed this glory on thee.

10   Strangers shall build up thy walls for thee, kings shall do thee service; great as my severity in chastising thee shall be my favour when I pardon
11   thee. Thy gates shall stand open continually, no need to shut them day or night; [1] make way for the wealth of the nations that shall flow
12   into thee, for the kings with their escorts! Every nation and kingdom that refuses thee homage shall vanish away, whole provinces empty
13   and forlorn. All the beauty of Lebanon shall be brought to thee, fir-wood and box-wood and pine-wood mingled together to adorn this place, my sanctuary; I will have honour paid to this, the resting-place of
14   my feet. See how they come bending low before thee, the race of thy former oppressors, how the men that once despised thee worship the ground thou hast trodden, calling thee The City of the Lord, Sion,
15   dear to the Holy One of Israel! Thou, the desolate, thou, the un-befriended, a place unvisited by man, shalt be the pride of ages, the
16   joy of succeeding generations; thou shalt have nations to suckle thee, kings to foster thee, and acknowledge at last that I, the Lord, am thy deliverer, the Lord that rules in Jacob has paid thy ransom.

17   I will exchange thy brass for gold, thy stone for silver, thy wood for brass, thy stone for iron; I will give thee peace itself to be thy
18   government, justice itself to be thy magistracy; there shall be no more talk of wrong in that land of thine, no tidings of wreck and ruin within those frontiers; all thy walls shall be deliverance, and all thy gates
19   renown. No longer wilt thou have the sun to shine by day, or the moon's beam to enlighten thee; the Lord shall be thy everlasting light,
20   thy God shall be all thy splendour. [2] No more, for thee, the setting of suns, the waning of moons, now that the Lord is thy everlasting light,
21   and the days of thy widowhood are over. Thy people, all guiltless now, shall inherit the land eternally, the flower I planted, the pride of my
22   workmanship. The meanest of them shall be ancestor to a thousand, the least regarded, to a great nation; swift and sudden shall be the doing of it, when once the hour is come.

CHAPTER SIXTY-ONE

THE Lord has anointed me, on me his spirit has fallen; he has sent me to bring good news to men that are humbled, to heal broken hearts,
2   promising the release of captives, the opening of prison doors, proclaiming the year of the Lord's pardon, the day when he, our God, will give us

---

[1] Apoc. 21.25.   [2] Apoc. 21, 23; 22.5.

3   redress. Comfort for every mourner; Sion's mourners, what decree should I make for them, what gift offer them? Heads shall be garlanded, that once were strewn with ashes; bright with oil, the faces that were marred with grief; gaily they shall be clad, that went sorrowing. Sturdy growths (men will say) that fulfil hope reposed in them,[1] pride of the
4   Lord's planting! Theirs to rebuild what long has lain desolate, repair the ruins of past days, restore the forsaken cities that were lost, we thought, for ever.

5   Strangers they shall be that tend your flocks for you, farm and vine-
6   yard alien hands shall till; for you, a higher name, a greater calling, priests and chosen ministers of the Lord our God. All the wealth of the
7   nations shall be yours to enjoy, their spoils shall be your boast; for double portion of shame and contempt, you shall be twice honoured
8   now. Twice happy that home-coming, eternal that content;[2] I am the Lord, that love to give each his due, resent the wrong, when men rob me of my sacrifice. Faithfully I will give them their recompense,
9   bind myself, now, by an eternal covenant. Such a race shall spring from them, as all the nations of the world shall acknowledge; none that sees them but shall know them for a people the Lord has blessed.
10   Well may I rejoice in the Lord, well may this heart triumph in my God. The deliverance he sends is like a garment that wraps me about, his mercy like a cloak enfolding me; no bridegroom so proud of garland
11   that crowns him, no bride of the necklace she wears. See how yonder earth gives promise of spring, how the garden seeds give promise of flower! And the Lord God will make good his promise for all the world to see; a spring-time of deliverance and renown.

CHAPTER SIXTY-TWO

FOR love of Sion I will no more be silent, for love of Jerusalem I will never rest, until he, the Just One, is revealed to her like the dawn,
2   until he, her deliverer, shines out like a flame. All the nations, all the kings of the nations, shall see him, the just, the glorious;[3] and a new

---

[1] 'Sturdy growths that fulfil hope reposed in them'; or possibly, 'that tell of protecting care.' It is not easy to be certain whether the word 'justice' in the original implies, here, faithfulness on the part of man or faithfulness on the part of God.

[2] The interpretation of this verse is obscure, whether in the Hebrew text or in the Latin.

[3] Instead of 'Just One,' 'the just' and 'the glorious,' the Hebrew text has 'justice' (*i.e.,* redress, restoration), 'deliverance' and 'glory.'

3 name shall be given thee by the Lord's own lips. The Lord upholds thee,
4 his crown, his pride; thy God upholds thee, his royal diadem. No longer
shall men call thee Forsaken, or thy land Desolate; thou shalt be called
My Beloved, and thy land a Home, now the Lord takes delight in thee,
5 now thy land is populous once again.[1] Gladly as a man takes home the
maiden of his choice, thy sons shall come home to thee; gladly the Lord
shall greet thee, as bridegroom his bride.

6   I have set watchmen, Jerusalem, upon thy walls, that shall never
7 cease crying aloud, day or night; you that keep the Lord in remembrance,[2] take no rest, nor let him rest neither, till he has restored
8 Jerusalem, spread her fame over all the earth. The Lord has sworn
by his own right hand, by that arm which makes known his power.
Never again shall thy enemies eat the harvest of thy corn-fields, alien
9 folk drink the wine thou hast toiled to win; harvester and waggoner,
here in my precincts, shall eat and drink together, praising the Lord.
10   Out, out through the city gates! Give my people free passage; a
road, there, a smooth road, away with the boulders on it! Raise a signal
11 for all the nations to see. To the furthest corners of the earth the Lord
proclaims it, A message to queen Sion: Look, where thy deliverer
comes, look, how they come with him, the reward of his labour, the
12 achievement of his task![3] A holy people they shall be called, of the
Lord's ransoming, and thou the city of his choice, no more forsaken.

CHAPTER SIXTY-THREE

WHO is this, coming from Edom, coming on the road from Bosra,
with garments deep dyed? Who is this, so gaily clad, marching so
valiantly?

I am one who is faithful to his promises, a champion bringing deliverance.[4]

2   And why are thy garments stained with red? Why dost thou go clad
like the men who tread out the wine-press?

3   None other has trodden the wine-press but I only; out of all the
nations, no champion came to stand at my side. I have been treading
them down in my anger, trampling on them, full of vengeance; their
blood that has been sprinkled on the clothes about me; I come in

---

[1] In the Hebrew text, the land is to be called not 'a Home,' but 'a Wife,' and
it is to be 'espoused,' not 'populous,' once again.

[2] 'Keep the Lord in remembrance'; that is, according to the Latin version,
remember him; according to the Hebrew text, remind him (of his promises).

[3] See note on 40.10 above.

[4] The speaker here is probably the Lord himself; cf. 59.16.

4 garments deep dyed. My heart told me the time had come for vengeance,
5 this was my destined year of ransom; looked I all around, there was
none to help me; vainly I called for aid. My own arm should bring the
6 deliverance I intended; my own indignation uphold me.[1] I have
trampled the peoples down in my anger, stunned them [2] with my fury,
brought down their strength to the dust.

7 Listen, while I tell again the story of the Lord's mercies, what renown
the Lord has won; all the Lord has done for us, all the wealth of blessings
his pardoning love, his abounding pity has lavished on the race of
8 Israel. They are my own people, he would say; my own children cannot
9 be false to me; and with that, he delivered them. In all their straits,
power of his was not straitened;[3] his angel, token of his presence,
brought them deliverance. In love and pity he ransomed them, lifted
them in his arms and raised them up, all through the days gone by.
10 Only when they rebelled against him, when they distressed the spirit
of his chosen servant,[4] he would turn their enemy, and fight against them.
11 And even yet he would bethink him of times past, of Moses, and the
people that once was his.

Where is he now, the God that led them through the sea, his flock
with his own appointed shepherds; gave his holy spirit to the man
12 of his choice?[5] Majestic power, that led Moses by the hand; that parted
13 the sea at their coming, to win his name renown. Through its waters
they passed, sure of their foothold as horse that is led through the
14 desert; carefully as driver on some treacherous hill-side, the Lord's
spirit guided his people. Thus didst thou bring them home, and win
15 thyself honour. Bethink thee now, in heaven; look down from the
palace where thou dwellest, holy and glorious. Where, now, is thy
jealous love, where thy warrior's strength? Where is thy yearning of
heart, thy compassion? For me, compassion is none.

16 Yet, who is our father, Lord, if not thou? Let Abraham disown

---

[1] Cf. 59.16, note.

[2] 'Stunned them'; literally, 'made them drunk.' Some Hebrew MSS read 'broke them in pieces.'

[3] There is a doubt, here, in the Hebrew text, whether we should read 'he was not afflicted (constrained)' or 'he was afflicted.'

[4] 'The spirit of his chosen servant'; literally, 'of his holy one,' which may refer to Moses in verse 11, to other national heroes (such as Josue and Moses) in this verse. But the Hebrew text has 'the spirit of his holiness,' which in Hebrew idiom is nearly equivalent to 'his holy spirit'; and this is the translation given by the Septuagint Greek (cf. Eph. 4.30).

[5] The second half of this verse is usually joined to the first, as if it were the thought in the mind of the person there mentioned. But, if so, we must understand 'Israel' as the subject of 'bethought himself,' which is a very abrupt transition.

us, Israel disclaim his own blood, we are thy sons still; is it not thy
17 boast of old, thou hast paid a price for us? And now, Lord, wouldst
thou drive us away from following thee, harden our hearts till worship
we have none to give thee? For love of thy own servants, relent, for love
18 of the land that by right is thine. Is it nothing to thee, enemies of thy
holy people should have the mastery, trample thy sanctuary down?
19 Fared we worse in old days, before ever we called thee King, ever took
thy holy name for our watchword?

CHAPTER SIXTY-FOUR

WOULDST thou but part heaven asunder, and come down, the hills
2 shrinking from thy presence, melting away as if burnt by fire; the
waters, too, boiling with that fire! So should the fame of thee go abroad
3 among thy enemies; a world should tremble at thy presence! Of thy
marvellous doing, we ourselves cannot bear the sight; so it was when
thou camest down, and the hills shrank away before thee, long ago.[1]
4 Such things as were never known from the beginning, as ear never
heard, eye never saw, save at thy command, thou, O God, hast made
5 ready for all that await thy aid. Graciously thou goest out to meet
them, loyal lovers of thine that keep thee ever in mind, ever follow
thy bidding.[2]
And now thou art angry with us; we have sinned; so it has been
6 a long while, and shall we find deliverance? We are men defiled; what
are all our claims on thy mercy? No better than the clout a woman
casts away; we are like fallen leaves, every one of us, by the wind of
7 our own transgressions whirled along. There is none left that calls
on thy name, that bestirs himself to lay hold of thee. Thou hidest
thy face from us, broken men caught in the grip of their wrong-doing.

---

[1] The Hebrew text can be translated so as to make this verse part of the
wish contained in verses 1 and 2; 'Oh that thou wouldst do marvellous things
such as we do not expect, while the hills shrank away before thee.' But the
verb does not mean 'expect'; it means 'hope for.' The use of the perfect tense,
'thou didst come down,' in the Latin is difficult to account for, unless we suppose it to be a reference to mount Sinai (Ex. 20.18, 19), suggested by the historical reminiscences of the foregoing chapter.

[2] The meaning of verses 4 and 5 is obscure. The Hebrew text of verse 4 is
usually taken to mean, 'No one has ever seen or heard of a God, other than
thee, that acts on behalf of those who wait for him (literally, for thee).'
But the construction is awkward, and the passage was early taken in the sense
which the Latin gives it; cf. I Cor. 2.9. It seems likely there has been some
corruption in the text. The end of verse 5 is very abrupt if we translate it as
a statement, 'and we shall be delivered.'

 8 Yet, Lord, thou art our father; we are but clay, and thou the craftsman
 9 who has fashioned us; wilt thou crush us, Lord, with thy anger, wilt
10 thou keep our sins ever in mind? We are thy people, all of us. A desert,
   the city thy chosen servant knew, a desert, the Sion we love; Jerusalem
11 lies forlorn. Given over to the flames, the house that was our sanctuary
   and our pride, the house in which our fathers praised thee; all that
12 we loved lies in ruins; Lord, wilt thou have patience still? Wilt thou
   keep silent still, and overwhelm us with calamity?

CHAPTER SIXTY-FIVE

SO ready I to answer, and ask they will not; so easy to be found, and
   search for me is none! A people that will not call on my name; else my
 2 own voice should whisper, I am here, I am close at hand.[1] Outstretched
   these hands of mine, all the day long, to a nation of rebels, straying this
 3 way and that as the mood takes them,   openly defying me. Shrines hidden
 4 away in gardens, altars of brick! See how they lodge in tombs, pass the
   night in the precincts of strange gods;[2] eat swine's flesh, and stew them-
 5 selves broth of forbidden things! And all the while so scrupulous: Touch
   of thine would defile me! What marvel, if my indignation smoulders yet?
 6 Nay, fire it is that burns continually. See where the decree stands written
   in my presence, This shall not be passed over; I will take vengeance, pour
 7 it out into their laps. Sin of yours, the Lord says, sin of your fathers, that
   sacrificed on mountain-tops, worshipped on the hill-sides in defiance of
   me; for all these I must repay due measure, poured out into the lap; that
   is my first task.

 8   Thus says the Lord: If one sound grape is found in a cluster, the
   cry is, Do not destroy it, there is a blessing in it. And I, for the sake
 9 of my true servants, will not destroy root and branch;   I will leave
   Jacob a stock to breed from, settlers enough in Juda for these mountains of mine; the men of my choice shall have their portion, my servant
10 shall dwell there. Flocks there shall be, folded on the Plain,[3] and
   cattle resting in the valley of Achor; of my people none shall be disap-
11 pointed that had recourse to me. But you that forsook the Lord, left
   his mountain sanctuary forgotten, spread a table for the Powers of

---

   [1] This verse may be interpreted in either of two ways: (i) that the Lord
offers mercy to the Gentiles, although they have not asked for it, or (ii) that he
offers mercy to the Jews, and yet they do not accept it. The latter sense is
probably foremost in the author's mind; St. Paul gives the opposite side of the
picture (Rom. 10.20, 21).
   [2] It was one of the heathen methods of divination to sleep in some reputedly
holy place and expect inspiration to be given by dreams.
   [3] The Plain, that is, Saron.

12 Fortune, and poured out wine at it,[1] fortune that awaits you is the
sword, you shall bow down to death. My call unanswered, my voice
13 unheard, you did ever what I forbade, chose ever what I hated. This,
then, is the sentence the Lord God pronounces; you shall be hungry,
while my servants have food, you shall be thirsty, while my servants
14 drink, you shall be disappointed, while my servants are glad. My
servants shall be light-hearted and sing, while you, with sad hearts,
15 cry aloud, groan in the heaviness of your spirits. A name you shall
leave behind you to serve my chosen people as a curse; the Lord God
takes full toll. For his own servants he will have a new name instead;
16 By the God of truth shall be the blessing men invoke, By the God of
truth shall be the oath men take, in this land of mine henceforward.[2]
Forgotten, the sorrows of past days, hidden away from my eyes.

17   See where I create new heavens and a new earth; old things shall
18 be remembered no longer, have no place in men's thoughts. Joy of
yours, pride of yours, this new creation shall be; joy of mine, pride
19 of mine, Jerusalem and her folk, created anew. I will rejoice in Jerusalem, take pride in my people, and the sound of weeping and lament
20 shall be heard among them no more. None shall die there unweaned
from life; never an old man but lives out his full time; young he dies
that dies a hundred years old; so brief a span, it shall be the curse pro-
21 nounced on a sinner.[3] Live they now to occupy the houses they built,
22 enjoy the fruit of the vines they planted, that once built houses for
others to occupy, planted what others should enjoy; my people shall
live to the age of trees and see the work of their own hands wear out
23 before them. Not in vain they shall toil, these, my chosen, nor beget
children to see them overwhelmed by calamity; their race the Lord
24 blesses, their children shall be spared to them. Answer shall come ere cry
25 for help is uttered, prayer find audience while it is yet on their lips. Wolf
and lamb shall feed together, lion and ox eat straw side by side, and the
serpent be content with dust for its food; all over this mountain, my sanctuary, there shall be no hurt done, the Lord says, no life shall be forfeit.

---

[1] In the Hebrew text, 'poured out wine to Destiny.'

[2] The name of Israel will be used as a curse, cf. the formula in Jer. 29.22.
(Some think the words which follow, literally 'And the Lord shall slay thee,'
are meant as an abbreviation for some such formula as 'May the Lord slay
thee as he slew Israel'). The faithful remnant will be given a different name
instead of Israel, and God himself will no longer be invoked under the familiar
name, 'the God of Jacob,' but as 'the God of truth' instead. The name, with its
painful associations, must be forgotten.

[3] Literally, 'There shall not be there (in the Hebrew text, from there) an
unweaned child of days (or years), or an old man who does not fill up his span
of life; for a young man of a hundred years shall die, and a sinner of a
hundred years shall be cursed.'

CHAPTER SIXTY-SIX

THUS says the Lord, Heaven is my throne, earth the footstool under my feet. What home will you build for me, what place can be my
2 resting-place?[1] Nothing you see about you but I fashioned it, the Lord says; my hand gave it being. From whom, then, shall I accept an offering?[2] Patient he must be and humbled, one who stands in dread of my
3 warnings. To the rest it is all one; slaughter they an ox, or murder a human victim,[3] cut sheep's throat, or dash out a dog's brains, make offering of meal, or of swine's blood, in my honour burn incense, or bless the name of a false god. In all this, it is but caprice guides their choice,
4 in all manner of abominations; trust me, at my own caprice I will choose the terrors I bring down upon them.[4] My call unanswered, my voice unheard, they did ever what I forbade, chose ever what I hated.
5   Listen to the word of the Lord, you that hold it in reverence! Foiled their hopes shall be, that hate and shun you because my name you bear; that say, Come, let us see the Lord reveal himself in majesty,
6 let us witness this triumph of yours! Hark, a stir of tumult in the city, a stir in the temple! It is the stir the Lord makes, as he brings retribution on his enemies!
7   Without travail, the mother has given birth; before her time a mother
8 of men.   Never till now was such a tale heard, such a sight witnessed; should a nation's pangs come upon it in a day, a whole people be born at once? Such are the pangs of Sion, such is the birth of her children.
9 What, says the Lord thy God, shall I, that bring children to the birth, want power to bring them forth? Shall I, that give life to the womb,
10 want strength to open it? Lovers of Jerusalem, rejoice with her, be glad for her sake; make holiday with her, you that mourned for her till now.
11 So shall you be her foster-children, suckled plentifully with her consolations, drinking in, to your hearts' content, the abundant glory that
12 is hers. Thus says the Lord, Peace shall flow through her like a river, the wealth of the nations shall pour into her like a torrent in flood; this shall be the milk you drain, like children carried at the breast,
13 fondled on a mother's lap. I will console you then, like a mother
14 caressing her son, and all your consolation shall be in Jerusalem; your

---

[1] Ac. 7.49.

[2] 'From whom shall I accept an offering?'; literally, 'to whom shall I have regard?' cf. Gen. 4.4.

[3] Literally, 'he who slays an ox (is as) he who murders a man,' &c.

[4] 'At my own caprice I will choose the terrors'; literally, ' I will choose the wanton outrages and the terrors.'

eyes feasted with it, your hearts content, vigorous as the fresh grass your whole frame.

Thus to his servants the Lord makes known his power; his enemies
15 shall have no quarter given them.   See, where the Lord comes with fire about him, with chariots that drive like the storm, angry his retribu-
16 tion, his vengeance like a scorching flame!   Fire and sword shall be
17 the world's purging, till the Lord has taken full toll.   Vainly they sought holiness, that would purify themselves in secret gardens, behind shut doors, and all the while ate flesh of swine and field-mouse and other meats abominable; one end there shall be for all of them, the Lord says.[1]

18   Trust me, I will hold assize upon all such deeds and devices of theirs; ay, upon all nations and races. All must come and see my glory
19 revealed,   and I will set a mark upon each of them. What of those that find deliverance? I have an errand for them, to be my messengers across the sea; to Africa, and to Lydia where men draw the bow, to Italy, and to Greece, and to the Islands far away.[2] They shall go out where men never heard of my name, never saw my glory yet, to reveal
20 that glory among the nations.   And out of all nations they shall bring your brethren back, an offering to the Lord, with horse and chariot, with litter and mule and waggon, to Jerusalem, the Lord says, to this
21 mountain, my sanctuary.   A bloodless offering this, for the sons of Israel to bring, in its sanctified vessel, to the Lord's house! And some among these newcomers, the Lord says, I will choose out to be priests and Levites.

22   This, too, he promises: Enduring your race and name shall be as the new heavens, the new earth I fashion, to stand continually in my
23 presence.   Month after month, sabbath after sabbath shall go by, and still all mankind shall come to bow down before me, the Lord says.
24 And ever as they leave the gates, mortal remains they shall see of the men that rebelled against me long since; a prey now, to worm undying, to fire unquenchable;[3] none that sees it but shall turn with loathing from the sight.

---

[1] The Hebrew text of verses 17 and 18, which differs from the Latin version, is probably corrupt, and has called forth a variety of interpretations.

[2] The geographical identifications found in the Latin text are by no means certain.

[3] Mk. 9.43, 45.

THE PROPHECY OF JEREMIAS

CHAPTER ONE

THESE are the words of Jeremias, son of Helcias, one of the priests
2 who dwelt at Anathoth, in the lands of Benjamin. The word of the
Lord came to him during the reign of Josias, son of Amon, over Juda,
3 in the thirteenth year of it; came to him during the reign of Josias'
son, Joachim, and did not cease till the men of Jerusalem went into
exile, when Sedecias, that was also son to Josias, had been reigning
eleven years and five months.

4 The word of the Lord came to me, and his message was: I claimed
thee for my own before ever I fashioned thee in thy mother's womb;
before ever thou camest to the birth, I set thee apart for myself; I
6 have a prophet's errand for thee among the nations. Alas, alas, Lord
7 God (said I), I am but a child that has never learned to speak. A child,
sayest thou? the Lord answered. Nay, I have a mission for thee to
8 undertake, a message to entrust to thee. Have no human fears; am
9 I not at thy side, to protect thee from harm? the Lord says. And with
that, the Lord put out his hand, and touched me on the mouth; See,
10 he told me, I have inspired thy lips with utterance. Here and now
I give thee authority over the nations; with a word thou shalt root them
up and pull them down, overthrow and lay them in ruins; with a word
thou shalt build them up and plant them anew.

11 Then the Lord's word came to me, Tell me, Jeremias, what is this
thou seest? A branch of a tree, I told him, with the eyes already open.[1]
12 Well seen, he answered; and I too have my eyes open, watching for
13 the opportunity to carry out the threats I utter. And again it came,
Tell me, what is this thou seest? A boiling caldron, said I, that is coming
14 from the north. And it is from the north, the Lord told me, that
15 calamity is brewing for all thy fellow countrymen. All the tribes the
northern kings rule I mean to muster, the Lord says; hither they will
march, and each will set up his throne where gate of Jerusalem stands,
16 or encircling wall, or fortified city of Juda. And there I will plead
my cause against the men of Juda, charging them with their rebellion
in forsaking me; in offering libation to gods not theirs, and worshipping
idols of their own making.

17 Up, then, gird thee like a man, and speak out all the message I give

---

[1] 'Eyes'; that is, buds. In the Hebrew text, there is a play upon the similarity
of the word 'to watch' and the word 'almond-tree', which is derived from it.

thee. Meet them undaunted, and they shall have no power to daunt
18 thee. Strong I mean to make thee this day as fortified city, or pillar
of iron, or wall of bronze, to meet king, prince, priest and common
19 folk all the country through; impregnable thou shalt be to their attack;
am I not at thy side, the Lord says, to deliver thee?

CHAPTER TWO

2 THEN the Lord's word came to me: Go and cry out so that all
Jerusalem may hear, with this message from the Lord of hosts:
What memories I have of thee, gracious memories of thy youth, of
the love that plighted troth between us, when I led thee through the
3 desert, alone in the barren wastes, thou and I! Israel was set apart for
the Lord, first-fruits vowed to be his revenue; he lay under a ban that
plucked them, and must rue his rashness, the Lord says.

4 Listen, then, to the Lord's word, men of Juda; listen, every clan
5 that bears the name of Israel, to the Lord's message: What fault did
they find in me, those fathers of yours, that they should keep their
6 distance from me, and court false gods, false as themselves? And
never a thought to ask where I, the Lord, was, that rescued them
from Egypt, and led them on their way through the desert, wild and
solitary, parched and dead, far from haunt of traveller and the homes
7 of men! Into a garden I brought you, to enjoy the fruits and the blessings
of it; and you had no sooner entered it than you must needs defile it,
8 my own land, turn my chosen home into a place abominable. Never
a priest to ask where I, the Lord, was; never a man of law but made
a stranger of me, never a ruler but played me false, never a prophet
but took Baal for his oracle, and had recourse to powers that were
9 impotent. Against you, the Lord says, my appeal still lies, and with
your children I will yet be at issue.

10 Sail the seas till you reach the isles of Cethim; send envoys out
to the wilds of Cedar; look for yourselves and make earnest enquiry,
11 to know if the like was ever heard! What nation ever changed its gods,
though gods indeed they were not? And should my people barter away
the glory that dwelt among them, for powers that power have none?
12 In horror and dismay witness, you heavens, the sight; crumble in
13 ruins![1] Two wrongs this people of mine committed; me they forsook,

---

[1] There is some doubt whether the text of this verse has been rightly preserved; the meaning of the Hebrew text is given above, since the Latin has
an unintelligible sentence: 'Be dismayed, ye heavens, over this, and crumble
in ruins, ye gates of it.'

the fountain of living water, and thereupon they dug cisterns of their own, leaking cisterns, that water had none to give them.

14 What, is the race of Israel a slave, a chattel, that it should pass from
15 hand to hand as the prize of war? Roaring lions have claimed it for
16 their prey; the land lies waste, the cities burnt and desolate. Even the
17 Egyptians have come from Memphis and Taphne, to strip thee bare; tell me, Israel, how came this? Was it not because thou hadst forsaken the Lord thy God, that till then had led thee? [1]

18 What, wouldst thou turn to Egypt, to Assyria, and slake thy thirst
19 with Nile or Euphrates? [2] Here is the very proof of thy wickedness, the measure of thy unfaithfulness; see how ill it has gone with thee, says the Lord, the God of hosts, ever since thou didst forsake the Lord
20 thy God, ever since thou didst banish the fear of me! It is an old tale, now, how thou didst break in pieces the yoke of my dominion, didst sever all the bonds between us, crying out, I will serve no more! Thou wast off to play the wanton, the nearest hill-top or secret forest for
21 thy bower. Alas, vineyard of mine, that I planted with such care, never a worthless shoot! How is it thou hast played me false, and art no vineyard of mine?

22 Ay, use nitre for thy cleansing, spread potash as thou mayst, foul
23 with guilt I shall still find thee, says the Lord God. Nay, never boast that thou art undefiled, to countryside gods hast no recourse; bethink thee of thy traffickings in Ben-Ennom valley, and read there the story
24 of thy doings. Camel never found its way so lightly; wild ass in its familiar desert, scenting its mate, never obeyed the fire in its blood more uncontrollably! Little search it needs to find thy haunts, as his
25 mate in spring-time. [3] Reckless of unshod feet, of parching throat, thou criest out despairingly, Return I cannot; to alien gods all my heart is vowed, and I must follow still!

26 Thief caught in the act has less cause to blush than the men of Israel,
27 king and prince, priest and prophet, with the rest. Stock of wood and block of stone they hailed as the father that had begotten them; on me they turned their backs, and gave me never a glance. And now,

---

¹ *vv.* 14–17. Some think these verses have been misplaced. If they refer to the times of Josias, they must be understood as addressed, not to the kingdom of Juda, but to that Northern country which, since the Ten Tribes went into exile, had been debatable ground between the empires of Assyria and Egypt.

² This verse is addressed to Juda, and refers to attempts made at the time to secure foreign alliances; cf. verse 36 below. For 'Nile' the Latin version gives 'turbid water,' translating instead of transliterating.

³ The last part of the verse is not easy to interpret. It runs, literally, 'Those who look for her will have no laborious search; they will find her in her month (according to the Latin, her monthly times).'

28 in their distress, it is Up, Lord, and bring us rescue! Where are those other gods thou madest for thyself? Bid them rise up and aid thee in the hour of peril; gods thou hadst a many; no city of thine, Juda,
29 but must have its own! And would you still implead me? Nay, says
30 the Lord, you have forsaken me, one and all. In vain I have smitten them, all those sons of Juda; still you turned your swords against the prophets, bloodthirsty as lions.

31   Out upon this age! Here is the Lord's message, give good heed to it. Have I shewn myself unfriendly to Israel, like a desert, like a land overcast by shadows, that my own people has resolved to keep its
32 distance, and come my way no more? What, should maid forget her jewels, bride her stomacher? And my own people, all these long days,
33 has forgotten me! What avails it to justify thyself, in hope of winning back my love, when thou thyself dost blazon so openly thy doings, thy
34 foul misdoings? There is blood on thy hands, the blood of friendless folk and innocent. It is not thieves I have found, but men guilty of
35 such crimes as these.[1] And still thou declarest thyself innocent of any fault, still thou biddest me withhold my vengeance! Come, let me answer thy plea of innocence.

36   How light a woman thou art, ever at thy old ways! Not less than
37 thy hopes of Assyria, thy hopes of Egypt shall be disappointed; thence, too, thou shalt come away wringing thy hands; all the confidence thou hast the Lord means to destroy; thou shalt make no shift with Egypt.

CHAPTER THREE

WHAT is the law of common life? Let wife that has been put away by her husband marry a second, can she afterwards return to the first? That were shame and defilement.[2] And thou with many lovers hast played the wanton; yet come back to me, the Lord says,
2 and thou shalt find welcome. Lift up thy eyes to the bare hills, and tell me, which of them has not been the scene of thy shame? Like a highway robber thou didst lurk by the road-side, waiting for thy lovers;

---

[1] *vv.* 33, 34. There is probably corruption in the text. In the Latin version it reads literally: 'Why dost thou strive to shew that thy way is good, in order to seek love, who moreover hast taught thy wickedness thy ways; and the blood of poor and innocent souls is found on thy wings? I have not found them in ditches, but over all the things which I have mentioned above.' In the Hebrew text, 'wings' means 'skirts'; and the word translated 'ditches' means housebreaking (Ex. 22.1). The translation given assumes a reference to verse 26 above.

[2] To the woman herself, according to the Latin version; to the whole country, according to the Hebrew text (cf. Deut. 24.4).

3 by thy heartless wantonness the whole land was defiled. I called thee
to account for it; heaven's dews were stanched, and the late rains did
4 not fall, and still never a blush on thy harlot's brow! Little wonder
thou shouldst have been crying out to me, since then, calling me father,
5 calling me the loved friend of thy girlhood's days; was there no quenching my anger? Would it smoulder on for ever? Ay, all this thou saidst,
but still wouldst go on sinning, still wouldst have thy way.

6 It was in the days of king Josias the Lord said to me: Israel's apostasy
thou hast seen, how she ever betook herself to the nearest high hill
7 or leafy wood, to play the wanton there; and how, when I called her
8 back to me in spite of it, she would not come. Now mark the treachery
of her sister Juda. She too had seen it all, how I had bidden apostate
Israel begone, and given her a writ of separation; and now treacherous
9 Juda, unabashed, went off in her turn to play the wanton. So wayward,
so wanton, she defiled all that land of hers, giving herself to lovers
10 made of wood and stone! After all the warnings I had given, Juda,
the treacherous, would never come back to me in good earnest, only
with lying professions, the Lord says.

11 And the Lord told me: Better than Juda's treachery, the apostasy of
12 Israel deserves to be acquitted. Carry this message of mine to the
north country: Come back to me, apostate Israel, the Lord says, and
there shall be no frown of mine awaiting you; I am merciful, the Lord
13 says, and vengeance shall not last for ever. Only acknowledge thy
fault, he tells thee, in deserting the Lord thy God and betaking thyself
14 to the bowers of strange lovers, deaf to my call. Wandering hearts,
the Lord bids you come back to him, and renew your troth; by ones
and twos, from this city or that, from this clan or that, he will claim
15 you for his own and bring you back to Sion; and you shall have shep-
16 herds of his own choice to guide you well and prudently. After that,
the Lord says, when all is growth and fertility, no longer shall you
have the Ark of the Lord's Covenant for your rallying-cry; from thought
and memory it will have passed away, nor any care shall be bestowed
17 on the fashioning of it. It is Jerusalem men will speak of as the Lord's
throne; there at Jerusalem all the nations of the world will meet in
the Lord's name, the false aims of their perverse hearts forgotten.
18 When that time comes, Juda and Israel will be united; together they
will come back from the north country to the land I gave your fathers
for their home.

19 Must I ever be offering thee sonship, and a land so fair that all the
peoples of the world might envy thee its possession? Must I ever be
pleading with thee to acknowledge me as thy father, and forsake my
20 guidance no more? Hitherto, the Lord says, nothing could I win

21 from Israel but a false jade's contempt. Now, from yonder hill-passes, another cry is heard; a cry of mourning and lament from the sons of Israel, over the wrong path they have chosen in forgetting the Lord

22 their God. Wandering hearts, come back to me, and all your rebel acts shall be pardoned.

23   See, we come to thee; art thou not the Lord our God? The many gods of hill and mountain side have played us false; we know it now; we know now that Israel must look to the Lord our God for deliverance.

24 Ever since the days of our youth all the hopes our fathers had, of flock and herd, of son and daughter, are lost; the worship of shame has

25 cheated us.[1] Lie we down with shame for our bed, and let reproach be all our covering; sinners from our youth upwards, we and our fathers before us, against the Lord our God; the Lord our God, and we would not listen to his voice!

CHAPTER FOUR

DO but retrace thy steps, Israel, and return to me, do but cast away the abominations that offend my sight, and in that mind

2 persist; let but thy oath, As the Lord is a living God! be a true oath, in loyal duty uttered; then shall all the nations learn to bless and to praise him.

3   And to the men of Juda, to Jerusalem, this is the Lord's message: Yours to drive a new furrow, nor sow any longer among the briers.

4 You must be circumcised afresh, men of Juda; citizens of Jerusalem, of heart's defilement rid yourselves, if you would not see my vengeance burst into flame unquenchable, as your scheming malice has deserved.

5   News for Juda, news that shall echo through Jerusalem; tell it out, sound the trumpet over the countryside! Loud be the cry raised, for

6 all to muster and to man the fortified cities! Raise the standard in Sion, and rally to it with all haste! Here is peril I am bringing upon

7 you from the north country, here is great calamity. Roused is the lion from his lair; he is astir, ready to prey on the nations; he is marching out to make earth a desert, and thy cities too shall be laid waste, and

8 stand there untenanted. Well may you gird yourselves with sackcloth, well may you beat the breast and cry aloud; fire of the Lord's vengeance

9 has not passed us by. When that day comes, the Lord says, heart of king

---

[1] Literally, 'Ever since the days of our youth shame has devoured the earnings of our fathers, their flocks and herds, sons and daughters.' But it is most probable that the word 'shame' stands here as a pious substitute for the name of the god Baal.

and heart of prince shall be dismayed; dumb-stricken the priest, the prophet unmanned.

10   Alas, alas, Lord God, said I,[1] can it be that thou hast deceived thy people, deceived Jerusalem, by telling them they should have peace, and here is the sword threatening our very lives?

11   When that time comes, verdict shall be passed on this people of mine, and on Jerusalem: My people's wanton ways are like the hot wind[2] that blows from the desert slopes, that will neither winnow nor sift.

12   And in return, I will summon to my side a wind that blows full, and
13   so I will plead my cause against them. An overshadowing cloud the invader shall be, his chariots outspread like the storm-wrack, his horses swifter than eagles. Alas the day, we are ruined!

14   Now, Jerusalem, as thy life thou lovest, rid thy heart of guile; wilt
15   thou never cease to harbour those false thoughts of thine? Here is news cried from Dan, here are monstrous tidings[3] from the hill-country
16   of Ephraim; tell it far and wide, Jerusalem has heard the bruit of her besiegers coming from a distant land, that even now raise their battle-
17   cry among the cities of Juda; even now they keep watch over the countryside about her, the Lord says, and all because she defied my
18   vengeance. Ill deeds and ill counsel of thine have brought all this upon thee; the due reward of thy wickedness, how bitter the taste
19   of it, how it wrings thy heart! Deep, deep rankles the wound; my very heart-strings echo lament; no rest is mine, since my ear caught
20   bray of trumpet and cry of battle. Tale upon tale of ruin; a whole land laid waste, no cabin or hovel spared, suddenly, all in a moment!
21   Always the sight of men fleeing, always the sound of the trumpet in my ears!

22   Ah, reckless people of mine, that would not acknowledge me; blind fools, for mischief so shrewd, in well-doing so untutored![4]

23   Earthward I looked, and all was void and empty; heavenward, and
24   in heaven no light shone; looked at mountain and hill-side, and saw
25   them stir and tremble; looked for some sign of man, and in vain; the
26   very birds in heaven had all taken flight. It was a garden I looked

---

[1] According to some manuscripts of the Septuagint Greek, the true reading is 'said they.' This would evidently improve the run of the context.

[2] The Hebrew text may also be interpreted as meaning 'A hot wind is coming in the direction of the daughter of my people.' But the use of language is in any case forced, and it may be doubted whether the true text of verses 11 and 12 has been preserved to us.

[3] Literally, 'the making known of an idol'; according to the Hebrew text, 'the making known of distress.'

[4] The sudden introduction of Almighty God as the speaker in this verse mars the unity of the passage, and some attribute it to textual error.

at, but a garden untenanted; no city in it but had perished at the Lord's
27 glance, before the frown of his vengeance. For it was so the Lord's
sentence ran; the whole countryside should be abandoned, and still
28 he will not have taken full toll. At his sentence, earth should mourn
and heaven grow dark with sorrow, yet of his decree there should
29 be no repenting; he would not go back from it. Everywhere, at the
noise of archer and horseman, the townsfolk flee away, take to the hills [1]
and climb their high rocks; never a town but is left deserted of its
30 inhabitants. And thou, Jerusalem, when thy turn comes to be despoiled,
what shift wilt thou make? Vain was it to dress in scarlet, and deck
thyself with chains of gold, and with antimony darken thy eyes; vain
were those arts, thy lovers are weary of thee now, and thy life is forfeit.
31 Cries of anguish I hear, as from a woman in the throes of travail; it
is queen Sion, gasping out her life, and crying with hands outspread,
Woe is me, I swoon away, here in the slaughter-house!

CHAPTER FIVE

GO the rounds of Jerusalem, search the streets of it with hue and
cry; and if you find one man there that faithfully does his duty,
2 and keeps troth, then the city shall be pardoned. Nay, though they
call on the living God to be their witness, they forswear themselves
none the less.
3 On faithfulness, Lord, thy eyes are set. And these, when thou smitest
them, are unrepentant still; when thou crushest them to earth, will
not heed reproof; brows are theirs unyielding as rock, and return they
4 will not. But indeed, thought I, perhaps they are poor men and foolish,
that have never learnt the divine command, or what their God requires
5 of them. I will go and have speech with the men of rank; what the
divine command is, what their God requires of them, these will surely
know. And these I found conspiring, as none other, to throw off the
6 yoke, to break through their bonds. What wonder if they are attacked
and despoiled by robbers, that leave the woods at night-time, stealthily
as lion or wolf or prowling leopard, to beleaguer their towns and catch
all who venture forth? So many their rebellions, so obstinate their
defiance!
7 For all this, how should I pardon thee? Thy sons have deserted me,
by gods that are no gods their vows are taken; full-fed with my bounty,
they left their wedded troth, to wanton in the bower of a mistress;
8 bold in their adultery as stallion at grass neighing for his mate. What,
shall I let all this pass me by, the Lord says; shall I not take my fill

---

[1] In the Hebrew text, 'thickets.'

10 of vengeance against such a nation as this? Scale those ramparts, and
fall to pillage, not taking full toll even yet; root out the slips of yonder
11 vine, the Lord will not claim them. Obstinately they have defied me,
12 the Lord says, Israel and Juda both; they disown me; Nay, they tell
one another, this is none of his doing, harm shall never befall us, we
13 shall have neither slaughter nor famine here; the prophets did but waste
breath, no word of revelation made to them; on their own heads be it!

14   Vain words; but not vainly the Lord, the God of hosts, has spoken;
flaming words of his he has entrusted to my lips, and fuel this people
15 shall be for their devouring. A nation from far away I am summoning,
even now, to the attack; a warlike nation, of ancient lineage, whose
very tongue shall be strange to thee, no word of it well understood;
16 greedily as the tomb their quivers gape, and they are warriors all.
17 They shall rob thee of harvest and of food, rob thee of son and daughter,
rob thee of flock and herd, rob thee of vine and fig-tree; and all the
strongholds, wherein thy hope lies, at the sword's point shall be over-
18 thrown. Yet even then, the Lord says, I will not take full toll of thee.
19 Ask you why the Lord has so much misused you, this is to be my
answer: Did you not forsake me, to worship alien gods in your own
land? Alien gods you shall worship in an alien land, for your punishment.

20   To Israel's race proclaim it, for all Juda to hear, Listen, foolish
folk and unperceiving, with sightless eyes, ears that had as well been
22 deaf! Have you no fear of me, the Lord says, will you stand unmoved
in my presence? Was it not I gave the sea its frontier of sand, by my
eternal decree inviolate? Vainly the waves boil and toss, they cannot
23 pass beyond it. A faithless heart, a rebellious heart this people of
mine has; in a moment they swerve aside from the path, and are gone;
24 never a thought of reverence for the Lord their God, who gives them
autumn and spring rains when the time comes, and secures them a
25 full harvest. It is your wrongdoing that has altered their course;
to guilt such as yours, blessings are denied.

26   Godless men there are among my people that lie in wait like any
27 fowler, but noose and trap of theirs is set to catch men. Never was
cage so full of birds, as their homes of wealth ill gotten; men of power
28 and riches, pampered and sleek, they defy my will past all bearing;
redress they deny to the widow, right to the orphan, justice to the
29 poor. What, shall I let all this pass me by, the Lord says, shall I not
30 take my fill of vengeance against such a nation as this? A wonder
31 this land has seen beyond all belief; here are prophets that utter a
lying message, priests that clap their hands in applause, and this people
of mine is well content. And what shift will you make when the end
comes?

CHAPTER SIX

R ALLY, tribesmen of Benjamin that live in the midst of Jerusalem;
at Thecua sound the trumpet, raise the standard on Bethacarem;
it is from the north peril may be seen coming, peril of great calamity.[1]
2 Poor Sion, all too fair she seems, all too delicate! Alas, what strange
shepherds are these, what troops that follow them? See how they
pitch their tents about her! See how many each has at his back, and
4 there must be pasture for them all! Handsel we the attack on the city;
to move now were best, and march up under the light of noon! Plague
upon it, the day is already spent, the shadows of evening lengthen
5 already; up, then, march we on by night, by night plunder their houses!
6 Down with yonder trees, the Lord of hosts says, and build siege-
works about Jerusalem; here is a city must be called to account for
7 all the oppression that is harboured there. Never cistern kept its waters
so fresh, as she her store of wickedness; no news from her but of wrong
8 and waste, no sight I see there but distress and violence. Jerusalem,
be warned in time; else my love thou shalt forfeit, and I will make
a ruin of thee, a land uninhabited.
9 Israel, says the Lord of hosts, is a vineyard for the gleaning; no
10 cluster shall be left; back with thee, vintager, to the baskets! Vain
appeal, whom shall I cite for witness of it? Oh that it should fall on
ears uncircumcised, oh that God's word should be slighted, and find
11 no welcome! Nay, but the divine anger burns within me, I can forbear
no longer. I must blurt out my message to all, children playing in
the streets, no less than warriors met in council; none shall be spared,
12 husband or wife, greybeard or man of many summers. Homes, lands
and wedded wives, all must pass into other hands; none that dwells
13 in Juda, the Lord says, but shall feel my vengeance. High and low,
ill-gotten gains they covet; treacherous the ways alike of prophet and
14 of priest; here lies my people grievously hurt, and they tend her unconcernedly; All's well, they say, all's well, when in truth all goes amiss.
15 Shamed they needs must be, that did so detestably; shamed, but never
ashamed, for indeed they have lost the power to blush;[2] theirs to fall

---

[1] The Latin version does not make clear, what is evidently intended, that
the men of Benjamin (to whose country the prophet belonged) are invited
to escape from Jerusalem, and hold their own in the hill country of the south.

[2] The text here apparently says, 'They are confounded, because they have
done abominably; or rather they are not confounded, they do not know how
to blush.' Probably the verb 'to be confounded' is used in two different senses,
(i) to be ignominiously disappointed of one's aim, (ii) to express shame, own
oneself in the wrong.

amid the common ruin, crushed to earth, the Lord says, when I call
all to account.

16   The Lord's message was, Halt at the cross-roads, look well, and
ask yourselves which path it was that stood you in good stead long
ago. That path follow, and you shall find rest for your souls. But follow
17 they would not; and next, I would set watchmen on the heights; let
them only listen, when these sounded the trumpet; but listen they
18 would not. To the nations, then, I proclaim it; let my doom be pro-
19 nounced in the public ear; all earth shall hear it. I mean to bring upon
this people of mine the punishment their scheming wickedness has
20 earned, so deaf to my calls, of my law so defiant. What avails it to
offer me incense from Saba, and the fragrant calamus that grows far
away? Unwelcome to me your burnt-sacrifice, undesired your victims.
21 This doom the Lord pronounces; I mean so to entangle this people
of mine that they shall stumble to their undoing all of them, father
and son together, neighbour with neighbour, friend with friend.
22   Here is a people marching from the north country, the Lord says,
23 a great nation from the world's end. Arrow and shield [1] they ply, and
their hard hearts pity none; loud their battle-cry as the roaring of
the sea. So they ride on, as warriors ride, poor Sion, thy enemies.
24 Unnerved our hands droop at the very rumour of it; grief overmasters
25 us, sharp as the pangs of travail; forbidden is the countryside, the
high roads untravelled; the drawn sword threatens, and peril is all
26 about us. Juda, poor widowed queen, put sackcloth about thee and
strew thyself with ashes; as for an only son make loud lament; without
warning the spoiler will be upon us.
27   I have a task for thee to perform among my people; thou shalt be
28 my trusty assayer, putting the quality of their lives to the test. These
faithless rulers that go about on their slanderous errands, what are
29 they but copper and iron, base metal all? Bellows have done their
work, the lead streams away in the fire, carrying nothing with it; vain,
30 smelter, thy toil, the dross remains unpurged. Refuse silver they shall
be called; has not the Lord refused them?

CHAPTER SEVEN

2   A MESSAGE came from the Lord to Jeremias, bidding him take
his stand at the temple gate, and there proclaim aloud: Listen to
this word of the Lord, men of Juda, that make your way in through these
3 gates to worship him. Thus says the Lord of hosts, the God of Israel,

---

[1] According to the Hebrew text, 'bow and javelin.'

Amend your lives and your likings, if you would have me dwell here
4 among you.   Misleading are those words all about you,   The temple
of the Lord, here,   The temple of the Lord, there; do not trust them.[1]
5 Will you but amend your lives and your likings, giving one man redress
6 against another,   not oppressing the alien, the orphan, the widow,
nor in these precincts putting innocent men to death, nor courting,
7 to your ruin, the gods of other nations,   then indeed I will make my
dwelling here among you, in the land which was my gift to your fathers
8 from the beginning to the end of time.   You put your trust in flattering
9 hopes, which can nothing avail you;   theft, murder, adultery, the false
oath, libations to Baal, the courting of alien gods that are no gods
10 of yours, nothing comes amiss,   if only you can come and stand in
my presence, here in this house, the shrine of my name, and tell yourselves you have made amends for all these your detestable doings!
11 What, does this house, the shrine of such a name, count for no more
than a den of thieves, in eyes like yours? Think you, the Lord says,
12 that eternal God has no eyes to see it?[2] Go and visit that sanctuary
of mine at Silo, where of old my power rested; look well, what havoc
I have made of it, to punish the misdeeds of Israel, that were my people
13 too.   Because of so much done amiss, the Lord says; because you would
not listen when I cried early at your doors, or answer any call of mine;
14 this house, shrine of my name and centre of your hopes, this home
15 I gave to you and to your fathers, shall fare as Silo fared.   All those
brethren of yours, the whole stock of Ephraim, I banished from my
presence, and you shall be banished in your turn.
16   Nor do thou, Jeremias,[3] think to plead for this people of mine, or
take up in their name the burden of praise and prayer; thwart my will,
17 thou shalt have no hearing.   Canst thou not see for thyself what ill
deeds are done in the townships of Juda, in the very streets of Jeru-
18 salem?   See the children gathering sticks, the father lighting a fire,
the mother kneading dough, and all to make cakes for the queen of
19 heaven! See how they offer libation to alien gods, to despite me!   Yet
not to me they do despite, the Lord says, rather to themselves; every
20 hope of theirs shall fail them.   This warning, then, the Lord God
sends them: Fury and indignation of mine are brewing against this

---

[1] The original runs, 'Do not trust in deceptive words, saying, The temple
of the Lord, the temple of the Lord, the temple of the Lord, these.' It is generally assumed, and the Latin version implies, that *spoken* words are meant.
The rendering given above supposes the existence of sign-boards here and
there, within view of the gate, marking where the temple precincts began.
[2] Literally, in the Latin version, 'I, I am, I have seen, the Lord says.' The
Hebrew text has merely, 'Behold, I also have seen it, the Lord says.'
[3] The word 'Jeremias' is not expressed in the original.

place, man and beast, woodland tree and growing crop; and when that fire is lit, there shall be no quenching it.

21 A message from the Lord of hosts, the God of Israel: No more be at pains to distinguish between burnt-sacrifice and offering; use for
22 your own eating the flesh of all alike! Burnt-sacrifices, offerings, not of these was my theme when I gave commandments to your fathers
23 at the time of their deliverance from Egypt;[1] my word of command to them was, Obey my bidding, if I am to be your God, you my people; follow the path I have marked out for you, as you hope to prosper.
24 And did they listen? Hearing they gave me none; their own whim, the false aim of their corrupt hearts was all the rule they lived by; still
25 turned their backs on me, and refused to look my way; so it has been since your fathers left Egypt, so it is yet. No day dawned but I was at
26 work betimes, sending my servants to prophesy to them, but still they would not listen, still hearing they gave me none; stubborn under my
27 yoke, they outdid their own fathers in wickedness. All this thou shalt say to them, but they will not listen to thee; thy call shall go unheeded.
28 Then tell them, Here is a people who will not listen to the voice of their own God, or accept reproof from him; loyalty is dead, the word is on their lips no more.

29 Cut off, Jerusalem,[2] those locks of thine, and cast them away from thee; loud let the hills echo with thy lament; on a guilty age, the Lord
30 has pronounced sentence of banishment and rejection. The men of Juda have defied my will, the Lord says; foul idols they have set up in the house that is the sanctuary of my name, and utterly profaned
31 it; in the valley of Ben-Ennom stands the hill-shrine of Topheth, where they sacrifice their own sons and daughters in the furnace, a
32 rite not of my bidding, not of my imagining. And now, the Lord says, a time is coming when no more will be heard of Topheth or Ben-Ennom; it will be called The Valley of the Slain; men will be finding room for their dead in Topheth, because other burying-ground is
33 none. Nay, Juda shall be carrion for birds that fly in air, for beasts
34 that roam the earth; and never a man left to drive them away. In the townships of Juda, in the streets of Jerusalem, cries of joy and mirth shall be heard no more, voice of bridegroom and of bride shall be heard no more; the whole land will have turned into a wilderness.

---

[1] *vv.* 21–23. The burnt-sacrifice was offered to God whole, unlike the other sacrifices (*e.g.*, the welcome-offering) in which the victim was shared between God and his worshipper. Here, the prophet ironically suggests that ceremonial distinctions of this kind may well be abandoned, since the sins of Juda have in any case made their offerings unacceptable. Verses 22 and 23 should probably be understood as implying, not that the moral law was anterior in time to the ceremonial precepts, but that it wholly overshadowed them in importance.

[2] The name is not expressed in the original.

CHAPTER EIGHT

ALL the tombs in Jerusalem will be rifled, the Lord say., when that day comes, tomb of king and prince of Juda's line, tomb of
2 priest and prophet, tomb of common citizen; naked their bones shall lie, with sun and moon and all the starry host to witness it, their gods aforetime; gods so loved, so well served, so hailed, so courted, so adored! Those bones there shall be none to gather, none to bury; they
3 shall lie like dung on the bare ground. And the living shall envy the dead; so poor a home shall be left, the Lord of hosts says, to the remnant of a guilty race, in the far lands to which I have banished them.
4   Give them this message from the Lord: A man falls but to rise, errs
5 but to retrieve his path; how is it that this rebellious people of mine at Jerusalem has rebelled so obstinately? They cling to their illusion,
6 and return no more. Listen I never so attentively, wholesome word I hear none; never a man that repents of his sin, asks himself what his life has been. No, each one follows his own bent, reckless as war-
7 horse charging into battle. Yet the kite, circling in air, knows its time; turtle-dove can guess, and swallow, and stork, when they should return; [1]
8 only for my people the divine appointment passes unobserved. What, still boasting that you are wise, that the Lord's law finds its home among you? Nay, but the scribes, with their false penmanship, have con-
9 strued all amiss. In all their wisdom, how disappointed, how bewildered, how entrapped! God's word they cast away, and wisdom left them.
10 Alien lords their wives shall have, alien masters their lands; (high and low, ill-gotten gains they covet; treacherous the ways alike of prophet
11 and of priest; here lies my people grievously hurt, and they tend her unconcernedly; All's well, they say, all's well, when in truth all goes
12 amiss. Shamed they needs must be, that did so detestably; shamed, but never ashamed, for indeed they have lost the power to blush; theirs to fall in the common ruin, crushed to earth, the Lord says,
13 when I call all to account).[2] When the time comes for gathering, the Lord says, grape is none on the vine, nor fig on the fig-tree; the very leaves are withered; and I have given them . . . what has passed them by.[3]

---

[1] The birds cannot be certainly identified; some would alter 'kite' to 'stork,' and 'stork' to 'crane.'

[2] *vv.* 10–12. The repetition of 6.13–15 may be intentional, but is more probably due to a copyist's error; they are wanting here in some Greek manuscripts.

[3] The last clause of this verse does not yield any natural sense, either in the Hebrew or in the Latin, and it seems likely that the text as we have it is defective.

14 Why do we linger here? Muster we, and man the stronghold, and wait there uncomplaining; silence the Lord our God has imposed on us, given us a draught to dull the senses; the Lord, whom our sins have
15 offended.[1] How we long for better times, and no relief comes to us;
16 for remedy at last, and danger still threatens! All the way from Dan the noise of horses reaches us, gallant chargers neighing in their pride, till earth trembles with the echoes of it; on they come, bearing ruin
17 to field and crop, to city and citizen! With such a serpent-brood I am plaguing you, the Lord says, charm is none shall rid you of its bite.
18 Grief beyond all grief, that bows down my heart within me! So cries my own people in its distress from a country far away. Does the Lord dwell in Sion no longer? Is she forsaken by her king?

And she? What of the idols, what of the alien gods that turned me into her enemy?
20 Harvest-time is over, summer is gone, and still no deliverance has
21 come to us. Wounded she lies, my own people, and is not her wound
22 mine? Shall I not go mourning, bewildered by grief? Grows the balm in Galaad no more, is the healer's art lost there, that the people I love should lie wounded, and the wound will not close?

CHAPTER NINE

WELL-HEAD were this head of mine, eyes of a fountain these eyes,[2] day nor night should serve me to weep enough for my
2 country's dead. Oh that some lodging-place in the wilderness for me were dwelling-place, far from the haunts of my own people, that are faithless lovers, rebel subjects all!
3 Deceitful tongues, treacherous as the hidden archer's bow, hearts that lord it over their fellow-countrymen, wrong leading to wrong,
4 and my claims forgotten! the Lord says. Neighbour of neighbour beware, kinsman let kinsman never trust; none goes about to over-
5 throw thee more craftily than brother of thine or friend. None but will overreach his fellow with lies; all their schooling is in falsehood,
6 all their striving for ill-gotten gain. In what a nest of treason thou

---

[1] 'Uncomplaining' and 'silence' represent a Hebrew verb which normally has that sense, but is interpreted by some, here and in a few other passages, as meaning 'to die.' 'A draught to dull the senses'; literally, 'waters of a root'; the potion so described in Hebrew is probably the 'gall' offered to our Lord at his Crucifixion (Mt. 27.34).

[2] 'Eyes' of a fountain, in the sense of openings. The Hebrew words for 'head' and 'eye' are also used for springs of water.

dwellest! And such treason, the Lord says, as will acknowledge no
7 claim of mine. This warning, then, he utters, the Lord of hosts: The
fire for them! They must be tried in the crucible; what other choice
8 has my faithless people left me? Tongues that wound like an arrow,
with deceit for poison, ever the smooth word of friend laying snare
9 for friend; what, shall I let all this pass me by, the Lord says; shall I
not take my fill of vengeance against such a nation as this?
10   Sad dirge be made for the hills, lament for all the wide pasture-
lands, that are scorched bare, and left untravelled; silent the herdsman's
call; birds that nested there, cattle that grazed there, fled and gone.
11   I mean to turn Jerusalem into a heap of dust, the lair of serpents;[1]
the cities of Juda shall stand desolate, with none to inhabit them.
12 Come now, who is wise enough to read the riddle, to what spokesman shall the Lord's proclamation be entrusted, when he tells us why
the land lies ruined, burnt up like the wilderness, and never a passer-
13 by? It is because they forsook the commandment I gave them, the
14 Lord says, would not heed my call or follow it; because they had
recourse to ill devices of their own, and to the gods of the country-
15 side, whose worship their fathers taught them. This doom, then,
the Lord of hosts pronounces, the God of Israel: On wormwood I will
16 feed this people of mine, gall shall be the drink I give them; far away
I will scatter them, in countries never they, never their fathers knew;
and the sword shall follow close behind, to exterminate them.
17   This too the Lord of hosts says, the God of Israel: Search all about,
and find mourners, mistresses of their craft, and such as will answer
18 your summons with all haste; no time let them lose in making dole for
19 us; weep every eye, be every eye-lid blubbered with tears. Listen
to Sion's lament: Alas, what scathe, alas, what shame! Our land lies
20 deserted, our homes in ruins! To you, women, the Lord's word comes;
this is matter for your hearing. To daughters of yours, neighbours of
21 yours, teach the sad melody of yonder lament; here is death looking
in at our windows, finding its way into our palaces, and soon there
will be no children playing out of doors, nor grown men passing to
22 and fro in the streets. A message from the Lord: Like dung they shall
lie on the ground, the corpses of the dead, like the sheaf left after reaping
is done, that none is at pains to gather.
23   This, too, is the Lord's message: Never boast, if thou art wise, of
thy wisdom, if thou art strong, of thy strength, if thou art rich, of
24 thy riches; boast is none worth having, save that insight which gives
knowledge of me; in all my dealings with mankind so merciful a Lord,

---

[1] The word in the Hebrew text here represented by 'serpents' is generally
translated 'jackals' by modern commentators.

the Lord says, so just, so faithful, and a lover of such dealings where they are found.[1]

25 A time of reckoning there shall be, the Lord says, for all the nations
26 that practise circumcision, Egypt, Juda, Edom, Ammon, Moab; they shall be all one with the desert folk that clip their foreheads bare. The whole world is uncircumcised; all have hearts uncircumcised, and Israel with the rest.[2]

CHAPTER TEN

LISTEN, men of Israel, to the Lord's utterance concerning you.[3]
2 Thus says the Lord: Do not learn to follow Gentile ways, or be
3 dismayed by portents in the heavens, as the Gentiles are. How empty the observances the heathen use! What is the stuff upon which the carver
4 works but a trunk of wood, felled by an axe out in the forest? Only he has tricked it out with gold and silver, hammer and nail must do their
5 work, lest it should fall to pieces. Idols cunningly plated as palm-trees,[4] yet dumb as they, and men must carry them to and fro, for movement they have none! To these give no reverence; they can neither mar nor make thee.
6 No, Lord, thou hast no rival; so great thou art, so great is the
7 sovereignty of thy name. King of all nations, how should we not fear thee in that majesty of thine? Boast the world as it will of wisdom
8 or of empire, none can rival thee. Ah, folly and blindness, ah, fond
9 teaching, lifeless as wood itself! Ay, bring plates of silver from Tharsis, gold from Ophaz, it is all man's work, fresh from the smithy; bring
10 robes of blue and purple, they are man's work still! But the Lord is God in good earnest, a God that lives, that has eternal dominion, and can make earth tremble with his frown, strike the nations powerless when he threatens them.

---

[1] This paragraph is thought by some to have been accidentally misplaced; it has little apparent connexion with its present context.

[2] *vv.* 25, 26. This appears to be the sense intended by a passage of considerable obscurity.

[3] *vv.* 1–25. It may be doubted whether this chapter is more than a collection of certain isolated utterances made by the prophet. Verses 2–16 read as if they were addressed to men already in exile, not to men threatened with exile as a punishment for their own idolatries.

[4] 'Cunningly plated as palm-trees'; literally, 'fashioned into the similitude of a palm-tree'; the plates of metal in which the wooden core of the idol was sheathed may have suggested the figure of a palm-trunk. But some understand the Hebrew text as meaning 'like a scare-crow in a garden of melons'; cf. Bar. 6.69.

11   No place on earth or under heaven, you must tell the nations, for gods that neither heaven nor earth could fashion.[1]

12   Power that made the earth, wisdom that orders nature, foresight
13   that spread out the heavens! At the sound of his voice, what mustering of the waters overhead! He summons up the cloud-wrack from the world's end, turns the lightning into a rain-storm, brings the winds
14   out of his store-house;[2] how puny, then, is man's skill, how sorry a thing is the carver's workmanship; after all his pains, only a lifeless
15   counterfeit! Fond imaginations, antic figures, when the time comes for
16   reckoning, they will be heard of no more. Not such the worship that is the heirloom of Jacob's line; their God is the God who made all things, Israel his patrimony, Javé, the God of hosts, his name.

17   Take up from the ground, poor besieged one, thy load of shame.[3]
18   This time, the Lord says, I mean to hurl them far away, the dwellers in this land, and great distress shall be theirs, that they may be found . . .[4]

19   Alas, for my wounding, for the grievous hurt that is mine! Hitherto
20   I had thought to bear my sickness, if this were all; but now what am I? A tent broken down, all its ropes severed: all my citizens have deserted me, and are no more to be found; who shall raise the pole, who shall
21   stretch the curtains now? And the cause of it? Unskilful shepherds that would have no recourse to the Lord; see how their art has failed
22   them, and all the flock is scattered far and wide! A sound comes to me that brings tidings with it, a great stir from the north country; all Juda is to become a desert, a lair for serpents[5] now.

23   Lord, I know it well enough, it is not for man to choose his lot;
24   not human wisdom guides our steps aright. Chasten me, Lord, but with due measure kept; not as thy anger demands, or thou wilt grind
25   me to dust. Pour out this indignation of thine upon the nations that do not acknowledge thee, on the tribes that never invoke thy name; by whom Jacob is devoured, devoured and devastated, and all his pride scattered to the winds.[6]

---

[1] This verse is phrased, not in pure Hebrew, but in the Aramaic dialect, as if it were written under the influence of the captivity.

[2] For the later part of this verse cf. Ps. 134.7.

[3] In the Hebrew text simply 'thy load.'

[4] It seems clear that there must be some omission at the end of this verse, whether we read 'that they may be found,' or (as in the Hebrew text) 'that they may find.'

[5] Or perhaps 'jackals' as in 9.11 above.

[6] Cf. Ps. 78.6, 7.

CHAPTER ELEVEN

2 HERE is a message which came from the Lord to Jeremias about the covenant: Listen well to the terms of it, and be the spokesmen
3 of it to all the race of Juda, all the citizens of Jerusalem.[1] This warning thou shalt give them from the Lord God of Israel: Cursed be the man
4 who will not obey the terms of this covenant, the commandment which I enjoined on your fathers when I rescued them from Egypt's furnace of iron. Give heed to my call, I told them, and do as I bid you; then you
5 shall be my people, and I will be your God. So would I fulfil the promise made on oath to their fathers before them; the promise of a land all milk and honey, that land which is yours to-day.
6 So be it, Lord, said I; and he bade me cry the message aloud all through the townships of Juda, all through the streets of Jerusalem:
7 Listen to the terms of this covenant, and keep them well; ever since I rescued them from Egypt I have been adjuring those fathers of yours,
8 day in, day out, to listen to me, and listen they would not. No hearing would they give me, but went each his own way, perverse as ever, till at last I must carry out the threats contained in this covenant, still proclaimed and still defied.
9 Why, the Lord said to me, here is a conspiracy among Juda's folk,
10 Jerusalem's folk! They have gone back to the old guilty ways of their rebellious fathers; they in their turn have betaken themselves to the worship of alien gods; my immemorial covenant with Israel and Juda
11 is void; they have rescinded it! And now, the Lord says, I mean to
12 visit them with punishment inevitable, punishment inexorable; let Juda and Jerusalem have recourse, if they will, to the gods they honour
13 with their sacrifices, it will avail them nothing in their distress. No township of thine, Juda, but must have its own deity, no street in Jerusalem but thou wouldst set up there altars abominable, where sacrifice is offered to the gods of the countryside!
14 Nor do thou, Jeremias, think to intercede for this people of mine, or take up in their name the burden of praise and prayer; when they
15 cry to me in their distress, hearing they shall have none. A people so well beloved, that so haunts my house, yet stained with crime! What, dost thou think the consecrated flesh will avail to rid thee of
16 thy wanton guilt?[2] An olive-tree, sturdy and fair and fruitful, so it

---

[1] 'The covenant'; this alludes, presumably, to the rediscovery of the Law under king Josias (IV Kg. 22.8). 'Spokesmen' implies that the rulers are addressed; the Septuagint Greek gives 'spokesman.'

[2] The Hebrew text here is untranslatable, and evidently corrupt.

was the Lord loved to think of thee; and now, at the sound of his majestic voice,[1] fire breaks out, and all those shoots are burned away.
17 Yes, it is the Lord of hosts, who once planted thee, that has now decreed the undoing of Israel and Juda, undoing for their own ill-doing, when they sacrificed to the gods of the countryside in defiance of me.
18 Thou, Lord, didst make it all known to me past doubt, warning me
19 beforehand of their devices. Hitherto, I had been unsuspecting as a cade lamb that is led off to the slaughter-house; I knew nothing of the plots they were hatching against me, as they whispered, Let us give him a taste of the gallows-tree;[2] let us rid the world of him, so
20 that his very name will be forgotten! But thou, Lord of hosts, true judge that canst read the inmost thoughts of man's heart, let me live to
21 see thee punish them; to thee I have made my plea known. And now the Lord has a word for yonder men of Anathoth, who conspired to kill me, and would have stopped me prophesying in the Lord's
22 name, on pain of my life. I will call them to account for it, says the Lord of hosts; by the sword their warriors shall perish, and their sons
23 and daughters by famine. None shall be left; woe betide the men of Anathoth, when the year comes for my reckoning with them.

CHAPTER TWELVE

LORD, I know well that right is on thy side, if I should implead thee, yet remonstrate with thee I must; why is it that the affairs of the wicked prosper; never a traitor double-dyed but all goes well
2 with him? Deep roots they strike, so firmly thou hast planted them, thrive and bear fruit; yet all the while their hearts keep thee at a dis-
3 tance, only their lips proclaim thee. Yet it is thy warrant, Lord, I hold; with favour thou regardest me, hast proof of my heart's loyalty; wilt thou not herd them together like sheep, and mark them down for
4 slaughter? How long must this land go in mourning, all the verdure of its fields be parched up, to avenge the ill-doing of its inhabitants? Neither beast nor bird left in it; and still their hope is, I shall not live to see their end come![3]
5 What, tired out so soon when thy rivals were on foot? And hast thou

---

[1] 'His majestic voice'; in the Hebrew text, 'a great tempest.'
[2] This is perhaps the best interpretation of the reading, adopted by the Vulgate and by the Septuagint Greek, 'let us put wood into his bread.' The Hebrew text gives, 'Let us destroy the tree in its bread'; that is, presumably, 'with its fruits,' but such an expression finds no parallel elsewhere.
[3] 'I shall not live to see their end come'; or possibly, 'God does not care what becomes of them.'

the mettle to challenge horsemen? Easy to keep thy confidence, here
6 on safe ground; what shift wilt thou make in the fens of Jordan? Even
by thy own clansmen, thy own father's kin, thou art betrayed; these too
will join in the hue and cry after thee; never trust soft words of theirs.[1]
7 Farewell, my home; I have done with my chosen people; the life
8 that was so dear to me I have handed over to its enemies.[2] My people
grown strange to me, as lion snarling in its forest lair; what marvel
9 if I am weary of it? My people grown strange to me as carrion-bird,
its mottled plumage all bathed in blood![3]
Gather here, beasts that roam the earth, eager for your prey.
10 Drovers a many have laid waste my vineyard, trampled down my
11 lands; the land I loved so, turned into a lonely wilderness! Desolate
they have made it, and desolate it mourns for me now; a very picture
12 of desolation, and all for the want of men with heeding hearts. No
track over the uplands but has seen the freebooters coming by; from
end to end of the country the sword of divine vengeance must pass,
13 leaving no peace for any living thing; where wheat was sown, the
harvest shall be of briers, where men hold lands, they shall get no
advantage of it; all your harvests shall disappoint you, so fierce the
Lord's anger burns.
14 And this message comes from the Lord to those ill neighbours of
his, that encroach upon the domain he has granted to his people of
Israel: I mean to uproot them from their homes, when I uproot the
15 men of Juda from the land that lies between them. Yet I will relent
towards them in their exile and have pity on them; to their scattered
16 homes and countries they shall all return. Then, if they will but learn
the traditions of my own people, and take their oaths by the Lord,
the living God, as they once taught my people to take oaths by Baal,
17 their fortunes shall be founded anew in the midst of Juda. But wherever
my call goes unheeded, the Lord says, that people's uprooting shall
be that people's undoing.

---

[1] *vv.* 5, 6. This is apparently the divine answer to the prophet's impatience
with the men of Anathoth; what he has experienced so far is nothing to the
disappointments which await him at Jerusalem. The fens (literally, the 'Pride')
of Jordan were a lair of wild beasts (49.19); it is not clear whether peril
from wild beasts or peril from flood is here envisaged.
[2] The way in which Jeremias has been treated by his fellow-citizens resembles
the way in which God has been treated as a stranger by his chosen people.
[3] The first half of verse 9 runs literally, 'Has my people become a speckled
bird to me, a bird dyed all over?' The Hebrew text gives, 'Has my people
become a speckled vulture to me? The (other) vultures around are against
it'; the Septuagint Greek, 'Is my people a hyena's cave to me, or a cave round
it?' Probably the true reading is lost.

CHAPTER THIRTEEN

2 THE Lord's word came to me: Go and buy a girdle of linen, and put it about thy loins, never yet soaked in water. Girdle I bought me
3 as the Lord had bidden, and wore it; and now the Lord spoke again:
4 Is the girdle bought and worn? Up, take it with thee to Euphrates river,
5 and hide it there in a crevice of the rock. So I went obediently, and hid
6 it away in the Euphrates. Many days afterwards, the Lord sent me on my travels again to the Euphrates, to recover the girdle hidden there at
7 his command; so thither I went, and unearthed the girdle from its hiding-
8 place, to find it all perished and useless. Whereupon the Lord's word
9 came to me, and this was his message: Not less the great pride of Juda,
10 the great pride of Jerusalem, must perish. Here is a rebellious people that will not listen to my call; they must needs take their own false path,
11 courting alien gods and submitting to their worship. No better, then, than yonder useless girdle; close as a man's girdle fits about his loins I had bound Israel and Juda to myself; my people they were to be, my renown and prize and pride; but no, they would not listen.[1]
12 Tell them this, too, from the Lord God of Israel: Flagons are for wine. And when they answer, it is no news to them that flagons are
13 for wine, give them this message from the Lord: Ay, but the people of this land, king of David's line sitting on David's throne, priest and prophet and citizens of Jerusalem every one, are flagons waiting to be
14 filled. I mean to bemuse them, as with wine, and then shatter [2] them; brother torn away from brother, and fathers from their children; ruth and respite none shall have, nor be spared in the common ruin.
15 Hear and heed and humble yourselves; it is the Lord who speaks.
16 Give God his due, ere the shadows fall, and your feet begin to stumble on the dark mountain ways. For day you shall long, but he will have
17 turned it into night; dark as death the lowering of the storm. Sirs, if you will not listen now, give me leave to hide myself away and bemoan your proud hearts; weep I must and wail, and my eyes run down with tears, if the Lord's flock is doomed to captivity.
18 To king [3] and queen-mother say this, Come down and take your

---

[1] *vv.* 1–11. According to the opinion of St Jerome, the events here described happened only in a vision.

[2] The Latin verb has rather the sense of 'scatter,' but this loses the idea of the parable.

[3] There can be no certainty which king is alluded to; if it was Joakim or Joachin, the 'cities of the south' may perhaps be the border-cities of Egypt (cf. IV Kg. 24.7).

19 places with the rest, discrowned of your royalty.   Shut off are the
cities of the south, entry is none; dispeopled lies Juda, of all her sons
20 dispeopled.   New-comers from the north country, look about you
and see! . . .¹
. . . Ah, Jerusalem, what has become of the flock once entrusted to
21 thee, thy honourable care? What wilt thou say when thou art called
to give account of it? Thy enemies are such as thou hast taught how
to attack thee; thy schooling has recoiled on thy own head; sharper
22 than travail-throes the anguish that shall overtake thee.   And wilt
thou find room for surmise, why this should have befallen thee? Doubt
not it is thy own wrong-doing that has stripped thee naked, and plunged
23 thee deep in defilement.   Sooner may Ethiop turn white, leopard's hide
24 unmarked, than Juda unlearn the lesson of ill-doing and amend.   Far
and wide I will scatter thy sons, like straws caught in the desert wind;
25 such is the fortune sent thee, such thy retribution exactly awarded,
because thou hast forgotten me, and in lying fables put thy trust.
26 That is why I will pull thy skirts about thy ears and manifest thy shame;
27 adulteries of thine, and lasciviousness, and all the guilt of thy debauchery,
the foul deeds I have seen done on hill-tops, in the open countryside.
Fie on thee, Jerusalem, that wilt not come back to me and be cleansed!
Shall it last for ever?

CHAPTER FOURTEEN

HOW the Lord answered Jeremias in the matter of the drought.
2 Lamentation in Juda, faint hearts and the dress of mourners
3 in the market-place, loud the cry that goes up from Jerusalem! Master
sends man to fetch water, but when cistern is reached, water is none;
back go the pails empty, and disappointed vexation veils its head.
4 Vexation, too, and veiled heads among the country folk, so languish
5 the fields for lack of rain; hind forsakes its new-born young, because
6 grass has failed it, and the wild ass on the hill-side gasps for air, croco-
7 dile-fashion,² eyes dim with the vain search for pasture.   What though
we have guilt to plead against us? For thy own honour, Lord, bring
8 us aid, rebel so often, yet confessing how we have wronged thee! Thou,
Israel's hope, in time of calamity its refuge still, wilt thou pass us

---

¹ In the Latin version, the new-comers from the north are addressed; the
Hebrew text, which is evidently faulty, gives, 'Lift thou your eyes, and see
thou the men coming from the north.' The connexion between the two halves
of the verse is in any case obscure, and there may have been an omission.
The word 'Jerusalem' is not expressed in the original until verse 27.
² Literally, 'as the dragons do.' Some would interpret, 'as the jackals do.'

by, like stranger in a land that is none of his, like some traveller that
9 will ask for a night's lodging and be gone? Why dost thou hang back
like a man irresolute, a warrior that has forgotten his strength? Lord,
thy dwelling-place is among us; thy holy name we bear; wilt thou
abandon us?
10   Hearts ever in love with wandering, never at rest, what answer
will the Lord make them? That his favour is not for them; at this hour
he keeps their guilt in memory, for all their misdoings calls them to
11 account. Nay, the Lord said to me, do not pray for the welfare of
12 such a people as this. Fast they, their prayers shall go unheard; offer
they burnt-sacrifice and victim, I will have none of it; sword, and
13 famine, and the pestilence shall wear them down. Alas, alas, Lord
God, said I, here are their prophets telling them they shall never see
sword drawn, famine shall be none among them; theirs shall be a
14 land of lasting content. These are but false promises, the Lord said,
that they utter in my name; warrant they never had from me, nor
errand, nor message; of false visions they tell you, and soothsayings,
15 and trickery, and their own hearts' inventions. Here is the Lord's
sentence upon prophets not of his sending, who speak to you in his
name of a land unhurt by sword or famine; by sword and famine those
16 prophets shall be devoured. Slain by sword and famine, the common
folk that listen to them shall lie in the streets of Jerusalem, with none
to bury them; wives and sons and daughters shall die with them; their
own misdoings shall be a flood to drown them.
17   This too thou shalt say to them . . .[1]
   . . . Weep, eyes, day and night, never resting, at the great hurt, the
18 grievous wound she suffers, my people, inviolable till now! Nothing
the countryside shews but massacre, nothing the city but faces pinched
with famine; prophet and priest are gone, in a land of strangers they
19 must ply their trade[2] now. Hast thou abandoned Juda once for all,
art thou weary of Sion? Past all healing thou hast wounded us; how
we long for better times, and no relief comes to us, for remedy at last,
20 and danger still threatens! Lord, we acknowledge our rebelliousness,
acknowledge our fathers' guilt, confess that we have wronged thee;
21 for thy own honour, do not shame us, do not drag thy own royal glory
in the dust; wilt thou forget, wilt thou annul the covenant that binds
22 thee? Grant rain, they cannot, the false gods of the heathen, the dumb

---

[1] It does not seem likely that the rubric 'This too thou shalt say to them'
applies to the very human remonstrances which follow; an omission or a dislocation in the text is more probable.
[2] This is definitely implied by the verb used in the Hebrew text; the Latin
version has obscured its significance.

skies have no showers of their own to give; for these, his creatures, wait we patiently on the Lord our God.

CHAPTER FIFTEEN

BUT it was thus the Lord answered me: Though Moses himself and Samuel made intercession for them, neither love nor liking would I have for this people of mine; banish them from my presence,
2 to go where they will. If they ask whither, give them this message from the Lord: Whom the plague beckons, to the plague; whom the sword, to the sword; whom famine, to famine; whom exile, to exile.
3 Escort they shall have of four kinds, the Lord says; the sword to slay and the dogs to tear them, birds in air and beasts on earth to devour
4 and make an end of them. All the kingdoms of the world shall be in a ferment [1] over them; so will I punish the ill deeds done in Jerusalem
5 by Manasses, son of Ezechias, when he was king of Juda. Nay, Jerusalem, who shall pity or bemoan thee, who shall turn aside, as he passes,
6 to wish thee well? Thou hast forsaken me, the Lord says, and wouldst journey with me no more; now my hand is raised to strike, and make
7 an end of thee; I am weary of wooing thee. Over the threshold of the land I blow my people away like chaff, bereaved, diminished, and
8 unrepentant still. Widows there be, countless as the sea-sand; where is now the warrior son? In broad daylight I send the roving spoiler
9 to strike terror into their cities. Sick at heart and faint she lies, that seven sons had borne; her noon is night, her hopes and her pride gone; and all that she has left, the Lord says, shall fall a prey to the sword in battle.
10 An ill day when thou, my own mother, didst bring me into the world! A world where all for me is strife, all is hostility; neither creditor I nor debtor to any man, yet they curse my name!
11 But the Lord answered, I promise that thou shalt leave behind thee good service done, and that in all distress and persecution I am coming
12 to thy side, to save thee from thy enemies. What, should iron and bronze be in league with the iron that comes from the north? [2]
13 . . . (All the riches and treasures of thy land shall be despoiled, in
14 punishment for all its guilt, and to no purpose; I am summoning

---

[1] According to the Hebrew text, 'in consternation.'

[2] *vv.* 11, 12. The sense of these two verses is doubtful, and the Latin does not agree well with the Hebrew text in some points. Verse 12 perhaps implies that Jeremias was accused of being hand in glove with the invaders (37.17); how could the 'pillar of iron,' the 'wall of bronze' (1.18) be in league with the iron yoke (28.14) of Babylon?

enemies to attack thee from a land far away; it is your own persons that shall be burnt up in the fires of vengeance my anger has kindled) [1] ...

15 Thou art my witness, Lord; bethink thee, and come to my defence against my persecutors; hold thy hand no longer, but claim me for
16 thy own; [2] if I have earned an ill name, it was in thy cause. When thy words were found, [3] how greedily I devoured them! Great joy and content those words gave to my heart, heart of a prophet that bears
17 thy name. Not for me the company of the merrymakers, I would not share in their boastfulness; under the threat of thy judgement I
18 sat alone, filled with boding thoughts. Why are those sad thoughts still with me? Is my hurt desperate, beyond all remedy? Did it cheat me, like some empty water-course, my hope in thee?
19 Draw [4] near to me, the Lord said, and I will draw thee to myself, to wait upon me. When thou hast learned to separate worth from dross, thou shalt be my true spokesman, and thou shalt draw others
20 to thyself, not let thyself be drawn to them. This people of mine shall find thee a stout wall of bronze, impregnable to their attack; am I not
21 at thy side, the Lord says, to protect and deliver thee? Let the wicked be never so powerful, I will engage for thy safety.

CHAPTER SIXTEEN

2 THE Lord's word came to me: With such a land for thy dwelling-
3 place, neither wive nor gender; for sons and daughters born in this land, for mothers who there gave them birth and fathers who
4 begot them, the Lord has ill news to hear. Die they of the plague, they shall lie like dung on the ground, unwept, unburied; meet they their end by sword or famine, birds in air and beasts that roam the
5 earth shall prey on the carrion of them. Where they hold wake for the dead, such is the Lord's bidding, never enter thou, condole and

---

[1] *vv.* 13, 14. These verses are repeated, in part, lower down (17.3); they hardly seem to be in place here. The words 'to no purpose' perhaps refer to the tribute exacted by Egypt (IV Kg. 23–35), which left the men of Juda with no means of buying off the Chaldeans.
[2] This is the best that can be made of the obscure (and perhaps corrupt) phrase, 'Do not take me in thy long-suffering.'
[3] 'When thy words were found'; this is usually taken as referring to pro-phetic inspiration; but no parallel is adduced for such a forced way of talking. It may be suggested that Jeremias is here referring to his feelings when the Book of the Law was rediscovered under king Josias. The Septuagint Greek reads 'from those who despise thy words' (connected with verse 15).
[4] Literally, 'turn,' throughout this verse.

console thou never; friendship of mine this people shall never have,
6 nor grace, nor mercy, the Lord says. Die rich, die poor in that country
of theirs, burial and wake they shall have none; never a limb gashed
7 or a head shaved to honour them; none shall break bread with the
mourner, nor give him a draught of wine for his comfort, though
8 father or mother he bewail. Nor enter thou where men feast, to sit
9 at meat and drink with them; this doom he utters, the Lord of hosts,
the God of Israel: You shall live to see the day when cries of joy and
mirth, voice of bridegroom and of bride, in this land are heard no
more.

10 This warning uttered, if they ask thee why the divine sentence is so
stern, wherein their guilt lies, what wrong they have done to the Lord
11 their God, tell them this in his name: It is because your fathers have
forsaken me, had recourse to alien gods, and submitted to the worship
12 of them, my claim renounced, my laws defied. And you have outdone your fathers in malice, each of you following the ill bent of his own
13 heart, and disobeying me. Exiles far from home, in a land neither
you nor those fathers of yours ever saw, you shall spend day and night
14 in the service of alien gods, without respite. (Ay, the Lord says, a time
is coming when the living Lord men swear by will no longer be the
15 God who rescued Israel from Egypt; the living God will be one who has
rescued Israel from the north country, and all the places of exile that
are now designed for you, restoring them to the home which was once
16 his gift to their fathers.[1]) Many fishermen I have, the Lord says, to
spread the nets for them; and after that many huntsmen, to hunt them
17 down among mountains and hill-sides and rocky caverns. Good watch
I keep on their doings, never lose sight of them; no guilt of theirs
18 can escape my scrutiny. Twice over they shall pay for guilt of theirs,
misdoing of theirs, the men that have profaned my own land with
dead idols, spread pollution through all my domain.

19 Strength and stronghold, Lord, refuge in time of peril, shall not
the Gentiles themselves come to thee from the ends of the earth, confessing that all their patrimony is but a heritage of lies, that their idols
20 cannot avail them? Shall men make gods for themselves, that gods in
truth are none?

21 Ay, it is the very lesson I mean to teach them now; that I act, and
act with power; they shall learn to know the name of Javé at last.

---

[1] *vv.* 14, 15. These verses are repeated later on (23.7, 8), and some think they
have been wrongly inserted here by accident.

CHAPTER SEVENTEEN

NOT more indelible were the guilt of Juda, if pen of steel or point of diamond had graven it with their hearts for tablet, or upon the
2 rim of their altars; indelible, while there are sons of theirs to remember where altar stood once and sacred tree, shrine in the thick forest, shrine
3 on the high hills; to offer sacrifice even yet in the open countryside. All the riches and treasures of thy land shall be destroyed, all its hill-shrines,[1]
4 in punishment for all its guilt. Lost to thee, the home that once I gave thee; in a land thou knowest not thou shalt be the slave of thy enemies; the fire of anger thou hast kindled in me can never be quenched.
5 Cursed shall he be, the Lord says, that puts his trust in man, and
6 will have flesh and blood to aid him, his thoughts far from God. Never shall the sight of better times greet him; forlorn as some bush of tamarisk out in the desert, he dwells in a parched waste, the salt plains
7 for all his company. Blessed shall he be that puts his trust in the Lord,
8 makes the Lord his refuge. Not more favoured is tree planted by the water's edge, that pushes out its roots to catch the moisture, and defies the summer heat; its green leaves careless of the drought, its fruit unfailing.
9 There is no riddle like the twists of the heart; who shall master
10 them?[2] Who but I, the Lord, that can see into man's heart, and read his inmost thoughts, to every life awarding what its doings have earned?
11 Partridge that fosters a brood not its own is fit emblem for the man that wins riches unjustly; when life is but half done, he must take leave of them, a fool to the last.
12 Where from the first supreme majesty sits enthroned, there lies our
13 sanctuary; thou, Lord, art Israel's hope; the men who forsake thee will be disappointed, the men who swerve from thy paths will be names written in sand; have they not forsaken that Lord who is the fountain
14 of living water? If I am to be healed, it is thou, Lord, must heal me; if I am to find deliverance, it is thou must deliver me; thou art all my
15 boast. What has become of the Lord's threat? (so men taunt me),
16 we are waiting to see it accomplished! But this was no hasty word of mine, I did but lead where thou leddest; it was no wish of mine that

---

[1] The mention of the hill-shrines here is probably due to a false reading; cf. 15.13.

[2] Literally, 'the heart of all men is perverse and inscrutable; who shall have knowledge of it?' The Hebrew text gives, 'the heart of man is perverse and diseased above all things; who shall have knowledge of it?'

calamity should befall mankind;[1] no word I uttered but had the warrant
17 of thy scrutiny.   Not for me thy terrors; the day of affliction is coming,
18 but I shall find refuge in thee.   They must be abashed, and I vindicated;
they must cower, while I stand confident. It is on them the day of
affliction will fall; reward them, then, with twofold hurt for the hurt
they did.

19   The Lord bade me go and take my stand at the People's Gate, where
the kings of Juda passed to and fro; and then, in turn, at the other
20 gates of Jerusalem.   This was to be my message from the Lord to
king and people of Juda, to every citizen of Jerusalem that used those
21 gates: No more, on peril of your lives, shoulder those packs of yours
22 and carry them through Jerusalem gates on the sabbath day.   Never
a load must leave your houses, nor any work be done, on the sabbath;
23 this was the command I gave to your fathers, only they would not
listen or pay heed, chafed under the yoke of discipline and refused
24 to obey me.   And you, the Lord says, will you obey? Rid these gateways of their sabbath burdens, keep the sabbath holy by resting from
25 work, and your kings and princes, David's own heirs, shall still go
riding through them, with horses and chariots, with their retinue
of nobles, with the men of Juda and Jerusalem's citizens in their train.
26 Evermore your city shall be populous; from the townships of Juda,
from your own countryside, from Benjamin, from plain and hill and
the waste lands of the south, men shall come with burnt-sacrifice
and victim and bloodless offering and incense to enrich the Lord's
27 temple.   Refuse to keep the sabbath holy, profane it with burdens
borne and burdens admitted through the gates, and I will set those
gates in a blaze that shall burn down all Jerusalem ere you can quench it.

CHAPTER EIGHTEEN

2 THE Lord's word came to Jeremias, bidding him betake himself
3   to the potter's house; there a divine message awaited him. So I
4 went to the potter's house, and found him working at his wheel; just
then, the thing of clay he was a-fashioning broke in his hands, and
5 he, as the whim took him, turned it into another thing of clay. Then
6 it was the Lord's word came to me: You are in my hands, men of
Israel, as the clay in the potter's; why may I not do as the potter did?
7 All at once to a nation here, a kingdom there, I pronounce my sentence,
8 for the uprooting and undoing of it, for its utter destruction. Let

---

[1] The word 'mankind' is not in the Hebrew text; its presence in the Latin
seems due to a false interpretation.

but that nation repent of the crimes I brought against it, I too will
9 repent of the punishment I thought to exact. All at once to a nation
here, a kingdom there, I promise restoration of its fortunes and new
10 life. Let but that nation defy my will, shut its ears to my claim, I too
will repent of all the fair promises I made it.
11   Be this, then, thy message from the Lord to Juda's folk, to the
citizens of Jerusalem: Ill days I have in store for you; all my plans
are laid; time that each one of you should return from the false path,
12 shape aims and thoughts anew. Ah no, they tell me, too late! Each
13 one clings to his own course, follows his own bent still. Search the
world over, the Lord says, where were ever such deeds heard of as
14 this deed Israel, false maid, has most foully done? What, shall the
snows of Lebanon melt from those wild peaks,[1] shall they be dried
15 up at their source, those icy torrents that flow down from it? Not
less strange that this people of mine should forget me, and resort to
vain sacrifices; that they should find their own paths too rough for
them, the tracks marked out so long ago, and journey on instead along
16 by-paths untrodden. Desolate their country shall lie, doomed to everlasting scorn; every passer-by will shudder at it, or toss his head in
17 derision. I will sweep them away before the enemy's onset, as the
east wind sweeps all before it; turn my back and never look their way
in the hour of need.
18   Hereupon they summoned a conclave to plot against me, Jeremias;
What, they said, would he have us believe we need no more priests to
expound the law, no more wise men to counsel us, no more prophets to
say their word? They thought to compass my death by their whisper-
19 ings; to all my warnings would pay heed no longer. Lord, give me
20 audience; listen to these pratings of my enemies. Must they make such
a return for my good will, laying a snare to take my life? Bethink thee,
how I ever stood up before thee to plead for them, to avert thy anger
21 from them. Henceforth leave their children to famish, or give them
up to butchery; may their wives be childless widows, their grown
men die of pestilence, their young men by the sword-thrust in battle;
22 let their homes ring with lamentation, a prey to the sudden onslaught
of robbers! Cunning the snare they laid, deep the pit they dug to entrap
23 me; but there is no hiding from thee, Lord, the designs they have on
my life. Do not forgive their malice, keep their guilt ever in thy sight;
cast them down to earth at thy presence, and in thy anger make an end
of them.

---

[1] Literally, 'before the rock of the field.' The text may be corrupt, and perhaps conceals a proper name.

CHAPTER NINETEEN

2 UP, the Lord said to me, and get thee a jar of earthenware; take it to the valley of Ben-Ennom, close to the Earthenware Gate, with elders of the people and some of the older priests for thy company;
3 there prophesy as I bid thee. To the dynasty of Juda, to all the citizens of Jerusalem, give this message from the Lord of hosts, the God of Israel: I mean to bring such calamity on this place, as shall ring in
4 the ears of all that hear it. The place that once was mine, now alienated by the rebels that dwell there; to alien gods they never knew, no fathers of theirs, no kings of Juda ever knew, they have done sacrifice in this
5 place, drenching it with the blood of the innocent. Here the gods of the countryside must have their hill-shrines, and children must be burnt as a sacrifice in their honour; a rite not of my prescribing, or enjoining, or
6 imagining. And now, the Lord says, a time is coming when it will no more be called Topheth, or the Valley of Ben-Ennom; it will be called the
7 Valley of the Slain. In this valley all the hopes of Juda and Jerusalem shall be poured away; at the sword's point they shall meet their enemy and fall into pitiless hands, and I will give leave to bird in air, beast on earth,
8 to prey on the carrion of them. A thing of horror and scorn this city shall be; no passer-by but will shudder at it, or hiss derision at the memory of
9 its sufferings. Nay, a pitiless enemy shall press the siege so hard, that I will leave them no food save the flesh of son and daughter; man shall eat man.
10   Then break that jar of thine, for all thy company to see, and give them this message from the Lord of hosts: Broken to pieces you shall be, nation and city, like yonder thing of clay that is past all repairing; men will be finding room for their dead in Topheth, because other burying-ground is
12 none. Such, the Lord says, is the doom I have pronounced on city and
13 citizens; Jerusalem itself shall be a Topheth, all the houses in it, and yonder palace where the kings of Juda reigned, as Topheth unclean; it was there, on the roof-tops, they sacrificed to all the host of heaven, and made offering to alien gods.
14   His errand at Topheth done, Jeremias took his stand in the temple
15 courts, and gave the people this message from the Lord God of Israel: All these threats against Jerusalem and her daughter cities I mean to perform; the punishment of a yoke refused, a call unheeded.

CHAPTER TWENTY

WHEN Jeremias uttered this prophecy, one of those who heard him was Phassur, son of Emmer, a priest who was entrusted with the
2 care of the temple. This Phassur gave Jeremias a beating, and put him in
3 the stocks at the upper gate of Benjamin, in the temple precincts, but next day released him. A new name the Lord has for thee, Jeremias told him, instead of Phassur; he means to call thee Danger-Everywhere.
4 Danger enough thou shalt have, the Lord says, thou and those friends of thine; with thy own eyes thou shalt see the enemy put them to the sword, when I make the king of Babylon master of Juda; to Babylon he will take
5 them, and put them to the sword there. All the wealth of this city, all the fruits of its toil, all that is of price, all the treasury of Juda's kings, those enemies shall have in their power, to plunder and carry off and take back
6 to Babylon with them. And thou, Phassur, with all thy household, shalt go into exile; to Babylon thou shalt go, in Babylon thou shalt die, and there find burial with all such friends of thine as listened to thy lying prophecy.
7 Lord, thou hast sent me on a fool's errand; if I played a fool's part, a strength greater than mine overmastered me; morn to night, what a
8 laughing-stock am I, every man's nay-word! Long have I prophesied, and still I clamoured against men's wickedness, and still cried ruin; day in, day out, nothing it earns me, this divine spokesmanship, but reproach
9 and mockery. Did I think to put the Lord out of my thoughts, and speak no more in his name, all at once it seemed as though a raging fire were locked up in my bosom, till I was worn out with it, and could bear no
10 more. For me, danger everywhere; so many crying, Denounce him, and that cry echoed by all the companions I trusted, as they kept close watch on me: Denounce him we will; he may be fooled yet! Then we can over-
11 master him, and take our vengeance! But the Lord stands at my side, a strong champion; fall and fail they must, and be disappointed of their hopes; fools, that cannot foresee shame eternal, shame indelible, awaiting
12 them! But thou, Lord of hosts, true judge that canst read the inmost thoughts of man's heart, let me live to see thee punish them; to thee I
13 have made my plea known.[1] Sing to the Lord yet, praise the Lord yet; he does not leave a defenceless life at the mercy of the wicked.
14 Cursed be the day of my birth! A time for cursing it was, not for bless-
15 ing, when my mother brought me into the world. Cursed be the man who told my father a son had been born to him, and brought gladness, ay,

---

[1] A repetition of 11.20 above.

16 gladness, into his heart! For that good news, be he rewarded with the
noise of battle-cry at morn, dirge at noon, like some city the Lord over-
17 throws in anger unrelenting! Why did he not slay me yet unborn, the
18 womb for my tomb, and frustrate my mother's hope eternally? Why
must I come out into the light of day, where only labour and sorrow
greet me, and in disappointed striving all my life is spent?

CHAPTER TWENTY-ONE

A ND this was the answer Jeremias had from the Lord, when king
Sedecias sent two envoys to consult him; their names were Phassur
2 son of Melchias, and Sophonias son of Maasias, a priest. The king sought
a divine oracle about the war then levied on him by Nabuchodonosor,
king of Babylon; would the Lord grant his people wondrous deliverance
3 as of old? Would the siege be raised? And Jeremias sent them back to the
4 royal presence, with this message from the Lord, the God of Israel: All
the strength you have put into the field,[1] to meet the king of Babylon and
your Chaldaean besiegers at a distance from the walls, I mean to force
5 back into the city and coop it up within. Then my arm shall be raised to
strike, then my power shall be exerted, but against you; I will be all anger,
6 all indignation, all resentment, smiting the inhabitants of this city with
7 a great pestilence that shall slay both man and beast. But not king
Sedecias; he shall be left alive, and some of his courtiers and his retinue,
some of the citizens will be left alive, plague and war and famine notwithstanding. And these shall fall into the hands of Nabuchodonosor, king of
Babylon, into the hands of a pitiless enemy, that will put them to the
sword without ransom, or ruth, or respite.
8   And this warning the Lord gives to the common folk: Here is choice I
9 offer you between life and death, take which course you will. To remain
in this city means death by sword, famine, or pestilence; leave it, and go
over to the investing army of Chaldaeans, and you shall be spared; you
10 shall have your lives for guerdon. For woe, not weal, I keep this city ever
in regard; the king of Babylon shall be master of it, and burn it to the
ground.
11   And for king and princes of Juda: Men of David's line, here is a mes-
12 sage from the Lord for your hearing. Learn betimes to make true award,
and rob the oppressor of his prey, or my vengeance will blaze out against
you, like fire that still burns and will not be quenched.
13   Now turn I to thee, the Lord says, proud city that hast thy dwelling-
place in the valley, between rock and plain. Boast you, its townspeople,

---

[1] Literally, 'all the weapons you have in your hands.'

14 that on you no stroke shall fall, none shall reach your lair? You shall be
called to account, the Lord says, as your ill-doings have deserved; in this
forest I will light such a fire as shall consume all around it.[1]

CHAPTER TWENTY-TWO

2 A MESSAGE from the Lord, I must betake myself to the royal palace,
and make proclamation there; Listen to a divine warning, king of
Juda though thou be, and heir to David's throne; it is for thee and thy
3 courtiers and thy retinue, all that claim entry here. Just sentence, the
Lord says, and right award; rob the oppressor of his prey; to alien, orphan
and widow do neither despite nor wrong; never, within these walls, be
4 innocence condemned to death. This warning if you obey, through these
palace gates the heirs of David and of David's throne, with horses and
5 chariots, courtiers and retinue, shall yet pass to and fro. Disobey, the
Lord says, and my own honour is engaged to make, of this palace, a ruin.
6 On the royal house of Juda this is the Lord's sentence: Growth I found
here once, generous as in Galaad or on Lebanon's height; now I have
7 sworn to make a desert of it, no place for the haunts of men.[2] Who shall
strike the blow, and with what arms, is decreed already; all those fair
cedars shall be cut down, and cast into the fire.

8 Nations a many shall pass by those ruins; and when a man asks his
neighbour what it meant, that the Lord should deal so hardly with a great
9 city like this, the answer will be, It was because they forsook the covenant
of the Lord their God, and worshipped alien gods, took alien gods for
their masters.

10 Not for the dead your tears, not for him bow your heads; if weep you
must, weep for him that must go and come again no more, never again see
11 the land of his birth! Sellum,[3] that followed his father Josias on the
throne of Juda, is leaving Jerusalem, the Lord says, and will never come
12 back to it; die he must in that country to which I have banished him,
and see this land no more.

13 Alas, for the palace that is built with gains ill gotten, for halls founded

---

[1] *vv.* 13, 14. These verses are generally understood as referring to Jerusalem. But the geographical description given hardly seems applicable, and it
is better to admit that the destination to which this particular prophecy was
addressed remains unknown.

[2] Literally, 'For the Lord says this about the house of the king of Juda:
Galaad thou to me, the summit of Lebanon; I swear to make thee a desert,
uninhabitable cities.'

[3] Sellum (also mentioned in I Par. 3.15) is usually identified with Joachaz
(IV Kg. 23.30).

only on wrong! Alas for the man that sets his fellow man vainly drudging,
14 and leaves his wages unpaid! A fine house I will make of it, says he, and
wide rooms in it! Here he will throw out a window, there he will panel
15 a wall with cedar, and paint it vermilion. Art thou hoping for a long
reign, that thou shouldst challenge comparison with the cedar?[1] Thy
father was one that ate and drank at his ease, gave every man his just due,
16 and was content; well for him that he gave the friendless and the poor
17 redress, as men will when they bethink themselves of me. Thou hast no
eyes, no thoughts, but for gain; for innocent men's undoing, for oppres-
18 sion, for the reckless pursuit of mischief. This, then, is the Lord's sentence upon Joachim, son to Josias and king of Juda: For him no cry shall
be made, Brother, what grief! Sister, what grief![2] For him no cry shall
19 be made, Ah, what a master! Ah, what renown! An ass's burial he shall
have, cast out, a stinking corpse, beyond the gates of Jerusalem.[3]

20   Get thee gone, faithless people, to Lebanon, and cry out there; fill
Basan with thy voice, and let Abarim[4] echo the cry again; ruin has over-
21 taken all those lovers of thine. In the days of thy ease, I gave thee warning, but thou wouldst not listen; it was ever thus from thy girlhood's days,
22 my voice went unheard. Drifting with the wind, the drovers thou once
didst follow, captive all those that once held thy love! Be ashamed at last,
23 and blush for all thy wickedness. High on Lebanon thy dwelling-place,
high in the cedars that nest of thine, piteous shall be thy moan when pangs
overtake thee, like the pangs of a woman in travail.

24   And of Joachim's son Jechonias, that is heir to the throne of Juda, the
Lord says this: Were he the signet ring on my right hand, I would cast
25 him off none the less. Thou hast sworn enemies to fear; Nabuchodonosor
26 king of Babylon, and his Chaldaeans, shall have the mastery of thee. Cast
away, thyself and the queen-mother who bore thee, into an alien land,
27 far from the land of your birth, to die there; ever longing for home, and
28 home returning never. What, is he but a broken piece of earthenware,

---

[1] The first half of this verse is generally interpreted as asking, Does Joachim
think that competitiveness in the matter of cedar panelling will make more
of a king of him? The translation given above, which follows the Latin, perhaps demands less of the imagination. 'Ate and drank at his ease,' *i.e.,* took
things as they came, instead of occupying himself with grandiose schemes;
cf. Eccl. 2.24 and *passim.*

[2] The use of the word 'sister' would suggest that the mourners are represented as condoling with one another upon their common loss; the sense being
'Alas, O my sister,' not 'Alas for my sister' (the common interpretation).

[3] See note on IV Kg. 24.6.

[4] For 'Abarim' the Latin version has 'the Passers-by,' translating the word
instead of transliterating it. 'Lovers' is understood by some to mean the kings
of Juda; others would understand it of foreign countries, like Egypt, with
which Juda had formed entangling alliances.

this Jechonias, a useless shard, that he should be thrown away, and his
29 sons with him, cast out into a land unknown? Alas, my country, alas,
30 alas, my country, bitter hearing the Lord sends thee: Write him down a
barren trunk, a life gone to waste; child of his race shall never mount
David's throne, or govern this realm of Juda.

CHAPTER TWENTY-THREE

OUT upon them, the Lord says, the shepherds who ravage and dis-
2 perse my flock, sheep of my own pasturing! This is the Lord's word
to the shepherds that guide his people: You are the men who have dispersed my flock, driven it to and fro, and made no account of it; account
3 you must give to me, the Lord says, for all you have done amiss. Then
will I reassemble all that is left of my flock, scattered over so many lands,
and restore them to their old pasture-ground, to increase and grow
4 numerous there; shepherds I mean to give them that will do shepherd's
work; fears and alarms shall be none to daunt them, and none shall be
5 missing from their full count, the Lord says. Nay, a time is coming, the
Lord says, when I will raise up, from the stock of David, a faithful scion
at last. The land shall have a king to reign over it, and reign over it
6 wisely, giving just sentence and due award. When that time comes, Juda
shall find deliverance, none shall disturb Israel's rest; and the name given
7 to this king shall be, The Lord vindicates us. In those days to come, says
the divine message, the living Lord men swear by will no longer be the
8 God who rescued Israel from Egypt; the living God will be one who
rescued Israel and brought them home from the north country, and from
all the places of exile he had once designed for them, to live in their own
land again.[1]
9 A message to the prophets: Crushed is the heart in me, and my whole
being trembles; my thoughts whirl like a drunken man's, bemused by a
10 divine presence, by awe of a divine voice. The whole land is a nest of
adulterers; their guilt it is that widows the countryside, parches the upland meadows; reckless their pursuit of mischief, through the power they
11 wield all goes amiss. Prophet and priest alike are impious; in my own
12 house, the Lord says, those ill doings of theirs are plain to view. Perilously they shall fare as one that walks by night in slippery places; falter
and fall they must; punishment awaits them, the Lord says, my audit-
13 year is at hand. For the prophets of Samaria how was it I lost all liking?[2]

---

[1] *vv.* 7, 8. See 16.14, 15.
[2] 'I lost all liking'; the Latin here probably means not 'I found foolishness,'
but 'I found insipidity,' which is an exact rendering of the Hebrew.

Because they were the spokesmen of Baal, and did but lead Israel astray,
14 that was my people. And now the same foul adultery I find in the prophets of Jerusalem, the same treacherous dealings; and the sinner is
encouraged to go on in his evil ways, till city and citizens, for me, are one
15 with Sodom and Gomorrha. A warning to you then, prophets, from the
Lord God of hosts, that he will give you wormwood to eat, gall to drink;
you, the fountain-head of that pollution which overflows all the land.
16 Do not listen, says the Lord of hosts, to the prophets who prophesy
only to fool you; fancy of theirs, not word of mine, inspires the utterance.
17 To my blasphemers they bring divine assurance that all shall go well
with them; never a man so set on his own false aims but they will tell him,
18 Harm shall never touch thee. Never a one of them privy to the Lord's
designs, never one looked and learned, listened and heard his message.
19 Like a whirlwind it will suddenly appear, the Lord's vengeance; will
20 break in storm over rebel heads. Nor shall the divine anger be appeased
till the blow has been struck and the decree executed; what his design
was, you shall know all too well, all too late.[1]
21 An errand these prophets ran, but none of mine; a message they gave,
22 but not of my sending. Privy to my design had they been, ah, then they
should have uttered my own warnings, and so I might have turned my
23 people aside from false paths, and erring thoughts! God am I, the Lord
24 says, only when I stand near, and not when I am far away? Where, he
would know, will you hide so close that he is not watching you, he, the
25 Lord, that fills heaven and earth? No word, he says, but reaches my ears
when one of these prophets gives false guidance in my name; I had a
26 dream, he will tell you, I had a dream! Will they never have had enough
27 of their lying divinations, their cheating fantasies? Dreams bandied from
mouth to mouth, for these would they have my people barter away the
28 memory of me, as their fathers did for Baal? Nay, let the dreamer be content to tell his dreams, and the prophet to whom my word comes utter
29 my word faithfully; chaff and grain must not be mingled. My word is a
30 fire, the Lord says, a hammer to break rocks in pieces; out upon the
prophets, I say, who proclaim divine utterances they have borrowed from
31 their fellow men;[2] out upon the prophets, I say, who let their tongues
32 wag and then cry, Oracle. Out upon the prophets, I say, who dream all
amiss and recount their dreams, leading my people astray with their lies
and their mummeries; yet errand or warrant they had none from me, the
Lord says, nor yet to this people of mine bring any advantage.

---

[1] *vv.* 19, 20. See 30.23, 24, where the same words are repeated; some think
they have been included by error in the present context.

[2] Literally, 'Steal my words each man from his neighbour,' but the context
(cf. verse 22 above) makes it clear that there is no allusion to *genuine* mes-
sages from Almighty God.

33 And if people, or prophet, or priest, should greet thee with the question, Pray, what burden [1] is the Lord taking up to-day? thy answer shall
   be, You are the burden I bear, the Lord says, and I mean to cast you
34 from my shoulders. Prophet, priest or simple citizen that asks thus about
   the Lord's burden does it at his own peril, and the peril of all his house-
35 hold; be content to ask friend or neighbour, What oracle, what message
36 has the Lord given? Do not speak any more of his burden. If you do, you
   lay a heavy charge upon yourselves, by bandying words with the living
37 God, the Lord of hosts, the God of Israel. Ask the prophet what the
38 Lord's oracle, what the Lord's message is; if you ask after the Lord's
   burden, this warning I give you from him: For your disobedience to the
39 message I sent, commanding you to use the word Burden no longer, I
   will make a burden of you, and carry you away, and leave you abandoned,
40 you and your city, my gift to you and to your fathers. You shall be a
   laughing-stock for ever, a by-word eternally; time shall never efface the
   memory of your shame.

CHAPTER TWENTY-FOUR

AFTER king Nabuchodonosor, of Babylon, had carried off the king of
Juda, Jechonias the son of Joachim, and taken him away to Babylon
with all his nobles, and all the carpenters and smiths in Jerusalem, the
Lord shewed me a vision. I saw two baskets of figs, set down at the gate
2 of the Lord's temple. The figs in one basket were of excellent nature,
like those which first ripen; in the other, most foul, so foul there was no
3 eating them. What seest thou, Jeremias? the Lord asked, and I told him,
Figs, the good ones excellent food, the foul ones very foul, too foul for
4 eating. Then the Lord's word came to me, A message from the Lord
God of Israel: This meaning the good figs have, that good will of mine
goes with the men of Juda I have banished from their homes, and sent
6 them away into the country of Chaldaea. I will smile on them once more,
and bring them back home, and all will be building now, not pulling
7 down, planting now, not uprooting. And I will give them a heart to know
me, to know Javé's name, once in good earnest they have retraced their
8 steps, and come back to me. And this meaning the foul figs have, that
could not be eaten, they were so foul. Doom like theirs I have in store for

---

[1] *vv.* 33–40. The Hebrews used the same word for (i) a load or pack, (ii)
the content of a divine revelation; see Is. 13.1 and *passim*. The people of Jerusalem, weary of Jeremias' continual pessimism, used to mock him by asking
what was the Lord's 'burden' (much as we talk about the burden of a song,
the burden of a complaint). This levity of theirs is here rebuked, and threatened with punishment.

Sedecias, king of Juda, the Lord says, and for his nobles, and for all those other men of Jerusalem that have either stayed in the city or taken up
9 their abode in Egypt. Bane [1] and burden they shall be to all the kingdoms of the world, a laughing-stock and a warning, a by-word and a name to curse by, in all the countries I have appointed for their banishment.
10 Sword and famine and pestilence I will let loose upon them, till none of them is left in this land, my gift to them and to their fathers.

CHAPTER TWENTY-FIVE

HERE is a message for the whole people of Juda, entrusted to Jeremias in the fourth year of Joachim's reign (that was son to Josias) in
2 Juda, the first of Nabuchodonosor's in Babylon. To all Juda, and to all
3 the citizens of Jerusalem, the prophet Jeremias delivered it: These twenty-three years, ever since the thirteenth year of Josias' reign, that was son to Amon, the Lord's word has been coming to me, and ever I was
4 early at your doors repeating it, but you would not listen. Early to your doors the Lord sent all those prophets that were servants of his, but hear-
5 ing there was none, nor heeding. False aims, he warned you, lead you by false paths astray; come back to me, and you shall dwell yet in this land, my gift to you and to your fathers from the beginning to the end of time.
6 Would you court slavery by worshipping alien gods, defy my vengeance
7 with your ill doings, till I plague you? But you would not listen to me,
8 the Lord says; ill was done yet, and my vengeance was yet defied. And
9 now, says the Lord of hosts, finding you disobedient still, I mean to summon all the nations of the north country, with Nabuchodonosor, that servant of mine that is king in Babylon; I, the Lord, will bid him march on this land and its citizens, and all its neighbours. I mean to make an end of them, and leave it a thing to provoke wonder and scorn, desolate for all
10 time. Never again cries of joy and mirth, never again the voice of bride-
11 groom and of bride, never a mill turning, never a lamp to shine. For seventy years this whole land shall be a desert and a portent, and the king of Babylon shall have all these peoples for his slaves.
12 Then, when seventy years have passed, I will call the king of Babylon to account, the Lord says, for all the wrongs he has done, with his people and with that Chaldaean country of his; that country in its turn I will
13 leave desolate for ever. The sentence I have pronounced against it shall be executed in full, all the doom Jeremias has foretold in this book of pro-
14 phecy against all the nations of the world. Great nations, proud kings,

---

[1] According to the Hebrew text, 'a source of shuddering.' The same word occurs in 15.4, where the Latin version translates 'ferment.'

have held Israel enslaved; now for their own lives, their own deeds, they too must make amends.[1]

15 The Lord of hosts, the God of Israel, bade me take the cup of vengeance that was in his hand, and give drink out of it to all the nations to
16 which my errand lay; drink it they should, and reel to and fro, bemused
17 by the threat of his sword let loose among them. So I took the cup from
the Lord's hand; nor was there any of the nations the Lord had sent me
18 to threaten but must drink of it. Jerusalem must drink, and the townships
of Juda, kings and nobles with the rest; the land was doomed to become
a desert, a thing of wonder and scorn, a name to be used in cursing, as it
19 is at this day. Pharao king of Egypt and all his court and his nobles must
20 drink, and all the mingled people of his realm. No king in the land of
Hus but must drink of it, nor among the Philistine cities, Ascalon, Gaza,
21 Accaron and Azotus, nor in Edom, Moab and Ammon, no king in Tyre,
23 and the Sidonian country, and the islands that lie beyond the sea. Dedan
24 must drink, and Thema, and Buz, and all the folk with shaven heads, all
25 the kings of Arabia, and the western desert kings.[2] Nor any king in
26 Zambri, Elam, and Media, nor any king in the north country, far or
near, but must pledge his neighbour; all the kings of the earth must have
their share, and Sesach [3] not till the last.

27 This message I was to give them from the Lord of hosts, the God of
Israel, Drink, besot yourselves, and then fall to vomiting; and topple over
at last, never to rise again, so well shall my sword do its work among you!
28 If they made to refuse the cup I offered them, this more I should add:
29 Nay, but drink you must, says the Lord of hosts; here am I beginning my
work of vengeance with that city which is the shrine of my name, and
shall you be acquitted, you others, and go scot-free? That shall never be,
says the Lord of hosts; to the sword if I appeal, it is for a whole world's
punishment.

30 With such words as these thou shalt prophesy to them: From on high,
from his holy dwelling-place, the Lord makes his voice heard, terrible as
lion roaring; as roar of lion against sheep-fold, and that fold his own!
Loud echoes his vintage-cry as he treads down all the dwellers on earth;

---

[1] *vv.* 12–14. Some think that these verses are wrongly inserted in their present context. And indeed, the order of the text from this point onwards remains
uncertain. The Latin version follows the Hebrew; but the Septuagint Greek
preserves quite a different tradition. The chapters which are numbered 26 to
31 in our text appear much later in the Greek, between ch. 50 and ch. 51, nor
do they appear in precisely the same order.

[2] For the Arab custom of cutting the hair back from the temples, cf. 9.26.
The meaning of the Hebrew text is probably 'the kings of the desert steppes'
rather than 'the western desert kings.'

[3] 'Sesach' is a cabalistic way of referring to Babylon; cf. 51.41. This item in
the catalogue, like certain others, is absent from the Septuagint Greek.

31 to the ends of the world it must echo; a whole world he calls to account,
impleads the whole race of men; The sword's point for my adversaries,
32 the Lord says.   From nation to nation, says the Lord of hosts, calamity
will spread, like a great whirlwind sprung up from the corners of the
33 earth,   and from end to end of it the bodies of the Lord's foes, unwept,
34 ungathered, unburied, shall lie like dung on the ground.   Cry out, make
loud lament, shepherds of the nations, and you, the lordliest among their
flocks; your day is done, slain you must lie there, unvalued as some
35 delicate vase broken to pieces.   For shepherds, and the pride of the flock,
36 no refuge now;   hark how they lament, shepherds and pride of the flock,
37 for pasture-grounds the Lord has laid waste!   Silent they lie now, once
38 happy fields, under ban of the Lord's vengeance.   Lion springs not from
his lair more suddenly; all their land lies waste, so pitiless the invader's
onset,[1] so pitiless the Lord's anger.

CHAPTER TWENTY-SIX

A T the beginning of Joachim's reign in Juda, that was son to Josias,
2 word came from the Lord,   and this was his bidding: Go and stand
in the temple porch, and there, to pilgrims from all the townships of Juda,
deliver the message I have entrusted to thee; no word of it do thou re-
3 trench.   It may be they will listen, and go astray no longer; then I will
4 forgo the punishment I have devised for their ill doings.   This divine
warning give them: Listen to me, and live by the law I have enjoined upon
5 you,   obeying the call of the prophets, those servants of mine whom I sent
6 early to your doors, upon an errand that went unheeded;   or this sanctuary, too, shall be deserted as Silo, and this city shall be an accursed
name, all the world over.

7   Priests and prophets and townsfolk heard it alike, this utterance of
8 Jeremias in the temple;   and when he had thus done the Lord's errand for
all the people to hear, priests and prophets and townsfolk laid hands upon
9 him, crying out, His life must pay for it!   What, would he threaten in the
Lord's name that this temple is to share Silo's doom, this city to be left
forlorn, uninhabited?   There, in the Lord's house, Jeremias must con-
10 front the anger of a whole people.   When they heard of it, the nobles of
Juda left palace for temple, and there held assize, at the approaches of the
11 New Gate.   Before these, and before the general assembly, priest and
prophet called for the death penalty; here was a man who had foretold, in
12 the public hearing, calamity for Jerusalem.   To nobles and to people

---

[1] For 'the invader' the Latin version has 'the dove,' which is a possible
translation of the Hebrew, but yields no satisfactory sense.

Jeremias had but one defence: Nothing have I said against temple or city
13 but what the Lord's errand bade me.   Come, do but amend your lives and
your likings, and listen to the Lord your God; he will spare you the doom
14 he has pronounced upon you.   As for me, I am in your hands; do with me
15 what you will, what you think right.   Only be sure of this, if you kill me,
you will bring the guilt of murder on yourselves, your city, and all that
dwell there; no word you have heard from me but has the Lord's true
warrant.

16   And this answer both nobles and townsfolk made to priest and prophet, There is no death sentence lies against this man; as the spokesman
17 of the Lord our God he has given us his message.   There were some of the
18 older citizens that rose to defend him publicly;   Remember the prophet
Michaeas of Morasthi, they said, in the days of king Ezechias, who told
the people of Juda: Sion shall be no better than a ploughed field, says the
Lord of hosts, Jerusalem but a heap of stones, the temple height only a
19 hanging wood.[1]   Did Ezechias king of Juda, or his subjects, thereupon
put him to death? Nay, they feared the Lord too well for that; went
about to appease his anger, so that he spared them the punishment he had
threatened. It were pity of our lives, did we so great a wrong!

20   Another prophet there was that came in the Lord's name, Urias, the
son of Semei, a man of Cariathiarim, and used no gentler language about
21 this city and country than Jeremias himself.   King Joachim, and all his
chieftains and his nobles, were for making away with him when they
22 heard such warnings;   and though he took alarm and fled to Egypt, royal
pursuivants were sent there under Elnathan, son of Achobor, to bring
23 him back;   whereupon king Joachim put him to the sword, and cast his
24 body away among the tombs of the common folk.   But Jeremias had a
friend in Ahicam, the son of Saphan, who would not let him be handed
over to the people and put to death.

CHAPTER TWENTY-SEVEN

AT the beginning of the new king's [2] reign in Juda, that was son to
2 Josias, word came from the Lord to Jeremias after this fashion.   The
Lord bade me make myself a yoke, band and bar, and put it about my
3 neck; let it be the answer, he said, given by Sedecias, king of Juda, to the
envoys that have come to him from the kings of Edom, Moab, Ammon,

---

[1] See Mic. 3.12.
[2] The Hebrew text, and all the versions except the Syriac, give the name of
the reigning monarch as Joachim. But it seems clear this must have been a
scribe's error; cf. verses 3 and 12, where Sedecias is mentioned instead.

4 Tyre and Sidon. This message thou shalt give them, for their masters,
5 from the Lord of hosts, the God of Israel: My strength it was, the exertion of my power, that made earth, made man and beast to walk on it; and
6 I give dominion over it to the man on whom my choice falls. And all these countries I have handed over to my servant Nabuchodonosor, king
7 of Babylon, making even the wild beasts subject to him; all the world must obey him, and his son and his grandson after him, until the time has run out, for him and for his land both; nations a many and great kings
8 shall pay him their homage. Nation or people that will not be vassal to Nabuchodonosor, will not bow to Babylon's yoke, I will punish with sword and famine and pestilence, until the last of them is left at his mercy.
9 Do not listen, then, to those prophets of yours, diviner and dreamer,
10 soothsayer and sorcerer, who bid you resist the king of Babylon; whither will they bring you, these lying prophecies? To a land far from your home,
11 to sentence of banishment, and your undoing. But let a nation once bow to the king of Babylon's yoke, and become his vassal, to that nation, the Lord says, I will leave its own fields to till, its own home to dwell in.
12 All this message I gave to Sedecias, king of Juda; Your lives shall be spared, I told him, if only you will bow your necks to the yoke,
13 letting king and people of Babylon be your masters; will you court death, king and people at once, from sword, famine, and pestilence, the Lord's
14 threat against all who refuse submission? To the prophets who declare you shall never be vassals of Babylon, give no heed; they are cheating you
15 with lies; warrant from me they have none, yet falsely claim to be my spokesmen, to your own casting away and undoing, and theirs moreover who so prophesy.
16 And this message I gave from the Lord to priests and people: Do not listen to those prophets of yours, who bid you expect the speedy return of the sacred treasures from Babylon. These are but lying prophecies;
17 do not let them deter you from submitting to the king of Babylon, your
18 only hope of safety; shall this city become a desert? Prophets if they be, spokesmen of the Lord if they be, let them rather plead with him, the Lord of hosts, that the treasures still left in temple and palace and city
19 may not find their way to Babylon too. Doom the Lord of hosts has decreed upon all of them, pillars and brazen basin and stands, and those
20 other treasures that remained here untouched, when Joachim's son Jechonias, that once reigned in Juda, was carried off to Nabuchodonosor's
21 capital at Babylon, with all the notables of this city and realm. This he would have you know, he, the Lord of hosts, the God of Israel, that all
22 the treasures left in temple, palace or city   shall be carried away to Babylon in their turn. There they shall remain, the Lord says, till the time comes for demanding an account of them, for bringing them back and setting them up again where they stood before.

CHAPTER TWENTY-EIGHT

SEDECIAS had then but lately come to the throne of Juda; it was the fourth year of his reign. In the fifth month of that year a prophet from Gabaon, Hananias son of Azur, came up to me in the temple, in full
2 sight of priests and worshippers. A message, he said, from the Lord of hosts, the God of Israel: So much for the king of Babylon's yoke! I have
3 broken it to pieces. Two years must run their course, and then all shall come back again here; all the temple treasures Nabuchodonosor took
4 away with him to his capital at Babylon, and the king of Juda too, Jechonias son of Joachim, with all the exiles from Juda Babylon now holds. I will bring them back, the Lord says, and break the yoke of the king of Babylon to pieces.
6   And the prophet Jeremias answered, Amen to that! Well indeed it were if the Lord would grant this prophecy of thine fulfilment, would bring all
7 the temple treasure home, and all the exiles at Babylon! Only, here is a
8 word for thy hearing, and for the general hearing no less. So many prophets before thy day and mine, so many nations, such proud empires
9 their theme, and all alike told of battle, of distress, of famine; here is one at last that brings good news! Why then, when his words come true, none
10 will doubt that his errand was from the Lord. At that, Hananias took the
11 band from Jeremias' neck and broke it, crying out before all the people, A message from the Lord! Thus, when two years have run their course, I will break the yoke which king Nabuchodonosor of Babylon has laid on
12 the necks of all the nations! And Jeremias said no more, but passed on.
   Thus did Hananias break the band on the neck of his fellow prophet;
13 and thereupon came the word of the Lord to Jeremias, Go and give Hananias this message from the Lord: Wooden yoke break, iron yoke
14 make! The Lord of hosts, the God of Israel, tells thee that he is putting a yoke of iron on the necks of all the nations, subjecting them to Nabuchodonosor king of Babylon. His subjects they shall be; even over the
15 wild beasts dominion is granted him. This, too, Jeremias said to his fellow prophet, Listen, Hananias; errand from the Lord thou hast none, thou
16 art cheating yonder people with false hopes. And this doom the Lord has uttered: I mean to banish thee from this earth altogether; thou shalt die
17 within the year, for this language of rebellion against the Lord. Hananias died that year, before seven months were over.

CHAPTER TWENTY-NINE

TO those other elders, priests and prophets who had already gone into exile, to all the citizens Nabuchodonosor had carried off with him 2 to Babylon, the prophet Jeremias sent a message in writing. Among these were king Jechonias and the queen-mother, and the chamberlains, and all that were of note in realm or capital; nor were any carpenters or smiths 3 left in Jerusalem. The new king of Juda, Sedecias, was sending Elasa, the son of Saphan, and Gamarias, the son of Helcias, on a mission to Nabuchodonosor at Babylon, and to their hands the letter of Jeremias was entrusted.

4 It ran thus: A message from the Lord of hosts, the God of Israel, to 5 the men of Jerusalem he has sent into exile at Babylon! I would have you build yourselves houses of your own to dwell in, plant yourselves gardens 6 of your own to support you, wive and gender, wed son and daughter so that they their in turn may breed, grow numerous, that are now so few, 7 there in your land of exile. A new home I have given you; for the welfare of that realm be ever concerned, ever solicit the divine favour; its welfare 8 is yours. And this warning he sends you, the Lord of hosts, the God of Israel; Never allow prophet and soothsayer that are of your company to 9 mislead you; his dreams let the dreamer abandon; prophets there are, the Lord says, that claim falsely to be my spokesmen, and warrant from 10 me have none. All but seventy years, he tells you, must have run their course before Babylon's time is up; then I will come to relieve you, and make good the promise of your return.

11 I have not lost sight of my plan for you, the Lord says, and it is your welfare I have in mind, not your undoing; for you, too, I have a destiny 12 and a hope. Cry out to me then, and your suit shall prosper; [1] plead with 13 me, and I will listen; look for me, and you shall find me, if you will but 14 look for me in good earnest. Find me you shall, the Lord says, and your sentence of exile shall be reversed; the same Lord who scattered them 15 among alien folk and in far countries will bring the exiles home. So much for your claim that [2] the Lord has revived the gift of prophecy among you, there in Babylon.

16 As for the king who now sits on David's throne, and the citizens who dwell here now, instead of sharing your exile, this is the divine sentence:

---

[1] 'And your suit shall prosper'; literally, 'and you shall go.' The verb seems to be used as in Jg. 4.24; the rendering 'and you shall go and plead with me and I will listen' breaks the run of the sentence.

[2] Literally, 'because you say that.' Some think the order of the text has become dislocated, and this verse ought to come between verses 20 and 21.

17 I mean to plague them, says the Lord of hosts, with sword and famine and
pestilence; of no more account will I make them than a basket of foul
18 figs, so foul there is no eating them.　Sword and famine and pestilence
shall follow at their heels; bane they shall be to all the kingdoms of the
world, a name to curse by, a thing of wonder and of scorn, a laughing-
19 stock among all the countries I have appointed for their banishment.　All
this, because they would not listen to any word of mine, the Lord says;
early to their doors I sent the prophets that were servants of mine, I, your
Lord, and could get no hearing.

20 　　Listen, then, to the Lord's decree, men of Jerusalem I have sent into
21 exile at Babylon.　This doom the Lord has pronounced upon Achab, the
son of Colias, and Sedecias the son of Maasias, false prophets both of
them, that speak to you as in my name; I mean to hand them over for
punishment to Nabuchodonosor king of Babylon, and that punishment
22 you shall witness for yourselves.　Wherever exiles from Juda are found
in the Chaldaean country, this shall be the curse they use: Such doom
the Lord give thee as he gave to Sedecias and Achab, that the king of
23 Babylon roasted over a fire!　This is great shame they have brought on
Israel, bedding with their neighbours' wives, and uttering in my name
counterfeit prophecies that had no warrant of mine; of these misdoings
I am judge and witness both.

24 　　And another message must be given to Semeias of Nehelam　from the
Lord of hosts, the God of Israel, about the letter he sent to the citizens
left in Jerusalem, and namely to the high priest Sophonias, the son of
26 Maasias, and his fellow priests.　This letter ran,　If the Lord would have
thee follow Joiada in the high priesthood, it was to make thee master of
his house, ready with stocks and gaol for any mad fellow that came a-
27 prophesying.　Why does Jeremias of Anathoth go unrebuked, and pro-
28 phesy among you still?　He has written to us here in Babylon for the very
purpose of telling us our exile shall be long; we must build ourselves
29 houses to dwell in, we must plant gardens to support us!　This letter was
30 read aloud to Jeremias by the high priest; and then it was that the Lord's
31 word came to Jeremias,　with a message he must send to the exiles: This
doom the Lord utters against Semeias of Nehelam.　Would he prophesy
in my name, a man that has no warrant from me, and give you confidence
32 in false hopes?　I will call Semeias of Nehelam to account for it, the Lord
says, and his children after him.　Man of his race there shall be none surviving among this people of mine, the Lord says, to see my bounty bestowed on it. Against me, the Lord, he has used the language of rebellion.

CHAPTER THIRTY

2 WORD came to Jeremias from the Lord, the God of Israel, bidding
3 him write down in a book the revelation made known to him. A
time is coming, the Lord says, when I will reverse the sentence of exile
against my people of Israel and Juda; I, the Lord, will restore them to
possession of the land I gave to their fathers.

4   This is the divine promise made to Israel and Juda: A cry of terror,
the Lord says, for all to hear! All is consternation, where all was peace.
6 Why, here is a riddle and a wonder; can motherhood fall to the lot of men
folk? Why is there none to be seen but goes by hand on loins, cheeks
7 blanched, like a woman in travail? Alas for pity, what a day is this, none
like it; what a time of distress for Jacob's race! Yet it shall leave them
8 unharmed. A promise they have from the Lord of hosts that he will
break the yoke they bear, when that day comes, and part their chains
9 asunder; no more shall they be at the mercy of alien masters, they shall
obey the Lord their God only, and that David-king of theirs whom he
will give them.

10   Have thou no fear, the Lord says, Jacob, that art my servant still; not
for Israel is danger brewing. From that far country of exile I mean to
restore thee, restore those children of thine; Jacob shall return, and live
11 at ease, every blessing shall enjoy, and enemies have none to fear; I am
at thy side, the Lord says, to protect thee. Of all the lands in which I have
dispersed thee I will take full toll, but not of thee; I would but chasten
thee with due measure kept, lest thou shouldst hold thyself altogether
12 acquitted. Poor Sion, thine is a wound past curing, a grievous hurt, the
13 Lord says; no man brings thee redress or remedy, salve to heal thee thou
14 hast none; thy old lovers think of thee no more, woo thee no more. A
shrewd blow I struck thee, unsparing of correction; so many thy mis-
15 doings, thy guilt so inveterate. Misdoings a many, and guilt inveterate,
these be the cause of thy hurt, and I the doer of it; and wouldst thou cry
16 out upon a grief there is no remedying? Only be sure of this, the enemies
that prey on thee shall themselves fall a prey to exile; spoiled thy spoilers
17 shall be, and all that plunder thee I will give up to plunder. Then I will
heal that scar of thine, the Lord says, cure thee of thy wounds; too soon
they called thee a neglected bride, Sion the unwooed!

18   Nay, says the Lord, I mean to bring tent-dwelling Jacob home, have
pity on those ruined walls, build the city anew on its height, set up the
19 temple and its ordinances anew; here songs of praise shall echo once
again, and cries of mirth. They shall increase, that hitherto had dwindled,
20 be exalted, that once were brought low. Then, as in days of old, the full

muster of the tribes shall have its place in my regard; who wrongs them
21 shall be called to account for it. A prince of their own race they shall
have, a home-born ruler, singled out by my own call to serve me; that
22 office, the Lord says, none may take on himself unbidden. You shall be
my own people, and I your own God.
23   Like a whirlwind it will suddenly appear, the Lord's vengeance; will
24 break in storm, and light upon rebel heads. Nor shall the divine anger be
appeased till the blow has been struck and the decree executed; what his
design was, will be known all too well, all too late.[1]

CHAPTER THIRTY-ONE

NO clan in Israel, the Lord says, but shall own me as its God when
2   that day comes, and all of them shall be my people. Out there in
the solitudes they have won pardon, those exiles the sword left untouched;
3 Israel shall find a home, the Lord says, the Lord, making himself known
from far away.[2] With unchanging love I love thee, and now in mercy I
4 have drawn thee to myself. Israel, poor homeless maid, I will build thy
fortunes anew; built anew they shall be, and thou shalt go forth once
5 more, thy tambour hung about thee, among the choir of dancers. Once
more thou shalt plant vineyards over the hill country of Samaria; planted
they shall be, and the men who planted them await the appointed time
6 before they gather the vintage.[3] Watchmen there shall be, when that day
comes, in the hill country of Ephraim that will cry aloud, Up, to Sion go
7 we, and there worship the Lord our God! Rejoice, the Lord says, at
Jacob's triumph, the proudest of nations greet with a glad cry; [4] loud echo
your songs of praise, Deliverance, Lord, for thy people, for the remnant
8 of Israel! From the north country, from the very ends of earth, I mean to
gather them and bring them home; blind men and lame, pregnant women
and women brought to bed, so great the muster at their home-coming.
9 Weeping they shall come, and I, moved to pity, will bring them to their
journey's end; from mountain stream to mountain stream they shall
travel, by a straight road where there is no stumbling; I, Israel, thy father
again, and thou, Ephraim, my first-born son.

---

[1] *vv.* 23, 24. These verses are repeated from 23.19, 20, and some think they
are wrongly inserted here, where the prophet is more concerned to reassure
his fellow-countrymen than to threaten them.
[2] 'Making himself known': according to the Latin, 'to me,' which follows
the Hebrew text; but the Septuagint Greek has 'to it,' *i.e.,* Israel.
[3] See Lev. 19.23–25.
[4] Literally, 'neigh against the head of the nations,' a phrase which cannot
be interpreted with certainty.

10   Listen, Gentiles, to the Lord's promise; his word must go out to the
islands that are far away; word that he who scattered Israel will gather
11   Israel in, will guard it faithfully as a shepherd guards his flock. The Lord
means to ransom Jacob, to grant deliverance from the tyrant's power.
12   The exiles will return, greeting mount Sion with cries of gladness; thronging in to take possession of the Lord's gifts, corn and oil and wine, increase of flock and herd. Revived their spirits shall be, like a garden when
13   the stream flows full; they shall hunger no more. Glad the maidens shall
dance, gladness there shall be for young and old alike; I will turn all their
14   sorrow into joy, comfort and cheer their sad hearts. Full-fed my priests
shall be with dainties; blessings my people shall have, the Lord says, till
they ask no more.

15   Now, the Lord says, a voice is heard in Rama, of lamentation and bitter
mourning; it is Rachel weeping for her children, and she will not be com-
16   forted, because none is left.[1] But thus he reassures thee: Sad voice,
lament, sad eyes, weep no more; I, the Lord, give thee promise of a re-
17   ward for thy working-days, a return from the enemy's country. A hope is
left for thee hereafter, the Lord says; to their own possessions thy sons
18   shall return. Doubt not I heard it, the cry of Ephraim forlorn: Lord, it
was thy task to chasten me, that must learn, like bullock untamed, to bear
the yoke; grant me return, and I will return to thee;[2] thou art the Lord
19   my God. Only when thou calledst me back to thyself did I repent; only
when my lesson was learnt did I cry out upon my shame.[3] How did I
blush with confusion, bearing the disgrace the sins of my youth had
20   earned! Why, what a favourite son is this Ephraim, what a spoilt child
of mine, that I should pronounce my doom on him, and care for him none
the less! In truth, my heart goes out to him; I will be merciful to him yet,
the Lord says.

21   Way-marks leave behind thee, sad trophies[4] be raising as thou goest, to
put thee in mind of the straight road thou hast trodden. Return thou
22   must, poor Israel, return thou must to these, thy own cities; fickle maid,
dally no longer. Here is a new order of things the Lord has established on
earth; weak woman is to be the protectress of man's strength.[5]

---

[1] *v.* 15. Cf. Mt. 2.18.

[2] 'Grant me return,' literally 'turn me'; 'I will return to thee,' literally, 'I
will turn'; and in the next verse, 'when thou calledst me back to thyself,' literally, 'at my turning.' The same verb is used in Hebrew, somewhat confus-
ingly, to express turning away and turning back, whether in a literal or in a
figurative sense.

[3] Literally, 'did I smite the thigh,' a Hebrew way of shewing humiliated regret.

[4] Literally, 'bitternesses,' the same word as in verse 15. But modern scholars
understand it here as meaning 'cairns,' and derive it from a different root.

[5] Literally, 'a female shall surround a male,' a phrase much discussed but
little elucidated by commentators.

23   A message from the Lord of hosts, the God of Israel: To town and
      countryside of Juda I will restore the exiled folk, and once again the
      greeting will be heard, A blessing on thee from the Lord, fair home of
24   true observance, holy mountain-side! Once again Juda and Juda's towns-
      folk shall dwell there; fields shall be tilled and flocks led out to pasture;
25   faint hearts shall be refreshed, and hunger's craving satisfied.
26   Ah, to wake upon such a sight! Then were sleep welcome.[1]
27   A time is coming, the Lord says, when I mean to enrich Israel's home,
28   Juda's home, with stock of men and of cattle both; jealous watch I will
      still keep over them, but not, as of old, to root up and to demolish, to
      scatter and lay waste and to do hurt; all shall be building, the Lord says,
29   all shall be planting now. When that time comes, no more shall be heard
      of the proverb, The fathers have eaten sour grapes, and the children's
30   teeth are being set on edge; tooth of eater shall ache now, and a man's
      own guilt shall be a man's own doom.[2]
31   A time is coming, the Lord says, when I mean to ratify a new covenant
32   with the people of Israel and with the people of Juda. It will not be like
      the covenant which I made with their fathers, on the day when I took
      them by the hand, to rescue them from Egypt; that they should break my
33   covenant, and I, their Lord, should abandon them. No, this is the cove-
      nant I will grant the people of Israel, the Lord says, when that time
      comes. I will implant my law in their innermost thoughts, engrave it in
34   their hearts; I will be their God, and they shall be my people. There will
      be no need for neighbour to teach neighbour, or brother to teach brother,
      the knowledge of the Lord; all will know me, from the highest to the low-
      est. I will pardon their wrong-doing; I will not remember their sins any
35   more.[3] A message from the Lord, from Javé, the God of hosts, the same
      who brightens day with the sun's rays, night with the ordered service
      of moon and star, who can stir up the sea and set its waves a-roaring;
36   All these laws of mine will fail me, he says, before the line of Israel fails
37   me; a people it must remain until the end of time. You have the Lord's
      word for it; When you can measure heaven above, he tells you, and
      search the foundations of earth below, then I will cast away the whole
      line of Israel, for all its ill deserving.
38   Behold, says the divine promise, a time is coming when the city shall
      be rebuilt in the Lord's honour, from Hanameel's Tower as far as the
39   Corner Gate; nay, in advance of that the limit of its range shall reach,
40   across Gareb hill, to take in Goatha, burial-ground and ash-pit and all
      the dead soil as far as Cedron brook, and eastward as far as the corner by

---

[1] What is the exact meaning of this phrase, or who is the speaker, cannot
be determined with certainty.
[2] Cf. Ez. 18.2.
[3] *vv.* 31–34. Cf. Heb. 8.8 sqq.

the Horsemen's Gate; all shall be consecrated to the Lord; tree shall not be uprooted there henceforward, nor house overthrown.

CHAPTER THIRTY-TWO

A MESSAGE came from the Lord to Jeremias during the tenth year of Sedecias' reign in Juda, the eighteenth of Nabuchodonosor's at
2 Babylon; the Babylonian army was besieging Jerusalem at the time, and Jeremias was a prisoner there, confined in the court that lay before the
3 royal palace. It was for his prophesying that king Sedecias had imprisoned him; what meant this threat from the Lord, of giving Jerusalem
4 over to capture by the king of Babylon? He had said, besides: King Sedecias of Juda shall not escape from the Chaldaeans; the king of Babylon shall have the mastery of him; they shall have speech together, meet
5 face to face.[1] To Babylon Sedecias shall go, and there remain till I have entered into a reckoning with him. All shall go amiss, if you join battle with the Chaldaeans.
6 And now Jeremias announced a new oracle the Lord had given him.
7 The Lord told me, he said, that my cousin Hanameel, son of Sellum, would come and ask me to buy in certain land of his at Anathoth, which
8 was my duty as his next of kin. And as the Lord foretold, so it fell out; Hanameel came to my prison doors, and said, Pray buy in that field of mine at Anathoth in Benjamin; thou art the rightful heir, and thy duty it is, as next of kin, to buy it from me. Then I knew that I had received
9 a divine warning, and buy it I did, this field at Anathoth, from Hanameel, that was son to my uncle Sellum. I paid him the price, that was but
10 seventeen pieces of silver; wrote and signed the deed, called in witnesses,
11 and weighed out the money on the scales. So here was the deed of possession sealed up, all its terms set down and attested, and characters
12 written without; all this I handed over to Baruch, son of Neri, son of Maasias, still in the presence of my cousin Hanameel, and the witnesses that had signed it, and the Jews who sat around me in the court where
13 I was confined. Before them all, I gave Baruch this charge: A message for thee from the Lord of hosts, the God of Israel: Take these two pieces of writing, the sealed deed within and the covering of it that is open to view, and keep them in some jar of clay, where they can remain long
15 without damage. This is what he would tell thee, he, the Lord of hosts, the God of Israel, that there shall yet be buying of house and field and vineyard, here in this land.
16 The deed once made over to Baruch, son of Neri, I prayed to the Lord
17 thus: Alas, alas, Lord God! Thou art the maker of heaven and earth, so

---

[1] See 34.3 below.

great is thy power, so wide thy reach; no task, for thee, is too difficult.
18 A thousandfold thou shewest thy mercy; yet, when thou dost punish,
into the son's lap the father's guilt overflows; how great, how strong is
19 the God of hosts! And Javé is his name. How sublime thy counsels, thy
thoughts how high above us! And still thou keepest watch over all man-
20 kind, ready to award each life what its own devices have earned. Such
deeds thou didst as are signs and portents to this day in the land of Egypt,
in Israel too and all the world over; didst win that renown which to this
21 day is thine.[1] Signs and portents there must be, and the exercise of thy
constraining power, and a great dread, before thou couldst rescue thy
22 people Israel from Egypt; then thou wouldst bestow upon them this land,
23 the home promised to their fathers, a land all milk and honey; they invaded it, they took possession of it. But to thy voice they would not listen,
thy law they would not follow; no duty thou hadst enjoined but lay neg-
24 lected, and all the calamities we see about us are the issue. Here are siege-
works raised to reduce the city; sword and famine and pestilence are
giving it over to the Chaldaeans for their prey; of all thou hast threatened
25 thou seest here the fulfilment. And now, Lord God, thou wouldst have
me buy land, and call in witnesses of payment made; now, when this city
lies at the mercy of the Chaldaeans!
26   Hereupon the word of the Lord came to Jeremias: Am I not the Lord,
the God of all that lives? How should any task be too difficult for me?
28   This is the Divine sentence;[2] I mean to hand over this city to capture
29 by the king of Babylon and his Chaldaeans; they shall take it by storm,
and set it alight, and burn all its houses to the ground; it was there, on the
roof-tops, they sacrificed to Baal, and made offering to alien gods in
30 despite of me. From their youth up, Israel and Juda have defied my will
unceasingly; even now, says the Lord, their ill doings are a provocation
31 to me. Anger and scorn this city of theirs has earned from me, nothing
else, from the day they built it to this day when I purpose that it shall
32 offend my sight no more; so long have Israel and Juda defied my vengeance with the wrong they did, king and prince, priest and prophet,
33 country-folk and citizens of Jerusalem; always the back turned, never
a glance my way, always the deaf ear, the warning unheeded, when I sent
34 early to their doors to bring them to a better mind! Have they not profaned that house which is the sanctuary of my name, by setting up their
35 idols in it? Have they not made hill-shrines for Baal in the valley of Ben-

---

[1] The beginning of this verse runs literally, 'Who hast set signs and portents in the land of Egypt to this day, and in Israel, and among mankind';
there is probably some slight corruption in the text.

[2] *vv.* 28–35. It may be doubted whether these verses appear here in their
true context; if we suppose that they belong elsewhere, verse 36 follows much
more naturally.

Ennom, and there initiated son and daughter with Moloch-rites that were never of my bidding? No thought was it of mine that they should do this foul deed, which has brought guilt on Juda.

36   What, then, of this city, doomed in your eyes to fall into the power of Babylon's king, through sword and famine and pestilence? This is the
37 message the Lord God of Israel sends to it: I mean to gather its people again, scattered over so many lands by the vengeance my fierce anger brought; restore them to this place, and bid them dwell there contentedly.
38 They shall be my people, I their God; one will they shall have, and journey by one way, living evermore in the fear of me, winning for them-
40 selves and for their sons a blessing. An eternal covenant I will make with them, nor ever cease to speed them; inspire their hearts with the fear of
41 me, that never swerves aside. My welcome task it shall be to prosper them, and root their stock firmly in this land of theirs; this shall be all my
42 love and liking. Threat of mine and promise of mine, the Lord says,
43 shall alike be fulfilled. This country of yours a desert, man nor beast to dwell in it, given up to the power of Babylon? So your fears tell you; but
44 there shall be buying of lands in it yet, the price paid, the deed executed, the bond sealed, witnesses called in, all over Benjamin and round about Jerusalem, all through the cities of Juda, by hill and plain and the uplands of the south; I mean to bring the exiles home again, says the Lord.

CHAPTER THIRTY-THREE

JEREMIAS was still confined to his prison in the court when the word
2 of the Lord came to him a second time. It ran: Thus says the Lord, that all this will do, all this will devise and determine, he whose name is
3 Javé: Cry out to me still, and thou shalt find audience; great mysteries
4 that lie beyond thy ken I will make known to thee. Ruined houses of Jerusalem, ruined palace of the kings of Juda, what has the Lord to tell thee about these? . . .
5   . . . to siege and sword. Come they to fight against the Chaldaeans, it is but to strew those earthworks with their own dead bodies; in anger and scorn I will smite them down, turning my back on the city they have stained with such guilt . . .[1]
6   Closed and cured those wounds shall be; I myself will heal them, grant
7 them peace and safety to their heart's content. The fortunes of Juda and

---

[1] *vv.* 4, 5. Although the Latin version conceals it, there is considerable confusion in the text here, which is probably due either to corruption or to omission.

Jerusalem I will reverse, and they shall be established as firmly as ever;
8 all the guilt that offends me purged away, all the wrong and despite they
9 did me forgiven.   My pride and prize, my renown and triumph, to be
their benefactor, so that all the world shall hear of it; everywhere the tale
of my bounty and my blessing shall strike awe and dread into men's
10 hearts.   Where all seems to your eyes but a desert, man nor beast left in
the townships of Juda and in Jerusalem, empty street, empty house,
11 empty byre,   there, says the Lord, you shall hear cries of joy and mirth,
voice of bridegroom and voice of bride. There you shall hear men singing,
Give thanks to the Lord, the Lord is gracious, his mercy endures for ever,
as they bring to his temple the offerings they have vowed. Your country's
doom shall be reversed, says the Divine promise, and all shall be as of old.
12 Juda and all its townships a desert, no living thing to dwell there?   Nay,
says the Lord of hosts, once again it shall be the abode of shepherds, a
13 resting-place for their flocks.   By hill and plain and the uplands of the
south, all over Benjamin and round about Jerusalem, all through the
cities of Juda, there shall be flocks passing to and fro, and their masters
a-counting them, the Lord says.
14   Behold, he says, a time is coming when I will make good my promise
15 to Israel and Juda;   the day will dawn, the time be ripe at last for that
faithful scion to bud from David's stock; the land shall have a king to
16 reign over it, giving just sentence and due award.   When that time comes,
Juda shall find deliverance, none shall disturb Jerusalem's rest; and the
17 name given to this king shall be, The Lord vindicates us.[1]   Never a man
18 wanting of David's line, the Lord says, to sit on Israel's throne;   never
a lack of priest and Levite to wait upon me, bring me burnt-sacrifice and
burn the bloodless offering and slaughter victims, day after day.
19   And the word of the Lord came to Jeremias,   giving him this message:
Please you annul my ordinance of day and night, let there be day-time
21 and night-time no more!   Only then will I annul the privilege granted to
my servant David, and there shall be heirs of his throne no more, Levites
22 and priests to wait on me no more.   My servant David, the Levites that
wait on me, these shall have a posterity countless as the stars of heaven,
23 measureless as the sea-sand.   This message, too, Jeremias had from the
24 Lord: Mark well how they declare, the folk among whom thou dwellest,[2]

---

[1] *vv.* 15, 16. Cf. 23.5, 6 above. In the present passage, the Hebrew text represents the name 'The Lord vindicates us' as given, not to the king, but to the
city of Jerusalem. The disparity is difficult to explain, and probably the manuscripts are at fault. The whole paragraph, verses 14–18, is lacking in the Septuagint Greek.
[2] Literally, 'this people.' If the text is sound, the reference cannot (in the
nature of the case) be to the Jews, but either to some foreign nation or, less
probably, to Israel as distinct from Juda.

that there are two families [1] the Lord has chosen, and both he has cast off;
25 so that they despise my own people, and no longer count it a nation. But
this is the divine answer: Laws if I have made none for day and night,
26 for heaven and earth no ordinances prescribed, then let it be thought
that I mean to cast Israel away, or depose the line of David from its head-
ship over all who spring from Abraham, Isaac, and Jacob. Trust me,
their doom shall be reversed, their lot shall be pitied.

CHAPTER THIRTY-FOUR

THE word of the Lord came to Jeremias at the time when king Nabuchodonosor of Babylon, at the head of his own army, with vassal kingdoms and peoples to aid him, levied war on Jerusalem and its daughter
2 cities. This was the message sent by the Lord God of Israel: Go and
warn Sedecias, king of Juda, in my name that I mean to hand over this
3 city to the Babylonian king, who will burn it to the ground. And add this
besides: Thou thyself wilt not escape from him; they will catch thee, sure
enough, and hand thee over to him; thou and the king of Babylon shall
have speech together, meet face to face, and to Babylon thou shalt go.
4 Wouldst thou but listen, King Sedecias of Juda, to the Lord's bidding! [2]
5 Die by the sword, he tells thee, thou should not; peaceful thy death
should be, and they should make such burning for thee as they made for
thy fathers that reigned before thee, raise such cries of lamentation, Alas,
6 what a king was this! This is my promise to thee, the Lord says. All
this king Sedecias of Juda must hear from the prophet Jeremias, there in
7 Jerusalem; and still the Babylonian army pressed hard on the city, and
on those other cities of Juda that were left, Lachis and Azecha; the rest of
the fortified cities had already been taken.
8   Here is another message the Lord entrusted to Jeremias, and this was
the occasion of it. King Sedecias had bound the citizens of Jerusalem by
9 a covenant; all alike were to set free their slaves and handmaids that were
of Hebrew blood; would they play the master to their own Jewish kins-
10 folk? On hearing the proclamation, nobles and common people alike had
agreed to release slave and handmaid, and exempt them from all service

---

[1] Probably the tribes of Juda and Benjamin; they may, however, be Israel
and Juda, or Levi and David (mentioned in the foregoing verses), or Jacob
and David (see verse 26 below).

[2] This might be translated, 'Listen to a message from the Lord, king Sedecias
of Juda!' But probably the promise made in the rest of the verse is meant to
be conditional upon Sedecias' obeying the Lord (and ceasing to resist the
invader).

11 henceforward; and this they did obediently enough; but afterwards they
   changed their minds, haled them off, men and women, and reduced them
12 to slavery once again. Then it was word came from the Lord to Jeremias,
13 and thus the divine message ran: Word from the Lord God of Israel!
   I made a covenant with your fathers, when I rescued them from their
14 place of bondage in Egypt. Seven years up, every slave sold in bondage
   to his fellow Hebrew must go free; six years of service, and then release.
15 Your fathers would not listen, turned a deaf ear to me; but you, to-day,
   have thought better of it, and done my will, proclaiming liberty to your
   fellow-countrymen; you have sworn it in my presence, in the house that
16 is the shrine of my name. And then you went back, and dragged my
   name in the dust! You would claim them afresh, men and women servants
   you had set free, now their own masters; they must be your servants and
   handmaids still.
17   This sentence, then, the Lord pronounces: You have not obeyed me,
   by granting freedom to your own brethren and neighbours, and here is
   the freedom I mean to grant you in return; freedom of the sword, freedom
   of the famine, freedom of the pestilence! A bane I will make you to all the
18 kingdoms of earth. I will have no more of them, the men who transgress
   my covenant, have no respect for the agreement they made in my own
   presence, the calf they cut in two and walked between the slices of it,
19 nobles of Juda and Jerusalem, chamberlains and priests, and all the com-
20 mon folk that passed between share and share. I mean to give them up
   into the hands of enemies that are sworn upon their lives; bird in air
21 and beast on earth shall prey upon that carrion of theirs. Sedecias, king
   of Juda, and his nobles, shall fall into the hands of pitiless enemies, the
22 armies of Babylon, that now give you a respite. These, at my command,
   shall march on this city again, lay siege to it, and capture it, and burn it
   to the ground; and I will make the townships of Juda into a desert, never
   a soul to dwell there.

CHAPTER THIRTY-FIVE

IN the reign of Josias' son Joachim, word came to Jeremias from the
2 Lord, Go, make thyself acquainted with the men of Rechab's clan; I
   would have thee entertain them in one of the treasury rooms at the
3 temple, and there set wine before them. So Jezonias, son of Jeremias, son
   of Habsanias was my guest, with his brethren and his sons and the whole
4 Rechabite clan; into the temple I brought them, to the apartment of
   Hanan's sons, that come down from God's servant Jegedelias. It was next
5 to the apartment of the door-keeper, Maasias the son of Sellum. Here I

set a bowl and goblet of wine before the men of Rechab's clan, and bade
6 them drink, but drink wine they would not. Our father Jonadab, said
they, the son of Rechab gave us a rule to live by. Wine neither we should
7 drink, nor any son of ours in perpetuity; no house build, no crops sow,
no vineyard plant or possess; in tents we were to live all our days, and
8 long those days should last in this land that was none of ours. As our
father Jonadab son of Rechab bade us live, so live we, so our wives and
9 sons and daughters live, drinking no wine at any time. Houses we build
10 none to dwell in, vineyards and fields and crops have none; tent-dwellers
11 we remain, true to every command of our father Jonadab; it was only
when king Nabuchodonosor of Babylon marched against us that we were
fain to take shelter in Jerusalem from threats of Chaldaean and Syrian;
that is why we make our abode in Jerusalem.
12 And now the Lord's word came to Jeremias: A message from the
Lord of hosts, the God of Israel! Go and tell all the men of Juda, all the
citizens of Jerusalem. Great marvel it is, the Lord says, you are so unruly
14 still, and will not heed my bidding. Here is Jonadab son of Rechab will
have his sons drink no wine, and his word holds; wine they drink none to
this day, for love of their father's rule; and I, that send word early to your
15 doors, can win no obedience. Early I sent them to your doors, the prophets that were servants of mine, bidding you come back from your straying, and shape your thoughts anew; have recourse no longer to the worship of alien gods, if you would dwell securely in this land, my gift to you
16 and to your fathers; but you gave me neither heed nor hearing. So loyal
the Rechabites to the commands of their father Jonadab, and my people
17 so disobedient! I mean, then, says the Lord of hosts, the God of Israel,
to punish the citizens of Jerusalem for warnings unheeded, for calls re-
18 fused, with all the punishments I have threatened. To the clan of Rechab
Jeremias gave this message from the Lord of hosts, the God of Israel:
For your obedience to your father Jonadab, for precept remembered and
19 for duty done, he, the Lord of hosts, the God of Israel, promises that
this line of Rechab and Jonadab, long as time lasts, shall never want a
posterity to do him service.

CHAPTER THIRTY-SIX

IN the fourth year of Josias' son Joachim, the Lord gave Jeremias this
2 commandment: Get thyself a scroll, and write down on it all the warnings I have uttered against Israel and Juda, and against the other nations
3 of the world, ever since I first spoke to thee under king Josias. Maybe,
when the men of Juda hear of all the mischief I mean to do them, they

will leave off their straying in false paths, and so I will overlook the guilt
of their wrong-doing.

4 So Jeremias sent for Baruch the son of Nerias; the Lord's utterances,
5 every one, Jeremias rehearsed and Baruch wrote down on the scroll. And
now Jeremias had an errand for him; I must keep my house, said he, go
6 into the Lord's temple I may not.[1] Do thou, on a fasting day, go there
instead, and read out some of the divine utterances I have dictated to
thee, in the temple itself, for all the citizens to hear, and all the men of
7 Juda besides, that have come in from their several townships. Maybe
their intercession will find its way into the Lord's presence; maybe they
will leave off their straying in false paths; here are grievous threats from
8 the Lord of angry vengeance against his people. So it was Baruch son of
Nerias, but in fulfilment of Jeremias' command, that took the scroll and
9 read out, there in the Lord's house, the Lord's message. It was the ninth
month, in the fifth year of Josias' son Joachim, when they proclaimed a
fast, that was to be kept in the Lord's presence by all the citizens and all
10 who had come in from the other towns of Juda. And there in the Lord's
house, from the apartment of Gamarias, whose father, Saphan, had once
been secretary, in the upper court, close by the entry of the new temple
11 gate, Baruch read out Jeremias' book of warning. No line he read of the
divine utterance but had an eager listener in Gamarias' son Michaeas,
12 who thereupon went down to the secretary's room, where he found all the
notables assembled. There was the secretary, Elisama; there were Dalaias
son of Semeias, and Elnathan son of Achobor, and Gamarias son of
Saphan, and Sedecias son of Hananias, and all the notables in general.
13 To these Michaeas repeated all he had heard Baruch read out from the
14 scroll in public; and Judi, son of Nathanias, son of Selemias, son of
Cushi, was sent on an errand to Baruch in the name of all present. Come
thither he must, and bring the scroll he had read thus publicly with him.
So it was Baruch, son of Nerias, that came before them, and the scroll
15 with him; they bade him be seated, and read it aloud to them, so read it
16 he did. When all the reading was over, they looked each at other in
amazement, and told Baruch all this must be brought to the king's ears.
17 Then they asked, How comes it that these are the words of Jeremias, and
18 yet of thy writing? Why, said he, Jeremias gave them out, as if he were
reading them aloud, and I sat by with paper and ink to write them down.
19 Go into hiding, they told him, thou and Jeremias with thee, and be sure
none knows where to find you.
20 Then they made their way into the palace court to find the king, leaving
the book there in the secretary's room. When they had brought their
21 news to his hearing, the king would have Judi fetch the book itself from

---

[1] Cf. Neh. 6.10.

Elisama's room; which he did, and read it out for the king to hear, and all
22 the courtiers that stood about him. Since it was the ninth month, Joachim
23 was in his winter parlour, and a brazier of coals in front of him; and when
Judi had read but three columns or four, he took his pen-knife and began
cutting the scroll into pieces, which he threw on to the brazier until the
24 whole book had perished in the flames. King and courtiers listened to all
25 these warnings, yet feared they never, nor rent their clothes; and although
Elnathan, Dalaias and Gamarias would have prevented Joachim from
26 burning the scroll, he would not listen to them. Jeremiel son of
Amelech,[1] Saraias son of Ezriel, and Selemias son of Abdeel were bidden
to attach the persons of the scribe Baruch and the prophet Jeremias; but
the Lord kept them in safe hiding.
27 And this was the Lord's word to the prophet Jeremias, when the king
burnt the scroll, and with it all the utterances he had dictated to Baruch:
28 Get thee another scroll, and write down on it whatever was contained in
29 the one king Joachim burnt. And to king Joachim give this message from
the Lord: Burn book and chide prophet, if thou wilt, for warning thee
that the king of Babylon will come back with all speed, and lay this coun-
30 try waste, leaving neither man nor beast to dwell in it. But this is the
Lord's doom against king Joachim of Juda: No son of his shall follow
him on the throne of David; his body shall be cast away in the open, to
31 bear the day's heat and the night frost. With guilt of his, with guilt of
household and court of his, I will reckon in full; all my unheeded threats
against Jerusalem and Juda shall be made good.
32 So Jeremias must get Baruch another scroll to write on, and all the contents of the book Joachim burnt must be dictated anew; much more was
added besides to enlarge it.

CHAPTER THIRTY-SEVEN

IN place of Jechonias, that was son to Joachim, Nabuchodonosor king
of Babylon would have Sedecias, another of Josias' sons, mount the
2 throne of Juda; but no heed would the new king give, nor his courtiers,
nor his subjects, to the warnings uttered in the Lord's name by the pro-
3 phet Jeremias. To him the king sent envoys, Juchal the son of Selemias
and the priest Sophonias, son of Maasias, bidding him pray to the Lord
4 their God for the common welfare. Jeremias was still free to come and
go as he pleased among his fellow-citizens; they had not yet imprisoned
him.

---

[1] 'The son of Amelech'; the Hebrew text is probably better understood as
meaning 'the king's son,' that is, a prince of the royal blood.

At this time, Pharao's army was on the march, advancing from the Egyptian frontier; and the Chaldaeans, this news reaching them, had
5 raised the siege of Jerusalem. So the Lord's word came to the prophet
6 Jeremias: Take back this message from the Lord God of Israel to the king who sent you to consult me. Back home to Egypt it shall march, the
7 army of Pharao that has come out in your support; whereupon the Chaldaeans will return to the attack, will capture this city and burn it to the
8 ground. Never cheat yourselves with the hope that the enemy will march
9 away and leave you alone; march away they will not, the Lord says. Low
· though you should lay every Chaldaean that takes the field against you, save for some few wounded, those wounded men shall rise up from their tents, and burn this city to the ground notwithstanding.
10 And now, while Pharao still threatened, and the Chaldaeans had raised
11 the siege, Jeremias took occasion to leave Jerusalem and make his way to Benjamin, where he must divide up some property in the presence of
12 his fellow-citizens. When he reached the Benjamin gate, the officer whose turn it was to mount guard there, Jerias, the son of Selemias, the son of Hananias, put the prophet under arrest, under the charge of deserting to
13 the Chaldaeans. In vain did Jeremias protest, What, I desert to the Chaldaeans? There is no truth in it! Jerias led him away into the presence
14 of the nobles; and these, in a rage, first had him beaten, then confined him in the house of the secretary, Jonathan, who had charge of the pris-
15 oners at this time. So came Jeremias to a dungeon cell, and long remained there.
16 It was king Sedecias who released him, sending for him and questioning him privately in the palace. Has the Lord any message for me? he asked. Yes, said Jeremias; that thou shalt be at the mercy of Nabuchodo-
17 nosor. Then he asked the king, What wrong have I done to thee, to thy
18 courtiers or thy subjects, that thou hast thrown me into prison? Tell me, how have they sped, those prophets of yours who foretold that the king of Babylon should never reach you, never invade this land of yours?
19 Listen to me, my lord king, I entreat thee, and look favourably on my suit. Do not send me back to the house of yonder secretary Jonathan, for
20 there I needs must die! So king Sedecias had him confined in the court
· without, and given a loaf of bread each day, with seasoning added,[1] as long as bread there should be in the city. And there Jeremias was left, among the prisoners in the courtyard.

---

[1] 'With seasoning added'; according to the Hebrew text, 'from the Street of the Bakers.'

CHAPTER THIRTY-EIGHT

STILL Jeremias would speak out before all the people; and among those who listened to him were Saphatias son of Mathan, Gedelias son of Phassur, Juchal son of Selemias, and Phassur son of Melchias.
2 This message they heard him proclaim from the Lord: To remain in this city means death by sword, famine and pestilence; go over to the Chal-
3 daeans, you shall have your lives for guerdon, and be spared. And this: Past doubt, the city will fall into the hands of the king of Babylon, by
4 right of capture. And they urged the king, these notables, to make an end of him; He goes about, said they, to weaken the resolve of the garrison, and of the people at large, by talking in this fashion; there is malice
5 here, not good will. He is at your disposal, king Sedecias answered; king
6 is none may withstand you. So they had their way with Jeremias; he should be left helpless in the cistern of Melchias the son of Amelech,[1] there in the court where the prisoners were kept. Into the cistern they lowered him with ropes; there was no water in it now, only mire, and into the mire he sank.

7 But there was an Ethiopian chamberlain at the court, named Abdemelech, that heard how Jeremias had been let down into the cistern; and as
8 the king was sitting at the Benjamin Gate, this Abdemelech came out
9 from the palace and remonstrated with him. My lord king, he said, here is foul wrong done to the prophet Jeremias; they have let him down into a cistern, where he will die of hunger, such lack of bread there is in the
10 city. Why then, said the king to Abdemelech the Ethiopian, take thirty [2] men with thee, and rescue Jeremias from the cistern while there is yet
11 life in him. So Abdemelech took the men with him, made his way into the palace, beneath the store-chamber, took old rags and clouts that lay mouldering there, and let them down by ropes to Jeremias in the cistern.
12 Here be torn things and mouldering, the Ethiopian said to Jeremias, but thou mayst put these under thy arm-pits, and the ropes under these
13 again. Jeremias obeyed, and they pulled them up by the ropes till he was clear of the cistern; but the courtyard was his prison still.
14 Then king Sedecias would have the prophet come to him by the third door of the palace, the one that leads to the temple. I have a question to
15 ask thee, he said to Jeremias; hide nothing from me. Why, Jeremias answered, if I tell thee what I know, thou wilt but kill me, and if I give
16 thee advice, thou wilt not heed it. But king Sedecias took a secret oath, As the Lord is a living God, the Lord who gave us this breath we breathe,

---

[1] See note on 36.26.
[2] Some suspect the word 'thirty' of being a copyist's mistake for 'three.'

17 slay thee I will not, nor hand thee over to thy mortal enemies. Thereupon Jeremias told him a message from the Lord, the God of hosts: Go out and give thyself up to Nabuchodonosor's chieftains, and thy life shall be safe, nor shall there be any burning of the city; thou and thine shall be spared.
18 If thou dost not give thyself up to them, then the Chaldaeans shall gain mastery of the city and burn it to the ground, and for thyself there is no
19 escaping them. Yet my heart misgives me, Sedecias told him, over the Jews that have already made their submission; what if I should be handed
20 over to these, and they wreak their spite on me? That shall not be, Jeremias answered. Give heed, only give heed, to this message from the Lord
21 I bear thee; so thou shalt speed well, and life be granted thee. Refuse to
22 yield, and here is the doom he has made known to me. Never a woman that is left in the palace of the kings of Juda but shall be spoil for the chieftains of the king of Babylon! And as they are led away, this shall be their lament: False friend fooled thee, and had the better of thee; feet fast
23 in the treacherous morass has left thee! Wife of thine and son of thine led away into the enemy's camp, and thou thyself powerless to escape; thyself the king of Babylon shall take prisoner, and burn thy city to the ground.
24   On peril of thy life, king Sedecias warned him, let none hear what has
25 passed between us. If it reach the ears of the nobles that we have had speech together, and they bid thee repeat what thou saidst, or what said the king, hiding nothing as thou holdest thy life dear, then be this thy
26 answer, Why, I pleaded my suit with the king's grace that he would not
27 have me sent back to Jonathan's house, to die there.[1] Come and ask him they did, and he answered as the king bade him; so with that they let him
28 be; nothing had been overheard. This imprisonment of Jeremias in the courtyard lasted until the taking of Jerusalem; for, sure enough, Jerusalem was taken.

CHAPTER THIRTY-NINE

SEDECIAS had been reigning for eight years and ten months in Juda when Nabuchodonosor king of Babylon led his armies to the siege of
2 Jerusalem; in the eleventh year, on the fifth day of the fourth month,
3 the gates were thrown open to him. In they marched, Neregel, Sereser, Semegarnabu, Sarsachim, Rabsares, (Neregel, Sereser), and Rebmag,[2]

---

[1] Some authors hold that Jeremias had in fact repeated, on this occasion, the appeal made in 37.19 above; otherwise he would not have been induced to adopt the king's expedient.

[2] Some of these names appear to have been repeated by a copyist's error. Rabsares and Rebmag are probably titles, not names.

and all the king of Babylon's other chieftains, and occupied the central
4 gate. Sedecias king of Juda and all his warriors fled at their approach, leaving the city at dead of night by way of the royal garden and the gate between the two walls; it was the desert road they took when they left it.
5 The Chaldaean army went in pursuit, and overtook Sedecias in the open plain of Jericho; captured him, and brought him before Nabuchodonosor at Reblatha, in the Emath country; and there sentence was pronounced
6 on him. Slain by the king of Babylon were all his sons, there in their father's sight; slain by the king of Babylon were all the nobles of Juda;
7 and as for Sedecias himself, his eyes were put out, and he was carried off,
8 loaded with chains, to Babylon. King's palace and poor man's house the Chaldaeans burnt to the ground, and threw down the walls of Jerusalem
9 in ruins. All the rest who survived, defenders and deserters alike, were carried off by Nabuzardan, the captain of the royal bodyguard, to Baby-
10 lon; he left none except the poorest of the inhabitants, landless men, in Juda, who found themselves enriched, that day, with vineyards and cisterns of their own.
11   This Nabuzardan, captain of the royal bodyguard, had orders from
12 king Nabuchodonosor about Jeremias; Take him under thy loving
13 charge, said he, and let him have what cheer he will. So here were Nabuzardan, captain of the royal bodyguard, and Nabusezban, and Rabsares, and Neregel, and Sereser, and Rebmag, and all the king of Babylon's
14 great chieftains, sending out to free Jeremias from his prison in the courtyard. And they entrusted him to the care of Godolias, son of Ahicam; with him Jeremias should dwell, and make his home among his own people.
15   While he was still in the courtyard prison, Jeremias had been entrusted
16 with a message from the Lord for the Ethiopian, Abdemelech: All my doom against this city, says the Lord of hosts, the God of Israel, I mean
17 to fulfil; ban it is and not blessing, and thou shalt live to see it; but to thee I will grant safety, the Lord says. Never shall dreaded foe have the
18 mastery, when I am there to deliver thee; thou art marked out for safety, that didst put thy confidence in me, the Lord says.

CHAPTER FORTY

TO Jeremias the word of the Lord still came, after the captain of the bodyguard, Nabuzardan, had set him at liberty. This happened at Rama, where he was singled out, still in chains, among the prisoners from
2 Jerusalem and Juda who were on their way to Babylon. As he took him apart from the rest, the captain of the bodyguard said to him, With calam-

3 ity the Lord thy God threatened this land of thine, and calamity he has brought upon it; his threat is fulfilled. What guilt was this, to refuse the
4 Lord obedience! And here is the issue. From thy hands I have struck the chains, as thou seest; bear me company, if thou wilt, to Babylon, and I will take good care of thee; if thou wilt not go my way, then abide where thou art. The whole land is at thy disposal, and thou art free to take thy
5 own path; none may constrain thee to go with me. Here is Godolias, son of Ahicam, son of Saphan, that is entrusted by the king of Babylon with the charge of all Juda; dwell with him if thou wilt, here among thy own people, or where thou hast a mind betake thee. And with that, the captain of the bodyguard furnished him with provisions, and made him a present
6 besides, and so took leave of him. It was to Godolias son of Ahicam, at Maspath, that Jeremias repaired, and dwelt with him among the remnant of the land's inhabitants.

7 　　Men, women, and children, to Godolias son of Ahicam the king of Babylon entrusted them, all these landless folk who had not been carried off into exile. And when the news of this appointment reached the army
8 chieftains, scattered here and there with their men, they rallied to Godolias at Masphath. Here were Ismahel, son of Nathanias, Johanan and Jonathan, sons of Caree, Sareas, son of Thanehumeth, the sons of Ophi from Netophathi, and Jezonias, son of Maachathi, all with men at their backs.
9 To these, chiefs and men alike, Godolias son of Ahicam son of Saphan took an oath. They need have no fear of living under Chaldaean rule; let them remain in the country as the king of Babylon's vassals, and all
10 should go well with them. I am living here in Masphath, said he, to take the orders sent me from Chaldaea; it is for you to gather in vintage and harvest and olive-yield, each of you abiding in the city he now occupies.
11 There were other Jews living in Moab, Ammon, Edom, and the countries round about; these, when they heard that the king of Babylon had left a remnant in Juda, and put Godolias, son of Ahicam, son of Saphan,
12 in charge of them, came back from the countries where they had taken refuge into Judaea, came to Godolias at Masphath; and abundant was the store they brought in, of grapes and grain both.

13 　　And now, at Masphath, Godolias was visited by Johanan son of Caree,
14 and the other chieftains from the countryside, with this warning: We have information that Ismahel, son of Nathanias, was sent here by Baalis, king of Ammon, to take thy life. But Godolias would not believe it.
15 When Johanan was at Masphath he took Godolias aside; Let me go and make away with Ismahel secretly, he urged; take he thy life, all the Jews that have rallied about thee will be scattered again, and Juda have a rem-
16 nant no more. But Godolias would have none of it; Nay, said he to Johanan, leave off thy purpose; it is but a false report thou tellest me concerning Ismahel.

CHAPTER FORTY-ONE

THE seventh month had come; and now Ismahel, son of Nathanias, son of Elisama, one of the royal princes and the king's vassals,[1] came with ten followers to Masphath, where Godolias was, and at Masphath 2 they sat at table together. There and then, at the sword's point, Ismahel and his ten men put Godolias to death. So perished Godolias, son of Ahicam, son of Saphan, that held the king of Babylon's warrant to rule 3 the country. Such Jews as were with Godolias at Masphath, such Chal-4 daean soldiers as he found there, Ismahel despatched at the same time. And 5 the day after Godolias' murder, before the news of it was out, came eighty pilgrims from Sichem, Silo, and Samaria, beards shaven, garments rent, in mourning all of them, with bloodless offerings and incense for 6 the Lord's temple. Out came Ismahel son of Nathanias from Masphath to meet them, and wept ever as he went; Welcome, said he, from Godolias 7 son of Ahicam! And when they had reached the middle of the town, just 8 by the cistern,[2] they were slain by Ismahel and his men; all except ten of them, who pleaded for their lives and told Ismahel they had a hoard of wheat, barley, oil and honey hidden away under their lands; these were 9 spared the fate of the rest. When he slew the companions of Godolias, Ismahel had thrown their bodies into the cistern; it was one which king Asa had made to defend the place against Baasa, king of Israel; now, Ismahel's massacre filled it to the brim.

10   Thus there was no longer a remnant at Masphath; the king's daughters, and all the other folk left there by Nabuzardan under the care of Godolias, Ismahel took off with him as his captives, and so would have marched 11 away into the Ammonite country. But Johanan, son of Caree, and the other army chieftains that were on his side, no sooner heard the ill news 12 of what Ismahel had done than they mustered all their men to give him 13 battle, and caught up with him at the pool of Gabaon. A welcome sight it was to Ismahel's company, when they saw Johanan, son of Caree, and 14 the other chieftains approaching; back went all the prisoners to Mas-15 phath, and threw in their lot with Johanan instead; Ismahel fled at the sight of him, and reached the Ammonite country with only eight men at his back.

16   Johanan and his fellow chieftains would not leave at Masphath this remnant they had rescued from Ismahel after the murder of Godolias, all

---

[1] This reads in the original, presumably by a copyist's error, as if it meant that Ismahel was accompanied by some of the king's vassals.

[2] Literally, 'into the middle of the cistern,' a phrase which can hardly have been intended.

the fighting men, the women and children, the eunuchs, who had re-
17 turned with them from Gabaon. They went off and made their home
for a time at Chamaam, near Bethlehem, thinking to take refuge in Egypt
18 from the vengeance of the Chaldaeans. From these they had much to fear,
now that Ismahel son of Nathanias had murdered Godolias son of
Ahicam, the king of Babylon's own representative in Juda.

CHAPTER FORTY-TWO

A ND now all the army chieftains, Johanan son of Caree and Jezonias
2 son of Osaias and their followers, high and low, came to consult
Jeremias. Look kindly, they said, on our request; we would have thee
intercede with the Lord thy God for this poor remnant, left so few in
3 number, as thou seest. Whither go we? What shift make we? Please it
4 the Lord thy God to make all this known to us. And the prophet Jeremias said, Your request shall be granted. Pray I will, as you bid me pray,
to the Lord your God, and his answer you shall hear in full, no word kept
5 hidden from you. And this promise they made on their part: The Lord
himself bear witness against us, unerring and unfailing, if we are not true
6 to every word of that message the Lord sends us through thy means. Be
it for weal or woe, it is the voice of the Lord our God; to him lies thy
errand, and him we will obey; heed we the commands of the Lord our
God, nothing can go amiss.
7   Ten days passed, and then the Lord's word came to Jeremias; Johanan
son of Caree he summoned to him, and all the army chieftains, and their
9 followers, high and low; and thus spoke to them: A message to you from
the Lord, the God of Israel! To him I went on your errand, and laid your
10 prayers before him. Wait on quietly, he says, in this land of yours, and
all shall be building now, not destroying, all shall be planting now, not
11 uprooting; amends enough is the calamity I have brought on you. What,
does the king of Babylon daunt you with his terrors? Of him have no fear;
danger from him is none, the Lord says, when I am at your side to pro-
12 tect you, and deliver you from his power. I will take pity on you now;
only pity shall you find, and on your native soil an abiding home.
13   But if you refuse to make it your home, if you disobey the divine com-
14 mand; if you are heard crying, No! To Egypt! There we will dwell,
where are no sights of bloodshed, no sound of trumpet-call, no famine to
15 be endured! then, last of the Jews, listen to this, the Lord's message!
This he tells you, he, the Lord of hosts, the God of Israel: If you turn
16 your faces towards Egypt, and thither repair to find a refuge, the sword
you dread shall overtake you, there in Egypt, the famine that haunts you

17 shall be with you still, there in Egypt, and in Egypt you shall die! None
   that turns his face towards Egypt for refuge but sword or famine or
   pestilence shall be the undoing of him; such calamity I mean to bring on
18 it as none shall survive, none shall escape. Thus says the Lord of hosts,
   the God of Israel: Go you to Egypt, my angry vengeance shall blaze out
   against you no less, than when you dwelt once at Jerusalem; yours shall
   be a name of execration and horror, a name to curse by and to revile, and
19 this land you shall never see more. Last of the Jews, this is the Lord's
   message: Go to Egypt you must not. Bear me witness, all of you, that
20 I have given you solemn warning this day. But no, you did but hoodwink
   yourselves; you would have me do your errand to the Lord our God, and
   so you promised, Pray to the Lord our God for us, make known to us
21 whatever is his divine will, and it shall be done; but now I have told it
   you, and where is your obedience to that divine will, to the message he
22 bade me deliver to you? Here then is full warning that the land where
   you mean to take refuge shall be the undoing of you, by war and famine
   and pestilence.

CHAPTER FORTY-THREE

SUCH was the errand upon which the Lord now sent Jeremias to his
people. And when Jeremias had delivered all this message to them
2 from the Lord their God, Azarias, son of Osaias, contradicted him;
Johanan, too, the son of Caree, and the other malcontents [1] held the same
language. Thou liest, they said, warrant thou hast none from the Lord
3 our God to prevent us taking refuge in Egypt; it is Baruch, son of Nerias,
who sets thee on, thinking to betray us to the Chaldaeans, and have us
4 put to death, or carried away to Babylon. Thus Johanan, son of Caree,
with the army chieftains and all their men in his support, refused to obey
5 the Lord's bidding and remain where they were in Juda. He and his
fellow chieftains took all the remaining Jews away with them; some of
these had been scattered in distant parts, but had now come back to live
6 at home with their wives and children; others, the king's daughters
among them, had been entrusted by Nabuzardan, the captain of the bodyguard, to Godolias, son of Ahicam, son of Saphan, that had the prophet
7 Jeremias and Baruch son of Nerias at his side. With all these at their
back they crossed the Egyptian frontier, in defiance of the Lord's bidding,
and made their way to Taphnis.
8   And at Taphnis the word of the Lord came to Jeremias: Take a load

---

[1] Literally, 'and all the proud men, saying.' The text is probably corrupt.

of great stones with thee, and go to the vault [1] under the brick wall by the gate of Pharao's palace at Taphnis; there bury them, with Jewish folk by
10 to watch thee. And this message thou shalt give them from the Lord of hosts, the God of Israel: I mean to summon one that is my servant, Nabuchodonosor king of Babylon, and set up a throne for him on these founda-
11 tions; where these stones lie buried, his canopy shall rise. He it is that shall come and doom the Egyptians; whom the plague beckons, to the
12 plague, whom exile, to exile, whom the sword, to the sword. The idols of Egypt he shall carry away into banishment, first setting light to their temples and burning them down. Lightly as shepherd dons cloak, he shall invest himself with sovereignty over its people, and unmolested go his
13 way,   breaking in pieces the statues that adorn Egypt's sun-temple, the shrines of Egypt burning to the ground.

CHAPTER FORTY-FOUR

HERE is a message that was sent through Jeremias to all the Jews living in Egypt, whether in Magdalus or Taphnis or Memphis or the
2 Phatures country: Thus says the Lord, the God of hosts: You have seen for yourselves what calamity I brought on Jerusalem and the cities of
3 Juda, how this day they are empty of inhabitants. By their own guilt they earned it, when they defied my vengeance, courting the sacrifices and the worship of alien gods they had never known till then, they and
4 you and your fathers alike. Early to your doors I sent those prophets that were servants of mine, bidding you leave off such foul doings of yours,
5 doings most hateful to me;   but heed and hearing they gave me none, still
6 went astray, to alien gods still made sacrifice. At last my angry vengeance blazed up, and lit such a fire in the townships of Juda, in the streets
7 of Jerusalem, as has left them, this day, a barren wilderness. And now, says the Lord of hosts, the God of Israel, what of yourselves? Would you fasten a noose round your own necks, court death for man and woman,
8 child and weanling, till remnant of Juda there is none? For rivals must I have images of your own making? Will you sacrifice to gods not yours, there in Egypt? Why would you take refuge there, to your own undoing, to be a name all the world should curse by and revile?
9   Have you forgotten them, ill deeds done in your fathers' days by king and queen, by man and wife, throughout Juda and the streets of Jeru-
10 salem? Alas, to this day there is no amending; no dread of me, no living by the divine law, by the rule I held up for a pattern to you and to your
11 fathers! Thus, then he threatens you, he, the Lord of hosts, the God of

---

[1] 'The vault'; this represents a noun in the Hebrew which is not found elsewhere. Modern commentators give the rendering 'mortar.'

Israel: It is my frown you shall see henceforward; the whole of Juda shall
12 be cut away. The remnant that looked to find a refuge in Egypt, in Egypt
shall perish, sword and famine their undoing, sword and famine for all
of them, high and low. Theirs shall be a name of execration and of won-
13 der, a name to curse by and to revile. Sword, famine and pestilence, so I
14 called Jerusalem to account, and so I will call Egypt to account; for
those Jewish survivors that have taken refuge in Egypt there is no escaping with their lives, no returning to Juda, home of their eager desire; only
fugitives shall return.

15 Jeremias did not go unanswered; there were men there who knew well
their wives made offering to alien gods; of the women themselves, many
were standing by. They had but one thought, all these exiles that were
16 making their home at Phatures in Egypt; Ay, so the Lord bids thee tell
17 us, but we will have none of it. Sworn we are, and by that oath we mean
to stand, that we will do sacrifice to the queen of heaven, and make offering of cakes to her, as we ever did, we and our fathers, kings and rulers
of ours, in the townships of Juda and in Jerusalem streets; bread we had
in those days to our heart's content, and all went well with us; bad times
18 we never saw. It is only since we left off doing sacrifice to the queen of
heaven, and paid tribute of cakes no more, that all is woe and want, sword
19 wasting us and famine. Sacrifice when we women make to the queen of
heaven, and pour libation to her, be sure our men-folk know in whose
honour cake is made, and wine is poured!

20 But Jeremias turned upon them all, men and women alike, all that had
21 given him his answer. Nay, said he, when you did sacrifice all through
Juda and in Jerusalem streets, and your fathers before you, king and noble
and plain citizen, be sure the Lord was heeding you, and marked it well.
22 It was when the Lord could bear no longer with false aims and foul deeds
of yours, that your land became a wilderness, a thing of wonder, a name
23 to curse by, a land empty of inhabitants, as it is this day. It was because
you sacrificed, in the Lord's despite, to false gods, because you would not
obey him, would not follow law and decree and ordinance of his, that all
the calamity of these times has come upon you.

24 This, too, Jeremias said to the crowd about him, and to their women-
folk besides: Jews of Egypt, listen to the message he sends you, he, the
25 Lord of hosts, the God of Israel. So you will be as good as your word;
sacrifice and libation you have vowed to the queen of heaven, and must
26 pay it; all is accomplished, will has turned into act! Then listen, Jews of
Egypt, to the doom which the Lord pronounces: By the honour of my
own name I have sworn it, the Lord says, never Jew shall be heard more
27 taking his oath by the living God, in all this land of Egypt! For woe,
not for weal, these eyes of mine shall watch over them, till sword and
28 famine have done their work, and Jew in Egypt is none. To Juda from

Egypt they shall return, such few as have escaped the sword's point, and the remnant that took refuge here shall learn to their cost whose prophecy
29 was fulfilled, theirs or mine. Here is a sign I mean to give you, the Lord says, here in this land, in proof that my threats shall be accomplished.
30 Thus says the Lord: I, that gave up Sedecias of Juda to Nabuchodonosor, his mortal enemy, will give up to his mortal enemies yonder Ephree,[1] that is now Pharao in Egypt.

CHAPTER FORTY-FIVE

WHEN Baruch, son of Nerias, had written down the words dictated to him by Jeremias, in the fourth year of Joachim's reign in Juda,
2 this comfort Jeremias gave him:[2] A message from the Lord, the God of
3 Israel, to thee, Baruch! Woe is thee, heavy is thy heart; sorrow upon
4 sorrow the Lord gives thee, and respite thou canst find none. Yet this message the Lord has for thee: Here am I destroying what my own hands
5 built, uprooting what my own hands planted; and for thee must it be all prizes? For prizes never look thou; enough for thee that, go thou where thou wilt, safe-conduct of thy life I am granting thee.

CHAPTER FORTY-SIX

2 HERE follows the doom which the Lord pronounced to the prophet Jeremias against the nations of the world. And first against Egypt, whose army stood at Charcamis, by the river Euphrates, under its king Pharao Nechao, and there was defeated by Nabuchodonosor king of Babylon, in the fourth year of Joachim's reign over Juda, that was son to Josias.
3 Buckler, there, and shield; march we to battle! Yoke steed, and, horsemen, mount; stand to your ranks, helmeted; scour lance, and don breast-
5 plate! What means it? Here be cowards turning their backs, here be great warriors slain; pell-mell they flee, and never a glance behind; peril is all
6 around, the Lord says. For the swift no escape, for the strong no prevailing; there in the north, by Euphrates banks, they fail and fall!
7 Can it be a river that comes up in flood, eddies are these of a foaming
8 torrent? Like river in flood, like foaming torrent marches Egypt to battle,
9 threatening to cover earth with its advance, drown city and citizen. Ay, mount horse, dizzily reel the chariot; way there for the warriors, Ethiop and Libyan with their great shields, men of Lydia that ply bow and shoot

---

[1] That is Apries, or Hophra, deposed by Amasis in 571 B.C.
[2] Cf. ch. 36.

10 arrow so well! Alas, not yours the day; this day the Lord, the God of hosts, has chosen for his day of vengeance, when he will take toll of his enemies; fed and glutted his sword shall be, drink deep of men's blood; here, on Euphrates banks, the Lord, the God of hosts, will claim his

11 sacrifice. Egypt, poor maid, to Galaad betake thee, to find balm for thy wounds! Salve after salve thou wilt try in vain; there is no healing thee.

12 Thy shame has come to all men's ears, earth echoes with thy lament; warrior leaned upon warrior of thine for support, and they fell both together.

13 And thus the Lord prophesied to Jeremias the coming of Nabuchodo-

14 nosor, king of Babylon, and his victory over Egypt. Here is news for Egypt; cry it in Magdalus, wake the echoes of Memphis, in Taphnis tell it abroad! Stand to arms, make ready for battle; thy border countries

15 have fallen a prey to the sword already! Why have thy warriors melted away? [1] Stand they could not, when the Lord was minded to overthrow

16 them. Many he brought to earth; stumbled they, man over his fellow, crying out, Up, to men of our own race return we, to the land of our birth; escape we from the invader's sword! [2]

17 What name shall we give to Pharao? Call him, Din of Battle at Last. [3]

18 By his own life he has sworn it, that King whose name is Javé, God of hosts; Pharao's conqueror is on the way, towering high as Thabor among the hills, as Carmel above the sea.

19 Poor maid of Egypt, an exile's pack provide thee! A lonely wilderness Memphis shall be, where none may dwell henceforward.

20 Fitting emblem of Egypt, a heifer lithe and graceful; from the north

21 a gad-fly [4] shall come to trouble her rest. But those mercenaries of hers that went to and fro like bullocks full-fed, see how they have turned about and taken flight all at once, none ready to stand his ground! The day has come when they are marked down for slaughter; they shall be

22 called to account at last. Loud her voice shall rise above the clash of bronze, [5] now that the invader's army draws near, pitiless as woodmen

23 that go a-hewing; forest is none so deep they shall not lay it bare, num-

---

[1] Literally, 'Why has thy strong one been thrown down' (in the Latin version, 'become rotten'). Some think there is an allusion to the god Apis here, perhaps concealed by a false reading.

[2] See note on 25.38.

[3] Literally, 'The (appointed) time has brought tumult.' The sense of the Hebrew is probably 'Tumult has passed its appointed time,' perhaps meaning that it is too late now to do anything about it.

[4] If 'gad-fly' is the right rendering of a word not found elsewhere, it is impossible not to suspect a reference to the Greek myth of Io (regularly identified with the Egyptian goddess Isis). Io was changed by Zeus into a heifer and pursued by a gad-fly as the result of Hera's jealousy.

[5] Literally, 'as if of bronze.' The Hebrew text gives 'as if of a serpent.'

24 berless as the locust-swarm.   Poor Egypt, all shame and confusion, prey
25 of the northern folk!   The Lord of hosts, the God of Israel, has pronounced his doom: I mean to have a reckoning now with Amon of
Thebes,[1] with Pharao and Egypt, with all its gods and all its kings, with
26 Pharao and all who trust in Pharao's aid!   I mean to give them up into
the hands of their mortal enemies, Nabuchodonosor king of Babylon and
his vassals; then Egypt shall have rest, as Egypt did of old.
27   Have thou no fear, the Lord says, Jacob, that art my servant still; not
for Israel is danger brewing. From that far country of exile I mean to
restore thee, restore those children of thine; Jacob shall return, and live
28 at ease, every blessing shall enjoy, and enemies have none to fear.   For
thee no terrors, Jacob that art my servant, the Lord says; am I not at thy
side? Of all the lands in which I have dispersed thee I will take full toll,
but not of thee; I would but chastise thee with due measures kept, lest
I should leave thee altogether acquitted.[2]

CHAPTER FORTY-SEVEN

A ND this doom the Lord pronounced to the prophet Jeremias
against the Philistines, before the defeat of Gaza by king Pharao.
2   Waters rising in the north,[3] the Lord says, a river that overflows its
banks, covering earth and earth's increase, city and citizen! Loud the
3 cries everywhere, a whole world in lament, as the sound of armed hosts
draws nearer, groan of chariot and rattle of wheels; listless hang hands,
4 father for son has never a glance to spare.   So comes the day when
Philistia shall be plundered, all of it, Tyre and Sidon of all their defenders
shall be stripped; Philistia the Lord despoils, and all that is left of the
5 island-dwellers from Caphtor.   Shorn heads in Gaza; Ascalon is silent
now, silent all their valleys. Long wilt thou bear the marks of thy mourn-
6 ing!   Rest thee, sword of the Lord! Back into thy scabbard, calm thyself,
7 and rest!   Nay, rest how should it? It holds the Lord's warrant to subdue
Ascalon and the sea-board country; there he has made tryst with it.

---

[1] The Latin version has read the name of the god Ammon as a common
noun, 'multitude'; and, somewhat strangely, identifies the town of No not
with Thebes, but with Alexandria, which was founded two centuries after
Jeremias' date.
[2] *vv.* 27, 28. A repetition of 30.10, 11.
[3] The mention of the north suggests that we are still dealing with the con-
quests of Nabuchodonosor. If so, the time-indication of verse 1 must be regarded
as having an *a fortiori* value; even before the invasion of Philistia by Pharao-
Nechao, Jeremias prophesied its invasion by Nabuchodonosor some years later.

CHAPTER FORTY-EIGHT

A ND thus to Moab speaks the Lord of hosts, the God of Israel. Alas
for Nabo, spoiled and shamed, for Cariathaim taken, the high fort-
2 ress humbled, a prey to alarms! For Moab, scant triumph; against Hesebon there are plots a-brewing, Away with it, a nation let it be no more!
3 Silence for thee, a long silence; the sword is at thy heels. From Oronaim
4 the cry goes up, rack and ruin everywhere; Moab lies crushed, let Segor
5 echo the cry! Weep they and wail, that climb the slopes of Luith; all
the way down from Oronaim their foes may hear it, the cry of desolation.
6 Fly he must that would escape with life, stripped though he be as the
7 desert tamarisk. Ill reposed that confidence in ramparts of thine, stores
of thine; taken thou shalt be like the rest, and Chamos go into exile, all
8 his priests and all his votary chiefs with him. Of all thy cities, none shall
be safe from the spoiler's entry; wasted thy valleys shall be, swept bare
9 the hill-sides; the Lord decrees it. Weave a coronal [1] for Moab; in the
flower of her pride she goes into exile, and all her cities lie desolate, none
to dwell there.
10   Cursed the man who goes about the Lord's work grudgingly, nor with
blood stains his sword!
11   Since those first days of his, ever was Moab too rich; he, that knew not
exile, is like a wine that has settled on its lees, never decanted; tang and
12 reek of it were never lost; a time is coming now, the Lord says, when
I mean to send certain stewards of mine that shall tilt those jars; draw
13 wine, drain goblet, and break jar to pieces! Chamos will play Moab false,
14 as Bethel played Israel false, when Israel trusted in its sanctuary. Ay,
15 boast on of your bravery, tell us you are warriors all! Yet Moab is laid
waste, its townships aflame, all the flower of its chivalry gone to their
16 death; so that king decrees, whose name is Javé, God of hosts. Not long
17 delayed, Moab's last hour; runs on swift feet his calamity. Mourn with
him, you that are his neighbours, you that are his familiars; so trusty a
rod broken, a staff so fair.
18   Poor maid of Dibon, come down from thy splendour and sit on the
parched ground; the spoiler of Moab has scaled thy heights, dismantled
19 thy walls; poor maid of Aroer, by the wayside linger and look around
20 thee; ask of the fugitives, How went the day? Alas, Moab's hope is lost;
Moab lies conquered. Loud be the cry of lament in Arnon, that tells of
21 fields laid waste; doom on the hill-country, on Helon, Jasa, and

---

[1] Literally, 'give a flower.' The Hebrew text is generally rendered 'wings,'
with 'flying' instead of 'flourishing' in the second part of the verse, but the
justification of this sense is doubtful.

22 Mephaath, Dibon, Nabo, and Beth-Diblathaim, Cariathaim, Beth-
24 gamul, Bethmaon, Carioth, and Bosra, and all the cities of Moab, far and
25 near. Blunted now is that horn, the Lord says, crushed that strong arm!
26 Senseless let him fall, that once for the divine power vaunted himself
27 a match; a laughing-stock let him be, that once, vomiting over his wine,
clapped hands in derision to make a laughing-stock of Israel! An interloper thou didst call him, and now, for this ill speaking of thine, thyself
28 shalt be cast into exile.[1] Leave your cities, Moabites, and take to the
hills; make the dove your model, that ever at the outermost edge of cave
will build her nest.

29 The boasting of Moab has long been in our ears,[2] as it was ever boast-
30 ful; proud, scornful, boastful Moab, with head so high in air! Well I
know, the Lord says, those high pretensions of hers, that have no
31 strength to warrant them, those dreams that never come true! So, from
one end of Moab to the other, there is dole and dirge, mournful hearing
32 for the men behind those walls of hardened brick. Jazer laments for thee,
vineyard of Sabama, and with Jazer I too will mourn; thy shoots reached
from Jazer itself to the Dead Sea and beyond; now, harvest of thine and
33 vintage of thine the spoiler has overrun. From the garden-lands of Moab
joy and triumph have died away; all the presses I have emptied of their
34 wine, no vintage-song, no treading the grapes as of old. The dirge goes
up from Hesebon, from Eleale and Jasa; goes up all the way from Segor
to Oronaim, like the lowing of heifer full-grown; foul grow the waters of
35 Nemrim. None will I leave in Moab, the Lord says, to worship at the
36 hill-shrines, or do sacrifice to its gods. For Moab my heart wails like the
wailing of flutes, wailing of flutes for those brick-walled cities of hers;
37 too high she aimed, and see, they lie in ruins. Every head is shorn, every
beard shaved in mourning; with bound [3] hands men go, sackcloth on their
38 backs. Roof-top and street in Moab is none but echoes with grief; I have
cast Moab away, the Lord says, like a jar past mending.
39 Lament for Moab in defeat, bowed heads for Moab's shame! A laugh-
40 ing-stock it will be and a by-word for all its neighbours. An eagle's flight
yonder conqueror has, the Lord says, and will sweep down on Moab too.
41 Now Carioth [4] is lost, and all the strongholds taken; cowed as woman's

---

[1] *vv.* 26, 27. The sense here is very doubtful. 'Interloper'; literally, 'thief';
the reference is perhaps to Israel's comparatively late arrival in Palestine.
[2] *vv.* 29–38. Most of these phrases are to be found, though some of them
in a different form, in chh. 15, 16 of Isaias. The simplest explanation seems
to be, that both prophets, at this point, wrote in certain appropriate lines from
an older poem. The 'walls of hardened brick' and the 'heifer full-grown' perhaps conceal proper names, Cir-heres and Eglath-Salisia.
[3] According to the Hebrew text 'lacerated' (in sign of mourning).
[4] Or perhaps the Hebrew word should be read as a common noun, 'cities.'

42 heart in child-bearing are those warrior hearts; Moab, that set the Lord
43 at defiance, shall be a people no more. Terror in front of its people, the
44 Lord says, trap and toil behind them; from terror flee thou, into trap
fall thou; from the trap free thee, toils shall fasten thee. Such shall be
45 my year of reckoning with the men of Moab, the Lord says. From the
toils escaped, who turns to Hesebon for shelter? Helpless he stands; such
a fire comes out from Hesebon, all Seon's capital aflame, till cheek and
46 head of blustering Moab are consumed. Alas, Moab, alas, people of
Chamos, for thy undoing! Gone into exile now thy sons and daughters! [1]
47 Yet a time shall come at last, the Lord says, when her lot shall be reversed.

Thus far the doom of Moab.

CHAPTER FORTY-NINE

AND thus the Lord speaks to the Ammonites: Did Israel, then, leave
no sons, no heirs to follow him? How comes it that Melchom boasts
2 possession of Gad, and worshippers of his dwell in yonder cities? A time
is coming, the Lord says, when Rabbath Ammon shall hear the din of
fighting, and shall be thrown down in ruins; when her daughter cities
shall be burnt to the ground, and Israel, so runs the divine promise,
3 shall drive out the intruder. Shall Hesebon mourn for Hai laid waste,
and the women of Rabbath for Rabbath make no lament? [2] Nay, put on
sackcloth, raise the dirge as you scatter among the hedge-rows; Melchom
4 goes into banishment, his priests and his votary chieftains with him. So
proud of thy valleys! Wasted away, now, is that vale of thine, pampered
maiden; confident in thy rich store, thou didst flatter thyself none should
5 come near to harm thee, but I mean to fill thee with dread, says the
Lord, the God of hosts, dread of all thy neighbours. Each man shall
take his own path, scattering in flight, and there shall be none to rally
6 the fugitives. Yet afterwards, the Lord says, I will bring the exiled sons
of Ammon back to their home.

7 And for Edom, this. No more is Theman wise, as of old, says the Lord
of hosts; the prudence of that breed is lost, its wisdom all gone to waste.
8 Flee away, men of Dedan, and never look behind you, or hide deep in
earth; I am bringing ruin upon Esau, calling him to account at last.
9 Here are such vintagers as will leave thee never a cluster, such night-

---

[1] *vv.* 45, 46. Here again the prophet seems to be quoting from an older poem,
which may or may not be the same as that already alluded to; cf. Num. 21.28; 29.

[2] The original runs simply, 'Mourn, Hesebon, for Hai is laid waste; lament,
daughters of Rabbath.' But it seems clear that Hesebon, which had no connexion
with the Ammonites, is only brought in by way of comparison. No town of Hai
is elsewhere mentioned east of the Jordan, and many think the text is corrupt.

10 robbers as will have their fill; mine to strip Esau bare, dig up his lairs
   till there is no hiding in them. The whole brood of him must be de-
11 stroyed, never a kinsman or neighbour left, that will say,[1] To my care
12 entrust thy orphans, to me let thy widows look for support. So many
   there are, the Lord says, that must drink the cup of vengeance all undeserving; and wouldst thou be spared, wouldst thou be acquitted?
13 Acquittal for thee is none; thou shalt drain it to the dregs. By my own
   honour I have sworn it, the Lord says, that Bosra shall be an empty
   wilderness, a name to revile and to curse by; that her daughter cities shall
   for ever be desolate.
14   Hue and cry the Lord has brought to my ears, that even now goes out
   among the nations, Muster we and march we against her; on to battle!
15 A little thing I mean thee to be in the world's eyes henceforward, un-
16 regarded among the nations; till now, pride and the insolence of thy
   heart deluded thee, so safe thy nest among the rock-crevices, so close thou
   didst cling to the mountain summits; but now, be thy eyrie high as the
17 eagle's, I will yet drag thee down, the Lord says.[2] A very desert Edom
   shall be; no passer-by but will stand amazed, and hiss derision at its
18 sufferings; not more ruinously Sodom fell, and Gomorrha, and their
19 neighbour cities, that lie uninhabited, far from the homes of men. See
   how lion from the fens of Jordan sallies out against yonder protected
   fold! Not less sudden the alarm shall be;[3] and the flock shall have a master
   of my own choosing. Match for me is none, there is none dare implead
20 me, no rival shepherd may challenge a claim like mine! Would you know
   what the Lord's design is for Edom, what plans he is devising against the
   homesteads of Theman? Why, he says, it will but need an array of weaklings to dislodge them,[4] pull their dwelling-place down about their ears!
21 And with the crash of that ruin earth shakes, far as the Red Sea ring the
22 echoes of it. An eagle's flight yonder conqueror has, to soar high and
   sweep down on Bosra; cowed as woman's heart in child-bearing are the
   warrior hearts of Edom.
23   And for Damascus, this. Hamath and Arphad see their hopes betray

---

[1] *vv.* 10, 11. The words 'that will say' are not expressed in the original, but
it seems necessary to supply them; otherwise the two verses are in direct contradiction, and the mention of 'neighbours' is inexplicable.

[2] *vv.* 14–16. The prophecy of Abdias opens with (substantially) the same
expressions, and Abd. 5 is a reminiscence of verse 9 above. The use of common material by the two prophets seems the most probable explanation; cf.
note on 48.29–38.

[3] Literally, 'I will suddenly make him run to it,' but the Hebrew text has,
'I will make him (Edom) suddenly run away from it.'

[4] Literally, 'the little ones of the flock will throw them down'; the Hebrew
text can be interpreted as meaning, 'they will throw down the little ones of
the flock.'

them; grievous the news that reaches them, and they are rocked on a sea
24 of doubt; anxiety gives them no respite. As for Damascus, her strength
has left her; no thought has she but for flight, daunted by her peril,
25 overcome, like woman in child-bearing, with sharp pangs. City so re-
26 nowned, home of such delights, must all abandon her? In her streets
they lie slain, all the flower of her youth, all her brave warriors lie silent
27 now, the Lord says; and such a fire I will light within Damascus walls
as shall feed on the palaces of Benadad.

28   And this for Cedar, and the realms of Asor, that were destroyed by
Nabuchodonosor king of Babylon. Word comes from the Lord: Up,
29 march against Cedar, despoil we these children of the East! Pillage there
shall be of home and herd, plundering of tents and gear and camels,
30 and cries of Danger everywhere. Flee away, wander far away, men of
Asor, deep, says the Lord, be your hiding-places! Here is Nabuchodonosor king of Babylon holding a council of war, devising plans against
you.

31   Up, march against a people that lives at ease, fearing no attack, the
Lord says; gates and bars they have none, dwelling there in the wilder-
32 ness; camels for your plunder, herds a many for your prey! Scattered
they shall be to all the winds, the folk that clip their foreheads bare, and
from every corner of their lands death shall threaten them, the Lord says.
33 Asor shall be a lair for serpents, a land for ever desolate; uninhabited it
shall lie, far from the homes of men.

34   And here is the doom the Lord pronounced to the prophet Jeremias
35 against Aelam, at the beginning of Sedecias' reign in Juda. A message
from the Lord of hosts! I mean to break the bows of yonder Aelamites,
36 wherein lies all their strength. Upon Aelam I will bid the winds blow
from the four corners of heaven, and before each scatter them like chaff,
37 till nation is none that has not seen their fugitives. Daunted the Aelamites shall be by the onset of their mortal enemies; my angry vengeance
I will let loose against them, the Lord says, and my sword shall go at
38 their heels till I have taken full toll of them. In Aelam I will set up my
39 throne, he says, and rid it altogether of kings and princes. Yet afterwards, so runs the divine promise, I will bring the exiled sons of Aelam
back to their home.

CHAPTER FIFTY

A ND here is the doom the Lord pronounced, with Jeremias for his
spokesman, against Babylon and Chaldaea.
2   Tell it out, proclaim it for all the world to hear; set up a trophy, and
cry the news, leave nothing untold! News of Babylon taken, and Bel
thwarted, and Merodach overcome; all the idols put to shame, routed, all

3 the false gods! Here is a people on the march from the north country
that shall attack Babylon and turn her land into a desert; man nor beast
shall dwell there, all are fled and gone.

4 So the day shall dawn, the time be ripe at last, the Lord says, when
Israel and Juda both together shall come back, weeping as they hasten on
5 their journey to find the Lord their God. For Sion every voice asking,
every face towards Sion turned, they will come back, and bind them-
6 selves to the Lord by an eternal covenant, never to be forgotten. My
people, all this while, has been but a flock gone astray; their shepherds led
them by false paths, and left them to roam the hill-side; hill and moun-
7 tain-side they crossed, and their own resting-place lay forgotten. None
passed by but preyed on them; nor did the oppressor's conscience smite
him; had they not set the Lord at defiance, that Lord who was the home
of their loyalty, the hope of their race?

8 Flee, Israel, from Babylon; from Chaldaea's land be foremost to depart,
9 like buck-goats that lead the way for their fellows. See what a confederacy of great nations I am mustering, there in the north country, to
besiege and take Babylon, death-dealing archers that never speed arrow
10 in vain! Chaldaea shall be a prize of war, the Lord says, and all her
11 spoilers be content. Ay, boast and brag, trample on my own domain,
12 like calves at grass or bellowing bull![1] Shame waits for the mother that
bore you, her pride must be lowered in the dust; least regarded of all
13 realms, a desert, pathless and parched! Doomed, all of her, by the Lord's
vengeance to empty desolation; no passer-by but shall stand amazed at
14 Babylon, or hiss derision at her sufferings. To your posts, archers, around
the walls of Babylon; shoot, never spare arrow; to the Lord her life is
15 forfeit. Now, raise the cry! Everywhere she is yielding; falls buttress and
gapes wall, the Lord is avenged! Ay, take your fill of vengeance, pay her
16 what she has earned. Leave none in Babylon to sow the fields, or carry
scythe in harvest-time; fled, each to his own, before the invader's sword,
fled, this way and that, to the countries of their birth.

17 Poor Israel, a flock so scattered! Lions have chased them away; first
the Assyrian king would prey on them, and since then yonder Nabu-
18 chodonosor, of Babylon, has mangled their bones! And now, says the
Lord of hosts, the God of Israel, I mean to have a reckoning with the
19 Babylonian king, and his realm, as once with Assyria. And Israel I will
restore to his home; Carmel and Basan shall be his pasture-ground
again, hill-country of Ephraim and Galaad his hunger shall content.
20 When that day dawns, the Lord says, when the time is ripe for it, guilt
shall be found in Israel no more, for the record of Juda's sins you

---

[1] The sense of the Hebrew text is probably 'heifer treading out the corn or
neighing stallion.'

shall search in vain; the remnant which I leave shall win my pardon.
21   March on, the Lord says, into the land of tyranny, and call its citizens
to account; bale and ban at their heels! All my command see thou
22 execute. Din of battle sounds through the land, and the crash of ruin;
23 rack and ruin everywhere! And this Babylon was once a hammer to smite
24 the world; now it lies by all the world abandoned! I laid a trap for thee,
Babylon, and thou wast caught unawares; thy long defiance of the Lord
25 has found thee out and overtaken thee at last. Now the Lord opens his
armoury, takes out from it the tools that shall wreak his vengeance; he,
the Lord of hosts, has work for them to do in the country of the Chal-
26 daeans. From the furthest confines of the land draw near; open a way for
the spoilers; pile up stones from the road in heaps; make an end of her,
27 leave nothing to survive.[1] An end of all her warriors, to the slaughter-
house with them! Woe betide them, their day has come, the time when
they must meet their reckoning.
28   Listen to the buzz of voices, as the fugitives escaped from Babylon
come back to Sion, spreading the news how the Lord has been avenged,
how the Lord's temple has been avenged.
29   Archers a many with bent bows, give them orders how the city must
fare: Stand about it in a ring, let never a man escape, pay it what its deeds
have earned; to Babylon do as Babylon did to others, the city that was
30 the Lord's enemy, defied the holy One of Israel. In her streets they lie
slain, all the flower of her youth, all her brave warriors lie silent now,
31 the Lord says.[2] Have at thee, says the Lord, the God of hosts; thy day
32 has come, the time when thou must meet thy reckoning! Stumbles the
tyrant and falls, with none there to raise him; and in those cities of his
I will kindle such a fire as shall consume all around it.
33   Thus says the Lord of hosts: Here is great wrong done to Israel and to
Juda both; he that has them holds them fast, and let them go he will not.
34 Yet they have a strong champion that claims them as his own; his name
is Javé, the God of hosts; right and redress he will bring them in such a
fashion as will shake earth,[3] and make the homes of Babylon tremble.
35 The sword it must be, the Lord says, for the men of Chaldaea, for citizen
36 of Babylon, and prince, and councillor; the sword for their wise men,
37 that shall be fools, and their brave men, that shall be cowards; the sword
for horse and chariot, the sword for all the mixed breed in it, that shall
be weak as women, the sword for all their treasure-houses, that shall be

---

[1] The Latin version here seems to have misunderstood the Hebrew text,
which refers to the opening of store-rooms and the piling up of their contents as
forfeit to the Lord and therefore unavailable for booty (Jos. 6.17, 18; 7.11, 12).
[2] Repeated from 49.26.
[3] 'Shake earth'; or perhaps (deriving the Hebrew verb from a different
root) 'bring repose to earth.'

38 given up to plunder. And for their waters, not a sword, but drought to
dry them up; is not this a land of idols, that loves to see portents befall? [1]
39 It shall be a lair for serpents and strange monsters,[2] a haunt of the ostrich,
but never again shall man dwell there; age after age, it shall never be
40 rebuilt; not more ruinously the Lord overthrew Sodom and Gomorrha
and their neighbour cities, that lie uninhabited, far from the homes of
men.[3]

41   Here is a people marching from the north country, the Lord says, a
42 great nation from the world's end, and vassal kings a many. Bow and
shield they ply, and their hard hearts pity none; loud their battle-cry as
the roaring of the sea. So they ride on, as warriors ride, poor Babylon,
43 thy enemies. Unnerved the king's hands droop at the very rumour of it;
44 grief overmasters him, sharp as the pangs of travail.[4] See how lion from
the fens of Jordan sallies out against yonder protected fold! Not less sudden the alarm shall be; and the flock shall have a master of my own choosing. Match for me is none, there is none dare implead me, no rival shep-
45 herd may challenge a claim like mine! Would you know what the Lord's
design is for Babylon, what plans he is devising against the realm of Chaldaea? Why, he says, it will need but an array of weaklings to dislodge
46 them, pull their dwelling-place down about their ears![5] Babylon has
fallen; earth trembles at the sound of it; a great cry goes up for all the
world to hear.

CHAPTER FIFTY-ONE

THUS says the Lord, I mean to let loose on Babylon, and the whole
2   of Defiance-land,[6] a destroying blast; winnowers of mine shall reach
Babylon and fall to winnowing it, till all the heaps are gone; an ill day for
3 Babylon, cut off on every side. Let not a man live to bend bow again,
or don breastplate for battle; never a warrior spare, army she must have
4 none left. Everywhere in countryside and street of Chaldaea the mangled

---

[1] There is here a play upon words in the Hebrew; 'sword' and 'drought'
differ only by a single point. The second half of the verse is of doubtful interpretation. Herodotus affirms (i.191) that Cyrus took Babylon by diverting the
course of the Euphrates.

[2] Literally, 'dragons and fig-fauns.' Cf. Is. 34.14, where the Latin version
renders the same Hebrew phrase 'demons and onocentaurs.' There can be
no certainty what creatures are really alluded to; some think wild cats and
jackals.

[3] Repeated from 49.18.

[4] *vv.* 41–43. Repeated from 6.22–24.

[5] *vv.* 44, 45. Repeated from 49.19–21.

[6] The Hebrew letters of this word form a cipher equivalent for the name
'Chaldaea.'

5 corpses lie; not altogether has Israel's God, the Lord of hosts, for-
6 saken her, and to that holy One of Israel the whole land is forfeit. Flee
away from the confines of Babylon, flee for your lives; would you meekly
accept her punishment? The time has come when the Lord will take
7 vengeance on her, he it is that sends this retribution. Babylon, that was
once a golden cup in the Lord's hand, for a whole world's bemusing!
8 Drank nations of that cup, how they reeled and tottered! And now, all
in a moment, Babylon herself falls to her ruin. Raise the dirge, go find
9 balm to heal those wounds of hers! Alas, we sought a cure for Babylon,
but curing her there was none; time it is we left her, and went back each
to his own land; towers heaven-high the measure of her punishment, and
10 is lost among the clouds. Come, then, since he has given us the redress
we needed, recount we in Sion the great doings of the Lord our God.
11   Whet arrow, and fill quiver; the Lord has put a resolve into the heart
of the Median king; he will have Babylon overthrown. The Lord shall
12 be avenged, his temple shall be avenged! Against Babylon's walls display
the standard, keep strict watch, post sentinels, lay ambush; the doom of
13 its folk, long since devised, long since denounced, he will execute. Land
by all those tributary streams so enriched, thy end is reached, thy thread
14 is spun. By his own honour the Lord of hosts has sworn it, thy enemies
shall swarm about thee like locusts, raising their vintage-song.
15   Power that made the earth,[1] wisdom that orders nature, foresight that
16 spread out the heavens! At the sound of his voice, what mustering of the
waters overhead! He summons up the cloud-wrack from the world's end,
turning the lightning into a rain-storm, bringing the winds out of his
17 store-house; how puny, then, is man's skill, how sorry a thing is the
18 carver's workmanship; after all his pains, only a lifeless counterfeit! Fond
imaginations, antic figures, when the time comes for reckoning, they
19 will be heard of no more. Not such the worship that is the heirloom of
Jacob's line; their God is the God who made all things, Israel his patrimony, Javé, the God of hosts, his name.
20   Great conqueror, the weapon I wield! By thy means I crush the nations,
21 undo empires;[2] crush horse and rider, chariot and charioteer, man and
23 woman, old and young, lad and lass, shepherd and flock, ploughman and
24 team, prince and ruler! And now I mean to repay Babylon, and all the
people of Chaldaea, for the wrongs they did, says the Lord, and your
25 eyes shall see it. Have at thee, stronghold of ruin, the Lord says, a whole
world's ruin! My hand is raised to smite thee, and tear thee from thy

---

[1] *vv.* 15–19. These verses are repeated from 10.12–16; it is not easy to see
how they are relevant in their present context.

[2] Some think Babylon itself is addressed, as having been previously the
instrument of the Divine vengeance. But it seems better to understand the
passage as referring to king Cyrus, like verse 11 above and verse 28 below.

26 rocky bed; a calcined heap thou shalt be, that never corner-stone, never foundation-stone shall yield; the Lord dooms thee to lie for ever desolate.
27 Display your standard for all the world to see, sound the trumpet far and wide, enrol the nations against her; make tryst with the kings of Ararat, Menni, and Ascenez, and count Taphsar among her enemies; like
28 locusts in bristling array swarm your cavalry. Plight all the nations to make war on her, the kings of Media with their chieftains and satraps,
29 all their wide dominion; a whole world in turmoil and travail with the stir of the divine resolve to crush Babylon, make Babylon an empty
30 desert. See how her warriors quit the field, to garrison their strongholds, how their valour dies away and grows womanish, how her roofs blaze,
31 the bars of her gates are shattered! Courier meets courier, post to post hands the tidings on; tell the king of Babylon how his capital has fallen,
32 length and breadth of it, the fords occupied, the reed-beds aflame, dis-
33 mayed the defenders. Thus says the Lord of hosts, the God of Israel: Babylon is a threshing-floor time has worn smooth; wait but a little, and it is ready for harvest.
34 Nabuchodonosor king of Babylon, how he has preyed on me, feasted on me, left me but an empty shell; a devouring monster that with kernel
35 fills his maw, throws husk away! Thus Sion, for her torn flesh, thus Jerusalem, for her blood spilt, arraigns Babylon and all yonder Chaldaean
36 folk; and now the Lord of hosts promises to maintain their quarrel, to redress their wrongs. I will turn her sea into desert sand, he tells you,
37 dry up her flow of waters; Babylon shall remain a heap of ruins, a lair for serpents, a thing of wonder and derision, and never a soul to dwell
38 in it. What though they rage like roaring lion, like young lion that tosses
39 his mane? I have a medicine for this thirst of theirs, to bemuse them and steal away their senses; they shall sleep on, the Lord says, with that
40 eternal sleep from which there is no waking. Never was lamb led to the
41 slaughter-house, never ram or buck-goat, so unsuspecting. Sesach [1] taken, the paragon of kingdoms fallen! Babylon turned into a sight of
42 horror for all the world to see! Babylon founded and gone, the waste
43 waves closing over her! All her cities a picture of desolation, an empty
44 desert, uninhabited, untrodden by mortal foot. Bel, too, the God of Babylon, I will call to account, and make him disgorge his treasures; no more shall pilgrims flock into his temple from distant lands; Babylon's defences are down.
45 You that are my own people, separate yourselves from her neighbour-
46 hood; else you shall be ever faint with alarms,[2] ever daunted by the news

---

[1] As in 25.26, a cipher name for Babylon.

[2] Literally, 'lest you should (continue to) be faint-hearted.' The common rendering (favoured by the Latin) 'Do not be faint-hearted,' is doubtful grammar and still more doubtful logic.

that reaches you, each year a fresh rumour of wrongs done in this land, of rulers struggling for pre-eminence.

47 A time is coming when I mean to have a reckoning with the idols of Babylon; the land will learn that they have played it false, when corpses
48 lie thick in the heart of it. Heaven and earth, and all they contain, will be triumphing over Babylon, says the Lord, as they see the spoilers
49 marching against her from the north country; through Babylon so many slain in Israel, of Babylon so many slain, in every corner of their land!
50 Come, linger not, you that have escaped the sword; exiled far away, bethink you still of the Lord, still let the thought of Jerusalem return to your hearts.
51 Alas, we are all confusion; what taunts we must listen to, shame-faced, now that the Lord's holy temple by alien intruders is defiled! [1]
52 A time is coming, the Lord says, when I mean to have a reckoning with those false gods of hers. Everywhere in Chaldaea there shall be wounded
53 men a-groaning; let Babylon scale the skies, fortify her walls heaven-high, they shall yet find their way in, the spoilers that do my errand, the
54 Lord says. Babylon shall be all lament, Chaldaea a crash of ruin; the mighty stir of the city will be drowned, when the Lord lays it waste, by
56 the surge of armies, wave upon wave, and the noise of their shouting. The spoiler has come upon Babylon; her warriors are caught in a trap, their bows are useless now; the Lord's vengeance is irresistible, and he pays
57 full measure. Bemused they shall be, prince and councillor and chieftain and ruler and warrior; all shall sleep eternally the sleep from which there is no waking; such is the decree of that King whose name is Javé, the God of hosts.
58 That wide wall of Babylon, says the Lord of hosts, shall be dismantled at last, those high gates burnt. So men labour for nothing; so the toil of nations perishes in the fire. [2]
59 And now Jeremias had an errand for Saraias, son of Nerias, son of Maaseias. When king Sedecias departed to Babylon, in the fourth year
60 of his reign, Saraias went with him as his principal spokesman. [3] Jeremias had written down on a single scroll all the doom that was to befall
61 Babylon, all the prophecy against Babylon aforegoing. When thou
62 reachest Babylon, he told Saraias, be sure thou readest all this. And say, in reading it: Lord, thou dost threaten this place with destruction; man
63 nor beast shall dwell there, it shall lie desolate for ever. Then, when thou

---

[1] This verse is generally understood as a protest from the exiles, who dare not return to Judaea from a sense of shame. But its appearance here is curiously inappropriate, and some suspect that, through accident, it has been misplaced.

[2] The second half of this verse is also found in Hab. 2.13.

[3] According to the Hebrew text, 'his chief of resting-place,' perhaps in the sense of quartermaster.

hast finished reading the scroll, tie a stone to it and sink it in the midst of
64 Euphrates; and this add: Thus Babylon shall sink, and rise no more out
of the calamity I mean to bring upon it; Babylon shall melt away.[1]
Here ends the prophecy of Jeremias.

CHAPTER FIFTY-TWO

SEDECIAS was twenty-one years old when he came to the throne,[2]
and his reign at Jerusalem lasted eleven years; his mother's name was
2 Amital, daughter of Jeremias of Lobna. He disobeyed the Lord's will,
3 as Joachim had; for now the Lord's anger hung over Juda and Jerusalem, ready to banish them from his presence. And Sedecias in his turn
revolted from the king of Babylon.
4   And now, in the ninth year of Sedecias' reign, on the tenth day of the
tenth month, Nabuchodonosor reached Jerusalem at the head of his
5 army. They surrounded it and threw up siege works about it, and so the
6 city continued beleaguered until king Sedecias' eleventh year. Then, on
the ninth day of the fourth month, when famine had broken out in the
7 city and the poorer folk had nothing left to eat, a breach was made in the
walls; and that night all the fighting men made their escape by way of the
gate between the two walls, by the royal garden, leaving the Chaldaeans
to continue the siege of the city. They chose for their flight the road which
8 leads to the desert, and in the desert by Jericho Sedecias was overtaken by
the Chaldaeans, who had set out in pursuit. All his retinue deserted him;
9 and so, a prisoner, the king was borne away to Reblatha, in the Emath
10 country, where Nabuchodonosor passed sentence on him. Slain by the
king of Babylon were all his sons, there in their father's sight; slain by the
11 king of Babylon, at Reblatha, were all the nobles of Juda; and as for
Sedecias himself, his eyes were put out, and he was carried off, loaded
with chains, to Babylon, where he remained a prisoner till the day of his
death.
12   On the tenth day of the fifth month in the nineteenth year of Nabuchodonosor's reign, the commander of his bodyguard, Nabuzardan, came
13 on his master's errand to Jerusalem, where he burned down temple and
palace and private dwellings too; no house of note but he set it on fire.
14 The troops he brought with him were employed in dismantling the walls

---

[1] The words 'Babylon shall melt away' represent what is probably an error
of copying in the Hebrew text.
[2] The whole of this chapter, except verses 28–30, is repeated from IV Kg.
24 and 25. There are a few very slight differences, some of which suggest
errors of transcription.

15 on every side of it. Then Nabuzardan carried off the remnants of the people that were left in the city, the deserters who had gone over to
16 Nabuchodonosor, and the common folk generally; leaving only such of
17 the poorer sort as were vine-dressers and farm labourers. Brazen pillars and brazen stands and the great basin of bronze that stood in the Lord's temple the Chaldaeans broke up, and took away all the bronze to Baby-
18 lon; for bronze, too, they carried away pot and fork, ladle and cup and
19 saucer, all the appurtenances of worship that were of bronze; for gold, too, and for silver, bowl and censer and urn and basin and lamp-stand
20 and spoon and goblet; nothing did Nabuzardan leave behind him. There was no reckoning the weight of bronze, when the two pillars, the great basin, and the twelve brazen calves supporting it, all set up by Solomon
21 in the temple, are included; each pillar was eighteen cubits high, twelve
22 cubits round, and four cubits thick, and they were hollow within. On each rested a brazen capital, five cubits in height, with network and pomegranate mouldings on the rim; the pattern of each was the same.
23 There were ninety-six pomegranates besides, making a hundred in all, and all had network around them.
24   Prisoners, too, Nabuzardan carried away with him, the two chief priests, Saraias and Sophonias, the three door-keepers from the tem-
25 ple, and among the citizens, the chamberlain who commanded the army, seven other courtiers who were left in the city, the secretary who was charged with the army and had the levying of recruits, and sixty
26 surviving citizens of the common sort. All these were carried away by
27 Nabuzardan to Reblatha, into Nabuchodonosor's presence; and there at Reblatha, in the Emath country, Nabuchodonosor put them to death. So
28 the men of Juda were exiled from their country. Three thousand and twenty-three Jewish citizens Nabuchodonosor banished in the seventh
29 year of his reign, and another eight hundred and thirty-two, from Jeru-
30 salem, in the eighteenth year of it; then, in his twenty-third year, seven hundred and forty-five were banished by Nabuzardan, the captain of the bodyguard; four thousand six hundred in all.
31   On the twenty-fifth day of the twelfth month, in the thirty-seventh year after king Joachim of Juda had been carried into exile, the new king of Babylon, Evil-Merodach, in this first year of his reign, gave redress
32 to his captive and released him from prison. Graciously did Evil-Mero-dach receive him, gave him a seat of honour above the other captive kings,
33 and relieved him of his prisoner's garb. All the rest of his life he was
34 entertained at the royal table; all the rest of his life he received, day by day, a perpetual allowance granted to him, as long as he should live, by the king's bounty.

THE LAMENTATIONS
OF THE PROPHET JEREMIAS

WHEN Israel was brought into captivity, and Jerusalem left deserted, the prophet Jeremias sat down there and wept, with this mournful lamentation following. And as he spoke, ever he sighed and moaned in the bitterness of his heart.

CHAPTER ONE

ALONE she dwells, the city erewhile so populous; a widow now, once a queen among the nations; tributary now, that once had provinces at her command.

2   Be sure she weeps; there in the darkness her cheeks are wet with tears; of all that courted her, none left to console her, all those lovers grown weary of her, and turned into enemies.

3   Cruel the suffering and the bondage of Juda's exile; [1] that she must needs dwell among the heathen! Nor respite can she find; close at her heels the pursuit, and peril on either hand.

4   Desolate, the streets of Sion; no flocking, now, to the assembly; the gateways lie deserted. Sighs priest, and the maidens go in mourning, so bitter the grief that hangs over all.

5   Exultant, now, her invaders; with her enemies nothing goes amiss. For her many sins, the Lord has brought doom on her, and all her children have gone into exile, driven before the oppressor.

6   Fled is her beauty, the Sion that was once so fair; her chieftains have yielded their ground before the pursuer, strengthless as rams [2] that can find no pasture.

7   Grievous the memories she holds, of the hour when all her ancient glories passed from her, when her people fell defenceless before the invader, unresisting before an enemy that derided them. [3]

8   Heinously Jerusalem sinned; what wonder if she became an outlaw? [4]

---

[1] Literally, this verse appears to imply that Juda has gone into exile *because of* affliction; and some think the reference is to refugee Jews in Egypt and elsewhere. But the word used for 'exile' really means 'deportation.'

[2] In the Hebrew text, 'stags.'

[3] Literally, 'her enemies derided her sabbath,' that is, her quiescence. The Hebrew text is generally interpreted as meaning that Sion, in her affliction, remembers her past glories; but the expression is obscure.

[4] 'An outlaw'; literally, 'unable to hold its ground'; but the word used in the Hebrew text implies ceremonial defilement.

How they fell to despising her when they saw her shame, that once flattered her! Deeply she sighed, and turned away her head.

9 Ill might skirts of her robe the defilement conceal; alas so reckless of her doom, alas, fallen so low, with none to comfort her! Mark it well, Lord; see how humbled I, how exultant my adversary!

10 Jealous hands were laid on all she treasured; so it was that she must see Gentiles profane her sanctuary, Gentiles, by thy ordinance from the assembly debarred.

11 Kindred was none but went sighing for lack of bread, offered its precious heirlooms for food to revive men's hearts. Mark it well, Lord, and see my pride abased!

12 Look well, you that pass by, and say if there was ever grief like this grief of mine; never a grape on the vineyard left to glean, when the Lord's threat of vengeance is fulfilled.[1]

13 Must fire from heaven waste my whole being, ere I can learn my lesson? Must he catch me in a net, to drag me back from my course? Desolate he leaves me, to pine away all the day long with grief.

14 No respite it gives me, the yoke of guilt I bear, by his hand fastened down upon my neck; see, I faint under it! The Lord has given me up a prisoner to duress there is no escaping.

15 Of all I had, the Lord has taken away the noblest; lost to me, all the flower of my chivalry, under his strict audit; Sion, poor maid, here was a wine-press well trodden down!

16 Pray you, should I not weep? Fountains these eyes are, that needs must flow; comforter is none at hand, that should revive my spirits. Lost to me, all those sons of mine, outmatched by their enemy.

17 Quest for consolation is vain, let her plead where she will; neighbours of Jacob, so the Lord decrees, are Jacob's enemies, and all around they shrink from her, as from a thing unclean.

18 Right the Lord has in his quarrel; I have set his commands at defiance. O world, take warning; see what pangs I suffer, all my folk gone into exile, both man and maid.

19 So false the friends that were once my suitors! And now the city lacks priests and elders both, that went begging their bread, and sighed out their souls for the want of it.

20 Take note, Lord, of my anguish, how my bosom burns, and my heart melts within me, in bitter ruth.[2] And all the while, sword threatens without, and death not less cruel within.

---

[1] The opening of this verse, in the Hebrew text, is of uncertain interpretation; some think the meaning is, 'May it never happen to you!' The vineyard metaphor used here and in verse 22 seems due to a mistaken interpretation in the Latin.

[2] Literally, 'for I am full of bitterness.' But the Hebrew text has, 'for truth it is that I have rebelled against thee.'

21   Uncomforted my sorrow, but not unheard; my enemies hear it, and rejoice that my miseries are of thy contriving. Ah, but when thy promise comes true, they shall feel my pangs!

22   Vintager who didst leave my boughs so bare, for my much offending, mark well their cruelty, and strip these too in their turn; here be sighs a many and a sad heart to claim it.

CHAPTER 2

ALAS, what mantle of cloud is this, the Divine anger has thrown over unhappy Sion? The pride of Israel cast down from heaven to earth; the ground where the Lord's feet once rested, now, in his anger, forgotten?

2   Blessed abodes of Jacob, by the Lord's unsparing vengeance engulfed; towers that kept Juda inviolable hurled to the ground in ruin; kingdom and throne dragged in the dust!

3   Crushed lay all the defences of Israel, under his displeasure; failed us, at the enemy's onset, the protection of his right hand; Jacob must be hedged about, as by flames of a consuming fire.

4   Deadly his bent bow, steady the play of his right hand assailing us; all that was fairest in poor Sion's dwelling-place needs must perish, under the fiery rain of his vengeance.

5   Enemies he counts us, and has engulfed the whole of Israel in ruin; gone the palaces, gone the strongholds; Alas, poor Sion! weeps man, weeps maid, with cowed spirits.[1]

6   Fallen, as it had been some garden shed, his own tabernacle; his own trysting-place with men he would pull down! Feast-day and sabbath should be forgotten in Sion; for king and priest, only anger and scorn.

7   Grown weary of his altar, from his own sanctuary turning away in abhorrence, the Lord has given up yonder embattled towers to the enemy; their cries ring through the temple like shout of holiday.

8   Heedfully the Lord went about his work, to strip the inviolable city of her walls; exact his measuring-line, busy his hand with the task of overthrow, till wall and rampart should lament their common ruin.

9   Idly the gates of her sag towards earth, bars riven and rent; king and chieftain are far away, exiled among the heathen; tradition is dead, nor any prophet learns, in vision, the Lord's will.

10   Jerusalem's aged folk sit there in the dust, dumb with sorrow; dust scattered over their heads, and sackcloth their garb; never a maid shall you see but has her head bowed down to earth.

---

[1] The Latin here describes God as filling Juda with 'humiliated men and humiliated women'; the sense of the Hebrew is rather 'lamentation and lament,' as in Is. 29.2.

11   **K**een anguish for the overthrow of an unhappy race, that dims eye with tears, that stirs my being to its depths, as my heart goes in boundless compassion! [1] Child and babe lie fainting in the streets.

12   **L**isten, how they ask where all the bread and wine is gone to! Wound they have none, yet there in the open streets you shall see them faint away, sighing out their lives on their mothers' bosoms.

13   **M**ight I but confront thee with such another as thyself! What queen so unhappy as Jerusalem, what maid as Sion desolate? How shall I comfort thee? Sea-deep is thy ruin, and past all cure.

14   **N**ever a true vision or a wise thy prophets have for thee, never shew thee where thy guilt rests, and urge thee to repentance; lies and lures are all the burden of their revealing.

15   **O**penly the passers-by deride thee, poor maid; clap hands, and hiss, and wag their heads at thee; So much, they cry, for the city that was once the nonpareil of beauty, pride of the whole earth!

16   **P**ale [2] envy mops and mows at thee; how they hiss and gnash their teeth! Now to prey on her carrion! What fortune, that we should have lived to see this day, so long looked for in vain!

17   **Q**uit is the Lord of his oath taken in times past, all his purpose is fulfilled; for thee, ruin relentless, for thy bitter enemy, triumph and high achievement.

18   **R**ound those inviolable defences, cry they upon the Lord in good earnest. Day and night, Sion, let thy tears stream down; never rest thou, never let that eye weary of its task.[3]

19   **S**leepless in the night watches raise thy song; flow thy heart's prayer unceasingly; lift ever thy hands in supplication for infant lives; yonder, at the street corner, they are dying of famine.

20   **T**hink well, Lord, is there any other people of whom thou hast taken such toll? Shall woman eat her own child, so tiny, hands can still clasp it? In the Lord's sanctuary, priest and prophet be slain?

21   **U**ntended they lie on the bare earth, the young and the aged; maid and warrior slain by the sword! This day of thy vengeance was to be all massacre, thou wouldst kill unsparingly.

22   **V**engeance this day all around me; what mustering of thy terrors,[4] as for a solemn assembly! Escape is none, nor any remnant left; of all I fondled and fostered, the enemy has taken full toll.

---

[1] Literally, 'my liver is poured out on the ground.'

[2] The Hebrew letters Phe and Ain are unaccountably transposed, here and in 3.46–51; 4.16 and 17.

[3] The first part of this verse is perhaps corrupt; the Hebrew text of it gives a rather improbable sense.

[4] Some think that we should interpret the Hebrew text as meaning '(some) of my neighbours,' not 'terrors.'

CHAPTER 3

AH, what straits have I not known, under the avenging rod! [1]
    Asked I for light, into deeper shadow the Lord's guidance led me;

3   **A**lways upon me, none other, falls endlessly the blow.

4   **B**roken this frame, under the wrinkled skin, the sunk flesh.

5   **B**itterness of despair fills my prospect, walled in on every side;

6   **B**uried in darkness, and, like the dead, interminably.

7   **C**losely he fences me in, beyond hope of rescue; loads me with fetters.

8   **C**ry out for mercy as I will, prayer of mine wins no audience;

9   **C**limb these smooth walls I may not; every way of escape he has undone.

10 **D**eep ambushed he lies, as lurking bear or lion from the covert;

11 **D**rawn aside from my path, I fall a lonely prey to his ravening.

12 **D**read archer, of me he makes a target for all his arrows;

13 **E**ach shaft of his quiver at my vitals taught to strike home!

14 **E**vermore for me the taunts of my neighbours, their songs of derision.

15 **E**ntertainment of bitter herbs he gives me, and of wormwood my fill,

16 **F**iles all my teeth with hard gravel-stones, bids me feed on ashes. [2]

17 **F**ar away is my old contentment, happier days forgotten;

18 **F**arewell, my hopes of long continuance, my patient trust in the Lord!

19 **G**uilt and suffering, gall and wormwood, keep all this well in memory.

20 **G**od knows it shall be remembered, and with sinking of the heart;

21 **G**age there can be none other of remaining confidence.

22 **H**is be the thanks if we are not extinguished; his mercies never weary;

23 **H**ope comes with each dawn; art thou not faithful, Lord, to thy promise?

24 **H**eart whispers, The Lord is my portion; I will trust him yet.

25 **I**n him be thy trust, for him thy heart's longing, gracious thou shalt find him;

26 **I**f deliverance thou wouldst have from the Lord, in silence await it.

27 **I**t is well thou shouldst learn to bear the yoke, now in thy youth,

28 **J**ust burden, in solitude and silence justly borne.

29 **J**oy may yet be thine, for mouth that kisses the dust,

30 **J**eering of the multitude, and cheek buffeted in scorn, bravely endured.

---

[1] There is no general agreement whether this chapter (and especially the concluding part of it) refers to the personal experiences of Jeremias, or describes poetically the misfortunes of the Jewish race.

[2] The sense given here is that of the Septuagint Greek; the Latin version gives in the first half, 'He has broken my teeth one and all'; the Hebrew text in the second half is usually rendered, 'he has bowed me down among the ashes.'

31   Know for certain, the Lord has not finally abandoned thee;
32   Kind welcome the outcast shall have, from one so rich in kindness.
33   Kin of Adam he will not crush or cast away wantonly;
34   Let there be oppression of the poor under duress,
35   Law's right denied, such as the most High grants to all men,
36   Lying perversion of justice, then he cannot overlook it.[1]
37   Man may foretell; only the Lord brings his word to pass;
38   Mingled good and evil proceed both from the will of the most High;
39   Mortal is none may repine; let each his own sins remember.
40   Narrowly our path scan we, and to the Lord return;
41   Never hand or heart but must point heavenward this day!
42   Nothing but defiant transgression on our part; and shouldst thou relent?
43   Over our heads thy angry vengeance lowered; smiting, thou wouldst not spare.
44   Oh, barrier of cloud, our prayers had no strength to pierce!
45   Offscouring and refuse of mankind thou hast made us,
46   Put to shame by the mocking grimaces of our enemies.
47   Prophets we had, but their word was peril and pitfall, and ruin at the last.[2]
48   Poor Sion, for thy calamity these cheeks are furrowed with tears;
49   Quell if thou wouldst the restless fever of my weeping,
50   Quickly, Lord, look down from heaven and pay heed to us,
51   Quite forspent, eye and soul, with grief Jerusalem's daughters bear.[3]
52   Relentless as hawk in air they pursued me, enemies unprovoked,
53   Reft me of life itself, sealed with a stone my prison door.
54   Round my head the waters closed, and I had given myself up for lost,
55   Save for one hope; to thee, Lord, I cried from the pit's depth,
56   Sure of thy audience; wouldst thou turn a deaf ear to sighs of complaint?
57   Summoned, thou didst come to my side, whispering, Do not be afraid.
58   Thine, Lord, to take my part; thine to rescue me from death;
59   The malice of my enemies to discover, my wrongs to redress.
60   Thrust away from thy sight, the grudge they bear me, the ill they purpose,
61   Unheard by thee their taunts, their whispered plottings?

---

[1] *vv.* 33–36. This is perhaps the least unnatural of the various interpretations suggested for this difficult passage. It assumes that the word 'wantonly' is emphatic, and that the end of verse 36 is a question, 'Does the Lord take no notice?'

[2] In the Hebrew text, 'Peril and pitfall, rack and ruin have overtaken us.'

[3] Literally, 'My eye has treated my soul harshly as the result of all the daughters of my city'; the text is perhaps corrupt.

62   Uttered aloud or in secret, their malice assails me from morn till night;
63   Up in arms, or met in secret conclave, ever against me they raise the
battle-song.
64   Visit them with the punishment their ill deeds have earned;
65   Veiled be those blind hearts with fresh blindness of thy own making;
66   Vanish from the earth their whole brood, ere thy vengeance leaves off
pursuing them!

CHAPTER 4

ALL dim, now, and discoloured, the gold that once shone so fair!
Heaped up at every street-corner lie hallowed stones.
2   Bright they shone once in all their renown, the men of Sion, and now
what are they? Little regarded as common earthenware, of the potter's
fashioning.
3   Cub of jackel [1] is fed at its dam's breast; and has my people grown unnatural towards its own children, like some ostrich in the desert?
4   Dry throat and parching tongue for babe at the breast; children asking
for bread, and never a crust to share with them!
5   Ever they fared daintily, that now lie starved in the streets; ever went
richly arrayed, and now their fingers clutch at the dung-hill.
6   Faithless Juda! Heavier punishment she must needs undergo than
guilty Sodom, that perished all in a moment, and never a blow struck.
7   Gone, the fair bloom of princely cheeks,[2] snowy-pure, cream-white,
red as tinted ivory,[3] and all sapphire-clear;
8   Here is no recognizing them, out in the streets, coal-black, skin clinging
to bones, dry as wood!
9   It were better to have fallen at the sword's point than yield thus to the
stab of hunger, wasted away through famine.
10   Juda brought low, and mother-love forgotten; that women should eat
their own children, cooked with their own hands!
11   Kindled at last is the Lord's anger; rains down from heaven the storm
of his vengeance, lighting a flame that burns Sion to the ground.
12   Little dreamed they, king and common folk the world over, that any
assault of the foe should storm Jerusalem gates;
13   Malice and lawlessness it was of priest and prophet, whereby innocent

---

[1] This is the accepted meaning of the word used in the Hebrew text, here
represented in the Latin by an obscure and inappropriate rendering.
[2] 'Princely cheeks'; the word 'Nazirite' can hardly be used in its technical
sense (Num. 6), and is better taken in its wider meaning of 'consecrated person.' That royal princes are referred to is only a conjecture based on the context.
[3] Literally, 'ancient ivory'; the Hebrew word perhaps means 'coral.'

men came to their deaths, that brought such punishment.

14 Now, as they walk blindly through the streets, they are defiled with blood; no help for it, gather their skirts about them as they may;

15 Out of my way! cries one to other; Back, pollution, do not touch me! The very Gentiles protest in alarm, Here is no place for them!

16 Protection the Lord gives them no longer, they are dispersed under his frown; the priesthood no honour claims, old age no pity.[1]

17 Quenched is the hope our eyes strained for, while hope was left us; looking for help so eagerly to a nation that had none to give!

18 Refuge for us in the treacherous highways is none; we are near the end; all is over, this is the end;

19 Swifter than flight of eagles the pursuit; even on the mountains they give chase, even in the desert take us by surprise.

20 Through our fault he who is breath of life to us, our anointed king, is led away captive;[2] under his shadow we hoped our race should thrive.

21 Until thy turn comes, shout on, Edom, triumph on, land of Hus; the same cup thou too shalt drink, and be drunken, and stripped bare.

22 Vengeful audit-day! Sion's account closed, recovered her fortunes; Edom called to account, discovered her guilt!

CHAPTER FIVE

BETHINK thee, Lord, of our ill case; see where we lie humiliated,
2 and seeing take pity! New tenants our lands have, our homes foreign
3 masters; orphaned sons of widowed mothers were not more defence-
4 less. Ours to buy the very water we drink, pay a price for every stick of
5 fire-wood; led hither and thither under the yoke, with no respite given,
6 we must make our peace with men of Egypt or Assyria, for a belly-full of
7 bread. So must we bear the guilt of our fathers, that sinned and are gone!
8 Slaves for our masters now, and none to ransom us; bread won out in the
10 desert, and at peril of our lives from the sword's point! What wonder if
our skins are burnt dry as an oven, seared by long famine?

11 Never a woman in Sion, never a maid in all Juda's cities, but has met
12 with dishonour; merciless hands hurry our princes to the gallows;
13 reverence is none for grey hairs. Toiling at the mill, the flower of our

---

[1] vv. 14-16. The interpretation of this passage is very doubtful. The Latin version is not always in accordance with the Hebrew text, and gives 'him' instead of 'them' in verse 15, perhaps with the idea that Almighty God is referred to (cf. verse 16).

[2] It is generally held that the literal and primary reference of this verse is to king Sedecias. The Hebrew text has, not 'through our fault,' but 'through the trap they have laid.'

14 youth, or staggering under loads of wood; ¹ never an old man left to sit
15 at the gate, or a young man to wake the echoes of the harp; gone, all our
16 mirth, all our music drowned in sadness. Alas, we are sinners; the
17 wreath has faded from our brows; there are sad hearts everywhere, and
18 dim eyes. What, does not the hill of Sion lie desolate, ravaged by the
foxes?

19 Lord, thou abidest ever; age after age thy throne endures; and wilt
thou still be forgetful of us, through the long years leave us forsaken?
21 Bring us back to thee, Lord, and let us find our home; bring back to us
22 the days of our youth; wouldst thou altogether abandon us, shall thy
indignation know no measure?

¹ The sense given is that of the Hebrew text; cf. Jg. 16.21.

THE PROPHECY OF BARUCH

CHAPTER ONE

THE words which follow were committed to writing in the country of Babylon. The writer of them, Baruch, was descended from Helcias,
2 through Nerias, Maasias, Sedecias and Sedei, and wrote in the fifth year, . . . on the seventh day of the month, at the time when the Chaldaeans
3 took Jerusalem and burnt it to the ground.[1] Baruch read this book of his aloud to Jechonias, son of Joachim, king of Juda. All the people, too,
4 flocked to hear the reading of it, nobles, and royal princes, and elders, and common folk high and low; all that were then living in the country of Babylon, near the river Sodi.

5 And as they heard it, all was weeping and fasting and prayer offered
6 in the Lord's presence; they made a collection of money besides, each
7 according to his means, which they sent to the chief priest, Joachim, son of Helcias, son of Salom, and his fellow priests and fellow citizens at
8 Jerusalem. . . . when he[2] travelled to Juda on the tenth day of Sivan, taking with him the sanctuary ornaments which had been removed from the temple, and were now to be restored. They were of silver; Sedecias,
9 the son of Josias, that now reigned in Juda, had had them made, when Jechonias, with the princes and all the nobles and many other citizens of

---

[1] It seems almost certain that the text is defective here; to mention the day of the month and not mention which month it was, would be most unusual. But probably the omission was a more considerable one. It is difficult to see how the events referred to in verses 6–8 could have happened in or near the year 587, when Jerusalem was burnt; it had been closely besieged for two years already. It looks as if these prophecies of Baruch had been dated over a period of years, like those of his master Jeremias (Jer. 1.2, 3), and only the earlier part of them had been sent to Jerusalem at the time indicated. The text will have run: 'in the fifth year of Sedecias' reign, right up to the eleventh year of it, the fifth month and the seventh day of the month, when the Chaldaeans took Jerusalem.'

[2] 'He' can hardly be Joachim; and the last mention of Baruch is too far away to justify a reference by pronoun. Another short deficiency in the text seems probable; the money was sent to Jerusalem 'by the hand of' some person named, Baruch or another. It is commonly assumed that Sedecias had made silver ornaments at Jerusalem, to replace the old ones which had been carried off; that these silver ones were carried off in their turn (on some unspecified occasion), and were then restored to Juda (for some unspecified reason). All this seems unduly elaborate. The gold ornaments were removed with Jechonias (IV Kg. 24.13), and at the same time all metal-workers were exiled (*ib.* 16). Sedecias, who was still in favour, had to get models made *not in Jerusalem but in Babylon;* and with these silver models the prophecy of Baruch, or rather such parts of it as had already been committed to writing, could conveniently be despatched.

Jerusalem, was carried off by Nabuchodonosor, king of Babylon, to his own country.

10 Here is money, they said, with which you are to buy victims for burnt-sacrifice, and incense; bloodless offerings [1] too you must make, and
11 amends for fault committed, at the altar of the Lord our God. You shall pray long life for king Nabuchodonosor of Babylon, and his son Bal-
12 tassar, that their reign on earth may last as long as heaven itself. May the Lord grant courage to all of us, and send us a gleam of hope; long thrive we under the protection of king Nabuchodonosor and his son Bal-
13 tassar, persevering loyally in their service and winning their favour! And intercede with the Lord our God for us exiles; against his divine will we
14 have rebelled, and to this hour he has not relented. Scan closely, too, this book we are sending to you; it is to be read aloud on feast days and
15 in times of solemn assembly. You shall make your prayer in these words following.

The fault was never with him, the Lord our God; ours the blush of shame, as all Juda this day and all the citizens of Jerusalem can witness.
16 With king and prince of ours, priest and prophet of ours the fault lies,
17 and with our fathers before us. We have defied the will of the Lord our
18 God; trust and loyalty we had none to give him, nor ever shewed him submission, by listening to his divine voice and following the commands
19 he gave us. Ever since the day when he rescued our fathers from Egypt we have been in rebellion against the Lord our God, straying ever further
20 from the sound of his voice; till at last, as these times can witness, bale and ban have caught us by the heels, the very same he pronounced to his servant Moses long ago, when he had rescued our fathers from Egypt and
21 was leading them on to a land all milk and honey. Unheeded, that divine voice, when message after message came to us through his pro-
22 phets; each must follow the whim of his own false heart, doing sacrifice to alien gods, and setting the will of the Lord, our own God, at defiance.

CHAPTER TWO

THAT is why the Lord our God has made good his threats against us; against the rulers of Israel, whether kings or nobles, and against the
2 common folk of Israel and Juda. Here was a threat made in the law of Moses, that went beyond all hitherto seen on earth, and yet in Jerusalem
3 it came true; that men would be eating the flesh of their owns sons and

---

[1] Literally 'manna,' but it is clear that the Septuagint Greek has confused two separate Hebrew words, and the Latin version has come to us through the Greek.

4 daughters! Neighbouring kings had the mastery, and in all the far countries to which the Lord had banished us, we became a thing of scorn and
5 horror. Slaves are we, that might have ruled; and the reason of it?
Because by sinning we offended the Lord our God, and left his voice
6 unheeded; his was never the fault; for us and for our fathers the blush
7 of shame, as this day can witness. No calamity has befallen us but he, the
8 Lord, had prophesied it; and still we would not sue for the divine mercy,
9 but each of us went on straying by false paths. That is why the Lord's
jealous care was for our undoing; he has but fulfilled what he threatened;
10 in all he has imposed upon us,[1] the Lord our God is without fault. It was
our fault if we would not listen to his warnings, would not follow the
divine commands which he set before us.

11 Lord God of Israel, whose constraining hand rescued thy people from
Egypt with portents and wonders, with sovereign power signally mani-
12 fested, and won thee renown that is thine yet, we are sinners! We have
13 wronged thee, revolted against every claim thou hast upon us. But oh,
would thy vengeance give over the pursuit! So wide thou hast parted us,
14 and we are left so few. Grant a hearing, Lord, to this our plaint and
plea; for thy own honour, be our rescuer still, and win over the hearts of
15 our captors; prove to the whole world that thou art the Lord our God,
16 that it was thy name Israel bore, and Israel's race yet bears. Look down
upon us, Lord, from the sanctuary where thou dwellest; thine be the
17 attentive ear, the watchful eye! Once breath has left body, and a man lies
18 in the grave, honour and devoir is none he can pay thee; but let a man be
downcast over his great misfortune, so that he goes bowed and tottering,
dim eyes and hungry belly, there, Lord, thou shalt have the honour that
is thy due.

19 Well for us, O Lord our God, as we pour out our supplications for thy
mercy, if we could plead that fathers of ours, kings of ours, did loyally
20 thy will. But no; thou hadst given them due warning, through those
prophets that were servants of thine, before letting thy angry vengeance
21 have its way, and the warning went unheeded.[2] Bow shoulder and bow
neck, said the divine voice, and be vassals to the king of Babylon; and the
22 land I gave to your fathers shall still be your home. Refuse to serve the
king of Babylon at my divine bidding, and Jerusalem with her daughter
23 cities shall mourn their loss; no more the cry of joy and mirth, no more
the voice of bridegroom and of bride; untrodden the whole land shall be,
24 and uninhabited. But all thy threats could not persuade them to be the

---

[1] This is usually understood of God's commandments, but the context suggests rather a reference to his chastisements.
[2] 'And the warning went unheeded'; these words are not in the original, but
are supplied here from the context in order to make the connexion between
verses 19 and 20 intelligible.

king of Babylon's vassals; thy servants prophesied in vain. And so thy
threats were performed; kings of ours and fathers of ours might not rest
25 quiet in their graves; their bones were cast out to endure sun's heat and
night frost, and great anguish they endured in their deaths, from the
26 sword, and famine, and pestilence.[1] As for the temple that was the shrine
of thy name, thou madest it into the thing it is this day, for Israel's sin,
for Juda's sin.

27 No greater proof we could have had of thy consideration, of that abun-
28 dant mercy [2] which is thine. And merciful was the promise thou didst
make to thy servant Moses, when thou badest him write down thy law
29 for Israel's acceptance. Out of all this thronging multitude, thou didst
say to him, what a sorry remnant of scattered exiles will be left, if my
30 voice goes unheeded! And go unheeded it will; this is a race that ever
spurns the yoke. What then if they come back to a right mind, there in the
31 country of their banishment? What if they learn to recognize that I, the
Lord, am their God (the heedful heart, the listening ear, are mine to give
32 them); what if they remember to honour me, to invoke my name, in their
33 exile? What if they follow the example of their fathers, that were sinners
before them, repent of their stubborn indifference and of all their ill
34 doings? Then they shall come home again; back to the country I promised to their fathers, Abraham, Isaac and Jacob; they shall be masters
35 of it, and their dwindled strength shall thrive anew. A fresh covenant
I will make with them, that shall last for ever; I their God, and they my
people; never again will I banish my people, the sons of Israel, from the
land I have made theirs.

CHAPTER THREE

LORD Almighty, God of Israel, here be lives in jeopardy, here be
2 troubled hearts, that plead with thee! Listen, Lord, and have mercy,
3 none so merciful as thou; pardon the sins that lie open in thy sight. Thou
4 reignest for ever; must we for ever be lost? Lord Almighty, God of
Israel, listen to the prayer Israel makes to thee from the grave![3] Our

---

[1] The Greek word used here (of which the Latin gives a literal rendering)
means 'a despatching of envoys,' and does not justify the translation 'banishment.' It is probably used here, as in Jer. 32.36, to represent the Hebrew word
for 'pestilence,' as something specially sent by Almighty God.

[2] In verses 19–26, the 'mercy' referred to consists in the warning issued to
the Jews against further resistance. In verses 27–35 the same mercy is shewn
in the promise of ultimate restoration.

[3] Literally, 'the prayer of the dead of Israel.' Some think this refers to prayer
offered by the dead on behalf of the living; others, that the race of Israel is,
by a metaphor, described as 'dead'; others, that the Hebrew text had simply
'the folk of Israel,' and that the Greek translator, having no vowel-points to
guide him, was deceived by the identical form of the two words.

fathers it was that defied the Lord their God, and gave no heed to him;
5 and to us, their sons, the punishment clings. Forget the wrong they did,
those fathers of ours; remember thy ancient power, thy own honour,
6 this day; only to thee, the Lord our God, shall praise of ours be given.
7 Why else hast thou inspired us with such dread of thee? Thou wouldst
have us learn to invoke thy name, to utter thy praise, here as exiles, in
proof that we disown the wrong our fathers did, when their sins defied
8 thee. Exiles we are this day, dispersed by thee to suffer scorn and reviling,
until we have made amends for all the wrong our fathers did when they
abandoned thee, abandoned the Lord our God.

9 Listen, Israel, to the warnings that shall bring thee life; give attentive
10 audience, if thou wouldst learn to be wise. What means it, Israel, that
11 thou findest thyself in the enemy's land, grown old in exile, unclean as
a dead body, no more taken into account than men who have gone down
12 into their graves? It is because thou hast forsaken the fountains whence
13 all wisdom comes. If thou hadst but followed the path God shewed thee,
14 thou mightest have lived in peace eternally. Learn where to find wisdom,
and strength, and discernment; so thou wilt find length of years, too,
15 and true life, and cheerfulness, and peace. Who can tell where wisdom
16 dwells, who has made his way into her store-house? What has become
of those heathen princes, who gained mastery of the beasts that roam the
17 earth, tamed the birds for their pastime; heaping up silver and gold,
man's confidence, man's interminable quest? How anxiously they toiled
for wealth! And now these devices of theirs are beyond our tracing.

19 They disappeared, went to their graves, and others succeeded them;
20 a younger generation saw the light and peopled the earth in its turn; but
21 still they could not find their way to the true wisdom, the path to it
was hidden still. Their children, too, clutched at it in vain, it was as far
22 as ever from their reach. In Chanaan, none had heard tell of it, in
23 Theman none had caught sight of it; even the sons of Agar, so well
schooled in earthly wisdom, even the merchants of Merrha and Theman,
with all their store of legend, their skill and cunning laboriously gained,
never found the track of true wisdom, or told us what its haunts were.
24 Israel, how wide is God's house, how spacious is his domain, large
26 beyond all bound, high beyond all measure! [1] The heroes of old were
nurtured there, men whose fame has come down to us from the beginning
27 of time, huge in stature, great warriors; but it was not these God had
28 chosen; they died without ever attaining true knowledge. Not for them
was the possession of wisdom, and in their folly they perished.
29 What man ever scaled heaven, gained wisdom there, and brought it

---

[1] *v.* 24 sqq. God's 'house' is usually identified as creation generally. But it
must be confessed that this reference to the giants belongs to a stream of tradition about which we know little.

30 back from the clouds? What man ever crossed the sea, and found it there,
31 brought it back like a cargo of pure gold? The path to it none may know,
32 the clue of it none may find. Only he who knows all things possesses it,
     only his mind conceives it. He it is who framed the abiding earth, and
33 filled it with cattle and four-footed beasts of every kind. It is on his
     errand that the light goes forth, his summons that it obeys with awe;
34 joyfully the stars shine out, keeping the watches he has appointed,   answer
     when he calls their muster-roll, and offer their glad radiance to him who
36 fashioned them. Such a God is ours; what rival will be compared to
37 him? He it is who has the key to all knowledge, and gave it to his servant
38 Jacob, to the well-loved race of Israel; not till then would he reveal
     himself on earth, and hold converse with mortal men.

CHAPTER FOUR

HERE is the book [1] in which you may read God's commandments, that
law of his which can never be abrogated; holding fast by it or for-
2 saking it, a man makes life or death his goal. Jacob, thy steps retrace,
    and this path follow, guiding thy steps by glow of the light that beckons
3 thee; this is thy pride, wouldst thou yield it up to another? Thy prize,
4 shall an alien race enjoy it? Israel, a blessed race is ours, that has know-
    ledge of God's will.
5   People of God, take courage, all that is left of Israel's muster-roll!
6 Sold as slaves though you be, he does not mean your ruin. He has given
    your enemies the mastery, none the less; had you not defied his ven-
7 geance? Had you not challenged the eternal power that made you, by
8 sacrificing to evil powers, that gods were none? To God that fostered
    you, what ingratitude, to Jerusalem that nursed you, what bitter pain!
9   Alas, she cried, as she saw the divine vengeance falling on you, listen,
    neighbour cities all, to my complaint; here is a heavy load of grief God
10 has charged me with! Sentence of banishment he, the eternal, has pro-
11 nounced upon my people, sons and daughters of mine; how joyously I
12 nurtured them, with what tears of anguish I saw them depart! And let
    none boast over my widowing, that so much have lost; if I am thus for-
13 lorn, it is because of my sons' transgression, that refused God's will; his
    claim disowned, his paths left untrodden; not for them the straight road
14 of loyal observance. Come, neighbours, tell we the sad tale again, how he,
    the eternal, would sentence these sons and daughters of mine to exile.
15 A cruel race he summoned to the attack from far away, men of an alien
16 speech; for old age they had no reverence, for childhood no pity; robbed
    widow of her darling sons, and left her desolate.

---

[1] Apparently in the sense that wisdom is to be identified with the divine law.

17 Alas, my children, look not to me for aid! He it is must save you from
19 the power of your enemies, who is the author of your calamity. Go your
20 ways, my children, go your ways; I am left desolate; the festal robe of
    happier times I have put aside, clothed myself in sackcloth as the sup-
21 pliants do; I will spend my days pleading with him, the eternal. Take
    courage, my children, and raise your voices, too, in appeal; from the
22 enemy's tyrant grasp the Lord shall deliver you. Upon him, the eternal,
    I pin evermore my hopes of your happiness, the holy God, evermore our
    deliverer! Light grows my heart, to think of the mercy he has in store for
23 you. With lamentation I bade farewell to you, and with tears; with joy
24 and triumph he will bring you back to me, and for ever; these neighbours
    of mine, that saw you banished at his decree, shall witness ere long a
    divine deliverance; what renown shall be yours when it comes, what
25 dawn unending! Bear patiently, my children, with the punishment that
    has overtaken you. What if thy enemy hunts thee down? Ere long thou
26 shalt see the ruin of him, set thy foot on his neck! Ah, the rough roads
    delicate feet of yours have travelled! Like a plundered flock the enemy
27 drove you. Yet take courage, my children, and cry out upon the Lord;
28 he, the author of your exile, has not forgotten you. Hearts that loved to
    stray, ten times more eagerly retrace your steps, and come back to him!
29 And he, that compassed your woe, in unfading joy will compass your
    deliverance.
30 Thyself, Jerusalem, take courage! He that called thee by thy name
31 brings thee comfort. Woe to the men that harassed thee, and triumphed
32 in thy ruin, woe to every city that enslaved and harboured children of
33 thine! No smile of content greeted the disaster of thy fall, but shall be
34 paid for with a sigh of desolation; the city that was once so populous, all
35 its boasting gone, all its pride of yesterday turned into lament! Long shall
    the fires of eternal justice smoulder there, long shall it be the haunt of
    devils.[1]
36 Turn thee about, Jerusalem, and look to the sun's rising; see what
37 rejoicing the Lord has in store for thee; sons of thine, in many lands
    lost to thee, gathered from east to west shall come back again, praising
    joyfully God's holy will.

CHAPTER FIVE

ENOUGH, Jerusalem; lay aside now the sad garb of thy humiliation,
and put on bright robes, befitting the eternal glory God means for

---

[1] The same Greek word is translated 'satyrs' in Is. 13.21. Some think the
reference is to wild goats.

2 thee; cloak of divine protection [1] thrown about thee, thy temples bearing
3 a diadem of renown.   In thee God will manifest the splendour of his
4 presence, for the whole world to see;   and the name by which he will call
5 thee for ever is, Loyalty rewarded, Piety crowned.[2]   Up, Jerusalem, to
   the heights! Look to the sun's rising, and see if thy sons be not coming
   to thee, gathered from east to west, joyfully acknowledging God's holy
6 will!   Afoot they were led off by the enemy; it is the Lord that shall lead
7 them home, borne aloft like royal princes.   He will have the ground made
   level; high mountain must stoop, and immemorial hill, and the valleys
8 be filled up, for Israel's safe passage and God's glory;   spinneys of every
   scented tree shall grow, by his divine command, to give Israel shade.
9 So merciful he is, and so faithful! In great content, their journey lit by
   the majesty of his presence, Israel shall come home.

CHAPTER SIX

Here follows a copy of the letter Jeremias sent to the prisoners whom the
king of Babylon was carrying off to his own country, with the warnings
God bade him give them.

FOR the assoiling of the sins by which you have offended God, you
shall now be carried off to Babylon, by Nabuchodonosor that is king
2 of it.   Babylon once reached, you shall have a long exile there, years
   a many, till seven generations [3] have passed; then I will grant you a safe
3 return.   And you must know that you will see, in that country, gods of
   gold and silver, gods of stone and wood, that are carried about on men's
4 shoulders; to the heathen, things of great dread.   Look well to it that you
   do not fall in with these alien customs, by the same fear overmastered.
5 What though a great throng of worshippers attends them, before and
   behind? Let your hearts whisper in adoration, To thee, Lord, all worship
6 belongs!   My angel is at your side, and your lives shall be held to account
   for it.[4]

---

[1] 'Divine protection'; literally 'justice,' that is, a renewal of the covenant
between Israel and their God, with the obligations of it fulfilled on either side.
    [2] Literally, 'Prosperity (which comes) of justice (see last note), and Honour
(which comes) of Piety.'
    [3] It is not easy to see how this computation is arrived at. Notoriously the exile
of Juda was expected to last seventy years. If, therefore, our versions correctly
represent the figures given in the original, and the word 'generation' has its
ordinary meaning, it would appear that the beginning of the exile is dated here,
not by the capture of Jerusalem in B.C. 598, but by the destruction of Samaria
in B.C. 722. This would give, roughly, seven generations of thirty years each
down to Zorobabel, or seven generations of forty years each down to Nehemias.
    [4] Literally, 'I will require your lives.' Some think this means, 'I will require

7   Puppets of gold and silver, speak they cannot, for all the craftsman has
8 given them tongues to speak with.   Ay, gold must go to their fashioning,
9 never was maid so bravely tricked out;   gods they are, and must wear
   golden crowns. And of this gold and silver the priests will steal some part
10 for their own uses,   and spend it on their minions; what the gods wore,
11 harlots wear, what harlots wore, the gods.[1]   From rust they cannot pro-
12 tect themselves, nor from the moth;   alas for the purple robes that deck
   them! And the temple dust lies thick upon them, so that their faces must
13 be wiped clean.   Here is an idol bearing a sceptre, human-fashion, as
   though it ruled the countryside, yet has it no power to kill the blas-
14 phemer;   another carries sword or axe, yet from alarm of war or of rob-
15 bers cannot defend itself; be sure, then, gods they are not.   Never fear
   them; broken jar a man throws away as useless can be matched with such
   gods as these.

16   There they sit in their temples, with eyes full of dust from the feet of
17 passers-by,   mewed up by their priests with bolt and bar for fear of rob-
18 bery, like king's enemy in his dungeon, dead man in his tomb;   of all the
   lights that burn before them, they see none; roof-beam is not more sense-
19 less.   Yet men will have it that serpents creep out of the earth and drink
   in the secrets of their hearts![2]   Worms, more like, that eat the idol up,
20 clothes and all, and it none the wiser.   Smoke of the temple blackens their
21 faces;   about their bodies and heads fly owl and swallow; birds hover and
22 cats prowl.   Be sure they are no gods; never fear them.

23   Fair, golden faces! Yet will they not shine on the worshipper, till he
   rub off the stains on them; cast once for all in a mould, without feeling.[3]
24 Cost what they will, there is never a breath of life in them;   never a pace

---

(or perhaps, according to the Greek, he will require) satisfaction from anyone
who takes your lives.'

[1] Literally, 'They give some of it to prostitutes, and deck out harlots, and
again when they have received it from harlots, they deck out their gods.' The
Greek has 'They give some of it to the harlots on the roof; and they deck out
the gods in clothes, like men, gods of silver and gold and wood.' Such a variation between the two versions must indicate that the Hebrew original was
very obscure, or that its text had suffered from corruptions. And indeed,
throughout this chapter it is impossible to feel that the versions have always
caught the meaning of the original exactly.

[2] Literally, 'And they say that serpents from the earth lick out their hearts,
while they eat them and their clothes, unfelt by them.' The Greek has 'creeping
things' instead of serpents. If the meaning of the original has been preserved,
the reference is perhaps to the belief in snakes as an incarnation of heathen
divinities; cf. Aristophanes, *Plutus* 736.

[3] Literally, 'The gold, too, which they have is for appearance; unless a man
rubs off the stains, they will not shine, and if it comes to that, they had no feeling
while they were being cast.' The Greek has, 'Unless a man rubs off the stains,
they will not cause to shine the gold with which they are beautified . . .' etc.

they walk, but must still be carried on men's shoulders, putting their
26 own worshippers to shame by the betrayal of their impotence. Fall they
to earth, they cannot rise from it, and though they be set up again, it is
in no power of their own that they stand. As well bring gifts to dead men
27 as to these; the victim thou offerest yonder priest will sell, or put to his
own use, nor ever a slice his wife cuts shall find its way to the sick and the
28 needy. Those offerings every woman may touch if she will, child-birth
and monthly times notwithstanding. And are these gods? Are these to be
29 feared? Things of silver and gold and wood, that have women for their
ministers, shall the divine name be theirs?

30   In their temples you shall find priests sitting by with clothes rent,
31 shaven and shorn, heads uncovered,   raising lament over their gods as at
32 a dead man's dirge. Vestments their idols wore they will carry away, to
33 dress their wives and children; so powerless are these gods to requite
injury or reward service done. Not theirs to make kings or unmake them,
34 grant riches, or wreak vengeance; the unpaid vow they cannot exact,
35 nor deliver men from death, and the tyrant's oppression,   give sight to
37 the blind, succour in time of peril,   shew mercy to the widow, or cheer
38 the orphan's lot. Things of wood and stone, gold and silver, no more
39 than rock on the mountain-side can they speed their worshippers; gods
do we reckon them, gods do we call them?

40   And indeed the Chaldeans themselves have but scant reverence for
these idols of theirs; hear they of a dumb child that can utter no word,
Bel's image must be brought to it and petitioned for the gift of speech;
41 as if the senseless thing which cannot move could yet hear them! Sense
42 neither god nor worshipper has, else god should find no worship.[1]   See
where their women sit in the streets, with ropes about them, each before
43 a fire of olive-stones,[2]   each waiting till some passer-by drags her away and
beds her, then taunting her less coveted neighbours, that have ropes
44 about them still! All lies, the worship of them, and shall they claim the
title of gods?

45   Carpenters made them and goldsmiths, only at the priests' whim; and
47 shall the handiwork of mortal craftsmen be divine? One day, their
48 descendants will reproach them with a legacy of imposture. Come war,

---

[1] *vv.* 40, 41. The meaning here is very uncertain. The Greek almost certainly
implies that Bel's image was brought to the patient, not the patient to the
image, and the meaning is perhaps that it was absurd to expect help from a
statue which had to be carried because it could not walk (cf. verse 25). There
are several differences between the Greek and the Latin; the Greek, for example, has 'sick person' in the masculine, whereas the neuter gender used in
the Latin presumably implies a child in arms.

[2] This ceremony of general prostitution is described by Herodotus, i.199; he
does not mention the fires of olive-stones (or bran, according to the Greek).

come peril, the priest thinks only of hiding himself and his gods both;
49 gods who shall think them, that from war and peril their own selves
50 cannot deliver? Recognize it at last they will, kings and peoples everywhere, that gods of wood, gold and silver are false gods, creatures of man,
51 not creators. Man's handiwork, with nothing in them of the divine, who
52 can doubt it? Not through them comes king to throne, comes rain to
53 country folk; redress wrong they may not, nor rid a people of tyranny;
54 dead crow hung between heaven and earth is not more powerless. Does
a temple catch fire? You shall see priests taking refuge in flight, and the
wooden gods, for all the silver and gold on them, burning among the
55 woodwork. Against the king's power, against the enemy's attack, they
can make no head; who shall reckon them or name them divine?

56   Wood and stone, gold and silver, how to protect themselves against
57 the superior strength of house-breaker and robber, that will carry off
sheathes of silver and gold, carry off the clothes from their backs, and
58 leave them powerless? Better some golden emblem of royal prowess, cup
of silver meant for use, not only for display, door of wood that keeps safe
59 the treasures of a house, than these deceiving idols![1] How fair to look
upon are sun and moon and stars! Yet theirs is loyal and useful service;
60 and so it is with yonder lightning, that dazzles the view. Everywhere
61 winds blowing, clouds drifting across the earth as God bade them, fulfil
62 an appointed task; an appointed task, too, has the heaven-lit fire that
burns mountain-side and forest. What beauty have the idols, or what
63 power, that they should be compared with any of these? Gods never
think them, gods never call them, that have no power to execute judge-
64 ment, to do men good or ill. And, since gods they are not, need is none
65 to fear them; can they pronounce a curse or a blessing on kings? Can
they startle the world with portents, shine like the sun, light up darkness
67 like the moon? Why, the very beasts are their betters, that know at least
how to take shelter for their own safety!

68   Fear we never the gods that ungod themselves so plainly! Wood and
silver and gold, that watch over the world as a scare-crow over a herb-
70 garden; wood and silver and gold, patient of the birds that perch on them
71 as bush of white-thorn, or corpse left to lie in a dark alley! From the
purple robes that rot on them, you may learn they are no gods; they, too,
shall be eaten away when their time comes, and be a disgrace to the countryside.

72   Well it is for God's loyal servants, that eschew idolatry, and live from
all censure far removed.

---

[1] Literally, 'So it is better to be a king making display of his power, or a
useful vessel in a house of which its owner is proud, or a door in a house
which guards its contents, than false gods.' The Greek adds, 'or a wooden
pillar in a palace' after the word 'contents.'

THE PROPHECY OF EZECHIEL

CHAPTER ONE

THIRTY years had passed;[1] it was the fifth day of the fourth month,
and I was sharing the lot of the exiles by the river Chobar, when
2 heaven opened, and I saw a vision of God. The fifth day of the month,
3 and the fifth year since king Joachim was banished. To the priest
Ezechiel, son of Buzi, the divine word came; there in the Chaldaean land,
by the river Chobar, the power of the Lord could reach him.
4   I looked round me, to find that a storm-wind had sprung up from the
north, driving a great cloud before it; and this cloud had fire caught
up in it, that fringed it with radiance. And there in the heart of it, in the
5 very heart of the fire, was a glow like amber, that enclosed four living
6 figures. These were human in appearance, but each had four faces, and
7 two pairs of wings. Either leg was straight-formed, yet ended in a calf's
8 hoof; they sparkled like red-hot bronze. On each of the four sides, human
arms shewed beneath the wings; faces and wings looked outwards four
9 ways.[2] Wings of each were held touching wings of other; and when they
10 moved, they did not turn round, but each kept an onward course. As for
the appearance of their faces, each had the face of a man, yet each of the
four looked like a lion when seen from the right, like an ox when seen
11 from the left, like an eagle when seen from above.[3] So much for their
faces; each had two wings spread out above him, those two which met his
12 neighbours' wings; with the other two he veiled his body. Each of them
marched straight forward, following the movement of a divine impulse,
13 never swerving as he marched. There was that, too, in the appearance
of the living figures which put me in mind of flaming coals, or of torches;
that was what I saw going to and fro in the midst of the living figures,
14 a glow as of fire, and from this glow lightning came out. So the living
creatures came and went, vivid as lightning-flashes.

---

[1] This must refer either to the prophet's age, or to some date artificially
chosen, *e.g.*, the rediscovery of the law under Josias.

[2] It is not easy to form a clear picture of what the prophet saw; but it seems
most probable that the four figures stood back to back in a square, the eight
upper wings all touching. If so, the 'four sides' will be the four sides of the
square, and each angel will have had one arm (or hand) shewing underneath
either of his lower wings.

[3] If the assumption made in the previous note is true, we can understand
why no reference is made to the appearance of the angelic body from behind;
we are given a view from above instead. But the Hebrew text and the other
versions omit the word 'above,' leaving the whole picture in considerable
confusion.

15   And as I watched the living figures, all at once wheels appeared close
16   to them, one at each of the four sides, of strange colour and form. All
      four were alike, the colour of aquamarine,[1] and each looked like a wheel
17   within a wheel. Moved they, it was ever one of the four ways the living
18   figures looked; and they did not turn round in moving. As for their size,
      their height was terrible to look upon; and the whole frame of them, all
19   round, was full of eyes. Onward the wheels moved, when the living
      figures moved onward, at their side; rose above the earth when the living
20   figures rose above it. They too had a living impulse in them, they too,
      whenever that impulse stirred them, must rise up and follow the way it
21   went; with the living figures, whose vital impulse they shared, the
      wheels too moved, and halted, and rose.
22   Over the living figures a vault seemed to rise, like a sheet of dazzling
23   crystal resting on their heads; under this vault each held two wings erect
      to meet his neighbour's. Each had two turned upwards to overshadow
24   him, and two turned downwards to veil his body.[2] When they moved,
      the sound of their wings reached me, loud as waters in flood or thunders
      from on high,[3] incessant as the hum of a great throng or an armed camp;
25   only when they came to rest did they lower their wings. A voice would
      come from the firmament over their heads; then they would halt, then
26   they would lower their wings.[4] Above this vault that rested on them,
      sapphire blue towered up into the form of a throne, nor did that throne
27   seem to be empty; a shape was there above it, as of one enthroned, and
      all about him it was filled with amber-coloured flame. Upwards from his
28   loins, downwards from his loins, an arch of light seemed to shine, like
      rainbow among the clouds on a day of storm; there was brightness all
      about him.

---

[1] Literally, 'a vision of the sea.' The Latin translators seem to have supposed,
here as in Is. 23.10 and elsewhere, that 'Tharsis' was a Hebrew word meaning
'sea.' (In 10.9 the rendering given is 'chrysolith'). Here, as in Ex. 28.20, it
evidently means some kind of precious stone, possibly jasper. It is doubtful
whether the phrase 'a wheel within a wheel' describes a wheel with an inner
circle joining its spokes in addition to the outside rim, or two wheels inter-
secting one another at right angles, forming a kind of approach to a sphere.

[2] The Hebrew text of this verse is perhaps corrupt; it seems to imply that
each angel used all four wings to veil his body, which is in contradiction with
all the other evidence this chapter provides. The statement in the Latin version that 'each of them veiled his body with two wings, and the other one was
veiled similarly' yields no acceptable sense.

[3] Literally, 'the voice of the most High'; it seems clear that thunder is referred to, cf. Apoc. 14.2.

[4] This is the sense given in the Latin version to a sentence in the Hebrew
which is obscure, and perhaps corrupt.

CHAPTER TWO

SO much I saw of what the Lord's glory is like; and seeing it, I fell down face to earth. And now I heard a voice, which said to me, Rise 2 up, son of man, I must have speech with thee.   And at his words, a divine force mastered me, raising me to my feet, so that I could listen to him. 3 Son of man, he told me, I am sending thee on an errand to the men of Israel, this heathen brood that has rebelled and forsaken me; see how my covenant has been violated by the fathers yesterday, the children to-day! 4 To brazen-faced folk and hard-hearted thy errand is, and still from the 5 Lord God a message thou must deliver,   hear they or deny thee hearing; rebels all, at least they shall know that they have had a prophet in their 6 midst.   Never fear them, son of man, never let rebuke of theirs dishearten thee; with the unbelieving and the unruly [1] thou must learn to live, scorpions ever at thy side; rebels all, they must not frighten thee, must 7 not dishearten thee.   Hear they or deny thee hearing, remonstrate with them thou must; they are a defiant brood. 8   Do my bidding, then, son of man; no rebel thou, like those others; 9 open thy mouth and eat what I give thee.   And with that, I saw a hand stretched out towards me, with a closed book in it; and this, when he opened it to my view, had writing on both sides of it; nothing was there but dirge and lamenting, nothing but cries of woe.

CHAPTER THREE

SON of man, he told me, eat thou must what eat thou canst; here is this roll for thy eating. After that, go and give my message to the sons 2 of Israel.   Thereupon I opened my mouth, and he gave me the scroll to 3 eat,   promising me safe digestion and a full belly with the gift; and indeed, 4 it was sweet as honey when I ate it.   Now, son of man, said he, to the men 5 of Israel betake thee, and give them my message.   Are they strange folk 6 that lisp and stammer,[2] these men of Israel? Ah, no;   nations there are a many that lisp and stammer, past thy understanding, but I am sending 7 thee to Israel instead. These might have listened to thee;[3]   hearing from

---

[1] The Hebrew text is generally interpreted as meaning 'thorns and briers.'

[2] Literally, 'of deep speech and unknown tongue'; in the Hebrew text, 'of deep lips and heavy tongue.' The language of the other Semitic races suggested an attempt to talk Hebrew under difficulties.

[3] Literally, in the Latin, 'If I were sending thee to these, they would be listening to thee.' The sense of the Hebrew text is probably, 'But no, I am sending thee to these (the Israelites). These (the other nations) would be listening to thee.'

Israel thou shalt have none; my word goes ever unheeded, so brazen-
8 faced they are and so hard-hearted, all the brood of them.   Yet eyes of
thine, I promise thee, shall outstare them, forehead of thine shall out-
9 brazen them;   flint nor adamant is more unyielding than the resolve that
shall inspire thee. Fear them not, nor shun their looks, rebels ever, rebels
all.

10   Then he said to me, Son of man, all the words I tell thee heed and hear;
11 then to captive Israel betake thee, and give them thy message in the name
12 of the Lord God, hear they or deny thee hearing. And with that, a sudden
transport seized me, and as I went, I heard the noise of a great stir behind
me.... Blessed be the glory of the Lord ... from the place where he was.[1]
13 Beat of wing against wing as the living figures moved onwards, and whirr
of the wheels that followed them, great stirring there was all about me;
14 and I, in a transport borne up and on, set out on my journey, unwillingly
enough, and vexed at heart, but the Lord's hand was there to hold me to
15 my purpose.   So I made my way to the settlement of exiles at Tel-Abib,[2]
near the river Chobar; and when I had found them, I sat there for seven
days in their company, dumb all the while with grief.

16   Then, when seven days had passed, the Lord's word came to me.
17 Son of man, he told me, I am posting thee here as a sentry, to give the
sons of Israel warning; no message I send thee but thou must pass it on in
18 my name.   Threaten I the sinner with doom of death, if word thou givest
him none, nor warnest him, as his life he loves, to have done with sinning,
die he shall as he deserves, but for his undoing thyself shalt be called to
19 account.   If thou warn him, and his rebellious sinning leave he will not,
20 die he shall as he deserves, and thou go free.   Or let the upright man
leave his innocence, and I take him unawares in his wrong-doing, dies he
for want of warning? Die he shall, his good deeds all forgotten, but thou
21 for his undoing shall be called to account.   Thine to warn the upright
man against the marring of his innocence; and he, sin avoiding, shall owe
his life to thy remonstrance; thy duty is done.[3]

22   Then the power of the Lord came over me, bidding me rise up and
23 keep tryst with him, out in the open plain.   Rise up I did, and when I
reached the open plain, there was the glory of the Lord rising above it,
24 such as I had seen it by the banks of Chobar; and I fell face to earth.   But
a divine force mastered me and raised me to my feet again. Now go

---

[1] If one consonant is altered, the Hebrew text would give the sense, 'I heard
the noise of a great stir behind me, as the glory of the Lord rose up from the
place where it was.'
[2] Tel-Abib (not the modern Tel-Aviv, in Palestine) is translated, instead
of being transliterated, in the Latin version; 'to the Mound of New Crops.'
[3] *vv.* 16–21. The sense of these verses, and in great part the actual language
of them, can be found repeated in ch. 33, and some think they have been misplaced here through an error.

25 within doors, he said, and shut thyself in there . . . And thou, son of man . . . here are bonds confining thee; closely thy fellow countrymen shall keep thee imprisoned, so that thou canst not escape from them.

26 And I, meanwhile, will keep tongue of thine fast fixed in thy throat; dumb thou shalt be, when thou wouldst fain expostulate with a rebellious brood.

27 Then, when my message I give thee, I will unseal thy lips, and thou shalt speak to that rebellious brood in the name of the Lord God, hear they or deny thee hearing.[1]

CHAPTER FOUR

AND now, son of man, go and get thee a tile; set it before thee and

2 make marks on it, to represent the city of Jerusalem. This thou art to beleaguer; siege-works built, mound raised, camp pitched, battering-

3 rams all around.[2] And therewithal get thee an iron cooking-pan, that shall make a ring of iron between thee and this city of thine; look closely as thou wilt, here is siege complete, So thou shalt beleaguer it; a sign, this, for the race of Israel.

4 This, too, thou must do; ever on thy left side lie down to sleep, weighing it down, day after day as thou sleepest upon it, with the guilt of

5 Israel; bear it thou must. Three hundred days of guilt-bearing I have

6 allotted thee, one day for every year of Israel's guilt; this done, Juda's guilt thou must bear for forty days yet, sleeping on thy right side; a day

7 for a year, for every year a day. And ever towards beleaguered Jerusalem thou shalt turn thy face, and hold thy arm stretched out, prophesying its

8 doom; I hold thee enchained, and never shalt thou turn from one side to other, till the days of thy siege are over.[3]

---

[1] *vv.* 24–27. There has perhaps been some fault in the manuscript transmission of these verses, which run very awkwardly. The Hebrew text has 'so that thou canst not go out among them' instead of 'so that thou canst not escape from them.'

[2] *vv.* 1, 2. It is not clear whether the prophet was to draw a map, or simply to write the name, of Jerusalem. The directions in verse 2 may be simply an anticipation of verse 3; the rim of the iron cooking-vessel was to represent the continuous cordon of besiegers.

[3] *vv.* 4–8. The word rendered 'to sleep' in the Latin may also mean 'to lie,' and it is generally understood that the prophet was to remain all day and all night in the same posture. The figures are extremely perplexing. We should have expected that the days would be equal in number with those of the siege, but this, according to IV Kg. 25, lasted about 500 days. The forty years fall short of the interval between the taking of Samaria in 722 and the taking of Jerusalem in 586. And we should expect the other figure to correspond with the number of years between the division of the Kingdom and the fall of Samaria, *i.e.*, about 410 years; instead of which the Hebrew text gives 390, and the Septuagint Greek 190.

9   For thy food, wheat thou must have by thee, and barley, and beans,
and lentils, and spelt, and vetch; all in one pan mix them, and make thee
bread, while thou art sleeping ever on the same side; for three hundred
10 and ninety days thou shalt eat it.[1]   Nine ounces shall be all thy daily food,
11 at set times apportioned, and water thou shalt drink at set times, two
12 pints by measure. Cooked in the ashes thy bread, like barley cakes, and
13 dung of man shall be thy fuel, for all to see. Polluted as this, the Lord
says, shall be the bread Israel eats, in the land I have decreed for his exile.
14   Alas, alas, Lord God, said I, here is a soul that never knew defilement;
from childhood's days, beast I never ate that died by chance or lay
15 mangled, nor ever did food unclean cross my lips. Be it so, he answered;
for dung of man droppings of cattle thou shalt have, and cook thy bread
16 with these. But be sure of this, son of man; I mean to cut off from Jerusalem every source of bread; weighed out to them their bread shall be,
17 and anxiously, measured out to them their water, and in great lack. And
at last, for want of bread and water, every man's face shall fall as he
looks at other, and they shall pine away in their guilt.

CHAPTER FIVE

AND next, son of man, to the sharp sword betake thee! A razor thou
must take, and pass it over head and beard both; then weigh thy hair
2 in the scales and make equal portions of it. A third of it thou shalt set
alight and burn up within this city of thine, when the days of its besieging
are over; a third thou shalt cut to pieces with the blade thou carriest,
round about it; and a third thou shalt scatter to the winds, for my un-
3 sheathed sword to go in pursuit. Of this last third, gather some few hairs
4 and secure them in the fold of thy cloak; yet even of these take some
away and throw them into the heart of the fire, to burn there; fire enough
to kindle the whole race of Israel![2]
5   Look you, says the Lord God, here is Jerusalem, that I have set down
6 at earth's very midst, the nations all about her, and she has defied my
will, than the very heathen more rebellious, defied my commandments,
as neighbouring peoples never did. My bidding they have cast to the
7 winds, followed never where my commandments led. All your neighbours, the Lord God says, outdone in wickedness, my paths untrodden,
my bidding unheeded! False even to the heathen traditions of yonder
8 countryside! Have at thee, says the Lord God; in thy very heart I will

---

[1] The different kinds of crop are probably meant to symbolize the simultaneous deficiency of all bread-stuffs; cf. verse 16.

[2] It is not clear what is meant by the last clause of this verse.

9 execute judgement for all the world to see; such punishment I will inflict
10 as never was before, never shall be again, for thy detestable doings. Men's
flesh men shall eat, father of son and son of father; then, when my sentence is executed, I will scatter all that is left of thee to the four winds.
11   As I am a living God, the Lord says, since thou hast not scrupled to
profane my sanctuary with vile things and detestable things a many, I
will make havoc of thee, and my eye shall not melt with pity; I will not
12 scruple in my turn. A third of thy sons shall die of pestilence, or with
famine pine away; a third shall fall in thy defence; a third I will scatter
13 to the four winds, and my sword unsheathed in pursuit. And at last, my
anger spent, my vengeance glutted, my grief healed, doubt they shall not
that the God whom they slighted has decreed it; my sentence shall take
14 full toll of them. Desolate, and the scorn of thy neighbours, so every
15 passer-by shall see thee. A name of scorn and reproach, a by-word thou
shalt be and a thing of horror, to all the nations about thee, when thy
16 punishment is done, so fierce the anger, so shrewd the blow; I, the Lord,
have decreed it. Hungry arrows [1] of mine shall fly abroad, dolorous and
deadly, for your minishing; famine that grows worse and worse as the
17 stocks of bread fail, and with the famine wild beasts to bereave you,
visitations of plague and violent death; and the sword, too, I will let
loose upon you; I, the Lord, have decreed it.

CHAPTER SIX

2   AND now the Lord's word came to me: Turn thy eyes, son of man,
towards the hills of thy own country, and prophesy their doom.
3 Mountains of Israel, thou shalt say, listen to the word of the Lord God;
here is a message from the Lord God to mountain and hill, to rocky slope
and river-bed. I mean to let the sword loose on you, pull shrine down,
4 overthrow altar, break column, pile corpses before the false god's feet;
5 before every idol, sons of Israel prostrate in death, before every altar,
6 the ground strewn with their bones. In all your confines, every city
desolate, every shrine wrecked and ruined; deserted and defaced the
altars, forlorn the idols, shattered the columns, obliterated all the work
7 of man; and ever the dead lying in the midst of you. Will you doubt,
then, that I am the Lord? [2]
8   I will leave a remnant of you; some shall escape the sword, to live on
9 among the Gentiles, dispersed far and wide; and these survivors, in their

[1] Literally, 'arrows of hunger,' but it seems likely that the other plagues
about to be mentioned are included, as well as the famine.
[2] *vv.* 6, 7. It is not clear whether we should take these verses as part of the
first paragraph (addressed to the mountains) or as part of the second (addressed to the Israelites themselves).

land of exile, shall once again bethink themselves of me. Wanton heart
that played me false, eyes that hankered still after idols, shall be tamed
now; they will look back with loathing on all the foul wrong they did,
10 and confess it was no empty boast, when I threatened this calamity.[1]
11   Clap hands and stamp feet, the Lord God says, and cry aloud, Out
upon the foul wrong the men of Israel did, that are now doomed to perish
12 by sword, famine and pestilence! Keep they their distance, the plague
shall smite them, come they to grips, the sword; safe behind the battlements, they shall die of famine; so shall my vengeance take toll of them.
13 Who shall doubt the Lord's power, when the dead lie thick at the feet of
your idols and about your altars; on hill-top and mountain height, in
forest covert and under spreading oak, where once men would burn frag-
14 rant incense to their false gods? Once the blow falls, I will make their
countryside, once so thickly inhabited, into a wilderness; Deblatha [2]
itself is not more forlorn. And who shall doubt the Lord's power?

CHAPTER SEVEN

2 THEN the Lord's word came to me: And thou, son of man . . .[3] A
    message to the land of Israel from the Lord God! For this land, for
3 every corner of it, here is doom, here is doom. Doom for thee at last;
I mean to wreak vengeance on thee, pass sentence on thy evil life, bring
4 home to thee thy foul deeds. Nor shall my eye melt with pity; I will not
spare. All thy evil life brought home to thee, all thy foul deeds confront-
5 ing thee; who shall doubt that it comes from the Lord? The blow, the
6 first blow has fallen, says the Lord God; all is over now, all is over; the
7 day dawns, and for thee doom comes with day. Dwellers in the land, this
is the end of you; your time is up, your day has come; a day when your
8 mountains shall echo with tumult, not with harvest-home.[4] Close at
hand, now, I will rain down my vengeance upon you, give my anger full
9 play, no crime unjudged, no weight of punishment unborne. Never
shall my eye melt with pity for thee; all thy evil life shall be accounted for,

---

[1] *vv.* 8–10. These verses seem to interrupt the thread of the chapter, and
some think they have been accidentally misplaced.

[2] No such place as Deblatha is elsewhere heard of, and there may be some
error in the text.

[3] It seems probable that there is some slight omission in the manuscripts here.

[4] *v.* 7. 'This is the end of you'; literally, in the Latin version, 'ruin has come
upon you,' but this is probably a guess, the word translated 'ruin' being of
quite uncertain significance. The root idea seems to be that of 'a garland.'
'When your mountains shall echo with tumult, not with harvest-home'; literally, 'of slaying (in the Hebrew, of tumult) and not of the glory (in the
Hebrew, of the shout) of the mountains.'

all thy foul deeds brought to light; and none shall doubt that I, the Lord,
punish.
10   It has come, the day has come; the wheel full circle,[1] the branch in full
11   bloom, pride bears its harvest.   Violence has grown up into a shoot of
rebellion . . . and not by their means, not through clamouring multitude
12   of theirs; rest they shall have none.   The time is up, the day of reckoning
come; who buys now, of his purchase shall have no joy, who sells now,
shall not feel his loss; the Lord's vengeance will overtake the whole
13   throng of citizens alike; [2] alas! here is property alienated for ever, though
buyer and seller count among the living yet.   The vision is for the whole
throng of citizens; there is no reversing it; never a man of that guilty race
shall survive.[3]
14   Sound the trumpet there, rally all to arms! But none goes out to war;
15   on the whole throng of citizens my vengeance has fallen; sword without,
pestilence and famine within; sword for the straggler, pestilence and
16   famine for the besieged.   Fugitives there shall be that make good their
flight, but these must take to the mountains, fluttered as the doves that
17   haunt their ravines, sinners all; hands that hang listless, knees weak as
18   water.   See where men go clad in sackcloth, trembling in every limb, with
19   downcast faces, and their heads shorn!   See where they cast their silver
out of doors, their gold on to the dung-hill; how should precious metal
speed them in this day of the Lord's vengeance? Hunger it sates not,
belly it fills not; and this, all the while, was the very occasion of their
20   guilt!   Did they not pride themselves on the beauty of their workmanship, was it not from this they made images of their detestable false gods?
21   And now there it lies, all defilement! Now I am giving it over to strangers
22   for spoil; the vilest of earth's inhabitants shall plunder it.   Still my eyes
shall be averted, while my own treasure-chamber is broken open, while
23   the enemy's pursuivants enter and profane it.   Make short work of it,[4]
24   a land where innocent lives are forfeit, a nest of wrong! The very refuse
of the heathen I will summon to dispossess them of their homes, to be

---

[1] 'The wheel full circle' is only a guess at the sense of the Hebrew phrase
'the garland (see note on verse 7) has gone out.' The text of this and the next
two verses is hopelessly obscure, and may well be corrupt.

[2] Literally, here and in verse 13, 'her multitude'; Jerusalem is presumably
meant.

[3] The sense of the first clause is perhaps that property which changes hands
now, in B.C. 586, will not revert to its owner at the time of jubilee (Lev. 25.13),
because the population will still be in exile. Some think 'the vision' should be
'the vengeance'; it is doubtful, in spite of Is. 55.11, whether 'shall not return'
can mean 'it is irreversible.' 'Never a man of that guilty race shall survive';
literally, in the Latin, 'a man shall not be strengthened in the wickedness of his
life,' but a comparison of the Hebrew text with the Septuagint Greek suggests
that the true meaning is 'a man in his wickedness shall not lay hold of life.'

[4] Literally, 'make a conclusion'; in the Hebrew text, 'make a chain.'

masters of their holy places, that proud boast of theirs [1] now for ever silenced.

25 Days of despair, when they will look about them for a respite, and
26 respite shall be none! Fresh anxieties still, and fresh alarms; vainly they ask the prophet for revelation; tradition among the priests, counsel among
27 the elders is none. Mourns king, princes go covered with dismay, numb with despair the common folk; ill they shall fare, that ill did, cruelly be judged, that were cruel judges; they shall know what manner of God they serve.

CHAPTER EIGHT

THE sixth year of King Sedecias [2] came; and on the fifth day of the sixth month, as I sat in my house with the elders of Juda for my
2 company, the power of the Lord God came over me there. I had a vision; a figure was there before me all aglow, fire beneath where his loins shewed, and from the loins upwards, brightness made visible, like amber
3 to see. It seemed as if an outstretched hand caught me by a lock of my hair; and with that, a force lifted me up between heaven and earth, and I was carried away in a divine transport to Jerusalem. There was the gateway of the inner court, looking northwards, and there was that image
4 of rival deity God sees and hates. There, too, was the bright presence of
5 Israel's God, as I had seen it earlier on the river plain; Son of man, he told me, look northwards; so northwards I looked from the altar-gate,
6 and saw the image of rival deity standing at the very entrance. Foul deeds a-doing, son of man, said he; little wonder if I was fain to withdraw from my sanctuary, where the men of Israel do me such wrong. But thou art not finished with them; thou hast fouler yet to see.

7 And with that, he brought me close up to the door of the court, where
8 I found a hole in the wall. Then he would have me dig through the wall;
9 so dig I did, and there was a door facing me. Now go in, he told me, and
10 see for thyself what foul deeds are done here. And when I went in to look, what should I find painted on the walls but likenesses of reptile and of beast! A very foul sight it was; no idol Israel worships but it was there;
11 and in front of these pictures stood Jezonias, the son of Saphan, with seventy elders of Israel about him, censer in hand each of them, so that a
12 thick cloud of incense went up. Now, son of man, he told me, thou canst see for thyself what work they make in the darkness, these elders of Israel, each hidden where hide he may; Fear is none, they say, the Lord

---

[1] Literally, 'the pride of the powerful'; this seems to be a phrase regularly applied to local sanctuaries (24.21, 30.18 below).
[2] 'Of King Sedecias' is not expressed in the original. So in 26.1; 29.1.

should see us; he has forsaken the land for good and all, the Lord has.

13   Thou hast not seen all yet, he told me; thou shalt see still fouler things
14 done; and he took me through the northern gate of the temple, and there
15 what found I but women that sat weeping for Adonis? Hast thou marked
16 it well, son of man? he asked. Prepare thyself for a sight fouler yet. Then
he took me into the inner court of the temple, and there, at the door of the
Lord's own house, between porch and altar, some five and twenty men
were standing with their backs to the temple, that worshipped the
17 eastern sun. Hast thou marked it well, son of man? he asked. And are
they not content, the men of Juda, with such detestable doings as these,
that they must provoke me further yet, filling the whole land with wrong?
18 See how they hold branch to nostril![1] For their busy wickedness, busy
shall my vengeance be; unmelting this eye, this heart unpitying, deaf
these ears to their cry of complaint.

CHAPTER NINE

THEN I heard him cry aloud, Make way there for the plagues that
2   must befall the city, for the weapon-bearers of death! And with that,
from the upper gate which looks northwards, I saw six men coming on
their way, and none of them but bore his deadly weapon; in their midst
walked another, clad in linen, with a writer's ink-horn at his girdle. All,
3 when they had entered, took their stand by the brazen altar; and now,
borne on cherub wings, the glory of Israel's God rose above the threshold
of the house, summoning him of the linen clothes and the ink-horn to
4 set about his task. Make thy way, the Lord said to him, all through the
city, from end to end of Jerusalem; and where thou findest men that weep
and wail over the foul deeds done in it, mark their brows with a cross.[2]
5 To the others I heard him say, Yours it is to traverse the city at his heels,
6 and smite. Never let eye of yours melt with pity; old and young, man and
maid, mother and child, all alike destroy till none is left, save only where
you see the cross marked on them. And begin first with the temple itself.
7   So they began with the elders in the court. Desecrate yonder temple,
said he, and fill its precincts with the slain; then go out on your errand.
8 So out they went, and now it was on the city their strokes came. And I,
left alone amid that carnage, fell face to earth; Alas, alas, Lord God,
cried I, wilt thou destroy all the poor remnant of Israel, pouring out thy

---

[1] We have no means of determining what is the sense of the phrase which
concludes this verse. Some think it is a forgotten proverb; others, that it refers
to idolatrous ceremonies.

[2] Literally, 'with a tau.' This was the last letter of the Hebrew alphabet,
and in the old script a cross was the symbol for it.

9 vengeance on Jerusalem thus? Nay, he told me, the guilt of Israel and Juda is past bound or measure; all bloodshed the countryside, the city all wrong-doing; The Lord has forsaken the land for good and all, say they;
10 fear is none the Lord will see it. And should eye of mine melt with pity?
11 Nay, they shall rue yet the false paths they have taken. And sure enough, the man clad in linen stood there with the ink-horn at his side to give account of himself, and reported, I have done thy errand.

CHAPTER TEN

AND now I looked up at the vault over the cherubim, and there was the hue of sapphire, and the likeness of a throne.
2   And his word came to the man clad in linen, Make thy way in where the whirring is loudest, beneath the cherubim, take a handful of the coals that lie there among them, and pour these out over the city. So I watched
3 him make his way in; and all the while, as he did so, the cherubs were standing close to the right of the temple, and the inner court was full of
4 smoke. And the brightness of the Lord's presence, cherub-throned, rose up above the threshold, till the house was all smoke, and all the precincts
5 filled with the divine radiance; and ever the beating of the cherubs' wings could be heard in the outer court, loud as the voice of the Omnipotent
6 heard in thunder.[1] There by the wheels stood the man clad in linen,
7 ready to receive the cherub-guarded flame as he was bidden; and one cherub, parting from the rest, reached hand out, took fire from the
8 midst, and gave it him; so he went on his errand. Cherub hand shewed under every cherub wing.
9   Such was the vision I saw; four wheels beside four cherubim, one by
10 each, and their colour shewed like aquamarine; all alike had the same
11 appearance, of a wheel within a wheel. Moved they to this quarter or that, they followed ever without ado the lead of the foremost; there was
12 no turning about when they moved. Eyes were everywhere, on body and neck and hand and wing and wheel too, for each cherub had its own
13 wheel. (It was these wheels I had heard spoken of as the whirring).[2]
14 Fourfold was the semblance of them, now cherub, now man, now lion,
15 now eagle. They rose aloft, these cherubim, (such living figures as I had
16 seen by Chobar; the wheels accompanying them as they went, never left behind, but still at their side when they spread their wings for flight,
17 resting when they rested, rising when they rose; these too had a living

---

[1] See note on 1.24.
[2] Literally, 'And in my hearing he called (to) the wheels (to) them rotation (in the Latin, rotatory).' This obscure phrase is perhaps best understood as a note on verse 2, where the same word is used in the Hebrew.

18 impulse in them),   and therewith the bright presence of the Lord left the
19 temple threshold, and stood there, cherub-throned.   With my own eyes
   I saw them, as they spread their wings and rose aloft; saw the wheels
   follow as they went; saw a halt made ¹ at the eastern gate of the temple,
20 and the Lord's bright presence resting above them.   Full well I knew
   that cherubs they were, these living figures I had seen bearing God's
21 throne by Chobar,   each with four semblances, and four wings, and
22 human hands shewing under their wings;   the same faces, the same looks,
   I had seen by Chobar, the same onward impulse of their journeying.

CHAPTER ELEVEN

THEREUPON a transport seized me, carrying me off to the gate of the
   temple that looks eastward; and here were twenty-five men, with two
   nobles, Jezonias son of Azur and Pheltias son of Benaias, plain to be seen
2 among them.   Son of man, the divine voice said to me, here are folk that
3 plot mischief, and give the city ruinous counsel. What, say they, have we
   not houses here newly built? We may lie as snug here as meat in a cook-
4 ing-pot.²   Tell them of their doom, son of man, tell them of their doom.
5   With that, the spirit of the Lord came full upon me, and bade me
   speak. This message I gave them from the Lord of hosts, These are your
6 own words, men of Israel; can I not read your hearts?   So many done to
   death in this city, you have filled all the streets of it with bodies of the
7 slain! You have peopled it with the dead, says the Lord God; their flesh
   it is shall line yonder cooking-pot; as for you, I will fetch you out of it.
8 The sword it is you dread, and to the sword I doom you, the Lord God
9 says;   out of it you shall come, and fall into the enemy's hands, and be
10 punished as you deserve.   Doomed to fall by the sword, up and down the
   countryside of Israel; then you shall learn what manner of God the Lord
11 is! Cooking-pot is none here to shelter you; up and down the country-
12 side you shall meet your sentence,   and learn what manner of God it is
   whose paths you have left untrodden, whose will you have disobeyed, to
   follow the ill customs of your neighbours!
13   So, in my vision, I prophesied, and while I was prophesying, Pheltias
   the son of Banaias sank down dead. Thereupon I fell face to earth, crying
   aloud, Alas, alas, Lord God, wilt thou take full toll of the remnant left
14 to Israel? But the Lord's answer came to me: Thou hast brethren, son

---

¹ Literally, 'I saw it (or, him) halt.' It is not easy to see what noun should
be supplied.
² The attitude here condemned is perhaps that of the citizens who refused
to surrender, trusting in the strength of their walls; cf. Jer. 21.9. For the
metaphor of the cooking-pot, cf. 4.3 above.

of man, thou hast brethren still. They are nearest of kin to thee that are far away, exiled sons of Israel. What though these dwellers at Jerusalem
16 cry, Keep your distance, the land is ours? Not such is the message the Lord God sends them; Far away I have banished them, says he, widely scattered them; yet, go they where they will, a sanctuary in little they
17 shall find in my companionship. Tell them this, from the Lord God, Lost among the peoples, I will gather you, scattered over the world, I
18 will muster you, and give you the land of Israel for your home. To it they shall find their way, and rid it of all that is foul, all that is abominable
19 there; one mind they shall have, and a new spirit shall fill their inmost being; gone the heart of stone, and a human heart theirs in place of it.
20 My paths they shall tread, my will jealously obey, they my people, and I
21 their God. Only where men's hearts are set on their own foul abominations, the Lord God says, they shall bear their punishment.

22   And now the cherubim spread their wings for flight, the wheels beside
23 them, the bright presence of the Lord above them; and that presence, withdrawn from the city's midst, came to rest upon the mountain height
24 eastwards of it. With that, a fresh transport seized me, and I was back among the exiles in Chaldaea, still in a trance, still full of the divine
25 impulse. So the vision faded from my eyes, and I told the exiles all the Lord had made known to me.

CHAPTER TWELVE

2 WORD came to me from the Lord: Son of man, thou dwellest among a brood of rebels, that have eyes to see with, ears to hear with, yet
3 see and hear nothing, so bent are they on rebellion. Do thou, then, son of man, provide thee with an exile's pack, and while it is daylight, let them see thee marching to and fro; in their full view, if those rebellious
4 eyes will but mark it, remove from one place to another, carrying those goods of thine with thee, as if ready for a journey. Then, at nightfall,
5 take thy leave in public, as if thou wert going into exile. Let them see
6 thee dig a hole through the wall of thy house, to escape by; let them see thee carried out on men's shoulders, darkness all around, blindfold, so that thou canst not view the land about thee. A portent of doom thou shalt be to the men of Israel.[1]

---

[1] Here, and in verses 7 and 12, the fugitive is represented by the Septuagint Greek, and by the Latin version, as being carried on men's shoulders; by the Hebrew text, as carrying his pack on his shoulders. It is doubtful whether the Hebrew verbs are rightly pointed; the more so, as they have no pronoun to express the object they refer to. The implication is perhaps that it will be impossible or unsafe for Sedecias to escape on horseback. Presumably he has his face muffled so as to be unrecognizable; the darkness is perhaps only the effect

7   His bidding was done; while daylight served, I brought my exile's pack out into the open; then, at nightfall, dug wall through and went out
8 on my dark journey, borne on men's shoulders, plain to view. And word
9 came to me from the Lord: What of the rebel brood? Have the Israelites
10 asked to know what thou meanest? This tell them from the Lord God, A princely burden! [1] Here went the prince that rules over Jerusalem, and
11 over all such Israelites as dwell in their native country. Tell them, This is your own doom I foreshadow; the men of Israel shall fare as I do, exile
12 and prison their lot, and he who rules among them shall be fain to escape in the darkness, borne on men's shoulders. They shall breach wall to make way for him, and he shall go with his face covered, so that he will
13 look on the land no more. But my net is spread; I have him in the noose; Babylon for him, the Chaldaean country for him; that land, too, he shall
14 not see, yet die in that land he must.[2] Retinue and bodyguard of his, nay, all his army, I will scatter to the four winds, with my naked sword at
15 their heels. Then at last they shall learn what manner of God I am, when they find themselves lost among the nations, dispersed all the world over!
16 A few shall survive, in despite of sword, famine, and pestilence, to tell these new neighbours of theirs what foul deeds they did; so shall the Gentiles [3] learn to know me.

17   Word came to me from the Lord: Son of man, tremble still when
19 bread thou eatest, nor ever drink water but with anxious fear; and this message send from the Lord God to thy countrymen that are left at home: Never citizen of Jerusalem, never inhabitant of Israel, but must eat in fear, put cup to his lips unmanned, till at last unmanned it lies, the whole
20 countryside around them, for their guilt that dwelt in it. Lonely the crowded streets, wasted the countryside must be, ere you learn to know me.

21   Word came to me from the Lord: What means this saying you have in
23 Israel, The days drag on, and never a warning comes true? Tell them this from the Lord God: Here is a proverb shall be heard in Israel no more; I mean to do away with it. Tell them the time is close at hand now
24 for the fulfilment of all my warnings. Vain vision and flattering hopes
25 Israel shall know no longer; the divine foretelling shall not wait for the divine fulfilling; in your own days, brood of rebels, you shall witness

---

of the blindfolding, since the escape must have taken place at twilight if the men of Israel were to see it.

[1] In the Hebrew text, there is a play upon words, the burden being 'that which is lifted up' and the prince 'he who is lifted up.' Curiously, the Hebrew text here represents Sedecias as being carried, the Latin as being weighed down with a burden.

[2] See IV Kg. 25.7.

[3] In the original simply 'they,' which can be read, less probably, as referring to the exiles themselves.

26 both, the Lord God says. And the Lord's word came to me: Fond hope
of Israel, that these should be distant things thou foretellest, the prophet
28 of a later age! Give them word from the Lord God: Warning of mine
knows no delay; here and now, the Lord says, it shall be accomplished.

CHAPTER THIRTEEN

2 WORD came to me from the Lord: Son of man, on the prophets
pronounce my doom, the prophets whom Israel heeds; would they
prophesy after their own devices? Give them this message from the Lord:
3 Out upon the reckless prophets, the Lord God says, that follow their own
4 whim, and vision have none! Poor Israel, that such foxes as these should
5 burrow among thy ruins! What did you to restore the fortunes of the
day, when the Lord's stroke fell? Not for you to man the breach, to
6 throw up a wall about Israel! [1] Vain vision and cheating hopes are theirs,
that warrant from me have none, yet speak in the Lord's name, and look
7 to see their word fulfilled; has the Lord spoken? Not the Lord, only your
8 empty dreams, your lying oracles. For these vain visions, these cheating
9 hopes of yours, have at you! says the Lord God. On false prophet and
sightless seer my hand is raised in judgement; never shall they take part
in the assembly of Israel, or have their names written in its muster-roll,
or find a home in Israel's land! So shall you learn what manner of God
the Lord is.
10 How dared they cheat my people with false hopes, crying, All's well,
when in truth all went amiss? My people, that strove to build a wall, and
here were the prophets plastering it with clay that had no straw in it!
11 Thine to warn these unskilful plasterers that the wall must needs crumble;
here is a rain-storm brewing, and I mean to ply it with a volley of great
12 hail-stones, and a tempestuous wind that scatters all before it; crumble
your wall, shall no one ask what became of the mortar that went to its
13 plastering? Like a temptestuous wind my anger shall break out, the Lord
God says; like the rain-storm my indignation shall be, and like a volley
14 of hail-stones my vengeance shall take toll of you; down shall come the
wall you plastered so ill, razed to earth, and all its foundations shewing,
overthrown to your common ruin; so you shall learn what manner of
15 God the Lord is. Wall nor plasterer my vengeance shall spare; Down
with the wall, my sentence is, and down with the plasterers that plastered
16 it so unworkmanly, Israel's prophets, that gave Jerusalem comfort, the
Lord says, promising all should be well when all went amiss.

---

[1] The military expressions in this verse are probably no more than a metaphor to illustrate the uselessness of the false prophets, like the building
metaphor which follows.

17   There are women, too, among this people of mine who would play the
prophetess as their own whim bids them. Turn upon these, son of man,
18 and tell them their doom: Out upon them, says the Lord God, the women
who stitch an elbow-cushion for every comer, make a soft pillow for the
heads of young and old! ¹ Men's lives are their prey; shall they cast a net
19 about the lives of Israelites, and save their own? For a handful of meal,
or a crust of bread, they will put me to shame ² before my own people;
will doom to life or death the undeserving, such credence they win from
20 a people ever credulous. Have at those elbow-cushions of yours, the Lord
God says, the nets yonder silly birds are caught in! I mean to snatch them
away from your grasp, and set the birds free, those lives you have
21 ensnared with your prophesying.³ Your pillows shall be torn in pieces;
I will rescue my people from your power, and they shall no longer be
yours to ensnare; then you will learn what manner of God the Lord is.
22 You have brought woe on innocent lives, when I was fain to comfort
them, confirmed the sinner in those evil ways that shall be his undoing;
23 now there shall be no more of your empty visions, there shall be no more
divinings; I mean to save my people from your clutches, and you shall
know the Lord's power at last.

CHAPTER FOURTEEN

AT a time when some of the Israelite leaders had come to visit me,
2   and sat closeted with me, this message I had from the Lord: Son of
man, here be folk that have cumbered their own hearts with false gods,
entangled their own feet with guilt; wouldst thou have me answer when
4 I am consulted by such as these? Speak to them, thou, and tell them this
from the Lord God: When a man of Israel's race comes to consult me

---

¹ *vv.* 17–23. This passage remains hopelessly obscure. Some have thought
that 'cushions' and 'pillows' are only a metaphor describing the false hopes
raised by these diviners. But more probably they were magical contrivances; if
the rare words used in the Hebrew have been rightly translated, we may
perhaps suppose that the enquirer slept on pillows that were stuffed with
magical herbs, etc., and took omens from his dream (cf., Virgil, *Aeneid*
vii.89). Even so, it is not clear whether these prophetesses were content to tell
people's fortunes, or whether (as the text seems to imply) they were in a
position to swear away innocent lives by false accusations.

² Literally, 'profane me,' an unusual expression. The meaning seems to be
that by fathering their impostures on divine revelation the prophetesses
brought religion into disrepute.

³ 'The nets yonder silly birds are caught in'; literally, 'by which you catch
flying souls'; 'set the birds free, those lives you have ensnared,' literally, 'set
free the souls you catch, souls for flying.' The Hebrew text is no less obscure
than the Latin.

through a prophet, his own heart yet cumbered with false gods, his own feet yet entangled with guilt, shall I, the Lord, give him answer in his
5 idolatry? [1] Nay, the faithless heart that leaves me for the worship of false
6 gods shall be Israel's undoing. This warning give them in the name of the Lord God: Come back to me, leave those idols of yours, have no eyes
7 henceforward for sights detestable! If a man of Israel's race, or any of alien breed among them, forsakes me, cumbers his heart with false gods, entangles his feet with guilt, and then comes to consult me through a
8 prophet, shall I, in my own name, answer him? Nay, that man, under my frown, shall become a warning and a by-word, lost to his people, and you
9 shall doubt the Lord's power no longer. Or, if, misguided, the prophet speaks, it is I, the Lord, that have guided that prophet amiss.[2] And thereupon I will exert my power, and rid my people Israel of his company;
10 both alike shall be held guilty, the prophet and his dupe; till Israel learns
11 to wander from me no more, stain itself with guilt no more. So they shall be my people, and I will be their God, says the Lord of hosts.
12   And word came to me from the Lord: Son of man, if a land lies deep in guilt, sin upon sin, and I cut off every source of bread, sending famine
14 upon it to slay man and beast, though three such men as Noe, Daniel, and Job were counted among its citizens, no life but theirs innocence of
15 theirs should save. If I send beasts to make a pathless wilderness of it,
16 none daring to pass for fear of their encounter, as I am a living God, the Lord says, man nor maid should those three rescue by their companion-
17 ship; in a desert land they alone should live. The sword if I let loose, bid
18 the sword pass through that land to destroy man and beast, as I am a living God, the Lord says, their own lives those three should ransom, and
19 neither man nor maid besides. Or if pestilence does my errand of punish-
20 ment, taking deadly toll of man and beast, though Noe dwell there, and Daniel, and Job, as I am a living God, the Lord says, only their own
21 lives they shall ransom, neither man nor maid besides. And what of Jerusalem, says the Lord God, when I send all four plagues on her at once, sword and famine and wild beast and pestilence, till men nor cattle

---

[1] At the end of this verse, and at the end of verse 7, the original would be more naturally rendered as a statement, not a question: 'I will give him answer.' This is usually understood as meaning, 'I will give him a practical answer,' *i.e.*, inflict punishments on him. But this leaves a great deal to the imagination, and there is no parallel for such use of language elsewhere. It is perhaps better, therefore, to translate by a question, as above, and treat verses 5 and 8 as depending loosely on their context.

[2] See III Kg. 22.21-23, where it will be observed that Almighty God is described as the author of an effect which was *directly* attributable to the angel. Here, as there, a false prophet is in question; and his guilt lies in the pride which makes him take some omen or presentiment, of a common sort, as proof that God is speaking through him.

22 are left alive there? A remnant only shall survive, sons and daughters
of your race led out into exile. When these reach you, and you find out
what manner of folk they are in thought and deed, for the sorrows of
Jerusalem you shall weep no more, though I have plagued her so abun-
23 dantly. From thought and deed of theirs you shall take consolation, nor
doubt it was with good reason I used her thus, says the Lord God.[1]

CHAPTER FIFTEEN

2 WORD came to me from the Lord: So much timber in the forest,
3 son of man! And what of the vine that grows wild there? What
avails the wood of it for any manner of craftsmanship? Who will use it to
4 make so much as a peg that pot or pan should hang from? And now it
has been thrown away to feed the fire; now either end is burnt up
altogether, and the middle of it no better than charcoal; of what use is it
5 now, that use had none even when it was whole? Half burned away, half
6 scorched, here is right unserviceable timber! And I, the Lord says, that
destined yonder wild vine to feed the oven, have decreed for the citizens
7 of Jerusalem no other destiny. My frown shall meet them yet; if they
have escaped the fire, it is to be consumed by fire anew. Under my frown,
8 they shall learn what manner of God I am; their land all pathless and
desolate, for their guilt's rewarding, says the Lord God.

CHAPTER SIXTEEN

2 WORD came to me from the Lord: And now, son of man, do thou
3 confront Jerusalem with the record of her misdoings. Tell her this,
in the name of the Lord God: Root of thee, stock of thee, spring from
yonder soil of Chanaan; an Amorrhite it was begot thee, a Hethite bore
4 thee. Born when thou wast, there was none to cut navel-string, in healing
water wash thee, with salt harden thee, wrap thee in swaddling-clothes;
5 never an eye melted with pity, none befriended thee; on the bare ground
6 thou wert cast away, a thing of abhorrence, that day of thy birth. Who

---

[1] *vv.* 22, 23. These verses imply, according to the common opinion, that the
exiles will recognize the justice of Jerusalem's fate, when they witness the
idolatrous behaviour of the new arrivals from that city. But it seems curious
that this recognition should be described as 'consoling' the exiles, and conceivably the prophet means us to think of the new arrivals as attesting, by their
amended lives, the good effects of the chastisement they have undergone.

but I found thee, as I passed on my way, blood-bespattered as thou wert, and trodden under foot; in that plight preserved thee, bade it live on, this defiled thing?

7 Swift as the wild blossoms I bade thee grow; grow thou didst and thrive, and camest to woman's estate, the breasts formed, new hair shew-
8 ing; and still thou wast all naked, and blushing for thy nakedness. Who but I came upon thee, as I passed on my way? And already thou wert ripe for love; cloak of mine should be thrown about thee, to hide thy shame; my troth I plighted to thee, the Lord God says, and thou wert
9 mine. Water to wash thee, all thy stains gone, oil I brought to anoint
10 thee; clad thee with embroidery, shod thy feet with leather; of fine linen
11 thy tiring should be, of silk thy wear. How I decked thee with orna-
12 ments! Bracelets for those arms, a collar for that neck; a frontlet on thy
13 brow, rings in thy ears, on thy head a crown magnifical. Of gold and silver thy adorning, of fine linen and silk and embroidery thy apparel, of wheat and honey and oil thy nourishment; matchless beauty, too, was
14 thine, such beauty as brought thee to a throne. All the world heard the fame of thy loveliness; I had made thee so fair, says the Lord God, utterly fair!

15 Fatal beauty, fatal renown, which emboldened thee to play the harlot,
16 lavish thy favours on every passer-by, and be his! That thou shouldst use those garments of thine to make curtains for thy hill-shrines, what
17 age can match the villainy of it? Silver and gold of mine, thy adornment and my gift, should they be turned into gods of male form, at thy harlot's
18 whim? And these wouldst thou clothe with thy own embroideries, offer
19 them the perfume and incense that was mine by right, set before them the bread, the oil, the honey I gave thee, to appease them with the smell of burnt-sacrifice? More happened besides, (he, the Lord God, reminds
20 thee); to these gods thou wouldst bring sons and daughters of thine and mine, consecrating them to death. Could not thy wanton desires rest
21 content, without immolating my own sons as victims to such as these?
22 Most foul deeds and most lecherous, that quite put thy youth out of mind, the days when thou wast naked, and overcome with shame, blood-bespattered and trodden under foot.

23 And at last, to crown thy misdoings (Fie on thee, fie on thee for shame!
24 says the Lord God), thou wouldst build thee a brothel, a common stew,
25 in every street; no cross-roads but should carry the blazon of thy har-lotry. O the dishonour done to thy beauty, when thou didst welcome
26 every passer-by to thy favours, insatiable in thy dalliance! With those lusty neighbours of thine, the Egyptians, thou wouldst play the wanton;
27 these should be my rivals! What wonder I should interpose, and abridge the rights thou didst enjoy, handing thee over for a prey to the maids of

Philistia, rivals of thy own, and such as blushed to witness thy ill-doings?[1]
28 It was not enough; thou must needs dally with the men of Assur, nor
29 might their dalliance content thee; thou wouldst extend thy trade as far
as Chaldaea, where all is for sale, insatiable to the last.[2]
30   Salve is none, says the Lord God, for such a heart as thine, set on fol-
31 lowing a harlot's ways. Never a cross-roads, never a street, but thou hast
set up some brothel for public resort; never harlot despised the lover as
32 thou his hire! Thine was the craving of the false wife, that must ever
33 bring a stranger between her husband's sheets. The price of love other
harlots claim, thou wouldst offer; gifts of thine should entice gallants
34 from every side to thy bower. Never did wanton the like, nor shall again;
it is out of all nature, a harlot that gives, not takes.
35   Here then, poor wanton, is the Lord's doom; this message he has for
thee. Because all thy bronze was put to such ill use,[3] because thou didst
wanton so shamelessly with those lovers of thine, idols most foul, in
37 whose honour the lives of thy own children were sacrificed, I mean to
have a reckoning with thee. All the gallants that have enjoyed thee, men
that love thee and men that hate, I will muster together; muster them
from all around, and then lay thy shame bare, expose thy nakedness for
38 all to see. Such punishment thou shalt have as unfaithful wives have,
39 or murderers; to my jealous anger thy life must make amends; I mean
to leave thee at their mercy. Ruined thy bower, ransacked thy brothel
shall be; thy garments stripped off thee, plundered thy fair adornment;
40 naked they shall leave thee, and overcome with shame. Hue and cry they
41 shall raise against thee, stone thee and put thee to the sword; house of
thine the flames shall not spare. Before all womankind they will make an
42 example of thee; no more dalliance, no more hired lovers now. Then at
last my vengeance shall be complete, my jealous anger appeased; thou
43 shalt have a respite from my ill will. So forgetful of thy youth, so
obstinate in thy provocations, what wonder if I pay thee what thou hast
earned? the Lord says. Yet even now I have not requited thee as thy
most foul crimes have deserved.

---

[1] Sennacherib claims, on an inscription, that he took certain towns from
Ezechias and handed them over to the Philistine princes.
[2] Literally, in the Hebrew text, 'And thou didst multiply thy harlotries to the
land of merchants (or, of Chanaan), as if to the Chaldaeans, and even with
that thou wast not satisfied.' The meaning can only be a matter of conjecture;
the Latin version, 'thou didst multiply thy harlotries with the Chaldaeans in
the land of Chanaan' is not likely to be right.
[3] Literally, 'thou didst pour out all thy bronze.' This can hardly mean money,
which is never thus described in the Old Testament; if the text has been correctly preserved, it is perhaps best to suppose a reference to the accessories of
heathen worship. But some would derive the word from a different root altogether, and give it the sense of 'thy favours.'

44   Like mother, like daughter; so runs the proverb, and of thee it shall be
45 spoken.   Thou art thy mother's daughter, that was false to husband and
child; false to husband and child were those sisters of thine; thy mother
46 a Hethite, thy father an Amorrhite, sure enough.   Here was thy elder
sister on thy right, Samaria, thy younger sister on thy left, Sodom, with
47 daughter towns both of them.   Didst thou follow their example, share
their misdoings? Nay, that was not enough for thee; it should go hard
48 but thou wouldst outdo them in their crimes.   As I am a living God, the
Lord says, never were Sodom and her daughters guilty as thou and thine.
49 Pride was the fault of her, this sister of thine; pride and a full belly; the
peace and plenty she and her daughters had, with no thought for the
50 poor that stood in need! So it was they rebelled against me, ever I must
51 see foul deeds done, till I rid myself of them, as thou seest.   Nor was
Samaria in her turn half so guilty as thou. It remained for thee to outvie
thy sisters in crime, till thy more abominable doings put them in coun-
52 tenance.   Their lesser guilt, that somewhat excuses them, is the measure
of thy shame; of that shame thou must bear the brand, while thy sisters
53 go free.   When I reverse the doom of exile against Sodom and her daughters, Samaria and her daughters, then, in their company, thy own exiles
54 shall return;   a sorry boast for thee, that thou hast cheered, in such
55 fashion, their loneliness!   Only when Sodom and her daughters, Samaria
and her daughters, to their former state return, is there any hope for
thy daughters and for thee.
56   Time was, when no mention of Sodom's name might soil thy proud
57 lips;   that was before thy own sins came to light, that now disgrace thee
before Syria's daughters, Philistia's daughters, thy watchful neighbours
58 north and south.   Now it is thy turn, the Lord God says, to undergo the
59 shame of thy guilt.   And this is his doom: [1] False to thy oath, thou hast
forsworn our covenant, and thou shalt have the punishment thou hast
60 earned.   That covenant I made with thee in thy youth shall not be for-
61 gotten; nay, I will ratify it eternally,   but humbled thou shalt be with
memories of past days, when thou must needs take thy sisters, older and
younger, to thyself. Daughters of thine they shall be, strangers to the
62 covenant no longer. My covenant thus ratified with thee, thou shalt know
63 my power at last;   remembering still, shamefaced and tongue-tied still,
even when I have pardoned all thy ill-doing, says the Lord God.

---

[1] *vv.* 59–63. The precise emphasis of this passage is a matter of dispute; the
rendering given above assumes that the reference to 'thy older and younger
sisters' alludes to the call of the Gentiles.

CHAPTER SEVENTEEN

2　WORD came to me from the Lord: A riddle, son of man, a parable
3　for the men of Israel to interpret! This shall be thy message from
the Lord God: A great eagle there was, strong of wing, long of limb;
thick and gay his plumage. And this eagle flew to Lebanon, where he
4　robbed cedar of cedar's very pith; tore away its crown of leaves and
5　carried it off to Merchant-land,[1] set it down in Traffic City. Then back
he flew to that same country, chose out both seed and seed-ground there;
6　it was on a level lawn by a brimming stream he planted it. When the
plant grew, it proved to be a spreading vine, low of stature, and ever
branch curled inwards and root struck downwards, yet vine it was, with
7　sprig that burgeoned, shoot that sprang. But now, here is a second eagle
comes in sight, another great eagle, strong of wing, thick-plumed; and
it seems as if the vine, in the garden where it grows, were stretching out
its roots, waving its tendrils, to ask this second eagle for water instead.
8　What, when it was planted in ground so fair, by waters so abundant, with
9　such promise of leaf and fruit, a vine so destined to greatness! Will any
good come of this? asks the Lord God. Nay, roots shall be plucked up,
fruit ravaged, branches left to wither; fade it must, nor is it like to need
10　great strength or many hands for its unearthing. Take root is not thrive;
rich soil or none, when the sirocco parches it, the vine must wither.
11　　Then the Lord's word came to me, bidding me ask the rebel brood,
Were they at a loss for the meaning of it? This tells how Nabuchodonosor
came to Jerusalem, carried off the king and princes and took them away
13　to Babylon; yet spared a prince of the blood royal, making a treaty with
him and exacting an oath of allegiance. All the flower of the citizens he
14　carried away; the kingdom should be submissive henceforward, and
15　rebel no more, should keep troth with him loyally.[2] Straightway the new
king revolted from Nabuchodonosor, and sent envoys to Egypt, asking
for horses, asking for the despatch of a great army in his support. Speeds
16　he, finds he deliverance? Should broken faith avail him? As I am a living
God, the Lord says, Babylon that made a king of him, Babylon that
trusted in his false oath of allegiance, shall be the place of his death.
17　Nor think that his enemy [3] will need great strength, a great muster of men,

---

[1] 'Merchant-land'; the Latin version here transliterates, 'Chanaan,' instead
of translating. Chaldaea is evidently meant.

[2] *vv.* 12–14. The Latin here, like the Septuagint Greek, has the verbs in the
future tense. But the reference is clearly to the banishment of Joachim, which
had already taken place, not to that of Sedecias.

[3] In the original, 'Pharao.' But it seems clear that the text is at fault; Nabuchodonosor, not Pharao, was the enemy. And although the Hebrew text can

to overcome him, mound here, trench there, and the loss of many lives;
18 for the man that did so ill, held his faith a light thing and broke the bond
19 he had set his hand to, there is no escape. This doom the Lord pronounces: As I am a living God, false troth and broken treaty shall be the
20 undoing of him! My net is spread; I have him in the noose; Babylon for
him! There I will call him to account for the dishonour he has done to
21 my name by his treachery; and all that escape with him, nay, his whole
army, must fall by the sword, or survive scattered to the four winds; you
shall learn what manner of God you worship.
22 And here is a message from the Lord God: Pith of the tall cedar I will
take and set it firm, young branch from its crest of branches I will snap
23 off, and plant it on a mountain that stands high above the rest. High in
the hill-country of Israel I will plant it, and there it shall grow into a great
cedar-tree; no bird on the wing but shall find rest under its shade, nestle
24 among its branches; till all the forest learns its lesson, that I, the Lord,
bring high tree low, raise low tree high, wither the burgeoning trunk,
give life to the barren. What the Lord promises, the Lord fulfils.

CHAPTER EIGHTEEN

2 WORD came to me from the Lord: Strange, that a proverb should be
current in Israel, The fathers have eaten sour grapes, and the child-
3 ren's teeth are being set on edge! As I am a living God, the Lord says,
4 this proverb shall be current in Israel no more. What, is not every soul
at my disposal, father and son alike? It is the guilty soul that must die.
5 Is a man loyal to me, does he live innocently and uprightly? Is he one
who never feasted at mountain-shrines, or looked for help to the false
gods that are worshipped in Israel; never came between his neighbour's
7 sheets or had commerce with a woman when she was defiled? Does he
keep clear of oppression, giving back the pledge he took from his neighbour, and seizing nothing by violence? Does he feed the hungry, clothe
8 the naked? Does he shun usury and extortion? Does he refuse the bribe,
9 and judge honestly between man and man? Does he follow my commandments, hold fast to my ordinances, as a true man should? Here is a loyal
servant of mine; life for him, he shall live on, says the Lord God.
10 But now, what if son he begets that is a man of violence, a murderer;
11 lends himself to any of those practices   which his father ever shunned? [1]

be read as implying that Pharao with his great army will not be able to save
Sedecias, this is not the sense required; cf., the parallel in verse 9 above.
    [1] *vv.* 10, 11. The text of the Hebrew is somewhat doubtful, and the grammar
of the Latin obscure. But 'which his father ever shunned' is probably the sense
originally intended. The rendering 'though not all of them' is possible, but
hardly attractive.

12 At hill-shrine eats he, wedded wife wrongs he, the friendless poor
oppresses; gets him ill gains, withholds the pledge, betakes himself to
13 false god and foul rite; a usurer besides and an extortioner. Shall he live
on? Nay, no life for him; he must die the death his foul crimes have
14 earned him. Son of his, in turn, warned by such a father's doom, for-
15 swears that ill example. Not for him the hill feast, the false gods of the
16 countryside, the adulterous bed; never a wrong done, a pledge withheld,
17 gain dishonestly come by; feeds he the hungry, clothes the naked, and
keeps clear of oppression, and usury, and extortion; what of him? Doer
of my will, keeper of my law, he shall not die for his father's sins; he
18 shall live on. His father, a man of wrong and violence, that deserved ill
19 of his countrymen, has paid for his guilt by death; would you have the
son, too, make amends for it? Nay, but here is a man upright and honest,
that holds fast by decrees of mine and obeys them; he must live on.
20   It is the guilty soul that must die; not for the son the father's punishment, nor for the father the son's; good shall befall the good, evil the evil.
21 It may be the wicked man will repent of all his sinful deeds, and learn
to keep my commandments, and live honestly and uprightly; if so, he shall
22 live on; life, not death, for him. All his transgressions shall be forgotten,
23 and his uprightness shall bring him life. What pleasure should I find in
the death of a sinner, the Lord God says, when he might have turned
24 back from his evil ways, and found life instead? It may be the innocent
man will lose his innocence, and begin to live as foul a life as that other
in his wickedness; if so, shall he be spared? No, all his upright life shall
be forgotten; a traitor, shall he not die in his treachery, a sinner in his sins?
25 And yet you say, The Lord is inconsiderate in his dealings! Listen, sons
26 of Israel; it is your dealings that are inconsiderate, not mine. The innocent man loses his innocence, and lives amiss; it is death I deal to him;
27 he dies for his guilty deeds. The wicked man abandons his wicked ways,
28 and learns to live honestly and uprightly; he wins life by it. He bethinks
himself, and turns away from his evil doings; there is life, not death, for
him.
29   What, should the sons of Israel hold the Lord inconsiderate? It is you
30 who are inconsiderate, men of Israel, not he. Each by his own life you
shall be judged, men of Israel, the Lord God says. Come back, and make
31 amends for all this guilt of yours, that shall else be your undoing; away
with them, your defiant rebellions against me; a new heart, a new spirit!
32 Why must you choose death, men of Israel? Die who will, his death is
none of my contriving, says the Lord God; come back to me, and live!

CHAPTER NINETEEN

2   THINE to raise a dirge over the princes of Israel: Prince, that
. . . mother of thine was a lioness indeed; where lions haunt, she
3 made her lair, among their whelps nursed her brood.[1] One cub she
reared that grew to lion's estate, learned to bring down his prey, to eat
4 men; the neighbours [2] heard of it, caught him, not scatheless, in their
5 pit, and carried him off in chains to Egypt. Baulked of her hopes, she
6 reared another, till it was a grown lion. This one, in turn, took his ease
7 like a lion among the rest; learned to bring down prey, eat men, of women
make widows, of cities a desert; dispeopled a whole land with his roaring.
8 At that, folk came from far and near [3] with nets to snare him, caught him
9 in their cruel toils and caged him. This one they led off in chains to the
king of Babylon; in Babylon he remained a prisoner, and his voice was
heard on the hill-sides of Israel no more.
10   Mother of that royal stock! Vine planted by the water-side, and in that
11 neighbourhood leafy and fruitful both, was never so fertile. Here was a
vine could yield sturdy boughs, sceptres for kings to govern with; high
12 grew the leaves, fair the branching tendrils. But vengeance fell upon it,
torn up and thrown away on the ground, the sirocco to wither its leaves;
13 faded and dry those strong boughs, till at last fire consumed them! It is
14 planted now far away, in the parched soil of a desert. Fire came out from
those branching boughs, that consumed all the fruit of it; never a sturdy
bough more, to be a king's sceptre. Make dole, then; here is good cause
for dole.

CHAPTER TWENTY

AND now it was the seventh year, the tenth day of the fifth month.
Some of the Israelite leaders had come to visit me, asking what was
2 the Lord's will, and sat closeted with me. And this message I had from
3 the Lord: Son of man, tell the leaders of Israel this from the Lord God:
Would you come to ask my will? As I am a living God, the Lord says,
4 you shall have no answer. Arraign them, son of man, arraign them for

---

[1] The two lions referred to are presumably Joachaz (IV Kg. 23.31) and
Joachin (IV Kg. 24.15). The mother referred to is probably the kingdom of
Juda. The absence of any rubric at the beginning of the chapter is curious, and
it does not follow naturally on chapter 18; some words may perhaps have
fallen out, or the whole chapter may have been accidentally misplaced.

[2] Literally, 'the nations.'

[3] Literally, 'nations came from the provinces.' It is a habit of Hebrew authors to read the application of a parable into the parable itself.

their crimes; tell them what foul things their fathers did before them.
5 This shall be thy message to them from the Lord God: Long ago I made
choice of Israel, plighted to Jacob my troth, when I made myself known
6 to them in the land of Egypt. I swore to be their own God, swore that
I would take them away to the home I had destined for them, a land all
7 milk and honey, the best of lands. Only, I told them, his darling idolatries each man must set aside; not for you to be contaminated with the
8 false gods of Egypt; I, the Lord, am your God. All was defiance and disobedience; idolatry still cherished, the worship of Egypt's gods still un-
forsaken. I was minded to let my anger have its way, glut my vengeance
9 on them, there in Egypt. But no, I would be their champion, for my own
honour's sake; the heathen all around, that had witnessed my coming to
10 deliver them, must not learn to hold my honour cheap. So from Egypt
I rescued them, and led them out into the desert.
11   There I gave them a law, made known to them the usages that bring
12 life; bade them share my sabbath rest, that should be a token between
13 me and them, a token that they were divinely set apart. What did Israel
then? Defied my anger, disobeyed my law, life-giving commandments
cast away, left my sabbath all unhonoured. Should I give vent to my
14 anger, and make an end of them, there in the desert? And let the heathen
see my work of deliverance half accomplished? For my honour's sake, I
15 must not. But I swore, out in the desert, that the promised land, all
16 milk and honey, best of lands, should never be theirs. My will defied,
my law forsaken, my sabbath neglected, a heart set on idols, they should
17 learn to rue; had not my pity spared them, they should have died there
18 and then, swallowed up in those wastes. To their sons, the desert-born,
warning I gave: Not for you your fathers' example, your fathers' tradi-
19 tions, the contamination of the false gods they worshipped. I, the Lord,
am your God; mine the laws you must follow, the usages you must
20 cherish and obey; my sabbath you must honour, in token that the Lord
21 is the God you worship. But they too, the sons, defied me; my laws
forsook, my life-giving usages forgot, my sabbaths profaned. There in
the desert I would have given vent to my anger, let my vengeance take
22 its toll of them, but still I held my hand; for my own honour, the heathen
23 must see my work of deliverance accomplished. But once more in the
desert I bound myself by an oath . . .[1] I would scatter them among all the
24 nations, spread them over the face of earth, men defiant of my will, contemptuous of my law, careless of my sabbath as ever, after the false gods

---

[1] It seems possible there has been an omission here, such as is very likely to
occur in a passage full of repetitions. Verse 24 seems to deal with an existing
situation (not with a future situation, like Deut. 4.27, etc.) ; and if so, the
threat of dispersal would more naturally be uttered against a people already
settled in Chanaan.

25 of their fathers hankering still. Laws they should have, but for their
26 harm, usages that brought, not life, but death; guilty, they should stain
themselves with fresh guilt by the very offerings they made, when they
consecrated their first-born to the fire; they must have proof of my
power at last.[1]

27 They blasphemed me (tell Israel from the Lord God), those fathers
28 of yours, and did me great despite. Scarce had I brought them into the
promised land, when the sight of high mountain here, thick forest there,
set them offering victims in honour of my rivals, burning incense, pour-
29 ing libations! Well might I ask them, Whither resort you? And hill-
resorts they are called to this day.[2]

30 Give the men of Israel, then, this message from the Lord God: Still
the same ways your fathers went, still the same itch for things abomin-
31 able? To this day, when you would make offering, you pass your sons
through the fire; guilt of idolatry stains you yet, and shall I make answer
to you, men of Israel? As I am a living God, the Lord says, you shall have
32 no answer from me! Never think I will allow you to worship wood and
33 stone like other races of men, your neighbours; as I am a living God, the
Lord says, I mean to reign over you, though it should need all the exercise of my constraining power, all the outpouring of my vengeance.
34 Rescued from many masters, summoned from many lands, you shall
serve me perforce, my power constraining you, my vengeance threaten-
35 ing you. I will lead you out into a desert world, and there plead my cause
36 against you, as I did with your fathers long ago, in the desert confines
37 of Egypt. I will force you under my sceptre, chain you to my covenant.
38 The rebels I will set apart, and though I summon them away from their
banishment, they shall never return to the land of Israel; then you will
39 know what manner of God you serve. Come, then, says the Lord God,
let each man have recourse to his own idol, and pay it due worship! If
that counsel you will not follow, nor drag my name in the dust with foul
rites and false gods . . .[3]
40 On that holy mountain of mine, the Lord God says, that high mountain

---

[1] *vv*. 25, 26. This passage cannot mean that Almighty God commanded the
sacrifice of children; cf. Jer. 32.35. The prophet implies, by a kind of ironical
exaggeration, that by refusing aid to his guilty people God drove them to become worshippers of Moloch, whose usages brought death instead of life.
'Laws they should have,' 'they should stain themselves'; literally, 'I gave them
laws,' 'I stained them.'

[2] This verse contains a (probably fanciful) derivation of the usual Hebrew
word for 'hill-shrines.' It is perhaps intended to emphasize the fact that the
shrines were still used in the prophet's own day, in spite of all the punishments Israel had experienced.

[3] It seems clear that there is an omission after this verse, unless indeed the
text of it has been incorrectly transmitted.

that looks down over Israel, all the race of Israel shall be my worshippers, favoured suitors in a favoured land ; first-fruit and tithe, all your hallow-
41 ings shall be awaited there. Rescued from so many masters, summoned from so many lands, you shall be a fragrant offering ; all my dealings with
42 you the heathen shall acclaim, and you yourselves shall recognize my power, restored to the land of Israel, the land I promised to your fathers.
43 False paths and foul misdoings you shall remember yet, and think with
44 loathing of what you were ; my power you shall know, men of Israel, says the Lord God ; and that I was your benefactor, not for your deserts, that erred and sinned, but for my own honour's sake.

45 　　Word came to me from the Lord : Look southward, son of man ; pour out thy complaint towards the noon-day sun, and let the southern wood-
47 lands hear thee prophesy. To the listening forest give this message from the Lord God : I mean to set thee alight, burn up green tree and dry ; unquenchable, that flame shall scorch the faces of all beholders, north-
48 ward and south alike ; plain enough it shall be for all the world to see that it was I, the Lord, set it ablaze, and there is no quenching it.
49 　　Alas for pity, Lord God, said I, they are complaining already that I speak to them only in parables !

CHAPTER TWENTY-ONE

2 　SO the Lord's word came to me, Why then, son of man, towards 　Jerusalem turn thee, pour out thy complaint sanctuarywards, and let
3 the land of Israel hear thee prophesy. And this be thy message to the land of Israel : Have at thee ! the Lord God says ; here is my sword un-sheathed to make an end of thy inhabitants, innocent souls and guilty.
4 In token that all alike must perish, northward and south alike, all the
5 world over, my unsheathed sword must go on its errand ; drawn it is,
6 plain for all the world to see, and there is no sheathing it. And there-withal I would have thee groan, as men groan that have an aching in the
7 loins, very piteously in the public view ; ask they the reason of it, thou wilt say, For ill tidings. Faint every heart shall be, when those tidings come, every hand shall hang listless ; cowed every spirit shall be, every knee flag. Those tidings are on the way, the Lord God says ; there is no averting it.

8 　　Word came to me from the Lord : Tell them, son of man, the Lord God has this message for thee to utter : Whetted the sword is, polished
10 the sword is, whetted for slaughter, polished to dazzle as lightning does. Never a tree but must fall at thy onset, woodman who art to overthrow
11 the sceptre my son wields.[1] Polished, for the hand to grasp it well, the

---

[1] Like much else in this chapter, the second half of the verse is obscure, and probably corrupt, in the Hebrew text.

sharp sword, the bright sword, which the slayer must needs handle!
12 Cry aloud, son of man, and bewail thee, that on my people it must fall,
and all the princes of Israel that are left; prince and people, doomed to
13 perish by the sword; smite on thy thigh most dolorously. A tried sword,
the Lord God says, and when yonder sceptre it has overthrown, brought
14 to nothing. . . .[1] Prophesy, then, son of man; smite hands together and
call for a second stroke and a third of the avenging sword; a sword of
15 massacre, that strikes men dumb, turns their hearts faint, and lays all
in ruin. Havoc wrought at every gate by the sharp sword, the sword
polished till it shines again, wrapped about the hilt for more ease of
16 smiting!   Sharp be thy blade; cut right, cut left, wherever thy lust
17 beckons thee!   I too will smite hands together, telling the tale of my
vengeance; I, the Lord, command thee.
18   Word came to me from the Lord: And now, son of man, draw a picture. A picture of two roads, both leading from a common point, by which
the sword of the Chaldaean king may travel. Here he is, planning his
course at the sign-post, where two roads meet, a city at the end of either.
20 Draw the two roads, one beckoning that sword to Rabbath, where the
21 Ammonites dwell, one to Juda, and Jerusalem the impregnable. There
stands the king of Babylon at the parting of the ways, taking omens;
there is shuffling of arrows, consulting of deities, searching of entrails.
22 Choose he the right, it is for Jerusalem; the battering-rams, the breach
made ere the slaughter can begin, the cries of battle, the assault on the
23 gates, the mound, the siege-works. Thy picture will shew him as a man
baffled by the omens given him, that remains idle, as if he were keeping
the sabbath rest.[2] Then he remembers the guilt; shall a guilty race go
free?
24   Ay, says the Lord God, still fresh is the memory of that guilt; open
rebels you are, and never a thought in your hearts but shews vile; capture
25 awaits you, that revive those memories still. And thou, perjured wretch
26 that rulest Israel, thy time has run out; off with head-band, off with
27 crown, symbols that honour the base, the noble degrade! I will wrest it
this way, wrest it that, as it was never wrested yet;[3] at last one shall
come that claims it of right, and to him I will give it.

---

[1] Once more the Hebrew text gives us no help, and grammar can only be restored to the Latin by assuming that there has been an omission in the original.

[2] The Hebrew text refers here not to keeping sabbaths, but to swearing
oaths; the sense of it is extremely doubtful.

[3] 'Symbols that honour the base, the noble degrade! I will wrest it this way,
wrest it that, as it was never wrested yet.' Literally, the Latin version runs: 'Is
not this the thing that has lifted up the low, abased the high? I will make it
guilt, guilt, guilt (or perhaps, inequality, inequality, inequality). And this has
not happened.' The Hebrew text appears to mean: 'This is not this! Lift up the

28   Prophesy, son of man, and give a message from the Lord God to the
men of Ammon, in answer to their taunts: Drawn be the sword, cried
29 they,[1] whetted be the sword and bright for its work of slaying! Nay,
sword of Ammon, it was but a vain dream, a lying augury, that it should
be thy office to fall on the necks of yonder doomed sinners, whose time
30 has run out. Back to thy sheath with thee, back to thy native soil; there,
31 in the land where thou wast fashioned, I will call thee to account. I
mean to pour out my vengeance on thee, blast thee with the fire of my
anger; barbarian foes shall have the mastery of thee, that are skilful only
32 to destroy. Fire shall feed on thee, earth run with thy blood, oblivion
bury thy name; I, the Lord, have given sentence.

CHAPTER TWENTY-TWO

2 WORD came to me from the Lord: Wilt thou not arraign them,
3   citizens of this murderous place, wilt thou not arraign them? Confront them with their foul misdeeds, and give them this message from
the Lord God: Here is a city that hastens her own end with open blood-
4 shed, soils herself with idols to her own undoing. Blood-spilth and idol-
filth have brought thy time nearer, shortened thy years; what marvel if I
5 let the heathen reproach thee, a whole world mock thee? What marvel
if men exult over thee, far and near, great only in thy misfortune, as thou
6 art renowned only for thy shame? No better title now to Israel's nobility,
7 than to fill those streets with blood! Home of wrong, where father and
mother are despised, the stranger oppressed, widow and orphan ill-used!
8 My sanctuary, how it is despised, my sabbath how profaned! Innocent
lives sworn away, feasting at the hill-shrines, and foul deeds done besides;
10 see where a father's bed is dishonoured, a woman pleads her defilement
11 in vain; neighbour comes lecherously between his neighbour's sheets,
father beds incestuously with his son's wife, brother mates with sister
12 sprung of the same blood! The murderer's hire, usury and extortion,
gains won by violence; and of me, the Lord God says, never a thought!
13 Well may I smite hands together, indignant at thy ill-gotten gains, thy
14 murderous doings; will thy courage be so high, thy arm so powerful,
when it is I that reckon with thee? What the Lord threatens, the Lord

---

low, abase the high! I will make it distortion, distortion, distortion. And this
was not.'
[1] The words 'cried they,' and 'sword of Ammon' in the next verse, are not
in the original; they have been inserted above as being necessary for the understanding of what the passage presumably means. It appears that the Ammonites had hoped to profit by the misfortunes of Israel, instead of which they
will be involved in a common ruin.

15 fulfils. Far will I banish thee, widely scatter thee, and bring the tale of
16 thy shame to an end; so I will claim my rights over thee for all the world
to see, and thou shalt learn at last my power.
17   And word came to me from the Lord: Son of man, where the race of
Israel shews in the heart of the furnace, nothing I find but dross; all is
copper, and tin, and iron, and lead; dross of silver where silver should be.
19 This warning, then, the Lord God has for them: I mean to shut you up
20 in Jerusalem, dross as you are; this shall be your furnace, silver and
copper and tin and iron and lead, all together; and I will light a fire to
smelt you. There my angry vengeance shall imprison you, and I will give
21 you respite for a little, and then melt you down. Beleaguered there, with
22 the fire of my anger to smelt you like silver in the furnace, you shall feel
the force of the Lord's vengeance at last.
23   Then word came to me from the Lord: Son of man, tell the land of
Juda that it is unclean, and, when my vengeance falls on it, rain it shall
25 have none. What of the prophets? [1] A sworn conspiracy; lions roaring
for their prey, the lives of men; wealth and treasure they must have; there
26 be widows everywhere. What of the priests? Priests, that despise
my law, violate my sanctuary, cannot tell sacred from profane, count
all one, clean or unclean; priests, that leave my own sabbath un-
27 regarded; am I not defiled by their company? What of the nobles?
28 Ravening wolves, all blood and murder, greedy for gain; and here are the
prophets with their untempered mortar, their vain dreams and false
auguries, crying a message from the Lord when message from the Lord
29 they have none. Great wrong the citizens themselves do, robbing where
they will, harrying the helpless poor, oppressing the stranger and deny-
30 ing him redress. Who would close the breach, intercede with me to spare
31 the land from ruin? Never a man was found! What wonder if I have
poured out my vengeance, burnt them up in my anger? It was but their
deserts I gave them, says the Lord God.

CHAPTER TWENTY-THREE

2 WORD came to me from the Lord: There were two women once,
3 son of man, daughters of the same mother, that went to Egypt and
played the wanton there, so wanton and so young! There those breasts
4 surrendered to the attack, virginity was ravished. For their names, the
elder was called Oölla, the younger Oöliba; both I espoused, and they
bore me sons and daughters. (Samaria and Jerusalem are the true names).
5   What did Oölla? She played me false, love-sick for the Assyrians that

---

[1] For 'prophets' the Septuagint Greek has 'princes,' which may well be the
true reading; only a difference of one letter is involved in the Hebrew, and the
prophets are to be mentioned in verse 28 below.

6 dwelt hard by, her paramours. Gay gallants were these, princes and noblemen that went clad in purple, and proudly they came riding, for they were
7 horsemen all. Among the flower of Assyrian chivalry was none but enjoyed her favours; and she, that courted all alike, soiled herself with their
8 idolatry. Alas, still unforgotten her dalliance in Egypt; the lovers that
bedded her in her youth, mishandled her virgin breast, plied her with their
9 debauchery! Love-sick for new paramours, into their keeping she should
10 be given up, the Assyrians should have the mastery of her. How they
stripped and dishonoured her, robbed her of sons and daughters both,
and then put her to the sword! Never fell such signal punishment upon
womankind.

11   That sight before her, what did the other sister, Oöliba? Why, she out-
12 went the first in her wantonness, more lascivious yet; she too cast shame
aside, gave herself to the gallants of Assyria that came riding by, horsemen all, princes and noblemen in their broidered cloaks, so young, so
13 fair! Light women both; I knew them now. This other would set no
bounds to her lust; her eye fell on some pictured wall, where the men of
15 Chaldaea stood portrayed, all in crimson. What girdles they had about
their loins, these men of Babylon, what gaily-coloured turbans they
wore! Sure, they must be princes, all of them, in their own Chaldaean
16 land! And with that, her eye fell a-doting on them, and she must send
17 them a message all the way to Chaldaea. So the Chaldaeans, too, were
her bed-fellows, dishonoured her with their embraces, till even she grew
18 weary of dishonour. Weary was I too, as once of her sister; the open
19 harlotry, the public shame! Must she still renew her unfaithfulness,
20 hanker still after those old debaucheries in Egypt, when she was love-
sick for gallants lusty as the wild ass, hot as stallions?

21   Alas, Oöliba, are they remembered still, the passions of thy youth,
far away in Egypt, when those breasts surrendered to the attack, that vir-
22 ginity was ravished? This doom, then, the Lord God pronounces on
thee: They shall be summoned to the attack, all those old lovers thou art
23 wearied of, beleaguer thee round about; all those Chaldaeans from Babylon, nobleman and prince and chieftain, all those gay gallants from
Assyria, captains and rulers, lords paramount and knights of renown!
24 What rattling of chariot-wheels, what hordes of warriors in breast-plate
and shield and helmet, mustered about thy walls! These shall be thy
25 judges; theirs the sentence thou must abide. Ministers of my jealous
anger, they shall cut nose and ears off thee, and there shall be sword-
strokes yet; carry off thy sons and thy daughters, and the fire shall have
26 work to do yet. They shall strip thee of thy clothes, rifle thy proud orna-
27 ments; gone the memory of thy harlotries in Egypt, no hankering for
them now, no thought of Egypt now!
28   Weary thou art and disdainful of them, says the Lord God, but they

29 shall have the mastery of thee; and they shall use thee cruelly enough; carry all thy harvest away, and leave thee stripped and humbled; lay bare
30 the secret of thy shame. Lust it is and lechery of thine that has brought thee to this pass; so wantonly didst thou court the heathen, till at last
31 their idolatry infected thee. Thy sister's counterpart, the cup of thy
32 sister's doom thou shalt inherit; deep thy cup shall be as hers, wide as
33 hers; full of mockery and reproach, so much it holds, full of dizziness and dismay, full of despair and melancholy, the cup of thy sister Samaria.
34 Drink it thou shalt, ay, drain it to the dregs, till thou art ready to devour
35 cup itself piecemeal, or mutilate thy own breasts in thy madness.[1] Me thou didst forget; on me thy back was turned; wanton and faithless, thou shalt be held to account.

36 Arraign them, son of man, the Lord God said to me; confront Oölla
37 and Oöliba with the record of their foul deeds. Blood-stained those adulterous hands; false gods they have taken for their paramours, and to
38 the greed of false gods sacrificed their own children and mine. Theirs to
39 defile my sanctuary, profane my sabbath; no sooner had they done offering their sons to false gods, than my sanctuary must be violated; so would
40 they treat me in my own house. And then they sent word to their paramours, summoning them from afar.

They came, those paramours; and thou, fresh from the bath, eyes
41 painted, all thy ornaments hung about thee, didst await them, sitting on a fine bed with a table before it; incense of mine, oil of mine was there.
42 What a stir was heard there, as of a great throng taking their ease! They had brought in a rabble of desert folk with them, and these must be
43 given bracelets for their arms, fine garlands for their heads. And I wondered whether she would grant them her favours, even she, that had
44 grown so old in unfaithfulness; but sure enough they went in, boldly as to a harlot's bed.[2]
45 Such lovers had Oölla and Oöliba, wantons both. Yet honest folk there be,[3] that can judge their deeds as adultery should be judged and
46 murder; adulterous they are and murderous both at once. Muster me a company of such men, the Lord God says, and let them make a fearful
47 example of these women, their prize. With stones from many hands, with swords from every side dispatch them; death for their children, the
48 fire for their homes! Rid we the land of its guilt; of such harlotry let all

---

[1] The text and meaning of this verse is doubtful.
[2] *vv.* 42–44. It can hardly be doubted that the Hebrew text as we have it is corrupt; no sense can be made out of it. The translation given above follows the Latin, which is somewhat less obscure.
[3] This may refer (by a metaphor) to the Chaldaeans, but more probably, in these concluding verses, the coming fate of Jerusalem is left out of sight, and appeal is made to the moral sense of the prophet's audience.

49 women beware! Wantonness punished, idolatry's guilt uncondoned; you shall know the Lord's power at last.

CHAPTER TWENTY-FOUR

AND so the ninth year came, and the tenth month, and the tenth day
2 of it. And the Lord gave me this message: Son of man, write down this day as The Day Itself.[1] This day, this very day, the king of Babylon
3 has closed his grip on Jerusalem. A riddle, a parable, for the rebellious brood! Tell them the Lord God this bidding gave thee: Set a pot on the
4 fire, but filling it first with water; slice after slice goes in, all that is best;
5 thigh and shoulder, the best joints of all, to fill the pot; and fat be the sheep that yields them. Pile high the fuel [2] beneath; now boil pot, and
6 see the stew, there in the heart of it! But ah, says the Lord God, what of the city that is stained with blood? It is no better than a pot covered with rust, that cannot be scraped off any longer; broken in pieces that must be
7 cast away one by one; never shall the lot fall upon it.[3] Blood plain for all to see, spilt on the polished rock, not on earth that might hide it away
8 under the dust; rock, not earth, so I would have it; blood unconcealed, to warrant my angry frown, my avenging punishments!
9 Out upon the blood-stained city, says the Lord God, the great pyre
10 I mean to kindle! Pile high the fuel for its burning! Why, how is this,
11 meat wasted, the whole dish charred, the very bones calcined? Empty of water it must be set on the coals, till it is red-hot, and copper melts away,
12 and the stain on it is burnt out, and it is rusty no more! Alas, it is but labour spent in vain; so deep is that rust, even the fire will not drive it
13 out.[4] A curse lies on this uncleanness of thine; purge thee I would, yet

---

[1] Literally, 'write down the name of this day, this very day.'

[2] The word translated 'fuel,' here and in verse 10, is in the Latin 'bones.' The Hebrew text has 'bones' here and 'wood' in verse 10; the two Hebrew words differ only by a single letter. There is some likelihood that the original had 'wood' in both places.

[3] The Hebrew text is obscure, and perhaps corrupt; as it stands, it must mean that the rusty pot was thrown away in pieces, not that it was emptied of the slices of meat. It is difficult to see why a 'lot' should fall upon it; unless indeed we are to think of it as so riddled with holes that it could not even be used as an urn for casting lots in.

[4] *vv.* 10–12. No certainty can be attained about the meaning of this passage. The Latin, but not the Hebrew text, has the word 'empty' in verse 11; it is rendered above 'empty of water,' on the assumption that we are meant to look back to verse 3. A cooking-vessel with no water in it—possibly because it has rusted away into holes—will char the meat that is put into it and afterwards be burnt through, so that it is left more useless than ever. But it is not clear that this is the meaning.

purged thou wilt never be, never till I have taken full toll of my ven-
14 geance on thee.   Such is my divine doom; come it must, executed it needs
must be; indulgence is none, nor mercy, nor pity; I will pay thee what thy
ill life, thy ill thoughts have earned.

15   The Lord's word came to me,   Son of man, I mean to smite thee down,
by taking away from thee what thou most lovest. Dole make thou none,
17 nor lament, shed never a tear.   Unmarked be thy sighing, with no funeral
grief made; thy head covered, thy feet shod, no veil on thy face, no cus-
18 tomary fare of mourners.   And so it was; that morning I uttered my word
to the people, and my wife died at set of sun. Next day, I did as the Lord
19 bade me,   and the people were all agog to know the meaning of what I
20 did.   Why, I told them, the Lord has spoken to me,   giving me a message
for the race of Israel: he means to profane his own sanctuary, that proud
boast of yours, which you love so, trembling ever for its safety. Sons and
daughters of yours, left behind at Jerusalem, will die at the sword's point.
22 As I do now, you will do then; no veils on your faces, no customary fare
23 of mourners;   heads covered, feet shod, you will make neither dole nor
lament, but languish ever under the load of your guilt, sighing each of
24 you in his neighbour's ear.[1]   In Ezechiel, says the Lord God, read your
own doom; when that day comes, you will be at pains to do as he does
now, your lesson learnt at last.

25   Yes, son of man, the day is coming when I will rob them of that
citadel of theirs, that proud boast of theirs, so well loved, the comfort of
their thoughts; rob them, too, of sons and daughters. And what of thy-
27 self?   Wait till a fugitive comes and tells thee the news;[2] then, when he
utters his message, utter thou thine, dumb no longer. So thou shalt be
the presage of their doom, and they shall learn my power at last.

CHAPTER TWENTY-FIVE

2 WORD came to me from the Lord: Son of man, turn thy regard
3 towards the Ammonites, and prophesy their doom.   Give Ammon
this message from the Lord God: Joy, joy! was thy cry when my sanctuary was profaned, Israel ravaged, the men of Juda carried off into
4 exile;   what shall be thy reward? The eastern folk shall enjoy thy lands;
sheep-cote of theirs, tent of theirs shall be found in thee, crop of thine
5 they shall eat, milk of thine drink;   camels lodged in Rabbath, and all
Ammon a pasture-land of sheep!   Thus you shall know what power is

---

[1] *vv.* 22, 23. Various reasons have been suggested for this absence of public
lament among the exiled community; fear of political consequences is perhaps
the simplest explanation.

[2] It seems to be implied that Ezechiel received no more revelations for his
own fellow-countrymen during the two years of the siege. Cf. 33.21.

6 mine. For clapping of hand and stamping of foot, and heart that re-
7 joiced at Israel's fall, that power shall be used in vengeance; all the
world shall have the pillaging of thee, till thou art a nation no longer,
a kingdom no longer; thy ruin shall teach thee what manner of God I am.
8 This doom, too, the Lord God pronounces: Boasted they, the Moabites
9 and the men of Seir, that Juda had gone the way of other lands? I will
lay open the valleys of Moab, that climb up from the cities, those frontier
10 cities, fair Bethjesimoth, and Beelmeon and Cariathaim; open them to
the men of the east in their pursuit of the Ammonites, and all shall be
11 overrun. Ammon shall be blotted out from the memory of mankind,[1] and
there is justice, too, awaiting the Moabites; they too shall learn my power.
12 And this: Ill did the Edomites to glut their malice, by taking their
13 revenge on Juda. This doom the Lord God pronounces: My hand is
raised to smite Edom, sparing neither man nor beast, making a desert of
it all the way from Teman in the south to Dedan, that shall be put to the
14 sword. My own people of Israel shall execute this sentence against Edom,
avenge for me the grudge I bear it; then it shall be seen how I punish my
enemies, the Lord God says.
15 And this: Rancour of the Philistines, that murderous toll would take,
16 old scores would settle! Against the Philistines, too, this hand is raised;
executed they shall be, the executioners;[2] the dwellers on the sea-coast,
17 all that is left of them, I mean to exterminate. Great havoc I mean to
make of them, unrelenting in my anger; such havoc as shall teach them
to know what the Lord is.

CHAPTER TWENTY-SIX

IN king Sedecias' eleventh year, on the first day of the . . . month,
2 word came to me from the Lord: Son of man, what was the cry of Tyre
over Jerusalem? Joy, joy, the toll-gate[3] of the world has been broken
3 down! It is mine now; I shall grow fat on Jerusalem's ruin! This doom
the Lord God pronounces: Have at thee, Tyre! I mean to bring hordes of

---

[1] *vv.* 9, 10. Literally, 'Behold, I will open up the shoulder of Moab from the
cities; from his cities, I say, and from his frontiers; (I will open up) those
famous (cities) of the earth, Bethjesimoth, Beelmeon and Cariathaim, to the sons
of the east with the sons of Ammon,' etc. It seems probable that the whole prophecy against Moab has come down to us in a faulty text; the mention of Seir
(Edom) in verse 8 comes too early, the mention of Ammon in verse 10 too late.

[2] 'The executioners'; that is, the Cerethites, a Philistine clan, 'cutters-down'
both by the derivation of their name, and by the office they enjoyed under the
early kings of Israel (II Kg. 8.18, III Kg. 2.25, 29).

[3] In the original simply 'the gate,' but it is difficult to see how Tyre could
have regarded Judea as her rival, except in the sense that it lay on the trade
route between the Gulf of Akabah (III Kg. 9.26, 22.49) and the Phoenician ports.

4 nations marching on thee, like wave upon wave of the sea. Walls of Tyre they shall break down, and towers of her overthrow; all the soil I will
5 scrape away from her, and leave her bare rock, doom her to be but an island where fisher-folk dry their nets: I, the Lord God, will give her over
6 as a prey to all the nations. Daughter-towns that stand in her territory shall be put to the sword, and learn my power at last.

7 Here is Nabuchodonosor of Babylon, the Lord says, a king that has kings for his vassals, marching from the north with horse and chariot,
8 with his knights and all his retinue, a great army of men, to put thy daughter-towns to the sword, compass thee with siege works and raise a
9 mound about thee. A barrier of shields he will raise under thy walls, ply engine and battering-ram against them, and bring down thy towers with
10 grappling-irons. Of horses such a company, as shall cover thee all with dust; with cries of horsemen and rattle of chariot-wheels entering thy
11 gates, thy walls shall ring again like the walls of a breached city. Never a street of thine but must echo with hoofs; butchered thy citizens shall be,
12 thy fair pillars cast down, thy wealth plundered, thy merchandise taken for spoil. Down shall come walls, palaces totter in ruins; stone and timber
13 and mortar of thine shall strew the seas. Hushed the murmur of thy
14 songs; never more the sound of harp shall be heard in thee. Bare rock thou shalt be, for fisher-folk to dry their nets on; there shall be no building thee again, says the Lord God.

15 This too: The very isles shall echo with the crash of thy fall, ring with
16 the cries of the wounded dying in thy streets. Down from their thrones they shall come, all the lords of the sea-harbours, throw robe aside, broidered coats lay down; wrapped in dismay they sit on the bare ground,
17 at the sudden fall of thee bewildered and amazed. And thus they shall sing thy dirge: What a doom was thine, sea-built city, far renowned!
18 Mistress of the seas, mother of a race that all held in dread! Day of terror, that affrights the very ships, fills the islands with alarm, to see no ships leave thy harbour now!

19 This too: Desolate thou shalt be, thy place among the lost cities; higher and higher yet the fathomless ocean shall rise about thee, swallowing thee
20 up under its waters. Among the dead thy place is, that go down into the grave, where time is not; entombed with those other ruined cities in the depths of earth, tenanted no longer. The living world shall see the glory
21 of my presence, but thou shalt have no part in it, thou shalt no longer be; who searches for thee will search evermore in vain, says the Lord God.[1]

---

[1] *vv.* 19–21. Actually the siege of Tyre lasted for thirteen years (cf. 29.18), and her commercial prosperity remained considerable for many centuries. Thus it seems clear that the sentence of overthrow, however well deserved in Ezechiel's time, was not literally executed, in the counsels of divine Providence, till much later.

CHAPTER TWENTY-SEVEN

2 AND word came to me from the Lord: Son of man, do thou thyself
3 sing the dirge over Tyre. A message from the Lord God to the city
that is built by the sea's gates, and trafficks with many peoples on many
4 shores! Thine was the boast of perfect beauty, the embosoming sea thy
frontier. A well-fitted ship thou wert, such as they build on yonder coast;
5 of fir-wood from Sanir thy outer planks, of Lebanon cedar thy mast,
6 oars shaped from Basan oak, thy thwarts of box-wood [1] from the western
7 islands, with marquetry of Indian ivory. Of broidered linen from Egypt
the sails they spread for thee, awning of blue and purple from the Grecian
isles gave thee shade.
8 　For thee, men of Sidon and of Arad manned the oar; thyself, Tyre,
9 gavest men of skill, thy own citizens, to be helmsmen. For thy dock-
yards,[2] all the grey-haired wisdom of Gebal was at thy command, and for
10 trafficking, never was ship or sailor in the world but visited thee. Warriors from Persia, from Lydia, from Africa, fought thy battles, with
11 shield and helmet decked thy walls; men of Arvad ringed the battlements, thy defenders, and the Gammadim,[3] too, were mounted on thy
towers, on thy walls hung their quivers; lacked nothing for thy adornment.
12 　And for the merchants that dealt with thee, how Carthage poured her
13 wealth into thy market-place, of silver and iron, of tin and lead! What
purveyors of thine were Ionia, Thubal, and Mosoch, with their slaves to
14 sell thee, their urns of bronze; and the men of Thogorma, with horse and
15 horseman and mule! The sons of Dedan were thy pedlars; riches came
to thee from the islands far away; ivory and ebony thou couldst win by
16 barter. Syria, too, for the multitude of thy wares, must trade with thee,
exposing in thy mart carbuncles, and purple, and embroidery, and lawn,
17 and silk, and rubies. Juda and Israel themselves had their yield to bring
thee, fresh wheat and balm and honey and oil and gum for thy stalls.
18 Damascus, for thy many goods, had much to exchange, rare wines and

---

[1] It seems almost certain that this word stood in the original, but, being rare,
was wholly misconstrued. Thus our present Hebrew text speaks of 'the daughter
of Assyria,' the Septuagint Greek of 'forest-shrine habitations,' and the Latin
version of 'small country-houses.' For 'western' the Latin version has 'Italian,'
but this is only a guess; Balearic box-wood is probably meant.

[2] In the Hebrew text 'to caulk thy leaks'; in the Latin version 'for the admin-
istration of thy varied equipment.'

[3] Who the Gammadim were, is unknown; some think they were the Cappa-
docians. The Latin version can hardly be right in identifying them with the
pygmies.

19 brightly dyed wool; Dan and Ionia and Mosel offered wrought iron for
20 sale, with cassia and calamus supplied thee. Dedan brought thee saddles;
21 Arabia and Cedar's chieftains were at thy call, driving in lamb and ram
22 and goat for thy purchasing. The merchants of Saba and Reema were
   thy merchants too, with spices and precious stones and gold to shew in
23 thy fairs; Haran, Chene and Eden, Saba, Assur and Chelmad, none of
24 them but exchanged traffick with thee; and how rich the variety of it, the
   coverlets of blue, the embroideries, the treasure-caskets wound about with
   cords, the cedar-wood, all for thy profit! [1]
25   But the ships, they were thy pedlars in chief; the ocean-going ships,
26 that gave thee thy wealth, gave thee thy sea-environed renown. Alas, that
   those oarsmen of thine should have ferried thee out into deep waters, for
27 the storm-wind to catch thee, out in the heart of the sea! All thy wealth
   and treasure and merchandize, thy mariners and helmsmen, dockyard
   masters and captains, all the warriors thou hast, and the common folk
   that dwell in thee, must sink down to the sea's depths in this day of thy
28 fall. Bewildered, all thy navy, with the helmsmen's shouts; down come
30 the rowers from their ships, mariner and pilot line the shore. Loud their
   wailing, bitter their cry, as they throw dust on their heads and sprinkle
31 themselves with ashes; heads are shaven, sackcloth is every man's wear;
32 woeful hearts are all around, and woeful lament. And a sad dirge they
   shall sing as they mourn over thee: City was none like Tyre, that now lies
33 forgotten in the depths of the sea! Peoples a many thy trafficking supplied; all the kings of the earth were richer for wealth of thine, enterprise
34 of thine; and now the sea has swallowed thee up; buried in the deep
   waters all the prosperity that was thine, all the citizens that thronged
35 thee. The island peoples, how they stood aghast at thy fall; the island
36 kings, how their faces fell at the news of thy shipwreck! How they hissed
   in derision, the traders of other nations! Only ruin is left of thee, for ever
   vanished and gone.

CHAPTER TWENTY-EIGHT

2 AND word came to me from the Lord: Son of man, give this message
   from the Lord God to the prince of Tyre: An ill day for thee, when
   thy proud heart told thee thou wast a god, enthroned god-fashion in the

---

[1] *vv.* 12–24. There is considerable uncertainty, all through this section, about
the identification of the nations mentioned and their wares. In verse 16 Aram
(Syria) is probably a mistake for Edom, which resembles it in Hebrew script;
the Edomite caravans would naturally bring eastern goods from the Red Sea.
Syria, under the name of Damascus, has a separate mention below. The text
at the beginning of verse 19 is almost certainly corrupt.

heart of the sea! Mortal man, thou hast played the god in thy own
3 thoughts. What if a Daniel thou wert for wisdom, no secret hidden from
4 thee? Skill and craft have brought thee power, lined thy coffers with
5 gold and silver; and this skill of thine, this pedlar's empire of thine, have
6 made thee proud of thy own strength. This doom, then, the Lord God
7 has for thee, man that wouldst play the god: I mean to embroil thee with
foreign foes, a warrior nation as none else, that shall draw sword on that
8 fair creature, thy wisdom, soil thy beauty in the dust! Dragged down to
9 thy ruin, wounded to thy death, there in the heart of the sea, wilt thou
still boast of thy godhead to the slayer, while his sword ungods thee?
10 Such my doom is for thee, death at an alien's hand, the uncircumcised for
thy company.
11   This too: Son of man, sing a dirge over yonder king of Tyre.[1] This be
thy message to him from the Lord God: The token, thou, of my con-
13 siderateness.[2] How wise thou wast, how peerlessly fair, with all God's
garden to take thy pleasure in! No precious stone but went to thy adorning; sardius, topaz, jasper, chrysolith, onyx, beryl, sapphire, carbuncle
and emerald; all of gold was thy fair fashioning. And thy niche [3] was pre-
14 pared for thee when thou wast created; a cherub thou shouldst be, thy
wings outstretched in protection; there on God's holy mountain I placed
15 thee, to come and go between the wheels of fire.[4] From the day of thy
16 creation all was perfect in thee, till thou didst prove false; false within
all these traffickings had made thee, and for thy guilt I must expel thee,
guardian cherub as thou wert, from God's mountain; between the wheels
17 of fire thou shouldst walk no longer. A heart made proud by its own

---

[1] *v.* 11. The 'king' of Tyre, to whom the foregoing ten verses were addressed,
was doubtless a historical figure. But it is not certain that we ought to read
verses 12–19 in the same connexion; the exaggerated phrases would suggest a
rhetorical apostrophe to the Tyrian god Melkarth ('King of the City'). Further,
it seems evident that the prophet identifies him (local king or local god) with
Satan, or some other fallen angel; cf. the reference to Lucifer in Is. 14.12.

[2] Literally, 'the seal of similitude.' The Latin, like the other versions, gives
a literal rendering of a confessedly obscure phrase in the Hebrew. The noun
translated 'similitude' occurs only here. It is the verbal noun of a verb meaning
to regulate, to adjust, to put in a right proportion. There are nineteen occurrences of the verb in Scripture, and nine of these are in chapter 18 above or in
chapter 33 below. It seems best, then, to assume that we have here a cross-
reference. The equitableness or considerateness of Almighty God in punishing
the just man who has turned sinner is illustrated by his treatment of the fallen
Angel, who is therefore described as a seal or token of (his) considerateness.

[3] Literally 'holes' (or just possibly 'flutes'). If the text is right, a niche meant
for a god's image is perhaps the nearest tolerable meaning.

[4] Literally, 'stones of fire.' But no plausible suggestion has been made as to
what-'stones of fire' could mean, and a very slight alteration in the Hebrew
word would give the sense of 'wheels,' readily understandable in view of numerous passages (*e.g.* 9.6 above).

beauty, wisdom ruined through its own dazzling brightness, down to
18 earth I must cast thee, an example for kings to see.   Great guilt of thine,
all the sins of thy trafficking, have profaned thy sanctuaries; such a fire
I will kindle in the heart of thee as shall be thy undoing, leave thee a heap
19 of dust on the ground for all to gaze at.   None on earth that recognizes
thee but shall be dismayed at the sight of thee; only ruin left of thee, for
ever vanished and gone.
20   This too: Son of man, turn thy regard towards Sidon, and prophesy
22 its doom. This message give it from the Lord God: Have at thee, Sidon!
Battle-field thy territory shall be of my renown! In her, too, my power
shall be made known, my sentence executed, my holiness vindicated.
23 Plague I mean to bring down on her and blood-letting both; the sword
everywhere, and wounded men dying in her streets, to prove what power
the Lord has.
24   No more shall the Israelites have scornful enemies round about, thorns
and briers to prick and hurt them; they shall know at last what manner
25 of God they serve. When I restore the scattered race of Israel from its
exile, the Lord God says, my holiness shall be vindicated for all the
world to see. The land I gave to my servant Jacob shall be thence-
26 forward its home; securely it shall dwell there, build houses, plant vineyards, fear no attack. It shall see every scornful neighbour punished, and
know at last what it is to have the Lord for its God.

CHAPTER TWENTY-NINE

IT was the tenth year of Sedecias, on the eleventh day of its tenth
2 month, when word came to me from the Lord: Son of man, turn thy
regard towards Pharao, king of Egypt, and prophesy his and all Egypt's
3 doom. This message give him from the Lord God: Have at thee, Pharao,
king of Egypt, great dragon that liest couched between thy streams,
4 boasting that yonder river is thy own, thou art a god, self-created! [1] Trust
me, I will bridle those jaws of thine, and all the fish in thy river I will
fasten to thy scales! Out of the river, fish clinging to scales, I will drag
5 thee, and leave thee aground in the desert, and thy fish too. None shall
go out to search for thy corpse, or bring it home; carrion it shall be for
6 beast on earth, for bird in heaven, and all the citizens of Egypt shall
learn my power. This, because thou didst prove a staff of cane to the men
7 of Israel; [2] grasped they that staff, it splintered, and there was an arm
wounded; leaned they on it, it broke, and their strength gave way under
them.

---

[1] Literally, 'thou didst make thyself,' but some think the sense is 'thou didst
make it (the river) for thyself,' cf. verse 9.
[2] Cf. Is. 36.6.

8   This doom, then, the Lord God pronounces: For thee, the sword; man
9 nor beast will I spare in thee;   a lonely desert thou shalt be, till thou hast
   learned what my power is, thou that wouldst be river's lord and river's
10 maker.   Out upon thee, out upon those streams of thine; a desert Egypt
   shall be, devastated by the sword, from Syene's tower to the marches of
11 Ethiopia;   man nor beast shall set foot in it till it has lain forty years
12 desolate.   Land of Egypt shall be as the desert lands are, cities of Egypt
   as the ruined cities are, for forty years uninhabited; and the men of
   Egypt shall be scattered wide as earth among the nations.
13   This too: At the end of forty years I will bring the Egyptians back
14 from their countries of exile,   restore them from banishment, and in
   Phatures, the land of their birth, give them a home once more; there they
15 shall be a kingdom of little account.   Least of the kingdoms Egypt shall
   be, no more hold up its head among the nations, too weak for empire now.
16 No more shall it raise hopes among the men of Israel, and bring upon
   them the guilt of finding a refuge there; they shall learn that I, the Lord,
   am their God.
17   It was on the first day of the twenty-seventh year [1] that word came to
18 me from the Lord: Son of man, here is great drudgery king Nabuchodonosor of Babylon has given his men in the assault upon Tyre; every head
   worn bald, every shoulder smooth, by the burdens they carried! A
19 thankless service it was they did me there, he and his army;   but now,
   says the Lord God, I will make use of Egypt to pay Nabuchodonosor his
   wages; all its great wealth he shall have, spoil for his spoiling, plunder for
20 his plundering, and so his men shall have their reward.   He has fought
21 my battles, and Egypt shall be his recompense, the Lord God says.   When
   that day comes, new life shall spring from the stock of Israel, and to the
   men of Israel thou shalt speak with unhampered utterance, to attest my
   divine power.

CHAPTER THIRTY

2 AND again word came to me from the Lord: Son of man, tell them
   their doom in the name of the Lord God, and bid them raise loud
3 lament: Alas, alas the day!   Nearer, nearer it comes, the Lord's reckoning
4 day, dawning in cloud; it is the heathen's turn now.   Egypt shall feel the
   sword, and far Ethiopia tremble to see Egypt's warriors dying, Egypt's
5 wealth carried away, the foundations of Egypt overthrown.   Ethiop and
   Libyan and Lydian, all that motley host, men of Chub and men that hold

---

[1] The other dates given in these chapters plainly refer to the reign of Sedecias, though this is not expressed in the original. Less certainty can be felt about
the 'twenty-seventh year'; cf. note on 1.1.

6 their lands under treaty, by that same sword shall perish. Such doom the Lord God pronounces; gone, all the props that supported her, gone her proud empire; all that lies beyond Syene, the Lord says, ravaged by the 7 sword! Land of Egypt shall be as the desert lands are, cities of Egypt as 8 the ruined cities are; my power they will never learn till I have spread 9 fire over their country, till all their allies have perished. When that day comes, there will be ships carrying news of my onset, to daunt the courage of Ethiopia; Egypt's doom approaching, they shall know it and be afraid.

10 This too: I mean to make an end of Egypt's prosperity, through king 11 Nabuchodonosor of Babylon; he and his army, in all the world is none fiercer, shall be let loose for the land's undoing, their swords drawn to 12 fill Egypt with dead. I will dry up the course of its rivers, and leave the land at the mercy of its bitter enemies; nothing in it but shall be ravaged 13 by alien hands; I, the Lord, have decreed it. Down shall come the idols of Memphis, the Lord God says, I will have no more false gods there, and prince in all the land shall be none. Such terrors Egypt shall know, 14 Phatures all in ruin, Taphnis afire, in Alexandria my doom executed. 15 Pelusium, her fortress, shall feel my vengeance, Alexandria be laid 16 waste; all Egypt shall be ablaze, such bitter throes Pelusium shall have, Alexandria such devastation, Memphis such hard straits day by day. 17 Their warriors put to the sword, Heliopolis shall be enslaved and Bubas- 18 tis; dark days there shall be at Taphnis, when I crush the power of Egypt there, and all the pride of her empire is gone; a city in darkness, 19 with all her women-folk carried off into exile. Such doom I will execute upon the Egyptians, and they shall know my power at last.

20 In the eleventh year of Sedecias, on the seventh day of the first month, 21 word came to me from the Lord: Son of man, I have left Pharao, king of Egypt, with his arm broken; bound up and healed it may not be, clout or bandage is none to wind about it and give it support, give it strength to 22 hold sword again. Out upon Pharao, king of Egypt, says the Lord God; that strong arm of his, that broken arm of his, I will disable, strike the 23 sword from his hand; dispersed among the nations Egypt shall be, 24 scattered to the winds. Strong arms I will give the king of Babylon, and a sword to wield, to Pharao broken arms, and the groans of dying men 25 for all his comfort. Nabuchodonosor strong, and Pharao disabled; my power shall be known, when my sword, in Babylon's hand, hangs over 26 Egypt; my power shall be known, when the men of Egypt are scattered wide as earth among the nations.

CHAPTER THIRTY-ONE

2 THEN, on the first day of the third month, word came to me from the Lord: Son of man, here is a message for Pharao, king of Egypt, and his retinue. Say to him, This greatness of thine, whose memory does it

3 recall? Not less powerful once was the Assyrian [1] king, a very cedar of Lebanon. How fair its boughs, yonder tree, its leaves how overshadow-

4 ing; what height, what thickness of growth about its top! Water nour- ished it, water came up from the depth beneath to sustain it, washed

5 about its roots and parted into runnels to feed the trees around. In all the countryside none rose so tall, had covert so thick, branches so wide;

6 none fed so deep. Among its boughs the birds nested, the beasts in their travail sought its shade; proud nations a many under Assyria's shelter

7 grew. So fair it was, so tall and spreading, there by the brimming water's

8 side, in God's own garden cedar could not overtop it, fir-tree match it for height, or plane-tree for shade. God's garden itself could not shew

9 such beauty: never a tree there, tree of Eden,[2] but must envy it the leafy loveliness that was my gift.

10 Alas, that he should aim too high, the Lord God says; alas for youth's

11 luxuriant promise, that swelled his heart with pride! I must needs hand him over to a conquering power, that should settle my reckoning with

12 him; he, the godless, homeless should be. Cut down, yonder tree, by alien woodmen, and left to lie on the hill-side, boughs choking the valleys, branches carried off by the mountain streams; vassal nations

13 abandoned his shelter, and he was all alone. In the fallen trunk birds

14 nested, under torn branches the wild beasts made their lair; never again should tree boast of its height, there by the river bank, overtopping the covert of the woods, never again should the waters nourish its pride. Death and the deep earth should await them all, mortal things to a mortal doom appointed.

15 Sad dirge was his, the Lord God says, at his down-going; the great depth was the shroud of him, its flooding streams hushed and stayed;

16 mourned Lebanon, and all the forest swooned away. How it echoed through the world, the crash of his fall! He too, like all mortal things, was for the earth at last; comfort for those others that were brought to earth

---

[1] Some think that the name of Assyria has crept in through an error in the text, and that Egypt itself, not Assyria, is being compared to the cedar-tree. In verse 6, there is no mention of Assyria in the original; it has been introduced for the sake of clearness, on the assumption that the text of verse 3 has been correctly preserved.

[2] Here, and in verses 16 and 18, the name 'Eden' has been translated ('pleas- ure') in the Latin version.

like himself, trees of Eden like himself, so noble, so fair, so well watered!
17 All alike must go down to the grave, the sword's way; his arm . . .[1]
18   . . . his shadow their protection against surrounding nations. And thou, in thy greatness and glory among Eden's trees so like him! Yet thou, like other Eden trees, must come down low as earth can bring thee; and the sword shall level thee with the uncircumcised in death. (Pharao is meant, and Pharao's retinue.) [2]

CHAPTER THIRTY-TWO

AND in the twelfth year, on the first day of the twelfth month, word
2 came to me from the Lord: Son of man, sing a dirge for Pharao, the king of Egypt, that counts for a lion among the nations: Monster thou art of the depths, holding up thy head in those rivers of thine, fouling the
3 waters of every trampled stream! This doom the Lord God pronounces: A net-work I have of many peoples that I will cast over thee, a seine that
4 will bring thee presently ashore. High on the beach I will leave thee aground, for all the birds to perch on thee, all the beasts to take their fill
5 of thee; flesh of thine shall strew the mountains, with blood of thine the
6 gullies shall overflow, reeking blood that drenches hill and chokes valley with its stream.
7   Thy light when I quench, muffled the skies shall be, the stars dim, the
8 sun beclouded, and the moon shall refuse her light; no luminary in heaven but shall go mourning for thee, and in that land of thine, the Lord God says, all shall be darkness.
9   Here shall be a challenge to many nations, in lands thou still knowest
10 not, when I tell them the story of thy downfall; peoples there shall be that gape in bewilderment, kings that tremble and quake at the story of thee. My sword they shall see flashing before their eyes, and each for his
11 own life shall tremble in the day of thy fall. Sword of the king of Baby-
12 lon shall reach thee, the Lord God says; tried warriors thy thronging multitudes shall cut down, pitiless hordes that shall harry the pride of
13 Egypt, scatter her wealth. The very beasts that roam beside your full stream I will destroy; never foot of man, hoof of beast shall sully it thence-
14 forward; clear those waters shall be as never they were, smooth as oil
15 the river's flow, the Lord God says; all Egypt, now, shall be desolate, all its busy life shall be still, when I smite the men that dwell in it, and

---

[1] There seems to have been either an error, or an omission, in the Hebrew text. The Latin rendering, 'the arm of each will sit under its shade' yields no good sense.

[2] According to the Septuagint Greek, the concluding words of the chapter should read 'So (it will be with) Pharao and all his retinue.'

16 teach them to recognize my power. Make dole, then; here is good cause;
Egypt shall have the world for her mourner, none but shall mourn for
Egypt and her lost greatness, says the Lord God.

17   And on the fifteenth day of the month, this: Son of man, a dirge now
for the common folk of Egypt; sing Egypt to her grave, and with her

19 those other proud nations that must go down into the dark: Measure not
thy beauty against another's; to thy grave get thee, and with the uncir-

20 cumcised take thy rest. The sword carries off all alike; once loose it, she

21 and all her multitudes must perish. From the tomb they greet the new-
comer, those great warriors, men of the uncircumcised races, allies once,

22 that now lie there, slain in battle.[1] Here is the Assyrian king with all his

23 muster-roll; how their graves ring him about, dead warriors all! Down
there in the dark, his grave and theirs around him, dead now in battle,

24 that once daunted the hearts of the living! Here are the Elamites, too,
lying about their king, men uncircumcised that made themselves feared
in life, and now lie in the pit beneath with all those others, stripped and

25 shamed as they were left on the battle-field; (here he lies, with his men
about him for monument, once so feared; stripped and shamed they lie,
Elamites uncircumcised, there in the dark, there amongst the slain).[2]

26 Uncircumcised, too, the king of Mosoch and Thubal, with all his retinue

27 buried around him, dead now and feared no longer; shall they not sleep
on there with the slain warriors, with the uncircumcised, still armed,
swords beneath their heads; their corpses lawless yet, and feared no

28 longer?[3] Thy place too, the place of thy slain warriors, is with the uncir-

29 cumcised in their ruin. King and chief of the Edomites[4] lie slain among

30 the uncircumcised, there in the dark; so do all the kings of the north,
and the Sidonians, dismayed now and trusting no more in their own

31 valour, stripped and shamed. Well may Pharao and his men be comforted by that sight over the multitude of their slain, the Lord God says.

32 He too, in this living world, wielded my terrors; he too lies there, the
Lord God says, slain in battle, with the uncircumcised about him.

---

[1] In this curiously repetitive passage, from here to the end of the chapter,
the Latin version follows the Hebrew text, which is here so different from the
Septuagint Greek as to suggest the possibility of a very early corruption in the
manuscripts.

[2] This verse does not appear in the Septuagint Greek at all.

[3] It is difficult to attach any sense to this verse unless it is treated as a question,
not a statement. 'Their corpses lawless yet'; literally, 'their lawlessnesses were
upon their bones'; the absence of circumcision is perhaps referred to.

[4] The mention of the Edomites (who practised circumcision) is unexpected.
According to the Septuagint Greek, we return in this verse and the next to the
Assyrians.

CHAPTER THIRTY-THREE

2 WORD came to me from the Lord: Son of man, tell thy fellow-
countrymen this: Plague I a country with war, some frontier-
3 dweller is chosen by the citizens to be their sentry. Let such a man spy
4 the invader's approach, and sound the alarm with his trumpet; whoever
hears it must give good heed, or else the enemy may catch him, and none
5 but himself to blame. What, hear trumpet, and pay no heed? The fault
6 is his. More cautious, he should have found safety. But what if sentry,
when he sees the invader coming, sounds no alarm to warn his neighbours? Here is some citizen overtaken by the enemy; well, his guilt
deserved it. But for his death I will hold the sentry accountable.
7   So it is with thee, son of man; for the whole race of Israel thou art
8 my watchman. Sinner if I threaten with death, and warning thou give
him none to leave off his sinning, die he shall, as he deserves to die, but
9 thou for his death shalt answer to me. If warning thou givest, and he will
not leave off his sinning, he dies by his own fault, and thou shalt stand
acquitted.
10   This be thy word, son of man, to the race of Israel: Think you no hope
of life is left, so burdened you are, so languish under the guilt of your
11 sins? This message give them from the Lord: As I am a living God, the
sinner's death is none of my contriving! I would have him leave his
sinning, and live on. Come back, come back from your ill-doing; why
12 must you choose death, men of Israel? And warn them, son of man,
warn thy fellow-countrymen that, once the upright man falls a-sinning,
his uprightness shall nothing avail him. Sinner that will leave his sinning,
no harm shall he have; upright man that sins, no life shall his uprightness
13 bring him. Promise I the upright he shall live on, he must not by his own
uprightness be emboldened to sin; forgotten, all his good deserts, his
14 guilt shall be his undoing. Threaten I the sinner with instant death, he
15 has but to repent of his sins, do innocently and uprightly, restore the
debtor's pledge, the ill-gotten gains, follow the life-giving law, forswear
16 ill-doing, and it shall be life, not death for him. Forgotten, all his ill-
17 deserving; innocent and upright, he shall live on. And yet they say, these
fellow-countrymen of thine, that the Lord's dealings are inconsiderate,
18 when in truth it is they that deal inconsiderately. Death for the upright
19 that is upright no more, and turns ill-doer; life for the sinner that will
20 leave his sinning, upright and innocent now! Will you still have it that
the Lord's dealings are inconsiderate? Nay, men of Israel, each of you
shall have his deserts.
21   It was in the twelfth year of the exile, on the fifth day of the tenth

month, that a fugitive came to me with the news that Jerusalem had
22 fallen. That night, the power of the Lord had visited me, to unseal my
lips in readiness for his coming; so now I could speak out, and was dumb
23 no longer. And a message came to me from the Lord: Son of man, what
are they saying, the folk that now inhabit yonder ruins of Israel? Enough
of us, they say, to be the true heirs of this land! Abraham was granted
25 possession of it when he was all alone.[1] Tell them this from the Lord
God: You, that cook your meat with the blood in it, that look to false
26 gods for aid, that thrive by murder, the land's heirs! You, that live by
the sword, that practise foul rites, that dishonour your neighbours' wives,
27 the land's heirs! This is the Lord's message to them: As I am a living
God, ruin-dwellers, the sword shall be your ruin! Or choose you the
open country, you shall be a prey to the wild beasts; choose you moun-
28 tain-fastness and cave, the pestilence shall take you. A lonely desert this
land shall be, all its proud boast at an end; the hill-country of Israel shall
29 lie desolate, untrodden by wayfarers; desert and desolate their land
must be, in punishment of all their foul doings, before they learn to
recognize my power.

30   And thou, son of man, listen to what they are saying of thee, as they
stand close to wall, huddled under doorway. Each says to other, Come
31 and find out whether the Lord has any message for us. Ay, they come
crowding about thee, this people of mine, and sit here closeted with thee,
listening to all thou sayest, but do thy bidding they will not. No, they
will have thee sing in their own tune,[2] and all their thought dwells upon
32 gains ill-gotten. As well had it been some tuneful air, sung excellently
33 well; better listeners thou couldst not have, nor less achievement. But
when thy words come true, as come true they shall, none shall doubt
that they have had a prophet in their midst.

CHAPTER THIRTY-FOUR

2 WORD came to me from the Lord: Now, son of man, prophesy
doom to the rulers of Israel, the shepherds of my flock. This be thy
message from the Lord God: Out upon Israel's shepherds, that had a

---

[1] The contrast, 'Abraham was but one, and we are many' appears somewhat
forced. It seems just possible that this paragraph is addressed, not to Jews, but
the heathen still living in Palestine, who were not descended from Abraham,
and here express their intention of disputing his inheritance. It is perhaps worth
noticing that the sin of eating meat with the blood in it (verse 25) is not elsewhere mentioned among the delinquencies of Israel.

[2] Literally, 'they turn them (thy words) into a song of their mouth.' The
Hebrew text seems to mean 'they make loves in their mouths,' but for 'loves'
the Septuagint Greek has 'lies.'

3 flock to feed, and fed none but themselves; the milk drank, the wool
wore, the fat lambs slaughtered, but pastured these sheep of mine never
4 at all! The wasted frame went unnourished, the sick unhealed; nor bound
they the broken limb, nor brought strayed sheep home, nor lost sheep
5 found; force and constraint were all the governance they knew. So my
sheep fell a-wandering, that shepherd had none; every wild beast fell
6 a-preying on them, and they scattered far and wide. All over the hills
they strayed, all over the countryside were scattered, this flock of mine,
7 and no search was made for them, no search at all. This doom, then, the
8 Lord pronounces on yonder shepherds: As I am a living God, I will have
a reckoning for sheep of mine carried off, sheep of mine the wild beasts
have preyed on, while they went all untended, with shepherds that would
not go in search of them, shepherds that no flock would feed, but them-
9 selves only. A word, shepherds, for your hearing, a message from the
Lord God: Out upon yonder shepherds! I will hold them answerable for
the flock entrusted to them, and they shall have charge of it no more,
feed themselves out of its revenues no more. From their greedy power
I will rescue it; no longer shall it be their prey.

11   This is what the Lord God says: I mean to go looking for this flock of
12 mine, search it out for myself. As a shepherd, when he finds his flock
scattered all about him, goes looking for his sheep, so will I go looking
for these sheep of mine, rescue them from all the nooks into which they
13 have strayed when the dark mist fell upon them. Rescued from every
kingdom, recovered from every land, I will bring them back to their own
country; they shall have pasture on the hill-sides of Israel, by its water-
14 courses, in the resting-places of their home. Yes, I will lead them out
into fair pastures, the high mountains of Israel shall be their feeding-
ground, the mountains of Israel, with soft grass for them to rest on, rich
15 feed for them to graze. Food and rest, says the Lord God, both these I
16 will give to my flock. The lost sheep I will find, the strayed sheep I will
bring home again; bind up the broken limb, nourish the wasted frame,
keep the well-fed and the sturdy free from harm; [1] they shall have a true
shepherd at last.

17   And what of you, my flock? I mean to do justice, the Lord God says,
among the beasts themselves, give redress against the rams and the buck-
18 goats. What, was it not enough to have stripped the pasture-lands with
your grazing, drunk all that was purest out of the stream, but you must
19 trample and foul all that was left? None but trampled fields must my
20 sheep graze, none but fouled waters drink? This is what the Lord God
21 says: I mean to see justice done between fat beast and lean. Thrust back

---

[1] 'Keep . . . free from harm'; the Septuagint Greek has 'destroy,' which
would involve only a very slight alteration in the Hebrew.

with side and shoulder, gored with the horn, all the weaker of them have
22 been driven away; but now I mean to protect this flock of mine against
your greed, give beast redress against its fellow.
23 ... They shall have a single shepherd to tend all of them now; [1] who
24 should tend them but my servant David? He shall be their shepherd, and
I, the Lord, will be their God, now that he rules them on earth; such is
25 my divine promise to them. Renewal of my covenant shall grant them
security; beasts of prey there shall be none, safe resting, now, in the
26 desert, safe sleeping in the woods; on my hill-sides they shall dwell, a
blessed people in a blessed home, rain in its season fall on them, and
27 blessings all the while. Wild trees their fruit, the earth its crops shall
afford; undisturbed they shall dwell on their own lands, acknowledging
my power at last, my power that severed strap of yoke, rescued them from
28 the tyrant's hand. Forgotten, the enemies that despoiled, the wild beasts
29 that preyed on them; they will live sheltered from all alarms. Once more
their renown shall burgeon; [2] never again the land starve with drought,
30 never the alien's taunts be heard. None shall doubt that I, the Lord their
God, am at their side, and they are my own people, the race of Israel, the
31 Lord God says. Flock of mine, the Lord God says, flock of my pasturing,
you are but men, [3] yet I, the Lord, am your God.

CHAPTER THIRTY-FIVE

2 WORD came to me from the Lord: Son of man, turn thy regard
3 towards the hill-country of Seir, and prophesy its doom. This be
thy message from the Lord God: Have at thee, Seir! My hand is raised
4 to smite thee; desert thou shalt be and desolate; when I have pulled down
thy cities and left thee in ruins, thou shalt know my power at last.
5 Relentless foe, didst thou not cut off Israel's retreat in its most need,
6 when doom closed round it? As I am a living God, the Lord says, to
bloodshed I doom thee, bloodshed shall hunt thee down, the very
7 bloodshed that liked thee so little. [4] Desolate and desert mount Seir

---

[1] The rest of the chapter, from this verse onwards, has a different setting and a different emphasis from what goes before; there may have been some omission or misplacement.
[2] Literally, in the Hebrew text, 'I will raise up a planting for them for renown.' This is usually interpreted as implying a successful development of afforestation; the rendering given above perhaps makes the sentence less frigid.
[3] Or possibly, 'you are men' (as opposed to dumb beasts). But in either case the contrast seems uncalled for, and there is some reason to doubt whether the text has been correctly preserved; the Septuagint Greek has simply, 'you are the sheep of my flock and I am your God.'
[4] Literally, 'I have created thee (or appointed thee; in the Latin, I will hand

8 shall be, none come and go there, every crest of it piled high with the
   slain. Slain they shall fall, thy warriors, by hill-slope and valley and
9 ravine, till thou art left solitary for all time, thy cities uninhabited; so
10 thou shalt witness my power. Two nations and two countries (thy boast
   was), and both are mine; [1] to me is left the enjoyment of them! for-
11 getting that I, the Lord, dwell there. As I am a living God, the Lord
   says, the rankling grudge that embittered thee thou shalt feel to thy cost;
   by the doom I execute upon thee, Israel shall learn to know me better;
12 and thou too shalt learn that I, the Lord, was listening, when thy
13 arrogance claimed the deserted hill-country for thy prey. I was listening
14 to all those defiant blasphemies of thine, and now, says the Lord God,
15 let all the world rejoice as it will, thou shalt lie desolate. Ruined utterly'
   they shall be, mount Seir and all Edom, that triumphed in the ruin of
   Israel; the Lord's power shall be made known at last.

CHAPTER THIRTY-SIX

A ND now, son of man, to the mountains of Israel address thy pro-
2   phecy, and give them my divine message, comforting them, in the
   name of the Lord God, for the taunts of the enemy, that think to claim
3 possession of their ancient strongholds. Thus shall thy word of prophecy begin: Desolate you lie, the Lord God says, and overrun by the
   invader; aliens have the lordship of you, and your name is on men's lips,
4 a byword of common talk. Yet here is word for you, mountains of Israel,
   from the Lord God; word from him for crag and hill, ravine and valley
   and barren upland, ruined wall and deserted city, empty now and a
5 mockery to their neighbours! On Edom, on all the Gentiles that fell to
   and feasted on lands of mine, marked them down for pillage, my jealous
6 love pronounces doom. A promise, then, from the Lord God to every
   mountain and hill, every upland and valley in the land of Israel! Till now,
   the Lord God says, you have been put to the blush before your neighbours,
7 but now my love and my indignation can contain itself no more. My oath
   upon it, the Lord God says, these neighbours of yours shall be put to the
   blush in their turn.

thee over) to blood, and blood shall pursue thee; I swear that thou hast hated
blood, and blood shall pursue thee.' The word 'blood' is not used in the Hebrew
in the sense of 'kinship'; and it is not easy to see why the Edomites are rebuked
for 'hating blood,' unless possibly in the sense that they closed their frontiers
at the time of Juda's defeat, to keep the war out of their own territory. But there
is reason to suspect that the text is corrupt.

[1] The 'two nations and two countries' are usually identified as Israel and Juda.
But it may be questioned whether the reference is not to Israel (generally) and
Edom; cf. Gen. 25.23.

8   But you, mountains of Israel, must burgeon anew, and grow fruit for
9   my own people to enjoy; their home-coming is not far off now. Watch
for me, I am coming back to you; soil of you shall be ploughed and sown
10 anew; and men, too, shall thrive on it, Israel's full muster-roll, peopling
11 the cities, restoring the ruins. Full tale you shall have of men and beasts
that thrive and multiply; I will make you populous as of old, more than
12 of old my blessings lavish, and you shall not doubt my power. Masters
you shall have, and those masters my people of Israel, your rightful
13 lords; never shall they want lands or you lords again. Till now, the Lord
God says, men have called thee a land that starves folk and empties
14 cradle;[1] henceforth, his will is that thou shouldst starve thy folk, be-
15 reave thy folk, no longer; scoff and taunt of heathen neighbours thou
wilt have none to bear, he says, nor lack men to till thee henceforward.

16   This too: Son of man, how the race of Israel profaned this country of
theirs, when they still dwelt in it, by their lives and their likings! Cast
18 clouts of woman were less defiling. What marvel if my vengeance was
let loose on them for all the blood that stained it, all the idols that polluted
19 it? What marvel if I drove them out among the nations, scattered them
20 wide as earth, as lives and likings of theirs had deserved? But alas,
wherever they went among the heathen, they brought my holy name into
ill repute; These are the Lord's people, folk said, and here they are, exiled
21 from the land he loves! Should I let my holy name go unhonoured,
among the heathen that harboured them?

22   Give Israel, then, this message from the Lord God: It is not for your
own sakes, men of Israel, that I come forward as your champion; it is for
the sake of my holy name, brought into disrepute among the Gentiles
23 who have crossed your path. That great renown of mine I mean to vindicate, that is now dragged in the dust among the Gentiles, dragged in the
dust because of you. The very Gentiles will recognize my power, the
Lord God says, when I proclaim my majesty in their sight by delivering
24 you.[2] I mean to set you free from the power of the Gentiles, bring you
25 home again from every part of the earth. And then I will pour cleansing
streams over you, to purge you from every stain you bear, purge you
from the taint of your idolatry. I will give you a new heart, and breathe
26 a new spirit into you; I will take away from your breasts those hearts

---

[1] Literally, 'Thou art a devourer of men, that bereavest (in the Latin, stiflest)
thy population.' This was perhaps a proverbial saying about Palestine (Num.
13.33). The suggestion here is probably that it was not fertile enough to support
a large number of inhabitants. But the reference may be to the misfortunes of
Israel in general.

[2] *vv.* 20–23. The suggestion is, not that the Israelites in exile brought disgrace on the true religion by their sinfulness, but that the heathen looked with
contempt on a God who seemed unable to protect his votaries.

27 that are hard as stone, and give you human hearts instead. I will make
my spirit penetrate you, so that you will follow in the path of my law,
28 remember and carry out my decrees. So shall you make your home in
the land I promised to your fathers; you shall be my people, and I will
29 be your God. I will set you free from the guilt which stains you; [1] I will
send my word to the harvest, and bid it come up abundantly, from
30 drought spare you; yield of tree and crop of earth I will multiply, and the
31 heathen shall taunt you no longer with your starving lot. Well may you
think with loathing of what you were, as your minds go back to false
32 paths and crooked aims you once followed! Be assured of it, the Lord
God says, it was for no deserts of yours I delivered you; blush still, men
of Israel, for your crimes, hang your heads still!
33   This too: A time is coming when I will set you free from the guilt
which stains you; when I will people your cities, rebuild your ruins;
34 when the deserted land shall be tilled anew. Desolate the passers-by saw
35 it once; now they will say, Why, it is a very garden of Eden, the countryside which once lay all uncultivated; the empty towns, all gone to rack
36 and ruin, are walled and populous! And the heathen shall know, such
heathen as are your neighbours still, that I, the Lord, rebuild ruin and
37 plant wilderness; what the Lord promises, the Lord fulfils. This boon,
says the Lord God, Israel shall yet have of me, as a flock thrives their
38 manhood shall thrive. See how the victim-herd throngs the streets of
Jerusalem on her feast-days! Yonder empty cities shall be thronged, too,
but with men; the proof of my divine power.

CHAPTER THIRTY-SEVEN

THE Lord's power laid hold of me, and by the spirit of the Lord
I was carried away and set down in the midst of the plain, which
2 was covered with bones.[2] Round the whole extent of them he took me,
3 heaped up high on the plain, and all of them parched quite dry. Son of
man, he said, can life return to these bones? Lord God, said I, thou know-
4 est. Then he bade me utter a prophecy over the bones: Listen, dry bones,
5 to the word of the Lord. A message to these bones from the Lord: I mean
6 to send my spirit into you, and restore you to life. Sinews shall be given
you, flesh shall grow on you, and skin cover you; and I will give you
breath to bring you to life again; will you doubt, then, the Lord's power?

---

[1] Literally, 'I will save you from your stains'; but in verse 33, 'I will cleanse
you from your guilt.'
[2] We should expect to find the date or place of the vision specified, and some
think there is an omission in the manuscripts.

7   So I prophesied as he had bidden me, and as I prophesied a sound came, and I felt a stirring, and the bones came together, each at its proper

8 joint; under my eyes the sinews and the flesh clothed them, and the skin

9 covered them, but there was no breath in them even now. Son of man, he said, prophesy now to the breath of life; give the breath of life itself this message from the Lord God: Come, breath of life, from the four winds,

10 and breathe on these slain men to make them live. So I prophesied as he had bidden me, and the breath of life came into them, so that they lived

11 again; and all rose to their feet, host upon host of them. Then he told me, Son of man, in these bones here thou seest the whole race of Israel. They are complaining that their very bones have withered away, that all hope

12 is lost, they are dead men. It is for thee to prophesy, giving them this message from the Lord God: I mean to open your graves and revive you,

13 my people; I mean to bring you home to the land of Israel. Will you doubt, then, the Lord's power, when I open your graves and revive you?

14 When I breathe my spirit into you, to give you life again, and bid you dwell at peace in your own land? What the Lord promises, the Lord performs; you will know that, he tells you, at last.

15   And word came to me from the Lord: Son of man, take two pieces of wood, and write on one, For Juda, and the tribes of Israel that take part with him; on the other, that is the stick of Ephraim, write, For Joseph,

17 and all the tribes of Israel that take part with him. Then join them together into the form of a single stick, so that they are united in thy

18 hand. And when thy fellow-countrymen would have thee tell them what

19 thou meanest by all this, give them this message from the Lord: Here is this stick of Joseph and his confederate tribes, with Ephraim at their head; I mean to join it with Juda's and make one stick of it; one stick now, and in my hand.[1]

20   And while thou art still holding the inscribed sticks, there in the

21 presence of thy fellow-countrymen, say this: A message from the Lord God! I mean to recall the sons of Israel from their exile among the Gentiles, gather them from every side and restore them to their home.

22 And there, in the hill country of Israel, I will make one nation of them, with one king over them all; no longer shall they be two nations under

23 two crowns. No more shall they be contaminated with idol-worship, and foul rites, and forbidden things a many; I will deliver them from the lands [2] that were once the haunts of their sinning, and make them clean

---

[1] The Latin version gives 'in his hand,' but probably meaning 'the Lord's hand,' and assuming a break in the quotation. The Septuagint Greek has 'in Juda's hand,' that is, 'with Juda at their head.'

[2] The word means 'dwelling-places' or 'places of assembly,' and is used in 8.3 above for an idol's pedestal. But probably those critics are right who think that, by a slight error of copying, our text gives us 'dwelling-places' instead of 'apostasies,' which is the reading of the Septuagint Greek.

24 again; they shall be my people, and I will be their God. They shall have
   one king over them, a shepherd to tend them all, my servant David; my
25 will they shall follow, my commands remember and obey. And their
   home shall be the home of your fathers, the land I gave to my servant
   Jacob; they and their children shall enjoy it, and their children's children,
26 in perpetuity, and ever my servant David shall be their prince. My
   covenant shall pledge them prosperity, a covenant that shall never be
   revoked; I will make them . . .¹ and give them increase, and set up my
27 sanctuary in their midst for ever. My tabernacle over them; they my
28 people, and I their God; proof to all the world that I, the Lord, have set
   Israel apart, I that dwell apart in their midst for ever.

CHAPTER THIRTY-EIGHT

2 WORD came to me from the Lord: Son of man, turn thy regard now
   towards Gog, Magog's country, that has the lordship of Mosoch
3 and Thubal, and prophesy its doom.² This be thy message to it from the
   Lord God: Have at thee, Gog, that hast the lordship of Mosoch and
4 Thubal! Trust me, I will turn thee about this way and that, bridle those
   jaws of thine! I will bring thee out to battle, with all thy army; with
   horses and mailed cavalry, with a great company that ply spear and shield
5 and sword. Persians shall be there, and Ethiopians, and Libyans, all with
6 shield and helmet, Gomer with his hordes, the men of Thogorma from
   the northern hills, mustered in full force; what an array thou hast about
7 thee! Now hold thyself in readiness, marshal thy own strength and the
   hordes that follow thee; thine is the leadership.
8   Long hence thy turn shall come; long years must pass before thou dost

---

¹ Or perhaps, 'I will give them'; in either case, it seems as if there had been
an omission in the manuscripts. The Latin version renders, but inexactly, 'I
will found them.'

² If our text, in this verse and the verse which follows, has been correctly preserved, we are here meant to think of Gog as a people, not as a person; if any
individual is mentioned, it is Magog. Mosoch and Thubal appear to be the
Moschi and Tibareni, from the southern shores of the Black Sea; a general
descent of barbarians is clearly envisaged, comparable to the Scythian invasions
of B.C. 630. But the nations mentioned in verse 5 suggest that the picture is one
of allegory, rather than of history, and the identifications of 'Gog' with the
Persian emperor Cambyses or with Antiochus Epiphanes are probably misplaced
ingenuity. What is meant by the 'Prince-head' or 'prince of the head' is not clear;
the expression is not elsewhere found, and it is perhaps worth observing that
it might easily be a false reading in the Hebrew for 'one who lifts the head' (*i.e.,*
restores the fallen fortunes) of a man or a community (Gen. 40.13, IV Kg. 25.27,
Zach. 1.21). Thubal and Mosoch are undergoing a kind of resurrection, cf. 32.26
above.

march on Israel; a land, now, recovered from its blood-letting; its hills, desolate till now, are repeopled with exiles from many shores, come back
9 to dwell there in security. Storm never rose so suddenly, cloud-wrack never darkened it so fearsomely, as thou with that host of thine, those
10 confederate hordes. What thoughts will be in thy heart that day, the
11 Lord God says, what foul design will be a-brewing? Why, thou wilt think to march on a land unfortified, a people dwelling free from all alarms, that walls about them have none, bolt nor bar to shut them in;
12 spoil for thy spoiling, plunder for thy plundering. Easily enough they are like to fall into thy hand, the ruins so lately rebuilt; the men restored from exile, that hold but the heart of the country,[1] and are already
13 enriched! Small wonder if the traders of Saba, Dedan and Tharsis, ravenous lions all, would know whether it is plunder thy heart is set on? Such a muster of men, it can but mean spoil; silver and gold to rifle, stock and stuff to carry away, ay, there is spoil behind this, and spoil worth the taking!

14 Prophesy, then, son of man, and make known to Gog this divine message: None better ware of it than thou, when my people of Israel is living
15 at peace, free from alarms! Then it is thou wilt come down from those northern heights, with thy hordes about thee, thy troops of cavalry, a
16 great muster, an army irresistible, sweeping down on my people of Israel like a cloud that overshadows the land. Offspring of that later age,
17 thou shalt march on yonder land of mine, so that in Gog's doom my power may be vindicated, and the heathen may learn what I am. Long years ago, the Lord God says, there were servants of mine that foresaw my will concerning thee, and even then warned Israel, in my name, of thy coming.

18 When Gog marches against Israel, the Lord God says, my indigna-
19 tion will contain itself no longer; jealous love and fierce anger of mine,
20 I swear it, shall throw all the land of Israel into commotion. Fish in sea, bird in air, beast on earth and all the creeping things of earth shall tremble at my presence, and the world of men, too, shall tremble; moun-
21 tains be overthrown, defences totter, walls come toppling to the ground. All through this hill-country of mine my word shall run, The sword! And with that, the Lord says, friend shall turn his sword against friend;
22 ordeal they shall have of pestilence and of blood-letting, of lashing storm and great hail-stones, fire and brimstone I will rain down upon them,

---

[1] Literally, 'that are inhabitants of the navel of the land (or, earth).' For the phrase, cf. Jg. 9.37; the suggestion seems to be that the newly-returned people is too small in numbers to occupy more than the central portion of its territory. There is no reason to think that Jerusalem is here being described as the centre of the habitable globe, although 5.5 above would help to justify such language.

23 all that great army and the hordes that follow with it. My greatness, my holiness, shall then be displayed for a world of nations to see, and they will recognize my power at last.

CHAPTER THIRTY-NINE

PROPHESY, then, son of man, the doom of Gog; be this the divine message thou givest him: Have at thee, Gog, that hast the lordship of
2 Mosoch and Thubal! This way and that I will turn thee, whistle thee on and bid thee leave thy northern heights, to march against the hill-
3 country of Israel; then I will strike yonder bow from thy left hand, spill
4 the arrows from thy right! Host and horde of thine shall fall with thee on the mountains of Israel, carrion for every bird in air, every beast on
5 earth; cast away on the bare ground thou shalt lie, such is my doom for
6 thee, the Lord God says. Such a fire I will light as shall reach Magog, and others besides, island-dwellers far away that have no thought of
7 peril; they too shall know my power. Among my own people of Israel my renown shall spread, and never more shall my holy name be dragged in the dust; the heathen shall know what manner of God it is that dwells apart in Israel.
8   When all is over and done, and my day of doom past, the townsfolk of Israel will come out to gather kindling-wood and fire-wood out of the spoils that were left; shield and spear, bow and arrow, staff and pole;
10 and they will be seven years a-burning. All that time, faggots will strew the countryside ungathered, and never axe will be laid to forest tree; weapons of war shall be all their fuel, spoil of the spoiler, plunder of the
11 plunderer, the Lord God says. Then, too, Gog shall have a burying-place named after him, there in Israel, none other than the Valley of the Wayfarers, east of the Dead Sea; a thing of wonder to all that pass by. There they shall bury Gog with all the rabble that came after him, and
12 Valley of Gog's Rabble the place shall be called. Seven months' work Israel shall have burying them, and cleansing the land from its defile-
13 ment; all the citizens shall take part in it, and shall commemorate that
14 day as the day on which I was vindicated, says the Lord God. Even when the seven months are over, some there will be whose office it is to search ever the countryside, finding those remains and burying them, to rid the
15 land of defilement; still they will be scouring those plains, and setting up a mark where they see men's bones lie, for the grave-diggers to bury them,
16 there in the valley of Gog's Rabble; Amona, that will be the name of it. And so the land shall be cleansed.
17   This too: Son of man, here is a message for every bird in air, every beast that roams the earth: Come all, come with haste, gather from every

side for the sacrificial feast I am making for you, a great feast on the
18 uplands of Israel, flesh to eat, blood for your drinking! Flesh of fighting
men, blood of the world's great ones; never was ram or lamb, never was
19 goat or bull, so well fed or so daintily! Glutted with fat, drunk you shall
20 be with blood, at this feast of mine; horse and brave rider, warriors of
high rank and low, are the cheer they shall have at my table, says the Lord
God.
21   In glory I will reveal myself to the Gentiles; the doom I have executed,
22 the power I have exerted, shall be for all to see; nor shall Israel doubt
23 thenceforward that I, the Lord, am their God. All the world shall know
why it was that Israel went into banishment, why I turned my back on
them and gave them up to massacre; that it was because they wronged
24 me and deserted me; that it was foul crime of theirs bade me disown
25 them. I mean to restore Jacob from exile, the Lord God says, and
extend my mercy to the whole race of Israel; the honour of my name
26 demands it. The disgrace, the punishment of all their guilt, they needs
must bear . . .[1]
    . . . when they are dwelling safely in their own land, free from all
27 alarms; when I have brought them back from banishment among
strangers, in hostile countries, and so, before the whole world's eyes,
28 retrieved my honour. They shall know at last that I, the Lord, am their
God: if it was I that drove them into captivity, it was I, too, that restored
29 them to their home, not a man of them left in exile. And I will turn away
from them no longer, I, that have poured out my spirit on the whole race
of Israel.

CHAPTER FORTY

IT was the tenth day of the month; the twenty-fifth year of our banishment, and the fourteenth since the fall of the city, was just beginning.
This was the precise day upon which the Lord's power came over me,
2 and I fell into a transport; in which transport, so the divine revelation
would have it, I was carried off to the country of Israel. There, I found
myself on the top of a very high mountain, that seemed to have a city
3 built on it, sloping away towards the south. Into this city I was taken,
and there met a man whose look dazzled the eye like bronze; he stood
4 there in the gateway, holding a flaxen cord and a measuring-rod. The
open eye, son of man, said he, the open ear, and mark well all I shew

---

[1] If the text has been correctly transmitted, it seems clear that some words
(perhaps not many) have dropped out. But it has been suggested that the word
'they must bear' might be a scribe's error for 'they shall forget.'

thee! Thou wast brought here to see, and tell the men of Israel what thou seest.[1]

5   There was an outer wall that ran round the whole building, which he measured with his rod, that was six cubits and a palm[2] in length; a rod's
6 thickness there was in the wall, and a rod's height; when he came to the gate at the eastern approach and had mounted the stairs of it, the entrance-way was spanned by a single rod, so it proved that the wall was
7 of a rod's thickness. Within were guard-chambers, three cubits square
8 and five cubits apart; then came an inner gateway, a rod's length deep;
9 then an inner entrance-hall, measuring eight cubits across, with pillars
10 two cubits thick. This eastern gateway had three guard-chambers on
11 each side, alike in size, and alike in size the pillars between them. The entrance of the gateway was ten cubits across, and the span of the gate-
12 way itself thirteen cubits; on either side the six-cubit guard-chamber
13 was set a cubit back. From gable-window of guard-room to gable-
14 window of guard-room opposite was twenty-five cubits.[3] (And he made the whole length of the colonnade sixty cubits, but this was measuring
15 right up to the pillars which stood out round the gateway); [4] the distance
16 from the outer gate to the inner was fifty cubits ... and slanting windows in the guard-chambers and in the thickness of the walls that separated them, all round the gateway; the hall, too, within had its windows all round, and there was a pattern of palm-trees on the pillars between them.
17   So he led me into the outer courtyard, which was surrounded by par-lours, that had the ground about them paved with stone; there were
18 thirty parlours standing in this strip of pavement. It stretched up to the gateways, and was broad as they were long; like them, it was on the level
19 of the ground. And now he measured the distance from the eastern gate to the inner courtyard, where they stood fronting one another; it was a hundred cubits.[5]

---

[1] All through this chapter, the descriptions are very obscure, and their inter-pretation is largely a matter of conjecture.

[2] The extra palm gives rise to some difficulty, unless it was a mere handle to hold the rod by. As a measure, the rod was equivalent to six cubits only (verses 7 and 12). The Hebrew text probably means that each cubit was the length of a forearm and a palm (cf. 43.13 below).

[3] Literally, 'And he measured the gate from roof of guard-chamber to roof of guard-chamber, a width of twenty-five cubits, door against door (or, opening against opening).'

[4] The rendering given above seems preferable to one which would suddenly introduce us to pillars sixty cubits high. But it does not look as if the text had been correctly preserved; we have been told nothing of these projecting columns, and there is no reason to think that the Hebrews used the expression 'he made' in our modern sense. It seems as if there must be a gap in the manuscripts at the end of verse 15.

[5] 'The eastern gate'; this description is given for the sake of clearness; in the

20 As with the east, so with the north; length and breadth he must
21 measure of the outer gate that looked northwards. This, too, was fifty
    cubits long and twenty-five broad; it had guard-chambers, three on each
22 side, pillar and hall like the other. Hall and windows and palm-tree
    pattern differed nothing from those of the eastern gate; all was the same,
23 from the seven steps of the approach to the hall within. As on the east,
    so on the north, the inner court had a gateway matching it, a hundred
24 cubits distant. And next he took me to the south, where there was a fresh
25 gate, which he measured, pillar of it and hall of it, as before; the same
26 windows about the hall, the same length and breadth; the seven steps,
    the hall at the further end, the pillars with a palm tree patterned on either
27 side. Here, too, a hundred cubits away, was a gateway on the south side
    of the inner courtyard.

28 It was through this southern gateway of it that we entered the inner
29 courtyard itself; a gateway with the same measurements as before, guard-
    chamber and pillar and hall. It had the same windows and window-
30 pillars, the same length and breadth, (and the porch round it was twenty-
31 five cubits long, five cubits broad.)[1] The pillars had the same pattern,
    but this time the hall was on the outer side of the gateway, and there
32 were eight steps instead of seven. Then he took me to the east side of the
33 inner court, with the same measurements, guard-chamber and pillar and
34 hall, window and window-pillar, length and breadth; the pillared hall
35 again facing the outer court, the steps eight in number. And next to the
36 northern gate, with the same measurements still, guard-chamber and
37 pillar and hall and windows and length and breadth; the pillared hall
    facing outwards, the eight steps.

38 . . . and each ante-chamber had a door, between pillars. This was
39 where they washed the victims for burnt-sacrifice; and in the hall of the
    entrance-way there were two tables on each side, for the slaying of the
    victims, whether it were a burnt-sacrifice, or some offering for a fault or
40 for a wrong done. On the outer side of the gateway, towards the north
    gate, and again on the opposite side, there were two more tables, close to
41 the hall. Thus altogether there were eight tables ranged along the side
42 of the entrance-way, all for sacrifice. And for the burnt-sacrifice there
    were four other tables of hewn stone, a cubit and a half square, and a

original it is 'the lower gate,' because (as the foregoing verse has explained)
the whole outer court was lower (by eight steps) than the inner court. At the end
of this verse, the original has 'eastwards and northwards'; the only possible
rendering of the words appears to be that given at the beginning of the new
paragraph.

[1] This verse is very difficult. The word 'porch' is the same as that elsewhere
rendered 'hall'; but the hall or lobby of each gate was not of the measurements
here stated; a portico jutting out from the building seems the only explanation
of the text as it stands.

43 cubit in height; here they laid the instruments needed for sacrifice and offering; they had ledges, too, curving upwards all round, a palm in breadth, for these tables must also hold the flesh of the victims.

44 In the inner court itself, beyond the gateway, the singers had their lodging, on the north side, facing south. There was a parlour, too, at the
45 side of the eastern gate, facing . . . north;[1] the one facing south, he told
46 me, was for the priests who kept watch over the temple, the one facing north for the priests who are busied with the service of the altar, Sadocite
47 Levites, that were the Lord's privileged ministers. The court, with the altar standing in it, was a hundred cubits square.
48 Then he led me to the porch of the temple; the jamb on either side was five cubits deep, and the width of the gate . . . three cubits on either side;[2]
49 the porch itself was twenty cubits long and eleven broad. As we climbed up the eight steps to it, there were columns facing us, one on either side.

CHAPTER FORTY-ONE

So he brought me into the temple, between pillars that were six cubits
2 square by tabernacle measure.[3] The door was ten cubits across, the recess behind the doorway five cubits on either side; the whole length
3 of the outer temple was forty cubits, and the width twenty. Then he went into the inner sanctuary, measuring the doorway, two cubits thick, the door, six cubits across, and the width of the recess behind the door-
4 way, seven cubits. Each side had the length of the side next to the outer temple, twenty cubits. Here, he said, all is holiness.
5 Then he measured the temple wall, which was six cubits thick; it was
6 flanked all round by rooms four cubits square. There were sixty of these rooms, in three storeys one on the top of another; and their upper storeys jutted out all round the temple wall, but keeping apart from it; the
7 temple wall must not be touched. And there was a round stair-case which went up in a spiral to this upper loft of the temple building, which projected outwards for that very reason; there was thus an easy passage from the lower to the middle, and from the middle to the upper storey.[4]

---

[1] 'Facing . . . north'; the context seems to imply an omission. The prophet must surely have written, 'facing south, and a corresponding parlour facing north.'

[2] According to the Septuagint Greek, we should read 'the width of the gate fourteen cubits, leaving a blank piece of wall on either side, three cubits in width.'

[3] This whole chapter is even more obscure than the last, and it is difficult to believe there have not been omissions, if not faults of copying, in the text.

[4] vv. 6, 7. Cf. III Kg. 6.5, 6; here, as there, it seems clear that the rooms at the side must have no architectural connexion with the sacred walls of the temple itself; beyond that, nothing is clear. The rendering above assumes the accuracy of the Latin version; it differs widely both from the Hebrew text and

8 The building, I saw, was all raised above the ground; the rod shewed
9 that the ground level of the rooms was six cubits up. The rooms were
at a distance of five cubits beyond the temple wall, and they enclosed
10 it all round;[1] and there was a close of twenty cubits' width between these
11 and a line of parlours which flanked the temple. The doors of the inner
rooms let out, to north and south, on a praying-walk,[2] five cubits in width,
which ran round the temple.

12 Round this again was the close of twenty cubits, and beyond that, on
the west, a pavilion seventy cubits by ninety, with a wall five cubits thick.
13 He shewed me that the temple was a hundred cubits long; the close with
14 the pavilion beyond it, including its walls, a hundred cubits long; the
eastern face of the temple, with the close on each side of it, a hundred
15 cubits long; and the breadth from side to side of the pavilion beyond the
close (with its galleries) a hundred cubits long . . .[3]

. . . and the inner sanctuary, and the halls that gave on to the court-
16 yard, the doorways, the slanting windows, the galleries that went round
on three sides, over the several doorways; all were completely panelled in
wood. The panelling ran right up to the windows, which it framed, right
17 up to the top level of the doorway; ran all the way round to meet the
18 inner sanctuary, keeping the same height within and without it. The
design was of alternate cherubs and palm-trees, and each cherub had two
19 faces, shewing like a man towards one palm-tree and like a young lion
20 towards the other; the same pattern ran all through the building, carved
cherubs and palm-trees on each wall from ground level to the height
of the door's lintel.

21 The entrance of the temple stood square, facing the inner sanctuary;
22 facing the altar, which was of wood, three feet high, and two feet across;
corners and slab and sides were all of wood. This, he told me, is the
23 table that stands in the Lord's presence.[4] Outer temple, inner sanctuary,

---

from the Septuagint Greek, which are unintelligible. It is not easy to see why
projecting upper storeys should have matched especially well with a spiral
stair-case. According to the Hebrew text, there were three storeys of thirty
rooms each; the Latin version may imply three storeys of twenty rooms, or two
storeys of thirty-three rooms each.

[1] The Hebrew text seems to imply that there was a five-foot wall outside
the rooms all round, as well as a six-foot wall inside. But it is not likely that so
many rooms should have been made receiving no light whatever.

[2] In the Hebrew text simply 'an open strip of ground.' This seems to have
been a narrow strip at the edge of the raised platform; the twenty-foot close
was on ground level.

[3] It looks as if there must have been an omission here, to account for the
sudden change of subject. 'With its galleries' is difficult to explain; we should
have expected 'including its walls.'

[4] This was presumably the altar of incense; some, however, identify it with
the table on which the sacred loaves were exposed (Ex. 25.23, 30.1).

24 had two doors each; and either door had leaves that folded together, two
25 leaves on each door, with the same pattern of cherubs and palm-trees
that the walls had. To match this, the outer porch was faced with thick
26 beams [1] reaching up to the level of the slanting windows; thick beams
figured with palm-trees in either recess . . . matching the width of the
rooms and of the temple walls.

CHAPTER FORTY-TWO

THEN he took me into the outer court again, the northern part of it,
and would have me enter the parlours that lay there, close to the
2 pavilion and to the northern side of the temple.[2] The long side of them,
3 facing the north door, was a hundred cubits, the breadth fifty; between
the twenty-cubit close of the inner court, and the paving of the outer,
4 they rose, gallery upon gallery, three storeys in all. In front of them was
a walk ten cubits wide, encroaching on the inner court by one cubit; [3]
5 all their doors faced the north. Here, the top rooms were narrower,
since they must make room for porticos at the side, built out over the
6 two lower storeys; these three-storeyed parlours had no columns in
front of them, like the parlours in the outer court,[4] but made up for it by
porticos that rose from the roof of the first two floors, (filling in the width
7 of the fifty cubits). Inner parlours faced outer only with fifty cubits of
8 their wall's length; in the outer court, the parlours were but fifty cubits
9 long, whereas those beside the temple were a hundred. These inner parlours were entered from below at their eastern end, from the outer court.
10 . . . in the thickness of the court's eastern wall . . . opposite the pavilion,
11 and here too there were parlours close to the pavilion.[5] Southern parlours, like northern, had a walk in front of them; had the same length and
12 breadth, were entered by doors of the same kind; the doors of these

---

[1] The Hebrew word translated 'thick beams' is of very doubtful significance.
The last words of the chapter are difficult to understand, whether in the Hebrew,
in the Greek, or in the Latin; if the text of them is right, it looks as if there had
been a fresh omission.

[2] *vv.* 1–12. Once more the original is very obscure, and the interpretation of
it far from certain.

[3] Literally, 'looking towards the inwards of a way of one cubit,' an expression
from which it is hard to derive any definite meaning. The Septuagint Greek
has, 'of a hundred cubits in length,' but this is probably a guess.

[4] The outer parlours are those mentioned in 40.17; where, however, perhaps
through some omission in the manuscripts, there is no mention of a colonnade.

[5] It can hardly be doubted that there is some serious disturbance in the text.
At the end of the verse, it is clear that the prophet and his guide have gone to
measure the southern parlours, corresponding to the northern parlours already
described.

parlours opened on a walk along their southern side, and the main entrance was approached at the eastern end, from the walk that faced the hall and the close.

13   These parlours, he told me, built to north and south beside the pavilion, are hallowed precincts, where the priests who sacrifice to the Lord may eat what is set apart for holy uses. All that is set apart, all the offerings made for fault and for wrong done, shall there be laid out, as on 14 holy ground. Nor, entering it, shall the priests leave it for the inner court all at once; here they must lay aside their vestments, for these, too, are hallowed, and put on other clothes before ever they mingle with the people.

15   With that, he made an end of measuring the precincts within, and led 16 me through the eastern doorway, to measure them from without. Along 17 the eastern side his reed measured five hundred cubits; five hundred 18 cubits along the northern side, and five hundred cubits along the south- 20 ern; westwards, too, the measure of it was five hundred cubits. All round the four quarters of the wind he would measure it, five hundred cubits in length as in breadth, this boundary between things sacred and things profane.

CHAPTER FORTY-THREE

2   THEN he took me to the eastern gate; and all at once, from the sun's rising, the bright presence of the God of Israel made entry there. Like the sound of waters in deep flood his voice was, and earth was lit 3 up with the splendour all around. Such was the appearance I had seen of him, when he came bent on the city's destruction, when I saw my 4 vision by the banks of Chobar; down fell I, face to earth. In it came 5 through the eastern gateway, the splendour of the Lord himself; and with that, a transport seized me, carrying me off into the inner court, where already the brightness of the Lord's presence filled the temple. 6 Thence it was I heard his voice speaking to me; and the man who stood at my side passed on the message.

7   Son of man, he told me, here is my throne; here eternally, in the heart of Israel, is my resting-place. No more shall Israel's folk, Israel's kings, drag my name in the dust with their infidelities, with the dead gods they 8 served, with their hill-sanctuaries.[1] Door next to door of mine, pillar to pillar, only a wall between us; and for the foul doings that dragged my

---

[1] Literally, 'with their fornications, with the ruins of their kings, and with their hill-sanctuaries.' St. Jerome understands this as meaning that worship at the hill-sanctuaries brought the kings of Juda to their ruin. But the word used in the Hebrew text means carcases, not ruins; 'with the carcases of their kings, their

9   name in the dust, my vengeance took full toll of them.[1] Bid they those
    infidelities, those dead gods farewell, I will make my eternal home here
10 in the midst of them.   Thine, son of man, to shame the men of Israel by
11 the sight of yonder temple; who measures the fabric of it, shall learn to
    blush for his misdeeds. Form and fashion of the temple, gates that lead
    in and out, all the plot of it do thou make known to them; and what
    observances they are that govern the ordering of it. All this they must see
    in writing, and so learn to keep its pattern ever unaltered, its laws ever to
    fulfil.

12   Wouldst thou know what the temple's charter is? No part of the moun-
    tain top that lies within its bounds but is my inmost sanctuary; that,
    nothing less, is the charter of the temple.

13   . . . These measurements the altar had,[2] measured by the true cubit,
    that is the width of a fore-arm and a palm; first came a gutter, of a cubit's
    depth and a cubit's width, ending in a lip a span broad all round; thus the
14 altar was drained. Above this gutter, which was at ground level, came the
    lower base, two cubits high and a cubit across; the upper base rose four
15 cubits above it, and was again a cubit wide. The altar proper was four
16 cubits high, with four horns projecting above it, and the sides of it were
17 square, twelve cubits by twelve. The base was also square, fourteen
    cubits by fourteen, and had a projecting rim half a cubit across; the
    groove under this was a cubit in height. The steps of the altar faced
    eastwards . . .

18   Son of man, he told me, when the altar is set up, ready for burnt-
    sacrifice and for blood-sprinkling, these ceremonies the Lord God would
19 have thee observe. A young bullock the priests must have, those priests
    of Sadoc's line that are my true ministers, for a transgression-victim.
20 Horns of the altar, and the four corners of its base, and the rim round
    about it, thou shalt smear with the victim's blood, to cleanse them and
21 purge them of fault, then take the victim itself to a place apart, beyond
22 the temple precincts, and there burn it. Next day, the transgression-
    victim shall be a male kid, without blemish; with this, as with the calf, the

hill-sanctuaries,' or possibly, 'with the carcases of their kings when they died.'
It has been supposed that Ezechiel is protesting against the burial of kings close
to the temple, as a profanation. But no such protest is found elsewhere, and we
have no evidence that the practice existed. The rendering given above assumes
that 'kings' is used for 'gods,' as (apparently) in Am. 5.26. 'Dead gods,' either
in the sense of 'dumb idols,' as in Lev. 26.30, or possibly in reference to the
worship of Adonis (see 8.14 above). But it seems likely that the manuscripts
may have been at fault, some copyist writing the word 'their kings' twice over
by accident.
    [1] The prophet is complaining, not that the royal palace adjoined the temple,
but that profane rites were celebrated just beyond its walls; see 8.8 above.
    [2] *vv.* 13–17. It seems possible that this passage has been accidentally mis-
placed. The terms used in it are of very doubtful interpretation.

23 altar must be purged; and when the purging is over, bullock and ram
24 must be offered, these too without blemish; when they have been
brought into the Lord's presence, and the priests have sprinkled them
25 with salt, they must be given to the Lord in burnt-sacrifice. Each day,
for seven days, goat and bullock and ram must be offered, all un-
26 blemished; purged and cleansed and hallowed the altar must be for
27 seven days, and when these are over, on the eighth day and ever afterwards, the priests may use it for burnt-sacrifice and welcome-offering of
yours, and I will look favourably on you, the Lord God says.

CHAPTER FORTY-FOUR

THEN he brought me back to the eastern gate of the outer precincts,
2 that was fast shut. Shut this gate must ever be, the Lord told me,
nor open its doors to give man entrance again, since the Lord, the God
3 of Israel, entered by it. Access to it is none, even for the prince himself;
sit there he may, to eat his share of the welcome-offering, but it is
through the hall at the other end of the gateway he comes and goes.
4 And so he took me towards the northern gate, in full view of the
temple; and all the temple was filled with the brightness of the Lord's
5 presence, a sight that brought me to my knees, face to earth. Give good
heed, son of man, the Lord said to me; the open eye, the open ear! Rule
and observance of the Lord's house I mean to tell thee; of the temple,
and who may approach it, of my sanctuary, and the manner of leaving it.
6 This message deliver, from the Lord God, to the rebel brood of Israel:
7 Will you never have done with insult, men of Israel, letting alien folk,
that in mind and body circumcision have none, profane my house by
entering the sanctuary? What avails it, to offer me bread, and fat, and
blood, when all the while these foul doings of yours violate my covenant?
8 The sacred charge committed to you went for nothing; guardians of my
own worship, in my own sanctuary, should be men of your choosing!
9 Place the alien may have, though body and mind be both uncircumcised,
in the commonwealth of Israel, the Lord says; place in my sanctuary he
10 has none. There be Levites that have forsaken the following of me, when
all the race of Israel went a-straying; that have betaken themselves to
11 false gods, and must needs do penance for their fault. What forbids they
should be sacrists and door-keepers of mine, temple attendants to prepare burnt-sacrifice, slay victim, and stand ministering in the people's
12 presence? Ministers of false worship, that betrayed Israel into guilt, they
have made me their sworn enemy, and must be held to account for it;
13 never may they come before me as priests, never touch consecrated gift

that is set apart for holy uses; disgraced they must needs be, penance
14 must needs bear; yet I would have them keep the doors of my house, and be charged with all the menial offices that belong to it.
15 The priests, the true Levites, shall be those sons of Sadoc that held fast by my temple worship when Israel left the following of me. Theirs to come forward as my ministers; theirs to wait upon my presence, offering
16 me fat and blood of victims, the Lord God says; theirs my sanctuary to enter, my table to approach, servants of mine that shall keep the charge
17 I gave them. Come they within the inner gate, they shall be all vested in linen; nothing of wool shall clothe them, when they serve me in the
18 intimacy of the inner court; mitres of linen on their brows, breeches of linen about their loins, with no such habiting as may bring them out in a
19 sweat. These vestments of office they must lay aside, and put away in the temple sacristy, when they go out to mingle with the people in the outer court; that holy contact is not for common folk; it is time they put on their workaday clothes instead.
20 They shall be at pains to cut their hair, not grow it long; yet cropped
21 their heads must not be. As for wine, a priest may not drink it when he is
22 soon to enter the sanctuary. Wed he, it must be a maid he weds, of Israelite birth; not rejected wife or widow, save it be the widow of another
23 priest. Their office it is, to teach the people what is clean and unclean,
24 what is holy and what profane; when dispute arises, to take their place at my judgement-seat and give award; my feasts with due rite and
25 ordinance to observe, my sabbaths to keep holy. Never shall they defile themselves with dead body's contact, save only it be father or mother,
26 son or daughter, brother or unwedded sister of theirs. Cleansed though
27 he be after such contact, a priest must wait for seven days yet, nor enter the inner court to do service in my sanctuary, the Lord God says, till he
28 has made an offering in amends for his fault. And for the priestly tribe, it must have no patrimony assigned to it; I am their patrimony, nor needs
29 he portion, whose portion is his God. Bloodless offering they shall eat, and the victim that is offered for a fault or a wrong done; theirs every gift
30 an Israelite vows to me, theirs the first of all first-fruits, and the residue of all you offer; and the first batch of your baking you must give to the
31 priest, to win his blessing for you and yours. Bird or beast that drops dead, or has been a wild thing's prey, the priest may not eat.

CHAPTER FORTY-FIVE

W HEN you set about the allotment of your territory, one strip you
must leave out, twenty-five thousand cubits by ten thousand,[1] a
hallowed strip of land that is to be the Lord's peculiar, all the length and
2 breadth of it hallowed. (Hallowed entirely one plot in it shall be, a square
plot of five hundred cubits each way, with fifty cubits' space for approach
3 all about it.) [2] Within the Lord's domain, a space of twenty-five thousand cubits by ten thousand, surrounding temple and sanctuary, must be
4 measured out   as dedicated to the priests, that serve the sanctuary and
worship in the Lord's presence; this shall be their home, this their sacred
5 enclosure. And for the Levites that serve the temple another like space
6 is to be measured out; twenty cells they shall have there.   Marching with
the sacred enclosure, there shall be a strip of twenty-five thousand cubits
by five thousand, where the common folk of Israel shall have their city and
7 their city's lands. And at either end of the enclosure, and of the city lands,
the prince shall have his domains, adjoining either end, and stretching
away to west and east as far as each of the tribal allotments stretches west-
8 wards and eastwards. He shall enjoy his own possessions on Israelite soil;
there shall be no more encroaching on the public rights; each tribe shall
be given its own territory, to have and to hold.

9   Will you never have enough, princes of Israel? the Lord God says.
Must it always be wrong and robbery, never right and redress? Right of
10 king and right of people he bids you determine once for all.   Let us have
11 true scales, a true ephi, a true bate;   let ephi and bate match, a tenth part
of a cor either of them; by the standard of the cor they shall be measured.
12 Let twenty obols go to the sicle, twice twenty sicles and fifteen besides
13 go to the mina.   And so let these be the tithings you pay; a sixth of an
14 ephi for every cor of wheat or barley,   and a tenth of a bate for every cor
of oil, (tenth of bate or hundredth of cor, since the cor is to measure ten
15 bates); [3]   and one ram you must contribute out of every two hundred that
feed in Israel's pasture-lands. That each may pay his scot, for bloodless

[1] 'Cubits'; the word is not expressed in the original, and some think that all
through this paragraph, except in the last clause of verse 2, the unit of measurement is not the cubit but the angel's rod, six cubits long. But since we know
that the temple precincts were five hundred cubits each way (42.20) and they are
described as 'five hundred each way' in verse 2 here, it seems best to assume
the cubit-standard throughout. 'By ten thousand'; the Septuagint Greek gives
twenty thousand, which would include the enclosure of the Levites (verse 5).

[2] Some think this verse has been misplaced, and should come after verse 4.

[3] The Hebrew text has probably suffered from corruption in this verse; the
Septuagint Greek gives ten per cent, not one per cent, as the rate of the oil-tithe.
The Latin does not yield any acceptable sense.

16 offering or burnt-sacrifice or welcome-offering, the Lord says,   this tax
17 the whole land of Israel owes to its prince.   And he, on Israel's behalf,
shall defray the cost of burnt-sacrifice, and bloodless offering, and libation, on feast-day and new moon and sabbath, whenever the folk of Israel
keep holiday; transgression-victim, and burnt-sacrifice, and welcome-
offering, he must provide them all.
18 On the first day of the year, the Lord God says, the sanctuary must
19 have a calf, without blemish, sacrificed for its purging.   Door-posts of the
temple, corners of the altar's base, door-posts of the inner court, the
20 priest shall smear with blood of the transgression-victim.   And the like
must be done again on the seventh day of that month, for faults committed unwittingly, through inadvertence; and so the temple shall be
21 purged clean.   On the fourteenth day of the first month you will keep the
22 paschal feast, and for a week eat bread without leaven.   On the feast
itself, the prince must provide a calf, in amends for fault of his own,
23 fault of his people;   and every day during the week seven calves and seven
rams without blemish, every day, too, a goat for a transgression-victim;
24 with each ram or goat a bushel of flour, and with each bushel of flour a
25 gallon and a half of oil.   The same provision he must make, of transgression-victim, burnt-sacrifice, bloodless offering, and oil, for the fifteenth day of the seventh month, and its week of holiday.

CHAPTER FORTY-SIX

EASTERN gate of the inner court, the Lord God says, must be shut
on the six working days, open on the sabbath; on the day of the new
2 moon, too, it shall be opened.   When it is opened, the prince shall come
in by way of the outer hall, and wait in the entrance till the priests have
done presenting burnt-sacrifice of his, welcome-offering of his; there on
the threshold he shall do reverence, and go his ways, but the gate shall
3 not be shut after him, not till the evening.   On sabbath days, and when
4 the moon is new, before this gate the people also shall do reverence.   Six
lambs and a ram, without blemish, are the prince's burnt-sacrifice to the
5 Lord every sabbath,   with a bushel of flour for the ram, and for the lambs
what bloodless offering he will; and of oil a gallon and a half to the bushel.
6 And when the moon is new, the same victims, and a bullock besides, un-
7 blemished as they;   with the bullock, too, a bushel goes as bloodless
8 offering, and the rest shall be as before.   Through the outer hall of the
9 gateway the prince comes and goes;   but on feast-days, when a great
throng comes into the Lord's presence, they must enter by one gate and
10 leave by the opposite, from north to south or south to north,   and the
11 prince, that worships in their midst, shall enter and leave as they.   And

for the bloodless offering, come feast-day, come holiday, it shall be made
12 as aforesaid. Will the prince make burnt-sacrifice or welcome-offering
of his own free will, the eastern gate shall be opened for him, as on the
sabbath, till burnt-sacrifice or welcome-offering is done; but when he
13 goes out, the gate shall be shut behind him. And there shall be daily
burnt-sacrifice; morning by morning he shall offer one of that year's
14 lambs, unblemished; of flour, morning by morning, the sixth part of a
bushel, and half a gallon of oil mingled with it; ever this bloodless offer-
15 ing is the Lord's due, continual and unalterable. Lamb and flour and oil,
morning by morning, an eternal sacrifice.
16   If the prince will make a gift of land to sons of his, the Lord God says,
17 their patrimony it is, held by right of inheritance; crown lands he cannot
alienate to any of his servants beyond the year of jubilee, when they must
18 needs return to him; the crown lands are entailed upon his sons. And at
no time shall he rob the people by violence of their rightful patrimony;
if he will endow his sons, out of his own patrimony let him do it; my
people must not be disinherited.
19   And now he took me through an entry close by the side of the gate,
which led to the northern row of priests' rooms round the sanctuary.
20 Where this reached its western end, there was a kitchen, which the
priests used, he told me, to boil the flesh of victims for a fault or a wrong
done, to bake the bloodless offering. They must not be carried out into
21 the courtyard; such holy contact was not for the people. Afterwards he
. took me into the outer court, round all the corners of it in turn, and
shewed me that there was a little garth in each of them; no corner but had
22 its garth; in each, there was a space of forty cubits by thirty, perfectly
23 matched. The wall enclosed them, and here, under an open roof,
24 kitchens were built. These kitchens, he told me, were used by the temple
attendants for cooking the welcome-offerings made by the people.

CHAPTER FORTY-SEVEN

AND last, he took me to the door of the temple itself, and shewed
me where a stream of water flowed eastwards from beneath the
threshold of it. Eastward the temple looked, and eastward these waters
flowed, somewhat to the temple's right, so as to pass by the southern side
2 of the altar. Through the northern gate he led me, and round the walk
that passed the outer gate, taking the eastern sun; and here, to the right
3 of the gate, the water gushed out. Eastward then he faced, the man of
the measuring-rod; measured a thousand cubits, and led me across a
4 stream that reached my ankles. Another thousand, and when I crossed

5 the stream it reached my knees; another thousand, and it was up to my waist, another thousand, and now it had become a torrent I might not
6 cross any longer, so high the waters had swelled, out of my depth. Mark it well, son of man, said he; and with that he brought me out on to the
7 bank again; when I reached it, I found that there were trees growing thick on either hand.

8   This stream, he told me, must flow eastward to the sand-dunes, and so fall into the desert; pass into the Dead Sea and beyond it, cleansing those
9 waters by its passage. Wherever it flows, there shall be teeming life once again; in the Dead Sea itself there will be shoals of fish, once this stream has reached it, this stream that heals all things and makes all things live.
10 Fisher-folk will line the shores of it, and there will be drying of nets all the way from Engaddi to Engallim, and fish there will be in great shoals,
11 varied in kind as the ocean fish are. Only the swamps and marshes about
12 it there is no cleansing; these shall turn into salt-pits. And on either bank of the stream fruit-trees shall grow of every kind; never leaf lost, never fruit cast; month after month they shall yield a fresh crop, watered by that sanctuary stream; fruit for man's eating, and medicinal leaves.

13   This message, too, the Lord God has for you, about the frontiers of the territory you are to divide among the twelve tribes; twelve, because
14 Joseph must have a double portion. I promised it to your fathers long ago; This land, I told them, shall be allotted to you.[1] And you must allot
15 it among yourselves in equal shares. These are to be its boundaries on the north; from Hethalon, on the Great Sea, across the pass which leads
16 to Sedada and Emath, by Berotha and Sabarim (where Emath marches
17 with Syria) and Hazar Tichon (near the Hauran country) to the Syrian frontier-town of Hazar Enan, its extreme limit inland. Ever northward
18 it stretches, this northern frontier of yours, till it reaches Emath. The eastern frontier is to be drawn between Hauran and what is now Syria, between Galaad and Israel proper, down the line of the Jordan to the
19 Dead Sea. Towards the south and the noon-day sun, the line stretches from Thamar to the Waters of Challenge at Cades, then follows the
20 Brook of Egypt to the sea; and on the west, it runs straight from the
21 Egyptian border to the Emath pass.[2] All this territory must be appor-
22 tioned between the tribes of Israel; then you will divide it up among

---

[1] The quotation is from Num. 34.2; the subject-matter of that chapter is the distribution of Chanaan between the tribes in the first instance.
[2] *vv.* 15–20. The text here is awkward, and perhaps partly corrupt; several of the place-names remain unidentified. What seems clear is that the length of the new kingdom (from north to south) is that of David's kingdom, including Syria ('Damascus' in the original) but not Emath on the north or Hauran on the east; the breadth of it is curiously shrunken, the whole of Transjordania being abandoned.

yourselves. Aliens will have their share in it, such aliens as have thrown in their lot with yours and bred amongst you; native Israelites you shall

23 count them, and allot them their portions in this tribe or that. Amidst the tribe which has given him shelter, each shall find a home, the Lord God says.

CHAPTER FORTY-EIGHT

AND here is a list of the tribal domains. First Dan, with its northern frontier on a line from Hethalon, across the Emath pass, to the Syrian frontier-town of Hazar Enan, and marching with Emath all the

2 way; its eastern limit . . . the sea.[1] Next, stretching from Israel's eastern

3 frontier to the sea, Aser; next, in like manner, Nephthali; next, in like

5 manner, Manasse; next, in like manner, Ephraim; next, in like manner,

7 Ruben; next, in like manner, Juda.

8   Next, in like manner, comes the strip of dedicated land you are to set apart; in breadth, twenty-five thousand cubits, in length, stretching from Israel's frontier to the sea like the rest; and in the heart of it, the sanc-

9 tuary. The Lord's own domain will be twenty-five thousand cubits by

10 ten thousand; and in this holy plot, measuring twenty-five thousand cubits north and south, ten thousand cubits east and west, the priests are

11 to dwell, with the sanctuary in their midst. Priests, I say, of Sadoc's line, that held fast by my observances and never went a-straying with

12 strayed Israel, as the other Levites did; first-fruit of the first-fruits their

13 domain shall be, the domain of the Levites marching with it. This neighbouring strip will be of the same size, twenty-five thousand cubits

14 by ten thousand; sell their land they may not, nor exchange it; the con-

15 secrated ground is unalienable. The remaining strip of five thousand cubits' breadth shall be for city's buildings and city's lands; the city

16 itself standing in the middle; north, south, east and west it shall measure

17 four thousand five hundred cubits; north, south, east and west it shall

18 have purlieus two hundred and fifty cubits deep. In length, it will fall short of the Lord's domain by ten thousand cubits on the east, and as much on the west; but this remaining space will be city lands, like the sanctuary lands, growing food for the needs of labouring men in the city;

19 these shall have the right to cultivate it, come they from what tribe they

20 will. All the length and breadth of this square of territory, twenty-five thousand cubits either way, shall be sanctuary enclosure and city lands;

21 beyond this square of sanctuary and city, all that is left of the dedicated

---

[1] It seems probable that the original text ran, 'Its eastern limit the eastern limit of Israel, its western limit the sea.'

domain, eastwards to the Jordan and westwards to the sea, shall belong
to the prince; the hallowed plot that surrounds the temple shall divide
22 his lands in two. Royal lands and Levite lands shall march with Juda,
royal lands and city lands with Benjamin.[1]

23 For the rest of the tribes, Benjamin comes first, stretching from Israel's
24 frontier on the east to the sea on the west; next, in like manner, Simeon;
25 next, in like manner, Issachar; next, in like manner, Zabulon; next, in
28 like manner, Gad. Gad shall be the southernmost, facing the noon-day
sun, with a frontier running from Thamar to the Waters of Challenge at
29 Cades, and along the Brook [2] to the Great Sea. Such shall be the territory allotted to Israel's tribes, the Lord God says, and thus allotted they
shall be.

30 And these are the city's limits; on the north side, measure four thou-
31 sand five hundred cubits; and here (for all must be named after Israel's
32 tribes) are three gates named after Ruben, Juda and Levi. As many on
33 the east, and here are gates named after Joseph, Benjamin, and Dan. As
many on the south, and here are gates named after Simeon, Issachar and
34 Zabulon. As many on the west, and here are gates named after Gad,
35 Aser and Nephthali. The whole circumference is one of eighteen thousand cubits. THE LORD IS THERE; such is the name by which the
city will be known ever after.

---

[1] The order of the words in this verse implies, what is not clearly stated elsewhere, that the Levite domain was on the north of the sacred enclosure, the city
lands on the south of it.

[2] As in 47.19; the Latin version has misread the word 'brook' as 'portion.'

THE PROPHECY OF DANIEL

CHAPTER ONE

WHEN Nabuchodonosor, king of Babylon, marched against Jerusalem and laid siege to it, in Joakim's third year as king of Juda,[1]
2 the Lord gave him the mastery. Not only Joakim fell into his hands, but
. . . some of the temple treasures,[2] which he carried off to Sennaar as offerings to his own god, and there, in the treasure house of his own god's
3 temple, bestowed them. Meanwhile, he had a command for Asphenez, his head chamberlain. He was to take under his charge certain young
4 Israelites, of royal or princely stock, in body well formed, handsome of mien, so well versed and grounded, so keen of wit, as they might be taught
5 lore and language of the Chaldaeans, and have places at his court. For three years they should have daily allowance of the king's meat and wine; then he would send for them.

6 Among these were four tribesmen of Juda, called Daniel, Ananias,
7 Misael and Azarias; the chamberlain had given them fresh names, Bal-
8 tassar, Sidrach, Misach and Abdenago. Daniel had resolved, neither meat nor wine from the royal table should sully his lips; and for this abstinence
9 he hoped to get leave from the head chamberlain; with such kindness and
10 pity God had touched his heart. But this would not serve; Nay, said he, what of the charge my lord king gave me, that you should have food and drink? It were as much as my life is worth, if he saw you haggard-cheeked
11 beside others of your own age. Hereupon Daniel went to Malasar, one of the other chamberlains, to whose care Asphenez had entrusted all four
12 of them.[3] Sir, said he, be pleased to put us on our trial. For ten days, give
13 us nothing but pulse to eat, water to drink, then compare our looks with the looks of those others who have fed on the king's bounty; judge by what
14 thou seest, and do with us what thou wilt. The challenge was accepted,
15 and the ten days' trial began; when it was over, never a one of the king's

---

[1] The capture of Jerusalem in Joakim's reign is vouched for by II Par. 36.6; the corresponding passage in IV Kg. 24.1 is perhaps defective. The dating here gives rise to difficulties; Nabuchodonosor had not yet acceded to the throne in the third year of Joakim (Jer. 25.1). Some think he is called 'king,' although still crown prince; others, that the 'reign' of Joakim is only dated from his revolt against Babylon, his position up to that time having been merely that of a viceroy.
[2] It seems probable, from what follows, that there has been an omission, and that the original text contained some account of persons (including Daniel and his companions) being removed to Babylon.
[3] The Septuagint Greek seems to preserve a different account of this incident, in which Malasar disappears from the story and it is Asphenez, after all, who grants Daniel's request.

16 pensioners shewed healthy and well nourished as they. After that, Malasar had their allowance of meat and wine, and they pulse.

17   Meanwhile, in all lore and learning, God made apt pupils of these four;
18 and of visions and dreams especially Daniel was master. And now, the
time of their probation over, Asphenez presented his pupils before Nabu-
19 chodonosor, who had speech with all of them; and no match was found
for Daniel, Ananias, Misael and Azarias; all must have places at court.
20 Never a question the king could propound, to make trial of their learning
and their quick wits, but they could answer it ten times better than any
21 diviner or sage in his kingdom. And still, up to the beginning of Cyrus'
reign, Daniel was . . .[1]

CHAPTER TWO

2 IN the second year of his reign,[2] Nabuchodonosor had a dream; and his
mind, between sleep and waking, was all distraught.[3] Diviner and sage,
soothsayer and astrologer must be summoned without more ado, to pro-
3 nounce on the royal dream; and when they were admitted to his presence,
he said to them, I have had a dream, but my mind is so distraught, I can-
4 not tell what it was. And the astrologers gave him answer.

IN ARAMAIC [4]

Long life to the king's grace! Be pleased to tell us what the dream was, and
5 it shall be interpreted. Why, said the king, I know no more than this;

---

[1] It seems probable that a few words have dropped out at the end of the
chapter, telling us that Daniel was 'in high favour,' or something of the kind.
The phrase 'Daniel was until the first year of Cyrus' is quite without parallel
in the Old Testament. Some, by a slight change in the text, would read 'Daniel
lived'; but it appears Daniel was still alive in the third year of Cyrus (10.1
below).

[2] It is difficult to see how Nabuchodonosor should still have been in the second
year of his reign, when Daniel and the others had already undergone three years
of training. The difficulty disappears if we suppose that he was only crown
prince when he marched on Jerusalem (see note on 1.1). But some think that the
years are computed in two different ways, chapter 1 reckoning from the day of
the king's accession and chapter 2 from the beginning of his first complete year.

[3] 'Between sleep and waking, was all distraught'; literally, in the Hebrew text,
'his spirit was bewildered, and his sleep took place upon him' (which is explained
as meaning, 'was all over for him'). The Septuagint Greek has, 'his sleep was
away from him,' the Latin version, 'his dream fled from him.' The Latin perhaps
implies that Nabuchodonosor had really forgotten his dream; but this is unnecessary to the story.

[4] It is, of course, possible to render, 'And the astrologers gave him his answer
in Aramaic,' but no plausible reason has been suggested for this sudden philo-
logical digression. Meanwhile, it is certain that, from this point up to the end of
chapter 7, the text given in the Hebrew Bible is not written in Hebrew properly
so called, but in the dialect called Aramaic (also used in I Esdras); hence it seems

dream and interpretation both you must needs tell me, or else your lives
6 must be forfeit, and your houses put to public use. Gifts and great honour
shall be your reward, if you will but tell me both. Come now, what dreamt
I, and what meant my dream?

7   Once again they demurred; would the king be pleased to recount his
8 dream to them, interpreted it should be forthwith. Nay, said the king, I
see how it is, you are trying shifts with me. You know well there is but
9 one way to it; dream of mine or doom of yours it must be. Some lying
story you have ready, that will suit your turn; how shall I know your inter-
10 pretation is right, if you cannot tell me what dream I saw? Nay, said they,
never a man on earth could do what the king's grace asks. Princes and
great rulers there have been a many, but none of them yet, from diviner,
11 sage or astrologer, expected so much! Here is riddle indeed thou wouldst
have us read for thee, lord king; where is counsellor can tell thee the
secret? Unless it were the gods only, and they walk not with men.

12   At this, the king was in such a taking of fury that he would have all the
13 wise men of Babylon put to death; and, once the warrant was out for the
extinction of them, there was hue and cry against Daniel and his fellows.
14 Arioch it was, the captain of the king's guard, that was commissioned to
rid Babylon of all its wise men, and from him Daniel would have the why
15 and wherefore of it; here was cruel work committed to him; what moved
the king's grace to be so absolute? And, when Arioch had made all clear to
16 him, into the king's presence he went, asking for more time to answer the
17 royal question. So, returning to his fellows, Ananias, Misael and Azarias,
18 he made all known to them, and would have them cry out upon the God
of heaven for better knowledge of his secret, without which both he and
they should perish in the general massacre of the wise men.

19   Then, in the night, the secret was revealed to Daniel, and he fell to
20 praising the God of heaven, with such words as these: Blessed be the
Lord's name from the beginning to the end of time; his are the wisdom
21 and the power; change and chance of our mortal life he rules, crowns one
man and discrowns another. Wisdom of the wise, skill of the skilful, what
22 are they but his gift? The hidden depths he can lay bare, read the secrets
23 of the dark; does not light dwell with him? God of our fathers, I give
thee thanks and praise for thus enabling, thus enlightening me; for
prayer answered, doubt resolved, and the king's thought revealed.

24   With that, he betook himself to Arioch, that was to slay the wise men,
and made suit to him, slay the wise men he should not. Thou hast but to

---

likely that the two words given above in capitals are merely a note intended to
warn the reader. The most probable account of this circumstance is that two
versions of the original text were current, one Hebrew and one Aramaic, and
that certain chapters which were lost in one had to be supplied from the other.

take me into the king's presence, said he, and the riddle shall be read.
25 Without more ado, Arioch granted his request; here was an exile from
26 Juda, he said, that would answer the royal question. Is this true? the king
asked of Daniel. Canst thou, Baltassar, tell me the dream and its meaning
27 both? And Daniel spoke out in the royal presence, Never wizard or sage,
28 never diviner or prophet, that can give the king's grace an answer! But
there is a God in heaven, king Nabuchodonosor, that makes hidden things
plain; he it is that has sent thee warning of what must befall long hence.
29 Let me tell thee what thy dream was, what visions disturbed thy sleep. As
thou wast lying there abed, my lord king, thy thoughts still turned on
future times; and he that makes hidden things plain revealed to thee what
30 the pattern of those times should be. If the secret was disclosed to me
also, it is not that I have wisdom beyond the wont of living men; I was
but the instrument by which the meaning of it was to be made known,
and a king's thoughts unravelled.
31   A vision thou hadst of a great image; what height, what splendour, how
32 terrible an aspect it was that confronted thee! Of fine gold the head,
33 breast and arms of silver, belly and thighs of bronze; of iron the legs, and
34 of the feet, too, part was iron, part was but earthenware. And as thou
wert watching it, from the mountain-side fell a stone no hands had quarried, dashed against the feet of yonder image, part iron, part clay, and
35 shattered them. With that, down came iron and clay, down came bronze
and silver and gold; chaff of the threshing-floor was never so scattered on
the summer breeze. They were gone, none knew whither; and stone that
had shattered image grew into a high mountain, filling the whole earth.
36   So much for the dream, and now we that know the secret of it [1] will tell
37 the king's grace what it means. Thou hast kings for thy vassals; royalty,
power, dominion and great renown the God of heaven has bestowed on
38 thee; every haunt of man and wild beast and flying bird he has given over
to thee, all alike he has made subject to thee; the head of gold, who else
39 but thou? Another and a lesser empire must follow thine, one of silver,
40 then another of bronze, still wide as the world; then a fourth, of iron,
breaking down and crushing all before it, as iron has power all-conquer-
41 ing, all-subduing.[2] But feet and toes of the image were part iron, part
clay; this fourth empire will be divided within itself. Foundation of iron

---

[1] 'We that know the secret of it'; in the original simply 'we.' It is to be supposed that Daniel was associating himself with his three fellow-pupils, who had
perhaps accompanied him to the court.
[2] Many authors identify the second empire with a 'Median' empire (cf. note
on 5.31 below), the third with Persia, and the fourth with Macedon. Others
identify the second with Persia, the third with Macedon, and the fourth with
Rome; the break-up of the (now divided) Macedonian empire began with the
victory of Paulus at Pydna, B.C. 168.

42 there shall yet be, from which it springs; sure enough, in the feet thou
sawest, earthenware was mixed with true steel. Yet was true steel mixed
with base earthenware, token that this empire shall be in part firmly estab-
43 lished, in part brittle. Iron and clay mingled; race of the conquerors shall
be adulterated with common human stock; as well mix clay with iron! [1]
44   And while those empires yet flourish, another empire the God of heaven
will bring into being, never to be destroyed, never to be superseded; con-
45 queror of all these others, itself unconquerable. This is that stone thou
sawest none ever quarried, that fell from the mountain-side, bringing
clay and iron and bronze and silver and gold to nothing; this was a revelation the king's grace had from the most high God himself of what must
come about; true was thy dream, and this, past doubt, the meaning of it.
46   With that, king Nabuchodonosor bowed down face to earth, and made
Daniel reverence; ay, he would have sacrifice offered to him, and incense,
47 and with these words greeted him: Doubt is none but this God of yours of
all gods is God, of all kings the master; he it is brings hidden things to
48 light, or how couldst thou have read the secret? Thereupon, he raised
Daniel to high rank, and showered riches on him; ruler he should be of
all Babylon's provinces, and over all its wise men have the pre-eminence.
49 But Daniel made suit to him, and it was Sidrach, Misach and Abdenago
that had Babylon under their charge; Daniel himself was the king's courtier still.

CHAPTER THREE

IT was this king Nabuchodonosor made a golden image, sixty cubits
high and six cubits broad, which he set up on the plain of Dura, in the
2 province of Babylon; and word went round in king Nabuchodonosor's
name, summoning all the governors, magistrates, judges, chieftains, rulers,
prefects and leading men from every part of his dominions, to be present
3 at the dedication of the image king Nabuchodonosor had set up. So they
gathered there, governors, magistrates, judges, chieftains, rulers, noblemen in high office, and leading men from every part, for the dedication of

---

[1] Literally, 'As thou sawest iron mixed with earthenware, so they shall mingle
themselves with the seed of men, but they shall not cohere, this with that, just
as iron will not mix with clay.' This is usually understood as meaning 'the rival
dynasties will enter into alliance with each other *by means of* royal marriages
(the seed of men), but they will not contrive to keep the peace.' All this is very
much out of tune with the allegory, which plainly implies that the fourth empire
in its later stages will be composed of a weaker and a stronger element within
itself, the two elements not really mixing. We must understand, then, that the
conquering power (whatever it may be) will fail to absorb and unify the conquered elements it is dealing with.

king Nabuchodonosor's image. And, as they stood before the image he
4 had set up, a herald cried lustily to men of all peoples, nations and lan-
5 guages: As soon as you hear the sound of horn, flute, harp, zither, dulcimer, pipe and other instruments of music, you are to fall down and wor-
6 ship the image of gold which king Nabuchodonosor has set up. Whoever
does not fall down in worship will be thrown, there and then, into the
7 heart of a raging furnace. No sooner, then, did the sound of horn, flute,
harp, zither, dulcimer, pipe and the rest reach the assembly than all of
them, whatever their tribe, people or language, fell down in worship of
king Nabuchodonosor's image.

8 It was then that certain Chaldaeans came forward with malicious accu-
9 sations against the Jews. They wished long life to king Nabuchodonosor,
10 and said, Lord King, thy command was that all men, at the sound of horn,
flute, harp, zither, dulcimer, pipe and the rest, should fall down and wor-
11 ship the golden image, on pain of being thrown into a raging furnace.
12 And here are certain Jews, entrusted by thee with the affairs of Babylon
province, to wit, Sidrach, Misach and Abdenago, who have set the royal
command at defiance, and will not reverence thy gods, or worship the
13 golden image thou hast set up. Upon this, Nabuchodonosor sent for
Sidrach, Misach and Abdenago in a transport of rage; and when they
14 were brought, without delay, into his presence, this was the threat king
Nabuchodonosor uttered: So Sidrach, Misach and Abdenago will not
15 reverence my gods, or worship this golden image of mine? Here is your
choice, then; either you will fall down and worship this image of mine
when the sound of horn, flute, harp, zither, dulcimer, pipe and the other
music reaches you, or then and there you shall be thrown into a raging
furnace. You are in my power; what God can deliver you?
16 Then Sidrach, Misach and Abdenago said to king Nabuchodonosor,
17 There is no need for any answer of ours to that question; thou wilt see for
thyself whether the God we worship is able to rescue us from the raging
18 fire, and from thy royal power. But, whether he rescues us or no, be
assured, sir king, here are men who do not reverence thy gods, or worship
19 any image of thine. At this, Nabuchodonosor fell into a rage; his features,
as he glared at Sidrach, Misach and Abdenago, were distorted with fury.
20 He would have the furnace heated seven times hotter than its wont; and
into this raging furnace he bade his chosen bodyguard throw Sidrach,
21 Misach and Abdenago with their feet shackled. So they were bound just
as they were, in breeches and turban, shoes and coat, and thrown into the
22 heart of the raging furnace; the king's order admitted no delay. So
fiercely was the furnace heated that those who threw them in were
23 burned to death. Meanwhile these three, Sidrach, Misach and Abdenago,
fell fast bound into the heart of the fires that raged in it.
24 And there, in the hottest of the flames, they walked to and fro, singing

25 to God their praises, blessing the Lord. There, as he stood in the heart of
26 the fire, Azarias found utterance, and thus made his prayer: Blessed art
   thou, Lord God of our fathers, renowned and glorious is thy name for
27 ever! In all thy dealings with us, thou hast right on thy side; so true to thy
28 promises, so unswerving in thy course, so just in thy awards! No punishment thou hast inflicted upon us, or upon Jerusalem, holy city of our
   fathers, but was deserved; for sins of ours, faithfulness and justice that
29 stroke laid on. Sinners we were, that had wronged and forsaken thee, all
30 was amiss with us; unheard thy commandments, or else unheeded, thy
31 will neglected, and with it, our own well-being! Nothing we had not
32 deserved, pillage of thy contriving, plague of thy sending, and at last the
   foul domination of godless foes, of a tyrant that has no equal on earth!
33 Tongue-tied we stand, that have brought disgrace on the livery of thy true
   worship.
34   For thy own honour, we entreat thee not to abandon us eternally. Do
35 not annul thy covenant, and deprive us of thy mercy. Think of Abraham
   that was thy friend, of thy servant Isaac, of Jacob whom thou didst set
36 apart for thyself; the men to whom thou didst promise that thou wouldst
   increase their posterity, till it was countless as the stars in heaven, or the
37 sand by the sea shore. Whereas now, Lord, we are of all nations the most
38 insignificant; all the world over, men see us humbled for our sins. In
   these days we are without prince or leader or prophet, we have no burnt-
   sacrifice, no victim, no offering; for us no incense burns, no first-fruits can
39 be brought into thy presence and win thy favour. But oh, accept us still,
40 hearts that are crushed, spirits bowed down by adversity; look kindly on
   the sacrifice we offer thee this day, as it had been burnt-sacrifice of rams
   and bullocks, thousands of fattened lambs; who ever trusted in thee and
41 was disappointed? With all our hearts, now, we choose thy will, we
42 reverence thee, we long after thy presence; for that clemency, that
43 abundant mercy of thine must we hope in vain? By some wondrous de-
44 liverance vindicate thy own renown; theirs be the vain hope, that
   would do thy servants an injury. Fools, that would match themselves with
45 omnipotence! Crush down their might; teach them that in all the world
   Lord there is none, God there is none, glorified as thou.
46   Meanwhile, their tormentors were not idle; naphtha and tow, pitch and
47 tinder must be heaped on the furnace, till the flame rose forty-nine cubits
48 above the furnace itself, breaking out and burning such Chaldaeans as
49 stood near it. But an angel of the Lord had gone down into the furnace
   with Azarias and his companions; and he drove the flames away from it,
50 making a wind blow in the heart of the furnace, like the wind that brings
   the dew. So that these three were untouched, and the fire brought them
51 neither pain nor discomfort. Whereupon all of them, as with one mouth,
   began to give praise and glory and blessing to God, there in the furnace,

52 in these words that follow: Blessed art thou, Lord God of our fathers, praised above all, renowned above all for ever; blessed is thy holy and

53 glorious name, praised above all, renowned above all for ever. Blessed art thou, whose glory fills thy holy temple, praised above all, renowned

54 above all for ever; blessed art thou, who reignest on thy kingly throne,

55 praised above all, renowned above all for ever. Blessed art thou, who art throned above the cherubim, and gazest down into the depths, praised

56 above all, renowned above all for ever. Blessed art thou, high in the vault of heaven, praised above all, renowned above all for ever.

57 Then they cried out upon all things the Lord had made, to bless him,

58 and praise him, and extol his name for ever. Bless the Lord they should,

59 the Lord's angels; bless him they should, the heavens, and the waters

61 above the heavens; bless him they should, the Lord's Powers. Bless him

63 they should, sun and moon, stars of heaven, each drop of rain and mois-

65 ture, and all the winds of God. Bless him they should, fire and heat,

67 winter cold and summer drought, dew and rime at morning, frost and

70 the cold air. Bless him they should, ice and snow, day-time and night-

72 time, light and darkness, lightnings and storm-clouds. And earth in its

75 turn should bless the Lord, praise him, and extol his name for ever. Bless

76 the Lord they should, mountains and hills, every growing thing that

77 earth yields, flowing fountains, seas and rivers. Bless him they should,

80 sea-monsters and all life that is bred in the waters, all the birds that fly in

81 heaven, wild beasts and tame, and the sons of men. Bless him Israel

84 should, priests of the Lord bless him, servants of the Lord bless him;

86 bless him they should, spirits and souls of all faithful men; bless him they

88 should, dedicated and humble hearts. And for Ananias, Azarias and Misael, well might they bless the Lord, praise him and extol his name for ever; here was the grave spoiled, death robbed of its prey, and ever they

89 were kept safe from the furnace, let its flames rage as they would. Give thanks to the Lord, they cried, the Lord is gracious; his mercy is eternal!

90 Bless the Lord, you that are his worshippers; he is God above all gods; praise him and give him thanks, whose mercy is eternal.[1]

91 Sore amazed was king Nabuchodonosor, and started to his feet; Tell me, he said to his courtiers, did we not cast three men into yonder furnace,

92 all closely bound? And when they answered, Sire, past doubt, he told them what he had seen; here were four men, that bonds wore none, walking to and fro in the heart of the fire, and never the worse. And such an

93 aspect he wore, the fourth of them, as it had been a son of God. With that, close went Nabuchodonosor to the furnace door, and cried, Come forth, Sidrach, Misach and Abdenago! Servants of the most high God,

---

[1] Verses 24–90 are found in the Septuagint Greek, but were unknown to the Aramaic text, it seems, even in the time of St. Jerome.

come out to me! So out came Sidrach, Misach and Abdenago, from the
94 fire's heart all of them; and with one accord governor and judge and
courtier clustered round them to look. Plain it was, the heat had no power
over them; never a hair singed, nor a coat shrivelled, nor any smell of burn-
95 ing marked its passage. And at that, Nabuchodonosor could contain himself no longer; Blessed be this God whom Sidrach, Misach and Abdenago
worship! Here were servants of his that trusted in him, and defied a king's
edict, ready to put their lives in peril, so they might be free men, worshipping no God but their own; and he has sent an angel to deliver them.
96 Hereby, then, I enact that if anyone blasphemes against the God of Sidrach, Misach and Abdenago, come he of what people, what tribe, what
race he may, he shall pay for it with his life, and his house be put to public
97 use. God there is no other that can grant such deliverance as this! And
be sure he promoted them to high rank in Babylon province.
98   King Nabuchodonosor to men of every race, tribe and tongue, dwell
99 they where they will, all health! Here be wondrous portents the most
100 high God has been manifesting, and in my person. And my will is to make
them known, portents most weighty, wonders most compelling; such a
reign as his lasts for ever, such power as his the ages cannot diminish.[1]

CHAPTER FOUR

ALL went well in my household; never was Nabuchodonosor's court
2   more flourishing. And then I had a dream that put me in fear; nor
3 waking thoughts gave my troubled wits repose. Thereupon I gave orders
that all the wise men of Babylon should appear before me, to interpret my
4 dream; diviner and sage, astrologer and soothsayer, all must assemble,
5 but never one of them could tell me the meaning of it. At last came
Daniel, one of their number, styled after my own god's name Baltassar,
and endowed by all the holy gods [2] with their spirit. To him I unfolded
6 my dream thus: Diviner is none, Baltassar, such as thou art; the spirit of
all the holy gods is in thee, and there is no mystery beyond thy ken. Tell
me, thou, what vision came to me in sleep, what events it boded.
7   Wouldst thou know, what fantasies disturbed my rest, this was what I
8 saw. Grew a tree from the heart of earth, beyond measure tall; a great
tree and a thriving; top of it reached the heavens, and the ends of the earth
9 had view of it. What fair leaves it had, what foison of fruit, enough to
cater for a whole world! Beast was none but might take shelter under it,

---

[1] Verses 98–100 should (and in some Greek manuscripts do) form part of the
next chapter.
[2] Or perhaps 'by the holy God'; so also in verses 6 and 15.

bird was none but might nest in its branches, and to all living creatures
10 it gave food. But as I lay watching in my dream, came down from heaven
11 one of the holy ones that mount guard there, and loud rang his message:
Down with yonder tree, lop branch, strip leaves, spill fruit! Let beast its
12 shade, bird its covert forsake! Yet leave the stock of it fast in earth.
Band of iron, chain of bronze! There on the soft meadow grass heaven's
13 dew wet him, pasture with the beasts find he; heart of man be changed
in him, beast's heart given him, till seven seasons there have found him,
14 and passed him by. Doom it is of the unsleeping ones, will and word of
the holy ones; live men and learn that he, the most High, of human kingship is overlord, gives it to whom he will, and holds none too base for the
having of it.

15   Thus dreamt I, the great king Nabuchodonosor. Make haste, Baltassar, and read me the riddle; wise man was none in my kingdom that
could tell me the meaning of it, but thou hast the spirit of the holy gods in
thee; thou canst unravel it.

16   But Daniel, Baltassar if you will, made no answer. For a whole hour, in
silence, he gave himself up to his thoughts, and right comfortless they
were. Nay, Baltassar, the king said at last, never lose heart over a dream,
and the interpretation of a dream! Lord king, said he, such dreams be for
17 thy enemies! To ill-wishers of thine bode they what they bode! A tree
18 tall and sturdy, top reaching the heavens, in all the world's view, fair
branches, fruit abounding, food for all, beasts sheltering, birds nesting
19 there, what is it, lord king, but thou? So great thy power has grown, it
20 reaches heaven; earth's bounds are the bounds of thy dominion. He
watches ever, that holy one thou sawest coming down from heaven; and
his word was, Down with the tree, away with it, yet leave the stock of it
rooted fast! Of iron band he spoke, and chain of bronze; of soft meadow
grass under the dews of heaven; of one that should have his pasture
among the beasts, till seven seasons had found him there, and passed him
21 by. Sentence from the most High this dream forbodes, and the king's
22 grace the subject of it. Far from the haunts of men thou shalt be driven
out, and among brute beasts thou shalt have thy dwelling; eat grass, ox-
fashion, and with heaven's dew be drenched, till seven seasons have passed
thee by; so learn thou must, that of all human kingship the most High is
23 overlord, and grants it where he will. If stock of tree is to be left rooted,
be sure thy throne shall be thine once again; but first thou must learn thy
24 lesson, that all power is from above. Deign, my lord king, to be advised
by me; with almsgiving, with mercy to the poor, for fault and wrong-
doing of thine make amends; it may be he will condone thy guilt.

25   All this king Nabuchodonosor underwent. A twelvemonth later, as he
27 walked to and fro on the roof of his palace at Babylon, he said aloud:
Babylon lies before me, the great city, the royal city I have built; sure

28 proof of my power, fair monument of my renown! And before the words
had died on his lips, came a voice from heaven: King Nabuchodonosor,
here is thy doom! Pass away from thee it must, that royal power of thine;
driven from the haunts of men, with beasts dwell thou, grass like the
cattle eat thou, till seven seasons have passed thee by, and learned thou
hast that the most High is overlord of all human kingship, to grant it
30 where he will. There and then fell the doom on Nabuchodonosor; thrust
him out they did, to feed on grass, and ever the dew of heaven drenched
him; thick as eagle's feathers his hair grew, and like birds' talons his nails.
31 When the appointed time was over, I lifted up my eyes to heaven, I,
Nabuchodonosor, and right reason came back to me. Blessed I then the
most high God, to the eternal gave glory and praise; such a reign as his
32 lasts for ever, such power as his the ages cannot diminish. Matched with
him, the whole world of men counts for nothing; in the heavenly powers,
as in our mortal lives, he accomplishes his will, and none may resist him,
33 none may ask his meaning. And when reason came back to me, back came
royal pomp and state, back came the beauty I once had; prince and senator waited on me, restored to my throne now in more magnificence than
34 ever. What wonder if I, Nabuchodonosor, praise this King of heaven,
extol and glorify him, so faithful to his promise, so just in his dealings?
Proud minds none can abase as he.[1]

CHAPTER FIVE

NOW turn we to king Baltassar, that made great cheer for courtiers of
his a thousand, each man drinking wine as his rank entitled him.[2]
2 And he, in his cups, would have the spoils of the old temple at Jerusalem
brought in, cups of gold, cups of silver that his father Nabuchodonosor
had carried away; king and court, wife and concubine should drink from
3 them. Brought in they were, all the spoils of Jerusalem; king and cour-
4 tier, wife and concubine, drank from those vessels; drank, and to their
own gods gave the praise, gods of gold and silver, bronze and iron, wood
and stone.
5 Then, in that hour, an apparition came to them. They saw the fingers

---

[1] It would seem that the story of Nabuchodonosor's dream must have been
current, from quite early times, in more than one version. The alternation, in
this chapter as it stands, between history and autobiography would by itself
suggest a compilation from sources. But it is also observable that the Septuagint
Greek, while agreeing as to the facts, tells the story throughout in quite different
words.

[2] In the Aramaic text, 'and (the king) drank wine in the presence of all the
thousand.'

of a man's hand writing on the plaster of the palace wall, full in the lamp's light; joints of a hand that wrote there the king could not choose but see.

6 All at once he changed colour, a prey to anxious thoughts; melted his heart
7 within him, and his knees knocked together. With a loud cry, he bade them summon the wise men of Babylon, sage and astrologer and diviner; and to these he made proclamation: Who reads me yonder writing, and tells me the meaning of it, shall go clad in purple, a gold chain about his
8 neck, and hold the third place in my kingdom. But when they came into the banqueting-hall, never a wise head among them could read the charac-
9 ters, nor tell the king what they meant; whereupon king Baltassar was in a great taking of fear, his cheeks paler yet, and his princes were no easier in mind than himself.

10 But now all this ado brought the queen-mother down into the banquet-ing-hall; Long life to the king's grace! cried she; here is no need for daunted
11 hearts and pale looks! One man thou hast in thy realm the holy gods in-spire; in thy father's time, good proof he gave of the wisdom and learning that were his. Did not thy father, king Nabuchodonosor, put him at the head of his wise men one and all, sage nor wizard nor astrologer nor soothsayer to match him? In such renown thy royal father held him, my
12 lord king; no common spirit is his, no common prudence and discern-ment, dreams to interpret, hidden things to reveal, spells to unbind. For his name, it is Daniel; thy father called him Baltassar. Let Daniel be sum-moned, and thy riddle shall not long go unread.

13 So Daniel was brought into the king's presence, and the king asked him if Daniel he were, one of the Jewish exiles his father had brought to Baby-
14 lon? Great things were told of him; that he had the spirit of the gods,
15 gave proof of skill, discernment and wisdom above the common. And here was certain writing, that had baffled sage and diviner called in to read
16 it; meaning of it they could not tell. If Daniel had skill indeed to reveal mysteries and unbind spells, let him read those characters and in-terpret them; robe of purple he should have, and a gold chain about his neck, and hold the third place in the kingdom.

17 But Daniel spoke out, there in the king's presence: Purple and gold keep for thyself; and for thy honours, let him have them who will. But for
18 the writing, I will read it willingly, and tell thee the meaning of it. Sir king, thy father was Nabuchodonosor; to him the most High gave royal
19 state, and splendid renown; for that renown of his, every people and race and tribe must tremble in awe of him; slew he, smote he, exalted he,
20 abased he, all he would. With that, his heart beat high; proud grew his will and obstinate; and the issue of it? From that throne he must come
21 down, be shorn of that glory; cast out henceforth from the haunts of men. Heart of beast the heart of him; dwelling-place of wild ass should be his, food of the ox; and the dews of heaven should drench him, till he had

learned that the most High is overlord of all human kingship, grants it to
22 whom he will. All this, Baltassar, thou knewest, yet son no more than
23 father would abate his pride; heaven's Ruler defying, thou wouldst bring
out yonder cups, the spoil of his temple, to serve wine for thee and thy
court, for wife and concubine. Gods of silver and gold, bronze and iron,
stone and wood, that cannot see or hear or feel, thou wouldst magnify;
for the God that holds thy life, thy fortunes, in his keeping, never a word
24 of praise. That is why the hand appeared to thee, fingers that wrote what
25 there stands written. This is the charactery of it: Mané, Thecel, Phares.
26 Mané betokens numbering; so many years allotted to thy empire, and now
27 God has brought them to an end. And thecel, weighing; the equal of his
28 benefits God demands, and has not found in thee. And phares, rending;
Persian and Mede shall be thy successors in the kingdom that is torn from
thy grasp.
29   With that, at the royal bidding, they clothed Daniel in purple, and
hung a chain of gold about his neck; proclamation, too, was made that he
30 held the third place in the kingdom. But that same night Baltassar, the
31 Chaldaean king, was slain, and his crown passed to Darius, a Mede, then
in the sixty-third year of his age.[1]

CHAPTER SIX

THIS Darius saw fit to appoint a hundred and twenty lords lieutenant,
2   who should govern the provinces of his empire; and over these, three
viceroys, of whom Daniel was one; governor should be answerable to vice-
3 roy, and the king take no hurt. Yet governor was none or viceroy that
4 could compare with Daniel, so richly God inspired him; and soon the
king's thought was, to put the whole empire under his care. Right gladly
would his rivals have found opportunity to discredit him in the king's
eyes; but no, handle or pretext they could find none, so faithful was he, so
5 far removed from all breath of suspicion. And at last they were fain to
admit, if charge was to be found against Daniel at all, keeping of his
God's law must be the ground of it.
6   So they took the king by surprise; Long life, they said, to the king's
7 grace! Here is a design upon which we are all agreed, viceroy and magistrate and governor and senator and judge; that an edict should go out

---

[1] If the event here referred to is the well-known capture of Babylon by Cyrus,
Darius the Mede should perhaps be identified with Gobryas, a general of his
who took command of the city after its capture. It is not impossible that a short-
lived 'Median' empire may have intervened between that of Babylon and that
of Persia, but the monuments reveal no trace of it; and the sacred writers appear
to regard the Medes and Persians as already, for political purposes, a single
nation.

under the royal seal forbidding thy subjects to make any request of god or man these next thirty days, save only of thyself. And if any man dis-

8 obeys, it shall be on pain of his life; he is for the lion-pit. May it please the king's grace to give this design of ours effect, and make the decree unalterable, under law of the Medes and Persians, the law there is no amending.

9 Draw up the edict he did, and signed it. As for Daniel, when he heard it was law, he took himself home; and now as ever, three times a day, he would open his chamber window towards Jerusalem eastwards, doing

11 reverence on bended knee and praising his God. Be sure they surprised

12 him at it, these enemies of his; found him a-praying to his God, and went off to remind the king of his edict. Had not a law been enacted, prayer there should be none to god or man those thirty days following, save to the king; and that on pain of the lions? Law it is, said he, and law of the

13 Medes and Persians there is no amending. Why then, they asked the king, what of Daniel, Daniel the Jewish exile, that for law and edict cares nothing? Three times a day he offers his God prayer.

14 Pitiful hearing was this for the king's ear; to save Daniel was all his

15 thought, and to that end he laboured till set of sun; but the trap they had devised was too crafty for him, and ever they put him in mind there was no help for it. By the law Medes and Persians use, let the king once make

16 a decree, there is no amending it. At last the king gave orders Daniel should be sent for and shut up in the lion-pit; So faithful a servant, he told

17 him, thy God must needs deliver. And with that, a stone was brought and set down at the pit's entrance, which the king sealed and his nobles

18 both; none might tamper with it. Home went the king, and supperless to bed; he would have no food brought him, and sleep he might not.

19 With the first light of day, the king was up and stirring; to the lion-

20 pit he hastened, and as he came up to it, he cried out most lamentably: Daniel, servant of the God that lives, has faithful service of thine availed

21 thee, rescued thee from the lions? Long life to the king's grace, Daniel

22 answered; angel of his did his errand, and stopped the lions' mouths. What harm should they do me, one that my God sees guiltless? And for

23 thyself, lord king, nought did I to earn thy displeasure. Right glad the king was to learn of Daniel's safety; be sure he gave orders they should bring Daniel up out of the pit, and out of the pit they brought him, un-

24 scathed from head to foot; such reward they have that trust in God. There-upon, at the king's bidding, they fetched his accusers, and thrust them into the lion-pit, their wives and children with them. But these never reached the floor of it, so quickly the lions fell upon them, and broke all the bones of them to nothing.[1]

---

[1] Cf. note on Mt. 1.25. The Septuagint Greek has, 'they fetched those two accusers of his,' *i.e.*, the two other viceroys alluded to in verse 2 above.

25   Then Darius sent out a proclamation to all the world, without distinc-
26 tion of nation, race or language, wishing them well, and enjoining this
   decree upon them, that all the subjects of his empire should hold the God
   of Daniel in awe and reverence. Here is a God that lives, he told them, a
   God that abides for ever; such a reign as his there is no overthrowing,
27 such power as his the ages cannot diminish. His to deliver, his to save,
   his to shew wondrous portents in high heaven and on earth beneath, the
   God who saved Daniel from the lions.
28   Let Darius reign, or Cyrus the Persian, this same Daniel throve yet.

CHAPTER SEVEN

IN the first year of the Babylonian king Baltassar, Daniel had a dream;
sleep he might, but still his thoughts were busy. The substance of this
dream he put on record, giving no more than the sum of it, in these words
following.
2   Night came, and brought with it a vision for my seeing. All the winds
3 of heaven, I thought, did battle over the wide sea, and out of it came four
4 great beasts, each of them different from the last. A lioness the first seemed,
   that yet had eagle's wings; but as I watched, these wings were plucked,
   and with that it rose up from the ground, standing on its feet like a man,
5 and a man's heart was given to it. Then rose up another by its side, this one
   like a bear; three rows of teeth it had in its mouth, and a summons came
6 to it, great part of mankind it should devour. What saw I next? A leopard
   it seemed, yet had a bird's wings, four of them, on its back, and four heads;
7 this beast it was that now attained dominion. But still I dreamed on, and
   a fourth beast saw at last, fiercer, and stranger, and more powerful yet.
   It had great teeth of iron, ready to crush and to devour, and ever what
   these spared it would trample down with its feet; match it those others
8 might not; and out of its head grew ten horns. Even as I watched them,
   a new horn grew up in the midst of the others, and three of them must be
   plucked away to make room for it; eyes it had, this new horn, like a man's
   eyes, and a mouth that talked very boastfully.
9   While I still watched, there were judgement-thrones a-setting; and one
   took his seat there crowned with age. White as snow his garments were,
10 and pure wool could not match his hair for whiteness; his throne all of
   flame, the wheels under it glancing fire; and ever from his presence a
   stream of fire came rushing onward. A thousand thousand they were that
   waited on his bidding, and for every one of these, a thousand others were
   standing there before him. Assize should be held now, and the records lay
11 open. And still I watched, to see what would become of the boasts yonder

horn had made; and all at once I was aware the beast itself had been slain,
12 and even the carcase of it had vanished, handed over to the flames; nor
might those other beasts enjoy power any longer, though life they should
13 enjoy for a while, until their turn came. Then I saw in my dream, how
one came riding on the clouds of heaven, that was yet a son of man; came
to where the Judge sat, crowned with age, and was ushered into his pre-
14 sence. With that, power was given him, and glory, and sovereignty; obey
him all must, men of every race and tribe and tongue; such a reign as his
lasts for ever, such power as his the ages cannot diminish.

15 By this, Daniel wrote, my heart was ill at ease; a dread sight it was, and
16 as I dreamed, my thoughts bewildered me. So I drew closer to one that
stood by, and asked to know the truth of all that had gone forward; he it
17 was that read the riddle for me, and thus he unravelled it; It is but earthly
18 kingdoms they betoken, these four great beasts thou hast seen; the servants of the most high God shall have dominion yet; theirs it shall be for
19 ever and for evermore. But I was minded to know the truth more fully;
what was the fourth beast, so different from all the rest, so dreadful; why
must it have teeth and claws of iron, to crush and to devour, to trample on
20 what was left? What of the ten horns on its head, and that other, before
which three of them fell, the horn that had eyes, and a mouth to boast
21 with, and grew greater than the rest? This horn it was I saw doing battle
against the servants of the most High, and getting the better of them,
22 until the Judge appeared, crowned with age, to give them redress, and
their turn came to have dominion.

23 And his answer was, this fourth beast was the fourth of those earthly
kingdoms, and the greatest of them all, to crush and devour and trample
24 down a whole world. Ten kings be the ten horns of that kingdom, and
after these another shall rise, more powerful yet, and three of them shall
25 bite the dust. Boastfully he shall challenge the most High, and do his servants despite; calendar and ordinance he shall think to set aside; for a
space of time, and for twice as long, and for half as long,[1] he must needs
26 have his way. Then assize shall be held on him, and all his power be taken
27 away, crushed down and forgotten for ever. Then what royalty, what
empire, what earth-embracing dominion shall be theirs, the people set
apart for the most High! Sovereignty everlasting; no monarch but must
bow to its yoke.[2]
28 So ended the revelation made to Daniel. Bewildered my thoughts were,
and my cheek pale, but I kept the memory of it faithfully in my heart.

---

[1] Literally, 'for a time, and times, and half a time.' This is traditionally interpreted as meaning three-and-a-half, that is, half of the mystical number seven.

[2] It must be confessed that the historical interpretation of verses 15–27 remains
wholly doubtful. It is not even clear whether the four beasts represent four suc-
cessive empires (like the statue in chapter 2), or four kingdoms existing simul-

CHAPTER EIGHT

TO me, to Daniel, another revelation came, besides that I had first
2   seen. It was now the third year of king Baltassar, and I was at the
town of Susa, in Aelam province, but it seemed, in my vision, it was by
3 the gate[1] of Ulai I stood. I looked at what lay before me, and what saw I,
at the edge of the marsh, but a ram standing there, with one high-branch-
4 ing horn, and another that grew up after it, but grew higher yet.   With
those horns it tossed every enemy that came to meet it; west and north
and south was never a beast could match it, or escape its attack; no wonder this ram carried all before it, and rose to greatness.
5   But now, as I looked, came a buck goat from the west country, earth
overshadowing, and spurning the ground beneath him; one horn this goat
6 had between the eyes of him, a horn of noble aspect. Close he came to the
ram, the great horned ram I had espied in yonder gateway, and bore down
7 upon it with very furious onslaught. So madly he charged that he overcame the ram and broke either horn of it with one blow; what shift could
it make now? Brought down it was and trampled under foot; there was no
8 rescuing it. So now it was the goat's turn to enjoy dominion; yet no sooner
had he reached his full strength, than the great horn was broken, and four
other horns must grow up in place of it, fronting the four winds of heaven.
9   It was from one of these a single horn now sprang; a little horn that
10 grew till it outrivalled south and east, aye, and the armies . . . For the
armies of heaven itself it proved a match, bringing heavenly powers down
11 to earth, stars down to earth, and trampling them under foot;   a match
even for the captain of those armies, that must lose the daily sacrifice
12 offered to him, and look on at the destruction of his sanctuary. Alas for
our guilt! That such a king, by armed force, should avail against the sacrifice, truth itself should dethrone, and should thrive yet, should prosper
13 yet! This complaint I heard one of God's servants making to another,
I know not who; and when that other asked how long a cessation of sacrifice the vision portended, how long the estranging guilt, and the defeat,
14 and the profanation, Night first, said he, morning after; two thousand
three hundred days it will be, ere the sanctuary is cleansed.[2]

---

taneously, *e.g.,* the four main divisions of the Macedonian empire after Alexander's death. The little horn is usually identified with Antiochus Epiphanes
(B.C. 176–164), the persecutor of the Machabees; but he was the eighth, not the
tenth of his line, and the explanations given of the 'three horns' displaced by him
seem curiously forced.

[1] According to the Hebrew text, 'the river,' and so in verse 16.

[2] Verses 9–14 (particularly verse 13 are very obscure, and may have suffered

15 But for me, for Daniel, that saw the vision, understanding of it was
16 none, till one appeared to me that had the semblance of a man, and a
voice hailed him from between Ulai gates; For thee it is, Gabriel, to make
17 the vision clear. Came he close, then, to where I was standing; but I, at
his coming, fell down in terror, face to earth. Heed thou well, son of man,
18 said he; what here thou seest, in the last days shall be accomplished. But
he spoke to one that lay swooning on the ground; so he must put out his
19 hand, and raise me to my feet. Then he went on: I mean to tell thee how
all shall fall out when the days of punishment are over; be sure the end of
20 them is fixed. Horned ram of thy vision rules over the Medes and Per-
21 sians; buck goat over the realm of Greece, and the great horn between his
22 eyes is first of the Greek kings. Those four others that grew after its
breaking are four kings that shall arise, fellow-countrymen of his, but not
23 his peers. These reigning, the world shall go from bad to worse, till a new
24 king comes to the throne, brazen-faced, a master of riddles. Great power
shall he wield, though of that first king not the peer, making havoc beyond
belief, thriving and prospering. Strength of arms nor holiness of life shall
25 rescue peoples from his will; all shall go well with crafty scheming of his,
till his heart grows proud, and he deals death all about him, when peril is
none. And at last with the Prince of princes he shall try conclusions; no
26 human hand it shall be that crushes him down at last. Night comes first,
then morning; but the revelation made to thee is a true one; seal it up, till
those last days when it must have effect.[1]
27 So much he told me; and for many days after I lay sick; when I was on
my feet again, I had the king's business to do, but still I was all dazed by
the vision, and there was no interpreting it.

---

from manuscript corruption. At the end of verse 9, the Septuagint Greek has
'the north'; the Hebrew text 'the splendour' (or possibly, 'the gazelle'); the
Latin version 'the armies.' Perhaps a word has dropped out, and we should
read either 'the armies of heaven,' as in verse 10, or 'the land of splendour' as
in 11.16. The reference to night and morning in verse 14 is generally interpreted, according to the Hebrew text, of the evening and morning sacrifices.
Some think that we should understand an interval of 1,150 days, involving 2,300
sacrifices.

[1] In verses 19–26, the great horn is evidently Alexander of Macedon, who
died in B.C. 323, and the little horn presumably Antiochus Epiphanes. The
Latin version gives two different translations of the same phrase in verses 22 and
24; but it seems likely that we ought to prefer a uniform interpretation; either
'not a match for Alexander's strength,' which suits the context best, or 'not by
means of their (his) own strength,' which is a more natural rendering of the
Hebrew. The description of Antiochus Epiphanes is not particularly recognizable.

CHAPTER NINE

THEN Darius-the Mede, son of Assuerus, was raised to the throne of
2 Chaldaea; and in the year when his reign began who but I, Daniel,
should discover, by the reading of old records, how to compute the seventy
years of Jerusalem's widowhood? Such doom the Lord had foretold to the
3 prophet Jeremias. And with that, I turned to the Lord my God; pray to
him I would, and sue for mercy, fasting ever, sackcloth and ashes still my
wear.
4 Prayed I then to the Lord my God, and made confession of my sins, in
these words following: Mercy, mercy, Lord God, the great, the terrible;
to those who love thee, so gracious, with those who keep thy command-
5 ments, troth keeping still! Sinned we have, and wronged thee, rebelled
we have, and forsaken thee, turned our backs on decree and award of
6 thine, nor heeded thy servants, the prophets, that spoke to us in thy name,
7 to king and prince and the common folk that gendered us. Fault with thee
is none; ours, Lord, to blush for the wrong-doing that has offended thee,
men of Juda, citizens of Jerusalem, Israel near at hand, Israel banished
8 far away, in what plight thou seest! Blush we, king and prince of ours,
9 fathers of ours that did the wrong; be it thine, O Lord our God, to have
10 mercy and to forgive. So far we have strayed from thee, so deaf to the
divine voice, when the prophets that served thee bade us follow thy law!
11 A whole people that would transgress thy command, turn a deaf ear to thy
calls! What wonder if it fell on us, drop by drop, the avenging curse God's
12 servant Moses wrote of? Our sins had deserved it, and if yonder unexampled punishment befell Jerusalem, it was but a threat fulfilled; warn-
13 ing we had of it, we and the princes that governed us. No misfortune
overtook us, but the law of Moses had foretold it; and yet, O Lord our
God, appease thy anger we would not, nor leave our sinning, nor bethink
14 ourselves, how well thy word thou keepest; what wonder if bane, not
blessing, the divine regard brought us? Be our punishment what it will,
not ours to find fault with the God we have disobeyed.
15 Thou art the Lord our God, whose constraining power rescued thy
people from the land of Egypt, who hast won thyself glory, too, in this our
16 day; we, Lord, have been sinners, we have shewn ourselves unworthy of
all thy faithful dealings with us. But wilt thou let thy indignant anger fall
on Jerusalem, on that holy mountain of thine? Too long, for our sins and
the sins of our fathers before us, all our neighbours have held Jerusalem,
17 and us thy people, in contempt. God of our race, give audience at last to
the prayer, the plea thy servant brings before thee; for thy own honour,
18 restore the sanctuary that now lies forlorn to the smile of thy favour. My

God, give ear and listen to us; open thy eyes, and see how desolate is this city of ours, that claims to be thy own. No merits of ours, nothing but thy

19 great love emboldens us to lay our prayers at thy feet. Thy hearing, Lord, and thy pardon; thy heed, Lord, and thy aid! For thy own honour, my God, deny thyself no longer to the city, the people that is called thy own![1]

20 Thus prayed I, thus did I confess my own sins, and the sins of my fellow Israelites, pouring out supplication, there in the presence of my God,

21 for that holy mountain which is his dwelling-place. And I was still at my prayer, when the human figure of Gabriel, as I had seen it at the beginning of my vision, flew swiftly to my side; it was the hour of the evening sacri-

22 fice when he reached me. And with these words he enlightened me:

23 Daniel, my errand is to instruct thee and give thee discernment. Even as thy prayer began, a secret was disclosed, and I am here to make it known to thee, so well heaven loves thee. Mark well, then, the message, and read

24 the revelation aright. It is ordained that this people of thine, that holy city of thine, should wait seventy weeks before guilt is done away, sin ended, wrong righted; before God's everlasting favour is restored, and the visions and the prophecies come true, and he who is all holiness receives his anoint-

25 ing. Be assured of this, and mark it well; a period of seven weeks must go by, and another period of sixty-two weeks, between the order to rebuild Jerusalem and the coming of the Christ to be your leader. Street and wall

26 will be built again, though in a time of distress; and then sixty-two weeks must pass before the Christ is done to death; the people will disown him and have none of him. Then the army of an invading leader will destroy both city and sanctuary, so that his taking away will mean utter destruc-

27 tion; only a ruin is to be left when that war is ended. High covenant he shall make, before another week is done, and with folk a many; but when that week has run half its course, offering and burnt-sacrifice shall be none; in the temple all shall be defilement and desolation, and until all is over, all is fulfilled, that desolation shall continue.[2]

---

[1] The prayer of Daniel has several points in common with that of the Jewish people in Bar. 1.15, 2.13.

[2] The traditional account given of verses 24–27 is, that Daniel interprets the seventy years of Israel's captivity as seventy weeks of years, and that the periods called 'weeks' are periods of forty-nine years, four hundred and thirty-four years, and seven years respectively, four hundred and ninety in all. The order to rebuild Jerusalem is, quite naturally, identified with that given in Neh. 2, and dated B.C. 445. This would explain the preoccupation with prophecies about 'the End' which characterizes the outlook of our Lord's contemporaries; Daniel's prophecy was to fall due within the course of that century. It must be admitted, however, that widely different views have been held about the application of the prophecy in detail. Modern commentators, who understand the whole passage as a reference to Antiochus Epiphanes, and the profanation of the Temple in B.C. 167, are driven to very unconvincing explanations of the time-periods

CHAPTER TEN

THEN, in the third year of Cyrus' reign, that was king of Persia, a fresh revelation was made to Daniel, who is also called Baltassar. Here is truth indubitable, and a great host . . . And right well he understood its meaning, little avails vision where understanding is none.[1]

2 For three weeks together I, Daniel, that saw it, had been making sad
3 cheer; for three weeks together dry bread was my diet, nor ever did meat
4 or wine cross my lips, nor oil anoint me. Came now the twenty-fourth day of the new year, and I stood by the banks of the great river, where it
5 is called Tigris. I looked up, and saw a man standing there clad all in
6 linen, and his girdle of fine gold. Clear as topaz his body was, like the play of lightning shone his face, and like burning cressets his eyes; arms and legs of him had the sheen of bronze, and when he spoke, it was like
7 the murmur of a throng. The vision was for me, for Daniel, alone; my companions never saw it; such fear overcame them, they were fain to hide
8 themselves, and I was left alone with this high vision for my company. No wonder if my spirits were cowed; pale grew my cheek, and all the
9 strength in me ebbed away. He spoke, and as I listened to that voice, I
10 swooned where I stood, and lay there, face to earth, till a hand touched me, giving fresh impulse to knee and wrist.
11 Daniel, he said to me, Daniel, so well beloved, up with thee, and heed thou well; I have an errand to thee. Yet for all he spoke thus to me, I
12 stood there trembling, and still he must allay my fears. Take heart, Daniel, said he; thy prayers did not go unheard. Prayer of thine it was beckoned me to thy side, from the very moment when thou didst set about
13 thy search for knowledge, by fasting in the presence of thy God; but these twenty-one days he who guards the realm of Persia has delayed my coming. At last Michael, one of the high lords, brought me aid, and there, at
14 Persia's court, I was left master of the field.[2] Now I am here to tell thee what shall befall thy people in the last days; long days must pass ere the revelation is accomplished.

---

involved. Verse 27 is very obscure, and the text seems to have suffered in transmission. 'All shall be defilement and desolation'; literally, 'there shall be abomination of desolation,' cf. Mt. 24.15.

[1] The attempts made to explain this verse as it stands are not such as to produce conviction, and it seems likely that there is some corruption or omission in the text.

[2] 'He who guards the realm of Persia'; the reference here, and all through the rest of the chapter, is to the guardian angels of the countries concerned, according to the common opinion. The last clause in this verse is of very doubtful interpretation.

15   Ever, as he spoke, I stood there dumb, and with eyes downcast, till
all at once a touch fell on my lips, like the touch of human hand.[1] Now
found I speech, to give yonder visitant his answer. Bethink thee, my
lord, I said, that sight of thee unknits my frame; strength in me is none.
17 How should slave bandy words with master? Not strength alone fails me;
18 the very breath will not come. Once again a hand seemed to touch me,
19 and words came to hearten me;   Nay, fears are not for thee, so well beloved; never harm befall thee! Take courage, and play a man's part! With
that, I found my strength again; Speak on, my Lord, said I; thou hast
20 put new heart into me. And he answered, Hast thou read, by this, the
secret of my coming to thee? I am even now on my way back to fight
against the lord of Persia; when I left him, what saw I but the lord of
21 the Greeks already on the march? Only I must shew thee first what is
written in the book of doom.[2]

Much is to do, and save for Michael, that is guardian of your race, I
have none to aid me.

CHAPTER ELEVEN

2   HIM to strengthen and uphold has been my task,[3] ever since Darius
the Mede began reigning. And now, doom to foreshew thee, a king
shall rise in Persia,[4] the fourth from this, rich in great revenue beyond all
the others; in the power such wealth gives him, he will set the whole
world in motion against the realm of Greece . . .
3   And a warrior king shall arise, winning such empire that there is no

---

[1] Literally, 'As it were the semblance of a son of man touched my lips.' This
would suggest, at first sight, the presence of a second angelic being, not yet
mentioned. But verse 19 probably implies that only one angel is referred to,
from verse 5 onwards.

[2] Verses 20, 21 do not read naturally, and some think the order of the original
text has become dislocated through an accident. 'The book of doom'; literally,
'the writing of faithfulness' (*i.e.,* certainty).

[3] 'Him' probably refers to Michael; but it might be understood of 'the lord
of Greece,' or even of Darius.

[4] This king is ordinarily identified with Xerxes (B.C. 485–465). But it is doubtful whether the Hebrew text should not be rendered 'shall set all in motion, the
(whole) realm of Greece'; and this might describe the provocation offered to
Philip of Macedon by Artaxerxes III; he might be called the fourth successor
of Artaxerxes I, in whose reign Jerusalem was rebuilt. If the interval (of more
than a century) between Xerxes and Alexander has been passed over in silence,
it may be a prophetic foreshortening of history, or conceivably there has been
an omission in the text.

4 resisting his will.[1] Divided that empire shall be, as soon as it is established, between the four quarters of heaven; not sons of his they shall be
that rule it, nor peers of his; besides these, foreign lords shall part his
5 dominions between them. The southern kingdom a strong ruler shall
have, but of his vassals one shall be mightier than he, and in dominion
6 excel him; wide, wide his domain; until at last these two make terms
between them, and, to seal their amity, daughter of Egyptian king to
Syrian king must pass.[2] Yet thrive she may not, nor dynasty of hers endure; herself in due time, with retinue of hers, faction of hers, must be a
7 victim. Not unavenged; scion of her own father's stock shall march on
8 Syria, and do battle, and prevail; shall carry off to Egypt the images of
Syria's gods, its treasures of silver and gold. Then, his rival mastered,
9 with that expedition he shall be content, and to his own kingdom return.
10   To Syria's heirs the quarrel is left; and now there are great hosts a-
mustering, under a new king that must ever be hurrying on, like river in
flood, returning with spirit to the charge, throwing all his forces into the
11 assault. See with what fury the Egyptian king takes the field against him,
rallies a great host of his own, and over Syria's host gains the mastery!
12 Captives a many, dead warriors a many, to gladden his heart, but all to
13 no purpose; back Syria comes, in greater force than ever, ranks filled, and
14 treasures swollen, with the years. All the world will be for picking a
quarrel with Egypt then; hot-heads there will be among thy own people
15 who think to fulfil the old prophecies thus, but to their cost. On marches
he, yonder Syrian king, raises mound, and makes fortified cities his own;
Egypt's vigour is all spent, never a halt, though its best warriors engage
16 him; irresistible he comes, to impose terms on his enemy, sets foot in
17 a noble land [3] and crushes it under his heel. How to gain secure possession of the whole kingdom? A bargain must be struck; gift of a royal
bride shall be the land's undoing! But no, that will not serve, never shall
18 it be his. To the sea-coast he turns his thoughts instead, and conquers
lands a many; puts to silence the author of his own disgrace, and covers
19 him with disgrace in his turn.[4] But at last, to his own province turning
back, he totters to his fall, and the fame of him is heard no more.

---

[1] In verses 3–19, the period from Alexander the Great to Antiochus the Great
is sketched in with considerable detail; verse 6 gives the history of Berenice,
daughter of Ptolemy II, and verse 17 that of Antiochus' daughter Cleopatra.

[2] 'Egyptian' and 'Syrian' are 'southern' and 'northern' in the original, all
through this chapter (though Egypt is mentioned by name in verses 8, 42 and 43).

[3] The 'noble land,' here and in verse 41, is usually understood as meaning
Palestine, though Egypt is a possible alternative in either case.

[4] This verse is very obscure, and in the Hebrew text untranslatable. We
should have expected some reference to the defeat of Antiochus by the Romans
at Magnesia (B.C. 190).

20 To a vile creature his throne must pass, of a throne unworthy; soon
21 shall his end come, and yet no blow struck in anger, or in battle.[1] And
    after him a man little thought of; royal investiture he has none, yet see
22 how stealthy his approach, what shifts he uses to win a throne![2] Down
    go strong armies, crushed before him, down goes covenanted chief;[3]
23 treaty first, and then treachery; of armed following he needs but little.
24 So he makes his way into rich cities that suspect no harm, outdoes father
    and grandsire both in havoc, so much wealth to plunder and to squander;
25 into strong cities, too, by crafty devices, while fortune serves. Power of
    his and policy of his he shall match at last against Egypt, with a great
    army at his back; alas, Egypt, what avails that great muster of warriors?
26 Craft wins the day; men that feed on thy royal bounty are thy own
27 undoing, and with great slaughter that army of thine is overborne. See
    where the two kings plot mischief at one table, liars both! But nothing
28 they shall achieve; not yet the appointed hour has come. Back goes the
29 king of Syria, enriched with spoil, wreaking his spite on God's covenant
30 as he journeys home; then, when the time is ripe, marches once again
    southwards. Yet speed he shall not as once he sped; here are Roman
    galleys [4] overtaking him, and he must return discomfited.
        And now, as he returns, he shall vent his spleen against the holy cove-
    nant in good earnest. The forsakers of that covenant have not escaped
31 his eye, and there are willing hands a many to help him profane the
    inviolable sanctuary, daily sacrifice annulling, spreading defilement and
32 desolation there. Fawning knaves, and traitors to the covenant! But
    those others, that their God acknowledge, shall go all the more boldly to
33 work, counsellors a few that give right counsel to many. Crippled they
34 shall be for a while, by sword and flame, by prison and plunder; then,
    even as they are falling, it will need but a little support, and the fickle
35 multitude will rally to their side. What if some of them should fall,
    those wise counsellors? Assayed let them be for a little, sifted, purged for
    a little; there shall be happier times yet.

---

[1] The Hebrew text describes this king as 'causing an exactor to pass through,'
presumably in allusion to II Mac. 3.7. But the Septuagint Greek, like the Latin
version, contains no such allusion.

[2] Throughout verses 21–45, the allusions are much less readily traceable than
in verses 3–19. Some parts of it at least are generally understood as referring to
Antiochus Epiphanes (B.C. 176–164), but for the most part it would be equally
applicable to any persecuting tyrant.

[3] 'Covenanted chief' perhaps means the high priest Onias III, deposed by
Antiochus in B.C. 175.

[4] So the Septuagint Greek, but the Hebrew text has simply 'ships of Chittim,'
i.e., from the West. It looks as if the versions had interpreted their original; it is
well known that Antiochus was warned off Egyptian soil by the Roman ambas-
sador Popilius Laenas.

36   As for the king, he shall have all his own way; in his pride, he will
think himself a match for any god, even of that God boast himself the
rival, who is above all gods, And still he shall thrive; vengeance is not
37 yet ready to overtake him; doom shall come when doom must. What are
his fathers' gods to him? Women's dalliance is all his concern; of gods he
38 recks little, that will set himself up over all. When his turn comes, it is
the god of Maozim [1] he will worship; for such a god, that never his
39 fathers knew, the gold, and the silver, and the precious jewels; with this
new-found god to aid him, he will make Maozim his stronghold, shower
honours and dignities upon its folk, make a present of lands to them.
40   Then comes the hour of destiny. Egypt shall declare war, and he, the
Syrian king, shall sweep down upon it with horse and chariot and a great
41 fleet. Which lands will he invade and conquer, which pass by, ere he
reach the noblest of them all? Ruined a many shall be, but Edom shall
42 escape his onslaught, and Moab, and the princedom of Ammon. A
country here he will attempt, a country there, and be sure Egypt shall not
43 go unscathed; gold and silver of Egypt, and all its precious treasures
shall come into his power. Then, as through Libya and Ethiopia he
44 makes his way, tidings shall come from east and north, to bring him back
45 with all his host, ready for havoc, ready for carnage. See where he sets
up his royal pavilion [2] betwixt sea and sea on yonder noble hill, yonder
sacred hill; reaches its very summit, and none brings aid! [3]

CHAPTER TWELVE

TIME, then, that Michael should be up and doing; Michael, that high
lord who is guardian of thy race. Distress shall then be, such as never
was since the world began; and in that hour of distress thy fellow-countrymen shall win deliverance, all whose names are found written when
2 the record lies open. Many shall wake, that now lie sleeping in the dust of
earth, some to enjoy life everlasting, some to be confronted for ever with
3 their disgrace. Bright shall be the glory of wise counsellors, as the
radiance of the sky above; starry-bright for ever their glory, who have
taught many the right way.
4   For thyself, Daniel, keep this revelation locked away; sealed up the

---

[1] 'Maozim'; or perhaps, 'fortresses.' But it is difficult to understand who
are meant by 'them' in verse 39 if Maozim is not a proper name. We do not meet
the name elsewhere; on the other hand, attempts to identify the 'god of fortresses' are not altogether convincing.

[2] The Latin version here transliterates, 'his pavilion Apadno.'

[3] The Hebrew text is generally understood as meaning 'he reaches his end,
and there is none to bring him aid.'

record of it must be until the hour appointed. Leave others to hasten to and fro, in search of knowledge.[1]

5 Thus he spoke; and now, looking up, I saw two others that stood there,
6 one on either bank of the stream.   But he, the man clad in linen, stood there yet over the river itself; and when I asked how long these wondrous
7 doings should last, it was from him I had my answer. Both hands raised to heaven, he swore by the God who lives for ever that there should be an end to it; it should last for a space of time, and for twice as long, and for half as long, no more. Strength of God's holy people must be broken
8 utterly; when that is over, all is over and done.[2] So I had my answer, but still could not tell the meaning of it; Ay, my Lord, I said, but what shall
9 be the end of it all? Nay, Daniel, said he, no more of this; needs must that this revelation be shut away and sealed up, till the appointed hour
10 comes;   and still there shall be chosen souls a many, that are purged by the fire's assaying, and still there are sinners that will not leave their sinning. The riddle, for these others, a riddle must remain, but wise
11 counsellors there be that will find the clue to it.   Of this be sure; after the time when the daily sacrifice is abrogated, and all becomes defilement
12 and desolation, twelve hundred and ninety days must pass.   Blessed shall his lot be that waits patiently till twelve hundred and thirty-five days are
13 over.[3] And for thyself, Daniel, go thy way . . . till the end; till the end of the days rest thou shalt, and rise to fulfil thy appointed destiny.[4]

CHAPTER THIRTEEN

2 THERE was a man called Joakim living in Babylon,   married to one Susanna, daughter of Helcias.[5] This was a woman of great beauty,
3 and one that feared God, so well had her parents, religious folk, schooled
4 their daughter in the law of Moses.   A rich man was Joakim, and had a fruit-garden close to his house; and he was much visited by the Jews,
5 among whom there was none more honoured than he.   There came a year in which those two elders of the people were appointed judges, of

---

[1] The last part of this verse cannot be rendered with any certainty.

[2] Here too the end of the verse is variously interpreted.

[3] The figures given in verses 11 and 12, like those given in 8.14, are mysteriously uncoordinated with the 'time, times and half a time' which is elsewhere given as the time-unit. Cf. Apoc. 12. 6,14 and 13.5, where the time-unit is consistent.

[4] This verse is very obscure, and perhaps corrupt. The latter part of it is usually interpreted as meaning that Daniel will die and rise again to happiness in a future life; but if so all the words in it are used in an unaccustomed sense.

[5] This chapter, with chapter 14, is preserved in the Septuagint Greek, but not in the Hebrew text.

whom the Lord said, Wickedness has sprung up in Babylon, and the
roots of it are those elders and judges who claim to rule the people.[1]

6   These two were often at Joakim's house, and all those who had disputes
to settle appeared before them there.

7   At noon, when the common folk had returned home, Susanna would
8   walk about in her husband's garden, and these two elders, who saw her
9   go in and walk there day after day, fell to lusting after her. Reason they
dethroned, and turned away their eyes from the sight of heaven; its just
10 awards they would fain have forgotten. The love that tortured both,
11 neither to other would disclose;   confess it for very shame they might not,
12 this hankering after a woman's favours;   yet day after day they seized the
opportunity to have sight of her. A day came at last when one said to the
13 other,   Home go we, it is dinner-time; and go they did, taking their
14 several ways;   yet both returned hot-foot to their watching-place, and
there met one another. So there was questioning on both sides, and out
came the story of their lust; and now they made common cause; at a
suitable time they would waylay her together, when she was alone.

15   They watched, then, for their opportunity; and she, as her custom was,
went out one day with two of her maids, and had a mind to bathe, there
16 in the garden, for it was summer weather,   and none was by except the
17 two elders; and they were in hiding, watching her. So she bade her
servants go and bring her oil and soap, and shut the garden door while
18 she was a-bathing. Her whim was obeyed; shut the door of the garden
they did, and went out by a back entrance to bring her what she had asked
19 for; they knew nothing of the elders that were hiding there within. And
these two, as soon as the servants were gone, rose from their hiding-place
20 and ran to her side. See, they told her, the garden door is shut, and there
is no witness by. We are both smitten with a desire for thy favours; come,
21 then, let us enjoy thee. Refuse, and we will bear witness that thou hadst
a gallant here, and this was the reason thou wouldst rid thyself of thy
hand-maidens' company.

22   Whereupon Susanna groaned deeply; There is no escape for me, she
said, either way. It is death if I consent, and if I refuse, I shall be at your
23 mercy. Let me rather fall into your power through no act of mine, than
24 commit sin in the Lord's sight. With that, Susanna cried aloud, and the
25 elders, too, began crying shame on her;   meanwhile, one of them ran to
26 the garden door and opened it. And now the servants of the house, hearing such outcry in the garden, came running in through the back entrance
27 to know what was afoot;   and they were greatly abashed when the elders
told their story; never before had Susanna been defamed thus.

28   When the morrow came, there was a throng of people in Joakim's

---

[1] Some think this is an allusion to Jer. 29. 21–23.

29 house, and the two elders were there, intent upon their malicious design against Susanna's life. They asked publicly that Susanna, daughter of
30 Helcias and wife to Joakim, should be sent for ; sent for she was, and
31 came out with her parents and her children and all her kindred. So
32 dainty she was, and so fair, these two knaves would have her let down
33 her veil, the better to enjoy the sight of her charms. All her friends, all
34 her acquaintances, were in tears. Then the two elders rose amidst the
35 throng, and laid their hands upon Susanna's head, while she, weeping, looked up to heaven, in token that her heart had not lost confidence in the
36 Lord. We were walking in the garden apart, said the elders, when this woman came out with two hand-maidens. She had the garden door shut
37 close, and sent the maidens away ; whereupon a young man, who had
38 been in hiding till then, came out and had his will with her. We, from a nook in the garden, saw what foul deed was being done, and ran up close,
39 so that we had full view of their dalliance ; but lay hold of the man we could not ; he was too strong for us, opening the garden door and spring-
40 ing out. The woman we caught, and asked her who her gallant was, but she would not tell us. To all this, we bear witness.
41   They were elders, they were judges of the people, and they persuaded
42 the assembly, without more ado, to pass the death sentence. Whereupon Susanna cried aloud, Eternal God, no secret is hidden from thee, nothing
43 comes to pass without thy foreknowledge. Thou knowest that these men have borne false witness against me ; wilt thou let me die, a woman inno-
44 cent of all the charges their malice has invented ? And the Lord listened
45 to her plea ; even as she was being led off to her death, all at once he roused to utterance the holy spirit that dwelt in a young boy there, called
46 Daniel. This Daniel raised his voice and cried out, I will be no party to
47 the death of this woman ; and when all the people turned upon him,
48 asking what he meant, he stood there in their midst, and said, Are you such fools, men of Israel, as to condemn an Israelite woman without trial,
49 without investigation of the truth ? Go back to the place of judgement ; the witness they have borne against her is false witness.
50   Eagerly enough the people went back, and the elders would have Daniel sit with them, such credit God had given him beyond his years.
51 He bade them part the two men, at a distance from each other, while he
52 questioned them. So parted they were, and when the first was sum-moned, thus Daniel greeted him: Grown so old in years, and years ill
53 spent ! Now, that past sinning of thine has found thee out, a man that perverts justice, persecutes innocence, and lets the guilty go free. Has not the Lord said, Never shalt thou put the innocent man, the upright
54 man, to death ? Thou foundest her ; good ; they met under a tree ; tell us what kind of tree. And he answered, Under a mastic-tree I surprised
55 them. The right word ! cried Daniel ; prized asunder thyself shall be,

56 when God bids his angel requite thee for this calumny. Then he had this one removed, and bade the other come near. Brood of Chanaan, said he, and no true son of Juda, so beauty ensnared thee? So lust drove thy heart
57 astray? Such approaches you have made, long since, to women of the other tribes, and they, from very fear, admitted your suit; but you could
58 not bring a woman of Juda to fall in with your wicked design. And now tell me, under what tree it was thou didst find them talking together?
59 Under a holm-oak, said he, I saw them. The right word again! cried Daniel. Saw thee asunder the angel of the Lord will, with the sharp blade he carries yonder; you are both dead men.

60 And with that, the whole multitude cried aloud, blessing God that is
61 the deliverer of those who trust in him. And they turned on the two elders, by Daniel's questioning self-accused of false witness; served they
62 must be as they would have served others, and the law of Moses obeyed;
63 so they put them to death. That day, an innocent life was saved. Good cause had Helcias and his wife to praise God for their daughter Susanna, good cause had Joakim and all his friends; no breath of suspicion assailed
64 her now. And as for Daniel, he was in high favour with all the people from that day forward.

65 When king Astyages became part of his line, it was Cyrus, the Persian, succeeded him.[1]

CHAPTER FOURTEEN

OF this king, Daniel was the courtier, and valued above all his other
2 friends. A great idol there was, that the men of Babylon worshipped; Bel was the name of it, and day by day it must be fed with thirty-two bushels of fine flour, and forty sheep, and of wine thirty-six gallons.
3 The king himself honoured it with the rest, and no day passed but he went to pay it reverence. A time came when he asked Daniel, that wor-
4 shipped no God but his own, why Bel he would not worship; and this answer Daniel made him, that for idols made by men's hands worship he had none, only for that living God that made heaven and earth, and
5 of all mankind held the sovereignty. What, cried the king, wilt thou have it Bel is not a living god? Hast thou no eyes for the great trencherman he
6 is, day in, day out, of food and drink both? Nay, my lord king, Daniel answered with a smile, give no heed to false tales. Clay he is within, and
7 bronze without; I warrant thee, eat he cannot. Whereupon the king, in high displeasure, summoned Bel's priests. You shall give account, said

---

[1] This verse evidently belongs to the next chapter. But it only gives us a loose historical reference; it was only after he had been king of Media for twelve years that Cyrus conquered Babylon.

he, of yonder revenues, and that on pain of your lives. Who is it has the
8 eating of them?   Prove to me it is Bel himself, and Daniel shall die
instead, that blasphemed him. As it pleases the king's grace, said Daniel.
9   Seventy of these priests there were, that had wives and children to
fend for besides. And when the king reached their temple, with Daniel
10 in attendance,   this challenge they offered: Withdraw we, as thou seest;
for thee it is, lord king, to set food, pour out wine, lock and seal door
11 with thy own hand.   To-morrow, come thou and find Bel fasting, we die
12 for it; or else Daniel dies, that so traduced us.   Lightly enough the challenge was made; had they not provided a hidden entrance-way, close
under the god's table, by which they came in and ate what eat they would?
13 So out they went, and the king set on Bel's viands with his own hand;
and what did Daniel? He would have his servants bring ashes, and scatter
them all over the temple floor, there in the king's presence. Which done,
14 all withdrew, leaving the door locked, and the royal seal upon it.   And
that night in they came as came they ever, priest and priest's wife and
priest's children, and left neither bite nor sup between them.
15   Next day, the king was early abroad, and Daniel with him.   What of
the seals, Daniel? the king asked. Are they safe? Ay, my lord king, safe
17 enough. What a cry was that the king gave, when he opened the door and
caught sight of the table within! A great god thou art, Bel, said he, and
18 no deceiver!   But Daniel smiled, and would not have the king go in yet;
Look about thee, he said, and ask thyself who it was left their prints on
19 yonder floor.   Why, cried the king, these be foot-prints of living men, and
20 women and children besides! With that, he fell into a rage;   priest and
priest's wife and priest's children must be taken into custody. And when
these had shewed him the door by which they came in and swept the
21 table bare of its offerings,   he put the whole company of them to death.
And as for Bel, he left him to Daniel's mercy, who threw down image
and temple both.
22   There was a great serpent, too, in those parts that was worshipped by
23 the folk of Babylon; and of this the king said to Daniel, here at least was
a god that lived; gainsay that he could not, and therefore he needs must
24 worship.   Nay, said Daniel, my own God I worship still; living God is
25 none but he. Here is no living God;   let me but have the royal warrant,
and I will make an end of it, and neither sword nor club to help me. So
26 the king gave his warrant,   and what did Daniel? Pitch and fat and hairs
he boiled all together, and with lumps of this fed the serpent, which
thereupon burst all to pieces; and, Here, said Daniel, is your god.
27   Angry men were the folk of Babylon when they heard of these doings,
and they made their way into the royal presence, crying out, Here is the
king himself turned Jew! Here is Bel overthrown, and the dragon slain,
28 and our priests massacred!   And when they found audience, Give up

Daniel to us, they said, or we will make an end of thee, and thy house-
29 hold with thee. The king, finding their onslaught so determined, gave
30 up Daniel to them against his will; and they threw him into a pit in
31 which lions were kept, where he spent six whole days. Seven lions there
were in the pit, and each day two human bodies were given them as food,
and two sheep; but now they were kept unfed, so that Daniel might be
their prey.

32 Far away, in Judaea, the prophet Habacuc had been making broth,
and crumbling bread in a great bowl, and was even now carrying it to
33 the reapers on the farm; when suddenly the angel of the Lord said to
him, Take this dinner thou hast prepared to Babylon, and give it to
34 Daniel; he is in the lion-pit. Lord, said Habacuc, I was never yet in
35 Babylon, and know nothing of any lion-pit there. Upon which the angel
of the Lord caught at his head and lifted him by the hair of it; then by
36 the force of his impulse, set him down in Babylon, close to the pit. So
Habacuc cried out, Daniel! Servant of God! The Lord has sent thee thy
37 dinner; come and take it. And Daniel said, Thou wouldst not forget me,
38 O God, wouldst not forsake such as love thee. So he rose and ate, while
the angel of the Lord brought Habacuc, all at once, back to his home.

39 When the seventh day came, the king went out to mourn for Daniel;
and now, reaching the pit and looking in, he saw Daniel seated there
40 among the lions. And at that, the king cried aloud, How great thou art,
O Lord, thou who art Daniel's God! And he took him out of the lion-pit,
41 and shut up there instead the men who had conspired to ruin him; and
42 in a moment, as he watched, the lions devoured them. Whereupon the
king said, Well may the whole world stand in awe of Daniel's God. What
deliverance he effects, what signal proofs of his power, here on earth,
the God who has rescued Daniel out of a den of lions!

THE PROPHECY OF OSEE

CHAPTER ONE

THIS is the message which came from the Lord to Osee, son of Beeri, during the reigns of Ozias, Joathan, Achaz and Ezechias in Juda, and during the reign of Jeroboam, son of Joas, in Israel.

2 When first the divine voice made itself heard through Osee, this was the command given him: Wanton wed thou, wantons breed thou; in a 3 wanton land thou dwellest, that keeps troth with its Lord never. So it was he came to marry Gomer, a daughter of Debelaim.[1] When he got her with child, and she bore him a son, This one, the Lord told him, thou 4 art to call Jezrahel; at Jezrahel the blood was spilt [2] for which, ere long, 5 Jehu's line must be punished, and Israel have kings no more; in Jezrahel 6 valley, my doom is, bow of Israel shall be broken. And next, she was brought to bed of a daughter; of whom the Lord said, Unbefriended call her, in token that I will befriend Israel no longer, heed them no 7 longer. To Juda I will be a friend yet, not with bow or sword of theirs delivering them, not in battle, with horse or horseman to give aid, but by the power of the Lord their God only.

8 Unbefriended, then, was the name of her; and after she was weaned, 9 once more Gomer conceived, and had a son. This time the command was, Call him Strange-folk; no longer shall you be my people, or I be your . . .[3]

10 . . . Measureless the race of Israel shall be and countless as the sand by the sea shore. In the very place where once the doom was uttered, You are but strangers to me, they shall be welcomed as sons of the living God. 11 As one people, Juda and Israel shall be rallied, under a leader of their common choice; and they shall come flocking from every corner of the land; such great doings there shall be at Jezrahel.

---

[1] It is not clear whether the transactions here described took place in real life, or in a vision.

[2] This perhaps refers to the massacres described in IV Kg. 10.1–11.

[3] It seems almost certain that there is an omission at the end of verse 9, the word 'God' being needed to complete the sense. It may be questioned whether the gap is not more considerable. We should expect more information about the history of Osee's family, to prepare us for the allusions of chapters 2 and 3; meanwhile, the abrupt change of situation in verses 10 and 11 appears to demand some kind of introduction. Some think verses 10 and 11 have been accidentally misplaced, and belong to the end of chapter 2.

CHAPTER TWO

GOD'S-FOLK and Befriended, these are the names they should have
2 by rights, brother and sister of yours. Blame her, blame your
mother, that she is no true wife of mine, nor I any longer her Lord. Must
she still flaunt the harlot's face of her, the wantonness of her breasts?
3 Must I strip her, leave her naked as babe new-born, leave her desolate
4 as the barren waste, the trackless desert, to die of thirst? Those children
of hers, must I needs leave them unpitied, the children of her shame?
5   Harlot mother of theirs brought reproach on the womb that bore them;
Haste I away, she said, to those gallants of mine, the gods of whose gift
6 bread comes to me, and water, wool and flax, oil and wine! See if I do not
hedge her way about with thorns, fence in her prospect, till way she can
7 find none! Then, it may be, when her gallants she courts in vain,
searches for them in vain, she will have other thoughts: Back go I to the
husband that was mine once; things were better with me in days gone by.
8   Yet I it was, did she but know it, that bread and wine and oil gave her,
9 gave her all the silver and gold she squandered on Baal. And now I
mean to revoke the gift; no harvest for her, no vintage; I will give wool
10 and flax a holiday, that once laboured to cover her shame; no gallant of
hers but shall see and mock at it; such is my will, and none shall thwart
11 me. Gone the days of rejoicing, the days of solemnity; gone is new moon,
12 and sabbath, and festival; vine and fig-tree blighted, whose fruit, she
told herself, was but the hire those lovers paid; all shall be woodland, for
13 the wild beasts to ravage as they will. Penance she must do for that hey-
day of idolatry, when the incense smoked, and out she went, all rings and
necklaces, to meet her lovers, the gods of the countryside, and for me,
the Lord says, never a thought!
14   It is but love's stratagem, thus to lead her out into the wilderness; once
15 there, it shall be all words of comfort. Clad in vineyards that wilderness
shall be, that vale of sad memory [1] a passage-way of hope; and a song shall
be on her lips, the very music of her youth, when I rescued her from
16 Egypt long ago. Husband she calls me now, the Lord says, Master no
17 longer; that name I stifle on her lips; master-gods of the countryside
18 must all be forgotten.[2] Beast and bird and creeping thing to peace pledge

---

[1] Literally, 'the vale of Achor,' see Jos. 7.26. It may be, however, that no historical allusion is intended; the valley in question is mentioned by Isaias (65.10)
in a quite general context.
[2] A Hebrew wife would address her husband as her *ba'al, i.e.,* 'proprietor';
the same word was used for those proprietary gods who were supposed to
control the harvest, the vintage, etc.

I ; bow and sword and war's alarms break I ; all shall sleep safe abed, the folk that dwell in her.

19 Everlastingly I will betroth thee to myself, favour and redress and
20 mercy of mine thy dowry ; by the keeping of his troth thou shalt learn to
21 know the Lord. When that day comes, heaven shall win answer, the Lord
22 says, answer from me ; and from heaven, earth ; and from earth, the corn
    and wine and oil it nourishes ; and from these, the people of my sowing.[1]
23 Deep, deep I will sow them in the land I love ; a friend, now, to her that
24 was Unbefriended ; to a people that was none of mine I will say, Thou
    art my people, and they to me, Thou art my God.

CHAPTER THREE

THE Lord's word came to me: To wife that will have gallants
a-courting her, shew thyself a lover yet. The Lord is yet Israel's
lover, that has no eyes but for alien gods, leaves grape for husk.[2]
2 So buy her back to me I must, fifteen pieces of silver paying for her
3 ransom, and a core and a half of barley. A long time thou must wait for
   me, I told her, thy wantonness leaving, yet still unwed ; and I will wait
   for thee as faithfully.
4 A long time the sons of Israel must wait, neither king nor prince to
   rule them, neither sacrifice nor shrine to worship at, neither sacred mantle
5 nor their own images to consult. Then they will come back, and to the
   Lord, their own God, betake them, and to David that is their true king ;
   the Lord, and the Lord's goodness, holds them spell-bound at last.

CHAPTER FOUR

LISTEN, sons of Israel, to a message from the Lord, notice of a suit
he prefers against all that dwell in this land of yours ; a land where
2 loyalty, and tenderness of heart, and knowledge of God is none. Curse
   they and lie, murder they and steal and live adulterously, till there is no
3 checking it ; never feud ends but another feud begins. What wonder the
   land lies widowed, and its folk dwindle ; gone, beast and bird, and the
4 sea-beach piled high with fish ? Nay, let us have no recriminations between man and man ; so should this people of thine fall to railing at their
5 priests ! Ruin for thee, sir priest, this day, and, come night, the prophet

---

[1] 'The people of my sowing'; literally, 'Jezrahel' (*i.e.,* God has sown). It seems clear that the word, an echo of the foregoing chapter, is used here as a kind of cipher-word for 'Israel.'
[2] 'Leaves grape for husk'; or perhaps 'offers raisin-cakes' idolatrously.

6 shall share thy ruin; [1] name of the mother that bore thee shall perish, as,
through thy fault, this people of mine perishes for want of knowledge.
Knowledge wouldst thou spurn, and shall not I spurn thy priesthood;
my law wouldst thou forget, and shall race of thine be spared oblivion?
7 Priests a many, and sins to match their number; shall that title bring glory
8 any longer, and not reproach? Fault if Israel committed, guilt if Israel
9 incurred, it was but the meat and drink such priests craved for. [2] Priest,
now, shall fare no better than people; he shall pay for his ill living, reap
10 what his false aims deserve; greed, that remained still unsated, wantonness, that could never have enough. Ah, faithless guardians, that you
11 should play your Lord false! [3] That dalliance, and wine, and revelry,
should so steal away your wits!

12 And what of my people? See where they have recourse to tree-stump or
senseless wand, for an answer to their perplexities! Lust for strange
13 worship swept them away, made them false to their troth with God; on
mountain and hill-side, under leafy shade of oak, poplar or terebinth,
falls victim, smokes incense of theirs. What wonder daughters should turn
14 harlot, wives play the wanton? Harlot daughter and adulterous wife
shall go unpunished; what did father and husband, but keep harlots' company, share revel with consecrated minions? Want wit, be sure a people
is ruined.

15 Wanton though Israel be, at least let Juda shun the wrong; not for
them the way that leads to Galgal, Bethaven's pilgrimage, or the oath
taken by the living God . . .[4]

16 Stubborn as frisking heifer, Israel turns away the head; would you have
17 the Lord feed him, like a cade lamb, unconfined? Wedded to idols, this
18 Ephraim; go his own way he must; here be revelers that will keep their
own company, here be idolaters in grain, and princes that dote still on
19 their own disgrace. Ay, but a storm is coming that shall carry them away
on its wings, to rue the unavailing sacrifice.[5]

---

[1] The text of verses 4 and 5 is barely translatable, and is widely suspected of
being corrupt. The word 'priest' only occurs once in the original, but there is
no telling whether it is meant to be the last word of verse 4 or the first of verse 5;
possibly it occurred in both places and, through inadvertence, was written once
instead of twice.
[2] Unless the prophet is using a somewhat violent metaphor, there is probably
an allusion to the sacrifices offered in expiation, when the law had been transgressed, and to the priests' share in them.
[3] The interpretation of this verse is very uncertain.
[4] It seems clear that the verse, as it stands, is incomplete, and some think a
reference to Bersabee has fallen out (cf. Am. 5.5). The reference to an oath, even
so, is puzzling; but cf. Am. 8.14.
[5] In verses 18 and 19, once more the accuracy of the Hebrew text may be
doubted; in verse 18, no sense can be made of it at all.

CHAPTER FIVE

P RIEST and people, hear and heed! And you, too, mark it well, men of
the court; whose but yours the blame, if there are snares on every
2 commanding height,¹ if Thabor itself is ringed with toils, and your
quarry is driven down to the depths? But to all alike comes the warning.
3 Think you that I have no eyes for Ephraim's wantonness? that Israel
4 escapes my scrutiny, Israel, so defiled? Return to the Lord? Not for such
hearts the message; lust for strange worship is there, and of the Lord they
5 reck nothing. Self-condemned, the pride of Israel; what wonder Israel
. . . and Ephraim should be entangled in guilt?² Juda itself shall not
6 escape their downfall. All their flocks and herds shall not win them
7 access to the Lord; he stands aloof from them, sinners that have defied
him; a bastard brood, that ere yonder moon rises new shall be disinherited
and brought to nothing.³
8   The trumpet, there, in Gabaa; at Rama sound for battle; let Bethaven
9 echo with the rallying-cry! Benjamin, to arms! Alas for Ephraim, in the
hour of punishment left forlorn! Mine to teach Israel's tribes a lesson
10 of faithfulness. And what of Juda's chieftains? A neighbour's land-mark
scrupled they never to remove; on these, too, the full flood of my ven-
11 geance shall come down. Poor Ephraim, ever since he set his face towards the mire, all is oppression with him, all is judgement gone amiss.
12 And all the while I, none other, wear away strength of Ephraim and Juda
13 alike; moth nor canker so surely! What did Ephraim, in his great sickness, what did Juda, bound hand and foot? To Assyria Ephraim would
despatch envoys, to yonder ruthless king; but heal you he could not, nor
14 unbind. Mine the encounter Ephraim has to fear, and Juda both; lion's
15 dam nor whelp mauls prey and carries it off so inexorably. All in a
moment come and gone whence I came! Who knows if weariness will
drive you back to my presence? ⁴

---

¹ The 'commanding height' may also be read as a proper name, Maspha.
It is not clear whether the hills are mentioned merely as a setting for the metaphor, or as places where idolatrous worship was in fact conducted.
² 'Israel' and 'Ephraim' are strict synonyms; it looks as if a verb might have
fallen out in the manuscripts.
³ Literally, 'They have begotten alien children; now a month shall devour
them with their territory,' an obscure phrase which is perhaps corrupt.
⁴ The situation in verses 8–15, is not easy to envisage. It would appear that a
common danger threatened the two kingdoms; Juda is invited to bring aid to
Israel (verse 8), but fails to do so (verse 9), and perhaps even takes advantage
of Israel's embarrassments to make territorial acquisitions (verse 10). It is hard

CHAPTER SIX

A Y, in their distress they will be waiting full early at my door; Back
2   to the Lord! will be their cry; salve he only can bring, that wounded
3 us; hand that smote us shall heal. Dead men to-day and to-morrow, on
the third day he will raise us up again, to live in his presence anew.
Acknowledge we, cease we never to acknowledge the Lord, he will reveal
himself, sure as the dawn, come back to us, sure as the rains of winter and
4 spring come back to the earth. What way will serve with you, men of
Ephraim? Juda, what way will serve? Ruth of yours is but momentary,
5 fades like the early mist, like morning dew. What wonder I should send
prophets first, to shape men to my will if they could, and then utter my
sentence of ruin? Believe me, this doom of thine shall be clear as daylight.
6 A tender heart wins favour with me, not sacrifice; God's acknowledging,
7 not victim's destroying; and these be very children of Adam, keep troth
8 they cannot, here is a land where my will is set at defiance.[1] What is
Galaad but a stronghold of idolatry, bedabbled with footprints of blood?
9 Nor much imports it, company of priests thou meet on Sichem road, or
troop of robbers thirsting for men's lives; be sure there is mischief afoot;[2]
10 foul deeds I see done in Israel.[3] Ephraim so wanton, Israel so defiled;
11 and, Juda, what of thyself? For thee, no harvest?[4]
    When I restore my people from exile . . .

CHAPTER SEVEN

W HEN I would grant[5] healing to Israel . . .
    Foul shews the guilt of Ephraim, Samaria's malice is plain to
view. What a workshop of wrong-doing is here, all thieving within doors,

---

to see whence the threat can have come, if not from Assyria; verse 13 therefore
probably indicates, not an appeal to Assyria for help, but an attempt to buy off
the invader, such as that made by king Menaham (IV Kg. 15.19).
    [1] There is considerable reason to think that the text of verses 7–11 has suffered
from corruption in the manuscript. Verse 7 reads literally, 'These, like Adam,
have sinned; they have behaved treacherously towards me there'—the last word
suggests that a place name should appear in the first half of the verse, possibly
Adom (Jos. 3.16).
    [2] This verse is untranslatable in the Hebrew text as it stands, and the Latin
version of it offers no grammatical construction.
    [3] Literally, 'in the house of Israel,' perhaps a false reading for 'in Bethel.'
    [4] Verse 11 remains wholly obscure; some think the latter part of it really
belongs to chapter 7.
    [5] So the Latin version, but the Hebrew text and the Septuagint Greek are more
naturally translated, 'When I grant.' It seems doubtful, therefore, whether the
first seven words of the verse really fit on to what follows.

2 all robbery without! Let them never complain I am too nice over the
chronicling of their misdeeds; why, they blazon these ill designs of theirs,
3 under my very eyes! King himself there is no pleasing but by villainy,
4 nor his nobles but by flattering speeches; false is every one of them to
his troth. What else is this whole realm but baker that lights his fire, and
then takes a rest from his kneading, leaves yeast to spread as it will?
5 Huzza for our king? [1] Ay, but see how the princes fall to their carousing,
6 and he himself reaches out for the wine, reckless as they! Their scheming
adds fuel to the fire; are there not plots afoot? Sleeps baker the long night
7 through, and morning finds him flaming hot like the rest. A very furnace
the city is; ruler may not abide nor king stand before the heat of it, and
8 never a man among them invokes my name! What wonder Ephraim
should throw in his lot with the Gentiles? No better than a girdle-cake is
Ephraim, baked only on one side.[2]
9   Foreign neighbours, all unawares, have drained the strength of him;
10 the dark locks, all unawares, dappled with grey; and even now self-
condemned stands the pride of Israel,[3] return to the Lord, recourse to the
11 Lord is none, even now. Never silly dove so lost her wits as this Ephraim,
12 now calling on Egypt, now turning to Assyria for aid! Fatal the journey;
my net I mean to spread over them, catch them as in the fowler's snare;
13 public the chastisement shall be, as public the warning. Dearly they
shall pay for their wandering from me, ruin follow on the heels of rebel-
14 lion; I their ransomer, and they so false! Never do their hearts cry out
to me; growl they like beast in den, or beast-like eat and drink and chew
15 the cud; me they have forsaken.[4] Now I chasten them, now I strengthen
16 their hands, and still they have no thought for me but of hatred; ever
they step back from the yoke,[5] like a twisted bow recoil.

---

[1] 'Huzza for our king!'; literally, 'The day of our king!'; cf. IV Kg. 9.13.

[2] The allegory from cooking seems to be a double one; the baker (apparently
the people of Israel) goes to sleep and lets the fire blaze up, instead of keeping
a moderate heat, and at the same time he does not finish kneading the dough,
so that the result is a half-baked state of things. The application is not easily
made; but perhaps the passage reflects the disappointment of God-fearing people
at the relapse of Jehu's dynasty into idolatry, after the overthrow of Achab's
Baal-worship. The ruling class, it seems to be intimated, are too strong for the
new sovereigns, and the old ways come back again.

[3] 'Self-condemned stands the pride of Israel'; the same words are used as in
5.5 above, but the Latin version here has 'The pride of Israel shall be humbled
before his very eyes.' It seems unlikely that we are meant to vary the interpretation in this way.

[4] Literally, 'And they did not cry out to me with their heart, but howled in
their beds, chewed the cud over wheat and wine, departed from me.' If 'chewed
the cud' is the right interpretation of the rare verb used, we must suppose that
the Israelites are being compared to dumb beasts. But it seems likely that the
text is corrupt.

[5] The Hebrew text is usually interpreted as meaning, 'they return, (but) not

Put to the sword their nobles must be, railing tongues the ruin of them. This the taunt that shall be uttered against them in the land of Egypt . . .

CHAPTER EIGHT

THE trumpet to thy mouth! Eagle's wings threatening the Lord's
2 domain! Conscious of faith forsworn, of my law defied, to me
3 Israel cries out, My God! cries out, We acknowledge thee![1] Estranged, poor Israel, from the good that was his, and the enemy pressing hard upon him.

4   Kings a many, and with no warrant from me; princes a many, that were none of my choosing; idols a many, of their own gold and silver
5 minted; here is cause enough for their undoing. Cast calf, Samaria, is yonder calf of thine; for this burning affront, it shall be long ere thou
6 canst find acquittal. Israel gave birth to it, this calf of Samaria, that came of man's fashioning, and god is none; it shall be beaten fine as filigree.

7   Sow the wind, reap the whirlwind; empty stook is empty bin, and here
8 if grain is any, alien folk shall have the grinding of it! Poor Israel, already engulfed, the heathen all around making a despised tool of him!
9 Lone as wild ass in the desert, to Assyria he betakes himself; if mate he
10 would, he must pay for his dalliance. Well, hire they mercenaries where they will, they shall be cooped up in their own land none the less, and have respite from the exactions of king and nobles both.[2]

11   So many the altars Ephraim has, and they shall increase his guilt, none
12 of them but shall increase his guilt; so many the laws I gave him, and all
13 alike went unrecognized. Appointed sacrifice[3] they still offer, flesh of the sacrifice still eat, but the Lord will have none of it; no more their guilt

---

upwards,' a phrase which leaves a good deal to the imagination. The latter part of the verse, if the text is genuine, can hardly be understood except on the supposition that some words have fallen out at the end of it.

[1] As before, it is difficult to feel certain that the text has been preserved in its original state. Literally, the passage reads: 'To thy palate the horn, like an eagle upon the house of the Lord, because they have overstepped my covenant and transgressed about my law, to me they shall cry out, My God, we recognize thee, Israel.'

[2] Literally, 'Even if they hire among the nations, now I will collect them, and they shall cease for a little from the burden of king of nobles.' Verses 7–10 are best explained if we suppose that Jeroboam II only won his victories against Syria at the price of calling in Assyrian aid; this meant burdening the people with taxation and, ultimately, forfeiting the national independence.

[3] 'Appointed sacrifice'; this seems the most probable translation of a rare word in the Hebrew text, for which the Latin version only gives us a rough equivalent.

shall go unrecorded, their sins unpunished; Egypt once again for them!
14 The God that made them forgotten, Israel builds shrine and Juda stronghold still; but the fire I am kindling shall fall upon Juda's cities, shall
devour them, citadel and all.

CHAPTER NINE

NO rejoicing, Israel, no cries of gladness now! Wouldst thou be like
the heathen, and rejoice that thou hast played thy God false, ever
selling thy favours to the first comer, in return for a full threshing-floor? [1]
2 Not for such reapers harvest and vintage; the wanton must go without
3 her wine; dispeopled, now, the Lord's territory, Ephraim back in Egypt
4 again, or tasting, among the Assyrians, unhallowed food. Libation shall
be none to win the Lord's favour, nor any sacrifice; bread of theirs shall
be as the bread mourners eat, defiling to the lips; fill their bellies it may,
5 but into the Lord's house it cannot enter. Alas, what shift will you make
6 when the great days come round, the Lord's festivals? Ruin fell on the
citizens, and they are gone; Egypt the home of them now, Memphis the
tomb of them; bowers that shone with silver the nettles have claimed,
burdocks grow in the doorways.
7 Close at hand the audit-day, the doom close at hand! And wouldst
thou know, Israel, why prophet is turned fool, and he can but rave now
that once was inspired? God's heavy plague is this for thy much sinning;
8 prophet of thine, watchman of thine, Ephraim, is a snare at every turn,
luring thee to thy ruin, and at God's decree; he stands there in God's
9 house, a plague to thee. So deep the canker of their sin; Gabaa itself
never knew worse wrong. For the remembered guilt of it they shall be
called to account. [2]
10 When I kept tryst with Israel long ago, rare the encounter, as of grapes
out in the desert, of spring figs a-ripening high up on the tree. And all at
once to Beelphegor they betook themselves, sold honour for shame,
11 caught foul contagion from the things they loved! Light as bird on
bough, Ephraim's glory has come and gone; womb is none that breeds,
12 or, breeding, bears; ay, though they should bring sons to manhood,
childless their race shall be, nameless among men.

---

[1] Literally, 'loving hire upon all the threshing-floors of wheat.' There can be
little doubt that the reference is to the worship of the countryside gods, or
Baalim, who were supposed to have a special influence over the harvest.
[2] The sense of verses 7–9 can only be guessed at, and most modern editors
suspect the text of corruption. In verse 8, 'God's decree' is 'my God's decree,'
and 'God's house' is 'his God's house' in the original. The mention of Gabaa
in verse 9 is explained by some as a reference to Jg. 19 and 20, but there can be
no certainty on the point.

13   Woe betide them indeed, when I withdraw my presence from them!
     Ephraim's land, so fair a garden, as I look out over it towards Tyre!
14 And must Ephraim rear her sons for the slaughter-house? [1]   Thy gift to
     them, Lord, what is the best gift they can have of thee?   A womb,
15 assuredly, that miscarries, and dried-up breasts!   See where, at Galgal,
     their offence comes to a head; there it is they have made an enemy of me.
     They shall dwell in my domain no longer, claim love from me no longer;
16 chieftains of theirs are no vassals of mine.   On Ephraim blight has fallen;
     withered the root now, wizened the fruit; beget they, doom of death is on
17 their offspring, so dearly loved.   Cast away, my God, from thy presence,
     because heed thee they would not, cast away to wander homeless through
     the world!

CHAPTER TEN

A SPREADING vine is yonder vine of Israel, and fruit of him matches
     leaf. Rich, fertile soil; alas, how rich in altars, in sacred trees how
2 fertile!   A race half loyal, half false, but the penalty must be paid in full;
     those altars God himself will devote to extinction, strip those trees bare. [2]
3   King we have none, you say; God we fear not; what of the great king?
4 What will he do to us?   All is vain promise and making of treaties; never
     a furrow in your land but shall yield the bitter fruit of punishment. [3]
5   Calf [4] of Bethaven, the folk of Samaria once honoured, what ado is
     here! Mourns people and writhes priest at the passing of its glory;
6 carried off, now, into Assyria, for the pleasure of a ruthless king; fooled
7 is Ephraim, Israel's hopes have played him false.   Like foam on the
8 river Samaria sees her king pass by; and with that, vanish the hill-shrines
     of false worship, Israel's darling sin; grows thorn and thistle on their
     altars; no prayer have the men of Israel now but that mountains should
     fall on them, hills should bury them alive.

---

[1] The use of language here is strained, and once more suggests the possibility
of corruption in the text. 'The slaughter-house' may refer to the worship of
Moloch (Jer. 32.35), or simply to the massacres that will accompany the capture
of Samaria.
[2] This verse is more easily understood if we suppose (as is most likely) that
the Israelites were not clear in their own minds whether the hill-shrines, etc.,
were devoted to the worship of the true God or not.
[3] Literally, 'For now they will be saying, We have no king, because we do not
fear God; what will the king do to (or, for) us? For now they speak perjured
words in making a treaty; therefore judgement springs up in their furrows like
hemlock.' It is hard to feel certain about the meaning or bearing of the passage.
[4] 'Calf'; so the Septuagint Greek. The Hebrew text, like the Latin version,
gives 'heifers,' followed by a masculine singular pronoun in the rest of the
sentence.

9   Old is the tale of Israel's guilt, old as what befell at Gabaa; there stood they unmoved; was it not at Gabaa the tide of battle reached them, battle against the champions of wrong? [1]

10   A jealous chastiser I will be to them; twofold their guilt, and many the
11 nations I will muster for their chastisement. Heifer that has learned the welcome task of the threshing-floor, such is Ephraim; that sleek neck of hers I have spared till now; now she is to be harnessed; when Juda goes a-ploughing, Jacob it shall be that breaks the clods for him. [2]

12   If mercy is to be the measure you reap by, seed of yours must be sown in right doing; there are fallow acres to be tilled. Not too late to have recourse to the Lord, waiting for him to come and bring [3] you redress!
13 But alas, shameful furrows [4] they were you traced, and what came of it? A harvest of wrong, fruit that cheated you in the tasting!

    So thou wouldst trust in thy own devices, in thy own warrior strength?
14 Believe me, there shall be turmoil among thy folk, and all thy strongholds shall fall, as fell Salmana before Jerobaal [5] when the day was won; fell
15 child, fell mother, dashed to pieces. So much shall yonder Bethel countervail the heinousness of your guilt!

CHAPTER ELEVEN

SOON fades the dawn; soon passes king of Israel. Israel in his boyhood, what love I bore him! Away from Egypt I beckoned him, henceforth my son. [6]

2   . . . They called them, the more they refused obedience; gods of the
3 countryside must have their victims, dumb idols their incense! [7] Yet it was I, none other, guided those first steps of theirs, and took them in my
4 arms, and healed, all unobserved, their injuries. Sons of Adam, they

---

[1] Cf. 9.9 above. Here, as there, some think the reference is to Jg. 20; but it may easily be to some incident not elsewhere recorded.

[2] The last part of this verse is usually translated, 'Juda shall plough, and Jacob shall break the clods for himself.' But the expression 'for himself' seems curiously inappropriate.

[3] The verb used in the Hebrew text may mean either 'rain down' or 'teach.'

[4] 'Shameful furrows'; it can hardly be a coincidence that the Hebrew verb used can mean either 'ploughing' or 'carving images.'

[5] According to the Hebrew text 'as Salman (quite differently spelt) destroyed Beth-arbel,' an event not elsewhere alluded to.

[6] The Hebrew text, at the end of the verse, is naturally understood as meaning, 'I called him to be my son.' If this is authentic, we must suppose that a different colour was given to it in early times; cf. Mt. 2.15. The Septuagint Greek has, 'I called his children.'

[7] Although the subject of verse 1 is continued, it looks as if one or two words had been accidentally omitted.

should be drawn with leading-strings of love; never wagoner was at more pains to ease bridle on jaw, fed beast so carefully.

5 Never again to Egypt; Assyria shall rule him now, the unrepentant;
6 already the sword is let loose in those towns of his, the brave shall engulf,
7 the wise shall devour. Can my people be reconciled with me? All hangs in doubt, until at last I put a yoke on all alike, never to be taken away
8 from them.[1] What, Ephraim, must I abandon thee? Must I keep Israel under watch and ward? Can I let thee go the way of Adama, share the doom of Seboim? All at once my heart misgives me, and from its embers
9 pity revives. How should I wreak my vengeance, of Ephraim take full toll?

God am I, not a man in the midst of you, the Holy One, that may not
10 enter those city walls;[2] the Lord must lead, and man follow.[3]

Loud he will call, like lion roaring, and at the sound of it, sons of his
11 will come trembling from the distant sea; fluttering like sparrow or dove from Egypt, from the Assyrian country, and in their own home, the Lord says, I will give them rest.
12 Ephraim so false, Israel so treacherous, all about me! But Juda governs his folk with God to aid him; Juda takes part with the holy ones, loyal yet.[4]

CHAPTER TWELVE

EPHRAIM, that would still play shepherd to the wind, still hunt in the track of the storm, and nothing hoard up but treachery, nothing but his own ruin! See him making treaties with the Assyrian, sending
2 tribute of oil to Egypt! On Juda's part the Lord takes up the quarrel, will call Jacob to account,[5] for ill deeds and ill designs rewarding him.

---

[1] Literally, 'The sword has begun in his towns, and shall consume his chosen ones, and devour their heads; and my people shall hang to my return; a yoke shall be put on them at the same time, which shall not be taken away.' The Hebrew text differs considerably, but is equally obscure.

[2] The first sentence of this verse may be read as a statement, 'I will not wreak my vengeance,' or as a question, 'Shall I not wreak my vengeance?' The remaining part reads literally, 'for I am God and not man in the midst of thee holy and I will not go into the city'; an obscure phrase, and perhaps corrupt.

[3] Literally, 'They shall go behind the Lord.' The rest of this verse, with verse 11, cannot easily be fitted into the context, and was perhaps misplaced.

[4] The language of this verse is curiously forced; if it has been correctly preserved, 'the holy ones' is perhaps best understood of the (non-rebellious) angels.

[5] Literally, 'And there is a quarrel to the Lord with Juda, and to the calling to account of Jacob.' In view of 11.12, it does not seem likely that the Lord's quarrel here is *against* Juda.

3   Here was one that took precedence of [1] his brother even in the womb;
4   strength was his, of celestial strength the rival. Did he not hold his own
     in contest with an angel, and prefer, with tears, his suit? Ay, and what
5   of that encounter at Bethel, when the promises came to us from him,
     the Lord of hosts, from Javé, name of renown?
6   Wouldst thou to thy God return? A tender heart keep thou must, and
     a right mind, and wait for thy God's help continually.
7   Is it the Chanaanite that carries false weights, and loves ill gotten gain?
8   Here is Ephraim boasting that he has grown rich, has found a false god to
     worship; will not these earnings of mine, thinks he, buy me out from the
     punishment I have deserved? [2]
9   I, the Lord, thy God in Egypt, and thy God still! Once again thou
10   shalt dwell in tents, as in the days when I kept tryst with thee; [3] once
     again I will bestow [4] utterance upon the prophets. Mine it is, by the
     prophets' means, to grant clear vision, to speak in parables.
11   If Galaad is all idolatry, vain the sacrifice of oxen that is made at Gal-
     gal; stone heaps their altars shall be, out in the plough-lands. [5]
12   Time was when Jacob fled to the Aram country; Israel worked for a
13   wife, and for that wife's sake loyally kept his troth. Time was, when the
     Lord rescued Israel from Egypt by a prophet's means, and, for that pro-
     phet's sake loyally preserved them. [6]
14   For bitter jealousy of mine Ephraim must pay the penalty; spurned
     Master spurns him now.

---

[1] 'Took precedence of'; literally, 'dogged the heels of.' The incident related
in Gen. 25.25 is cited here as an example, not of Israel's treachery, but of God's
favour for his own people.

[2] The meaning of these verses 7 and 8 is obscure, and much disputed.

[3] That is, when the Tabernacle of Appointment went with Israel through
the desert. Or, possibly, the sense may be 'as in the days of solemn observance,'
i.e., the Feast of Tent-dwelling (Lev. 23.34).

[4] The Latin version here has 'And I used to bestow'; but a reference to the
past seems out of place here.

[5] The language of this verse is strained, and the sense doubtful; some think
there is an error in the manuscripts. The Hebrew for 'stone-heaps' is *gallim,*
and there is possibly a play upon words.

[6] Little can be said for certain about these verses, except that those editors are
wrong who would print verse 12 after verse 5, and verse 13 after verse 10.
Evidently they must be taken together, but it is hard to see the force of their
minute parallelism; possibly there is an allusion to Assyria and Egypt as
places of exile; cf. 11.11.

CHAPTER THIRTEEN

S POKE Ephraim,[1] all Israel trembled at his word; how else came they,
2 for Baal's worship, to barter away life itself? And they are busy yet
over their sinning; melt down silver of theirs to fashion models of yonder
images, craftsman copying craftsman's design! And of such models they
3 say, The man who would do sacrifice has but to kiss these calves.[2] Fades
the memory of them, light as early mist or morning dew, light as chaff
on the threshing-floor, smoke from the chimney, when high blows the
wind!
4 And all the while I am the Lord thy God [3] ... from the land of Egypt;
5 God thou shalt own no other, other deliverance is none; out in the desert,
6 out in the parched wastes, owned I thee. Fatal pasturing! With food
came satiety, and with satiety pride, and with pride forgetfulness of me!
7 Now their way lies to Assyria, and on that road I will meet them again,
8 their enemy now, watchful as lion or leopard; bear robbed of its young
should not tear open breast more cruelly, lion devour more greedily;
they shall be a prey, now, to the wild beasts.
9 Alas, Israel, undone! Who but I can aid thee? Thy king, where is he?
Now, if ever, from end to end of thee thou hast sore need of king and
11 princes both; king and court thou didst demand of me, and gift of mine
was never so grudgingly made, so angrily withdrawn.
12 Trust me, it is stored away, it is jealously preserved, the record of
13 Ephraim's sinning. Pangs like the pangs of travail shall come upon him;
or say he is babe ill-guided, that shall thrive never when it comes to the
birth.[4]
14 From the grave's power to rescue them, from death to ransom them;
I, death's mortal enemy, I, corruption's undoing! [5]

---

[1] 'Ephraim' is here the tribe of that name (to which Jeroboam I belonged),
not, as elsewhere, a synonym for the twelve tribes in general.

[2] The Latin version gives no satisfactory sense in the last clause; it translates,
'Sacrifice, O men that worship calves,' or possibly, 'Sacrifice men, you that worship calves.'

[3] After 'the Lord thy God' the Septuagint Greek has 'that holds heaven in
place and is earth's Creator, whose hands made all the host of heaven. Warrant
thou hast none from me to follow such worship; I it was that rescued thee ...'

[4] The metaphor here is confused, and the details of it cannot be determined
with certainty.

[5] Literally, 'I will free them from the hand of the grave, I will ransom them
from death; O death, I will be thy plague, O grave, I will be thy devouring.'
But many editors read the first part of this as a question, implying a threat; and
translate the second part, 'Come, death, where are those plagues of thine?
Where is that destroying power of thine, corruption?' as if Almighty God was

15   Pity? My eyes are closed to it; these, that now have a share among
their brethren, shall feel the Lord's vengeance, a burning desert wind that
shall dry up their brooks, foul their springs, lay waste the store-houses
where they hoard their treasure.

CHAPTER FOURTEEN

DEATH to Samaria, that has provoked her God's anger! Death at the
sword's point; children dashed headlong, ripped open the womb!
2   Come back, Israel, to the Lord thy God; it is sin that has caused thy
3 overthrow.   Come back, men of Israel, with a plea ready on your lips:
Pardon all our guilt, and take the best we have in return;[1] the praises be
4 utter shall be our victims now.   No longer we will find refuge in Assyrian
help, mount our men on horses from Egypt;[2] no longer will we give the
name of gods to the things our own hands have made; thou art the friend
of the friendless who trust in thee.
5   I will bring healing to their crushed spirits;[3] in free mercy I will give
6 them back my love; my vengeance has passed them by.   I will be morning
dew, to make Israel grow as the lilies grow, strike roots deep as the forest
7 of Lebanon.   Those branches shall spread, it shall become fair as the
8 olive, fragrant as Lebanon cedar.   None that dwells under the protection
of that name but shall come back to me; corn shall be theirs in plenty,
and they will grow like one of their own vineyards, famed as the vintage
9 of Lebanon itself.   The false gods of Ephraim are forgotten; mine to
answer his prayer and tend him, ever-green as a fir-tree; from me all thy
10 increase comes.   All this the wise discern, the thoughtful understand;
straight paths the Lord has shewn us for his friends to walk in; who
leaves them shall stumble to his ruin.

---

calling on his creatures to assail unrepentant Israel. The Septuagint Greek has
'where,' instead of 'I will be,' and a reminiscence of its language is to be found
in I Cor. 15.55.

[1] 'Take the best we have in return'; literally, 'take good,' that is, perhaps, the
praises mentioned in the following clause; the phrase is unusual.

[2] 'From Egypt' is not expressed in the original, but is almost certainly intended; cf. Is. 31.1.

[3] The Hebrew text has here, as in Jer. 3.22, 'their apostasies.'

THE PROPHECY OF JOEL

CHAPTER ONE

THIS message came from the Lord to Joel, the son of Phatuel.
2 Citizens, hear and heed, ruler and commoner alike! Tell me, what happenings are these, in your days and in your fathers' days unmatched,
3 a tale you must needs hand on to your children, and they to theirs, and
4 theirs to a fresh generation yet? That locusts, breed upon breed of them, so ravage yonder countryside, Swarmer devouring what Spoiler, Ruin-
5 all what Gnaw-all has left? [1] Weep they and wail, the tipplers that must be ever at their cups, for the sweet wine they drank, and shall drink no more!
6 Alas, my country, how valiant an enemy is this, in number past all counting, that comes to invade thee; lion nor lion's whelp has teeth can
7 grind so pitilessly. Spoiled thy vineyards lie, stripped of the very bark thy
8 fig-trees; bare and blanched and ruinous every bough. Weep bitterly,
9 then, as maid that goes clad in sackcloth, untimely widowed; in the Lord's house, bread nor wine is offered now; for the priests, the Lord's
10 own ministers, no office now but tears. Desolate the land lies, every
11 field forlorn; crops ravaged, the vine thirsty, strengthless the oil. Alas, for husbandman's labour lost, for vintage-song turned to lament! Alas
12 for harvest perished, for vineyard withered, and drooping fig-tree! Pomegranate, and palm, and apple, no tree in the wood but fades there; what wonder? Has not joy faded in human hearts?
13 Mourn, priests, and lament; in mourners' garb go about your work at the altar; ministers of God, to his presence betake you, and there, in sackcloth, keep vigil; your God's house, that offering of bread and wine
14 has none! Then proclaim a fast, assemble the folk together, ruler and commoner alike summon to the temple, and there for the Lord's help cry
15 lustily. Woe betide us this day! The day of the Lord is coming; his the
16 dominion, his the doom. Even where we stand, in the temple of our God,
17 the festal cheer abolished, all the contentment, all the rejoicing! Beast on dung-heap rots; barn-wall gapes, and store-house lies in ruin, the hope
18 of harvest gone; echoes byre with lowing of bewildered cattle, that

---

[1] The Latin here mentions four destructive agencies—the caterpillar, two kinds of locust, and the blight. The Hebrew text is ordinarily understood as giving four different kinds of locust, or four different names for the locust. It is impossible to say with certainty whether the prophet, from 1.4 to 2.11, is describing a hostile invasion under the metaphor of a locust-swarm, or a locust-swarm under the metaphor of a hostile invasion.

19 pasture have none; even the flocks dwindle. What help, Lord, but thine?
20 Parched are the upland meadows, every tree scorched in the forest; to
thee even the wild beasts make their dumb appeal, from dry river-beds,
from upland pastures laid bare.

CHAPTER TWO

THE trumpet, there, in Sion! On yonder mountain-height, my sanctuary, sound the alarm! Tremble, fellow-countrymen, one and all;
2 the day of the Lord is coming, coming so soon. Day of gloom and darkness, day of cloud and storm; spread out, like dawn over the hills, this
great, this valiant army; never was the like since time began, never shall
3 be, while the ages run their course. Fire running greedily before them,
and a track of flame behind; in front, a land that could match Eden for
loveliness, and where they have passed, nothing but a desert waste; escape
4 from them is none. Horse nor horseman so terrible of aspect, so speedy
5 in advance; hark to the noise of them, as they spurn the hill-slopes! Din
of chariots is not so loud, nor crackling of flames that feed on stubble;
6 a valiant army, all arrayed for battle! What wonder if whole nations
7 groan at their coming, everywhere pale cheeks? [1] Bravely they hasten to
8 the attack, warrior-like scale the wall; unswerving they press on, never
one jostling with another, so well keeps each one his course; storm the
9 loop-hole [2] unhurt; and now, the city breached, mount wall, climb
house-top, enter by windows, the thief's way.
10   Before that army, quakes earth, and heaven rocks; dark grow sun and
11 moon, and the stars withhold their radiance; with his own voice the Lord
heralds its coming. Wide it stretches, that host of the Lord, valiant it is,
and ever ready to do his will. O great, O terrible day of the Lord; who
shall find strength to bear it?
12   Time now, the Lord says, to turn the whole bent of your hearts back
13 to me, with fasting and with mourners' tears. It is your hearts, not the
garments you wear, that must be torn asunder. Come back to the Lord
your God; he is ever gracious and merciful, ever patient and rich in par-
14 don; threatens he calamity, even now he is ready to forgive. Who knows
but he will relent, and be appeased; cast one glance behind him, and,
enough for his own due of bread and wine-offering, spare us largesse yet?
15   The trumpet, there, in Sion! Here is fasting proclaimed, [3] the citizens

---

[1] See note on Nahum 2.10.

[2] 'Storm the loop-hole'; literally, 'fall through windows,' but the Hebrew
text reads, 'fall (or plunge) among weapons.'

[3] Grammatically (if the text is sound) verses 15–17 imply a command; dra-
matically (as verses 18 and 19 shew) they imply that the command has been
carried out.

16 assembled; the folk summoned, the cleansing rites performed, the elders
   met; weanling must be there and babe unweaned, groom leave his
17 chamber and bride her bower. Hark how the priests, that wait upon the
   Lord, make lament between porch and altar, crying aloud: Spare thy
   people, Lord, spare them; thy chosen people, do not put them to the
   shame of obeying heathen masters! Wilt thou let the Gentiles ask, What
   has become of their God?

18   People of a land well loved, he spares us yet. His answer comes, Here
   is corn and wine and oil to your hearts' content; no more will I let the
20 nations mock you. Far he shall be driven from your lands, the northern
   invader; out in the trackless desert he shall lie, vanguard to eastern, rearguard to western sea, and nothing more shall assail you but stench and
21 stink of him, this enemy that did so wondrously. Fear no more, land of
22 Israel; in the Lord's wondrous doings triumph and rejoice! Fear no
   more, beasts that roam the countryside; grass grows on the upland
   meadows! There is fruit on the trees again; vine nor fig-tree ever bore so
23 lustily. Rejoice, men of Sion, and triumph in the Lord your God; proof
   he gives you of your restoration to favour,[1] making the winter and the
24 spring rains fall, as in time past. Now the threshing-floor shall be piled
25 with wheat, and the presses overflow with wine and oil. Profitless years,
   when the locust ravaged you, Gnaw-all and Ruin-all and Spoiler, they
26 shall be made good. Eat you shall to your hearts' content, praising the
   name of the Lord your God for his wondrous protection; never again
27 shall Israel go away disappointed. I will make myself known among you,
   I, the Lord your God, who alone am God; Israel cheated of their hopes
   never again!

28   And afterwards? Afterwards I will pour out my spirit upon all mankind, and your sons and daughters will be prophets. Your old men shall
29 dream dreams, and your young men see visions; everywhere servants
30 of mine, handmaids of mine, inspired to prophesy! I will shew wonders
31 in heaven, and on earth blood, and fire, and whirling smoke. The sun
   will be turned into darkness and the moon into blood before the day of
32 the Lord comes, the great, the terrible day. And never a soul shall call
   on the Lord's name but shall find deliverance; here on mount Sion, here
   in Jerusalem there shall be refuge; for a remnant, a remnant of the Lord's
   own summoning, there shall be deliverance at last.

---

[1] 'Proof of your restoration to favour', literally, 'a teacher of justice.' Some
would understand the Hebrew text as meaning, 'winter rain to (produce) the
restoration of your fortunes.' But it almost seems as if the prophet had made
a deliberate play upon words: 'He gives you a show-er of (the way to) restoration, makes the winter shower and the spring rain fall.'

CHAPTER THREE

2 PERILOUS those times shall be, when the hour has come for reversing my sentence against Juda and Jerusalem. Into the valley of Josaphat I will herd the heathen folk, one and all, and there hold assize over them for the wrong they did to my people, to Israel, my own domain. People of mine they scattered through the world, land of mine they parcelled out
3 between them. Must they be awarded by lot, such captives, and then sold cheap, boy-slave for a harlot's hire, girl-slave for the draining of a
4 wine-stoup? What, would you chaffer with me, men of Tyre and Sidon, men from the pale of Philistia? Must there be barter and exchange between us? Nay, if you will have exchanges with me, look to it that the
5 reward does not fall on your own heads, swift and sudden! [1] Would you carry off silver of mine and gold, lay up the choicest of my treasures in
6 yonder temples? Citizens of Jerusalem, men of Juda's breed, would you
7 sell them to Grecian masters, far away from their home? See if I do not summon them back from exile that was of your contriving, and, for that
8 service done, pay you in your own coin; make over son and daughter of yours to these same men of Juda, slaves they can barter at will to the remote Sabaeans; I, the Lord, have decreed it.
9 Cry it to the nations, they should do sacrifice and muster their tried
10 warriors for battle; rally they, march they, all that bear arms. Plough-share beat into sword, spade into spear; weakling is none but must sum-
11 mon up his manhood now! To arms, to the rendez-vous, nations all
12 about; doom of the Lord awaits you, warriors all! Up, up, to Josaphat's valley betake you; here, upon all neighbouring peoples, I will hold assize.
13 The sickle, there! Harvest is ripe already. Down to the vineyard with you! Are not the vats full, the presses overflowing? Has it not come to a head, the measure of their wickedness?
14 Thronging, thronging they come, in yonder valley to try their destiny,
15 appointed trysting-place of a divine audit; dark grow sun and moon,
16 light of the stars is none. Loud as roaring of lion speaks the Lord in thunder from his citadel at Jerusalem, till heaven and earth quake at the sound. To his own people, the sons of Israel, refuge he is and strong-
17 hold; doubt you shall have none thenceforward that I, the Lord your God, have my dwelling-place at Jerusalem; a holy city Jerusalem shall be, never again shall alien foe breach the walls of her.
18 Drip now with sweet wine the mountain slopes, bathed in milk the up-

---

[1] The interpretation of this verse in detail is not altogether clear; the general sense is evidently that Almighty God demands to be indemnified for the loss he is represented as having suffered when his people were sold as slaves.

land pastures; never a stream in all Juda but flows full and strong. What
fountain is this that comes out from the Lord's temple, and waters the
19 dry valley of Setim? A lonely ruin Egypt shall be, and Edom a desert
waste; here was great wrong done to Jewry's people, here unoffending
20 lives were taken. For Juda, for Jerusalem, there shall be peace undis-
21 turbed, long as time shall last; for these, guilt of blood that went still
unpardoned shall be pardoned now; here, in Sion, the Lord will have his
dwelling-place.

THE PROPHECY OF AMOS

CHAPTER ONE

HERE tells Amos, one of the shepherd folk at Thecua, what visions he had concerning Israel. In Juda, Ozias was then reigning, in Israel,
2 Jeroboam son of Joas, and it was two years before the earthquake. Loud as roaring of lion, said he, the Lord will speak in thunder from his citadel at Jerusalem; forlorn they lie, yonder pastures the shepherds loved once, the heights of Carmel all shrivelled away.

3 A message from the Lord: Thrice forfeit Damascus, and forfeit once
4 again,[1] that rode rough-shod over the men of Galaad;[2] fall fire on
5 Azael's court, to burn down all the strongholds of Benadad! Broken Damascus gate shall be, nor any be left to dwell in Aven's plain, or rule over Eden valley; far off, at Cir,[3] the Syrian folk shall go into banishment, the Lord says.

6 This, too: Thrice forfeit Gaza, and forfeit once again, that secured for
7 the men of Edom their full toll of captives;[4] fall fire on Gaza's walls, to
8 burn down all its strongholds! None shall dwell in Azotus, none rule over Ascalon; upon Accaron, too, my stroke shall fall; every trace of Philistia vanished and gone, the Lord God says.

9 This too: Thrice forfeit Tyre, and forfeit once again, that gave Edom its full toll of captives, as though bond there were none between brethren;
10 fall fire on its walls, to burn down its strongholds!

11 This too: Thrice forfeit Edom, and forfeit once again, that would hunt down his own brother at the sword's point; unnatural cruelty, so to hug
12 his enmity, nor ever let rancour die down; fire fall on Theman, to burn down the strongholds of Bosra!

13 This, too: Thrice forfeit Ammon, and forfeit once again, that so

---

[1] Literally, 'For three offences of Damascus, and for four, I will not bring it back.' The verb is variously explained: 'I will not restore Damascus to prosperity,' 'I will not recall the sentence I have pronounced,' etc.

[2] 'Rode rough-shod over the men of Galaad'; literally, 'threshed Galaad with iron threshers.'

[3] The situation of Cir is unknown; but the Latin version can hardly be right in rendering it as Cyrene.

[4] Here and in verse 9, it is usually explained that first the Philistines, then the Phoenicians, invaded Israel, and sold the prisoners they took to the Edomites. But such a notion is both historically and geographically improbable. It seems much simpler to understand that the Edomites invaded Israel (see verse 11) from the south-east, and neither the Philistines on the south-west nor the Phoenicians on the north-west would allow Israelite refugees to cross their frontiers. This would be described in Hebrew idiom as 'shutting up Israel into the hands of the Edomites.' Cf. Abd. 14.

14 coveted Galaad's lands, every mother's womb he would rip open; fire
fall on Rabba's walls, to burn down its strongholds! Hark to the bray of
15 battle, blustering of the storm-wind! Into exile Melchom [1] shall go,
with all his retinue.

CHAPTER TWO

THIS, too: Thrice forfeit Moab, and forfeit once again, that burned
2 the king of Edom's bones to dust; [2] fall fire on Moab, to burn down
all the strongholds of Carioth! With tumult and the bray of trumpets,
3 Moab shall go to his death; ruler of theirs I will strike down in their
midst, and all his vassals shall perish with him, the Lord says.
4   This, too: Thrice forfeit Juda, and forfeit once again, that spurned
the Lord's law and left his bidding undone, so mazed were they by the
5 false gods their fathers had gone a-courting; fire fall on Juda, to burn
down all the strongholds of Jerusalem!
6   And this, too: What of Israel? Thrice forfeit Israel like the rest, and
forfeit once again, that for a debt, though it were but the price of a pair
7 of shoes, will make slaves of poor, honest folk. Ground in the dust, the
poor man's rights, shouldered aside, the claim of the unbefriended! See
8 where father and son, to my name's dishonour, bed with one maid! See
where they lie feasting beside the altar, at the very shrine of their God,
no cloak there but is some borrower's pledge, no stoup of wine but is
some debtor's forfeit!
9   Was it for such men as these I exterminated the Amorrhites, a race
tall as the cedar, hardy as the oak, root and fruit of them doomed to
10 destruction? These are the men I rescued from Egypt, guided them, all
those forty years, through the wilderness, to make the domain of the
11 Amorrhites theirs! Tell me, men of Israel, the Lord says, what avails it
that I should call sons of yours, from their boyhood's days, to serve me
12 as prophets and Nazirites? Ever you tempt the Nazirites with wine, ever
13 you forbid the prophet to raise his voice in prophecy. Henceforth, you
shall seek my help in vain; waggon-axle overladen with sheaves groans
14 not so reluctant as I! Speed shall be no profit to the speedy, strength to
15 the strong; warrior shall not escape, nor bowman stand firm; fleet of
16 foot and well-mounted horseman shall have no deliverance; a day is

---

[1] For 'Melchom' the Hebrew text, probably by an error, reads 'their king.'

[2] It seems unlikely that the words 'burned the king of Edom's bones to dust'
represent what the prophet wrote. Nowhere else in the Old Testament is one
heathen nation reprimanded for its conduct to another; nowhere else is crema-
tion treated as an atrocity. And the denunciation of the Edomites in 1.11 does
not prepare us for a sympathetic reference to them.

coming, the Lord says, when tried valour shall be fain to throw arms away, and take flight.

CHAPTER THREE

T HIS, then, is the Lord's message to you, men of Israel, to the whole
2   race I rescued from Egypt: Nation is none I have claimed for my own, save you; and guilt of yours is none that shall go unpunished.
3   Tryst there must be, if friends will meet and journey together; prey there must be, ere lion will roar in the forest, lion's whelp growl in its
5 lair; bird is not pinned to the ground, without fowler to snare it, nor
6 trap released without a catch made. Sounds trumpet in the streets, men do well to be afraid; if peril is afoot in the city, doubt not it is of the
7 Lord's sending. Never does he act, but his servants, the prophets, are in
8 the secret. Roars lion, who but will tremble? Comes the divine warning, who but will prophesy? [1]
9   Raise a cry from the house-tops, there in Azotus, there in Egypt's land: To the hills about Samaria betake you, and look deep into the heart of her,
10 what turbulent doings are there, what wrongs men suffer! In yonder palaces, the Lord says, that are store-houses of oppression and rapine,
11 honest doing is all forgot. This doom, then, the Lord God utters: Distress and siege for such a land as this! All thy fastnesses shall be dis-
12 mantled, all thy palaces spoiled. Wilt thou have lion disgorge his prey? Pleased enough the shepherd, if a pair of legs he recover, a mangled ear! They shall fare no better, the Israelites that lie on a corner of the mattress
13 at Samaria, and have their bed at Damascus.[2]   A message for you, says
14 the Lord, the God of hosts, a warning for the sons of Jacob! I will have a reckoning with the rebellions of Israel, a reckoning with those altars of theirs at Bethel, that shall have the horns of them cut off and hurled to
15 the ground; on summer dwelling of yours and winter dwelling my hand shall fall, houses of ivory and houses of the common folk, all shall lie in ruin, the Lord says.

---

[1] The meaning of this difficult passage seems to be that there is no smoke without fire; the lesser judgements already experienced by Samaria (4.6–11) are sure proof that it has incurred God's anger, and worse calamity is to follow.

[2] The insinuation is not clear, perhaps a general warning against luxury is intended (cf. verse 15). But this seems to be the natural rendering of a sentence that has produced a wide variety of interpretations. It runs, literally: 'So shall the sons of Israel be dragged out, that dwell in Samaria on the corner of a bed, and in Damascus . . . a couch.' There is no evidence that the stuff called 'damask' was known, or was so called, in Amos' time.

CHAPTER FOUR

HERE is word for you, pampered cattle that dwell at Samaria, the poor wronging, the friendless folk spurning, and ever crying out
2 upon your husbands, Wine, there! We would drink! Never let me be called holy, the Lord God says, if doom does not overtake you for this; see if you be not trussed on spears, and your children given up to feed
3 the cooking-pan! [1] Leave the city walls you must, the Lord says, one by this breach, one by that, and be cast away in Armon.
4 On with you to Bethel, and defy me, thence to Galgal, and repeat
5 defiance there; morning victims, tithes on the third day, bread, leavened bread, for thank-offering, gifts of devotion publicly proclaimed! [2] Have your will, men of Israel, says the Lord God, have your will.
6 What would you? Never a city left but men's teeth were idle, never a village but bread lacked there, and you would not come back to me, the
7 Lord says. It was three months to harvest, and rain I denied you; or rain fell on one city, and not on the next, one village had a drenching and the
8 next was dry, till one city must supply water for three neighbours, and
9 water had none, and you would not come back to me. You would not come back to me, the Lord says, when sirocco I sent, and mildew, and the locust preyed on garden and vineyard, fig and olive-tree of yours;
10 you would not come back to me, when with Egypt's pestilence [3] I slew you, when your warriors fell at the sword's point, and your horses were carried off, and never a camp of yours but the stench of it plagued your
11 nostrils; you would not come back to me, when ruin threatened, swift as the divine stroke that ruined Sodom and Gomorrha, and you yourselves were like a brand saved from the burning.
12 Now I have worse, Israel, in store for thee; [4] when that worse comes,
13 prepare thou must, Israel, to meet thy God. He is here, that fashioned the hills and made the winds; he is here, that gives man warning of his designs, that turns dawn into darkness, and sets his feet on the highest heights of earth; Javé, the God of hosts, is the name of him.

---

[1] Literally, 'they shall lift you up on poles (or, spears), and that which you leave behind (or, that which is left of you) in boiling pots.' We might compare Jer. 19.9, or possibly Ez. 11.7. But the meaning of the Hebrew text is probably different: 'he will lead you away with hooks, with barbed prongs such as fisherfolk use, all that is left of you.'

[2] See Ex. 23.18.

[3] See Deut. 7.15, 28.27.

[4] Literally, 'I will do *this* to thee,' the nature of the punishment being left vague, as is the common formula, 'May the Lord do to me (that is, punish me) thus and more than thus.'

CHAPTER FIVE

PLEASE you then listen to the dirge I raise for you, men of Israel:
2 Fallen she is, never to rise again, Israel, the unsubdued; stretched at
3 full length she lies there forsaken! Ay, the Lord God says, but a hundred
citizens, but ten villagers left to you, city that marched out a thousand,
village a hundred strong!

4 Yet warning the Lord gave to the race of Israel: On peril of your lives,
5 to my aid betake you! Not to Bethel, not to Galgal's ring-shrine, or
Bersabee pilgrimage; a long road yonder circle shall lead you, a road that
never returns; house of God shall not avail you, that is home of idols
6 now! On your lives, to the Lord betake you, as you would not see all
7 Joseph ablaze, quenchless fire raging over Bethel! And still you poison
the springs of justice, still in the dust fling honour away.

8 . . .[1] Creator he of Arcturus and Orion; dawn brings he out of darkness, and turns night to day, beckons to the waters of the sea, and over
9 the surface of earth spreads them, Javé his name! At his glance falls ruin
on the strong, devastation on the stronghold.

10 Ill looks he will earn at yonder city gate, that finds fault; the wise word,
11 there, is a thing abominable. Yet, trust me, it shall nothing avail you,
this harrying of the poor, and taking toll of the best they have. Houses
of stone you build you shall never dwell in, sunny vineyards you plant
12 you shall drink of never. Your often misdoing, your heinous guilt, never
think I am blind to it; innocence hated, the bribe taken, the poor refused
13 their rights at the judgement-seat! And should wisdom keep silence in
14 times like these, ill times like these?[2] Set your minds on right, that now
are set on wrong-doing; so you shall find life, so your boast shall come
15 true that the Lord, the God of hosts, is with you. Shun wrong, cherish
the right, justice enthrone at your judgement-seat; then there is hope that
the Lord, the God of hosts, will have mercy on some remnant of Joseph's
line.

16 This doom he utters, he, the Lord of hosts, he, our Master: Market-
place or street is none but shall echo with wailing and cries of woe;
country-folk, and such as are skilled in mourning, they shall call in to
17 make dirge and dole;[3] dirge, too, the vineyards shall sing; all this, when

---

[1] Both grammar and logic seem to demand that some thought should be supplied here, which our existing manuscripts do not express.

[2] This sentence may be read either as a statement or as a question; if it is a
statement, no satisfactory account of it has yet been devised.

[3] At the end of this verse, the Latin seems to be a correction of a text unintel-

18 I make my way through your midst, the Lord says. Fools, that wait eagerly for the day of the Lord's coming! Think you it shall serve your turn? Nay, it is the Lord's day of triumph, not yours; dawn it must, but
19 in darkness, not in light. Speeds he well, that shuns lion and meets bear? Has he joy of his home-coming, that leans hand on wall, and all at once
20 is bitten by a viper? And for you, that day brings darkness, not the light you craved for; no radiance haunts about it, only gloom.
21   Oh, but I am sick and tired of them, your solemn feasts; incense that
22 goes up from your assemblies I can breathe no longer! Burnt-sacrifice still? Bloodless offerings still? Nay, I will have none of them; fat be the
23 victims you slay in welcome, I care not. O to be rid of the singing, the harp's music, that dins my ear!
24   ... And like waters rolling in full tide, like a perennial stream, right and justice shall abound ...
25   What, men of Israel, did you spend forty years in the desert, ever for
26 me your burnt-sacrifice, ever for me your offerings; and now would you have Moloch for your king, a star for your god, carry shrine of theirs,
27 idolatrous image you made of them, hither and thither?[1] What wonder if I banish you beyond Damascus far away? Dooms you with his own sign-manual the Lord, the God of hosts.

CHAPTER SIX

POOR fools, that in Sion or high Samaria take your ease, and fear nothing! That lord it over the Gentiles, and pass proudly through
2 Israel's domain,   bidding us make our way to Chalane, and thence to noble Emath, or go down to Gath, where the Philistines are, and see if land of theirs be fairer, borders of theirs be wider, than these of ours.
3 Poor fools, with the evil day ever at arm's length, wrong enthroned ever

---

ligible in the Hebrew. But it may be questioned whether the corruption does not go deeper.
    [1] Literally, 'And took up (or, will take up) Siccuth (or, the booths) your king (or, of Moloch), and Ciun (or, the image, or, the pedestal) of your images, the star of your God (or, gods), which you made for them.' The meaning of the sentence has been much disputed, and the general reference to Israel's idolatrous habits in Ac. 7.42 does not help to clear up the difficulty. Many suspect a reference to the Assyrian worship of the planet Saturn; but it should be observed that Amos does not, as a rule, tax the Israelites with worshipping false gods; rather with an idolatrous and unspiritual approach to their own religion. It is not improbable that the text has suffered from an early corruption, like the beginning of chapter 6.

4 close at hand!¹ Sleep they on beds of ivory, sprawl they at table, eating
5 the best lambs flock can provide, calves fattened at the stall; and ever
must harp and voice nicely accord, ay, very Davids they think them-
6 selves for musical invention! All their drinking is from the bowl, all
their ointment of the best, and what care they for Joseph's ruin?
7 Lead their folk they shall, but into exile; the revel must break up at
8 last. By my divine power I swear it, says the Lord God of hosts, pride of
yours shall weary me, great houses of yours shall offend my sight, no
9 longer; city and citizens, I will leave you at the enemy's mercy. Be there
ten men left alive in a house, death shall take toll of them . . .²
10 . . . Kinsman that comes to take him away must burn him first, and so
carry his bones without. Ho, there! cries he to one that lurks in the inner
11 rooms, hast thou any left? And when he hears the task is over, bids him
say no more, unless it be to call the Lord's name to memory³ . . .
12 A word from the Lord, and all shall be a gaping ruin, palace and cot-
13 tage both. Strange, if yonder mountain crags men should climb on horseback, or plough with oxen!⁴ Stranger still, that people of mine should
14 poison the springs of right and justice, all wormwood now! And still
you boast over some conquest of little worth;⁵ To what greatness, you
15 say, valour of ours has brought us!⁶ Trust me, men of Israel, the Lord
God of hosts says, I mean to embroil you with such an enemy as shall

---

¹ The language of the Hebrew text is curiously forced all through verses 1–3,
and it is difficult to feel certain that manuscript errors have not interfered with
it. Verse 2 must be taken as the utterance, not of the prophet, but of the boastful
Samaritan leaders; otherwise the logic of the passage is wholly obscure. For the
mention of Sion (if the text is rightly preserved) cf. 2.4, the only other threat
against Juda in the whole book; cf. 7.12 below.

² There seems to be a gap, both in grammar and in logic, at the end of this
sentence, which suggests a manuscript omission: e.g., the mention of the number
ten would be more readily intelligible if the text ran, 'Be there ten men left alive
in a house, nine of these shall die.' We should expect also to hear what kind of
danger (perhaps battle) they had escaped, to fall into some other danger, perhaps
that of pestilence. If a reference to plague has dropped out, it would explain the
allusion to burning in verse 9; the Israelites did not ordinarily burn their dead.

³ The exact bearing of this vivid passage escapes us, perhaps because the true
context of it has not been preserved. 'Say no more, unless it be to call the Lord's
name to memory'; the Latin means, and the Hebrew text may mean, 'Hush! No
mention must be made of the Lord's name.' But no plausible reason has been
produced for such a taboo; nor does it appear that there was any immediate
danger of the divine name being introduced into the conversation.

⁴ By a very slight change in the Hebrew text it is possible to get the reading,
'or plough the sea with oxen.'

⁵ 'Of little worth'; or possibly, 'Of Lodabar,' a place-name (II Kg. 9.4). The
prophet may intend a play upon words, as we might upon the name 'Littleworth.'

⁶ Literally, 'Have we not by our own strength taken to ourselves horns?' The
Hebrew word for horns, Carnaim, was also a place-name (I Mac. 5.26).

crush the life out of you, from Emath pass to the brook that bounds the desert.

CHAPTER SEVEN

THIS was a vision the Lord God shewed me; here were locusts a-making, just at the time when the aftergrowth was coming up, after
2 the king's crop had been carried. Short work had these made of all the land yielded; Ah, Lord God, said I, be merciful! How should Jacob sur-
3 vive, the puny creature he is? And with that, the Lord relented; Happen
4 it shall not, said he. And a second vision the Lord God shewed me, how he would summon them to ordeal by fire; fire should devour the waters
5 below the earth, and devoured some part of them were. Ah, Lord God,
6 said I, for pity! How should Jacob survive, the puny creature he is? And with that, the Lord relented again; Happen it shall not, said he.
7   But now the Lord shewed me a third vision; a plastered wall, and the Lord himself standing by it with a trowel [1] in his hand, asking me if I
8 could see what he had there. Why, Lord, I said, a plasterer's trowel! Ay, he answered, and here, in full view of Israel's folk, that trowel I lay
9 aside; cementing they shall have from me no more. Hill-shrines of Aven [2] shall tumble down, sanctuaries of Israel be laid waste; at the sword's point I will try conclusions with the race of Jeroboam.
10   Hereupon, a message came to Jeroboam, king of Israel, from Amasias that was priest at Bethel. Here is Amos, said he, raising revolt against thee in the realm of Israel; there is no room in all the land for such talk
11 as his; Jeroboam to die at the sword's point, Israel to be banished from
12 its native country! And this was his counsel to Amos, Sir prophet, get thee gone; in Juda take refuge if thou wilt, and there earn thy living by
13 prophecy. Prophesy here in Bethel thou mayst not, where the king's chapel is, and the king's court.

---

[1] The Hebrew word rendered in the Latin by 'trowel' more probably means a plumb-line, which Almighty God threatens to apply against Israel; that is, he will proceed strictly against them, he will not pass over (their sins) any more (cf. 8.2, where the same words are used).

[2] The Latin version gives 'hill-shrines of Aven (or, the Idol),' exactly as in Os. 10.8 (cf. Am. 1.5). In verse 16 below it gives 'Bethaven (or, House of the Idol)', exactly as in Os. 4.15, 5.8, 10.5. Our present Hebrew text gives 'hill-shrines of Isaac' and 'house of Isaac'; it is supported by the Septuagint Greek (which, however, translates the word as 'laughter'); this, too, was St Jerome's reading. It almost looks as if there had been some early uncertainty in the manuscripts, due perhaps to scrupulous reluctance, on a scribe's part, to write down some name connected with heathen worship (like 'Baal'). It may be pointed out that 'house of Isaac' is a phrase nowhere else used—it would necessarily include Edom —and that Isaac is never mentioned by the prophets, except in Jer. 33.26.

14   What, said Amos, I a prophet? Nay, not that, nor a prophet's son
     neither; I am one that minds cattle, one that nips the sycamore-trees;
15   I was but tending sheep when the Lord took me into his service. It was
16   the Lord bade me go and prophesy to his people of Israel. He has a mes-
     sage for thee: Thou wilt have no prophesying against Israel, no word
17   dropped against Bethaven? Here, then, is the divine doom pronounced
     on thee: Wife of thine, here in the city streets, shall be dishonoured; sons
     and daughters of thine shall die at the sword's point; lands of thine shall
     feel the measuring-rope. And for thyself, on unhallowed soil death awaits
     thee, when Israel is banished, as banished it needs must be, from the land
     of its birth.

CHAPTER EIGHT

THEN the Lord God shewed me another vision, of a hook [1] such as
2   they use for fruit-gathering. And when he asked, could I see what
     he had there, Why, Lord, I said, a grappling-hook for fruit-trees! Ay,
     said he, and right autumn it is for my people of Israel; no further chance
     shall they have of repentance.
3   Day of doom! How shriek the hinges of yonder temple gates; then,
     what massacre! Everywhere deep silence falls.[2]
4   Here is word for you, oppressors of the poor, that bring ruin on your
5   fellow citizens in their need; you that long for new moon and sabbath
     to be at an end, for trading to begin and granary to be opened, so you
     may be at your shifts again, the scant measure, the high price, the false
6   weights! You that for a debt, though it were but the price of a pair of
     shoes, will make slaves of poor, honest folk; you that sell refuse for
7   wheat! By Jacob's ancient renown the Lord swears it, crimes of yours
8   shall remain for ever unforgotten. Well may the earth quake over such
     doings, to the hurt of all that dwell in it; everywhere mount up, and
9   shift, and sink, like Egypt's river in flood. Day of doom, says the Lord
     God, when there shall be sunset at noon, and earth shall be overshadowed
10   under the full light! All your feasting turned to lament, all your songs
     to dirge and dole; not a loin but goes clad in sackcloth, not a head but is
     shaved bald; never was such mourning made, though it were for an only
     son; bitter the day, bitter its ending .
11   A time is coming, says the Lord God, when there shall be great lack
     in the land, yet neither dearth nor drought. Hunger? Ay, they shall
12   hunger for some message from the Lord, yet go they from eastern to
     western sea, go they from north to south, making search for it every-

---

[1] 'A hook'; according to the Hebrew text, 'a basket.'
[2] The sense of this verse is uncertain, and a manuscript error seems probable.

13 where, message from the Lord they shall have none. Thirst, ay, they
14 shall thirst, fair maid and brave warrior both. Fools, that by the shame
of Samaria take their oaths, pin their faith to Dan's worship or Bersabee
pilgrimage! Here is fall there is no amending.

CHAPTER NINE

AND now I saw the Lord standing above the altar; Smite column
there, he cried, lintel there dislodge, nest of ill-gotten gains! [1] To the
last man, the sword must take its toll; refuge shall be none. Flee they,
2 never a fugitive shall escape; from the pit beneath I will dig them up,
3 from heaven above I will drag them down; hide they on Carmel's
heights, I will search and seize them, lurk they in the sea's depths, my writ
4 runs there; maw of monster shall devour them. Let enemy drive them
into exile, even there the sword shall be my pursuivant; watch and ward
I keep over them, never doubt it, but to their undoing.
5 ... The Lord God of hosts, whose touch melts earth, to the hurt of all
that dwell in it, makes it everywhere mount up and sink, like Egypt's
6 river in flood; his the arched stairway of heaven, his the knitted frame of
earth; beckons he to the waters of the sea, and over the earth spreads
them, Javé his name!
7 Ethiop or Israelite, what care I? the Lord says. God that brought you
here from Egypt was God that brought the Philistines from Caphtor,
8 brought the Syrians from Cir! [2] Divine regard that watches ever this
kingdom, marks ever its guilt; I will blot it out, believe me, from the face
of the earth.
And blot out the name of Jacob altogether? Nay, not that, the Lord
9 says. At my command, the whole world shall be a sieve, to sift the race
of Israel as corn is sifted in the riddle, and never a grain [3] cast out loose
10 on the bare ground; at the sword's point they shall die, all the guilty that
are found among my people; the guilty, who now flatter themselves that
11 evil shall never come next or nigh them. Then, I mean to rebuild the
fallen dwelling-place of David, all its breaches made good, all its ruins
12 restored; it shall stand once more as it stood long ago; empire it shall
13 have over the Edomites, and all the Gentile folk I claim for my own. A

---

[1] 'Nest of ill-gotten gains'; the meaning of this phrase is very doubtful.

[2] The Latin version here gives Cappadocia for Caphtor, and Cyrene for Cir,
as elsewhere. The identification is by no means probable.

[3] 'Never a grain'; the word used is of doubtful significance. But the meaning
seems to be that all the Israelites will go into captivity, and this will be a sieve
to separate the good from the worthless among them; none will escape, as a
grain of corn might escape by being thrown carelessly over the sieve's edge.

time is coming, the Lord says, when ploughman shall tread on the heels of reaper, sower's task begin ere vintager's is ended; never a mountain-side but shall run with sweet wine, never a hill but its rugged nature shall
14 be tamed.[1] I will bring back my people of Israel from its exile, to rebuild ruined cities and dwell there, plant vineyards and drink of them, till
15 gardens and eat the fruits of them. Firm root they shall take in their native soil, never again to be torn away from the home I have given them, says the Lord, thy own God.

---

[1] 'Its rugged nature shall be tamed'; literally, in the Latin version, 'it shall be cultivated'; in the Hebrew text, 'it shall melt.'

THE PROPHECY OF ABDIAS

HERE follows the vision of Abdias. What doom does the Lord God
pronounce on Edom? What bruit is this has reached our ears, what
embassage has been sent abroad among the nations? Up, march we out to
2 engage him in battle![1] Sorry the lot I have given thee among the peoples
3 of the world, no better than a thing of contempt; yet, dwelling where
thou dost in the clefts of the rocks, thou art puffed up with pride; high
thou hast built thy throne, and thinkest there is none can drag thee down
4 to earth. Build thy eyrie high as the eagle, nest, if thou wilt, among the
5 stars, I will yet drag thee down thence, the Lord says. Strange, the
silence that has fallen upon Edom! Thieves were they, midnight robbers,
that had assailed thee, at least they had been content to carry off what
needed them, some gleanings at least those vintagers would have left thee!
6 But now, see how Esau is ransacked, how all his treasury is rifled! See
how the very folk that are in league with thee drive thee back to thy own
frontier, thy own confederates playing thee false, pressing thee hard!
Stabbed from beneath by boon companions of thy own? Thou art a fool
for thy pains.
8 Day of doom, the Lord says, when wise man shall be none in Edom,
9 nor any prudent counsellor on all Esau's hill-side; dismayed the warriors
of Theman shall be, till slaughter leaves all the mountains of Esau deso-
10 late. What wonder if hopes of thine come to nothing, name of thine perish eternally, that didst assail thy own brother, Jacob, with murderous
11 wrong? Hast thou forgotten the day when thou stoodest aloof, while the
enemy disarmed his ranks, while aliens thronged through yonder gates, and
parcelled out Jerusalem by lot, thyself making common cause with them?
12 What, look on idly, when fortune turns against that brother of thine;
13 nay, triumph over Juda's fall, boast of his calamity? He overthrown, and
thou wouldst find thy way in at the gates of my own city; he overthrown,
and thou wouldst rejoice at his discomfiture; he overthrown, and thou
14 wouldst offer him battle? Thou wouldst take up thy post in the breach,
and cut off the fugitive, bar the way to the straggler, when all is lost?
15 Be sure of this, a time is soon coming when the Lord will summon all
the nations to their account; then, as thou didst, it shall be done to thee,
16 in thy own coin thou shalt be paid. The cup of vengeance you, my people,
have drunk, there on that mountain which is my sanctuary, all the
heathen shall drink henceforward; drink, ay, drink deep, and fall into
17 forgetfulness, as if they had never been. But here, on mount Sion, all

---

[1] It seems possible that some of these early verses are a quotation from an
earlier prophecy, which is also cited by Jeremias (49.9 and 14–16).

shall be deliverance, all shall be holiness, and their spoilers the men
18 of Jacob shall despoil.   A fire Jacob shall be, a living flame the sons of
Joseph, and Esau's race stubble before their onset ; the spark once kindled,
all shall be consumed, and of Esau's race no memory be left ; the Lord
decrees it.
19   Hill-country of Esau shall fall to the southern folk, and Philistia to the
men of the plain ; all that is Ephraim and Samaria now shall be theirs, and
20 Galaad shall be made over to Benjamin.   Warriors of Israel, banished
far away, shall hold all the Chanaanite lands, Sarepta their northern
frontier, men of Jerusalem, come back from the shores of Bosphorus to
21 claim the cities of the south.   No lack of champions Sion shall have, to do
justice on the mountains of Edom ; and of that empire the Lord himself
shall be sovereign ruler.

THE PROPHECY OF JONAS

CHAPTER ONE

2 THE Lord's voice came to Jonas, the son of Amathi: Up, and to the great city of Nineve make thy way; I would have thee preach to
3 them; great guilt of theirs claims my cognizance. Rise up he did, but his thought was, he would escape to Tharsis, and there avoid the Lord's scrutiny. So he made his way to Joppa, and there, sure enough, was a ship bound for Tharsis; passage-money was paid, and aboard went Jonas with the rest of them, sailing for Tharsis to be out of the Lord's way.
4 But now the Lord sent out a boisterous wind over the sea, that raised a great tempest there, and the ship was like to have been broken all to
5 pieces. Sore afraid the mariners were, and loud they called upon their god; ay, and fell to throwing the tackle overboard, to lighten ship. And what of Jonas? He had gone down into the ship's hold, and fallen fast
6 asleep. But that would not serve; up came the captain and asked what he meant, to lie there sleeping? Up, said he, and cry out upon thy God! Who knows but God will take pity on us, and grant us our lives yet?
7 By this, the ship's company were of another counsel; Nay, said one to other, cast we the lot, and so find out how it is that such peril has befallen
8 us! Cast lots they did, and Jonas was singled out. Tell us, they cried, for whose sake [1] it is that we are come into such peril! Tell us what thy errand is, whence thou art journeying and whither, what nation it was
9 gave thee birth. I am a Hebrew, he told them, and worship the Lord,
10 the God of heaven, that made the sea and the dry land both. And when they heard (for he told them all) that this was a man who would escape from the Lord's sight, they were in a great taking of fear. What ailed
11 thee? they asked. And how must we use thee, if we would have yonder seas calmed for us? (Even as they spoke, the waves grew more angry yet.)
12 Why, said he, take me up and throw me over the ship's side; doubt there is none, I am the cause of all this peril that has befallen you.
13 What would you? They fell to the oars, but could nothing avail; ever
14 angrier grew the seas about them. And at last they cried out upon the Lord; Take we this man's life, they said, let it not be to our own undoing! Do not charge us with the death of an innocent man, thou who hast so
15 manifested thy divine will! And with that, they took Jonas up, and threw him over the ship's side. All at once, the raging of the sea was stilled;

---

[1] 'For whose sake'; that is, probably, 'in vengeance for whom,' the assumption being that Jonas was a murderer (Ac. 28.4). But this clause is omitted by the best manuscripts of the Septuagint Greek, and it may possibly be a footnote on the similar clause in verse 7, accidentally included in the text.

16 what fear fell on those mariners! What sacrifices they made, what vows
they offered to the Lord!

CHAPTER TWO

AND what of Jonas? At the Lord's bidding, a great sea-beast had
swallowed him up; and there, in the belly of it, three days spent he
2 and three nights. This was the prayer which Jonas made to the Lord
3 his God, there in the belly of the sea-beast: Call I on the Lord in my
peril, redress he grants me; [1] from the very womb of the grave call I, thou
4 art listening to me! Here in the depths of the sea's heart thou wouldst
5 cast me away, flood of thine, wave of thine sweeping over me, till it
seemed as if I were shut out from thy regard: yet life thou grantest me;
6 I shall gaze on thy holy temple [2] once again. Around me the deadly waters
close, the depths engulf me, the weeds are wrapped about my head;
7 mountain caverns I must plumb, the very bars of earth my unrelenting
prison; and still, O Lord my God, thou wilt raise me, living, from the
8 tomb. Daunted this heart, yet still of the Lord I would bethink me;
9 prayer of mine should reach him, far away in his holy temple! Let fools
10 that court false worship all hope of pardon forgo; mine to do sacrifice in
thy honour, vows made and paid to the Lord, my deliverer!
11   And now, at the Lord's bidding, the sea-beast cast Jonas up again,
high and dry on the beach.

CHAPTER THREE

2 A SECOND time the Lord's voice came to Jonas: Up, and to the
great city of Nineve make thy way; there preach, what preach I bid
3 thee. That voice he obeyed; rose up and took the road for Nineve, a great
4 city indeed, three days' journey from end to end. And when he had
advanced into it as far as one day's journey would carry him, he began
5 crying out, In forty days, Nineve will be overthrown. With that, the
Ninevites shewed faith in God, rich and poor alike, proclaiming a fast
6 and putting on sackcloth; nay, the king of Nineve himself, when word of
it reached him, came down from his throne, put on sackcloth, and sat

---

[1] Verses 3–10: Cf. Ps. 119.1; 17.7; 41.8; 30.23; 68.2; 141.4; 142.4; 17.6; 30.7;
116.17, 18; 3.9. The occurrence of such a cento proves how complete a body of
psalms was in existence at the time when this book was written.
    [2] The temple here alluded to is presumably the temple at Jerusalem, although
Jonas is usually regarded as belonging, not to Juda, but to the northern kingdom
(IV Kg. 14.25).

7 down humbly in the dust. And a cry was raised in Nineve, at the bidding
of the king and his nobles, A fast for man and beast, for herd and flock;
8 no food is to be eaten, no water drunk; let man and beast go covered
with sackcloth; cry out lustily to the Lord, and forsake, each of you, his
9 sinful life, his wrongful deeds! God may yet relent and pardon, forgo
10 his avenging anger and spare our lives. Thus, when God saw them
amending their lives in good earnest, he spared them, in his mercy, their
threatened punishment.

CHAPTER FOUR

AS for Jonas, he took it sore amiss, and was an angry man that day.
2 And thus he made his prayer to the Lord: See if this be not the very
thought I had, far away in my own country! Good cause had I to seek
refuge at Tharsis from such an errand as this. I knew from the first what
manner of God thou art, how kind and merciful, how slow to punish,
3 how rich in pardon, vengeance ever ready to forgo. A boon of thee, Lord!
4 take away this life of mine; I had rather die than live. Why, the Lord
said, what anger is this? [1]
5 Jonas had left the city, and sat now under a little arbour he had made
for himself on the east of it, waiting there in the shade to see what doom
6 would fall on Nineve. And now, at the Lord God's bidding, an ivy-plant
grew up over Jonas' head, to give him shade and shelter after his toiling;
7 and great joy he had of his ivy-plant. But when the morrow dawned,
came at God's bidding a worm, that struck at the plant's root and killed
8 it. Up rose the sun, and at the Lord's bidding the sirocco came; here was
Jonas with the sun's rays beating on his head, and all of a sweat. Now
indeed his heart's prayer was, he might die; Better death than life, said he.
9 Why, said the Lord, what anger is this over an ivy-plant? Deadly angry
10 am I, Jonas answered, and no marvel either. Great pity thou hast, the
Lord said, for yonder ivy-plant, that was not of thy growing, and no toil
11 cost thee; a plant that springs in a night, and in a night must wither! And
what of Nineve? Here is a great city, with a hundred and twenty thousand folk in it, and none of them can tell right from left, all these cattle,
too; and may I not spare Nineve?

---

[1] The exact force of the Hebrew idiom used here is uncertain. Some think it
means, 'Hast thou good reason to be angry?'; others would translate, 'Art thou
very angry?'

THE PROPHECY OF MICHAEAS

CHAPTER ONE

THIS message came from the Lord to Michaeas the Morasthite, during the reigns of Joathan, Achaz and Ezechias in Juda; this revelation was made to him concerning Samaria and Jerusalem both together.

2 A word for you, nations far and near; let the whole world give audience, and all the world contains! Listen to this indictment the Lord God

3 brings, from his high throne all beholding. See, where the Lord comes out from his dwelling-place; and, as he makes his way down, the topmost

4 peaks of earth for his stairway, melt hills at his touch, melt valleys like wax before the fire, like water over the steep rocks flowing away!

5 Alas, what betokens it? What but Jacob's going astray, what but guilt of Israel's line? Head and front of Jacob's sinning Samaria needs must

6 be, sure as Jerusalem is Juda's place of pilgrimage.[1] In ruin Samaria shall lie, a heap of stones in the open countryside, a terrace for vineyards; all down yonder valley I will drag the stones of her, till her very

7 foundations are laid bare. Shattered all those idols must be, burnt to ashes the gauds she wears; [2] never an image but shall be left forlorn; all shall go the way of a harlot's wages, that were a harlot's wages from the first.

8 For this, should I not raise the dirge aloud? Barefoot go I and stripped;

9 jackal nor ostrich cries out more lamentably. Hurt is here past all cure, that to Juda itself must spread; Jerusalem itself, mart of my own country-

10 side, shall feel the blow. Gate of Gath[3] must never hear the news, hushed

---

[1] In the original, the latter part of this verse reads simply, 'What is the crime of Israel; is it not Samaria? And what are the hill-shrines of Juda, are they not Jerusalem?' The sense of the phrase cannot be determined with certainty.

[2] 'The gauds she wears'; literally, 'the wages of a harlot,' as in the concluding part of the sentence. The prophet seems to regard the meretricious accessories of Samaritan worship not as a gift from man to God, but as a gift from God to man (possibly in allusion to the idea that false gods were responsible for Israel's prosperity, cf. Os. 2.5). The end of the verse is perhaps merely a proverb, 'lightly come, lightly go,' used of wealth won on easy terms.

[3] Gath seems to have been wrested from the Philistines by Ozias (II Par. 26.6); Michaeas points out that this and the neighbouring towns will once more be lost to Juda as the result of the Assyrian invasion. He plays upon the names of these towns by a series of rough assonances, of which the rendering given above may afford some idea. Unfortunately, the text of verses 10–15 seems to have been much disturbed; the meaning of the Hebrew is doubtful in several cases, and the Latin version, like the Septuagint Greek, yields no satisfactory sense, even where it can be construed as grammar. The Latin version also represents most of the place-names by common nouns. It is, therefore, the sense of the Hebrew text that is given here.

be the sound of weeping; afar at Beth-aphra cast the dust on your heads.
11 Away with you, Shaphir's folk, shivering and shamed; of coming and
going in Saanan sign is none; mourning of Beth-ezel . . . has taken the
12 ground from under your feet.   Marred, now, are the anxious hopes of
Maroth; so ruthless the Lord's decree against yonder gates of Jerusalem.
13 Recklessly at Lachis [1] harness they steed to chariot; Lachis, that first
betrayed poor Sion into guilt, that was Israel's mistress in wrong-doing!
14 Marriage-dower this daughter of thine, Moreseth-gath, shall cost thee;
15 here is Achsib, too, for the royal policy how rude a set-back!   Thy
marches, Maresa, shall be ridden once again; to Odollam . . .
16   . . . Israel's glory shall come.[2] Such pride in thy children! Shaven bare
thy brow; vulture itself is not so bald; alas, for sons of thine exiled far
away!

CHAPTER TWO

OUT upon you, that lie awake over dreams of mischief, schemes of ill,
and are up at dawn of day to execute them, soon as your godless
2 hands find opportunity!   Covet they house or lands, house or lands by
robbery become theirs; ever their oppression comes between a man and
3 his home, a man and his inheritance.   And I, too, the Lord says, am
devising mischief, mischief against the whole clan of you; never think to
shake it off from your necks and walk proudly as of old; ill days are
4 coming.   A by-word then they shall make of you, dirge and dole raise over
you most dolorously: Stripped, stripped bare! My country's bounds
removed! Come he but once again, that so parcels out our lands, all is
5 lost to me!   Trust me, when lands are allotted among the Lord's people,
never shall one of yonder clan have rope to throw.[3]
6   Prophets, leave your prophesying; word of prophecy is never for such
7 as these, never may shame overtake them.[4]   What, cry they of Jacob, is
the Lord so easily offended? Are his designs indeed so unfavourable? Nay,

---

[1] The allusion to Lachis as specially responsible for Juda's misdoings has not
been convincingly explained.

[2] It seems impossible to find any meaning in the phrase, 'the glory of Israel
shall come to Odollam,' and the text of the verse may well have suffered in transmission.

[3] Literally, 'thou shalt not have a man to throw a rope.' It is difficult to see
what is the singular subject addressed as 'thou,' unless it be the clan mentioned
in verse 3, though indeed we might have expected a feminine preposition to
follow it.

[4] Verses 6–11 are very obscure, and some critics think the text has suffered
from considerable faults of copying. Verse 6 begins, in the Hebrew text, 'Do not
prophesy, they will prophesy, they will not prophesy to these,' and in the Latin
version, 'Do not speak speaking, it will not drip upon these.'

certain it is, if a man will follow the straight path, award of mine shall
8 prosper him; but what of you? Has not this people of mine long counted
you enemies, rising up to arraign you? Robbers, that will have cloak and
9 coat both; what marvel if simple folk are up in arms against you? My
people! And you would dispossess its women of the homes they loved,
10 take away from its children . . . my glory for ever.[1] Do you, in your turn,
rise up and go your ways; no resting-place shall you have here; corruption most foul the guilt of this land shall breed in it.
11   Alas, that I should be one beckoned by the spirit, and not rather some
forger of lies! Wine and revel to inspire him, he might prophesy, and a
12 people such as this take him for an oracle: Trust me, Jacob, I mean to
assemble thee in full strength, rally all that is left of Israel in one place,
thronging like sheep in fold, like herd in byre, hum of voices echoing all
13 around; where the breach has been made ready for them, break they out
and pass on their way, sally forth with a king to lead them, with the Lord
at their head![2]

CHAPTER THREE

B UT no, this is my word to you, chieftains of Jacob's line, rulers of
2 Israel: Who should acclaim justice, if not you? Alas, that you should
be the foes of right, the friends of wrong! Beasts of prey, that will have
3 skin and flesh both, leave nothing save the bare bone. My people! And
you will gnaw flesh of them, tear skin of them, break bones of them;
4 cut them to pieces, meat for your pot, roast for your oven! What marvel,
if the Lord will not listen to such cry as yours, turns his back on you in
your distress, for your ill deserving?
5   And this message the Lord has for prophets that guide my people
amiss, prophets that must have their mouths filled ere they will cry, All's
well! sop thou must give them, else thou shalt be their sworn enemy.
6 Visions would you see, all shall be night around you, search you the
skies, you shall search in the dark; never a prophet but his sun is set, his

---

[1] It seems difficult to believe that the text has not suffered here, either by corruption or by omission.

[2] Verses 11–13 are usually printed as if a fresh paragraph began with verse 12.
But verses 12 and 13, in that case, wholly interrupt the run of the passage, and
the note of encouragement is particularly out of place here. The rendering given
above assumes that verses 12 and 13 are the utterance of the imaginary false
prophet, verse 1 of the next chapter being the message which Michaeas, as a true
prophet, is forced to deliver. It is doubtful whether there is any reference here
to a return from exile; the situation envisaged seems rather to be a sortie from
a besieged stronghold (cf. IV Kg. 25.4).

7 day turned into twilight! Seers that see nothing, baffled diviners, acknow-
8 ledge they, finger on lip, word from God is none.   But here stands one
that is full of the Lord's spirit; vigour it lends me, and discernment, and
boldness, fault of Jacob to denounce, guilt of Israel to proclaim.

9   A word with you, chieftains of Jacob's line, rulers of Israel, that hold
10 right abominable, and all justice pervert;   that build up strength of Sion,
11 fortunes of Jerusalem, with deeds of bloodshed and of wrong!   Never a
judge but has his price; never a priest tradition teaches, but for hire;
never a prophet but must have his hand lined with silver! And all the
while, how lean they on the Lord! Is not he in their midst? How should
12 harm befall them?   Trust me, for such guilt as yours I will turn mount
Sion into plough-lands; standing heaps of stones that were once Jerusalem, and brushwood of the high forest growing over the Temple hill.

CHAPTER FOUR

THE Temple hill![1] One day it shall stand there, highest of all the
mountain heights, overtopping the peaks of them, and the nations will
2 flock there together.   A multitude of peoples will make their way to it,
crying, Come, let us climb up to the Lord's mountain peak, to the house
where the God of Jacob dwells; he shall teach us the right way, we will
walk in the paths he has chosen. The Lord's command shall go out from
3 Sion, his word from Jerusalem,   and he will sit in judgement on the
nations, giving his award to peoples far away. Sword they will fashion
into ploughshare and spear into pruning-hook; no room there shall be
4 for nation to levy war against nation, and train itself in arms.   At ease
you shall sit, each of you with his own vine, his own fig-tree to give him
shade, and none to raise the alarm; such blessing the Lord of hosts pro-
5 nounces on you.   Let other nations go their own way, each with the name
of its own god to rally it; ours to march under the banner of Javé, our
God for ever and for evermore![2]

6   When that time comes, the Lord says, I will gather them in again and
take them to myself, flock of mine that go limping and straggling, ever
7 since I brought calamity on them;   lame shall yet be a stock to breed
from, and wayworn shall grow into a sturdy race; here in Sion they shall
8 dwell, and the Lord be king over them, for ever henceforward. And thou,
the watch-tower of that flock, cloud-capped fastness where the lady Sion

---

[1] *vv.* 1–3. The same words occur at the beginning of Is. 2. Since Michaeas was
Isaias' contemporary, it seems probable that both prophets are quoting from
some older fragment of literature.
[2] Literally, 'All peoples will walk each in the name of its god, but we will
walk in the name of Javé our God for ever and for evermore.'

reigns, power shall come back to thee as of old, once more Jerusalem shall be a queen.

9 When that time comes! At this present time, what anguish is this constrains thee? Have king and counsellor played thee false, that the pangs
10 of travail take hold on thee? Sorrow thou well mayst, lady of Sion, and labour as any woman brought to bed; city thou must needs leave, and lodge in the open countryside, nay, to distant Babylon thou must journey;[1] there it is thou wilt find deliverance, there it is the Lord will
11 ransom thee from the power of thy enemies. At this present time, how many the nations that gather about thee, crying, Death to the adulteress!
12 Feast we our eyes on Sion's downfall! Little they know God's thoughts; little they guess that he is but storing them up, like wheat on the thresh-
13 ing-floor! Up, lady of Sion, and set about the threshing of them! Horn of iron, hoof of bronze he will give thee, to grind all that conspiracy of nations to dust. Forfeit to the Lord their ill-gotten gains shall be; nothing of theirs but must be his, who is master of the whole earth.

CHAPTER FIVE

AT this present time, what is left thee but to muster thy roving bands, daughter of an outlaw king? Hard siege presses us now; smitten on the cheek, now, is the ruler of Israel.[2]
2 Bethlehem-Ephrata! Least do they reckon thee among all the clans of Juda? Nay, it is from thee I look to find a prince that shall rule over Israel. Whence comes he? From the first beginning, from ages untold![3]
3 Marvel not, then, if the Lord abandons his people[4] for a time, until

---

[1] The mention of Babylon suggests, to the modern reader, the Captivity, which took place a century later. Michaeas' own contemporaries will have imagined that they were going to take refuge in Babylon as in a friendly country (IV Kg. 20.12).

[2] The beginning of this verse reads literally, 'Now thou shalt be laid waste, daughter of freebooters'; in the Hebrew text, 'thou shalt be laid waste' is 'form thyself into bands' (or possibly 'cut thyself,' i.e., in sign of mourning). Thus both the meaning of the verse and its historical background are obscure; but conceivably the prophet is preaching guerrilla warfare, and reminding his fellow-countrymen that this was, in early days, king David's experience.

[3] Our present Hebrew text reads, 'Thou (art) too small to be among the clans of Juda'; but there may have been an alternative reading, 'thou art not small among the clans of Juda.' This would account for the rendering given in Mt. 2.6, without making it necessary to suppose that the translator of St Matthew's Aramaic was guilty of an error. 'From ages untold'; literally, 'from the days of eternity,' but this is a phrase used somewhat loosely by Hebrew authors (cf. 7.20 below), and no certain theological inferences can be based on it.

[4] Literally, 'he abandons them,' but the sense is presumably that given.

she who is in travail has brought forth her child; others there are, bre-
4 thren of his,[1] that must be restored to the citizenship of Israel. Enabled
by the Lord his God, confident in that mighty protection, stands he, our
shepherd, and safely folds his flock; fame of him now reaches to the
5 world's end; who else should be its hope of recovery? What though the
Assyrian invade our country, trample down our strongholds? Seven
leaders of men we shall find to marshal us, and an eighth yet in reserve;
6 sword in hand, they shall herd the men of Assyria, naked steel for the land
of Nemrod! Invade they, trample they as they will, he shall be our
deliverance.
7   Poor remnant of Jacob, lost among that multitude of peoples! Yet
thrive it shall; does not the grass thrive, with dew and shower from the
Lord to water it, nor looks for man's tending, unbeholden to our human
8 toil? Poor remnant of Jacob, among those heathen multitudes lost! Yet
lion amid the forest herds, lion's whelp amid flock of sheep, finds not
9 easier passage, brings not down more inexorably his prey. High triumph
thou shalt have over thy enemies; perish all that bear thee ill will!
10 * All other help, the Lord says, shall then be denied thee; gone, horse
11 and chariot of thine, the cities lost, ruined the strongholds. Sorcery thou
12 shalt have none to trust in, nor divinings; gone idol and sacred pillar of
13 thine, nor any of thy own imaginings left thee to worship; uprooted the
14 woods of thy false worship, fallen the cities. Only then shall my fierce
anger find its scope, only then fall my vengeance upon the nations that
defied me.

CHAPTER SIX

LISTEN to this message I have from the Lord: Up, and to the mountains make thy complaint, let the hill-sides echo with thy voice!
2 Listen they must, yonder sturdy bastions of earth, while the Lord im-
3 pleads his people; Israel stands upon its trial now. Tell me, my people,
4 what have I done, that thou shouldst be a-weary of me? Answer me. Was
it ill done, to rescue thee from Egypt, set thee free from a slave's prison,
5 send Moses and Aaron and Mary to guide thee on thy way? Bethink
thee, what designs had Balach, king of Moab, and how Balaam the son
of Beor answered him . . . from Setim to Galgala; and canst thou doubt,
then, the faithfulness of the Lord's friendship? [2]

---

[1] Apparently the brethren of the Messianic prince; the Septuagint Greek gives
'their brethren,' but this is probably guesswork.
[2] It seems probable that some words have been lost here; Setim and Galgala
are not connected in any way with Balaam's prophecy, but are, respectively, the
last camping-ground of Israel before, and its first camping-ground after, the
passage of Jordan.

6 How best may I humble myself before the Lord, that is God most high? What offering shall I bring? Calf, think you, of a year old, for my 7 burnt-sacrifice? Fall rams by the thousand, fattened buck-goats by the ten thousand, will the Lord be better pleased? Shall gift of first-born for 8 wrong-doing atone, body's fruit for soul's assoiling? Nay, son of Adam, what need to ask?[1] Best of all it is, and this above all the Lord demands of thee, right thou shouldst do, and ruth love, and carry thyself humbly in the presence of thy God.

9 So comes the divine voice to yonder city; best he shall thrive, that stands in awe![2] Listen, fellow tribesmen, to that voice; which of you dares 10 acclaim it? What of homes unhallowed, that hide yet the ill-gotten gain,[3] 11 the false measure that calls down my vengeance? Here the uneven scales, 12 there the bag of short weights, and shall I hold you acquitted? City where the rich are ever busy with oppression, where all is treachery, and 13 a man has a tongue in his mouth only to deceive! Thy turn, now, to feel 14 my lash; thy guilt is thy undoing. Thine to eat, and eating, never have thy fill; for all alike, now, the same affliction.[4] Thine to enslave, but thy slaves never to keep; those thou hast, I mean to make over to the sword. 15 Sow shalt thou, and never reap, press olive, and never anoint thee, tread 16 grape, and no wine drink. Commands of Amri thou wouldst obey, not mine, Ahab's purposes, not mine, fulfil; their bidding if thou wouldst follow, what marvel that I should mark thee down for ruin, Jerusalem for the hiss of scorn? Shame of its own origins the people that is mine must bear.[5]

CHAPTER SEVEN

YOUR tears for Sion! Not more pitiful work is gleaning when the vintage is done; never a cluster to eat; for the ripe figs belly craves

---

[1] 'What need to ask?'; literally, 'I will tell thee,' but in the Hebrew text 'he has told thee' (or possibly, 'it has been told thee').

[2] 'Stands in awe'; literally, 'stands in awe of thy name.' This verse is very obscure in the Hebrew text, and its interpretation remains uncertain.

[3] 'The ill-gotten gain'; literally, 'the embers of ill-gotten gain,' but it would appear that the Latin version and the Septuagint Greek have here misunderstood a word in the original.

[4] The Hebrew word here rendered 'affliction' occurs nowhere else, and the rendering given in the Latin is perhaps only a conjecture. In the second part of the verse, the Hebrew text is generally understood as referring, not to enslavement, but to the removal of wives, children, etc., into a place of safety.

[5] The concluding words of the chapter read literally, 'You shall bear the reproach of my people.' Some think this means, 'You (the rich) shall bear the reproach of my people in general'; others suppose that there is a slight error in the manuscripts, and that we should render, 'You shall bear the taunts of the (heathen) nations.'

2 in vain. Fled is piety, vanished honesty, from human kind; murderous plots afoot; the hunt is up everywhere, man spreading his nets for man.
3 Ever the wrong done, and fair names devised for it; ruler must have his benevolence, and judge his gratuity, and tyrant makes known what is his
4 earnest wish; they know well how to wrap it up.[1] Cruel as thorns they be, that are kindliest of them, close as thorn-edge, that are honest above the rest. Surely this is the day thy watchmen foretold, surely thou wilt call them to account; not long delayed their last extremity!
5 Trust no man, give thy heart to no man, though he be friend and counsellor of thine; against the wife that lies on thy bosom, guard the
6 entry of thy lips; here, where son fools father, and daughter her mother, and son's wife her mother-in-law, where a man's own household are his
7 enemies! On the Lord my eyes are set; it is to God I look for my protection; my own God, and will he deny me audience?
8 City that Sion hatest, never triumph over her fall; fall I, it is but to
9 rise again, sit I in darkness, the Lord will be my light. The Lord's displeasure I must bear, I that have sinned against him, till at last he admits my plea, and grants redress. Out into the light he will bring me, to find
10 him faithful still. Sore abashed that enemy of mine shall behold it; only yesterday she was crying, What is become of thy God now? Welcome the sight, when she is trampled down like mire in the streets![2]
11 Day of pell-mell disorder it shall be, the day of thy walls' rebuilding;
12 a day when folk shall resort to thee from all the lands that lie between Assyria and the towns of Egypt, between Egypt and . . . Euphrates,
13 between sea and sea, mountain-range and mountain-range.[3] By then, the whole countryside will be lying desolate, such reward the inhabitants
14 of it have earned by their ill-doing. With that staff of thine, gather thy people in, the flock that is thy very own, scattered now in the forest

---

[1] The interpretation of this verse is difficult; the meaning given above seems to fit the Latin best.

[2] We have no means of determining whether the last thirteen words are part of what the rival city used to say about Sion, or part of what Sion will say about the rival city.

[3] The passage is obscure, and there is some reason to doubt whether the text has been preserved accurately. It runs literally, 'Day for the building of thy walls, that (is a) day the limit is removed far off; that (is a) day and he (or, people) shall come all the way to thee, all the way from Assur and the cities of Mazor, all the way from Mazor and to the River, and the sea from the sea and the mountain the mountain.' 'Limit' can hardly mean 'frontier,' a notion which is always expressed elsewhere by a different word (over two hundred times in the Old Testament). The phrase 'limit is removed' is a jingle of words, probably meant to suggest confusion, like our 'higgledy-piggledy.' Mazor is translated as a proper noun ('fortress') in the Latin version. It is hard to see why the space between Assyria and Egypt should be regarded as different from the space between Egypt and the Euphrates; possibly something has dropped out.

glades, with rich plenty all around them; Basan and Galaad for their
15 pasture-grounds, as in the days of old.   Now for such wondrous evidences
16 of power as marked thy rescuing of them from Egypt! Here is a sight to
make the Gentiles hold their valour cheap, stand there dumb; ay, and why
17 not deaf too? Let them lick the dust, serpent-fashion, crawl out from
their homes, like scared reptiles, in terror of the Lord our God; much
cause they shall have to fear him.

18   Was there ever such a God, so ready to forgive sins, to overlook faults,
among the scattered remnant of his chosen race? He will exact vengeance
19 no more; he loves to pardon. He will relent, and have mercy on us,
20 quashing our guilt, burying our sins away sea-deep.   Thou wilt keep thy
promise to Jacob, shew mercy to Abraham, thy promised mercies of long
ago.

THE PROPHECY OF NAHUM

CHAPTER ONE

WHAT burden for Nineve? Here is matter revealed to Nahum the
2 Elcesite. A jealous lover the Lord is, and takes full vengeance; full
vengeance the Lord takes, no stranger, he, to indignation; nor spares
3 rebel, nor forgets the wrong. Bide his time he may, but power lacks not;
guilty is guilty still. Storm and whirlwind are the path he treads, cloud-
4 wrack the dust he spurns; the sea at his rebuke dries up, streams turn
into a desert, Basan withers away, and Carmel, all the leaf of Lebanon
5 fades. Shrink and shrivel they, mountain-top and hill-side, before him;
6 quakes earth at his coming, and all the world of men with it. Alas, when
the blow of his resentment falls, who may confront that fierce anger unmoved? Here is vengeance poured out like fire, to melt the hard rock!
7 None so gracious as the Lord, no strength like his in the hour of distress; do but trust him, and he will keep thee in his care . . .
8 . . . Flood-tide shall overwhelm the site of it;[1] ever his enemies find
9 darkness at their heels. Think not, by shifts of yours, to thwart the Lord's
will; believe me, he will take full toll, there shall be no second visitation.
10 Close be it as thicket of thorns, yonder conspiracy over the cups, all at
once, like scorched stubble, they shall be consumed.[2]
11 Here is one of thy number devising rebellion against the Lord, folly's
12 counsellor. But thus the Lord says: Be they in full muster? At least there
are over many of them; they must be shorn of their strength. It will pass;
13 once chastened is chastened enough,[3] and now I mean to shatter that
yoke of his that lies on thy back, tear thy chains asunder . . .
14 For thee, this doom the Lord has; race shall never spring from thee to
bear thy name, nor in the temple of thy god any images be left, cast or

---

[1] Since there is no noun in verse 7 to which the words 'of it' can conceivably
refer, the suspicion naturally arises that there may have been an accidental
omission in the text.

[2] Some modern scholars, by means of altering and transposing the text, make
verses 1–10 into part of an abecedarian poem; i.e., one in which the first verse
in the Hebrew begins with Aleph, the second with Beth, and so on (cf. e.g.,
Ps. 24). There is some reason to think that Ps. 9 was originally abecedarian, and
the traces of it were confused by subsequent editing (as happened with the Hymn
of Friday Lauds). But a careful examination of the present chapter suggests that
the apparent traces of arrangement may be due to mere coincidence.

[3] The meaning of the Hebrew text here is uncertain, and many scholars think
it corrupt. It runs, literally, 'Thus the Lord says: Are they complete? (or, If they
are complete) even so they are many; and even so they will be shaved. And it
(or, he) will pass, and I have afflicted thee but I will not afflict thee any more'.

carven; and I will write it on thy tomb-stone, thou wast nothing worth.[1]

15   See where they bring good news on the mountain heights, proclaiming that all is well! Now, Juda, keep holiday; paid be thy vows; mocking enemy shall pass through thee no more; never a one left.[2]

CHAPTER TWO

HERE is an enemy at thy gates that scatters all before him; here is close siege, no entry but must be guarded; gird thee well, summon

2 up all thy strength! Honour of Juda the Lord retrieves now, and honour of Israel both, that have seen the spoiler ransack them, strip vineyard

3 bare.[3] Bright flash that enemy's shields, warriors of his go clad in scarlet; dart like flame his chariots as he goes to the attack, dizzily sways char-

4 ioteer. How jostle they in the streets, those chariots, hurtle they in the open market-place; dazzle they like flame of torches, like the lightning that comes and goes!

5   Alas, for the muster-roll of the king's vassals,[4] fallen as they went about their task! Swiftly they manned the walls, but the engines were in place

6 already. Open, now, stands the water-gate, crumbles yonder temple into

7 dust. Alas, for warriors of Nineve gone into exile, for maids of hers led away,[5] that sigh and moan like ring-doves in the bitterness of their heart!

8 Nineve, welcome sight as pools of water to the fugitive;[6] stay, stay! But

9 never a one looks back. Out with silver, out with gold of hers; store is

10 here of costly stuff beyond price or reckoning! Roof to cellar rifled and

---

[1] This verse is evidently addressed not to Juda but to Assyria, and some think it has been accidentally misplaced.

[2] Verses 11–15. Some part, or all, of verses 11–15 may refer to the invasion of Sennacherib (IV Kg. 18 sqq.).

[3] Meaning and bearing of this verse are obscure; it tells us that the Lord will restore, or perhaps remove, or perhaps requite, the excellency, or perhaps the pride, of Jacob, and also that of Israel. 'Jacob' is a strict equivalent of 'Israel' as a rule; here, if the text is sound, it can only be conjectured that Jacob stands for Juda, and Israel for the ten tribes. Some think the whole verse has been accidentally misplaced.

[4] Literally, 'he will remember (or perhaps mention) his princes.' There is no evidence that the verb can mean 'to summon,' and the phrase is so awkward that we may be tempted to suspect the prophet wrote something else; e.g., 'his menfolk, his princes.'

[5] The word rendered 'warriors' in the Latin more probably refers, perhaps by a proper name, to some queen or goddess; the word used for 'maids' has, everywhere else, the sense of female attendants.

[6] 'Nineve, welcome sight as pools of water to the fugitive'; the Hebrew text here differs from that of the Septuagint Greek, and of the Latin, but the literal sense is probably, 'Nineve is a pool of water; water is she, and they fugitives.' The meaning of the verse can only be conjectured.

ransacked! Sore hearts are here, and knees that knock together, loins that
11 go labouring, and pale cheeks.[1]   Lair of lion, and nursery of his whelps,
what trace is left of thee, once so secure a retreat, his haunt and theirs?
12 Cub nor lioness should want, so preyed he, so mauled he, so filled with
13 plunder of his forays the den where he lay.   Have at thee! says the Lord
of hosts; yonder chariots shall be burnt to ashes; whelps of thine shall die
at the sword's point, plunder of thine be swept off the face of earth; and
for thy heralds, their voices shall be heard no more.

CHAPTER THREE

OUT upon thee, city of blood, full fed with treason and rapine, yet
2 still at prey!   What sounds are these? Crack of whip, whirring of
3 wheels, beat of horse-hoof, rattle of chariot. Mounts horseman,   flash like
lightning sword and spear; what carnage! How cumbered the earth with
4 slain! Dead bodies past counting; the living stumble over the dead.   Harlot so unwearied in thy harlot's ways, so fair, so full of witchery, too long
hast thou betrayed a nation here, a tribe there, with sorcery of thine,
5 harlotry of thine;   and now I will be even with thee, says the Lord God
of hosts. I mean to set thy skirts flying about thy ears, and lay bare the
6 naked shame of thee, for all the kingdoms of the world to see;   pelted thou
shalt be with things abominable, and foully bemocked; such a public
7 show I will make of thee,   passer-by will be fain to shun thee; Nineve
fallen, says he, and never a tear! Search where I will, never a friend to
8 comfort thee! [2]   Here was another city, No-Ammon,[3] fair as thyself; she
too was built on the river-side, water all about her; the sea her mart, the
9 sea her defences.   Hers the Ethiop land, hers was Egypt; wanted there
10 strength yet, African and Libyan were at her side;   yet thy fate was hers,
exile, and captivity, and children at every street's turning dashed to death;
honour and rank condemned to the lot's mercy, and the chain's grip!
11   Bemused and helpless with fear, looking about for succour against the
12 invader, so she was, so thou shalt be.   At a touch thy bastions shall fall,
like ripe figs that drop into the eater's mouth, soon as tree is shaken;

---

[1] 'Pale cheeks'; literally, 'faces like the blackness of a pot.' We may compare
Joel 2.6, where the Latin renders the same phrase, 'all faces shall be turned into
a pot.' The literal meaning of the Hebrew text is that they will gather some
kind of complexion perhaps best described as 'lividness'; the noun does not
occur anywhere else.

[2] It is not clear where the comments of the supposed passer-by come to an end.

[3] No or No-Ammon is commonly identified with (Egyptian) Thebes, the 'sea'
being understood as referring to the Nile. The Latin version gives 'Alexandria,'
which involves a manifest anachronism.

13 woman-hearted the defenders, the gates wide open to the enemy's on-
14 rush, touchwood the bars of them. Water, there, water for a siege! Raise
the battlements higher yet! Down to the clay-pit with thee, tread the
15 mortar, put thy hand to the brick-mould! Fire shall consume thee none
the less, the sword cut thee off, hungry as locust to devour.
16   Thrive thou as locust thrives or grasshopper, ay, let thy enterprises [1]
outnumber the stars in heaven, what avails it? Early hatches locust, early
17 flies away. Forgotten, the high lords, forgotten, the princelings,[2] as they
had been locusts, and brood of locusts, that cling to yonder hedge-row
in the chill of morning, and are gone, once the sun is up, who knows
18 whither? Gone to their rest thy marshals, king of Assyria; thy vassals lie
silent in the dust; out on the hills the common folk take refuge, with none
19 to muster them. Wound of thine there is no hiding, hurt of thine is
grievous; nor any shall hear the tidings of it but shall clap their hands
over thee, so long thy tyrannous yoke has rested on so many.

---

[1] In the Hebrew text, 'thy merchants.' A change of one letter would give 'thy
foot-soldiers.'

[2] The words rendered 'high lords' and 'princelings' are rare words of uncertain significance. The Latin has 'guardians' and 'little ones,' but it seems likely
that state officials of some kind are meant.

THE PROPHECY OF HABACUC

CHAPTER ONE

THIS burden following was revealed to the prophet Habacuc.
2 Lord, must I ever cry out to thee, and gain hearing never? Plead
3 against tyranny, and no deliverance be granted me? Must I nothing see
but wrong and affliction; turn where I will, nothing but robbery and
oppression; quarrels everywhere, everywhere contention raising its head?
4 What marvel if the old teachings are torn up,[1] and redress is never to be
found? Innocence by knavery circumvented still, and false award given!
5 Have you no eyes for the world about you? Look upon it with wonder
and awe; in your own days here be strange deeds a-doing, so strange, a
6 man would scarce credit them if they were told in story.[2] What a nation
is this I am spurring on to battle, the Chaldaean folk, so implacable, so
swift! Ready to march the wide world over, so there be lands, not theirs,
7 to covet! A grim nation and a terrible; arbiter of right and claim is none
8 but they. Not leopard so lithe as horse of theirs, not wolf at evening so
fast; wide the sweep of their horsemen, that close in, close in from afar,
9 flying like vultures hungry for their prey. Plunderers all; eager as the
10 sirocco their onset, whirling away, like sandstorm, their captives.[3] Here
be men that hold kings in contempt, make princes their sport; no fortress
but is a child's game to such as these; heap they up the sand, it is theirs.
11 Veers wind, and he is gone; see him fall down and ascribe the victory to
his god![4]
12 But thou, Lord, my God and all my worship, thou art from eternity!
And wilt thou see us perish? Warrant of thine they hold, take their
strength from thee, only to make known thy justice, thy chastening
13 power![5] So pure those eyes, shall they feast on wrong-doing? Wilt thou

---

[1] 'Are torn up'; according to the Hebrew text, 'have lost their vigour'. The
reference to teaching (that is, of the Law) shews that these verses refer to misdoings among God's own people. But the prophet only cites these as an instance
of man's inhumanity to man in general.

[2] These verses, 5–11, put into the mouth of Almighty God, are a preface to
Habacuc's own protest against the barbarity of the Chaldaeans. Probably,
although they are cast into the prophetic form, they represent facts which had
already taken place at the time when this prophecy was made; Habacuc seems
to have lived under the captivity (Dan. 14.32).

[3] The Hebrew text here is obscure; some think it means the Chaldaeans had
their faces set towards the east, or perhaps simply 'forward.'

[4] Literally, 'Then a wind (or spirit) will be changed, and he (or it) will pass
by, and he will fall down; this is the strength of his god.' The Hebrew text,
which is slightly different, gives a doubtful sense and is perhaps corrupt.

[5] It is not clear whether this means God has raised up the Chaldaeans in order

brook the sight of oppression, look on while treason is done? Innocence
14 the prey of malice, and no word from thee? As well had men been fishes
15 in the sea, or creeping things, that ruler have none! And indeed it nothing spares, hook of yonder Chaldaean; seine and drag he spreads for all,
16 and great joy has he of his sport. Nay, seine must have its victims, incense
be offered to drag; whom else thanks he for the rich fare on his plate,
17 viands most dainty? Trust me, wider still yonder net shall be flung;
sword of his will never have done with massacre.

CHAPTER TWO

WHAT message, then, is entrusted to me? What answer shall I make
when I am called to account? Here on the watch-tower my post
shall be; stand I on the battlements, and await his signal.
2   Write down thy vision, the Lord said, on a tablet, so plain that it may
3 be read with a glance; a vision of things far distant, yet one day befall
they must, no room for doubting it. Wait thou long, yet wait patiently;
4 what must be must, and at the time appointed for it. Foul air the doubter
breathes; by his faith he lives, who lives right.
5   Tyrant, like drunkard, is mocked by false dreams of glory.[1] See him
whet his appetite, not death itself nor the grave more insatiable; gather up
6 a tribe here, a nation there, heap his plate with them! One day, what a
by-word they will make of him! What riddling taunts shall be hurled at
him! As here follows:
So thou wouldst hoard up the possessions that are none of thine, load
7 thyself with base dross,[2] and it should go on for ever? All unawares the
8 foe shall spring, worry thee, harry thee, make a helpless prey of thee. So
many lands thou hast plundered, plundered thyself shalt be; enough
nations are left for that; for men's blood shed, and for fields ravaged,
plundered the city shall be, and all that dwell there.[3]

---

to punish the Jews, or in order to exhibit his justice by punishing, later, the
Chaldaeans themselves.
[1] Literally, 'Behold, the breath (or life) of him who is incredulous will not be
straight within him, but the just man will have life in his faith. And as wine
deceives the drinker, so shall a proud man be, and he will not be adorned.' The
Latin here is evidently trying to restore sense to a passage unintelligible in the
Hebrew text. The word 'faith' in the Old Testament usually means faithfulness
(to one's word); here the context suggests that it means confidence .
[2] 'Base dross'; literally, 'thick mud,' a mistaken attempt to identify a Hebrew
word which means 'borrowers' pledges.' In the next verse, the verb 'worry' or
'bite' is, in Hebrew, closely allied to a word meaning 'usury.'
[3] Here and in verse 17 below the Latin version has probably misunderstood
the Hebrew construction, referring 'the city and all that dwell there' not to
Babylon but to her victims.

9   Ill-gotten gains thou wouldst amass to deck that house of thine; make
10 it an eyrie, too high for envious hands to reach? Nay, with this undoing
of many peoples thou hast done thy own house despite, thy own life is
11 forfeit; stone from ruined wall cries out against thee, and beam from
gaping roof echoes the cry.
12   City thou wouldst found, city's walls build up, with deeds of blood-
13 shed and of wrong? What, has not the Lord of hosts uttered his doom,
toil of nations shall feed the fire, and all their labour be spent for nothing?
14 It is the Lord's glory men must learn to know, that shall cover the earth,
flooding over it like the waters of the sea.[1]
15   Thou wouldst pour out a draught for thy neighbour, a draught thy own
hand has poisoned; bemuse him as with wine, to leave him stripped and
16 bare? This was to cover thyself with shame, not with glory; drink thou
in thy turn, and grow dizzy! A round for thee, now, from yonder cup the
Lord holds in his hand; how shamefully is that glory of thine bespewed!
17 Wrong done to Lebanon, scathe of the roaming beasts, shall recoil on
thee; fear shall overtake them,[2] city of thine and all that dwell there, for
men's blood shed, and for fields ravaged.
18   What avails image, that carver should be at pains to carve it? In metal
his own hands have melted shall a man put his trust? Cheating likenesses,
19 dumb idols all! And thy prayer was, stock and stone should wake up and
come to thy aid, senseless things that cannot signify their will;[3] nay,
breath in their bodies have none, for all they are tricked out with gold and
silver!
20   And all the while, the Lord is in his holy temple. Keep silence, earth,
before him

CHAPTER THREE

A PRAYER of the prophet Habacuc for Shigionoth.[4]
2 I have heard, Lord, the tale of thy renown, awe-stricken at the divine
power thou hast. Reveal that power in these latter days, in these latter
days make it known once more! And though we have earned thy anger,

---

[1] Verses 12–14 seem to be a cento of quotations; cf. Mic. 3.10, Jer. 51.58, Is. 11.9.

[2] Literally, 'it shall frighten them'; the last word is masculine in the Latin, feminine in the Hebrew. The Hebrew text of this verse is very obscure, and may well be corrupt.

[3] 'Signify their own will'; literally 'teach.' If the text is sound, the contrast must be with the true God as Lawgiver.

[4] 'For Shigionoth' appears to be a musical direction, of uncertain meaning. The Vulgate Latin renders 'for faults of inadvertence.'

3 bethink thee of mercy still. God coming near from Theman, the holy
One from yonder hills of Pharan! See how his glory overspreads heaven,
4 his fame echoes through the earth; the brightness that is his, like light
5 itself, the rays that stream from his hand, masking its strength; pestilence
6 his outrider, the wasting sickness [1] in his train! There stood he, and
scanned the earth; at his look, the nations were adread; melted were the
everlasting mountains, bowed were the ancient hills, his own immemorial
7 pathway, as he journeyed. I saw the Ethiop quail in his tent,[2] the dwellings of Madian astir with terror.

8 Is it the rivers, Lord, that have awaked thy anger; should it be the
rivers? Or has the sea earned thy vengeance, that thou comest thus
9 mounted on thy horses, on thy victorious chariot; that bow of thine
brought into full play, which grants to Israel the assurance of thy suc- /
10 cour? [3] Earth is torn into ravines; the mountains tremble at the sight.
Fierce falls the rain-storm, the depths beneath us roar aloud, the heights
11 beckon from above; sun and moon linger in their dwelling-place; [4] so
bright thy arrows volley, with such sheen of lightning glances thy spear.
12 Nay, if thou ride through the world so angrily, with thy disdain striking
13 the nations dumb, it is to rescue thy own people, rescue thy own anointed
servant, that thou goest out to battle. Down fall the turrets in yonder
14 castle of godlessness, down sink the foundations to their very base; lights
thy ban on its princes, on the heads of its warriors, eager now to overthrow me, confident now as some petty tyrant who oppresses the poor in
15 secret. Over the sea, over the ooze beneath its waves, thou hast made a
path for thy horses to tread.
16 Such was the tale that set my whole frame trembling; at the rumour of
it my lips quivered with fear; there was a faintness overcame my whole
being, my steps faltered as I went. Now with tranquil heart let me await
this day of doom; upon the enemies of our people it is destined to fall.[5]

---

[1] 'The wasting sickness'; this is the rendering of the new Latin Psalter; the
Vulgate Latin translates, 'the devil.'

[2] Literally, 'the tents of Ethiopia under affliction.' The Vulgate gives a less
probable rendering, 'the tents of Ethiopia (requited) for their guilt.'

[3] 'Which grants to Israel the assurance of thy succour'; literally, 'the promises
which thou hast made to the tribes,' see Gen. 49.24. The new Latin Psalter has
'thy quiver so full of arrows,' a reading based on certain manuscripts of the
Septuagint Greek.

[4] 'The heights beckon from above; sun and moon linger in their dwelling-
place'; the new Latin Psalter reads (with certain manuscripts of the Septuagint Greek) 'the sun forgets to dawn in splendour, the moon lingers in her bower'.

[5] This is the rendering given by the new Latin Psalter; no satisfactory sense
is offered by the Vulgate here: 'Let rottenness enter into my bones, and fester beneath me, that I may have rest in the day of affliction, that I may go up to this
people of ours which is girded for battle.'

17 What though the fig-tree never bud, the vine yield no fruit, the olive fail,
   the fields bear no harvest; what though our folds stand empty of sheep,
18 our byres of cattle? Still will I make my boast in the Lord, triumph in
19 the deliverance God sends me. The Lord, the ruler of all, is my stronghold; he will bring me safely on my way, safe as the hind whose feet echo
   already on the hills.

   (For the chief singer, to the harp's music).[1]

---

[1] The musical direction here printed in brackets is omitted in the new Latin
Psalter; the Vulgate has confused it with the text of the canticle.

THE PROPHECY OF SOPHONIAS

CHAPTER ONE

TO Sophonias, that was descended from Ezechias through Amarias, Godolias and Chusi, this message came from the Lord, at the time when Josias son of Amon reigned in Juda.

2 Fall to I must, and weed yonder plot of ground, the Lord says; rid it, says he, of man and beast, of bird in air and fish under water; and down
4 shall the godless come too, never a man left alive upon it. All Juda, all the citizens of Jerusalem, shall feel the stroke. Not a trace shall they leave behind, yonder gods of the countryside, acolyte and priest of
5 theirs not a memory; forgotten, all that worship the host of heaven from the roof-tops, all that worship . . .,[1] take they their oaths to the
6 Lord, or swear they by Melchom; forgotten, all that turn their backs on the Lord, and will neither seek nor search for him.

7 Silence, there, to greet the Lord! Here is day of his appointing, here is great sacrifice of his preparing; all his guests bidden, all their cleansing
8 done. The Lord's sacrifice! A day of reckoning it shall be, king and
9 prince I will call to account, all that go clad in foreign bravery, all that spurn yonder threshold,[2] and fill the house of the Lord their God with
10 deeds of treachery and wrong. What an outcry that day, the Lord says, from the Fishmongers' Gate, what lamenting from the New Town! How
11 the hill-sides will echo to the noise of your ruin! Ay, lament indeed, you that dwell in Mortar Valley; of the merchant folk no more is heard; here is an end of all that trafficked in silver.

12 Time, then, to call for lamps, and search Jerusalem through! Trust me, I will find them out, spoiled natures, like wine that has settled on its lees, the men who think to themselves, From the Lord nothing is to hope,
13 nothing to fear. Ransacked their wealth shall be, and their homes ruined; houses they build they shall never dwell in, vineyards they plant they
14 shall drink of never. Nearer, nearer comes the great day of the Lord's reckoning, ay, and soon; bitter the bruit of its coming; here is peril to cow
15 the bravest heart. Day of vengeance, day of strain and stress, day of ran-
16 sack and ruin; dim and dark, overcast with cloud and storm! City is none so well fortified, pinnacle is none so high in air, but shall hear braying of
17 trumpets and the battle-cry. Guilty wretches, they shall grope in the
18 dark, flesh and blood of them cheap as dust and dung; silver and gold of

---

[1] It is difficult to explain the run of this verse except on the supposition that a word has been lost; e.g., 'on the hill-tops,' or 'at the forest shrines.'

[2] It is uncertain what is meant by 'leaping over the threshold'; probably it was some superstitious practice (cf. I Kg. 5.5.)

them powerless to buy off the Lord's present vengeance. Burns through the land the fire of his slighted love; takes full toll, and speedily, of all that dwell there.

CHAPTER TWO

2   B AND together, men of a nation so little loved, bind yourselves in one; ere resolve can bear fruit, like flying chaff passes the day.[1] Before the divine vengeance falls on you, before the day of divine retribution comes,
3   to the Lord betake you! To honest doing and patient suffering betake you, men of humble heart wherever you be, men obedient to his will; it may be, when the hour of the Lord's vengeance comes, you shall find refuge.

4   Gaza and Ascalon to rack and ruin left, Azotus stormed ere the day is
5   out, root and branch destroyed is Accaron! Out upon the forfeited race [2] that holds yonder strip of coast-land; the Lord's doom is on it, the little Chanaan of the Philistines; wasted it shall be, and never a man to dwell
6   in it. There on the coast-land shepherds shall lie at ease, there shall be
7   folds for flocks; and who shall dwell there? The remnant that is left of Juda's race; there they shall find pasturage, when the Lord their God brings them relief, restores their fortunes again.

8   And what of Moab, what of Ammon? Doubt not I have heard the blasphemous taunts they uttered against my own people, as they encroached
9   upon its borders. As I am a living God, says the Lord of hosts, the God of Israel, no better shall Moab and Ammon be than Sodom and Gomorrha, all waste and brushwood and salt-pits, for ever desolate; of my own people enough remnant shall be left, a nation still, to plunder and to
10 conquer them. Pride that would mock and overreach his own people he,
11 the Lord of hosts, knows how to punish; see what terror he strikes into them! Peak and pine they, gods of the other nations; rise they from their places, one by one, to adore him, island-dwellers of the world.
12 You too, men of Ethiopia, shall feel my sword.
13 That hand shall stretch out northward, and make an end of Assyria;
14 Nineve shall be left forlorn, a trackless desert. Flocks shall lie down there . . . all the wild things of earth; [3] bittern and hedgehog make their

---

[1] This passage appears to be addressed to the Jewish people scattered about the world. There is considerable obscurity about the sense, perhaps due to corruption of the text. 'Ere resolve can bear fruit, like flying chaff passes the day'; the Latin version has, 'Before the command brings forth the passing day like chaff,' which yields no appropriate sense. For 'resolve' cf. Jg. 5.15; the phrase is no doubt a proverb.

[2] In the Hebrew text, 'the Cerethite race.'

[3] It looks as if there was some slight omission here; the word for 'flock' in the Hebrew is only used of domesticated animals.

dwelling in its doorways, bird-song there shall be in the windows, and
15 raven perched on lintel; so ebbs the strength of it. And this was the proud
city that dwelt so free from alarms, thinking to herself, Here I stand,
with no rival; a desert now, lair of the wild beasts! Hisses the passer-by in
mockery, and shakes his fist.

CHAPTER THREE

2 OUT on the rebellious city, the defiled city, so full of wrong! [1] Never
the call heard, the warning heeded; trust in the Lord is none; nay,
3 they would keep God at a distance. Here be rulers no better than ravening lions, judges like wolf that prowls at night, and not a bone left on the
4 morrow; prophets that are heedless men and treacherous, priests that
5 profane the sanctuary and do violence to the law. And all the while the
Lord is there in the midst of it! Not his the blame; never morning passes
but he makes known his award for their enlightening, without fail; and
6 still injustice goes on unashamed! Short work I have made of other
nations; crumbling battlements, unfrequented streets, their cities lie
7 ruined and forlorn, with none to dwell in them; Ah, thought I, now at
least thou wilt learn to fear me, wilt profit by the warning! Here at least
is a city that may be left habitable, send them what plagues I may! But no,
early and late they would be at their perverse doings still!
8 Hope, then, is none,[2] till the day, long hence, when I will stand revealed; [3] what gathering, then, of the nations, all kingdoms joined in one!
And upon these, my doom is, vengeance shall fall, fierce anger of mine
shall fall; the whole earth shall be consumed with the fire of my slighted
9 love. And after that, all the peoples of the world shall have pure lips,
invoking one and all the Lord's name, straining at a single yoke in the
10 Lord's service. From far away, beyond Ethiop rivers, my suppliants
shall come to me, sons [4] of my exiled people the bloodless offering shall
11 bring. No need, then, to blush for wayward thoughts that defied me;
gone from thy midst the high-sounding boast; no room, in that mountain
12 sanctuary of mine, for pride henceforward; a poor folk and a friendless

[1] The Latin version gives 'the redeemed city, the dove,' but this seems due to a
faulty understanding of the Hebrew text. Cf. Jer. 25.38.
[2] Literally, 'Therefore thou must wait for me,' but the verb commonly expresses an attitude of pious longing, and it looks as if the faithful remnant, not
the generality of the Jewish people, were being addressed.
[3] Literally, 'the day when I will rise up thenceforward'; the Hebrew text has
'the day when I will rise up and catch my prey,' the Septuagint Greek, 'the day
when I will rise up to bear witness.'
[4] In the Hebrew text, 'daughters'; there is some ground for suspecting a faulty
reading in the manuscripts.

I will leave in thy confines, but one that puts its trust in the Lord's name.
13   The remnant of Israel, strangers now to treachery and wrong, the true
word ever on their lips! Yonder flock may graze and lie down to rest, none
14 to dismay it.   Break into song, fair Sion, all Israel cry aloud; here is com-
15 fort, Jerusalem, for thy royal heart.   Thy doom the Lord has revoked, thy
enemy repulsed; the Lord, there in the midst of thee, Israel's king! Peril
16 for thee henceforth is none.   Such is the message yonder day shall bring
17 to Jerusalem: Courage, Sion! What means it, the unnerved hand?   Thou
hast one in the midst of thee, the Lord thy God, whose strength shall
deliver thee. Joy and pride of his thou shalt be henceforward; silent till
now in his love for thee, he will greet thee with cries of gladness.
18   Truants that were lost to the covenant I will reclaim; of thy company
19 they are, thou shalt be taunted with them no longer; [1] only for thy persecutors that hour shall be the hour of doom. Lame sheep medicined, and
strayed sheep brought home! Lands that despised them shall hear name
20 and fame of them now.   Name and fame you shall have, all the world
over, the Lord says, when I call you back and gather you in; when you see
the fortunes of Israel retrieved at last.

---

[1] Here again, in verses 17 and 18, most modern editors question the soundness
of the Hebrew text; in the Latin version, the difficulties are partly disguised.

THE PROPHECY OF AGGAEUS

CHAPTER ONE

IT was in the second year of Darius' reign, on the first day of the sixth month of it, that a message came from the Lord through the prophet Aggaeus; came to Zorobabel, son of Salathiel, that was governor of Juda,

2 and to the high priest, Josue son of Josedec. And thus it ran: Word from the Lord of hosts to his people, that will not restore his temple, but cry,

3 Too early yet! Listen, the Lord said to them through the prophet

4 Aggaeus, is it not too early yet for you to have roofs over your heads,

5 and my temple in ruins? Think well on it, says the Lord of hosts; here is much sown, and little reaped, nor eating brings you a full belly, nor wine a merry heart; such clothes you wear as leave you shivering, such

7 wages win as leak out at purse's bottom! Think well on it, says the Lord

8 of hosts; up to the hill-side with you, fetch timber and restore my temple,

9 if content me you will, the Lord says, if honour me you will! So much attempted, so little attained; store you brought into your houses withered at my breath; would you know the reason for it? says the Lord of hosts. Because to your own houses you run helter-skelter, and my temple in

10 ruins! That is why the skies are forbidden to rain on you, earth to afford

11 its bounty; ban of barrenness lies on plain and hill, wheat and wine and oil and all the earth yields, man and beast and all they toil to win.

12 What made they of it, Salathiel's son Zorobabel, and the high priest, Josue son of Josedec, and all the people with them? That voice they could not choose but heed, that message from the Lord their God sent to them by the prophet Aggaeus, and they were sore adread of the divine warning.

13 Yet here was divine encouragement; Aggaeus, the Lord's own mes-

14 senger,[1] gave them the Lord's own assurance he was at their side. So the Lord put heart into them, governor and priest and people alike; and they set to work building up the temple of the Lord God of hosts.

CHAPTER TWO

THIS was on the twenty-fourth day of the sixth month, in the second year of Darius.

2 Afterwards, on the twenty-first day of the seventh month, the Lord

3 sent another message through the prophet Aggaeus. To Zorobabel, and

---

[1] Literally, according to the Latin version, 'Aggaeus, an angel from among the angels of the Lord,' but this is probably due to a misunderstanding of the Hebrew text.

4 Josue, and all the people with them his word was: Tell me, those of you
who saw this house in its former brightness, what make you of it now?
5 It is no better in your eyes than a very nothing. Take heart, Zorobabel;
Josue, son of Josedec, take heart! And you, too, people of the land, the
Lord of hosts bids you put heart into the work; is not he, the Lord of
hosts, at your side?

6   ... the promise I gave when you escaped from Egypt; my own spirit
shall be among you, do not be afraid.[1]

7   A little while now,[2] the Lord of hosts says, and I mean to set heaven and
8 earth, sea and dry land rocking; stirred all the nations shall be, hither
shall come the prize the whole world treasures,[3] and I will fill this temple
with the brightness of my presence, says the Lord of hosts.

9   Silver or gold, what matters it? the Lord of hosts says. Both are mine!
10 Bright this new temple shall be, he tells you, as never the first was; here,
he tells you, his blessing shall rest.

11   Then, on the twenty-fourth day of the ninth month, in this second
year of king Darius, another message came from the Lord to the prophet
12 Aggaeus, bidding him, in the name of the Lord of hosts, make enquiry
13 of the priests upon a matter touching the law. And the question was
this: Here is one carries consecrated meat in the fold of his garment, and
with this same fold chances to touch bread or broth, wine or oil, or what
food you will; does this food become consecrated thereby? And the
14 priests said No. Why then, Aggaeus went on, let some other man touch
this food, one that is contaminated by the contact of a dead thing, will the
food be defiled? And they answered, Defiled it is.

15   Then Aggaeus opened his mind to them: Here is a whole people, a
whole race, the Lord says, that shews defiled under my scrutiny. Never
16 an enterprise of theirs, never an offering they bring, but is defiled. But

---

[1] It looks as if some words had fallen out between these verses 5 and 6, including a verb to govern 'the promise.' Some editions print the end of verse 5 as a
parenthesis, and make the sentence run: 'The Lord of hosts bids you take heart
and perform (is not he, the Lord of hosts, at your side?) the word which I
covenanted with you when you escaped from Egypt.'

[2] Literally, 'a single little while,' but the addition gives no satisfactory sense.
The Hebrew text is difficult, and perhaps corrupt; the Septuagint Greek gives
'(only) once more,' a phrase interpreted in Heb. 12.26 as looking back to the
experience of Israel when the law was given on mount Sinai (Ex. 19).

[3] Literally, 'the object of the whole world's desire shall come.' The Septuagint
Greek has, 'the choice (treasures) of the whole world shall come.' Either of these
might represent the peculiar language of the Hebrew text, 'they shall come, the
object of the whole world's desire' (which could just be rendered, 'they shall
come to the object of the whole world's desire,' i.e., the temple). 'The brightness
of my presence'; literally, 'glory,' but the word, when used in connexion with the
temple, regularly implies a theophany; (cf. III Kg. 8.11, Ez. 10.4).

now, mark well how you thrive henceforward. Whilst none would be at
17 pains to set pillar on base, here in the Lord's temple, how fared it with
yonder twenty-bushel heap of corn? Look closer, and it was but ten
bushels. Did you think to press fifty quarts into the vat? There were but
18 twenty. Sirocco I sent and mildew, smote all your crops with hail, and
19 you would not come back to me, the Lord says. Mark well how you
thrive henceforward, from this twenty-fourth day of the ninth month,
20 when you laid the foundations of the Lord's temple;[1] mark it well. Not
yet has the corn ripened, not yet have vine and fig, pomegranate and
olive, had time to blossom; but on all these my blessing lies henceforward.
21 And this further message Aggaeus had from the Lord, on that twenty-
22 fourth day of the month, for Zorobabel, the governor of Juda: Earth and
23 heaven both I mean to set rocking; royal thrones shall be overturned,
and the power of Gentile kingdoms brought to nothing; overthrown they
lie, chariot and charioteer, down come horse and rider, friend turning his
24 sword against friend; but thou, son of Salathiel, says the Lord of hosts,
thou, Zorobabel, art my servant still; on that day I will take thee to my
side, keep thee there, close as signet-ring; it is a divine choice that has
fallen on thee, says the Lord of hosts.

---

[1] This had been done in some sort much earlier, under king Cyrus (Esd. 3.10),
but the work was interrupted, and doubtless had to start again from the beginning.

THE PROPHECY OF ZACHARIAS

CHAPTER ONE

IT was in the second year of Darius' reign, and the eighth month of it, that a message from the Lord came to the prophet Zacharias, son of
2 Barachias, son of Addo. And thus it ran: Beyond question, your fathers
3 incurred the Lord's displeasure; and now this word thou must proclaim from the Lord of hosts, Come back to me, he bids you, and I, he pro-
4 mises, will come back to your side. Prophets there were long since, that warned those fathers of yours in his name, they should turn away from ill living and rebellious thoughts; yet neither heed nor hearing, he says,
5 would they give me; not for you to follow their example. Gone, the men of an earlier day; prophets that spoke to them might not live on for ever,
6 but warning of mine, promise of mine, entrusted to the prophets that were my true servants, live on yet. See how the fulfilment of them over-took your fathers, till at last they must needs repent, must acknowledge the Lord of hosts had not threatened them, sinners and rebels, in vain!
7   Then, on the twenty-fourth day of Sabath, which is the eleventh month, word came from the Lord afresh, and once more it came to
8 Zacharias, son of Barachias, son of Addo. A vision appeared to me in the night, of one that was mounted on a sorrel horse, at a stand among the myrtle-trees, down in the Valley; and never a horse in all his company but
9 was sorrel, roan or white. Scarce had I asked, My Lord, what be these? when the angel that inspired me [1] promised he would shew me the mean-
10 ing of it; and with that, my answer came from him who stood among the myrtle-trees, These have gone out on the Lord's errand, patrolling the
11 earth. And to him, now, the angel of the myrtle-wood, those others made their report: All earth we have patrolled, said they, and everywhere is
12 safety, everywhere is rest. Ah, Lord of hosts, my angel monitor said, wilt thou never relent, never take pity upon Jerusalem and the towns of Juda?
13 Here be seventy years come and gone. And with that, the Lord answered
14 him; gracious his words were, gracious and full of comfort. Cry it abroad, now, my monitor said to me, this message from the Lord of
15 hosts: Jealous, right jealous my love for Sion's hill, deep, full deep my anger against the heathen that are so well content! I would have punished
16 Jerusalem but lightly, it was these drove home the blow. And now, the Lord says, I am for Jerusalem again, bringing pardon with me; temple shall be built there for the Lord of hosts, Jerusalem shall see mason's

---

[1] Literally, 'the angel who spoke in (or, by means of) me.' The Hebrew text can also be rendered, 'the angel who spoke to me' (cf. Num. 12.6 and 8). But see note on 2.3 over.

17 plummet busy once again. And this, too: A promise from the Lord of
hosts! Yonder towns shall yet overflow with riches; Sion shall yet receive
comfort, Jerusalem be the city of my choice.

18 Then I looked up, and what saw I? Here were four horns; [1] and when
I asked my guide what they should be, he told me, Upon these horns Juda,
20 and Israel and Jerusalem were tossed about. After that, the Lord sent
21 me another vision of four blacksmiths; What errand, said I, have these?
Why, said he, yonder horns made such havoc of Juda till now, never a
man might lift his head; what should be the blacksmiths' errand but to
turn them back? [2] Polled they must be henceforward, the heathen folk
that once tossed Juda to the winds.

CHAPTER TWO

2 WHEN next I looked up, I saw a man there that carried a measuring-
line; so I asked him, whither he was bound? For Jerusalem, said
3 he, to measure length and breadth of it. And at that, my angel monitor
would have gone out on his errand, but here was a second angel come out
4 to meet him. [3] Speed thee, said he, on thy way, and tell that pupil of
thine: [4] So full Jerusalem shall be, of men and cattle both, wall it shall
5 have none to hedge it in; I myself, the Lord says, will be a wall of fire
around it, and in the midst of it, the brightness of my presence.

6 Away, away, from the north country get you gone, the Lord says; what
7 if I have scattered you, far as the four winds? Away with thee, Sion;
8 captive wouldst thou dwell with captive Babylon? This promise the
Lord of hosts makes: After . . .

. . . glory,[5] I hold his warrant against the nations that plunder you;

---

[1] The horns evidently represent four (or perhaps two) enemies of the Jewish
people, but they cannot be identified with certainty.

[2] 'Turn them back'; literally, 'scare them away.' It seems probable that there
is an error in the manuscripts, and that some word more appropriate to the
activities of blacksmiths originally appeared there.

[3] Although the prophet is given direct vision, it seems that he only understands
the meaning of it through the medium of the angel who 'speaks in him' (cf. 1.9).
This angel monitor comes and goes between heaven and earth (5.5), he 'goes
out' from the divine presence, exactly like the deluding spirit in III Kg. 22.22,
with some revelation about the measuring of Jerusalem, but is intercepted on his
way by the assurance that the city needs no measuring.

[4] Literally, 'that young man' or 'that child.' Conceivably the reference is to the
man mentioned in verse 1, but more probably Zacharias is the 'child,' not in
years but in experience (III Kg. 3.7).

[5] No plausible explanation has been suggested to account for the words 'after
glory,' and it seems likely there has been an omission in the manuscripts; the
more so, because Almighty God is the speaker in verse 8, and not in verse 9.

9 apple of my eye [1] he touches, that touches you. Lift I my hand, they shall
be at your mercy that are your masters now; doubt shall be none it was
the Lord who sent me.

10   Sion, poor maid, break out into songs of rejoicing; I am on my way,
11 coming to dwell in the midst of thee, the Lord says. There be nations
a many that shall rally that day to the Lord's side; they, too, shall be
people of mine, but with thee shall be my dwelling.

Doubt there shall be none it was the Lord of hosts sent me to thy aid.[2]
12 Juda the Lord shall claim for his own, his portion in a holy land; still
Jerusalem shall be the city of his choice.

13   Be silent, living things, in the Lord's presence; yonder in his holy
dwelling all is astir.

CHAPTER THREE

ANOTHER vision the Lord shewed me; here was an angel of his, and
before this angel stood the high priest Josue, with the Accuser at his
2 right hand bringing accusation against him. But to the Accuser the divine
answer came, The Lord rebuke thee, Satan; the Lord, that makes choice
of Jerusalem, rebuke thee! What, is not this a brand saved from the
3 embers?[3] Then, for he saw Josue standing there in his presence very
4 vilely clad, the angel gave it out to his attendants they should take away
these vile rags from him; Guilt of thine, said he, I have set by; thou shalt
5 have new garments to wear instead. A clean mitre they should give him
besides. And so, when the new mitre was on his head and the new gar-
6 ments were about him, the angel of the Lord rose up and gave Josue his
7 commission: My beckoning follow thou, my commands keep thou,
people of mine thou shalt govern, house of mine shalt have in thy charge,
8 and in their company, that here stand about thee, shalt come and go. This
for the hearing of the high priest Josue, and others his co-assessors, names
of good omen all.[4]

9   Time is I should bring hither my servant, that is the Dayspring. Stone
is here I will set before yonder Josue; a stone that bears seven eyes, device
of my own carving, says the Lord of hosts. All the guilt of this land I will
10 banish in a single day. That shall be a day of good cheer, the Lord of
hosts says, friend making glad with friend under vine and under fig-tree.

---

[1] For 'my eye' the Hebrew text gives 'his eye.'
[2] The sudden change of speaker perhaps indicates that, all through this chapter, we are reading a series of prophetic fragments, not a continuous prophecy.
[3] Cf. Am. 4.11. The idea is not, in all probability, that of something rescued
from a conflagration, but that of a log which is saved from overnight to light this
morning's fire—Josue is a link between the pre-exilic and the post-exilic period.
[4] The meaning of verses 8–10 will have depended on some kind of symbolism

CHAPTER FOUR

ONCE the angel monitor roused me to my senses, as though I had
2 lain asleep; Now, said he, what seest thou? Why, I said, here is a
lamp-stand meets my eyes, all of gold. A bowl this lamp-stand has at the
top of it, and from the bowl run seven pipes, to feed the seven lamps that
3 crown it. And there are two olive-trees hanging over it, one to the right
4 and one to the left of the bowl. Then in my turn I asked a question of
5 the angel, Tell me, what does all this mean? What, said my monitor,
canst thou not recognize it? Not I, my Lord, I answered.
6   And thereupon the angel told me . . .
       . . . Word from the Lord to Zorobabel: [1] By arms, by force nothing
7 canst thou; my spirit is all, says the Lord of hosts. Vain is towering
height of thine, great mountain; down to plain's level thou must stoop at
Zorobabel's coming; stone from thee he must quarry and smooth to be his
8 coping-stone, how fair, how fair! [2] This message, too, I had from the
9 Lord: Yonder temple hand of Zorobabel has founded, hand of Zorobabel shall finish. No more you shall doubt that I come to you on the
10 Lord's errand. Humble fortunes of yesterday who dared belittle? Rejoice they now, to see plummet at work in Zorobabel's hand . . .
       . . . What should they be, those seven, but eyes the Lord has, glancing
this way and that to scan the earth?
11   Then I asked him about the two olive-trees, to right and left of the
12 lamp-stand; and there was more I would know, What of the two olive-
shoots, close beside the two golden taps that feed yonder pipes of gold? [3]
14 What, said he, canst thou not tell? Not I, my Lord, I answered. What

---

with which we are no longer conversant. 'Names of good omen'; literally, 'names
of sign.' 'The Dayspring' seems a translation from the Septuagint Greek, which
is ambiguous; probably, in accordance with the Hebrew text, it meant 'The
Branch.' See further 6.12 below, and note. It is not clear whether the 'stone' is a
fresh metaphor for describing God's servant, or needs some other explanation.
[1] Verses 6–10 seem to interrupt the thread of the narrative, and some think
they have been accidentally misplaced.
[2] Literally, in the Latin, 'And he shall bring out a primary stone, and shall
equalize grace to the grace of it'; in the Hebrew text, 'And he shall bring out
the stone, the top, a roaring, Grace, grace to it.' It seems likely that the text has
been badly preserved.
[3] The Hebrew text seems to imply that there were two shoots communicat-
ing between the olive-trees and the pipes, as if to feed the lamps with oil. But
the text is difficult, and perhaps corrupt, nor does this image fit in well with verse
14. Taking the Latin as it stands, we may perhaps conjecture that the two trees
represent the priesthood and the kingship, the two shoots (not mentioned earlier)
representing Josue and Zorobabel respectively.

should these be, he said, but the two newly-anointed ones that stand in his presence, who is Master of the whole earth?

CHAPTER FIVE

ONCE again I looked up, and there before me was a scroll, that had
2 wings to fly with. So when he asked, what saw I, A scroll, I said,
3 that flies past, twenty cubits long and ten broad. Here is ban, said he, that runs all the world over; thief is none, perjurer is none but shall be
4 judged [1] by the tenour of it. It shall go out under my warrant, says the Lord of hosts, making its way into house of thief, house of perjurer that wrongs my name, and clinging close till it makes an end of all, wood-work and stone-work both.
5 Again the angel visited me, and bade me look well at the revelation that
6 was sent me. What is it? I asked. Bushel-measure is this, he told me; And it is nothing other, said he, than guilt of theirs,[2] spread abroad over the
7 whole earth. Then he lifted up the cover, that was a talent's weight of
8 lead, and what should I see but a woman sitting there within? Godless-ness, he told me, is the name of her; and with that he thrust her back into
9 the barrel, and fastened down the cover of lead. And now, looking up, I saw two other women appearing, that had wings spread out to the wind, strong as a hawk's wings; and these carried the barrel off, midway
10 between heaven and earth. When I would know whither they carried it,
11 the angel told me, To Sennaar, where it must have a shrine built for it; there it must be set up, and rest on a pedestal of its own.

CHAPTER SIX

ONCE more yet I looked up, and had a vision of four chariots, coming
2 out of a pass between two mountains that were all of bronze. Of the
3 horses, the first pair were bay, the second black, the third white, the
4 fourth a sturdy pair of roans. And when I asked of my angel monitor
5 what these might be, Here be four winds, he told me, going out on their errand; their place is in his presence, who is Master of the whole earth.
6 So out they went, chariot drawn by black horses turning northwards;
7 the white followed these, and the roans turned southwards, the sturdiest pair of all . . .

---

[1] Instead of 'judged' the Hebrew text has 'declared innocent'; it can hardly be doubted that there has been some error of copying.

[2] 'Guilt of theirs,' presumably that of the Jews during their captivity. The Latin version here, following the Hebrew text, gives 'eyes' instead of 'guilt'; but 'guilt' is the rendering of the Septuagint Greek, and a very slight error in Hebrew script would account for the mistake.

... Went out on their errand,[1] fain to traverse the whole world through.

8 And a great cry came to me,[2] See, where they reach the north country! All is well in the north country, my heart is content.[3]

9 And a message from the Lord came to Zacharias: From yonder emissaries of the exiled Jews, Holdai, Tobias and Idaias, toll thou must take; this very day bestir thee, and make thy way to the house of Josias, son of

11 Sophonias, whither they have repaired, newly come from Babylon. Gold and silver thou must take from them, and make crowns, to crown the high

12 priest, Josue son of Josedec . . .[4] This message thou shalt give him from the Lord God of hosts: Here is one takes his name from the Dayspring;[5] where his feet have trodden, spring there shall be. He it is shall rebuild

13 the Lord's temple; builder of the Lord's temple, to what honours he shall come! On princely throne he sits, throne of a priest beside him,[6]

14 and between these two, what harmony of counsel! For Helem, Tobias, Idaias, and Hem the son of Sophonias, the crowns they gave[7] shall win remembrance in the temple of the Lord.

15 Men shall come from far away, to work at the temple's rebuilding; you shall not doubt, then, it was the Lord of hosts gave me my warrant. Will you but heed the voice of the Lord your God, this shall be your reward . . .[8]

---

[1] It seems likely that there is some defect in the text, which makes no mention of the bay horses, and implies (as it stands) that the roans first went southwards, and then went out in an unspecified direction.

[2] Literally, 'he cried and said to me,' the subject of the verb remaining unexpressed.

[3] Literally, 'they have given my spirit rest in the north country.' The sense is perhaps that they had executed vengeance (cf. Ez. 5.13); but the interpretation of the allegory must have depended on a situation with which we are no longer familiar.

[4] It is possible that two crowns at once were set on the head of Josue, to convey some mystical lesson. But it is more natural, especially in view of what follows, to infer that some words have dropped out of the text, indicating that the second crown was for Zorobabel.

[5] 'The Dayspring,' as in 3.8 above, is 'the Branch' (or, 'the Shoot') in the Hebrew text. It seems clear that the first half of Zorobabel's name is referred to. 'Where his feet have trodden'; literally, 'from under him.'

[6] The Latin and the Hebrew are ambiguous here; the meaning may be 'he shall be priest on his throne,' or 'a priest shall be on his throne.' The latter sense is given by the Septuagint Greek, and those authors who adopt the rival interpretation are at a loss to explain what is meant by 'these two.'

[7] Literally, 'the crowns,' but it seems fairly clear that the same persons are referred to as in verse 10, though with some curious differences of nomenclature.

[8] The form of the sentence in the Hebrew text suggests that the obedience of the Jewish people will produce some effect which still remains to be expressed; if so, we have to suppose another gap in the manuscripts.

CHAPTER SEVEN

IN the fourth year of Darius' reign, another message from the Lord
came to Zacharias; it was on the fourth day of Casleu, the ninth month.
2 This was the occasion of it; here was Sarasar, with Rogommelech and
others of his company, sending envoys to implore the Lord's favour.[1]
3 A question they put to the priests, there in the temple of the Lord of
hosts, and to the prophets besides: Must I yet mourn, yet rid myself of
defilement, when the fifth month comes round, as my wont has been
4 these many years past?[2]   Then came this message to me from the Lord of
5 hosts: Ask this, of priests and people both; was it indeed fast of mine
you kept, all these seventy years, the fifth month and the seventh observ-
6 ing ever with fasting and lament, you, that when food and drink were
set before you, shared them with none?[3]
7   Bethink you, what warnings gave he by the prophets of an earlier day,
when Jerusalem was yet safe and prosperous, she and the cities about her,
populous the western valleys, populous the hill-country of the south.
8 (Such was the word the Lord sent to Zacharias).[4] A message from the
Lord of hosts: Come now, the true award, the tender heart that pities a
10 neighbour's need! Widow and orphan, the alien and the friendless,
11 wrong no more; brother against brother plot no more! And would they
listen? Shrank every shoulder from the burden, deaf ears they turned
12 him, hardened their hearts to adamant. Heed his law they would not;
heed they would not, when the Lord of hosts inspired those older prophets to speak in his name. What wonder if his divine anger was
13 aroused? What wonder, says the Lord of hosts, if cry of theirs, like
14 warning of mine, went unheard? So it was I scattered them in unknown
. countries, left their land a desert, where none came or went; a land so
fair, by its own inhabitants laid waste.

---

[1] The interpretation of this verse is very doubtful; the persons referred to are
not mentioned elsewhere.

[2] The fifth month was that in which Jerusalem had fallen; it had evidently
been a time of fasting during the Captivity; now that the temple is in building,
they ask, should the commemoration cease?

[3] Literally, in the Latin, 'And when you ate and drank, did you not eat and
drink for yourselves?'; in the Hebrew text, 'And when you ate and when you
drank, were not you the eaters and you the drinkers?' A general accusation of
selfishness is perhaps intended; cf. Deut. 16.14 and elsewhere.

[4] Some think the words were included here by accident; if not, they are a
somewhat confusing repetition of the rubric in verse 1. It is clear that they interrupt the run of the paragraph; verses 9 and 10 are a message delivered (in the
first instance) not by Zacharias but by the older prophets mentioned in verse 7.

CHAPTER EIGHT

2 THIS word, too, came from him: A message from the Lord of hosts!
3 Great ruth have I for Sion, and sore it grieves me. To Sion I will
return, so runs his promise, and make in Jerusalem my home; The loyal
city, men shall call her, and that mountain where dwells the Lord of
4 hosts, The holy mountain. This, too: Trust me, there shall yet be aged
folk in the streets of Jerusalem, men and women both, that go staff in
5 hand, they are so bowed with years; thronged they shall be, those
6 streets, with boys and girls at play in the open. And this: Hard to believe? So now they find it, poor remnant of a people; but should I, the
7 Lord of hosts, find it hard to perform? And this, too: See if I do not
8 rescue my people from the east country and the west, bring them back
to dwell here, in the midst of Jerusalem; they my people, and I their God,
in troth and loyalty either to other bound.
9   A message from the Lord of hosts! Take courage, then, you that still
hold fast by[1] the commands the prophets gave you, when the foundations of yonder house were a-laying, and the Lord of hosts had no temple
10 yet. Before that time, labour went unrewarded, for man and beast; so
hard pressed were you, none might come or go in safety; every man, in
11 those days, I left at his neighbour's mercy. But now, says the Lord of
12 hosts, this remnant of my people shall enjoy better fortune; a happier
seed-time is theirs. Its fruit the vineyard shall yield, the land its harvest,
13 heaven its rain, and all for this remnant to enjoy. Breed of Juda, breed
of Israel, by-words of misfortune once, when heathen folk fell to cursing
their enemies; happy deliverance, they shall be names of blessing now!
14 Your fears vanquish, go bravely on; he, the Lord of hosts, gives you his
warrant for it. Time was, says he, when your fathers had roused my
15 anger, and I was ever planning mischief against you; no respite then!
To-day, for the good estate of Juda and Jerusalem plan I no less eagerly;
16 vanquish your fears. And for your part, this do: deal honestly with your
neighbours, give ever in your market-place the true, the salutary award;
17 harbour no ill thoughts one against another, nor set your hearts on the
oath falsely sworn; every deed of wrong is hateful to me, the Lord says.
18   And word came to me from the Lord of hosts, bidding me say this in
19 his name: Fasts you kept ever, when three months of the year, or four,
six months or nine were gone, shall be all rejoicing and gladness for the
men of Juda now, all high festival, will you but love true dealing and

---

[1] Literally, 'listen to'; but the people of Juda could not be listening, there and
then, to prophecies uttered two years earlier.

20 peaceful ways.[1] This promise I give you from the Lord of hosts: What
21 alien throngs, from what far cities, shall make pilgrimage yet! And ever,
     as fresh towns they reach, says pilgrim, Come with us, and welcome;
     court we the divine favour, to the Lord of hosts repair we; says towns-
22 man, Go with you I will. No nation so populous, no kingdom so strong,
     but shall betake itself to Jerusalem, to find the Lord of hosts and court
23 his divine favour. This, too: A time is coming, when there is never a man
     of Jewish blood but shall have ten Gentiles at his heels, and no two of the
     same speech; clinging all at once to the skirts of him, and crying, Your
     way is ours! The tale has reached us, how God is there to protect you.

CHAPTER NINE

BURDEN of the Lord's doom, where falls it now? On Hadrach's
2 land; ay, and Damascus shall be its resting-place; perilously near is
3 Emath, and yonder cities of Tyre and Sidon, so famed for wisdom. This
     Tyre, how strong a fortress she has built, what silver and gold she has
4 amassed, till they were common as clay, as mire in the streets! Ay, but
     the Lord means to dispossess her; cast into the sea, all that wealth of hers,
5 and herself burnt to the ground! At the sight of it, how Ascalon
     trembles, how Gaza mourns, and Accaron, for hopes belied; no chieftain
6 in Gaza, no townsfolk left in Ascalon now; in Accaron dwells a
7 bastard breed. So low will I bring the pride of yonder Philistines; snatch
     the blood-stained morsel from their mouths, the unhallowed food theirs
     no longer; [2] servant of our God he shall be that is left surviving, a clans-
8 man [3] in Juda; so shall Accaron be all one with the Jebusite. I have
     sentinels that shall march to and fro, guarding this home of mine, and
     none shall take toll of it henceforward; my eyes are watching now.
9   Glad news for thee, widowed Sion; cry out for happiness, Jerusalem
     forlorn! See where thy king comes to greet thee, a trusty deliverer; see
     how lowly he rides, mounted on an ass, patient colt of patient dam![4]
10 Chariots of thine, Ephraim, horses of thine, Jerusalem, shall be done
     away, bow of the warrior be unstrung; peace this king shall impose on the
     world, reigning from sea to sea, from Euphrates to the world's end.
11   How should they be ransomed, but by the blood of thy covenant with

---

[1] A delayed answer to the question mooted in 7.3 above.
[2] Some think this verse implies that the Philistines will be converted to Jewish
customs, abstaining from meat with blood in it and other forbidden food. But it
may be Philistia is compared to a beast of prey; cf. Am. 3.12.
[3] Literally, 'a chieftain,' but this makes the sense difficult; some scholars, by
a different pointing of the Hebrew text, would read 'a clan.'
[4] Literally, 'and a colt, the foal of an ass'; the implication seems to be that
the king will come in less than royal state. See Mt. 21.5.

12 me, those thy fellow-countrymen, in waterless dungeons bound? To these
    sheltering walls, O patient prisoners, return; you have my warrant, double
13 recompense shall be granted you.   Bow of mine is Juda, Ephraim my
    shafts employ; Greece, look to thy sons when I match the sons of Sion
14 against them, sword in a warrior's hand! See him there, in visible form,
    high above them, the Lord God, that volleys down shaft of his lightning,
15 sounds with the trumpet, rides on the storm-wind of the south! He, the
    Lord of hosts, will be their protection; with sling-stones for teeth, flesh of
    men eat they, drink blood like revellers at their wine; not sacrificial bowl,
16 nor altar's horns, so drenched with blood.   His own people, his own
    sheep, will not the Lord God in that hour defend them? His own sacred
    trophy themselves shall be, to this land of his beckoning all men's eyes; [1]
17 a people how blessed and how fair! [2]   So well with corn and wine
    furnished, both man and maid shall thrive. [3]

CHAPTER TEN

FOR rain in spring whom but the Lord entreat we? He it is, none
    else, fashions the storm-cloud, waters the crops on this farm or that.
2 Vain the false god's foretelling, vainly diviner cheats us, and dreams
    delude; comfort they have none to give; such ways Israel has followed,
3 like a flock of sheep untended, and to its cost. What marvel if my anger
    blazed out against the shepherds? A reckoning I must have with yonder
    buck-goats; ay, the Lord of hosts would keep strict count of his flock, the
    sons of Israel.
4   Who but Israel is the proud charger I will ride into battle? Corner-
    stone, he, of the building, peg of the tent's rope, bow that shall win the
5 day; spoilers of the world he, none other, shall send forth. Warriors they
    shall be that go out to battle trampling all before them in the mire; does
    not the Lord go out to battle at their side? Well mounted, their enemies
6 could yet nothing win.   Such aid the men of Juda shall have, the sons of
    Joseph such deliverance; in pity I will restore them, and all shall be as it
    was before I cast them off from me; I am the Lord their God, shall I not
7 heed them? Ephraim, of great warriors the peer! Glad all hearts shall be,

---

[1] Literally, 'And the Lord their God will deliver them in that day, like the
flock of his people, because (they shall be like) stones of sanctification that are
lifted up as a standard over his land.'

[2] 'A people how blessed and how fair'; literally, 'What is the goodness of it
and what is the beauty of it!' Or possibly 'of him,' but the word 'beauty' would
be out of place in this context.

[3] The reference of verses 11–17 is obscure; the conflict between Jewish and
Greek culture did not make itself felt until nearly three hundred years after
Zachary's time.

as when the wine-cup goes round; children of his shall acclaim the sight, and triumph lustily in the Lord.

8 Flock of my ransoming, see how they gather at my call! Thriving now
9 as they throve long since, yet scattered through the world, in those distant lands they shall remember me; with spirits revived, they and their
10 children shall return. Back from Egypt, back from Assyria I will summon them, rally them, to Galaad and Lebanon bring them home; and that
11 home shall be too small for them. Crossed, yonder straits, the sea's wave checked, depths of the river disappointed of their prey! Assyria's pride
12 brought low, empire of Egypt cut down! In the Lord they shall find strength, under his protection come and go; so runs the divine promise.

CHAPTER ELEVEN

FLING thy gates wide, Lebanon, for the fire to come in, and devour
2 thy cedars! Lament, neighbour pine-tree, for cedar overthrown; here be lordly ones plundered; lament, oaks of Basan, for the secret forest that
3 is cut down! Hark, how the shepherd-folk lament, their fine mantle [1] gone, how roars lion for the thickets of Jordan stripped!
4 This message the Lord my God sent me: [2] To this flock that is a-fatten-
5 ing for slaughter thou must play the shepherd. What, would they slay without remorse, yonder lords of the flock, sell carcase, and thank the
6 Lord that so enriches them; are there shepherds so unmerciful? Nay, I will be unmerciful too, the Lord says, to all that dwell on earth; I will leave every son of Adam at the mercy of his neighbour, or the king that rules over him, and no redress shall they have from me henceforward!
7 Poor sheep fattening for slaughter, take charge of your flock I must; and two staves I made me, for the better tending of it, one I called Beauty,
8 and the other Cords. Before a month was up, of three shepherds I had rid them, yet had I no patience with them, and they of me grew no less
9 weary. No more will I tend you, said I; perish all of you that will perish, be lost all that will be lost; and for the residue, let them devour one
10 another; I care not. With that, I took up the staff I called Beauty, and cut it in two; in token that my covenant with all the world should be null.
11 Null it was thenceforward; and doubt they might not, the starvelings of the flock that looked up to me, the Lord's word had come to them.

---

[1] The word used in the Hebrew text may mean either 'mantle' or 'magnificence.' In the present context, it may perhaps refer to the shade of the trees, now lost to the shepherds through felling; the beasts have similarly been robbed of their covert in the thickets (literally, 'the pride') of the Jordan valley.

[2] No plausible account has been given either of the meaning of this prophecy (verses 4–17), or of the occasion upon which it was delivered.

12   ... And now, said I, pay me my wages, if pay you will; if not, say no
13   more. So they paid me for my wages thirty pieces of silver. Why, the
Lord said, here is a princely sum they rate me at! Throw it to the craftsman yonder. So there, in the Lord's temple, I threw the craftsman my
thirty pieces of silver ...¹
14   Then I took my other staff, Cords, and cut it in two; in token that all
15   brotherhood was at an end between Juda and Israel.² And the Lord said,
16   Gear of a foolish shepherd thou must take to thee now. See if I do not
find me such a shepherd for this land of theirs, as will leave lost sheep
uncounted, strayed sheep unsought, hurt sheep unhealed; and such as are
left whole, feed he will not, but eat ever the fattest of them, tearing only
17   the hoofs away. Out upon the false shepherd ³ that abandons his flock!
Sword shall pierce the arm of him, and the right eye of him, till arm is
withered and eye darkened quite.

CHAPTER TWELVE

B URDEN of the Lord's doom, where falls it now? On Israel. Word
from the Lord, who spread heaven out, founded earth, fashions the
2   life that beats in man! This is my decree, that Jerusalem's walls (ay, and
the whole of Juda shall man those ramparts) be offered to all the nations
3   round about for a fatal cup; ⁴ to all the world Jerusalem shall be a stone
immoveable; lift it who will, shall be torn unmercifully. See where they
4   muster to the attack, all the kingdoms of the world! Time now, the Lord
says, to dazzle steed and craze rider's wits; for Juda, the sunshine of my
5   regard, the heathen must ride in darkness. Vainly do yonder chieftains
of Juda look to the garrison of Jerusalem to be their succour, in the
6   strength of the Lord their God; chieftains of Juda themselves shall be my
instruments then, fire-brand in the forest, spark among the dry sheaves,
to devour all the nations right and left of them. Jerusalem shall stand,
7   when all is over, where Jerusalem stood; but to the country folk of Juda

---

¹ It is not easy to see who could be the employers mentioned in such a context,
and it may even be doubted whether these two verses have not been misplaced.
In Mt. 27.9, 10, where they are quoted in a considerably different form, Jeremy,
not Zachary, is mentioned as their author. But see note there.
² If the text is correctly preserved, this part of the parable looks as if it referred to a situation several centuries earlier than Zachary's time.
³ Literally, 'shepherd that is an idol,' or perhaps (according to the Hebrew
text) 'shepherd of nothingness.'
⁴ Literally, 'Behold, I will make Jerusalem a lintel of drunkenness to all
peoples round about; ay, and Juda, too, shall be in the siege against Jerusalem.'
In the Hebrew text, a cup is probably meant rather than a lintel; and the second
half of the verse runs, 'Ay, and against Juda, too, it shall be, in the siege (or,
stronghold) against Jerusalem.'

the Lord grants deliverance first; clan of David, citizens of Jerusalem, shall not boast themselves better than the rest.

8   When that day comes, lowest fallen among the people shall seem royal as David's self, and David's clansmen a race divine, as though an angel of the Lord marched at their head.[1]

9   Never a nation that marched on Jerusalem but I will hunt it down, when that day comes, and make an end of it.

10   On David's clan, on all the citizens of Jerusalem, I will pour out a gracious spirit of prayer; towards me they shall look, me whom they have pierced through.[2] Lament for him they must, and grieve bitterly; never was such lament for an only son, grief so bitter over first-born dead.

11   When that day comes, great shall be the mourning in Jerusalem, great
12 Adadremmon's mourning at Mageddo;[3] the whole land in mourning, all its families apart. Here the men of David's clan, yonder their women,
13 here the men of Nathan's, yonder their women, here the men of Levi's, yonder their women, here the men of Semei's, yonder their women;
14 apart they shall mourn, whatever families there be, and all their women-folk apart.

CHAPTER THIRTEEN

WHEN that day comes, clansmen of David and citizens of Jerusalem shall have a fountain flowing openly, of guilt to rid them, and of defilement.

2   A time shall come, says the Lord of hosts, when I will efface the memory of the false gods; the very names of them shall be forgotten;
3 banish, too, the false prophets, and the unclean spirit they echo.   Dares one of them prophesy again, all men will turn against him, even the parents that begot him; Still at thy lying, and in the Lord's name? Thou shalt die for it! And with a javelin's thrust father and mother take the life they gave.

4   When that day comes, never a prophet but shall rue the false vision he
5 trusted in. Deceitful garb of sackcloth each one shall throw aside;   No prophet am I, but a simple peasant, that grew up to follow Adam's trade![4]

---

[1] Verses 8–14, with the whole of chapter 13, seem to form a collection of prophetic fragments rather than a continuous prophecy.

[2] A variant reading in some manuscripts gives 'him' instead of 'me.' On critical grounds, it is less plausible, but it seems to have been current in very early times (see Jn. 19.37; also Apoc. 1.7).

[3] The reference may be to II Para. 35.25; but many battles were fought in the neighbourhood of Mageddo.

[4] The meaning of the second half of this verse is quite uncertain.

6   Ask they, What wounds be these in thy clasped hands? [1] Thus wounded
was I, he shall answer, in the house of my friends.[2]
7   Up, sword, and attack this shepherd of mine, neighbour of mine, says
the Lord of hosts.[3]
    Smite shepherd, and his flock shall scatter; so upon the common folk
8 my vengeance shall fall.   All over this land, the Lord says, two thirds of
them are forfeit to destruction, only a third shall be left to dwell there;
9 and this third part, through fire I will lead them; purged they shall be as
silver is purged, tried as gold is tried. Theirs on my name to call, their
plea mine to grant; My own people, so I greet them, and they answer,
The Lord is my own God.

CHAPTER FOURTEEN

THE Lord's appointed time is coming, when spoil of thee shall be
2   divided in thy midst. All the nations of the world I will muster to the
siege of Jerusalem; taken the city shall be, and its houses pillaged, and its
women-folk ravished; of the defenders, half will go into exile, and leave
3 but a remnant in the city.   And then the Lord will go out to battle against
4 those nations, as he did ever in the decisive hour. There on the mount of
Olives, that faces Jerusalem on the east, his feet shall be set; to east and
west the mount of Olives shall be cloven in two halves, with a great chasm
between, and the two halves shall move apart, one northward, one south-
5 ward.   Down the clefts of that sacred hill-side you shall flee, each of them
now leading to the next; flee as you fled before the earthquake, in Ozias'
time, that reigned over Juda; on, on he comes, the Lord my God, with all
his sacred retinue.
6   Light there shall be none that day, all shall be frost and cold; [4] one day

---

[1] Literally, 'between thy hands,' a difficult phrase most inadequately interpreted by some moderns as meaning 'on thy back.' If the sacred author had meant
'between thy arms,' he would surely have said so, as in IV Kg. 9.24.

[2] Literally, 'my lovers'; elsewhere in the Old Testament this word always
refers to false gods, as the 'lovers' with whom Israel committed adultery. If the
false prophet is referred to, it is not easy to see what injuries he had sustained,
why any question was asked about them, what answer was expected, or what
was meant by the answer given.

[3] 'Neighbour'; the word is not likely to be what the prophet wrote. Elsewhere
it is only a legal term meaning 'a second party.' The second half of the verse
may be a continuation of the first; but if so the direction 'Smite!' cannot be
addressed to the sword, which would require a feminine, not a masculine forma-
tion of the verb.

[4] The sense of this verse is doubtful, and it seems possible the text needs
emendation; perhaps the prophet wrote 'there shall be neither light nor darkness, heat nor cold.'

there shall be, none but the Lord knows the length of it, that shall be neither daylight nor dark, but when evening comes, there shall be light. 8 Then a living stream will flow from Jerusalem, half to the eastern, half 9 to the western sea, winter and summer both; and over all the earth the 10 Lord shall be king, one Lord, called everywhere by one name. What shall be the land's frontiers? The desert, and Geba, and Remmon that is south of Jerusalem. What of the city? It shall be built up high, and its true limits keep, from gate of Benjamin to main gate and corner gate, 11 from tower of Hananeel to the king's wine-press. A populous city, no ban resting on it thenceforward; a secure dwelling-place.

12 And what of the visitation that shall smite down the assailants of Jerusalem? Wasted away the flesh of them, till they can keep their feet no 13 longer; wasted away eye in socket and tongue in mouth; with great tumult of mind the Lord will bemuse them that day, each of them laying 14 hands on his fellow, brother engaging brother in fight. Juda meanwhile, shall set about the regaining of Jerusalem,[1] and find the spoils of every neighbouring people amassed there, gold, and silver, and of raiment 15 great abundance; but as for horse and mule, camel and ass, and all the cattle in yonder camp, these will have perished by the same plague as their masters.

16 Yet of all the nations that sent their armies against Jerusalem there shall be some remnant left; and these, year by year, shall make pilgrimage, to worship their King, the Lord of hosts, and keep his feast of Tent-17 dwelling. Come and worship their King they must, the Lord of hosts; 18 else no rain shall fall on them, all the world over. What then of Egypt's folk, that rain have none? What if they refuse to go on pilgrimage? Why, for their neglecting of this feast, the same plague shall fall on them which 19 the Lord sent on the heathen armies aforesaid.[2] Be it Egypt, or be it any other nation, that will not keep the feast of Tent-dwelling, punished it shall be in this fashion or in that.

20 Spoils from the enemy's bridle-rein shall be consecrated on that day to the Lord's service, till there is never pot or pan in his temple but rivals 21 the altar's bowls for costliness![3] Nay, never pot or pan in all Jerusalem

---

[1] 'Set about the regaining of Jerusalem'; in the original simply 'fight against Jerusalem.' But it is clear from the context that we have gone back to the situation described in verse 2, where Jerusalem is enemy-occupied. The Vulgate here gives the form 'Judas,' instead of the more usual form 'Juda,' perhaps with the idea that Judas Machabaeus is referred to.

[2] The Hebrew text is obscure, and perhaps corrupt, but it seems most likely that the sense given above was the general sense of it. The Latin version gives no satisfactory meaning here.

[3] Literally, 'On that day that which is on the horse's bridle shall be holy to the Lord, and the caldrons in the Lord's house will be like bowls before the altar.' The Hebrew text is usually interpreted as meaning that the bells on the trappings

but shall be consecrated to the Lord of hosts, for any who will to come and take it and seethe victim in it; trafficking there shall be no more in the Lord's temple, when that day comes.[1]

of the horses (it is difficult to see what horses) will be inscribed, 'Holiness to the Lord.'

[1] This verse seems to imply that only consecrated vessels might be used in seething the victim before a sacrifice; and further, that some charge was made by the Temple authorities for the use of the vessels in question.

THE PROPHECY OF MALACHIAS

CHAPTER ONE

HERE follows burden of the Lord's doom for Israel, that was entrusted to Malachias.

2 Oh, but I have dealt lovingly with you! the Lord says. Would you know,
wherein I shewed my love, this tell me; was not Esau brother to Jacob?

3 Yet to Jacob I proved myself a friend, the Lord says, no friend to Esau;
I have made a waste of yonder mountain-side, of all his lands a dragon-

4 haunted desert. Ay, but, says Edom, what if we have fallen on evil days?
Give us time to repair the ruins! Trust me, says the Lord of hosts, as fast
as they build, I will pull down; land of rebellion men shall call it, brood

5 the Lord hates, and for ever. Glad sight, to make you cry God praise
from end to end of Israel!

6 Son to father, servant to master gives his due. Your father I, where is
the honour, your master I, where is the reverence you owe me? Such complaint the Lord of hosts makes, and to whom? To you, priests, that care

7 so little for my renown. Ask you what care was lacking, when the bread
you offer at my altar is defiled, ask you what despite you have done me,

8 when you hold the Lord's table a thing of little moment? What, no harm
done, when victim you offer in sacrifice is blind? No harm done, when it
is lame or diseased? Pray you, says the Lord of hosts, make such a gift to
the governor yonder, will he be content? Will he make favourites of you?

9 Ay, says the Lord of hosts, the guilt is yours. To the divine presence
betake you, and sue for pardon; which of you finds favour with him?

10 Never a man of you but must be paid to shut door, light altar-fire; no
friends of mine, says the Lord of hosts, no gifts will I take from such as

11 you. No corner of the world, from sun's rise to sun's setting, where the
renown of me is not heard among the Gentiles, where sacrifice is not
done, and pure offering made in my honour; so revered is my name, says

12 the Lord of hosts, there among the Gentiles; [1] and you? That you should
hold it so cheap! That you should think to yourselves, The Lord's table
is desecrated now; it makes no matter what food lies there, or what fire

13 burns it! Weary work, say you, and dismiss it with a sigh. Beast mangled,
beast gone lame, beast that is ailing you present to me, and the bloodless
offering with it. And should the Lord of hosts accept the gift you make
him?

---

[1] It is difficult to know whether the prophet, in reference to his own day, is
speaking there of the heathen sacrifices (as if they were offered, unwittingly, to
the true God), or of such sacrifices as were performed by the Jewish exiles, in
various (but hardly in numerous) parts of the world.

14   Cursed be the knavery that offers the Lord gelt beast, when vows are a-
     paying, and all the while there is an entire beast left at home! [1] Offers it to
     the Lord of hosts, the great King, no name in all the world so terrible!

CHAPTER TWO

2   IT is for you, priests, to see that this law of mine is obeyed.   Give me
    neither heed nor hearing, says the Lord of hosts, let my name go un-
    honoured, and with sore distress I will visit you; falls my curse on all the
    blessings you enjoy, falls my curse . . .,[2] to the punishing of your heed-
3   lessness.   Arm of yours I will strike motionless, bury your faces in dung,
    ay, the dung of your own sacrifices, and to the dung-pit you shall go.
4   So you shall learn your lesson; my law I gave you, says the Lord of hosts,
5   in token of my covenant with Levi's family.   Live they should and thrive,
    but the fear of me I enjoined upon them; none but should fear, and hold
6   my name in reverence.   Faithfully they handed on tradition, the lie never
    on their lips; safe and straight was the path they trod at my side, and
7   kept many from wrong-doing.   No utterance like a priest's for learning;
    from no other lips men will expect true guidance; is he not a messenger [3]
8   to them from the Lord of hosts?   That path you have forsaken; through
    your ill-teaching, how many a foothold lost! Nay, says the Lord of hosts,
9   you have annulled my covenant with Levi altogether.   What wonder if
    I have made you a laughing-stock, a thing contemptible in all men's
    sight, priests that so ill kept my command, so compliantly gave award?
10   Have we not all one Father, did not one God create us all? No room,
    then, for brother to despise brother, and unmake the covenant by which
    our fathers lived.[4]
11   Here is great wrong in Juda, here are foul deeds done by Israel and
    Jerusalem! [5] Juda, that was once content to be set apart for the Lord, has
    profaned that holy estate, allied himself by wedlock with an alien god.
12 Doer of such a deed, set he or followed the ill example, shall be lost to the

---

[1] 'Gelt,' literally, 'spoilt'; 'entire,' literally, 'male.' Some such contrast is evidently intended; cf. Lev. 22.24.
[2] The repetition, 'falls my curse,' is difficult to explain, except on the supposition that a word or two has dropped out in the manuscripts.
[3] Here, as often elsewhere, the Latin translates 'angel.'
[4] This verse does not seem closely connected either with what precedes it or
with what follows it. The prophet may have been thinking of other misde-
meanours, such as those mentioned in Neh. 5.
[5] This difficult passage, verses 11–16, is generally understood as referring to
the intermarriage of the Jews with surrounding nations; cf. Esd. 9 and 10. But
Malachy's protest is concerned only with foreign brides, not with foreign bride-
grooms; and he seems only to envisage those cases in which a Jewish wife has
been divorced to make room for a Gentile rival.

dwelling-place of Jacob, for all his offerings made to the Lord of hosts.
13 And anon, weeping and wailing, you drench the Lord's altar with your
tears! What marvel if I heed your sacrifices no more, gift of yours is none
14 can appease me? And the reason of it? Because the Lord bears witness to
her wrongs, that wife of thy manhood's age, whom now thou spurnest,
15 thy partner, thy covenanted bride! Yet doer of this is the same man as
ever, the will of him is unchanged; he asks nothing better, now as before,
than to breed a God-fearing race; to that will, men of Juda, keep true.
16 Spurn her not, the wife of thy manhood's age; what though the God of
Israel gives thee leave to send her away if she suits thee ill? Garment of
her, says the Lord of hosts, is yet stained with the wrong thou didst her.
Will of thine forgo not, wife of thine spurn not.[1]
17   Oh, but the Lord is aweary of your doings! And little wonder, when
you think so amiss of him; telling yourselves, Foul is fair in the Lord's
sight, and wrong-doing well likes him; God that judges us is none.

CHAPTER THREE

SEE where I am sending an angel of mine, to make the way ready for
my coming! All at once the Lord will visit his temple; that Lord, so
longed for, welcome herald of a divine covenant. Ay, says the Lord of
2 hosts, he is coming; but who can bear the thought of that advent? Who
will stand with head erect at his appearing? He will put men to a test
3 fierce as the crucible, searching as the lye that fullers use. From his
judgement-seat, he will refine that silver of his and cleanse it from dross;
like silver or gold, the sons of Levi must be refined in the crucible, ere
4 they can offer the Lord sacrifice duly performed. Then once more the
Lord will accept the offerings of Juda and Jerusalem, as he did long since,
5 in the forgotten years. Come I to hold assize, not slow to arraign the
sorcerer, the adulterer, the forsworn, all of you that deny hired man his
wages, widow and orphan redress, the alien his right, fearing no vengeance from the Lord of hosts.
6   In me, the Eternal, there is no change, and you, sons of Jacob, are
7 unperished still. What though you have refused my claims, left them

---

[1] Literally, 'Did not one man do (or, make)? And his spirit is left surviving.
And what does one man seek, except the seed of God? Guard therefore your
spirits, and do not despise the wife of thy youth. When thou hatest her, dismiss
her, says the Lord, the God of Israel; but wrong shall cover her (or, his) garment, says the Lord of hosts. Guard your spirits, and do not despise.' The
Hebrew text, which gives 'his (not her) garment,' is even more obscure throughout; and numerous explanations have been suggested, without throwing much
light on the passage.

unhonoured, as your fathers did before you? Nay, says the Lord of hosts, you have but to relent towards me, and I, in my turn, will relent. Would
8 you know the manner of it, bethink you that it is not for man to wrong God, as you wrong me; out of all question you wrong me, over your
9 tithes and first-fruits. Ay, here is sworn conspiracy;[1] it is myself you
10 wrong, the whole brood of you! Do but carry your tithe into the tithe-barn, for my temple's needs, and see if I do not open the windows of
11 heaven for you, rain down blessing to your hearts' content! Ban of mine shall fall on the locust,[2] and to your crops he shall do no harm; nowhere
12 in all your countryside, I promise you, shall vine cast its fruits; the envy of all nations you shall be, says the Lord of hosts, a land of content.
13 And now, says the Lord of hosts, your complaints have had their way
14 with me. Complain you did: Who serves God serves him for nothing; what reward is ours for keeping command of his, attending with sad mien
15 the Lord of hosts? Here are proud folk more to be envied than we, ill-
16 doers that yet thrive, abusers of his patience that escape all harm! So they used to talk among themselves, his true worshippers, till at last the Lord gave them heed and hearing; and now he would have a record kept in his presence of all that so worshipped him, all that prized his renown.
17 Dear they shall be to me, says the Lord of hosts, when I declare myself at
18 last; never to loyal son was father more gracious; then you shall think better of it, and know them apart, the just that serve God and the sinners that are none of his.

CHAPTER FOUR

TRUST me, a day is coming that shall scorch like a furnace; stubble they shall be before it, says the Lord of hosts, all the proud, all the wrong-doers, caught and set alight, and neither root nor branch left them.
2 But to you that honour my name there shall be a sunrise of restoration, swift-winged, bearing redress; light-hearted as frisking calves at stall you
3 shall go out to meet it,[3] ay, and trample on your godless enemy, spurning them like ashes under foot, on that day when the Lord of hosts declares himself at last.
4 Yours to keep the law ever in mind, statute and award I gave to

---

[1] Literally, 'You are cursed with a curse' (the Latin, however, has 'with distress'). The meaning seems to be, not that Juda is under a divine curse (which would destroy the logic of the sentence), but that the Jews have bound themselves under a curse to offer God resistance (cf. Jg. 21.1 and 18).

[2] Literally, 'the devourer.'

[3] Literally, 'But to you that fear my name a sun of justice shall rise, and healing in her wings; and you shall go out, and leap like calves from the stall.'

5 assembled Israel through Moses, that was my servant. And before ever
that day comes, great day and terrible, I will send Elias to be your
6 prophet; he it is shall reconcile heart of father to son, heart of son to
father; else the whole of earth should be forfeit to my vengeance.[1]

---

[1] It is not clear what kind of disagreement between the older and the younger
generation, or perhaps between the past and the present, is indicated. 'The whole
of earth,' or perhaps, 'the whole land.'

THE FIRST BOOK OF MACHABEES

CHAPTER ONE

NOW turn we to Alexander son of Philip, the Macedonian, that was the first to reign over all Greece. This Alexander marched out from his own land of Cethim, and overcame Darius, king of the Medes and

2 Persians. Battles he waged a many; nor any fortress might hold out

3 against him, nor any king escape with his life; and so he journeyed on to the world's end, spoiling the nations everywhere; at his coming, silence

4 fell on the earth. So great the power of him, so valiant his armies, what

5 wonder if his heart grew proud? All those lands conquered, all those

6 kings his tributaries! Then, all at once, he took to his bed, and the know-

7 ledge came to him he must die. Whereupon he summoned the noblest of his courtiers, men that had shared his own upbringing, and to these,

8 while he had life in him yet, divided up his kingdom. So reigned Alexander for twelve years, and so died.

9 And what of these courtiers turned princes, each with a province of his

10 own? Be sure they put on royal crowns, they and their sons after them,

11 and so the world went from bad to worse. Burgeoned then from the stock of Antiochus a poisoned growth, Antiochus the second, that was called the Illustrious. He had been formerly a hostage at Rome, but now, in the hundred and thirty-seventh year of the Grecian empire, he came

12 into his kingdom. In his day there were godless talkers abroad in Israel, that did not want for a hearing; Come, said they, let us make terms with the heathen that dwell about us! Ever since we forswore their company,

13 nought but trouble has come our way. What would you? Such talk

14 gained credit, and some were at pains to ask for the royal warrant; whereupon leave was given them, Gentile usages they should follow if

15 they would. With that, they must have a game-place at Jerusalem, after

16 the Gentile fashion, ay, and go uncircumcised; forgotten, their loyalty to the holy covenant, they must throw in their lot with the heathen, and become the slaves of impiety.

17 And now that he was firmly established on his throne, Antiochus would

18 be lord of Egypt, and wear two crowns at once. So, with overwhelming force, with chariots and elephants and horsemen and a great array of

19 ships, he marched on Egypt, and levied war against king Ptolemy, that

20 could not hold his ground, but fled away, leaving many fallen. So Antiochus made himself master of all the strongholds in Egypt, and

21 ransacked it for spoil; then, in the hundred and forty-third year, he

22 turned his victorious march against Israel. With all that great army of

23 his he came to Jerusalem and entered the sanctuary in royal state; the
golden altar, the lamp-stand with its appurtenances, the table where
bread was set out, beaker and goblet and bowl, curtain and capital and
24 golden facings of the temple, all alike were stripped. Silver nor gold was
spared, nor any ornament of price, nor hoarded treasures could he but
25 find them; and thus laden he went back to his own country, first shedding
a deal of blood, and speaking very blasphemously.

26 Loud mourning there was in Israel, mourning in all the countryside;
27 wept ruler and elder, pined man and maid, and colour fled from woman's
28 cheeks; bridegroom took up the dirge, bride sat in her bower discon-
29 solate; here was a land that trembled for its inhabitants, a whole race
covered with confusion.

30 Two years passed, and then the king sent his chief collector of revenue
to visit the cities of Juda. To Jerusalem he came, with a great rabble at
31 his heels, and won credence with idle professions of friendship. Then
he fell suddenly on the town and grievously mishandled it, slaying Israel-
33 ites a many, plundering the city and setting fire to it. Houses and en-
34 circling walls of it were thrown down in ruins, women and children
35 carried off into slavery, cattle driven away. And as for David's Keep,
they enclosed it with high, strong walls, and strong towers besides, to
36 serve them for a fortress; garrisoned it with a godless crew of sinners like
themselves, and made it fast, storing it with arms and provisions, besides
37 the plunder they had amassed in Jerusalem, which they bestowed there
38 for safety. Alas, what peril of treachery was here, what an ambush laid
39 about the holy place, what devil's work against Israel! What a tide of
40 guiltless blood must flow about the sanctuary, till it was a sanctuary no
more! Little wonder if the inhabitants of Jerusalem took to flight, leaving
their city to strangers; mother so unnatural her own children must
41 forsake. Her sanctuary a desert solitude, her feasts all lament, her
42 sabbaths derided, her greatness brought low! Her pride was the measure
of that abasement, her glory of that shame.

43 And now came a letter from king Antiochus to all the subjects of his
realm, bidding them leave ancestral custom of this race or that, and be-
44 come one nation instead. As for the heathen, they fell in readily enough
45 with the royal will; and in Israel itself there were many that chose slavery,
46 offering sacrifice to false gods and leaving the sabbath unobserved. Both
in Jerusalem and in all the cities of Juda the king's envoys published this
47 edict; men must live by the law of the heathen round about, burnt-
48 sacrifice, offering and atonement in God's temple should be none, nor
49 sabbath kept, nor feast-day. And, for the more profanation of the sanc-
50 tuary, and of Israel's holy people, altar and shrine and idol must be set
51 up, swine's flesh offered, and all manner of unhallowed meat; children
be left uncircumcised, and their innocent lives contaminated with rites

52 abominable; till the law should be forgotten, and the divine precepts fashioned anew. Durst any neglect the royal bidding, he must die.

53 Through the whole of his dominions the king's writ ran, and commis-
54 sioners were appointed besides to enforce it; no city of Juda but was
55 ordered to do sacrifice. Many there were, traitors to the divine law, that
56 took their part, and much mischief they did, driving the men of Israel
57 to seek refuge in hiding, where refuge was to be had. It was on the twenty-fifth of Casleu, in the hundred and fortieth year, that king Antiochus set up an idol to desecrate God's altar; [1] shrines there were in every
58 township of Juda, offering of incense and of victims before house doors
59 and in the open street; never a copy of the divine law but was torn up and
60 burned; if any were found that kept the sacred record, or obeyed the
61 Lord's will, his life was forfeit to the king's edict. Month by month such deeds of violence were done, in all townships where men of Israel dwelt,
62 and on the twenty-fifth of the month sacrifice was made at the shrine that
63 overshadowed the altar. Death it was for woman to have her child cir-
64 cumcised in defiance of the king; there in her own house she must be hung up, with the child about her neck, and the circumciser, too, must
65 pay for it with his life. Many a son of Israel refused the unclean food,
66 preferring death to defilement; and die they must, because they would
67 not break God's holy law. Grievous, most grievous was the doom that hung then over his people.

CHAPTER TWO

IN those days it was that Mattathias came forward, son of John, son of Simeon, a priest of Joarib's family; he was for Jerusalem no more, but
2 would take up his dwelling on the hill-side at Modin. Five sons he had,
3 John, that was also called Gaddis, Simon (or Thasi), Judas (or Macha-
5 baeus), Eleazar (or Abaron), and Jonathan (or Apphus) and these saw well what foul things were a-doing in Juda's country and the city of Jeru-
7 salem. Alas, what needed it, cried Mattathias, I should have been born into such an age as this? To see my people and the holy city alike brought
8 to ruin, to sit by while the enemy overcame her, and in her very sanctuary the alien had his will? Temple of hers like a churl's lot disregarded,
9 rare treasure of hers into exile carried away; young and old, in the open
10 streets of her, put to the sword! Never a race in heathendom but may
11 parcel out her domains, grow rich with the spoil of her! Gone, all her
12 fair adornment; the mistress is turned maid; laid waste, yonder sanc-
13 tuary, that was our prize and pride, by Gentile feet dishonoured! And would we live yet?

---

[1] Cf. Dan. 11.31, Mt. 24.15.

14 With that, they tore their garments about them, Mattathias and his
15 sons, and went clad in sackcloth, mourning right bitterly. And now the
pursuivants of king Antiochus came to Modin; take refuge there who
might, he must do sacrifice none the less, and burn incense, and leave the
16 following of God's law. Out went the folk of Israel to meet them, some
complaisantly enough, but Mattathias and his sons firm in their resolve.
17 And they singled out Mattathias from the rest; A man of mark, said they,
18 and a great chieftain thou; brethren and sons thou hast a many. Wilt
thou not be the first to come forward and do the king's bidding, with the
whole world, and the men of Juda everywhere, and what is left of Jerusalem? To be the king's friend, thou and thy sons with thee, gold and
19 silver and much else for thy reward! Loud rang the answer of Mattathias: What though king Antiochus have the whole world for his vassals?
Obey the edict who will, forsaking the custom his fathers lived by,
20 both I and son of mine, both I and clansman of mine, will obey the law
21 handed down to us. Mercy of God! What needs it we should leave his
22 will undone, his claims unhonoured? To deaf ears king Antiochus proclaims the sacrifice; we swerve not from the law's path, right or left.
23 Before he had done speaking, a Jew came to offer the false gods sacrifice, there in full view of all, before the altar at Modin, as the king bade.
24 Mattathias took fire at the sight of it; one heave of anger his heart gave,
and his zeal for the law could contain itself no longer; there on the altar
25 the sacrificer was slain. Nor spared he the pursuivant of king Antiochus
26 that enjoined it; the altar, too, he pulled down. Not Phinees himself
struck a better blow for the law, when he slew Zamri, the son of Salom! [1]
27 And now Mattathias raised a cry in the city, Who loves the law? Who
28 keeps the covenant unbroken? Out with you, and follow me! So fled
he with his sons into the hill-country, leaving his possessions behind,
there in the city.
29 Many there were that went out into the desert at this time, for love
30 of truth and right; took children and women-folk and cattle with them
31 and settled down there, castaways in a flood of misfortune. But news of it
reached Jerusalem, and the king's men that were in David's Keep; here
were rebels lurking in the waste country, and drawing many over to their
32 side. So they went out in pursuit, and offered battle; on a sabbath day,
33 as it chanced.[2] What, still stubborn? cried they. Come out, and yield
34 yourselves to the king's pleasure; your lives shall be spared. But the
Jews' answer was, come out and yield to the king's pleasure they might
35 not; law of the sabbath rest forbade it. So the attack began in good

---

[1] Cf. Num. 25.7.
[2] The words 'as it chanced' are not in the original, but it does not seem to be
implied that the king's men chose the sabbath day for making their assault.

36 earnest; but the Jews made no resistance, never a stone flew, never a
37 hiding-place of theirs was put in a state of defence; Die we all, they said,
   innocent men, and let heaven and earth bear witness, it was for no fault
38 of ours we died. Thus, because it was a sabbath day when the attack was
   made, these men perished, and their wives and children and cattle with
   them; a thousand human lives lost.

39   Great grief it was to Mattathias and his company when they heard
40 what had befallen them; and now there was high debate raised: Do we as
   our brethren did, forbear we to give battle for our lives and loyalties, and
41 they will soon make an end of us! Then and there it was resolved, if any
   should attack them on the sabbath day, to engage him, else they should
   be put to death all of them, like those brethren of theirs in the covert of
42 the hills. Now it was that the Assidaeans rallied to their side, a party that
43 was of great consequence in Israel, lovers of the law one and all; and all
   who would escape from the evils of the time, made common cause with
44 them, and came to their assistance. So, mustering their forces, they
   wrought indignant vengeance upon sinners that were false to the law, till
45 they were fain to take refuge among the heathen; wherever they went,
46 Mattathias and his company, they threw the altars down, and whatever
   children they found uncircumcised, from one end of Israel to the other,
47 they circumcised by right of conquest.[1] Ere long, they drove the
48 tyrant's minions before them, and to such good purpose that Gentile
   was none, king though he were, could restrain the law's observance;
   against their onslaught the powers of evil could not make head.

49   Meanwhile, the life of Mattathias was drawing to an end. And this
   charge he gave to his sons: Here be days when tyrant and blasphemer
50 have their will, when all is calamity and bitter retribution. The more
   reason, my sons, why you should be jealous lovers of the law, ready to
51 give your lives for that covenant your fathers knew. Your fathers, what
   deeds they did in their time! Great glory would you win, and a deathless
52 name, let these be your models. See how Abraham was tested, and how
53 trustfulness of his was counted virtue in him; see how Joseph in ill fortune was true to the commandment still, and came to be ruler of all
54 Egypt. Here was Phinees, our own father, that grew hot in God's cause,
55 and earned the right of priesthood inalienable; and Josue, that for his
56 loyalty was given command of Israel; and Caleb, that spoke out in the
57 assembly, what broad acres were his! David, for the tender heart of him,
58 left a dynasty that fails not; for Elias heaven opened, that was champion
59 of the law; by faith Ananias, Azarias and Misael overcame the furnace,
60 nor Daniel's innocence might ravening lions devour. No generation but

---

[1] It is not clear whether we are meant to understand that Gentile as well as
Jewish children were circumcised.

62 proves it; want they never for strength that trust in God. What, would
63 you fear the tyrant's threats? In dung and worms his glory shall end; all
   royal state to-day, and to-morrow there shall be no news of him; gone
   back to the dust he came from, and all his designs brought to nothing!
64   Nay, my sons, take courage; in the law's cause rally you, in the law's
65 annals you shall win renown. Here is your brother Simon, trust me, a
66 man of prudence; to him ever give heed, he is your father now. And here
   is Judas Machabaeus, from boyhood's days a warrior; let him be your
67 leader, and fight Israel's battles. All lovers of the law make free of your
68 fellowship; bring your country redress, and pay the Gentiles what they
69 have earned; yet heeding ever what the law enjoins. With that, he gave
70 them his blessing, and became part of his race. He was a hundred and
   forty-six years old when he died; his sons buried him where his fathers
   were buried, at Modin, and great lament all Israel made for the loss of
   him.

CHAPTER THREE

A ND now his son Judas, that was called Machabaeus, came forward
2   to succeed him; nor any of Judas' clan, nor any that had taken his
   father's part, but lent him their aid still; right merrily they fought Israel's
3 battle. Here was one that brought his race renown; as great a warrior as
   ever donned breastplate, or armed himself for the fight, or drew sword
4 to save his camp from peril; lion-hearted his deeds, not lion itself more
5 relentless in pursuit. Traitors he ever sought out and hunted down, ever
6 with fire-brand the oppressors of his people dislodged, till enemy was
   none but was daunted by the fear of him, traitor was none but fled in
7 confusion, so well sped he the work of deliverance. Great deeds, that
   kings rued bitterly, Jacob with exultation heard, posterity holds blessed
8 evermore! From city to city he went, ridding Juda of its law-breakers,
9 averting the vengeance guilt of theirs had deserved; no corner of earth
   but he was renowned there, for one that had been able to rally a doomed
   people.
10   How sped Apollonius, that mustered a great force, of Gentiles and
11 Samaritans both, to fight against Israel? No sooner Judas heard of it,
12 than he met and routed and slew him; fell many and fled more, leaving
   their spoils behind them. The sword of Apollonius Judas himself carried
   away; and this it was he evermore used in battle.
13   And next it was Seron, captain of the armies in Syria, heard what a
14 great retinue and faithful following Judas had; and nothing would serve,
   but he must win renown and high favour at court by crushing Judas, and

15 all other his companions that defied the king's edict. So he made all
ready, and marched in with a strong muster of the ungodly at his heels,
16 to be even with the men of Israel. As far as Bethoron pass they reached,
and there Judas met them with his company, no better than a handful.
17 These, when they saw such a host facing them, were for counsels of prudence; What, they said to Judas, should we offer battle to foes so many
18 and so strong, faint as we be from a day of hungry marching? Nay, said
Judas, nothing forbids great numbers should be at the mercy of small;
what matter makes it to the God of heaven, few be his soldiers or many
19 when he grants deliverance? Armed might avails not to win the day; vic-
20 tory is from above. What though they come to meet us in the proud confidence of superior strength, and think it an easy matter to slay us, slay
21 our wives and children, plunder our goods? Life and loyalty at stake, we
22 will offer battle none the less; and he, the Lord, will crush them to earth
23 at our coming; never be afraid. And with that, all unawares, he fell upon
Seron and his army, that were crushed, sure enough, by his onslaught;
24 all down the pass of Bethoron he gave them chase, down into the plain,
and eight hundred of them had fallen before ever they took refuge in the
country of the Philistines.

25 By this, the neighbouring peoples had begun to take alarm, so formid-
26 able did Judas and his brethren appear to them, and the renown of him
reached the king's court; all the world was talking of Judas and his vic-
27 tories. An angry man was king Antiochus when the news came to him;
he sent word round, and had all his army summoned together, a brave
28 array, be sure of it. The treasury must be opened, to provide the troops
29 with a whole year's pay, and keep them in readiness for every need. Why,
what was this? So heavily had Juda suffered, so great the discord he had
aroused by the abolishing of its ancient usages, that scant revenue had
30 come in from it, and the treasury was in default! Whence, now, to defray
the cost of that largesse he had made so often, and with so lavish a hand?
31 Here was the king in great confusion of mind; and his thought was, to
march into Persia and take toll of those countries; great store of money
32 he might there amass. But he left Lysias behind, that was a man of high
rank and royal blood; he was to administer all the business of the king-
33 dom, from Euphrates down to the Brook of Egypt, and have charge of
34 the young prince Antiochus, until the king's return. Half his army he
entrusted to Lysias, and the elephants besides; and he signified all that
35 he would have done, concerning Juda and Jerusalem particularly. A
force must be sent to overpower all that fought for Israel, or were yet left
in Jerusalem, and make a clean riddance of them; no trace of these must
36 be left; all through the country settlers must be brought in from abroad,
37 and the lands distributed to them. With that, the king left his capital of
Antioch, taking the remainder of his army with him; it was the hundred

and forty-seventh year of the empire. Soon he was across Euphrates
river, and on the march through the high countries.

38 Three generals Lysias appointed for the task; Ptolemy son of Dorymenes, Nicanor and Gorgias, nobles all that were high in the royal favour;
39 with forty thousand foot and seven thousand horse they were to march on
40 Juda and make an end of it, as the king had ordered. So out they went,
with all this army at their back, marched in, and pitched their tents near
41 Emmaus, down in the valley. Be sure the traders all about were apprised
of their coming, and made their way into the camp with great sums of
silver and gold, and a retinue of servants besides, thinking to buy Israelite slaves; levies, too, from Syria and Philistia made common cause with
the invader.

42 Judas, then, and his brethren found that matters had gone from bad to
worse; here were the enemy encamped within their frontiers; they heard,
besides, what orders the king had given for the destruction and taking
43 away of their people. And the word went round among them, Now to
restore the lost fortunes of our race; now to do battle for people of ours,
44 sanctuary of ours! So a general assembly was called; they must make
45 ready for the fight, and pray besides, to win mercy and pardon. Not at
Jerusalem; Jerusalem lay there, no city but a desert waste, nor any of her
sons came and went; her sanctuary defiled, her citadel garrisoned by the
alien, she was but a haunt of the Gentiles. Sad days for the men of Jacob;
46 pipe nor harp sounded there now. At Maspha, then, they gathered,
looking across towards Jerusalem; time was when Maspha, too, had its
47 place of prayer. All that day they fasted, and wore sackcloth, and covered
their heads with ashes, and tore their garments about them.

48 What sights were these? Here, lying open, was a copy of the law, such
as the heathen were ever making search for, . . . the counterpart of their
49 own images.[1] Here they had brought priestly vestments, and offering of
first-fruits and tithes; here Nazirites were gathered, ripe and ready for
50 the payment of their vows. And a loud cry rose to heaven, What shall we
51 do for these, thy votaries? Whither escort them now? Sanctuary of thine
is all profanation and defilement, priesthood of thine all misery and
52 despair. And now, see where the heathen muster their armies to destroy
53 us! Needs not we should tell thee, how murderous their intent. Lord, but
54 for thy aid, how shall we resist their onslaught? Loudly their voices, and
loud the trumpets rang.

55 Thereupon Judas chose out who should be their leaders, one with a
thousand, one with a hundred, one with fifty, one with ten men to follow

---

[1] As the sentence stands, it can only mean that heathen pursuivants had confiscated the scriptures, as being objects of veneration to the Jews no less than
idols were to themselves. But it seems possible that the text is deficient.

56 him; he sent home, too, all such as the law holds exempt; all that had but
just built house, or married wife, or planted vineyard, and whoever had
57 no stomach to the fight.[1] Then they moved camp, and pitched their tents
58 southward of Emmaus. Now for girded loins, cried Judas, and brave
hearts! By to-morrow's light, you must engage yonder heathen, sworn
59 enemies to us, and to the ground we hold sacred. Better die in battle,
60 than live to see our race and our sanctuary overpowered. Be it what it
may, heaven's will be done!

CHAPTER FOUR

THAT night, a detachment of five thousand foot and a thousand
picked horsemen left their lines, under the command of Gorgias,
2 thinking to reach the Jewish camp and strike a sudden blow at it; for
3 guides, they had men of the Jerusalem garrison. But Judas had word of
it; out he went, and all his valiant company with him, to attack the main
4 body of the king's army at Emmaus, while the defences of the camp were
5 yet scattered. So Gorgias, making his night attack on the camp of Judas,
and finding it empty, made no doubt they had given him the slip, and fell
6 to scouring the hill-country for them; meanwhile, came day-break, and
there was Judas down in the valley. True, there were but three thousand
7 at his back, for defence and attack very ill arrayed; and here was this
army of heathen folk, both strong and well protected, with cavalry cir-
8 cling about them, men bred to war! But Judas cried to his fellows, What,
would you be daunted by the numbers of them? Would you give ground
9 before their attack? Bethink you, what a host it was Pharao sent in pursuit of our fathers, there by the Red Sea, and they escaped none the less.
10 Now, as then, besiege we heaven with our cries; will not the Lord have
mercy? Will he not remember the covenant he had with our fathers, and
11 rout, this day, yonder army at our coming? No doubt shall the world
have thenceforward, but there is one claims Israel for his own, and
grants her deliverance.

12 And now the heathen folk caught sight of them as they advanced to the
13 attack, and left their lines to give battle. Thereupon Judas' men sounded
14 with the trumpet, and the two armies met. Routed the Gentiles were,
15 sure enough, and took to their heels across the open country, sword of
the pursuer ever catching the hindmost. All the way to Gezeron they
were chased, and on into the plains by Idumaea,[2] Azotus and Jamnia,

---

[1] See Deut. 20.5–8.
[2] For 'Idumaea' some Greek manuscripts read 'Judaea.' Neither reading gives
a good sense, and it seems possible that the name of Accaron, or some other
Philistine town, has been accidentally miswritten.

16 with a loss of three thousand men. When Judas and his army came back
17 from the pursuit, Not yours, he told them, to run greedily after the
18 spoils of the camp; there is battle still awaiting us over yonder. Not far
     away, in the hill-country, lie Gorgias and his army; first meet you and
     beat you the enemy, and then you shall fall to your pillaging unafraid.
19 Even as he spoke, they were ware of a company that watched them from
20 the hill-side. But by now the camp was on fire, and it needed no more
21 than the smoke of it to warn Gorgias of his defeat; that sight took the
     heart out of Syria, the more so when it proved that Judas and his army
22 were in the valley, all appointed for battle, and they fled for their lives,
23 down into the plain of Philistia. So to the pillaging of the camp Judas
     returned; what gold and silver they found there, what garments of blue
24 and sea-purple, what rich treasures! Be sure there was singing of songs
     on their homeward journey, as they praised God in heaven, God who is
25 gracious, whose mercy endures for ever. Here was a day of signal deliver-
     ance for Israel.
26   And what of Lysias? News reached him, through the survivors, of what
27 had befallen, and he was both sick and sorry at the hearing; his own
28 will crossed, and his master's command ill carried out! So, in the fol-
     lowing year, he made a muster of sixty thousand picked men, with five
29 thousand horse, to crush the rebellion; into Judaea they marched, and
30 encamped at Bethoron, where Judas met them with ten thousand.[1] At
     the sight of their great numbers, this was Judas' prayer: Blessed art thou,
     Saviour of Israel, who didst make use of thy servant David, a giant's
     onset to overthrow! Victory thou didst give, over an invading army, to
31 Saul's son Jonathan and the squire that bore him company! So may
32 yonder host, left at Israel's mercy, unlearn its confidence in strength and
     in speed; strike terror into them, let their manhood melt away, as they
33 tremble at the approach of doom; sword of thy true lovers be their un-
34 doing, triumph-song of thy worshippers their dirge! With that, battle
     was joined, and of Lysias' men, five thousand were left dead on the field.
35 What should he do? Here were his troops fled in disorder, here was Judas
     in command of brave men, that would as soon have an honourable death
     as life itself. Back he went to Antioch, and there levied soldiers for a
     greater expedition yet against Judaea.
36   And now Judas and his brethren had but one thought; the enemy van-
     quished, they would betake themselves to Jerusalem, to cleanse and
37 restore the sanctuary. So the whole army fell into rank, and they climbed
38 the hill of Sion together. What saw they? The holy place desolate, the
     altar profaned, charred gates, courts overgrown with brushwood, like

---

[1] For 'Judaea' the Greek manuscripts have 'Idumaea,' and for 'Bethoron,'
'Bethsura.' Cf. verse 61 below.

39 forest clearing or mountain glen, the priests' lodging in ruins. Upon this, there was rending of garments, and loud lament; dust they cast on their
40 heads, and fell face to earth, sounded the bugle, and raised their cries to heaven.
41 And what did Judas? First, he sent a force to engage the citadel's gar-
42 rison, while the holy place was a-cleaning; then he chose priests, with-
43 out blot or blemish, and true lovers of the law besides, who thereupon cleansed the sanctuary, nor any stone that was polluted with idolatry but
44 they had it away into a place unclean. And next, he must concern him-
45 self with the altar of burnt-sacrifice, that was now all defiled. And it was good counsel they took; the altar must be destroyed, else the day when the Gentiles polluted it should be remembered to their shame. So destroy
46 it they did, and laid up the stones in a place apt for their purpose, there on the temple hill. Here they must remain, until the coming of a prophet that should give sentence, what was to be done with them.
47 Then they raised a new altar in place of the old, using stones that had
48 never felt the pick, as the law bade; [1] repaired shrine and inner walls, and
49 rid both temple and temple courts of their defilement. New appurtenances, too, the temple must have, lamp-stand, incense-altar and table
50 be restored to it; incense be put on the altar, lamps kindled to light the
51 holy place, loaves set out on the table, and veils hung up; then at length
52 their task was accomplished. On the twenty-fifth of Casleu, the ninth month, in the hundred and forty-eighth year, they rose before daybreak,
53 and offered sacrifice, as the law bade, on the new altar they had set up.
54 This was the very month, the very day, when it had been polluted by the Gentiles; now, on the same day of the same month, it was dedicated anew,
55 with singing of hymns, and music of harp, zither and cymbals. There-upon all the people fell down face to earth, to adore and praise the
56 heavenly author of their felicity; and for eight days together they cele-brated the altar's renewal, burned victim and brought welcome-offering with glad and grateful hearts.
57 They decked the front wall of the temple, at this time, with gold crowns and escutcheons, consecrated the gates and the priests' lodging anew, and
58 furnished it with doors; and all the while there was great rejoicing among the people; as for the taunts of the heathen, they were heard no more.
59 No wonder if Judas and his brethren, with the whole assembly of Israel, made a decree that this feast should be kept year by year for eight days together, the feast-day of the altar's dedication. [2] Came that season, from the twenty-fifth day of Casleu onwards, all was to be rejoicing and holi-
60 day. At this time, too, they fortified the hill of Sion, with walls and

---

[1] See Ex. 20.25.
[2] Cf. Jn. 10.22.

61 strong towers all about; never more should Gentile feet profane it.   Judas
put a garrison there, and would have it strong enough to command
Bethsura; a bulwark Israel must have against attack from the frontiers of
Edom.

CHAPTER FIVE

2 GREAT indignation had the Gentiles that lived round about, when
they heard that altar and temple were standing as of old.   Their first
thought was to rid their own territory of Jacob's breed, and all at once
3 they set about to murder and harry them.   So Judas must needs take arms
against them, Esau's race in Idumaea, and the men of Acrabathane, that
were keeping Israelite folk under strict siege; and signally he defeated
4 them.   Nor might he overlook Bean's tribe and the treachery they shewed,
5 ever catching Israel at unawares by laying an ambush in his path.   These
he chased into their strongholds and besieged them there; laid them
under a ban [1] and burned the strongholds to the ground, with their de-
6 fenders in them.   Then he crossed over into Ammon, where he came upon
strong resistance and a great muster of men, that had one Timotheus for
7 their leader; often he engaged them, and as often put them to rout; when
8 he had defeated them,   and taken Gazer with its daughter townships, he
marched back into Judaea.

9 But by this all the heathen folk in the country of Galaad were making
common cause against their Israelite neighbours, eager to be rid of them.
10 And these, taking refuge in the stronghold of Datheman,   sent dispatches
to Judas and his brethren.   Here be all the neighbours, they wrote, banded
11 together for our destruction.   Even now, Timotheus at their head, they
12 are setting about the reduction of this our fortress;   come speedily to the
13 rescue; they have taken cruel toll of our lives already.   Slain, all those
clansmen of ours that had their dwelling in the Tubin country, carried
away, their wives, their children, and their goods; nigh upon a thousand
warriors then and there have perished.

14 This letter was still in the reading, when all of a sudden came other
envoys from Galilee, their garments rent about them; their message was,
15 Ptolemais, Tyre and Sidon were up in arms together, and all Galilee was
16 overrun with heathen folk, bent on massacre.   Grave tidings, these, for
Judas and his people; met they in high debate, and took counsel how they
17 might best aid their brethren in peril of assault.   And now Judas must
share the command with his brother Simon; Pick thy men, said he, and
18 make for Galilee, while Jonathan and I march into Galaad.   Part of his
army he left to defend Judaea, with Joseph son of Zachary and Azarias

---

[1] Cf. Jos. 6.17, 18 and other passages.

19 for its captains; Here is your charge, said he; and see to it that you do not
20 embroil yourselves with the Gentiles while we are gone. To Simon and
   to Galilee three thousand men were allotted; to Judas and to Galaad eight
21 thousand. As for Simon, when he reached Galilee, full many a battle he
   must fight with the Gentiles, that he drove ever before him, till he pur-
22 sued them at last to the very gates of Ptolemais. Of the enemy, some
23 three thousand fell, and his men had the spoiling of them; the Israelites
   that dwelt in Galilee and Arbata he took home with him, and their wives
   and children and all they had; great rejoicing there was when he brought
   them back safe to Judaea.
24   Meanwhile Judas Machabaeus and his brother Jonathan had crossed
25 the Jordan, and marched for three days through the desert. There the
   Nabuthaeans came to meet them, and told them of all that had befallen
26 their brethren in the Galaad country; how there were many whom their
   fellow citizens had brought to bay in such great fortified cities as Barasa,
27 Bosor, Alima, Casphor, Mageth and Carnaim; besides many others cut
   off in the rest of the Galaadite towns. And to-morrow, he was told, the
   heathen mean to occupy these cities with their army, seizing upon the
28 Israelites and making an end of them. Whereupon Judas and his men
   suddenly turned aside from their course into the desert of Bosor, and took
   the city; all its men-folk he put to the sword, and carried off the spoil of
29 it, and burned it to the ground. At night-fall they continued their jour-
30 ney, and reached the Israelite stronghold.[1] What a sight was this that met
   their eyes, when day broke! A great rabble of men past all counting, that
   brought up scaling-ladders and engines, as if they would take the strong-
31 hold by storm. Here was the battle fairly begun; the cry of them went
   up to heaven, loud as clarion-call, and a great cry, too, was raised within
32 the city. Now, cried Judas to his men, now to fight for your brethren's
33 deliverance! And hard at the enemy's heels he followed, with three companies of warriors that blew trumpets as they went, and cried aloud in
34 prayer. The name of Machabaeus once heard, how fled Timotheus'
   army at his approach! How grievous the blow that fell on them, when
35 eight thousand fell in a single day! Once more Judas turned aside, to
   Maspha; took it by storm, slew men of it, took spoil of it, burned it to the
36 ground; then on to seize Casbon, and Mageth, and Bosor, and the remaining cities of Galaad.[2]

----

[1] The word 'Israelite' is not in the original; but evidently the stronghold was
either that mentioned in verse 11 above, or else one in which the Israelites of
Bosor had taken refuge.
[2] There is some uncertainty about the names here; 'Casbon' is perhaps the
'Casphor' of verse 26, and 'Bosor' should perhaps be identified with the 'Barasa'
(in the Greek, Bossora) of the same verse. Bosor has already been destroyed in
verse 28.

37 Yet, when all was done, Timotheus put another army into the field,
38 and encamped close by Raphon, across the stream. What learned Judas
   from the scouts he had sent forward? Here were all the neighbouring
39 tribes assembled in great force, with hired support from Arabia besides,
40 ready to engage him; so out he marched to offer battle. Wait we, said
   Timotheus to his captains, till Judas and his army reach yonder stream.
   Cross he and challenge us, we may not speed; beyond doubt he has the
41 mastery of us. Fear he the passage, and encamp on the further side, then
42 cross we boldly, the day is ours. But Judas, when he drew near the
   ravine, had muster-masters in attendance by the stream, that were
   charged to let none linger behind, but send every man across into battle.
43 So he crossed, challenging them, and all the army at his heels, and sure
   enough the Gentile host was routed at their coming; threw arms away,
44 and sought refuge in the temple at Carnaim.[1] Upon taking the city, he
   burned its temple to the ground with all that were sheltered in it; so was
   Carnaim vanquished, and could make head against Juda no more.
45 And now Judas gathered all the Israelites in the Galaad country, high
   and low, with their wives and children, a whole army of them, to come
46 back with him to Juda. They journeyed safely as far as Ephron, that was
   a great city and well fortified, the very gate of Juda; turn to right or left
47 they might not, their road lay through the heart of it. And what must
   they do, the townspeople, but stand to the defence of it, and barricade the
   entrance with great boulders! Thereupon Judas made peaceful overtures
48 to them; Grant us leave, said he, to make our way through your country
   to ours, nor any harm shall befall you; we ask but the right of passage, and
49 on foot. But open the gates they would not; so Judas made a cry through
50 the camp, every man should go to the assault,[2] there where he stood; and
   go to the assault they did, the fighting men of his company. All day and
   all night they attacked the city, and Judas was given the mastery of it.
51 Never a male creature there but was put to the sword; the city was
   plundered and pulled down; and so he passed on through the streets of
52 it, all paved with dead men. Jordan they must still cross, there by the
53 great plain that faces Bethsan; and to the last Judas went ever to and fro,
   rallying the stragglers and encouraging the people on their journey, till
54 the land of Juda was reached. Glad and merry were men's hearts as they
   climbed up Sion mountain, and there offered burnt-sacrifice in thanks
   for their safe home-coming, with never a life lost.[3]

---

[1] Verses 40–43. It is not clear whether Timotheus was testing the courage of his
opponents, or taking an omen from the course of events (cf. I Kg. 14.9, 10).
Perhaps we are not meant to picture the crossing as taking place unopposed.

[2] 'Go to the assault'; literally, according to the Greek, 'to encamp,' but cf. the
use of the corresponding Hebrew verb in Jos. 10.31 and elsewhere.

[3] Literally, 'Because none of them had fallen until all returned safe and
sound,' cf. note on Mt. 1.25.

55 So fought Judas and Jonathan in Galaad, and their brother Simon in
56 Galilee at the gates of Ptolemais; meanwhile, what of Joseph son of
Zachary, and Azarias, that had charge of the garrison? News came to them
57 of victories gained, and great deeds done, and nothing would serve but
they must make a great name for themselves too, by offering battle to the
58 Gentiles round about. So orders went out to the army, to march on Jam-
59 nia, where Gorgias and his men came out to meet them. Back fell Joseph
and Azarias to the frontiers of Judaea in great disorder, with a loss to
61 Israel of two thousand men; such defeat they brought on our arms, because they would not listen to Judas and his brethren, but must be great
62 warriors like the rest. Not of that race they sprang that should afford
Israel deliverance.

63 But as for Judas and his company,[1] they were held high in honour,
both among Israelite folk, and wherever the renown of them was heard;
64 all flocked to greet them with cries of acclaim. But still he and his
brethren would be on the march, reducing the men of Edom in the south
country; on Hebron and its daughter townships the blow fell, neither
66 wall nor tower of it but was burned to the ground. Then he moved
camp, to march on Philistia, and would make his way through Samaria.[2]
67 Priests there were that took up arms and fell in battle that day, rashly
68 desirous of a warrior's renown.[3] And now Judas turned aside to Azotus,
in the country of the Philistines; altars he pulled down, images of their
gods burned to ashes, gave up their cities to plunder, and so came back
again to the land of Juda.

CHAPTER SIX

KING ANTIOCHUS was still on his journey through the high countries, when he heard tell of a city in Persia called Elymais, renowned
2 for its treasures of silver and gold; here was a temple of great magnificence, that had golden armour in it, breastplate and shield left there by
3 Philip's son, Alexander of Macedon, the first emperor of Greece. Thither
he marched, intent on seizing the city and plundering it; but seize it he
4 might not, because the townsfolk had news of his purpose, and came out

---

[1] 'Judas and his company'; the Latin here has 'the men of Juda,' which yields
no good sense, 'Juda' and 'Israel' being convertible terms at this period. The
Greek has, 'the man Judas and his brethren.'
[2] 'Samaria' is probably a false reading for Maresa, which lay on the route
between Edom and the Philistines.
[3] Most of the Greek manuscripts have a different and very curious reading,
'Priests there were that fell in battle that day, because he (Judas?) desired to
play the warrior, with which design he went into action unadvisedly.'

to offer battle. So he was put to the rout, and must take himself back to
Babylon, grievously disappointed.

5 And here, in the Persian country, a messenger reached him with tidings
6 from Juda. Fled were his armies, and Lysias, that erstwhile marched out
with so brave a retinue, had left the Jews masters of the field. Now they
were strong and well-armed, such spoil they had taken from the armies
7 they overthrew ; gone was that defiling image he had set up over the altar
at Jerusalem ; high walls, as of old, protected the sanctuary ; nay, they had
made shift to fortify his own stronghold of Bethsura.

8 What news was this! The king was all bewilderment and consternation ; he took to his bed, fallen into a decline for very sadness that his hopes
9 had failed him.   Long time he languished under the double burden of his
10 grief, and knew at last he was a-dying. So he called his friends about him,
and bade them farewell ; Here is sleep quite gone from me, said he ; so
11 dazed is this heart of mine with doubt unresolved.   Thus runs my
thought : How comes it that I have fallen upon such evil times, such a
flood of calamity as now engulfs me ; I, that in the days of my greatness
12 loved men well, and was well beloved? And now returns the memory of
all the havoc I made in Jerusalem, spoil of gold and silver I robbed from
13 it, doom of mine against the townsfolk, and for no fault. Past all doubt,
here is the source of all those miseries that have come upon me ; look you,
14 how I die consumed of grief, in a strange land! Then he sent for Philip,
one of his trusted friends, and gave all the kingdom into his charge ;
15 crown and robe and ring he delivered to him, bidding him seek out prince
16 Antiochus, and bring him up as heir to the throne. Then and there died
king Antiochus, in the hundred and forty-ninth year of the Grecian
17 empire. And Lysias, hearing of his death, crowned this same prince
Antiochus, that he had brought up from boyhood, giving him the name of
Eupator.

18 Meanwhile, what of the Jews that dwelt about the holy place? Here
was the garrison of the citadel hemming them in, seeking ever to do them
19 injury, and to sustain the Gentile cause. So Judas was fain make an end
20 of them, and summoned the whole people to rally for the siege. Rally
they did, and began the siege in the hundred and fiftieth year, with much
21 contriving of catapults and engines. But some of the defenders slipped
22 out ; and these, with traitors of Israelite stock to support them, went off
to gain the king's audience. Wilt thou never bring redress, they asked,
23 and do our brethren right? Jews are we, that resolved we would be loyal
24 to thy father, his policy furthering, his will obeying. What came of it?
Our own fellow Israelites would have no more of our company, slew all
25 they could lay hands on, robbed us of our possessions. Not us only, but
26 all the country about them, their violence threatens ; even now they
stand arrayed against the citadel at Jerusalem, ready to take it by storm,

27 and have fortified Bethsura. Forestall their plans thou must, and
speedily, or they will go further yet, and there will be no holding them.
28   Angered by these tidings, the king sent for all his trusted friends, for
29 his army captains and his commanders of horse; mercenaries, too, were
30 hired from foreign countries, and from the islands out at sea, till he
could put a hundred thousand foot and twenty thousand horse into the
31 field, besides thirty-two elephants, inured to war. Through Edom they
marched, and invested Bethsura; long they held it besieged, and built
engines to attack it, but these, by a brave sally, the defenders burned to
ashes.
32   Meanwhile, Judas drew away from the citadel, and encamped at Beth-
33 zacharam, close to the king's army. Ere dawn broke, the king was astir,
and his men marching hot-foot towards Bethzacharam, where the armies
34 made ready for battle, with a great blowing of trumpets. As for the ele-
35 phants, they were blooded to battle with juice of grape and mulberry, and
so divided here and there among the troops. A thousand foot-soldiers
were assigned to each, in coat of mail and helmet of bronze; with each
36 went five hundred picked horsemen; these were waiting ready for every
beast at its station, and must go wherever it went, never leaving its side.
37 On the back of every beast was a strong protecting tower of wood, cunningly fitted; and thirty-two valiant men were appointed to do battle
from this height, over and above the Indian that was the beast's driver.[1]
38 The remainder of the cavalry were stationed on either wing, to daunt the
oncoming host with a clamour of trumpets,[2] and harass them as they
39 stood tight packed in their ranks. Brightly the sun shone down on
shield of gold, shield of bronze, till all the mountain-side gave back the
40 glancing rays of them, and dazzled like points of fire. Part of the king's
army was drawn up on the heights, part on the level plain; warily they
41 came on and in good order; and ever, as they went, murmur of voices,
tramp of feet, and clash of arms daunted the countryside around them, so
42 great yonder army was, and so valiant. But Judas and his men closed
with them, and gave battle; and of the king's soldiers, there were six
hundred that fell.
43   What did Eleazar that day, the son of Sauran?[3] Here was one of the
beasts that went decked in royal trappings, and towered high above the
44 rest; There rides the king, thought he, and with that, he gave his life, to
win deliverance for his country, and for himself imperishable renown.

---

[1] The meaning of the original is, that each elephant carried no less than
thirty-two fighting men. The statement is perhaps due to some error in the
copying of the Greek manuscripts.
[2] There is no mention of trumpets in the Greek original. But the text is
obscure, and perhaps corrupt.
[3] In the Greek, 'Eleazar Sauaran,' perhaps a corruption of 'Abaron' (2.5 above).

45 Bravely he ran up to it, there in the heart of the press, slaying to right
46 and left of him, men falling on either side, till he could creep in between
the very feet of the elephant; crouched there, and dispatched it, and so,
crushed by its fall to earth, died where he lay.

47   But now, finding the royal forces so strong, and so determined in their
48 attack, the Jews withdrew from the encounter. To Jerusalem the king's
men followed them, and now here was the king entrenched against Judaea
49 and mount Sion itself. With the defenders of Bethsura he had made
terms; yield up the city they must, so ill were they victualled for a siege,
50 in a year when the land lay fallow;[1] thus Bethsura was in the king's
51 hands, and he put a garrison there. But it was against the holy place itself
that he turned his arms, and long he beleaguered it; what catapults he
brought to bear on it, what engines! Flew fiery darts, flew stone and
javelin and arrow from mangonel and arbalest, and the slings took their
52 turn. As for the Jews, they met engine with engine, and fought on day
53 after day; but the seventh year had come round, and what store was
left in the city had been eaten up by the new citizens rescued from Gen-
54 tile. countries, so food was none to be had. Only a few defenders were
left in the holy place now; the rest, overtaken by famine, had dispersed
to their homes.

55   But Lysias could not wait; he had news from Antioch. That same
Philip, whom king Antiochus, on his death-bed, had appointed to bring
56 up the young prince as heir to the throne, was now returned at the head
of his army from the land of the Medes and Persians, and would fain take
57 charge of the realm. So Lysias must betake himself to the king and his
generals, with such words as these: Our plight grows daily worse; scant
food is left us, and here is a fortress well defended; all the business of the
58 realm claims our care. What remains, but to make friendly advances,
59 offer terms to the besieged and to all their countrymen? Give we leave
they should follow their own customs as of old, which customs neglect-
60 ing, we have brought all this ill-will and all this trouble upon us. King
and chieftain fell in with his design; offer peace they did, and the offer
61 was accepted. So, upon terms with the king and his generals, the Jews
62 gave up their stronghold; and what must the king do, once he had set
foot on mount Sion and discovered the strength of its defences, but
63 break his oath, and have all the walls of it pulled down! Then, with all
haste, he took leave of it, and returned to Antioch, where he found Philip
in possession, and levied war on him, taking the city by storm.

---

[1] Cf. Lev. 25.4.

CHAPTER SEVEN

IT was now, in the hundred and fifty-first year, that Demetrius, the son of Seleucus, escaped from Rome and landed with a small retinue at one
2 of the sea ports, where he was proclaimed king. No sooner had he set foot in the palace of his ancestors, than his men laid hold of Antiochus
3 and Lysias, meaning to bring them into his presence. But he was warned
4 of it, and gave it out, sight of them he would have none; so they were dispatched by the troops, and Demetrius established himself on the royal throne.
5   To him came certain Israelites, enemies of the law and of religion, with
6 Alcimus at their head, a man who coveted the high-priestly office. And thus, in the royal presence, they defamed their own people: Here be Judas and his brethren have made away with all thy friends, and driven
7 us out of our country! Do but send some trusted agent to survey the scene of it, the havoc this man has wrought upon our own persons and upon the king's domain; ay, and to punish his partisans, with all who
8 comfort them. The king's choice fell on Bacchides, a courtier that was
9 loyal to him, and had charge now of all the realm east of Euphrates. Of the havoc wrought by Judas he should be judge, and with him went the traitor Alcimus, now confirmed in the high priesthood; thus should the royal vengeance fall on Israel.
10   So they took the road, and reached the land of Juda with a great army at their heels. Envoys they sent out, to cheat Judas and his brethren with
11 fair promises; but from these they got no hearing; the sight of their
12 retinue was enough. It was a company of scribes that went out to meet
13 Alcimus and Bacchides, asking for honourable terms; of all Israel, the
14 Assidaeans were foremost in demanding peace; Here is a priest of Aaron's
15 line, said they, in yonder company, fear we no treachery from him. Fair promises he made them, and swore they should take no harm, nor their
16 friends neither; and they took him at his word. And what did he? A full sixty of them he seized and put to death in one day. Not idly the word
17 was written, Bleeding corpses of thy true lovers they have strewn about
18 on every side of Jerusalem, and there was none to bury the dead. After this, all alike dreaded the new-comers and shrank from them; here was neither trust nor troth, when covenant and sworn promise went for
19 nothing. So Bacchides left Jerusalem and pitched his camp at Bethzecha, where he made search and laid hands on many that had deserted from his own army; some of the Jews he massacred besides, and had their bodies
20 thrown into the Great Cistern; then he left the whole country in Alcimus' charge, with troops to maintain him. So off went Bacchides to his master,

21 and Alcimus remained to make the best of his high priesthood. Be sure all the malcontents in Judaea rallied to his side, and took possession of the country, to Israel's great mischief.

23   Little it liked Judas, to see Alcimus and his crew mishandling the men
24 of Israel as never the Gentiles had; from end to end of Juda he passed, executing vengeance on such as had left his cause, till they might take the
25 field no longer. Everywhere Judas and his company had their way, and the sight of it warned Alcimus he was no match for them; so he, too, went
26 back to the king, loud in his complaints. Thereupon the king sent out an army for the people's undoing, with Nicanor at the head of it, that was one of his most notable princes, and had a grudge against Israel to satisfy.
27 This Nicanor, reaching Jerusalem with a great array, made peaceful over-
28 tures to Judas and his brethren, but treacherously; Need is none there should be blows given between us, he said. Let me come with a handful
29 of men, and parley we together under safe conduct. Come he did, and the greeting between them was friendly enough, but Judas was like to have
30 been seized, then and there, by the enemy; and when he had proof of Nicanor's treachery, he went in dread of him and would parley with him no longer.

31   Nicanor, then, his plot being now manifestly discovered, would take to
32 the field; it was close to Capharsalama that he engaged Judas, and his army, routed with a loss of five thousand men, must needs take refuge in
33 the Keep of David.[1] It was after this that Nicanor made his way to mount Sion, where some of the priests and elders came out to greet him in friendly fashion, and shew him how burnt-sacrifice was offered there on
34 the king's behalf. But nothing could they get from him but mockery and contempt; he did despite to their sacred persons, and sent them away with
35 threats. In his anger, he swore to them nothing would serve but he should have Judas and Judas' army at his mercy; if not, he would burn the temple down, as soon as ever he returned in safety. So, in high disdain,
36 he left them; and the priests must take themselves back within the walls,
37 where they stood before altar and temple, praying very mournfully. Lord, they said, thou hast chosen this house to be the shrine of thy name; here
38 thy people should offer prayer, and sue for thy favour. Do thou avenge thyself on chieftain and army both; die they at the sword's point! Wouldst thou forget their blasphemy; should they escape with their lives?
39   After this, Nicanor left Jerusalem, and pitched his camp at Bethoron,
40 where he was met by a fresh army from Syria; Judas, in his camp at

---

[1] According to Josephus, who usually follows the sacred narrative closely, it was Judas who was defeated and forced to take refuge in Jerusalem; this would accord better with what follows, and it seems possible that the text has been incorrectly preserved.

Adarsa, had but three thousand men. And this was the prayer Judas
41 prayed: Time was, Lord, when Sennacherib's men were loud in their
blasphemy, and thy angel must go out to smite them down, a hundred
42 and eighty thousand of them. This day a new enemy overwhelm with
our onslaught, and let all the world know what comes of threatening thy
holy place; for his ill-doing, ill requite him!
43   It was the thirteenth of Adar when the two armies met; sure enough,
Nicanor's army was overwhelmed, and himself the first to fall in the
44 encounter; whereupon the rest, seeing their leader gone, cast weapons
45 away and took to their heels. For a whole day the pursuit of them went
on, all the way from Adazer to the approaches of Gazara, and ever there
46 were trumpets sounding the hue and cry. Out came Jewish folk from all
the villages round about, to head them off,[1] till at last they turned at bay
47 and fell at the sword's point all of them, never a man left. Spoil of them
was plundered where they lay; as for Nicanor, the Jews cut off the head
from his body, and that right hand he lifted up so defiantly, and took
48 them away, to be hung up in full sight of Jerusalem. Glad men they were
49 that day, and kept high festival, decreeing that never thenceforward
50 should the thirteenth day of Adar go unobserved. And for a little while
the land of Juda had peace.

CHAPTER EIGHT

JUDAS had heard tell of the Romans, and their renown. Here was a
powerful nation, that would entertain overtures none the less from
such as craved their friendship, plighting their word faithfully. A power-
2 ful nation indeed; what battles they had fought, what exploits achieved
3 yonder among the Galatians, their conquered vassals now! In Spain,
too, they had done great feats of arms; and at last, by policy and patient
striving, won over the whole country, made themselves masters of all the
4 silver and gold that was mined there. Came peoples from far away, kings
from the furthest corners of earth, to offer battle, they were overwhelmed
and signally defeated; those nearer at hand were content to pay yearly
5 tribute. Had they not crushed and conquered Philip, and Perseus king of
6 the Greeks, and all others that had levied war upon them? And what of
Antiochus the Great, that ruled all Asia, and came against them with a
hundred and twenty elephants, with horsemen and chariots, and a great
7 array besides? The Romans overcame him, caught him alive, and
demanded both from him and from his heirs rich tribute, and hostages,
8 with other conditions of surrender; took away from him India, Media,

---

[1] 'To head them off'; the Latin has 'and tossed them with the horn,' probably
through a misunderstanding of the word used in the Greek text.

and Lydia, that were his most cherished provinces, and gave them to
9 king Eumenes instead. Later, word came that the men of Hellas were for
10 marching in and making an end of them; what was the issue of it? One
of the Roman generals was sent out to engage them; fell many in battle,
wives and children were carried off into exile, goods plundered, the land
conquered, its fortresses destroyed, and they are slaves to this day.
11 So it was with all the kingdoms and islands that defied their will; the
12 Romans crushed them and took their lands away. But to their friends,
that would live at peace with them, they were ever good friends in return.
Kingdoms both far and near became their vassals, nor any that heard
13 their name but feared it; helped they any man to a throne, the throne
was his; their good will lost, his throne was lost too; so high was their
renown.
14 Yet, with all this, was never one of them that wore crown, or went clad
15 in purple for his own aggrandizement. A senate-house they would have,
where a council of three hundred and twenty met day by day, providing
16 ever for the good estate of the commonalty; and every year they would
entrust one man with the rule and governance of their whole country, the
rest obeying him, without any debate or contention moved.[1]
17 So now Judas made choice of two envoys, Eupolemus, son of John, son
of Jacob, and Jason, son of Eleazar; to Rome they should go, and there
18 make a treaty of good will and alliance. Rome's task it should be to rid
them of the Grecian yoke; from the Greeks it was plain they could expect
19 nothing better than grinding slavery. So, after long journeying, to Rome
they came, and were admitted to the senate house, where they gave their
20 message as follows: We have been sent to you by Judas Machabaeus and
his brethren, and by our countrymen at large, to make a treaty of alliance
with you; fain would they be enrolled among your confederates and
21 friends. This proposition liked the Romans well; and they wrote back
to the Jews on tablets of bronze, that should be kept in Jerusalem to serve
23 them for a memorial, to this effect: Well speed they at all times, the
Roman and the Jewish peoples, by sea and land alike; far removed from
24 either be alarm of war, assault of the enemy! Yet if war befall, and
threaten the Romans first, or any ally of theirs in any part of their domin-
25 ions, such aid the Jewish people shall give as the occasion demands,
26 ungrudgingly. For the needs of the enemy they shall nothing find or furnish, be it corn, or arms, or money, or ships, according to the agreement
made at Rome; and they shall observe these undertakings with no
27 thought of their own advantage. In like manner, if the Jews be first
threatened, it shall be for the Romans to give aid as the occasion demands,

---

[1] These verses record only the impression which had reached Judas; it is not
necessarily accurate in all points.

28 most willingly; providing neither corn nor arms, money nor ships, to any
that take part against them, according to the agreement made at Rome; [1]
29 and they shall observe these undertakings honourably. Upon these terms
30 the Romans and the Jewish people are agreed; if hereafter it should be
the will of both parties [2] to enlarge or to restrict them, they may do so at
their discretion, and such enlargement or restriction shall have force
31 accordingly. As for the wrong done by king Demetrius, we have sent him
warning, What meanest thou, to burden with so heavy a yoke the Jewish
32 people, our friends and allies? Let them complain of thee once more, and
we will surely give them redress, by land and sea levying war against thee.

CHAPTER NINE

WHILE this was afoot, news came to Demetrius that Nicanor and
his men had perished in the encounter. But he would still have his
way; Bacchides and Alcimus should be sent back to Judaea, and the
2 northern command [3] of his army with them. Marching out along the Galgala road, they encamped at Masaloth in Arbella; the town was surprised,
3 and many of its inhabitants massacred. Then, in the first month of the
4 hundred and fifty-second year, they began an attack on Jerusalem, moving their camp to Berea. It was a force of twenty thousand foot and two
5 thousand horse; Judas, encamped at Laisa, had three thousand picked
6 followers with him, but these were greatly daunted when they saw what
heavy odds were against them, and began to desert their lines, till no
7 more than eight hundred of them were left. One by one they slipped
away, and raise fresh levies he might not, with the battle so hard upon his
8 heels; what wonder if Judas lost heart, and was unmanned? Yet said he
to the remnant that was left him, Up, go we to the attack, and try con-
9 clusions with the enemy! In vain they sought to dissuade him; Speed we
may not, they said; let us save our skins now, we may yet join hands with
10 our brethren, and do battle hereafter; why, we are but a handful! Nay,
said Judas, that may I never do; what, shew them our backs? If our time
is come, die we manfully in our brethren's cause, nor suffer any foul blot
to fall on our name!
11 By this, the opposing army had moved forward out of its lines, and
stood fronting them; here were the two bodies of horse, the slingers and

---

[1] The Latin has, 'according to the agreement made by the Romans.'

[2] 'Both parties'; according to the Latin version, 'either party,' but such a stipu-
lation would make the whole treaty ineffectual.

[3] 'The northern command'; literally, 'the right wing.' Presumably this means
the right extremity from Demetrius' point of view.

archers going on before the rest, and the choice troops that would bear
12 the shock of the encounter; here was Bacchides himself, on the right
wing. This side and that the phalanx drew nearer, with a great blowing of
13 trumpets, and Judas' men, they raised a great cry on their own part, till
the earth rang again with the noise of the two armies. Thus begun, the
14 battle went on from morning till dusk. On the right, where he saw
Bacchides' army was strongest, Judas made the attack, and all the most
15 valiant of his men with him; broke their line, and chased them all the
16 way to mount Azotus. But now those on the left, seeing their right wing
17 routed, cut off Judas and his men from the rear; now indeed the battle
18 grew fierce, and there were many fell wounded on either part, till at last
Judas fell, and with that, all the rest took to their heels.

19   As for his body, his brothers Jonathan and Simon recovered it, and so
20 buried him where his fathers were buried, in the city of Modin. Great
21 lament all Israel made over him, and long they mourned him; Here is
a great warrior fallen, they said, that once brought his people deliverance!
22 What other battles Judas fought, deeds did, greatness achieved, you shall
not find set down here; too long the record of them.

23   Once Judas was dead, there was no corner in Israel but treason began
24 to shew its face there, and lawlessness to abound; under such leadership
the whole country, at this time much distressed by famine, went over to
25 Bacchides. Good care he took to choose out godless men, that should
26 have the governance of his territory; and these raised a hue and cry after
Judas' partisans, haling them before Bacchides to be punished and used
27 despitefully; never, since prophecy died out among them, had the men
28 of Israel known such distress. And now all that had loved Judas rallied to
29 Jonathan instead; Since thy brother's death, they told him, none is left
to take the field against our enemies as he did, this Bacchides and all else
30 that bear a grudge against our race.[1] There is but one way of it; this day
we have chosen thee to be our ruler, our chieftain, to fight our battles for
31 us. So, from that day forward, Jonathan took command, in succession
32 to his brother Judas. Bacchides no sooner heard of it than he marked him
33 down for death; but of this Jonathan had warning, and took refuge, with
his brother Simon and all his company, in the desert of Thecua. It was
34 there, by Asphar pool, they halted; and it was there that Bacchides, well
informed of their movements, crossed Jordan at the head of his army and
came upon them, one sabbath day.

35   This was the manner of it. Jonathan had sent his brother John, that was
in command of the camp followers, on an errand to his good friends the
Nabuthaeans. They had brought a deal of their household stuff with

---

[1] The meaning of the Greek text is, 'all those of our own race that bear a
grudge against us.'

36 them; would the Nabuthaeans take it into safe keeping? But, as they
went, some of Jambri's folk came out from Madaba, seized John and all
37 that he had with him, and went off with them. Afterwards, Jonathan and
Simon heard that the men of Jambri had a great wedding toward; they
must bring home the bride from Nadabatha,[1] and with much pomp, be-
38 cause her father was a notable Chanaanite chief. So, to avenge the death
of their brother John, they climbed the hill-side and lay in ambush there.
39 What a sight was this met their eyes! All manner of rout and display; the
bridegroom, his friends and his brethren, passing on their way to the
trysting-place, with beating of drums, and making of music, and all
40 manner of warlike array! Then rose they up from their ambush and laid
about them, till many fell wounded, and the rest fled into the hills, leaving
41 all their spoil behind them. So turned they wedding mirth into funeral
42 dirge, to avenge the murder of their brother, and withdrew to the banks
of Jordan again.[2]

43   Hearing of these alarms, Bacchides marched down to Jordan bank one
44 sabbath day, in great force. Up now! cried Jonathan to his men; engage
45 our enemy we must. Gone is the vantage we had till now; here is armed
force confronting us, and all around us is Jordan stream, Jordan banks
46 full of marshes and thickets; escape is none. Cry we rather upon heaven,
47 for deliverance out of the enemy's hand. So the battle was joined; and
here was Jonathan exerting all his strength to deal a blow at Bacchides,
48 who declined the encounter! What did Jonathan then? With all his company, he leapt into Jordan. So now, to reach them, the enemy must swim
49 for it across the stream.[3] A thousand men of his following Bacchides lost
that day, and was fain to return to Jerusalem.

50   After this, they took to fortifying the cities of Judaea with high walls
and barred gates, making strongholds at Jericho, Ammaum, Bethoron,
51 Bethel, Thamnata, Phara and Thopo; here garrisons were set, for the
52 harrying of Israel. Bethsura, too, Bacchides fortified, and Gazara, and
53 the Citadel itself, keeping all of them well manned and provisioned; ay,
and the great men of all the country round must yield up their children
54 as hostages, to be held in Jerusalem citadel for safe keeping. Then, in the
second month of the hundred and fifty-third year, came an order from

---

[1] 'Nadabatha'; the Latin version has 'Madaba,' presumably a copyist's error.
[2] *vv.* 35–42. This incident is given by Josephus as if it followed the events
described in verses 43–49; but he has probably misunderstood the sequence of
the narrative. In verse 35, the Latin version seems to suggest that Jonathan asked
the Nabuthaeans for the loan of their equipment, but the account given in the
Greek text is more natural.
[3] Literally, 'and they swam across the Jordan to them.' The Greek text has
'and they did not swim across the Jordan to them.' The meaning, in either case,
can only be a matter of conjecture.

Alcimus, the dividing wall of the temple's inner court should be dismantled. The Prophets' Building [1] he had already cleared away, and be-
55 gun the dismantling, when himself was smitten down, and all his plans interrupted. Dumbstricken and palsied, he never spoke again, even to dis-
56 pose of his goods, but died there and then, in great torment.
57 Alcimus dead, Bacchides was for Judaea no longer; away he went to the
58 king's court, and for two years the land was at peace. But ere long there was conspiracy afoot among the godless party; here were Jonathan and his men living secure of their safety; came Bacchides in again, he might
59 seize them all, and make one night's work of it. To Bacchides, then, they
60 went, and imparted their scheme to him; whereupon he raised a great army for marching on Judaea, but first sent word to his partisans there, bidding them seize Jonathan and his company for themselves. Word went
61 abroad, and the plan miscarried; it was Jonathan [2] seized fifty notables of Judaea, that were the authors of the conspiracy, and put them to death.
62 Then, with Simon and the rest of his following, he removed to Bethbessen, out in the desert, and set about rebuilding it, to make a stronghold for them.
63 Bacchides had news of this; mustering his whole force, and sending
64 word to his Jewish supporters, he marched in and pitched his camp so as to command Bethbessen. Long time he besieged it, and brought up
65 engines against it; meanwhile, Jonathan had left his brother Simon in command of the city, and was roaming the countryside. When he came
66 back, it was with a band of men at his heels; smote he Odares and his clan, smote he the men of Phaseron where they lay encamped; everywhere
67 laid about him, and still gained strength.[3] As for Simon and his company,
68 they made a sally out of the town, and set fire to the engines; afterwards they engaged Bacchides himself, and worsted him, so that he must pay
69 dearly for plot and tryst of his that came to nothing. So enraged was he with the malcontents whose counsel had brought him into Judaea, he put many of them to death, and was for marching home again with the rest of
70 his following, when Jonathan, hearing of it, sent envoys to offer peace,
71 and an exchange of prisoners. This offer he gladly accepted, and carried out the terms of it, giving his word he would do Jonathan no more injury
72 as long as he lived, and restoring all the prisoners he had ever taken in the land of Juda. So he took himself back to his own country, and never
73 came that way again. Israel had a respite from fighting at last, and

---

[1] The Prophets' Building (literally, Work) was presumably the name given to some part of Zorobabel's temple; no allusion is made to it elsewhere.

[2] The name Jonathan is not given, but it seems the natural one to supply in the context. Josephus, perhaps through a misinterpretation, attributes the massacre to Bacchides.

[3] Verses 65, 66. The original here is strangely worded, and perhaps corrupt.

Jonathan took up his dwelling at Machmas, whence he ruled the people thenceforward, ridding the land of godless folk altogether.

CHAPTER TEN

AND now, in the hundred and sixtieth year, came Alexander, a son of Antiochus Epiphanes, and took possession of Ptolemais, where he
2 was received with royal honours. A great force king Demetrius levied,
3 when he heard of it, and went out to give him battle; at the same time, he
4 wrote to Jonathan, in such loving terms as should flatter his dignity. No time to be lost, thought he, in making friends with this man, before he
5 takes to comforting Alexander against us; for wrong done to himself, and
6 his brother, and all his race, he bears us a grudge yet. So he empowered Jonathan to muster an army, and to make weapons of war, as the ally of Syria; the hostages, too, in the citadel were to be given back to him.
7 When Jonathan came to Jerusalem, and read this letter aloud, not to
8 the townsfolk only, but to the citadel garrison, great was the fear fell on all who listened; here was Jonathan commissioned to levy troops by
9 the king's own order! The hostages were surrendered without more ado,
10 and given back to their parents; and he himself took up his quarters in
11 Jerusalem, where he set about building up the city and repairing it. It was the walls needed rebuilding, so he told his workmen; on every side, the hill of Sion must be defended with hewn stone; and punctually they
12 obeyed him. As for the alien folk that guarded the strongholds Bacchides
13 had left, they fled incontinently; what matter if their posts were aban-
14 doned? They were for home. Only Bethsura was garrisoned now, and that by traitors to God's law and commandment; it was all the refuge they had.
15 King Alexander heard of these overtures made by Demetrius; heard, too, the story of Jonathan and his brethren, battles fought, and deeds
16 done, and labours endured. Why, said he, this man has not his match
17 anywhere; time it is we should court his friendship and alliance. With
18 that, he wrote him a letter, and these were the terms of it: King Alex-
19 ander, to Jonathan his brother-prince, greeting! We have heard tell of
20 thee, a man so valiant, and so well worthy of our friendship; in token whereof, we appoint thee high priest of thy own race henceforward, and to have the title of the King's Friend. With that, he sent him a purple robe and a gold crown; Take ever our part, said he, and hold fast the bond
21 of friendship. So, when the seventh month came round, in the hundred and sixtieth year, Jonathan clad himself with the sacred vesture at the feast of Tent-dwelling; an army he levied besides, and made weapons of war in great abundance.

22   Sick and sorry Demetrius was when he heard of these doings; Here is
an ill day's work, said he, to let Alexander forestall us in making alliance
24 with the Jews, to his great comfort! From me, too, they shall have a message of entreaty, they shall have honours and gifts; the Jews shall be my
25 good friends yet. And thus he wrote: King Demetrius, to the people of
26 the Jews, greeting! Here is welcome news we have of you; right well you
have kept troth with us, honouring the treaty when you might have taken
27 part with our enemies. In that loyal mind continue, and your good
28 offices shall not go unrewarded; much immunity you shall enjoy, much
largesse receive.

29   By these presents, I exempt both you and all Jews from the poll-tax;
salt-tax and coronation dues I remit and forgo, with my right to a third
30 part of your seed-corn, and half your fruit-crop. From this day forward,
now and for ever, I resign all this; from Juda and from the three cantons
31 of Samaria and Galilee[1] lately added to it, there shall be no toll taken. For
Jerusalem, it shall be a place set apart, a free city with its own confines,
32 mistress of its own tithe and tribute; nor claim I any rights over the
citadel there, I make it over to the high priest, to garrison it as he will.
33 All persons of Jewish blood that were taken away as prisoners from Juda
shall now be set free gratuitously, and no distraint made on their revenues
34 or cattle. Feast-day and new moon and sabbath, and all other such
solemnities as are appointed to be observed, with the three days before
and after the feast itself, shall be days of immunity and respite for all the
35 Jews in my realm; nor any business done or debate moved to their detri-
36 ment at such times. In the king's army, Jews may be enrolled up to the
number of thirty thousand, paid according to the common rate of the
royal troops; and the same shall be free to serve in all the fortified towns
37 of our empire. Jews may be employed besides in all positions of trust,
and appointed governors,[2] yet live still by their own laws, that have royal
38 sanction in the land of Juda. The three cantons taken from Samaria and
added to Judea shall be accounted part of Juda, under a single government, with no allegiance but to the high priest.

39   Ptolemais, with all the country that lies about it, I hereby convey as a
free gift to the temple precincts at Jerusalem, to defray the temple ex-
40 penses.[3] To this gift I add a sum of fifteen thousand silver sicles yearly,
41 out of the royal dues that belong to me. With this sum, arrears shall be
made good in payments for the temple building, withheld till now by
42 such as had charge of the matter; and restitution made, to the priests now

---

[1] 'Samaria and Galilee,' here evidently treated as a single unit; the three dis-
tricts concerned had actually been Samaritan (verse 38).

[2] 'And appointed governors'; according to the Greek text, 'and let their
governors be men of their own race.'

[3] A fine touch; cf. verse 1.

in office, for the five thousand sicles that were confiscated year by year
43 from the temple treasury.[1] Debtor to the king, whatever be the charge
against him, that takes sanctuary in the temple or its precincts, shall be
left at liberty, and no distraint made upon goods of his within these
44 dominions. Payment shall be made besides from the royal treasury for
45 the finishing and repairing of the temple fabric; as also for building up
and making strong the walls of Jerusalem, and restoring the fortresses of
Judaea.

46   But in vain were such promises made to Jonathan and the Jewish folk,
nor credence found they any nor assent. Could they forget all the mischief Demetrius had done in Israel, all the tyranny they had endured?
47 Alexander it was had all their good wishes; his was the first offer of terms
48 that reached them, and all the while it was his cause they cherished. By
this, Alexander had mustered a great force, and marched against Deme-
49 trius. When the two kings met, it was Demetrius' men took to their
50 heels, and Alexander gave chase, pressing them hard; fiercely the battle
raged till sun-down, and before the day was over, Demetrius fell.

51   Hereupon Alexander sent an embassy to Ptolemy, king of Egypt,
52 addressing him in these terms following. Take notice I have returned to
my kingdom, and sit now on the throne of my fathers, in full possession
of my princely rights. Would I regain Syria, needs must I should over-
53 throw Demetrius; overthrow him I did, on field of battle, with all his
54 army, and here I sit in his place. And should we not be upon terms of
friendship, thou and I? Let me have thy daughter to wife; a niggardly
55 wooer thou shalt not find me, nor she either. And what answer made
king Ptolemy? An auspicious day, said he, this day of thy return to the
56 land and throne of thy fathers! Boon thy letter asks of me thou shalt
have; but first meet we together, face to face, yonder at Ptolemais; there
57 will I pledge my word to the articles thou namest. So here was king
Ptolemy come from Egypt, with his daughter Cleopatra, all the way to
58 Ptolemais, in the hundred and sixty-second year; and there king Alexander met him and took his daughter Cleopatra to wife, and they held the
wedding with great magnificence, as kings will.

59   King Alexander had sent word to Jonathan, he should come and keep
60 tryst with him; so to Ptolemais Jonathan went, and met the two kings
there. Gifts a many he made them, of silver and gold and much else, and
61 was high in favour with them. It chanced that certain Israelites, pestilent
fellows of the traitorous party, came there to bring charges against him.
62 But to these the king would not listen; he would have Jonathan change
his garments, and go clad in purple, and when this was done, a seat he

---

[1] *vv.* 41, 42. The Latin here differs from the Greek text, which is less intelligible.

63 must have beside the king himself. Take him out into the heart of the
city, Alexander said to his vassals, and there make proclamation, none
may bring charge against him on any pretext, or in any fashion molest
64 him. No thought had his accusers, when they heard such proclamation
made, and saw Jonathan there dressed in purple, but to escape, one
65 and all, as best they could; he himself was loaded with honours, enrolled
among the king's chief friends, and made a prince, with a share in the
66 governance of the kingdom. So Jonathan made his way back to Jerusalem undisturbed, and well content.

67   Then, in the hundred and sixty-fifth year, came Demetrius, son of that
other Demetrius, from the island of Crete, and landed in his native coun-
68 try; ill hearing indeed for Alexander, who returned at once to Antioch.
69 Demetrius [1] gave command of his army to Apollonius, that was governor
of Coelesyria, and a great array it was he levied. From Jamnia, where he
took up his quarters, this Apollonius sent word to the high priest Jona-
70 than: What, wilt thou defy us, and all alone? Here am I mocked and
71 flouted by the resistance offered me, up yonder in the hills! Nay, if such
confidence thou hast in thy own resources, come down and meet us in the
72 plain; try we conclusions there! Trust me, I am master of the field; what
I am, what my troops are, thou shalt learn upon a little enquiry; stand
thou canst not, they will tell thee, before onslaught of ours. Twice, on
73 their native soil, thy fathers fled in disorder, and wilt thou make head
against such an array of horse and foot, here in the plain, where rock is
none, nor gravel-bed, to aid thy flight?

74   Roused by this challenge, Jonathan marched out from Jerusalem with
a muster of ten thousand men; his brother Simon joined hands with him;
75 and together they appeared before the gates of Joppe. Enter they might
76 not, for Apollonius had a garrison there, but must needs attack it; whereupon the citizens took alarm, and themselves opened the gates. Thus
77 came Joppe into the power of Jonathan; the news reached Apollonius,
and he brought up three thousand horse, with a great array of men be-
78 sides. To Azotus he marched, as if he meant to pass them by, but all the
while he was luring them on into the plain; [2] in horse lay his strength and
his confidence. To Azotus Jonathan followed him, and battle was joined.
79   Apollonius, by a secret feint, had left a thousand horsemen encamped
80 in their rear; so all at once Jonathan found himself cut off by an ambush.

---

[1] It seems possible that the word 'Demetrius' may have been inserted for the
sake of clearness; Josephus treats Apollonius throughout as fighting on the side
of Alexander (in spite of verse 88).

[2] 'All the time he was luring them on into the plain'; this seems to be the
meaning of the Greek text, although Joppe and Azotus were both on the sea-
board, far away from any hill-country. The Latin has 'immediately he went out
into the plain,' which yields no satisfactory sense.

81 Round his army they rode, casting javelins into the ranks, from morning
till night-fall; but ever it stood firm, at Jonathan's bidding, till the horses
82 were tired out at last. Then, the force of the cavalry once spent, out
came Simon with his troops to attack the main body, which thereupon
83 broke and fled. Scattered over the open country, in vain they rallied at
84 Azotus, and took refuge in the precincts of their god Dagon; both Azotus
and all the neighbouring cities Jonathan burnt and plundered, and
Dagon's temple, with all that took shelter there, was burnt with the rest.
85 So perished, by sword and fire, some eight thousand men; as for Jonathan, he had no sooner encamped before Ascalon, than the townsfolk
opened the gates to him, and gave him honourable welcome.

87 So Jonathan came back to Jerusalem, and the army behind him, laden
88 with spoils. More than ever, when he heard of it, did king Alexander
89 heap honours upon him; a buckle of gold he sent him, ever the gift kings
make to men of blood royal, and Accaron, with all the countryside about
it, granted him for his domain.

CHAPTER ELEVEN

AND now Ptolemy, king of Egypt, levied a great army, countless as
sand on the beach, and a fleet besides; to win Alexander's realm his
2 treacherous design was, and add it to his own. To Syria he came, full of
fair speeches, and all the towns opened their gates to welcome him; such
welcome Alexander himself had prescribed; was not the king of Egypt
3 his father-in-law? And never a town king Ptolemy entered, but he left
4 a guard of soldiers there. When he reached Azotus, here was Dagon's
temple burnt, here was the town itself and all its neighbourhood in ruins;
the dead lay unburied, where they fell in battle, or in heaps by the road-
5 side. All this they shewed him, and told him, with malicious intent, how
6 it was Jonathan's doing; but no word said king Ptolemy. As for Jonathan,
he went to meet the king at Joppe, with a deal of pomp; there they greeted
7 one another, and passed the night, nor would Jonathan return to Jerusalem till he had escorted the king as far as the river called Eleutherus.

8 All the cities of the sea-coast, as far as maritime Seleucia, king Ptolemy
9 occupied, and with no friendly purpose towards Alexander; it was to
Demetrius he sent envoys instead. Come, said he, a pact between us! My
daughter thou shalt have in Alexander's place, and therewithal the throne
10 of thy fathers; here is an ill son-in-law I have chosen, that went about
11 but now to kill me! Thus, to find pretext for dethroning his rival, king
12 Ptolemy defamed him; took his daughter away, and gave her to Demetrius. His estrangement from Alexander now come to an open breach,
13 what must he do next but enter the city of Antioch, and there assume the

14 double crown, as ruler of Egypt and Asia both? As for Alexander, that
15 was then in Cilicia, quelling a revolt in those parts, he came out to do
   battle when the news reached him; but Ptolemy brought up his army,
16 met him with a superior force, and routed him. Thus Egypt had the
17 mastery; and when Alexander fled to Arabia for refuge, Zabdiel, an
18 Arabian, cut off his head and sent it to the conqueror. Three days later,
   Ptolemy himself lay dead; whereupon the garrisons he had left in the
19 towns were massacred by the citizens, and the royal power passed to
   Demetrius in this, the hundred and sixty-seventh year.

20   Now it was that Jonathan mustered the men of Judaea to deliver an
   attack on the Gentile citadel in Jerusalem; engines a many they brought
21 against it. Nor wanted there Jews of the godless party, traitors to their
22 own race, that went off and told Demetrius it was being attacked; the
   news greatly angered him, and he hastened to Ptolemais, bidding Jona-
23 than raise the siege and come to meet him without more ado. This
   message notwithstanding, Jonathan would have the siege go forward;
   certain elders of Israel, and certain of the priests, he chose out to bear
24 him company, and so put his own life in peril, going off to meet the king
   at Ptolemais, with gold and silver and garments and other gifts in great
25 number. He was received graciously enough; let his own traitorous
26 fellow-countrymen bring what accusations they would, the king would
   not be behind his predecessors in making much of Jonathan, for all his
27 courtiers to see. He was confirmed in the high priesthood, and what
   other high dignities he held aforetime, and declared besides the chief of
   the king's friends.

28   And now Jonathan had a favour to ask; exemption from tribute for
   Judaea, and the three cantons, and Samaria with its neighbouring town-
29 ships;[1] he promised in return a payment of three hundred talents. To
   this the king agreed, writing thus to Jonathan upon the matter raised:
30 King Demetrius, to his brother prince Jonathan, and to the people of the
31 Jews, greeting. We send you herewith, for your better information, a copy
   of the instructions we have given to our cousin Lasthenes in your re-
32 gard. King Demetrius, to Lasthenes, his good father, greeting. Whereas the people of the Jews have ever been trusty friends to us, our pleasure
34 it is to reward them for the loyalty they have shewn us. We therefore
   confirm them in the possession of all Judaea, the three cities of Ephraim,
   Lydda and Ramathan, that formerly belonged to Samaria, and all their
   neighbouring townships . . . to all those who do sacrifice at Jerusalem;
   instead of the yearly revenues hitherto set apart for the king from harvest

---

[1] 'The three cantons, and Samaria with its neighbouring townships'; some
think this is a copyist's error for 'the three cantons which had belonged to
Samaria, with their neighbouring townships,' cf. verse 34.

35 and fruit-gathering.[1] Tithe and tribute that was ours we also remit to them; nor lay any claim to the salt-pits, or the crowns which from time
36 to time were bestowed upon us. Of all this we give them a full discharge,
37 that shall be valid in perpetuity. See to it that a copy of this decree shall be made, and handed over to Jonathan, who shall set it up in a public place on the holy mountain.

38   Here, then, was the whole realm at peace under Demetrius' rule, nor any rival had he; what must he do but disband all his soldiers and send them home, except the foreign troops he had levied from the islands out at sea? Bitterly they hated him for it, the men who had served under his
39 fathers; and there was one Tryphon that took good note of these discontents in the army. This Tryphon was formerly of Alexander's faction, and now he had recourse to Emalchuel, the Arabian, that had care of
40 Alexander's son Antiochus.   Much persuasion he used with him, to let Antiochus return to his father's throne; much told him of Demetrius, and how the soldiers were disaffected against him.

41   Time passed, and Tryphon was in Arabia still.   Meanwhile, Jonathan was urgent with king Demetrius to withdraw the garrisons from Jerusalem citadel and the other strongholds, where they bore arms yet, and
42 against Israel. Nay, answered Demetrius, that I will do and more; great honours I have in store, for thee and for thy people both, when the time
43 is ripe for it. For this present, it were well done to send troops for my
44 own protection; here is all my army revolted from me! Three thousand picked men Jonathan dispatched to Antioch, to the king's side, and right
45 glad he was at their coming. What though the citizens, a hundred and twenty thousand strong, were banded together against his royal person,
46 driving him to take refuge within the court, and occupying the city streets
47 in warlike fashion? He had but to call the Jews to his aid, and they rallied at his summons; posted themselves here and there about the
48 streets, and in one day slew a hundred thousand men, setting fire to the town besides. Spoil there was for the winning, that day when they saved
49 the king's life. The townsfolk, when they saw how easily the Jews got the mastery of them, had no more stomach for fighting; they were loud in
50 their entreaties: A truce! A truce! Havoc enough yonder Jews have
51 made of us and of the city! And so, flinging away their weapons, they came to terms. Prince and people both had good proof, by now, of the Jews' valour; back they went to Jerusalem high in repute among the Syrians, and laden with spoils.

52   Demetrius, now firmly established on the throne, his dominions all at

---

[1] The sentence is obscure, and perhaps the text has been inaccurately transmitted. For 'Ephraim' the Greek has the form 'Aphaerema,' which the Latin interprets as a common noun, 'sequestration.'

53 peace,   recked little enough of his promises; from Jonathan he was estranged altogether, left his services unrecompensed, and much mischief
54 did him besides.   It was now that Tryphon came back, and with him
the young prince Antiochus, that took the style of king and had himself
55 crowned;   all the disbanded armies of Demetrius rallied to them, and
56 turned upon their former master, who fled routed before them;   Tryphon,
meanwhile, got possession of the elephants, and Antioch fell into his
57 hands.   Thereupon came a letter from the young Antiochus to Jonathan,
confirming him in the high priesthood, and in possession both of Judaea
58 and of the three cantons; he was acclaimed as the king's friend,   and a
present of golden cups sent for his use, with the right to drink out of gold
59 ware, to dress in purple, and to carry the golden buckle.   His brother
Simon, too, was made lord of the sea-coast, from Tyre to the frontiers of
Egypt.
60   And now Jonathan was on the march, across the river, patrolling the
cities everywhere, with all the armies of Syria gathered to aid him. . . .
He came to Ascalon, where the townsfolk welcomed him with all honour;[1]
61 came to Gaza, where they shut the gates on him, and he must needs
undertake the siege of it. But when he had spread fire and rapine through
62 the countryside,   the men of Gaza asked for terms, which he gave them,
carrying off their sons as hostages to Jerusalem. Then he went on patrol-
63 ling the country, all the way to Damascus.   News reached him that the
chiefs of Demetrius' faction were making head at Cades, in Galilee, with
a whole army to support them, and their design was to remove him from
64 office. So he went to meet them, leaving his brother Simon in charge of
Judaea.
65   As for Simon, he made an assault upon Bethsura, and kept it for a long
66 while besieged,   till at last it obtained terms of surrender; he rid the place
of its defenders and took over the command of it, putting in a garrison of
67 his own. Meanwhile, Jonathan was encamped by the waters of Genesar;
here, on the plain of Asor, they were on the watch before day-break,
68 when they saw the enemy's force coming to meet them over the level
plain. These had an ambush ready for him on the hill-side, and as he
69 advanced to meet the main body,   the men in ambush sprang up, and
70 engaged him. At this, all Jonathan's supporters took to their heels; none
stood their ground but Mathathias son of Absalom and Judas son of

---

[1] It is hardly possible to give any satisfactory account of the text as it stands.
'The river,' by all analogy, must be the Euphrates; why should Jonathan march
so far afield? And how, in doing so, did he arrive at Ascalon, some forty miles
west of Jerusalem? Conceivably there has been some disturbance in the text,
which may have read originally, 'And he (Antiochus) began patrolling the cities
across the river, with all the armies of Syria gathered to aid him; and Jonathan
marched out and came to Ascalon . . .'

71 Calphi, that had the marshalling of his men. What marvel if Jonathan
tore his garments about him, and strewed earth on his head, and betook
72 himself to prayer? Afterwards, he offered battle afresh, and routed his
73 enemies; as the fight went on, his own men that had deserted their ranks
rallied to him, and joined in the pursuit all the way to Cades, where they
74 encamped once more. In that day's fighting, three thousand of the Gentiles fell; and so Jonathan made his way back to Jerusalem.

CHAPTER TWELVE

HERE was a posture of affairs suited Jonathan well enough; yet would
he send delegates to confirm and renew his alliance with the Ro-
2 mans; Lacedaemon, too, and other countries should have letters of the
3 same tenour. To Rome, then, his messengers went, gained audience of
the senate, and told how the high priest Jonathan and the Jewish people
4 had sent them to renew their old treaty of friendship; and the Romans
gave them such letters of recommendation to this country or that, as
should bring them home to Juda under safe conduct.
5 The message Jonathan sent to the men of Sparta was in these terms
6 following. The high priest Jonathan, with the elders and priests and all
7 the people of the Jews, to their brethren the Spartans, greeting. Long
since, your king Arius wrote to our own high priest Onias claiming kin-
8 ship between us, as witness the copy here subjoined; an honourable
welcome Onias gave to this messenger of yours, and accepted the proposal
9 of friendly alliance. For ourselves, we have little need of such friendship;
10 seek we comfort, it is in the sacred books committed to our charge. Yet
we thought it best to treat with you for the renewal of this brotherly compact, before any estrangement should arise between us; your embassy to
11 us is of long ago. Never feast-day passes, nor day apt for remembrance,
but you are remembered, as brothers should be, in sacrifice and prayer
12 we offer; renown of yours is pride of ours still. In wars and calamities
much involved of late, powerful kings for our neighbours and our
14 enemies, we would not embroil you, nor other allies of ours, in these
15 quarrels. Now, by the grace of heaven, we are delivered; our enemies lie
16 crushed; delegates of ours, Numenius son of Antiochus and Antipater,
are on their way to Rome, friendship and alliance of former days to con-
17 firm afresh; and should we send them with no errand to you, no greet-
18 ing, no word from us of brotherhood revived? Pray you, send us fair
answer in your turn.
19 And, for Arius' letter to Onias, thus the copy of it ran, Arius, king of
21 the Spartans, to the high priest Onias, greeting. Spartan and Jew, written
22 record shews it, come of one blood, Abraham's. Apprised of this, we

23 would fain know how you do; pray tell us. And take this message in return, Cattle and whatever else is ours, is yours, and yours ours; of that, the bearer of this letter brings you assurance.

24 Then came news to Jonathan that the chiefs of Demetrius' faction were
25 returning to the attack, and in greater force than ever; so out he marched, and met them in the Amathite country; respite he would not give them,
26 to invade his own. Spies of his went out into the enemy's camp, and
27 reported, all was ready for a night attack; so, when the sun was down, Jonathan would have his men keep watch, ready armed all night for
28 battle, and posted sentries round his lines. The enemy, hearing of such preparedness on their part, took alarm and let cowardly counsels pre-
29 vail;[1] they were at pains to leave watchfires burning in their camp, so that Jonathan and his men, deceived by the glow of light, knew nothing
30 of their plans till morning; and when he gave chase, it was too late to
31 catch them; already they had crossed the river Eleutherus. Thereupon he turned his attack against the Zabadeans, an Arabian tribe, defeating
32 them and taking spoils from them; and so, harnessing his waggons,
33 pressed on to Damascus, patrolling all the country round about. Meanwhile, Simon had marched out to Ascalon and the neighbouring strong-
34 holds; thence he turned aside to Joppe, and took possession of it; rumour had reached him, the townsfolk would yield the citadel to Demetrius' party, and he must have a garrison there of his own.

35 When Jonathan returned, he summoned the elders of the people, and
36 took counsel with them, how best to raise strongholds in Judaea, and build up walls in Jerusalem itself. Height these must have, above all, between the Citadel and the rest of the town; he would have it cut off
37 from the rest, standing by itself, with no opportunity to buy and sell. A great muster there was for the city's rebuilding; and where the wall had tumbled down, over the ravine on the east, he made it good; it is the part
38 called Caphetetha. Meanwhile, Simon rebuilt Adiada in the Sephela and fortified it; bolt and bar it should have thenceforward.

39 And what of Tryphon? Lordship of all Asia he coveted, and a royal
40 crown; it should be Antiochus' turn next. The danger was, Jonathan would refuse his assent, and resort to arms; Jonathan first he must seize
41 and put to death. So he moved his quarters to Bethsan, where Jonathan came out to meet him with forty thousand men, picked warriors all of
42 them, at his back. Here was a great retinue; and Tryphon, daunted by
43 this show of force, was fain to give him an honourable welcome. He would admit Jonathan among his closest friends, and bestow gifts on him;
44 let Jonathan give orders, and Tryphon's soldiers would obey. Then he

---

[1] 'Let cowardly counsels prevail'; literally, 'were dismayed in their hearts,' but the context shews that in fact they beat a retreat.

asked, What needs it, such a host of men should go campaigning, when
45 threat of war is none? It were better to disband them, and choose out a
few for thy own retinue. That done, bear me company to Ptolemais; city
and strongholds and troops and officers I will hand over into thy charge;
it was on that errand I came.
46 What did Jonathan? He fell into the trap, sent his men back to Juda,
47 and kept but three thousand under arms; of these, he left two thousand
48 in Galilee, and took but a thousand in his company. No sooner had he
entered Ptolemais than the townsfolk shut the gates behind him, secured
49 his person, and put his retinue to the sword. Horse and foot Tryphon
sent out to Galilee, to find the rest of his followers in the Great Plain,
50 and make an end of them; but these, hearing that Jonathan and his men
had been caught and murdered, resolved to put a bold front on it, and
51 marched in battle array. Finding them ready to sell their lives dearly,
52 their pursuers abandoned the chase, and all reached Juda safe and sound.
For Jonathan and his companions they made great dole, and loudly all
53 Israel echoed their lament. Neighbouring people was none but went
54 about to overthrow them, and no wonder; their chieftain, their champion
gone, now was the time to fall upon them, and rid earth of their memory.

CHAPTER THIRTEEN

AND what did Simon, when he heard that Tryphon had levied a strong
2 force, for Juda's invasion and overthrow? Here was all the people
in a great taking of fear; so he made his way to Jerusalem and there
3 gathered them to meet him. And thus, to put heart into them, he spoke:
Need is none to tell you what battles we have fought, what dangers
endured, I and my brethren and all my father's kin, law and sanctuary
4 to defend. In that cause, and for the love of Israel, my brothers have
5 died, one and all, till I only am left; never be it said of me, in the hour
6 of peril I held life dear, more precious than theirs! Nay, come the whole
world against us, to glut its malice with our ruin, race and sanctuary,
7 wives and children of ours shall find me their champion yet. At these
8 words, the spirit of the whole people revived; loud came their answer,
9 Brother of Judas and Jonathan, thine to lead us now! Thine to sustain
our cause; and never word of thine shall go unheeded!
10 Thereupon, he summoned all the fighting men together, and pressed
on to have the walls of Jerusalem finished, till it was fortified all about;
11 and he sent Jonathan, son of Absalom, to Joppe, at the head of a force
newly raised; the garrison was disbanded, and a new captain held it now.
12 Meanwhile, Tryphon had left Ptolemais, with a great army at his heels,

13 marching on Juda; and with him went Jonathan, his prisoner. He found
14 Simon encamped at Addus, that looks out over the plain; here was
Jonathan's brother Simon taking his place, and offering battle. Envoys
15 were sent out to make his excuses: Hold we the person of thy brother
Jonathan, it is because he is in default to the royal treasury over his deal-
16 ings with it. Thou hast but to send a hundred talents of silver, and his
two sons, to be surety he will not play us false when we release him, and
17 he is a free man. Well Simon knew it was treacherously spoken; yet he
gave orders, both money and hostages should be surrendered. A bitter
18 grudge Israel's people would bear him, if they had cause to say, For
19 want of money paid over and surety given, Jonathan must die! Sent they
were, the boys and the money both, but all was treachery; Jonathan never
came back.

20   And now Tryphon invaded Juda, bent on its undoing; his troops must
fetch a compass by the road that leads round to Ador, and, march they
21 where they would, Simon and his army were at their heels. Word came
to him from the defenders of Jerusalem citadel, he should make his way
22 across the desert without more ado, and bring them supplies; and that
same night he had all his cavalry in readiness for the march, but there was
a great fall of snow, and come he might not . . . into the country of
23 Galaad.[1] When he reached Bascaman, then and there he put Jonathan
24 and his sons to death; and with that, he turned about, and went back to
his own country.

25   There lay the bones of Simon's brother Jonathan, till he sent to fetch
26 them, and gave them burial at Modin, the city of his fathers. Loud lament
27 all Israel made for him, and long they bemoaned him. Over the graves of
his father and his brethren Simon raised a towering monument, of hewn
28 stone behind and before; then, with father and mother and his four
29 brethren in mind, he built seven pyramids, in rows; and all about were
great columns, carved with armour and ships; an abiding memorial, and
30 a landmark to mariners at sea. Such was the tomb he raised at Modin,
31 and it may be seen to this day. Meanwhile, as they were journeying to-
32 gether, Tryphon murdered the young king Antiochus by artifice, and
succeeded to his throne, wearing the crown of all Asia; great mischief it
was he did to his country.

33   All the fortresses of Judaea Simon repaired, building them up with
high tower and stout wall, with bolt and bar; and never a garrison but had
34 provisions laid up in store. Then he chose out envoys and sent them to
king Demetrius, praying that the land might enjoy immunity after the

---

[1] It seems clear from the context that some words have dropped out. The Greek
text has, 'and come he might not, because of the snow. So he moved camp and
went into the country of Galaad.' But the passage may originally have indicated
what reasons Tryphon had for abandoning his campaign in Judaea.

35 tyrannous actions of Tryphon.[1] When king Demetrius answered the
36 request, he wrote in these terms following. King Demetrius to the high
priest Simon, the friend of kings, and to all the elders and people of the
37 Jews, greeting. Crown of gold and robe of scarlet you sent us were faithfully delivered. Great favour we mean to shew you, by sending word to
38 the king's officers to respect the remissions granted you. The decrees we
made concerning you are yet in force; and, for the strongholds you have
39 built, they shall be yours. Fault of yours in the past, witting or unwitting,
is condoned; coronation tax you owed, and all other tribute that was due
40 from Jerusalem, is due no longer. Fit be they for such enrolment, Jews
shall be enrolled in our armies, and ever between us and you let there be
peace!
41   Thus, in the hundred and seventieth year, Israel was free of the Gen-
42 tile yoke at last; and this style the people began to use, were it private
bond or public instrument they indited, In the first year of Simon's high
priesthood, chief paramount and governor of the Jews.
43   Then it was that Simon marched on Gaza,[2] and beleaguered it with
44 his army; built engines, and forced an entry into one of the towers. Out
into the streets they sallied, that manned the engine, and there was a fine
45 commotion in the city; here were the townsfolk, with their wives and
children, mounting the walls with their garments rent about them, and
46 crying aloud, Simon should give them quarter; great were their fault,
47 greater still his clemency! At that, Simon relented; harry them to the
death he would not, but he drove them out of the city, and cleansed all
the houses where idols had stood; then, with singing of psalms and giving
48 of thanks, he made his entry; and now all defilement must be put away,
and such citizens it must have as did what the law commanded. After
that, he fortified it, and made his own dwelling there.
49   And what of the Gentiles that were left in Jerusalem citadel? Enter
Jewish territory or leave it they might not, buy or sell they might not, so
50 that they were hard put to it for food, and many died of famine. At last
they cried out to Simon, he should give them quarter, and give them
quarter he did, but drove them out, and cleansed the citadel of its pollu-
51 tion. On the twenty-third day of the second month, in the hundred and
seventy-first year, in came the Jewish folk singing praise and bearing
palm-branches, with music of harp, and cymbals, and zither; of such ill

---

[1] 'After the tyrannous actions of Tryphon'; literally (in the Greek text), 'because all the actions of Tryphon were seizures.' The meaning is perhaps that
Simon now recognized all the actions of Tryphon as usurpations of power; it is
evident from what follows that he was not sure of his position; had the Jews, by
their support of a pretender, forfeited the privileges granted in 11.33–37?
[2] Josephus is perhaps right in reading 'Gazara' (less than twenty miles from
Jerusalem) instead of 'Gaza'; cf. 14.7.

52 neighbours Israel was now rid. Every year, Simon proclaimed, holiday
53 should be kept at this time; and he fortified that part of the temple mountain which was close by the citadel; here he dwelt, and his followers with
54 him. And now here was his son John grown into a brave warrior; him
   Simon put at the head of the whole army, with his quarters at Gazara.

CHAPTER FOURTEEN

THE year following, what must Demetrius do but muster his army and
betake himself to Media, where he would raise levies for the war
2 against Tryphon? When Arsaces, king of the Medes and Persians, had
news of it, he gave orders to one of his chieftains, the invader must be
3 taken alive and brought into his presence. The order was obeyed; the
Syrian king, routed and captured, was brought before Arsaces, who put
him safely in prison.
4   Thus, during Simon's days, the whole land of Juda was at peace. Ever
his people's good sought he, and ever by willing hearts was obeyed and
5 honoured. With great state he took possession of Joppe as a harbour,[1]
6 and so found access to the islands out at sea. How wide spread he the
7 frontiers of Israel, how firmly held its possessions, captured how many
of its foes! Gazara and Bethsura he won, ay, and the Citadel itself, ridding
8 it of all defilement; there was no resisting his power. In his day, every
man farmed his own lands in security, soil of Juda yielded its crops, and
9 the trees their fruit; sat old men in the market-place, busy over the
common weal, and young men wore the livery of their glorious cam-
10 paigning. Never a city but he furnished it with store of provisions; a bulwark each of them should be of sturdy defence. What wonder if the story
11 of his renown was noised to the world's end? Such peaceful times
12 brought he to his country, when all Israel kept high holiday, every man
with his own vine and fig-tree for shade, and enemy was none to daunt
13 them; domestic malice undone, foreign tyranny shattered all around!
14 Among his own folk, what comfort he gave the friendless, how scru-
15 tinized the law, what short work made of traitor and malcontent; how
adorned the sanctuary, how increased the number of its treasures!
16   To Rome, to Sparta itself, came tidings of Jonathan's death, and was
17 heard right sorrowfully. When they learned that his brother Simon had
been made high priest instead, master now of the land and all its cities,

---

[1] This is perhaps the best interpretation of a difficult phrase, 'With all his
glory he received Joppe to be a harbour.' For the language used, cf. 10.58,
II Mac. 5.20. Joppe had been captured by Jonathan (10.76), and remained at
least nominally in Jewish possession (12.33; 13.11); Simon's achievement, according to verse 34 below, was to fortify it.

18 they wrote to him on tablets made of bronze, to renew the treaty of
   friendship they had with his brethren, Judas and Jonathan, before him; [1]
19 and their letters were read out before the whole assembly at Jerusalem.
20 The Spartans wrote in these words following: The rulers and commonalty of Sparta, to the high priest Simon, the elders and priests and all
21 the people of the Jews, greeting. Welcome news your ambassadors have
22 brought us, of fame and credit and prosperity you enjoy. And their
   errand stands recorded in our public annals; how Numenius son of
   Antiochus and Antipater son of Jason came to renew our old treaty of
23 friendship with you; how the people resolved to give them fair greeting,
   and to lay up a copy of their report in the public archives, that should
   preserve the memory of it among the Spartan people; and how an account
   of all this was sent to the high priest Simon.
24 Numenius was sent on a further mission to Rome, bearing a great target of gold, a thousand minas in weight, to renew the alliance there. And
   when all this reached the ears of the people . . .[2]
25 . . . Men began to ask, how they could shew their gratitude to Simon,
26 and to his sons? Here was one that had restored the fortunes of his race,
   and rid Israel of its foes. So they gave him exemption from public burdens, and inscribed their decree on tablets of bronze, fastened to pillars
   which were set up on mount Sion.
27 And thus the inscription ran: On this eighteenth day of Elul, in the
   hundred and seventy-second year of the Greek empire, the third of
28 Simon's high priesthood, there was a high assembly held of priests and
   people, clan chiefs and elders of the whole nation, that had before them
   these considerations following. All through the long wars of our country,
29 Simon and his brethren, sons of Mattathias, of Jarib's clan, put their lives
   in peril, and fought for law and sanctuary against the common enemy,
30 much glory winning for their own nation. When Jonathan, that had
31 rallied the people and been their high priest, became a part of his race, enemies thought to invade the country and crush the power of it, violate its
32 holy places; and Simon it was withstood them. Champion of his people's
   cause, much he spent to arm its warriors, and furnish them with pay.
33 Juda's cities he fortified, and others besides; Bethsura on the frontiers,

---

[1] The implication appears to be that both Rome and Sparta sent answers in
the manner described.
[2] Verse 24. It would be natural to assume that the end of this verse refers to
the Roman people; and the Clementine Vulgate, without any manuscript authority, actually inserts the word 'Roman.' But the proceedings of verses 25 sqq.
are evidently those of the Jewish people. There is a want of sequence in the
narrative as it stands, and it seems possible that verses 15–24 of chapter 15
originally stood here, and were accidentally misplaced; if so, 'all this' will refer
to the Roman dispatches.

34 once a stronghold of the enemy, garrisoned now by Jews, Joppe on the sea coast, and Gazara in the Azotus region; Gazara, too, once hostile, with Jewish troops manned he, and in each town made provision for repairs to be done.

35 The people, seeing him so loyal a lover of his country's renown, made him their ruler and high priest; no less was due to such exploits, public service so faithfully done, such constant ambition for his people's honour.

36 In his days it was, and by his means, the land was rid at last of Gentile intruders; not least the garrison of David's own Keep at Jerusalem, that by their sallying out profaned the sacred precincts, and much defiled

37 their purity; a Jewish garrison he set there, to guard both city and coun-

38 tryside, and built Jerusalem walls yet higher. High priesthood of his,

39 king Demetrius must needs acknowledge, bestowing on him the title of king's friend, and loading him with honours. What could he do else?

40 Here was Rome itself greeting the Jewish folk as allies, good friends, and

41 kinsmen, welcoming the envoys of Simon with civic state. Here were the Jews, priests and people both, agreed that he should rule them, granting him the high priesthood [1] by right inalienable, until true prophet they

42 should have once more. Their ruler he should be, and guardian of their temple; appoint officer and magistrate, master of ordnance and captain

43 of garrison, and have charge of the sanctuary besides. Him all must obey, in his name deeds be drawn up, all the country through; of purple

44 and gold should be his vesture. Of the rest, both priests and people, none should retrench these privileges, nor gainsay Simon's will, nor con-voke assembly in the country without him; garment of purple, buckle

45 of gold, none should wear; nor any man defy or void this edict, but at his peril.

46 The people's pleasure it was to ennoble Simon after this sort; and Simon, he would not say them nay; high priest, and of priests and people

48 leader, governor and champion, he would be henceforward. So they had the decree inscribed on tablets of bronze, and set up plain to view in the

49 temple precincts; and a copy of it they put by in the treasury, in the safe keeping of Simon and his heirs. [2]

---

[1] The Machabaean high priesthood seems to have been regarded as an emergency dispensation. For the mention of the prophet, cf. 4.46.

[2] Verses 45–49. We should perhaps take these verses as part of the decree itself; otherwise verse 48 seems a needless repetition of verse 26.

CHAPTER FIFTEEN

NOW turn we to Demetrius' other son, Antiochus.[1] He it was directed a letter, from the islands over sea, to Simon, high priest and ruler
2 of the Jews, and to the whole nation; and this was the tenour of it. King Antiochus, to the high priest Simon and to the people of the Jews, greet-
3 ing. Here is the kingdom of my fathers overrun by ill folk; I mean to challenge them, and bring back the old ways. To this end, I have made a
4 great levy of mercenaries, and built ships of war; passage I needs must have through yonder territory, ere I can take vengeance for lands of mine
5 ravaged, cities of mine laid waste. This grant, then, I make thee; exemption, such as thou hadst, in the name of former kings, from public offer-
6 ings and all other payment due to me; the right of minting money within
7 thy own borders; for Jerusalem, enjoyment of her sacred liberties; of weapons thou hast made, strongholds thou hast built, the undisturbed
8 possession. Never a claim the king has, or shall have hereafter, on his
9 subjects, but to thee it is remitted; and, when the kingdom is ours, such honours we will bestow as shall make thee, and thy race, and its sanctuary, renowned all the world over.
10 So, in the hundred and seventy-fourth year, Antiochus returned to his native country, and the armies rallied to him, until Tryphon had but a
11 small following left; all down the sea coast he fled, with Antiochus at his
12 heels, till he reached Dora; and ever he saw the toils closing round him,
13 now his troops had played him false. With a hundred thousand foot, and
14 eight thousand horse, Antiochus came to the gates of Dora and began the siege of it; his ships, too, blockaded the coast, so that it was cut off by land and sea alike; enter it none might, nor leave it . . .
15 And now here were Numenius and his fellow envoys come back from Rome,[2] with a copy of despatches sent out to kings and nations every-
16 where, and this was the tenour of them. Lucius, the Roman consul, to
17 king Ptolemy, greeting. Envoys we have but now received in audience from a friendly country, to wit, Judaea; the people of the Jews, with their high priest Simon, had sent to renew their old treaty of alliance with us,
18 and had made us a present besides, a golden target of a thousand minas
19 weight. Agreed we then to warn kings and nations everywhere, they should not hurt or assault the Jewish people, its cities and countryside,
20 nor comfort its enemies; and for the target of gold, our pleasure was to
21 accept the gift of it. If then there be malcontents from Judaea sheltering

---

[1] Antiochus was son to the Demetrius whose death is recorded in 10.50, brother to the Demetrius first mentioned in 10.67.
[2] Verses 15–24. See note on 14.24.

among you, our bidding is you should hand them over to the high priest
22 Simon, for such punishment as the Jewish law prescribes. Copies of this
decree have been sent to Demetrius, Attalus, Ariarathes and Arsaces,
23 and to these countries following: Lampsacus, Sparta, Delos, Myndos,
Sicyon, Caria, Samos, Pamphylia, Lycia, Halicarnassus, Coos, Side,
24 Arados, Rhodes, Phaselis, Gortyna, Cnidus, Cyprus and Cyrene. A
further copy has been sent to the high priest Simon and to the Jewish
people . . .

25   Once again [1] king Antiochus laid siege to Dora, bringing fresh force to
bear, and devising fresh engines; and ever he kept Tryphon hemmed in,
26 so that escape was none. Thereupon Simon despatched two thousand
picked men to aid in the siege, with silver and gold and a deal of tackle
27 besides; but accept them the king would not; all his promises were forgot,
28 and Simon a stranger now. Athenobius it was, one of the king's friends,
that came to treat with him, and this was the message he bore: Cities of
29 mine you hold, Joppe, and Gazara, and Jerusalem citadel; lands about
them you have laid waste, and done Syria much mischief besides, en-
30 croaching everywhere on my domain. Needs must you should hand over
31 cities you have occupied, revenues of Gentile lands you have detained, or
else five hundred talents of silver in exchange, and five hundred more to
compensate for damage done and revenue lost; if not, we will come and
overpower you by force of arms.
32   So came Athenobius, the king's friend, to Jerusalem, where he saw
what state Simon kept, much display of gold and silver, and a great
throng of attendants, till he was dazzled at the sight. Yet delivered he his
33 errand; to which Simon made this answer: Other men's fief seized we
never, nor other men's rights detain; here be lands that were our father's
34 once, by enemies of ours for some while wrongfully held; opportunity
35 given us, should we not claim the patrimony we had lost? As for thy talk
of Joppe and Gazara, these were cities did much mischief to people and
land of ours; for the worth of them, thou shalt have a hundred talents if
36 thou wilt. Never a word said Athenobius, but went back to the king very
ill pleased, and told him what answer was given; of Simon's court, too,
and of all else he had seen.
37   Antiochus was in a great taking of anger; here was Tryphon newly
38 escaped by ship to Orthosias! He must needs leave the sea coast in charge
39 of Cendebaeus, with a strong command both of horse and foot, while
himself gave Tryphon chase. This Cendebaeus had orders to advance

---

[1] Some Greek manuscripts have 'on the second day,' instead of 'once again,'
but this is probably a correction, designed to clear up a difficulty. Nothing has
been said which implies that the siege described in verse 14 had come to an end;
and it is not easy to account for the mention of a second siege, unless we suppose
a gap in the manuscript which has been accidentally filled up by verses 15–24.

and threaten Judaea; Gedor [1] he should fortify, and there make himself
40 fast, the better to levy war on Juda. So he marched away to Jamnia, and
set about harassing the Jews; now it was an inroad, with prisoners
carried away, now a massacre; and all the while he was fortifying Gedor.
41 Cavalry he quartered there, and other troops besides, to sally out and
patrol the roads into Judaea; the king would have it so.

CHAPTER SIXTEEN

IT was not long before John came up from Gazara, to tell his father
2 Simon how ill Cendebaeus was using their fellow-countrymen. And at
that, Simon must have his two elder sons present, Judas and John both,
and made the command over to them. Still young we were, he said, I and
my brothers and my father's kin, when we began that war on Israel's
enemies which is being fought yet; under our banners once and again
3 came victory, and the day was saved for Israel. I am an old man now, and
it is yours to do what I and brother of mine did; march out, fight in our
people's cause, and heaven's aid be with you!
4   Twenty thousand warriors John [2] chose out from the rest, and cavalry
to support them, and away they went to fight Cendebaeus. That night
5 they spent at Modin, and on the morrow, when they left it for the valley,
what a huge array was this, both of horse and foot, encountering them!
6 And a mountain torrent flowed in between. When John brought his
army to the opposite bank, and found his men had little stomach for the
crossing, he made the passage first, leaving the rest to follow at his heels;
7 then drew them up by companies, with the cavalry in between, so greatly
8 did the enemy's cavalry outnumber them. And now the sacred trumpets
sounded the charge; fled Cendebaeus, fled his army at their onslaught,
and many were left dead on the field; for the rest, they were fain to take
9 refuge behind their walls again. John went in pursuit, for all his brother
Judas had been wounded in the battle, and chased them as far as the walls
10 of Cedron ... which he had fortified.[3] Nor might they find shelter in the
strongholds of the Azotus territory; he burnt these to the ground; a toll
of two thousand men he had taken before he returned victorious to Jerusalem.

---

[1] 'Gedor' is 'Cedron' in the Greek text, here and in verse 40 below, to correspond with verse 9 of the following chapter.
[2] The name John is not mentioned in the original, either here or in verses 6 and
7 below. But it is plain that either John or Judas is meant, and 13.54 seems to give
the best grounds for a decision.
[3] Verse 9. It is grammatically impossible to make Cendebaeus the subject of the
verb 'he had fortified,' as the sentence stands. It seems likely that there is some
slight error or omission in the manuscripts.

11   Turn we now to Ptolemy, son of Abobus, that was in charge of all
12 Jericho plain, and had a purse well lined with silver and gold; was he not
13 the son-in-law of a high priest?[1] But higher still his ambition ran; he
    would make himself master of the whole country; murder he plotted for
14 Simon and his sons together. It was in Sabath, the eleventh month, of
    the hundred and seventy-seventh year, that Simon came down to Jericho,
    as ever he visited all the cities of Judaea in his great care for them; and
15 his sons Mattathias and Judas went with him. And there, in a castle he
    had built for himself, Doch is the name of it, the son of Abobus gave
    them treacherous welcome. A great feast he made, but he had men wait-
16 ing in readiness, and with these, when Simon and his sons had drunk
    deep, he took arms, broke into the banqueting-chamber, and slew both
17 father and sons, with certain of their retinue. Never saw Israel so
    treacherous a deed, or good service so ill rewarded.
18   News of all this was sent by Ptolemy to the king, and in writing; his
    plea was, an army should be sent out in support of him, and the country,
    with all its cities and all the tribute that came from them, given into his
19 charge. Others of his men he despatched to Gazara; John must be put to
    death, he wrote, and for the captains, they should have silver and gold
20 and good recompense, would they but rally to his side; others again were
21 to take possession of Jerusalem, and of the temple hill. But too late; a
    messenger had reached John at Gazara, telling him his father and
22 brothers were dead, and himself too marked down for slaughter; where-
    upon he took alarm in good earnest; their murderous errand known, he
    seized his executioners and made an end of them.
23   What else John did, and how fought he, brave deeds done, and strong
24 walls built, and all his history, you may read in the annals of his time,
    that were kept faithfully since the day when he succeeded his father as
    high priest.

---

[1] 'Of a high priest'; Josephus understands this as referring to Simon himself.
But it does not seem likely that the author should have suppressed his name in
verse 12, only to mention it in verse 13; nor does he mention the circumstances of
affinity as adding to the heinousness of the crime (cf. verse 17). Possibly some
other name has dropped out, e.g., that of Alcimus.

THE SECOND BOOK OF MACHABEES

CHAPTER ONE

TO their brethren, the Jews of Egypt, those of Jerusalem and Judaea
2 send brotherly greeting and good health.[1] God speed you well, the
covenant he made with his true worshippers, Abraham, Isaac and Jacob,
3 never forgetting; reverent hearts may he give you, brave and generous to
4 perform his will; with law and precept of his enlarge your thoughts, and
5 send you happiness; may he listen to your prayer, and be gracious, and in
6 the hour of peril never forsake you! Take courage, then; we in this land
7 are praying for you. Time was, in the hundred and sixty-ninth year, when
Demetrius was a-reigning, we ourselves were writing to you in the midst
of suffering and alarms. Much had we to undergo, when Jason would
8 betray his own country, his own people; here was the gateway burnt to
the ground, here were innocent lives forfeited. Cried we upon the Lord,
and all our prayers were answered; burnt-sacrifice and bloodless offering
were made, lamps lighted, and loaves set forth in the temple as of old!
9 Look to it, then, you make bowers and keep holiday in this month of
10 Casleu.[2] Written in the hundred and eighty-eighth year.

The common folk of Jerusalem and Judaea,[3] their council of elders, and
I, Judas, to Aristobulus, of the anointed priestly race, that was master of
11 king Ptolemy, and to the Jews of Egypt, greeting and health. Great
thanks we owe to God, that from the extreme of peril has delivered us; ay,
12 though we had such a king for our adversary, as could bring in hordes
of men from Persia, both us and our holy city to subdue.[4]

13 What became of him, think you, the general that marched away into
Persia with a countless army at his heels?[5] He met his end in the temple of

---

[1] Verses 1–9. The first, it would seem, of a series of fragments prefixed to the
book proper. If the date given at the end belongs to it, it must have been written
about the year 125 before Christ, after the death of Simon.

[2] Here and in verse 18 the feast alluded to is not the feast of Tent-dwelling
(Lev. 23.34), but that of the Dedication (I Mac. 4.59, Jn. 10.22) at which it
appears that the same ceremonies were used.

[3] Verses 10–18. The date mentioned in verse 10 probably belongs to the earlier
fragment, since the ancients usually dated their letters at the end, cf. 11.21, 33, 38
below. If so, this second fragment, undated, will have been written by Judas
Machabaeus to Aristobulus, tutor of the Egyptian king Ptolemy Philomotor,
some forty years earlier than verses 1–9.

[4] Verses 11, 12. The Latin here seems designed to make sense of a passage
untranslatable, and probably corrupt, in the Greek text.

[5] Verses 13–16. If Antiochus Epiphanes is meant, the description of him as
'the general' is highly suspicious. It seems possible that no name was mentioned
in the original, and that the word 'Antiochus' was twice introduced by a copyist,

14 Nanea, through guile of the priests that served it. Thither Antiochus had come with his friends, putting it about that he would wed the goddess, and laying claim to a great part of her treasures under the title of dowry.

15 The priests, then, had the money laid out in readiness; into the precincts he came, with a meagre retinue, and they, now that Antiochus was within,

16 shut the temple gates. Thereupon, letting themselves in by their secret door, they killed the general and his company with throwing of stones, cut them limb from limb, and threw down the severed heads of them to

17 the populace without. Blessed, upon every account, be this God of ours,

18 that denies protection to the sinner! We, then, on this twenty-fifth day of Casleu, mean to solemnize the purification of the temple, and hold ourselves bound to notify you of it, so that you too may keep holiday, with making of bowers. ...

... And of the fire imparted to us, when Nehemias offered sacrifice at

19 the re-building of temple and altar.[1] Long ago, when our fathers were being carried off into the Persian country, priests of the true God that held office in those days took away the fire from the altar, and hid it down in the valley, in a pit both deep and dry, so well guarding their secret that

20 none might know where it was to be found. Years passed, and God's will was that Nehemias should come back, holding the Persian king's warrant. Nehemias it was that had search made for the fire, and by the grandsons of those very priests that hid it; but they made report, fire they could find

21 none, only a puddle of water.[2] And what did Nehemias? He would have some of the water drawn and fetched to him; with this water, once the sacrifice was laid on the altar, both the wood and the offerings themselves

22 must be sprinkled. Sprinkled they were, and when the sun shone out, that till now was hidden by a cloud, all at once a great fire blazed up, astonishing the beholders.

mistakenly anxious to identify the unnamed figure. If so, the fate we are concerned with is that of some general in command of Antiochus's army; his own is described, quite differently, in 9.5 below.

[1] The Latin makes a single sentence of the whole verse, but by dint of concealing what is evidently a gap in the Greek text. The end of the second fragment seems to have been lost; and also the beginning of a third fragment, which occupies the rest of the chapter. The identity of Nehemias seems doubtful; the well-known governor of that name restored the walls of Jerusalem nearly a century after the rebuilding of the Temple. But a Nehemias is mentioned in I Esd. 2.2, Neh. 7.7, among the exiles who returned with Zorobabel. The description 'Nehemias the priest' in verse 21 is probably due to an error in our present Latin text.

[2] The 'fire' hidden in the pit was presumably a smouldering log, such as might be buried away at night to be re-lit in the morning. The 'thick water' found on the site was evidently something different, and there is no reason to think that its properties, natural or supernatural, belonged to the 'fire' originally deposited there.

23 To prayer fell the priests all around, while sacrifice was done, Jonathan
24 to lead them,[1] and the rest answering; to prayer fell Nehemias, and this
was the manner of his praying: Lord God, that all things madest, the ter-
25 rible, the strong, the just, the merciful, king gracious as none else; none
else so kindly, none else so just, as thou, the almighty, the eternal! Israel
from all peril thou deliverest, thou didst make choice of our fathers, and
26 set them apart for thyself. For the whole nation of Israel receive our sacri-
27 fice; all are thine; thy own domain keep inviolate. Bring home the exiles;
captives of the heathen conqueror set free; to the despised, the outcast,
28 grant redress; let the world know what a God is ours! Crush the oppres-
29 sor, the tyrant that so mishandles us, and to thy own sanctuary, as Moses
foretold, thy own people restore!
30 Then, till the sacrifice was consumed, the priests went on with their
31 singing of hymns; and when all was finished, Nehemias would have them
32 drench great stones with the water that was left. Thereupon, a flame
broke out from them, but died away when the altar fires blazed up again
33 over yonder.[2] The news travelled, till the Persian king himself was told
how water appeared where exiled priests had hidden the fire, how, with
34 this water, Nehemias and his company had bathed the sacrifice. Good
heed he gave to the matter, and after due examination fenced the ground
35 in with a shrine, in witness of what befell there. Largesse the priests
had, and many were the gifts passed from hand to hand, when the truth
36 of the matter was proved.[3] As for the place, Nehemias himself called it
Nephthar,[4] which means Purification; but the vulgar call it Nephi.

CHAPTER TWO

YOU shall also find it set down in the dispositions made by the prophet
Jeremias, that he bade the exiles rescue the sacred fire, in the manner
2 aforesaid.[5] Strict charge he gave them, the Lord's commandments they

[1] Jonathan was not the high priest, but the leader of a course of priests (Neh. 12.14).

[2] Verses 31, 32. The Greek text here is very doubtful, and perhaps indicates not that the water was poured out on stones, but that stones were used to block up the hidden pool.

[3] In the Greek text, no mention is made of the priests; the Persian king exchanged gifts with his favourites, by way of celebrating the event (cf. Apoc. 11.10).

[4] The word Nephthar can hardly be what the author wrote; there is no such root signifying purification.

[5] Verses 1–19. These verses seem to be a continuation of the fragment pre-served in the foregoing chapter. Nothing in the prophecy of Jeremias, as we have it, relates the circumstances here mentioned, although verse 2 is possibly a reference to Bar. 6.

should keep ever in mind, nor let false gods, all gold and silver and fine
3 array, steal away their hearts; with much else to confirm them in their
4 regard for the law. And here, in this same document, the story was told,
how a divine oracle came to Jeremias, and he must needs go out, with
tabernacle and ark to bear him company, to the very mountain Moses
5 climbed long ago, when he had sight of God's domain.[1] A cave Jeremias
found there, in which he set down tabernacle and ark and incense-altar,
6 and stopped up the entrance behind him. There were some that followed;
no time they lost in coming up to mark the spot, but find it they could
7 not. He, when they told him of it, rebuked their eagerness; Nay, said he,
the place must remain ever unknown, till the day when God brings his
8 people together once more, and is reconciled; then, divinely, the secret
shall be made manifest. Then once again the Lord's majesty shall be seen,
and the cloud that enshrines it; the same vision that was granted to Moses,
and to Solomon when he prayed that the great God would have his temple
9 on earth; Solomon, the master of wisdom, that in his wisdom offered
sacrifice to hallow the temple he had made.
10   Prayed Moses, prayed Solomon, and fire came down from heaven to
consume the burnt-sacrifice. ...
11   ... Uneaten, Moses said, the victim for fault, and so the fire must consume it. ...
12   ... No other mind had king Solomon, that for eight days would continue his dedication feast.[2]
13   With all this, dispositions Nehemias made, records Nehemias kept, are
in full agreement. He it was founded a library, and there collected histo-
ries of king and prophet, and of David himself; dispatches, too, the kings
14 had sent, and inventories of gifts made. And now Judas in his turn has
recovered all such records as were lost to us through the late wars, and
15 they are here in our keeping; would you be in possession of these, you
have but to send and fetch them.
16   Meanwhile, we notify you by these presents of that cleansing ceremony
17 we mean to perform; do us the courtesy to keep holiday on your part. See
what deliverance God has sent to his people, restoring to us our common
18 domain, our sovereignty, our priesthood, our holy way of living! Think
you not he will fulfil, ere long, the promise made in his law; take pity on

---

[1] Some of the actions described by the Hebrew prophets may have taken place
only in a vision, not in actual life, cf. e.g., Jer. 13.1–7. The mountain is no doubt
Phasga (Deut. 34).
[2] Verses 10–12. It is difficult to make any continuous sense out of these verses
as they have come down to us, and it seems possible that a considerable portion
of the letter has here been lost. The missing part might have explained what was
the relevance of this long excursion into past history, which has no immediate
bearing on Judas and the re-dedication of the temple.

us, that are scattered wide as heaven, and on this hallowed soil reunite us?
19 What meant they else, those great perils overcome, that sanctuary purified
at last? . . .
20   Speak we of Judas Machabaeus and his brethren, and how the great
21 temple was purified, and the altar hallowed anew; [1] of the battles they
fought against Antiochus, called the Illustrious, and Eupator, that was
22 his son. Speak we of heavenly manifestations, sent to encourage the champions of Jewry, till at last, though so few, they won back their country,
23 and put the hordes of heathendom to flight. Speak we of that temple, the
most famous in all the world, by their means recovered, of a city set free,
of forgotten laws re-established, and how the Lord, in his great complai-
24 sance, shewed them mercy. All this, the argument of five books Jason of
Cyrene wrote, we have been at pains to abridge within the compass of a
single volume.
25   What would you? There be books a many, and they are hard put to it
that would trace the course of history, for the abundance of the matter
26 therein comprised. And my aim was, if a man would read, read he should
and with relish; would a man study, without great ado he should be able
27 to commit all to memory; and so I would serve every man's turn. But for
me, that undertook the business of abridgement, think you it was light
28 labour? Nay, here was a task all watching and sweat; yet shoulder the
burden I would; host that prepares a banquet must work for other men's
29 pleasure, and earn nothing but their thanks. Full information would you
have about this or that, I remit you to my author; for myself, I will be
30 true to my own pattern of shortness. When a house is first in building,
needs must the architect should bestow pains on every part of it; not such
the painter's care, he will pick out the surfaces that are most apt for adorn-
31 ment. And so, methinks, it is here; to expatiate, to digress, to indulge
32 curiosity on every point, is for the arch-historian; your epitomist will ask
33 leave to study brevity, and let long disquisitions be. And now, to our
matter! Here is preface enough; it were ill done to draw out the preamble,
and leave our story cramped for room.

---

[1] Verses 20–33. The book proper begins with this preamble, in which the author
is concerned, not to shift the responsibility for his statements on to Jason of
Cyrene, but to justify himself in selecting certain incidents for recital, and
omitting the rest. The exact sense of the Latin is hard to determine; it is here
interpreted in conformity with the Greek text.

CHAPTER THREE

TIME was, the holy city was a home of content; ever the laws of it were well kept; such a high priest they had, Onias, a devout man, and one
2 that hated evil. In those days, king and chieftain held the place much in
3 reverence, and with rich gifts endowed the temple; did not Seleucus, king
4 of Asia, defray all the cost of maintaining its sacrifices? Yet one citizen there was, Simon the Benjamite, the temple governor, that had lawless
5 schemes afoot, do the high priest what he would to gainsay him. And at last, when overcome Onias he might not, what did he? To Apollonius he betook himself, the son of Tharseas, that was then in charge of Coelesyria
6 and Phoenice, and gave him great news indeed; here was the treasury at Jerusalem stocked with treasures innumerable, here was vast public wealth, unclaimed by the needs of the altar, and nothing prevented but it should fall into the king's hands.
7 No sooner did Apollonius find himself in the royal presence than he told the story of the rumoured treasure; and at that, the king sent for Heliodorus, that had charge of his affairs, and despatched him with orders
8 to fetch the said money away. This Heliodorus set out on his journey without more ado, under colour of making a progress through the towns of Coelesyria and Phoenice, but with the king's business still in mind.
9 And when he reached Jerusalem, and there received a gracious welcome from the high priest, he made no secret of the information he possessed,
10 or of his errand, and he would know the truth about these moneys. A plain account the high priest gave him; some were moneys deposited on
11 trust, for the maintenance of widows and orphans; there were some, too, belonging to Hyrcanus son of Tobias, a man of repute. The information was maliciously laid, nor did the whole sum amount to more than four
12 hundred talents of silver, and two hundred of gold. Men had reposed their confidence in a city and a temple renowned throughout the world, for the high opinion they had of its sanctity; and should he play them
13 false? It was not to be thought of. But Heliodorus stood upon the terms of his commission; delivered to the king the money must be, there was no other way of it.
14 So the appointed day came, when he would visit the temple and take
15 order in the matter; what a stir there was then in the city! Priests, in their sacred vesture, cast themselves down before the altar, and cried out upon heaven; would not he, whose law enjoined safe-keeping, keep pro-
16 perty safe for its rightful owners? And for the high priest himself, the very aspect of him was heart-rending; such a change of look and colour
17 betrayed his inward feelings; grief and horror were stamped on his

18 features, and to all that saw him he seemed a broken man. Folk streamed out of their houses in droves, to make public intercession in the hour of
19 their country's disgrace; sackcloth about their waists, the women thronged the streets, and maids that might not go abroad must yet run
20 to the housetops, or peer out at windows, to see Onias pass. Heavenward
21 they raised their hands, each one of them, in prayer; and pity it was to see how common folk about him were sharing the high priest's agony of suspense.
22 Here, then, was a whole city praying Almighty God, no loss might
23 befall the men who had trusted them; and here was Heliodorus carrying out his design, already arrived at the treasury with his body-guard in
24 attendance. All at once the spirit of God, the omnipotent, gave signal proof of its presence; daunted by the divine power they trembled and
25 stood irresolute, these ministers of wrong. What saw they? A horse, royally caparisoned, that charged upon Heliodorus and struck him down with its fore-feet; terrible of aspect its rider was, and his armour
26 seemed all of gold. Two other warriors they saw, how strong of limb, how dazzling of mien, how bravely clad! These stood about Heliodorus and fell to scourging him, this side and that, blow after blow, without
27 respite. With the suddenness of his fall to the ground, darkness had closed about him; hastily they caught him up and carried him out in his
28 litter; a helpless burden now, that entered yonder treasury with such a rabble of tipstaves and halbardiers! Here was proof of God's power most
29 manifest. There he lay, by heaven's decree speechless and beyond hope
30 of recovery; and all around men were praising the Lord, for thus vindicating the honour of his sanctuary. In the temple, where all had been anxiety and turmoil until heaven declared itself, all was rejoicing and contentment now.
31 It was not long before friends of Heliodorus were entreating Onias to call down mercy from the most high, on one that was now at death's
32 door. This was anxious news for the high priest; what if the king should suspect the Jews of foul play? Offer sacrifice he did for the man's re-
33 covery, and with good effect. He was yet at his prayers, when those two warriors, in the same brave attire, stood by Heliodorus again; Thanks thou owest, they said, to the high priest Onias; at his instance, the Lord
34 grants thee life; God's scourge thou hast felt, God's wondrous power
35 be ever on thy lips. And with that, they were seen no more. Be sure this Heliodorus offered God sacrifice; ay, and made vows a many for his preservation, and thanked Onias besides; then he marched his army back
36 to the king. Everywhere he testified how great a God was this, what
37 strange things his own eyes had witnessed; and when the king himself
38 asked what manner of emissary he should next send to Jerusalem, Why, said he, some enemy of thine, some rebel that plots against the kingdom.

Escape he with his life, I warrant he will come back to thee soundly
beaten. Past doubt, there is some divine influence haunts yonder place;
39 watch and ward he keeps over it, that has his dwelling in heaven, to be
the plague and the undoing of all who come that way upon an errand of
mischief.
40   Such is the tale of Heliodorus, and of the treasury's preserving.

CHAPTER FOUR

AND now, what must Simon do, the same that had drawn men's eyes
to his country with stories of treasure, but fall to slandering Onias?
Onias it was, by his way of it, had egged Heliodorus on,[1] and been the
2 author of the mischief. So true a patriot, that well loved his race, well
guarded the divine law, and he must be branded with the name of traitor!
3 The feud grew worse, till at last there were murders done, and Simon's
4 faction answerable for it. Here was the public peace much endangered;
here was Apollonius, the governor of Coelesyria and Phoenice, adding
fuel to the flame of Simon's malice;[2] what marvel if Onias had recourse
5 to the king? Little enough it liked him to bring an ill name on his fellow
citizens; yet common good of the Jewish folk he must needs have in mind;
6 how should quiet times return, or Simon's madness be cooled, unless the
king took order in the matter?
7   But king Seleucus was done with life now, and the throne passed to
Antiochus, called the Illustrious. And here was a brother Onias had, called
8 Jason, that coveted the office of high priest. This Jason went to the new
king, and made him an offer of three hundred talents out of its revenue,
9 besides eighty from other incomings. Let leave be granted him to set up a
game-place for the training of youth, and enrol the men of Jerusalem as
citizens of Antioch, he would give his bond for a hundred and fifty more.
10 To this the king assented; high priest he became, and straightway set about
11 perverting his fellow countrymen to the Gentile way of living. Till now,
the Jews had followed their own customs, under royal privilege; it was
John that won it for them, father of that Eupolemus, who afterwards
went in embassage to Rome, to make a treaty of alliance. But Jason
would abrogate these customs; common right should be none, and
12 great wrong should find acceptance instead. This game-place of his he

---

[1] 'Egged Heliodorus on'; some think the word used in the Greek has a quite
different meaning from the usual, and that Onias was accused of having
attacked Heliodorus with violence (cf. 3.32).

[2] Verse 4. 'Adding fuel to the flame of Simon's malice'; literally, 'raving to
increase Simon's malice,' but this curious phrase is probably due to a copyist's
mistake.

did not scruple to set up in the very shadow of the Citadel, and debauch [1] all that was noblest of Judaea's youth.

13 Mischief in the bud, think you, when such alien Gentile ways came in? Nay, here was flower and fruit of it; and all through the unexampled villainy of one man, this Jason, that high priest was none, but rather an

14 arch-traitor. Why, the priests themselves had no more stomach for serving the altar; temple scorned, and sacrifice unheeded, off they went to the wrestling-ground, there to enter their names and win unhallowed

15 prizes, soon as ever the first quoit was thrown! What glory their fathers had handed down to them! And fame such as the Greeks covet was all

16 their ambition now. Alas, here was a perilous contest awaiting them; Greek fashions they would follow, and Greeks would be, that Greeks

17 should have ere long for their enemies, ay, and conquerors. There is no

18 breaking God's laws without paying the price; time will show that. When the quinquennial games were being held at Tyre, in the king's presence,

19 this vile Jason it was sent some of his wretches [2] with a gift of three hundred silver pieces to do honour to Hercules. True it is, the bearers of them asked they should not be spent on sacrifice, but on some other need

20 that was more befitting; yet Jason's meaning was, Hercules should have them, and if they went to the building of the fleet, it was thanks to Jason's envoys.

21 Afterwards, Apollonius the son of Menestheus was despatched to Egypt, for the enthroning of king Ptolemy Philometor. Well Antiochus knew that he was disaffected towards the royal policy, and there was his own safety to be considered . . . He passed on to Joppe, and so to Jeru-

22 salem,[3] where Jason and the whole city welcomed him in state, with carrying of torches and great huzza'ing. And so he led his army back to Phoenice.

23 Three years later, Jason would send to the king certain moneys, together with a report on affairs of moment; and for this errand he chose

24 Menelaus, brother to that Simon we have before mentioned. Access thus gained to the king's person, Menelaus was careful to flatter his self-conceit; then, outbidding Jason by three hundred talents of silver,

25 diverted the high-priestly succession to himself. Back he came to Jerusalem, with the royal warrant to maintain him, yet all unworthy, with a

---

[1] 'Debauch'; the Latin says he exposed them in brothels, but the obscure phrase used in the Greek, 'he brought them under the hat' is usually interpreted as meaning that he encouraged them to wear the broad-brimmed Greek *petasus* as a symbol of devotion to Hermes, the patron deity of athletics.

[2] 'Wretches'; the word found in our Latin text is probably a copyist's error for 'supplicators,' i.e., religious representatives.

[3] This sentence, in the original, is of unexampled obscurity. It runs, 'And when Apollonius son of Menestheus had been sent to Egypt for the enthroning

26 tyrant's cruel heart, more wild beast than high priest. Thus was Jason
supplanted, that had supplanted his own brother, and was driven to take
27 refuge in the Ammonite country; as for Menelaus, he got the office he
coveted, but never a penny paid the king of all he had promised, how-
28 ever urgent Sostratus might be, that was in command of the citadel. For
all exaction of tribute this fellow was answerable; and so it fell out that
29 both of them were summoned to court, Menelaus leaving his high priesthood to his own brother, Lysimachus, and for Sostratus . . . he became
governor of Cyprus.[1]
30   It befell at this very time that the men of Tharsus and Mallus made an
insurrection; so little it liked them that a gift should be made of their
31 cities to Antiochis, the king's paramour. Post-haste the king went off to
appease them, leaving one of his courtiers, Andronicus, to be viceroy.
32 Here was Menelaus' opportunity; he had gold ornaments with him, that
he had stolen out of the temple, and now, giving some of these as a present to Andronicus, he sold the rest at Tyre and other cities in the
33 neighbourhood. Of these doings, one man had clear proof, and thereupon denounced him: Onias, that had now taken refuge in Daphne
34 sanctuary, close by Antioch. What did Menelaus? He gained the ear of
Andronicus and demanded that Onias should pay for it with his life. So
the viceroy himself paid Onias a visit, swore friendship and overcame
his suspicions; then, when he had left sanctuary, without scruple of con-
35 science put him to death. Here was great matter of indignation, and not
among the Jews only; the very heathen took it amiss, so great a man
36 should meet so unworthy an end. No sooner was the king back from
Cilicia than the citizens of Antioch, Jew and Gentile both, assailed him
37 with complaints about the murder of an innocent man; whereat Antiochus himself was heartily grieved, ay, and moved to tears of pity, such
38 memories he had of Onias' well-ordered, honourable life. Anon he fell
into a rage, stripped Andronicus of his purple, and would have him led
away all through the streets, till he reached the very spot where he had
lifted his impious hand against Onias. There the sacrilegious wretch
perished, by the divine vengeance worthily requited.
39   Meanwhile, word had gone abroad at Jerusalem, how Lysimachus was
ever robbing the temple, by Menelaus' contrivance. Great store of gold

---

of king Ptolemy Philometor, Antiochus, realizing that he (who?) was estranged
from his (whose?) past deeds, felt anxious for his own safety. And for that
reason (what reason? Or perhaps, 'from that place,' but what place?) he (who?)
came to Joppe, and then rounded up at Jerusalem.' It seems possible that the
text has been inaccurately transmitted.
[1] According to the Greek text, Sostratus left his own office in charge of Crates,
'who was (afterwards?) over the Cyprians.' The island of Cyprus belonged at
this time to Egypt, and only came into the Seleucid empire some years later.

was lost already; but now there was a rising of the common folk against
40 Lysimachus, whose numbers and their rage increasing, he was fain to
put some three thousand men under arms, with one Tyrannus at their
head, that was far gone in years, and no less in folly. Lysimachus it was
41 that first resorted to violence; but the rabble, when they saw what he
would be at, caught up stones or stout clubs for the attack, and some of
42 them pelted him with cinders. When they had wounded some of his
retinue, and felled others to earth, the rest took to their heels; and there,
close beside the treasury, this robber of the temple was done to death.
43 And next, they must implead Menelaus himself on the same charge.
44 Three envoys from the council of elders brought the whole matter before
45 the king, when he visited Tyre, and Menelaus was as good as lost. What
did he? With the promise of a great bribe he secured the good word of
46 Ptolemy, son of Dorymenes;[1] Ptolemy it was waylaid the king, as he
rested from the heat in a covered walk of his, and put him from his pur-
47 pose. So now Menelaus, that was at the root of all the mischief, must go
scot free, and his unhappy accusers, that might have cleared themselves
easily enough before a court of bloodthirsty Scythians,[2] with their lives
48 must pay for it. Here were men come to plead for their own city, their
own people, their own temple treasures, and must they be hurried off to
49 undeserved punishment? Even the Tyrians thought shame of it, and in
50 princely fashion gave them burial. So, through the avarice of the great,
throve Menelaus still, and his wickedness went from bad to worse, to his
countrymen's undoing.

CHAPTER FIVE

AT this time Antiochus was preparing once more for a campaign
2 against Egypt. And all about the city of Jerusalem, by the space
of forty days together, there were strange sights appearing. High up in
air, horsemen were seen riding this way and that, in vesture of gold,
3 and spears they carried as if they went to battle; now riding in ordered
ranks, now engaged in close combat. In long array they moved past,
shields and helmeted heads and drawn swords; flew javelin and flashed
4 golden harness, a whole armoury of shining mail. No wonder if the
prayer was on all men's lips, good not ill such high visions might portend.
5 And now a false rumour went abroad, Antiochus had come by his
death. Jason's ears it reached, and all at once, with full a thousand men

---

[1] Verse 45. The words 'son of Dorymenes' appear in the Greek text, but not in
the Latin; they are inserted here to distinguish this Ptolemy (cf. I Mac. 3.38)
from the king of Egypt mentioned in verse 21 above.

[2] 'Scythians,' a barbarous race then inhabiting Russia.

at his back, he delivered an assault upon the city. Let the townsfolk man the walls as they would, at last it fell, and Menelaus must take refuge
6 within the citadel. As for Jason, he fell upon his own fellow-countrymen, and that without mercy. His own flesh and blood to vanquish, what was this but shameful defeat? Ay, but to him friend was foe, were there spoil
7 for the winning! Yet high priesthood he got none; disappointed of his
8 scheming, back he must go to the Ammonite country, and there, marked down for death by king Aretas of the Arabians, fled from city to city. An outlaw, hated and shunned by his kind, of a whole land, of a whole
9 race, the common foe, he was driven out into Egypt; and so making his way to Lacedaemon, as if to find refuge there by right of kinship, died miserably. In exile he died, that had brought exile on so many;
10 cast away without dirge or dole, that left so many tombless; in a strange land unburied, that might have rested in his fathers' grave.

11   Here was news to make the king doubt whether the Jews were loyal to him, and back he came from Egypt in a great taking of rage. He occupied
12 the city, and that by force of arms; then he bade his troops go about killing, with no quarter for any they met; let a man but shew his face on
13 the house-top, he must be slaughtered with the rest. Fell young and old alike; children with their mothers must die, nor maidenhood was spared,
14 nor helpless infancy. By the end of three days, eighty thousand had been massacred, forty thousand held as prisoners, and as many more sold into slavery.

15   Nor might all this content him; with Menelaus for his guide, that was traitor to faith and folk, what must he do but make his way into God's
16 temple, holier in all the world is none? What, should those sacred ornaments, dedicated by kings and peoples for the more splendour and worthiness of it, be caught up in his impious hands, pawed and defiled by his
17 touch? Surely he had taken leave of his wits, this Antiochus; how should he know that this sanctuary, for once, would lack the divine protection? And only because, for a little, God's anger was provoked by sins of the
18 men that dwelt there! Free had they been from the meshes of such guilt, Antiochus, too, should have been greeted with a drubbing, as Heliodorus was, the man king Seleucus sent to rob the treasury, and
19 should have learned to leave his rash purpose. But what would you?
20 People it was God chose, and city for people's sake; chastisement that fell on the people, city must rue, and anon share its good fortune. He, the omnipotent, the ruler of all, would leave Jerusalem forlorn in his anger, would raise her to heights of glory, his anger once appeased.

21   Antiochus, then, came away from the temple a thousand and eight hundred talents the richer; and back he went to Antioch, all at reckless speed; he had not scrupled to sail his fleet over the plain, march his troops
22 across the sea, his heart so swelled with pride in his doings. As for the

Jewish folk, he left viceroys of his own to harry them; in Jerusalem Philip,
23 that was a Phrygian born, and outdid his own master in cruelty; at
Garizim Andronicus and Menelaus, heaviest burden of all for the folk
24 to bear. But he would do worse by the Jews yet; or why did he send out
Apollonius, the arch-enemy, and a force of twenty-two thousand, to cut
25 off manhood in its flower, women and children to sell for slaves? This
Apollonius, when he reached Jerusalem, was all professions of friendship, and nothing did until the sabbath came round, when the Jews kept
26 holiday. Then he put his men under arms, and butchered all that went
out to keep festival; to and fro he went about the streets, with armed
fellows at his heels, and made a great massacre.
27 Meanwhile Judas Machabaeus, and nine others with him, went out
into the desert, where they lived like wild beasts on the mountain-side;
better lodge there with herbs for food, than be party to the general defilement.

CHAPTER SIX

NOT long after, the king despatched one of the senators at Antioch,
with orders he should compel the Jewish people, custom of their
2 fathers and law of their God to forsake. The temple at Jerusalem must be
profaned, and dedicated now to Jupiter Olympius; as for the temple on
Garizim, the Samaritans were to call it, as well they might,[1] after Jupiter
3 the god of strangers. What a storm of troubles broke then upon the
4 commonwealth, most grievous to be borne! All riot and revelry the
temple became, once the Gentiles had it; here was dallying with harlots,
and women making their way into the sacred precincts, and bringing in
5 of things abominable; with forbidden meats, to the law's injury, the
6 very altar groaned. Sabbath none would observe, nor keep holiday his
7 fathers kept; even the name of Jew was disclaimed. Instead, they went
to sacrifice on the king's birthday, though it were ruefully and under
duress; and when the feast of Liber came round, make procession they
8 must in Liber's honour, garlanded with ivy each one. And now, among
all the neighbouring cities, a decree went out, wherein the Ptolemies[2]
were the prime movers; all alike should constrain the Jews to do sacri-
9 fice, and those that would not fall in with Gentile ways, with their lives
must pay for it.

---

[1] 'As well they might'; literally, 'according as they were.' The author seems to
be taunting the Samaritans with their Gentile origin. But the Greek might mean
'according as they gained their request'; Josephus alleges that the Samaritans
themselves asked leave of the king to re-dedicate their temple.
[2] 'The Ptolemies'; the Greek has 'Ptolemy,' cf. note on 4.45.

10 Here were sights to be seen most pitiable. Two mothers there were, denounced for the circumcision of their own sons; what, think you, befell them? Both must be driven through the streets, with the children hung
11 about their breasts, and cast headlong from the battlements! At another time, Philip had information that certain Jews were meeting in caves near at hand, to keep the sabbath there without remark. Not one of these would lift a hand to help himself, so great care they had of the day's observance, and all were burned to death.
12 Reader, by these tales of ill fortune be not too much dismayed; bethink thee, all this came about for the punishment of our race, not for its
13 undoing. A mark of signal favour it is, when the Lord is quick to chastise,
14 nor lets the sinner sin on unreproved. See how he deals with other nations, waiting patiently to take full toll when the hour comes for
15 judgement! Not so with us; for our guilt he will not delay reckoning,
16 and claim strict vengeance at last. Towards us, his mercy is inalienable;
17 chastise us he will with adversity, but forsake us never. So much, reader, for thy warning; and now go we back to our history.
18 Here was Eleazar, one of the chief scribes, a man of great age and of noble features, being required to eat swine's flesh; but though they held
19 his mouth open they could not force him to eat. He would rather die gloriously than live defiled; on he went, of his own accord, to the place
20 of torture, scanning every step of the path that lay before him. He must endure all in patience, rather than taste, for love of life, the forbidden
21 meat. Old friends among the bystanders, out of misplaced kindness, took him aside and urged him to send for meat of some other kind, which he could taste without scruple; he could pretend to have obeyed the king's
22 will by eating the sacrilegious food, and his life should no longer be for-
23 feit. Such kind offices old friendship claimed; but he thought rather of the reverence that was due to his great age, of his venerable grey hairs, of a life blamelessly lived from childhood onwards. True to the precepts of God's holy law, he answered that they would do better to send him
24 to his grave and have done with it. It does not suit my time of life, said he, to play a part. What of many that stand here, younger than myself, who would think that Eleazar, at the age of ninety, had turned Gentile?
25 To gain a brief hour of this perishable life, shall I play a trick on them, shall I disgrace this hoary head of mine and bring down a curse on it?
26 Man's sentence here I may avoid if I will, but God's almighty hand,
27 living or dead, escape I may not. Let me take leave of life with a good
28 grace, as best suits my years, bequeathing to men younger than myself an example of courage; meeting, with ready resolve, an honourable death, for the sake of laws holy and august as ours are. And so without more
29 ado he was led away to his torturing; his executioners were in a rage, that but now had been gentle with him; pride, they would have it, spoke

30 here. And this was the last sigh he uttered, as he lay there dying under the lash, Lord, in thy holy wisdom this thou well knowest; I might have had life if I would, yet never a cruel pang my body endures, but my soul
31 suffers it gladly for thy reverence. Thus he died, not only to those younger men he spoke of, but to our whole race, leaving the pattern of a brave and honourable death.

CHAPTER SEVEN

SEVEN brothers there were, that lay under arrest, and their mother with them; these too were tortured at the king's command, to see if whip and thong would not make them eat swine's flesh, for all their
2 scruples. And thus spoke out one of them in the name of the rest: Why dost thou put us to the question? What secret wouldst thou learn? Of this be sure, we had rather die than break the divine law given to our
3 fathers. The king, in a rage, would have fire-pan heated, and caldron of
4 bronze; heated they were, and then he passed judgement upon this same spokesman. Tongue of him should be cut out, scalp torn off, hands and
5 feet mutilated, while mother and brethren stood by to see it; then, so maimed, he was for the fire; they should roast him alive in a caldron. There stood the rest with their mother, each heartening other to die
6 bravely; God sees true, said they, and will not allow us to go uncomforted. Did not Moses prophesy as much, even in his song of remonstrance, He will comfort his servants? [1]
7 So died the first, and now the second must make sport for them. When the hair was torn from his head and the skin with it, they asked, Would
8 he eat, or must his whole body pay for it, limb by limb? And he answered in good round Hebrew,[2] eat he would not; whereupon he, in his turn,
9 suffered like the first. Ay, miscreant, he said with his last breath, of this present life it lies in thy power to rob us; but he, who is ruler of the whole world, he, for whose laws we perish, will raise us up again, and to life
10 everlasting. And now they had their will with the third, who was no sooner bidden than he put forth tongue and hands very courageously;
11 Heaven's gift these be, he said, and for God's law I make light account
12 of them, well assured he will give them back to me. Well might they marvel, king and courtiers both, at one so young that recked so little of
13 his sufferings. Such was the manner of his passing; the fourth, too, when
14 with like tortures they assailed him, died with these words on his lips:

---

[1] Deut. 32.36.

[2] 'In good round Hebrew,' that is, in the Aramaic dialect, as if to clinch his attitude of defiance by refusing to address his persecutors in Greek.

Man's sentence of death, what matters it, so there be hope in God, that shall raise up the dead? For thee, resurrection to new life shall be none.
15 And when the fifth was put to the question, he looked Antiochus in the
16 face, thus warning him: Mortal, at thy own whim free to govern thy
17 fellow men, think not God has abandoned this race of ours! Wait but
a little, and good proof thou shalt have of his sovereign power, such tor-
18 ment thee and thine awaits. So they came to the sixth, and this was his
dying utterance: Never flatter thyself with vain hope; speed we amiss,
it was our own doing, that sinned against our God. Strange be his deal-
19 ings with us, yet think not thou to defy God unpunished.
20   And here was the greatest marvel of all, by honest folk ever to be kept
in mind, that the mother of seven children should be content to lose
21 them all in one day, for the hope she had in God's mercy. What gen-
erosity of mind was this, that could temper her womanly feelings with a
man's thoughts! One by one, in the speech of her own country, she put
22 heart into them; Into this womb you came, she told them, who knows
how? Not I quickened, not I the breath of life gave you, nor fashioned
23 the bodies of you one by one! Man's birth, and the origin of all things,
he devised who is the whole world's Maker; and shall he not give the
breath of life back to you, that for his law's sake hold your lives so cheap?
24   What should Antiochus do? Here was defiance of his authority, here
were tones of remonstrance that liked him little. The youngest son lived
yet; for him, what encouragement, what royal assurances of wealth and
happiness! Would he but leave the law of his fathers, he should be the
25 king's friend, and have weighty matters entrusted to him. But yield the
boy would not; till at last the king beckoned the mother apart; mother
26 of son should be the saviour yet. Much ado he had to win her, but
27 she agreed at last, counsel her son she would. And a fine trick she
played on the bloodthirsty tyrant, leaning over her son and counselling
him in her own native speech, to this effect: Nine months in the womb
I bore thee, three years at the breast fed thee, reared thee to be what thou
28 art; and now, my son, this boon grant me. Look round at heaven and
earth and all they contain; bethink thee that of all this, and of mankind
29 too, God is maker. Of this butcher have thou no fear; claim rightful
share among thy brethren in yonder inheritance of death; so shall the
divine mercy give me back all my sons at once.
30   Before ever she had finished speaking, the boy cried out, What dallying is this? To the king's law I own no allegiance; rule I live by is the
31 law we had through Moses. Arch-enemy of the Jewish race, thinkest
32 thou to escape from God's hand? Grievously if we suffer, grievously we
33 have sinned; chides he for a little, the Lord our God, he does but school,
does but correct us; to us, his worshippers, he will be reconciled again.
34 But thou, miserable wretch, viler on earth is none, wouldst thou vent thy

rage on those worshippers of his, and flatter thyself with vain hopes none
35 the less? Trust me, thou shalt yet abide his judgement, who is God
36 almighty and all-seeing. Brief pains, that under his warrant have seised
my brethren of eternal life! And shalt not thou, by his sentence, pay the
37 deserved penalty of thy pride? As my brethren, so I for our country's
laws both soul and body forfeit; my prayer is, God will early relent towards this nation, while thou dost learn, under the lash of his torments,
38 that he alone is God. And may the divine anger, that has justly fallen on
our race, with me and these others be laid to rest!
39   No wonder if this last, that so baffled the king's rage, was more bar-
40 barously used than all the others; yet kept he ever his confidence in the
41 Lord, and made a clean end of it. And at length, when all her sons were
gone, it was the mother's turn to die.
42   Enough! Of idolatrous sacrifice and inhuman cruelty you shall hear no
more.

CHAPTER EIGHT

NOW turn we to Judas Machabaeus and his company. Secretly they
made entry into the villages, whence they summoned both kinsman
and friend of theirs; ay, and rallied many more, that were yet true to the
2 Jewish faith, till they had mustered an army of six thousand men. And
ever they besought the Lord, he would look with favour on a race down-
3 trodden, have pity on a temple defiled by the heathen. Their city was
like to be razed to the ground; would he watch the ruin of it unmoved?
4 Would he be deaf, while bloodshed cried out for vengeance? Cruel
murders of innocent childhood, his own honour dragged in the dust,
would he not mark all this, and be roused to indignation?
5   By this, the divine anger had given place to clemency; and to all the
heathen round about Machabaeus and his company were an infliction
6 past bearing. On village or town of theirs he would fall suddenly, and
burn it to the ground; by seizing some point of vantage, once and again
7 he put their forces to the rout; going about these forays at night-time for
8 the most part, till the fame of his valour spread far and wide. What was
to be done? Here was a man that grew ever in strength, and still his
enterprises throve. At last Philip was fain to send dispatches, calling on
Ptolemy, the governor of Coelesyria and Phoenice, to further the king's
9 business. And he, without more ado, chose one of his best friends,
Nicanor son of Patroclus, and sent him out to exterminate the Jewish
race altogether. For which purpose, he armed full twenty thousand men,
a rabble of all nations; and Gorgias should be at Nicanor's side, a soldier
that had much experience in the wars.

10   Nicanor's purpose it was, to sell the Jewish people for slaves, and
thereby reimburse the king for a tribute of two thousand talents he must
11 needs pay to Rome. So, before aught else was done, he sent word to the
towns on the sea coast, crying a sale of Jewish captives, and offering
them at ninety for the talent; so little did he guess what divine vengeance
12 was to overtake him. No sooner did Judas hear of Nicanor's coming,
13 than he gave warning of it to the Jews who bore him company. Some
of these, cowardly souls that put no trust in God's awarding, took refuge
14 in flight; the rest made shift to sell all the goods they yet had, crying out
upon the Lord to deliver them from such an impious wretch as would
15 sell them first, and conquer them after. Themselves if he nothing regarded, let him remember at least the covenant made with their fathers;
the renown, too, of that holy name they bore!

16   As for Machabaeus, he called together the seven thousand that followed him, and warned them they should make no terms with the enemy,
nor be affrighted by a great rabble of men coming against them in so ill
17 a cause. Courage! he said; bethink you of the sanctuary their insults
have outraged, of a city wronged and mocked, of immemorial traditions
18 overthrown! What gives them confidence? Weapons of war, and their
own daring. Ours to trust in his omnipotence, who with a single nod
19 both these our adversaries and the whole world besides can undo. He
put them in mind, moreover, of God's signal mercy shewed to their
forefathers; how Sennacherib's army perished, a hundred and eighty
20 thousand strong; how they fought the Galatians at Babylon, with Macedonian allies whose heart failed them at the encounter, and six thousand
Jews, alone but for heaven's aid, made havoc of a hundred and twenty
21 thousand men, much to the common advantage.[1] With such words as
these he put heart into them, till they were ready to die for law and
country's sake.

22   And now he put the several commands of his army in charge of his
brethren, Simon, Joseph and Jonathan, entrusting one thousand five
23 hundred men to each; Esdras [2] was bidden read aloud from the sacred
writings, and the watchword was given, God's Aid. And with that, out
24 went Judas at the head of his army, and engaged the enemy. Such help
the Almighty gave them, they cut down more than nine thousand men;
and the rest of Nicanor's disabled forces must needs take to their heels.
25 All the money that had been paid for their enslaving fell into Jewish
26 hands, and they gave the enemy chase far and wide, only time hindering
them; the sabbath was coming on, and pursue further they might not.

---

[1] No other record of this engagement has been preserved to us.
[2] For 'Esdras' the Greek text has 'Eleazar,' meaning presumably Judas'
brother. If the Latin reading is right, Esdras must be some person not elsewhere
mentioned.

27 Arms and spoils of the fallen they gathered in, and so fell to keeping the sabbath, blessing the Lord for the deliverance he had sent that day, the
28 first refreshing dew of his mercy. The sabbath day over, they gave a share of the spoils to crippled folk, orphans and widows; they and theirs
29 should have the rest. And when this was done, they made public intercession, beseeching the Lord, that was so merciful, to be reconciled with his servants for good and all.
30　Other invaders they slew, twenty thousand of them and more, under Bacchides and Timotheus; and when they seized their high fortresses, and had spoil to divide in plenty, once more cripples and orphans and widows, and the aged folk too, must have a share to match their own.
31 Weapons of war they gathered with all care, and bestowed where they were most needed; it was the rest of the spoil they carried back to Jeru-
32 salem. At this time they slew Philarches, that had been of Timotheus' company, a man stained with crime, and many ways a persecutor of the
33 Jewish people. There was Callisthenes, too, that had burnt down the gates of the sanctuary; when all Jerusalem was rejoicing over the victory, he took refuge within doors, and they burnt the place down about his
34 ears; he too was served right for his godless doings. As for Nicanor, that was the arch-villain of all, and would have sold the Jews to a thou-
35 sand slave-dealers, the very men whose lives he held so cheap had now, by divine aid, humbled him to the dust. Robe of office he must lay by, and slink by country ways all unattended to Antioch. A fine home-
36 coming, this, with the loss of a whole army! Where were the Jewish captives that should have paid off the tribute to Rome? He was fain to confess, now, that the Jews had God himself for their protector, and, would they but keep his laws, there was no conquering them!

CHAPTER NINE

ANTIOCHUS himself, at this time, had a sorry home-coming from
2 Persia. He had made his way into the city they call Persepolis, thinking to plunder its temple and of itself have the mastery; but the common folk ran to arms and routed him. So he was a man defeated and disgraced
3 when he reached Ecbatana, and there news came to him of how Nicanor
4 had fared, and Timotheus. And now, in a great taking of rage, he would make the Jews suffer for the ignominy of his own defeat; on, on his chariot must be driven, and never a halt in the journey, with the divine vengeance ever at his heels. Had he not boasted, Jerusalem was his goal, and he would bury the Jewish race under the ruins of it?
5　The Lord, Israel's God, how should aught escape his scrutiny? The

words were barely uttered, when he smote Antiochus with such a hurt, there was neither remedying nor discovering it. A deadly griping it was
6 that took him, with cruel torment of the bowels; fitting reward for one that had often tortured his fellows, and to the marrow, in unexampled
7 fashion. Even so, he would not leave his wicked purpose; with pride undiminished, still breathing out fiery threats against the Jewish folk, he pressed forward on his errand, till of a sudden, in full career, down fell he from his chariot, and never a limb but was racked grievously by
8 the fall. What a living proof was this of God's power, when he was struck to earth, and must finish his journey by litter, one that boasted, till now, he could rise beyond man's measure, the sea's waves govern,
9 and weigh mountains in the balance! Bred worms at last in that sinful body, and he lived yet, though miserably enough, to see his own flesh
10 rot away, till his own men could not bear the foul stench of him; it was but yesterday the very stars seemed within his reach, and never a man now would carry so foul a burden.
11   What marvel, if the swelling pride of him ebbed away, and heaven's judgements brought him to himself? With every moment his anguish
12 grew, and the foul breath of his disease was past his own bearing. Alas, said he, to God all must bow; mortals we are, and god ourselves we may
13 not. Nay, he made suit to the Lord, vile wretch though he were, hoping
14 all in vain to win mercy. Forgotten, his haste to lay Jerusalem in ruins,
15 and make a cemetery of it; a free city it should be thenceforward. Grudge the Jewish folk burial, give their carrion to bird and beast, make an end of them, children and all? Nay, such high privileges they should have
16 as the townsfolk of Athens itself. And for that sacred temple he had stripped bare, with choice gifts he would enrich it, furnishing it as never before, and defraying, from his own purse, all the cost of its sacrifices.
17 Stay, he would become a Jew himself, would go the rounds of earth, proclaiming everywhere the divine power!
18   But all to no avail; the vengeance of God, well earned, had overtaken him, and find relief he might not. So now, despairing of that, he wrote
19 to the Jews in very humble fashion, as here follows.[1] To his loyal Jewish subjects Antiochus, their king and general, sends greeting, health, and
20 happiness! Thrive you and yours, and fare prosperously, I am well con-
21 tent. For myself, I am in ill case, yet think ever kindly of you. On my way home from Persia, so grievous a distemper has fallen upon me,
22 needs must I should take order for the public safety. Despair I will not;
23 there is good hope yet of my recovery. But this thought weighs with me; when he went a-campaigning in the high countries, my father gave

[1] Verses 18–27. It seems probable that this proclamation was sent to all Antiochus' subjects, the Jews receiving it among others. The document referred to at the end of verse 25 is no longer extant.

24 out who was to succeed him; should aught go amiss, and ill tidings come, every governor in his own province must know his duty without fear of

25 confusion. And here be princes all about, I know it well, waiting upon events and ready to go with the times. Heir to the throne, then, I needs must designate. Again and again, when I set out for the high countries, I entrusted my son Antiochus to the general care. And now this written

26 commission I have sent him . . . As you love me, then, bethink you of those benefits you have received, both publicly and in private; keep faith,

27 each and all of you, with me and with my son. I doubt not he will shew himself his father's true heir, ever courteous, and kindly, and easy of approach.

28 So died he, wretchedly enough, the murderer, the blasphemer, out in the hill country far away from home. Cruel the blow that struck him

29 down, as he had ever been cruel in his dealings. His body was brought home again; Philip, his foster-brother, came back with it, and then took refuge in Egypt with Ptolemy Philometor, so little he trusted the young prince Antiochus.

CHAPTER TEN

MEANWHILE, God aiding, Machabaeus and his followers had
2 recovered both temple and city. Down came the altars Gentile folk
3 had set up in the open streets, down came the shrines, and the temple was purged of its defilement. They made a fresh altar, struck fire from flint, and offered sacrifice again after two years' intermission; rose incense,
4 burned lamp, loaves were set out on the sacred table once more. Then, bowing down to earth, they made petition to the Lord, never again such calamity might overtake them; sin if they did, himself in his great mercy should chastise them, not hand them over into the cruel power of blas-
5 phemous enemies. It so fell out, that the temple was purified on the twenty-fifth day of Casleu, the very time of its profanation by the Gen-
6 tiles. Eight days of rejoicing they kept, with such ceremonies as belong to the feast of Tent-dwelling; it was a feast of tent-dwelling indeed they had kept a while back, when they lodged like beasts among the hill-side
7 caverns! Now that God had made the way clear for his temple's cleans-ing, what wonder if they set up in his honour branches, and green boughs,
8 and arbours of palm? What wonder if a decree was passed, by common consent, all Jewry should keep the festival year by year?
9 Now the story is told, how Antiochus called the Illustrious came by
10 his end, turn we to his son, Antiochus Eupator, that was born of a very ill father; [1] record we in brief the history of his reign, and the hazards of

---

[1] The Greek word 'Eupator' means 'born of a noble father.'

11 war that went with it. Upon his accession, this king entrusted all the business of the realm to one Lysias, commander of the forces in Phoenice
12 and Coelesyria. With Ptolemy, that was called Macer, we are concerned no more; fain would he have made amends to the Jews for the wrong done
13 them, and kept their friendship, but for that very reason he was denounced to Eupator by his courtiers. He was a traitor, they said, twice over, false to his trust, when Philometor left him in charge of Cyprus, and now weary of his new allegiance to Antiochus! Whereupon he put an end
14 to his own life by poison. When Gorgias was given command of the district, he was for ever making war on the Jews, with mercenaries to aid
15 him; and there were natives of the country besides,[1] well entrenched in their strongholds, that gave welcome to deserters from Jerusalem, and so fanned the flames of enmity.

16   And now the followers of Machabaeus, after prayer made for the di-
17 vine assistance, delivered an attack upon the Edomite strongholds. These, by a very courageous assault, they occupied, and cut down all they met,
18 putting not less than twenty thousand men to the sword; but there were two fortresses yet remaining, into which the survivors threw them-
19 selves, well provided with means of defence. Machabaeus himself went off to fight other battles of greater moment, leaving Simon, Joseph and Zacchaeus, with a strong force under their command, to carry on the
20 siege. And here the avarice of Simon's men was their undoing; for a bribe of seventy thousand silver pieces, they allowed some of the de-
21 fenders to escape. Machabaeus no sooner heard of it, than he summoned the leaders of the people, and arraigned the guilty men in their presence; what, would they sell their brethren's lives, by letting the enemies of
22 their race go free? So he put these traitors to death; and for the strong-
23 holds, he conquered both of them at a blow, so carrying all before him by force of arms, that twenty thousand of the defenders perished.

24   But Timotheus could not be content with one defeat at the hands of the Jews; he would bring in hordes of foreign soldiery, and cavalry from
25 Asia, threatening Judaea with slavery. At his coming, the party of Machabaeus fell to prayer; earth on their heads, sackcloth about their
26 loins, they lay prostrate at the altar's foot, entreating the Lord he would espouse their quarrel, and their foes should be his; the law had promised
27 it. Then, this supplication made, they took up arms and marched out, leaving the city far away in their rear, nor ever halted till they were close
28 to the enemy's lines. Soon as the dawn broke, they engaged; on the one side, all trust in the Lord, valour's best pledge of victory and fairer times; on the other, naught but human eagerness to inspire courage.
29 Hard went the day, and, so it seemed to the enemy, heaven itself took

---

[1] 'Natives of the country'; literally, in the Latin version, 'Jews,' but this is probably a copyist's mistake for 'Edomites,' the reading found in the Greek text.

30 part. Five horsemen came riding, with splendid trappings of gold, to lead the Jews onward; and two of these served Machabaeus for escort, cover- ing him with their shields to keep all hurt away from him. With shaft of theirs, lightning of theirs, dazzled and dismayed, the enemy fell to
31 earth; twenty thousand and five hundred of them perished that day, besides six hundred of the cavalry.

32 As for Timotheus, he took refuge in Gazara, a strong fortress that was
33 under the command of Chaereas. Four days together, Machabaeus and
34 his men eagerly pressed on the siege of it; but the defenders were con- fident in its strength; loud their defiance was, and very blasphemous the
35 words they uttered. Stung by these taunts, twenty warriors of Macha- baeus' company made a bold attack on the wall as the fifth day was dawn- ing, and, by the fierceness of their onslaught, made shift to climb it;
36 others, following at their heels, fell to burning tower and gateway alike,
37 and made a bonfire of the blasphemers. For two whole days they ran- sacked the fort, and at last came upon Timotheus [1] in his hiding-place; so they made an end of him, his brother Chaereas and Apollophanes
38 perishing with him. When all was over, they sang hymns of praise and gave thanks to the Lord, that had done marvellous things for Israel, and granted them victory.

CHAPTER ELEVEN

IT was but a short respite they had; Lysias, a kinsman of Antiochus that was regent and managed his affairs for him, was not a little con-
2 cerned over these happenings, and he marched on Judaea at the head of eighty thousand men, with all the cavalry he could muster. Here was a
3 city worth the capture, for Gentile folk to dwell in; here was a temple that would yield a fine spoil, as temples did everywhere; a priesthood,
4 too, that might be put up for sale year after year. Of all this he be- thought him, never of God's avenging power; blindly he trusted in his foot-soldiers by the ten thousand, his horsemen by the thousand, in his
5 elephants that numbered four score. Upon marching into Judaea he first reached Bethsura,[2] that stood in a narrow pass five furlongs away from Jerusalem, and laid siege to the citadel of it.
6 What did Machabaeus and his fellows, when they learned that the siege of the fortresses was already begun? Most piteously they besought the Lord, amid the tears of a whole populace, a gracious angel he would

---

[1] If the text here is sound, the Timotheus mentioned in 12.2 is a different person.
[2] If the reading 'Bethsura' is correct, the reference must be to some other fortress of that name, not to the well-known Bethsura, more than ten miles away.

7 send out for Israel's deliverance. Then they armed for battle, Machabaeus himself the first of all, as he summoned the rest to share with him
8 the hour of danger, for the relief of their brethren. So, in good heart,
they set out together, and before they left Jerusalem a vision came to
them; of a rider that went before them in white array, with armour of
9 gold, brandishing his spear. How they blessed God's mercy, all of them,
at the sight! How their courage rose, a match for all it should encounter,
10 men or wild beast or walls of iron! They marched on, ready for battle,
11 sure now of a heavenly champion, and of the Lord's favour; and when
they charged the enemy, they were very lions for valour. At their onslaught, fell eleven thousand of the foot, fell a thousand and six hundred
12 of the horse; and the whole army took to its heels, for the most part
wounded and disarmed; Lysias himself, ingloriously enough, turned and
fled.

13 Yet good sense he lacked not; great loss he had sustained, and, let the
Hebrews continue to rely for aid upon divine Omnipotence, he saw
14 there was no conquering them. So he wrote, offering to conclude hon-
15 ourable terms with them, and secure them the king's friendship. As for
Machabaeus, he consented to what Lysias asked, having no thought but
for the common good; and the written terms he proposed to Lysias in
the Jewish people's name received the royal assent.

16 The letter sent to the Jews by Lysias was after this manner: Lysias,
17 to the people of the Jews, all health! Your envoys, John and Abesalom,
handed me a written petition, and desired that I would give effect to the
18 terms of it. All that needed to be known, I have made clear to the king's
19 grace, and he has granted what grant he could. Doubt not I will be a
good suitor in your cause hereafter, so you abide loyal to the king's
20 interest. Meanwhile, I have given a verbal message to your envoys and
21 mine, which they will impart to you. Farewell. Given on this twenty-
fourth day of Dioscorus, in the hundred and forty-eighth year.

22 And of the king's own letter, the tenour was this: King Antiochus, to
23 his good cousin Lysias, all health! Now that our father has found his
place among the gods, it is for us to see that our subjects live at peace,
24 and go quietly about their business. But of one nation, the Jews, we
hear that they resisted our father's will, who would have had them con-
form to the Greek way of living; to their own tradition they hold fast,
and their plea is, we should grant them the enjoyment of their rights in
25 the matter. And whereas we would have this nation live peaceably like
the rest, we enact and decree that their temple should be restored to them,
26 and that they should follow the custom of their forefathers. Do us the
kindness, then, to send word and give them assurance of this; our will
made known, let them take heart, and order their own affairs contentedly.
27 To the Jews themselves the king wrote as follows: King Antiochus, to

28 the elders and people of the Jews, all health! Thrive you as well as our-
29 selves, we are well content. Menelaus has brought us word, you would
fain have free intercourse with the men of your race who dwell in these
30 parts ; [1] and we hereby grant safe conduct to all of you that would travel
31 here, up to the thirtieth day of Xanthicus . . . That the Jewish folk may
eat what food they will, use what laws they will, according to their
ancient custom ; and if aught has been done amiss through inadvertence,
32 none of them, for that cause, shall be molested. We are sending Mene-
33 laus besides, to give a charge to you. Farewell. Given on the fifteenth
day of Xanthicus, in the hundred and forty-eighth year.
34   The Romans, too, wrote to them after the manner following ; Quintus
Memmius and Titus Manlius, envoys of Rome, to the Jewish people, all
35 health! The privileges Lysias has granted you in the name of his royal
36 cousin, we hereby ratify. Other matters he has remitted to the king's
decision ; take counsel among yourselves, and let us know at once what
your mind is, if you would have us order all to your liking. Even now we
37 are on the road to Antioch ; write speedily, to let us know how you are
38 minded. Farewell. Given on the twenty-fifth day of Xanthicus, in the
hundred and forty-eighth year.

CHAPTER TWELVE

SO all was agreed upon ; Lysias was for the court again, and the Jewish
2   folk went back to their farms. But neither rest nor respite might they
have while Timotheus [2] and Apollonius, son of Gennaeus, were left at
their posts ; Hieronymus, too, and Demophon, and Nicanor that ruled
in Cyprus.
3   This was a very foul deed done by the men of Joppe ; they fitted out
certain vessels of theirs, and would have the neighbouring Jews go aboard,
with their wives and children, for all the world as if there were no grudge
4 between them. It was the common wish of their fellow-citizens ; how
should the Jews gainsay it? They were lovers of peace, and cause for
suspicion had none. Yet once they were on the high seas, they were cast
5 overboard and drowned, a full two hundred of them. Such tidings of
cruel murder done upon men of his own race, Judas could not hear
unmoved ; mustering his followers, and calling upon God, that judges
6 aright, to speed him, he marched out against the slayers of his brethren ;

---

[1] Verses 29–31. The situation is not made fully clear, either in the Greek text
or in the Latin. There seems to be a gap between verses 30 and 31, perhaps due
to a mistake in the manuscripts. The allusion to faults committed 'through inadvertence' is perhaps only a diplomatic formula for granting a general amnesty.
[2] For Timotheus, see note on 10.37.

at dead of night he burned down their wharves, and set all the ships
7 ablaze, nor any man that escaped the fire but was put to the sword. This
done, he left them, but threatening he would return, and leave none alive
8 in Joppe. He had word, too, that the men of Jamnia meant to do the
9 same by the Jews in their part; so he fell on Jamnia, too, by night, and
burnt both wharves and ships there; the light of that blaze was seen at
Jerusalem, thirty miles off. . . .
10   Nine furlongs they had marched, on their way to meet Timotheus,
when an Arab force engaged them, of five thousand foot and five hundred
11 horse.[1] Stern was the encounter, but with God's help they won the day;
and the defeated remnant of the Arabs asked Judas for quarter, promising
12 a grant of pasture-lands, with other advantages. And, beyond doubt,
they could be many ways serviceable to him; so he made terms with
them. They swore friendship, and the Arabs went back to their tents.
13   A city there was called Casphin, moated and walled about for its
defence, and held by a rabble of many races; this, too, Judas attacked.
14 Such trust the defenders had in the strength of their ramparts, and their
plentiful supplies of food, they carried themselves recklessly, hurling
taunts at Judas, with blasphemies and other talk little fit to be uttered.
15 But Machabaeus to that King made appeal, who needed neither engine
nor battering-ram, in Josue's day, to bring Jericho down in ruins; a fierce
16 attack he delivered upon the walls, and, so God willed, became master
of the city. The slaughter in it was past reckoning; there was a pool hard
by, of two furlongs' breadth, that seemed as if it ran in full tide with the
blood of slain men.
17   It needed a march of ninety-five miles to bring them to Charax, where
18 the Jews were whom they call Tubianaeans. Yet could they not come
up with Timotheus; he had retired, with nothing achieved, leaving a
19 strong garrison in one of the forts there; which garrison of his, ten
thousand strong, was destroyed by two of Machabaeus' captains, Dosi-
20 theus and Sosipater. Machabaeus himself, with six thousand men at his
heels, divided into companies, pressed on against Timotheus, that had a
hundred and twenty thousand foot, and two thousand five hundred horse,
21 under his command. At the news of Judas' coming, Timotheus was fain
to send on women, children, and stores, to Carnion, an impregnable
22 fortress and one difficult of approach, so narrow the pass was. And now
the first of Judas' companies came in sight, and with it the presence of
the all-seeing God.[2] What fear fell upon the enemy, how they scattered

---

[1] The mention of Timotheus and of the Arabs would suggest that this incident
took place beyond Jordan, rather than in the Jamnia neighbourhood. It seems
possible there is a gap in the text.

[2] The Greek implies that the divine presence was in some way visibly manifested.

23 in flight, stumbling over their own fellows, wounded by the point of their own swords! And all the while Judas pressed them hard, the scourge of ill-doers; thirty thousand of them that day he slaughtered.
24 As for Timotheus, he fell into the hands of another force, under Dositheus and Sosipater; of these he begged earnestly for his life, telling them of Jewish hostages in his keeping, their own fathers and brothers, that
25 would get no quarter if he came by his death. Many were the pledges he gave, covenanting for the restoration of these hostages, and at last, for love of their brethren, they let him go free.
26   Judas went on to Carnion, where the enemy lost twenty-five thousand
27 men, routed and slain; thence to Ephron, a fortified city, where stout warriors of many different breeds manned the walls most valiantly, well
28 provided with engines and weapons. Yet strength is none can hold its own against the Omnipotent; to him the Jews made appeal, and so took
29 the city, killing twenty-five thousand of the defenders. And thence to
30 Scythopolis, at seventy-five miles' distance from Jerusalem; but here the Jews themselves bore witness, how kindly their neighbours used them, and how honourably they carried themselves even in troublous times.
31 Thanking all such, and desiring them they would continue their good offices towards the Jewish folk, the army returned to Jerusalem, to keep the festival of the Weeks.
32   Then, after Pentecost, they marched away to meet Gorgias, that was
33 in command of Idumaea;[1] it was but a muster of three thousand foot
34 and four hundred horse.[2] Battle was joined, and some few Jews fell.
35 As for Gorgias, one Dositheus, a great warrior that was in Bacenor's company of horse, kept close on his heels and would have taken him alive; but one of the Thracian horsemen fell upon him and cut off his
36 arm at the shoulder, so Gorgias escaped safe to Maresa. A long fight Esdrin's company had of it, and were full weary, when Judas called upon
37 the Lord to succour them and lead them onwards, battle-hymn and battle-cry raising in his own language; and so he put Gorgias' army to the rout.
38   And now, recalling his men from the pursuit, he made his way to the city of Adollam; the week had gone round, and here, duly cleansed from
39 defilement, they kept the sabbath. Next day, with Judas at their head, they went back to recover the bodies of the slain, for burial among their
40 own folk in their fathers' graves; and what found they? Each of the fallen was wearing, under his shirt, some token carried away from the false gods of Jamnia. Here was defiance of the Jewish law, and none

---

[1] 'Idumaea' is probably a copyist's error for 'Jamnia'; the context seems to indicate that this engagement was fought in the Philistine country.

[2] 'It was but a muster of'; literally, 'And he marched out with,' but who? Grammatically it should be Gorgias, but most commentators think Judas is referred to.

41 doubted it was the cause of their undoing; none but praised the Lord for
42 his just retribution, that had brought hidden things to light; and so they
fell to prayer, pleading that the sin might go unremembered. Judas himself, their gallant commander, gave public warning to his men, of fault
they should evermore keep clear, with the fate of these transgressors
43 under their eyes. Then he would have contribution made; a sum of
twelve thousand silver pieces he levied, and sent it to Jerusalem, to have
sacrifice made there for the guilt of their dead companions. Was not this
well done and piously? Here was a man kept the resurrection ever in
44 mind; he had done fondly and foolishly indeed, to pray for the dead, if
45 these might rise no more, that once were fallen! And these had made a
46 godly end; could he doubt, a rich recompense awaited them? A holy and
wholesome thought it is to pray for the dead, for their guilt's undoing.

CHAPTER THIRTEEN

IT was in the hundred and forty-ninth year news came to Judas that
2 Antiochus Eupator was marching on Judaea in great force. Lysias was
at his side, that was lord protector and managed the affairs of the realm,
and with him were a hundred and ten thousand foot, five thousand horse,
3 twenty-two elephants, and three hundred scythed chariots. Menelaus,
too, must be of their company, and ever it was treacherous advice he
gave to Antiochus; not that he cared for his country's safety, but he had
4 designs upon the high priesthood still. And hereupon the King of all
kings brought this guilty wretch into ill favour with his master Antiochus,
who (upon Lysias' averring, here was the true source of all their mis-
adventures) would have him apprehended and put to death according
5 to the custom of the place where they were quartered. There is here a
tower fifty cubits in height, rising sheer above a heap of ashes that sur-
6 rounds it; from its walls the author of sacrilege is thrust forward to his
7 death by the common impulse of the bystanders. This, then, was the
doom of Menelaus; by this law the law-breaker met his end, and lay
8 there unburied. A fitting reward, this, for one that had done so many
outrages upon God's altar; fire of it and ashes of it are sacred, and it was
by ashes Menelaus went to his death.
9 Yet still the king pressed forward on his mad career, as if he would
10 prove himself a worse enemy of Jewry than his father; and Judas, when
the news came to him, bade the people entreat God night and day he
11 would come to their rescue, as ever he was wont hitherto. Here was
great peril, they should be deprived at one blow of law, of country, and
of sanctuary; would he allow blaspheming Gentiles to lord it again over

12 his people, that had but now won a little breathing-space? Entreat the Lord they did, and with one accord, for his mercy; wept they and fasted, and kept on their knees for three days together. Then Judas gave them
13 the word to arm, and himself called the elders to a council; his plan was, he told them, to march out and engage the king before he could reach Judaea and overpower the city, and the issue of it he would leave to the
14 Lord's good pleasure. So, committing all to God, the world's creator, and bidding his men fight bravely, even to the death, for law, temple,
15 city, country and kinsmen, he pitched his camp at Modin. The watchword he gave them was, Victory lies with God; and now, choosing out the best of his fighting men, he made a night attack upon the royal quarters. Four thousand men they slew in the camp, and the greatest of all the
16 elephants, with the crew that rode him, and so went back in triumph, leaving the camp all confusion and dismay.
17 After this daybreak victory, won under God's protection, the king had taste enough of Jewish valour, and set about to reduce the strongholds
19 by policy. And first he would deliver an attack upon Bethsura, a fortress
20 of the Jews, but ever he was thrown back and repulsed with great loss, so
21 well did Judas supply the garrison with all they needed. There was one Rhodocus in the Jewish army that betrayed secrets to the enemy, but,
22 upon enquiry made, he was apprehended and put under arrest; so the king was fain to parley with the defenders of Bethsura, and, upon agreed
23 terms, the siege of it was raised. Thus did he try conclusions with Judas, and had the worst of it; news came to him besides that Philip, whom he had left in charge at Antioch, was levying revolt against him. So, in great consternation of mind, he must needs throw himself on the mercy of the Jews, submitting under oath to the just terms they imposed on him. In token of this reconciliation, he offered sacrifice, paying the
24 temple much reverence and offering gifts there; as for Machabaeus, the king made a friend of him, and appointed him both governor and
25 commander of all the territory from Ptolemais to the Gerrenes. When he reached Ptolemais, he found the citizens much incensed over this treaty made, and angrily averring the terms of it would never be kept;
26 until at last Lysias must go up to an open stage, and give his reasons; whereby he calmed the indignation of the people, and so returned to Antioch. Such was the king's march upon Judaea, and such his homecoming.

CHAPTER FOURTEEN

THREE years later, came tidings to Judas and his company that Demetrius, son of Seleucus, was on the throne. This Demetrius, with a body of resolute followers and with ships to support him, had landed at Tripolis, in a part of the country well suited to his purpose,

2 and had wrested the whole kingdom from Antiochus, and from Lysias his general.

3 Now turn we to one Alcimus, that had been high priest formerly, but had wilfully incurred defilement in the days when folk began consorting with the Gentiles.[1] Little hope was left him, he should live to present

4 himself at the altar again; and now he had recourse to king Demetrius, in the hundred and fiftieth year. He came with gifts, a gold crown and a palm branch, and wreaths that had been better employed in the service

5 of the temple.[2] No word said he on the first day of his arriving; but ere long opportunity was given him of carrying out his impious design. He was called into counsel by Demetrius himself, and asked what resources the Jews had, or what purposes in view, that gave them such

6 confidence. And this was his answer: It is the faction of the Assideans, with Judas Machabaeus at their head, that will ever be fanning the flames

7 of war, and moving revolt, and destroying the peace of the realm. Thou seest here a man robbed of the high priesthood, his rightful inheritance.

8 And the cause of my coming is, first, the loyalty I have to the king's own interest, but not less, the love of my own fellow-countrymen; by the false

9 aims of a faction the whole of our race is brought into utter misery. Do but satisfy thyself, my lord king, that all is as I have said, and then, with

10 that kindliness the world knows so well, take order concerning them. No peace the commonwealth may have, while Judas lives.

11 Such was the opinion he gave, and the courtiers, that had little love

12 for Judas, fell to egging Demetrius on; he, with all haste, despatched one of his generals to Judaea, Nicanor, that was in command of the

13 elephants. His orders were, to take Judas alive, to disperse his company,

14 and of our glorious temple to make Alcimus high priest. The Gentiles whom Judas had chased out of the country flocked, now, to Nicanor's side, confident that the miserable ruin of the Jews would be the founda-

15 tion of their own prosperity. As for the Jews, when they heard Nicanor was on the march, with all this rabble of alien folk, they cast earth on

---

[1] 'Began consorting'; the Greek text has, 'refused to consort.'
[2] 'That had been better employed in the service of the temple'; literally, 'that seemed to belong to the temple.' The sense of the Greek text is probably 'such as were customarily used in the service of the temple.'

their heads and betook themselves to prayer. Was it not God's appointment, his people he should evermore preserve? Was he not wont to pro-
16 tect them with signal marks of his favour? And now orders came to them
from their leader; they must be on the march..Their mustering-place was
17 a fortress called Dessau, to which Simon, Judas' brother, had withdrawn after a brush with the enemy, who daunted him by the suddenness of their advance.[1]

18 But Nicanor had heard much about the valour of Judas' men, and how
nobly they fought in their country's quarrel; no wonder if he shrank from
19 the arbitrament of the sword, and sent envoys to meet them, Posidonius,
20 Theodotius and Matthias, with an offer of terms. After a deal of negotia-
tion, Judas referred the matter to the general voice, and all were agreed
21 upon accepting the offer of friendship. So the day was fixed for a secret
conference to be held between them; thrones of honour were brought
22 out and set ready, and you may be sure Judas had armed men posted in
waiting, to forestall any sudden treachery on the enemy's part; but their
23 parleys ended happily enough. Nicanor was now lodged in Jerusalem,
and did there no manner of hurt; all the rabble he had brought with him
24 were dispersed to their homes. Towards Judas he shewed unaffected
25 friendship, such a liking he had taken for the man; ay, and encouraged
him to take a wife and beget children; so Judas married, and took his
ease, and ever he lived on close terms with Nicanor.

26 And what of Alcimus? Little it liked him to see all this good-will
between the two of them, and their treaty-making; to Demetrius he
betook him, and charged Nicanor with disaffection; was he not purposing
27 to hand over his command to Judas, a traitor against the realm? Vile
accusations, that threw Demetrius into a great taking of fury; he wrote
to Nicanor, he was very ill content with the peace made, and would have
28 Machabaeus sent to Antioch in chains without more ado. Here was
Nicanor left in great confusion of mind; it went against the grain with
29 him to cancel the treaty with Judas, that had nothing wronged him, yet
30 run counter to the king's will he might not. So he began looking for an
opportunity of carrying out his orders; and Machabaeus, remarking that
a coolness had sprung up, and their meetings were less courteous than
hitherto, made sure this behaviour of his boded no good. Whereupon he
gathered some of his company, and went into concealment.
31 So Nicanor found himself quite outwitted; and he must needs make

---

[1] Verses 16, 17. There is perhaps some fault here in the manuscripts; the Greek
text reads literally, 'And, the leader having commanded it, he (who?) immediately moved his camp from there (from where?), and made contact with them
(with whom?) at the village of Dessau. But Simon, the brother of Judas, had
engaged Nicanor, but slowly, having come to grief through the sudden silence of
the enemy.'

his way into the high and holy precincts of the temple, where even then
the priests were offering their accustomed sacrifice. Judas, he said, must
32 be handed over to him; and when they, upon oath, denied all knowledge
33 of his hiding-place, what did Nicanor? He pointed to the temple, and
swore that if Judas were not handed over to him in chains he would raze
yonder sanctuary to the ground, demolish the altar, and consecrate its
34 precincts anew to Bacchus. With that, he left them; and the priests,
lifting up their hands to heaven, called upon the God that was ever the
35 champion of their race, with such prayer as this: Lord of all, that need
of thy creatures hast none, thy will it was to have thy dwelling-place
36 among us! Holy thou art, and of all holy things the master; this house,
that was so lately cleansed of its defilement, keep thou for ever undefiled.
37   It was this Nicanor that received information against one of the elders
at Jerusalem, named Razias, a true patriot and a man of good repute; for
38 the love he bore it, men called him the father of the Jewish people. Long
time this man had held to his resolve of keeping aloof from the Gentiles,
39 ready to put life and limb in jeopardy, so he might persevere. And now,
as if to give public proof of hatred towards the Jews, Nicanor sent five
40 hundred men to take him alive; shrewder blow was none he could deal
41 them, than to beguile such a man as this. And when this great company
set about to force an entry into his dwelling, breaking down the door
and calling out for firebrands, cut off from all escape, what did Razias?
42 He thrust a sword into his own body, counting it better to die honourably
than to fall into the hands of sinners, and suffer outrage unworthy of a
43 free-born man.[1] The hasty blow missed its aim; and now, with a rabble
of men pouring in through the doors he made gallantly for the outer wall,
and never hesitated to cast himself down, there in the heart of the crowd.
44 You may be sure they made room for his coming, and he fell on the very
45 joints of his neck; yet, breathing still, he rose to his feet undaunted;
blood streaming from his mortal wounds, he made his way through the
46 press of men, till he stood on a sheer rock above them. And there, for
now he had no blood left in him, he laid hold of his own entrails, and
with both hands cast them into the crowd beneath, calling upon the Lord,
giver of life and breath, to restore these same to his body; and so died.

---

[1] Some have attributed this action of Razias to a special inspiration; but we
are at liberty to suppose he was not conscious of a divine law against self-
destruction, and to admire his courage accordingly.

CHAPTER FIFTEEN

WHEN Nicanor was told, Judas was in the Samaritan country, he would have pressed home the attack against him, there and then,
2 on the sabbath day. But the Jews gainsaid him, for there were Jews that fought, unwillingly enough, under his orders. What, said they, wouldst thou fight beast-fashion, without mercy? This holy day respect thou needs
3 must, in his honour that is God all-seeing. Why, where is he then, said the impious wretch, this God who would have sabbath kept? In the
4 heavens? In heaven he is, sure enough, they answered, the living Lord
5 our master, that gave orders the seventh day should be observed. So be it, said he, and I am your master on earth, and my orders are, To arms, and despatch the king's business! Yet carry out his design they would not.
6 Such an empty braggart was this Nicanor, he thought to make a single
7 victory of it, over all the Jews at once; Machabaeus on his side kept ever
8 his confidence, yet with the sure hope, God would bring him aid. And for his men he had the same encouragement; let them never be daunted by the onslaught of the heathen, but rather bethink them of heaven's
9 mercies in time past, and look to God Omnipotent for victory. Of the
· law and the prophets he spoke to them, and reminded them of their old
10 battles, till all were eager for the fight; nor was it enough to arouse their ardour; he shewed them, too, how treacherous the heathen had proved,
11 and how forsworn. Thus it was his care to arm them, not with shield or spear for their defence, but with excellent words of good cheer.
A dream of his he told them, most worthy of credence, that brought
12 comfort to one and all. And what saw he? Onias, that had once been high priest, appeared to him; an excellent good man this, modest of mien, courteous, well-spoken, and from his boyhood schooled in all the virtues. With hands outstretched, he stood there praying for the Jewish folk.
13 Then he was ware of another, a man of great age and reverence, nothing
14 about him but was most worshipful; who this might be, Onias told him forthwith: Here is one that loves our brethren, the people of Israel, well; one that for Israel and for every stone of the holy city prays much; God's
15 prophet Jeremias. And with that, Jeremias reached forward to Judas,
16 and gave him a golden sword; This holy sword take thou, he said, God's gift; this wielding, all the enemies of my people Israel thou shalt lay low.
17 A most noble harangue, and one very apt to rouse the emulation of his followers, and to stiffen their courage. No wonder if they resolved they would put it to the touch, and manfully engage the enemy; valour should decide all. Was not the holy city, was not the temple itself in jeopardy?
18 For wives and children, for brethren and kindred, their concern was

less; of the perils they dreaded, profanation of the temple was first and
19 foremost.   And what of those who were left in the city? No common
20 anxiety they felt for these others that were going into battle.   Now was
the hour of decision; the enemy was at the gates, drawn up in full array;
here were the elephants, here was the cavalry, posted at points of van-
21 tage.   Judas, when he saw the number of his assailants, how manifold
were their appointments, how fierce the temper of the beasts, was fain
to lift hands heavenward, and to the Lord make his appeal; the Lord,
that is wondrous in his doings, and at his own pleasure crowns right, not
22 might, with victory.   And this was the manner of his praying: Lord, in
the days of Ezechias thou didst send thy angel, and take toll of a hundred
23 and eighty-five thousand in the camp of Sennacherib!   Ruler of heaven,
24 some friendly angel of thine this day escort us;   dread and dismay let thy
outstretched hand inspire, to the confusion of yonder blasphemers that
levy war on thy holy people! And so he brought his prayer to an end.
25   By this, Nicanor's army was coming forward to the attack, with blow-
26 ing of trumpets and with songs of battle.   But Judas and his company
27 went to meet them calling still upon God for his succour;   and ever while
hand fought, heart prayed. Such joy had they of God's present assistance,
28 they cut down a full thirty-five thousand of the enemy;   when they let
be, and returned in triumph from the pursuit, news greeted them Nicanor
29 himself had armed for the fight, and lay there dead.   What a cry was
then raised, what a stir, what hymns they sang, in the speech of their
own country, to God Omnipotent!
30   And Judas? Not for nothing had he devoted body and soul, this long
while, to the service of his fellow countrymen! Nicanor's head, and one
of his arms cut off from the shoulder downwards, he bade them carry to
31 Jerusalem;   and there he called the tribesmen together, ranged the priests
about the altar, and sent his summons to the heathen that garrisoned
32 the citadel.   Head and hand he shewed them of the godless Nicanor, the
hand that was stretched out so boastfully against the holy temple of the
33 Almighty,   bidding them cut the blaspheming tongue in pieces and cast
34 it to the birds, nail the rash hand to the temple's face.   None but praised
the Lord of heaven at the sight; Blessed be the Lord, they cried, that has
35 kept his house undefiled still!   As for Nicanor's head, Judas hung it at
the top of the citadel, to be a clear and evident token, how God gives
36 aid.   And all with one consent made a decree, never should that day pass
37 unobserved;   they would keep holiday on the thirteenth of the Syrian
month Adar, which is the eve of Mardochaeus' feast.[1]
38   Such was the history of Nicanor; and since that time the city has been
39 in Jewish possession. Here, then, I will make an end of writing;   if it

---
[1] See Est. 9.17 and 18.

has been done workmanly, and in historian's fashion, none better pleased
than I; if it is of little merit, I must be humoured none the less.[1] Noth-
40 ing but wine to take, nothing but water, thy health forbids; vary thy
drinking,[2] and thou shalt find content. So it is with reading; if the
book be too nicely polished at every point, it grows wearisome. So here
we will have done with it.

---

[1] 'I must be humoured none the less'; according to the Greek text, 'I have
done as well as I could.' Divine inspiration is something superadded to, not a
substitute for, human labour and human self-criticism.
[2] For 'vary thy drinking' the Greek text has 'mix both together'; and the rest
of the sentence is a (somewhat obscure) recommendation of style.

Appendix

THE BOOK OF PSALMS

Translated from the Latin text of the Pontifical Biblical Institute

PSALM ONE

BLESSED is the man who does not guide his steps by ill counsel, or turn aside
2 where sinners walk, or, where scornful souls gather, sit down to rest; the man
whose heart is set on the law of the Lord, on that law, day and night, his thoughts
3 still dwell. He stands firm as a tree planted by running water, ready to yield its
4 fruit when the season comes, not a leaf faded; all that he does will prosper. Not
5 such, not such the wicked; the wicked are like chaff the wind sweeps away. Not
for the wicked, when judgement comes, to rise up and plead their cause; sinners
6 will have no part in the reunion of the just. They walk, the just, under the Lord's
protection; the path of the wicked, how soon is it lost to sight!

PSALM TWO

WHAT means this turmoil among the nations? Why do the peoples cherish
2 vain dreams? See how the kings of the earth stand in array, how its rulers
make common cause, against the Lord, and against the King he has anointed,
3 crying, Let us break away from their bondage, rid ourselves of the toils! He who
5 dwells in heaven is laughing at their threats, the Lord makes light of them; and
6 at last, in his displeasure, he will speak out, his anger quelling them: Here, on
mount Sion, my sanctuary, I enthrone a king of my own choice.
7 Mine to proclaim the Lord's edict; how he told me, Thou art my son; I have
8 begotten thee this day. Ask thy will of me, and thou shalt have the nations for
9 thy patrimony; the very ends of the world for thy domain. Thou shalt herd them
10 like sheep with a crook of iron, break them in pieces like earthenware. Princes,
11 take warning; learn your lesson, you that rule the world. Tremble, and serve the
12 Lord, rejoicing in his presence, but with awe in your hearts. Kiss the rod, do not
brave his anger, and go astray from the sure path. When the fire of his vengeance
blazes out suddenly, happy are they who find their refuge in him.

PSALM THREE

(A psalm David wrote, when he fled before his son Absalom.)

2 SEE how they surround me, Lord, my adversaries, how many rise up in arms
3 against me; everywhere voices taunting me, His God cannot save him now.
4 Yet, Lord, thou art the shield that covers me, thou art the pride that keeps my
5 head erect. I have but to cry out to the Lord, and my voice reaches his mountain
6 sanctuary, and there finds hearing. Safe in God's hand I lay down, and slept,
7 and have awoken; and now, though thousands of the people set upon me from
8 every side, I will not be afraid of them. Bestir thyself, Lord; my God, save me;
9 thine to smite my enemies on the cheek, thine to break the fangs of malice. From
the Lord all deliverance comes; let thy benediction, Lord, rest upon thy people.

PSALM FOUR

(To the choir-master. On stringed instruments. A psalm. Of David.)

2 WHEN I call on thy name, listen to me, O God, and grant redress; still, in
time of trouble, thou hast brought me relief; have pity on me now, and hear
3 my prayer. Great ones of the world, will your hearts always be hardened, will you
4 never cease setting your heart on shadows, following a lie? To the souls he loves,
be sure the Lord shews wondrous favour; whenever I call on his name, the Lord
5 will hear me. Tremble, and sin no more; take thought, as you lie awake, in the
6 silence of your hearts. Offer sacrifices with due observance, and put your trust
7 in the Lord. There are many that languish for a sight of better times; do thou,
8 then, Lord, shew us the sunshine of thy favour. Never did rich harvests of corn
9 and wine bring gladness like the gladness thou puttest into my heart. Even as I
lie down, sleep comes, and with sleep tranquillity; what need, Lord, of aught but
thyself to bring me confidence?

PSALM FIVE

(To the choir-master. On the flute. A psalm. Of David.)

2 LORD, listen to my plea, let me not sigh in vain; pay heed to my cry of petition,
my King, my God. To thee, Lord, my prayer goes up, early to win thy audience;
4 early in the morning I lay my petition before thee and await thy pleasure. No
6 evil thing claims thy divine assent; with thee baseness cannot dwell; nor rebellion hold its ground at thy coming. Thou hatest the wrongdoer, and wilt bring
the liar to destruction; blood-thirsty and treacherous men the Lord holds in
8 abhorrence. I, then, encompassed by thy mercy, will betake myself to thy house,
and in reverence of thee bow down before thy sanctuary.
9 Lord, do thou lead me with faithful care; clear show the path, while I walk
10 beset by enemies. In their speech no truth can be found; their hearts are all
11 treachery, their mouths gaping tombs; flattering is ever on their lips. Thy
scourge, O God! Cheat them of their hopes, cast them out in all their wickedness;
12 have they not defied thee? But for all those who trust in thee there is joy and
everlasting triumph; welcome protection they have from thee, true lovers of thy
13 name. Lord, thou givest thy benediction to the just; thou dost throw thy loving-
kindness about us like a shield.

PSALM SIX

(To the choir-master. On stringed instruments. Over the octave.
A psalm. Of David.)

2 LORD, when thou dost reprove me, let it not be in anger; when thou dost
3 chastise me, let it not be in displeasure. Lord, pity me; I have no strength left;
4 Lord, heal me; my limbs tremble; my spirits are altogether broken; Lord, wilt
5 thou never be content? Lord, turn back, and grant a wretched soul relief; as
6 thou art ever merciful, save me. When death comes, there is no more remember-
7 ing thee; none can praise thee in the tomb. I am spent with sighing; every night
8 I lie weeping on my bed, till the tears drench my pillow. Grief has dimmed
my eyes, faded their lustre now, so many are the adversaries that surround me.
9 Depart from me, all you that traffic in iniquity; the Lord has heard my cry of
11 distress. O prayer divinely heard, O boon divinely granted! All my enemies
will be abashed and terrified; taken aback, all in a moment, and put to shame.

PSALM SEVEN

(A lament of David's, which he sang to the Lord because of Chus, the Benjamite.)

2 O LORD my God, my confidence is in thee; save me from all my pursuers,
3 and grant me deliverance: must I fall a helpless prey to the lion, be torn in
4 pieces, with none to bring me aid? O Lord my God, if I too have been at fault,
5 if these hands are stained with guilt; if I have been a false friend, and not rather
6 spared even those that wronged me, then indeed let some enemy overtake me
with his relentless pursuit, trample me to earth, and level my pride with the dust!
7 Lord, rise up in thy anger, countervail the malice of my enemies; bestir thyself,
8 O Lord my God, in defence of the laws thou thyself hast given us. All the nations
9 will gather about thee, if thou wilt come back to thy throne and rule them, the
Lord judging the nations! Give me redress, Lord, in my uprightness, in all the
10 innocence of my heart. Surely thou wilt put an end to the wrong-doing of the
wicked, and prosper the innocent; no thought or desire of ours can escape the
11 scrutiny of thy Divine justice. From the Lord, refuge of true hearts, my pro-
12 tection comes. God judges ever true; day by day his indignation mounts up;
13 if they do not repent, his sword will flash bright; he has bent and aimed his bow;
14 deadly are the weapons he is preparing for them; he has barbed his arrows with
15 fire. Here was a heart pregnant with malice, that conceived only spite, and gave
16 birth only to shame! Here was one who dug a pit and sunk it deep, and fell into
17 a snare of his own setting! All his spite will recoil on himself, all his violence will
18 fall on his own head. I will ever thank the Lord for his just retribution, singing
praises to the name of the Lord, the most High.

PSALM EIGHT

(To the choir-master. To the mood of the song. The Wine-presses.
A psalm. Of David.)

2 O LORD, our Master, how the majesty of thy name fills all the earth! Thy
3 greatness is high above heaven itself. Thou hast made the lips of children,
of infants at the breast, vocal with praise; to confound thy enemies; to silence
4 malicious and revengeful tongues. I look up at those heavens of thine, the work
5 of thy hands, at the moon and the stars, which thou hast set in their places; what
is man that thou shouldst remember him? What is Adam's breed, that it should
6 claim thy care? Thou hast placed him only a little below the angels, crowning
7 him with glory and honour, and bidding him rule over the works of thy hands.
8 Thou hast put them all under his dominion, the sheep and the cattle, and the
9 wild beasts besides; the birds in the sky, and the fish in the sea, that travel by the
10 sea's paths. O Lord, our Master, how the majesty of thy name fills all the earth!

PSALM NINE

(To the choir-master. To the mood of the song, Mut Labben.[1]
A psalm. Of David.)

2 L ORD, I give thee all the thanks of my heart, recounting thy wonderful doings;
3 glad and triumphant in thee, I will sing psalms to thy name, O God most
4 high. See how my enemies turn back, how they faint and melt away at the sight

[1] Some of the Hebrew words used in these title-headings are of quite unknown
significance; these, in the new version of the Psalter, are simply transliterated.

5 of thee! Thou hast given me redress and maintained my cause; thou art there
6 on thy throne, seeing justice done. Thou hast checked the heathen in their
course; thou hast brought the wicked to nothing, blotting out their name for all
7 time. Spent is the enemy's power, doomed to everlasting ruin; the memory of
8 them has died with the fall of their cities. But the Lord abides for ever on the
9 throne of judgement he has prepared, still judging the world rightly, still award-
10 ing each people its due; the Lord is a stronghold to the oppressed, a stronghold
11 in time of peril. Those who acknowledge thy name, Lord, can trust thee; never
was man forsaken that had recourse to thee.
12 Sing, then, to the Lord, who dwells in Sion, tell the Gentiles of his great deeds;
13 how he, the avenger of blood, cares for the afflicted, does not forget them when
14 they cry to him. Have pity on me, Lord, look upon all that I suffer at my enemies'
15 hands; thou who didst ever rescue me from the gate of death, to proclaim thy
16 praises at the gate of thy loved Sion, to exult in thy saving power. The heathen
have been caught in their own deadly devices; their feet have been trapped in the
17 very toils they had laid; now it will be seen how the Lord defends the right, how
18 the wicked contrive their own undoing. To the place of death the wicked must
19 return, heathens that have no thought of God. He does not forget the helpless;
20 their time will come; the patience of the afflicted will not go for nothing. Bestir
thyself, Lord, let not human strength prevail; let the heathen stand upon their
21 trial before thee; let the heathen, too, feel thy terrors, and learn they are but men.
22 Lord, why dost thou stand far off? In days of affliction, why dost thou make
23 no sign? The hearts of the oppressed burn within them, so triumphant is the
24 schemer that has entrapped them; so proud of his wicked end achieved, still
25 robbing men, blaspheming and despising the Lord. God there is none to punish
26 me, the sinner thinks in his pride, and makes that thought his rule; still, as he
goes on prospering, he banishes thy laws from his mind, and makes light of his
27 enemies. Endless time, he thinks, cannot shake his untroubled existence. His
mouth overflows with curses, and calumny, and deceit; his tongue is a storehouse
29 of dissension and mischief. Ambushed he lies at the village gate, to kill unawares
30 the man who never wronged him; his eyes are continually on his prey; like a lion
in its lair, he watches from his hiding-place, to surprise his defenceless foe, safe
31 in the net. So he catches him in the toils; stands there bowing and scraping, till
32 the prey falls by his onset. Why not? he thinks to himself, God has forgotten
about it; God still turns his face away, and sees nothing.
33 O Lord God, bestir thyself, lift up thy hand; do not forget the helpless. Why
35 is the sinner allowed to defy God, to think he will never exact punishment? But
in truth thou seest it; thou hast eyes for misery and distress, and wilt take them
into thy keeping. The destitute are cast on no care but thine; to thee only the
36 orphan looks for redress. Break down the power of the wicked oppressor, punish
37 his ill-doing, and let him be seen no more. The Lord will reign for ever and ever,
38 while you, the heathen, will vanish from the land he loves. The sighing of the
defenceless has found audience; thou wilt heed them and bring courage to their
39 hearts, wilt give redress to the fatherless and the persecuted; mortal man shall
make himself feared no longer.

PSALM TEN

(To the choir-master. Of David.)

2 MY trust is in the Lord; how is it that you say to your friend, Escape, like a
3 frightened sparrow, to the hill-side? Escape; the rebels have strung their
bows, have arrows ready in the quiver, to shoot from their hiding-places at an

4 unoffending heart; they have thrown down all thou hadst built; what hope, now, for the just man?
5   Is not the Lord in his holy shrine, the same Lord whose throne is in heaven,
6 whose eye watches, whose glance can appraise, the deeds of men? Innocent or sinful, he reads every heart, and the friends of wrong-doing are his enemies.
7 Pitilessly his weapons rain down upon the offenders; burning coals, and brim-
8 stone, and scorching wind; such is the draught he brews for them. The Lord is just, and just are the deeds he loves; none but upright souls shall enjoy his presence.

PSALM ELEVEN

(To the choir-master. Over the octave. A psalm. Of David.)

2 LORD, come to my rescue; piety is dead; in a base world, true hearts have grown
3 rare. None but exchanges empty forms of speech with his neighbour; every-
4 where false hearts and treacherous lips. Those treacherous lips, that tongue with
5 high-sounding phrases; Lord, rid the earth of them! With our tongues, they say, we can do great things; our lips are good friends to us; we own no master.
6 Now, says the Lord, I will bestir myself, on behalf of the helpless who are so ill used, of the poor who cry out so bitterly; I will win them the redress they long
7 for. The promises of the Lord are true metal, like silver that is tested in the
8 crucible, the stains of earth gone, seven times refined. Yes, Lord, thou wilt watch over us, and keep us ever safe from these evil days.
9   See how the wicked come and go all around us, how they rise to greatness, this base breed of men!

PSALM TWELVE

(To the choir-master. A psalm. Of David.)

2 LORD, must I still go all unremembered, must thy look still be turned away
3 from me? Each day brings a fresh load of care, fresh misery to my heart; must
4 I be ever the sport of my enemies? Look upon me, O Lord my God, and listen
5 to me; give light to these eyes, before they close in death; do not let my enemies
6 claim the mastery, my persecutors triumph over my fall! I cast myself on thy mercy; soon may this heart boast of redress granted, sing in praise of the Lord, my benefactor.

PSALM THIRTEEN

(To the choir-master. Of David.)

THERE is no God above us, is the fond thought of reckless hearts; warped natures everywhere and hateful lives! There is not an innocent man among
2 them. The Lord looks down from heaven at the race of men, to find one soul that
3 reflects, and makes God its aim; but no, all have missed the mark and rebelled
4 against him; an innocent man is nowhere to be found. What, can they learn noth-ing, all these traffickers in iniquity, who feed themselves fat on this people of mine,
5 as if it were bread for their eating, and never invoke the Lord's name? What
6 wonder if fear unmans them, when the Lord takes the part of the innocent? Easily
7 you thought to outwit the friendless; see, the Lord is his refuge! Oh, that it might dawn over Sion, Israel's deliverance! Day of gladness for Jacob, day of Israel's triumph, when the Lord restores the fortunes of his own people.

PSALM FOURTEEN

(A psalm. Of David.)

WHO is it, Lord, that will make his home in thy tabernacle, rest on the moun-
2 tain where thy sanctuary is? One that guides his steps without fault, and gives
3 to all their due; one whose heart is all honest purpose, who utters no treacherous
4 word, never defrauds a friend, or slanders a neighbour. He scorns the reprobate,
keeping his reverence for such as fear God, and is true, come what may, to his
5 pledged word; lends without usury, and takes no bribe to condemn the innocent.
He who so lives will stand firm for ever.

PSALM FIFTEEN

(A miktam. Of David.)

KEEP me safe, Lord; I put my trust in thee. The Lord, whom I own as my
3 God, confess that in him is all my good! There are faithful souls in this land
4 of his; wondrous delight he gives me in their companionship. What do they do
but lay up fresh store of sorrows, that betake themselves to alien gods? Not with
these will I pour out the blood of sacrifice; I will not take forbidden names on my
5 lips. No, it is the Lord I claim for my prize, the Lord who fills my cup; thou,
6 and no other, wilt assure my inheritance to me. Portion is none were more to my
liking; welcome the lot's choice!
7 Blessed be the Lord, who schools me; late into the night my inmost thoughts
8 chasten me. Always I can keep the Lord within sight; always he is at my right
9 hand, to make me stand firm. Glad and merry am I, heart and soul of me; my
10 body, too, shall rest in confidence that thou wilt not leave my soul in the place
11 of death, or allow thy faithful servant to see corruption. Thou wilt shew me the
way of life, make me full of gladness in thy presence; at thy right hand are delights that will endure for ever.

PSALM SIXTEEN

(A prayer. Of David.)

LORD, to my just complaint give ear; do not spurn my cry for aid. Listen to this
2 prayer of mine; they are no treacherous lips that make it. At thy judgement
3 seat I claim award; unerring thy scrutiny. Wilt thou read my heart, drawing near
4 in the darkness to test me as if by fire, thou wilt find no treachery in me. Never
have these lips been led astray by man's evil example; still to thy law's pattern
5 thy warnings kept me true; still in thy paths my steps were firmly planted, my
feet did not stumble.
6 And now I cry to thee, the God who ever hearest me; turn thy ear towards me,
7 and listen to my plea. Thy mercy, thy signal mercy shew; none ever sought
8 sanctuary at thy right hand in vain. Protect me as thou wouldst the apple of thy
9 own eye; hide me under the shelter of thy wings, safe from the evil-doers who
wrong me.
10 See how my enemies close about me mercilessly, their hearts shut to pity, a
11 boast on their lips! Even now their stealthy tread closes in on me, as they watch
12 their opportunity to bring me down; better had a lion caught me, eager for its
prey, a young lion that waits hidden in its lair.
13 Bestir thyself, Lord; forestall him and throw him to the ground; bare thy
14 sword, and save me from the evil-doer, raise thy hand, to rescue me from the

hands of mortal men! Mortal men indeed, that have all their portion here on earth; whose desires thou dost satisfy with treasures from thy store, so that their
15 children, too, live in abundance, and leave riches for new heirs to enjoy. As for me, I will come with upright heart into thy presence, and when thy glory dawns, I shall be well content.

PSALM SEVENTEEN

(To the choir-master. Of David, the servant of the Lord. He addressed to the Lord the words of this song, on the day when God delivered him from the hand of Saul, and from the hands of all his enemies; as follows:)

2 SHALL I not love thee, Lord, my only defender? The Lord is my rock-fastness, my stronghold, my rescuer; to God, my hiding-place, I flee for safety; he is my
4 shield, my weapon of deliverance, my refuge. Praised be the Lord! When I invoke
5 his name, I am secure from my enemies. All about me surged the waves of death,
6 deep flowed the perilous tide, to daunt me; the grave had caught me in its toils,
7 deadly snares had trapped my feet. One cry to the Lord, in my affliction, one word of summons to my God, and he, from his sanctuary, listened to my voice; the complaint I made before him found a hearing.
8 Earth thereupon shivered and shook, the very foundations of the hills quailed
9 and quaked at his anger; at the fiery smoke that breathed from his mouth and
10 nostrils, kindling coals to flame. He bade heaven stoop, and came down to earth,
11 with a dark cloud at his feet; he came, cherub-mounted, borne up on the wings
12 of the wind, shrouded in darkness, canopied with black rain-storm and deep
13 mist. Then, while coals were kindled at the brightness as he came, the Lord
15 sent his thunder from heaven, the most High let his voice be heard. How they scattered when he rained down his arrows on them, how they fled in confusion
16 before the volleys of his lightning! The sea's bed came to light, the very foundations of the world were laid bare, when thou didst threaten them, Lord, when
17 thou didst blow upon them with the breath of thy anger. Then he reached down
18 from heaven, caught hold of me, rescued me from that flood, saved me from
19 triumphant malice, from the enemies that held me at their mercy. Evil days,
20 when they faced me at every turn! Yet the Lord stood by me, and brought me out into freedom again; his great love befriended me.
21 So, for my faithfulness, the Lord would requite me, as he sees me guiltless in
22 act, he would make return. Have I not kept true to the Lord's paths? Have I not
23 been ever loyal to my God? No law of his, but I have kept it before my eyes; no
24 task he laid upon me have I refused; ever stainless in his presence, ever watchful
25 to keep myself clear of guilt, ever faithful, ever guiltless in act, the Lord has
26 requited me. Lovingly wilt thou treat those who love thee, with the loyal keep
27 troth; pure of heart the pure of heart shall find thee, the cunning thou wilt over-
28 reach. To humble folk thou wilt bring deliverance; the proud, with their haughty
29 looks, thou wilt bring down to earth. It is thou, Lord, that keepest the lamp of
30 my hopes still burning; shinest on the darkness about me, O my God. In thy strength I will engage a host of the enemy, in my God's strength their defences overleap.
31 Such is my God, unsullied in his dealings; his promises are like metal tested
32 in the fire; he is the sure defence of all who trust in him. Who but the Lord is
33 God? What other refuge can there be, except our God? It is he that girds me with
34 strength, bids me go on my way untroubled. He makes me sure-footed as the
35 deer, and gives me the freedom of the hills; these hands, through him, are skilled
36 in battle, these arms are a match for any bow of bronze. Thy saving power, Lord,

37 is my defence, thy right hand supports me; thy tender care fosters me. Through
38 thee, my steps are untrammelled as I go, my tread never falters; I can overtake
the enemies I pursue, and never turn home till I have made an end of them;
39 I can beat them to their knees, and hurl them down at my feet. Thou girdest me
about with a warrior's strength; whatever power challenges me, thou dost subdue
41 before me, putting my enemies to flight, and throwing all their malice into con-
42 fusion. Loudly they cry out to the Lord, bereft of aid, but he makes no answer
43 to their cries. I can crush them to pieces, like the dust which the wind blows
along; I can trample them down like mire from the streets.
44   Nor was it enough, of domestic broils to rid me; a world should be my vassal;
45 new realms should pay me homage, quick to do my bidding. See where they
come, the alien born, come slinking out of their strongholds, pale of cheek, to
47 cringe before me. Blessed be the living Lord who is my refuge, praised be the God
48 who delivers me! It is thou, my God, that bringest me redress, that bendest
49 peoples to my will, that savest me from the spite of my enemies: so that I am
50 high above the reach of their assaults, proof against their violence. Then, Lord,
I will give thee thanks in the hearing of all the nations, singing in praise of thy
51 name; victory thy mercy grants to the King thou hast anointed, to David, and
David's line for ever.

PSALM EIGHTEEN

(To the choir-master. A psalm. Of David.)

2 SEE how the skies proclaim God's glory, how the vault of heaven betrays his
3 craftsmanship! Each day echoes its secret to the next, each night passes on to
4 the next its revelation of knowledge; no word, no accent of theirs that does not
5 make itself heard, till their utterance fills every land, till their message reaches
6 the ends of the world. In these, he has made a pavilion for the sun, which comes
out as a bridegroom comes from his bed, and exults like some great runner who
7 sees the track before him. Here, at one end of heaven, is its starting-place, and
its course reaches to the other; none can escape its burning heat.
8   The Lord's perfect law, how it brings the soul back to life; the Lord's unchal-
9 lengeable decrees, how they make the simple learned! How plain are the duties
which the Lord enjoins, the treasure of man's heart; how clear is the command-
10 ment the Lord gives, the enlightenment of man's eyes! How sacred a thing is the
fear of the Lord, which is binding for ever; how unerring are the awards which
11 the Lord makes, one and all giving proof of their justice! All these are more
precious than gold, than a hoard of pure gold, sweeter than the honey, dripping
12 from its comb. By these I, thy servant, live, observing them how jealously! And
yet, who knows his own frailties? If I have sinned unwittingly, do thou absolve
14 me. Keep me ever thy own servant, far from pride; so long as this does not lord
15 it over me, I will yet be without fault, I will yet be innocent of the great sin. Every
word on my lips, every thought in my heart, what thou wouldst have it be, O Lord,
my defender, my redeemer!

PSALM NINETEEN

(To the choir-master. A psalm. Of David.)

2 THE Lord listen to thee in thy time of need, the power of Jacob's God be thy
3 protection! May he send thee aid from his holy place, watch over thee, there
4 on mount Sion; may he remember all thy offerings, and find savour in thy burnt-

5 sacrifice. May he grant thee what thy heart desires, crown thy hopes with fulfil-
6 ment. So may we rejoice at thy deliverance, rallied in the name of the Lord our
7 God; abundantly may he grant thy prayer. Shall I doubt that the Lord protects
   the king he has anointed, will listen to him from his sanctuary in heaven? Is not
8 his right hand strong to save? Let others talk of horses and chariots; our refuge
9 is in the name of the Lord our God. Stumbled and fallen they, while we stand firm
10 on our feet. O Lord, save the king, and hear us in the hour when we call upon
   thee.

PSALM TWENTY

(To the choir-master. A psalm. Of David.)

2 WELL may the king rejoice, Lord, in thy protection, well may he triumph in
3   thy saving power! Never a wish in his heart hast thou disappointed, never a
4 prayer on his lips denied. With happy auguries thou dost meet him on his way,
5 dost set a crown of pure gold on his head. Prays he for life? Long continuance
6 of his reign thou dost grant him; to last unfailing till the end of time. Great is the
   renown thy protection has won for him; glory and high honour thou hast made
7 his. An everlasting monument of thy goodness, comforted by the smile of thy
8 favour, he stands firm, trusting in the Lord; the favour of the most High is with
   him.

9   Ay, but thy enemies—they shall feel thy power; that right hand will not leave
10 their malice unpunished. At thy frown, they will wither away like grass in the
11 oven; whirled away by the Lord's anger, burnt up in its flames. Thou wilt rid
12 the land of their breed, their race will vanish from the world of men. See how
13 all their false designs against thee, all their plots come to nothing! Thou wilt
   rout them; bent is thy bow to meet their onslaught.
14 Stand high above us, Lord, in thy protecting strength; our song, our psalm,
   shall be of thy greatness.

PSALM TWENTY-ONE

(To the choir-master. A psalm. Of David.)

2 MY God, my God, why hast thou forsaken me? Loudly I call, but my prayer
3   cannot reach thee. Thou dost not answer, my God, when I cry out to thee
4 day and night, thou dost not heed. Thou art there none the less, dwelling in the
5 holy place; Israel's ancient boast. It was in thee that our fathers trusted, and
6 thou didst reward their trust by delivering them; they cried to thee, and rescue
7 came; no need to be ashamed of such trust as theirs. But I, poor worm, have no
8 manhood left; I am a by-word to all, the laughing-stock of the rabble. All those
   who catch sight of me fall to mocking; mouthing out insults, while they toss their
9 heads in scorn, He committed himself to the Lord, why does not the Lord come
   to his rescue, and set his favourite free?

10 What hand but thine drew me out from my mother's womb? Who else was
11 my refuge when I hung at the breast? From the hour of my birth, thou art my
12 guardian; since I left my mother's womb, thou art my God! Do not leave me now,
13 when trouble is close at hand; stand near, when I have none to help me. My
   enemies ring me round, packed close as a herd of oxen, strong as bulls from Basan;
14 so might a lion threaten me with its jaws, roaring for its prey. I am spent as spilt
   water, all my bones out of joint, my heart turned to molten wax within me;
16 parched is my throat, like clay in the baking, and my tongue sticks fast in my
17 mouth; thou hast laid me in the dust, to die. Prowling about me like a pack of

dogs, their wicked conspiracy hedges me in; they have torn holes in my hands
18 and feet; I can count my bones one by one; and they stand there watching me,
19 gazing at me in triumph. They divide my spoils among them, cast lots for my
20 garments. Then, Lord, do not stand at a distance; if thou wouldst aid me, come
21 speedily to my side. Only life is left me; save that from the sword, from the
22 power of these dogs; rescue me from the very mouth of the lion, the very horns of
the wild oxen that have brought me thus low.
23   Then I will proclaim thy renown to my brethren; where thy people gather,
24 I will join in singing thy praise, Praise the Lord, all you that are his worshippers;
25 honour to him from the sons of Jacob, reverence to him from Israel's race! He
has not scorned or slighted the appeal of the friendless, nor turned his face away
26 from me; my cry for help did not go unheeded. Take what I owe thee, my song
of praise before a great assembly. I will pay my vows to the Lord in the sight of
27 his worshippers; the poor shall eat now, and have their fill, those who look for
28 the Lord will cry out in praise of him, Refreshed be your hearts eternally! The
furthest dwellers on earth will bethink themselves of the Lord, and come back
29 to him; all the races of the heathen will worship before him; to the Lord royalty
30 belongs, the whole world's homage is his due. Him shall they worship, him only,
31 that are laid to rest in the earth, even from their dust they shall adore. I, too,
shall live on in his presence, and beget children to serve him; these to a later age
32 shall speak of the Lord's name; these to a race that must yet be born shall tell the
story of his faithfulness, Hear what the Lord did.

PSALM TWENTY-TWO

(A psalm. Of David.)

2 THE Lord is my shepherd; how can I lack anything? He gives me a resting-
place where there is green pasture, leads me out to the cool water's brink,
3 refreshed and content. As in honour pledged, by sure paths he leads me; dark
be the valley about my path, hurt I fear none while he is with me; thy rod, thy
5 crook are my comfort. Envious my foes watch, while thou dost spread a banquet
6 for me; richly thou dost anoint my head with oil, well filled my cup. All my life
thy loving favour pursues me; through the long years the Lord's house shall
be my dwelling-place.

PSALM TWENTY-THREE

(Of David. A psalm.)

THE Lord owns earth, and all earth's fulness, the round world, and all its
2 inhabitants. Who else has built it out from the sea, poised it on the hidden
streams?
3   Who dares climb the mountain of the Lord, and appear in his sanctuary? The
guiltless in act, the pure in heart; one who never set his heart on lying tales, or
5 swore treacherously to his neighbour. His to receive a blessing from the Lord,
6 mercy from God, his sure defender; his the true breed that still looks, still longs
for the presence of the God of Jacob.
7   Swing back, doors, higher yet; reach higher, immemorial gates, to let the King
8 enter in triumph! Who is this great King? Who but the Lord, mighty and strong,
9 the Lord mighty in battle? Swing back, doors, higher yet; reach higher, im-
10 memorial gates, to let the King enter in triumph! Who is this great King? It is
the Lord of Armies that comes here on his way triumphant.

PSALM TWENTY-FOUR

(Of David.)

2 ALL my heart goes out to thee, O Lord my God. Belie not the trust I have in
3 thee, let not my enemies boast of my downfall. Can any that trust in thee be
4 disappointed, as they are disappointed who lightly break their troth? Direct my
5 way, Lord, as thou wilt, teach me thy own paths. Ever let thy truth guide and
6 teach me, O God my deliverer, my abiding hope. Forget not, Lord, thy pity, thy
7 mercies of long ago. Give heed no more to the sins and frailties of my youth,
8 but think mercifully of me, as thou, Lord, art ever gracious. How gracious is the
9 Lord, how faithful, guiding our strayed feet back to the path! In his own laws he
10 will train the humble, in his own paths the humble he will guide. Jealous be thy
keeping of covenant and ordinance, and the Lord's dealings will be ever gracious,
11 ever faithful with thee. Kindly be thy judgement of my sin, for thy own honour's
sake, my grievous sin.
12 Let a man but fear the Lord, what path to choose he doubts no longer. Much
14 joy he shall have of his lands and to his heirs leave them. No stranger the Lord
15 is, no secret his covenant, to his true worshippers. On the Lord I fix my eyes
16 continually, trusting him to save my feet from the snare. Pity me, Lord, as thou
17 seest me friendless and forlorn. Quit my heart of its burden, deliver me from
18 my distress. Restless and forlorn, I claim thy pity, to my sins be merciful.
19 See how many are my foes, and how bitter is the grudge they bear me. Take
my soul into thy keeping; come to my rescue, do not let me be disappointed of my
21 trust in thee. Uprightness and purity be my shield, as I wait patiently, Lord,
22 for thy help. When wilt thou deliver Israel, my God, from all his troubles?

PSALM TWENTY-FIVE

(Of David.)

L ORD, be thou my judge; have I not guided my steps clear of wrong? Have I
2 trusted in the Lord, only to stumble on my path? Test me, Lord, put me to
3 the proof; assay my inmost desires and thoughts. Ever I keep thy mercies in mind,
4 ever thy faithfulness bears me company. I have not consorted with false men,
5 or joined in plotting evil; I have shunned the company of the wicked, never sat
6 at my ease with sinners. With the pure in heart I will wash my hands clean, and
7 take my place among them at thy altar, there making thy praises known, telling
8 the story of all thy wonderful deeds. How well, Lord, I love the house where thou
9 dwellest, the shrine of thy glory! Lord, never count this soul for lost with the
10 wicked, this life among the blood-thirsty; hands ever stained with guilt, palms
11 ever itching for a bribe! Be it mine to guide my steps clear of wrong; deliver me
12 in thy mercy. On sure ground my feet are set; where his people gather I will join
in blessing the Lord's name.

PSALM TWENTY-SIX

(Of David.)

T HE Lord is my light and my deliverance; whom have I to fear? The Lord
2 watches over my life; whom shall I hold in dread? Vainly the malicious close
about me, as if they would tear me in pieces, vainly my enemies threaten me;
3 all at once they stumble and fall. Though a whole host were arrayed against me,

my heart would be undaunted; though an armed onset should threaten me, still
4 I would not lose my confidence. One request I have ever made of the Lord, let
me claim it still, to dwell in the Lord's house my whole life long, resting content
5 in the Lord's goodness, gazing at his temple. In his royal tent he hides me, in
the inmost recess of his royal tent, safe from peril. On a rock fastness he lifts me
6 high up; my head rises high above the enemies that encompass me. I will make
an offering of triumphant music in this tabernacle of his, singing and praising the
Lord.
7   Listen to my voice, Lord, when I cry to thee; hear and spare. True to my
9 heart's promise, I have eyes only for thee; I long, Lord, for thy presence. Do not
hide thy face, do not turn away from thy servant in anger, but give me still thy
10 aid; do not forsake me, do not neglect me, O God, my defender. Father and
11 mother may neglect me, but the Lord takes me into his care. Lord, shew me the
way thou hast chosen for me, guide me into the sure path, beset as I am with
12 enemies; do not give me over to the will of my oppressors, when false witnesses
13 stand up to accuse me, breathe out threats against me. My faith is, I will yet
14 live to see the Lord's mercies. Wait patiently for the Lord to help thee; be brave
and let thy heart take comfort; wait patiently for the Lord.

PSALM TWENTY-SEVEN

(Of David.)

TO thee, my Lord, my refuge, I cry aloud, do not leave my cry unanswered;
2 speak to me, or I am no better than a dead man, sinking to the grave. Listen,
Lord, to my plea as I call upon thee, as I raise my hands in prayer towards thy
3 holy temple. Do not summon me, with the wicked, before thy judgement-seat;
with men who traffic in iniquity, men who talk of peace to their neighbours, while
4 their hearts are full of malice. For them, the reward of their own acts, their
5 own evil ways; as they did, be it done to them, in their own coin repaid. Of the
Lord's acts, the Lord's ways, they took no heed; ruin be theirs, ruin irreparable.
6   Blessed be the Lord's name, my plea is heard; the Lord is my strength and
shield. Trusting in him, I found redress; there is triumph in my heart, on my
8 lips the song of praise. The Lord defends his own people, protects the king he
9 has anointed. Lord, save thy people, bless thy own chosen race; be their shepherd, evermore in thy arms upholding them.

PSALM TWENTY-EIGHT

(A psalm. Of David.)

SONS of God, make your offering to the Lord; an offering to the Lord of honour
2 and glory, an offering to the Lord of the glory that befits his name; worship
3 the Lord, in holy vesture habited. The voice of the Lord is heard over the waters,
4 when the glorious God thunders, the Lord, thundering over swollen waters; the
5 Lord's voice in its power, the Lord's voice in its majesty. The Lord's voice, that
6 breaks the cedars; the Lord breaks the cedars of Lebanon; bids Lebanon and
7 Sarion leap high as a bullock leaps, breed of the wild ox. The Lord's voice kindles
8 flashing fire; the Lord's voice makes the wilderness rock; the Lord, rocking the
9 wilderness of Cades. The Lord's voice sets the oak-trees a-swaying, strips the
deep forest bare. Meanwhile, in his sanctuary, there is no sound but tells of his
10 glory. Out of a raging flood, the Lord makes a dwelling-place; the Lord sits en-
11 throned as a king for ever. And this Lord will give strength to his people; the
Lord will give his people his own blessing of peace.

PSALM TWENTY-NINE

(A psalm. A hymn for the feast of the temple's dedication. Of David.)

2 PRAISE to thee, Lord, thou hast taken me under thy protection, and baulked
3 my enemies of their will; I cried out to the Lord my God, and thou didst
4 grant me recovery. So didst thou bring me back, Lord, from the place of shadows,
5 rescue me from the very edge of the grave. Sing praise to the Lord, then, faithful
6 souls, invoke his name with thankfulness. For a moment lasts his anger, for a life-
time his love; sorrow is but the guest of a night, and joy comes in the morning.
7 I, too, had thought, in time of ease, Nothing can shake me now; such power
and state, Lord, had thy mercy granted me. Then thou didst turn thy face away
9 from me, and I was at peace no more. Lord, I was fain to plead with thee, cry
10 upon God for pity: How will it profit thee to take my life? I can but go down into
the grave; and will this dust give thanks to thee, or acknowledge, there, thy faith-
11 fulness? Listen, Lord, and spare; Lord, let thy aid befriend me. With that, thou
didst turn my sadness into rejoicing, thou hast undone the sackcloth I wore, and
13 girded me about with gladness. So may this heart never tire of singing praises;
O Lord my God, I will give thanks to thee for ever.

PSALM THIRTY

(To the choir-master. A psalm. Of David.)

2 TO thee, O Lord, I look for refuge, never let me be ashamed of my trust; in thy
3 faithful care, deliver me. Grant me audience, and make haste to rescue me;
4 my hill-fastness, my stronghold of defence, to save me from peril. Thou dost
strengthen and defend me; thou, for thy own honour, dost guide and escort me;
5 by thee protected, I shall escape from the snare that lies hidden in my path. Into
thy hands I commend my spirit; thou, God ever faithful, wilt claim me for thy-
7 self. Let fools provoke thee by the worship of false gods; for me, no refuge but the
8 Lord. I will triumph and exult in thy mercy; it was thou didst pity my weakness,
9 and save me when I was hard bestead; before the enemy's toils could close around
me, the open plain lay at my feet.
10 And now, Lord, have compassion on my distress; vexation has dimmed my
11 eyes, frets me away, soul and body. My life is all grief, my years are but sighs;
12 for very misery, my strength ebbs away, my frame is wasted. Openly my foes
deride me; even to my neighbours I am a thing of utter scorn; my friends are
13 adread, and the passer-by shuns my contact; I am lost to memory, like a dead
14 man, discarded like a broken pitcher. On every side their busy whispering comes
to my ears; peril all around, so powerful the conspiracy that threatens my life.
15 And still, Lord, my trust in thee is not shaken; still I cry, Thou art my God, my
fate is in thy hand; save me from the enemy's power, save me from my pursuers!
17 Smile on thy servant once more, and deliver me in thy mercy; Lord, do not let
me plead in vain. Disappoint the wicked of their hopes, hurl them down thwarted
19 into the abyss; let silence fall on those treacherous lips, that spoke maliciously
of the innocent in the days of their pride and scorn!
20 What treasures of loving-kindness, Lord, dost thou store up for the men who
21 fear thee, rewarding their confidence for all the world to see! Thy presence is a
sanctuary, to hide them away from the world's malice; thy tabernacle a refuge
22 from its noisy debate. Blessed be the Lord; so wondrous is his mercy, so strong
23 the wall of his protection. I thought, bewildered, that thy watchful care had lost
sight of me; but I cried out to thee, and thou thereupon didst listen to my plea.

24 Love the Lord well, you who worship him; the Lord keeps faith with his servants,
25 and repays the actions of the proud above measure. Take heart, keep high your
courage, all you that wait patiently for the Lord.

PSALM THIRTY-ONE

(Of David. A maskil.)

BLESSED are they who have their faults forgiven, their transgressions buried
2 deep; blessed is the man who is not guilty in the Lord's reckoning, the heart
3 that hides no treason. While I kept my own secret, evermore I went sighing, so
4 wasted my frame away, bowed down day and night by thy chastisement; still my
5 strength ebbed, faint as in mid-summer heat. At last I made my transgression
known to thee, and hid my sin no longer; Fault of mine, said I, I here confess
6 to the Lord; and with that, thou didst remit the guilt of my sin. Let every devout
soul, then, turn to thee in prayer when hard times befall; rise the floods never
7 so high, they shall have no power to reach it. Thou art my hiding-place, when
I am sore bestead; songs of triumph are all about me, and thou my deliverer.
8 Friend, let me counsel thee, trace for thee the path thy feet should tread; let
9 my prudence watch over thee. Do not be like the horse and the mule, senseless
creatures which will not come near thee unless their spirit is tamed by bit and
10 bridle. Again and again the sinner must feel the lash; he who trusts in the Lord
11 finds nothing but mercy all around him. Just souls, be glad, and rejoice in the
Lord; true hearts, make your boast in him.

PSALM THIRTY-TWO

2 TRIUMPH, just souls, in the Lord; true hearts, it is yours to praise him. Give
thanks to the Lord with the viol's music, praise him with a harp of ten strings.
3 For him let a new song be sung; give him of your best, sound the harp lustily.
4 The Lord's word is true, he is faithful in all his dealings; faithfulness he loves,
6 and the just award, the whole earth overflows with the Lord's goodness. It was
the Lord's word that made the heavens, the breath of his lips that peopled them;
7 he it is who stores up the waters of the sea as in a cistern, treasures up all its
8 waves. Let the whole earth hold the Lord in dread, let all the inhabitants of the
9 world stand in awe of him; he spoke, and they were made, he gave his command,
10 and their frame was fashioned. At the Lord's bidding, a nation's purposes come
11 to nothing, a people's designs are thwarted; his own designs stand firm for ever;
generation after generation, his will does not swerve.
12 Blessed the nation that calls the Lord its own God, the people he has chosen
13 out to be his! Looking down from heaven, he watches all mankind, his dwelling-
15 place has the whole world in view; he has fashioned each man's nature, and
16 weighs the actions of each. There is no protection for kings in powerful armies,
17 for warriors in abundant prowess; nor shall horses bring thee the mastery, brute
18 strength that cannot save. It is the Lord, watching over those who fear him and
19 trust in his mercy, that will protect their lives, will feed them in time of famine.
20 Patiently we wait for the Lord's help; he is our strength and our shield; in him
22 our hearts find contentment, in his holy name we trust. Lord, let thy mercy
rest upon us, who put all our confidence in thee.

PSALM THIRTY-THREE

(Of David, when he feigned madness at the court of Abimelech, so that Abimelech sent him away, and he escaped.)

2 AT all times I will bless the Lord; his praise shall be on my lips continually.
3 Be all my boasting in the Lord; listen to me, humble souls, and rejoice. Come,
5 sing the Lord's praise with me, let us extol his name together. Did I not look to
6 the Lord, and find a hearing; did he not deliver me from all my terrors? Ever
look to him, and in him find happiness; here is no room for downcast looks.
7 Friendless folk may still call on the Lord and gain his ear, and be rescued from
8 all their afflictions. Guardian of those who fear the Lord, his angel encamps at
9 their side, and brings deliverance. How gracious the Lord is! Taste and prove it;
10 blessed is the man that learns to trust in him. It is for you, his chosen servants,
11 to fear the Lord; those who fear him never go wanting. Justly do the proud fall
into hunger and want; blessing they lack not that look to him.
12 Know, then, my children, what the fear of the Lord is; come and listen to my
13 teaching. Long life, and prosperous days, who would have these for the asking?
14 My counsel is, keep thy tongue clear of harm, and thy lips free from every treacher-
15 ous word. Naught of evil cherish thou, but rather do good; let peace be all thy
16 quest and aim. On the upright the Lord's eye ever looks favourably; his ears are
17 open to their pleading. Perilous is his frown for the wrong-doers; he will soon
18 make their name vanish from the earth. Roused by the cry of the innocent, the
19 Lord sets them free from all their afflictions. So near is he to patient hearts, so
20 ready to defend the humbled spirit. Though a hundred trials beset the innocent,
21 the Lord will bring him safely through them all. Under the Lord's keeping, every
22 bone of his is safe; not one of them shall suffer harm. Villainy hastes to its own
undoing; the enemies of innocence will bear their punishment.
23 The Lord will claim his servant as his own; they go unreproved that put their
trust in him.

PSALM THIRTY-FOUR

(Of David.)

LORD, espouse my quarrel; disarm the enemies who rise in arms against me;
2 grip target and shield, bestir thyself in my defence. With poised lance, bar
4 the way against my pursuers; whisper in my heart, I am here to save thee. For
my mortal enemies, shame and disappointment; for my ill-wishers one and all,
5 ruin and remorse; chaff before the wind, with the angel of the Lord to scatter
6 them, benighted and bemired on their way, with the angel of the Lord in pursuit!
7 Wantonly they have spread their nets for me, wantonly they have dug the cruel
8 snares; now let sudden doom overtake them, their own nets enmesh, their own
9 snare entrap them! Mine to triumph in the Lord, to boast of the aid he brings me;
10 this be the cry of my whole being, There is none like thee, Lord; who else rescues
the afflicted from the hand of tyranny, the poor, the destitute, from his oppressors?
11 See how perjured witnesses have come forward, to browbeat me over charges of
12 which I know nothing; how they have repaid my kindness with cruelty, and left
13 me friendless! Time was, when these were sick; what did I then? Sackcloth was
14 my wear; rigorously I kept fast, prayed from my heart's depths. I went my way
sadly, as one that mourns for brother or friend, bowed with grief, as one that
15 bewails a mother's loss. And now it was my turn to reel under fortune's blows;
what did they? Gleeful they met, and plotted to attack me unawares; tore at me

16 without ceasing, baited and mocked me, gnashing their teeth in hatred. Lord,
wilt thou look on unheeding still? Wilt thou leave my life at the mercy of these
18 roaring lions? Let me live to praise and thank thee before the multitude that
19 throngs thy courts. No more the leer of triumph in the eye of yonder treacherous
foe, that wantonly assails me!

20   In all their whispering, never a word of peace; they will still be plotting against
21 the land's repose. See how they mop and mow at me, crying out, Joy, joy that
22 we should have lived to see this! Thou too, Lord, hast seen it, do not pass it by
23 in silence; Lord, do not abandon me. Bestir thyself and take my part, give me
24 speedy redress, my Lord and my God. As thou art just, O Lord my God, give
25 thy award for me, never let them triumph over me; never let them think, All
26 goes well, and boast that they have made a prey of me. Disappoint them, fill
them with confusion, the men who delight in my misfortune; cover them with
27 shame and self-reproach, the enemies that triumph over me. Joy and gladness
be theirs, who applaud my innocence; Praise to the Lord! be their cry, the Lord
28 who defends his servant. And all day long, for thy just awarding, this tongue
shall make known thy praise.

PSALM THIRTY-FIVE
(To the choir-master. Of David, the Lord's servant.)

2 DEEP in his heart the sinner hears the whispering of evil, and loses sight of the
3   fear of God; flatters himself with the thought that his misdoings go un-
4 discovered, earn no reproof. No word on his lips but is cruel and false; never a
5 noble thought, a kindly deed. He lies awake plotting mischief, and lends himself
to every evil course, never weary of wrong-doing.

6   Lord, thy mercy is high as heaven; thy faithfulness reaches to the clouds; thy
justice stands firm as the everlasting hills, the wisdom of thy decrees is deep as
8 the abyss. Lord, thou dost give protection to man and beast, so rich is thy divine
mercy; under the shelter of those wings the frail children of earth will find con-
9 fidence. With thy rich store thou wilt nourish them, bid them drink deep at thy
10 fountain of contentment. In thee is the source of all life; thy brightness will break
11 on our eyes like dawn. Still let thy mercy dwell with those who acknowledge thee,
12 thy favour with upright hearts; do not suffer the proud to trample on me, the
13 wicked to dispossess me. See what a fall awaits the wrong-doers, how they are
cast down to earth, and can keep their feet no more!

PSALM THIRTY-SIX
(Of David.)

ART thou impatient, friend, when the wicked thrive; dost thou envy the lot of
2   evil-doers? they will soon fade like the grass, like the green leaf wither away.
3 Be content to trust in the Lord and do good; live on thy land, and take thy ease,
4 all thy longing fixed in the Lord; so he will give thee what thy heart desires.
5 Commit thy life to the Lord, and trust in him; he will prosper thee, making thy
7 honesty clear as the day, the justice of thy cause bright as the sun at noon. Dumb
and patient, to the Lord's mercy look thou, never fretting over the man that has
8 his own way, and thrives by villainy. End thy complaints, forgo displeasure, do
9 not fret thyself into an evil mood; the evil-minded will be dispossessed, and
10 patient souls, that wait for the Lord, succeed them. Forbear yet a little, and the
11 sinner will be seen no more; thou wilt search in vain to find him, while patient
souls are the land's heirs, enjoying great peace.
12   Gnashing his teeth with envy, the wrong-doer plots against the innocent, and

cannot see his own turn coming; but the Lord sees it, and laughs at his malice.
14 How they draw the sword, how they bend the bow, these sinners, to bring ruin
15 on helpless poverty, to murder the upright; swords that will pierce their own
16 hearts, bows that will break in pieces! Innocence, ill endowed, has the better of
17 the wicked in their abundance; soon fails the strength of their arms, and still the
18 Lord has the just in his keeping. Jealously the Lord watches over the lives of the
19 guiltless; they will hold their lands for ever, undismayed by adversity, in time
20 of famine well content. Knavery will yet come to an end; like the spring's finery
21 they will die, the Lord's enemies, vanish away like smoke. Let the sinner borrow,
22 and never repay, still the good man will be a generous giver; win the Lord's
23 blessing, and the land is thine, his ban is death. Man's feet stand firm, if the Lord
24 is with him to prosper his journey; he may stumble but never fall, with the Lord's
25 hand in his. Now youth is past, and I have grown old; yet never did I see the good
26 man forsaken, or his children begging their bread; still he lends without stint,
27 and men call down blessings on his posterity. Offend no more, rather do good,
28 and be at rest continually; the Lord is ever just, and will not abandon his faithful
29 servants. Perish the sinner, forgotten be the name of the evil-doer, but these will
hold their land, and live on it always at rest.

30 Right reason is on the good man's lips, well weighed are all his counsels; his
32 steps never falter, because the law of God rules in his heart. Sinners lie in wait,
33 plotting against the life of the innocent; but the Lord will never leave him in
34 their power, never find him guilty when he is arraigned. Trust the Lord, and
follow the path he has chosen; so he will set thee up in possession of thy land, and
35 thou wilt live to see the wicked come to ruin. Until yesterday, I saw the evil-
36 doer throned high as the branching cedars; then, when I passed by, he was there
37 no longer, and I looked in vain to find him. Virtuous men and innocent mark
38 thou well; he that lives peaceably will leave a race behind him, while sinners are
39 rooted out every one, and their graceless names forgotten. When affliction comes,
40 the Lord is the refuge and defence of the innocent; the Lord will aid and deliver
them, rescue and preserve them from the power of wickedness, because they put
their trust in him.

PSALM THIRTY-SEVEN

(A psalm. Of David. For a memorial.)

2 THY reproof, Lord, not thy vengeance; thy chastisement, not thy condemna-
3 tion! Thy arrows pierce me, thy hand presses me hard; thy anger has driven
away all health from my body, never a bone sound in it, so grievous are my sins.
5 My own wrong-doing towers high above me, hangs on me like a heavy burden;
6 my wounds fester and rankle, with my own folly to blame. Beaten down, bowed
8 to the earth, I go mourning all day long, my whole frame afire, my whole body
9 diseased; so spent, so crushed, I groan aloud in the weariness of my heart. Thou,
11 Lord, knowest all my longings, no complaint of mine escapes thee; restless my
heart, gone my strength; the very light that shone in my eyes is mine no longer.
12 Friends and neighbours that meet me keep their distance from a doomed man;
13 old companions shun me. Ill-wishers that grudge me life itself lay snares about
14 me, threaten me with ruin; relentlessly their malice plots against me. And I, all
15 the while, am deaf to their threats, dumb before my accusers; mine the unheeding
16 ear, and the tongue that utters no defence. On thee, Lord, my hopes are set; thou,
17 O Lord my God, wilt listen to me. Such is the prayer I make, Do not let my
18 enemies triumph over me, boast of my downfall. Fall full well I may; misery
19 clouds my view; I am ever ready to publish my guilt, ever anxious over my sin.
20 Unprovoked, their malice still prevails; so many that bear me a grudge so wan-

21 tonly, rewarding good with evil, and for the very rightness of my cause assailing
23 me. Do not fail me, O Lord my God, do not forsake me; hasten to my defence,
O Lord, my only refuge.

PSALM THIRTY-EIGHT

(To the choir-master, Idithun. A psalm. Of David.)

2 IT was my resolve to live watchfully, and never use my tongue amiss; still, while
3 I was in the presence of sinners, I kept my mouth gagged, dumb and patient,
4 impotent for good. But indignation came back, and my heart burned within
5 me, the fire kindled by my thoughts, so that at last I kept silence no longer.

Lord, warn me of my end, and how few my days are; teach me to know my own
6 insufficiency. See how thou hast measured my years with a brief span, how my
life is nothing in thy reckoning! Nay, what is any man living but a breath that
7 passes? Truly man walks the world like a shadow; with what vain anxiety he
8 hoards up riches, when he cannot tell who will have the counting of them! What
9 hope then is mine, Lord? In thee alone I trust. Clear me of that manifold guilt
10 which makes me the laughing-stock of fools, tongue-tied and uncomplaining,
11 because I know that my troubles come from thee; spare me this punishment; I
12 faint under thy powerful hand. When thou dost chasten man to punish his sins,
gone is all he loved, as if the moth had fretted it away; a breath that passes, and
13 no more. Listen, Lord, to my prayer, let my cry reach thy hearing, and my tears
win answer. What am I in thy sight but a passer-by, a wanderer, as all my
14 fathers were? Thy frown relax, give me some breath of comfort, before I go
away and am known no more.

PSALM THIRTY-NINE

(To the choir-master. Of David. A psalm.)

2 PATIENTLY I waited for the Lord's help, and at last he turned his look to-
3 wards me; he listened to my plea, drew me up out of a deadly pit, where the
mire had settled deep, and gave me a foothold on the rock, with firm ground to
4 tread. He has framed a new music on my lips, a song of praise to our God, to fill
5 all that stand by with reverence, and with trust in the Lord. Happy is the man
whose trust is there bestowed, who shuns the rites of strange gods, the lure of lies.
6 O Lord my God, how long is the story of thy marvellous deeds! Was ever care
7 like thine? How should I tell the tale of those mercies, past all numbering? No
sacrifice, no offering was thy demand; enough that thou hast given me an ear
ready to listen. Thou hast not found any pleasure in burnt-sacrifices, in sacrifices
8 for sin. See then, I said, I am coming to fulfil what is written of me, where the
9 book lies unrolled; to do thy will, O my God, is all my desire, to carry out that
10 law of thine which is written in my heart. And I told the story of thy just dealings
11 before a great throng; be witness, Lord, that I do not seal my lips. Thy
just dealings are no secret hidden away in my heart; I boast of thy faithful protection, proclaim that mercy, that faithfulness of thine for all to hear it.
12 Lord, do not withhold thy pity from me; thy mercy and faithfulness that have
13 ever been my shield. I am beset with evils past numbering, overtaken by my sins;
they fill my prospect, countless as the hairs on my head; my courage fails me.
14 Deign, Lord, to set me free; Lord, give heed and help. Disappointment and
shame be theirs, who lay plots against my life; may they slink away covered with
16 confusion, who now rejoice over my downfall. Joy, joy! is their cry; dumb-
17 stricken let them stand, their hopes belied. Rejoicing and triumph for all the souls
that look to thee; Praise to the Lord, will ever be their song, who now long for thy

18 aid. I, so helpless, so destitute, and the Lord is concerned for me! Thou art my champion and my refuge; do not linger, my God, do not linger on the way.

PSALM FORTY

(To the choir-master. A psalm. Of David.)

2 BLESSED is that man who takes thought for the poor and the destitute; the
3 Lord will keep him safe in time of trouble. The Lord will watch over him, and give him long life and happiness on earth, and baulk his enemies of their
4 will. The Lord will sustain him when he lies bed-ridden, turn all to health in his sickness.
5 Lord have mercy on me, is my prayer; bring healing to a soul that has sinned
6 against thee. Bitterly my enemies taunt me; How long, they ask, ere he will die,
7 and his name be forgotten? When one comes to visit me, he comes with smooth
8 words, his heart full of malice, ready to go out and plot against me. There they
9 stand, my enemies, talking of me in whispers, devising hurt; Here is a foul plague
10 loosed on him; he will leave his bed no more. Why, the very man I trusted most, my own intimate friend, who shared my bread, has lifted his heel to trip me up.
11 Lord, have mercy on me; give me back health, and let me requite them! Proof
13 of thy favour, my enemies are baulked of their triumph; thou dost befriend my innocence; nevermore wilt thou banish me from thy presence.
14 Blessed be the Lord God of Israel, from the beginning to the end of time, Amen, Amen.

PSALM FORTY-ONE

(To the choir-master. A maskil. Of the sons of Core.)

2 O GOD, my whole soul longs for thee, as a deer for running water; my whole
soul thirsts for God, the living God; shall I never again make my pilgrimage
4 into God's presence? Morning and evening, my diet still of tears! Daily I must
5 listen to the taunt, Where is thy God now? Memories come back to me yet, melting the heart; how once I would join with the throng, leading the way to God's house, amid cries of joy and thanksgiving, and all the noise of holiday.
6 Soul, art thou still downcast? Wilt thou never be at peace? Wait for God's help; I will not cease to cry out in thankfulness, My champion and my God.
7 In my sad mood I will think of thee, here in this land of Jordan and Hermon,
8 here on Misar mountain. One depth makes answer to another amid the roar of the floods thou sendest; wave after wave, crest after crest overwhelms me.
9 Would he but lighten the day with his mercy, what praise would I sing at evening
10 to the Lord God who is life for me! Thou art my stronghold, I cry out to him still; hast thou never a thought for me? Must I go mourning, with enemies
11 pressing me hard; racked by the ceaseless taunts of my persecutors. Where is
12 thy God now? Soul, art thou still downcast? Wilt thou never be at peace? Wait for God's help; I will not cease to cry out in thankfulness, My champion and my God.

PSALM FORTY-TWO

O GOD, sustain my cause; give me redress against a race that knows no piety;
2 save me from a treacherous foe and cruel. Thou, O God, art all my strength; why hast thou cast me off? Must I go mourning, with enemies pressing me hard?
3 The light of thy presence, the fulfilment of thy promise, let these be my escort, bringing me safe to thy holy mountain, to the tabernacle where thou dwellest.
4 There I will go up to the altar of God, the giver of triumphant happiness; thou art

5 my own God, with the harp I hymn thy praise. Soul, art thou still downcast?
Wilt thou never be at peace? Wait for God's help; I will not cease to cry out in
thankfulness, My champion and my God.

PSALM FORTY-THREE

(To the choir-master. Of the sons of Core. A maskil.)

2 O GOD, the tale has come to our ears—have not our fathers told it?—of the
3 great things thou didst in their time, in days long ago; it was thy power that
gave them a home by rooting out the heathen, crushing and dispossessing nations
4 to make room for them. It was not by their own sword that our fathers won the
land, it was not their own strength that brought them victory; it was the work of
5 thy hand, thy strength; thy smile shone upon them, in proof of thy favour. I too
6 have no King, no God, save thee; who else sent deliverance to Jacob? Through
thee we routed our enemies; under thy protection we crushed their onslaught.
7 Not in my bow I trusted, not to my sword I looked for safety; thine it was to
9 save us from our enemies, and cover their malice with confusion. In God was
ever our boast; his name we praise unceasingly.
10   And now? Now, O God, thou hast disowned us, and put us to shame, by refus-
11 ing to go into battle with our armies. Thou dost put us to flight before our
12 enemies; our ill-wishers plunder us as they will. Thou hast made us like sheep
13 sold for food, scattered here and there among the heathen; thou hast bartered
14 away thy people without profit, asking no rich amends for thy loss. Thou hast
turned us into a laughing-stock for our neighbours, mocked and derided by all
15 who dwell around; till the heathen make a by-word of us, and Gentiles toss their
16 heads at us in scorn. Ever my disgrace confronts me; my cheeks are covered with
17 blushes, as I hear nothing but reproach and reviling, see none but enemies, none
but persecutors.
18   All this has come upon us, and it was not that we had forgotten thee. We have
19 not been untrue to thy covenant, or withdrawn our hearts from thee, that we
20 should let our steps wander away from thy paths. And all the while thou wouldst
21 bring us low, anguish on every side, darkness hanging over us. If we had forgotten the name of our own God, and spread out our hands in prayer to the gods
22 of the alien, would not he know of it? He can read the secrets of men's hearts.
23 No, it is for thy sake that we face death at every moment, reckoned no better than
24 sheep marked down for slaughter. Bestir thyself, Lord, why dost thou sleep on?
25 Awake, do not banish us from thy presence for ever. How canst thou turn thy
26 face away, without a thought for our need and our affliction? Our pride is bowed
27 in the dust; prostrate, we cannot lift ourselves from the ground. Arise, Lord, and
help us; in thy mercy, claim us for thy own.

PSALM FORTY-FOUR

(To the choir-master. Melody: The Lilies. To the sons of Core. A maskil. A
love-song.)

2 JOYFUL the thoughts that well up from my heart, the King's honour for my
3 theme; my tongue flows readily as the pen of a swift writer. Thine is more than
mortal beauty, thy lips overflow with gracious utterance; the blessings God has
4 granted thee can never fail. Gird on thy sword at thy side, great warrior, gird
5 thyself with all thy majesty and all thy beauty; ride on triumphant, in the name
6 of faithfulness and justice. Dread counsel thy own might shall give thee; so sharp
are thy arrows, subduing nations to thy will, daunting the hearts of the king's

7 enemies. Thy throne, O God, endures for ever and ever, the sceptre of thy
8 royalty is a rod that rules true; thou hast been a friend to right, an enemy to
wrong, and God, thy own God, has given thee an unction to bring thee pride
9 beyond any of thy fellows. Thy garments are scented with myrrh, and aloes, and
10 cassia; from ivory palaces there are harps sounding in thy honour. Daughters of
kings come out to meet thee; at thy right hand stands the queen, in Ophir gold
11 arrayed. (Listen, my daughter, and consider my words attentively; thou art to
12 forget, henceforward, thy own nation, and the house of thy fathers; thy beauty,
now, is all for the king's delight; he is thy Lord, and worship belongs to him.)
13 The people of Tyre, too, will have its presents to bring; the noblest of its citizens
14 will be courting thy favour. She comes, the princess, all fair to see, her robe of
15 golden cloth, a robe of rich embroidery, to meet the King. The maidens of her
16 court follow her into thy presence, all rejoicing, all triumphant, as they enter the
17 king's palace! Thou shalt have sons worthy of thy own fathers, and divide a
18 world between them for their domains. While time lasts, mine it is to keep thy
name in remembrance; age after age, nations will do thee honour.

PSALM FORTY-FIVE

(To the choir-master. To the sons of Core. Melody: The Virgins. A song.)

2 GOD is our refuge and stronghold; sovereign aid he has brought us in the hour
3 of peril. Not for us to be afraid, though earth should tumble about us, and the
4 hills be carried away into the depths of the sea. See how its waters rage and roar,
how the hills tremble before its might! The Lord of hosts is with us, the God
of Jacob is our refuge.
5   But the city of God, enriched with flowing waters, is the chosen sanctuary of
6 the most High, God dwells within her, and she stands unmoved; with break of
7 dawn he will grant her deliverance. Nations may be in turmoil, and thrones totter,
8 earth shrink away before his voice; but the Lord of hosts is with us, the God of
9 Jacob is our refuge. Come near, and see God's acts, his marvellous acts done on
10 earth; how he puts an end to wars all over the world, the bow shivered, the
11 lances shattered, the shields burnt to ashes! Wait quietly, and you shall have
proof that I am God, claiming empire among the nations, claiming empire over
12 the world. The Lord of hosts is with us, the God of Jacob is our refuge.

PSALM FORTY-SIX

(To the choir-master. Of the sons of Core. A psalm.)

2 CLAP your hands, all you nations, in applause; acclaim your God with cries
3 of rejoicing; The Lord is high above us, and worthy of dread; he is the sove-
4 reign Ruler of all the earth; he has tamed the nations to our will, bowed the Gen-
5 tiles at our feet, claimed us for his own portion, Jacob the fair, the well beloved.
6 God goes up, loud are the cries of victory; the Lord goes up, loudly the trumpets
7 peal. A psalm, a psalm for our God, a psalm, a psalm for our King! God is
9 King of all the earth; sound the hymn of praise! God reigns over the heathen,
10 God sits enthroned in holiness. The rulers of the nations throw in their lot with
us, that worship Abraham's God; a God so high, he has all earth's princes for his
vassals.

PSALM FORTY-SEVEN

(A song. A psalm. Of the sons of Core.)

2 THE Lord is great, great honour is his due, here in the city where he, our God,
3 dwells. Fair rises the peak of his holy mountain, the pride of the whole world,

4 and the true pole of earth, mount Sion, the city of the great King; within those
5 walls, God has proved himself a sure defence. See how the kings of the earth
6 have made common cause, and met there in arms! At the sight of her all was
7 bewilderment, and confusion, and dismay; fear took hold of them, sudden as the
8 throes of a woman in travail; not more ruinously on ocean-going ships falls the
9 east wind. Here, in this city of the Lord of hosts, the city of our own God, we
have proved the tale long since told us, that God upholds her for all eternity;
10 sheltered in thy temple, we give thanks for our deliverance. O God, wherever thy
12 name is known on earth, thy praise is told, ever just in thy dealings; well may
the hill of Sion rejoice, well may the townships of Juda triumph, at the decrees
13 which thou, Lord, hast executed. Walk about Sion, make the round of her towers,
14 and count the number of them; mark well the defences that are hers, pass all
15 her strongholds in review; then give the word to the next generation, Such is the
God, who is our God for ever and ever; our Shepherd eternally.

PSALM FORTY-EIGHT

(To the choir-master. Of the sons of Core. A psalm.)

2 LISTEN, you nations far and wide; let all the world give hearing, poor clods
4 of earth, and men nobly born, for rich and poor the same lesson. Here are
5 wise words, thoughts of a discerning heart; mine to overhear mysteries, and
reveal, with the harp's music, things of deep import.
6 What need have I to be afraid in troubled times, when malice dogs my heels
7 and overtakes me, malice of foes who trust in their own strength, and boast of
8 their great possessions? No man can deliver himself from his human lot, paying
9 a ransom-price to God; too great is the cost of a man's soul; never will the means
10 be his to prolong his days eternally and escape death. True it is, wise men die;
12 but reckless fools perish no less; their riches will go to others, and the grave will
be their everlasting home. Age after age, they will live on there, under the fields
13 they once called their own. Short is man's enjoyment of earthly goods; match
him with the brute beasts, and he is no better than they.
14 Fatal path, that ensnares the reckless! Pitiful end of the men that love life!
15 There they lie in the world beneath, huddled like sheep, with death for their
shepherd, the just for their masters; soon, soon their image fades, the grave for
16 its tenement. But my life God will rescue from the power of that lower darkness,
17 a life that finds acceptance with him. Do not be disturbed, then, when a man
18 grows rich, and there is no end to his household's magnificence; he cannot take
all that with him when he dies, magnificence will not follow him to the grave.
19 While life lasts, he calls himself happy: None but will envy my success; but soon
21 he will be made one with the line of his fathers, never again to see the light. Short
is man's careless enjoyment of earthly goods; match him with the brute beasts,
and he is no better than they.

PSALM FORTY-NINE

IT is the Lord God that speaks; his message goes out to all the earth, from the
2 sun's rise to its setting. Out of Sion, in perfect beauty, God comes, revealed;
he will keep silence no longer. Before him goes a raging fire; there is a whirling
4 storm round about him. So, from on high, he summons heaven and earth to
5 witness the judgement pronounced on his people: Muster in my presence my
6 faithful servants, who honour my covenant still with sacrifice. The heavens themselves pronounce him just, God who is our judge.

7 Listen, my people, to these words of mine, listen, Israel, to the protestation
8 I make thee; I, the God thou ownest as God. I do not find fault with thee over
9 thy sacrifices; why, all day long thy burnt-offerings smoke before me. But the
10 gifts I accept are not cattle from thy stock, or buck-goats from thy folds; I own
already every wild beast in the forest, the hills are mine, and the herds that people
11 them. There is no bird flies in heaven, no life stirs in the countryside, but I know
12 of it. If I am hungry, I will not complain of it to thee, I, who am master of earth
13 and all that earth contains. Wouldst thou have me eat bull's flesh, and drink the
14 blood of goats? The sacrifice thou must offer to God is a sacrifice of praise, so
15 wilt thou perform thy vows to the most High. So, when thou criest to me in time
of trouble, I will deliver thee; then thou shalt honour me as thou wilt.
16 But thus, to the sinner, God speaks: How is it that thou canst repeat my com-
17 mandments by rote, and boast of my covenant with thee, and thou, all the while,
hast no love for the amendment of thy ways, casting every warning of mine to the
18 winds? Swift thou art to welcome the thief who crosses thy path, to throw in thy
19 lot with the adulterers. Malice wells up from thy lips, and thy tongue is a ready
20 engine of deceit; thou wilt sit there in conclave, speaking evil of thy brother,
21 traducing thy own mother's son. Such were thy ways, and should I make no sign?
Should I let thee think I am such as thou? Here is thy reproof; here is thy indict-
22 ment made plain to thee. Think well on this, you that forget God, or his hand
23 will fall suddenly, and there will be no delivering you. He honours me truly,
who offers me a sacrifice of praise; live aright, and you shall see the saving power
of God.

PSALM FIFTY

2 (To the choir-master. A psalm. Of David, when the prophet Nathan came to
reproach him for his adultery with Bethsabee.)

3 HAVE mercy on me, O God, as thou art ever rich in mercy; in the abundance
4 of thy compassion, blot out the record of my misdeeds. Wash me clean,
5 cleaner yet, from my guilt, purge me of my sin, the guilt which I freely acknow-
6 ledge, the sin which is never lost to my sight. Thee only my sins have offended;
it is thy will I have disobeyed; thy sentence was deserved, and still when thou
7 givest award thou hast right on thy side. For indeed, I was born in sin; guilt was
8 with me already when my mother conceived me. But thou art a lover of faithful-
9 ness, and now, deep in my heart, thy wisdom has instructed me. Sprinkle me
with a wand of hyssop, and I shall be clean; washed, I shall be whiter than snow;
10 tidings send me of good news and rejoicing, and the body that lies in the dust
shall thrill with pride.
11 Turn thy eyes away from my sins, blot out the record of my guilt; my God,
bring a clean heart to birth within me; breathe new life, true life, into my being.
13 Do not banish me from thy presence, do not take thy holy spirit away from me;
14 give me back the comfort of thy saving power, and strengthen me in generous
15 resolve. So will I teach the wicked to follow thy paths; sinners shall come back
16 to thy obedience. My God, my divine Deliverer, save me from the guilt of blood-
17 shed! This tongue shall boast of thy mercies; O Lord, thou wilt open my lips,
18 and my mouth shall tell of thy praise. Thou hast no mind for sacrifice, burnt-
19 offerings, if I brought them, thou wouldst refuse; here, O God, is my sacrifice,
a broken spirit; a heart that is humbled and contrite thou, O God, wilt never
20 disdain. Lord, in thy great love send prosperity to Sion, so that the walls of Jeru-
21 salem may rise again. Then indeed thou wilt take pleasure in solemn sacrifice,
in gift and burnt-offering; then indeed bullocks will be laid upon thy altar.

PSALM FIFTY-ONE

2 (To the choir-master. A maskil. Of David, when Doeg, the Edomite, came and
told Saul, David went into Abimelech's house.)

3 WILT thou still take pride, infamous tyrant, in thy power to harm? Evermore
4 thou settest thy heart on mischief; thy words are razor-edged, and thou a
5 traitor. Cruelty, never kindness, is thy study, treason, never honest speech; well
7 thy false lips love the word that brings men to ruin. And will not God destroy
thee utterly, root thee up, drive thee from thy home, till thy stock is known among
8 living men no more? Honest folk will watch, and wonder, and taunt him then;
9 So much for the man who would have none of God's help, but relied on his store
10 of riches, and found his strength in knavery? And I? rooted like a fruitful olive-
11 tree in the house of my God, I will trust for ever in his divine mercy; I will give
thee eternal thanks for all thou hast done, and boast, as men should ever boast,
of thy name, the faithful for my company.

PSALM FIFTY-TWO

(To the choir-master. The Melody, Mahalat. A maskil. Of David.)

2 THERE is no God above us, is the fond thought of reckless hearts. Warped
natures everywhere and hateful lives, there is not an innocent man among them.
3 God looks down from heaven at the race of men, to find one soul that reflects,
4 and goes in search of him; but no, all have missed the mark and rebelled against
5 him; an innocent man is nowhere to be found. What, can they learn nothing, all
these traffickers in iniquity, who feed themselves fat on this people of mine, as if
6 it were bread for their eating, and never invoke God's name? What wonder if
fear unmans them, where they have no cause for fear? Where are the foes that
hemmed thee round? God has scattered their bones far and wide, forgotten as his
7 enemies must ever be. Oh, may Sion bring deliverance to Israel! Day of gladness
for Jacob, day of Israel's triumph, when God restores the fortunes of his own
people.

PSALM FIFTY-THREE

2 (To the choir-master. For stringed instruments. A maskil. Of David, when the
men of Ziph told Saul that David was in hiding among them.)

3 LORD, by the virtue of thy name deliver me, let thy sovereign power grant me
4 redress; give a hearing, Lord, to my plea; let me speak, and know thou art
5 listening. Scornful foes take arms against me, fierce foes that grudge me life itself,
6 with no thought of God to check them. Ah, but God is here to help me; the Lord
7 has my safety in his keeping. Let the blow recoil on my persecutors; ever faithful
8 to thy word, do thou overthrow them. So will I joyfully offer thee sacrifice, and
9 praise thy name, Lord, as praised it must ever be; who else has delivered me
from all peril, and let me see the downfall of my enemies?

PSALM FIFTY-FOUR

(To the choir-master. For stringed instruments. A maskil. Of David.)

2 GIVE audience to my prayer, O God; do not spurn this plea of mine; hear
4 and grant relief. No rest I find in my distress, daunted ever by the hue and
5 cry of godless enemies, whose malicious spite would compass my ruin. My

6 heart is full of whirling thoughts; the fear of death stands over me; trembling
7 and terrified, I see perils closing round me. Had I but wings, I cry, as a dove
8 has wings, to fly away and find rest! Far would I flee; the wilderness should be
9 my shelter, so I might find speedy refuge from the whirlwind and the storm.
10   Plunge them deep, Lord, in ruin, bring dissension into their councils! Do I not
11 see, already, violence and sedition in the city? Day and night they make the
   round of its walls, and all the while there is wrong and oppression at the heart of
12 it, its treacherous heart; cruelty and cunning walk ever in its streets. Had some
   enemy decried me, I could have borne it patiently; some open ill-wisher, I could
14 have sheltered myself from his attack. But thou, my second self, my familiar
15 friend! How pleasant was the companionship we shared, thou and I; how lov-
16 ingly we walked as fellow pilgrims to the house of God! May death overtake
   them, may the abyss swallow them up alive, their homes, their hearts so tainted
   with evil!
17   Still I will call upon God, and the Lord will save; still at evening and morn
   and noon I will cry aloud and make my plea known; he will not be deaf to my
19 appeal. He will win my soul peace, will rescue me from attack, when many take
20 part against me. He, the God who reigned before time was, will listen to me,
21 will bring them low. Never a change of heart, never the fear of God; not one
22 but will turn against his friend, break his pledged word. Smooth as butter their
   looks, when their hearts are all hatred; soft as oil their speech, yet never was
   drawn sword so deadly.
23   Cast the burden of thy cares upon the Lord, and he will sustain thee; never
24 will he let thee stumble, his servant if thou be. These, O God, thou wilt sink
   in a pit of ruin; the blood-thirsty, the treacherous, will not live out half their days;
   but I, Lord, will put my trust in thee.

PSALM FIFTY-FIVE

(To the choir-master. Melody: Yonat Elem Rehoquim. Of David. A miktam.
When the Philistines had him in their hands at Gath.)

2 HAVE mercy on me, O God, downtrodden evermore by man's cruel oppres-
3 sion; evermore my enemies tread me under foot, so many there are to make
4 war upon me. In thee, the most High, I will put my trust when peril overtakes
5 me. I claim God's promise; my trust is in God, no mortal threat can daunt me.
6 Evermore they traduce me, have no thought but for my undoing; conspire in
8 secret, watching my steps as they plot against my life! O God, requite their
9 treachery; trample on the Gentiles in thy anger. My wandering life none knows
10 as thou; no tear of mine but thou dost hoard and record it. One cry raised to thee,
11 and my enemies are driven back; shall I doubt God is on my side? I claim God's
12 promise; my trust is in God, man's threats cannot daunt me. The vows which
14 thou claimest from me, O God, my sacrifice of praise shall fulfil; hast thou not
   saved my life from every peril, my feet from every slip? And shall I not enjoy
   God's favour, while the light of life is with me?

PSALM FIFTY-SIX

(To the choir-master. Melody: Do not destroy. Of David. A miktam. When he
took refuge from Saul in a cave.)

2 HAVE mercy on me, O God, have mercy on me; here is a soul that puts its
   trust in thee, I will take refuge under the shelter of thy wings, till the storms
3 pass by. I will cry out to the most high God, the God who has ever befriended

4 me: may he send aid now from heaven to deliver me, and bring confusion on my
5 oppressors; his mercy, his faithfulness be my speed! Fallen among lions I, that
hungrily eat men's flesh; here are envious teeth that bite deeper than spear or
6 arrow, tongues sharp as any sword. O God, mount high above the heavens, till
7 thy glory overshadows the whole earth. See where they have laid a snare for my
8 feet, to bring me low, dug a pit in my path; may it be their own undoing! A true
9 heart, my God, a heart true to thy service; its song, its music are for thee! Wake,
10 all my skill, wake, echoes of harp and viol; dawn shall find me watching; so will
I give thee thanks, Lord, for all the world to hear it, sing psalms while the
11 Gentiles listen, of thy mercy, high as heaven itself, of thy faithfulness, that
12 reaches to the clouds. O God, mount high above the heavens, till thy glory overshadows the whole earth.

PSALM FIFTY-SEVEN

(To the choir-master. Melody: Do not destroy. Of David. A miktam.)

2 NOBLES all, are they honest words you utter? And you, common folk, do you
3 make just award? See how you devise treachery in your hearts, deal out to
4 this land nothing but oppression! Sinners that left the womb only to go a-straying;
5 renegades and liars their mothers bore them! They are venomous as serpents,
6 as the asp that turns a deaf ear and will not listen to the snake-charmer's music,
7 skilful player though he be. My God, break their cruel fangs; Lord, shatter
8 their jaws, strong as the jaws of lions. Like spilt water let them run to waste,
9 shoot none but harmless arrows; melt into nothing, the snail's way, perish
10 like the untimely birth that sees never the light of the sun. Green stalks the whirl-
11 wind carries away, while yonder pot still waits for fuel! The innocent man will
triumph at the sight of their punishment, as he dips his hands in the blood of the
12 evil-doer; Sure enough, men will say, innocence has its reward, sure enough,
there is a God who grants redress here on earth.

PSALM FIFTY-EIGHT

(To the choir-master. Melody: Do not destroy. Of David. A Miktam. When Saul
had his house watched, so as to put him to death.)

2 O GOD, deliver me from my enemies, rescue me from their assaults; thwart
4 their treacherous designs, disappoint their lust for blood. See how they plot
against my life, how strong is their confederacy! Yet never, Lord, through any
5 fault or offence of mine; unprovoked, they rush to the attack. Bestir thyself, come
6 to my side and witness my wrongs. Lord of hosts, God of Israel, awake; a world
7 chastise, and shew the treacherous no mercy. See how they come back at night-
8 fall, like yelping dogs, to prowl about the city! Tongues that boast, lips that rail,
9 as if none could hear them; and all the while thou, Lord, makest light of them,
10 thou, in whose esteem all the nations are as nothing. To thee I look, the God
11 who strengthens me, the God who watches over me; my God, and all my hope
of mercy.
12 With that divine aid, may I triumph over my enemies. Smite them down, my
God, before they compass the overthrow of my people; let that power of thine
13 overawe and crush them, my protector, my Master! Down with the guilty
tongues, the boastful lips; let their own pride ensnare them, their cursing and their
14 lies. Ruinous, ruinous be thy vengeance, overwhelming them; shew them that
15 there is a God who rules over Jacob, rules over the utmost ends of the earth. Back
16 come they at nightfall, like yelping dogs, and prowl about the city; far and wide

they will roam in search of their prey, and snarl with rage when they go unfed at
17 last. And I, ere long, will be proclaiming thy greatness, will be triumphing in
the mercy thou hast shewn me, thou, my stronghold and my refuge in my hour
18 of peril. To thee I will sing, the God who strengthens me, the God who watches
over me, my God, and all my hope of mercy.

PSALM FIFTY-NINE

(To the choir-master. Melody: Lily of the Law. A miktam. Of David. To be
2 used for teaching. This was when he marched against the Syrians of Naharaim
and Soba, and Joab on his way home defeated the men of Edom in the Valley
of Salt, twelve thousand of them.)

3 TOO long, O God, hast thou disowned us, and scattered our armies in flight;
4 thy wrath forgo, and bring us back to our own. Heal the wounds of the land
5 thou hast shaken and torn asunder, the land that trembles still. Heavy the burden
thou didst lay on us; such a draught thou didst brew for us as made our senses
6 reel. But now thou hast set up a standard to rally thy faithful servants, and to
7 protect them from the archers' onset; now bring aid to the men thou lovest, give
our prayer answer, and lift thy right hand to save.
8 God's word came to us from his sanctuary, In triumph I will divide up Sichem,
9 and parcel out the valley of Tents; to me Galaad, to me Manasse belongs;
10 Ephraim is my helmet, Juda the staff I bear. Now Moab, too, shall be my drudge;
11 over Edom I will claim my right; I will lead the Philistines away in triumph. Such
was the oracle; but now who is to lead me on my march against this fortress, who
12 is to find an entrance for me into Edom, when thou, O God, hast disowned us, and
13 wilt not go into battle with our armies? It is thou that must deliver us from peril;
14 vain is the help of man. Only through God can we fight victoriously; only he can
trample our oppressors in the dust.

PSALM SIXTY

(To the choir-master. For stringed instruments. Of David.)

2 LISTEN, Lord, to this cry of appeal; do not let my prayer go unheeded, though
it be from the ends of the earth that I call upon thee. When my heart misgives
4 me, thou wilt set me high up on a rock, thou wilt bring me repose; thou, my only
5 hope, my strong tower against the assault of my enemies. Oh let me dwell for
6 ever in thy tabernacle, let me take refuge under the shelter of thy wings! Lord,
thou hast listened to my prayer, a domain thou hast given me where thy name
7 is held in awe. Year upon year do thou add to the king's reign; while generations
8 come and go, may his life still last. For ever may he reign under God's favour;
9 let mercy and faithfulness be his escort. Eternally I will sing thy praises, day
after day perform my vows.

PSALM SIXTY-ONE

(To the choir-master. Melody: Idithun. A psalm. Of David.)

2 NO rest has my soul but in God's hands; to him I look for deliverance. I have
no other stronghold, no other deliverer but him; safe in his protection, I fear
4 no deadly fall. Still one man my enemies single out for their onslaught, not
5 gaping hedge or ruinous wall more ripe for overthrow; from my safe fastness they
would fain dislodge me, ready liars that speak me fair, but ever with a curse in

6 their hearts. Yet even now, my soul, leave thyself in God's hands; all my trust
7 is in him. He is my stronghold and my deliverer, my protector, bidding me stand
8 unmoved. God is all my defence and all my boast; my rock-fastness, my refuge
9 is in God. Israelites, put ever your trust in him, and lay the homage of your
  hearts at his feet; God is our defence.
10   Man is a breath that passes; in Adam's sons there is no trust; high in the
11 scales they rise, weighed all together and lighter than a breath. Put your faith
   in extortion no more, boast no more of plunder; set never your heed on mount-
12 ing store of riches. Not once, but twice I have heard God's voice of warning;
13 all power is God's. To thee, Lord, mercy belongs; thou wilt repay every man
   the reward of his deeds.

PSALM SIXTY-TWO

(A psalm. Of David. This was when he was in the desert of Juda.)

2 O GOD, thou art my God; how eager my quest for thee, body athirst and soul
3   longing for thee, like some parched wilderness, where stream is none! So
  in the holy place, I contemplate thee, ready for the revelation of thy greatness,
4 thy glory. To win thy favour is dearer to me than life itself; my songs of praise
5 can no more be withheld. So, all my life long, I will bless thee, holding up my
6 hands in honour of thy name; my heart filled, as with some rich feast, my mouth,
7 in joyful accents, singing thy praise. My thoughts shall go out to thee at dawn, as
8 I lie awake remembering thee, and the protection thou hast given me. Gladly
9 I take shelter under thy wings, cling close to thee, borne up by thy protecting
10 hand. In vain do my enemies plot against my life, soon to be swallowed up in the
12 depths of earth, a prey to the sword, carrion for jackals! The king shall triumph
   in God's protection, blessed as they are ever blessed who take their vows in his
   name; silence shall fall on the lips that muttered treason.

PSALM SIXTY-THREE

(To the choir-master. A psalm. Of David.)

2 O GOD, listen to my prayer when I plead with thee, save me from the threats of
3   my mortal foe. Thine to defend me from this conspiracy of malice, this
4 throng of evil-doers; the tongues that wound like a sharpened sword, the
5 poisoned words aimed at me, like arrows. Stealthily they attack the innocent:
6 suddenly, from a safe vantage-point, they wound him. See them pledged to an
  infamous resolve, plotting to lay snares for me, sure that they will go unseen!
7 With what care they hatch their designs, planning treason double-dyed! Let the
8 thoughts of man's heart be deep as they will, yet God has arrows, too, to smite
9 them with, sudden wounds to deal them; all their conspiring plays them false.
10 Scornfully the onlookers shake their heads, awe-stricken every one; who but will
11 acclaim God's power, who but will ponder his great acts? Honest men will rejoice
   and put their trust in the Lord; upright hearts will not boast in vain.

PSALM SIXTY-FOUR

(To the choir-master. A psalm. Of David. A song.)

2 O GOD, thou shalt yet have praise in Sion; to thee let the vow be paid, hearer
4   of prayer. To thee all mankind must look for pardon, weighed down by its
5 sinfulness till thou dost forgive. Blessed the man on whom thy choice falls, whom

thou takest to dwell with thee in thy own domain! Fill these hearts with love of
6 thy house, with awe of thy holy temple.   Wonderful the miracles thou shewest
when in mercy thou dost hear us, O God our Saviour; at the bounds of earth, far
7 over the seas, in thee we hope.   What power girds thee about! In thy strength
8 the mountains stand firm;   thou dost calm the raging of the sea, raging sea-
9 billows, ay, and the turmoil of angry nations.   Thy portents strike terror at the
10 world's end, fill the lands of sunrise and sunset with rejoicing.   And now thou
hast brought relief to this land of ours, hast watered and greatly enriched it; deep
11 flows the channel whence thy divine providence grants us food;   long time thou
dost prepare it, watering the furrow, loosening the clods, multiplying the grain.
12 Thy bounty it is that crowns the year; where thy feet have passed, the stream of
13 plenty flows; flows through the desert pastures, till all the hill-sides are gaily
14 clad,   herds throng the fields, and the valleys stand deep in corn; the shout of joy
everywhere, everywhere the hymn of praise.

PSALM SIXTY-FIVE

(To the choir-master. A song. A psalm.)

2 LET the whole world keep holiday in God's presence, sing praise to his name,
3 pay homage to his glory!   Cry out to God, What dread, Lord, thy acts inspire!
How great is that might of thine, which makes thy enemies cringe before thee!
4 Let the whole earth worship thee, sing of thee, sing praises to thy name.   Come
near, and see what God does, how wonderful he is in his dealings with human
6 kind,   how he turns the sea into land, and lets men cross a river dry-shod; ours
7 to rejoice in his mercy.   In that power of his he reigns for ever, and has eyes for
8 what the Gentiles do; let rebellious souls tame their pride.   Bless the name of our
God, you Gentiles, echo the sound of his praise.
9   God's will is we should live yet; he does not suffer our steps to falter.   Yes,
11 Lord, thou hast put us to the proof, tested us as men test silver in the fire; led us
12 into a snare, and bowed our backs with trouble,   while human masters rode us
down; our way led through fire and water, yet in the end thou hast granted us
13 relief.   See, I come into thy house with burnt-offerings, to pay thee all the vows
14 these lips have framed, this mouth has uttered, when trouble came upon me.   Fat
burnt-offerings of sheep shall be thine, and the smoke of ram's flesh; bullocks and
16 goats shall be thy sacrifice.   Come and give ear, all you who worship God, while I
17 tell of the great mercies he has shewn me;   how this voice of mine cried out to him,
18 this tongue did him honour.   Would God listen to me, if my heart were set on
20 wrong?   And God has listened to me; given heed to my cry for succour.   Blessed
be God, who does not reject my prayer, does not withhold his mercy from me.

PSALM SIXTY-SIX

(To the choir-master. For stringed instruments. A psalm. A song.)

2 MAY God be merciful to us, and bless us; may he grant us the favour of his
3 smile.   Make known thy will, O God, wide as earth; make known among all
4 nations thy saving power.   Honour to thee, O God, from the nations, honour from
5 all the nations!   The Gentiles, too, may rejoice and be glad; a whole world abides
6 thy judgement, and the Gentiles, too, obey on earth thy sovereignty.   Honour
7 to thee, O God, from the nations, honour from all the nations!   The land has
8 yielded its harvest;   such bounty God, our own God, affords.   God grant us ever
his blessing, and may earth, far and wide, do him reverence.

PSALM SIXTY-SEVEN

(To the choir-master. Of David. A psalm. A song.)

2 LET God bestir himself, needs must his foes be scattered, their malice take
3 flight before his coming. Vanish the wicked at God's presence as the smoke
4 vanishes, as wax melts at the fire, while the just keep holiday and rejoice at the
5 sight of him, glad and content. Sing, then, in God's honour, praise his name with
   a psalm; a royal progress through the wilderness for the God whose name is
6 Javé! Triumph in his presence; he is a father to the orphan, and gives the widow
7 redress, this God who dwells apart in holiness. This is the God who makes a
   home for the outcast, restores the captives to a land of plenty, leaves none but the
   rebels to find their abode in the wilderness.
8   O God, when thou didst go forth at the head of thy people, on that royal pro-
9 gress of thine through the desert, how the earth shook, how the sky broke at God's
10 coming, how even Sinai shook, when the God of Israel came! And on this thy
   own land, O God, thou sendest rain abundantly; all parched it lies, and thou
11 dost bring it relief. Pasture-land of thy own flock; and shouldst thou not make
   bounteous provision here, O God, for thy pensioners?
12   Word has come from the Lord, good news borne on a multitude of lips:
13 Routed the kings, routed their armies; they have left their spoils for housewives to
14 carry away; never shone silver so bright on a dove's feathers, never gold so fair
   on a dove's wings; and you, all the while, resting quiet among the sheep-folds!
15 White fell the snows on Salmon, when the Lord put kings to rout.
16   Basan's hills are high, Basan's hills are rugged; must you turn your eyes,
   rugged hills, towards God's mountain, and envy what you see? The mountain
18 where God loves and will ever love to dwell. See where God comes, with chariots
   innumerable for his escort; thousands upon thousands; comes from Sinai to this his
19 sanctuary. Thou dost mount up on high, thou dost capture thy spoil, and men mus'
   be thy tribute; will they or no, yonder heathen must have the Lord God for their
20 neighbour. Blessed be the Lord now and ever, the God who bears our burdens,
21 and wins us the victory. Our God is a God of deliverance; Javé is a Lord who
22 saves from peril of death. God will smite the heads of his enemies, smite the
23 proud locks of the men who live at ease in their wickedness. I will restore my
   people, the Lord says; I will restore them to their land, from Basan, from the
24 shore of the high seas. Soon the blood of thy enemies will stain thy feet, never a
25 jackal that follows thee but shall lick its prey. Thou comest, O God, a mark for
26 all eyes; he comes, my God and my king, to visit his sanctuary. Before him go the
   singers, and the minstrels follow, while the maids play on their tambours between:
27 Give praise to the Lord God in this solemn assembly, sons of Israel! Here is Benjamin, youngest of the tribes, that marches in the van; here are the chieftains
   of Juda with the companies, chieftains, too, from Zabulon, chieftains from
   Nephtali.
29   Shew thy power, O God, shew thy Divine power, perfect thy own achievement
30 among us; to honour thy temple at Jerusalem, kings shall bring gifts before thee.
31 Tame the wild beasts of the marshes, fierce bulls that lord it over the peaceful
   herd of nations; down fall they, bringing silver pieces for their ransom. Scatter
32 the nations that delight in war, till Egypt sends hither her princes, till Ethiopia
33 makes her peace with God. Kingdoms of the earth, raise your voices in God's
34 honour, sing a psalm to the Lord; a psalm to God, who mounts on the heavens,

35 the immemorial heavens, and utters his word in a voice of thunder: Pay honour
to God, the God whose splendour rests over Israel, who holds dominion high
36 among the clouds. Awe dwells about him in his holy place! The God of Israel
gives his people strength and courage; blessed be God!

PSALM SIXTY-EIGHT

(To the choir-master. Melody: The Lilies. Of David.)

2 O GOD, save me; see how the waters close about me, shoulder-high! I am
like one who sticks fast in deep mire, with no ground under his feet, one who
4 has ventured out into mid-ocean, to be drowned by the storm. Hoarse my throat
with crying wearily for help; my eyes ache with looking up for mercy to my God.
5 Countless as the hairs on my head are my wanton enemies, I am no match for the
oppressors that wrong me. Should I make amends to them, I, that never robbed
6 them? O God, thou knowest my frailties, no fault of mine is hidden from thy
7 sight. Master, Lord of hosts, shall ill fortune of mine bring shame to those who
8 trust in thee, make men repent of looking for aid to thee, the God of Israel? It is
for thy sake that I have met with reproach, that I have so often blushed with con-
9 fusion, an outcast among my own brethren, a stranger to my own mother's child-
10 ren. Was it not jealousy for the honour of thy house that consumed me; was it
not uttered against thee, the reproach I bore?
11 What more could I do? I humbled myself before them by fasting; and that, too,
12 was matter for finding fault; I dressed in sackcloth, and they made a by-word of
13 me. Idlers in the market-place taunt me; the drunkards make a song of me over
14 their wine. To thee, Lord, I make my prayer; never man more needed thy good
will. Listen to me, O God, full of mercy as thou art, faithful as thou art to thy
15 promise of aid. Save me from sinking in the mire, rescue me from my enemies,
16 from the deep waters that surround me; let me not sink under the flood, swal-
17 lowed up in its depths, and the well's mouth close above me. Listen to me, Lord,
18 of thy gracious mercy, look down upon me in the abundance of thy pity; do not
turn thy face away from thy servant in this time of trouble, give a speedy answer
19 to my prayer. Draw near in my distress, and grant deliverance; relieve me, so
20 hard pressed by my enemies. Lord, thou knowest how they reproach me, how I
21 blush with shame; thou seest how many are my persecutors. Heart-broken with
that shame, I pine away, looking round for pity, where pity is none, for comfort,
22 where there is no comfort to be found. They gave me gall to eat, and when I was
23 thirsty they gave me vinegar to drink. Let their feast be turned into a trap, a net
24 to catch them and theirs; ever the blind eye be theirs, ever the halting loin. Pour
out thy anger upon them, let them be overtaken by the tide of thy vengeance;
26 let their dwelling-place be deserted, their tents for ever uninhabited. Who is it
they persecute? A man already afflicted by thee; hard was my hurt to bear, and
28 these have added to it. Do thou add guilt to guilt in their reckoning; let them
29 never claim thy acquittal; let their names be blotted out from the record of
the living, and never be written among the just.
30 See how friendless I am, and how distressed! Let thy help, O God, sustain me.
31 I will sing in praise of God's name, herald it gratefully; a more acceptable sacrifice, this, to the Lord than any young bullock, for all its promise of horn and
33 hoof. Here is a sight to make the afflicted rejoice; to cheer men's spirits in their
34 quest for God. The Lord listens to the prayer of the destitute; he does not forget
35 his servants in their chains. To him be praise from sky, earth and sea, and from
36 all the creatures that move about them. God will grant deliverance to Sion; the

cities of Juda will rise from their ruins, inhabited now and held firmly in posses-
37 sion, an inheritance for the race that serves him, a home for all true lovers of his
name.

PSALM SIXTY-NINE

(To the choir-master. Of David. A commemoration.)

2 DEIGN, O God, to set me free; Lord, make haste to help me. Disappoint
them, put them to the blush, the enemies who plot against my life! Baffled
4 let them go their way, that rejoice over my ill-fortune; slink away in confusion,
5 that crowed over me so loud! Triumphant joy be theirs, who long for thee;
Praise to the Lord, be ever their song, who look eagerly now for thy succour.
6 Thou seest me helpless and destitute; my God, help me. Thou art my champion
and my deliverer; Lord, do not delay thy coming.

PSALM SEVENTY

2 TO thee, O God, I turn for succour; may I never be disappointed! Rescue and
3 deliver me, faithful as thou art; listen to my cry for succour. Let me find
in thee a rock-fastness, a citadel of defence; I have no other stronghold, no other
4 refuge, but thee. Rescue me, Lord, from the power of the wicked, from the
5 grasp of lawlessness and oppression; thou, my God and Master, the hope and
6 confidence of my youth. Thou hast upheld me from birth, thou hast guarded me
7 ever since I left my mother's womb; ever in thee was my trust. Men stare at me
8 now as a strange portent, so signal the protection thou hast given me. And evermore praise was on my lips, my constant theme thy glory.
9   Do not cast me off now, in my old age; slowly my strength ebbs, do not thou
10 forsake me. A mark thou seest me for envious eyes and tongues; they conspire
11 together, and whisper, God has abandoned him; now is the time to overtake and
12 seize him; no one can bring him rescue now. O God, do not keep thy distance
13 from me; hasten, my God, to aid me. Defeat their plot against my life, and bring
it to nothing; cover my ill-wishers with confusion and shame.
14   Still will I hope on, praising thee ever more and more. Day in, day out, these
lips shall tell of thy faithfulness, of thy saving power, and find no end to them;
16 thy divine wonders, thy matchless justice, Lord, proclaim. It is thou, O God,
that hast inspired me ever since the days of my youth, and still I am found
18 telling the tale of thy wonders. O God, do not fail me, now when I am old
and grey-headed, till I have made known the proofs of thy power to this, to all
19 the generations that will follow; that faithfulness of thine which reaches up, O
God, to the heavens, so signally made manifest. There is none like thee, O God,
20 none like thee. Ah, how often thou hast burdened me with bitter trouble! And
still thou wouldst relent, and give me back life, and bring me up again from the
21 very depths of the earth. Lift my head high; turn back, and comfort me. So true
to thy word, and shall I not give thee thanks with psalm-music, praise thee on the
23 harp, O God, the Holy One of Israel? Gladly these lips will sing of thee, this
24 heart, which owes thee its deliverance. Day in, day out, I will repeat the story of
thy faithfulness, what shame fell, what confusion, on the men who sought to
wrong me.

PSALM SEVENTY-ONE

(Of Solomon.)

GRANT to the king, O God, thy own skill in judgement; the inheritor of a
2 throne, may he be just, as thou art just; may he give thy people right awards,
3 and to thy poor, redress. Such the harvest his subjects shall reap, peace on every
4 mountain, justice on every hill-side. Watch and ward he will keep over the friend-
5 less, protect the children of the poor, and crush the oppressor. Ageless as sun or
6 moon he shall endure; kindly as the rain that drops on the meadow grass, as the
7 showers that water the earth. Justice in his days shall thrive, and the blessings
of peace; and may those days last till the moon shines no more.
8 From sea to sea, from the great river to the ends of earth, his sway shall reach.
9 In his presence rebels shall bend the knee, all his enemies will be humbled in the
10 dust; gifts shall flow in from the lords of Tharsis and the islanders, tribute from
11 the kings of Arabia and of Saba; all kings must needs bring their homage, all
12 nations serve him. He will give the poor redress when they cry to him, destitute
13 folk, with none to befriend them; in their need and helplessness, they shall have
14 his compassion. Their lives he will take into his keeping, set them free from the
15 claims of usury and oppression, dearly avenge their blood. Long life shall be his,
and gold from Arabia shall be given him; men will pray for him continually, bless
16 his name evermore. The land shall have good store of corn, high up the hill-sides,
rustling like the woods of Lebanon; shall multiply its citizens like grass on the
17 ground. For ever let his name be used in blessing, a name to endure while the sun
gives light; in him all the tribes of the earth shall be enriched, all the nations shall
extol him.
18 Blessed be the Lord God of Israel, who does wonderful deeds as none else,
19 and blessed for ever be his glorious name; all the earth shall be filled with his
glory, Amen, Amen.

PSALM SEVENTY-TWO

(A psalm. Of Asaph.)

WHAT bounty God shews, what divine bounty, to the upright, to the pure
2 of heart! Yet I was near losing my foothold, felt the ground sink under my
3 steps, such heart-burning had I at seeing the good fortune of sinners that defy his
4 law; for them, never a pang; healthy and sleek their bodies shew. Not for these
to share man's common lot of trouble; the plagues which afflict human kind still
6 pass them by. No wonder if pride clings to them like a necklace, if they flaunt,
7 like fine clothes, their wrong-doing. From those pampered hearts what malice
8 proceeds, what vile schemes are hatched! Ever jeering, ever talking maliciously,
9 throned on high they preach injustice; their clamour reaches heaven, and their
false tales win currency on earth.
10 Enviously the men of my own race look on, to see them draining life's cup to
11 the full; Can God, they ask, be aware of this? Does the most High know of all
12 that passes? Look at these sinners, how they live at peace, how they rise to great-
13 ness! Why then, thought I, it is to no purpose that I have kept my heart true, and
14 washed my hands clean in pureness of living; still, all the while, I am plagued
15 for it, and no morning comes but my scourging is renewed. Was I to share their
thoughts? Nay, that were to put the whole company of thy children in the wrong.
16 I set myself to read the riddle, but it proved a hard search, until I betook myself

to God's sanctuary, and considered, there, what becomes of such men at last.
18 The truth is, thou art making a slippery path for their feet, ready to plunge them
19 in ruin; in a moment they are fallen, in a storm of terrors vanished and gone.
20 And thou, Lord, dost rise up and brush aside all their imaginings, as a waking
man his dream.
21   What if my mind was full of bitterness, what if I was pierced to the heart? I
22 was all dumbness, I was all ignorance, standing there like a brute beast in thy
23 presence. Yet ever thou art at my side, ever holdest me by my right hand. Thine
25 to guide me with thy counsel, thine to welcome me into glory at last. What
else does heaven hold for me, but thyself? What charm for me has earth, here at
26 thy side? This frame, this earthly being of mine must come to an end; still God
27 will be my heart's stronghold, eternally my inheritance. Lost those others may be,
28 who desert thy cause, lost are all those who break their troth with thee; I know
no other content but clinging to God, putting my trust in the Lord, my Master;
within the gates of royal Sion I will be the herald of thy praise.

PSALM SEVENTY-THREE

(A maskil. Of Asaph.)

O GOD, hast thou altogether abandoned us? Sheep of thy own pasturing, must
2 we feel the fires of thy vengeance? Bethink thee of the company thou hast
gathered, long ago; of the tribe thou hast chosen to be thy own domain; of mount
3 Sion, where thou hast thy dwelling-place. Hither turn thy steps, where all is
ruin irretrievable; see what havoc thy enemies have wrought in the holy place,
4 how their malice has raged in thy very precincts, setting up its emblems for a
5 trophy of conquest. Blow after blow, like woodmen in the forest, they have plied
6 their axes, brought it down, with pick and mallet, to the ground. They have set
8 fire to thy sanctuary, sullied the dwelling-place of thy glory in the dust. They
think to destroy us like one man, sweep away every shrine of God in the land.
9 Our own emblems are nowhere to be seen; there are no prophets left now, none
10 can tell how long we must endure. O God, shall our enemy taunt us everlastingly,
11 shall blasphemy still defy thy name? Why dost thou withhold thy hand? That
right hand of thine, must it always lie idle in thy bosom?
12   Mine is a King who reigned before time was; here on earth he was the means
13 to bring deliverance. What power but thine could sunder the shifting sea, crush
14 the power of the monster beneath its waters; shatter Leviathan's power, and give
15 him up as prey to the sea-beasts? Thou didst open up fountains and streams of
16 water; thou, too, madest the swollen rivers run dry. Thine is the day, thine the
17 night; moon and sun are of thy appointment; thou hast fixed all the bounds of
earth, madest the summer, madest the cool of the year.
18   Wilt thou take no heed, when thy enemies taunt thee, and in their recklessness
19 set the name of Javé at defiance? Must the dove be the vulture's prey? Souls
20 unbefriended, but for thee, wilt thou leave us quite forgotten? Bethink thee of thy
21 covenant; everywhere oppression lurks, or walks openly through the fields. Do
not let the humble go away disappointed; teach the poor and the helpless to exalt
22 thy name. Bestir thyself, O God, to vindicate thy own cause; do not forget the
23 taunts which reckless men hurl at thee, day after day; do not overlook them, the
triumphant shouts of thy enemies, the ever growing clamour that here defies thee.

PSALM SEVENTY-FOUR

(To the choir-master. Melody: Do not destroy. A psalm. Of Asaph. A song.)

2 WE praise thee, O God, and, praising thee, call upon thy name, tell the story
3 of thy wondrous deeds. When the time is ripe, I will judge strictly; earth
5 rocks to its fall, and all that dwell on it; I alone support its fabric. Rebel no more,
6 I cry to the rebels, Abate your pride, to the transgressors; would they match
7 themselves against the most High, hurl defiance at God? Look east, look west,
8 it will avail you nothing; no help comes from the desert, or the high hills; it is
9 God who rules all, humbling one man and exalting another. In the Lord's hand
foams a full cup of spiced wine; he holds it to men's lips, that must empty it
10 to the dregs, sinners everywhere must drink them. Evermore will I triumph,
11 singing praises to the God of Jacob; mine to crush the pride of every sinner,
and raise high the courage of the just.

PSALM SEVENTY-FIVE

(To the choir-master. For stringed instruments. A psalm. Of Asaph. A song.)

2 IT is in Juda God makes himself known, in Israel that his name is extolled;
3 there, in Salem, he makes his abode, dwells in Sion. It was there he broke the
5 archers' volleys, broke shield, and sword, and battle array. How princely was
6 thy dawning over the everlasting hills! Brave hearts, foiled of their purpose,
they slept their long sleep; lay there, no hand stirring, the warriors in their pride;
7 lay there, chariots and horsemen, overthrown, God of Jacob, at thy word of
rebuke.
8 Who can resist thee, so terrible, so sudden in thy anger? Loud rings in heaven
10 the doom thou utterest; earth trembles and is silent when God rouses himself
11 to execute his sentence, giving redress to those who are scorned on earth. Its
madness tamed, Edom shall do thee honour; to thee the spared remnant of Emath
12 shall keep holiday. To the Lord your God let vows be made and paid; bring gifts
13 from every side to God, the terrible; he it is that cows the hearts of princes,
feared among all the kings of the earth.

PSALM SEVENTY-SIX

(To the choir-master. Melody: Idithun. Of Asaph. A psalm.)

2 A CRY to my God in loud appeal, a cry to my God, to win his hearing! To the
Lord I look when distress comes upon me; in his presence I lift up my hands
4 amid the darkness, never wearied; grief like mine there is no comforting. Of God
5 I bethink me, yet sighing still; of God I muse, yet ever faint-hearted. Sleepless
6 that thought holds me yet bewildered and dumb. I reflect upon days long past,
7 the immemorial years possess my mind; deep musings occupy my thoughts at
8 midnight, never will my mind be at rest. Can it be that God will always leave us
9 forsaken, will never shew us again his old kindness? Can his favour desert us
10 altogether, his promise be set aside eternally? Can God forget to be gracious, can
11 anger move him to withhold his mercy? For me, I tell myself, this sorrow was
reserved; the most High has altered the fashion of his dealings with men.
12 To remember all the Lord has done, to recall those wonderful acts of thine,
13 long ago! To ponder over all thy doings, pass thy wonders in review! Thy
path, O God, is hedged about with holiness; what god is great as our God is

15 great? Thy own wonderful acts acclaim thy Deity; even to the Gentiles thou
16 wouldst make thy power known, by forcing them to set free thy people, the
17 sons of Jacob and of Joseph. The waters saw thee, O God, the waters trembled
   at the sight of thee, moved to their inmost depths; how the waves roared, how
18 the clouds volleyed rain, what echoes from their midst! To and fro thy arrows
19 passed, thy crackling thunders rolled, till all the world shone with thy lightning,
20 and the troubled earth shook. Thy way led through the sea, the deep tide made
21 a road for thee, and none may read the traces of thy passage, where thou, with
   Moses and Aaron for thy shepherds, didst bring thy people out on their journey.

PSALM SEVENTY-SEVEN

(A maskil. Of Asaph.)

   LISTEN, my people, to this testament of mine, do not turn a deaf ear to the
2 words I utter; I speak to you with mysteries for my theme, read the riddles of
3 long ago. It is a story often heard, well known among us; have not our fathers
4 told it to us? And shall we keep it back from their children, from the generation
   which follows? Speak we of God's praise, of his great power, of the wonderful
5 deeds he did. He gave Jacob a rule to live by, framed for Israel a law, com-
6 manding our fathers to hand on the message, so that a new generation might
   learn it; sons would be born to take their place, and teach it to their own sons
7 after them. They were to put their trust in God, ever remembering his divine
8 dealings with them, ever loyal to his commands; they were not to be like their
   fathers, a stubborn and defiant breed, a generation of false aims, of a spirit that
   broke faith with God.
9   So it was that the sons of Ephraim, bow in hand, were routed in the day of
10 battle. They were false to God's covenant, refused to follow his law, as if they
   had forgotten all his mercies, all those wonderful deeds of his they had witnessed.
12 Had not their fathers seen wonders enough in Egypt, on the plains of Tanis,
13 when he parted the sea to let them pass through it, making its waters stand firm
14 as a mound of earth; when he led them with a cloud by day, with glowing fire all
15 through the night? He pierced the rock, too, in the desert, and slaked their thirst
16 as if from some deep pool, bidding the very stones yield water, till fountains
   gushed from them, abundant as rivers.
17   And still they went on offending him, there in the wilderness, rebelling against
18 the most High, challenging God in their thoughts to give them the food they
19 craved for. Defiantly they asked, Can God spread a table for us in the wilder-
20 ness? True, he smote the rock, and made water flow from it, till the stream ran in
21 flood, but can he give bread too, and provide meat for his people? All this the Lord
   heard, and his indignation blazed out; its mounting fires Jacob had fed, its fury
22 must break on Israel. What, had they no faith in God, no trust in his power to
23 save? He laid his command upon the clouds above them, threw open the doors
24 of heaven, and rained down manna for them to eat. The bread of heaven was his
25 gift to them; man should eat the food of angels, and so their want should be
26 supplied abundantly. Next, he summoned his east wind from the sky, let loose the
27 fury of the southern gale, raining down meat on them thick as dust, birds on the
28 wing, plentiful as the sea-sand. Into their very camp it fell, close about their
29 tents; and they ate, and took their fill. All they asked, he granted them; even
31 now, their craving was satisfied. But while the food was yet in their mouths God's
   anger against them reached its height, and slew their lordliest, brought them
   low, all the flower of Israel.
32   Yet, with all this, they continued to offend him; all his wonderful deeds left

33 them faithless still. And ever he took away their lives untimely, hurried their
34 days to an end. When he threatened them with death, they would search after
35 him, feel their need of God once more; they would remind themselves that it was
God who had protected them, his almighty power that had delivered them.
36 But still they were lying lips, they were false tongues that spoke to him; their
38 hearts were not true to him, no loyalty bound them to his covenant. Yet, such
is his mercy, he would still pardon their faults, and spare them from destruction;
again and again he curbed his indignation, to his vengeance would not give
39 place. He would not forget that they were flesh and blood, no better than a breath
40 of wind, that passes by and never returns. How often the desert saw them in
41 revolt against him, how often, in those solitudes, they defied his anger! Always
new challenges to God's power, new rebellions against the Holy One of Israel.
42   Had they forgotten all he did for them, that day when he set them free from the
43 power of their oppressor, all those miracles among the men of Egypt, those por-
44 tents in the plain of Tanis, when he turned all their streams, all their channels
45 into blood, so that they could not drink? He sent out flies, to their ruin, frogs to
46 bring devastation on them, gave all their harvest over to the caterpillar, their
47 tillage to the locust, sent hail on their vineyards, frost on their mulberry-trees,
48 let the hail have its way with their cattle, the lightning with their flocks. He let
his anger loose on them in all its vehemence; what rage, what fury, what havoc,
50 as the angels of destruction thronged about them! So, the way made ready for
his vengeance, he took toll of their lives, doomed even their cattle to the pesti-
51 lence; on every first-born creature in Egypt, on the first-fruits of increase in
52 all the dwellings of Cham, his stroke fell. Then, like a shepherd, he set his own
53 people on their way, led them, his own flock, through the wilderness; guided
54 them in safety, free from all alarm, while the sea closed over their enemy. So
he brought them to that holy land of his, the mountain slopes he took, with his
55 own right hand for title; so he drove out the heathen at their onset, parcelled out
the land to them by lot, to each his own inheritance, bidding the tribes of Israel
dwell where the heathen had dwelt before them.
56   These were the men who defied the most high God, and rebelled against him;
57 would not observe his decrees, but turned away and broke faith with him as their
58 fathers had done, like a bow that plays the archer false; made mountain shrines,
59 to court his anger, carved images, to awake his jealousy! The Lord heard the
60 bruit of it, and burned with anger, cast Israel away in bitter scorn; he forsook
61 his tabernacle in Silo, that tabernacle where once he dwelt among men. Plunder,
now, in the enemy's hands, the ark that is shrine of his strength and majesty;
62 he would leave his people at the mercy of the sword, disdain his own inheritance.
63 Their young men fed the flames, and the maidens must go unwed; their priests
fell by the sword, and never a widow left to mourn for them.
65   Then suddenly, like a man that wakes up from sleep, like some warrior that
66 lay, till now, bemused with wine, the Lord roused himself; he smote his enemies
67 as they turned to flee, branded them for ever with shame. But he refused, now,
to make his dwelling with Joseph, it was not the tribe of Ephraim he would
68 choose; he chose the tribe of Juda, and the hill of Sion, there to bestow his love.
69 And there he built his sanctuary, immovable as heaven or earth, his own un-
70 changing handiwork. He chose David, too, for his servant; took him away from
71 herding the sheep; bade him leave off following the ewes that were in milk, and
72 be the shepherd of Jacob's sons, his own people, of Israel, his own domain. His
was the loyal heart that should tend them, his the skilful hand that should be
their guide.

PSALM SEVENTY-EIGHT

(A psalm. Of Asaph.)

O GOD, the heathen have broken into thy inheritance; they have profaned the
2 temple, thy sanctuary, and left Jerusalem in ruins. They have thrown the
corpses of thy servants to feed all the birds of heaven; wild beasts prey on the
3 carrion of the just; blood has flowed like water on every side of Jerusalem, and
4 there was none to bury the dead. What a triumph was this for the nations that
5 dwell around us; how have our neighbours mocked and derided us! Lord, must
we always taste thy vengeance, must thy jealous anger still burn unquenched?
6 Pour out this indignation of thine upon the nations that do not acknowledge thee,
7 on the kingdoms that never invoke thy name; see how they have made Jacob
8 their prey, and left his dwelling-place in ruins! Forget the long record of our
sins, and haste in mercy to our side; never was need so sore as this.
9 O God, our Saviour, help us; deliver us, Lord, for the glory of thy name, pardon
10 our sins for the sake of thy own renown! Shall the heathen ask, What has become
of their God? Shall our eyes never witness thy vengeance upon the Gentiles, that
11 open vengeance thou wilt take for thy servants' blood? Could but the groaning
of the captive reach thy presence! Thy arm has not lost its strength; from our
12 bonds deliver us, a race doomed to die. Pour out seven-fold retribution into the
laps of our neighbours, for all the insults, Lord, which they have put upon thee;
13 and we, thy own people, sheep of thy pasturing, will give thee thanks for ever,
echo, from one generation to the next, the story of thy renown.

PSALM SEVENTY-NINE

(To the choir-master. Melody: The Lily of the Law. Of Asaph. A psalm.)

2 GIVE audience, thou that art the guide of Israel, that leadest Joseph with a
shepherd's care. Thou who art enthroned above the Cherubim, reveal thyself
3 to Ephraim, Benjamin, and Manasse; exert thy sovereign strength, and come to
4 our aid. O God, restore us to our own; smile upon us, and we shall find deliver-
5 ance. Lord God of hosts, wilt thou always turn away in anger from thy servants'
6 prayer; daily wilt thou allot us, for food, for drink, only the full measure of our
7 tears? Thou hast made us a coveted prize to our neighbours, enemies mock at
8 our ill fortune! O God of hosts, restore us to our own; smile upon us, and we
9 shall find deliverance. Long ago, thou didst bring a vine out of Egypt, rooting
10 out the heathen to plant it here; thou didst prepare the way for its spreading,
11 and it took root where thou hadst planted it, filled the whole land. How it overshadowed the hills, how the cedars, divinely tall, were overtopped by its branches!
12 It spread out its tendrils to the sea, its shoots as far as the great river. Why is it
that in these days thou hast levelled its wall, for every passer-by to rob it of its
14 fruit? See how the wild boar ravages it, how it gives pasture to every beast that
15 roams! God of hosts, relent, look down from heaven, look to this vine, that needs
16 thy care. Revive the stock which thy own hand has planted, branches that by
17 thee throve, and throve for thee. Death be in thy frown for the men that have
18 cut it down and burned it. Thy chosen friends, a race by thee thriving, and
19 thriving for thee, O let thy hand protect them still! Henceforth we will never
20 forsake thee; grant us life, and we will live only to invoke thy name. Lord God
of hosts, restore us to our own; smile upon us, and we shall find deliverance.

PSALM EIGHTY

(To the choir-master. Melody: The Winepresses. Of Asaph.)

2 REJOICE we all in honour of the God who aids us; cry out with gladness to the
3 God of Jacob. Ring psaltery, and tambour, beat the harp, sweetly sounding,
4 and the zither! A new month, and a full moon; blow the trumpet loud, to grace
5 our festival! Duty demands it of Israel; the God of Jacob has decreed it, made
it a law for Joseph, since the day he left Egypt, and gained the further shore. In
7 a tongue unknown the message came to me; I have eased his shoulder of the
8 burden, freed his hands from the slavery of the hod! Such deliverance I brought,
when thou didst cry out to me in thy misery; gave thee audience under a canopy
of cloud, and tested thee at the Waters of Rebellion.
9 Give heed, my people, to this warning of mine; Israel, wouldst thou but listen!
10 Then let no strange worship find a home with thee; never let thy knees be bowed
11 to an alien God; am not I the Lord thy God, I, who rescued thee from Egypt?
12 Open thy mouth wide, and thou shalt have thy fill. So I spoke, but my people
13 would not listen; Israel went on unheeding, till I was fain to give their hard
14 hearts free play, let them follow their own devices. Ah, if my people did but
15 listen to me! Did Israel but take me for their guide! How lightly, then, would
16 I bring their enemies low, smite down their persecutors! The very men that were
once the Lord's enemies would be cringing at his feet; such, for ever, should be
17 their destiny; Israel should have full ears of wheat to nourish them, and honey
dripping from the rock to their heart's content.

PSALM EIGHTY-ONE

(A psalm. Of Asaph.)

SEE, where he stands, the Ruler of all, among the rulers assembled, comes
2 forward to pronounce judgement on the rulers themselves! Will you never
3 cease perverting justice, espousing the cause of the wicked? Come, give redress
4 to the poor and the friendless, do right to the afflicted and the destitute; to you
need and poverty look for deliverance, rescue them from the hand of wickedness.
5 But no, ignorant and unperceiving, they grope their way in darkness; see how
6 unstable are the props of earth! Gods you are, I myself have declared it;
7 favoured children, every one of you, of the most High; yet the doom of mortals
8 awaits you, you shall fall with the fall of human princes. Bestir thyself, Lord,
bring the world to judgement; all the nations are thy own domain.

PSALM EIGHTY-TWO

(A song. A psalm. Of Asaph.)

2 BE silent, Lord, no longer. O God, do not keep still now, do not hold back
3 now! What turmoil among thy enemies; how their malice lifts its head! Busily
they plot against thy people, compass the ruin of the men thou hast in thy keeping.
5 Come, they whisper, let us put an end to their sovereignty, so that the very name
6 of Israel will be remembered no more. All are agreed, all alike are ranged in con-
7 federacy against thee; here Edom lies encamped, there Ismael; Moab, too, and
8 the Agarenes; Gebal, Ammon and Amelec, the Philistines, and the folk that
9 dwell at Tyre. Even Assyria has made common cause with them, lends her aid
to these children of Lot.

10   Do to these what thou didst to Madian, to Sisara and Jabin at the brook of
11 Cison; the men who died at Endor, rotted there like dung on the ground. May
their princes fare as Oreb fared, and Zeb; may the doom of Zebee and Salmana
13 be the doom of all their chieftains. And did they think to make God's chosen
14 portion their spoil? My God, send them whirling this way and that, like leaves,
15 like straws before the wind. See how the fire burns up the forest, how its flames
16 scorch the mountain-side! So let the fury of thy onset rout them, thy fury dismay
17 them. Let their cheeks blush crimson with shame, Lord, till they come to sue
18 for thy favour; confusion and dismay be theirs for ever, for ever let them be
19 abashed and brought to nothing, till they, too, know the meaning of Javé's name,
acknowledge thee as the most high God, the Overlord of earth.

PSALM EIGHTY-THREE

(To the choir-master. Melody: The Winepresses. Of the sons of Core. A psalm.)

2   LORD of hosts, how I love thy dwelling-place! For the courts of the Lord's
house, my soul faints with longing. The living God! at his name my heart, my
4 whole being thrills with joy. Where else should the sparrow find a home, the
dove a nest for her brood, but at thy altar, Lord of hosts, my king and my God?
5 How blessed, Lord, are those who dwell in thy house! They will be ever praising
6 thee. How blessed is the man who finds his strength in thee! Where there are
7 hearts set on pilgrimage, the parched ravine turns into a water-course at their
8 coming, new-clad by the bounty of returning rain. So, at each stage refreshed,
they will reach Sion, and have sight there of the God who is above all gods.
9   Lord of hosts, listen to my prayer; God of Israel, grant me audience! God,
ever our protector, do not disregard us now; look favourably upon him whom
11 thou hast anointed! Willingly would I give a thousand of my days for one spent
in thy courts! Willingly reach but the threshold of my God's house, so I might
12 dwell no more in the abode of sinners! Sun to enlighten, shield to protect us, the
Lord God has favour, has honour to bestow. To innocent lives he will never refuse
13 his bounty; Lord of hosts, blessed is the man who puts his confidence in thee.

PSALM EIGHTY-FOUR

(To the choir-master. Of the sons of Core. A psalm.)

2   WHAT blessings, Lord, thou hast granted to this land of thine, restoring
3 Jacob's fortunes, pardoning thy people's guilt, burying away the record of
4 their sins, all thy anger calmed, thy fierce displeasure forgotten! And now, God
6 of our deliverance, do thou restore us; no longer let us see thy frown. Wouldst
thou always be indignant with us? Must thy resentment smoulder on, age after
7 age? Wilt thou never relent, O God, and give fresh life, to rejoice the spirits
8 of thy people? Shew us thy mercy, Lord; grant us thy deliverance!
9   Let me listen, now, to the voice of the Lord God; it is a message of peace
he sends to his people; to his loyal servants, that come back, now, with all their
10 heart to him. For us, his worshippers, deliverance is close at hand; in this
11 land of ours, the divine glory is to find a home. See, where mercy and faithful-
12 ness meet in one; how justice and peace are united in one embrace! Faithfulness
13 grows up out of the earth, and from heaven, redress looks down. The Lord, now,
14 will grant us his blessing, to make our land yield its harvest; justice will go on
before him, deliverance follow where his feet tread.

PSALM EIGHTY-FIVE

(A prayer. Of David.)

2 TURN thy ear, Lord, and listen to me in my helplessness and my need. Protect a life dedicated to thyself; rescue a servant of thine that puts his trust in thee.
3 In thee, my own God; have mercy, O Lord, for mercy I plead continually; com-
5 fort thy servant's heart, this heart that aspires, Lord, to thee. Who is so kind and
6 forgiving, Lord, as thou art, who so rich in mercy to all who invoke him? Give a
7 hearing, then, Lord, to my prayer; listen to my plea when I cry out to thee in a
8 time of sore distress, counting on thy audience. There is none like thee, Lord,
9 among the gods; none can do as thou doest. Lord, all the nations thou hast made
10 must needs come and worship thee, honouring thy name, so great thou art, so
marvellous in thy doings, thou who alone art God.
11   Guide me, Lord, thy own way, thy faithful care my escort; be all my heart's
12 direction reverence for thy name. O Lord my God, with all my heart I will
13 praise thee, eternally hold thy name in honour for the greatness of the mercy
14 thou hast shewed me, in rescuing me thus from the lowest depths of hell. And
now, O God, see how scornful foes have set upon me, how their dread con-
15 spiracy threatens my life, with no thought of thee to restrain it! But thou, Lord,
art a Lord of mercy and pity, patient, full of compassion, true to thy promise.
16 Look upon me and be merciful to me; rescue, with thy sovereign aid, one whose
17 mother bore him to thy service! Shew me some token of thy favour; let my
enemies see, abashed, how thou, Lord, dost help me, how thou, Lord, dost comfort me.

PSALM EIGHTY-SIX

(Of the sons of Core. A psalm. A song.)

2 HIS own building amidst the inviolate hills, the Lord loves Sion walls better
3 than any other home in Israel. How high a boast, city of God, is made for
4 thee, Mine it is to reckon the folk of Egypt, of Babylon, too, among my citizens!
5 Philistines, Tyrians, Ethiopians, all must claim Sion as their birthplace; None
was ever born, the proverb shall run, that did not take his birth from her; it was
6 the most High, none other, that founded her. This was their birthplace, the
7 Lord shall write over the muster-roll of the nations; nor any but shall tell her
praises with song and dance, each claiming from her its only origin.

PSALM EIGHTY-SEVEN

(A song. A psalm. Of the sons of Core. To the choir-master. Melody: Mahalat. For singing. A maskil. Of Heman the Ezrahite.)

2 LORD God, day and night I cry bitterly to thee; let my prayer reach thy
4 presence, give audience to my entreaty, for indeed my heart is full of trouble.
5 My life sinks ever closer to the grave; I count as one of those who go down into
6 the abyss, like one powerless. As well lie among the dead, men laid low in the
grave, men thou rememberest no longer, cast away, now, from thy protecting
7 hand. Such is the place where thou hast laid me, in a deep pit where the dark
8 waters swirl; heavily thy anger weighs down on me, and thou dost overwhelm me
9 with its full flood. Thou hast estranged all my acquaintance from me, so that
they treat me as a thing accursed; I lie in a prison whence there is no escape,

10 my eyes grow dim with tears. On thee I call, to thee stretch out my hands, each
day that passes.

11   Not for the dead thy wonderful power is shewn; not for pale shadows to return
12 and give thee thanks.   There in the grave, how shall they recount thy mercies;
13 how shall they tell of thy faithfulness, now that life is gone? How can there be
talk of thy marvels in a world of darkness, of thy favour in a land where all is
14 forgotten? To prayer, Lord, fall I lustily; it shall reach thee, while there is
15 yet time. Why dost thou reject my plea, Lord, and turn thy face away from me?
16 Ever since youth, misery and mortal sickness have been my lot; wearily I have
17 borne thy visitations; I am overwhelmed with thy anger, dismayed by thy threats,
19 that still cut me off like a flood, all at once surrounding me. Friends and neighbours gone, a world of shadows is all my company.

PSALM EIGHTY-EIGHT
(A maskil. Of Ethan the Ezrahite.)

2 HERE is a song to put the Lord's mercies on record for ever; ages will pass, and
3 still these words of mine shall proclaim thy faithfulness. Charter of everlasting mercy thy own lips have given; there, in the heavens, thy faithful promise
4 rests: I have made a sworn covenant with my chosen servant David: To all time
I will make thy posterity continue, age after age I will bid thy throne endure.

6   And are not those heavens, Lord, witnesses of thy wonderful power, of thy
7 faithfulness, before the court of the holy ones? Who is there above the clouds to
8 rival the Lord; where is the Lord's like among all the sons of God? How is God
feared, in that assembly of the holy ones; how great he is, how high in reverence
9 above all that stand about him! Lord God of hosts, who can compare with thee;
in the power, Lord, that is thine, in the faithfulness that everywhere attends thee?
10 It is thou that dost curb the pride of the sea, and calm the tumult of its waves;
11 wounded lies Rahab at thy feet, by the strong arm that has routed thy enemies.
12 Thine are the heavens, thine the earth; author, thou, of the world and all it holds.
13 The north wind and the south are of thy fashioning; thy name wakes the glad
14 echoes of Thabor and Hermon. God of the strong arm, the sure, the uplifted
15 hand, right and justice are the pillars of thy throne; mercy and faithfulness the
heralds of thy coming.

16   Happy is the people that knows well the shout of praise, that lives, Lord, in
17 the smile of thy protection! Evermore they take pride in thy name, rejoice over
18 thy just dealings. What else but thy glory inspires their strength? What else but
19 thy favour bids us lift our heads? From the Lord, the Holy One of Israel, that
royal protection comes which is our shield.

20   Long ago, in a vision, thou didst make a promise to thy faithful servants. Thou
saidst, I have crowned you a warrior king, chosen out among the common folk
21 a man to honour. Here was my servant David; on him my consecrating oil has
22 been poured. My hand shall never leave him unprotected, my arm shall give him
23 courage; no enemy shall take him unawares, no envious rival have power, hence-
24 forth, to crush him; beaten down, every foe, at his onset, baffled, all their ill will.
25 My faithfulness and mercy shall go with him; by my favour he shall rise to pre-
26 eminence. I will make his power rest on the sea; to the streams of the great river
27 his hand shall reach out. Thou art my Father, he will cry out to me, thou art my
28 God, my stronghold and my refuge; and I will acknowledge him as my first-born,
29 overlord to all the kings of earth. I will continue my favour towards him for ever,
30 my covenant with him shall remain unbroken; I will give him a posterity that
31 never fails, a throne enduring as heaven itself. Do his children forsake my law,
32 to follow paths not mine; do they violate my decrees, leave my will undone? Then

they shall feel the rod for their transgressions, I will scourge them for their sin,
34 but I will not cancel my gracious promise to him; never will I be guilty of un-
35 faithfulness, never will I violate my covenant, or alter the decree once spoken.
36 Pledged stands my inviolable word, I will never be false to David; his posterity
shall continue for ever, his royalty, too, shall last on in my presence like the sun;
38 like the moon's eternal orb, that bears witness in heaven unalterable.
39   And now? Now thou hast only loathing and scorn for us; heavy thy hand
40 falls on him thou hast anointed. Spurned lies the covenant thou didst make
41 with thy servant, thou hast dishonoured his royalty in the dust, broken down
42 all the walls about him, and made a ruin of his stronghold, till he is plundered
43 by every passer-by, a laughing-stock to all his neighbours. Thou hast granted
44 aid to the attacking armies, triumph to all his enemies, foiling the thrust of his
45 sword, and denying him thy succour in battle. Thou hast robbed him of the
46 bright glory that once was his; thou hast cast down his throne to earth, cut his
manhood short before its time; confusion overwhelms him.
47   Lord, wilt thou always turn thy face away so obdurately, will the flame of thy
48 anger never be quenched? Remember how frail a thing I am, how brief a destiny
49 thou hast granted to all Adam's sons. Where is the man that can live on, and
leave death untasted; can ransom his life from the power of the world beneath?
50 Lord, where are those mercies of an earlier time, promised so faithfully to David?
51 Remember how a world's taunts assail thy people, and this one heart must bear
52 them all; shall they hurl taunts, Lord, these, thy enemies, after the man thou thyself hast anointed?
53   Blessed be the Lord for ever. Amen, Amen.

PSALM EIGHTY-NINE

(A prayer. Of Moses, the man of God.)

2 L ORD, thou hast been our refuge from generation to generation. Before the
hills came to birth, before the whole frame of the world was engendered, from
3 eternity to eternity, O God, thou art. And wilt thou bring man to dust again, that
4 thou sayest, Return, children of Adam, to what you were? In thy sight, a thousand
years are but as yesterday, that has come and gone, or as one of the night-watches.
5 Swiftly thou bearest our lives away, as a waking dream, or the green grass that
7 blooms fresh with the morning; night finds it faded and dead. Still thy anger
8 takes toll of us, thy displeasure denies us rest, so jealous thy scrutiny of our
9 wrong-doing, so clear our hidden sins shew in the light of thy presence. Day after
day vanishes, and still thy anger lasts; swift as a breath our lives pass away.
10 What is our span of days? Seventy years it lasts, eighty years, if lusty folk we be;
for the more part, toil and frustration; years that vanish in a moment, and we are
11 gone. Alas, that so few heed thy vengeance, measure thy anger by the reverence
12 we owe thee! Teach us to count every passing day, till our hearts find wisdom.
13   Relent, Lord; must it be for ever? Be gracious to thy servants. For us thy
15 timely mercies, for us abiding happiness and content; happiness that shall atone
16 for the time when thou didst afflict us, for the long years of ill fortune. Let these
17 eyes see thy purpose accomplished, to our own sons reveal thy glory; the favour
of the Lord our God smile on us! Prosper our doings, Lord, prosper our doings
yet.

PSALM NINETY

2 C ONTENT if thou be to live with the most High for thy defence, under his
Almighty shadow abiding still, him thy refuge, him thy stronghold thou
3 mayst call, thy own God, in whom is all thy trust. He it is will rescue thee from

4 every treacherous lure, every destroying plague. His wings for refuge, nestle thou
5 shalt under his care, his faithfulness thy watch and ward. Nothing shalt thou have
6 to fear from nightly terrors, from the arrow that flies by daylight, from pestilence
that walks to and fro in the darkness, from the death that wastes under the noon.
7 Though a thousand fall at thy side, ten thousand at thy right hand, it shall never
8 come next or near thee; rather, thy eyes shall look about thee, and see the reward
of sinners.
9 He, the Lord, is thy refuge; thou hast found a stronghold in the most High.
10 There is no harm that can befall thee, no plague that shall come near thy dwelling.
11 He has given charge to his angels concerning thee, to watch over thee wheresoever
12 thou goest; they will hold thee up with their hands lest thou shouldst chance to
13 trip on a stone. Thou shalt tread safely on asp and adder, crush lion and serpent
under thy feet.
14 He trusts in me, mine it is to rescue him; he acknowledges my name, from me
15 he shall have protection; when he calls upon me, I will listen, in affliction I am
16 at his side, to bring him safety and honour. Length of days he shall have to
content him, and find in me deliverance.

PSALM NINETY-ONE

(A psalm. A song. On the sabbath day.)

2 SWEET it is to praise the Lord, to sing, most high God, in honour of thy name;
3 to proclaim thy mercy and faithfulness at daybreak and at the fall of night.
4 Here is a theme for ten-stringed harp and viol, for music of voice and zither; so
delightsome, Lord, is all thou doest, so thrills my heart at the sight of all thou hast
6 made. How magnificent is thy creation, Lord, how unfathomable are thy pur-
7 poses! And still, too dull to learn, too slow to grasp his lesson, the wrong-doer
goes on in his busy wickedness. Still he thrives, makes a brave show like the grass
9 in spring, yet is he doomed to perish eternally, whilst thou, Lord, art for ever
10 exalted on high. Vanished away thy enemies, Lord, vanished away, and all their
busy wickedness scattered to the winds!
11 Strength thy power gives me, that gives strength to the wild oxen; refreshes me
12 as with the touch of pure oil. Blessed are these eyes with the sight of my enemies'
13 downfall, these ears with the tidings of insolent malice defeated. The innocent
man will flourish as the palm-tree flourishes; he will grow to greatness as the
14 cedars grow on Lebanon. Planted in the temple of the Lord, growing up in the
15 very courts of our God's house, the innocent will flourish in a green old age, all
16 freshness and vigour still; theirs to proclaim how just is the Lord my refuge, his
dealings how clear of wrong.

PSALM NINETY-TWO

THE Lord reigns as king, robed in majesty; royalty the Lord has for robe and
2 girdle. He it was that founded the solid earth, to abide immovable. Firm stood
3 thy throne ere ever the world began; from all eternity, thou art. Loud the rivers
4 echo, Lord, loud the rivers echo, crashing down in flood. Magnificent the roar
of eddying waters; magnificent the sea's rage; magnificent above these, the Lord
5 reigns in heaven. How faithful, Lord, are thy promises! Holy is thy house, and
must needs be holy until the end of time.

PSALM NINETY-THREE

2 IN thy divine vengeance, Lord, in thy divine vengeance stand revealed! Judge
3 of the world, mount thy throne, and give the proud their deserts! Must it be the

4 sinners still, Lord, the sinners still that triumph? Shall there be no end to the
5 prating, the rebellious talk, the boastfulness of wrong-doers? See, Lord, how
6 they crush down thy people, afflict the land of thy choice, murder the widow and
7 the stranger, slay the orphan! And they think, The Lord will never see it, the God
8 of Israel pays no heed. Pay heed, rather, yourselves, dull hearts that count among
9 my people; fools, learn your lesson ere it is too late. Is he deaf, the God who
10 implanted hearing in us; is he blind, the God who gave us eyes to see? He who
gives nations their schooling, who taught man all that man knows, will he not
11 call you to account? The Lord looks into men's hearts, and finds there illusion.
12   Happy, Lord, is the man whom thou dost chasten, reading him the lesson of
13 thy law! For him, thou wilt lighten the time of adversity, digging a pit all the
14 while to entrap the sinner. God will not abandon his people, will not desert his
15 chosen land; ere long, his justice will reappear in judgement, claiming all upright
16 hearts for its own. Who takes my part against the oppressor? Who rallies to my
17 side against the wrong-doers? It is the Lord that helps me; but for that, the grave
18 would soon be my resting-place. Still, when my foothold seems lost, thy mercy,
19 Lord, holds me up; amid all the thronging cares that fill my heart, my soul finds
20 comfort in thy consolation. What part have these unjust judges with thee, that
21 make mischief in the name of law? Let them harry the just as they will, pass sen-
22 tence of death upon the innocent, the Lord will be my defence, in my God I shall
23 find a rock-fastness still. He will punish the wrong, destroy them in their wickedness; doubt not the Lord our God will destroy them.

PSALM NINETY-FOUR

COME, friends, rejoice we in the Lord's honour; cry we out merrily to God,
2 our strength and deliverer; with praises court his presence, singing a joyful
3 psalm! A high God is the Lord, a king high above all the gods; beneath his hand
5 lie the depths of earth, his are the mountain peaks; his the ocean, for who but he
6 created it? What other power fashioned the dry land? Come in, then, fall we
7 down in worship, bowing the knee before God who made us. Who but the Lord
is our God? And what are we, but folk of his pasturing, sheep that follow his
beckoning hand?
8   Would you but listen to his voice to-day! Do not harden your hearts, as they
9 were hardened once at Meriba, at Massa in the wilderness. Your fathers put me
10 to the test, challenged me, as if they lacked proof of my power, for forty years
together; from that generation I turned away in loathing; These, I said, are ever
11 wayward hearts, these have never learned to obey me. And I took an oath in
anger, They shall never attain my rest.

PSALM NINETY-FIVE

SING the Lord a new song; in the Lord's honour, let the whole earth make
2 melody! Sing to the Lord, and bless his name; never cease to bear record
3 of his power to save. Publish his glory among the heathen; his wonderful acts
4 for all the world to hear. How great is the Lord, how worthy of honour! What
5 other god is to be feared as he? They are but fancied gods the heathen call
6 divine; the Lord, not they, made the heavens. Honour and beauty are his escort;
worship and magnificence the attendants of his shrine.
7   Tribes of the heathen, make your offering to the Lord, an offering to the Lord
8 of glory and homage, an offering of glory to the Lord's name; bring sacrifice,
9 come into his courts, worship the Lord in holy array. Before the Lord's presence

10 let the whole earth bow in reverence; tell the heathen, The Lord is king now, he
   has put the world in order, never to be thrown into confusion more; he gives
11 the nations a just award. Rejoice, heaven, and let earth be glad; let the sea, and
12 all the sea contains, give thunderous applause. The fields, and all the burden
   they bear, full of expectancy; no tree in the forest but will rejoice to greet its
13 Lord's coming. He comes to rule the earth; brings the world justice, to every
   race of men its promised award.

PSALM NINETY-SIX

THE Lord reigns as king; let earth be glad of it, let the isles, the many isles,
2 rejoice! See where he sits, clouds and darkness about him, justice and right
3 the pillars of his throne; see where he comes, fire sweeping on before him, burn-
4 ing up his enemies all around. In the flash of his lightning, how shines the world
5 revealed, how earth trembles at the sight! The hills melt like wax at the presence
6 of the Lord; his presence, whom all the earth obeys. The very heavens proclaim
7 his faithfulness; no nation but has sight of his glory. Shame upon the men that
   worship carved images, and make their boast of false gods! him only all the
   powers of heaven, prostrate, adore.
8   Glad news for Sion, rejoicing for Juda's townships, when thy judgements, Lord,
9 are made known; art thou not sovereign Lord of earth, beyond measure exalted
10 above all gods? They are the Lord's friends, who were never friends to wrong;
   souls that are true to him he guards ever, rescues them from the power of evil-
11 doers. Dawn of hope for the innocent, dawn of gladness for honest hearts!
12 Rejoice and triumph, just souls, in the Lord, of his holy name publish everywhere
   the renown.

PSALM NINETY-SEVEN

(A psalm.)

SING the Lord a new song, a song of wonder at his doings; how his own right
2 hand, his own holy arm, brought him victory. The Lord has given proof of his
3 saving power, has vindicated his just dealings, for all the nations to see; has
   remembered his gracious promise, and kept faith with the house of Israel; no
4 corner of the world but has witnessed how our God can save. In God's honour
   let all the earth keep holiday; let all be mirth and rejoicing and festal melody!
5 Praise the Lord with the harp, with harp and psaltery's music; with trumpets of
   metal, and the music of the braying horn! Keep holiday in the presence of the
7 Lord, our King; the sea astir, and all that the sea holds, the world astir, and all
9 that dwell on it; the rivers echoing their applause, the hills, too, rejoicing to see
   the Lord come. He comes to judge the earth; brings the world justice, to every
   race of men its due award.

PSALM NINETY-EIGHT

THE Lord is king, the nations are adread; he is throned above the Cherubim,
2 and earth trembles before him. Great is the Lord who dwells in Sion, sover-
3 eign ruler of all peoples! Let them all praise that great name of thine, a name
4 terrible and holy. He reigns in might, that right loves, to all assuring redress,
5 giving the sons of Jacob doom and award. Praise, then, the Lord our God, and
6 bow down before his footstool; that, too, is holy. Remember Moses and Aaron,
   and all those priests of his, Samuel and those others who called on his name, how
7 the Lord listened when they called upon him. His voice came to them from the

8 pillar of cloud; so it was they heard the decrees, the command he gave them. And
   thou, O Lord our God, didst listen to them, and they found thee a God of pardon;
9 yet every fault of theirs thou wert quick to punish. Praise the Lord our God, and
   do worship on the holy mountain where he dwells; the Lord our God is holy.

PSALM NINETY-NINE

(A psalm. For thanksgiving.)

2 LET the whole earth keep holiday in God's honour; pay to the Lord the homage
3 of your rejoicing, appear in his presence with glad hearts. Learn that it is the
   Lord, no other, who is God; his we are, he it was that made us; we are his own
4 people, sheep of his own pasturing. Pass through these gates, enter these courts
5 of his, with hymns of praise, give him thanks, and bless his name. Gracious is the
   Lord, everlasting his mercy; age after age, he is faithful to his promise still.

PSALM ONE HUNDRED

(Of David. A psalm.)

2 OF mercy and of justice my song shall be; a psalm in thy honour, Lord, from
   one that would guide his steps ever more perfectly. Ah, when wilt thou grant
3 me thy presence? Here in my house I would live with stainless heart; no ill purpose clouding my view, the transgressors of the law my enemies. None such will
4 I have at my side; here treachery shall find no place, knavery no countenance;
5 of whispered calumny, death shall be the reward; on scornful looks and proud
6 thoughts I will have no mercy. To plain, honest folk in the land I will look for
7 my company; my servants shall be such as follow the path of innocence. No
   welcome here for schemers, no standing in my presence for men who talk deceit-
8 fully. Mine, as the days pass, to root out from the land every guilty soul, till I
   purge the Lord's city of all evil-doing.

PSALM ONE HUNDRED AND ONE

(A prayer for the friendless man, when he is troubled, and is pouring out his
griefs before the Lord.)

2 O LORD, hear my prayer, and let my cry come unto thee. Do not turn thy
   face away from me, but lend me thy ear in time of affliction; give me swift
4 audience whenever I call upon thee. See how this life of mine passes away
5 like smoke, how this frame wastes like a tinder! Drained of strength, like grass
6 the sun scorches, I leave my food untasted, forgotten; I am spent with sighing,
7 till my skin clings to my bones. I am no better than a pelican out in the desert,
8 an owl on some ruined dwelling; I keep mournful watch, lonely as a single
9 sparrow on the house top. Still my enemies taunt me, in their mad rage make a
10 by-word of me. Ashes are all my food, I drink nothing but what comes to me
11 mingled with my tears; I shrink before thy vengeful anger, so low thou hast
12 brought me, who didst once lift me so high. Like a tapering shadow my days
   dwindle, wasting away, like grass in the sun!
13   Lord, thou endurest for ever, thy name, age after age, is not forgotten; surely
   thou wilt bestir thyself, and give Sion redress! It is time, now, to take pity on
15 her, the hour has come. See how thy servants love her even in ruin, how they
16 water her dust with their tears! Will not the heathen learn reverence, Lord,
17 for thy glorious name, all those monarchs of the earth, when they hear that

18 the Lord has built Sion anew; that he has revealed himself there in glory, has
19 given heed to the prayer of the afflicted, neglects their appeal no more. Such
legend inscribe we for a later age to read it; a new people will arise, to praise
20 the Lord; the Lord, who looks down from his sanctuary on high, viewing earth
21 from heaven, who has listened to the groans of the prisoners, delivered a race
22 that was doomed to die. There will be talk of the Lord's name in Sion, of his
23 praise in Jerusalem, when peoples and kings meet there to pay him their homage.
24 Here, on my journey, he has brought my strength to an end, cut short my days.
25 What, my God, wilt thou snatch me away, my life half done? Age after age thy
26 years endure; it was thou, Lord, that didst lay the foundations of earth when
27 time began, it was thy hand that built the heavens. They will perish, but thou
wilt remain; they will all be like a cloak that grows thread-bare, and thou wilt lay
28 them aside like a garment, and exchange them for new; thou art unchanging, thy
29 years can never fail. The posterity of thy servants shall yet hold their lands
in peace, their race shall live on in thy keeping.

PSALM ONE HUNDRED AND TWO

(Of David.)

2 BLESS the Lord, my soul, unite, all my powers, to bless that holy name. Bless
3 the Lord, my soul, remembering all he has done for thee, how he pardons all
4 thy sins, heals all thy mortal ills, rescues thy life from deadly peril, crowns thee
5 with the blessings of his mercy; how he contents all thy desire for good, restores
6 thy youth, as the eagle's plumage is restored. The Lord's acts are acts of justice,
7 every wronged soul he offers redress. The Lord, who told Moses his secrets,
who shewed the sons of Israel his power!
8 How pitying and gracious the Lord is, how patient, how rich in mercy! He
10 will not always be finding fault, his frown does not last for ever; he does not treat
11 us as our sins deserve, does not exact the penalty of our wrong-doing. High as
12 heaven above the earth towers his mercy for the men that fear him; far as the
13 east is from the west, he clears away our guilt from us. For his own worshippers,
14 the Lord has a father's pity; does he not know the stuff of which we are made,
15 can he forget that we are only dust? Man's life is like the grass, he blooms and
16 dies like a flower in the fields; once the hot wind has passed over, it has gone,
17 forgotten by the place where it grew. But the Lord's worshippers know no be-
18 ginning or end of his mercy; he will keep faith with their children's children, do
19 they but hold fast by his covenant, and live mindful of his law. The Lord has
20 set up his throne in heaven, rules with universal sway. Bless the Lord, all you
angels of his; angels of sovereign strength, that carry out his commandment,
21 attentive to the word he utters; bless the Lord, all you hosts of his, the servants
22 that perform his will; bless the Lord, all you creatures of his, in every corner
of his dominion; and thou, my soul, bless the Lord.

PSALM ONE HUNDRED AND THREE

(For David himself.)

BLESS the Lord, my soul; O Lord my God, what magnificence is thine! Glory
2 and beauty are thy clothing. The light is a garment thou dost wrap about thee,
3 the heavens a curtain thy hand unfolds. The waters of heaven are thy ante-
chamber, the clouds thy chariot; on the wings of the wind thou dost come and
4 go. Thou wilt have thy angels be like the winds, the servants that wait on thee
like a flame of fire.

5 The earth thou hast planted on its own firm base, undisturbed for all time.
6 The deep once covered it, like a cloak; the waters stood high above the mountains,
7 then cowered before thy rebuking word, fled away at thy voice of thunder, leaving
9 the mountain heights to rise, the valleys to sink into their appointed place! And
to these waters thou hast given a frontier they may not pass; never must they flow
10 back, and cover the earth again. Yet there shall be torrents flooding the glens,
11 water-courses among the hills that give drink to every wild beast; here the wild
12 asses may slake their thirst. The birds of heaven, too, will roost beside them;
vocal is every bough with their music.
13 From thy high dwelling-place thou dost send rain upon the hills; thy hand
14 gives earth all her plenty. Grass must grow for the cattle; for man, too, she must
15 put forth her shoots, if he is to bring corn out from her bosom; if there is to be
wine that will rejoice man's heart, oil to make his face shine, and bread that will
16 keep man's strength from failing. Moisture there must be for the forest trees, for
17 the cedars of Lebanon, trees of the Lord's own planting. Here it is the birds build
18 their nests; the stork makes its home in the fir branches; finds refuge there such
as the goats find in the high hills, the rock-rabbit in its cave.
19 He has given us the moon for our calendar; the sun knows well the hour of his
20 setting. Thou dost decree darkness, and the night falls; in the night all the forest
21 is astir with prowling beasts; the young lions go roaring after their prey, God's
22 pensioners, asking for their food. Then the sun rises, and they slink away to lie
23 down in their dens, while man goes abroad to toil and drudge till the evening.
24 What diversity, Lord, in thy creatures! What wisdom has designed them all!
There is nothing on earth but gives proof of thy creative power.
25 There lies the vast ocean, stretching wide on every hand; this, too, is peopled
26 with living things past number, great creatures and small; the ships pass them
on their course. Leviathan himself is among them; him, too, thou hast created to
27 roam there at his pleasure. And all look to thee to send them their food at the
28 appointed time; it is through thy gift they find it, thy hand opens, and all are
29 filled with content. But see, thou hidest thy face, and they are dismayed; thou
takest their life from them, and they breathe no more, go back to the dust they
30 came from. Then thou sendest forth thy spirit, and there is fresh creation; thou
dost repeople the face of earth.
31 Glory be to the Lord for ever; still let him take delight in his creatures. One
glance from him makes earth tremble; at his touch, the mountains are wreathed
33 in smoke. While life lasts, I will sing in the Lord's honour; my praise shall be his
34 while I have breath to praise him; Oh, may this prayer with him find acceptance,
35 in whom is all my content! Perish all sinners from the land, let the wrong-doers
be forgotten! But thou, my soul, bless the Lord. Alleluia.

PSALM ONE HUNDRED AND FOUR

PRAISE the Lord, and call upon his name; tell the story of his doings for all
2 the nations to hear; greet him with song and psalm, recount his acts of miracle.
3 Triumph in that holy name; let every heart that longs for the Lord rejoice. On
the Lord, on the Lord's greatness still let your hearts dwell, on the Lord's presence
5 be your hearts set. Remember the marvellous acts he did, his miracles, his sen-
6 tences of doom; are you not the posterity of Abraham, his own servant, sons of
7 that Jacob on whom his choice fell? And he, the Lord, is our own God, wide though
8 his writ runs through all the world. He keeps in everlasting memory that covenant
9 of his, that promise which a thousand ages might not cancel. He gave Abraham
10 a promise, bound himself to Isaac by an oath; by that law Jacob should live, his

11 Israel, bound to him with an eternal covenant. To thee, he said, I will give the
12 land of Chanaan, a portion allotted to thee and thine. So few they were in number;
13 only a handful, living there as strangers! And ever they passed on from country
14 to country, the guests of king or people; but he suffered none to harm them; to
15 kings themselves the warning came; Lay no hand on them, never hurt them,
servants anointed and true spokesmen of mine.

16   And now he brought famine on the land, cutting off all their supply of bread.
17 But he had sent an envoy to prepare the way for them, that very Joseph, who was
18 sold as a slave. Fetters held his feet, the yoke galled his neck, but he proved a
20 true prophet at last, the Lord's accomplished word to vindicate him. Then the
21 king sent to release him; the proud ruler of many peoples set him free, and
appointed him master of his household, lord of all the possessions that were his.
22 Joseph should teach his courtiers to be as Joseph was, should train his aged coun-
23 sellors in wisdom. So it was that Israel came into Egypt, that Jacob dwelt as an
alien in the country of Cham.

24   Time passed, and he gave his people great increase of numbers, till it out-
25 matched its rivals. And in these he wrought a change of heart; they grew weary
26 of his people's presence, devised ruin for his worshippers. And now he sent his
27 servant Moses, and Aaron, the man of his choice, to bring about those signs,
28 those miracles of his which the country of Cham would witness. Dark night he
29 sent to benight them, and still his warnings went unheeded. He turned their
30 supply of water into blood, killing all the fish; frogs swarmed out of the ground,
31 even in their royal palaces; at his word, flies attacked them, and gnats all their
32 land over; hail was the rain he gave them, and it brought fire that burned up
33 their countryside; he shattered their vines and fig-trees, broke down all the
34 wood that grew in their domains. He gave the word, and locusts came, grass-
35 hoppers, too, past all numbering, eating up all the grass they had, eating up all
36 the crops their land yielded. Then, his hand fell upon Egypt's first-born, on
37 the first-fruits of all they had engendered; and so he brought his people out,
enriched with silver and gold, no foot that stumbled among all their tribes.

38   Glad indeed was Egypt at their going, such fear of them had overtaken it. He
spread out a cloud to cover them, that turned to fire in the darkness, lighting their
40 journey. Quails came, when they asked for food; he satisfied their desire, too,
41 with bread from heaven, and pierced the rock so that water flowed down, running
42 streams in the wilderness. So well did he remember that holy promise of his,
43 made to his servant Abraham; in joy and triumph he led them out, his chosen
45 people, and gave them the lands of the heathen for their own. There, on soil
Gentile hands had tilled, his commandments should be kept sacred, his law should
reign. Alleluia.

PSALM ONE HUNDRED AND FIVE

(Alleluia.)

2 PRAISE the Lord, the Lord is gracious; his mercy endures for ever;   what
tongue can recount all the great deeds of the Lord, can echo all his praise?
3 Blessed are they who abide ever by his decrees, ever do the right! Remember me,
Lord, with loving thoughts towards thy people, come and strengthen me with thy
5 aid, to witness the prosperity of thy chosen servants, to rejoice with thy people
that rejoices, to share the glory of thy own domain.
6   We have taken part in our fathers' sins; we are guilty men, rebels against thee.
7 So it was with our fathers in Egypt; unremarked, thy wonderful doings, unremembered, thy abundant mercies; even at the Red Sea they must prove rebellious.

8 Yet, for his own honour, to make known his power, he delivered them, checking the Red Sea, so that it dried up, and leading them through its depths as safely as
10 if they trod the desert sands. From a cruel tyrant's grasp he rescued them,
11 claimed them for his own; and the water overwhelmed their pursuers, till not
12 one of them was left. They believed, then, in his promises, sang songs, then, in
13 his honour, but soon they forgot what he had done, and could not wait upon his
14 will. They must needs give way to their cravings in the wilderness, challenge
15 God's power, there in the desert, till he granted their will, then sent a wasting
16 sickness to plague them. Faction raised its head in the camp against Moses,
17 against Aaron, the Lord's chosen priest; and now earth gaped, swallowing up
18 Dathan, overwhelming Abiron and his conspiracy; fire broke out in their com-
19 pany, and the rebels perished by its flames. They made a calf, too, at Horeb,
20 casting a golden image and worshipping it, as if they would exchange the
21 glory that dwelt among them for the semblance of a bullock at grass. So little
they remembered the God who had delivered them, those portents of his in
22 Egypt, strange things seen in the land of Cham, terrible things down by the Red
23 Sea! What wonder if he threatened to make an end of them? But Moses, the man
of his choice, stood in the breach to confront his anger, to ward off destruction.
24 And now they poured scorn on the land of their desire, distrusting his promise;
25 the camp was all disaffection. So the Lord, finding they would not listen to his
26 voice, lifted his hand and threatened to smite them down, there in the wilderness;
27 they should be lost among the peoples, scattered wide through the world. They
dedicated themselves to Beelphegor, in honour of the dead gods sat down to
29 feast; till their wicked ways roused God's anger, and a plague fell upon them.
30 Nor might the destruction cease, till Phinees rose up and made amends, winning
himself such title to God's favour as shall be remembered, age after age, eternally.
32 They provoked his anger, too, at the waters of Meriba, so that Moses was pun-
33 ished for their sake; because, in his heart's bitterness, he broke out into open
complaint.
34 Not theirs to root out the heathen, as the Lord had bidden them; they mingled
36 with the heathen instead, and learned their ways; worshipping carved images, to
37 their own undoing, sacrificing their sons and daughters in honour of devils.
38 Innocent blood, the blood of their own sons and daughters, was poured out in
39 worship to the idols of Chaanan; with blood the whole land was polluted, so
40 heinous the guilt of its people, so wanton their ways. Then God's anger blazed
41 up against his people, his chosen race became abominable to him, and he handed
42 them over to the Gentiles; despised slaves, they were oppressed by their enemies,
43 bowed down under the yoke. Again and again he brought them deliverance, but
ever there were fresh shifts to provoke him, there was fresh guilt to drag them in
44 the dust. And still, when he saw their distress, when he heard their appeals to
45 him, the thought of his covenant availed them; in his great mercy he would relent;
46 their very captors should be moved to pity.
47 Deliver us, O Lord our God, and gather us again, scattered as we are among the
heathen, to praise thy holy name, to triumph in thy renown.
48 Blessed be the God of Israel from all eternity to all eternity; let all the people
cry, Amen, Alleluia.

PSALM ONE HUNDRED AND SIX

2 PRAISE the Lord, the Lord is gracious; his mercy endures for ever; be this the
3 cry of men the Lord has rescued, rescued them from the enemy's hand, and
gathered them in from sunrising and sunset, from the north country and the
south.

4 Some have wandered in parched deserts, missing the way to the city that was
5 their home, hungry and thirsty, so that their spirits died within them. So they
7 cried out to the Lord in their trouble, and he relieved their distress, guiding them
8 surely to the place where they should find a home. Praise they the Lord in his
9 mercies, in his wondrous dealings with mortal men; poor souls that were thirsty,
contented now, poor souls that were hungry, satisfied now with all good.

10 Some lay where darkness overshadowed them, helpless in bonds of iron; their
punishment for rebelling against God's decrees, for thwarting the will of the most
12 High. Their hearts bowed down with sorrow, none else to aid their faltering
13 steps, they cried out to the Lord in their trouble, and he relieved their distress,
14 rescuing them from darkness, from the shadows, tearing their chains asunder.
15 Praise they the Lord in his mercies, in his wondrous dealings with mortal men;
16 the Lord who has shattered the gates of brass, riven the bonds of iron.

17 Some for their own fault must needs be humbled; for their guilt they lay
18 sick, with no stomach for food, close to death's door. So they cried out to
20 the Lord in their trouble, and he relieved their distress, uttered the word of
21 healing, and saved them from their peril. Praise they the Lord in his mercies, in
22 his wondrous dealings with mortal men; theirs to offer him sacrifice in thanksgiving, and proclaim joyfully what he has done for them.

23 Some there were that ventured abroad in ships, trafficking over the high seas;
24 these are men that have witnessed the Lord's doings, his wonderful doings amid
25 the deep. At his word the stormy wind rose, churning up its waves; high up
towards heaven they were carried, then sank into the trough, with spirits fainting
27 at their peril; see them reeling and staggering to and fro as a drunkard does, all
28 their seamanship forgotten! So they cried out to the Lord in their trouble, and he
29 relieved their distress, stilling the storm into a whisper, till all its waves were
30 quiet. Glad hearts were theirs, when calm fell about them, and he brought
31 them to the haven where they longed to be. Praise they the Lord in his mercies,
32 in his wondrous dealings with mortal men; let them extol his name, where the
people gather, glorify him where the elders sit in council.

33 Here, he changes rivers into desert sand, wells into dry ground; land that once
35 was fruitful into a salty marsh, to punish its people's guilt. There, he turns the
36 wilderness into pools of water, desert ground into springs; and establishes hungry
37 folk there, so that they build themselves a city to dwell in, sow fields, and plant
38 vineyards, and reap the harvest; he blesses them, so that their numbers increase
39 beyond measure, and to their cattle grants increase. Once, they were but few,
40 worn down by stress of need and ill fortune; but now the same power that shames
41 proud chieftains, and keeps them wandering in a pathless desert, has rescued the
42 poor from need, their households thrive like their own flocks. Honest men will
43 rejoice to witness it, and malice will stand dumb with confusion. Heed it well, if
thou wouldst be wise; be these thy study, the mercies of the Lord.

PSALM ONE HUNDRED AND SEVEN

(A song. A psalm. Of David.)

2 A TRUE heart, my God, a heart true to thy service; I will sing of thee and
3 praise thee. Wake, my heart, wake, echoes of harp and viol; dawn shall
4 find me watching. Let me give thanks, Lord, for all the world to hear it, sing
5 psalms while the Gentiles listen, of thy mercy, high above heaven itself, of
6 thy faithfulness, that reaches the clouds! O God, mount high above the heavens
7 till thy glory overshadows the whole earth. Now bring aid to the men thou lovest,

8 give our prayer answer, and lift thy right hand to save. God's word came to us
from his sanctuary: In triumph I will divide up Sichem, and parcel out the valley
9 of Tents; to me Galaad, to me Manasse belongs; Ephraim is my helmet, Juda
10 the staff I bear. Now Moab, too, shall be my drudge; over Edom I will claim my
11 right; I will lead the Philistines away in triumph. Such was the oracle; but now
who is to lead me on my march against this fortress, who is to find an entrance for
12 me into Edom, when thou, O God, hast disowned us, and wilt not go into battle
13 with our armies? It is thou that must deliver us from peril; vain is the help of
14 man. Only through God can we fight victoriously; only he can trample our
oppressors in the dust.

PSALM ONE HUNDRED AND EIGHT

(To the choir-master. Of David. A psalm.)

2 GOD that guardest my renown, do not leave me unbefriended; there are
3 malicious lips, treacherous lips, that decry me; whispering against me, hedg-
4 ing me about with a conspiracy of hatred, in unprovoked attack. On their side,
5 all calumny in return for love, on mine all prayer; kindness is repaid with injury,
love with ill will.
6 An ill master let him have, and an accuser ready at his side; let him leave the
8 court of judgement a doomed man, pleading with heaven in vain. Swiftly let his
9 days come to an end, and his office be entrusted to another; orphancy for the
10 children, widowhood for the wife! Driven from a ruined home, to and fro let
11 his children wander, begging their bread, while eager creditors eye his goods, and
12 strangers divide the fruits of his toil. May no friend be left to do him a kindness,
13 none to have pity on his defenceless kin; a speedy end to his race, oblivion for his
14 name before a generation passes! Still may the sin of his fathers be remembered
15 in the Lord's sight, his mother's guilt remain indelible; still may the Lord keep it
16 in mind, and wipe out their memory from the earth. Did he himself keep mercy
in mind, when he persecuted the helpless, the destitute, the grief-stricken, and
17 marked them down for death? Cursing he loved, upon him let the curse fall; for
18 blessing he cared little, may blessing still pass him by. Let cursing wrap him
about, sink like water into his inmost being, soak, like oil, into the marrow of his
19 bones! Let it be the garb he wears, cling to him like a girdle he can never take off.
20 So, in their own coin, may the Lord repay them, my accusers that defame me
21 so cruelly. But do thou, my Lord and Master, take my part, to defend thy own
22 honour; no mercy is so tender as thine. Deliver me in my helpless need; my
23 heart is pierced through with anguish. Like a tapering shadow I depart, swept
24 away like a locust on the wing. My knees are weak with fasting, my strength
25 pines away unnourished. They make a laughing-stock of me, toss their heads in
26 derision as they pass by. Help me, O Lord my God; deliver me in thy mercy;
27 prove to them that my woes are a visitation from thee, sent by no hand but thine.
28 Bless me, thou, and let them curse as they will; disappoint my adversaries, and
29 grant thy servant relief. Let these, my accusers, be covered with shame, wrapped
30 in the mantle of their own confusion. Loudly will I give the Lord thanks, praise
31 him before multitudes that listen; the Lord who has stood at the right hand of the
friendless, brought redress to an innocent soul misjudged.

PSALM ONE HUNDRED AND NINE

(Of David. A psalm.)

TO the Master I serve the Lord's promise was given, Sit here at my right hand
2 while I make thy enemies a footstool under thy feet. The Lord will make thy
empire spring up like a branch out of Sion; thou art to bear rule in the midst of
3 thy enemies. From birth, princely state shall be thine, holy and glorious; thou art
4 my son, born like dew before the day-star rises. The Lord has sworn an oath
5 there is no retracting, Thou art a priest for ever in the line of Melchisedech. At
6 thy right hand, the Lord will beat down kings in the day of his vengeance; he
will pass sentence on the nations, heap high the bodies, scatter far and wide the
7 heads of the slain. Let him but drink of the brook by the wayside, he will lift
up his head in victory.

PSALM ONE HUNDRED AND TEN

(Alleluia.)

ALL my heart goes out to the Lord in praise, before the assembly where
2 the just are gathered. Chant we the Lord's wondrous doings, delight and
3 study of all who love him. Ever his deeds are high and glorious, faithful he abides
4 to all eternity. Great deeds, that he keeps still in remembrance! He, the Lord, is
5 kind and merciful. In abundance he fed the men who feared him, keeping his
6 covenant for ever. Lordly the power he shewed his people, making the lands of
7 the heathen their possession. No act but shews him just and faithful; of his decrees
8 there is no relenting. Perpetual time shall leave them changeless; right and truth
9 are their foundation. So he has brought our race deliverance; to all eternity stands
10 his covenant. Unutterable is his name and worshipful; vain without his fear is
learning. Wise evermore are you who follow it; yours the prize that lasts for ever.

PSALM ONE HUNDRED AND ELEVEN

(Alleluia.)

A BLESSED man is he, who fears the Lord, bearing great love to his command-
2 ments. Children of his shall win renown in their country; do right, and thy
3 sons shall find a blessing. Ease shall dwell in his house, and great prosperity;
4 fame shall ever record his bounty. Good men see a light dawn in darkness; his
5 light, who is merciful, kind and faithful. It goes well with the man who lends in
6 pity, just and merciful in his dealings. Length of days shall leave him still un-
7 shaken; men will remember the just for ever. No fear shall he have of evil tidings;
8 on the Lord his hope is fixed unchangeably. Patient his heart remains and stead-
9 fast, quietly he waits for the downfall of his enemies. Rich are his alms to the
needy; still his bounty abides in memory. The Lord will lift up his head in tri-
10 umph; ungodly men are ill content to see it. Vainly they gnash their teeth in
envy; worldly hopes must fade and perish.

PSALM ONE HUNDRED AND TWELVE

(Alleluia.)

PRAISE the Lord, you that are his servants, praise the name of the Lord
2 together. Blessed be the Lord's name at all times, from this day to all eternity;

3 from the sun's rise to the sun's setting let the Lord's name be praised continually.
4 The Lord is sovereign king of all the nations; his glory is high above the heavens.
5 Who is like the Lord our God, so high above us, that stoops to regard both heaven
7 and earth, lifting up the poor from the dust he lay in, raising the beggar out of
8 his dung-hill, to find him a place among the princes, the princes that rule over his
9 people? He gives the barren woman a home to dwell in, a mother rejoicing in
her children.

PSALM ONE HUNDRED AND THIRTEEN

(Alleluia.)

WHEN Israel came out of Egypt, and the sons of Jacob heard no more a
2 strange language, the Lord took Juda for his sanctuary, Israel for his own
3 dominion. The seas fled at the sight they witnessed, backward flowed the stream
4 of Jordan; up leapt, like rams, the startled mountains, up leapt the hills, like
5 yearling sheep. What ailed you, seas, that you fled in terror; Jordan's stream,
6 what drove thee back? Why did you leap up like rams, you mountains, leap up, you
7 hills, like yearling sheep? Let earth thrill at its Master's presence; it is he that
8 comes, the God of Jacob, who turned the rock into pools of water, the flint-stone
into a springing well.
9   Not to us, Lord, not to us the glory; let thy name alone be honoured; thine the
10 merciful, thine the faithful; why must the heathen say, Their God deserts them?
11 Our God is a God that dwells in heaven; all that his will designs, he executes. The
heathen have silver idols and golden, gods which the hands of men have fashioned.
13 They have mouths, and yet are silent; eyes they have, and yet are sightless; ears
15 they have, and want all hearing; noses, and yet no smell can reach them; hands
16 unfeeling, feet unstirring; never a sound their throats may utter. Such be the
17 end of all who make them, such the reward of all who trust them. It is the Lord
18 that gives hope to the race of Israel, their only help, their only stronghold; the
Lord that gives hope to the race of Aaron, their only help, their only stronghold;
19 the Lord that gives hope to all who fear him, their only help, their only strong-
20 hold. The Lord keeps us in mind, and grants us blessing, blesses the race of
21 Israel, blesses the race of Aaron; all those who fear the Lord, small and great
22 alike, he blesses. Still may the Lord grant you increase, you and your children
23 after you; the blessing of the Lord be upon you. It is he that made both heaven
24 and earth; to the Lord belongs the heaven of heavens, the earth he gives to the
25 children of men. From the dead, Lord, thou hast no praises, the men who go down
26 into the place of silence; but we bless the Lord, we, the living, from this day to
all eternity.

PSALM ONE HUNDRED AND FOURTEEN

(Alleluia.)

2 MY heart is aflame, so graciously the Lord listens to my entreaty; the Lord,
3 who grants me audience when I invoke his name. Death's noose about me,
4 caught in the snares of the grave, ever I found distress and grief at my side, till
5 I called upon the Lord, Save me, Lord, in my peril. Merciful the Lord our God
6 is, and just, and full of pity; he cares for simple hearts, and to me, when I lay
7 humbled, he brought deliverance. Return, my soul, where thy peace lies; the
8 Lord has dealt kindly with thee; he has saved my life from peril, banished my
9 tears, kept my feet from falling. Mine to walk at ease, enjoying the Lord's
presence, in the land of the living.

PSALM ONE HUNDRED AND FIFTEEN

2 I TRUSTED, even when most I bewailed my unhappy lot; bewildered, I said,
3 Man's faith is false; but the Lord's mercies have never failed me; what return
4 shall I make to him? I will take the cup that is pledge of my deliverance, and
5 invoke the name of the Lord upon it; I will pay the Lord my vows in the presence
6 of all his people. Dear in the Lord's sight is the death of those who love him;
7 and am not I, Lord, thy servant, born of thy own handmaid? Thou hast broken
8 the chains that bound me; I will sacrifice in thy honour, and call on the name of
10 the Lord. Before a throng of worshippers I will pay the Lord my vows, here
in the courts of the Lord's house, here, Jerusalem, in thy heart.

PSALM ONE HUNDRED AND SIXTEEN

(Alleluia.)

P RAISE the Lord, all you Gentiles, let all the nations of the world do him
2 honour. Abundant has his mercy been towards us; the Lord remains faithful
to his word for ever.

PSALM ONE HUNDRED AND SEVENTEEN

(Alleluia.)

G IVE thanks to the Lord; the Lord is gracious, his mercy endures for ever.
2 Echo the cry, sons of Israel; the Lord is gracious, his mercy endures for ever.
3 His mercy endures for ever, echo the cry, sons of Aaron; his mercy endures for
5 ever; echo the cry, all you who are the Lord's worshippers. I called on the Lord
6 when trouble beset me, and the Lord listened, and brought me relief. With the
7 Lord at my side, I have no fear of the worst man can do; with the Lord at my
8 side to aid me, I shall yet see my enemies baffled. Better trust the Lord than
9 rely on the help of man; better trust the Lord than rely on the word of princes.
10 Let all heathendom ring me round, see, in the power of the Lord I crush them!
11 They cut me off from every way of escape, but see, in the power of the Lord
12 I crush them! They swarm about me like bees, their fury blazes up like fire
13 among thorns, but see, in the power of the Lord, I crush them! I reeled under the
14 blow, and had well-nigh fallen, but still the Lord was there to aid me. Who but
the Lord is my protector, my stronghold; who but the Lord has brought me
deliverance?
15 The homes of the just echo, now, with glad cries of victory; the power of the
16 Lord has triumphed. The power of the Lord has brought me to great honour,
17 the power of the Lord has triumphed. I am reprieved from death, to live on and
18 proclaim what the Lord has done for me. The Lord has chastened me, chastened
19 me indeed, but he would not doom me to die. Open me the gates where right
20 dwells; let me go in and thank the Lord! Here is the gate that leads to the Lord's
21 presence; here shall just souls find entry. Thanks be to thee, Lord, for giving me
22 audience, thanks be to thee, my deliverer. The very stone which the builders
23 rejected has become the chief stone at the corner; this is the Lord's doing, and it
24 is marvellous in our eyes. This day is a holiday of the Lord's own choosing;
greet this day with rejoicing, greet this day with triumph!
25 Deliverance, Lord, deliverance; Lord, grant us days of prosperity! Blessed is
he who comes in the name of the Lord! A blessing from the Lord's house upon
27 your company! The Lord is God; his light shines out to welcome us; marshal the

procession aright, with a screen of boughs that reaches to the very horns of the
28 altar. Thou art my God, mine to thank thee, thou art my God, mine to extol
29 thee. Give thanks to the Lord; the Lord is gracious, his mercy endures for ever.

PSALM ONE HUNDRED AND EIGHTEEN

AH, blessed they, who pass through life's journey unstained, who follow the
2 law of the Lord! Ah, blessed they who cherish his decrees, make him the
3 whole quest of their hearts! Afar from wrong-doing, thy sure paths they tread.
4 Above all else it binds us, the charge thou hast given us to keep. Ah, how shall
6 my steps be surely guided to keep faith with thy covenant? Attentive to all thy
7 commandments, I go my way undismayed. A true heart's worship thou shalt
8 have, thy just awards prompting me. All shall be done thy laws demand, so
thou wilt not forsake me utterly.
9 Best shall he keep his youth unstained, who is true to thy trust. Be thou the
whole quest of my heart; never let me turn aside from thy commandments.
11 Buried deep in my heart, thy warnings shall keep me clear of sin. Blessed art thou,
13 O Lord, teach me to know thy will. By these lips let the awards thou makest ever
14 be recorded. Blithely as one that has found great possessions, I follow thy decrees.
15 Bethinking me still of the charge thou givest, I will mark thy footsteps. Be thy
covenant ever my delight, thy words kept in memory.
17 Crown thy servant with life, to live faithful to thy commands. Clear sight be
19 mine, to contemplate the wonders of thy law. Comfort this earthly exile; do not
20 refuse me the knowledge of thy will. Crushed lies my spirit, longing ever for thy
21 just awards. Chastener of the proud, thy curse lies on all who swerve from thy
22 covenant. Clear me of the reproach that shames me, as I was ever attentive to
23 thy claims. Closeted together, princes plot against me, thy servant, that thinks
24 only of thy decrees. Claims lovingly cherished, decrees that are my counsellors!
25 Deep lies my soul in the dust, restore life to me, as thou hast promised. Deign,
now, to shew me thy will, thou who hast listened when I opened my heart to thee.
27 Direct me in the path thou biddest me follow, and all my musing shall be of thy
28 wonderful deeds. Despair wrings tears from me; let thy promises raise me up
29 once more. Deliver me from every false thought; make me free of thy covenant.
30 Duty's path my choice, I keep thy bidding ever in remembrance. Disappoint me,
32 Lord, never, one that holds fast by thy commandments. Do but open my heart
wide, and easy lies the path thou hast decreed.
33 Expound, Lord, thy whole bidding to me; faithfully I will keep it. Enlighten
35 me, to scan thy law closely, and keep true to it with all my heart. Eagerly I long
36 to be guided in the way of thy obedience. Ever let my choice be set on thy will,
37 not on covetous thoughts. Eyes have I none for vain phantoms; let me find life
38 in following thy way. Establish with me, thy servant, the promise made to thy
39 worshippers. Ease me of the reproach my heart dreads, thou, whose awards are
40 gracious. Each command of thine I embrace lovingly; do thou in thy faithfulness
grant me life.
41 For me too, Lord, thy mercy, for me too the deliverance thou hast promised!
42 Fit answer for those who taunt me, that I rely on thy truth. Faithful thy pro-
44 mise, let me not boast in vain; in thy covenant lies my hope. For ever and for
45 evermore true to thy charge thou shalt find me. Freely shall my feet tread, if
46 thy will is all my quest. Fearlessly will I talk of thy decrees in the presence of
47 kings, and be never abashed. Fain would I have all my comfort in the law I love.
48 Flung wide my arms to greet thy law, ever in my thoughts thy bidding.

49 Go not back on the word thou hast pledged to thy servant; there lies all my
50 hope. Good news in my affliction, thy promises have brought me life. Ground
52 down by the scorn of my oppressors, never from thy law I swerve aside. Gracious
53 comfort, Lord, is the memory of thy just dealings in times long past. Great ruth
54 have I to see wrong-doers, and how they abandon thy law. Gone out into a land
55 of exile, of thy covenant I make my song. Gloom of night finds me still thinking
56 of thy name, Lord, still observant of thy bidding. Guerdon I ask no other, but
the following of thy will.

57 Heritage, Lord, I claim no other, but to obey thy word. Heart-deep my sup-
59 plication before thee for the mercies thou hast promised. Have I not planned
60 out my path, turned aside to follow thy decrees? Haste such as mine can brook
61 no delay in carrying out all thy bidding. Hemmed in by the snares which sinners
62 laid for me, never was I forgetful of thy law. Hearken when I rise at dead of
63 night to praise thee for thy just dealings. How well I love the souls that fear thee,
64 and are true to thy trust! How thy mercy fills the earth, Lord! Teach me to do
thy will.

65 In fulfilment of thy promise, Lord, what kindness thou hast shewn thy servant!
66 Inspire, instruct me still; all my hope is in thy covenant. Idly I strayed till thou
68 didst chasten me; no more shall thy warnings go unheeded. Indeed, indeed thou
69 art gracious; teach me to do thy bidding. In vain my oppressors plot against me;
70 thy will is all my quest. Inhuman hearts, curdled with scorn! For me, thy law is
71 enough. It was in mercy thou didst chasten me, schooling me to thy obedience.
72 Is not the law thou hast given dearer to me than rich store of gold and silver?

73 Jealous for the handiwork thou hast made, teach me to understand thy com-
74 mandments. Joy shall be theirs, thy true worshippers, to see the confidence I
75 have in thy word. Just are thy awards; I know well, Lord, it was in faithfulness
76 thou didst afflict me. Judge me no more; pity and comfort thy servant as thou
77 hast promised. Judge me no more; pardon and life for one that loves thy will!
78 Just be their fall, who wrong me scornfully; thy law is all my study. Joined to
80 my company be every soul that worships thee and heeds thy warnings. Jealously
let my heart observe thy bidding; let me not hope in vain.

81 Keeping watch for thy aid, my soul languishes, yet I trust in thy word. Keeping
watch for the fulfilment of thy promise, my eyes languish for comfort still delayed.
83 Kitchen-smoke shrivels the wine-skin; so waste I, yet never forget thy will.
84 Knowest thou not how short are thy servant's days? Soon be my wrongs redressed.
85 Knaves will be plotting against me still, that are no friends to thy law. Knaves
87 they are that wrong me; bring aid, as thy covenant stands unchanging. Keep
88 thy bidding I would, though small hope of life they had left me. Kind as thou
ever wert, preserve me; then utter thy bidding, and I will obey.

89 Lord, the word thou hast spoken stands ever unchanged as heaven. Loyal to
91 his promise, age after age, is he who made the enduring earth. Long as time lasts,
92 these shall stand, obeying thy decree, Master of all. Lest I should sink in my
93 affliction, thou hast given thy covenant to be my comfort. Life-giving are thy
94 commands, never by me forgotten. Lend me thy aid, for thine I am, and thy
95 bidding is all my quest. Let sinners go about to destroy me, I wait on thy will.
96 Look where I may, all good things must end; only thy law is wide beyond
measure.

97 My delight, Lord, is in thy bidding; ever my thoughts return to it. Musing still
99 on thy commandments, I have grown more prudent than my enemies. More
100 wisdom have I than all my teachers, so well have I pondered thy decrees. More
101 learning have I than my elders, I that hold true to thy charge. Mindful of thy
102 warnings, I guide my steps clear of every evil path. Meek under thy tuition, thy

103 will I keep ever in view. Meat most appetizing are thy promises ; never was honey
104 so sweet to my taste. Made wise by thy law, I shun every path of evil-doing.
105   No lamp like thy word to guide my feet, to shew light on my path. Never will
107 I retract my oath to give thy just commands observance. Nothing, Lord, but
108 affliction, never the saving help thou didst promise me? Nay, Lord, accept these
109 vows of mine ; teach me to do thy bidding. Needs must I carry my life in my
110 hands, yet am I ever mindful of thy law. Nearly the snares of the wicked caught
111 my feet, yet would I not swerve from thy obedience. Now and ever thy covenant
112 is my prize, is my heart's comfort. Now and ever to do thy will perfectly is my
      heart's aim.
113   Out upon the men that play traitor to the law I love! Other defence, other
115 shield have I none ; in thy law I trust. Out of my path, lovers of wrong ; I will
116 keep my God's commandments. Only let thy promised aid preserve me ; do
117 not disappoint me of the hope I cherish. Only do thou sustain me in safety,
118 looking ever to thy will. Obey thee who will not, shall earn thy disdain ; idle is
119 all their scheming. Outcasts they are that profane the land with wrong ; for me,
120 thy law is enough. Overcome is my whole being with the fear of thee ; I am
      adread of thy judgements.
121   Protect the justice of my cause ; never leave me at the mercy of my oppressors.
122 Pledge thyself still to befriend me ; save me from the oppression of my enemies.
123 Pining away, I look for thy saving help, the faithful keeping of thy promises.
124 Pity thy own servant, and teach him thy decrees. Perfect in thy own servant's
126 heart the knowledge of thy will. Put off the hour, Lord, no more ; too long thy
127 commandment stands defied. Precious beyond gold or jewel I hold thy law.
128 Prized be every decree of thine ; forsworn be every path of evil-doing.
129   Right wonderful thy decrees are, hard to read, and well my heart heeds them.
130 Revelation and light thy words disclose to the simple. Rises ever a sigh from my
132 lips as I long after thy covenant. Regard and pity me, as thou hast pity for all that
133 love thy name. Rule thou my path as thou hast promised ; never be wrong-doing
134 my master. Rescue me from man's oppression, to wait henceforth on thy bidding.
135 Restore to thy servant the smile of thy living favour, and teach him to know thy
136 will. Rivers of tears flow from my eyes, to see thy law forgotten.
137   So just, Lord, thou art, thy awards so truly given! Strict justice and utter faith-
139 fulness inspire all thy decrees. Stung by love's jealousy, I watch my enemies
140 defy thy bidding. Shall not I, thy servant, love thy promises, tested and found
141 true? Still despised and disinherited, I do not forget thy charge. Stands thy
143 faithfulness eternally, thy law for ever changeless. Sorrow and distress have
144 fallen on me ; in thy commandments is all my comfort. Sentence eternal is thy
      decree ; teach me the wisdom that brings life.
145   Thy audience, Lord, my whole heart claims, a heart true to thy trust. To thee
147 I cry, O grant deliverance ; I will do all thy bidding. Twilight comes, and I awake
148 to plead with thee, hoping ever in thy promises. Through the night my eyes
149 keep watch, to ponder thy sayings. Thine, Lord, to listen in thy mercy, and
150 grant life according to thy will. Treacherous foes draw near, that are strangers
151 to thy covenant. Thou, Lord, art close at hand ; all thy awards are true. Taught
      long since by thy decrees, I know well thou hast ordained them everlastingly.
153   Unblessed is my lot ; look down and rescue me, that still am mindful of thy
154 law. Uphold my cause, and deliver me ; true to thy promise, grant me life. Un-
156 known thy mercy to the sinner that defies thy bidding. Unnumbered, Lord, are
157 thy blessings ; as thy will is, grant me life. Under all the assaults of my oppressors,
158 I keep true to thy charge. Unhappy I, that watch thy warnings to the sinner
159 go unheeded! Up, Lord, and witness the love I bear thy covenant ; in thy mercy

160 bid me live! Unchanging truth is thy word's fountain-head, eternal the force
of thy just decrees.
161   Vexed by the causeless malice of princes, my heart still dreads thy warnings.
162 Victors rejoice not more over rich spoils, than I in thy promises. Villainy I abhor
164 and renounce; thy law is all my love. Votive thanks seven times a day I give thee
165 for the just awards thou makest. Very great peace is theirs who love thy law;
166 their feet never stumble. Valiantly, Lord, I wait on thee for succour, keeping
167 ever true to thy charge. Vanquished by great love, my heart is ever obedient to
168 thy will. Vigilantly I observe precept and bidding of thine, living always as in
thy sight.
169   Wilt thou not admit my cry, Lord, to thy presence, and grant me thy promised
170 gift of wisdom? Wilt thou not countenance my plea, redeem thy pledge to deliver
171 me? What praise shall burst from my lips, when thou makest known thy will!
172 What hymns of thankfulness this tongue shall raise to the author of all just de-
173 crees! Wouldst thou but lift thy hand to aid me, that take my stand on thy
174 covenant! Weary it is, Lord, waiting for deliverance, but thy law is my comfort.
176 When will thy just award grant redress, that I may live to praise thee? Wayward thou seest me, like a lost sheep; come to look for thy servant, that is mindful
still of thy bidding.

PSALM ONE HUNDRED AND NINETEEN

(A song of ascents.)

2 NOT unheeded I cry to the Lord in the hour of my distress. Lord, have pity
3 and deliver me from the treacherous lips, the perjured tongue. Perjurer, he
4 will give thee all thy deserts and more; sharp arrows from a warrior's bow,
5 blazing faggots of broom. Unhappy I, that live an exile in Mosoch, or dwell
6 among the tents of Cedar! Long banished here among the enemies of peace,
7 for peace I plead, and their cry is still for battle.

PSALM ONE HUNDRED AND TWENTY

(A song of ascents.)

2 I LIFT up my eyes to the hills, to find deliverance; from the Lord deliverance
3 comes to me, the Lord who made heaven and earth. Never will he who guards
4 thee allow thy foot to stumble; never fall asleep at his post! Such a guardian has
5 Israel, one who is never weary, never sleeps; it is the Lord that guards thee, the
6 Lord that stands at thy right hand to give thee shelter. The sun's rays by day,
7 the moon's by night, shall have no power to hurt thee. The Lord will guard thee
8 from all evil; the Lord will protect thee in danger; the Lord will protect thy
journeying and thy home-coming, henceforth and for ever.

PSALM ONE HUNDRED AND TWENTY-ONE

(A song of ascents. Of David.)

WELCOME sound, when I heard them saying, We will go into the Lord's
2 house! Within thy gates, Jerusalem, our feet stand at last; Jerusalem, built as
4 a city should be built that is one in fellowship. There the tribes meet, the Lord's
5 own tribes, to give praise, as Israel is ever bound, to the Lord's name; there the
6 thrones are set for judgement, thrones for the house of David. Pray for all that
7 brings Jerusalem peace! May all who love thee dwell at ease! Let there be peace

8 within thy ramparts, ease in thy strongholds! For love of my brethren and my
9 familiar friends, peace is still my prayer for thee; remembering the house of the
Lord our God, for thy happiness I plead.

PSALM ONE HUNDRED AND TWENTY-TWO

(A song of ascents.)

2 UNTO thee I lift up my eyes, unto thee, who dwellest in the heavens. See how
the eyes of servants are fixed on the hands of their masters, the eyes of a maid
on the hand of her mistress! Our eyes, too, are fixed on the Lord our God, waiting
3 for him to shew mercy on us. Have mercy on us, Lord, have mercy on us; we
4 have had our fill of man's derision. Our hearts can bear no more to be the scorn
of luxury, the derision of the proud.

PSALM ONE HUNDRED AND TWENTY-THREE

(A song of ascents. Of David.)

2 IF the Lord had not been on our side, Israel may boast, if the Lord had not
3 been on our side when human foes assailed us, it seemed as if they must have
4 swallowed us up alive, so fierce their anger threatened us. It seemed as if the
5 tide must have sucked us down, the torrent closed above us; closed above us the
6 waters that ran so high. Blessed be the Lord, who has not let us fall a prey to
7 those ravening mouths! Safe, like a bird rescued from the fowler's snare; the
8 snare is broken and we are safe! Such help is ours, the Lord's help, that made
heaven and earth.

PSALM ONE HUNDRED AND TWENTY-FOUR

(A song of ascents.)

THOSE who trust in the Lord are strong as mount Sion itself, that stands
2 unmoved for ever. The hills protect Jerusalem; so the Lord protects his
3 people, now and for ever. Domain of the just! No longer shall godless men bear
4 rule in it; else the just, too, might soil their hands with guilt. Deal kindly, Lord,
5 with the kindly, with the true-hearted. Feet that stray into false paths the Lord
will punish, as he punishes wrong-doers; but upon Israel there shall be peace.

PSALM ONE HUNDRED AND TWENTY-FIVE

(A song of ascents.)

WHEN the Lord gave back Sion her banished sons, we walked like men in a
2 dream; in every mouth was laughter, joy was on every tongue. Among the
3 heathen themselves it was said, What favour the Lord has shewn them! Favour
4 indeed the Lord has shewn us, and our hearts are rejoiced. Deliver us, Lord,
from our bondage; our withered hopes, Lord, like some desert water-course
6 renew! The men who are sowing in tears will reap, one day, with joy. Mournful
enough they go, but with seed to scatter; trust me, they will come back rejoicing,
as they carry their sheaves with them.

PSALM ONE HUNDRED AND TWENTY-SIX

(A song of ascents. Of Solomon.)

2 VAIN is the builder's toil, if the house is not of the Lord's building; vainly the
guard keeps watch, if the city has not the Lord for its guardian. Vain, that
you should be astir before daybreak, and sit on over your tasks late into the night,
you whose bread is so hardly won; is it not in the hours of sleep that he blesses the
3 men he loves? Fatherhood itself is the Lord's gift, the fruitful womb is a reward
4 that comes from him. Crown of thy youth, children are like arrows in a warrior's
5 hand. Happy, whose quiver is well filled with these; their cause will not be set
aside when they plead against their enemies at the gate.

PSALM ONE HUNDRED AND TWENTY-SEVEN

(A song of ascents.)

2 BLESSED thou art, if thou dost fear the Lord, and follow his paths! Thyself
shall eat what thy hands have toiled to win; blessed thou art; all good shall be
3 thine. Thy wife shall be fruitful as a vine, in the heart of thy home, the children
4 round thy table sturdy as olive-branches. Let a man serve the Lord, such is the
5 blessing that awaits him. May the Lord who dwells in Sion bless thee; mayest
6 thou see Jerusalem in prosperity all thy life long. Mayest thou live to see thy
children's children, and peace resting upon Israel.

PSALM ONE HUNDRED AND TWENTY-EIGHT

2 SORE have they beset me even from my youth (let this be Israel's boast);
sore have they beset me even from my youth, but never once outmatched
3 me. I bent my back to the oppressor, and long was the furrow ere the plough
4 turned; but the Lord proved faithful, and cut the bonds of tyranny asunder.
5 Let them be dismayed and routed, all these enemies of Sion. Let them be like the
7 stalks on a house-top, that wither there unharvested; never will they be grasped
8 in the reaper's hand, or fill the gleaner's bosom, no passer-by will say, The Lord's
blessing on you; we bless you in the name of the Lord.

PSALM ONE HUNDRED AND TWENTY-NINE

(A song of ascents.)

2 OUT of the depths I cry to thee, O Lord; Master, listen to my voice; let but
3 thy ears be attentive to the voice that calls on thee for pardon. If thou, Lord,
4 wilt keep record of our iniquities, Master, who has strength to bear it? Ah, but
5 with thee there is forgiveness; be thy name ever revered. I wait for the Lord, for
6 his word of promise my soul waits; patient as ever watchman that looked for the
7 day. Patient as watchman at dawn, for the Lord Israel waits, the Lord with
8 whom there is mercy, with whom is abundant power to ransom. He it is tha
will ransom Israel from all his iniquities.

PSALM ONE HUNDRED AND THIRTY

(A song of ascents. Of David.)

LORD, my heart is not lifted up, my eyes not raised from the earth; my mind
2 does not dwell on high things, on marvels that are beyond my reach. Bear
me witness that I kept my soul ever quiet, ever at peace. The thoughts of a child
3 on its mother's breast, a child's thoughts were all my soul knew. Let Israel trust
in the Lord, henceforth and for ever.

PSALM ONE HUNDRED AND THIRTY-ONE

(A song of ascents.)

2 IN David's reckoning, Lord, let not his patient care be forgotten, the oath he
3 swore to the Lord, the vow he made to the great God of Jacob: Never will I come
beneath the roof of my house, or climb up into the bed that is strewn for me;
4 never shall these eyes have sleep, these eye-lids close, until I have found the Lord
6 a home, the great God of Jacob a dwelling-place. And now, at Ephrata, we have
7 heard tidings of what we looked for, we have found it in the plains of Jaar; now
8 to go into his dwelling, pay reverence at his footstool! Up, Lord, and take pos-
9 session of thy resting-place, thou and the ark which is shrine of thy glory! Let
thy priests go clad in the vesture of innocence, thy faithful people cry aloud
with rejoicing.
10   Think of thy servant David, and do not refuse audience to the king thou hast
11 anointed. Never will the Lord be false to that inviolable oath he swore to David:
12 I will raise to thy throne heirs of thy own body; if thy sons hold fast to my covenant, to the decrees which I make known to them, their sons too shall reign on
13 thy throne for ever. The Lord's choice has fallen upon Sion, this is the dwelling
14 he longed for: Here, for ever, is my resting-place, here is my destined home.
15 Trust me, I will bless her with abundant store, the poor shall have bread to their
16 heart's content; I will clothe her priests in the vesture of triumph, cries of rejoic-
17 ing shall echo among her faithful people. There the stock of David shall bud,
18 there shall a lamp burn continually for the king I have anointed. I will cover his
enemies with confusion; on his brow the crown I gave shall shine untarnished.

PSALM ONE HUNDRED AND THIRTY-TWO

(A song of ascents. Of David.)

GRACIOUS the sight, and full of comfort, when brethren dwell united.
2 Gracious as balm poured on the head till it flows down on to the beard; balm
3 that flowed down Aaron's beard, and reached the very skirts of his robe. It is as
if dew like the dews of Hermon were falling on this hill of Sion; here, where the
Lord grants benediction and life everlastingly.

PSALM ONE HUNDRED AND THIRTY-THREE

(A song of ascents.)

COME, then, praise the Lord, all you that are the Lord's servants; you that
2 wait on the Lord's house at midnight, lift up your hands towards the sanc-
3 tuary and bless the Lord. May the Lord who dwells in Sion bless thee, the Lord
who made heaven and earth!

PSALM ONE HUNDRED AND THIRTY-FOUR

(Alleluia.)

2 PRAISE the Lord's name; praise the Lord, you that are his servants, you who
3 stand in the house of the Lord, in the courts where our God dwells. Praise to
4 the Lord, a Lord so gracious, praise to his name, a name so well beloved. Has not
the Lord made choice of Jacob, claimed Israel for his own?
5 Doubt it never, the Lord is great; he, our Master, is higher than all the gods.
6 In heaven and on earth, in the sea and in the deep waters beneath us, the Lord
7 accomplishes his will; summoning clouds from the ends of the earth, rain-storm
8 wedding to lightning-flash, bringing winds out of his store-house. He it was
9 that smote the first-born of the Egyptians, man and beast alike; what wonders
and portents, Egypt, thou didst witness, sent to plague Pharao and all his servants!
10 He it was that smote nation after nation, and slew the kings in their pride, Sehon
king of the Amorrhites, and Og the king of Basan, and all the rulers of Chanaan,
12 and marked down their lands for a dwelling-place where his own people of Israel
should dwell.
13 Lord, thy name abides for ever; age succeeds age, and thou art ever unforgotten.
14 The Lord defends his people, takes pity on his servants. What are the idols of the
16 heathen but silver and gold, gods which the hands of men have fashioned? They
17 have mouths, and yet are silent; eyes they have, and yet are sightless; ears they
18 have, and want all hearing, never a breath have they in their mouths. Such the
19 end of all who make them, such the reward of all who trust them. Bless the Lord,
20 sons of Israel, bless the Lord, sons of Aaron, bless the Lord, sons of Levi, bless
21 the Lord, all you that are the Lord's worshippers. Here, in Sion his dwelling-
place, here, in Jerusalem, let the Lord's name be blessed.

PSALM ONE HUNDRED AND THIRTY-FIVE

(Alleluia.)

2 GIVE thanks to the Lord for his goodness, his mercy is eternal; give thanks to
3 the God of gods, his mercy is eternal; give thanks to the Lord of lords, his
4 mercy is eternal. Eternal his mercy, who does great deeds as none else can; eternal
6 his mercy, whose wisdom made the heavens; eternal his mercy, who poised earth
7 upon the floods. Eternal his mercy, who made the great luminaries; made the
9 sun to rule by day, his mercy is eternal; made the moon and the stars to rule by
night, his mercy is eternal.
10 Eternal his mercy, who smote the Egyptians by smiting their first-born; eternal
12 his mercy, who delivered Israel from their midst, with constraining power, with
13 his arm raised on high, his mercy is eternal. Eternal the mercy that divided the
14 Red Sea in two, eternal the mercy that led Israel through its waters, eternal the
16 mercy that drowned in the Red Sea Pharao and Pharao's men. And so he led his
people through the wilderness, his mercy is eternal.
17 Eternal the mercy that smote great kings, eternal the mercy that slew the kings
19 in their pride, Sehon king of the Amorrhites, his mercy is eternal, and Og the
21 king of Basan, his mercy is eternal. Eternal the mercy that marked down their
22 land to be a dwelling-place; a dwelling-place for his servant Israel, his mercy is
23 eternal. Eternal the mercy that remembers us in our affliction, eternal the mercy
25 that rescues us from our enemies, eternal the mercy that gives all living things
26 their food. Give thanks to the God of heaven, his mercy is eternal.

PSALM ONE HUNDRED AND THIRTY-SIX

WE sat down by the streams of Babylon and wept there, remembering Sion.
2   Willow-trees grow there, and on these we hung up our harps when the men
who took us prisoner cried out for a song. We must make sport for our enemies;
4 A stave, there, from the music they sing at Sion! What, should we sing the Lord's
5 song in a strange land? Jerusalem, if I forget thee, perish the skill of my right
6 hand! Let my tongue stick fast to the roof of my mouth if I cease to remember
7 thee, if I love not Jerusalem dearer than heart's content! Remember, Lord, how
the sons of Edom triumphed when Jerusalem fell; O'erthrow it, they cried, o'er-
8 throw it, till the very foundation is left bare. Babylon, pitiless queen, blessed be
9 the man who deals out to thee the measure thou hast dealt to us; blessed be
the man who will catch up thy children, and dash them against the rocks!

PSALM ONE HUNDRED AND THIRTY-SEVEN

(Of David.)

MY heart's thanks, Lord, for listening to the prayer I uttered; angels for my
2   witnesses, I will sing of thy praise. I bow down in worship towards thy
sanctuary, praising thy name for thy mercy and faithfulness; thy own honour
3 and thy pledged word thou hast vindicated for all the world to see. To thee
I appealed, and thou didst listen to me, didst fill my heart with courage.
4 All the kings of the earth, Lord, will praise thee now; were not thy promises made
5 in their hearing? Their song shall be of the Lord's doings, how great is his
6 renown, the Lord, who is so high above us, yet looks with favour on the humble,
7 looks on the proud too, but from far off. Though affliction surround my path, thou
dost preserve me; it is thy power that confronts my enemies' malice, thy right
8 hand that rescues me. My purposes the Lord will yet speed; thy mercy, Lord,
endures for ever, and wilt thou abandon us, the creatures of thy own hands?

PSALM ONE HUNDRED AND THIRTY-EIGHT

(To the choir-master. Of David. A psalm.)

2 LORD, I lie open to thy scrutiny; thou knowest me, knowest when I sit down
3   and when I rise up again, canst read my thoughts from far away. Walk I or
4 sleep I, thou canst tell; no movement of mine but thou art watching it. Before
5 ever the words are framed on my lips, all my thought is known to thee; rearguard
6 and vanguard, thou dost compass me about, thy hand still laid upon me. Such
wisdom as thine is far beyond my reach, no thought of mine can attain it.
7   Where can I go, then, to take refuge from thy spirit, to hide from thy view?
8 If I should climb up to heaven thou art there; if I sink down to the world beneath,
9 thou art present still. If I could wing my way eastwards, or find a dwelling be-
10 yond the western sea, still would I find thee beckoning to me, thy right hand
11 upholding me. Or perhaps I would think to bury myself in darkness; night should
12 surround me, friendlier than day; but no, darkness is no hiding-place from thee,
with thee the night shines clear as day itself; light and dark are one.
13   Author, thou, of my inmost being, didst thou not form me in my mother's
14 womb? I praise thee for my wondrous fashioning, for all the wonders of thy
15 creation. Of my soul thou hast full knowledge, and this mortal frame had no
mysteries for thee, who didst contrive it in secret, devise its pattern, there in the

16 dark recesses of the earth. All my acts thy eyes have seen, all are set down already in thy record; my days were numbered before ever they came to be.
17   A riddle, O my God, thy dealings with me, so vast their scope! As well count the sand, as try to fathom them; and, were that skill mine, thy own being still
19 confronts me. O God, wouldst thou but make an end of the wicked! Murderers,
20 keep your distance from me! Treacherously they rebel against thee, faithlessly
21 set thee at defiance. Lord, do I not hate the men who hate thee, am I not sick at
22 heart over their rebellion? Surpassing hatred I bear them, count them my sworn
23 enemies. Scrutinize me, O God, as thou wilt, and read my heart; put me to the
24 test, and examine my restless thoughts. See if on any false paths my heart is set, and thyself lead me in the ways of old.

PSALM ONE HUNDRED AND THIRTY-NINE

(To the choir-master. A psalm. Of David.)

2 RESCUE me, Lord, from human malice, save me from the lovers of oppression,
3 always plotting treachery in their hearts, always at their quarrelling; tongues
5 sharp as the tongues of serpents, lips that hide the poison of adders. Preserve me Lord, from the power of sinful men, save me from these lovers of oppression who
6 are plotting to trip my feet. What hidden snares they set for me, these tyrants, what nets they spread to catch me, what traps they lay in my path!
7   To the Lord I make my appeal, Thou art my God, listen, Lord, to the voice that
8 pleads with thee. My Lord, my Master, my strong deliverer, it is thou that
9 shieldest my head in the day of battle. Lord, do not let malice have its way with
10 me, do not prosper its evil designs. They carry their heads high as they close
11 in around me; let their conspiracy prove its own undoing; let burning coals rain
12 down on them, be they cast into a pit whence they shall rise no more. Not long the blasphemer's time on earth: misfortune will overtake the oppressor unawares.
13 Can I doubt that the Lord will avenge the helpless, will grant the poor redress?
14 Honest men will yet live to praise thy name; upright hearts to enjoy the smile of thy favour.

PSALM ONE HUNDRED AND FORTY

(A psalm. Of David.)

COME quickly, Lord, at my cry for succour; do not let my appeal to thee go
2 unheard. Welcome as incense-smoke let my prayer rise up before thee; when
3 I lift up my hands, be it acceptable as the evening sacrifice. Lord, set a guard on
4 my mouth, post a sentry before my lips; do not turn my heart towards thoughts of evil, and deeds of treachery; never let me take part with the wrong-doers,
5 and share the banquet with them. Rather let some just man deal me heavy blows; this shall be his kindness to me; reprove me, and it shall be balm poured over me; such unction never will this head refuse. Their injuries I will still greet with a prayer ...
6   ... My words have won their hearts, a people that had seen their chieftains
7 hurled down the rock-face, a people whose bones lie scattered at the grave's mouth, like seed when the earth is cloven into furrows.
8   To thee these eyes look, my Lord, my Master; in thee I trust; let not my life
9 be forfeit. Preserve me from the ambush they have laid for me, from the snares
10 of the wrong-doers. Into their own net, sinner upon sinner, may they fall, and I pass on in safety.

PSALM ONE HUNDRED AND FORTY-ONE

(A maskil. Of David, when he was in the cave. A prayer.)

2
4 LOUD is my cry to the Lord, the prayer I utter for the Lord's mercy, as I pour out my complaint before him, tell him of the affliction I endure. My heart is ready to faint within me, but thou art watching over my path. They lie in ambush
5 for me, there by the wayside; I look to the right of me, and find none to take my
6 part; all hope of escape is cut off from me, none is concerned for my safety. To thee, Lord, I cry, claiming thee for my only refuge, all that is left me in this world
7 of living men. Listen, then, to my plea; thou seest me all defenceless. Rescue me
8 from persecutors who are too strong for me; restore liberty to a captive soul. What thanks, then, will I give to thy name, honest hearts all about me, rejoicing to see thy favour restored!

PSALM ONE HUNDRED AND FORTY-TWO

(A psalm. Of David.)

LISTEN, Lord, to my prayer; give my plea a hearing, as thou art ever faithful;
2 listen, thou who lovest the right. Do not call thy servant to account; what
3 man is there living that can stand guiltless in thy presence? See how my enemies plot against my life, how they have abased me in the dust, set me down in dark
4 places, like the long-forgotten dead! My spirits are crushed within me, my heart
5 is cowed. And my mind goes back to past days; I think of all thou didst once,
6 dwell on the proofs thou gavest of thy power. To thee I spread out my hands in prayer, for thee my soul thirsts, like a land parched with drought.
7 Hasten, Lord, to answer my prayer; my spirit grows faint. Do not turn thy face
8 away from me, and leave me like one sunk in the abyss. Speedily let me win thy
9 mercy, my hope is in thee; to thee I lift up my heart, shew me the path I must
10 follow; to thee I fly for refuge, deliver me, Lord, from my enemies. Thou art my God, teach me to do thy will; let thy gracious spirit lead me, safe ground under
11 my feet. For the honour of thy own name, Lord, grant me life; in thy mercy
12 rescue me from my cruel affliction. Have pity on me, and scatter my enemies; thy servant I; make an end of my cruel persecutors.

PSALM ONE HUNDRED AND FORTY-THREE

(Of David.)

2 BLESSED be the Lord, my refuge, who makes these hands strong for battle, these fingers skilled in fight; the Lord who pities me and grants me safety, who shelters me and sets me at liberty, who protects me and gives me confidence,
3 bowing down nations to my will. Lord, what is Adam's race, that thou givest
4 heed to it, what is man, that thou carest for him? Like the wind he goes, like a shadow his days pass.
5 Bid heaven stoop, Lord, and come down to earth; at thy touch, the mountains
6 will be wreathed in smoke. Brandish thy lightnings, to rout my enemies; shoot
7 thy arrows, and throw them into confusion! With heavenly aid, from yonder
8 flood deliver me; rescue me from the power of alien foes, who make treacherous
9 promises, and lift their hands in perjury. Then, O my God, I will sing thee a

10 new song, on a ten-stringed harp I will sound thy praise; the God to whom kings must look for victory, the God who has brought his servant David rescue.
11 Save me from the cruel sword, deliver me from the power of alien foes, who make treacherous promises, and lift their hands in perjury.
12 So may our sons grow to manhood, tall as the saplings, our daughters shapely
13 as some column at the turn of a building, it may be, the temple itself. Our garners full, well stored with every kind of plenty, our sheep bearing a thousand-fold,
14 thronging the pasture in their tens of thousands, our oxen straining at the load;
15 no ruined walls, no exile, no lamenting in our streets. Happy men call such a people as this; and is not the people happy, that has the Lord for its God?

PSALM ONE HUNDRED AND FORTY-FOUR

(Praises. Of David.)

A ND shall I not extol thee, my God, my king; shall I not bless thy name for
2 ever and for evermore? **Blessing** shall be thine, day after day; for ever and
3 for evermore praised be thy name. **Can** any praise be worthy of the Lord's
4 majesty, any thought set limits to his greatness? **Down** the ages the story of thy
5 deeds is told, thy power is ever acclaimed; each magnifies thy unapproachable
6 glory, makes known thy wonders. **Fearful** are the tales they tell of thy power,
7 proclaiming thy magnificence; grateful their memory of all thy goodness, as they
8 boast of thy just dealings. **How** gracious the Lord is, how merciful, how patient,
9 how rich in pity! **Is** he not a loving Lord to his whole creation; does not his mercy reach out to all that he has made?
10 Joining, then, Lord, in thy whole creation's praise, let thy faithful servants
11 bless thee; let them publish the glory of thy kingdom, and discourse of thy power,
12 making that power known to the race of men, the glory, the splendour of that
13 kingdom! **No** age shall dawn but shall see thee reigning still; generations pass, and thy rule shall endure. **O** how true the Lord is to all his promises, how high
14 above us in all his dealings! **Prostrate** though men may fall, the Lord will lift them up, will revive their crushed spirits.
15 Quietly, Lord, thy creatures raise their eyes to thee, and thou grantest them,
16 in due time, their nourishment, ready to open thy hand, and fill with thy blessing
17 all that lives. **So** faithful the Lord is in all he does, so gracious in all his dealings.
18 The Lord draws near to every man that calls upon him, will he but call upon him
19 with a true heart. **Utter** but the wish, you that fear the Lord, and he will grant
20 it, will hear the cry, and bring aid. **Vigilantly** the Lord watches over all that love
21 him, marks down the wicked for destruction. **While** these lips tell of the Lord's praise, let all that lives bless his holy name, for ever, and for evermore.

PSALM ONE HUNDRED AND FORTY-FIVE

(Alleluia.)

2 P RAISE the Lord, my soul; while life lasts, I will praise the Lord; of him, my
3 God, shall my songs be while I am here to sing them. **Do** not put your trust in
4 princes; they are but men, they have no power to save. As soon as the breath leaves his body, man goes back to the dust he belongs to; with that, all his designs will
5 come to nothing. **Happier** the man who turns to the God of Jacob for help, puts
6 no confidence but in the Lord his God, maker of heaven and earth and sea and all
7 they contain; the God who keeps faith for ever, who redresses wrong, and gives
8 food to the hungry. The Lord, who brings release to the prisoner, the Lord,

who gives sight to the blind, the Lord, who comforts the burdened, the Lord, who
9 befriends the innocent! The Lord, who protects the stranger, who defends
10 orphan and widow, who overturns the counsel of the wicked! The Lord, reigning
for ever, thy God, Sion, reigning from age to age! Alleluia.

PSALM ONE HUNDRED AND FORTY-SIX

(Alleluia.)

PRAISE the Lord; the Lord is gracious; sing to our God, a God who so claims
2 our love; praise is his right. The Lord is rebuilding Jerusalem, is calling the
3 banished sons of Israel home; he it is that heals the broken heart, and binds up
4 its wounds. Does he not know the number of the stars, and call each by its name?
5 How great a Lord is ours, how magnificent his strength, how inscrutable his
6 wisdom! The Lord is the defender of the oppressed, and lays the wicked low in
7 the dust. Strike up, then, in thanksgiving to the Lord, with the harp's music
8 praise our God; the God who curtains heaven with cloud, and lays up a store of
rain for the earth, who clothes the mountain-sides with grass, with corn for man's
9 need, gives food to the cattle, food to the young ravens that cry out to him. Not
11 the well-mounted warrior is his choice, not the swift runner wins his favour; the
Lord's favour is for those who fear him, and put their trust in his divine mercy.

PSALM ONE HUNDRED AND FORTY-SEVEN

2 PRAISE the Lord, Jerusalem; Sion, exalt thy God! He it is that bolts thy gates
3 fast, and blesses thy children, who dwell safe in thee; that makes thy land a
4 land of peace, and gives thee full ears of wheat to sustain thee. See how he issues
5 his command to the earth, how swift his word runs! Now he spreads a pall of
6 snow, covers earth with an ashy veil of rime, doles out the scattered crusts of ice,
7 binds the waters at the onset of his frost. Then, at his word, all melts away; a
8 breath from him, and the waters flow! This is the God who makes his word
9 known to Jacob, gives Israel ruling and decree. Not such his dealings with any
other nation; nowhere else the revelation of his will. Alleluia.

PSALM ONE HUNDRED AND FORTY-EIGHT

(Alleluia.)

2 GIVE praise to the Lord in heaven; praise him, all that dwells on high. Praise
3 him, all you angels of his, praise him, all his armies. Praise him, sun and
4 moon; praise him, every star that shines. Praise him, you highest heavens, you
5 waters beyond the heavens. Let all these praise the Lord; it was his command
6 that created them. He has set them there unaging for ever, given them a law
which cannot be altered.
7 Give praise to the Lord on earth, monsters of the sea and all its depths; fire
9 and hail, snow and mist, and the storm-wind that executes his decree; all you
10 mountains and hills, all you fruit trees and cedars; all you wild beasts and cattle,
11 creeping things and birds that fly in air; all you kings and peoples of the world,
12 all you that are princes and judges on earth; young men and maids, old men and
13 boys together; let them all give praise to the Lord's name. His name is exalted as
14 no other, his praise reaches beyond heaven and earth; and now he has given fresh
strength to his people. Shall not his faithful servants praise him, the sons of Israel,
the people that draw near to him? Alleluia.

PSALM ONE HUNDRED AND FORTY-NINE

(Alleluia.)

S ING the Lord a new song; here, where the faithful gather, let his praise be
2 heard. In him, the maker of Israel, let Israel triumph; for him, the ruler of
3 Sion, let Sion's children keep holiday; let there be dancing in honour of his name,
4 music of tambour and of harp, to praise him. Still the Lord shews favour to his
5 people, still he relieves the oppressed, and grants them victory. In triumph let
6 thy faithful servants rejoice, rejoice and take their rest. Ever on their lips they
bear the high praise of God, ever in their hands they carry two-edged swords,
7 ready to take vengeance upon the heathen, to curb the nations, to chain kings,
9 and bind princes in fetters of iron. Long since their doom is written; boast
it is of his true servants that doom to execute. Alleluia.

PSALM ONE HUNDRED AND FIFTY

(Alleluia.)

P RAISE God in his sanctuary, praise him on his sovereign throne. Praise him
3 for his noble acts, praise him for his surpassing greatness. Praise him with the
4 bray of the trumpet, praise him with harp and zither. Praise him with the tam-
5 bour and the dance, praise him with the music of string and of reed. Praise him
with the clang of the cymbals, the cymbals that ring merrily. All creatures that
breath have, praise the Lord. Alleluia.